BLACK WOMEN IN AMERICA

SECOND EDITION

BLACK WOMEN

IN

AMERICA

SECOND EDITION

Editor in Chief

Darlene Clark Hine

VOLUME 2

H–Q

OXFORD
UNIVERSITY PRESS
2005

OXFORD
UNIVERSITY PRESS

Oxford University Press, Inc., publishes works that further
Oxford University's objective of excellence
in research, scholarship, and education.

Oxford New York
Auckland Cape Town Dar es Salaam Hong Kong Karachi
Kuala Lumpur Madrid Melbourne Mexico City Nairobi
New Delhi Shanghai Taipei Toronto

With offices in
Argentina Austria Brazil Chile Czech Republic France Greece
Guatemala Hungary Italy Japan Poland Portugal Singapore
South Korea Switzerland Thailand Turkey Ukraine Vietnam

Copyright © 2005 by Oxford University Press, Inc.

Published by Oxford University Press, Inc.
198 Madison Avenue, New York, New York, 10016
http://www.oup.com

Oxford is a registered trademark of Oxford University Press

Library of Congress Cataloging-in-Publication Data

Black women in America / Darlene Clark Hine, editor in chief.--2nd ed.
p. cm.
Includes bibliographical references and index.
ISBN-13: 978-0-19-515677-5 (alk. paper)
ISBN-10: 0-19-515677-3 (alk. paper)
1. African American women--Encyclopedias. I. Hine, Darlene Clark.
E185.86.B542   2005
305.48′896073--dc22

2005001532

ISBN-13 (vol. 1): 978-0-19-522374-3   ISBN-10 (vol. 1): 0-19-522374-8
ISBN-13 (vol. 2): 978-0-19-522375-0   ISBN-10 (vol. 2): 0-19-522375-6
ISBN-13 (vol. 3): 978-0-19-522376-7   ISBN-10 (vol. 3): 0-19-522376-4

Printing number: 9 8 7 6 5 4 3 2 1

Printed in the United States of America
on acid-free paper

BLACK WOMEN IN AMERICA

SECOND EDITION

H

HAIR. For African American women, hair has long been entwined with issues of beauty, class, cultural acceptance, and citizenship. Depending on the historical period, the texture of hair may tell a story about how an African American woman feels about herself in relation to the prevailing standards of beauty; its care might provide an opportunity to become economically self-sufficient, and its styling could speak to political beliefs and ideologies. The history of African American women's relationship to hair and beauty culture is richly complicated and reflects the complexities of African Americans' connections to both African and African American culture. It is a relationship as old as the presence of those women in the United States, and any attempt to understand its significance must start with the arrival of African women in America.

Early Hair and Beauty Practices

When African women first arrived in America, they drew upon their West African roots and artistry to create hairstyles and beauty standards reflecting their own culture. For their beauty and grooming rituals, many continued to rely on African practices, which included braiding hair in traditional patterns and using berries and herbs for skincare preparation. Over time, dominant beauty constructs in white American culture replaced these African-inspired ideals of beauty. However, such standards were often at odds with the body types and hair textures of most African American women. Nonetheless, some enslaved women and men became proficient in European beauty care techniques by serving as beauticians or barbers for their owners, and some free blacks in both the North and the South made their living as hairdressers for white customers.

For many enslaved African American women, however, hair-grooming aids were of a more practical nature. For example, in an interview conducted by the federally funded Works Progress Administration (WPA), one formerly enslaved African American man, Amos Lincoln, commented about hair styling practices in slave communities, specifically on why so many African American women wore bandanas to cover their hair: "All week they wear they hair all roll up with cotton. . . . Sunday come they com' the hair out fine. No grease on it. They want it naturally curly."

Lincoln's description was of a natural precursor of the contemporary practice of African American women rolling their hair and setting it under a dryer. The tightly wrapped bandanna served as an absorbent of perspiration that dried quickly and "trained" hair growth.

Though many African American women may have used natural methods such as combining the use of bandanas, the sun, and their own sweat to groom their hair, by the 1830s, the merchandising of hair care products manufactured by white companies and designed specifically to straighten African American hair became widespread. The technique that these straightening products advised was to shampoo the hair and lay it out flat. The consumer was then to apply a hair straightening solution and use a hot flat iron to iron it in. When shampooed and laid out, one might assume that the hair of many African American women was not long enough to iron, and, indeed, one of the most common beauty complaints amongst these women was burned scalps. Many young women suffered from baldness. Clearly, early hair-straightening methods were far from safe.

To make matters worse, when African American women did attempt to bring their appearances into line with conventional, or white, notions of beauty, they only exacerbated their woes. Despite such difficulties, many African American women continued to use such products in order to straighten their hair and came to believe that if they were successful, they could change their social circumstances and become more easily accepted in American culture and society.

This was a message African American women saw in late nineteenth-century advertisements for hair and beauty products. Because hair texture could be changed through the use of specific beauty products, such products aimed at changing the texture of African American hair had wide-ranging consequences in the dominant, as well as the African American, culture and society. A look at early messages connecting straight hair with cultural mobility explains why many African American women were willing to endure potentially damaging hair-grooming techniques.

Nineteenth-Century Beauty Advertisements

Late-nineteenth- and early-twentieth-century beauty care companies resorted to the commonly held racial beliefs

CANDIS DARDEN, photographed on 1 August 1939. (The Library of Virginia.)

and maintained them in their advertisements, even those aimed at African American audiences. Advertisements for hair straighteners marketed by white companies suggested that only through changing their physical features would consumers of African descent be afforded class mobility within African American communities and social acceptance by the dominant culture.

This negative message was particularly overwhelming for African American women because advertisements, even in African American newspapers and periodicals, did not feature any other products aimed at enhancing African American beauty. While advertisements for the dominant population featured a wide range of beauty products, including girdles, and other types of body-shaping garments, as well as different lotions and ointments aimed at making skin appear softer and more youthful, advertisements aimed at African American women were primarily for products that promised to straighten their hair.

By the turn of the century, advertisements for one such product, "Oxonized Ox Marrow," were staples in African American newspapers. These advertisements featured a bold headline stating "Wonderful Discovery, Curly Hair Made Straight By Original Oxonized Ox Marrow." The featured image was of an African American woman. In the "before" drawing, her hair was shown literally standing on end, while the "after" drawing portrays the hair as neatly combed and styled. The advertising copy proclaims, "This wonderful hair pomade is the only safe preparation in the world that makes kinky or curly hair straight." Similarly, an advertisement for "Black Skin Remover and Hair Straightener" shows the "before" drawing outlined in ink so dark that one cannot see the model's individual features clearly. However, her forehead slopes forward sharply, and her nose is broad and short. Her hair is short, quite curly, and appears uncombed. The "after" drawing is supposed to show the change that will occur once the product is used. The woman's skin is now white, and her hair has become long, straight, and neatly styled. Furthermore, her nose has become long and quite aquiline while her forehead no longer slopes forward as drastically as in the previous drawing. Not only has her skin color and hair texture changed, but also her bone structure has followed suit.

While the manufacturers of hair straightening products urged African American women to straighten their hair in order to foster societal acceptance, many African Americans, even then, argued that straightened hair amounted to a disavowal of their African ancestry. The issue of beauty standards and of their effects upon African Americans was an integral part of nineteenth-century discussions of "black pride" that linked beauty products and practices to a call for imagery able to combat damaging cultural representations of African Americans.

For example, in the 11 March 1853 editorial, "White Is Beautiful," appearing in *Frederick Douglass' Paper*, William J. Wilson told readers: "We despise, we almost hate ourselves, and all that favors us. Well we scoff at black skins and woolly heads, since every model set before us for admiration has a pallid face and flaxen head." While Wilson was concerned with the psychological effects of internalized oppression and the need for a more "authentic" representation of the self, Martin Freeman decried the lengths to which African Americans would go in an attempt to approximate Anglo-Saxon standards of personal beauty. In an April 1859 article in the *Anglo-African Magazine*, he offers a vivid description of practices and a stern critique of those who choose to imitate European standards of beauty:

The child is taught directly or indirectly that he or she is pretty, just in proportion as the features approximate the Anglo-Saxon standard. Hence flat noses must be pinched up. Kinky hair must be subjected to a straightening process— oiled, and pulled, twisted up, tied down, sleeked over and pressed under, or cut off so short that it can't curl, sometimes the natural hair is shaved off and its place supplied by a straight wig. Thick lips are puckered up and drawn in. Beautiful black and brown faces by the application of rouge and lily white powder, are made to assume unnatural tints, like the livid hue of painted corpses. (Freedman, 4)

Given that hair and beauty products before 1906 consisted primarily of products such as "Black Skin Remover and Hair Straightener" and "Oxonized Ox Marrow," it is perhaps not surprising that cultural discussions about the meaning of using such products tended to chastise African American women for wanting straight hair. However, it should be noted that numerous beauty-care companies were owned and operated by African American women between 1906 and 1919, and their advertisements tended to shift the significance of African American women's hair styling practices from beauty, upward mobility, and social acceptance, to concerns with health, styling versatility, hair length, and economic well-being.

Twentieth-Century African American Women: Advertising Beauty

One early-twentieth-century hairdresser, known only as Madame Newell, exemplified this difference in her $100 offer to anyone proving that her chosen product did not stimulate hair growth when used as directed. Writing in the *St. Louis Palladium* in 1906 she adds, "Now don't you be satisfied with simply having your hair made to look beautiful, but grasp for all there is in the Crowning Glory of Woman—and let her grow yours." Significantly, African American women were not addressed as if they somehow lacked what was necessary to prosper in American society. Instead, the focus was on health as well as a reference to "hair as a woman's crown and glory."

In addition, others urged African American women to become hairdressers and earn money for themselves. In a 1908 issue of the *St. Louis Palladium*, Madame J. Nelson told readers they need not "struggle along in uncongenial employment with long hours and short pay. Educate yourself to do work that has little competition; isn't it better to spend a half-hour daily and qualify yourself to do work that everyone else cannot do. The fields are large."

Perhaps the most well-known hairdresser from this period was Madam C. J. Walker, an African American woman who began her business with only $2 and came to amass over $1 million before her death in 1919. By that time, she was said to have helped over 100,000 women begin careers as hairdressers.

While African American intellectual leaders were either downplaying the importance of outward physical beauty, or raging at those who tried to imitate white beauty, agents for hair straightening systems were selling their products door-to-door. Agents were often members of the communities in which they sold the products and served

as visual images of African American female beauty. The presence of these women, themselves users of the products sold door-to-door, was perhaps the best marketing tool available to demonstrate visually and more effectively than could a newspaper advertisement that a particular product actually worked.

As a result, the agents offered images of African American beauty and hair styling options that could lead to feelings of trust. If the products proved unsatisfactory, someone was available and could be held responsible for the unfortunate effects.

By the middle of the twentieth-century, hair had come to mean a variety of things to and for African American women. The advent of hair straightening was even a source of political tension, including claims that straightening hair amounted to race hatred. Nevertheless, a clear majority of African American women straightened their hair. It came to be an accepted and, indeed, often preferred form of grooming for African American women. And, significantly, large numbers had careers as hairdressers, thus enabling them to support themselves and their families.

Natural Hair Styles and Political Protest

The loudest twentieth-century protest against the use of European beauty standards and styling periods for African American women came during the 1960s and was a direct result of the civil rights and Black Power movements. As the "black is beautiful" slogan became more popular, African Americans across the country began to embrace hairstyles and beauty techniques that emphasized essential African American characteristics. Unstraightened hairstyles came to define what was considered most acceptable and appropriate for African American women. Most memorable was the Afro, a popular natural hairstyle for both men and women in the late 1960s and early 1970s. Once again, appearing as "black" as possible became a mark of status within the community, especially among younger African Americans.

Indeed, as the civil rights movement became the Black Liberation, or Black Power movement in the mid-1970s, to wear an Afro was to link oneself with nationalist sentiments in both the African American community and America at large. The Afro denoted black pride and became synonymous with activism and political consciousness. This sentiment moved sharply against the prevailing integrationist ideology and evinced a belief that the gains of the civil rights movement were not broad enough. It is this dichotomy that led one author, Gloria Wade-Gayles, to observe:

An activist with straight hair was a contradiction. A lie. A joke, really. The right to tout the movement gospel of self-esteem carried with it the obligation to accept and love one's self naturally. Our appearance had to speak the truth before our lips stretched to sing songs. Never again, I decided, would I alter my hair. In its natural state, my hair would be a badge, a symbol of my self-esteem and racial pride. (Wade-Gayles, 20)

Hairstyles were no longer regarded as mere personal choices about aesthetics or as opportunities to provide employment for African American hairdressers. By the 1960s, hairstyles had become clear political statements about how connected the wearer was to African American communities and were thought to indicate the depth of the wearers' sense of pride in her own blackness.

Along with the Afro, braided styles also became more popular. However, unlike the Afro, thought to be a clear indication of black pride, braids were often more highly prized because of the opportunity for closeness and touching associated with achieving the style. The closing pages of Shirley Ann Williams's novel, *Dessa Rose*, center on the main character, Dessa, braiding her child's hair and "remembering" her life.

> I missed this when I was sold away from home. . . . The way the womens in the Quarters used to would braid hair. Mothers would braid children heads—girl and boy—until they went into the field or for as long as they had them. This was one way we told who they peoples was, by how they hair was combed. . . . Child learn a lot of things setting between some grown person's legs, listening at grown peoples speak over they heads. This is where I learned to listen, right there between mammy's thighs, where I first learnted to speak, from listening at grown peoples talk. (Williams, p. 234)

This scene in *Dessa Rose* highlights one of the important aspects of hair as it relates to African American culture: the act of styling hair as both a social and learning occasion.

A similar moment is highlighted in Karla Holloway's recollections of braiding her daughter's hair:

> When my daughter was a child, I braided her hair on the front porch. In twilight hours or warm summer mornings I worked intricately braided patterns into Ayana's hair, trying to capture some of that precious childhood time when my sisters and I could not have been closer to our mother or grandmothers Celia and Marguerite than we were when they were braiding our hair. We sat propped between their strong legs, our shoulders leaning against their soft thighs, feeling touched and safe. Those were times when our bodies and theirs, intimately intertwined and held by the web of their fingers and our hair, were sweetly cared for, and immeasurably valued. (Holloway, pp. 70–71)

If within African American culture, literary and recollected, the act of braiding came to symbolize closeness, comfort, and community, by the 1990s, once the results of such practices came into public conflict with the dominant culture, the style often came to exemplify the continuing political significance of hair for African American women.

Contemporary African Women's Hair: 1980–Present

The 1980s and 1990s saw a broad spectrum of African American hair and beauty styles. This included the resurgence of braids, often in designs that imitated traditional West African styles. Straightened hair became popular again in a wide range of short and long styles, while the new jeri curl used a chemical process to create loose, wet, curls, a style popular with both men and women. They also chose dreadlocks, twists, fades, and other styles that took advantage of African American hair's natural texture. Although hair styling choices became far more numerous, the reality of hairstyles as overtly political images remained unresolved and continued to shape cultural interactions between African American women and American culture.

For example, in November of 1998, a public drama over hair, its meaning, and relationship to African American identity erupted when a white elementary schoolteacher in Brooklyn was charged with racism, threatened with bodily harm, suspended, and subsequently reassigned to another school because she assigned a book entitled *Nappy Hair* for her students to read. The book was supposed to build self-esteem in children with such hair, but a group of black parents objected to the title, illustrations, and the book's assumption that hair of that type could or should be seen as a positive.

Another incident involved nine-year-old Meghan Smith in 1996. At the time, Meghan was a third grader at Grace Christian School in Brandon, Florida. One day in December, she left home with her hair neatly braided in twelve cornrows that climbed up the curve of her head and were bunched in a ponytail at the crown of her head with a little white barrette. When Meghan arrived in her classroom, the teacher immediately sent her to the office of the principal, who sent her home. School administrators first informed Meghan and then her parents that she was in violation of the schools dress code, which forbade "extreme" hairstyles that might distract students and disrupt learning. The officials said the hairstyle clashed with the spiritual and educational mission of the school; they labeled the cornrows a fad and told Meghan not to return to school until she changed the style.

Although Meghan did not know it, her school forbade cornrows, dreadlocks, hair ornaments, and designs shaved into the hair. There was no explanation offered for banning these particular hairstyles. School administrators decided that Meghan was attempting to make an undefined political or cultural statement with her hairstyle. Such statements, the administrators said, would not be tolerated. Meghan returned to school a few days later with her hair straightened and was readmitted to her class.

While hair is a genetically determined physical feature, its care and styling is quite clearly influenced by cultural concerns. What makes hair a unique and revealing "natural" feature in the exploration of the expressive culture of African American women is the cultural value placed upon the ease with which it can be altered, and a largely self-determined willingness and ability to do with it what one will: dread, cornrow, perm, dye, press. While some styling choices are born of a desire to look like somebody one admires, or to adhere to a look desirable in a particular political or social position, hairstyles and the cultural interactions that produce them speak to larger concerns as well. They reflect African American women's experience in the United States.

See also Beauty Culture *and* Walker, Madam, C. J. (Sarah Breedlove).

BIBLIOGRAPHY

Banks, Ingrid. *Hair Matters: Beauty, Power and Black Women's Consciousness*. New York: New York University Press, 2000.

Craig, Maxine Leeds. *Ain't I a Beauty Queen: Black Women, Beauty and the Politics of Race*. New York: Oxford University Press, 2002.

Freedman, Martin. "Beauty." *Anglo African Magazine*, April 1859.

Harris, Juliette, and Pamela Johnson, eds. *Tenderheaded: A Combbending Collection of Hair Stories*. New York: Pocket Books, 2001.

Herrera, Carolina. *Nappy Hair*. New York: Knopf, 1997.

Holloway, Karla. *Codes of Conduct: Race Ethics and the Color of Our Character*. New Brunswick, NJ: Rutgers University Press, 1995.

Rooks, Noliwe. *Hair Raising: Beauty, Culture and African American Women*. New Brunswick, NJ: Rutgers University Press, 1996.

Wade-Gayles, Gloria. "The Making of a Permanent Afro." *Catalyst: A Magazine of Heart and Mind*, Summer 1988.

Williams, Shirley Anne. *Dessa Rose*. New York: Harcourt Brace Jovanovich, 1984.

—NOLIWE ROOKS

HALE, MAMIE ODESSA (b. 1911; d. 1968); healer.

The public health career of the nurse and midwife Mamie Odessa Hale demonstrates the importance black women have played in helping to improve the health of black Americans, particularly in the South. Hale's training of the "granny" midwives of Arkansas proved to be her lasting gift to public health.

Born in Pennsylvania, Mamie Odessa Hale attended a teachers college and later worked as a public health nurse in Pittsburgh, eventually leaving that career to attend the Tuskegee School of Nurse-Midwifery in Alabama, from which she graduated in 1942. Tuskegee, famous and infamous in black health history, played an important role as an institution dedicated to improving the health of poor rural blacks. The institution opened one of the first black nurses training programs in 1892 and served as a major educational institution in providing both training for black professionals and health programs for southern blacks.

The Nurse-Midwifery program opened in 1941, and before it closed in 1946, the program produced twenty-five graduates, including Hale. In health programs in the 1920s, often funded by the Sheppard-Towner Act, southern states hired public health nurses to help train midwives. In these cases, white nurses usually trained black midwives. The experience of Arkansas midwives would be different, with Hale providing essential training to both white public health nurses and black and white midwives. The Arkansas State Board of Health recruited Hale after her graduation and certification as a nurse-midwife to help improve maternal-child care programs in the state and ultimately to help lower its infant mortality rate. Efforts to train midwives in Arkansas dated back to 1925, but with the hiring of Hale, the Board of Health found a highly trained nurse practitioner capable of improving the state's midwifery practice.

Despite gains in reducing infant mortality rates in general across the country, black babies died in higher numbers than did white babies, and reductions in infant mortality rates were the lowest in Alabama, Arkansas, Mississippi, and Tennessee. In Arkansas, the majority of all babies were born without any attention from physicians or hospitals.

In the segregated South, black midwives—often known as "granny" midwives—delivered more than 25 percent of all babies and more than 50 percent of black babies. Even though many black midwives were illiterate, they held positions of respect in poor rural communities. They provided the majority of the health care within each community and were viewed as community leaders and guardians of customs and culture. Government health officials found it easier to train these women than to make fundamental changes in the health care delivery system.

In its initial midwife regulation, the state of Arkansas requested midwives to possess a permit, but did not require any training. In 1940, this voluntary system requested that Arkansas midwives have a physical examination, a Wasserman test (for syphilis), and a clean practice bag. They were also asked to sign pledge cards and submit forms to the State Health Department. Mirroring national programs, the Arkansas midwife training program focused on making the practice of midwives aseptic, or germ free.

A 1941 Committee on the Study of Midwifery revealed how badly these voluntary regulatory efforts had failed. More than a third of the midwives practicing in 1941 did not have a permit and, moreover, had never possessed one. The report noted that, of the 142 deaths in childbirth of black women, all but 35 could probably have been avoided with better delivery conditions. Problems with infant mortality continued. In 1943, 10 percent of Arkansas babies died in their first year, with most of these deaths occurring in the first month and many after only a day. The poor maternal mortality rate continued for black women in the 1940s. The State Department of Health slowly moved to address this problem, finally acknowledging the vital role midwife training would play in improving black health conditions. A 1945 report recommended the State Board of Health adopt mandatory midwife registration, with a penalty imposed for those who failed to comply.

Mamie Hale started her work with granny midwives at the Crittendon County Health Department in 1942. She was promoted to the position of midwife consultant for the Maternal and Child Health Division of the Arkansas Health Department in 1945. It was in this position that Hale used all her Tuskegee training to hire and educate public health nurses for a midwifery training program. The Arkansas infant and maternal care programs received funding from the federal Children's Bureau. Health Department officials wanted all practicing midwives to hold permits, which depended on the successful completion of the midwife training program and an examination. "Nurse" Hale started training granny midwives in four county health departments in 1946.

The program consisted of seven lessons, and Hale also accompanied the midwives on visits to their patients' homes. She held informational meetings for parent groups to inform them of the improved services, and the midwives she trained encouraged better prenatal care for their patients. The lessons devised by Hale demanded she be inventive and responsive to local conditions. Three-fourths of the midwives could not read or write, and only a small minority could correctly fill out a birth certificate. Hale used songs, movies, pictures, and practical demonstrations to teach the midwives. Like other public health midwife training programs, Hale's instruction emphasized making the birth process cleaner. She demonstrated how to use warm newspapers to keep the birthing bed clean and encouraged the midwives to use beds rather than floors. Hale gave the midwives practical explanations that helped improve sanitation. She showed them how to bake the tape that was used to remove the infant's cord, telling them to keep the tape in the oven the same amount of time as a small baked potato.

Many of the practicing midwives were between sixty and eighty years of age. Most felt that they had been "called" to the practice of "catchin' babies." Hale played upon these sentiments and incorporated religious elements into her lessons. Meetings were often held in local churches and included hymn singing and prayer. One of Hale's biggest challenges was to change the midwives' sometimes dangerous superstitious practices while still respecting folk beliefs that caused no harm and may even have had positive psychological effects, such as the notion that placing an ax under the woman's bed would alleviate her pain. Other lessons encouraged illiterate midwives to enlist the aid of family members who could write in order to properly fill out birth certificates. Hale

recommended midwives make at least three prenatal visits, during which the midwife and pregnant woman could discuss how the birth would occur and what the pregnant woman's diet was. These visits also allowed the midwife to assess the woman's condition.

Hale encouraged the midwives to set good practice standards, which included limiting their caseload, working cooperatively with local doctors, and promoting physician follow-up examinations after the birth. Later sessions addressed the sanitary preparation of midwives' practice bags, with Hale demonstrating how to sterilize items the women would use. Hale also urged the midwives to make certain that their bags contained all the necessary items, such as clean newspapers, string to tie the baby's cord, and ampoules of silver nitrate for the baby's eyes. Hale discouraged the use of rubber gloves, and instead advocated meticulous hand-washing techniques to attain an aseptic birthing environment. Hale sometimes used a thirty-pound dummy to demonstrate birth techniques and the proper way to sterilize instruments. During lessons, Hale sometimes wore a clean white apron and hat, the proper attire for births.

Mamie Odessa Hale gained the respect of the local midwives and the white nurses and doctors with whom she worked. So great was the respect accorded to her that white nurses traveling with her refused to eat in segregated restaurants. By 1948 Hale had helped to establish new maternal health clinics in eleven Arkansas counties. Public health nurses helped identify trained midwives, and of the 569 midwives receiving annual permits, 482 of them delivered over 5,000 babies. Hale's educational program convinced many of the state's midwives to enter the modern era, leaving some of their older ways behind them. Hale successfully helped change midwife practice in the state. In part because of her efforts, the death rate for Arkansas's black women and babies fell from seventy-six deaths in 1940 to forty-three in 1950. Hale taught black midwives to deliver better care, but she also taught their patients to expect better care, a contribution that secured her place in the legacy of black women healers.

See also Nursing.

BIBLIOGRAPHY

Bell, Pegge L. "Hale, Mamie Odessa." In *Black Women in America: An Historical Encyclopedia*, edited by Darlene Clark Hine, Elsa Barkley Brown, and Rosalyn Terborg-Penn. Brooklyn, NY: Carlson, 1993.

Bell, Pegge L. "'Making Do' with the Midwife: Arkansas's Mamie O. Hale in the 1940s." *Nursing History Review*, Vol. 1 (1993): 155–167.

Hine, Darlene Clark. *Black Women in White: Racial Conflict and Cooperation in the Nursing Profession, 1890–1950*. Bloomington: Indiana University Press, 1989.

Smith, Susan L. *Sick and Tired of Being Sick and Tired: Black Women's Health Activism in America, 1890–1950*. Philadelphia: University of Pennsylvania Press, 1995.

—AMY M. HAY

HAMER, FANNIE LOU (b. 6 October 1917; d. 14 March 1977), civil rights activist. "I'm sick and tired of being sick and tired." The famous and radical words of Fannie Lou Hamer expressed how many black Americans had come to feel by the 1960s. Her speeches and songs influenced everyone who heard and saw her. For many Americans, Fannie Lou Hamer symbolized the best of what the civil rights movement could be.

Fannie Lou Townsend was born to Jim and Ella Townsend in rural Montgomery County, Mississippi. Ella and Jim Townsend moved to Sunflower County, Mississippi, when Fannie Lou was two years old, and the child received her early education there. At the age of six, Fannie Lou began working in the cotton fields and worked many long years chopping and picking cotton until the plantation owner, W. D. Marlow, learned that she could read and write. In 1944 she became the time and record keeper for Marlow, and in 1945 she married Perry Hamer, a tractor driver on the Marlow plantation. For the next eighteen years, Hamer worked as sharecropper and time keeper on the plantation, four miles east of Ruleville, Mississippi, where she and Perry made their home. All this changed in 1962 when Hamer suffered economic reprisals after an unsuccessful attempt to vote in the county seat of Indianola. Familiar with the physical violence that would often follow economic reprisals, and having received threats, Hamer left her family to stay with friends. The move did not end the threat of violence, however, and Hamer and her friends miraculously escaped rounds of gunshots fired into the friends' home when a person or persons unknown discovered her presence there.

Despite this intimidation, Hamer became an active member of the Student Nonviolent Coordinating Committee (SNCC) in Ruleville. She took the literacy test several times in order to repeatedly demonstrate her right to vote. In 1963, she became a field secretary for SNCC and a registered voter; both put her life in jeopardy. From this point onward, Hamer worked with voter registration drives and with programs designed to assist economically deprived black families in Mississippi.

The youngest of twenty children whose parents seldom were able to provide adequate food and clothing, Hamer saw a link between the lack of access to the political process and the poor economic status of black Americans. She was instrumental in starting Delta Ministry, an extensive community development program, in 1963. In 1964 she took part in the founding of the Mississippi Freedom Democratic Party (MFDP), becoming vice chairperson and a member of its delegation to the Democratic National Convention in Atlantic City, New Jersey, in order to challenge the seating of the regular all-white Mississippi delegation. The challenge failed despite a compromise

FANNIE LOU HAMER at the Democratic National Convention, 27 August 1968. For many Americans, she symbolized the best of the civil rights movement. (© Bettmann/Corbis.)

offered by Hubert Humphrey and Walter Mondale that would have seated two nonvoting MFDP members selected by Humphrey. Instead, the MFDP's actions resulted in an unprecedented pledge from the national Democratic Party not to seat delegations that excluded black delegates at the convention in 1968.

Also in 1964 Hamer unsuccessfully ran for Congress. Because the regular Democratic Party refused to place her name on the ballot, the MFDP distributed a "Freedom Ballot" that included all of the candidates' names, black and white. Hamer defeated her white opponent, Congressman Jamie Whitten on the alternative ballot, but the state refused to acknowledge the MFDP vote as valid. In 1965 Hamer, Victoria Gray, and Annie Devine appealed to the Congress, arguing that it was wrong to seat Mississippi's representatives, who were all white, when the state's population was 50 percent black. The three women watched as the House voted against the challenge, 228 to 143.

Hamer remained active in civic affairs in Mississippi for the remainder of her life and was a delegate to the Democratic National Convention in 1968 in Chicago. Her founding in 1969 of the Freedom Farms Corporation (FFC), a nonprofit venture designed to help needy families raise food and livestock, was a response to the economic plight of black Americans in Mississippi. The FFC also provided social services, minority business opportunity, scholarships, and grants for education. When the National Council of Negro Women started the Fannie Lou Hamer Day Care Center in 1970, Hamer became its board's chairperson. In 1976, even as she struggled with cancer, Hamer served as a member of the state executive committee of the United Democratic Party of Mississippi.

Fannie Lou Hamer in an interview in 1965 said "I was determined to see that things were changed." Paraphrasing John F. Kennedy, she continued, "I am determined to give my part not for what the movement can do for me, but what I can do for the movement to bring about a change." On being tired, Hamer put it best:

> I do remember, one time, a man came to me after the students began to work in Mississippi, and he said the white people were getting tired and they were getting tense and anything might happen. Well, I asked him, "how long he thinks we had been getting tired?" I have been tired for forty-six years, and my parents was tired before me, and their parents were tired; and I have always wanted to do something that would help some of the things I would see going on among Negroes that I didn't like and I don't like now.

Hamer consistently stated that she had always wanted to work to transform the South because she saw her parents work so hard to raise twenty children. Once, her father bought two mules after much sacrifice, and simply because this meant he might experience semi-independence from the landowner, his mules were poisoned. Hamer said she never understood this kind of hatred, but fighting it gave her courage.

Fannie Lou Hamer's frankness, determination, courage, and leadership abilities made her a memorable figure in the 1960s civil rights struggle, particularly in the MFDP challenge to the Democratic Party in August 1964, and especially in its challenge to white southern members of the party.

Fannie Lou Hamer received wide recognition for her part in bringing about a major political transformation in the Democratic Party and for raising significant questions that addressed basic human needs. In 1963 the Fifth Avenue Baptist Church in Nashville, Tennessee, presented her with one of the first awards that she received, for "voter registration and Hamer's fight for freedom for

mankind." Among her numerous awards, she received the National Association of Business and Professional Women's Clubs National Sojourner Truth Meritorious Service Award, a tribute to Hamer's strong defense of human dignity and fearless promotion of civil rights. Delta Sigma Theta Sorority awarded her a life membership. Many colleges and universities honored her with honorary degrees, including Tougaloo College in 1969.

Fannie Lou Hamer gave numerous speeches across the country into the 1970s. She suffered with cancer, but she continued to accept invitations to speak about the issue most dear to her, basic human rights for all Americans. Indeed, she remained tired of being sick and tired until her life ended. She died of cancer at Mound Bayou Community Hospital in Mississippi.

See also Civil Rights Movement.

BIBLIOGRAPHY
"Autobiography of Fannie Lou Hamer." Fannie Lou Hamer papers, Amistad Research Center, New Orleans, LA.
Carson, Clayborne. *In Struggle: SNCC and the Black Awakening of the 1960s* (1981). Cambridge, MA: Harvard University Press, 1995.
DeMuth, Jerry. "Tired of Being Sick and Tired." *Nation*, 1 June 1964.
De Veaux Garland, Phyl. "Builders of a New South." *Ebony*, August 1966.
Golden, Marita. "The Sixties Live On: The Era of Black Consciousness Is Preserved as a State of Mind." *Essence*, May 1985.
Hamer, Fannie Lou. Personal interviews, 1964, 1965.
Ladner, Joyce A. "Fannie Lou Hamer: In Memoriam." *Black Enterprise*, May 1977.
"Life in Mississippi: An Interview with Fannie Lou Hamer." In *Afro-American History: Primary Sources* (1965), edited by Thomas R. Frazier. Chicago: Dorsey Press, 1988.
Locke, Mamie E. "Is This America? Fannie Lou Hamer and the Mississippi Freedom Democratic Party." In *Women in the Civil Rights Movement: Trailblazers and Torchbearers, 1941–1965* (1990), edited by Vicki L. Crawford, Jacqueline Anne Rouse, and Barbara Woods. Bloomington: Indiana University Press, 1993.
Norton, Eleanor Holmes. "Woman Who Changed the South: Memory of Fannie Lou Hamer." *Ms.*, July 1977.
Reagon, Bernice Johnson. "Women as Culture Carriers in the Civil Rights Movement: Fannie Lou Hamer." In *Women in the Civil Rights Movement* (1990), edited by Vicki L. Crawford, Jacqueline Anne Rouse, and Barbara Woods. Bloomington: Indiana University Press, 1993.

—LINDA REED

HAMILTON, GRACE TOWNS (b. 10 February 1907; d. 18 June 1992), politician, activist. Grace Towns Hamilton is best known as the first African American woman to serve in the Georgia legislature. Throughout her political career, Hamilton upheld the ideals of interracial cooperation, but her continued activism reflected her faithful commitment to political empowerment and the improvement of social conditions for African Americans.

Born in Atlanta, Georgia, Hamilton was the eldest of the four surviving children of George Towns and Nellis McNair

Towns. Raised in the close-knit community of Atlanta on the campus of Atlanta University, Hamilton was protected during her early life from the racism that was common throughout much of Georgia. Within the Towns's home, education, church, community involvement, and service to the black race were emphasized. Hamilton's mother, a housewife and committed volunteer for the African American branch of the Young Women Christian Association (YWCA), played a role in Hamilton's later community activism and personal involvement with the YWCA. Her father, a professor of English and pedagogy at Atlanta University, was also politically active and served as Hamilton's early political and professional mentor.

Hamilton entered high school in 1919 at Atlanta University's Preparatory Department, the only high school for African Americans in the city, and then only for those who could afford it. In 1927, she finished her bachelor of arts at Atlanta University, moving soon after to Columbus, Ohio, to attend Ohio State University to pursue a master's degree in psychology.

Columbus sparked the major transformation of Hamilton's life. She moved from her secure Atlanta community of family and friends to the cold racial climate of Ohio. Although she found a job as a girl's work secretary in the African American branch of the YWCA, Hamilton quickly discovered that job opportunities for educated blacks were limited to teaching, factory work, postal service, and preaching. Despite anti-segregation laws, many white theaters, restaurants, hotels, and lunch counters still barred African Americans.

After finishing the written requirements for her master's degree, Hamilton was awarded her psychology degree in 1929. A year later, at the age of twenty-three, Hamilton married Henry Cooke Hamilton. They immediately moved to Memphis, Tennessee, where both of them landed teaching positions at LeMoyne College. Shortly thereafter, in 1931, she gave birth to their only daughter, Eleanor. In 1934 Hamilton was terminated from her teaching duties when LeMoyne sought to limit teaching positions to one per family, reserving most jobs for men.

Laying the foundation for later political work, Hamilton became the first woman executive director of the Atlanta Urban League (AUL) in 1934. Under her leadership, housing became a central issue, as did school funding, voter registration, improved medical care, and the training of physicians. In 1947, the health of Atlanta's black population caught Hamilton's attention as she fought to highlight the exclusion of blacks from many of the whites-only city hospitals. It was the tragic death of a close friend who was injured in a car accident and died because of the color of her skin that made Hamilton double her efforts for the integration of Atlanta's Grady Memorial Hospital. Despite the major improvements she

made for blacks in Atlanta through her work with the AUL, Hamilton grew tired of the sexism she constantly battled within the organization. She retired from the AUL in September 1960 at the age of fifty-three.

Following her departure from the AUL, Hamilton returned to the YWCA, accepting a part-time consulting position in community relations. In 1963 she was appointed by Georgia governor Carl Sanders to serve on the Committee on the Status of Women, her introduction into the Georgia legislature. Shortly afterward, following a Supreme Court decision requiring reapportionment of all congressional and legislature districts, a special election was held in June 1965. Hamilton was elected to the Georgia House of Representatives. A historical landmark, this election inspired black women's involvement in state legislature not only in Georgia but also throughout the deep South.

Much of Hamilton's power in the Georgia legislature stemmed from her practical approach to race and politics, a contrast to the growing militancy among young African Americans during much of the 1960s. Through her pragmatism, Hamilton represented the Vine City area of Georgia most effectively. In 1968 Hamilton challenged the Atlanta government to revise the Atlanta City charter, hoping to make the city's governing apparatus more workable and representative for African Americans. She introduced a bill to create the Atlanta Charter Commission, which was accomplished in June 1971.

The Atlanta Charter Commission redrew Atlanta's political map, reducing the number of at-large seats and requiring that council members live in the districts they represented. These changes seriously limited black representation and power in the city. Shortly after the redistricting, Maynard H. Jackson was elected the first black mayor in Atlanta or any other major city in the South.

Hamilton began to arouse opposition when she authored a bill to shorten county-commissioner terms from four to two years. She was defeated and was deprived of her position on the Fulton-Dekalb Hospital Authority in reprisal. She then opposed the recommendations of a Georgia Reapportionment Committee. Finally, she supported Walter Mondale in the 1984 Democratic presidential campaign, rather than Jesse Jackson. In 1984, at the age of seventy-eight and close to retirement, Hamilton filed for reelection, seeking a final term in the Georgia legislature. However, she suffered defeat to a young Chicago native, Mabel Thomas, who claimed 2,502 votes to Hamilton's 1,013.

In 1988 Emory University honored the strides made by Hamilton, inaugurating a lecture series on her behalf, the first such series named for a black woman within a major university. Two years later, Emory went further to create distinguished chairs named for Hamilton in both the Sociology and African American Studies departments.

Described as "a healer, a communicator, and a bridge builder," Grace Towns Hamilton died at the age of eighty-five.

BIBLIOGRAPHY

Spritzer, Lorraine N., and Jean B. Bergmark. *Grace Towns Hamilton and the Politics of Southern Change*. Athens: University of Georgia Press, 1997.

Aldridge, Delores. "Grace Towns Hamilton." In *Black Women in America: An Historical Encyclopedia*, edited by Darlene Clark Hine, Elsa Barkley Brown, and Rosalyn Terborg-Penn. New York: Carlson, 1993.

"Grace Towns Hamilton, a Fighter for Those Less Fortunate." African American Registry. http://www.aaregistry.com/african_american_history/688/Grace_Hamilton_a_fighter_for_those_less_fortunate.

—SOWANDE' MUSTAKEEM

HAMILTON, VIRGINIA ESTHER (b. 12 March 1936; d. 19 February 2002), writer. Virginia Hamilton wrote books in every genre except poetry. Her fiction and nonfiction garnered nearly every major award in children's literature, including the Newbery Award, the children's literature equivalent of the Pulitzer Prize, and the Hans Christian Andersen Award, considered the Nobel Prize for children's literature. She was the first children's author designated a recipient of the MacArthur Foundation's Genius Award. Her literary legacy became an integral part of the children's literature canon. Her work challenged and defied prevailing ideas about girls and women, race and ethnicity, class, geography, language, and narrative structure. Hamilton routinely took artistic risks and pushed the boundaries of children's literature.

Hamilton was the fifth and youngest child of Kenneth James Hamilton and Etta Belle Perry Hamilton in Yellow Springs, Ohio. She attended a rural elementary school and high school. She received a scholarship to attend Antioch College for her undergraduate degree. She later enrolled at Ohio State University and the New School for Social Research. Hamilton moved to New York City in the 1950s. She met and married Arnold Adoff, a Jewish teacher in Harlem and a critically acclaimed writer. He served as Hamilton's manager. They were the parents of a daughter, Leigh, later an opera singer, and a son, Jamie, who would become a children's book author and musician.

Hamilton's novel *Zeely* signaled the emergence of a new black aesthetic in children's literature. The novel's protagonist, Elizabeth, also called Geeder, is mesmerized by a six-foot-tall woman, Zeely, whose height, regal bearing, physical features, and gorgeous black skin remind her of the pictures of Africans found in old magazines lying around her uncle's attic. Together, Zeely and Geeder strike up a friendship that involves discussions about various topics, including the role of the individual and how to maintain one's identity despite external pressures. The

VIRGINIA HAMILTON was the first children's author to receive the MacArthur Foundation's Genius Award. Her works have become part of the canon in children's literature. (Photograph by Ron Rovtar, from Arnold Adoff.)

book's imagery suggests many of the tropes associated with women's fiction: closeness to nature, birth, and the home. The novel also explores female empowerment, challenges to male dominance, and a rejection of violence against animals. Some critics consider the novel the first feminist children's novel. But *Zeely* was radical, too, in its belief that black women and girls, especially those with darker skin, are beautiful and intelligent.

Other novels and biographies followed, including *The House of Dies Drear* (1968), *The Time-Ago Tales of Jadhu* (1969), *The Planet of Junior Brown* (1971), *W. E. B. Du Bois* (1972), *Time-Ago Lost: More Tales of Jadhu* (1973), and *M. C. Higgins, the Great* (1974). The books covered genres from mystery, folktales, contemporary realistic fiction, and biographies to a melding of fantasy and contemporary realistic fiction. Hamilton's Justice Trilogy depicts the fantastic adventures of a girl-seer, her brothers, and neighbors in a blending of traditional science fiction and fantasy with black mythology. These books and subsequent publications showed that Hamilton's artistic goals were to present unique ideas, capture the oral storytelling cadences of stories she had heard as a child, offer stories of hope and truth, and present what she called "the known, the remembered, and the imagined."

M. C. Higgins, the Great was the first children's novel written by a black author to win the Newbery Medal. The story takes place in the mountains of Ohio as Hamilton's characters face a pending ecological disaster and depicts the first love between M. C. and a teenaged girl who travels by herself in search of authentic examples of local music. In addition to the Newbery Medal, Hamilton was also awarded the *Boston Globe–Horn Book Magazine* Award, the National Book Award, the Lewis Carroll Shelf Award, and the International Board on Books for Young People Award, a rare accumulation of accolades for a single children's book.

Hamilton wrote extraordinary essays about her craft and her aesthetic and cultural views. She rejected ideas about minorities or minority cultures and argued, instead, for the idea of parallel cultures, equal yet different from each other. Many scholars of children's literature accepted Hamilton's ideas as they attempted to document the history of black children's literature, advocate its continued publication, and urge its inclusion in literary canons.

Over the years, Hamilton also developed the idea of liberation literature, the purposes of which were to entertain, educate, and encourage social action. The novels and biographies included in this category present the experiences of blacks through the prism of a progressive, critical eye. The folktale collections *The People Could Fly* and *Many Thousand Gone* introduced readers to the experiences of slavery and liberation in vivid imagery, stunning detail, and imaginative language. Hamilton created dialects that artfully contested the crude or insulting representations of black dialects often found in literature written by non-blacks.

Hamilton possessed the profound ability to tell a story from the perspective of girls and women. *Willie Bea and the Time the Martians Landed* presents a circle of women, sisters, who gather at the family homestead during Halloween. Their kitchen conversation shows women reveling in each other's company and young girls gaining access to a sacred sisterhood by listening in the shadows. *Sweet Whispers, Brother Rush* captures the anguish of a girl-woman who must care for an ill brother as her mother works as a housekeeper, a job that requires her to often be absent. Biracial and multiracial identity is presented in all its complexity in *Arilla, Sun Down, Plain City*, and *Bluish*.

A Little Love is one of the few portraits of disabled teens written by a black author. These teens also explore their sexuality and independence. *White Romance* examines the world of rock music and drugs. *Cousins* and *Second Cousins* capture the sometimes competitive relationships among relatives that can result in tragedy. *Childtimes* experiments with narrative structure as well as ideas about time and shifts among past, present, and future.

Hamilton also reinvigorated the folktale genre. The collection *Her Stories* is a fulfillment of Hamilton's desire to honor the women storytellers in her family and those of her acquaintance. The illustrations by Leo and Diane Dillon that appeared throughout the text were an almost perfect blend of text and illustration. The cover was particularly striking, as black women ranging in color from mahogany to ivory fan out from the stern of a boat. The powerful visual imagery continued with the text as female characters outwit devils, slave owners, and wily animals.

Hamilton was known for the thoughtful essays that she shared with audiences at various conferences such as those sponsored by the American Library Association, International Reading Association, and the National Council of Teachers of English. She challenged her listeners to respect children's abilities to cope with complex ideas and unfamiliar ways of telling stories. She exhorted them to view the "other" and the marginalized in new ways through her notions about parallel cultures. Equally important, she urged them to read literary works that presented a diverse, complex group's "hopescape." Hamilton succeeded in her dream of creating a unique body of literature that entertained, offered hope, educated, and challenged the reader to accept her often innovative style.

BIBLIOGRAPHY

Hamilton, Virginia. "On Being a Black Writer in America." *Lion and the Unicorn* 10 (1986): 15–17.

Hamilton, Virginia. "The Known, the Remembered, and the Imagined: Celebrating Afro-American Folk Tales." *Children's Literature in Education* 18 (Summer): 67–75.

Hamilton, Virginia. "The Mind of a Novel: The Heart of the Book." *Children's Literature Quarterly* 8 (Winter 1983): 10–13.

Mikkelsen, Nina. *Virginia Hamilton.* Detroit: Twayne, 1994.

Muse, Daphne. "The World She Dreamed, Generations She Shared, Visions She Wrote: A Tribute to Virginia Hamilton (1936–2002)." *New Advocate* 15 (Summer 2002): 171–173.

Rochman, Hazel. "The *Booklist* Interview: Virginia Hamilton." *Booklist* 88 (1 February 1992): 1020.

—Violet J. Harris

HANSBERRY, LORRAINE VIVIAN (b. 19 May 1930; d. 12 January 1965), playwright. Lorraine Hansberry was a celebrated black playwright who was born in Chicago, Illinois, and died in New York City at the age of thirty-four after a scant six years in the professional theater. Her first produced play, *A Raisin in the Sun*, has

LORRAINE HANSBERRY. Her play *A Raisin in the Sun* was an immediate success when it was first produced and has become an American classic. (Eva Jessye Collection, Pittsburg State University, Kansas; Special Collections Department, Leonard H. Axe Library.)

become an American classic, enjoying numerous productions since its original presentation in 1959 and many professional revivals during its twenty-fifth anniversary year in 1983–1984. The Broadway revival in 2004 brought the play to a new generation, and earned two Antoinette Perry (Tony) Awards for individual performances. The roots of Hansberry's artistry and activism lie in the city of Chicago, her early upbringing, and her family.

Early Years

Lorraine Vivian Hansberry was the youngest of four children; seven or more years separated her from Mamie, her sister and closest sibling, and two older brothers, Carl Jr. and Perry. Her father, Carl Augustus Hansberry, was a successful real estate broker who had moved to Chicago from Mississippi after completing a technical course at Alcorn College. A prominent businessman, he made an unsuccessful bid for Congress in 1940 on the Republican ticket and contributed large sums to causes supported by the National Association for the Advancement of Colored People (NAACP) and the Urban League. Hansberry's mother, Nannie Perry, was a schoolteacher and later ward committeewoman who had come north from Tennessee after completing teacher training at Tennessee Agricultural and Industrial University. The Hansberrys were at the center of Chicago's black social life and often entertained important political and cultural figures who were visiting the city. Through her uncle, Leo Hansberry, professor of African History at Howard University, Hansberry made early acquaintances with young people from the African continent.

The Hansberry's middle class status did not protect them from the racial segregation and discrimination characteristic of the period, and they were active in opposing it. Restrictive covenants, in which white homeowners agreed not to sell their property to black buyers, created a ghetto known as the "black metropolis" in the midst of Chicago's South Side. Although large numbers of black Americans continued to migrate to the city, restrictive covenants kept the boundaries static, creating serious housing problems. Carl Hansberry knew well the severe overcrowding in the black metropolis. He had, in fact, made much of his money by purchasing large, older houses vacated by the retreating white population and dividing them into small apartments, each one with its own kitchenette. In doing so, he earned the title "kitchenette king." This type of tiny, functional apartment became the setting in *A Raisin in the Sun*, just as the struggle for better housing drove its plot.

Hansberry attended public schools, graduating from Betsy Ross Elementary School and then from Englewood High School in 1947. Breaking with the family tradition of attending southern black colleges, Hansberry chose to attend the University of Wisconsin at Madison, moving from the ghetto schools of Chicago to a predominantly white university. She integrated her dormitory, becoming the first black student to live at Langdon Manor. The years at Madison focused her political views as she worked in the Henry Wallace presidential campaign and in the activities of the Young Progressive League, becoming president of the organization in 1949 during her last semester. Her artistic sensibilities were heightened by a university production of Sean O'Casey's *Juno and the Paycock*. She was deeply moved by O'Casey's ability to universalize the suffering of the Irish without sacrificing specificity and later wrote: "The melody was one that I had known for a very long while. I was seventeen and I did not think then of writing the melody as I knew it—in a different key; but I believe it entered my consciousness and stayed there." She would capture that suffering in the idiom of the Negro people in her first produced play, *A Raisin in the Sun*. In 1950 she left the university and moved to New York City for an education of another kind.

In Harlem she began working on *Freedom*, a progressive newspaper founded by Paul Robeson, and turned the world into her personal university. In 1952 she became associate editor of the newspaper, writing and editing a variety of news stories that expanded her understanding of domestic and world problems. Living and working in the midst of the rich and progressive social, political, and cultural elements of Harlem stimulated Hansberry to begin writing short stories, poetry, and plays. On one occasion she wrote the pageant that was performed to commemorate the *Freedom* newspaper's first anniversary. In 1952, while covering a picket line protesting discrimination in sports at New York University, Hansberry met Robert Barron Nemiroff, a student of Russian Jewish heritage who was attending the university. They dated for several months, participating in political and cultural activities together. They married on 20 June 1953, at the Hansberry home in Chicago. The young couple took various jobs during these early years. Nemiroff was a part-time typist, waiter, Multilith operator, reader, and copywriter. Hansberry left the *Freedom* staff in 1953 in order to concentrate on her writing and for the next three years worked on three plays while holding a series of jobs: tagger in the garment industry, typist, program director at Camp Unity (a progressive, interracial summer program), teacher at the Marxist-oriented Jefferson School for Social Science, and recreation leader for the handicapped.

A sudden change of fortune freed Hansberry from these odd jobs. Nemiroff and his friend Burt d'Lugoff wrote a folk ballad, "Cindy Oh Cindy," that quickly became a hit. The money from that song allowed Hansberry to quit her jobs and devote herself full time to her writing. She began to write *The Crystal Stair*, a play about a struggling black family in Chicago that would eventually become *A Raisin in the Sun*.

Drawing on her knowledge of the working class black tenants who had rented from her father and with whom she had attended school on Chicago's South Side, Hansberry wrote a realistic play with a theme inspired by Langston Hughes. In his poem "Harlem," he asks: "What happens to a dream deferred? . . . Does it dry up like a raisin in the sun? . . . Or does it explode?" Hansberry read a draft of the play to several colleagues. After one such occasion, Phil Rose, a friend who had employed Nemiroff in his music publishing firm, optioned the play for Broadway production. Although he had never produced a Broadway play before, Rose and his coproducer David S. Cogan set forth enthusiastically with their fellow novices on this venture. They approached major Broadway producers, but the "smart money" considered a play about black life to be too risky for Broadway. The only interested producer insisted on directorial and cast choices that were unacceptable to Hansberry, so the group raised the cash through other means and took the show on tour without the guarantee of a Broadway house. Audiences in the tour cities—New Haven, Connecticut, Philadelphia, and Chicago—were ecstatic about the show. A last-minute rush for tickets in Philadelphia finally made the case for acquiring a Broadway theater.

Celebrity

A Raisin in the Sun opened at the Ethel Barrymore Theatre on 11 March 1959 and was an instant success with both critics and audiences. The New York critic Walter Kerr praised Hansberry for reading

the precise temperature of a race at that time in its history when it cannot retreat and cannot quite find the way to move forward. The mood is forty-nine parts anger and forty-nine parts control, with a very narrow escape hatch for the steam these abrasive contraries build up. Three generations stand poised, and crowded, on a detonating-cap (*New York Herald Tribune*, 12 March 1959).

Hansberry became a celebrity overnight. The play was awarded the New York Drama Critics Circle Award in 1959, making Lorraine Hansberry the first black playwright, the

A Raisin in the Sun. Left to right: Ruby Dee, Sidney Poitier, and Diana Sands, in a scene from the first production, 1959. (© Bettmann/Corbis.)

youngest person, and only the fifth woman to win that award.

In 1960 the NBC producer Dore Schary commissioned Hansberry to write the opening segment for a television series commemorating the Civil War. Her subject was to be slavery. Hansberry thoroughly researched the topic. The result was *The Drinking Gourd*, a television play that focused on the effects that slavery had on the families of the slave master and the white poor as well as the slave. The play was deemed too controversial by NBC television executives and, despite Schary's objections, was shelved along with the entire project.

Hansberry was successful, however, in bringing her prize-winning play, *A Raisin in the Sun*, to the screen a short time later. In 1959, a few months after the play opened, she sold the movie rights to Columbia Pictures and began work on drafts of the screenplay, incorporating several new scenes. These additions, which were rejected for the final version, sharpened the play's attack on the effects of segregation and revealed with a surer hand the growing militant mood of black America. After many revisions and rewrites, the film was produced with all but one of the original cast and released in 1961.

In the wake of the play's extended success, Hansberry became a public figure and popular speaker at a number of conferences and meetings. Among her most notable speeches was one delivered to a black writers' conference sponsored by the American Society of African Culture in New York. Written during the production of *A Raisin in the Sun* and delivered on 1 March 1959—two weeks before the Broadway opening—"The Negro Writer and His Roots" is in effect Hansberry's credo. In her speech, Hansberry declared that "all art is ultimately social" and called upon black writers to be involved in "the intellectual affairs of all men, everywhere." As the civil rights movement intensified, Hansberry helped to plan fund-raising events to support organizations such as the Student Nonviolent Coordinating Committee (SNCC). Disgusted with the red baiting of the McCarthy era, she called for the abolition of the House Un-American Activities Committee. Later she criticized President John F. Kennedy's handling of the Cuban missile crisis, arguing that his actions endangered world peace.

In 1961, amid many requests for public appearances, a number of which she accepted, Hansberry began work on several plays. Her next stage production, *The Sign in Sidney Brustein's Window*, appeared in 1964. Before that, however, she finished a favorite project, *Masters of the Dew*, adapted from the Haitian novel by Jacques Romain. A film company had asked her to do the screenplay; however, contractual problems prevented the production from proceeding. The next year, seeking rural solitude, Hansberry purchased a house in Croton-on-Hudson,

forty-five minutes from Broadway, in order to complete work on *The Sign in Sidney Brustein's Window*.

Early in April 1963 Hansberry fainted. Hospitalized at University Hospital in New York City for nearly two weeks, she underwent extensive tests. The results suggested cancer of the pancreas. Despite the progressive failure of her health during the next two years, she continued her writing projects and political activities. In May 1963 she joined the writer James Baldwin, the singers Harry Belafonte and Lena Horne, and other black and white individuals in a meeting in Croton to raise funds for SNCC and a rally to support the southern freedom movement. Although her health was in rapid decline, she greeted 1964 as a year of glorious work. On her writing schedule, in addition to *The Sign in Sidney Brustein's Window*, were *Les Blancs*, *Laughing Boy* (a musical adaptation of the novel), *The Marrow of Tradition*, *Mary Wollstonecraft*, and *Achnaton*, a play about the Egyptian pharaoh. Despite frequent hospitalization and bouts with pain and attendant medical conditions, she completed a photo-essay for a book on the civil rights struggle titled *The Movement: Documentary of a Struggle for Equality* (1964).

In March 1964 she quietly divorced Robert Nemiroff, formalizing the separation that had occurred several years earlier. Only close friends and family had known; their continued collaboration as theater artists and activists had masked the reality of the personal relationship. Those outside their close circle only learned of the divorce when Hansberry's will was read in 1965.

Throughout 1964 hospitalizations became more frequent as Hansberry's cancer spread. In May she left the hospital to deliver a speech to the winners of the United Negro College Fund's writing contest in which she coined the famous phrase, "young, gifted, and black." A month later, she left her sickbed to participate in the Town Hall debate "The Black Revolution and the White Backlash," at which she and her fellow black artists challenged the criticism by white liberals of the growing militancy of the civil rights movement. She also managed to complete *The Sign in Sidney Brustein's Window*, which opened to mixed reviews on 15 October 1964 at the Longacre Theatre. Critics were somewhat surprised by this second play from a woman who had come to be identified with the black liberation movement. Writing about people she had known in Greenwich Village, Hansberry had created a play with a primarily white cast and a theme that called for intellectuals to get involved with social problems and world issues.

Lorraine Hansberry's battle with cancer ended at University Hospital in New York City. She was just thirty-four years old. Her passing was mourned throughout the nation and in many parts of the world. The list of senders of telegrams and cards sent to her family reads like a who's who of the civil rights movement and the American theater.

The Sign in Sidney Brustein's Window closed on the night of her death.

Hansberry left a number of finished and unfinished projects, among them *Laughing Boy*, a musical adapted from Oliver LaFarge's novel; an adaptation of *The Marrow of Tradition* by Charles Chesnutt; a film version of *Masters of the Dew*; sections of a semiautobiographical novel, *The Dark and Beautiful Warriors*; and numerous essays, including a critical commentary written in 1957 on Simone de Beauvoir's *The Second Sex* (a book that Hansberry said had changed her life). In her will, she designated Nemiroff as executor of her literary estate.

Hansberry's reputation continued to grow after her death in 1965 as Nemiroff, who owned her papers, edited, published, and produced her work posthumously. In 1969 he adapted some of her unpublished writings for the stage under the title *To Be Young, Gifted, and Black*. The longest-running drama of the 1968–1969 off-Broadway season, it toured colleges and communities in the United States during 1970–1971. A ninety-minute film based on the stage play was first shown in January 1972.

In 1970 Nemiroff produced on Broadway a new work by Hansberry, *Les Blancs*, a full-length play set in the midst of a violent revolution in an African country. Nemiroff then edited *Les Blancs: The Collected Last Plays of Lorraine Hansberry*, published in 1972 and including *Les Blancs*, *The Drinking Gourd*, and *What Use Are Flowers?*, a short play about the consequences of nuclear holocaust. In 1974 *A Raisin in the Sun* returned to Broadway as *Raisin*, a musical, produced by Robert Nemiroff; it won an Antoinette Perry (Tony) Award.

In 1987, *A Raisin in the Sun*, with original material restored, was presented at the Roundabout Theatre in New York, the Kennedy Center in Washington, DC, and other theaters nationwide. In 1989 this version was presented on national television. The year 2004 saw the first Broadway revival of the play. With the hip-hop star Sean "P. Diddy" Combs in the lead role of Walter Lee, the show attracted a large and diverse audience. For her performance as Lena Younger, Phylicia Rashad won the first Tony for best performance by an actress in a drama ever awarded to an African American woman. Audra McDonald won her fourth Tony for best featured actress for her role as Beneatha.

In March 1988, *Les Blancs*, much of the original script restored, was presented at Arena Stage in Washington, DC, the first professional production in eighteen years.

Hansberry made a significant contribution to American theater, despite the brevity of her theatrical life and the fact that only two of her plays were produced during her lifetime. *A Raisin in the Sun* was more than simply a "first" to be commemorated in history books and then forgotten. The play was the turning point for black artists in the professional theater. Authenticity and candor combined with timeliness to make it one of the most popular plays ever produced on the American stage. The original production ran for 538 performances on Broadway, attracting large audiences of white and black fans alike. Also, in this play and in her second produced play, Hansberry offered a strong opposing voice to the drama of despair. She created characters who affirmed life in the face of brutality and defeat. Walter Younger in *A Raisin in the Sun*, supported by a culture of hope and aspiration, survives and grows; and even Sidney Brustein, lacking cultural support, resists the temptation to despair by a sheer act of will, by reaffirming his link to the human family.

With the growth of women's theater and feminist criticism, Hansberry was rediscovered by a new generation of women in theater. Indeed, a revisionist reading of her major plays reveals that she was a feminist long before the second wave of the women's movement surfaced. The female characters in her plays are pivotal to the major themes. They may share the protagonist role, as in *A Raisin in the Sun*, where Mama is co-protagonist with Walter; or a woman character may take the definitive action, as in *The Drinking Gourd*, in which Rissa, the house slave, defies the slave system and black stereotypes by turning her back on her dying master and arming her son for his escape to the North. In *The Sign in Sidney Brustein's Window*, Sidney is brought to a new level of self-awareness through the actions of a chorus of women—the Parodus sisters. Likewise, the African woman dancer is ever present in Tshemabe Matoeseh's mind in *Les Blancs*, silently and steadily moving him to a revolutionary commitment to his people. Hansberry's portrayal of Beneatha as a young black woman with aspirations to be a doctor and her introduction of abortion as an issue for poor women in *A Raisin in the Sun* signaled early on Hansberry's feminist attitudes. These and other portrayals of women challenged prevailing stage stereotypes of both black and white women and introduced feminist issues to the stage in compelling terms. Documents uncovered beginning in the 1980s revealing Hansberry's homosexuality and sensitivity to homophobic attitudes have further increased feminist interest in her work.

A reprint of *A Raisin in the Sun* and *The Sign in Sidney Brustein's Window*, edited by Robert Nemiroff (1987), contains material restored to both scripts, a foreword by Nemiroff, an appreciation by Frank Rich, and critical essays by Amiri Baraka and John Braine. Hansberry's published works appear in various English language editions as well as in French, German, Japanese, and other languages. The unfinished *Toussaint* appears in *Nine Plays by Black Women*, edited by Margaret B. Wilkerson (1968).

[This entry was originally published in *Notable Women in the American Theatre: A Biographical Dictionary*, edited by A. M. Robinson, V. Roberts, and M. S. Barranger (1989).]

BIBLIOGRAPHY

Anderson, Michael, et al. *Crowell's Handbook of Contemporary Drama*. New York: Crowell, 1971.

Bigsby, C. W. E. *Confrontation and Commitment: A Study of Contemporary American Drama 1959–1966*. London: MacGibbon & Kee, 1967.

Carter, Steven R. *Hansberry's Drama: Commitment amid Complexity*. New York: Penguin, 1991.

Guy-Sheftall, Beverly. "Simone de Beauvoir and *The Second Sex*: An American Commentary." In her *Words of Fire: An Anthology of African-American Feminist Thought*. New York: New Press, 1995.

"Lorraine Hansberry: Art of Thunder, Vision of Light." *Freedomways* 19 (1979).

Matlaw, Myron. *Modern World Drama: An Encyclopedia*. New York: Dutton, 1972.

May, Robin. *A Companion to the Theatre: The Anglo American Stage from 1920*. New York: Hippocrene, 1973.

McGraw-Hill Encyclopedia of World Drama. New York: McGraw-Hill, 1972.

Mitchell, Loften. *Black Drama: The Story of the American Negro in Theatre*. New York: Hawthorn, 1967.

Rigdon, Walter, ed. *Biographical Encyclopaedia and Who's Who of the American Theatre*. New York: Heineman, 1966.

Who's Who of American Women, 1964–1965. Chicago: Marquis, 1963.

Who Was Who in America, 1961–1968. Chicago: Marquis, 1968.

—MARGARET B. WILKERSON

HARLEM RENAISSANCE.

HARLEM RENAISSANCE. In the history of art and culture, some periods glow with a light that illuminates all the rest. Whether we talk about the Mauve Decade, Bloomsbury, or Paris in the 1920s, there is a sense that extraordinary personalities and forces somehow coalesced—with the intangible addition of what we call style—in a way that changed the world. The Harlem Renaissance is one of those periods in America, and its effect has yet to be fully explored.

Langston Hughes always believed that the flowering began when Florence Mills took over Broadway in the black musical *Shuffle Along* in 1921. Within the decade, Ethel Waters would become the highest-paid woman, black or white, on the Broadway stage. Bessie Smith, Alberta Hunter, and the other great blues queens sold millions of records and created a new style of performance. The Lafayette Players, founded by Anita Bush, began to produce serious drama in Harlem, starring black actors. Black writers such as Hughes himself, Zora Neale Hurston, Countee Cullen, James Weldon Johnson, Nella Larsen, Arna Bontemps, Dorothy West, Jean Toomer, and Claude McKay were not only on the lists of some of the best publishing companies in the country but they were also on the A-list for New York's most prestigious literary parties. "In some places," wrote Bontemps, "the autumn of 1924 may have been an unremarkable season. In Harlem, it was like a foretaste of paradise." The literary and artistic paradise

ZORA NEALE HURSTON wrote works that included folklore, anthropology, autobiography, and fiction. She also collaborated with Langston Hughes in creating a play, *Mule Bone*. (© Corbis.)

continued for a decade and a half, and, in music, Harlem was heaven for a long time to come.

Unfortunately, history's perception is that most of the deities in the Harlem firmament were men. It has taken decades to reestablish the importance and value of the many black women who contributed to that shining moment in African American history.

The Origins

People have speculated endlessly about the origins of the Harlem Renaissance. Most agree that the Great Migration—the movement of tens of thousands of black Southerners into the North to find work and escape oppression—had a lot to do with it. Those emigrants from a land of cotton fields, country churches, and lynch mobs brought with them a rich culture of storytelling. They brought the blues. And they brought the experience of being in the majority, even if it was a severely persecuted majority. They knew what it was like to grow up in a black community, with a black preacher, a black teacher, and a black moral leader, and they brought that consciousness with them to the cities of the North. They brought it to Harlem.

Some of it was probably coincidence. It would not have been the first time that a number of remarkably talented people happened to gather within the borders of one city or one neighborhood. One or two wildly gifted writers, a sculptor with a new vision, a musician with a new sound—these would be enough to attract others.

Certainly, the Harlem Renaissance was caused, in part, by a redefining of black culture in America. W. E. B. Du Bois and Alain Locke were, at the time, encouraging African Americans to look to their roots in Africa and in the folk traditions of the American South. They talked about art created by, for, and in the vicinity of black people. Young artists responded, writing about their history as well as their own lives and experiences. They began to turn away from the standards and limitations of European American literature in order to celebrate their own cultural heritage. They also began to write fiercely and with passionate intensity about the oppression of their people.

But other thinkers contributed to the excitement of the times. Ida B. Wells-Barnett was the passionate voice of protest and activism. She continued to provide the yeast of outrage to African America's cultural ferment as she supported Timothy Thomas Fortune in his efforts to resuscitate the National Afro-American League and Marcus Garvey in his Universal Negro Improvement Association. Until she died in 1931, Wells-Barnett constantly reminded the Renaissance that lynchings and riots were still happening around the country and that violence lay always just below the surface of African American culture.

Nannie Helen Burroughs likewise kept things stirred up. Having been put under government surveillance during World War I because of her militancy and her criticism of President Woodrow Wilson's weakness on the lynching issue, she still traveled around the country denouncing all forms of oppression, including African colonialism. She also stressed the strength of African American culture in combating the deleterious effects of continuing racism.

Other women public intellectuals, many of whom had come out of the powerful black women's club movement of the late nineteenth and early twentieth centuries, wrote and spoke with an eloquence and force that they could not have employed only a decade before. And one of the major players of the coming civil rights movement was in Harlem itself. The famous Baker of the Harlem Renaissance is Josephine Baker, who became America's most no-

torious expatriate. But Ella Josephine Baker, who would be instrumental in virtually every action of the civil rights movement of the 1950s and 1960s, including the founding of the Student Nonviolence Coordinating Committee (SNCC), was national director of the Young Negroes Cooperative League in Harlem. She also worked with the Harlem Housewives Cooperative and the NAACP.

Although the Harlem Renaissance has been seen primarily as a literary and artistic movement, it can, with a slight shift, be viewed as part of a greater cultural phenomenon, the emergence in New York City and other urban centers of African Americans as figures of importance. And, although not as visible to the white community as their male counterparts, black women created an intellectual and political basis within the black community for the phenomenon known as the Harlem Renaissance.

The Entertainers

Most studies of this period focus on the writers. It is an understandable approach because of the quality of the work done during the Renaissance. But it is an approach that lends immediately to an undervaluation of the role of black women. A great deal of the cachet of African Americans in New York City during the 1920s derives from entertainers, and the greatest of these were women. This may sound like an overstatement until one looks at the names involved.

This was the era of the blues queens—Bessie Smith, Ma Rainey, Alberta Hunter, and Ethel Waters. They transformed American music and brought the real power of black women into the cultural mainstream for the first time. The first blues recording was made in 1920 by Mamie Smith. It was called "Crazy Blues," and it surprised everyone by selling thousands of copies. This success is said to have been the beginning of the highly lucrative "race records" industry, which later gave birth to rhythm and blues. After Mamie Smith's hit, the other blues queens stepped up to the recording mike and became the stars of American music. Classic blues became the soundtrack for the Harlem Renaissance.

This was also the period of the first black superstar, Florence Mills, whose funeral parade brought out 150,000 people into the streets of Harlem. She emerged on the scene when she took over for the original ingenue in Noble Sissle and Eubie Blake's *Shuffle Along*, which took ragtime onto the Broadway stage and into the consciousness of white audiences. The show made her a star and she went on to do *Plantation Revue* and then, in London, *Dover Street to Dixie*. In England, she was seen as an important artist, for her strangely sweet singing and remarkable dancing. When she returned to New York, Florenz Ziegfeld tried to make her a Follies star, but she refused the opportunity. She was deeply committed to her race and, instead, created an all-black revue. *From Dixie to Broadway* was another hit. Then Mills became the first African American to headline at the Palace Theatre. Finally, she took *Blackbirds of 1926* to London. She pushed herself too hard, however, postponing needed surgery to keep working. She died in New York in 1927, at the age of only thirty-one.

Following on the heels of Mills was a star of a different kind. Where Mills was a diminutive charmer who performed almost entirely onstage, Ethel Waters was a tall, strong-boned blues singer who knew the nightclub circuit like the back of her hand. She was already a minor star when Irving Berlin heard her sing at the Cotton Club in Harlem. He immediately offered her a role in his show *As Thousands Cheer* (1933), writing her four songs. She thus became the first black performer to appear on Broadway in an otherwise all-white show. One of the songs Berlin wrote for her was "Suppertime," in which a woman fixes dinner for her family while she grieves for her husband, who has been lynched that day. Such a powerful musical expression of anti-lynching sentiment would not emerge again until Billie Holiday's rendition of *Strange Fruit* five years later.

After two years in the show, Waters became the biggest black star on Broadway since Mills. She would become even bigger. She continued her success as a singer in clubs, with some of the best bands in the country, and on the musical stage. But she transformed Broadway in 1939 when she performed a dramatic role in Dorothy and Du-Bose Heyward's *Mamba's Daughters*. The first black actress to star on Broadway in a dramatic role, she was a huge success, both critically and popularly. Waters played the role of Hagar with such honesty and power that the critics were stunned, with the sole exception of the influential Brooks Atkinson, critic for the *New York Times*. He did not like the play or Waters's performance in it. But a group of theater professionals disagreed so thoroughly with him that they took out an ad in the *New York Times*. The ad was an extraordinary tribute to Waters's achievement. It was signed by, among others, Judith Anderson, Tallulah Bankhead, Dorothy Gish, Carl Van Vechten, and Burgess Meredith. After reading it, Atkinson went back to see *Mamba's Daughters* again and changed his opinion.

On the club scene, the lesbian singer Gladys Bentley became a cult star. Wearing her trademark tuxedo and top hat and performing in a speakeasy on 133rd Street, she fascinated the intellectual and artistic set of New York City with her obscene parodies of popular songs. The sculptor Isamu Noguchi did a life mask of her. Langston Hughes sang her praises, as did Eslanda Robeson. Bentley even announced to the press her marriage to a white woman lover.

These women brought both black glamour and black soul to New York. It can be argued, with great validity, that they were as important to the popularity of African American culture in the New York City of the 1920s and 1930s as the male writers whose names would become so familiar.

Alongside the Great White Way

In Harlem itself, black women brought theater to the community. During the entire period of the Renaissance, Anita Bush's Lafayette Players presented serious drama to the people of Harlem. Bush was the daughter of a Broadway tailor. After working in the comedies of Bert Williams and George Walker, she became determined to found a company in which she and other black actors would perform without singing, dancing, and mugging. All-black casts brought the best and the most popular plays to the Lafayette Theatre for seventeen years. A great many of the plays were the same plays that were being done on Broadway with all-white casts. They did *The Count of Monte Cristo*, *Dr. Jekyll and Mr. Hyde*, and *Madame X*. They did the Jewish comedy *Potash and Perlmutter*. They did anything and everything that white actors did. They simply did it in Harlem. An article in *Billboard* in August 1921 predicted that black actors would soon be accepted in all areas of theater, including serious drama, and offered as evidence the performances at the Lafayette Theatre. The article went on to report the favorable reactions of a white producer who was "profuse in encomiums," and a white actor who was so thrilled with the company's work that she went backstage to compliment the players. But the important reaction to the Lafayette Players came from the black community. When it became clear that black audiences wanted, needed, and were willing to pay for serious theater, a group of black capitalists formed the Quality Amusement Corporation, which sponsored the Lafayette Players, sent them on tour, and formed black theaters in other cities.

Over the seventeen years of its existence, the Lafayette and its offshoots changed black acting. With a place to develop their skills and talents, black actors began to thrive, at least artistically. And the larger theater world soon heard from such Lafayette Players as Abbie Mitchell, Evelyn Ellis, Evelyn Preer, Edna Thomas, Laura Bowman, and Inez Clough. In 1917 several of the Lafayette Players appeared at the Garden Theatre in a trio of short plays by the white poet Ridgely Torrence—*The Rider of Dreams*, *Granny Maumee*, and *Simon the Cyrenian*.

In American theater histories this show is remembered, when it is remembered at all, for its playwright. The theater critic and historian Emory Lewis called Torrence "the first white playwright who presented blacks with artistry and truth." However, at the time, the show was considered a triumph primarily for the cast. Critics of the time were hugely impressed by the quality of the performances. Robert Benchley, critic for the *Tribune*, raved. George Jean Nathan, leading critic of the day, put *two* of the actors—Opal Cooper and Inez Clough—on his list of the ten best male and the ten best female performers on Broadway that year.

Another black woman who set the theatrical stage for the Harlem Renaissance was Rose McClendon. One of the few black women to win recognition on Broadway, she served on the board of the Theatre Union, which ran the Civic Repertory Theatre on West 14th Street in New York City. She also directed plays for the Harlem Experimental Theatre and organized the Negro People's Theatre, whose first production was a black version of Clifford Odet's social protest play, *Waiting for Lefty*. When Franklin Roosevelt's Works Progress Administration (WPA) initiated the Federal Theatre Project (FTP) to help theater professionals survive the Great Depression, McClendon was appointed codirector of the Negro Unit, with white director John Houseman. She served in that capacity until her death from cancer.

In her honor, the first important black theater in New York since the Lafayette Players was called the Rose McClendon Players. It was founded in 1937, and with her spirit of commitment to excellence in theater and equality for black performers, the modern black theater movement was born. Ossie Davis and Ruby Dee were in the group. So were Jane White, Helen Martin, and others who would have long, distinguished careers in the black theater. The Rose McClendon Players performed for five years. When it folded, several of its members became involved in the founding of the American Negro Theatre, training ground for Rosetta LeNoire, Alice Childress, Isabel Sanford, and Clarice Taylor, as well as for such male stars as Sidney Poitier and Harry Belafonte. The theater produced eighteen plays over the decade of its existence, including Katherine Garrison's *Sojourner Truth*.

The theater's biggest hit was *Anna Lucasta*, a play with an interesting history. It was originally written to be performed by a white cast, dealing as it did with a Polish family. But its author, Philip Yordan, was unable to find a producer to commit to it. Abram Hill, artistic director of the American Negro Theatre, suggested to Yordan that the play could be adapted for an all-black cast. It was, and the production, with Hilda Simms as Anna, was a smash hit in Harlem. Also in the cast was Alice Childress, soon to make her name as one of the first successful black woman playwrights.

There was another step to take, however, in creating a black theater. Black leader W. E. B. Du Bois called for "native drama," plays about black people written by black people.

> The plays of a real Negro theatre must be: *One: About us*. That is, they must have plots which reveal Negro life as it is. *Two: By us*. That is, they must be written by Negro authors who understand from birth and continual association just what it means to be a Negro today. *Three: For us*. That is the theatre must cater primarily to Negro audiences and be supported and sustained by their entertainment and approval. *Fourth: Near us*. The theatre must be in a Negro neighborhood near the mass of ordinary Negro people.
>
> (Du Bois, p. 134)

He backed up his call with the power of the NAACP's *Crisis* magazine, which he edited. With the editor of the National Urban League's *Opportunity* magazine, Charles S. Johnson, he held a contest for one-act plays. The prize would be publication in one of the two magazines and a cash award.

The first contest was held in 1925. That year, two of the three winning plays that appeared in *Crisis* were by women—Ruth Gaines-Shelton's *The Church Fight* and Myrtle Smith Livingston's *For Unborn Children*. Four of the seven *Opportunity* winners were written by women—Zora Neale Hurston's *Colorstruck* and *Spears*, May Miller's *The Bog Guide*, and Eloise Bibb Thompson's *Cooped Up*. In the two years that followed, before the contest was discontinued, awards were won by Eulalie Spence, Marita Bonner, and Georgia Douglas Johnson.

Du Bois also founded the Krigwa Players, a black theater company based in Harlem. Companies of Krigwa Players were formed in other cities as well, and many of the plays performed in the short history of this endeavor were by black women. Mary P. Burrill's *Aftermath* was produced by the New York Krigwa Players and appeared in the David Belasco Little Theatre Tournament in 1928. Three of Eulalie Spence's plays were produced by the theater—*Foreign Mail*, *Fool's Errand*, and *Her*. The first two were published by Samuel French. In Baltimore, the Krigwa Players produced the plays of May Miller and Georgia Douglas Johnson. Many other black women saw their plays produced on the stages of the Krigwa Players during the 1920s.

The Writers

The one woman whose name appears on most lists of Harlem Renaissance writers is Zora Neale Hurston. It is staggering to see the names that are left off such a list, including Dorothy West, Jessie Fauset, Georgia Douglas Johnson, Angelina Weld Grimké, Alice Dunbar-Nelson, Nella Larsen, and many others.

Most of these women did not make the A-list when it came to parties thrown by white patrons for the artists and intellectuals of the Harlem Renaissance. And they did not make the A-list when it came to books written about the Renaissance for decades. Then, in the 1970s, in the wake of the women's movement, critics and historians began to look more closely at their writing. Whole bodies of work were rediscovered and reputations reconstructed.

Hurston was first to find her new audience. During the Renaissance, she had shared some of the spotlight with her friends, who included many of the black male writers

JESSIE REDMON FAUSET, shown here c. 1920, was a multifaceted and influential figure in the Harlem Renaissance. She wrote four novels as well as poetry, essays, and reviews and was a guiding spirit behind *Crisis*, the official publication of the NAACP. (© Corbis.)

She wrote two critically acclaimed novels about the black middle class. Georgia Douglas Johnson, another middle-class black woman, was criticized for her first book of poetry, which did not deal sufficiently with racial issues, and then praised for her second, which did. Some of the same issues arose with poet Anne Spencer, a protégé of James Weldon Johnson. Although Spencer was included in virtually every anthology of black poetry during this period, her poetry was not distinctively racial in character, although she was politically militant in her private life.

Gwendolyn Bennett was part of the backbone of the New Negro movement. As an artist, she exhibited her paintings and illustrated covers for *Crisis* and *Opportunity*. Her poetry was widely read and praised. As assistant editor of *Opportunity*, she wrote a literary gossip column called Ebony Flute. A frequent contributor to both these influential magazines was Marita Bonner, who was part of the "S" Salon that met every week at Georgia Douglas Johnson's. Among her most influential works was the essay "On Being Young–a Woman–and Colored."

In addition to being an important writer of short stories, Dorothy West published a literary magazine, *Challenge*, which promoted Harlem Renaissance writers. It was not until the 1940s that she began to write novels, one reason that she was not given her due for so long as part of the Renaissance.

The Artists

In 1925, Alain Locke edited a book called *The New Negro* in which he declared that black artists had developed no school of Negro art. He asserted that African American artists should do two things. First, they should look toward Africa to explore their "ancestral arts." Second, they should develop the "Negro physiognomy," or physical features, in their work. In fact, Meta Vaux Warrick Fuller had begun doing the first two decades earlier, and May Howard Jackson had been doing the second for almost that long. The idea had grown from the art and was articulated by this critic to inspire black artists.

Meta Vaux Warrick Fuller was born in 1877 in Philadelphia and attended the Pennsylvania Museum School for the Industrial Arts. She studied in Europe, where she was praised and encouraged by Auguste Rodin. When she began having private exhibitions of her work, the Paris press called her the "delicate sculptor of horrors" because of the grotesque nature of her portrayals. The only American artist in one Paris exhibit, she showed her *Head of John the Baptist* and *The Impenitent Thief on the Cross*. She even had a one-woman show sponsored by S. Bing, patron of Aubrey Beardsley, Mary Cassatt, and Henri de Toulouse-Lautrec. But when she returned to the United States, she found few buyers for her work. Gradually, she developed a following among wealthier African Americans, but in 1910

of the time. But she was never interested in the party line. She refused to be defined by either race or gender and seldom talked specifically about "race relations," a subject that did not particularly interest her. She was interested in black people and their lives, their relationships with each other, and their inner struggles. At least part of the reason that white critics and other white people did not find her particularly interesting during her lifetime was that she did not find them of any real interest, either.

Nella Larsen was the first African American to win a creative writing award from the Guggenheim Foundation.

a warehouse containing her tools and sixteen years worth of her work burned to the ground.

Three years later, Fuller created the *Spirit of Emancipation* for the New York celebration of the Emancipation Proclamation. It was a startlingly new conception for the time. As Judith N. Kerr put it, "Fuller had also not chosen to favor the female figure with Caucasian features, indicating her heightened race consciousness." From that time until her death in the 1960s, Fuller created sculptures with powerful African American themes. In 1921, she created *Ethiopia Awakening* for New York City's "Making of America" Festival, a powerful symbol of the African past and the new future for black Americans.

Born the same year as Fuller, in the same city, May Howard Jackson attended the Pennsylvania Academy of Fine Arts and studied with renowned artists for four years. She then married a math teacher and set up her own studio at home. She did not travel to Europe to study the classics, as was common among artists at the time. Instead, she began doing sculptures of the people around her. In her own style, she focused on the many faces of the African American racial mix. At a time when all races were portrayed in the style, and with the features, of the classical tradition, her realistic portrayals of African features were shocking. They were seen as evidence that she was untrained and untalented. This reaction to her work created in Jackson a deep bitterness that would mar her life.

Not many other black women benefited from the interest in African American art that helped a number of black men gain entry into galleries and private collections during this time. But the sculptural tradition established by Fuller and Jackson was continued by Nancy Elizabeth Prophet, Augusta Savage, Beulah Ecton Woodard, and Selma Burke. The painters who came to prominence were Laura Wheeler Waring and Lois Mailou Jones.

Music

At the time of the Harlem Renaissance, concert music was in flux. Just as some black composers were beginning to be taken seriously in the European tradition, the call went out for music that explored the roots of the African American experience. Black woman composers reacted in different ways. Nora Douglas Holt, who began composing just before the ideological shift of the Renaissance, held steadfastly to the position that black popular music forms had no place in serious composition. Florence Price, on the other hand, came along just as ideas and approaches were changing. Her compositions had names such as "Dances in the Canebrakes," "Arkansas Jitter," and "Bayou Dance." Her student Margaret Bonds followed in her footsteps. Undine Smith Moore also worked in the spirit of the Renaissance with choral works such as *Striving after God*, *Mother to Son*, *Hail Warrior*, and *Daniel, Daniel, Servant of the Lord*, most of which were inspired by or arrangements of spirituals. Shirley Graham Du Bois was both a musician and writer. Her musical works included *Little Black Sambo*, a children's opera, and another opera, *Tom Tom*.

One of the most visible black women in music during the Renaissance was Eva Jessye. She came to prominence as choral director of Virgil Thomson's landmark opera *Four Saints in Three Acts*. A few years later, in 1935, George Gershwin chose her as choral director of *Porgy and Bess*. She was also choral director of the all-black film *Hallelujah*, directed by King Vidor in 1927. She arranged spirituals for her Eva Jessye Choir and wrote a folk oratorio, *Paradise Lost and Regained*, and a folk drama, *The Chronicle of Job*.

Personalities

Some black women were a crucial part of the ambience of the Harlem Renaissance even though they did not write, paint, or compose. One of the most colorful of these was A'lelia Walker, daughter of beauty tycoon Madam C. J. Walker. A'lelia created a salon at her home on 136th Street which was dubbed the "Dark Tower" after Countee Cullen's column in *Opportunity*. There, black artists hung their paintings, and writers came to talk about their latest work. Walker also entertained lavishly at the Villa Lewaro, an Italianate home built for her late mother in Irvington-on-Hudson, New York. In addition to black artists and writers such as James Weldon Johnson, Zora Neale Hurston, Langston Hughes, Countee Cullen, Florence Mills, Rudolph Fisher, Charles Gilpin, Bruce Nugent, Aaron Douglas, and Jean Toomer, her guests included European dignitaries and white Americans of influence.

In a different way, Eunice Hunton Carter contributed to the cachet of African Americans in New York during these years. A lawyer in private practice in New York in the early 1930s, she was appointed by Mayor Fiorello La Guardia as secretary of the Committee on Conditions in Harlem after the race riots of 1935. This led to a job with New York County District Attorney William D. Dodge, whereby she began to notice patterns in the testimonies of prostitutes in the magistrate's court. She suspected mob involvement but could not convince Dodge of this, so she went to Special Prosecutor Thomas E. Dewey. He hired her to assist in his investigation of racketeering and organized crime. She was the only woman among the "Twenty Against the Underworld," as the press called them. She was also the only African American on the prosecutorial team. Soon, she was almost as famous as Dewey. Her charisma added to the glow cast by the artists and writers of Harlem.

The Harlem Legend

It was the redefinition of what it means to be an African American that made the Harlem Renaissance a lasting influence instead of just a stylish moment. In the terrible years that were yet to come, when the Jim Crow South defied all modern ideas of humane behavior, African Americans would be sustained and strengthened by a different vision of themselves and their possibilities. The style, however, was very much there. The Cotton Club with its "high yaller" chorus girls. The jazz musicians with their hot music and cool attitudes. The rent parties where a quarter toward someone else's rent could buy you a whole night of food and dancing. Even the celebrities who left—Paul Robeson to Hollywood, Josephine Baker to Paris—somehow remained part of the Harlem legend.

For everyone in Harlem—male or female, old or young—there were two lives. There was the daytime, when people engaged in the dreary, often grim, struggle to survive in a white world. And there was the night, when darkness softened reality. In the night, there were dreams and there was music and there was also the knowledge that often these are the necessities, the real tools of survival. Perhaps that was the great secret of the Renaissance in the end. For, as the poet Claude McKay wrote of Harlem in 1940, "Where can you find so many people in pain and so few crying about it?"

BIBLIOGRAPHY

Benjamin, Tritobia Hayes. Introduction to Visual Arts Volume, *Facts on File Encyclopedia of Black Women in America*. New York: Facts on File, 1997.

Bontemps, Arna, ed. *Harlem Renaissance Remembered*. New York: Dodd, Mead, 1972.

Campbell, Mary. *Harlem Renaissance: Art of Black America*. New York: Abrams, 1987.

Du Bois, W. E. B. "Krigwa Players Little Negro Theatre." *The Crisis* 32 (July 1926): 134–136.

Floyd, Samuel. *Black Music in the Harlem Renaissance: A Collection of Essays*. New York: Greenwood, 1990.

Hine, Darlene Clark, and Kathleen Thompson. *A Shining Thread of Hope: The History of Black Women in America*. New York: Broadway Books, 1998.

Hughes, Langston, and Milton Meltzer. *Black Magic: A Pictorial History of the African-American in the Performing Arts*. New York: Da Capo Press, 1990.

Lewis, David L. *When Harlem Was in Vogue* (1981). New York: Penguin Books, 1997.

Lewis, Emory. *Stages: The Fifty-year Childhood of the American Theatre*. Englewood Cliffs, NJ: Prentice-Hall, 1969.

Lewis, Samella S. *Art: African American*. New York: Harcourt, Brace, Jovanovich, 1994.

Locke, Alain, ed. *The New Negro* (1925). New York: Atheneum, 1992.

McKay, Claude. *Harlem: Negro Metropolis*. New York: E.P. Dutton, 1940.

Roses, Lorraine Elena, and Ruth Elizabeth Randolph. *The Harlem Renaissance and Beyond: Literary Biographies of 100 Black Women Writers, 1900–1945*. Boston: G.K. Hall, 1990.

Schoener, Allon, ed. *Harlem on My Mind: Cultural Capital of Black America, 1900–1968*. New York: Random House, 1969.

Wintz, Cary. *Black Culture and the Harlem Renaissance*. Houston, TX: Rice University Press, 1988.

—KATHLEEN THOMPSON

HARPER, FRANCES ELLEN WATKINS (b. 24 September 1825; d. 22 February 1911), internationally recognized journalist and the nineteenth century's most prolific African American novelist and best-loved African American poet, known as the "bronze muse." For sixty-eight years, Harper wrote, recited, and published poetry and fiction, essays, and letters, all designed to delight and to teach people how to live lives of high moral purpose and dedicated social service.

But the publication of over a dozen books and innumerable poems, essays, and stories was only a part of her efforts to work for what she called "a brighter coming day." Harper was an active member of the Underground Railroad, one of the first African American women to be hired as an abolitionist lecturer, a founder of the American Woman Suffrage Association, a member of the national board of the Women's Christian Temperance Union, and an executive officer of the Universal Peace Union. She was a founding member of the National Association of Colored Women in 1896, the director of the American Association of Educators of Colored Youth, and a tireless worker for the African Methodist Episcopal Church and the National

FRANCES HARPER was—among other things—a member of the Underground Railroad, an abolitionist, a renowned journalist, a poet, a suffragist, and a founding member of the National Assocation of Colored Women. This print is captioned "Mrs. F. E. W. Harper, author and lecturer." (Ohio Historical Society: The African-American Experience in Ohio.)

Colored Women's Congress. By word and by deed, she became such a symbol of empowering and empowered womanhood that women across the nation organized F. E. W. Harper Leagues or named local chapters of national organizations after her, like the many Frances E. Harper Women's Christian Temperance Unions. She was judged a "Woman of Our Race Most Worthy of Imitation," listed in *Daughters of America; or, Women of the Century*, and was included in *Patriots of the American Revolution*. In his 1911 memorial tribute, the president of the Universal Peace Union, Alfred H. Love, reported that she had "acquired the title of 'Empress of Peace and Poet Laureate.' "

Frances Ellen Watkins was born to free parents in the slave city of Baltimore, Maryland, but by the age of three she was an orphan. It was a loss to which she was never reconciled. In a letter to a friend many years later, she wrote: "Have I yearned for a mother's love? The grave was my robber. Before three years had scattered their blight around my path, death had won my mother from me. Would the strong arm of a brother have been welcome? I was my mother's only child." In comparison with the majority of black Americans of that time, however, Watkins lived a privileged life. She was reared by relatives and attended the prestigious William Watkins Academy for Negro Youth, an institution founded by her uncle and noted for its emphasis upon biblical studies, the classics, and elocution, as well as for the political leadership and social service of its graduates. As a young woman, Watkins was noted for her industry and intelligence. By the age of fourteen, she had acquired an education superior to that of most nineteenth-century women of any color or class in the United States. She had gained a reputation locally as a writer and a scholar, but when she left the academy, the best employment she could obtain was as a seamstress and babysitter for the owners of the local bookstore.

Baltimore was never a comfortable place for free black people to live, and by 1850 it had become perilous indeed. When her uncle closed his school and moved his family to Canada, Watkins moved to Ohio and became the first female faculty person at the newly established Union Seminary, the precursor to what is now Wilberforce University. In his annual report of 1851, principal John M. Brown noted that "Miss Watkins . . . has been faithful to her trust, and has manifested in every effort a commendable zeal for the cause of education; and a sacrificing spirit, so that it may be promoted." After Union Seminary, she taught in Little York, Pennsylvania. Then, in 1853, she moved to Philadelphia in order to devote herself entirely to the abolitionist cause. The exact nature of her involvement there is not known, but it is known that she lived with the William Still family, whose home was the main depot of the Philadelphia Underground Railroad. She frequented the local antislavery offices, where she learned

both the theory and practice of that organization, and she published several poems and essays in the *Christian Recorder*; Frederick Douglass's paper, the *Liberator*; and other periodicals.

By 1854 Watkins was in New Bedford, Massachusetts, lecturing on antislavery and equal rights and, shortly thereafter, was employed by the Maine Anti-Slavery Society as a traveling lecturer. Watkins's travels took her throughout New England and southern Canada and as far west as Detroit and Cincinnati. She became a highly popular speaker and earned accolades from journalists, who applauded her highly articulate and "fiery" speeches yet reported her delivery as "marked by dignity and composure" and "without the slightest violation of good taste." Watkins often incorporated her own poetry into her lectures. This, combined with her regular publication in various newspapers and magazines, helped to create her national reputation as a poet. Thus, when *Poems on Miscellaneous Subjects* was published in 1854, it was printed in both Boston and Philadelphia, sold over ten thousand copies in three years, and was enlarged and reissued in 1857. Most likely it was her considerable contribution to the antislavery efforts that has made many scholars refer to her as an abolitionist poet, but this volume, and all of her subsequent collections, contained poems on a variety of subjects. In addition to well-known antislavery poems such as "The Slave Mother," "The Fugitive's Wife," and "The Slave Auction," the poems in *Poems on Miscellaneous Subjects* deal with issues such as religion, heroism, women's rights, black achievement, and temperance. Some of the poems are responses to contemporary writers such as Harriet Beecher Stowe and Charles Dickens. Some are reinterpretations of Bible stories. Others comment on events such as the murder of Elijah Lovejoy in 1837, the Methodist church's expulsion of one of its ministers because of his antislavery stance, and the news report about a slave in Tennessee who was beaten to death because he would not testify about an escape attempt by other slaves.

The major themes of Harper's early writing and lectures are those that she expounded throughout her career: personal integrity, Christian service, and social equality. Far from repeating homilies and slogans, however, the full corpus of her work reveals a unique blend of idealism and pragmatism, faith and philosophy. Though she consistently wrote of being "saved by faith," of looking for "light in darkness," and of believing that "the pure in heart shall see God," she also spoke crisply, even stridently, about the need for mass political action, the virtues of civil disobedience and economic boycotts, and the occasional necessity for physical confrontation. She argued that it was not enough to express sympathy without taking action. According to the Philadelphia press, she was one of the most liberal and able advocates of her day for the Underground Railroad and the slave. She was a longtime friend and colleague to activists such as Sojourner Truth, Susan B. Anthony, Frederick Douglass, and Henry Highland Garnet, and she remained a staunch and public supporter of John Brown after the failure of his raid on the Harpers Ferry arsenal in 1859. Her personal hero was Moses. In the serialization of her long dramatic poem *Moses: A Story of the Nile* (1869), she commented, "I like the character of Moses," because "he is the first disunionist we read about in the Jewish scriptures."

Hers was neither an assimilationist nor a separationist creed; Watkins preferred education over violence. She believed, as the title of one of her early essays declared, "We Are All Bound Up Together." The burdens of one group were "The Burdens of All" and, as the poem of that name makes clear, without interracial cooperation, no group will be spared:

The burdens will always be heavy,
The sunshine fade into night,
Till mercy and justice shall cement
The black, the brown and the white.

Yet Watkins recognized the contradictions and complexities of issues and was not afraid to take controversial stands or to compromise when necessary. For example, she worked assiduously with the American Equal Rights Association, but when the racism of Elizabeth Cady Stanton, Susan B. Anthony, and other white feminists became apparent in their disparaging remarks about black men, she sided against them, urged the passage of the Fifteenth Amendment allowing blacks to vote even though it excluded women, and ultimately contributed to the dissolution of that group and the formation of the American Woman Suffrage Association. Watkins made her position widely known. She believed in equal rights for all, but if there had to be a choice between rights for black Americans and rights for women, then she would not encourage any black woman to put a single straw in the way to prevent the progress of black men. She took this stance even though she also argued that her own close observation had shown that women are the movers in social reform, that while men talk about changes, the women are implementing them.

In 1860 Watkins married Fenton Harper, a widower with three children. They moved to a farm outside Columbus, Ohio, and they had a daughter, Mary. Marriage and family responsibilities left her little time to lecture or to write, but during the Civil War years Frances Harper did continue to speak out and to publish occasionally. Fenton Harper died in 1864 and that same year Frances returned to full-time lecturing. For the next several years, she traveled continuously throughout the North and in every southern state except Texas and Arkansas, lecturing and working for the Reconstruction effort. Papers throughout the nation advertised her appearances, reported on her travels, and published her letters about her experiences. Despite her hectic schedule, Harper did some of her most experimental writing in the postbellum years. In 1869 she published a serialized novel, *Minnie's Sacrifice*, in the *Christian Recorder*. In *Moses: A Story of the Nile*, she retells the Old Testament version of the Hebrews' Egyptian captivity and exodus. *Sketches of Southern Life* (1872), a pioneering effort in African American dialect and folk characters that narrates the story of slavery and Reconstruction through a series of poems told by "Aunt Chloe" is considered by many critics to be her most innovative and best literary contribution. In 1873 Harper began writing for the *Christian Recorder* a series of fictionalized essays called "Fancy Etchings." Using a cast of characters whose conversations upon current events and social mores served to expose the issues and propose solutions, Harper pioneered the journalistic genre that others such as Langston Hughes were to make popular a half century later.

Her experimentation with new literary techniques supplemented but did not replace her preference for lyrical ballads. Nor did her writing detract from her social involvement. In 1871 Harper arranged for the publication of the twentieth edition of *Poems on Miscellaneous Subjects* and of the first collection of her published poetry since 1857, a volume simply titled *Poems*. About that time, she bought a house in Philadelphia, and 1006 Bainbridge became her address until she died. She had become a homeowner, but Harper was rarely at home. She was in great demand as a speaker for lecture series and as a delegate to numerous conventions. She helped develop Sunday schools and Young Men's Christian Association groups in the black community and worked for the rehabilitation of juvenile delinquents, as well as the security of the aged and infirm. In 1873 she became superintendent of the Colored Section of the Philadelphia and Pennsylvania Woman's Christian Temperance Union, and in 1883 she became national superintendent of work among blacks. In this capacity she tried to help those who wished to join the white groups and those who preferred to organize themselves separately. For Harper it was a matter of coalition building. She recognized and did not apologize for racism among some of the individuals with whom African Americans might need to affiliate but declared this a "relic . . . from the dead past." Her comments in "The Woman's Christian Temperance Union and the Colored Woman" (written for the January 1888 edition of the *African Methodist Episcopal Church Review*) are typical of her stance on this issue. In writing about the southern white women who would not work in harmony with black women, Harper satirizes their pretentiousness and makes it clear that, in failing to acknowledge their common interests, these women are not only risking their political future but also their Christian rewards:

> Let them remember that the most ignorant, vicious and degraded voter outranks, politically, the purest, best and most cultured woman in the South, and learn to look at the question of Christian affiliation on this subject, not in the shadow of the fashion of this world that fadeth away, but in the light of the face of Jesus Christ. And can any one despise the least of Christ's brethren without despising Him?
>
> (p. 316)

On issues of joint concern, Harper believed in and worked with coalitions, but her priorities were always with the progress and elevation of African Americans. Two of her serials, *Sowing and Reaping: A Temperance Story* (1876–1877), whose title says it all, and *Trial and Triumph* (1888–1889), a story about the black middle class during the post-Reconstruction period, were written to that end. It was *Iola Leroy; or, Shadows Uplifted* (1892), a work that the *African Methodist Episcopal Church Review* called the crowning effort of her life, which became her best-known novel. Weaving her story from threads of fact and fiction, Harper wrote to correct the record on slavery and Reconstruction, to inspire African Americans to be proud of their past and diligent in their work toward a greater future, and to persuade all Americans that a stronger sense of justice and a more Christlike humanity was essential to the peace and prosperity of the United States. Incorporating the patterns of antebellum slave narratives and of novels such as William Wells Brown's *Clotel* (1853), Frank J. Webb's *The Garies and Their Friends* (1857), and Albion W. Tourgée's *The Royal Gentleman* (1881) and *Bricks without Straw* (1880), while refuting the themes of works such as Thomas Nelson Page's *In Ole Virginia* (1887), Harper hoped to demonstrate yet again the utility of beauty. *Iola Leroy* appears to have been Harper's last long literary project. After that work, she published at least five collections of poetry: *The Sparrow's Fall and Other Poems* (c. 1894), *Atlanta Offering: Poems* (1895), *The Martyr of Alabama and Other Poems* (c. 1895), *Poems* (1900), and *Light beyond the Darkness* (n.d.). However, these are generally rearrangements of previously published volumes supplemented by previously uncollected works.

At the beginning of the twentieth century, Harper declared the beginning of a "woman's era" and clearly intended to be a part of that brighter coming day. She traveled less and published infrequently, but her counsel and her concern continued to be eagerly sought. During her last years, Harper was often sick. Believing that, because of her failing health and her old age, she would not be able to support herself, many people offered her a place to live and continuing care. Always, Harper gently but firmly declined, saying that she had always been independent, that she loved her liberty, and that she would support herself without charity, as she had always done.

Harper died 22 February 1911. Her funeral was held at the First Unitarian Church in Philadelphia. She is buried in Eden Cemetery. Her record stands as a testimony to the strength, courage, and vision of African American women who wrote and worked for a brighter coming day. In *Sowing and Reaping*, Harper describes one of her characters as "a firm believer in the utility of beauty." Had she been talking about herself, she could not have chosen a more apt phrase.

BIBLIOGRAPHY

Bacon, Margaret Hope. "One Great Bundle of Humanity: Frances Ellen Watkins Harper (1825–1911)." *Pennsylvania Magazine of History and Biography* (January 1989).

Carby, Hazel V. *Reconstructing Womanhood: The Emergence of the Afro-American Woman Novelist*. New York: Oxford University Press, 1987.

Christian, Barbara. *Black Woman Novelists: The Development of a Tradition, 1892–1976*. Westport, CT: Greenwood Press, 1980.

Daniels, Theodora Williams. "The Poems of Frances E. W. Harper." Master's thesis, Howard University, 1937.

Filler, Louis. "Frances Ellen Watkins Harper." In *Notable American Women*, vol. 2, edited by Edward T. James. Cambridge, MA: Belknap Press, Harvard University Press, 1971.

Harper, Frances Ellen Watkins. "The Woman's Christian Temperance Union and the Colored Woman." *African Methodist Episcopal Church Review* 4.8 (January 1888).

Harris, Trudier, and Thadious Davis, eds. *Afro-American Writers before the Harlem Renaissance*. Vol. 50 of *Dictionary of Literary Biography*. Detroit: Gale, 1986.

Logan, Rayford W., and Michael R. Winston, eds. *Dictionary of American Negro Biography*. New York: Norton, 1982.

Love, Alfred H. "Memorial Tribute to Mrs. Frances E. W. Harper." *Peacemaker and Court of Arbitration*, June–July 1911.

McDowell, Deborah E. "The Changing Same: Generational Connections and Black Women Novelists." *New Literary History* (Winter 1987).

Redding, J. Saunders. *To Make a Poet Black* (1939). Ithaca, NY: Cornell University Press, 1988.

Still, William. *The Underground Rail Road* (1872). Chicago: Johnson Publishing, 1970.

Washington, Mary Helen, ed. *Invented Lives: Narratives of Black Women, 1860–1960*. Garden City, NY: Anchor Press, 1987.

Williams, Kenny J. *They Also Spoke: An Essay on Negro Literature in America, 1787–1930*. Nashville, TN: Townsend Press, 1970.

—FRANCES SMITH FOSTER

HARRIS, BARBARA (b. 12 June 1930), religious leader, civil rights activist. Barbara Clementine Harris was born in Philadelphia and spent her formative years receiving her religious education at Saint Barnabas Church. While attending the Philadelphia High School for Girls, Harris established a young adults group at Saint Barnabas. The organization quickly became the largest youth group in the city.

BARBARA C. HARRIS, the first woman to become a bishop in the Episcopal church. She was ordained in 1989. (Photograph by Robert Burgess, from Episcopal Diocese of Washington.)

After graduating from high school in 1948, Harris took a position with Joe V. Baker and Associates, a black-owned public relations firm. Her responsibilities included editing a publication that promoted historically black colleges representing white companies in predominantly black communities. She performed her duties so effectively that, after ten years of employment, she became president of the firm, a position she enjoyed until 1968, when she assumed the head position of Sun Oil Company's community relations department.

Although Harris achieved career success, she continued her activism within the church. She participated in the Dismas Society, a group formed to visit and befriend prison inmates and sometimes conducted religious services for them. Harris participated in this voluntary program for the next fifteen years. She also served as a board member of the Pennsylvania Prison Society. The lack of activism among the congregants at Harris's church led her to reconsider her affiliation. After receiving the blessings

of the rector, Harris left Saint Barnabas to join the Church of the Advocate, a center for grassroots mobilization.

Located in North Philadelphia, the Church of the Advocate was led by the Reverend Paul Washington, a rector known for his political activism. His church provided transportation to the famous march in Selma, Alabama, where Harris and other members of the congregation joined Martin Luther King Jr. Three years later, in 1968, congregants invited members of the Black Panthers to a convention in the organization's honor. That same year, Harris lobbied for the inclusion of women in a newly formed association of black Episcopal ministers called the Union of the Black Clergy, later changed to the Union of Black Episcopalians, following the acceptance of women such as Barbara Harris. These extracurricular activities did not prevent Harris from serving in the vestry, volunteering at a soup kitchen, or helping to desegregate an orphanage, though they did reaffirm her commitment to social justice and to the church, her spiritual and political base.

In 1974 Harris protested against the prohibition against women serving as ordained priests. This gender discrimination led the Philadelphia native to contemplate becoming a priest, as indeed she did, in 1980. Before attaining this position, Harris had compiled an impressive résumé. She attended Villanova University from 1977 to 1979 and the Urban Theology Unit in Sheffield, England. In 1979 she was ordained a deacon, after which she underwent training for the position at the Church of the Advocate, before finally becoming a priest. From 1980 to 1984 Harris served as a priest-in-charge at Saint Augustine-of-Hippo in Norristown, Pennsylvania, and then attended Hobart and William Smith Colleges in 1981. She served as a prison chaplain while also working in small parishes. Harris used her position as executive director of the Episcopal Church's publishing company and the Church's publication, *The Witness*, as vehicles for social change and protest. Within the pages of *The Witness*, Harris condemned the firebombing of abortion clinics and advocated on behalf of people suffering from Acquired Immune Deficiency Syndrome (AIDS). Her advocacy also extended to African Americans and other ethnic minorities, women, and the impoverished.

Harris sought to ascend in the religious hierarchy, and her progress was aided by participants at the Lambeth Conference, a meeting of the Anglican order held once a decade. Conference attendants passed a resolution in 1976 to allow the ordination of female bishops. In 1989 the Massachusetts Episcopal diocese nominated Harris. Tremendous controversy arose over her leftist views and her lack of a traditional education, but the dispute was inspired at least in part by her race and gender. Harris was, however, confirmed as a bishop. She became a symbol of gender equality in Christianity as a whole. During her thirteen-year tenure, Harris focused on social issues and reconciliation. She retired on 1 November 2002.

BIBLIOGRAPHY

"Barbara Harris: A Spiritual First!" The African American Registry. http://www.aaregistry.com/african_american_history/1196/Barbara_Harris_a_spi.

"History-making Bishop Barbara Harris Retires." *The Christian Century*, 20 November 2002.

Rosellini, Lynn. "The First of the 'Mitered Mamas': Bishop Barbara Harris Doesn't Even Want to Be One of the Boys." *U.S. News and World Report*, 19 June 1989.

—DAWNE Y. CURRY

HARRIS, MARCELITE JORDON (b. 6 January 1943); soldier, political appointee. Marcelite Jordon Harris, a graduate of Spelman College in Atlanta, Georgia, served as a White House aide to President Jimmy Carter. She was also the first and only black woman to earn the rank of general in the United States Air Force. While the native Texan may not have been eligible for the title of Georgia's "favorite daughter," Atlanta Mayor Andrew Young was impressed enough to declare a Marcelite J. Harris Day on 30 May 1988. She was presented with the key to the city of Detroit in 1990. The city of Houston, Texas, designated 11 February 1991 as Marcelite J. Harris Day. Marcelite J. Harris made it to the top of her field and in the process accumulated a succession of firsts.

Marcelite Jordon was born in Houston, Texas. She earned a BA in Speech and Drama from Spelman College in 1964 and a BS in Business Management from the University of Maryland in 1986. After teaching in the Head Start program in 1964 and 1965, Harris joined the U.S. Air Force. Her initial assignments in administration were unchallenging, so she applied for the maintenance specialty hoping to repair airplanes. After two unsuccessful attempts, Harris was admitted into the military occupational specialty of maintenance. She was the first woman aircraft maintenance officer in the U.S. Air Force. Then, in December 1988, Harris became the first female wing commander of the Air Training Command at Keesler Air Force Base in Gulfport, Mississippi. The air force school at this command trained thousands from all branches of the military in computer science, communications, avionics, electronics, and air traffic control. To bring her own training up to date, Harris attended Central Michigan University, the University of Maryland, Harvard University, and the National Defense Institute, among others.

General Harris was a highly decorated officer, receiving the Air Force Commendation Medal with oak leaf clusters, the Presidential Unit Citation, the Air Force Commendation Unit Award with "V" device and eight oak leaf clusters, and the Republic of Vietnam Gallantry Cross with Palm.

She was also recognized with many civilian honors, including the Woman of the Year award from the National Organization of Tuskegee Airmen. She was honored for contributions to the Department of Defense by the National Political Congress of Black Women and as Black Woman of Courage by the National Federation of Black Women Business Owners. She also received the Ellis Island Medal of Honor.

At the time of her retirement in 1997, Harris was the highest-ranking female officer in the air force. In 2002 she accepted the challenging position of chief of staff to the chancellor of the New York Public Schools, continuing the tradition of her family's involvement with education.

BIBLIOGRAPHY

Darby, Joe. "Woman Rises High in the Air Force." *New Orleans Times Picayune*, 4 December 1988.

Kertes, Tom. "Gen. Marcelite Harris, Chief of Staff, Dept. of Ed." *Spotlight on Schools*, December 2002.

"Marcelite J. Harris." U*X*L Biographies. U*X*L, 2003. Detroit: Gale, 2004.

—LINDA ROCHELLE LANE

HARRIS, PATRICIA ROBERTS (b. 31 May 1924; d. 23 March 1985), first African American woman to serve as a U.S. cabinet secretary. Honored in 2000 with a postal stamp bearing her portrait, the politician and civil rights advocate Patricia Roberts Harris was a leader in trying to bring about improvements and progress for disadvantaged people. Her career culminated in being named the secretary of Housing and Urban Development (HUD) by President Jimmy Carter in 1977.

Patricia Roberts was born in Mattoon, Illinois, to Bert and Hildren Roberts. She and her brother were raised by their mother after her father left the family when she was still a young child. Racked by economic hardships, Roberts's mother knew that education was the means to gaining a better life and continually stressed its importance to her daughter. Roberts followed her mother's advice, and after finishing her secondary education in Chicago, Roberts entered Howard University's School of Liberal Arts in 1941, from which she graduated summa cum laude four years later. While at Howard she participated in civil rights sit-ins aimed at desegregating the Little Palace Cafeteria in Washington, DC.

After completing her studies, Roberts returned to Chicago and began working for the Young Women's Christian Association and then became executive director of Delta Sigma Theta sorority. She also met and married William Beasly Harris, an attorney. With his encouragement, she decided to attend law school at George Washington University in 1957. Her stellar performance there resulted in her graduating at the top of her class in 1960.

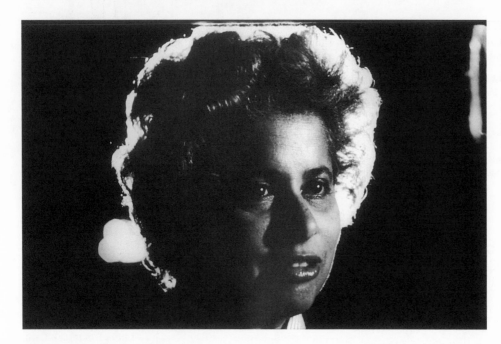

PATRICIA ROBERTS HARRIS, shown here at a women's caucus during the Democratic National Convention, New York City, 1980, had an outstanding academic and political career. (© Bettye Lane.)

After graduating, Harris joined the appeals and research staff of the criminal division of the U.S. Department of Justice and then in 1961 began working as a part-time law lecturer at Howard. By 1963 she had been promoted to a full-time position, making her one of two women on Howard's law faculty. From 1965 to 1967 she went on leave from Howard to accept an appointment by President Lyndon Johnson to serve as ambassador to Luxembourg. Her efforts while there earned her the Order of the Oaken Crown for diplomatic service. Upon her return to the United States she worked full time at Howard and served as an alternate U.S. delegate to the twenty-first and twenty-second General Assemblies of the United Nations and as the alternate to the twentieth Plenary Meeting of the Economic Community of Europe.

In 1969 Harris was appointed dean of Howard University School of Law, a position she held for only a month because of student and faculty conflicts. Afterward she worked for the Washington, DC–based legal firm of Fried, Frank, Harris, Shriver & Kampleman. In 1977, after eight years of private practice, she accepted an appointment by President Jimmy Carter as secretary of Housing and Urban Development (HUD). During the Senate confirmation hearings for the position held in 1976, she was questioned as to whether she knew anything about the poor. Her response appeared in every major newspaper in the country:

> You do not understand who I am. . . . I am a black woman, the daughter of a Pullman car waiter. I am a black woman who even eight years ago could not buy a house in parts of the

District of Columbia. I didn't start out as a member of a prestigious law firm, but as a young woman who needed a scholarship to go to school. If you think I have forgotten that, you are wrong.

As secretary of HUD Harris installed a "new order" tilting toward cities and poor people. John F. Bauman characterized Harris as a strong-willed and gifted individual whose goal was to use her post to make the urban agency a servant of the inner-city poor rather than a tool of the building industry, which dominated HUD at that time. As she stated in *From Tenements to the Taylor Homes*, Harris considered housing as "the single most important physical component of national urban policy." Her vision was for HUD to lead urban neighborhood revitalization, end the concentrated clusters of poor people, and promote rehabilitation by preserving existing housing and making cities a reasonable alternative to suburban living. She fought for the resources to enlarge the number of certified Section 8 (government subsidized) housing units, to expand the Section 312 housing rehabilitation program, and to modernize public housing.

After Harris had served as HUD secretary for three years, President Carter named her secretary of the Department of Health, Education, and Welfare, a position she filled until the arrival of the Reagan administration in 1982. That year she ran for mayor of Washington, DC, but was defeated by Marion S. Barry. In 1983 she joined the faculty of George Washington University. She taught there for less than two years before dying of cancer on 23 March 1985. In President Carter's tribute to her he remarked that she was "a fine lady and Cabinet officer, sensitive to the needs of others and an able administrator . . . an inspiration to . . . everyone who knew her."

BIBLIOGRAPHY

Bauman, John F., Roger Biles, and Kristin M. Szylvian, eds. *From Tenements to the Taylor Homes: In Search of Urban Housing Policy in Twentieth-Century America*. University Park: Pennsylvania State University Press, 2000. Chapter 21 contains a discussion and critique of the Carter-Harris housing policies.

"Her Stamp on History." *Jet*, 1 November 1999, 4. Brief article about Harris's inclusion in the U.S. Postal Service's Black Heritage stamp series in 2000.

Obituary. "Patricia R. Harris, Carter Aide, Dies." *New York Times*, 24 March 1985.

"Patricia Harris." *African American Biographies* 2 (1994): 328–330.

"Patricia Roberts Harris." *DISCovering Multicultural America*. Detroit: Gale Research, 1996.

—MONA E. JACKSON

HARSH, VIVIAN GORDON (b. 27 May 1890; d. 17 August 1960), librarian and historian. She was called "the Lieutenant" by some of her colleagues and a taskmaster by many of the young people who did their research at the Chicago Public Library branch she headed. Yet Vivian G. Harsh was revered by a generation of prominent black writers and scholars. She was eulogized as "the historian who never wrote," yet she succeeded in building one of the most important research collections on black history and literature in the United States.

Vivian Gordon Harsh grew up in the world of Chicago's Old Settlers, the tightly knit community of pioneer black families in the city. The year after she graduated from Wendell Phillips High School on Chicago's South Side, Harsh began working for the only employer she would ever have, the Chicago Public Library. She started as a junior clerk in December 1909, rising slowly through the ranks during her first fifteen years of service. By 1921 she had graduated from Simmons College Library School in Boston, and on 26 February 1924, she became the first African American appointed as a branch librarian for the Chicago Public Library.

In the late 1920s George Cleveland Hall, then chief of staff at Provident Hospital and one of the founding members of the Association for the Study of Negro Life and History headed by Carter G. Woodson, began pressing the Chicago Public Library to open a branch in the rapidly expanding South Side black community. Hall convinced the philanthropist Julius Rosenwald to donate land for the branch, but Hall died before construction was completed.

On 18 January 1932, the building, named the George Cleveland Hall branch, was opened to the public with Vivian G. Harsh as its first head librarian. Harsh had been active in the Association for the Study of Negro Life and History since the mid-1920s, a time when the first Chicago

VIVIAN HARSH was a pioneering bibliophile and collector. The Vivian G. Harsh Collection of Afro-American History and Literature, Chicago Public Library, is named in her honor. (Austin/Thompson Collection, from Woodson Regional Library, Chicago.)

celebrations of Negro History Week sparked widespread community interest in the topic.

Opening day created a sensation in the community as thousands flocked to see the new library. In its holdings was a small but significant collection of books on black history and literature, which Harsh called the Special Negro Collection. Even before the opening of the library, Harsh had received a fellowship from the Rosenwald Foundation to supplement her studies at the Graduate Library School of the University of Chicago with travels to other black history collections. Harsh began to collect rare books, pamphlets, and documents on her journeys. Among the first donations to the Special Negro Collection were three hundred books from the library of Dr. Charles

Bentley, a Chicago dentist and one of the founders of the Niagara Movement.

Aided by the Hall branch children's librarian, Charlemae Hill Rollins, Harsh tirelessly expanded the collection through subsequent Rosenwald Foundation grants, donations from supportive patrons, and her own purchases. The work continued throughout the 1930s, despite persistent antagonism from the Chicago Public Library's administration, which did not believe that public funds should be expended on such a project.

As the collection's reputation spread, the library became a meeting place for young black writers and artists. The Works Progress Administration's (WPA) Federal Writers Project launched a study called "The Negro in Illinois." Headed by Arna Bontemps; the library served as its unofficial headquarters. Many young scholars were attracted to the library's "Book Review and Lecture Forum," begun by Harsh in 1933. Its semimonthly meetings continued for twenty years and featured an impressive array of black speakers, including Richard Wright, Langston Hughes, Zora Neale Hurston, Arna Bontemps, Gwendolyn Brooks, Horace Cayton, William Attaway, Margaret Walker, Alain Locke, and St. Clair Drake.

By the 1940s the Hall Branch library had taken its place among the constellation of black cultural, political, and intellectual institutions clustered in the South Side community. Fiction writers and poets, social scientists and artists, musicians and journalists all participated in the activities coordinated by Harsh. The library served as one of the centers for a cultural flowering later known as the Chicago Renaissance.

Harsh encouraged the writers who spoke at the forum to help build the Special Negro Collection. Langston Hughes, a regular visitor to the collection in the 1940s, donated the typescripts and galley proofs of his autobiographical work *The Big Sea.* When Richard Wright's *Native Son* was published, he returned to the library to present Harsh with an inscribed copy, and he credited the collection with enriching his knowledge of the black experience. Arna Bontemps, faced with the shutdown of the Federal Writers Project in 1942, gave Harsh nearly one hundred boxes of research from the unfinished "Negro in Illinois" study.

Throughout the 1930s and 1940s Harsh was active in community and professional organizations. She served on the board of the Parkway Community Center and participated in the work of the National Association for the Advancement of Colored People, the Young Men's Christian Association, and the Young Women's Christian Association, and was a member of the influential Sixth Grace Presbyterian Church. She continued to work in the Association for the Study of Negro Life and History, and played a central role in the organization's 1936 convention, held in Chicago. After a serious illness and a period of depression, Harsh retired on 10 November 1958. She had never married and had no children, yet when she died two years later, her funeral was crowded with friends and former library patrons.

In 1970 the Chicago Public Library renamed the Special Negro Collection as the Vivian G. Harsh Collection of Afro-American History and Literature. By 1975 it had moved to the new Carter G. Woodson Regional Library, where a large photograph of Harsh hung near one of Woodson. The collection grew to some seventy thousand volumes, with important holdings of rare black journals and newspapers and an outstanding collection of archival materials on Illinois black history.

As a black bibliophile and collector, Harsh's achievements complement the work of Arthur Schomburg, Jesse Moorland, and other pioneers in the field. Even in the face of bureaucratic opposition and tight Depression-era finances, Harsh was able to institutionalize her collection. Her greatest legacy is the extraordinary milieu she created, a meeting place that helped develop the work of so many black writers and scholars.

BIBLIOGRAPHY

Joyce, Donald Franklin, ed. *Dictionary Catalog of the Vivian G. Harsh Collection of Afro-American History and Literature, the Chicago Public Library.* Boston G.K. Hall, 1978.

Joyce, Donald Franklin. "Vivian G. Harsh Collection of Afro-American History and Literature, Chicago Public Library." *Library Quarterly,* Winter 1988.

"Notes from the Branches." *Chicago Public Library Staff News,* September 1931.

Ottley, Roi. "Hall Library Becomes Negro Cultural Center." *Chicago Tribune,* 21 February 1954.

"Resignation of Miss Vivian G. Harsh." *Proceedings of the Board of Directors of the Chicago Public Library,* 27 October 1958.

Slaughter, Adolph J. "Historian Who Never Wrote: The Vivian Harsh Story." *Chicago Defender,* 29 August 1960.

—MICHAEL FLUG

HATS. *See* Millinery.

HEALTH. "Of all the forms of inequality, injustice in health is the most shocking and most inhuman," said Dr. Martin Luther King Jr. in Chicago on 25 March 1966. For black women, this form of injustice has ranged from the horrors of the Middle Passage to disproportionately high rates of heart disease and breast cancer death.

The Middle Passage

The story of the systematic destruction of the physical and mental health of the African American population began in the seventeenth century with the advent of the slave trade. The first merchant ships came to Africa for gold, but later the gold became human bodies. The opening of the American colonies, with their vast natural resources and endless rich farmlands, created a great demand for labor—cheap labor, slave labor. The slave trade thrived and continued to grow well into the nineteenth century.

African men, women, and children were captured and taken from their homes. They were chained together and loaded like livestock into the cargo holds of European merchant ships. In some cases, one naked body was stacked on top of another. Deprived of adequate food, light, and other necessities, their health often failed. Africans survived the journey, when they survived, on almost nothing. Human waste was everywhere, and they were forced to live in it. They were exposed for the first time to European diseases: tuberculosis, diphtheria, and small pox, among others. Africans had no immunity to these diseases, and the death toll was enormous. Less than half of those on the slave ships survived, and many arrived at their destination barely alive. The slave trade fostered one of the factors that helps explain the disparity in mortality rates between black and white Americans even into the twenty-first century—the unbridled use of black people as commodities.

Volumes could be written about the irreparable damage, both physical and mental, caused by the violent transplantation of a people to another culture. The transplant was followed by a "seasoning" period, usually in the Caribbean, that involved all means of physical deprivation and cruelty. Once Africans reached the United States, those who were healthy were put up for auction. The auctions were a dehumanizing examination, by the white community, of the naked bodies of these African people. This process extracted a huge psychological and physical toll on the slaves, as women were separated from their husbands, children, and friends. Once a black woman was sold, she became the complete and indisputable property of her white owner.

During the colonial period in the North, some enslaved people worked on farms, in shops, or in homes, many times in much the same conditions as would indentured servants. On the plantations of the antebellum South, however, the situation was quite different and especially destructive to the health of black women.

Plantation Life

Only the hardiest survived the Middle Passage and the seasoning process. Once purchased by a plantation, Africans lived under the harshest conditions. The adjustment to new, colder climates was difficult. Infection and respiratory diseases were common. Overcrowded slave quarters, lack of sanitation, contaminated drinking water, and poor nutrition combined to create ideal conditions for the spread of disease. The average diet provided calories but only limited nutrition. Nutritional diseases, such

as rickets and scurvy, were not uncommon, and without adequate vitamins most slaves had a poor resistance to all diseases.

Compared to whites, Africans suffered a much higher death rate from accidents and infectious diseases. The list of diseases that were prevalent, often in epidemic proportions, includes tuberculosis, pneumonia, rheumatic fever, yellow fever, typhoid fever, cholera, and smallpox. Of course, many other illnesses claimed lives. For instance, many Africans contracted hookworm from walking barefoot over fields covered with compost containing human feces. Others developed tapeworm by eating tainted meat.

Since most slave women worked more than did men, they were at greater risk for health problems brought on by exhaustion and general physical debility. After pointing out that women usually worked side by side with men, doing the same work and the same amount of work in the fields, the historian Brenda Stevenson writes, "some males did perform more physically strenuous work, but women generally worked more—spinning, weaving, nursing, and cooking once their field work was over, to say nothing of the child care and domestic work they did in the quarters." Men were also given, as a matter of routine, more and better food. Women were often compelled by their owners to share their smaller portions with their small children.

In addition, enslaved women were seldom relieved of their duties while pregnant. According to Richard Steckel, "women continued to work almost until delivery, at least during seasonal peaks in the demand for labor." This and other health factors on the plantation commonly resulted in miscarriages and stillbirths. Many more black women died in childbirth than did women in the white landowner population. Infant and childhood mortality rates were high. Most black children did not reach their fifth birthday.

Obviously, this was more than a race problem; it was socioeconomic as well. Poor white women were victims of some of the same health conditions and disease patterns. However, they were not subject to the level of violence inflicted on black slaves as a matter of course. Again, Stevenson indicates that, "slave masters and overseers made no distinction in the ways they punished male and female field slaves. It was a brutal, disfiguring, health-threatening attack." Black women were also subject to terrible sexual violence, from sexual humiliation during beatings to rape.

An appalling example of the violence inflicted on black women occurred in the health field itself. The antebellum years were a time of medical progress, particularly in the area of surgery. Dr. Marion Sims is referred to in medical books as the "Father of Gynecology." It is seldom mentioned that he developed his surgical procedures on

Featuring Hospital and Clinic Founders

● **Virginia M. Alexander** (1900–1949) founded the Aspiranto Health Home in Philadelphia. She was born in Philadelphia and attended the University of Pennsylvania and the Woman's Medical College of Pennsylvania (MD, 1925). She interned at Kansas City (Missouri) General Hospital and was its first woman hospital staff member. In 1928 she returned to her hometown and in 1931 founded the Aspiranto Health Home, which provided care to the poor of Philadelphia, with a special emphasis on children and pregnant women. She was also on the courtesy staff of the Woman's Medical College of Pennsylvania. She continued her education, graduating with a master's degree in public health from Yale University in 1937. She was then appointed physician-in-charge of women students at Howard University Medical School and worked for the U.S. Department of Health. During World War II she provided health care to iron and coal miners in Birmingham, Alabama. While there she developed lupus. After the war she returned to private practice in Philadelphia; however, she lived only a few more years, dying from lupus in 1949.

● **Regina Benjamin** (1956–) has spent her life caring for her community and advising others on how to make rural health care work. Born in Mobile, Alabama, she attended Xavier University (BS, Chemistry, 1979) and the University of Alabama at Birmingham (MD, 1984). She funded her schooling by joining the National Health Service Corps (NHSC) and fulfilled her agreement with the corps by working at a clinic in Irvington, Alabama. In 1990 she opened her own private clinic in the nearby small town of Bayou La Batre. She attended Tulane University and earned her MBA (1991) in order to be able to manage the clinic more effectively. She also registered her practice as a rural health clinic, thereby making federal funds available. Most recently, in 2003 her clinic became a not-for-profit organization, in the hope that this would bring much-needed grant money into the clinic.

The lack of health care in rural areas is an ongoing crisis in America. Because of her success, Benjamin has become not only a national hero but a renowned consultant on rural health care. She conducted a nationwide conference on how to open and maintain rural clinics and speaks on the topic across the country. She also serves on national, state, and local boards in order to further her goal of providing health care to poor and isolated Americans. In 2002 she became the first black and the first woman to be named president of the Alabama Medical Association. Among her many honors, in 1995 she was chosen as the Person of the Week by ABC News.

● **Lucy Hughes Brown** (1863–1911) founded the Cannon Hospital and Training School for Nurses (later named McClennan-Banks Hospital). She was also the first female doctor to establish a practice in South Carolina and the first black woman doctor licensed to practice in North Carolina. Born in North Carolina, she attended Scotia Seminary before enrolling in the Woman's Medical College of Pennsylvania, from which she graduated in 1894. She practiced medicine in North Carolina for two years before moving to Charleston, South Carolina. A year after she arrived, in 1897, she established the Cannon Hospital and became head of the hospital's nursing program. She also edited its journal, the *Hospital Herald: A Journal Devoted to Hospital Work, Nurse Training, and Domestic and Public Hygiene*, and was secretary of the Cannon Hospital Association. Unfortunately, she suffered from poor health and retired from the practice of medicine only seven years later.

● **Rebecca J. Cole** (1846–1922) co-founded the Women's Directory Center of Philadelphia, which offered both medical and legal help to poor women. She was also the first black woman to graduate from the Woman's Medical College of Pennsylvania, becoming, in 1867, the second black woman doctor in the country. Born in Philadelphia, she graduated from the Institute for Colored Youth in 1863. After obtaining her medical degree, she joined Elizabeth Blackwell (the first female doctor in the country) and began working as the resident physician and sanitary visitor at the New York Infirmary for Women and Children. She left New York and for a short time had a practice in Columbia, South Carolina. Ultimately, she returned to her hometown and practiced in South Philadelphia. In 1873 Cole and Dr. Charlotte Abbey opened the Women's Directory Center. Some sources report that in 1899 she moved to Washington, DC, and became the superintendent of a home established by the Association for the Relief of Destitute Colored Women and Children. At some point she returned to Philadelphia, where she died in 1922.

● **Georgia Dwelle** (1884–1977) founded the Dwelle Infirmary. It was the first successful black hospital, as well as the first obstetric hospital for black women in Atlanta. It also housed Georgia's first venereal disease clinic for African Americans. Born in Albany, Georgia, and raised in Augusta, Georgia, she was the daughter of a former slave who had bought his own freedom as well as his mother's. Dwelle attended the Walker Baptist Institute and Spelman Seminary before obtaining a medical degree from Meharry Medical College in1904. She scored 100 percent in nine out of ten subjects on the Georgia state medical exam. In 1906 she moved to Atlanta and established a private practice in a poor section of the city. In 1920 the Dwelle Infirmary officially opened. Ultimately, it became a full-fledged hospital and stayed in operation until 1949. During that entire period the hospital did not lose a single patient. After 1949 Dwelle moved to Chicago. In her later years she was a member of the Children's Adoption Commission of New York and the Women's International League for Peace and Freedom.

● **Matilda Arabella Evans** (1872–1935) founded two hospitals (one to replace the other, which had been destroyed by fire). They were in operation from 1901 to 1918. (See individual entry: Evans, Matilda Arabella.)

● **Marilyn Hughes Gaston** (1939–) founded two different medical care services, the Cincinnati Comprehensive Sickle Cell Center and the Lincoln Heights Community Health Center, before moving on to become a leader in the field of public health. Born in Cincinnati, she attended Miami University in Ohio (BA, Zoology, 1960) and the University of Pennsylvania (MD, 1964). She opened her first health center in Lincoln Heights, an all-black city near Cincinnati, and served as the director from 1969 to 1972. She then founded and served as director of the Cincinnati Comprehensive Sickle Cell Center (1972–1976). After her husband, Alonzo Gaston, accepted a job in Washington, DC, she went to work at the NIH as a medical expert with the Sickle Cell Center in the National Heart Lung and Blood Institute (1976–1979). While there she helped develop the national sickle cell screening test for infants, which has saved thousands of lives. She joined the U.S. Public Health Service in 1979 and became the director of the Division of Medicine for the Bureau of Health Professions in 1989. She became an assistant surgeon general when she was named director of the Bureau of Primary Health Care in 1990. She retired from government service in 2002. Among her many awards and honors, Gaston is the recipient of the AMA's Dr. Nathan Davis Award for Career Public Service (2000) and has published the enormously popular book *Prime Time: The African American Woman's Guide to Midlife Health and Wellness* (2001), co-authored with Dr. Gayle K. Porter. She is currently the Chief Medical Officer for the National Minority Health Month Group.

● **Millie E. Hale** (1881–1930) founded a hospital and much more. Born in Nashville, Tennessee, she attended the Graduate School for Nurses in New York City and Fisk University (BA, 1927). In 1916 she established, with her husband, Dr. John Henry Hale, Nashville's first year-round hospital for African Americans, the

Millie E. Hale Hospital. After it became an unqualified success, Hale expanded the hospital's services to include free medical services for poor patients and relief for their families. In addition, she helped establish a nurse training department and published a newspaper that reported on the health needs of the community. Still seeing a need in the community, she and her husband converted their house into a community center that included, among other services, a free clinic. She also donated land to create playgrounds for children and managed a community grocery store. She died in 1930 in the hospital she founded.

● **Sarah Garland Boyd Jones** (1865–1905) founded Women's Central Hospital in Richmond, Virginia. In addition, she was the first woman to be licensed to practice medicine in that state. Born in Albemarle County, Virginia, she attended the Richmond Normal School, graduating in 1883. She worked as a teacher until she enrolled in the Howard University Medical School in 1890. In 1893 she was certified by the Virginia State Medical Board and she opened a practice in Richmond with her husband. Five years later, the couple established the twenty-five-bed Women's Central Hospital (also called the Richmond Hospital). It was the first hospital in the city for African Americans. In 1901 a nurse training school was added to the facility (it closed in 1920). When Jones died in 1905, she was still the sole black woman doctor in the state. In 1912 her hospital became incorporated as the Sarah G. Jones Memorial Hospital.

● **Alice Woodby-McKane** (1863–1946) founded the first hospital in Monrovia, Liberia, in 1895, with her husband, Dr. Cornelius McKane. Born in Pennsylvania, she attended Hampton Institute (1884–1886) and the Institute for Colored Youth (1886–1889). She continued her education at the Woman's Medical College of Pennsylvania, graduating in 1892. For a short time she had a practice in Augusta, Georgia, and at the same time taught at the Haines Institute. In 1893, after her marriage, she moved to Savannah and, with her husband, founded a training school for nurses. The following year they left for a two-year stay in Liberia. When she returned to Savannah, she founded the McKane Hospital for Women and Children. She moved again in 1900, this time to Boston, where she had a private practice and taught nurses at Plymouth Hospital. Politically active, she was a member of the Republican Party and a precinct leader and delegate at the party's state convention. In addition, she was a director of the South End Cooperative Bank. She died in 1946.

enslaved women who had not been anesthetized, on the assumption that black women did not feel pain in the same way or to the same degree that white women did. He is said to have operated on one woman nearly twenty times.

Black women and white women also had considerably different access to healthcare. Enslaved people had little treatment except that provided by their own healers, who used traditional African medicine. This often proved futile against previously unknown conditions and ailments. In essence, for the vast majority of African Americans, life remained a combination of harsh treatment, overcrowding, exposure to cold, ongoing diseases, and early death. Healthcare did not include hospitals, physicians, or any other health professionals. There were no "pesthouses" for those with contagious illnesses. Some slaves were fortunate enough to have owners who would pay for this substandard care.

Health in the Jim Crow South

After the Civil War, formerly enslaved people were released from bondage with nothing—no resources and few skills. Although some free health clinics were established for blacks, the dearth of black physicians made the care they offered questionable. Toward the end of the antebellum years, a meager amount of progress had been made in medical education for blacks. The first black physician, Dr. James Smith, graduated from medical school in 1837. Educated in Europe, Smith returned to the United States to find the possibility of a medical practice virtually nonexistent.

In 1860, historically black Howard University opened its Medical Department. In the forty-five years that followed, a dozen black medical schools attempted to create programs similar to the one offered at Howard. According to Michael Byrd, black physicians increased in number from 909 in 1890 to 3,409 in 1910, mainly from the increase in black schools, translating into an approximate doctor-patient ratio for blacks of 1:3000; the white doctor-patient ratio was 1:770, a significant difference. Such numbers translated into suffering, neglect, and deaths for the black population.

Byrd states, "this tiny handful of professional individuals in no way substituted for, nor represented, the huge number of black healers, providing 'hands-on care' for the black communities." This level of care existed well into the Reconstruction era. A dozen black medical schools were opened following the Civil War, and the two existing black universities opened medical departments. In the end, however, white society's restrictions and limitations forced ten of the schools to close. The little progress made was almost entirely halted by the development of the American Medical Association. This professional organization was

Access to Healthcare

Healthcare coverage in this country has slowly become a privilege of the rich or "well employed." In the population as a whole, one in six people was uninsured in the early twenty-first century. This number was much greater for those at or below the poverty level, among whom are many black women. According to *An American Health Dilemma*, by Michael Byrd, three-fourths of the African American population was uninsured or underinsured in the early twenty-first century.

Access to healthcare coverage involves interrelated barriers. The most obvious is financial, as blacks make up proportionately the largest part of the low-income population. A second barrier is distrust by the black community of the white bureaucratic world, a distrust that is historically justified. Finally, communication with those who administer and deliver healthcare is often poor. For low-income African Americans on assistance or Medicaid, the assistance may start with a white middle-class social worker. Often it is difficult to establish trust and a working relationship. The barrier to healthcare may also include hospitals and physicians who accept only limited numbers of welfare patients or no Medicaid patients at all. The reality of Medicaid is that there have been loopholes in the legislation, which have allowed doctors to refuse Medicaid patients or limit the number they serve. With new high-cost technology, hospitals have been adversely affected by Medicaid patients. During the 1990s in Chicago, ten hospitals that accepted the bulk of Medicaid patients were forced to close.

Possibly the worst part of the story regarding access to healthcare is that blacks (both poor working and middle class) have been losing ground. The strides made as a result of the civil rights legislation of the 1960s came to an abrupt halt after 1975. The disparity of healthcare coverage between African Americans and the white population has increased over the past two decades into the early years of the twenty-first century. The impact on low-income black women has been highly destructive. It has meant postponing diagnosis, postponing treatment, accepting a lesser quality of care, and failing to follow through on treatment. In brief, the lack of healthcare coverage, and therefore the access to quality healthcare, has meant a diminished quality of life for large portions of the African American population.

—Diane Epstein

highly political and self-serving, furthering segregation for many years through restrictions and covenants to exclude blacks. In 1910, Abraham Flexner published a report on American and Canadian medical schools, sponsored by the Carnegie Foundation and under the supervision of the American Medical Association. It was highly critical of medical schools in general and black medical schools in particular. In pursuit of a higher level of professionalism in medicine, the AMA began to insist on stricter admission requirements and more sophisticated laboratory facilities in schools. To refuse the AMA's recommendations was to lose grants and other funding and be forced to close. In no more than a decade, most of the black medical schools and training facilities were gone. Howard and Meharry Medical College, in Nashville, Tennessee, were the only medical schools approved for funding by Flexner and the AMA, and they were the only ones left.

Throughout the Jim Crow period, a substandard system of medical care continued to exist for African Americans. Dispensaries and clinics for blacks were also scarce, usually funded by black women's organizations, churches, and other groups within the black community. At the time of the Civil War and the Reconstruction era, the mortality rate per 10,000 was 95 for whites and 146 for blacks. As late as the 1920s, life expectancy for blacks at birth was 45.3 years. By the time they were ten years old, life expectancy for African American males and females fell to 39 years, significantly lower than for whites.

Inadequate or scarce healthcare for African Americans was considered "normal" in the order of things. The basic infrastructure of racially segregated and class-exclusive healthcare delivery was still in place through the first half of the twentieth century. Life span, mortality rates, and incidence of disease remained grossly unequal for African Americans. There were, too, a number of health concerns related to medical abuses that can only be called egregious. These, unfortunately, continued well into the second half of the twentieth century.

In her biography of Fannie Lou Hamer, Chana Kai Lee reports that Hamer was involuntarily sterilized when she underwent surgery for a small stomach cyst. Lee points out that this was not an uncommon occurrence for black women in the South. Indeed, as a result of "eugenics" laws passed in a number of states, as many as twenty-five thousand involuntary sterilizations were performed on black women. During the 1950s, some state legislatures proposed bills that would have forced sterilization on any woman who was receiving welfare payments and had a second child.

Life and Health in the North

The Jim Crow South was not the only place black women and their families suffered from the effects of poverty and discrimination on their health. The Great Migration of the early twentieth century brought tens of thousands of southern blacks into the northern urban centers. African Americans in these cities experienced a degree of overcrowding and unhygienic conditions that, if anything, surpassed that of the rural South, nor did they escape the violence that had always haunted their lives.

A new health hazard entered the lives of black women: the northern ghetto. In 1890, 95 percent of all African

Mental Health

Depression, lack of self-esteem, and anger have become a normal part of life for many black women. They are the result of negative history and current society stressors. History has created a generally "inferior view of self" for all blacks. But black women also have the highest numbers at or below the poverty line and live in a world that values not only whiteness, but maleness and affluence as well. There is little doubt that the stressors in a poverty environment, coupled with racism, make black women particularly vulnerable to emotional disorder.

However, statistics on mental health among black women are unreliable, influenced by the biases of white mental healthcare professionals. The term "emotional disorder"—an inability to cope with one's world—is far more often used with reference to the white population. This might not make sense on the surface, since African Americans generally have a higher incidence of many of the by-products of emotional problems, such as substance abuse. The answer is in the eyes of the healthcare worker. Social workers, psychologists, and psychiatrists are likelier to label a black woman with "serious" disorders, such as schizophrenia, than to do so for white women, for whom they are likely to use the term "depressive disease" or "emotional disturbance."

Statistics published on the incidence of mental illness are also influenced by a woman's socioeconomic level. The more affluent the sufferer, the more likely she is to seek private help, and accurate numbers are not necessarily available for those in private care. The poor are more likely to be found in hospitals, in public clinics, or in government-funded programs, making them far easier to count.

In addition, a black woman who has sought out treatment has probably reached a more extreme state of disturbance. This is the product of generations of thoroughly justified black fears of abuse in systems and institutions, as well as a lack of funds for better options. Racism and sexism make the potential for poor mental and physical health among black women very high. Unfortunately, the possibility for receiving adequate help is very low. Psychological care is even more underfunded and fraught with red tape than medical care.

Major research needs to take into account the causes for emotional illness in black women. Furthermore, results need to be analyzed with regard to gender, race, and socioeconomic factors along with African American traditions and other dimensions of life. Social workers who are the first line of defense for health assistance need better training in recognizing the needs of a specific population.

For more information, see Marilyn Martin, *Saving Our Last Nerve: The Black Woman's Path to Mental Health* (Roscoe, IL: Hilton Publishing, 2002).

—DIANE EPSTEIN

Americans lived in the South, mostly in rural areas. By the 1960s, 90 percent lived in the North, almost all in urban areas. Many of them had jobs that paid more than they could have imagined in the South, but life also cost more. Complicating matters was that most black women could not get jobs in the factories of the North. They found themselves cleaning white women's houses, a job that was all-too familiar to them. Because housing was segregated, black families lived crowded together in separate neighborhoods. Conditions that were brutal for most of the working poor were even worse for African Americans.

These neighborhoods became known as ghettos, and if African Americans had left the South in part to escape violence, they soon found that they had been unsuccessful. During one summer in 1919, there were twenty-two race riots in the cities of America. The violence, along with overcrowding, unsanitary conditions, and poverty, meant that blacks again faced astronomical rates of maternal death, infant mortality, and infectious diseases.

The first real improvements in the health status of black women did not occur until the Civil Rights movement of the late 1950s and the 1960s, and especially with the passage of the Civil Rights Act of 1964. This act outlawed segregation in places of "public accommodation" such as theaters, restaurants, and hotels. It banned discriminatory practices in employment and housing, and ended segregation in public places, including schools. Unfortunately, places of "public accommodation" did not include hospitals and medical offices, but significant advances were made because of the "federal financial assistance" provision. From that point on, receipt of funds from the federal government required any hospital, clinic, or other medical service provider to eliminate racial discrimination. Unfortunately, under pressure from the South, legislators went to great lengths to limit the definition of "federal financial assistance" in order to preserve the right to discriminate in private medical practices. Nonetheless, the enlargement of medical services to the African American public was hugely significant.

The passage of Medicare and Medicaid was yet another positive step in health services for the black and elderly. There was finally a formal admission that "separate was not equal." But real access to improved medical care was slow and hard won. For one thing, there were not enough doctors and back-up health professionals to make up for the deficit caused by years of neglect. And laws alone did not ensure equality.

A second and equally important driving force in healthcare progress was the Women's Movement that gained momentum in the 1960s. The movement placed a great deal of emphasis on the need for research into and education about those diseases that affected women most, such as breast, cervical, and ovarian cancer, and on reforms in reproductive issues.

Forced sterilization was also finally addressed. Ruth Sidel, in *Women and Children Last*, states, "In the early 1970s reports began to surface of forced sterilization of women on welfare and women receiving care in publicly funded hospitals. Suits were filed and regulations passed." However, according to Helen Rodriguez-Trias, whom Sidel cites, these regulations, "were largely ineffective and unknown or ignored." The number of sterilizations of nonwhite, low-income women rose in the 1970s, and an organization, the Committee to End Sterilization Abuse (CESA), was formed. Eventually, the department of Health, Education, and Welfare (HEW) developed guidelines to put a stop to this appalling practice.

The Twenty-First Century Condition

At the beginning of the twenty-first century, there were still serious problems for black women in every area of medicine and health. With regard to cancer, African American women, like other groups, were more vulnerable to some forms of cancer than others. Black women continued to have a particularly high incidence of cervical, ovarian, and lung cancer. The risk of death for African American women with breast cancer was 67 percent higher than for Caucasian women, even though black women had a lower incidence of the disease. However, in the early years of the twenty-first century, that trend may be changing. As of 2003, black women were no longer less likely than were white women to have mammograms.

The Cancer Institute has stated that black women make up the lowest level of the socioeconomic strata, with all the health consequences related to that dubious distinction. Among these women, smoking, obesity, poor nutrition, lack of exercise, and lack of knowledge about disease were common. Many women in this category also lacked the money or insurance to obtain adequate medical help. This segment of society was most likely to wait before seeking medical help and least likely to follow through on medical instructions. Obviously, the Medicaid program was not sufficient to overcome the health deficits of poverty.

Black maternal deaths remained 3.4 times higher than white maternal deaths, and the infant mortality rate was 2.5 times higher for blacks than for whites. However, according to the annual "Vital Statistics" article in *Pediatrics* magazine in 2002, "From 1990 to 2002, the use of timely prenatal care increased by 6 percent (to 88.7 percent) for non-Hispanic white women, by 24 percent (to 75.2 percent) for black women, and by 28 percent (to 76.8 percent) for Hispanic women, thus narrowing racial disparities." The disparity in life expectancies narrowed, too. The life expectancy for a black woman in the early twenty-first century was 75.5, as compared to 80.2 for white women.

A four-year study conducted by Ashish K. Jha revealed that black women were twice as likely as were white women to suffer from heart disease, but were less likely to be given standard drugs for prevention and treatment. Black women were nine times more likely to contract

HIV than were white women and a third more likely to have diabetes.

An examination of these statistics should remind us that disparities in the healthcare received by black women is part of a class issue as well as a race issue. Since a considerably larger percentage of African Americans lived near or below the poverty level, numbers on the whole are skewed. Numbers for disease and death rates comparing only middle-class black women with middle-class whites would probably be much closer. But it is also important to remember that poverty is a health risk too many black women continue to face.

Growing up a black woman was not without its advantages, however. Young black women were much less likely to suffer from an eating disorder. In a study of more than one thousand black women aged nineteen to twenty-four, there were no cases of anorexia detected, and the rate of bulimia was one-sixth that of white women of the same age. Also, black women were increasingly more likely to report domestic abuse to their doctors than were white women. They were also more likely to resist.

One of the most significant health problems African American women have faced over the centuries is violence, as we have seen, and that continues to be true. A 2004 report by the Violence Policy Center revealed that more than 3 of every 100,000 black women were murdered in 2001, compared with 1 of every 100,000 white women. Domestic violence was the leading cause of death for African American women in the fifteen- to thirty-four-year-old age range. Of these deaths, 53 percent were inflicted with guns.

It is not only the violence inflicted upon themselves that affects black women. They must deal every day with the danger faced by their children and the men they love, from gang violence to police brutality. The atmosphere of violence contributes to such conditions as hypertension, obesity, substance abuse, and other stress-related illnesses. It simply is not healthy to live in a violent world. Addressing that concern is probably the highest priority in healthcare for black women from all walks of life.

BIBLIOGRAPHY

Arias, Elizabeth. "Annual Summary of Vital Statistics." In *Pediatrics* 112.16 (December 2003): 1215.

"Black Women's Cardiac Care Trails That of White Women." In *Patient Care Management* 19.11 (November 2003): 10.

Braithwaite, Ronald L., and Sandra E. Taylor. *Health Issues in the Black Community*. San Francisco: Jossey-Bass Publishers, 1992.

Byrd, Michael W., and Linda A. Clayton. *An American Health Dilemma, Volume I: A Medical History of African Americans and the Problem of Race: Beginnings to 1900*. New York: Routledge Press, 2000.

Byrd, Michael W., and Linda A. Clayton. *An American Health Dilemma, Volume II: Race, Medicine, and Health Care in the United States 1900 to 2000*. New York: Routledge Press, 2000.

Crawford, Jewel, Wade W. Nobles, and Joy DeGruy Leary. "Reparations and Health Care for African Americans: Repairing the Damage from the Legacy of Slavery." In *Should America Pay?*, edited by Raymond A. Winbush. New York: Harper Collins, 2003.

Johnson, Audreye E. *The Black Experience: Considerations for Health and Human Services*. Chapel Hill: School of Social Work, University of North Carolina, 1981.

Jones, Alma R. "Racial/Ethnic Differences in the Self-Reported Use of Screening Mammography." In *Journal of Community Health* 28.2 (October 2003): 171.

Nuland, S. B. *Doctors: The Biography of Medicine*. New York: Knopf, 1988.

Striegel-Moore, Ruth. "Eating Disorders in White and Black Women." In *American Journal of Psychiatry* (July 2003).

"The Cycle of Violence." *Essence* 34.10 (February 2004): 34.

—DIANE EPSTEIN

HEDGEMAN, ANNA ARNOLD (b. 5 July 1899; d. 17 January 1990), educator, activist. Anna Arnold was born in Marshalltown, Iowa. She grew up in an Irish neighborhood in Anoka, Minnesota, a small town without any signs of poverty and without a black community. Raised in a religious household, she was taught to read at home by her mother and did not attend school until the age of seven. Anna was in high school before she first realized that hers was the only black family in town.

Early Career

After she graduated from high school in June 1918, her father sent her to Hamline University, a Methodist college in St. Paul, Minnesota. Because she lived with white friends of her father's, Arnold never knew whether, as Hamline's first black student, she would have been accepted in the dormitory. Her best friend at college was white, and her sense of her race was only incidental in her life. The fact that she was female, however, did limit her choice of a career, because teaching was the only occupation open to women at the time. Anna Arnold did her practice teaching at Hamline, learning only later that she would not have been allowed to do so at St. Paul High School because of her race.

Deciding she wanted to teach in the South, Arnold found a teaching job at Rust College, a black school in Holly Springs, Mississippi. Her first experience with segregation came on the train trip south in September 1922, when she was forced to change to the "colored" coach at Cairo, Illinois. Not only was racial segregation a constant affront in the South, but Rust College was also sex segregated. Arnold lived with the women students, serving as their chaperone when they needed to go into town. As was the case in many other southern towns, Holly Springs's black grade school was inferior and, because town leaders assumed that black children neither needed nor were capable of high school training, there was no black high school. Consequently, in addition to its college offerings, Rust maintained a grade school and high school for black

ANNA ARNOLD HEDGEMAN was an educator, public servant, and civil rights activist who worked to improve race relations and to better the lives of Harlemites. (Schomburg Center for Research in Black Culture, New York Public Library.)

students. Many came from sharecropping families, so they could not begin classes until after harvest, and they left early in the school year for spring planting. Parents paid tuition out of their often-meager earnings.

Disillusioned by southern segregation, Arnold decided to return to the Midwest to teach in 1924. After learning that racism prohibited her from getting a teaching job in the North, Arnold accepted a position with a YWCA in Springfield, Ohio, beginning in fall 1924. The Springfield YWCA was segregated according to neighborhood and lacked a gym, swimming pool, cafeteria, and adequate

staff. Arnold found it difficult to give black children confidence in the face of such discrimination and even more difficult to give lectures on race relations because there were no relations. Yet the national YWCA was ahead of its time, even hiring black executives, and Arnold's relationship with the YWCA, where she helped develop a variety of international programs in education, lasted on and off for twelve years.

Having spent time in the summer of 1926 in the freer atmosphere of New York, Arnold was eager to return. Requesting a transfer from the national YWCA, she became the executive director of a black branch in Jersey City. There, black Americans were represented on all committees, and there were even a few black teachers in the public schools. Her days off were spent in Harlem, where she became acquainted with the culture of the Harlem Renaissance at A'Lelia Walker's soirées. In 1927 Anna Arnold became membership secretary of the Harlem YWCA. Endowed by the Rockefellers, the Harlem YWCA had a well-equipped physical plant, a business school, a beautician training program, an employment agency, and meeting rooms. Because African Americans were barred from white branches of the YWCA just as they were from other public accommodations, this branch was particularly important to the community. For two years Arnold had a good job and was surrounded by black colleagues and friends. The Great Depression, however, brought more difficult times. The branch's membership shrank dramatically as people could no longer afford to pay for its services. Yet the community was now faced with the reality of starvation and a burgeoning Harlem population that had increased more than 600 percent in twenty-five years.

In fall 1933 Arnold became the executive director of the black branch of the Philadelphia YWCA. She made the black branch a vital part of the life of the community but only stayed one year. She returned to New York City in November 1933 to marry Merritt A. Hedgeman, a concert artist, an interpreter of black folk music and opera, and a former member of the Fisk Jubilee Singers. By this time, her parents and siblings had also settled in New York. By fall 1934 the city's Emergency Relief Bureau had begun to hire a few black supervisors, and Anna Hedgeman began working for the agency as the city's first consultant on racial problems, serving Jews and Italians as well as black Americans. In fall 1937 the Emergency Relief Bureau became the Department of Welfare, whereupon Hedgeman resigned and accepted the directorship of the black branch of the Brooklyn YWCA. She used this position to organize a citizens' coordinating committee to seek provisional appointments for black Americans to the Department of Welfare. They secured the first 150 provisional appointments the city had ever given to the black community. With the aid of white women on the race relations committee of the Federation of Protestant Churches, Hedgeman also succeeded in expanding employment opportunities for black clerks in Brooklyn department stores. Hedgeman resigned from the Brooklyn YWCA, however, after her activities became a point of contention with the central board. Her organizing tactics—including picket lines and challenges to the old guard leadership—proved too militant.

Anna Hedgeman continued to lobby for change. She defended the picketing of a local defense plant that refused to hire black workers on the grounds that government contracts should be denied to contractors who discriminate against black workers. She joined the civilian defense program as a race relations assistant. Then she joined A. Philip Randolph's March on Washington Committee, designed to fight segregation and discrimination against African Americans in defense industries and the military. In 1944 Randolph offered Hedgeman the job of executive director of the National Council for a Permanent Fair Employment Practices Committee (FEPC). Be-

cause she had come to believe that permanent legislation was needed to outlaw discrimination in employment, Hedgeman took the job, moved to Washington, DC, and began to lobby on behalf of FEPC. The National Council was unable to obtain a permanent FEPC, and after a major legislative drive in 1946 failed, Hedgeman resigned to become dean of women at Howard University.

In summer 1948 Congressman William L. Dawson, vice chair of the Democratic National Committee, asked Hedgeman to join the presidential campaign of Harry Truman by becoming executive director of the national citizens' committee to raise funds among African Americans. Pollsters predicted that Truman would lose, and Hedgeman was reluctant to align with racist southern Democrats, but Dawson had supported FEPC, and Hedgeman accepted the offer. After the election, Hedgeman received a patronage appointment as assistant to Oscar R. Ewing, administrator of the Federal Security Agency, later the Department of Health, Education and Welfare. She was sworn in on 12 February 1949, the first black American to hold a position in the Federal Security Agency administration. At the request of Ambassador Chester Bowles, Hedgeman spent three months in India in 1952 as an exchange leader for the State Department. She resigned upon her return to the United States, following the Republican victory in the presidential election.

Hedgeman returned to New York City after a ten-year absence and was met by a Harlem delegation that urged her to delve into city politics. So, on 1 January 1954, when Robert F. Wagner invited her to be a mayoral assistant, she accepted. Hedgeman was responsible for eight city departments, acting as their liaison with the mayor, and she remained in the post until 1958. As the first black woman at the cabinet level, Hedgeman gave speeches, represented the mayor at conferences and conventions, hosted United Nations' visitors to the city, and participated in weekly cabinet meetings. In 1955, when Mayor Wagner was on a European tour, Hedgeman was designated as his representative at the tenth-anniversary meeting of the United Nations in San Francisco. In 1956, she was invited on a study tour of Israel and the Middle East through the American Christian Committee on Palestine. Because she was a board member of the United Seamen's Service, she continued on to Munich, Germany, where she chaired a panel at the International Conference of Social Work as a representative of the Seamen's Service. In the same capacity, she attended the International Conference of Social Work in Japan in 1958. Hedgeman served as secretary to the board of the United Seamen's Service from 1955 to 1960.

Further Challenges

By fall 1958, frustrated by City Hall's lack of response to black concerns and the black community, Hedgeman accepted the offer of S. B. Fuller to join his cosmetics firm as a public relations consultant and an associate editor and columnist for the *New York Age*, one of the oldest black papers in the United States.

In 1960 a group of black and Puerto Rican reformers asked Hedgeman to run for Congress as an insurgent from the East Bronx. She ran, but she lost.

That same year, Hedgeman was invited to be the keynote speaker at the First Conference of African Women and Women of African Descent held in Accra, Ghana in July. She also became a consultant for the division of higher education of the American Missionary Association to help six black colleges prepare for their centennial anniversaries in 1966, and she had her own radio program, "One Woman's Opinion," on a New York City station.

In February 1963 Hedgeman played a key role in conceptualizing the 1963 March on Washington as a joint effort. A. Philip Randolph had called for a march on Washington for job opportunities to be held in October 1963. When Hedgeman learned that Martin Luther King Jr. was planning a march for that July to pressure public opinion on behalf of a strong civil rights bill, she suggested that they combine efforts into a March on Washington for Jobs and Freedom to be held in August. Hedgeman was the only woman on the organizing committee of the march; indeed, the heads of all the sponsoring organizations and all of the proposed speakers were male, even though women had played major roles in fundraising. While plans for the march were taking shape, Hedgeman was appointed to the newly formed commission on religion and race of the National Council of Churches as coordinator of special events. The intent of the commission was to mobilize the resources of Protestant and Orthodox churches to work against racial injustice in American life. Her first assignment was to relate the March on Washington to this renewed commitment of Protestant churches to justice for all. In this capacity, Hedgeman was asked to help mobilize thirty thousand white Protestant church leaders to march. About a third of the 250,000 marchers were white; some credit for that figure certainly belongs to Hedgeman.

In 1965, granted a leave from the commission on religion and race, Hedgeman campaigned unsuccessfully for president of the City Council of New York on the Reform Democratic ticket. She was the first woman and the first black woman to run for the office. In 1968 she unsuccessfully ran in the Democratic Party primary for an assembly seat.

On 31 December 1967 Hedgeman retired from her work with the National Council of Churches. She and her husband established Hedgeman Consultant Services in 1968. Their clients included educational institutions and civic, business, and community organizations.

The recipient of many honors and awards for her work in race relations, Hedgeman garnered, among others, the Frederick Douglass Award from the New York Urban League, the National Human Relations Award from the State Fair Board of Texas, and awards from the Schomburg Collection of Negro Literature and the American Federation of Labor-Congress of Industrial Organizations (AFL-CIO). She received citations from the National Association for the Advancement of Colored People (NAACP), the Southern Christian Leadership Conference (SCLC), the National Council of Negro Women, and United Church Women. In 1948 she was awarded an honorary doctorate of humane letters by Hamline University, the first woman graduate of Hamline to be so honored. In 1983, she received a "pioneer woman" award from the New York State Conference on Midlife and Older Women. Hedgeman was also a board member of the National Council of Christians and Jews. In 1964 she published her autobiography and study of black leadership, *The Trumpet Sounds*, following it with an assessment of the civil rights movement from 1953 to 1974, *The Gift of Chaos* (1977).

In later years, Hedgeman used a restaurant at 22 West 135th Street as her unofficial office and meeting place for friends during the breakfast and dinner hours. From there, she continued her efforts to improve conditions for the people of Harlem.

Despite her indisputable accomplishments, Hedgeman never received the recognition due her. Partly from her own desire to better her situation and partly forced by circumstances, she constantly changed jobs, never remaining in one long enough to achieve prominence as a leader. Still, her long career as a civil rights advocate deserves further attention.

BIBLIOGRAPHY

Hedgeman, Anna Arnold. *The Gift of Chaos: Decades of American Discontent*. New York: Oxford University Press, 1977.

Hedgeman, Anna Arnold. *The Trumpet Sounds: A Memoir of Negro Leadership*. New York: Holt, Rinehart and Winston, 1964.

Obituaries: *New York Amsterdam News*, 10 February 1990, and *New York Times*, 26 January 1990.

Pfeffer, Paula F. *A. Philip Randolph: Pioneer of the Civil Rights Movement*. Baton Rouge, LA: Louisiana State University Press, 1990.

ARCHIVAL SOURCES

Anna Arnold Hedgeman's papers are in the Schomburg Center for Research in Black Culture, New York Public Library, New York.

—PAULA F. PFEFFER

HEIGHT, DOROTHY IRENE (b. 24 March 1912), activist, author. Widely recognized and honored as one of the great civil rights and women's rights leaders of contemporary history, Dorothy Irene Height spent decades inspiring and leading countless organizations in the struggle for equality and human rights for all people. To

DOROTHY HEIGHT was a leading figure in the Young Women's Christian Association and the fourth president of the National Council of Negro Women. She is shown here with the labor leader A. Philip Randolph, at a banquet c. 1970–1974. (Library of Congress, A. Philip Randolph Collection.)

mark her ninety-second birthday on 24 March 2004, Dorothy Irene Height was awarded the Congressional Gold Medal by President George W. Bush. The ceremony in the Capital Rotunda in Washington was to honor her lifetime of achievements and service to the country as one of the preeminent social justice and civil rights activists of her time.

In her memoir, *Open Wide the Freedom Gates*, Height chronicles her life and work for justice, equality, and opportunity for women and black families. In it, she recounts her close relationship with Eleanor Roosevelt and Mary McLeod Bethune, as well as her encounters with

W. E. B. Du Bois and Martin Luther King Jr., among others. She also details her efforts and love for the YWCA, her more than forty years at the helm of the National Council of Negro Women (NCNW), and her role at the 1963 March on Washington, a defining moment in history.

Born in Richmond, Virginia, Height moved to Rankin, Pennsylvania, a small town near Pittsburgh, with her family when she was four years old. In the early 1900s, when blacks from the South were migrating North for jobs in the steel mills, her mother, a nurse, and her father, a contractor, sought a better life up North.

Height grew up in a household where politics and volunteerism prevailed, instilling in her a sense of responsibility and integrity in working with others. Educated in the Rankin public schools, Height established herself early as a dedicated student with exceptional oratorical skills. With a $1,000 scholarship for winning a national oratorical contest sponsored by the Elks and a record of scholastic excellence, Height entered New York University, where she went on to earn both the bachelor's and master's degrees in Educational Psychology in four years. She did postgraduate work at Columbia University and the New York School of Social Work.

Having graduated in 1933 at the height of the Great Depression, Height turned her attention to the needs of the poor in New York City. While working as a social worker for the New York City Welfare Department, she was the first black American chosen to deal with the Harlem riots of 1935. It was during this time that Height became one of the young leaders of the National Youth Movement of the New Deal era and began to develop her collaborative leadership style. She joined the United Christian Youth Movement, became president of the New York State Christian Youth Council, chaired the Harlem Youth Council, and represented youth in the National Negro Congress founded by A. Philip Randolph.

Turning Point

When Height realized that her extracurricular activities with youth organizations were what she enjoyed most, she resigned from the New York City Welfare Department. As her work as a human rights and civil rights advocate unfolded, Height began to understand her life's purpose. Since that time in the 1930s, Height worked tirelessly toward ending discrimination, reforming the criminal justice system, protecting children, spearheading voter registration drives, and recognizing the rights of women.

From her position with the Harlem Young Women's Christian Association (YWCA) and within the United Christian Youth Movement (UCYM), Height worked inside and outside the system, grappling with tough social, political, and religious issues. But the turning point in her life came on 7 November 1937, when Mary McLeod Bethune, founder and president of the NCNW, noticed the young woman, then assistant director of the Harlem YWCA, who was escorting Mrs. Roosevelt into an NCNW meeting. Bethune invited Height to join her quest for women's rights, and Height heeded the call. Thus began her dual role as YWCA staffer and NCNW volunteer, roles she would fill for the next forty years. Under the guidance of Bethune—who was her mentor, friend, and inspiration—Height organized voter registration drives in the South, testified repeatedly before Congress on social issues, and worked tirelessly on issues most important to women of the time, such as housing, job programs, and food drives.

At the YWCA, Height tackled the challenging issues of racism, discrimination, and segregation in the YWCA and the country. She quickly rose through the YWCA ranks from 1937 until she retired in 1977. As vice chair of the UCYM of North America, she was chosen as one of ten American youth delegates to the World Conference on Life and Work of the Churches in Oxford, England. Two years later, in 1939, Height was a YWCA representative to the World Conference of Christian Youth in Amsterdam, Holland. These early international experiences and activities as a leader of the youth movement left her with heightened confidence and the conviction that her goals and vision should be broadened to a global human rights perspective.

By the early 1950s, Height's leadership and understanding of the need to move the woman's agenda beyond the boundaries of the United States were evident. She successfully integrated and significantly expanded the work of human rights and social justice wherever an assignment took her. As a YWCA staff member, she represented the NCNW at a meeting of the Congress of Women in Port-au-Prince, Haiti, in connection with Haiti's bicentennial exposition. While there, she arranged for the initiation of the first international chapter of Delta Sigma Theta sorority.

In 1952 Height arranged a four-month visiting professorship at the University of Delhi's School of Social Work, which was founded by the YWCA of India, Burma, and Ceylon, to learn firsthand the needs of Indian women. In 1958, she was one of thirty-five members in a Town Meeting of the World on a special people-to-people mission to five Latin American countries. Because of Height's skills as a trainer and her understanding of the needs and struggles of women, she was sent by the YWCA to study the training needs of women's organizations in five West African countries.

Height held positions at the YWCA's Emma Ransom House in Harlem and the Phyllis Wheatley Branch in Washington, DC, two local segregated branches. But she returned to New York City to assume responsibility at the national level for developing leadership training activities for volunteers and staff and programs to promote interracial and ecumenical education. In 1965 she founded and served as director of the Center for Racial Justice for the National Board of the YWCA.

The YWCA owed much to Height for her persistent agitation for the YWCA to provide equal opportunity and facilities for all women and for the programs, policies, and training that she fought for while she was a staff member of the National Board. In 2000, Height's contributions were acknowledged when the YWCA established the Dorothy I. Height Racial Justice Award. One of the first awards was presented to President Bill Clinton in 2000 for his strong antidiscrimination policies.

The Civil Rights Era

Height, often known as the "grande dame" of the civil rights movement, served in the leadership of two other major women's organizations devoted to social change. As president of Delta Sigma Theta from 1947 to 1956, she carried the sorority to a new level of organizational development. Her leadership training skills, social work background, and knowledge of volunteerism benefited the sorority as it moved into a new era of activism on the national and international scenes. From the presidency of Delta Sigma Theta, she was elected president of the NCNW in 1957, a position she held until she assumed the position of chair and president emerita in 1998. As NCNW president, Height led a crusade for justice for black women and worked to stress the importance of the black family.

In the 1960s, Height placed NCNW on an issue-oriented course of action, helping out at Freedom Schools, promoting voter education drives in the North and voter registration drives in the South, and establishing dialogue between black and white women. NCNW, working with interracial and interfaith teams of women from the YWCA, National Council of Jewish Women, the League of Women Voters, the National Council of Catholic Women, United Church Women, and the American Association of University Women, sponsored "Wednesdays in Mississippi" to establish lines of communication in the community and across racial and regional boundaries. Height labored tirelessly to provide hope for inner-city children and their families, to increase the visibility and status of women in society, and to open doors for advancing educational and career development opportunities for black women in the 1970s.

As a self-help advocate, Height was instrumental in the initiation of NCNW-sponsored food drives, child care and housing projects in Mississippi, and career and educational programs that embodied the principles of self-reliance. In the late 1960s when Mississippi officials threatened to disqualify Head Start teachers, NCNW established the Fannie Lou Hamer Day Care Center in Ruleville, Mississippi, to provide child care for working mothers. The Bethune Museum and Archives for Black Women, the first institution devoted to preserving black women's history, was able to get the 102nd Congress to designate the Bethune Council House, the first national NCNW headquarters, a national historic site.

Working closely with Martin Luther King Jr., Roy Wilkins, Whitney Young, A. Philip Randolph, and James Farmer, Height—the only woman in the so-called "big six" group—participated in virtually all the major civil and human rights events from the 1960s on. President John F. Kennedy appointed her in 1961 to the President's Commission on the Status of Women. In 1964 Height was awarded the Myrtle Wreath of Achievement by Hadassah for her contributions to the interfaith, interracial, and ecumenical movements for over thirty years. A year later, in 1965, the National Council of Jewish Women honored her, along with Vice President Hubert H. Humphrey, with the John F. Kennedy Memorial Award.

In 1966 Height served on the council to the White House Conference "To Fulfill These Rights." During the mid-1960s she traveled to Israel to participate in a twelve-day study mission sponsored by the Institute on Human Relations of the American Jewish Committee, attended an Anglo-American Conference on Problems of Minority Integration held by the Ditchley Foundation, and encouraged President Lyndon Johnson to appoint African American women to subcabinet posts. In 1968 Height received the Lovejoy Award, the highest recognition by the Grand Lodge, IBPO Elks of the World, for her outstanding contribution to human relations. In 1969 she was awarded the Ministerial Interfaith Association Award.

Later Years

In the 1970s Height significantly expanded her internationalism. By 1974 she was a delegate to the United Nations Educational, Scientific, and Cultural Organization (UNESCO) Conference on "Woman and Her Rights" held in Kingston, Jamaica. That same year, *Ladies' Home Journal* named her "Woman of the Year" in human rights, and the Congressional Black Caucus presented Height with the William L. Dawson Award for "decades of public service to people of color and particularly women." In 1975 she conducted a seminar and participated in the Tribunal at the International Women's Year Conference of the United Nations at Mexico City. As a result of the Mexico City experience, the NCNW, under Height's leadership, was awarded a grant from the United States Agency for International Development to hold a postconference study tour that arranged for women from the United States, Africa, South America, and the Caribbean to visit with rural women in Mississippi. In 1975 Height established the NCNW International Division to promote relationships with women's organizations, especially in African countries. NCNW opened its first international office, the West Africa Regional Office, in Dakar, Senegal, and signed a Twinning agreement with the Federation of Senegalese Women and the National Union of Togolese Women, as a collaborative model between African and African American women's organizations. Under the auspices of the United States Information Agency, Height lectured in South Africa after addressing the National Convention of the Black Women's Federation of South Africa near Johannesburg in 1977.

As a promoter of positive images of the black family, Height turned her attention in the 1980s to developing programs to strengthen black family life. NCNW opened new offices in locations including New Orleans, Louisiana, and the Jamaica neighborhood of Queens, New York, to provide services to youth, and in Atlanta to provide parent teacher training. In 1986 Height conceived and organized the Black Family Reunion Celebration in seven cities to reinforce the historic strengths, education, and traditional values of the African American family. A continuing program of NCNW, the Celebration was later held in Washington, DC, and often drew over 500,000 people annually. Over the years, the Celebration made a difference in the lives of over 14 million family members and citizens, who went on to organize their own family reunions to celebrate and honor their heritage.

During the administration of President George Herbert Walker Bush, Height was appointed to the advisory council of the White House Initiative on Historically Black Colleges and Universities, and Secretary Louis Sullivan appointed her to the Department of Health and Human Services' National Advisory Council on Aging. During the 1990s, after almost forty years at NCNW, Height was able to realize her dream to establish NCNW as a permanent national presence in the nation's capital by purchasing a building on Pennsylvania Avenue in Washington, DC. Under her leadership, NCNW, which led the movement for voting rights and desegregated education, achieved tax-exempt status, raised funds from thousands of women in support of erecting a statue of Bethune in a federal park, developed several model national and community-based programs that were replicated by other groups, addressing issues ranging from teenage parenting to "banks" that addressed hunger in rural areas in the South, and reorganized NCNW in 1994 to "center in" on advancing black women by establishing the National Centers for African American Women and the Dorothy I. Height Leadership Institute at its new headquarters building.

Height received more than thirty-five honorary degrees from educational institutions worldwide, including New York University, Central State (Ohio), Harvard, Lincoln (Pennsylvania), Princeton, and Tuskegee universities, and Morehouse, Smith, Spelman, and Mount Holyoke colleges. Her contribution to furthering human rights was widely recognized. In their book *The African American Century: How Black Americans Have Shaped Our Country*, published in 2000, Cornel West and Henry Louis Gates Jr. cited Height as one of the hundred most influential African Americans of the twentieth century because of her role as a valued adviser on human and civil rights issues to First Lady Eleanor Roosevelt.

Height received the Franklin Delano Roosevelt Freedom Medal from the Franklin and Eleanor Roosevelt Institute; the Essence Award, 1987; the Caring Award by the Caring Institute, 1989; the Stellar Award, the Camille Cosby World of Children Award, and the Olender Foundation's Generous Heart Award, all in 1990, and the Spingarn Medal from the National Association for the Advancement of Colored People (NAACP) and induction into the National Women's Hall of Fame, both in 1993. President Ronald Reagan presented her with the Citizens Medal Award for distinguished service to the country in 1989. In 1994 President Clinton presented her with the

Presidential Medal of Freedom, the nation's highest civilian distinction.

In many ways, Height's achievements measure the liberation of black America, the advancement of women's rights, and the efforts to lift up the poor and the powerless. For the greater part of the twentieth century and the beginning of the twenty-first century, she led the struggle for equality and human rights for all people. By the age of twenty-five, she had a sense that she had to work for justice. As a result of her extraordinary leadership in advancing women's rights, her dedication to the liberation of black America, and her selfless determination and abiding faith that right will prevail, Height carried out the dream of her friend and mentor, Mary McLeod Bethune, to leave no one behind. During her seven decades of public life as dream giver, earth shaker, and crusader for human rights, Dorothy Irene Height made a difference.

See also Civil Rights Movement; Civil Rights Organizations; and Young Women's Christian Association.

BIBLIOGRAPHY

Gates, Henry Louis, and Cornel West. *The African American Century: How Black Americans Have Shaped Our Country*. New York: Free Press, 2000.

Height, Dorothy. *Open Wide the Freedom Gates: A Memoir*. New York: Public Affairs, 2003.

Ifill, Gwen. "Freedom's Gatekeeper." *American Legacy* (Spring 2004): 33–43.

—ELEANOR HINTON HOYTT

HERMAN, ALEXIS M. (b. 16 July 1947), activist. As a community activist, businesswoman, and political manager, Alexis Herman has devoted her life to resolving labor issues and advocating for American workers. Throughout her thirty-five-year career, Herman has been successful in translating her experiences with workers into effective labor policy. Having dealt with both gender and racial discrimination herself, Herman has dedicated her life to exposing institutional barriers and developing policies based on "common sense ideas that improve the bottom line."

Alexis Margaret Herman was born in Mobile, Alabama. After graduating from Heart of Mary High School in 1965, Herman moved to Wisconsin, where she attended Edgewood College. In 1967 she transferred to Spring Hill College in Mobile before going on to Xavier University in New Orleans, where in 1969 she received her BS. Herman later did graduate work at the University of South Alabama while pursuing a career in community activism.

Herman's early career provided a base of experience and knowledge about the needs of American laborers that would benefit her future business and political endeavors. She took a position as a community worker with the socially progressive religious organization Interfaith in

ALEXIS HERMAN, photographed on 23 October 2000, when she was secretary of labor. (© Pace Gregory/Corbis Sygma.)

remarkable abilities with people. Like many great politicians, she knew how to exercise tact and form personal contacts, abilities that would increase as she grew older. She held this post until the end of the Jimmy Carter administration in 1981. During the Reagan era, she took a break from formal political involvement and started a marketing and management company in Washington, DC. Specializing in the development of marketing strategies, organizational analysis, and human resource management, A. M. Herman and Associates helped Herman gain experience with public- and private-sector labor issues.

In 1989 Herman reentered politics as chief of staff of the Democratic Party's national committee, and two years later she became deputy chair. In November 1992, Herman was recruited as deputy chair of the Clinton-Gore Presidential Transition Office. When Bill Clinton took office in 1993, he appointed Herman assistant to the president and director of the White House office of public liaison, where she earned a reputation as Clinton's "Miss Fix-it."

In 1997 Herman became the first African American Secretary of Labor and one of only a few women to head the department. It took the Senate almost four months to confirm her appointment, during which she was subjected to a barrage of politically motivated accusations. Three months into her term, however, Herman proved her mettle when she successfully facilitated negotiations between United Parcel Service (UPS) management and the Teamsters, bringing an end to a decade-long labor conflict. As secretary of labor, Herman focused on developing, promoting, and implementing practical policies designed to help American workers gain the skills necessary to compete in the job market. As the nation's "ultimate job councilor," Herman focused on three policy objectives: job training, education, and skills development. She also spearheaded efforts to rid the workplace of discrimination and harassment based on race, ethnicity, and gender.

Throughout her career, Herman was consistently recognized for her community work, business acumen, and political savvy. She received the First Woman Award from the Negro Business and Professional Women's Clubs of Atlanta (1976) and the Scroll of Distinction from the National Association of Negro Business and Professional Women's Clubs. She was also honored by various labor and civic organizations for her support of anti-discrimination measures. In addition to these awards, Herman received honorary doctorate degrees from Xavier University, Central State University, and Lesley College.

After completing her term as secretary of labor, Herman refocused her attention on corporate consulting, serving as chair and chief executive officer of New Ventures Inc., director of Cummins Inc., Presidential Life Insurance Company, and MGM Mirage. Herman also

1969 before becoming a social worker for Catholic Social Services and an outreach worker for the Recruitment Training Program in Pascagoula, Mississippi. One of her important achievements during this time was integrating her former high school, Heart of Mary. Between 1972 and 1977 she worked with disadvantaged women workers, first as director of the Black Women Employment Program South Regional Council, then as director of the Minority Women Employment Program in Atlanta. She also served as a consulting supervisor for the Department of Labor Recruitment Training Program.

At the age of twenty-nine, Herman became the youngest woman to direct the U.S. Department of Labor Women's Bureau and the highest ranked African American in the Department of Labor. She was quickly recognized for her chaired the Coca-Cola task force on human resources and the Toyota Motor Sales diversity advisory board. In 2003 she took a position on the board of directors for Entergy corporation.

BIBLIOGRAPHY

"Alexis Herman." African American Publications. http://www. nativepubs.com/Apps/bios/0017HermanAlexis.asp?pic=none.

Garson, Regina. "Alexis Herman." Women's Village. IMDiversity.com. http://www.imdiversity.com/villages/woman/Article_Detail.asp? Article_ID=672.

Herman, Alexis. Speech presented for Women Work, 2001 National Conference, 8 November 2001.

"Secretary of Labor: Alexis Herman." Bill Clinton. Presidency in History. American President. http://www.americanpresident.org/ history/billclinton/cabinet/labor/alexisherman/h_index.shtml.

—JAIME MCLEAN

HERNANDEZ, AILEEN CLARKE (b. 23 May 1926), activist, educator. The career of Aileen Clarke Hernandez was a long and varied one. Her work as a student activist, a union organizer and officer, a college instructor, a president of the National Organization for Women (NOW), an urban consultant, a businesswoman, and a community organizer was characterized by a lifelong commitment to one goal: ending the discrimination that historically had limited the lives and aspirations of African Americans and other ethnic minorities, women, and the poor and underprivileged.

Aileen Hernandez was born Aileen Clarke in Brooklyn, New York, to Charles Henry Clarke Sr. and Ethel Louise Hall Clarke, immigrants from Jamaica. A graduate of the Brooklyn public schools, Hernandez won a scholarship to Howard University in Washington, DC, in 1943. Shocked by the rampant racial discrimination of the time, she became an active member of the Howard University Chapter of the National Association for the Advancement of Colored People (NAACP), picketing segregated theaters and restaurants. She also took part in other extracurricular activities, including theater groups, the campus choir, and the modern dance group. Hernandez edited the campus newspaper during her junior and senior years and wrote a column on campus affairs for the *Washington Tribune*.

Aileen Hernandez received her degree in Sociology and Political Science from Howard University in 1947, graduating magna cum laude. Later that year, she did graduate work in Comparative Government at the University of Oslo, Norway.

In 1950 Hernandez moved to California to begin a year of training at the labor college of the International Ladies Garment Worker's Union (ILGWU), an innovative internship program designed to recruit and train a new generation of labor leaders. After the internship, Hernandez was assigned to the Los Angeles Office of the ILGWU, where she worked as a shop organizer and assistant educational director until 1959 and as director of public relations and education for the pacific coast region from 1959 to 1961. In 1960 she toured six South American countries as a specialist in labor education for the State Department, lecturing on the American political system, labor unions, and the status of women and minorities.

Hernandez received her MA in Public Relations, with honors, at California State University in 1961. That same year, she left the ILGWU to serve as campaign coordinator for the future senator Alan Cranston's successful campaign for the office of California state controller. In 1962 she was appointed assistant chief of the California Fair Employment Practice Commission by Governor Edmund Brown.

In 1965 President Lyndon B. Johnson appointed Aileen Hernandez one of the original five commissioners of the Equal Employment Opportunity Commission (EEOC). The commission was created by the Civil Rights Law of 1964 to enforce laws banning job discrimination on the basis of race, color, sex, religion, or national origin. Hernandez served on the commission for eighteen months before returning to California to found an urban and management consulting firm in San Francisco.

In 1967 Hernandez was appointed the Western vice-president of the National Organization for Women, and in March 1970, she became the organization's second president, succeeding founder Betty Friedan. In the spring of that year, Hernandez and NOW member Representative Shirley Chisholm testified before a Senate subcommittee on the proposed Equal Rights Amendment to the Constitution. On 26 August 1970, NOW was part of coalition of women's groups that sponsored the nationwide Women's Strike for Equality. The event featured demonstrations and rallies in more than ninety cities across forty-two states.

Believing that black women have an inherent interest in both the black liberation and women's liberation struggles, Hernandez sought to bring the two movements closer together. Soon after resigning the NOW presidency in 1971, Hernandez helped found and lead a minority task force to search for ways to increase minority participation in the organization. Throughout the 1970s, however, she grew increasingly frustrated with NOW's continuing failure to act on the task force's suggestions and to address the needs of minority women.

In a 1979 minority task force report, Aileen Hernandez accused NOW of refusing to confront issues of racial inequity. Later that year, after the national convention elected an all-white slate of officers for the second year in a row, Hernandez resigned from NOW and called on all of its nonwhite members to leave the organization until it confronted its own racism.

After leaving NOW, Hernandez founded, organized, and participated in numerous groups devoted to fighting racial and sexual discrimination and promoting social justice. Among her many affiliations, she was the co-chair of the National Urban Coalition, the chair of the Working Assets Money Fund and of the Coalition for Economic Equality and a founding member of both the National Women's Political Caucus and Black Women Organized for Political Action. She served on the boards and advisory committees of organizations that included the American Civil Liberties Union, the NAACP, the Campaign against Poverty, the National Institute for Women of Color, and the California Academy of Sciences.

Hernandez taught and lectured at several branches of the University of California, as well as at San Francisco State University. She also continued her consulting work as president and CEO of her own firm, Aileen C. Hernandez Associates. Its clients included United Airlines, Standard Oil, United Parcel Service, the University of California and the city of Los Angeles.

BIBLIOGRAPHY

Giddings, Paula. *When and Where I Enter: The Impact of Black Women on Race and Sex in America.* New York: Morrow, 1984.

Medea, Andra. "Aileen Clarke Hernandez." In *Facts on File Encyclopedia of Black Women in America*, edited by Darlene Clark Hine. New York: Facts on File, 1997.

Moritz, Charles, ed. *Current Biography Yearbook 1971.* New York: H. W. Wilson, 1971.

Oleck, Joan. "Aileen Clarke Hernandez." In *Contemporary Black Biography: Profiles from the International Black Community.* Vol. 13, edited by Shirelle Phelps. Detroit: Gale, 1997.

Richardson, Francine, ed. *Who's Who of American Women.* New Providence, NJ: Marquis Who's Who, 2002.

—ROBERT W. LOGAN

HILL, ANITA (b. 30 July 1956), lawyer, activist, author. When Anita Hill stood before the Senate committee and testified that she had been sexually harassed by Supreme Court nominee Clarence Thomas, she initially expected to be believed. As a lawyer, she expected to be questioned. She did not, however, expect to be virulently attacked, to trigger national debates, and finally to emerge as a leading voice on standing up to the abuse of power. In short, she expected to have her say, not to change the nation.

Anita Hill was born on her parents' farm near Lone Tree, Oklahoma. When she was young, the house did not have running water, and a telephone was not installed until she was a teenager. She was the youngest of thirteen children of Albert and Irma Hill, who were hardworking, religious people. Uneducated themselves, they believed education was the way for their children to get ahead. Anita attended public schools and became the valedictorian of her high school class, which had a white majority. At a time when integration was still exceptional in Oklahoma, Hill was a popular girl with both black and white friends.

Hill won a National Merit Scholarship, which she used to attend Oklahoma State University, where she majored in Psychology. However, an internship with a local judge convinced her to try law. She won an NAACP scholarship for law school at Yale University, where she graduated in 1980. After graduation, she accepted a job at the Washington law firm of Ward, Harkrader, and Ross, but soon accepted a new posting as Clarence Thomas's personal assistant. At the time, Thomas worked in the Department of Education, heading the Office of Civil Rights. He was soon promoted to chairman of the Equal Employment Opportunity Commission, and he offered Hill a promotion to follow him.

Within a year, Hill found herself in the hospital with stress-related stomach problems. Soon afterward, she decided to go back to Oklahoma and become the civil rights

ANITA HILL, lawyer, activist, and author, speaking at the Leadership Conference, Manhattan, New York, in 2002. (© Najlah Feanny/Corbis Saba.)

professor at Oral Roberts University's Law School. After three years the school reorganized and relocated to Virginia. At that time Hill opted not to leave her home state, but to become a professor in the University of Oklahoma Law School at Norman. Having won tenure in only four years, Hill could look forward to a quiet and successful life as a local law school professor. Then, in 1991, her old boss Clarence Thomas was nominated to the Supreme Court.

Thomas was nominated to take the seat of Thurgood Marshall, a famed civil rights lawyer and prominent jurist. There were doubts about Thomas's qualifications from the start of the nomination process. With only one year's experience as a judge, Thomas was considered by many to be no more than a well-connected Republican, someone who would vote a political line and limit African American influence rather than advance it. Moreover, rumors circulated about Thomas's having sexually harassed female staff members. After an investigative committee asked Hill about her experiences working for Thomas, she was called to Washington to testify.

This poised and dignified woman went before the Senate committee to describe a pattern of sexual harassment under her old boss, describing behaviors that would be unacceptable for a factory supervisor, much less a judge in the highest court in the country. For instance, she reported Thomas talking to her about pornographic movies and sex acts. The entire country became riveted by the scandal. This was no longer just about Hill and Thomas. The hearing touched off a national firestorm of debate about how men and women should treat each other, what behavior is demeaning and what is acceptable, and why an intelligent, powerful woman might endure on-the-job humiliation. Many men felt the issue was absurd. Many felt Hill was speaking for every woman in the country.

The debate was still in progress on Capital Hill when Thomas's backers counterattacked, implying that Hill was crazy, vindictive, maniacal, a jealous woman out for blood or a disturbed woman with a twisted fantasy life. Thinking the issue was a question of veracity, Hill had a lie detector test performed by a former FBI agent. She passed. Thomas declined the same test. However, the lie detector didn't settle anything. Instead, the former FBI agent's credibility was attacked. All in all, it was one of the shabbier moments in American history. Despite fierce pressure, Hill would not change her story. Despite these questions, Thomas won the appointment by a narrow margin and was installed as a member of the Supreme Court.

Hill went back to her job at Norman, but by now she had made some powerful enemies. She received death threats. Conservatives mounted a crusade to get her fired from her position. A state representative called her a "cancerous growth" and, since she had tenure and could not be fired, proposed a bill to eliminate the entire law school. Under fire, the law school dean and the university president stepped down. Hill and a close ally finally resigned in 1997.

The depth and breadth of the personal attacks were remarkable. In 1993, two years after the hearings, David Brock published a book, *The Real Anita Hill*. Touted as an exposé and favorably reviewed in the *New York Times* and the *Washington Post*, it was a forthright smear job. Working with innuendos and half-truths, Brock tried to discredit Hill as, in his own words, "a little bit nutty and a little bit slutty." The book was a national best seller. Meanwhile, more serious reporters dug through the evidence and came to a very different conclusion. Jane Mayer of the *New Yorker* and Jill Abramson of the *Wall Street Journal* published a book in 1994 called *Strange Justice: The Selling of Clarence Thomas*. They not only found that the preponderance of evidence supported Hill, but uncovered signs of widespread suppression of evidence. Among their findings were that another female employee had stated that she had been harassed by Thomas; she waited in Washington to testify but was never called. One of the issues in the hearing revolved around Thomas's supposed interest in pornography, something his supporters denied as inconsistent with his churchgoing ways. However, the local video store manager reported that Thomas regularly checked out pornography and asked his opinion in making choices. The store owner was also not called to testify.

Most telling of all, in 2002 David Brock published another book, *Blinded by the Right: The Conscience of an Ex-Conservative*. In this new book, Brock confessed that his previous book on Hill had been a smear. Brock himself called it "a witches' brew of fact, allegation, hearsay, speculation and invective." Having had a change of heart, Brock came to deeply regret what he had done. He sent a copy of his new book to Hill, along with a personal apology.

Hill was hard-pressed to withstand these attacks when so many people did not believe her. But her family, though deeply conservative in religious matters, believed her and her own religious faith gave her courage. Although she described herself as "deeply wounded" at the time, her inner toughness asserted itself. She said, "I just could not let this destroy me. It doesn't mean I didn't feel beat up a lot of the time, but I just refused to be undone." Hill received some twenty thousand letters, both for her and against her, which she still keeps stored in the basement of her house.

After leaving the University of Oklahoma in 1997 Hill wrote her own book, *Speaking Truth to Power*. After that book came out, she received a phone call from Brandeis sociology professor Shulamit Reinharz, then head of the

Women's Studies program. Reinharz had read Hill's book, thought it was "brilliant" and decided to bring her to teach at Brandeis. Hill started at Brandeis in the fall of 1998 as a visiting professor in the Women's Studies program. The following year she became a professor with Brandeis's Heller School, where she teaches both graduate and undergraduate courses focusing on race, class, and gender issues.

The repercussions from the Hill-Thomas hearings had a ripple effect across the country. In Illinois, Senator Alan Dixon, one of the prominent senators in the hearing, was defeated in his own primary by a black female candidate, Carol Mosley Braun. Braun went on to become the first black woman in the Senate. Hill's testimony also caused new standards to be created around sexual harassment, with legislation enacted around the nation.

No longer a quiet Oklahoma professor, Hill now follows a busy speaking schedule. Apart from her duties at Brandeis, she has lectured at Harvard, Yale, and other prominent universities. Hill also brought out a collection of essays, *Race, Gender, and Power in America: The Legacy of the Hill-Thomas Hearings*, which she coedited with Emma Coleman Jordan.

BIBLIOGRAPHY

Brock, David. *Blinded by the Right: The Conscience of an Ex-Conservative*. New York: Three Rivers Press, 2002.

Brock, David. *The Real Anita Hill*. New York: Free Press, 1993. This was the book that was later retracted by the author. Useful as an example of the attacks against Hill.

Graves, Florence George. "The Complete Anita Hill." *Boston Globe Magazine*, 19 January 2003. An in-depth interview with Anita Hill.

Hill, Anita. *Speaking Truth to Power*. New York: Doubleday, 1997. Hill's view of the Hill-Thomas proceedings, with a final chapter of suggestions of how to improve Senate hearings.

Hill, Anita, and Emma Coleman Jordan, eds. *Race, Gender, and Power in America: The Legacy of the Hill-Thomas Hearings*. New York: Oxford University Press, 1995. A compendium of essays on the interplay of these powerful forces in the U.S.

Mayer, Jane, and Jill Abramson. *Strange Justice: The Selling of Clarence Thomas*. Boston: Houghton-Mifflin, 1994. A well-documented investigative study of the hearings.

—ANDRA MEDEA

HINE, DARLENE CLARK (b. 7 February 1947), historian, writer. A scholar of national renown, Darlene Clark Hine has published pathbreaking scholarship; introduced and developed new and existing fields of scholarly inquiries; provided leadership for various groups of scholars; and mentored and trained several generations of historians. She served as president of the Organization of American Historians (2001–2002) and the Southern Historical Association (2002–2003). During her productive, decades-long career as a professional historian, Hine has taught at eight different universities, published several books, cowritten and coedited a dozen scholarly volumes, edited three major works, written more than fifty journal articles and chapters in anthologies, presented more than sixty papers in professional venues, lectured at universities all over the United States, and served on countless programming, advisory, and nominating committees and editorial boards. Since the mid-1980s, Hine has received numerous grants, awards, and honors, including honorary doctorates from Purdue University and Buffalo State College, the *Detroit News* Michiganian of the Year Award (2002), and honor as One of the Outstanding College Leaders of the Twentieth Century from *Black Issues of Higher Education*.

Darlene Clark Hine was born in Morley, Missouri, but spent her formative years on her maternal grandparents' farm in Villa Ridge, Illinois. During her junior year of undergraduate study, she decided to become a history major; she earned her BA in 1968 from Roosevelt University in Chicago. Seven years later, Hine earned her PhD from Kent State University. From 1972 until 1974 she taught at South Carolina State College. From 1974 until 1987 Hine worked in various capacities at Purdue University. From 1974 until 1979 she was an assistant professor of history. In 1979 she became an associate professor. From 1981 until 1986 she served as vice provost, becoming one of the few black women to hold such a position at a Big Ten university. In 1985 Hine was promoted to full professorship. Two years later, she became a John A. Hannah Professor at Michigan State University. Hine has been a full-time, tenured historian at two major, Big Ten universities for twenty-five years combined, and since the mid-1980s, she was also a visiting professor at six universities.

Hine has been a prolific scholar who altered the course of African American historiography and significantly contributed to two major subfields of U.S. history: black professional class history before the classic civil rights movement and black women's history. She also promoted the study of African descendants' history and culture within a global context, as evidenced in the comparative black history PhD program that she initiated after arriving at Michigan State. In her first monograph, *Black Victory: The Rise and Fall of the White Primary in Texas*, first published in 1979, Hine unearthed and analyzed the processes by which Judge William Hastie, Thurgood Marshall, the NAACP, and a host of lesser-known, yet equally important, Afro-Texan professionals, lawyers, community-based movers and shakers, and political activists struggled against "systematic disenfranchisement" from the mid-1920s until the mid-1940s.

Accepting the challenges of the Indianapolis public school teacher Shirley Herd and the Indianapolis section of the National Council of Negro Women, in the early and mid-1980s, Hine entered the field of black women's history while simultaneously generating new ideas in

DARLENE CLARK HINE with Volume II of *Black Women in America: An Historical Encyclopedia*, First Edition. The woman shown on the cover is Anna Julia Cooper. (Austin/Thompson Collection.)

African American history in general. She published *When Truth Is Told: A History of Black Women's Culture and Community in Indiana, 1875–1950* (1981); edited *Black Women in the Nursing Profession: An Anthology of Historical Sources* (1985); coedited *Black Women in the Middle West Project: Comprehensive Resource Guide, Illinois and Indiana* (1985) and *Eyes on the Prize: History of the Civil Rights Era, a Reader* (1987); coordinated a major American Historical Association conference on the state of black history and edited the papers, presented in *The State of Afro-American History: Past, Present, Future* (1986); and published more than a dozen articles.

In 1989 Hine published *Black Women in White: Racial Conflict and Cooperation in the Nursing Profession, 1890–1950*, a project that transformed her scholarship. Hine analyzed the effect of racism on the development of the nursing profession, focusing particularly on black nurses. Viewing black nurses' lives as representing a collective microcosm of black professional history during the era of Jim Crow segregation and paying close attention to the intersections of race, class, and gender, Hine explored black nurses' struggles to survive, dignify their labor, and uplift their communities.

In the 1990s Hine helped to edit diverse reference materials on black women's history, including resource guides, anthologies, and a sixteen-volume series on black women in U.S. history, *Black Women in the United States, 1619–1989.* Most influential of these was the two-volume *Black Women in America: An Historical Encyclopedia* (1993), which led the way to a blossoming of scholarship in the field.

In 1996 Hine published *Hine Sight: Black Women and the Re-Construction of American History*, a collection of essays written during a fourteen-year period, reflecting the evolution of her thinking about black women "as historical subjects and as members of the academic community." In 1996 Hine also published *Speak Truth to Power: Black Professional Class in United States History*, a multi-layered volume that illuminates the development of the black professional class from slavery through the late twentieth century while challenging its readers to reconsider familiar ideas about class, race, gender, and community formation in American culture.

Following *Speak Truth to Power*, Hine coedited four volumes of essays in the field of African American history. She was a coauthor of *A Shining Thread of Hope*, a general history of black women, with Kathleen Thompson, and two African American history textbooks with William C. Hine and Stanley Harrold. She also published significant articles and chapters in anthologies, and revised and re-released *Black Victory* with additional essays by herself, Steven F. Lawson, and Merlina Petrie. Hine continued to develop her creative conceptualizations of black women's history and black professional class history. In an essay in the *Journal of American History*, "Black Professionals and Race Consciousness: Origins of the Civil Rights Movement, 1890–1950," Hine expanded upon her theory of parallelism and explored "obscure" physicians' and nurses' strategies of resistance during the pivotal World War II era.

Hine's presidential address at the Southern Historical Association, "The Corporeal and Ocular Veil: Dr. Matilda

A. Evans (1872–1935) and the Complexity of Southern History," acknowledged an important black woman physician. Her scholarship on black professionals and twentieth-century African American history challenged coming generations of black historians while contributing to a new, refreshing body of historical scholarship on black leaders during what Hine dubbed the "proto-civil rights movements."

BIBLIOGRAPHY

Hine, Darlene Clark. "Editor's Preface." In *Black Women in America: An Historical Encyclopedia*, edited by Darlene Clark Hine, Elsa Barkley Brown, and Rosalyn Terborg-Penn. Brooklyn, NY: Carlson, 1993.

Hine, Darlene Clark. "The Future of Black Women in the Academy: Reflections on Struggle." In *Black Women in the Academy: Promises and Perils*, edited by Lois Benjamin. Gainesville: University Press of Florida, 1997.

Hine, Darlene Clark. *Hine Sight*. Brooklyn: Carlson, 1994.

Hine, Darlene Clark. "The Making of Black Women in America: An Historical Encyclopedia." In *U.S. History as Women's History: New Feminist Essays*, edited by Linda Kerber, Alice Kessler-Harris, and Kathryn Kish Sklar. Chapel Hill: University of North Carolina Press, 1995.

Hine, Darlene Clark. "Reflections on Race and Gender Systems." In *Historians and Race: Autobiography and the Writing of History*, edited by Paul Cimbala and Robert F. Himmelberg. Bloomington: Indiana University Press, 1996.

—PERO GAGLO DAGBOVIE

HIP HOP. Hip hop culture evolved from the rap music genre. Rap was commercial, hip hop conscious. Rap says, "I love rhyme." Hip hop vows, "I'm in love with rhyme culture." Hip hop is a place where people of all colors come to create African American music, rap, dance, graffiti, and fashion. Whereas some listeners considered rap a 1970s musical art form, hip hop is language, a mode of dress, attitude, politics, lifestyle, and—above all—stance. Hip hop is musical style. Its attire has included baggy jeans, flop hats, sneakers, brand-name knock-offs, and haute couture of a generation ranging from preteen to thirty year olds.

To be hip has meant to understand, like, or dig. To hop has been to put one's own swerve on something, using the existing as a point of departure. Hip hop has inspired sexual appetites, hairstyles, child-rearing, to name a few. Hip hop politics has espoused what's hot for the minute. Today's lifestyle may embrace midrift maternity tops. Tonight's flavor might be Afrocentric garb. Tomorrow, a baseball cap with a widow's net and pleather (plastic leather) suit may be the move. With hip hop, it's all good. Hip hop activists have supported reparations for descendants of African American slaves. Junk food junkies and strict vegans have marked—yet not limited—the hip hop diet. All things considered, the hip hop spectrum must be painted with a broad stroke.

The position of women in hip hop culture has been complex and problematic. Since the culture has been, at its heart, African American, the music, styles, and attitudes have seemed to reflect the multifaceted relations between men and women in at least one portion of the African American community. In an important sense, hip hop has consciously and outrageously rejected the "respectability defense" for both men and women. Women in hip hop have struggled with the freedom and the exploitation it has offered.

How the Music Is Made

Hip hop music was born as a live, record-scratching idiom at parties and clubs. It can be traced through 1940s hep, 1950s cool, 1960s hip, 1970s ice cold, 1980s solid, and 1990s hip hop. Hip hop's foundation includes turntablist, abstract, bass, blues, gangsta-rap, gospel, independent or underground, jazz, new jack swing, old school, reggae, and ska. Hip hop's roots run as deep as the West African griot, and the form has taken inspiration from the 1970s rap of Gil Scott Heron, Nikki Giovanni, Millie Jackson, and other spoken word poets. After years of raiding their parents' and grandparents' attic record collections, hip hoppers emerged with a new sound. Hip hoppers deconstructed 78s, LPs, and 8-track tapes in the name of inventing themselves and reinventing art forms, lick-by-lick.

Sampling, a hip hop staple, is the practice of quoting riffs, phrases, or entire songs as a foundation over which new lyrics are arranged. Early sampling was done in the name of teaching African American music history via serving old beats to new listeners. More buckets were dipped at the Motown well than any other label. This was due primarily to vintage Motown's classic storytelling chops. Unlike classical "Variations on a theme," sampling often uses unauthorized, direct quotes that fuel plagiarism lawsuits. Aretha Franklin, Gladys Knight, Billie Holiday, Millie Jackson, Betty Wright, James Brown, Marvin Gaye, Stevie Wonder, and the O-Jays' greatest hits propped up Angie Stone, Erykah Badu, India Arie, and many other young artists.

From the record industry's perspective, hip hop has been lucrative because talk, as it were, is cheap. Hip hoppers have taken existing hit beats (music), floated rhymes over them, making the tracks good to go: instant, freeze-dried hits and re-hits. No new composition, per se, is needed, no composer to pay. Half pennies on the dollar have been paid to artists, many of whom relinquished power of attorney to agents and record company executives because of their lack of business savvy.

The First Women of Rap

As early as 1974, rhythm and blues singer Millie Jackson set the stage for women in rap with her spoken-word

✏ In Charge of It All

Female rap and pop performers of the twentieth and early twenty-first centuries assumed unprecedented control of their professional careers. The rapper MC Lyte is credited with being the first to do so, but many groups and solo artists soon followed. Among the earliest and most successful female rappers, Salt, of the group Salt-N-Pepa, produced a number of tracks on the 1990 album *Blacks' Magic* and then went on to produce and write for the group 4-Play. *Brand New*, released in 1997, was entirely written, arranged, and produced by the group. Salt-N-Pepa also founded Jireh Records in 1995.

Indeed, the number of hip hop stars with their own independent labels or who started sub-labels within the major companies was remarkable. Missy "Misdemeanor" Elliot's label, through Elektra, was The Gold Mine, Inc. Lisa "Left Eye" Lopes's label created Left Eye Productions, and Lil' Kim founded Queen Bee Records, to mention but a few.

Queen Latifah was perhaps the early twenty-first century's best known hip hop entrepreneur. Her entertainment empire, Flava Unit Entertainment, started out as a management and recording company but expanded to include film and television production. Flava Unit artists included Naughty By Nature, Outkast, and LL Cool J. In 2002 Queen Latifah and her partner Shakim Compere again set out to create a revolution within the music industry. After a hiatus, they reopened Flava Unit Records, but with a significant and unheard of alteration. The artists recording with Flava Unit would now be the label's partners, royalties would be split 50/50, and the artists would own their master recordings after any recording costs were recouped. As Queen Latifah told AllHipHop.com, "Everybody else has owned us, here's your chance to own yourself."

Queen Latifah also typified another element of the successful contemporary singer. She became a movie star and a spokesperson for Revlon cosmetics. Beyonce Knowles, another example of the powerful black woman pop star, conquered the marketing end of the modern music career when she became a pitchwoman for Pepsi. She made the transition to feature films with *The Fighting Temptations*.

Alicia Keys also exemplified the new power taken by young musicians at the turn of the twenty-first century. She took control of her career when she was only sixteen. At the time she was signed by Columbia Records, she insisted that she be allowed to produce her own album, a brave move for an established artist, much less one cutting her virgin effort. Erykah Badu summed it up well when she told Michael Gonzales of *Essence* magazine in 1997:

"You can't go into the music business and say 'Aw, I just want to sing, I don't care.' If you're not prepared, you'll get jacked. It's beautiful and new to be spiritual, but I'm going to take advantage as well. Since I'm in demand and I'm the boss, I'm going to get everything that's due me."

—Hilary Mac Austin

monologues on *Caught Up*, an album that received a Grammy nomination. In 1976, Sharon Jackson of the Bronx became Sha Rock, the only woman in the rap group Funky Four. The following year, the Mercedes Ladies became the first all-female hip hop crew. In 1978, "Vicious Rap," one of the first rap records ever recorded, featured the teenage daughters of producer Paul Winley—Paulette Tee and Sweet Tee. But the first hugely influential woman in hip hop history was Sylvia Robinson, a former rhythm and blues singer who founded the first rap label, Sugar Hill. Her first release, "Rapper's Delight," by the male Sugarhill Gang, was hip hop's first hit record.

It was another R & B singer, Angie Stone, who created Sugar Hill's first all-female group. She renamed herself MC Angie B and teamed up with Cheryl "The Pearl" Cook and Gwendolyn "MC Blondie" Chisolm. The three looked more like a sequined sixties girl group than a rap group, but they created a mix of rap and song that foreshadowed the future of hip hop. In the 1980s, East Coast MCs blasted positive messages influenced by black nationalists. Queen Lisa Lee was featured on Afrika Bambaataa's "Zulu Nation Throwdown." In 1981, Sha Rock went on *Saturday Night Live* as part of Funky4+1, the first rap group to appear on national television, and the next year Lisa Lee rhymed in the underground hip hop movie *Wild Style*. She would appear again in 1984, this time with Sha Rock and Debbie Dee, in the movie *Beat Street*.

None of these early contributions by women could have prepared the hip hop nation for the next development, the birth of the "gangsta bitch." The group UTFO (Un-Touchable Force Organization, consisting of three male rappers) released "Roxanne, Roxanne," in which a group of guys taunt a hard-to-get girl. In response, producer Marlon "Marley Marl" Williams recorded a fourteen-year-old girl's answer to the boys. The girl was Lolita Shanté Gooden, soon to be known as Roxanne Shanté. The record was "Roxanne's Revenge," and it started what *Vibe* magazine called "the longest-running series of answer records in the annals of hip hop, an ongoing 'battle on wax' that resulted in over ninety different releases." It also sold more than a quarter of a million copies in New York alone.

Ironically, UTFO threatened to sue Shanté for sampling their music to launch her career. The lawsuit was abandoned when UTFO realized Shanté's response had sparked 120 catfight rebuttals that resuscitated "Roxanne, Roxanne" and UTFO's career. Like a 1980s real-life version of the 1960s TV show *To Tell the Truth*, the insatiable audience demand was simple: "Will the Real Roxanne please stand up?"

Roxanne Shanté had a decade in the limelight before she was worn down by one of the great dangers of hip hop storytelling. Because the rhymers were often characters in their own—and each other's—rhymes, reality could become confused with fiction. Shanté became the woman that other women loved to hate and to attack on their records. By sixteen, she was trying to handle a baby, a high-powered career, and wall-to-wall hostility. At twenty-five, she dropped out of sight, along with the Real Roxanne, Roxanne-Roxanne, and all the others whose careers fed on the feud. The next wave of female hip hoppers wrote their own lyrics and beats and chose their own styles, including Salt 'N Pepa, Queen Latifah, MC Lyte, Nikki D., and Monie Love from the United Kingdom.

Salt 'N Pepa (SNP) hit the scene in 1987 with the *Hot, Cool & Vicious* album. Cheryl "Salt" James and Sandi "Pepa" Denton, along with their personal DJ, Dee Dee "Spinderella" Roper, turned the rap music industry on its ear by putting five albums on the charts. SNP achieved shock value by creating a female counterpart to the wild dancing, posing, and attitude of male hip hop crews. *Black's Magic* was the first album on which the trio exercised production control, and it had three major hits. "Let's Talk about Sex" became an AIDS public service announcement for ABC and the state of New York. It preceded *A Blitz of Hits*, the multi-platinum *Very Necessary*, and *Brand New*. SNP contributed the title track to the 1995 benefit album *Ain't Nothing but a She Thing*. They also founded Jireh Records.

The year 1987 also saw the first million-selling record by a female rap group, J. J. Fad's "Supersonic"; the first all-female rap compilation, *B-Girls Live & Kickin'*; and the beginning of another feud, this one between rhymer Antoinette and soon-to-be-star MC Lyte. That year also saw black women searching for their place in a genre that had belittled and abused them but was increasingly taking center stage in their culture.

There have been at least three definitions of power for women in hip hop. There has been the power of competitive toughness, of an un-gendered persona that rejects feminine vulnerability. There has been the power of dignity, which came out of a history of inner strength among black women. And there has been the power of sexuality, which hearkens back to women's position in virtually all underground cultures. Individual women in hip hop have usually chosen one of these sources of power as their inspiration.

Competing Head-On

The career of MC Lyte was marked by her head-on attack on sexism and misogyny in rap. By choosing a sexually neutral persona, she demanded that attention be paid to her words and her talents instead of her body, while still utterly rejecting respectability and the role of the "nice girl." Her first album, *Lyte as a Rock* (1989), included "10% Dis," a response to a recorded attack by Antoinette, "I Got an At-

titude." But the Brooklyn-based Lyte aimed much of her rhyme at out-of-control male egos and libidos. Lyte's *Ain't No Other* (1993) features tough talk and innovative music (phat beats). *Bad as I Wanna Be* lived up to Lyte's claim. It is propped up by Lyte's *Badder Than B-fore*, and *Seven-Seven* CDs. Excellent singles include "I am the Lyte," the rowdy "Shut the Eff Up, Hoe," and "Kickin' 4 Brooklyn."

Lyte helped make the soundtrack for *Set it Off*, the utmost in rap albums. The movie features a Lyte protégé, Queen Latifah, whose career flourished beyond most of her contemporaries. Lyte also opened doors for Missy Elliot and others. Lyte's canon earned her a permanent page in the hip hop annals.

Mary Jane Blige was born in the Bronx. A chain of events including a karaoke demo recording led her to Uptown Records and Sean "P-Diddy" Combs. Combs launched Blige's career, billing her as the "Queen of hip hop." Blige backed up the claim by selling two million copies on her debut album in 1992. Her slamming, B-girl thuggery ignited many solo albums, including *Dance for Me*, *No More Drama*, *Mary*, *Tour*, *Share My World*; and soundtracks for *Waiting to Exhale* and *Prison Song*. Despite her raw exterior, Mary J. had a soft side that she bared repeatedly in the name of giving it all up to her audience. This thread can be traced from classics like "I'm Going Down" through groove-grinding jams like "Let No Man Put Asunder." Blige described her music as hip hop-gospel simply because her message was "good news." Not only could Blige sling it with the best of male MCs, but she also collaborated with female artists such as Aretha Franklin, Gladys Knight, Lauryn Hill, and her home-girl, Lil' Kim.

Da Brat was born Shawntae Harris in Chicago. She began as a drummer in her church choir—hence, the title of her debut CD, *Funkdafied* (1994), a play on the word sanctified. *Funkdafied* billed the foul-mouth church-girl as a female Snoop Doggy Dog and sampled the Isley Brothers' single "Between the Sheets" for the mega-hit title track. Her follow-up CD, *Anutha Tantrum*, poked fun at critics who dismissed Brat as Jermaine Duprey's pawn. Record sales of *Unrestricted* deemed Brat a force to be reckoned with.

Defining Dignity

Queen Latifah announced her stance with her name. Dana Owens chose the power of the monarch and the power of African tradition when she became Queen Latifah and titled her debut album *All Hail the Queen*. As she put it in her inspirational book *Ladies First*, "A queen is a queen when riding high, and when clouded in disgrace, shame, or sorrow, she has dignity. Being a queen has very little to do with exterior things. It is a state of mind." With help from MC Lyte, Latifah recorded regularly. No album is more arresting than the Queen's 1998 *Order in the Court*, featuring her trademark crown of blazing fire and fellow rapper Nikki D.

Latifah was one of the first black woman rappers to diversify and reinvent herself as an actor, talk show host, producer, and investor. Her role in the television situation comedy *Living Single* gave her the exposure she needed to survive. Along the way, she helped redefine standards of beauty in America via fashion spreads for such brands as Lane Bryant and Reebok. She even garnered an Academy Award nomination for her role in the 2002 film *Chicago*, a role she won over such competitors as Bette Midler, Rosie O'Donnell, and Madonna—all white actors.

Lauryn Hill was born in South Orange, New Jersey. The singer-actor-producer holds the female record for winning five Grammys in one year. The *Miseducation of Lauryn Hill* CD came after Hill produced songs and a video for Aretha Franklin (*A Rose is Not a Rose*) and Common. Hill was one of the three-member Fugees with two male MCs, but later reemerged as an acoustic folk singer for her sophomore album, *MTV Unplugged*. The double CD presents Hill's love of her son and hip hop, and her bittersweet bout with life in the fast lane. She features stream of consciousness sermonizing and coffeehouse folk singing.

Sister Souljah (née Lisa Williamson) was a rapper, author, and activist. She studied American history and African American studies at Rutgers University, Cornell University, and University of Salamanca in Spain. She actually became better known for her politics than for her rap. Souljah moved further into social activism, and her grassroots organization came to touch thousands of urban youths through summer hip hop camps and other educational activities.

Bahamadia was often praised for not appealing to the lowest common denominator of hip hop. This Philadelphian was born Antonio Reed. Her Arabic name is a fusion of Badia, which means "original creation," and Hamd'allah, which means "praise be to God." Her *Kollage* album, which sampled Marvin Gaye and the Isley Brothers, debuted in 1996. Inspired by religious ideals, her 2000 CD *B. B. Queen* (Beautiful Black Queen) results from biblical passages that helped her transform sexual urges into creative energy. The album salutes regular folks through diverse topics such as thrift shopping, lullabies, serial killers, and sex scandals. Bahamadia's "Pep Talk" single is about energy that flows from the vagina. Other albums include *Total Wreck*, *I Confess*, *Uknowhowwedo*, and collaborations with the Roots, Lauryn Hill, and Sade. Bahamadia is a mother of two and has hosted the B-sides radio show.

Graphic Sexuality

Kimberly "L. Kim" Jones was one of hip hop's most controversial figures. The lady of a thousand faces—one of them a dead ringer for female impersonator Rupaul Charles—she represented the cadre of female hip hoppers who opted for the power of graphic sex, instead of dignity. The former homeless teenager made a name for herself with X-rated rhymes on her debut album, *Hardcore* (1996), and her *Notorious KIM* received serious parental advisory warnings. She was the only female member of Junior MAFIA. When the charge was made that women in hip hop were giving black women a bad name, Lil' Kim's name often came up first.

Foxy Brown was another controversial figure in hip hop. Born Inga Marchand in Brooklyn, she took her stage name from a seventies blackploitation film starring Pam Grier. Foxy's act was full of sex-charged lyrics, even on her first CD, *III Na Na* (1996). Her *Fever* and *Broken Silence* earned the parental advisory rating. Partner-in-rhyme collaborations included BWA (Bitches with Attitudes) with Gangsta Boo and Mia X, often hailed as a female anthem. One trait that endeared Foxy to audiences was that she allowed them to glimpse the pain of living the high life.

Next Generation

Eve of Destruction (Eve Jihan Jeffers), Yo Yo, Erykah Badu, Missy "Misdemeanor" Elliot, Gangsta Boo, Khia Chambers, Queen Pen, Meshell N'degéocello, Rah Digga (Rashiya Fisher), Sugar-T, and Mia X were among the women who used hip hop for personal and cultural expression. Some hip hop women had short lives, including Aaliyah (1979–2001) and TLC's Lisa "Left-eye" Lopes (1972–2002), whose eye was usually covered by her signature bangs or an eye patch. Aaliyah died in a plane crash over Bermuda. Left Eye was killed in a car wreck in Honduras. Both were canonized by fans and the media.

Other women have clearly been on the hip hop track—or have hoped to be—to the kind of stardom enjoyed by Queen Latifah and male rappers like Ice T and Snoop Dogg. There has been a great deal of money in hip hop. There has also been a great deal of cultural meaning. There has been opportunity for African American young people that recalls the days of doo-wop groups and Motown, and there has been cultural pressure that often undermines the best efforts of parents to give their children educations and futures.

Despite criticism of their lyrics and videos, hip hoppers have claimed to deliver messages that elicit positive awareness. Without a doubt, hip hop has appealed to people across ethnic, social, economic, generational, and international borders. Moreover, hip hop has been largely responsible for the resurgence and popularity of poetry among young people.

BIBLIOGRAPHY

Harris, James. Telephone Conversations with the Author. Interview by Regina Harris Baiocchi. Chicago, 2002.

Muhammad, Angelique. Telephone Conversations with the Author. Interview by Regina Harris Baiocchi. Chicago, 2002.

Patterson, Ama. E-mail Conversations with the Author. Interview by Regina Harris Baiocchi. Chicago and New York, 2002.

Vibe Magazine, ed. *Hip hop Divas*. New York: Three Rivers Press, 2001.

DISCOGRAPHY

Various Artists. *Fat Beats & Bra Straps*. Produced by Zenobia Simmons. Rhino Records, 1997. Three compact disc set.

—REGINA HARRIS BAIOCCHI

HISTORIANS. On 23 March 1925, roughly thirty years after W. E. B. Du Bois became the first African American historian to receive a PhD, at the age of sixty-six, feminist pioneer, educator, and social activist Anna Julia Cooper, who lived from 1858 to 1964, became the fourth black woman to receive a PhD and the first to receive a PhD within the fields of History and Romance Languages. She earned her doctorate of philosophy from the prestigious University of Paris, the Sorbonne. Her dissertation, written in French, was titled "L'Attitude de la France dans la question de l'esclavage entre 1789 et 1848" ("The Attitude of France on the Question of Slavery between 1789 and 1848"). Cooper conducted meticulous research at the Library of Congress, various French archives, and the Bibliothèque Militaire while immersing herself in the relevant secondary source materials. The leading French historians M. Sagnac, M. Cestre, and M. C. Bougle questioned her during her dissertation defense. Cooper's achievements were remarkable on many levels. The author of the first major black feminist manifesto, *A Voice from the South* (1892), Cooper did not conform to the "cult of true womanhood," the prevalent ideology that a woman's place was in the domestic or private sphere. Cooper directly challenged the leading male spokespersons of the Progressive era for their sexism, declaring "only the BLACK WOMAN can say 'when and where I enter . . . then and there the whole *Negro race enters with me.*'" She maintained this stance throughout her life.

Anna Julia Cooper was an outspoken advocate for the higher education of women and she embraced the National Association of Colored Women's "Lifting as We Climb" motto. She earned her BA and MA degrees in Mathematics and as a doctoral student she studied literature, history, languages (French, Latin, and Greek), and phonetics. She was indeed multidisciplinary in her intellectual approach. Like Du Bois, she combined her knowledge and expertise in history with other fields of intellectual inquiry to forge an original worldview. Moreover, she earned her doctorate while serving as guardian to five grandnieces and grandnephews. Though largely unnoticed in French and U.S. academic circles, Cooper's dissertation candidly critiqued France's and the western world's slaveholding past. Her fundamental argument was that slavery had profoundly impacted French revolutionary political culture and that the French revolutionaries' reluctance to critique slavery fundamentally contradicted their ideas. The tone of Cooper's study is polemical at times, yet she adhered to the historical profession's standards of her times.

The history of black women historians, formally trained like Cooper and self-proclaimed like many others, constitutes a dynamic narrative, challenging readers to revisit the lives and works of lesser known black women scholars and reconceptualize conventional definitions of what makes an historian. Black women historians can be subdivided into four main groups: (1) Progressive-era novelists who published fiction which critically addressed important historical subject matter; (2) self-taught, non–PhD holding historians or "historians without portfolio" who produced insightful, accessible, and practical scholarship from the turn of the century until the classic civil rights movement; (3) accomplished and professionally trained scholars, namely Dorothy Porter Wesley and Shirley Graham Du Bois, who, though not formally trained as historians, published historical monographs and engaged in rigorous historical research; and (4) professionally trained, PhD–holding historians.

Early Black Women Historical Writers

The first distinguishable group of black women historians emerged during the late 1800s and the first half of the twentieth century. During the late nineteenth century, several Progressive-era black women novelists, social activists, schoolteachers, and scholars published significant historical scholarship. During the Harlem Renaissance and the Great Depression, black women "historians without portfolio" published noteworthy historical scholarship. From its founding through the 1950s, the Association for the Study of Negro Life and History (ASNLH) organization provided black female teachers, activists, and professionally trained scholars with a vital arena in which to study and disseminate African American history. Yet, in the decade after Cooper earned her PhD, no black women appear to have earned a PhD in History. This drought in the 1930s was followed by a decade in which the numbers of black female historians increased significantly. In 1940 Marion Thompson Wright became the first black woman historian to earn a PhD in the United States from Columbia University. Other black women followed in her footsteps. In the 1940s, six black women received PhDs in History. Following the modern civil rights movement and the Black Power era, the number of black women historians increased. The Association of Black Women Historians, whose constitution was drafted in 1980, became the first organization for professional black women historians, bringing together the key

Featuring Early Scholars

● **Sadie Tanner Mossell Alexander** (1898–1989) was the second African American woman in the United States to receive a doctoral degree and the first to receive a PhD in economics. She went on to become the first African American woman to enter the bar and practice law in the state of Pennsylvania. (See individual entry: Alexander, Sadie Tanner Mossell.)

● **Delilah Leontium Beasley** (1872–1934) published the groundbreaking book, *The Negro Trail-Blazers of California*. Born in Cincinnati, Ohio, she first published in the *Cleveland Gazette* when she was only twelve. Her first column appeared in the *Cincinnati Enquirer* when she was fifteen. After her parents died when she was in her teens she worked at a variety of jobs in several towns, ultimately becoming a masseuse. After moving to California in 1910 she sat in on history classes at the University of California, Berkeley, but never enrolled. She spent at least nine years carefully researching, compiling, and writing her book. *Negro Trail-Blazers* was finally finished in 1919, and although professional historians including Carter G. Woodson criticized it, it went on to become an essential resource on the history of African Americans in California. While she was working on *Negro Trail-Blazers* Beasley became a news contributor with the *Oakland Tribune*. In 1923 she began to publish her weekly Sunday column titled "Activities among Negroes." In addition she successfully lobbied the white press in the area not to use the words *darkie* and *nigger*, as well as to capitalize *Negro*. She died in 1934 in San Leandro, California.

● **Letitia Woods Brown** (1915–1976) was an early scholar of African American history. She was born in Tuskegee, Alabama, and earned a BA from Tuskegee (1935), an MA from Ohio State University (1937), and a PhD from Harvard University (1966). She taught throughout her life starting in the Macon County school system when it was still segregated. She moved on to teach at Tuskegee, Lemoyne-Owen College in Memphis, and Howard University. She ultimately became a member of the American Studies Department at George Washington University. One of the earliest scholars to explore the African American experience in detail, she wrote *Free Negroes in the District of Columbia, 1790–1846* (1972). In addition to teaching and writing she was a member of the restructuring committee of the American Historical Association which was formed in the early 1970s to reorganize the association. She was also a senior Fulbright scholar, and worked to establish the Schlesinger Library's oral history project on African American women. After her death the Association of Black Women Historians created the Letitia Woods Brown Memorial Publication Prizes to acknowledge her contribution to African American history.

● **Fanny Jackson Coppin** (1837–1913) was named the principal of Philadelphia's Institute for Colored Youth in 1869. She is the first black woman in the nation to head an institution of higher learning. (See individual entry: Coppin, Fanny Jackson.)

● **Caroline Stewart Bond Day** (1889–1948) was one of the first African Americans if not the first to receive an advanced degree in anthropology. She studied interracial families in the 1930s. Born in Montgomery, Alabama, she grew up in Boston, Tuskegee, Birmingham, Selma, Alabama, and Washington, DC. She attended Atlanta University where she earned a bachelor's degree. She then moved on to Radcliffe College, but Radcliffe would not accept her bachelor's from Atlanta, so she studied for two more years and received a second BA in 1919. After college she became a member of the faculty first at Prairie View College, and then at Atlanta University. During this period she also published a variety of prose and poetry both fiction and nonfiction. In 1927 she returned to school, and entered Harvard's Graduate School of Anthropology. She received her MA in 1932. Her thesis on the history of interracial families, A Study of Some Negro–White Families in the United States, was published by Harvard's Peabody Museum of Archeology and Ethnology. Although the book has been criticized in the years since for its methodology, it and the auxiliary research Day collected are valuable historical resources. Suffering from a chronic heart ailment, Day retired after she finished the book. She died in 1948 in Durham, North Carolina.

● **Eva Dykes** (1893–1986) was one of the first three African American women to receive a PhD in 1921. Born in Washington, DC, she attended Howard University (BA, English, summa cum laude, 1914). She moved on to Radcliffe College where in 1917 she was magna cum laude and Phi Beta Kappa, and received a second BA. Staying on at Radcliffe she pursued her English studies and, in 1918 received an MA, and in 1921 her PhD in English philology. Her dissertation was titled "Pope and His Influence in America from 1715 to 1850." She then left the academy and began teaching at Dunbar High School in Washington, DC. In 1929 she joined the faculty at Howard University as an associate professor of English. Only a year later, she was named the best all-around teacher by the College of Liberal Arts. In 1945 Howard gave her the Alumni Award for Distinguished Postgraduate Achievement. In 1946 Oakwood College in Huntsville, Alabama, hired her to head its English department. She was named chair of the accreditation quest committee in 1958. In 1973 the college named its new library the Eva Beatrice Dykes Library. She retired in 1975. In addition to her teaching duties Dykes published *Readings from Negro Authors for Schools and Colleges* (1931) and *The Negro in English Romantic Thought* (1942). She died in 1986 in Hunstville, Alabama.

● **Drusilla Dunjee Houston** (1876–1941) is best known for the publication of *Wonderful Ethiopians of the Ancient Cushite*

Empire, Book 1: Nations of the Cushite Empire, Marvelous Facts from Authentic Records. The book boldly proclaimed an African origin of civilization. (See individual entry: Houston, Drusilla Dunjee.)

● **Camille Lucie Nickerson** (1887–1982) taught audiences as well as students the value of African American folk music through her performance and study of Creole music. Born in New Orleans, Louisiana, she received a BA and MA from the Oberlin Conservatory of Music. There she became a member of the Pi Kappa Lambda National Music Honor Society. Her master's thesis was on Creole music, which was throughout her life the primary focus of her scholarship and teaching. She left Ohio and returned to New Orleans to teach with her father in the Nickerson School of Music. Many of her students became music teachers themselves. In 1926 Nickerson joined the faculty of Howard University where in addition to her work as professor of piano, and continued scholarship on Creole music she founded the Junior Department of the Howard University School of Music. In addition to her work in the academy, in 1917 she founded the B Sharp Music Club in New Orleans, which still exists. In 1921 the club affiliated itself with the National Association of Negro Musicians, an organization that Nickerson also served as president (1935–1937). Both with the club and on her own, Nickerson had a career as a concert musician. She billed herself as the "Louisiana Lady" and showed thousands of Americans the power and beauty of traditional African American music. She died in Washington, DC, in 1982.

● **Mary Jane Patterson** (1840–1894) was the first black woman to earn a bachelor's degree from an American college. She was born in Raleigh, North Carolina, but moved to Oberlin with her family when she was sixteen. After she graduated from Oberlin College in 1862 she moved to Philadelphia and went to work in the Female Department of the Institute for Colored Youth. In 1869 she moved to Washington, DC, to work at the new Preparatory High School for Colored Youth (Dunbar High School). Two years later she became its first black principal. She remained in that position until 1884. In addition to her work at Dunbar, Patterson was involved in establishing industrial schools for black women and helped found the Home for Aged and Infirm Colored People. She died on 24 September 1894.

● **Lucy Stanton Day Sessions** (1831–1910) is the first known African American woman to graduate from college. Born in Cleveland, Ohio, to free mulatto parents, she was raised in an atmosphere of education and antislavery activism. She entered the Ladies Literary Course at Oberlin College in 1848. This course was similar to a BA but required no mathematics, Greek, or Latin and was only two years long. When Sessions graduated in 1850 she presented an essay, "A Plea for the Oppressed," which signaled her lifelong activism in various reform movements. She then became principal of a school for African Americans in Columbus, Ohio, for a short time before returning to Cleveland and marrying William Howard Day. In 1854 she published her first story in her husband's antislavery newspaper, the *Alienated American.* In 1856 she moved to the black community of Buxton, Ontario, and lived there until her husband left her in 1859, at which point she returned to Cleveland. After the Civil War ended she was sent by a local abolition association to teach in Georgia. In 1871 the American Missionary Association hired Sessions to teach at a school in Fayette, Mississippi. She remained in Fayette, divorced her first husband, and married Levi Sessions. In 1884 they went to Chattanooga, where Sessions taught, became president of the colored chapter of the Women's Christian Temperance Union, and was a grand matron of the Grand Order of the Eastern Star and an officer of the National Aide Women's Relief Corps. Sessions moved for the last time in 1903 when she relocated to Los Angeles. She died there in 1910.

● **Georgiana Simpson** (1866–1944) was the first black woman in America to earn a PhD. Born in Washington, DC, she graduated from the city's Normal School, and in 1885 became an elementary school teacher. Later she traveled to Germany to study its language and literature. After her return to DC, she began to teach German at Dunbar High School. During her summers off from teaching she continued to expand her knowledge by attending programs at Harvard and the University of Chicago. She earned her BA in German from the latter institution and, in 1921 her PhD as well. Although Sadie Alexander and Eva Dykes also earned PhDs the same year, Simpson's came first. Simpson then began postdoctoral work in the French language and French literature. In 1924 she edited Grangon La Coste's *Toussaint L'Ouverture.* In 1931 she joined the faculty of Howard University, and she taught there until her retirement eight years later. She died in 1944. The National Association of Black Professional Women honored her with an achievement award in 1976.

● **Eileen Jackson Southern** (1920–) was the first black female tenured full professor at Harvard College, and she chaired Harvard's African American Studies Department from 1975 to 1979. She is also the mother of African American ethnomusicology. (See individual entry: Southern, Eileen Jackson.)

● **Merze Tate** (1905–1996) was the first African American woman to receive an advanced degree from Oxford University. She provided exceptional instruction to students, who remembered her years later as a wonderful role model and rigorous teacher. (See individual entry: Tate, Merze.)

figures within the black female historical profession. Since then, especially in the course of the mainstreaming of black women's history in the 1980s and 1990s, black women historians proliferated. As black women's history became more sophisticated and popular, many black women acquired prominence in the American historical profession. Several successive generations of black female historians during the late nineteenth and throughout the twentieth century laid the foundations for the current contributions of black women historians and the present state of the study of black women's history.

During the late nineteenth century, the Progressive-era black women novelists Frances Ellen Watkins Harper, living from 1825 to 1911 and Pauline Hopkins, living from 1859 to 1930, wrote "female-centered," seemingly unthreatening, "domestic novels" which critically addressed controversial issues and events in U.S. history, such as slavery, the Civil War, and Reconstruction. As Carter G. Woodson would stress more than a decade after these writers' novels appeared, Harper and Hopkins argued that history was instructive because of its direct connection with the present and future. In 1892, Harper's widely circulated *Iola Leroy; or, Shadows Uplifted* addressed many of the complex issues surrounding slavery, the wartime South, Emancipation, Reconstruction, and the historical social responsibility of black reformers. Similarly, Hopkins's *Contending Forces: A Romance Illustrative of Negro Life North and South* (1900) and *Winona* (1902) discussed the historical realities faced by blacks during the antebellum era, Emancipation, and Reconstruction. From 1900 to 1902, Hopkins published two dozen biographical sketches on well-known African American men and women in the *Colored American Magazine*. In 1905 Hopkins also published a thirty-one-page booklet, *A Primer of Facts Pertaining to the Early Greatness of the African Race and the Possibility of Restoration by Its Descendants—with Epilogue*. Other Progressive-era black women offered their interpretations of history in nonfiction works. In 1894, Gertrude E. H. Bustill Mossell, living from 1855 to 1948, editor, journalist, and feminist, first published *The Work of the Afro-American Woman*, an historical and contemporary assessment of black women intellectuals' and activists' monumental accomplishments since the era of the American Revolution. Joanne Braxton has posited that this volume "was, for the black woman of the 1890s, the equivalent of [Paula] Giddings' work of the 1980s—in sum, a powerful and progressive statement."

In the first several decades of the twentieth century, many self-taught black female historians contributed noteworthy autobiographical accounts and popular histories to U.S. and African American historiography. In 1902 Susie King Taylor, living from 1848 to 1912, published the only black woman's account of the Civil War. *A Black Woman's Civil War Memoirs* recounted her experiences as a laundress and a nurse behind Union lines from about 1862 until 1865. Though not as widely known as Taylor, the Washington, DC, public school teacher Laura Eliza Wilkes, living from 1871 to 1922, also contributed to U.S. military history, becoming the first black woman to chronicle the history of blacks in the military from the colonial era through the War of 1812 in *Missing Pages in American History: Revealing the Services of Negroes in the Early Wars of America* (1919).

In 1919 the journalist and social activist Delilah Leontium Beasley, living from 1872 to 1934, published *The Negro Trail Blazers of California*. Beasley was committed to challenging the notion that blacks had not contributed to California's history. Ahead of her time, she drew attention to the African American experience in the West; she employed methodologies of modern historians. Beasley conducted meticulous research at various archives and libraries, interviewed black Californians, examined newspapers, combed through personal papers and memorabilia, and contacted counties in California requesting any materials dealing with African Americans. Several years after Beasley's study appeared, the sociologist Elizabeth Ross Haynes, living from 1883 to 1953, published *Unsung Heroes*, a 279-page collection of biographical sketches of black historical leaders. Several years later, in 1923, her MA thesis, "Negroes in Domestic Service in the United States," was published in the *Journal of Negro History*. In the 1920s and 1930s, the progressive social reformer Elizabeth Lindsay Davis, born in 1855, published two illuminating historical narratives of the lives and works on black clubwomen, *The Story of the Illinois Federation of Colored Women's Clubs* (1922) and *Lifting as They Climb* (1933). The latter study constitutes the first major effort at chronicling the contributions of the National Association of Colored Women. It is more than four hundred pages long and is subdivided into seven main parts, covering more than three decades of history, activities, and leadership. As Wanda Hendricks has noted, "much of what we currently know about the early club work of African American women is due to the commitment of Elizabeth Lindsay Davis." In the mid-1920s, the self-taught historian Drusilla Dunjee Houston, living from 1876 to 1941, became the first black woman to extensively examine ancient African history in her *Wonderful Ethiopians of the Ancient Cushite Empire* (1926). Houston's study stands as a precursor to the modern black American Afrocentric tradition which has flourished since the Black Power era.

Organizing Historians under the ASNLH

When Houston's book appeared, black women historians, both professionally trained and self-taught, came together under the umbrella of the ASNLH. Woodson welcomed black women into his black history movement and supported their efforts to legitimize and popularize the study of black culture. Black women teachers, club women, librarians, self-taught historians, and social activists all played vital roles in the activities of the ASNLH, especially by the 1930s. Between 1916 and 1950, several outspoken black female leaders and scholars contributed to the *Journal of Negro History*, including Mary Church Terrell, Alice Dunbar-Nelson, Elizabeth Ross Haynes, Dorothy Porter, Zora Neale Hurston, and Mary McLeod Bethune. From the outset, women performed essential behind-the-scenes work in the association's infrastructure. After the founding of Negro History Week in 1926, black women organized activities in schools such as book displays and pageants, promoted annual celebrations and observances, and established active ASNLH branches, history clubs, and study groups throughout the country.

At the state and local levels, black women like Sylvia Tucker, Wilhelmina Crosson, and Jane Dabney Shackelford were among the key organizers and participants in the association's annual meetings, activities, and overall work. During the 1930s and 1940s, Tucker was a key activist in the association's Detroit branch. Founded in 1924, the Detroit branch thrived under Tucker's leadership. Under her guidance and fundraising skills, the Detroit branch grew to an impressive fifteen hundred members. She also introduced association chapters to other parts of Michigan such as Flint, Lansing, Ann Arbor, and Grand Rapids. Tucker has been remembered as being a "spark plug," a "dynamic leader," and "Miss Negro History." Crosson, a member of the *Negro History Bulletin*'s editorial board, a Boston public school teacher, and a member of the ASNLH's executive council, was one of Woodson's most engaged female field researchers. She conducted exhaustive research on the African presence in Mexico during the World War II era. Shackelford, a schoolteacher from Terre Haute, Indiana, and the author of the very popular *The Child's Story of the Negro* (1938), was "immortal" in Woodson's opinion. In addition to writing several children's books on African American history, she was an enthusiastic and energetic promoter of black history as the head of the Indiana Negro Historical Society, an association branch in Terre Haute, Indiana.

Women's clubs often sponsored events, hosted dinners, and organized the daily activities for the visiting ASNLH conferees. Black women attended all of the association annual meetings, contributed to the lively discussions, and many outspoken black women activists and intellectuals presented papers at association annual meetings, including Sadie Mossell Alexander, Nannie Helen Burroughs, Charlotte Hawkins Brown, and Jane Edna Hunter. In 1935, Lucy Harth Smith and Mary McLeod Bethune became the first black women elected to the ASNLH's executive council.

From 1936 until 1952, Bethune served as the president of the ASNLH. She was a skilled publicist and an adroit fund-raiser for the organization. She was an unwavering supporter of Woodson's quest to popularize black history. As association president, Bethune delivered addresses at annual meetings, five of which were published in the *Journal*. She argued that black historians needed to arm black children with the knowledge of their past, while underscoring black America's humanity to white society.

Black women were especially active in making the association's *Negro History Bulletin* a successful vehicle for the dissemination of black history to schools and to a general black readership. From its inception in October 1937, black women occupied significant positions on the magazine's editorial staff. The *Bulletin* served as an important forum for debate and discussion among female teachers. Images of black women were common in the *Bulletin*. Black women were also in charge of the *Bulletin*'s popular "Children's Page." For many years, the renowned artist Lois Mailou Jones worked as the magazine's artist and "Children's Page" coordinator.

As the association matured during the 1930s and 1940s, a cadre of professionally trained black women historians emerged. Other black women, namely Dorothy Burnett Porter Wesley, living from 1905 to 1995, and Shirley Graham Du Bois, living from 1896 to 1977, used their professional training to promote black history. The 1940s proved a watershed for professional black women historians. In this decade alone at least six black women earned PhDs in History. These scholars shared some important traits. Born in the early twentieth century, these trailblazers received their training from some of the most prestigious institutions in the country, often becoming the first black woman to earn doctorates at their respective institutions. They often used the *Journal of Negro History* and the *Journal of Negro Education* as outlets for their scholarship. Like their contemporaries John Hope Franklin and Benjamin Quarles, these women tended to write very objective history, a strategy dictated by their times. Not surprisingly, none focused on black women's history. These women often served as mentors for younger black female scholars and they interpreted their roles as teachers very seriously, often pioneering new strategies of education. As female historians, they had to develop mechanisms to cope with the sexism and racism prevalent in American academia. Elsie Lewis's advisor had to seek help from her white advisor in order to gain access to the Arkansas State Archives. Others, like Marion Thompson Wright, had to overcome great obstacles in order to gain promotion and tenure. At the same time, these women were politically and ideologically diverse. Helen G. Edmonds, for instance, was committed to the National Republican Party at a time when most black spokespersons were moving toward the Democratic Party.

Contributions from Related Fields

Unlike their Progressive-era predecessors, Dorothy Burnett Porter Wesley and Shirley Graham Du Bois received extensive training in academic areas other than history and used their expertise to generate significant historical scholarship. From 1930 until 1973, Porter Wesley served as the chief curator for the Moorland-Spingarn Research Center. Constantly underfunded, Porter Wesley developed into a very resourceful and persistent collector and promoter of African descendants' history and culture. In 1973, her colleague Benjamin Quarles praised her, declaring "without exaggeration, there hasn't been a major black history book in the last 30 years in which the author hasn't acknowledged Mrs. Porter's help." Henry Louis Gates Jr.'s discovery of Hannah Craft's *The Bondwoman's Narrative* (written circa 1850s and brought to publication by Gates in 2002) owed a great debt to Porter Wesley; this manuscript was part of her personal collection. Porter Wesley was also a published historian. Before the modern civil rights movement, she compiled many comprehensive bibliographies on black history, her earliest being *A Selected History of Books by and about Negroes* (1936) and *Negro American Poets: A Bibliographic Checklist of Their Writings* (1945). In addition, during the 1930s, 1940s, and 1950s, Wesley published articles on antebellum black activists in the *Journal of Negro Education* and the *Journal of Negro History*.

While they are in the same subgroup, Shirley Graham Du Bois and Porter Wesley adopted divergent approaches to black history. Graham Du Bois's contributions as an historian have been overshadowed by her social and political activism. Yet, between 1944 and 1976, she published thirteen biographies of famous historical figures in African American history, half of which were published between 1944 and 1955. Creative, accessible to a broad readership, and often based upon careful examinations of the available documentation, Graham Du Bois's biographies that were produced during the era of segregation demonstrate her abilities as an historian.

Black Women Historians on College Faculties

In 1940, Marion Thompson Wright, living from 1902 to 1962, became the first black woman to earn a doctorate in history in the United States. Her dissertation, *The Education of Negroes in New Jersey*, was published in 1941 by the Columbia University Teacher's College Series. After graduating magna cum laude from Howard University in 1927, she earned her MA degree at Howard in Education. In the 1930s, she enrolled in a doctoral program in History and Education at Columbia Teacher's College, where she studied under Merle Curti. While pursuing her doctorate during the Great Depression, Wright worked as a case supervisor for the Newark Department of Public Welfare.

In 1940, she joined the faculty at Howard University, setting high standards for her students while inspiring younger black women to consider becoming historians. While at Howard, Wright published articles on blacks in New Jersey in the *Journal of Negro History*, the *Journal of Negro Education* (for which she served as the book review editor), and the *Journal of Educational Sociology*.

Wright's scholarship remains important in the field. Despite significant pioneering accomplishments, Wright faced significant gender discrimination. Her struggle for tenure and promotion to the rank of full professor was long and hard. But her research was important in helping to expose the negative impact of discrimination on U.S. culture, and it helped influence New Jersey's new constitution and the public school desegregation cases decided by the Supreme Court in 1954.

In 1941 Lulu M. Johnson earned a doctorate in History from Iowa State University. Her dissertation was titled "The Problem of Slavery in the Old Northwest, 1787–1858." This Rockefeller Foundation fellow published a manual entitled *The Negro in American Life* and taught at West Virginia State College. In the same year that Johnson received her degree, Merze Tate became the first black woman to earn a PhD in Government and International Relations from Harvard University. Though not formally trained as an historian, Tate embraced an interdisciplinary approach. In the 1940s she taught courses in History and published several historical monographs, such as *The Disarmament Illusion: The Movement for a Limitation of Armaments to 1907* (1942) and *The United States and Armaments* (1948). In 1943, Susie Owen Lee received a PhD in history from New York University. She completed a dissertation titled "The Union League of America: Political Activity in Tennessee, the Carolinas, and Virginia, 1865–1870." Three years later, Elsie Lewis earned a PhD in History from the University of Chicago. She completed her dissertation on the secession movement in Arkansas. This Fisk University graduate published an intriguing article, "The Political Mind of the Negro, 1865–1900," in the *Journal of Southern History* in 1955. She was also active within the predominantly white Southern Historical Association. Like Wright, Lewis became an important member of Howard University's History Department, serving as acting chairman for six years.

Helen G. Edmonds, living from 1911 to 1995, received her PhD in History in 1946 from Ohio State University. In 1951 she published her dissertation, *The Negro and Fusion Politics in North Carolina, 1894–1901*, a detailed examination of African Americans' role in politics in North Carolina during the pivotal 1890s. Many well-respected reviewers welcomed Edmonds's monograph. Decades later, she published a study on blacks in the government, *Black Faces in High Places: Negroes in Government* (1971). Edmonds was among the few black historians born during the Progressive era who wrote a monograph focusing on black history during the civil rights movement. Edmonds was also an important presence at North Carolina Central University in Durham, North Carolina. She worked there from 1941 until she retired in 1977. She held a host of positions at NCCU, serving at one point as the chair of the Department of History. A steady supporter of the National Republican Party, she served in the Department of State, the Department of Defense, the National Advisory Council of the Peace Corps, and even as a U.S. delegate to the United Nations. In this case, she preceded Mary Frances Berry, who held U.S. governmental positions during the 1980s and 1990s. The John Hope Franklin Research Collection of African and African American Documentation at Duke University houses the Helen G. Edmonds Papers, 1951–1976, containing four thousand items. In the late 1940s Margaret Nelson Rowley closed out the decade for professionally trained black female historians, earning a PhD from Columbia University.

Civil Rights–Era Historians

During the civil rights movement, several black women historians who came of age in the 1940s remained involved in the profession. Yet, much like the 1930s, the 1950s were challenging years for black women historians. According to the historians August Meier and Elliot Rudwick, the number of black women who earned doctorates during the 1940s "seems to have been a transitory phenomenon and a substantial flow of Negro women PhDs into history does not appear to have resumed until the late 1960s." Lorraine Williams, living from 1923 to 1996, was among the few black women to earn doctorates in History the 1950s. Williams received her doctorate from American University in 1955. Her focus was on American intellectual history. After earning her BA and MA degrees from Howard University in the mid 1940s, she started her career at her alma mater; she began by teaching a survey course in Social Services and ultimately became a full professor and was chair of the Department of History. During her career, she edited or coauthored eight monographs and published a half a dozen articles, several of which appeared in the *Journal of Negro Education*, a popular outlet for black women historians. Williams was also a social activist. During the 1960s she "taught in an experimental program for disadvantaged students" at Howard. In addition, she was active in organizations such as the Urban League, the National Council of Negro Women, the Black Woman's Agenda, the American Council of Human Rights, and the NAACP. According to Rosalyn Terborg-Penn and Janice Sumler-Edmond, Williams was a "pioneering female professor and university administrator" who "mentored hundreds of students" and helped popularize the *Journal of Negro History*, for which she served as editor. In

1977, she edited a popular monograph, *Africa and the Afro-American Experience: Eight Essays.*

Towards the end of the civil rights movement and the emergence of the Black Power era, few black women earned PhDs in history. Among them was Mary Frances Berry, who received a PhD in Constitutional History from the University of Michigan in 1966. Berry also earned a doctorate of Jurisprudence. Berry "both writes and makes history," Genna Rae McNeil has noted. Among her mentors were the Howard University professors Elsie Lewis and Lorraine Williams. During the 1970s, she published several important articles and monographs. Her classic volume published during the Black Power era was *Black Resistance/White Law: A History of Constitutional Racism* (1971). Berry also held various administrative positions in the 1970s, and beyond, at major research institutions.

The ABWH and Formally Trained Black Women Historians

By the 1970s, many key developments had contributed to the rise of professionally trained black female historians. During the Black Power era, black student activism reached a peak and thousands of black students at predominantly white institutions initiated the Black Studies movement. The study of history was considered one of the most important disciplines. A budding Black Women's History and Studies movement coincided with these trends. Many black women historians and scholars published major studies on black women during the post–Black Power era 1970s and 1980s. Among those to contribute important historical scholarship on black women in the 1970s were Angela Davis, Gerda Lerner (a white female), Sharon Harley, Rosalyn Terborg-Penn, Debra L. Newman, and Darlene Clark Hine. This revisionist scholarship, epitomized by Harley and Terborg-Penn's anthology *The Afro-American Woman: Struggles and Images* (1978), signaled the emergence of this field. Another important development occurred in 1979 when black women historians created the Association of Black Women Historians, Inc. (ABWH). In 1977 Terborg-Penn, Eleanor Smith, and Elizabeth Parker called for the creation of this organization and in February 1979, the governing rules, regulations, and foundations of the organization were in place.

In 1980 the ABWH's constitution was adopted and the organization was incorporated. The organization's first national director was Terborg-Penn. According to Francille Rusan Wilson, the ABWH has a "dual identity," serving as a "professional home for black women who are historians, and the central location of support of historical research on black women." In the words of one of its early members, "the ABWH became the institutional infrastructure of the black women's history movement just as the Association for the Study of Negro Life and History ... served as the organizational foundation for the Black History Movement." Since the 1980s, the group has engaged in practical work such as networking, mentoring younger scholars in the field, defining the field of black women's history, promoting scholarship and research within black women's history, and offering support for black women historians.

The 1980s and 1990s witnessed watershed developments in black women's history and the black female historical profession. In the 1980s important monographs were published in the field of black women's history, including Hine's *When the Truth Is Told: Black Women's Culture and Community in Indiana, 1890–1950* (1981) and *Black Women in White: Racial Conflict and Cooperation in the Nursing Profession, 1890–1950* (1989); Dorothy Sterling's *We Are Your Sisters: Black Women and the Nineteenth Century* (1984); Beverly Guy-Sheftall's *"Daughters of Sorrow": Attitudes towards Black Women, 1880–1920* (1984); Paula Giddings's *When and Where I Enter: The Impact of Black Women on Race and Sex in America* (1984); Deborah Gray White's *Ar'n't I A Woman?: Female Slaves in the Plantation South* (1985); Jacqueline Jones's *Labor of Love, Labor of Sorrow: Black Women, Work, and the Family from Slavery to the Present* (1986); Jacqueline Rouse's *Lugenia Burns Hope: Black Southern Reformer* (1989); and Cynthia Neverdon-Morton's *African American Women and the Advancement of the Race in the South, 1895–1925* (1989). White's path-breaking monograph on black women slaves in the plantation South was one of the first major studies in black women's history. Her research and publication possessed enormous implications for the field. Her monograph challenged the many male-centered studies on U.S. slavery. Prior to the publication of *Ar'n't I A Woman?*, historians ignored the distinctly unique female slave experience. White's study contributed to the development of microstudies within the dynamic slavery historiography. White also demonstrated to her colleagues, as she stressed in a 1987 *Journal of American History* article, that a careful examination of manuscript collections and the WPA Slave Narrative Collection could help "rescue black women from their submergence and invisibility."

By the 1980s black women historians were in key positions at leading colleges and universities throughout the nation. Among those high-ranking black female historians active during the Reagan years were Mary Frances Berry (who even sued the fortieth president), Elsa Barkley Brown, Bettye Collier-Thomas, Paula Giddings, Sharon Harley, Evelyn Brooks Higginbotham, Darlene Clark Hine, Nell Irvin Painter, Linda Reed, Rosalyn Terborg-Penn, and Deborah Gray White. In the late 1980s, three black women historians received chaired professorships: Berry, Geraldine R. Segal Professor of American

Social Thought at the University of Pennsylvania; Painter, Edwards Professor of American History at Princeton; and Hine, John A. Hannah Professor of History at Michigan State University.

In the 1990s black women's history acquired legitimacy as a recognized field of scholarly inquiry. In the spring of 1990 Mary Frances Berry served as the president of the Organization of American Historians, the first black woman to achieve such a recognition within the historical profession. Moreover, Darlene Clark Hine built upon the works of black women who entered the field in the 1970s and 1980s. With others, and in collaboration with the publisher Ralph Carlson, she institutionalized and validated black women's history. During the 1990s not only were more key monographs published by black women historians than ever before, but important research materials were also made accessible. The sixteen-volume *Black Women in the United States* (1990), *Black Women in America: An Historical Encyclopedia* (1993), and *"We Specialize in the Wholly Impossible": A Reader in Black Women's History* (1995) are among those efforts. Among the significant monographs by black women historians of the 1990s are Evelyn Brooks Higginbotham, *Righteous Discontent: The Women's Movement in the Black Baptist Church, 1880–1920* (1993); Elizabeth Clark-Lewis, *Living In, Living Out: African American Domestics in Washington, DC, 1910–1940* (1994); Stephanie Shaw, *What a Woman Ought to Be and Do: Black Professional Women Workers during the Jim Crow Era* (1996); Nell Irvin Painter, *Sojourner Truth: A Life, a Symbol* (1996); Tera Hunter, *To 'Joy My Freedom: Southern Black Women's Lives and Labors after the Civil War* (1997); Rosalyn Terborg-Penn, *African American Women and the Struggle for the Vote, 1850–1920* (1998); Wanda Hendricks, *Race, Gender, and Politics in the Midwest: Black Club Women in Illinois* (1998); Jane Rhodes, *Mary Ann Shadd Cary: The Black Press and Protest in the Nineteenth Century* (1998); Deborah Gray White, *Too Heavy a Load: Black Women in Defense of Themselves, 1894–1994* (1999); and Chana Kai Lee, *For Freedom's Sake: The Life of Fannie Lou Hamer* (1999). Other recent studies by black women historians include Ula Yvette Taylor, *The Veiled Garvey: The Life and Times of Amy Jacques Garvey* (2002); and Johnnetta Cole and Beverly Guy-Sheftall, *Gender Talk: The Struggle for Women's Equality in African American Communities* (2003). Following in the footsteps of Mary Frances Berry and other black female historians who have risen to high administrative positions, Darlene Clark Hine marked several important milestones by becoming president of the Organization of American Historians (2001–2002) and also president of the Southern Historical Association (2002–2003).

Many promising black women historians were also born during the Black Power era. Often mentored by the black women historians who came of age during the civil rights and Black Power movements, these black women historians of the "hip-hop generation" began to make their names known in the early twenty-first century.

The history of black women historians constitutes a dynamic narrative. It is a history of struggle, perseverance, and great accomplishments. In the early twentieth century, when the Organization of American Historians and the Southern Historical Association were founded, few would have ever imagined that black women would rise to serve as their presidents. The achievements of black women historians gives credence to Nannie Helen Burroughs's dictum, "we specialize in the wholly impossible."

BIBLIOGRAPHY

Beasley, Delilah L. *The Negro Trail Blazers of California*. New York: G. K. Hall, 1997.

Boyd, Melba Joyce. Discarded Legacy: *Politics and Poetics in the Life of Frances E. W. Harper, 1825–1911*. Detroit: Wayne State University Press, 1994.

Burstyn, Joan N. *Past and Promise: Lives of New Jersey Women*. Syracuse, NY: Syracuse University Press, 1997.

Cooper, Anna Julia. *Slavery and the French Revolutionists (1788–1805)*. Lewiston, NY: E. Mellen, 1988.

Cooper, Anna Julia. *A Voice from the South*. New York: Oxford University Press, 1988.

Crocco, Margaret Smith. "Shaping Inclusive Social Education: Mary Ritter Beard and Marion Thompson Wright." In *Bending the Future to Their Will*, edited by Margaret Smith Crocco and O. L. Davis Jr. Lanham, MD: Rowman & Littlefield, 1999.

Crocco, Margaret Smith, Petra Munro, and Kathleen Weiler. *Pedagogies of Resistance: Women Educator Activists, 1880–1960*. New York: Teachers College Press, 1999.

Dagbovie, Pero Gaglo. "Black Women, Carter G. Woodson, and the Association for the Study of Negro Life and History, 1915–1950." *Journal of African American History* 88 (Winter 2003): 21–41.

Daniel, Walter G. "A Tribute to Marion Thompson Wright." *Journal of Negro Education* (Summer 1963).

Davis, Elizabeth L. *Lifting as They Climb*. Washington, DC: National Association of Colored Women, 1933.

Edmonds, Helen G. *The Negro and Fusion Politics in North Carolina, 1894–1901*. Chapel Hill: University of North Carolina Press, 1951.

Greene, Harry Washington. *Holders of Doctorates among American Negroes*. Boston: Meador, 1946.

Gruesser, John Cullen, ed. *The Unruly Voice: Rediscovering Pauline Elizabeth Hopkins*. Urbana: University of Illinois Press, 1996.

Harley, Sharon, and Rosalyn Terborg-Penn, eds. *The Afro-American Woman: Struggles and Images*. Port Washington, NY: National University Publications, 1978.

Hine, Darlene Clark. "Black Women's History at the Intersection of Knowledge and Power." In *Black Women's History at the Intersection of Knowledge and Power*, edited by Rosalyn Terborg-Penn and Janice Sumler-Edmond. Acton, MA: Tapestry, 2000.

Hine, Darlene Clark. *Hine Sight: Black Women and the Re-Construction of American History*. Brooklyn, NY: Carlson, 1994.

Hine, Darlene Clark, ed. *The State of Afro-American History: Past, Present, and Future*. Baton Rouge: Louisiana State University Press, 1986.

Hine, Darlene Clark, Elsa Barkley Brown, Tiffany R. L. Patterson, and Lillian S. Williams, eds. *Black Women in United States History*. Brooklyn, NY: Carlson, 1990.

Hopkins, Pauline. *Contending Forces: A Romance Illustrative of Negro Life North and South*. New York: Oxford University Press, 1988.

Horne, Gerald. *Race Woman: The Lives of Shirley Graham Du Bois*. New York: New York University Press, 2000.

Houston, Drusilla Dunjee. *Wonderful Ethiopians of the Ancient Cushite Empire*. Oklahoma City, OK: Universal Publishing, 1926.

Hutchinson, Louise Daniel. *Anna J. Cooper: A Voice from the South*. Washington, DC: Smithsonian Institution Press, 1981.

"In Memoriam and Tribute: Dr. Lorraine A. Williams, 1923–1996." *Journal of Negro History* 82.1 (Winter 1997): 180.

Johnson, Madison Arvil, and Dorothy Porter Wesley. "Dorothy Porter Wesley: Enterprising Steward of Black Culture." *Public Historian* 17.1 (Winter 1995): 15.

Meier, August, and Elliott Rudwick. *Black History and the Historical Profession, 1915–1980*. Urbana: University of Illinois Press, 1986.

Mossell, N. F. *The Work of the Afro-American Woman* (1908). New York: Oxford University Press, 1988.

Patterson, Martha H. "'Kin' o' Rough Jestice fer a Parson': Pauline Hopkins's Winona and the Politics of Reconstructing History." *African American Review* 32 (1998).

Price, Clement Alexander. *Dr. Marion Thompson Wright: A New Jersey Pioneer*. http://njtimes.rutgers.edu/wright.htm.

Tate, Claudia. *Domestic Allegories of Political Desire: The Black Heroine's Text at the Turn of the Century*. New York: Oxford University Press, 1992.

Taylor, Susie King. *A Black Woman's Civil War Memoirs: Reminiscences of My Life in Camp with the 33rd U.S. Colored Troops, Late 1st South Carolina Volunteers* (1902). New York: Wiener, 1988.

Terborg-Penn, Rosalyn, and Janice Sumler-Edmond, eds. *Black Women's History at the Intersection of Knowledge and Power: ABWH's Twentieth Anniversary Anthology*. Acton, MA: Tapestry, 2000.

Thorpe, Earl E. *Black Historians: A Critique*. New York: Morrow, 1971.

White, Deborah Gray. "Mining for the Forgotten." *Journal of American History* 74 (June 1987): 237–242.

Wilkes, Laura E. *Missing Pages in American History*. Washington, DC: R. L. Pendleton, 1919.

Wilson, Frances Rusan. "Our Foremothers' Keepers: The Association of Black Women Historians and Black Women's History." In *Black Women's History at the Intersection of Knowledge and Power*, edited by Rosalyn Terborg-Penn and Janice Sumler-Edmond. Acton, MA: Tapestry, 2000.

Wright, Marion Thompson. *The Education of Negroes in New Jersey*. New York: Teachers College, Columbia University, 1941.

—PERO GAGLO DAGBOVIE

HISTORICALLY BLACK COLLEGES AND UNIVERSITIES.

Even though the majority of African American students at the beginning of the twenty-first century, nearly 64 percent, were enrolled in predominantly white institutions (PWIs), black colleges and universities remained important sites for the education of thousands of black students.

In 2000, some 227,000 black students enrolled in historically black colleges and universities (HBCUs), and these institutions continued to produce a disproportionate number of black college graduates. Census data indicate that 15 million students were enrolled in U.S. colleges in 2000, nearly 750,000 of them African Americans. The Integrated Postsecondary Education Data System Survey of the U.S.

Department of Education showed a total of 3,328,038 degrees awarded in the academic year 1997–1998. During this period, one in four black graduates (27.4 percent) received their bachelor's degrees from HBCUs, while one in six (15.7 percent) received master's degrees or their first professional degrees (16.8 percent). While women outnumbered men in undergraduate colleges throughout the United States, the gender gap was especially high among black students, including those at HBCUs. At Howard University, for example, women outnumbered men by nearly two to one. According to the National Center for Education Statistics, more than one million black women were enrolled in degree-granting institutions in 2000 compared to 635,000 black men.

Beginnings

The history of black women in the academy begins with the efforts of Myrtilla Miner, a young white woman from New York who, during the 1850s, led the first organized effort to provide higher education for black women, an effort that came to be called the Miner Normal School for Colored Girls and was later named Miner Teachers College. With the end of the Civil War came the emergence of coeducational colleges for former slaves and the coming of higher education for black women on a broad scale. Between 1865 and 1900, a number of black colleges were established in the South, largely by religious organizations eager to increase the number of black teachers and ministers; these included Fisk and Shaw University, founded in 1865; Howard University, Atlanta University, Morehouse College, and Morgan State University, founded in 1867; and Tougaloo College, founded in 1869.

At the same time, a few attempts were made to establish black women's seminaries. Of those, the experiments in Atlanta, Georgia, and Greensboro, North Carolina, had an enduring effect on the history of black women's higher education. Spelman was founded in 1881, and Bennett, initially a coeducational institution, in 1873. Newly emancipated slaves provided the land on which the college would later stand, and Lyman Bennett donated ten thousand dollars for the construction of one of the earliest buildings on campus. In the early years, Bennett trained men for careers in the ministry and women for careers in education. In 1926 Bennett College was reorganized when the Women's Home Mission Society expanded its educational program to include black women. Two other black colleges, Scotia Seminary and Tillotson, were founded for women but later became coeducational. A Presbyterian school for girls located in Concord, North Carolina, Scotia became a junior college in 1932 when it merged with Barber College for Women in Anniston, Alabama, and was renamed Barber-Scotia College. In 1955 a white man entered the college, ending

its long tradition as a women's institution. The American Missionary Association founded Tillotson as a coed college in 1875. In 1925, faced with declining enrollment among men and eager to help elevate the status of African American women, the board decided to convert the college to a women's institution. Tillotson remained a women's college until 1935, when its president, Mary E. Branch, began to enroll male students once again. Branch remained president until her death in 1944, one year after the college received accreditation from the Southern Association of Schools and Colleges.

Getting to the Top

Too often ignored, the saga of black women institution builders is a heroic one. It began in 1820 when Sarah Mapps Douglass, a Philadelphia teacher, opened a private school for black children and in 1853 assumed responsibility for running the Girls' Department of the Institute for Colored Youth in Philadelphia. It was one of the first institutions of higher education for African Americans. Fannie Jackson Coppin, who graduated from Oberlin College in 1865, became principal of the institute in 1869. She was the first African American woman to head an institution of higher learning. Mary McLeod Bethune, the most well known of these educators, became the first black woman college president when she founded Daytona Educational and Industrial Training School, which evolved into a four-year college known as Bethune-Cookman, where she served as president from 1904 until 1942.

Still, black women college presidents, even at black women's colleges, were rare, a reflection of the persistent male control of historically black colleges and universities. When Willa Player became president of Bennett College in 1955, she became the first black woman to head a college for black women, an office she filled for eleven years. During Player's presidency, in 1957, Bennett was accredited by the Southern Association of Colleges and Schools. In 1987, Gloria Randle Scott, then vice president for academic affairs at Clark College in Atlanta, Georgia, became the second black woman president of the college. When Johnnetta Betsch Cole assumed the presidency of Spelman College, also in 1987, she became the first black woman to head the oldest historically black college for women; she later won the distinction, as president of Bennett College for Women, of being the only black woman in the United States to have been president of the only two historically black colleges for women. In 1987 Niara Sudarkasa became the first black woman president of Lincoln University in Pennsylvania.

There was a paucity of women administrators at historically black colleges, as well. Still, black women made some progress. In the 1970s Harriet Trader was vice president for academic affairs, and Clara Adams was dean of the

Fɪsᴋ Uɴɪᴠᴇʀsɪᴛʏ in Nashville, Tennessee. Shown here is the junior normal class, c. 1890–1906. (Library of Congress.)

graduate school, later vice president for academic affairs, at Morgan State University. At Howard University in the 1970s, Lorraine Williams became vice president for academic affairs. Black women became deans of women earlier than did women at majority institutions (except for women's colleges). Early examples are Lucy Slowe in the 1920s at Howard University, Merze Tate at Barber-Scotia in the 1940s, and Thelma Bandon at Morgan State in the 1950s. Also worthy of note was the appointment of Patricia Roberts Harris as the first black woman to head a law school, at Howard University in 1969.

Despite these shortcomings, black colleges and universities have produced a large number of extraordinary women graduates; they include Congresswoman Barbara Jordan (Texas Southern University); the Olympic gold medalist for track, Wilma Rudolph (Tennessee State University); Patricia Roberts Harris, the activist and scholar Mary

Frances Berry, and the actors Debbie Allen and Phylicia Rashad (Howard University); the writer Alice Dunbar Nelson and the Brown University president Ruth Simmons (Dillard University); the opera diva Leontyne Price (Central State University in Ohio); the singer and composer Bernice Johnson Reagon of Sweet Honey in the Rock, the writer Alice Walker, and the children's crusader Marian Wright Edelman (Spelman College); the artists Lois Mailou Jones and Elizabeth Catlett, the Nobel laureate in literature Toni Morrison, the opera star Jessye Norman, and the 2003 Rhodes Scholar Marianna Ofosu (Howard University); the poet Nikki Giovanni and the civil rights activist Diane Nash (Fisk University); and Oprah Winfrey (Tennessee State University). Howard University also has the distinction of having produced several black women politicians: mayors Sharon Pratt Dixon (Washington, DC) and Shirley Franklin (Atlanta, Georgia) and the congressional delegate Eleanor Holmes Norton (Washington, DC).

Despite a growing body of research on HBCUs, there has been little scholarship on the gender issues that influence and shape these institutions. A number of questions emerge in this regard: How well do black women faculty and administrators at HBCUs succeed compared to their male counterparts? Does an examination of rank, tenure, and promotion reveal black women to be at parity with black men and other women on campus? Are their curricula gender-sensitive and sufficiently attentive to the experiences of black women? Do HBCUs adequately support the advancement of women administrators and the research development of faculty? Is there adequate support for the appointment of black women presidents at these institutions? In what ways are the specific developmental needs of women students addressed? What do black women have to say about the climate of their institutions with respect to its treatment of women?

Scholars have given some attention to the education of and climate for black women at HBCUs. Allen, Epps, and Haniff's 1989 research reveals that "developmental profiles of black males evidenced advantage relative to black females" on HBCU campuses. Their study found that black female HBCU students felt less competent and tended to be less assertive, compared to their male peers. The study further maintained that black female students at HBCUs were more willing to take on roles that made them seem less competent in order to appear less threatening to males.

Other studies indicate that black female students at coed colleges tend to be less assertive than their male peers. One study revealed that some women faculty and administrators are reluctant to discuss with researchers issues of climate, mentoring, parity in employment, and the nature of the professional development opportunities at their particular institution for fear that their candor would reveal their identities. The survey asked about the types of discrimination respondents might have experienced, including the most serious incident they had experienced on campus. More than 45 percent indicated that they had been discriminated against based on their gender; 7.8 percent reported discrimination based on age; 7.9 percent reported ethnic discrimination; 3.9 percent claimed discrimination based on disability; and 5.9 percent noted that they had been discriminated against based on sexual preference. Some indicated that mentoring on their campus was minimal, and most indicated that pay equity and opportunities for advancement favored men. In this regard, the respondents reported gender-bias experiences similar to those encountered by women on PWI campuses, but to a more limited extent.

African American women continued to struggle for parity with all men and white women in higher education. Despite their increased matriculation rates, they continued to be located at the bottom of the employment ladder in pay, administrative appointments, tenure and tenure-track positions, as well as associate and full professor ranks in the faculty within higher educational institutions in general. Even at the turn of the twenty-first century, increased attention to the situation of women at HBCUs was necessary so that a clearer picture could be formed of the extent to which black colleges and universities have managed or not to eradicate the vestiges of male dominance and sexism that permeate higher education.

There are many reasons why it is important to engage in a more systematic study of the situation of women at HBCUs. It would illuminate the issue of gender discrimination and oppression at these institutions. HBCUs were established to provide educational opportunities for blacks who were systematically excluded from formal education due to slavery, racial segregation, and discrimination. Because of the urgency of racial matters, there has been a reluctance to discuss the manner in which women have been treated at HBCUs. However, a range of gender issues at HBCUs demands critical and in-depth examination.

BIBLIOGRAPHY

Allen, Walter R., Edgar Epps, and Nesha Haniff. "Determining Black Student Academic Performance in U.S. Higher Education: Institutional versus Interpersonal Effects." *International Perspectives on Education and Society* 1 (1989): 115–136.

Barton, Paul E. "Students at Historically Black Colleges and Universities: Their Aspirations and Their Accomplishments." Princeton, NJ: Educational Testing Service, 1977.

Guy-Sheftall, Beverly, ed. *Words of Fire: An Anthology of African American Feminist Thought*. New York: New Press, 1995.

Moses, Yolanda T. "Black Women in Academe: Issues and Strategies, Project on the Status and Education of Women." Washington, DC: Association of American Colleges and Universities, 1989.

—BEVERLY GUY-SHEFTALL
—FLORENCE B. BONNER

HOLIDAY, BILLIE (b. 7 April 1915; d. 17 July 1959), jazz singer. Billie Holiday never won a jazz popularity poll during her lifetime. Readers of *Metronome*, *Melody Maker*, and *Down Beat* magazines consistently chose Holiday second, third, even tenth after Ella Fitzgerald, Mildred Bailey, Helen O'Connell, and Jo Stafford, all of whom, with the exception of Fitzgerald, were white, and all of whom sang with commercially popular big bands.

Among jazz critics and historians, however, there is little question that Billie Holiday was the greatest jazz singer ever recorded. Coming into her own a generation after classic blues singers like Bessie Smith, Holiday created a place for herself outside the limited confines of the "girl singer" role within the big band, setting standards by which other jazz singers continued to be judged and influencing singers as diverse in style as Sarah Vaughan, Frank Sinatra, Carmen McRae, and Lena Horne.

Holiday began recording in the 1930s during the emergence of the big band or swing band style of jazz. Although her work with Count Basie attests to her ability to perform

BILLIE HOLIDAY, "Lady Day," photographed on 23 March 1949 by Carl Van Vechten. (Library of Congress.)

with such ensembles, her style was better suited to small combos in which she found the freedom to be a jazz soloist. Recordings made during the twenty-six years of her career reveal her skill as a re-composer of melody and a rhythmic innovator, the hallmarks of a skilled jazz improviser.

Humble Beginnings

Born Eleanora Fagan in Philadelphia, Pennsylvania, to teenaged parents, Holiday grew up in Baltimore, Maryland, and ostensibly took her first name from her screen idol, Billie Dove. Her father, later a guitarist with Fletcher Henderson's orchestra, never lived with the family, and Holiday was raised by her mother and other relatives. Her childhood was marked by deprivation, cruelty, and sexual abuse, and she spent a year at the Catholic-run House of the Good Shepherd for Colored Girls. As a teenager she rejoined her

mother, who had moved to New York City, and she may have worked for a time as a prostitute while learning her craft as a singer.

The beginnings of Holiday's career are unclear. She claimed not to read music, but family friends remember her singing as a child, and by her early teens she was performing for tips and jamming with other musicians in Baltimore's waterfront entertainment district. In her autobiography, *Lady Sings the Blues*, Holiday stresses the early influences of recordings by Louis Armstrong and Bessie Smith. Although not a traditional blues singer, Holiday certainly shared with classic blues singers like Smith an emotional identification with her text, a gift for emphasizing particular words and syllables in performance, and a fondness for slow tempos. Similarly, although she did not imitate Louis Armstrong's vocal scatting technique, as did Ella Fitzgerald, Holiday's singing was marked by the rhythmic flexibility and swing characteristic of Armstrong's trumpet performances. Holiday was not a big-voiced belter like Armstrong or Smith, but she used the distinctive timbre and limited range of her voice to their best advantage, producing solos marked by subtlety and nuance.

By 1931 Holiday was singing in New York City accompanied solely by piano. For a time, she was part of a show featuring bassist George "Pops" Foster and tap dancer Charles "Honi" Coles. In 1933 John Hammond, a white jazz record producer and critic, heard the then eighteen-year-old Holiday singing in Monette Moore's club accompanied by the house pianist, Dot Hill. Hammond immediately wrote about her in the British journal *Melody Maker*, describing the individual vocal style and delivery that set Holiday apart from other singers of the time.

Hammond, who as a record producer was always looking for new talent, arranged for Holiday to record, and she cut two sides in 1933. Ironically, Hammond recorded Holiday within twenty-four hours of producing Bessie Smith's final recordings. Although Holiday's sidemen included well-known and established white performers Jack Teagarden, Benny Goodman, and Gene Krupa, the songs she was given to record, "Your Mother's Son-in-Law" and "Riffin' the Scotch," were second-rate tunes. However, for her first time in front of a recording microphone, accompanied by musicians she did not know and in a musical and racially integrated manner to which she was unaccustomed, the teenaged Holiday sounded assured and confident, if lacking in the rhythmic freedom that marked her later work.

Before Holiday returned to a recording studio in 1935, she took part in Duke Ellington's short film depiction of African American life, *Symphony in Black*. Holiday performed "Big City Blues," a twelve-bar blues chorus sung during the second scene, entitled "A Triangle," and her brief appearance demonstrated her musical growth as a singer with a captivating stage presence. While it was not uncommon for popular white female singers, such as Doris Day and Rosemary Clooney, to make the transition to Hollywood and the film industry, black women's opportunities were limited. Holiday made one other screen appearance in *New Orleans* (1946). Playing opposite her musical mentor Louis Armstrong, she performed three numbers in an otherwise demeaning role as the singing maid to the white, blond leading lady, Dorothy Patrick.

In July 1935 Hammond arranged for Holiday to return to the recording studio accompanied now by the black pianist Teddy Wilson and his pickup ensemble. Holiday found that these musicians and their spontaneous approach suited her style. She particularly enjoyed working with Count Basie's sideman, the saxophonist Lester Young, who began recording with her in 1937 and whose approach was ideal for providing instrumental responses and counter melodies during her solos, as in "When a Woman Loves a Man" and "I'll Never Be the Same." Holiday credited Young with giving her the nickname "Lady Day," by which she was known from then on, a name that seemed to symbolize her desire for the racial respect and gender benefits accorded to white middle- and upper-class women.

Between 1935 and 1938, Holiday released some eighty titles on the Brunswick label marketed to the black jukebox audience, earning a reputation as a one-take artist who learned material quickly and had a fantastic ear. Although she was rarely given well-known songs to record, Holiday's performances demonstrated her improvisatory skill and contributed to her growing popularity with nightclub audiences. In 1935 she made the first of many successful appearances at Harlem's Apollo Theater. By 1936 she was recording under her own name, as well as with Teddy Wilson.

Basie and Further Success

John Hammond also championed the work of Count Basie, and in 1937 he took Basie to hear Holiday and encouraged him to take her on as a singer with his band. Basie enthusiastically agreed, and Holiday performed with the band for a year. Due to contractual problems the two were not able to record together, but three air checks from Savoy and Meadowbrook Ballroom radio performances show that Holiday was capable of meeting the rhythmic challenges of one of the hottest bands of the era. The reasons given for her departure vary, depending on the source, but Holiday and Basie remained friends, and she made occasional appearances with the band in the 1940s.

Holiday went on to perform with the white clarinetist Artie Shaw and his band in 1939, becoming one of the first black performers to perform with an all-white ensemble onstage and in public, not just on recordings. Contrac-

tual problems again kept Holiday from recording with the band, and her time with Shaw's band was fraught with tensions over her style, which remained less popular with his audiences (who were used to a mainstream pop style), and especially over racial politics. Shaw hired the white performer Helen Forrest as a backup singer when establishments refused to allow Holiday to perform with the all-white ensemble or when conflicts over Holiday's approach to her material arose, and that did little to alleviate tensions. Holiday's descriptions of her time with Shaw, particularly on tour, formed some of the most poignant parts of her autobiography. She describes the difficulty of obtaining food and lodging for herself as well as her experiences in public with white male band members, who often assumed she was a prostitute.

By 1939, when she was just twenty-four, Holiday had gained significant recognition through her appearances at Café Society, a club opened by Barney Josephson in December 1938 for the express purpose of providing entertainment to integrated audiences. It was within this context that Holiday came to be identified with the song "Strange Fruit." Written under the pseudonym Lewis Allan by Abel Meeropol, "Strange Fruit" is about lynching; in it, lynched bodies are described as "strange fruit," the "bitter crop" of southern racial politics. The song was unusual for the directness of its message, and many critics, including Hammond, were uncomfortable with Holiday's adoption of it as a kind of anthem, which she performed in a dramatic manner. Columbia Records held her contract at the time and was unwilling to record "Strange Fruit," but Holiday managed to record the song on Milt Gabler's independent Commodore label. The recording sold well, with one of Holiday's blues numbers, "Fine and Mellow," on the flip side. Following her time at Café Society, Holiday became a much-sought-after performer in New York City and elsewhere. "Strange Fruit" remains one of the earliest examples of jazz protest songs.

In 1944 Holiday signed with Decca, a label with a reputation for mainstream popular music rather than for jazz but the label for which Gabler then worked. Holiday decided she wanted strings as part of her backup ensemble, and Gabler complied. "Lover Man," her first recording in this new style, became her best-selling record to date. During her six years with Decca, Holiday recorded her own compositions, "God Bless the Child" and "Don't Explain." She also had success with the material of other writers, recording songs like "Good Morning, Heartache," by Irene Higginbotham, as well as some standards.

In 1947 Holiday entered a private clinic to try and kick her drug habit, but some three weeks after her discharge, she was arrested for drug possession. The circumstances surrounding her arrest remain unclear, but rather than receive further treatment, as was typically allowed white celebrity addicts, Holiday was sentenced to a year and a day at the Federal Reformatory for Women at Alderson, West Virginia. She served nine and one-half months, and upon her release for good behavior, New York City authorities revoked her cabaret card, making it impossible for her to perform in local clubs. Holiday was forced to look for work outside New York City and in special concert venues in the city, such as at Carnegie Hall and on national and European tours.

Decca records let Holiday's contract lapse in 1950, and she was without a recording label until 1952, when she signed with Norman Granz's Verve label. Granz wanted Holiday's recordings to recapture the spontaneity of her earlier sessions with Teddy Wilson, and so she shed the rehearsed orchestral arrangements of the Decca releases. With the formidable backup talent of Oscar Peterson, Bobby Tucker, Ben Webster, Paul Quinichette, Harry "Sweets" Edison, and others, Holiday recorded almost one hundred songs for Granz. Although these recordings share the informality of the Brunswick releases, Holiday's material consisted of standards, like "Blue Moon" and "Stormy Weather," as well as remakes of some of her earlier numbers, such as "What a Little Moonlight Can Do," recordings that allowed her listeners to hear how she reworked her material over time.

In 1958 Holiday recorded her last and most popular album, *Lady in Satin*, featuring lush string arrangements by Ray Ellis. Holiday's voice is noticeably different from the one captured in her Verve releases. Its cracked, harsh timbre, so apparent when accompanied by the strings, led several critics to call it her worst album. Holiday's talent shines through, however, and her rhythmic flexibility and careful shaping of the text remain as true as ever.

Prior to her *Lady in Satin* release, Holiday made one other recording that stands as a testament to her career as a jazz soloist. In December 1957 she took part in a special CBS program, *The Sound of Jazz*. Produced by Robert Herridge with the advice of Whitney Balliett and Nat Hentoff, the show presented nine live performances by the leading jazz musicians of the time. Holiday performed her own "Fine and Mellow" blues with assisting solos by Ben Webster, her old friend Lester Young (just days before his death), Vic Dickerson, Gerry Mulligan, Doc Cheatham, Coleman Hawkins, and Roy Eldridge. Gerry Mulligan's presence integrated the otherwise all-black ensemble. Holiday performed in a circle with the other musicians. Her singing is true and rhythmically flexible, and she takes obvious delight in the work of the others. On her remaining choruses, she enters, not as a singer carrying the blues text, but as a distinctive soloist in the jazz ensemble.

Billie Holiday died in New York City from the long-term effects of drug addiction. She was forty-four years old. A lifelong Roman Catholic, she was buried in Saint Raymond's Catholic Cemetery in the Bronx. Thousands of friends and fans attended her requiem mass held at Saint Paul the Apostle Cathedral. Years later, Holiday's life and musical legacy benefited from the critical attention of black feminist historians, such as Angela Y. Davis, and other scholars interested in her position as a black professional woman and in her distinctive autobiographical voice. *Time* selected her recording of "Strange Fruit" as its "Song of the Century" in 1999, offering the fitting tribute that in it, "history's greatest jazz singer comes to terms with history itself."

See also **Jazz.**

BIBLIOGRAPHY

"The Best of the Century." *Time*, December 31, 1999, 73–76.

Chilton, John. *Billie's Blues*. New York: Da Capo, 1975.

Davis, Angela Y. *Blues Legacies and Black Feminism: Gertrude "Ma" Rainey, Bessie Smith, and Billie Holiday*. New York: Pantheon Books, 1998.

Holiday, Billie, and William Dufty. *Lady Sings the Blues* (1956). New York: Penguin, 1984.

Margolick, David. *Strange Fruit: Billie Holiday, Café Society, and an Early Cry for Civil Rights*. Philadelphia: Running Press, 2000.

O'Meally, Robert. *Lady Day: The Many Faces of Billie Holiday*. New York: Arcade, 1991.

Schuller, Gunther. *The Swing Era: The Development of Jazz, 1930–1945*. New York: Oxford University Press, 1989.

White, John. *Billie Holiday: Her Life and Times*. New York: Universe Books, 1987.

Williams, Martin. *The Jazz Tradition*. New York: Oxford University Press, 1983.

VIDEOS

Duke Ellington and His Orchestra. Jazz Classics JCVC 101, 1987.

Lady Day: The Many Faces of Billie Holiday. Masters of American Music Series, Kultur International Films, 1991.

Lester Young and Billie Holiday. Jazz and Jazz Video, Vidjazz 12, 1990.

The Long Night of Lady Day. BBC television, 1985.

The Sound of Jazz. Vintage Jazz Classics, 1990.

SELECTED DISCOGRAPHY

Billie Holiday—The Complete Decca Recordings. Decca 2 compact discs (1991).

Billie Holiday—The Legacy. Columbia 3 compact discs, 47724 (1991).

The Billie Holiday Songbook. Verve/Polygram Records 823246-2 (1986).

—SUSAN C. COOK

HOOKS, BELL (b. 24 September 1952), writer, essayist. The intrepid bell hooks has been one of America's premier social critics, although often incorrectly categorized as merely a black feminist. It would be more accurate to characterize her as a public intellectual engaged in the arts of literary, film, and popular cultural criticism and committed to the struggle against racism, sexism, classism, and homophobia. Many of her writings, interviews, and public speeches identified these dominant discourses

BELL HOOKS, as an intrepid writer and essayist, has been one of America's premier social critics, committed to the struggle against racism, sexism, classism, and homophobia. (Courtesy of William Morrow/An Imprint of HarperCollins Publishers. Photograph by Marion Ettinger.)

as serious impediments designed to inhibit people from realizing a fuller understanding of themselves and their fellow human beings. Hooks sought to dismantle these dominant political discourses by exposing their use in art, literature, and film. Meanwhile, hooks encouraged those most damaged by these ideas, such as black women, to join this struggle, believing strongly that the elevation of black womanhood will result in the liberation of blacks and American society itself.

Bell hooks was born Gloria Jean Watkins in Hopkinsville, Kentucky, and reared by two working-class parents. It was in this context that hooks' combative disposition toward racism, sexism, and classism took root. She later recalled her awakening in her memoir *Bone Black: Memories of Girlhood* (1996). Unlike many other intellectuals coming of age in the civil rights era, hooks had many encounters with elementary and high school teachers who accommodated rather than opposed the racism that informed segregation.

Meanwhile, she was introduced to sexism in the more private setting of her own family when her father forced her mother to leave their home at gunpoint after suspecting her of infidelity.

The combination of this violent family altercation with the accommodative sensibilities of local teachers convinced the young hooks that she resided within an oppressive social order, one that required blacks to subordinate themselves to whites, wives to their husbands, and children to their mothers. Most terrifying to the author was her mother's willingness to submit to a system that suggested men submit to god, women to men, and children to their parents. Troubled by her mother's capitulation, hooks proclaimed that she would not follow the same path. She unequivocally would "not obey." To reaffirm this newfound conviction, hooks adopted the name of her great grandmother—a rebellious woman who had refused to yield to racist and sexist societal pressures.

Hooks was the beneficiary of many years of formal education, acquiring her bachelors, masters, and doctoral degrees in English from Stanford University (1973), the University of Wisconsin (1976), and the University of California at Santa Cruz (1983), respectively. She went on to accept teaching positions at Oberlin College, Yale, and the City College of New York. This long association with institutions of higher learning did not, however, undermine her conviction that to engage in a struggle against racism and the dehumanizing effects of capitalism, one must not lose oneself and one's audience in the pursuit of intellectual self-aggrandizement. To this end, hooks has often written pieces that appear in both academic and popular periodicals for the purpose of reaching a large number of black readers.

Hooks designed her numerous publications to encourage readers to combat the intertwined notions of white supremacy and capitalist patriarchy and the institutions these discourses of domination support. She developed this position in *Ain't I a Woman: Black Women and Feminism* (1983), honed it in *Killing Rage: Ending Racism* (1995), and intensified her assault on these ideas in subsequent books, articles, and public discussions. *Ain't I a Woman* described the relationship between racism and sexism within the overlapping feminist and abolitionist movements of the nineteenth century. Hooks contended that white feminists who initially identified their struggle for political recognition with the antislavery movement prior to the Civil War disengaged from any sort of mutual liberation struggle with blacks during postwar debates over voting rights. In short, these white feminist leaders were willing to accept the exclusion of "inferior" black men and women from the political franchise, while they believed "superior" white women should be awarded this privilege. According to hooks, this feminist strategy resulted in the continued "defeminization" of black women, the disfranchisement of black women and men, the intensification of preexisting tensions between white women and black working class women, and the strengthening of white supremacist capitalist patriarchy. Consequently, the racism of white feminists weakened the overall thrust of their nineteenth-century liberation movement.

Hooks further asserted that the tendency of white feminist to "evoke" white supremacy hobbled the feminist movement in the twentieth century as well. This information pushed hooks toward a conclusion that became the fundamental premise of many of her publications and speeches. Although they have addressed a plethora of issues, ranging from the Nazi art of Leni Riefenstahl to "gangsta" rap, hooks' conclusion remained the same: until men and women involved in feminist struggle closed ranks against the ideas of white supremacist capitalist patriarchy, the movement would never regain a sense of "progressive revolutionary momentum." Therefore, it was imperative that male and female feminists overcome white supremacist modes of thinking and acting.

BIBLIOGRAPHY

hooks, bell. *Ain't I a Woman: Black Women and Feminism*. Boston: South End Press, 1981.

hooks, bell. *Bone Black: Memories of Girlhood*. New York: Henry Holt, 1996.

hooks, bell "Sexism and Misogyny: Who Takes the Rap? Misogyny, Gangsta Rap, and *The Piano*." *Race & Ethnicity*, 4 March 1994. http://eserver.org/race/misogyny.html.

hooks, bell. *Killing Rage: Ending Racism*. New York: Henry Holt, 1995.

hooks, bell. *Wounds of Passion: A Writing Life*. New York: Henry Holt, 1997.

hooks, bell. "The Feminazi Mystique." *Transition* 73 (1997).

—AMY GRANT

HOPE, LUGENIA BURNS (b. 19 February 1871; d. 14 August 1947), activist, community leader, and suffragist. Lugenia Burns Hope spent her formative years in St. Louis, Missouri, and later Chicago, Illinois. The last of seven children, she was able to attend school, where she focused on photography, printing, drawing, sculpting, and business management. When her family's economic situation changed, however, she was forced to quit school and work full time. She worked with several charitable settlement groups for more than twelve years, including the Kings Daughters and Hull-House in Chicago, which helped develop her interest in community building and public service.

In 1893 Lugenia Burns met John Hope, a native Georgian and a theological student at Brown University. They married during the Christmas holidays of 1897 and then moved to Nashville, Tennessee, where John Hope had accepted a professorship at Roger Williams University. During their one-year stay in Nashville, Lugenia Hope became involved in community activities through her relationship with families such as the Crosthwaits and the Napiers, and she taught physical education and arts and crafts classes to the female students at Roger Williams University. However, because of John Hope's desire to return to his native Georgia, the Hopes moved in 1898 to Atlanta, where he had accepted a position as an instructor in classics at Atlanta Baptist College, later Morehouse College. For the next thirty-five years, the Hopes lived on campus, beginning in Graves Hall, a dormitory, and ending in the president's house as John Hope's career took him from the classroom to the office of the presidency.

Lugenia Hope immediately became involved in the West Fair community as a result of the conferences on African American life that were hosted by Atlanta University and that featured W. E. B. Du Bois and Gertrude Ware. Spurred on by conference sessions on child welfare, Hope and a core group of women began to organize kindergartens and daycare centers for working mothers of the West Fair community. The group persuaded Atlanta Baptist College to donate land for playgrounds for neighborhood children. Later, as their community work grew, the core group organized themselves into the Neighborhood Union, Hope's most important legacy.

For twenty-five years, Hope led the Neighborhood Union as it became an international model for community building and race and gender activism. Adopting the motto "Thy Neighbor as Thyself," the union offered services to Atlanta's African American communities that were not provided by the state, county, or city. The union divided into zones, districts, and neighborhoods in order to ascertain the cultural, medical, educational, recreational, social, religious, and economic needs of the city. Students from the local black colleges—Morehouse, Spelman, and Atlanta University—were instrumental in organizing classes for young and elderly citizens.

The union participated in the drive for equal education, instruction, and facilities, supporting black students as they organized community-wide and citywide rallies and confrontations. The union joined with many prominent male leaders, churches, and local organizations to fight the discrimination of separate-but-equal education. Their efforts to educate black Atlantans about the double and triple sessions of black schools, the shortage and low pay of black teachers, the poor physical condition of the school buildings, and the limited funds appropriated to black schools led to successful campaigns to block bond issues in municipal elections. Limited successes enabled the African American community to appreciate the importance of being organized and united in order to overcome the odds.

As the Neighborhood Union grew, Hope acquired a national reputation as a social reformer and community leader. She took her place alongside Mary Church Terrell,

LUGENIA BURNS HOPE (back row, right) with members of the International Council of Women of the Darker Races, founded in 1920. Earlier, in 1908, she founded the Neighborhood Union, a community service organization whose motto was "Thy Neighbor as Thyself." (Neighborhood Union Collection, Atlanta University Center, Robert W. Woodruff Library.)

Mary McLeod Bethune, Charlotte Hawkins Brown, Margaret Murray Washington, Nannie Helen Burroughs, and other African American women who were fighting for equal rights and freedom. In the southern network of African American female activists, Hope was a major force in challenging racism and initiating interracial cooperation.

Hope's interracial work is best illustrated by two separate campaigns: the creation of African American Young Women's Christian Association (YWCA) branches in the South, and the antilynching movement, especially her alliance with Southern Methodist women and the Association of Southern Women for the Prevention of Lynching (ASWPL). In both campaigns, Hope believed that she and her counterparts, representing more than 300,000 black southern women, could speak without reservation in order to bring about immediate change.

They first challenged the racist policies of the YWCA, which did not allow African American autonomy, and threatened to withdraw from the movement and to return to their churches as bases of support. Hope worked for years to eliminate discriminatory practices and to demand black women's participation in administrative functions. Her steadfastness often led to charges of inflexibility and hampering the progress of racial harmony and compromise, but Hope did not relent. She continued the struggle until the direction of black YWCAs in the South was controlled from the national office in New York and not the regional and state offices. Southern black women were soon able to determine the types of young women they would help and the areas where their services were most needed, a right that was not guaranteed prior to 1924.

While working on the second campaign, to outlaw lynching, Hope came to believe that southern white women did not accept enough responsibility for the continued use of lynching in the region. Given the widespread assertion that lynching "protected white womanhood," Hope and her network expected enlightened southern white women to do more than speak out against this so-called act of chivalry and merely hint at feminist jargon. They expected them to control their husbands, sons, brothers, uncles, and grandfathers, who were maliciously murdering black men. They also expected white women to include the rape of black women in their view of female liberation. The manner in which black domestics were treated in some white women's homes, not to mention their low wages, were important issues for black southern women determined to awaken southern progressive white women to the fact of their own racism.

Joining with such figures as Jessie D. Ames, Hope tried to convince this group that the most expedient measure was a national bill to prohibit lynching, one that called for the prosecution of local law officials in towns where such acts occurred. Championing states rights, however, Ames and the ASWPL opposed federal intervention, believing that state laws prohibiting lynching would be more likely to pass local legislatures and to be enforced by local law enforcement officials. As a result, Hope came away with deep misgivings about southern white women's commitment to equality and the elimination of racism, but she forced them to face their own role as participants and as beneficiaries of racism.

Lugenia Hope was a member or official in several of the traditional race protest organizations. For example, in 1932, she was first vice president of the Atlanta chapter of the National Association for the Advancement of Colored People (NAACP). In this capacity, she created citizenship schools, establishing six-week classes on voting, democracy, and the Constitution that were taught by professors of Atlanta University. The success of the Atlanta program triggered citizenship classes in other branches. That same year, Hope was nominated to receive the Spingarn Award, the NAACP's highest honor.

The strategies developed by Hope were reused in the civil rights movement of the 1950s and 1960s. Representatives of the Student Nonviolent Coordinating Committee (SNCC) and the Congress of Racial Equality (CORE) canvassed the South, educating rural and urban African Americans about their rights and voting procedures and enabling them to become politically active. The Highlander School/Center in Monteagle, Tennessee, used citizenship training to prepare many of the activists who led heroic efforts to repeal Jim Crow laws in the South. Although the connection is seldom made, the civil rights movement had its origin in the political activism of early twentieth-century women such as Hope and those in the Neighborhood Union.

Hope, the mother, wife, and "first lady" of Morehouse College, had to split time with Hope the social activist and reformer. She supported her husband's work as professor, college president, spokesman for the YWCA, race leader, and educator. She traveled with her husband nationally and abroad, especially on fund-raising trips, and when the opportunity arose, she persuaded him to accept the position of president of Atlanta University. Having helped to establish Morehouse College, he could now help create new opportunities for more black students and at the same time build a major black higher educational center, the Atlanta University Center. Creating the country's first African American graduate school was the opportunity of a lifetime, one that Lugenia Hope believed her husband could not overlook or decline.

In relation to the young men of Morehouse, Hope followed the African American female tradition of the "other mother," nurturing these young men as she took time to acquaint them with their different world. By forcing them to take lessons in etiquette and to work with young children through the Neighborhood Union programs, Hope was instrumental in creating the mystique of the Morehouse man.

After John Hope's death in 1936, Hope moved to New York City, to Chicago, and then to Nashville to be near relatives. When she died, her ashes were thrown from the tower of Graves Hall over the campus of Morehouse College.

Lugenia Hope exemplified the strong-spirited race woman who worked for racial justice in the early years of the twentieth century. She was a determined woman who recognized and utilized her abilities and who expected the same from others. She succeeded as a leader because of her ability to work with diverse groups of people and because of her great executive skills. She was successful in African American communities because of her access to the white power structure and her ability to use that access. Poor and voiceless black Atlantans expected her to be their voice at board and city council meetings. Thus, part of her appeal was her radical, yet undaunted, activism; the other was her genuine love and concern for all children and her willingness to struggle to improve their lives.

Hope's radical style of activism made her far more outspoken than her peers, more demanding, and less willing to compromise on the issues of racial justice and gender equality. She was more accusatory, and more direct, in interracial meetings than were most of her colleagues. In fact, her voice spoke what other black women felt but could not risk saying. Her peers praised her courage, her frankness, and the forthright manner in which she exposed deceit, prejudice, and injustice. Her refusal to allow misunderstandings and injustice to pass unchallenged sometimes cost her support and allies, but because of Hope the African American women's agenda was always clear, its priorities always visible.

Lugenia Hope's dominating nature also cost her allies within the Neighborhood Union. Oral and written accounts of the union's successes and failures reflect a respect and fear of Hope, for the group always deferred to her. Under her leadership, however, the community witnessed major reforms, including the establishment of the first African American high school in 1924 and the first public housing for African Americans in the country.

Whether her steadfast and forthright leadership was politically correct is debatable. It did, however, take its toll on Hope's health, and it did put a strain on her family.

Lugenia Hope was a product of Victorian America, and she struggled to improve the image of her class against those whose actions she viewed as immoral and a detriment to the race. She imparted and enforced her values on others so that they could use them to clean up their lives and uplift the race. At the same time, she presented an alternative to the southern white view of conciliatory, conservative black southerners. She openly opposed segregation and discrimination, and her efforts helped the growth of racial cooperation and intra-racial solidarity in the New South of the late twentieth century.

BIBLIOGRAPHY

Lerner, Gerda. "Early Community Work of Black Clubwomen," *Journal of Negro History*, April 1974.

Lerner, Gerda, ed. *Black Women in White America* (1972). New York: Vintage Books, 1992.

Neverdon-Morton, Cynthia. *Afro-American Women of the South and the Advancement of the Race, 1895–1925*. Knoxville: University of Tennessee Press, 1989.

Rouse, Jacqueline A. "The Legacy of Community Organizing: Lugenia Burns Hope and the Neighborhood Union." *Journal of Negro History*, Summer/Fall 1984.

Rouse, Jacqueline A. *Lugenia Burns Hope: Black Southern Reformer*. Athens: University of Georgia Press, 1989.

Torrence, Ridgley. *The Story of John Hope*. New York: Macmillan, 1948.

COLLECTIONS

John and Lugenia Burns Hope Papers, Woodruff Library, Atlanta University Center, Atlanta, Georgia.

Neighborhood Union Collection, Woodruff Library, Atlanta University Center, Atlanta, Georgia.

—JACQUELINE A. ROUSE

HOPKINS, PAULINE ELIZABETH (b.1859; d. 19 August 1930), writer. Born in Portland, Maine, to William and Sarah Allen Hopkins, Hopkins was the great-grandniece of poet James Whitfield. Her mother was a descendant of Nathaniel and Thomas Paul, who founded Baptist churches in Boston. When Hopkins was a child, her family moved to Boston, where the young girl attended elementary and secondary school, eventually graduating from Girls High School.

Hopkins's writing talents emerged when she was only fifteen and entered a writing contest sponsored by Boston's Congregational Publishing Society. The contest was supported by William Wells Brown, an escaped slave who wrote one of the first African American novels, *Clotel* (1853). Brown wished to promote temperance, believing it to be a virtue that would enhance the black community. Hopkins's essay, an eloquent, if moralistic, response to the contest theme, "The Evils of Intemperance and Their Remedy," won the first prize of ten dollars.

Hopkins was only twenty years old when she completed her first play, *Slaves' Escape: or The Underground Railroad*. Just one year later, on 5 July 1880, *Slaves' Escape* was produced at Boston's Oakland Garden by the Hopkins Colored Troubadours. The play is a musical comedy celebrating the bravery and ingenuity of those slaves, such as Harriet Tubman and Frederick Douglass, who escaped bondage. The cast included Hopkins's mother, stepfather, and Hopkins herself, who later achieved fame as "Boston's Favorite Colored Soprano."

For twelve years, Hopkins performed with the Colored Troubadours. During this time, she wrote another play, titled *One Scene from the Drama of Early Days*, dramatizing the biblical story of Daniel in the lion's den. At this point, she decided to leave the stage and train herself as a stenographer to better support her writing. In the 1890s, she worked at the Bureau of Statistics and developed a career as a public lecturer.

At the turn of the century, Hopkins became instrumental in the development of a new publication, *The Colored American Magazine*. Aimed at a predominantly African American audience, *The Colored American* contained short stories, articles, and serialized novels, all designed to entertain and educate. The magazine was a medium for African American writers to demonstrate their talents. Hopkins was not only a founding member and editor of *The Colored American* but she also published three novels, seven short stories, and numerous biographical and political sketches there. The sketches, which reflect her skill as a dramatist, flesh out the positive fictional images that appear in her fiction by applauding the achievements of luminaries such as William Wells Brown, Sojourner Truth, Harriet Tubman, and Frederick Douglass.

In May 1900, the first issue of *The Colored American* carried her short story "The Mystery Within Us." At the same time, the Colored Co-operative Publishing Company, a Boston firm that produced the magazine, brought out Hopkins's *Contending Forces: A Romance Illustrative of Negro Life North and South*. *Contending Forces* showcased the themes and techniques that inform all of Pauline Hopkins's fiction. In her effort to present "the true romance of American life . . . the history of the Negro," Hopkins employs strategies used in popular historical romances of her day. Suspenseful, complicated plots involving superhuman heroes, imperiled heroines, and incomparable villains inform the audience about African American history and common social issues. *Contending Forces* is an ambitious story about several generations of an African American family from their pre–Civil War Caribbean and North Carolina origins to their later life in the North. The plot involves Will and Dora Smith, brother and sister, and their friend Sappho Clark, with whom Will falls in love. In addition to the formula plot of boy meets girl, boy loses girl, boy marries girl, the narrative dramatizes essential American historical realities: slavery, lynching, hidden interracial blood lines, post-Reconstruction voting disenfranchisement, and job discrimination against African Americans.

Underlying these themes and techniques is Hopkins's announced purpose in the preface to *Contending Forces* "to raise the stigma of degradation from my race." To that end, her black characters are admirable, intelligent, and, often, educated. Writing at a time when African American writers struggled with the nearly inescapable color prejudice that exalted an ideal of beauty based on Anglo Saxon features, skin, and hair, Hopkins invariably described her heroines as light-skinned, sometimes so much so that they themselves were unaware of their racial origins. Sappho Clark, and the characters in much of Hopkins's fiction, exemplified the cultural contradictions in which African American writers were often caught in their efforts to recast black cultural identity.

Hopkins's three other novels, all serialized in *The Colored American*, employ additional romance techniques. Cliffhangers, episodes concluding with an unresolved question, such as who the murderer really was, enticed the reader to anticipate the next issue of the magazine. Mistaken identities and disguise typify these novels, as do outrageous coincidences, supernatural occurrences, and evil schemes.

Hagar's Daughter: A Story of Southern Caste Prejudice, serialized in 1901 and 1902, is a generational novel like *Contending Forces*. The characters in *Hagar's Daughter* are, however, mostly white. Anticipating later romance novels and soap operas, *Hagar's Daughter* concerns a glamorous leisure class preoccupied with clothes, gambling, and intrigue. In each generation, an adored, beautiful woman, fully entrenched in a white, wealthy culture, discovers herself to be black, forcing her to cope with racism and rejection. *Hagar's Daughter* strongly implies that wealth and status do not equate with ethics. Moreover, the novel concludes with a bitter indictment of American racism, even among white Americans supposedly sensitive to racial issues.

Winona: A Tale of Negro Life in the South and Southwest, serialized in 1902, is an historical romance set during slavery. Hopkins surrounds the love story about a black woman and an antiracist white Englishman with dramatic incidents involving slave traders, the Underground Railroad, and John Brown's Free Soilers. Judah, a militant black man described as "a living statue of a mighty Vulcan," stands proudly at the center of the novel, symbolizing African Americans' positive historical roles during slavery. Judah not only embodies resistance against slavery, but he also transmits Hopkins's notion that African Americans should always resist oppression.

Of One Blood: or The Hidden Self, serialized in 1902 and 1903, explores Hopkins's belief that blacks should revere their African origins. Reuel, who has never identified himself as black, visits Africa. There, he becomes aware of the superiority of African civilization and culture and begins to embrace his heritage. Reuel's emergence as a descendent of African kings underscores Hopkins's belief that African Americans should ignore racist messages of inferiority. *Of One Blood* not only encouraged racial pride for African Americans, but it also voiced a Pan-African vision, unifying and celebrating black people all over the world.

During the time that Hopkins serialized her novels in *The Colored American*, she published seven short stories in the magazine. The stories echo many themes and techniques found in her novels. The unmasking of black characters passing for white, such as those in "As the Lord Lives, He Is One of Our Mother's Children" and "A Test of Manhood," reiterated Hopkins's insistence that racial barriers are irrational. Black characters are extraordinary and ethical, contributing to Hopkins's urge to create positive images of African Americans. The stories contain the devices of romance and popular fiction, such as coincidence and the supernatural. Hopkins's stories, like her sketches, complement the aims and tactics of her novels to form a coherent body of work.

Hopkins's contributions to *The Colored American* included her voluminous fiction and nonfiction, her editorial talents, and her business skills. Hopkins promoted the magazine through Boston's Colored American League, which she founded. She also went on tour in 1904 to promote the magazine.

When Booker T. Washington bought *The Colored American* in 1903, however, Hopkins's influence began to fade. By September 1904, her dissatisfaction with this situation, combined with her poor health, led her to resign. During the next fifteen years, Hopkins published several other pieces, including "The Dark Races of the Twentieth Century" (1905) and the novella *Topsy Templeton* (1916). At the time of her death, she was a stenographer for the Massachusetts Institute of Technology.

Hopkins died "when the liniment-saturated red flannel bandages she was wearing to relieve the neuritis she suffered were ignited by an oil stove in her room," as Ann Allen Shockley wrote. Equally tragic was the critical neglect she suffered afterward. Despite her impressive career as a poet, playwright, novelist, essayist, lecturer, editor, and actor, Hopkins was virtually forgotten until Shockley rediscovered her work in 1972. Afterwards, Hopkins's reputation gradually reemerged. A feminist and Pan-Africanist dedicated to celebrating and preserving her racial history, Hopkins prefigured such writers as Jessie Fauset, Zora Neale Hurston, and Alice Walker. Moreover, her work is as serious, timely, and accessible today as it was a century ago.

BIBLIOGRAPHY

Allen, Carol. *Black Women Intellectuals: Strategies of Nation, Family, and Neighborhood in the Works of Pauline Hopkins, Jessie Fauset, and Marita Bonner*. New York: Garland, 1998.

Campbell, Jane. *Mythic Black Fiction: The Transformation of History*. Knoxville: University of Tennessee Press, 1986.

Campbell, Jane. "Pauline Elizabeth Hopkins." In *Dictionary of Literary Biography 50: Afro-American Writers before the Harlem Renaissance*, edited by Trudier Harris and Thadious M. Davis. Detroit: Gale, 1986.

Carby, Hazel V. *Reconstructing Womanhood: The Emergence of the Afro-American Woman Novelist*. New York: Oxford University Press, 1987.

Gruesser, John, ed. *The Unruly Voice: Rediscovering Pauline Elizabeth Hopkins*. Urbana: University of Illinois Press, 1996.

Patterson, Martha. "Remaking the Minstrel: Peculiar Sam and the Post Reconstruction Black Subject." In *Black Women Playwrites: Visions on the American Stage*, edited by Carol P. Marsh-Lockett. New York: Garland, 1999.

Rohrbach, Augusta. "To Be Continued: Double Identity, Multiplicity, and Antigenealogy as Narrative Strategies in Pauline Hopkins's Magazine Fiction." *Callaloo* 22.2 (Spring 1999).

Shockley, Ann Allen. "Pauline Elizabeth Hopkins: A Biographical Excursion into Obscurity." *Phylon* 33 (Spring 1972): 22–26.

Somerville, Siobhan. "Passing through the Closet in Pauline E. Hopkins's Contending Forces." In *No More Separate Spheres! A Next Wave American Studies Reader*, edited by Cathy N. Davidson and Jessamyn Hatcher. Durham, NC: Duke University Press, 2002.

Tate, Claudia. "Pauline Hopkins: Our Literary Foremother." In *Conjuring: Black Women, Fiction, and Literary Tradition*, edited by Marjorie Pryse and Hortense J. Spillers. Bloomington, IN: Indiana University Press, 1985.

—JANE CAMPBELL

SHIRLEY HORN, jazz vocalist and pianist. In 2003, at age sixty-six, after a career of nearly fifty years, she released a new CD, appropriately titled *May the Music Never End*. (Photofest.)

HORN, SHIRLEY

HORN, SHIRLEY (b. 1 May 1937), jazz singer. Shirley Horn was born in Washington, DC. Her parents held civil servants' jobs, and her father also drove a taxi part-time to support the family. Even before Horn began kindergarten, her parents recognized that their daughter possessed musical talent but were unable to pay for piano lessons. Fortunately, Horn's uncle was a physician, and he agreed to pay for her music lessons. With his financial support, Horn was able to attend Howard University's school for musically gifted children, where she was the only girl in her class.

Despite being, in her words, "an oddity," Horn never lost her passion to play music, and she worked hard to develop her skills. In fact, her love of music inspired her to secretly take a job playing the piano at a local jazz club before she was of legal age to work. One night, a male patron brought a large turquoise-colored teddy bear into the club. He sent word to Horn that, if she sang "Melancholy Baby," he would give her the teddy bear. Horn agreed and, soon after, an item about her performing in the club appeared in the local newspaper. Upon discovering her daughter's secret activities, Horn's mother made her quit.

Upon finishing high school, Horn was accepted at both Julliard and Xavier Universities, but her parents could not afford either, and the uncle who had previously financed her piano lessons had died. At the age of eighteen, Horn made the decision to pursue her jazz interests and become a professional performer in Washington. In *Madame Jazz*, Horn described her determination to succeed as a jazz musician despite the lack of help from her male counterparts: "The guys didn't help me in Washington. And it did-n't make a darn bit of difference to me. Not one gig for me came from them. . . . But I got older and bolder. And I decided to get into this crap. And I got their jobs."

In 1956, at the age of nineteen, Horn married Shep Deering. Four years later, she released her first album, *Embers and Ashes*, and became accepted in the music world as a singer. For about ten years after that, she worked close to her home in Washington so that she could raise her daughter, born in 1959. She spent several years singing in jazz clubs throughout the United States. Horn also toured and recorded with jazz artists such as Quincy Jones, Branford Marsalis, Wynton Marsalis, and Toots Thielemans.

Although she always enjoyed a following, Horn's career experienced a resurgence in the latter part of the 1980s when she signed with the Verve label. In 1987, she released her first album with Verve, *I Thought about You*. Soon after, Horn became what one writer in the *Philadelphia Tribune* called a "worldwide phenomenon." Her other classic albums include her 1992 recording, *Here's to Life*, which held the number one spot on Billboard's jazz chart for seventeen weeks. In 1998, Horn won a Grammy for her album *I Remember Miles*, recorded as a tribute to her mentor, the legendary trumpeter Miles Davis.

After a career spanning nearly fifty years, Horn continued to record jazz music. In 2003, at the age of sixty-six, Horn released a new CD, appropriately titled *May the Music Never End*. The title is even more significant in light of the fact that Horn struggled against cancer and the severe diabetes that cost her the loss of her right foot. Horn received numerous awards in honor of her outstanding talent, including the Billie Holiday award in 1990 and the Phineas Newborn Jr. Award in 1999, honoring her lifelong contributions to jazz. When speaking of her long and successful career, Horn gave no indication of retiring from the music business. "The secret," she maintained, "is I have a lot of music in me. And the music has to come up and out. I love the music. Music gives me everything. May the music never end."

BIBLIOGRAPHY

Bessman, Jim. "May the Music Never End." *Billboard*, 12 July 2003.

Bryant, Steve. "The History of Shirley Horn." *Philadelphia Tribune*, 13 February 1998.

Gourse, Leslie. *Madame Jazz: Contemporary Women Instrumentalists.* New York: Oxford University Press, 1995.

"Jazz Singer Shirley Horn Wins New Fans with CD, *May the Music Never End*." *Jet*, 22 September 2003.

Nahigian, Alan. "Sounding the Horn." *Down Beat*, May 1999, 18.

"Shirley Horn." *Who's Who Among African Americans*. 15th ed. Detroit: Gale, 2002.

—MONA E. JACKSON

HORNE, LENA (b. 17 June 1917), entertainer, jazz singer. The great-granddaughter of a freed slave, Lena Calhoun Horne was born in Brooklyn, New York. Her father was a gambler and a racketeer, her mother a struggling actress. Both of them, however, came from respectable middle class families, and, as a girl, Horne was surrounded by that respectability. She and her parents lived with her paternal grandparents, Edwin and Cora Horne, until her mother and father divorced when she was three.

Edwin Horne was a co-founder of the United Colored Democracy, a lobbying group. Cora Calhoun Horne was a suffragist and a bold defender of black rights. "My grandmother took me to her meetings," said Horne in an interview for *I Dream a World*,

> "from the time I was little until I was fifteen. She was in the Urban League, the NAACP, and the Ethical Culture Society. I was surrounded by adult activities. . . . if I hadn't had that from her, then the other side of my life, which was more bleak, might have finished me."
>
> (Lanker, p. 77)

There are probably few other Hollywood legends who were members of the National Association for the Advancement of Colored People at two years old.

Unfortunately, Horne was not able to stay permanently with her grandmother. When she was about seven, she rejoined her mother and spent the next few years traveling with her as she pursued her career as an actress. They had no home and, because of Jim Crow laws, could seldom find a hotel to stay in. They slept in the homes of relatives, friends, and even strangers, a common practice in the Southern black community, where hospitality stretched to try to fill the void created by prejudice. Horne then spent several years in Brooklyn, living with relatives, attending the Brooklyn public schools and the Girls High School. When she was fourteen, her mother remarried, returning from a tour in Cuba with a new husband, Miguel Rodriguez. The new family moved to a poor section of the Bronx, having been rebuffed by Brooklyn's black middle class.

LENA HORNE, a legendary performer, photographed at a rehearsal at the Minskoff Theater in New York City, 30 October 1975. (© Bettye Lane.)

When she was sixteen, Horne had to quit school. Her mother had become very ill, and the household needed money. A friend of her mother's, Elida Webb, was choreographer at the Cotton Club and got Horne a job, solely on the basis of her spectacular looks. The singing and dancing lessons she had taken as a proper young lady in her grandparents home were useful, but Horne started studying music in earnest. She said later that she was never a natural singer and that it took a lot of hard work and a number of years for her to hone her skills. In the meantime, she danced in the chorus on bills with Count Basie, Cab Calloway, Billie Holiday, and Ethel Waters. However, when she was only seventeen she was cast in *Dance with Your Gods* (1934) on Broadway. At eighteen, she left the Cotton Club for good to be a singer with Noble Sissle's Society Orchestra in Philadelphia. Her father was not far away, operating a hotel in Pittsburgh. The two became reacquainted, and he remained an important part of her life until he died.

On the road with the orchestra, Horne was constantly confronted with the harsh realities of racism. Possibly to escape, at nineteen, she married a friend of her father's, Louis Jones, who was twenty-eight. They remained married for four years, long enough for Horne to bear two children. In 1939 she took a starring role in the revue *Blackbirds of 1939*, and in 1940 she left her husband. When she went to New York, she left her children with their father so that she could make a start and find a place for the three of them to live. Late in the year, she became chief vocalist for the Charlie Barnett band and began recording. Able to provide a home for her children, she went back to Pittsburgh to get them, but Jones would give up only her daughter. Horne agreed to settle for visiting rights with her son. The separation from him was a source of sorrow for her the rest of her life.

Charlie Barnett was one of the first white band leaders to hire African American musicians, but singing and traveling with his band was a difficult experience for Horne. She was often unable to stay in the same hotel with the rest of the band. She frequently was barred from a theater's dressing room and had to change in the bus. She was even prevented from sitting with white members of the band between songs.

While with Barnett's band, Horne started recording. One of her most popular early records, "Haunted Town," was made with Barnett. Next, she went to the Café Society Downtown, an engagement that might be said to have made her name. There she met Paul Robeson and Walter White, both on the same night. Both of them, as her friends, helped increase her awareness of the political struggles of black people. She also met and started dating boxer Joe Louis. Within the year, she got an offer of a booking at the Trocadero Club in California.

Hollywood

The decision to accept the offer and go to Hollywood was a difficult one. Horne knew it might lead to work in films, but she had serious doubts about battling what she expected would be the rampant racism of the film community. Walter White persuaded her that she would be doing a service to her people if she could break into films. He made her think of the possibility as a challenge. Sure enough, two months after arriving in Los Angeles Horne was auditioning for Metro-Goldwyn-Mayer (MGM). Soon she was signing a seven-year contract with a starting salary of $200 per week and a clause saying she did not have to perform in stereotypical roles. "My father had them scared to death. I think that was the first time a black man had ever come into Louis B. Mayer's office and said, 'I don't want my daughter in this mess.' He was so articulate and so beautiful, they just said, 'Well, don't worry.' "

The problem was how to use her. She lost her first chance for a speaking role in a mixed-cast movie because she was too light-skinned. She did not get another shot until 1956. All her performances in between were guest spots in which she only sang. These scenes never included the principals of the film in any important way and were easily edited out so that the films could be shown in southern theaters. Horne did one speaking part at MGM, in an all-black film entitled *Cabin in the Sky* (1943), and she was lent out for another, *Stormy Weather* (1943).

The guest spots had a tremendous effect. Her job, as Walter White had seen it, was to change the American image of black women, and she did. She fit white society's standards of beauty as well as the most beautiful white women, but she was clearly a woman of color. She was also a woman of great charm and dignity who was conscious of her position as a representative of black America. Her choices about the way she presented herself were influenced by that role. It seemed important at the time to show that a black woman did not have to sing spirituals or earthy, overtly sexual laments; Horne sang Cole Porter and Gershwin. It seemed important that a black woman could be cool, glamorous, and sophisticated; Horne always looked as though she had stepped out of the pages of *Vogue*.

When not singing on screen, she was singing in clubs. Horne had staying power. During the 1940s, she commanded as much as $10,000 a week at the clubs. Her recordings—including "Birth of the Blues," "Moanin' Low," "Little Girl Blue," and "Classics in Blue"—were highly successful, and she was in demand on the radio. During World War II, she traveled extensively to entertain the troops, an experience that was not always salubrious. There are many versions of the story about one of her performances, at Fort Riley, Kansas. She stepped onstage and saw that German prisoners of war were seated in front of African American soldiers. Some versions of the story say she walked out, some that she stayed, and some that she walked down the aisle, past the Germans, and serenaded the black soldiers. In an interview in 1997 in *U.S. News and World Report*, Horne said, "To set the record straight, I did walk out. I went immediately to the local office of the NAACP and filed a complaint. As a result, MGM Studios pulled me off the USO tour. So I began to use my own money to travel and entertain our troops."

In 1947, Horne secretly married Lennie Hayton, whom she had been seeing for years. Hayton was white, and Horne's position as a symbol for African Americans rose up to haunt her again. She did not reveal her marriage until 1950, and when she did, her mail was filled with hate letters from white racists and bitter reproaches from black Americans. It was a reaction she had anticipated. "Isn't it ironic?" she said in a 1965 *Ebony* article. "For three years I preferred to let the world think I was a woman living in sin than admit that I had married a white man."

At the beginning of the 1950s, Horne was at the top of her form. By 1948 she received $60,000 a week for appearing at the Copacabana in New York. In 1950 she made her first television appearance, on Ed Sullivan's *Toast of the Town*. In 1956 she had her first speaking role in a mixed-cast film, *Meet Me in Las Vegas*. In 1957 she starred on Broadway for the first time in *Jamaica*. However, she lost the film role she had most hoped for, the mulatto Julie in *Show Boat*, to her friend Ava Gardner. Her marriage to Hayton may have been the deciding factor in her loss of the role, but Horne took it as a sign that Hollywood had nothing to offer her. Also, because she remained loyal to friends who were being blacklisted for supposed Communist sympathies, particularly Paul Robeson, she was eventually blacklisted herself from television work. Her second appearance in that medium was nine years after her first, on *The Perry Como Show* in 1959.

During the 1960s, Horne, like many others, became more and more involved in civil rights. She was at the March on Washington in 1963. In the atmosphere of change, she also separated from her husband. "I took a chance," she told *Ebony* in 1968. "I said, 'Lennie, I'm going through some changes as a black woman. I can't explain them. I don't know what they're going to mean, what they're going to do to me, but I've got to be by myself to work it out.' " They remained apart for three years and then came back together to go on with their twenty-four year marriage. In the meantime, Horne toured for the National Council of Negro Women, speaking to black women all over the South. Her autobiography, *Lena*, which she wrote with Richard Schickel, appeared in 1965.

In 1970 Horne's father died, followed, in just a few months, by her son, Teddy, who was just thirty years old

and the father of a family. Less than a year later, her husband died. The next few years were filled with grief and sorrow. She had lost the two people she most depended on and three of the people she most loved.

In 1974 Horne was back on Broadway, performing with Tony Bennett. Four years later, she played Glinda, the Good Witch, in the film *The Wiz*. On 30 April 1981, at the age of sixty-four, she opened on Broadway with *Lena Horne: The Lady and Her Music*, which became the longest-running one-woman show in Broadway history and won her a special Tony Award, the New York City Handel Medallion, the Drama Desk Award, and a Drama Critics' Circle citation.

Horne continued to appear on television regularly and to record. She appeared in *That's Entertainment III* in 1994, saying "I never felt like I really belonged to Hollywood. At that time, they didn't know what to do with me, a black performer." In 1994 Blue Note released her "We'll Be Together Again" and in 1995 "An Evening With Lena Horne," recorded live at New York's Supper Club, won her a Grammy. In 1996, she stopped the show at a tribute concert for her old friend Billy Strayhorn. Her album *Lena Horne: Being Myself* came out in 1997 and was received with praise and gratitude by critics and the public. She received both an Image Award and the Spingarn Medal from the NAACP, as well as the Kennedy Center Award for Lifetime Contribution to the Arts. In 1979 she accepted an honorary doctorate from Howard University, and in 1998, she received the same honor from Yale. She also received the Ella Award for Lifetime Achievement by the Society of Singers. In 1996, Public Broadcasting's *American Masters* series presented "Lena Horne: In Her Own Voice," a documentary of her life. In 2003 Sony Pictures Television, along with ABC and Storyline Entertainment, announced that it would be making a film biography of Horne, starring Janet Jackson and based on Horne's autobiography, *Lena*.

It is difficult to assess the historical importance of Lena Horne's life and work. In part, this is because she was so remarkably contemporary. Thinking of her as a historical figure strains the imagination. Her image as a beautiful, proud, self-assured black woman suggests that nothing, not even history, could or would dare impinge on her. She responded to this idea when she talked about the time she struck a white man in a Hollywood nightclub for a racist insult. The incident was widely reported by journalists.

Later, Horne said that she got telegrams from black people saying that they never knew she had the same problems they did.

Lena Horne's position as a symbol of and for her race worked hand in hand with racism to limit her possibilities as a performer and a person. However, she managed to transcend those limitations to carve out a remarkable stage, film, and recording career and a life of personal fulfillment.

BIBLIOGRAPHY

Bhan, Esme E. "Lena Horne." In *Notable Black American Women*, edited by Jessie Carney Smith. Detroit, MI: Gale Research, 1992.

Bogle, Donald. *Blacks in American Films and Television: An Encyclopedia*. New York: Garland, 1988.

Bogle, Donald. *Brown Sugar: Eighty Years of America's Black Female Superstars*. New York: Harmony Books, 1980.

Buckley, Gail Lumet. *The Hornes: An American Family*. New York: Knopf, 1986.

Feinstein, Herbert. "Lena Horne Speaks Freely." *Ebony*, May 1963.

"Horne at 80: She's Weathered the Storms." *U.S. News & World Report*, 30 June 1997.

Horne, Lena. "My Life with Lennie." *Ebony*, November 1965.

Lanker, Brian. *I Dream a World: Portraits of Black Women Who Changed America*. New York: Stewart, Tabori & Chang, 1989.

Matsumoto, Nancy, and Tom Gliatto. "Horne of Plenty." *People Weekly*, 6 July 1998.

Monti, Gloria. "Lena Horne receives honorary degree." *Yale Film News*, Fall 1998.

Pierce, Ponchitta. "Lena Horne at 51." *Ebony*, July 1968.

"Young Negro with Haunting Voice Charms New York with Old Songs." *Life*, 4 January 1943.

—KATHLEEN THOMPSON

HOUSTON, DRUSILLA DUNJEE (b. 20 June 1876; d. 8 February 1941), historian, journalist, and teacher. One of the most important African American women in the history of Oklahoma, Drusilla Dunjee Houston was a multifaceted figure who, at one time or another during her wide-ranging career, was an educator, self-trained historian, elegist, black clubwoman, and journalist. Her writings span three different literary periods: the race writers, the Black Women's Era (1890–1900), and the Harlem Renaissance. Despite voluminous writings, both journalistic and historical, for more than four decades, Houston remains one of the most overlooked of all African American women writers.

One of ten siblings of former slaves, the Reverend John William Dunjee and Lydia Dunjee, Houston was born in Harpers Ferry, West Virginia. Her family lived in Myrtle Hall on the grounds of the Storer College, a school for freedmen in the Shenandoah Mission, where her father was the financial officer during Reconstruction. Commissioned by the American Baptist Home Missionary Society, Reverend Dunjee built and/or pastored Baptist churches for blacks in rural areas throughout the South, New England, and the Midwest. His last church was Tabernacle Baptist Church in Oklahoma, where he brought the family during the second land run in 1892. Houston was deeply influenced by her devout Baptist family upbringing, and, like her father, was a fierce "race" warrior who spent a lifetime dedicated to the uplift of blacks in Oklahoma.

Houston is best known for the publication of Wonderful Ethiopians of the Ancient Cushite Empire, Book 1: Nations of the Cushite Empire, Marvelous Facts from Authentic Records. The book boldly proclaimed an African origin of civilization in 1926, a year when twenty-three African Americans were lynched. Wonderful Ethiopians was intended to be the first in a three-volume set and is best described as a "recuperative narrative" in the Originists—subset of the Authentists—tradition. That is, it is part of a body of literature written by black writers referred to as Nile Valley scholars, Egyptologists, or African World scholars. Houston is the only woman in this tradition, among such prominent black male writers as Yosef ben-Jochannan, John Henrik Clarke, John G. Jackson, St. Clair Drake, Ivan Van Sertima, and Cheikh Anta Diop. Her hope was that the book would refute white claims of the inferiority of black Americans, heal the psychological wounds of slavery, and ease the continued racism of the early twentieth century. Shortly after publication, Wonderful Ethiopians enjoyed a wide readership throughout the country, the Caribbean, and parts of Europe. Aided by the National Association of Colored Women's Clubs (NACW), the book was also studied in black women's study groups across the country. Despite its shortcomings—largely a lack of bibliography and footnotes—the book remains a classic historical text that contributes to the historiography of ancient Africa.

In the early 1900s there were nearly fifty newspapers and forty magazines and periodicals published by African Americans, and women played a central role in their publication. In the tradition of her father's post-Emancipation newspaper, the *Harper's Ferry Messenger*, Houston had a newspaper career that spanned nearly three decades, beginning in 1914 with the *Bookertee Searchlight* in Okmulgee, Oklahoma. In 1917 she joined with her brother Roscoe Dunjee, a nationally known civil rights activist, to produce the *Oklahoma Black Dispatch*; and toward the end of her life, she wrote for the *Arizona Journal and Guide*. Most of her work was with the *Black Dispatch*, where for more than two decades she turned her often scathing pen and tart tongue on racial inequality and injustice. In the mid-1920s she launched a syndicated newspaper column with the Associated Negro Press and became well known across the country. Like other African American women journalists, Houston also wrote on such racial uplift issues as negative stereotyping of black women, self-reliance, temperance, education, home building, and the creation of sustainable organizations. She also espoused these same and other themes from lecture platforms across the country. Houston wrote several different columns, most notably one titled the "Wondrous History of the Negro," in which she celebrated the lives of such prominent African Americans as Blanche K. Bruce,

Frederick Douglass, and Mercer Langston, among many others, all of whom were regular visitors to the Dunjee home.

Houston, an active club woman, helped her community to create sustainable organizations and pool their collective efforts to support the needy among them. She skillfully utilized her columns in the *Black Dispatch* to argue for the creation of racially autonomous institutional structures in the Baptist Church, public schools, clubs, mutual benefit societies, and businesses. An ardent proponent of economic nationalism, she devoted numerous columns that urged women to restrict their spending to absolute necessities purchased within the black community. She responded to every major incident that imperiled blacks in Oklahoma, including racism in the Kellyville train disaster, environmental racism in the way blacks were forced to build their homes in known floodplains, and lynchings throughout the state. Immediately after the Tulsa Race Massacre of 1921, Houston defied armed marshals and bravely walked the streets of the Greenwood District, gathering information to report on the disaster and later to call for financial and moral support for the Tulsa victims

There was essentially no women's movement of any consequence in Oklahoma in which she was not involved. Her oftentimes lengthy editorials in the *Black Dispatch* served as a nerve line for organizations of which she was either the founder or a founding member, including the YWCA, NAACP, Red Cross, the Civic League, the Federated Colored Women's Clubs chapter of the National Association of Colored Women's Clubs (NACW), and the Oklahoma Business League, all providing social and economic uplift for early Oklahoma blacks. At a time when women were expected to be subservient to husbands, Houston was fiercely independent in her marriage to the wealthy businessman Price Houston. A strong believer in financial investments, Houston owned and managed a dry goods store, had extensive real estate holdings, and created her own educational institutes to teach and train others.

To Houston, the Baptist church was pivotal in the life of the black community. She was a devout Baptist and she played an important role with the Oklahoma Baptist State Convention in the development of a school for black women and girls. In 1917 she moved to Sapulpa, Oklahoma, to become principal of the first Baptist Training School for Girls, also known as the Baptist College. The Baptist Training School was the first school in the Oklahoma territories for black women and girls and was one of the most important early educational institutions in Oklahoma. Houston brought to that job a fluency in German and Latin, considerable skills in curriculum development, and membership in the Oklahoma State Teachers organization, from which she received numerous awards

for her teaching. She was also an accomplished musician, having studied music at Northwestern Conservatory of Music in Minnesota.

After five years, Houston left the Training School because of her husband's illness. Continuing her service to young black boys and girls, to whom she referred as "acres of diamonds," Houston worked with numerous state-run agencies to protect their interests. She served as religious director and supervisor at the State Home for Boys in Oklahoma, saying that she went there to "make men out of hazards." Other schools she initiated or directed included the McAlester Seminary for Girls, which she operated for twelve years, and her own private school, the Vocational Industrial Institute.

Like her mother, Houston was plagued by tuberculosis throughout much of her adult life. She succumbed to the disease in 1941 in Phoenix, Arizona, attended by her only living child, Florence. It is believed that because of the shame and stigma associated with tuberculosis, Houston was very secretive and often asked not to be publicly recognized for her work. Her obituary in the *Black Dispatch* was brief. The epitaph on her gravestone is simple and true to her beliefs, stating only that "To Die Is to Gain."

Houston's life is celebrated by at least two scholarship funds: the Uncrowned Queens, Drusilla Dunjee Houston Scholarship Fund under the auspices of the Uncrowned Queens Institute for Research and Education on Women, Inc., and one administered by the Association of Black Women Historians. The Institute is named after a poem written by Houston in 1917, "America's Uncrowned Queens." Future publication of Houston manuscripts discovered at the beginning of the twenty-first century will shed further light on her contribution to black women's history and firmly establish that her contribution to the African American women's social, religious, and literary tradition is highly significant. To continue to ignore Houston's contribution, we would be, as Anna Julia Cooper said more than a century ago: "blinded by the loss of sight in one eye and unable to detect the full shape of the black women's American historical literary tradition."

—PEGGY BROOKS-BERTRAM

HOUSTON, WHITNEY (b. 9 August 1963), singer, actor. One of the most successful pop singers of all time, Whitney Houston is the only recording artist to have seven consecutive singles reach number one on the charts. By the early 2000s, she had sold 120 million albums and 50 million singles, and even managed to make a million-seller out of *The Star Spangled Banner*—twice.

Whitney Houston was born in Newark, New Jersey, to John and Emily (Drinkard) Houston. Her mother was the R&B and gospel singer popularly known as Cissy Houston, and at the time of Whitney's birth, her father was the executive secretary of the Newark Central Planning Board.

Houston began singing in church, appearing with the New Hope Baptist Church of Newark choir from the time that she was nine. When she was fifteen, she performed with her mother at a benefit concert at Carnegie Hall and began appearing with her at local clubs, as well as singing backup vocals for recordings by Lou Rawls and Chaka Khan. After graduating from high school in 1981, Houston signed with Tara Productions, a talent management company. She recorded advertising jingles and appeared on albums by the Neville Brothers, Material, and Paul Jabara.

Clive Davis, the founder and head of Arista Records, saw Houston perform in 1983 and offered her a recording contract, launching a creative partnership that would last for seventeen years. Davis worked personally with Houston, spending two years and more than $250,000 building up to the release of her first solo album, *Whitney Houston*. The publicity included television appearances, showcase engagements, a promotional film, and duet recordings

WHITNEY HOUSTON, the singer and actress, is one of the most successful pop musicians of all time and the only recording artist to have seven consecutive singles reach number one on the charts. (Photofest.)

with Teddy Pendergrass and Jermaine Jackson. When it came time to record the album, Davis assembled a team of proven hit-makers to write and produce the songs. Davis himself chose the songs and the order they would appear in. The album built slowly after its release, taking a year to reach the top of the charts, propelled by a series of hit singles and videos that included "Saving All My Love for You," "How Will I Know?," and "The Greatest Love of All." In 1986 Houston won her first Grammy Award, for Best Pop Vocal Performance on "Saving All My Love for You."

The popularity of the album notwithstanding, it received decidedly mixed reviews. Near universal praise for the beauty and power of Houston's voice was tempered by some critics' disappointment with the plain pop format of the songs, which allowed for little of the gospel style expressiveness she displayed in live appearances.

The overwhelming success of *Whitney Houston*, which remained in the Top 10 longer than any previous album in history, caused the release of her second album, *Whitney*, to be delayed for six months. *Whitney*, the first album by a female recording artist to debut at number one, yielded four chart-topping singles. Although it failed to sell as well as her first two albums, *I'm Your Baby Tonight* (1990) was certified double platinum.

In 1992 Whitney Houston married Bobby Brown, a star of "New Jack Swing," a musical style that combined contemporary soul and some of the elements of hip-hop. In 1993 their daughter, Bobbi Kristina, was born.

In 1992 Whitney Houston co-starred in the hit movie *The Bodyguard* with Kevin Costner, playing a pop singer. The soundtrack album, featuring six songs sung by Houston, sold more than 15 million copies. The biggest hit from the album was Houston's take on Dolly Parton's "I Will Always Love You," which held the number one spot on Billboard's Hot 100 chart for fourteen weeks and garnered Houston two of the three Grammy awards she won in 1994.

Houston's other movies include *Waiting to Exhale* (1995), with Angela Bassett and Gregory Hines, directed by Forest Whitaker, and *The Preacher's Wife* (1996) with Denzel Washington. Both movies yielded best-selling soundtrack albums, replete with new Whitney Houston hits, and Houston revealed a natural, charming acting style. The 1998 album *My Love Is Your Love*, which Houston co-produced with Clive Davis, generated the kind of towering sales figures that, combined with a string of four hit singles, would have been exceptional in the career of nearly any other singer. It was the norm for Whitney Houston.

Show business performers at the top of their field inevitably find their private lives becoming the subject matter of tabloid television and newspapers. In Houston's case the process was accelerated by a series of well-publicized events. Bobby Brown was arrested frequently during the years of their marriage on charges relating to drugs, unsafe driving, disorderly conduct, and repeated violations of parole for a drunken driving incident in 1996. In January 2000, Whitney Houston was stopped by guards at a Hawaiian airport, who found a small amount of marijuana in her bag, but she left the scene to avoid further questioning. Later that year she was fired from performing at the Academy Awards by the director Burt Bachrach.

Houston has cancelled a number of high-profile appearances at the last minute. Her gaunt appearance and seeming unsteadiness at a tribute to Michael Jackson in 2001 led to widespread rumors that she was dying and false reports of her death. In 2002 her father's entertainment company, which handled her business affairs, sued Houston for $100 million, claiming it had been denied payment for services rendered.

In a December 2002 television interview with Diane Sawyer, Houston admitted to abusing cocaine, marijuana, and prescription drugs, but claimed that the problem was in the past. Although the interview was intended to sweep away the rumors, to some observers Houston's demeanor and comments raised more questions rather than offered answers.

One week later, Arista released Houston's eighth album, *Just Whitney*. In what was widely interpreted as a display of fan loyalty to a beleaguered star, the album sold more copies during its first week than any previous Whitney Houston album, but then failed to sustain the kind of sales that characterized her previous releases. On the other hand, the Diane Sawyer interview the previous week had drawn 21.3 million viewers. A great many people still seemed to care about the well-being of this legendary singer.

BIBLIOGRAPHY

de Moraes, Lisa. "Whitney's Weird Chat Gives ABC Fat Ratings." *Washington Post*, 6 December 2002.

Larkin, Colin, ed. *The Virgin Encyclopedia of R&B and Soul*. London: Virgin Books, 1998.

Moritz, Charles, ed. *Current Biography: Yearbook 1986*. New York: H. W. Wilson, 1986.

Whitney Houston Platinum Club. WhitneyHouston.com. http://www.whitneyhouston.com/news/index.html.

—ROBERT W. LOGAN

HUNTER, ALBERTA (b. 1 April 1895; d. 17 October 1984), blues singer and composer whose career spanned seven decades. "I've got the world in a jug, the stopper's in my hand," are among the powerful closing lines of the blues composition "Down Hearted Blues," made famous as one of the most popular songs of the blues music era of the 1920s. The tune was the first recording of the legendary blues singer Bessie Smith and was written by two other classic blues music stars, Lovie Austin and Alberta Hunter. Out of this triad of Tennessee-born African American

ALBERTA HUNTER had a long and successful career as a blues and jazz singer, beginning at age fifteen, and was also a composer. She made a successful comeback in 1977, at age eighty-two, and then continued performing and recording until her death. (Photofest.)

female musicians, it was the incomparable Alberta Hunter who lived on through six more decades of entertainment history and prompted a resurgence of classic blues in the late 1970s that brought the black music creation to a whole new audience.

Born in Memphis, Tennessee, Hunter was the second child of a Charles Hunter, porter, and Laura Hunter, a domestic and laundress. Abandoned by her father, Alberta and her elder sister La Tosca were raised by their mother and their maternal grandmother, Nancy Peterson. Although not completely impoverished, Hunter did live through a difficult childhood and was supported by Laura's income as a domestic in a local brothel. Hunter was also plagued by sexual abuse at the hands of an elder male family friend and a local school principal. It was this destruction of her innocence that caused Hunter's distrust of many male figures and prompted her to "just stay away from men" as she remarked in interviews with Frank C. Taylor for the biography *Alberta Hunter*. The abuse may have prompted Hunter to forge closer relationships with women in general. Although not a publicly professed lesbian, Hunter would have select, long-standing relationships with women in her adult years.

In the many moves Hunter and her family made throughout Memphis during her childhood, it was the 1903 move to the city's famed Beale Street that brought Hunter close to the beckoning sounds of fledgling blues and jazz music. By the early 1900s, Beale Street was home to churches, shops, saloons, and theaters—all patronized, managed, and often owned by African Americans. As a hub of black musical and recreational activity and the home to the musician W. C. Handy, the first composer of written blues music, Beale Street soon became known as the street where "blues began." The combination of the songs that emanated from Beale Street and reports from a family friend that songstresses could earn ten dollars a week in Chicago sparked the desire in Hunter to become a vocalist. Weary of her hand-to-hand existence and determined to succeed, Hunter lied about her age so that she could use a child railway pass and, without permission from her mother, relocated to Chicago at the age of sixteen in 1911. In accordance with black female relocation patterns during the migration era, Hunter sought out a family friend, Ellen Winston, who initially boarded Hunter and helped her find domestic employment.

From 1911 to 1921, Hunter rose to the top of the black music scene in Chicago. She initially launched into the world of song by lying about her age again to work as a singer in the vice-filled bars of the city. Hunter performed blues tunes and popular songs and soon learned about the jazz music craze when, in 1917, she became a regular at the Dreamland nightclub on Chicago's Southside. Future jazz legends, including the trumpeter King Oliver and the cornet-player Louis Armstrong, frequented the Dreamland, and Hunter not only became acquainted with rising jazz stars but also came to be known as "Southside's Sweetheart." More than a vocalist, Hunter began to compose popular blues tunes with pianist Lovie Austin, including "Down Hearted Blues" and "Chirpin' the Blues." On stage, Hunter used her soprano voice to weave the lyrics of a song into a vocal tapestry and draw audiences into her tales of how "You Can Take My Man, But You Can't Keep Him Long" or how she had the "Bleeding Hearted Blues," and the "Michigan Water Blues."

In 1921 Hunter cut her first recordings with Pace and Handy's Black Swan Records, the first African American–owned recording company. She later went on to record at Paramount, Okeh, Victor, Gennett, Prestige, and Columbia, and circumvented exclusive, binding contracts by working under the names of Josephine Beatty, Mae Alix, Helen Roberts, and Alberta Prime. Hunter became an important factor in the blues music craze led by black female entertainers in the 1920s. The classic, or vaudeville, blues performance often consisted of a female vocalist backed by a bass, piano, drum, and brass instrument, and it was the classic genre that reached the height

of its popularity in the 1920s. A performance or recording by one of the reigning classic blues queens (including Hunter, Bessie Smith, Ma Rainey, Ethel Waters, and Mamie Smith) drew the attention of southern and northern African Americans alike, and represented how southern working class musical culture could be transmitted to northern cities as a result of black migration patterns.

As the 1920s progressed, Hunter traveled to New York City and landed a part in the 1923 Broadway musical *How Come?* shortly after her arrival. Searching for the acceptance and opportunities black entertainers of the time had been able to find in Europe, Hunter journeyed to London and won the part of Queenie in *Show Boat* at the Drury Lane Theatre in 1928. Alongside her leading man, the African American actor, activist, and vocalist Paul Robeson, Hunter enjoyed the praises of European royalty and garnered international acclaim. Hunter enjoyed the relative freedom and escape from American race relations that Europe had to offer and remained a fixture in the London and Paris entertainment scene until 1939, while simultaneously developing a repertoire of songs in French, Dutch, Italian, and German. She later continued her international performances when she entertained U.S. troops during World War II and the Korean War. When not performing abroad, Hunter returned to the United States to record and perform, and eventually she worked with the black singer and actress Ethel Waters when they were both cast in the Broadway drama *Mamba's Daughters* in 1939.

During the rise of Hunter's career, her personal life went through various transformations. She married Willard Townsend in 1919 and divorced him in 1923. She also reportedly had long-standing relationships with several female companions, yet still devoted much of her attention to providing for her mother. With the death of Laura Hunter in 1954, Hunter lost her desire to entertain. She subsequently studied nursing and devoted her life to a career as a scrub nurse at Goldwater Hospital on Roosevelt Island in New York. Hunter was as dedicated to her medical career as she was to her musical craft and did not leave nursing until the hospital administration retired her in 1977 at the age of eighty-two.

Although Hunter was absent from the entertainment scene for more than twenty years, she started performing the blues again at the Cookery in Greenwich Village in October 1977. Her initial appearances heralded her comeback into the music scene as an octogenarian and sparked a flurry of musical activity between 1977 and 1984. Hunter played select venues across the nation, reissued some of her earlier recordings and compositions, and released a series of new live recordings that included "My Handy Man Ain't So Handy No More" and "Amtrak Blues." Hunter was met with wonderful reviews and scores of new audiences longing to hear her suggestive tunes in her expressive new alto voice.

Hunter's presence in the world of entertainment continued to live on long after her death in 1984. In September 2001 the musical *Cookin' at the Cookery*, which recounts Hunter's life and music, opened in Lowell, Massachusetts. The show continued its run into the coming years, which is a true testament to Hunter's artistry and her influence on contemporary generations of entertainers. Apparently, both new and old aficionados of black music believed that the blues entertainer Alberta Hunter left this earth still holding the "world in a jug, with the stopper in her hand."

See also **Blues**.

BIBLIOGRAPHY

Harrington, Richard. "Singer Alberta Hunter, Made Comeback at 82." *Washington Post*, 19 October 1984.

Harrison, Daphne Duval. *Black Pearls: Blues Queens of the 1920s*. New Brunswick, NJ: Rutgers University Press, 1988. An insightful study of the classic blues women and the significance of blues culture. Includes a biographical chapter on Hunter.

Kernis, Mark. "It's Alberta: Grandmama of the Blues." *Washington Post*, 5 January 1979.

McKee, Margaret, and Fred Chisenhall. *Beale Black and Blue: Life and Music on Black America's Main Street*. Baton Rouge: Louisiana State University Press, 1981. One of the best collections of oral histories to focus on the history of Beale Street and its key performers.

Taylor, Frank C., and Gerald Cook. *Alberta Hunter: A Celebration in Blues*. New York: McGraw-Hill, 1987. One of the most comprehensive biographical studies of Hunter to date.

Wilson, John S. "Alberta Hunter, 89, Cabaret Star, Dies." *New York Times*, 19 October 1984.

—MICHELLE R. SCOTT

HUNTER, CLEMENTINE (b. December 1886; d. 1 January 1988), folk artist. "If Jimmy Carter wants to see me, he knows where I am. He can come here." This reply to President Carter's invitation that she come to Washington for the opening of an exhibition of her work is vintage Clementine Hunter. Her disregard for fame and the famous was part of her special charm and did not change, even after she became known worldwide for her colorful folk paintings of black life in the Cane River region of northern Louisiana.

Hunter was born on Hidden Hill Plantation, near Cloutierville, Louisiana. Her mother, Mary Antoinette Adams, was the daughter of a slave who was brought to Louisiana from Virginia. Her father, John Reuben, had an Irish father and a Native American mother. Hunter considered herself a Creole. When she was a teenager, she moved with her family from Hidden Hill to Yucca Plantation, which was renamed Melrose, seventeen miles south of Natchitoches, Louisiana. She lived and worked at Melrose until 1970, when the plantation was sold; then she moved to a small trailer a few miles away, where she lived until her death.

CLEMENTINE HUNTER became renowned for her folk paintings of black life in northern Louisiana. She is shown here c. 1970. (From the collection of Shelby R. Gilley, Gilley's Gallery, Baton Rouge, Louisiana; Herbert Stemley, photographer.)

Charles Dupree, the father of Hunter's first two children—Joseph (Frenchie) and Cora—died about 1914. In January 1924, Clementine married Emmanual Hunter, by whom she had five children: Agnes, King, Mary (called Jackie), and two who died at birth. Emmanual Hunter died in 1944. Clementine Hunter outlived all her children except Mary.

Hunter's mentor was François Mignon, a French writer who lived on Melrose Plantation from 1938 to 1970. According to Mignon, Hunter did her first painting in 1939. From then until a few months before her death, she painted continually, on any surface she could find. Her output was prodigious; estimates are that she completed more than five thousand paintings. Like many folk artists, however, Hunter painted the same scenes over and over. Her works roughly fall into five thematic categories: work scenes from plantation life, recreation scenes, religious scenes, flowers and birds, and abstracts. The quality of her work varies greatly, but her paintings are prized for their vibrant colors and whimsical humor.

The first exhibit of Hunter's work was at the New Orleans Arts and Crafts show in 1949. After three exhibits in the 1950s, her work received little attention until the early 1970s, when it was shown at the Museum of American Folk Art in New York City (1973) and in the Los Angeles County Museum of Art's exhibit "Two Centuries of Black American Art" (1976). In the last fifteen years of her life, Hunter had many one-woman shows at colleges and galleries throughout Louisiana. She was featured on local and national television shows and was included in two oral black-history projects (Fisk University, 1971; Schlesinger Library, Radcliffe College, 1976). She also was part of the photographic portrait exhibition "Women of Courage by Judith Sedwick," shown in 1985 in New York and Boston. That same year, Hunter was awarded an honorary doctor of fine arts degree from Northwestern State University of Louisiana in Natchitoches. Although the quality of Hunter's paintings is uneven, the historical value of her work is beyond question.

BIBLIOGRAPHY
Bailey, Mildred Hart. "Clementine Hunter." In *Four Women of Cane River: Their Contributions to the Cultural Life of the Area.* Natchitoches: Northwestern University of Louisiana, 1980.
Mignon, François. *Plantation Memo: Plantation Life in Louisiana, 1750–1970, and Other Matters.* Baton Rouge: Claitor's, 1972.
Mills, Gary B. *The Forgotten People: Cane River's Creoles of Color.* Baton Rouge: Louisiana State University Press, 1977.
Read, Mimi. "Clementine Hunter: Visions from the Heart." *Dixie Magazine,* New Orleans *Times-Picayune* Sunday Supplement, 14 April 1985.
Ryan, Bob, and Yvonne Ryan. "Clementine Hunter: A Personal Story." *Louisiana Life* (September–October 1981).
Wilson, James L. *Clementine Hunter: American Folk Artist.* Gretna, LA: Pelican, 1988.

ARCHIVES AND SPECIAL COLLECTIONS
Hunter's work is held as part of the François Mignon Collection, James Register Collection, Melrose Collection, and Thomas N. Whitehead Collection, among others. Archival resources are available at the Cammie G. Henry Research Center, Eugene P. Watson Memorial Library, and the Northwestern State University of Louisiana, Natchitoches.

—ANNE HUDSON JONES

HUNTER-GAULT, CHARLAYNE (b. 27 February 1942), journalist. Charlayne Hunter-Gault achieved notoriety in 1961 when she and Hamilton Holmes became the first African American students to attend the University of Georgia-Athens. In the years following her internationally famous matriculation, Hunter-Gault grew weary of being known as "Charlayne Hunter, the pioneer." She wanted to use the news, as opposed to just being in the news, in order to help people ask questions based on good information.

Charlayne Hunter was born in Due West, South Carolina, to Althea Hunter. Charlayne's father and namesake, Charles S. H. Hunter Jr., was a chaplain in the U.S. Navy. His frequent and extended tours of duty left the abridged Hunter family to spend much of Charlayne's childhood in the southern United States. From 1954 to 1959, Charlayne Hunter attended Henry McNeal Turner High School in Atlanta, Georgia. Her ambition to be a college-trained reporter was a reasonable one, given her honor-student status and editorship of the school newspaper. However, Hunter's admission to the University of Georgia was hampered by dissenting white Georgians. While a group of civil rights leaders navigated the desegregation process on behalf of Hunter and fellow applicant "Hamp" Holmes, Hunter left the south for Wayne State University in Detroit, Michigan. A year and a half went by before Hunter's place at the University of Georgia was secured.

After she returned to Georgia to attend the university, Hunter found work as a summer intern with the *Louisville Times.* The first black person to hold a job with the paper, Hunter relied on her writing experience as an intern for an African American circular based in Atlanta, the *Inquirer.* She earned her BA in journalism in 1963, married a white classmate, Walter Stovall, and again went north, this time for a job at the *New Yorker,* where she was the first African American on the magazine's staff. In 1967 a Russell Sage Fellowship supported Hunter's study of social science at Washington University in St. Louis, Missouri. During her fellowship year, Hunter covered the Poor People's Campaign in Washington, DC, and edited articles for *Trans-Action* magazine. Her next professional assignment, as a metropolitan reporter for the *New York Times,* coincided with a second marriage and the birth of her second child.

During Hunter's tenure at the *Times,* she worked as the Harlem bureau chief. Hunter's coverage of the urban black community was honored with the National Urban Coalition Award for Distinguished Urban Reporting. Concluding almost a decade of African American firsts, Hunter left the *Times* and joined *The MacNeil/Lehrer Report* at the Public Broadcasting System (PBS) in 1978. In 1983, PBS promoted her to national correspondent for the show's new franchise as *The MacNeil/Lehrer NewsHour.* Hunter-Gault spent almost two decades with the show. In 1997 she moved to Johannesburg, South Africa, leaving the *NewsHour.*

On 11 May 2003, Charlayne Hunter-Gault, Johannesburg bureau chief of CNN, gave the commencement address for the School of Communication/Kogod School of Business at American University (AU). In her speech, Hunter-Gault did not chronicle the events of her decision to desegregate the University of Georgia during the civil rights movement. She did not mention the articles she had

CHARLAYNE HUNTER-GAULT with Hamilton Holmes at their graduation from the University of Georgia on 3 June 1963. They were the first African Americans to attend that university. (National Archives; Joe McCary, Photo Response Studio.)

written for *Life*, *Ms.*, *Essence*, and *Vogue* nor her numerous other accomplishments, including two Emmys, two Peabody awards, two awards from the Corporation for Public Broadcasting, the Journalist of the Year Award from the National Association of Black Journalists, the *Good Housekeeping* Broadcast Personality of the Year award, the American Women in Radio and Television award, Amnesty International's Media Spotlight Award, and the African-American Institute award for outstanding coverage of Africa. She also called no attention to the Charlayne Hunter-Gault Africa Journalism Fellowship, established in her name by the AllAfrica Foundation, in association with the All Africa Global Media. Instead, she stressed the significance of having a good memory, a memory not necessarily of planned victories and firsts, but rather of the "dance," of a life spent taking care of business, especially when it calls for courage to break down barriers.

BIBLIOGRAPHY
Hunter-Gault, Charlayne. *In My Place*. New York: Vintage Books, 1992.
Rose, Thomas, and John Greenya. *Black Leaders: Then and Now, A Personal History of Students who Led the Civil Rights Movement in the 1960's—And What Happened to Them*. Garret Park, MD: Garrett Park Press, 1984.
Smith, Jessie Carney. "Hunter-Gault, Charlayne." In *Black Women in America: An Historical Encyclopedia*, edited by Darlene Clark Hine. Brooklyn: Carlson Publishing, Inc., 1993, 595–96.

—LATRESE EVETTE ADKINS

HUNTON, ADDIE WAITES (b. 11 June 1875; d. 21 June 43), activist. Born in Norfolk, Virginia, Addie Waites Hunton was educated first in the public schools of Boston and later at Philadelphia's Spencerian College of Commerce. In 1889 she graduated from Spencerian College, the only African American student in her senior class. She spent the next four years working as a teacher and school administrator at A&M College of Alabama. In 1893, Addie Waites married William Alphaeus Hunton Sr. Although Addie had a career, she decided to give it up to become her husband's helpmate. She devoted her married years mainly to her husband's work and their two children, Alphaeus Hunton Jr. and Eunice Hunton Carter. On the eve of her husband's death in November 1916, Addie Waites Hunton became an activist, a race woman, and a peace reformer.

In 1915, at the age of forty, Hunton was invited by Jane Addams to join the newly organized Woman's Peace Party (WPP), which in 1919 became known as the Women's International League for Peace and Freedom (WILPF). Hunton accepted Addams's invitation, which she viewed as another chance to fight for racial justice. From 1915 until her death in 1943, Hunton repeatedly linked race with peace in both domestic and international issues.

A few months after America entered World War I in 1917, the War Department began to deploy troops to Europe. Black combat troops were among the first to arrive in France, and many others were later sent to Germany and other parts of Europe where military life was, for the most part, no better than it had been in America. Black men were confined to segregated units and subjected to the racist behavior of their white colleagues.

Despite this treatment, black men were determined to fight for their country at any cost. When some African Americans heard about the treatment of black soldiers, they decided to go to Europe to engage in war work. Addie Hunton was one such concerned citizen.

Hunton believed that she was a crusader on a quest for democracy who was answering the call to help her people. As a black woman, Hunton felt responsible for representing to the French what it was like to be a black woman in America. She felt that black men needed the comfort that could only be offered by those who understood their pain.

Once Hunton reached France, she noticed that, while the official heads of the Young Women's Christian Association (YWCA) at Paris were considerate and courteous to their black constituency, the attitudes of many of the white secretaries in the field were deplorable. They came from all parts of America and brought their native prejudices with them. Consequently, Hunton and her black colleagues of the YWCA worked hard, visiting wounded soldiers in hospitals, teaching illiterates to read and write, lending an ear to the soldiers who wanted to tell their stories of joy or sorrow, serving them food and refreshments, cleaning the huts and leave areas. Black women engaged in war work performed duties, Hunton contended, for which they were peculiarly fitted.

For the next decade, Hunton devoted most of her energy to international issues. In doing so, she continued to root her search for peace in the politics of race. In 1926, for example, she served on an unofficial investigatory commission on the American occupation in Haiti. Her findings were chronicled in two chapters of *Occupied Haiti*, a valuable study for the U.S. State department. She was also a delegate to the Pan African Congresses of the 1920s and raised money for the Congresses through an organization she founded called the Circle for Peace and Foreign Relations.

In the early 1930s Hunton again focused her attention on domestic race issues when she took the lead in the antilynching crusade and the Scottsboro Case. Lynching, which had steadily decreased during the first thirty years of the twentieth century, was on the rise. The increase, in large part, was due to the bitter competition for jobs during the economic recession and World War II, violent racism, and growing intolerance. When African Americans were driven from traditional areas of employment, competition for scarce relief monies increased, and many who administered New Deal programs in the South openly encouraged hostility toward blacks seeking work. In response, Hunton urged the WILPF to publicly endorse a federal antilynching bill. However, despite the peace groups' efforts as well as those of Hunton and other all-black organizations, Congress did not pass a federal antilynching law. Regardless, Hunton continued her fight for an antilynching law. But in the early 1930s, Hunton campaigned to stop another racial injustice, the Scottsboro incident.

Hunton urged the WILPF to help free the nine Scottsboro boys, who had been accused of raping two young white women. To Hunton and to most intelligent observers, the young men had been proven without a doubt to be innocent. She based her judgment on eyewitness accounts and the contradictory statements of the alleged victims. Despite Hunton's conviction, the WILPF initially refused to become involved, citing a lack of evidence. The WILPF's unwillingness to become involved did not prevent Hunton from taking on this cause. An active member of the NAACP, she devoted most of her time as a member of the organization during the 1930s to fight for the Scottsboro Nine. Hunton had been disappointed with WILPF's inaction on several key race-based issues and decided that she could be more effective fighting for peace and freedom either within an all-black organization or completely outside of an organized interracial structure. Meanwhile, Hunton continued to fight for the Scottsboro Nine until the Alabama courts began to free them in 1937.

After the Scottsboro Nine case, Hunton's health began to fail. She lived the remainder of her life, when she could, continuing her lifelong struggle for peace and freedom. Many of her colleagues and friends saw her passing as a great loss to the world. Addie Waites Hunton had become known by all who knew her as a race woman and peace activist.

BIBLIOGRAPHY
Blackwell-Johnson, Joyce. "African American activists in the Women's International League for Peace and Freedom, 1920s–1950s." *Peace and Change: Journal of Peace Research* 23, no. 4 (October 1998): 466–482.

Hunton, Addie Waites. *A–K Biography*, Swarthmore College Peace Collection, Swarthmore College, Bertha McNeill Papers, Box 1.

Hunton, Addie Waites. *William Alphaeus Hunton: A Pioneer Prophet of Young Men*. New York: International Publishers, 1938.

Hunton, Addie, and Kathryn Johnson. *Two Colored Women with the American Expeditionary Forces*. Brooklyn, NY: Eagle Press, 1920.

MacLachlan, Gretchen. "Addie Waites Hunton." In *Black Women in America: An Historical Encyclopedia*, edited by Darlene Clark Hine. Bloomington: Indiana University Press, 1994.

Schott, Linda. *Reconstructing Women's Thoughts: The Women's International League for Peace and Freedom before World War II*. Stanford, CA: Stanford University Press.

—JOYCE BLACKWELL-JOHNSON

HURSTON, ZORA NEALE (b. 7 January 1891; d. 28 January 1960), writer. Born in the all-black town of Eatonville, Florida, Zora Neale Hurston was the fifth of

ZORA NEALE HURSTON, shown beating a hountar, or mama drum, in 1937. She was a folklorist and anthropologist, and also a writer of fiction; her most famous novel, *Their Eyes Were Watching God*, was published the same year that this photograph was taken. (Library of Congress.)

gender and where she had the opportunity to develop her own individuality. This idyllic childhood was shattered by the death of her mother around 1904 and the disintegration of her family. Hurston's father sent her off to boarding school, and her sisters and brothers scattered into marriages, schools, and journeys of their own. Her father's remarriage several months after her mother's death catapulted Hurston out of the safe world of Eatonville.

A Writer's Foundation

For several years, Hurston wandered from job to job and lived in the homes of family members and strangers. She worked as a maid in a traveling Gilbert and Sullivan theater company. While working as a maid and a manicurist, she finished her high school education at Morgan Academy in Baltimore, Maryland, and her college education at Howard University in Washington, DC, and she earned a graduate degree from Barnard College in New York City. With the assistance of such luminaries as Charles S. Johnson and Alain Locke, she published several short stories in *Opportunity* magazine, including "Drenched in Light" in December 1924, "Spunk" in June 1925, and "Muttsy" in August 1926. In collaboration with other writers, including Langston Hughes and Wallace Thurman, Hurston edited the short-lived magazine *Fire!*, in which her short story "Sweat" appeared in November 1926. In 1930, in collaboration with Langston Hughes, she wrote a play entitled *Mule Bone*, a comedy about African American life, but it was never performed during her lifetime. After developing her skills as an anthropologist, Hurston wrote a volume of folklore, *Mules and Men*, which was not published until 1935, and a second volume of Caribbean folklore, *Tell My Horse*, published in 1938. Hurston then turned her attention to the novel.

In 1934 Hurston published *Jonah's Gourd Vine*, a work loosely based on the life of her parents, particularly her father. Her masterpiece, *Their Eyes Were Watching God*, was published in 1937; *Moses, Man of the Mountain* in 1939; and *Seraph on the Suwanee*, the least successful of her writings, in 1948. Equally important in Hurston's canon was her autobiography, *Dust Tracks on a Road*, published in 1942.

In these novels, set within an all-black or mostly black background, Hurston rejects color and race identity as important to her situation, although the implications of these factors are woven skillfully into her work. It is in the response to the reality of race and racism that this all-black community comes into existence. Yet within this world, Hurston brings forward gender as critical in influencing African Americans' ability to come to self-realization. She creates characters who deal with gender in an African American, rural, middle-class world. Poverty is not at the core of their problem, as it is for the

eight children of John Hurston, a minister, and Lucy Potts Hurston. In her autobiography, Hurston described her childhood as a safe and secure world where her imagination was unencumbered by the restrictions of race or majority of African Americans. Rather, their struggle is for an internal sense of freedom—of spirit and body. In Hurston's novels, this struggle of African Americans for both spiritual and physical freedom is carried out behind the walls of segregation.

Although Hurston presented gender as central to identity, her works also revealed the construction of race and its relationship to class. The tension among color, class, and gender is revealed further in her autobiography, *Dust Tracks on a Road*. Shaping and molding these meditations on gender, race, color, and class is Hurston's search and struggle for freedom—freedom as an artist, as a woman, as an African American, freedom as a space to be enlarged upon. The questions of how to be black without being limited by that reality, how to be woman without the constraints of womanhood, and how to remain true to both of these identities and still be an educated artist plagued Hurston all her life.

For Hurston, African American culture had its own internal logic and moral code. She did not challenge the ideology of racism by attempting to prove the humanity of African Americans, but rather she attacked the power of the dominant culture to represent African American people negatively. Hurston challenged and contested the notion that the integrity of the African American race needed defending and that the responsibility for this defense must be borne by each individual black person. She believed that such a burden originated from essentially the same racist ideas: that is, that black people were deficient and had to be uplifted for approval by the dominant society, and that each representative Negro must assume the burden of both uplifting and defending the race even at the cost of personal wishes and needs. These views were developed and shaped to a considerable extent by her anthropological training at Barnard College under the direction of the renowned anthropologist Franz Boas. Boas believed in the value and legitimacy of all cultures and trained his students to discover the internal logic of the cultures they studied. Hurston, one of his most devoted students, was strongly influenced by this perspective, which led her to reject the prevailing notion of black culture as inferior and immoral. For Hurston, the race needed no improvement or justification.

Hurston also contested the gender conventions that required a ladylike image for women, confining them to both the private sphere of marriage and motherhood and the public sphere of nurturing roles as teachers, nurses, and other homespun heroines uplifting the African American race. She refused to be a female "race man," at least in her public persona. This defiance is embedded in both her artistic and autobiographical writings. Unlike characters in the novels of two of her contemporaries, Richard Wright and Jessie Fauset, Hurston's characters are not engaged in race relations. They seek to build, quite deliberately, worlds where African American people concern themselves with life issues outside the control and purview of white institutions. Race moves from an all-controlling factor to one that influences but does not wholly determine day-to-day existence. Instead, Hurston's characters struggle through life in spite of race, drawing on their own communities and culture for strength and direction. They focus on gender, family, and community in an effort to find space for the individual. This view of race is in sharp contrast to the reality of her life, during which white patrons required demeaning behavior of her before granting the financial support she needed to complete her work. Yet Hurston looked to her own strengths in her private struggle in gender, family, and community relationships in which she sacrificed marriage, family connections, motherhood, and community acceptance in order to become a scholar and artist.

Hurston was a rural, southern, black woman attempting to be an artist in a world controlled by white people and men. Her struggle, as evidenced by her artistic, ethnographic, and autobiographical writings, dealt with how love is possible, how color can liberate and imprison at the same time, how ambiguous an identity it is to be an American, how genius can or cannot be borne, and how womanhood can both adorn and strangle a life. Hurston refused to be confined by gender and racial roles. Her critics misunderstood her public behavior and also missed the meaning of her scholarly and artistic production. It is in her novels that one finds the key to her understanding and confusion surrounding the realities of gender, race, and class.

In the introduction to her folklore collection, *Mules and Men*, Hurston provides insight into the mind of black rural people. Black people:

> are most reluctant at times to reveal that which the soul lives by and the Negro, in spite of his open-faced laughter, his seeming acquiescence, is particularly evasive. . . . The Negro offers a feather-bed resistance. That is, we let the probe enter, but it never comes out. It gets smothered under a lot of laughter and pleasantries.

Hurston suggests that this "onstage" consciousness of African Americans was distinctly different from their "offstage" consciousness. She argued for a deliberate deception constructed by African Americans that would establish mental protection from the intrusion of the outside world. If African Americans could not protect themselves totally from physical and economic exploitation, they could resist intrusion into their inner lives, into their soul: "I'll set something outside the door of my mind for him to play with and handle. He can read my writing but he sho' can't read my mind."

Mules and Men and Hurston's other folklore writings are humorous and informative collections of the conversations, sermons, and joke-telling as well as the cultural behavior, religious customs, and local characters in Florida and Louisiana. The humor and seeming triviality of the stories conceal important discussions on gender and race in community life. The discourse on race is far different from the one found in the dominant culture. In this discourse, race is not a badge of inferiority; instead, it is a trick to be played on the arrogant, a way of referencing race and class, and a way of protecting the inner lives of black people. Gender tensions rest uneasily beneath an apparent male dominance in these tales, and a sensitivity to color is also evident. These folktales establish Hurston's understanding and respect for African American culture and her acute awareness of racial and gender constructions in rural culture.

Their Eyes Were Watching God

Hurston's most famous and popular novel was *Their Eyes Were Watching God*, published in 1937 and set in the all-black world of Eatonville, Florida. The central character is a woman, Janie, who struggles to realize her true self in a world where self-definition is filtered through race and gender. It is an African American world to be sure, but within that world there are those who seek their identity, and therefore their freedom, in models drawn from the white, male-dominated world outside of Eatonville. The idioms and foundation for their freedom are sought in that external world and are then interpreted within a black context. Janie's grandmother, her first two husbands, and some members of the community seek to impose lifestyles and definitions of self on Janie that restrict and confine her. Hurston explores and unpacks the basis of spiritual and physical freedom in this story.

Freedom in this work is intimately tied to the question of land and how land is a symbol for freedom, yet land must be shared in common. Janie sees the world through community eyes, and that structures how she conceives love, ownership of property, justice, and labor. For Janie, freedom remains an elusive quest as long as she is outside or above the black community. Only when she is part of a whole community, one in which men and women work in concert with the human needs of each other, can she be free to be herself.

Throughout the narrative, freedom for Nanny Crawford, Logan Killicks, and Jody Starks, people central to Janie's life, is defined in material terms. For Janie, freedom means love and fulfillment, and she first witnesses both in the pollination of the pear tree. For Nanny, who has only known the horrors of slavery and the meaning of women's oppression, the major concern and fear is that Janie will live a similar life of despair and deprivation. She

knows that women have often been a "spit cup" for men and white folks. Marriage and security represent freedom for Nanny and escape for Janie. Deprived of material security, Nanny knows that property and class offer protection in the white world and position in the black world. It is not that she wants to make Janie literally "like white folks"; she wants what white represents. She forces Janie, therefore, to marry the aged but well-off Logan Killicks.

Killicks takes Janie to a lonely and isolated existence; she is simply another piece of property. She is not free to be a person, and neither is he. Killicks stifles Janie, and the environment robs her of any life-giving force. At last, Janie runs away with the handsome Jody Starks, hoping to find her freedom in his promise of love. Jody plans to be a big man with a big voice. He buys land, builds a town, installs himself as the head official, and puts Janie on a pedestal. She sits on the pedestal that Nanny envisioned for her, just as alone and unsatisfied as she was on Killicks's farm. Janie is not permitted to take part in the stories that the local folk participate in because she serves as a showpiece for Jody.

Slowly, the marriage dies from a lack of connectedness. Jody's deathbed scene after twenty years reveals the price he paid to be a "big man with a big voice." Janie insists that he know the mistake he made before he dies. With skillful use of dialect, Hurston captured the rhythm and texture of the African American cultural spirit as Janie forces Jody to witness their life together:

> You wouldn't listen. You done lived wid me for twenty years and you don't half know me atall. And you could have but you was so busy worshippin' de works of yo' own hands, and cuffin folks around in their minds till you didn't see uh whole heap uh things you could have had.

In spite of Jody's anguish and wish for silence, Janie insists on having her say. "You wasn't satisfied wid me the way Ah was. Naw! Mah own mind had tuh be squeezed and crowded out tuh make room for yours in me."

Jody dies as "the icy sword of the square-toed one had cut off his breath and left his hands in a pose of agonizing protest." Janie ponders their life together and the price Jody paid for his power and success: "'Dis sittin in the rulin chair is been hard on Jody,' she muttered out loud. She was full of pity for the first time in years. Jody had been hard on her and others, but life had mishandled him too." Starks had bought land and set himself above the people; he was not a part of them. He had not labored with or loved with them. His model of freedom and leadership had been drawn from outside the community.

After Jody dies, Janie is materially secure. She enters into a relationship with Teacake, a penniless younger "ne'er-do-well," and with him she finds her freedom, not as a possessor of land but as part of a community connected to the land and laboring on the land. It is a self-actualized community. The home that Teacake and Janie share on the "muck" is alive with people. They come to gamble, tell stories, and listen to music. Janie is a part of the life there, and she wonders what Eatonville would think of "her blue denim overalls and heavy shoes? The crowd of people around her and a dice game on her floor!" Here she can listen and laugh and tell her own stories. Life on the "muck" shows people in motion—singing, talking, playing. It is a community where conflict occurs only when idioms based on color and class enter and are filtered through gender.

A careful reading of her texts reveals that, for Hurston, real freedom can only occur in a whole, self-actualized community. She explores this discussion of the meaning of freedom in texts constructed within the black world. The white world encases this world to be sure, intruding at times with its values and definitions, but Hurston focuses squarely on the black world, and this shapes her understanding of freedom, gender, and race. It is an idealized world, one in which Hurston works out her views of race, class, and gender. By using this approach, Hurston addressed how gender relations are constructed in this world, the role that class plays in gender identity, and how the ways of talking about these issues are embedded in folk material. What she discovered is that while many sought their identity in the values of white society, others struggled for self-realization in the "muck" of the African American world.

Dust Tracks on a Road

Hurston's discussion of these issues connects with the larger discussion going on in the world inhabited by African Americans: How should women manage their encounters with men and other women? How should men and women deal with Jim Crow in the North and South? How can one move up in social class and deal with the jagged edges of social mobility? How should one think about humble origins? Writers and activists such as Anna Julia Cooper, W. E. B. Du Bois, Ida B. Wells-Barnett, James Weldon Johnson, Langston Hughes, and others pondered these concerns in their writings. Huge numbers of southern peasants and northern workers were also pondering these concerns as they moved to urban communities in the North and South and struggled to define freedom in spiritual and material terms. These questions, too, are taken up in Hurston's autobiography, *Dust Tracks on a Road*.

When J. B. Lippincott approached Hurston in 1941 with the idea of writing her autobiography, her response was less than enthusiastic. She was uncomfortable exposing her inner self to the world and initially resisted the idea. The request came in the middle of her career, she protested, and her career was hardly over. Two books of

folklore, two novels, and a series of articles and short stories had established her as a major literary figure. Despite her success, Hurston remained dependent on patronage for her writing and artistic endeavors. Financial stability continued to be elusive. Her only means of earning additional money was to comply with Lippincott's request for the autobiography.

Katherine Mershon, a wealthy friend in California, offered her a place to live and work on the autobiography, so Hurston moved there from New York in the spring of 1941. She completed a draft of the manuscript by mid-July. However, rewriting took over half a year. Her biographer, Robert Hemenway, has suggested that much rewriting became necessary after the bombing of Pearl Harbor because Hurston disliked the colonial and imperialist implications of World War II. Her dislike of war was evident in her satirical comments about American marines who "consider machine gun bullets good laxatives for heathens who get constipated with toxic ideas about a country of their own" and Americans who sang "Praise the Lord and Pass the Ammunition." Lippincott deleted such passages from the final version of her autobiography. What remained and was finally published in November 1942 was a document that some argued was the most problematic piece in Hurston's canon.

Dust Tracks on a Road is a simulated story of Hurston's life. Facts are often missing or distorted. For example, Hurston portrays herself as younger than she actually was when her mother died. She states that she was nine years old, but census records establish her age as probably thirteen. *Dust Tracks on a Road* is her life played out in full view of the white world, the world that defined images and determined which works received acceptance. It was a world in which only primitive black people were authentic. It is the life of a woman resisting the confinement of rigid gender conventions that required the appearance of submission by women to male and white authority. In this work, Hurston attempted to discuss an idyllic childhood where neither race nor poverty was central; a disrupted family caused by the death of her mother that sent her wandering in search of education and self; the creation of a woman scholar and artist aided by patrons; and a southern individual who would not be contained or transformed. She attempts to do this in a manner acceptable to a white audience that was a necessary part of the story. What emerges from this autobiography is what her former employer, the writer Fannie Hurst, called a "woman half in shadow."

Navigating between the black and white worlds was not an easy task. If she exposed the pain and anger that black women invariably felt when trying to enter doors blocked by racism and sexism, no admittance would ever have been possible. Hurston's entrance into the privileged world of academic degrees would have been forever denied. Her dilemma was to unblock that passageway and at the same time retain the essence of herself that included her southern identity and her intellectual independence. In commenting on her years at Barnard, she referred to herself as Barnard's sacred black cow. She once stated, "I feel most colored when I am thrown against a sharp white background." Her essays, "How It Feels To Be Colored Me" (1928), "The Pet Negro System" (1943), and "My Most Humiliating Jim Crow Experience" (1944), are testimony to her understanding that racism confined and restricted and that the struggle for a healthy existence is a lifelong engagement for African Americans.

Later Years

The decades of the 1940s and 1950s were not easy for Hurston. After the publication of *Seraph on the Suwanee* in 1948, she struggled to write a novel about Herod the Great, which she never completed. She left the literary world of New York and returned to Florida, where she continued to write articles for various newspapers and magazines. She had little money, and by the mid-1950s her health had begun to deteriorate.

Hurston spent some of the last years of her life responding to the U.S. Supreme Court's 1954 decision to desegregate public schools. On 11 August 1955 the *Orlando Sentinel* in Florida, published a letter Hurston had written to express her disapproval of the court decision. For most African Americans and Euro-Americans alike, the decision represented the culmination of over fifty years of struggle to end segregation by law. For Hurston, the decision was deplorable and an insult to her people. Hurston defended the job done by African American teachers, arguing that unless there was some quality or facility in white schools that could not be duplicated in black schools, there was simply no reason to desegregate. She contested, "I can see no tragedy in being too dark to be invited to a white school social affair. The Supreme Court would have pleased me

more if they had concerned themselves about enforcing the compulsory education provisions for Negroes in the South as is done for white children."

Embedded in these comments was the fierce racial pride that others had thought was missing from her consciousness. Recognizing that her comments would not be well received by the civil rights leadership, Hurston defended her views and made clear the basis for her opposition. She stated, "Them's my sentiments and I am sticking by them. Ethical and cultural desegregation. It is a contradiction in terms to scream race pride and equality while at the same time spurning Negro teachers and self-association."

During the last decade of her life, Hurston fell into obscurity—she was poor, ill, alone, but still proud. She remained virtually unknown for two decades after her death in 1960. Her burial in an unmarked commoner's grave belied the genius of a gifted and rich life that had once captured the hearts and minds of thousands. Her life and work yield a mosaic of gender, racial, and class images that reveals much about the mental state, social realities, and political tensions of African American life.

BIBLIOGRAPHY

Awkward, Michael, ed. *New Essays on* Their Eyes Were Watching God. New York: Cambridge University Press, 1990.

Bloom, Harold, ed. *Zora Neale Hurston's* Their Eyes Were Watching God. Philadelphia: Chelsea House, 1986.

Glassman, Steve, and Kathryn Lee Seidel, eds. *Zora in Florida.* Orlando: University of Central Florida Press, 1991.

Hemenway, Robert. *Zora Neale Hurston: A Literary Biography.* Urbana: University of Illinois Press, 1977.

Howard, Lillie P. *Zora Neale Hurston.* Boston: Twayne, 1980.

Kaplan, Carla, ed. *Zora Neale Hurston: A Life in Letters.* New York: Doubleday, 2002.

Nathiri, N. Y. *Zora!: Zora Neale Hurston, A Woman and Her Community.* Orlando, FL: Sentinel Communications, 1991.

Turner, Darwin T. *In a Minor Chord.* Carbondale: Southern Illinois University Press, 1971.

Wall, Cheryl, ed. *Zora Neal Hurston's* Their Eyes Were Watching God: *A Casebook.* New York: Oxford University Press, 2000.

—TIFFANY R. L. PATTERSON

I

INCARCERATED WOMEN. Black women have been incarcerated since the beginning of this nation's history and have constituted the largest percentage of imprisoned women throughout U.S. history. During the American colonial period jails were developed that closely mirrored those established in England, from which many of the colonists came. They brought their customs, traditions, and religious beliefs to America, which influenced the penal and incarceration systems of the colonies. As colonial society developed, prison rules became especially closely related to the religious beliefs of the settlers and were strictly enforced when applied to women offenders—a characteristic still common in today's criminal justice system.

Slavery was another tradition settlers brought to America. Slavery necessitated a large degree of social control. Prior to the Civil War, African American slaves were imprisoned in plantation-built jails and punished by the slave master, who had unlimited power, including the use of capital punishment. African American slaves were punished, without trial, for real and imaginary crimes that included running away, stealing, assaulting an overseer, or disobeying an order. On rare occasions, female runaway slaves were held in municipal jails until their masters claimed them. During this period, there were separate courts for blacks and whites. Although the summary judgment of the slave owners prevailed on the plantations, the governing classes found it necessary to pass laws that were sanctioned in the "Negro Court." Punishments handed out in the Negro Court for crimes committed by slaves were not applicable to whites who committed the same crimes. When blacks were found in jails outside the plantation prior to the Civil War, they had already been subjected to the laws of the Negro Court and were usually awaiting trial for felonies.

The literature on the early history of prisons indicates that women comprised a small percentage of the prison population. This small percentage was given as a reason not to build separate institutions for women until much later in the nineteenth century. For instance, the Maryland State Penitentiary, which opened in 1811, was one of the earliest state prisons established in the United States and serves well as a representative example. Women were admitted to the penitentiary at its initial opening, and both men and women were housed in the same institution until 1921, though the rules governing the management of the facility stipulated that prisoners were to be separated by sex. Both men and women in jails and prisons were confined to filthy quarters. States other than Maryland, such as Massachusetts and Michigan, also confined men and women in the same institutions. In Wisconsin and Illinois, the women's building and adjacent yard were within the walls of the state prison and were not used for the intended purpose, but rather to ease overcrowding among male prisoners. Many prison scandals involving harsh and violent treatment, overcrowding, and rape or impregnation by prison guards and inmates occurred as a result of men and women being housed together in penal institutions, which led public supporters to urge the building of separate prisons for men and women. In Maryland, blacks and whites were housed in the same institutions until the 1830s, when the addition of a new dormitory made it feasible to separate female prisoners by race. Within these early prison systems, black women were housed primarily in penitentiaries where there was no hope of rehabilitation, while white women were housed in reformatories where the ultimate goal was to reenter society.

At the time its state penitentiary opened, Maryland, which had a sizable free black population and a sizable slave population, was divided by industrial and agricultural interests, as well as by opinions on the institution of slavery. The Maryland legislature passed a number of statutory provisions during the antebellum period that affected the length and type of sentences imposed on black women. For example, in 1817, legislation was passed that provided that the minimum sentence to the penitentiary for a black person must exceed one year. An 1858 supplement required that free blacks convicted of larceny and other crimes be sentenced not to prison, but rather to public sale.

Vernetta D. Young, in "All the Women in the Maryland State Penitentiary," also indicates that before the Civil War there was a disproportionate percentage of black women held in the prisons of the northeastern and the midwestern states. In the South, where the institution of slavery already confined most of the African American population, few black females or males were held in prison before the Civil War. Incarcerated women averaged twenty-one years or older; they were unmarried, working-class, and mostly sentenced for property crimes. Furthermore, Butler reports that the prison registers of Louisiana, Texas, Kansas, Nebraska, and Montana show that female inmates were usually young and uneducated. During the antebellum period, 953 female prisoners were imprisoned in Maryland State Penitentiary, at an average of about 19 women per year. There were more than twice as many black female prisoners (70 percent) as white female prisoners (30 percent). The only time that white female inmates outnumbered black female inmates in the Maryland State penitentiary was in the early history of the institution, with white women accounting for 75 percent of the female prison population in 1812 and 64 percent in 1813. In fact, more than one half of all white female prisoners were incarcerated early in the history of the institution, between 1812 and 1818, compared to just 21 percent of black female prisoners. Also, during the colonial period, serious property crimes accounted for the incarceration of the largest proportion of both black and white female prisoners in the Maryland State penitentiary. In the case of black women in the Maryland State penitentiary during the colonial period, 73 percent were incarcerated for property crimes, 13 percent for felonies, 10 percent for miscellaneous offenses, and 4 percent for violent crimes. In the case of white female offenders, 48 percent were incarcerated for property offenses, 42 percent for miscellaneous offenses, 8 percent for felonies, and 2 percent for violent crimes.

Moreover, in the Maryland State penitentiary black women served more time in prison than white women. During the antebellum era, 38 percent of black female inmates served one year or less, 29 percent served two years, 26 percent served between three and five years, and 6 percent served six years or more. In the case of white female inmates, 68 percent served one year or less, 14 percent served two years, 16 percent served between three and five years, and 2 percent served six years or more.

Black Women Imprisoned during the Civil War Period

White women accounted for the largest proportion of the female prison population at the beginning of the Civil War (83 percent in 1859 and 100 percent in 1860) in the Maryland State penitentiary. It should be noted that during these two years, only thirteen women were imprisoned in the Maryland State penitentiary, six in 1859 and seven in 1860. In Maryland, black women outnumbered white women for three of the five years from 1861 to 1865. Two points should be noted. First, most of the

inmates were received later in the Civil War. Second, as the U.S. moved toward the end of the war, black female inmates as a proportion of the total female population increased. Even though the Maryland State penitentiary received only 114 female prisoners, black women accounted for 68 percent of the total population—about the same as during the pre–Civil War years. Female inmates in male prisons in the northeast and midwest were used to provide domestic chores for the maintenance of the institutions and sexual services for the guards and male inmates. Two things, at least, were equitable during the Civil War period: roughly equal numbers (89 percent of white women and 90 percent of black women) were incarcerated for property crimes, and 50 percent of black female inmates and 53 percent of white female inmates served one year or less.

Black Women Imprisoned during the Post–Civil War Period

Throughout the post–Civil War period, black female prisoners once again outnumbered white female prisoners. The Maryland State penitentiary received 136 female prisoners, at an average of 34 women per year—a significant increase from the average received in the preceding time periods. Black women accounted for 90 percent of the total population (123 inmates) and white women accounted for 10 percent (13 inmates). The proportion of black women in the female prison population also grew during the post–Civil War period, to 90 percent (up from 70 percent during the antebellum period and 68 percent during the war). In 1910 New York and Massachusetts reformatory populations were approximately 95 percent white females, while Indiana reported 72 percent. In reformatories where most whites and very few blacks were confined, the common practice of the old southern plantation lessee programs prevailed. Black women prisoners were assigned to the laundry while white women were given paid office jobs.

The nature of crimes committed also differed between the populations: 77 percent of white women were incarcerated for offenses such as violence, vagrancy, felonies, and other miscellaneous offenses while 90 percent of black women were incarcerated for property crimes. Also during the post–Civil War period, 63 percent of black female inmates and 85 percent of white female inmates served a term of one year or less.

Following the Civil War, southern states found themselves lacking the manpower to rebuild large plantations and cities ravaged by Union armies. Southern policymakers began crafting laws that would surely be broken by the multitude of hungry and homeless former slaves. For example, the state of Missouri passed the so-called "pig law," which defined the theft of property worth more than

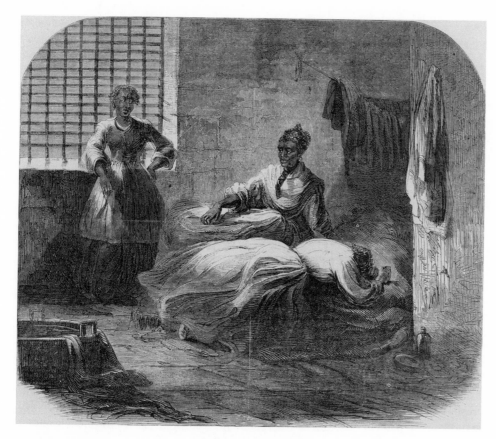

WOMEN IN JAIL IN WASHINGTON, DC. From *Frank Leslie's Illustrated Newspaper*, 28 December 1861. This front-page illustration was captioned "Secrets of the prison-house—a cell in the female department of the Washington jail.—From a sketch made on the spot by our special artist, Mr. Lumley." The accompanying story was about "the confinement of negroes . . . for no other cause than their color," a practice against which the newspaper was crusading. (Library of Congress.)

$10,000—including cattle and swine—as grand larceny, punishable by five years of hard labor. Once these laws were broken by displaced and hungry former slaves, the southern states were able to impress the convicts into a form of legalized slavery. Black females constituted the largest number of women imprisoned under these laws and funneled into the lease system, which allowed for a fixed per capita consideration to be paid to the state, in exchange for the state providing prisoners to private employers, called lessees, who could work them at will. These black women were put to work in the large, decaying plantation cotton fields or assigned to millwork sewing in a large central building. The lease system was very profitable for the southern states; there was, needless to say, a lot of brutality and neglect. The women in the lease system could become a financial liability to the new "masters," who were held marginally accountable for these women's food, clothing, and medical care. In order to reduce the liability, some female prisoners were literally worked to death. Furthermore, to assure that the southern prisons would continue to have an abundance of free black labor, judges often refused to send white women to prison and penalized black women more severely than white women. Moreover, when white women were imprisoned, they were treated better than black

women even in penal institutions where the population was predominantly African American.

The Imprisonment of Black Women in the Twentieth Century

By the twentieth century the "pig laws" had been replaced by unethical enforcement practices. For instance, pro bono attorneys who were overworked and uninterested in the black women they represented did little to defend their clients, resulting in many of the women being imprisoned. In comparing the number of black women in penitentiaries and reformatories in 1923 in the United States, the results of a segregated system were apparent. In 1923 incarcerated black women accounted for 48 percent of the female prison population. Moreover, scholars have noted that compared to white women who committed comparable crimes, black women were more likely to be sent to the state penitentiary, serve their full sentence, and be excluded from pardon procedures. The majority of prisons built between 1930 and 1966 were built with the reformatory model as the goal for white women, while black women were confined to farm camps to perform arduous physical labor. By 1971 thirty-four states had completely separate facilities for women, while two federal institutions also housed women. In 1992 fourteen federal institutions housed women and every state contained at least one state prison (with the exception of New Hampshire and West Virginia, which boarded out female inmates to neighboring state prisons or housed them in county jails).

The state prison system has not changed a great deal since the legal end of segregation, with the exception of its scale. In the late twentieth century, the women's prison population was made up of primarily poor, uneducated black women. During the period from 1985 through 1989, 43 states opened a total of 54 new adult correctional facilities, including 119 prisons, 12 camps, and 23 other facilities for men and women. These new facilities represented 89,000 beds. Between 1980 and 1993 the number of women in prison increased by 313 percent, while the comparable increase for men was 182 percent. Women represented the fastest-growing group in prison, growing almost twice as fast as the male prison population. In 1994 Congress allocated $22 billion to the Federal Bureau of Prisons partly to build additional federal prison facilities and for the hiring of new correctional officers. Among women who were federal prisoners in 1997, whites numbered 3,665 and blacks numbered 2,466; however, the rate of incarceration was higher for blacks. Despite the fact that black men comprised 48.7 percent of the male prison population while black women comprised 49.2 percent of the total female prison population, society has paid little attention to the large percentage of black women in prison. Similarly, the number of black women incarcerated in state prisons has grown at a much faster rate than the number of white women.

Throughout U.S. history, the same crimes committed by white women and black women have generally earned black women longer and harsher sentences. The dragnet cast by current sentencing policies and practices are bringing into U.S. prisons nonviolent, first-time petty criminals who are disproportionately black. The increase in the black female prison population can largely be attributed to drug law violations (for which black women are more likely than white women to be imprisoned). Interestingly, white women are more likely to test positive for opiates—which belong to the class of dangerous and addictive drugs—while black women are more likely to test positive for marijuana—a much less dangerous and nonaddictive drug. Both groups are equally likely to test positive for cocaine use. In addition, black women are also more likely to be property offenders than white women.

It has been claimed that the disparity between the incarceration of black and white women is due to black women committing crimes that are more similar to those of men than those of women. Yet, a closer examination of women's offenses tells us that the crimes committed by black women are very much like crimes committed by white women. In fact, the high rate of black female incarceration suggests that racial bias and discrimination are the primary factors contributing to the disproportionate imprisonment of black women. Fishman provides a succinct description of the stereotype that helps to perpetuate bias and discrimination:

> The legacy of slavery also provided images of black women with some gender-specific criminal traits. They were frequently described as wanton, hot-blooded, highly sexed, and erotic, as well as very fertile. Because black women had been forced to do the same hard labor as black men, they also were perceived as possessing an excess of such masculine characteristics as toughness and aggressiveness. They were thought to be assaultive, murderous, uncompassionate, physically strong, and capable of physical abuse. This sexual objectification and defeminization of Black women persists today. ("Images of Crime and Punishment—The Black Bogeyman and White Self-Righteousness")

Until bias and discrimination are eliminated from the criminal justice system, the percentage of black women being imprisoned will continue to increase.

The United States' too-typical response to the crises of drug abuse, unemployment, under-education, mental illness, and the like is not to deal with those social ills, but to find a way to control female prisoners who have no voice as to where they live, sleep, or eat. Unfortunately, due to the overcrowding of America's prisons, correctional services have begun to reinstate the lease system that in the past failed to protect the rights of its female inmates. When the female prison population began to increase in 1985 (jumping from 1,345 inmates to 49,154 inmates in 1994) so did the number of privately managed prisons. The enticement for prison officials is the savings per female prisoner. In the United States in 1991 there were fifteen private prison lessee corporations that managed male, female, and juvenile inmates. Five of these prison lessee corporations were exclusively for female inmates and nine had a mixed population. Considering past experiences with the lease system, this return to privatizing prisons will undoubtedly lead to black female inmates again being neglected and abused. Policies must be developed to create intervention and prevention programs for undereducated, poor black women in order to help them obtain skills and employment so that they can fulfill their basic needs and avoid becoming a part of the prison system.

BIBLIOGRAPHY

Adamson, C. "Punishment after Slavery: Southern State Penal System 1859–1895." In *The Imprisonment of African American Women: Causes, Conditions, and Future Implications*, edited by Catherine Fisher Collins. Jefferson, NC: McFarland, 1983.

Butler, A.M. "Still in Chains: Black Women in Western Prisons, 1865–1910." *Western Historical Quarterly* 20 (1989): 19–35.

Evitts, W. J. *A Matter of Allegiances: Maryland from 1850 to 1861.* Baltimore, MD: Johns Hopkins University Press, 1974.

Freedman, Estelle. "Their Sister's Keepers: A Historical Perspective of Female Correctional Institutes in the U.S. 1870-1900." *Feminist Studies* 2 (1), 1974: 77–95.

Fisher Collins, Catherine. *The Imprisonment of Black Women: Causes, Conditions, and Future Implications.* Jefferson, NC: McFarland, 1997.

Fishman, Laura. "Images of Crime and Punishment—The Black Bogeyman and White Self-Righteousness." In *Images of Color, Images of Crime: Readings*, edited by Coramae Mann and Marjorie Zatz. Los Angeles: Roxbury, 1998.

Gilbert, Evelyn. "Crime, Sex, and Justice: African American Women in U.S. Prisons." In *Harsh Punishment: International Experiences of Women's Imprisonment*, edited by Sandy Cook and Susanne Davies. Boston: Northeastern University Press, 1999.

Lekkerkerker, Eugenia. *Reformatories for Women in the United States.* Groningen, Netherlands: J. B. Wolters, 1931.

Pollock-Byrne, J. *Women, Prison, and Crime.* Belmont, CA: Wadsworth Thomson Learning, 2002.

Rafter, Nicole. *Partial Justice: State Prisons and Their Inmates 1800–1935.* Boston: Northeastern University Press, 1985.

Schewber, C. "Beauty Marks and Blemishes: The Cold Prison as a Microcosm of Integrated Society." *Prison Journal* 64 (1): 3–15.

Sellin, J. T. *Slavery in the Penal System 1896–1930.* New York: Elsevier, 1976.

Shugg, W. *A Monument to Good Intentions: The Story of the Maryland Penitentiary, 1804–1999.* Baltimore: Maryland Historical Society. 2000.

Young, Vernetta D. "All the Women in the Maryland State Penitentiary." *Prison Journal* 81 (1), 2001: 113–133.

—LUCINDA M. DEASON

INDEPENDENT ORDER OF ST. LUKE.

Rising from a long tradition of social activism and community self-help organizations, the Independent Order of St. Luke became one of the most successful mutual benefit societies in a period of American history commonly seen as the nadir of race relations. Through the Order of St. Luke, middle-class, educated African American women exerted a level of influence and leadership denied them in mainstream American society and fought to advance opportunities for both African American women and the African American community as a whole.

The Independent Order of St. Luke was founded in Maryland in 1867 by Mary Prout. By 1880, it had spread to New York and Virginia. Originally conceived as a so-called mutual benefit society interested primarily in issues of women's sickness and death, the Order later diversified. In 1895, at the recommendation of a young woman named Maggie Lena Walker, a juvenile division was created to provide programs for community youth. Despite this expansion, by 1899 the Order was in decline, with only 1,080 paying members, an inadequate staff, and a debt ($400) that far exceeded the treasury reserve ($31.61). William Forrester, Right Worthy Grand Secretary since 1869, declined reappointment and was replaced by the energetic and determined Walker. She was intent on enlisting women to assist her in leadership, and by 1901 six out of the nine executive board members were women: Patsie K. Anderson, Frances Cox, Abigail Dawley, Lillian H. Payne, Ella O. Waller, and Walker herself. Under this new leadership, the Order of St. Luke flourished. Within twenty-five years, the Order had built up a cash reserve of $70,000, constructed a three-story headquarters, and boasted a staff of fifty-five, with 145 field agents spread across twenty-eight states. In the same period, membership rose to over 100,000.

Walker drastically altered the fortunes of her organization by redirecting its focus to that of the economic uplift of the African American community. The 1896 Supreme

MAGGIE LENA WALKER, c. 1900, when she began to transform the Independent Order of St. Luke into a highly successful and effective organization. (Valentine Richmond History Center, Virginia.)

Court ruling in the case of *Plessy v. Ferguson* had sanctioned segregation and paved the way for dehumanizing Jim Crow laws. Choosing a course of self-help in an era when no other form of help was forthcoming, Walker and the women of the Order of St. Luke worked to strengthen the financial power of African American women and their communities. In 1903 Walker founded the Saint Luke Penny Savings Bank in Richmond, becoming the first woman bank president in the United States. The bank catered to those with limited financial resources and was supported early and in large numbers by female clients. In 1905, in another dramatic stroke, twenty-two female members of the Order of St. Luke founded the Saint Luke Emporium, a department store that served the interests of the African American community and offered employment and business training to African American women. Although the Emporium was forced out of business in 1912, it represented an important attempt to build African American self-sufficiency.

The Independent Order of St. Luke also branched out into politics and activism. The *St. Luke Herald* was founded in 1902 under the editorship of Lillian Payne. The paper attacked segregation laws, lynching, and the dearth of educational opportunities for young African Americans. The women of Saint Luke were also actively involved in the 1904 streetcar boycott in Richmond, part of a six-year struggle on the part of African Americans across the South to reverse Jim Crow laws. As historians August Meier and Elliot Rudwick have pointed out, what was remarkable about the streetcar boycotts was not the success of the protests, but rather that they came at a time when white hostility toward blacks was reaching its zenith and African American leaders, following the example of Booker T. Washington, were preaching accommodation. After Congress passed the Nineteenth Amendment in 1919, Walker led a campaign to register African American women voters. By the 1920 Richmond elections, 80 percent of the eligible African American voters were women.

In an influential essay, Elsa Barkley Brown argued that the Independent Order of St. Luke, through the leadership of Maggie Lena Walker, served as an early model for "womanism," a belief that issues of race and gender are inseparable. The Order sought to create opportunities for African American women outside the home, which Walker believed would benefit not only the women of the community but also the men. While the Order of St. Luke was a women's organization, Walker ensured that its membership policies remained egalitarian, admitting people of both sexes.

The accomplishments of the women of the Independent Order of St. Luke serve as a reminder that it is often those who are most marginalized who are best able to articulate both the failings of the society that excludes them and the direction in which that society must travel if it is to become more just. Faced with a double oppression, as women and as African Americans, they embodied an ideal of community that remains instructive for a nation still struggling with problems of oppression and inequality at the beginning of the twenty-first century.

See also Walker, Maggie Lena.

BIBLIOGRAPHY

Brown, Elsa Barkley. "Womanist Consciousness: Maggie Lena Walker and the Independent Order of Saint Luke." *Signs* (Spring 1989): 610–633.

Cash, Floris Barnett. *African American Women and Social Action: The Clubwomen and Volunteerism from Jim Crow to the New Deal, 1896–1936.* Westport, CT: Greenwood Press, 2001.

Dabney, Wendell Phillips. *Maggie L. Walker and the I. O. of Saint Luke; the Woman and Her Work.* Cincinnati, OH: Dabney Publishing, 1927.

Meier, August, and Elliott Rudwick. "The Boycott Movement Against Jim Crow Streetcars in the South, 1900–1906." *Journal of American History* 55 (March 1969): 756–775.

Salem, Dorothy, ed. *African American Women: A Biographical Dictionary.* New York: Garland, 1993.

—ADAM EWING

INGRAM, ROSA LEE (b. ?; d. c. 1980), cause célèbre. Rosa Lee Ingram became the focus of national and international attention following her 1948 conviction for murder in rural southwest Georgia. The granddaughter of slaves and the recently widowed mother of twelve children, Ingram was accused of killing a white man on the small farm both worked as sharecroppers. Hers was one of several southern criminal cases taken up by the National Association for the Advancement of Colored People (NAACP) and the Civil Rights Congress (CRC) in the late 1940s. Rosa Lee Ingram served as a symbol of the many outrages and daily indignities black women suffered in the rural south—from rape and sexual assault to the unrelenting, demeaning reminders of second-class citizenship.

The news coverage of Ingram's appeal portrayed her as having merely defended herself against lewd advances, a case of self-defense. But Ingram's own description of the events suggests that her neighbor John Stratford's death resulted from a more nuanced contest of wills. Ingram's mules and hogs sometimes wandered into Stratford's adjacent fields. Livestock could quickly destroy crops, and a man living on narrow margins would certainly demand satisfaction. Add to that John Stratford's frequent and unsolicited advice to Ingram, near constant since her husband's death, and what emerges is a human drama in which race and gender trump class in the lives of two families, both barely eking a living from sandy soil.

And so one November morning in 1947, John Stratford, rifle in hand, walked the field road that lay between his and the Ingrams' house to finish an angry confrontation started earlier that day. He threatened to kill Ingram and her mules, cursed her, and rapped his gun about her head and shoulders. According to Ingram, she wrested the gun from the old man's hands and returned his assault in kind. Exactly what happened next remains controversial, and whether it was she or one or more of her several sons who dealt the deathblow remains unknown. In the end, it mattered little. As both the NAACP and the CRC knew, in southern courts a black woman could never prevail in a case bound to inflame the passions of the white community.

Following a one-day trial, Ingram and two of her minor sons were sentenced to death. Local NAACP leaders asked the state's chief NAACP lawyer, A. T. Walden, to assist with an appeal. In Atlanta, under the auspices of the Citizens' Defense Committee, which had formed after the 1946 lynching of a black World War II veteran and three others in Walton County, the Ingrams's defense took on a decidedly political tone. An *Atlanta Daily World* interview with Ingram in the Dougherty County jail (made notorious during demonstrations by the Student Nonviolent Coordinating Committee in Americus and Albany in the 1960s) attracted the attention of the national Negro press. Front-page stories in the *Pittsburgh Courier* and the Communist *Daily Worker* broadcast nationwide news of the Ingrams's appeal. Phone calls, telegrams, and letters flooded the offices of the several county sheriffs who had custody of the Ingrams at different points during the proceedings, the trial court judge, and the prosecutor. All demanded the defendants' release.

By the time of the hearing, the CRC had organized a protest in Washington, DC, calling for federal intervention. Vivian Carter Mason, vice-president of the Congress of American Women, who had gained prominence in the National Council of Negro Women, led a delegation of women to Americus, where they joined members of the CRC, the NAACP, and members of the black press who gathered to observe motions for a new trial. White authorities found the presence of more than two hundred "strangers" unnerving. Not since Reconstruction had the district seen such a powerful demonstration of black citizens' insistence on full participation in civil affairs. Mason's statement in the *Atlanta Daily World* of 21 March 1948 captured the moment for many:

> every Negro woman in the United States is on trial with Rosa Ingram. . . . Negro women have died too many deaths for their right to life. They have suffered too long for their honor and a chance to raise their children without shame. This struggle we won't give up.

The hearing did not result in the new trial the Ingrams and their defenders sought. Instead, the judge commuted Ingram and her sons' sentences to life in prison. A subsequent Georgia Supreme Court appeal likewise failed. None of the procedural issues surrounding the prosecution, from jury exclusion to uninformed consent, had been properly raised at the original trial.

The NAACP and the CRC vowed to continue the fight to free Rosa Ingram and her sons. For a number of years the CRC and its several Ingram defense and women's committees, one headed by Mary Church Terrell, sponsored annual biracial pilgrimages of women to Georgia's state capital. But their efforts waned as time passed and as both organizations turned to other struggles. Ingram became eligible for parole in 1955 and was quietly released in 1959.

For Ingram, the events that made her a symbol of racial, gender, and class oppression remained a profoundly personal tragedy. On parole, Rosa Lee Ingram returned to obscurity and a life punctuated by poverty and declining health. Her death brought modest notice in the *Atlanta Daily World*, the newspaper that broke the story on her case.

BIBLIOGRAPHY

Georgia Supreme Court Case File #16263, Georgia Department of Archives and History; Elijah Lewis Forrester Papers, Richard B. Russell Library, University of Georgia.

Papers of the Civil Rights Congress, Schomberg Research Center of the New York Public Library.

Papers of the National Association for the Advancement of Colored People, Library of Congress.

Shadron, Virginia. "Popular Protest and Legal Authority in Post–World War II Georgia: Race, Class, and Gender Politics in the Rosa Lee Ingram Case." PhD diss., Emory University, 1991.

—Virginia A. Shadron

INTERNATIONAL AFFAIRS. As national security adviser and secretary of state to George W. Bush, Condoleezza Rice has moved beyond the U.S. borders and undeniably affected world politics. Rice, however, is not the first black woman to concentrate her efforts on international affairs. It has been only recently that black women have begun to gain a foothold in the main avenue for international policy-making inside the U.S. government, the State Department. However, since the nineteenth century, indeed since before the Civil War, African American women have been crossing geographic and cultural boundaries.

Early Internationalism

Much of the involvement by black women in international affairs has been directed toward focusing the eyes of the world, or at least of Europe, on the plight of African Americans in the United States, as in the case of black women such as Ellen Craft and Sarah Parker

Remond in the era before the Civil War. Nancy Gardner Prince was an early exception. She traveled to Russia with her husband in 1824 and, during her nine and a half years there, distributed Bibles and helped found an orphanage. She traveled to Jamaica twice, in 1840 and 1842, in an unsuccessful attempt to found a school for girls. In this way she was a precursor of the African American woman missionary.

After the Civil War, black women as well as men were primarily active internationally in missionary work. Their work centered in Africa, as did that of many of their successors. These women founded schools and hospitals as well as churches. Among them was Dr. Georgia Washington Patton, one of the first two black women to graduate from Meharry Medical College. She worked as a medical missionary for two years in Liberia. In the late 1890s, Dr. Alice Woodby-McKane and her husband, Dr. Cornelius McKane, spent two years in Liberia and founded the first hospital in that country. Fanny Jackson Coppin traveled to South Africa with her husband in 1902. Her influence on the missionaries there can be seen in the building of the Fanny Jackson Coppin Girls Hall at Wilberforce Institute in Cape Town. Amanda Berry Smith traveled for years in Europe, India, and West Africa. She spent eight years just in Liberia, where she advocated for education for women and children while leading revivals and promoting temperance.

Both the temperance and suffrage movements led even more black women, particularly club women, into the international arena. Like the abolitionist speakers, much of their work was focused on bringing international attention to bear on the hypocrisies in American policy toward African Americans. And, as in many national and international organizations before and since, black women had to fight to belong and fight to be heard.

Featuring Ambassadors

● **Carol Moseley Braun** (1947–) served as ambassador to New Zealand and Samoa. (See individual entry: Braun, Carol Moseley.)

● **Aurelia E. Brazeal** (1943–) has served as ambassador to three countries and is the first African American woman career Foreign Service officer to be promoted into the Senior Foreign Service. Born in Chicago, she grew up in Atlanta and attended Spelman College (BA, 1965), Columbia University (master's, International Affairs, 1967), and the John F. Kennedy School at Harvard University (1972–1973). She joined the Foreign Service in 1968 and was posted variously to Uruguay, Paraguay, and Argentina. In 1984 she was named deputy director of the Economic Office at the U.S. Embassy in Japan. In 1987 she became the minister counselor of economics at the same embassy. In 1990 she became the first U.S. ambassador to Micronesia and in 1993 took the position of ambassador to Kenya. She was the deputy assistant secretary for East Asian and Pacific Affairs (1996–1998) and dean of the Senior Seminar (1998–1999) before being named dean of the new Leadership and Management School of the Foreign Service Institute (1999–2002). As of 2004, she was serving as U.S. ambassador to Ethiopia.

● **Ruth A. Davis** (1943–) was named ambassador to Benin in 1992 and is the first black woman to direct the Foreign Service Institute. Born in Phoenix, she attended Spelman College (BS, Sociology, 1966), the University of California at Berkeley (MS, Social Work, 1968), the Senior Seminar of the Foreign Service Institute (1993), and the Aspen Institute. She joined the Foreign Service in 1969 and was posted to Zaire, Kenya, Japan, and Italy. She was later a senior watch officer at the Operations Center at the State Department. In 1984 she was named chief of training and liaison at State's Bureau of Personnel. In 1987 she returned overseas as consul general in Barcelona, Spain. After her service as ambassador to Benin, she was named principal deputy assistant secretary of Consular Affairs (1995) and became the first African American director of the Foreign Service Institute (1997). During her tenure there she established the Leadership and Management Institute. In 2001 she was named director general of the Foreign Service, becoming the highest-ranking black woman in the history of the State Department. Davis has received numerous awards for her service, including two Presidential Distinguished Service Awards (1999 and 2002) and the Secretary's Distinguished Award (2003). She was also the first African American to receive the Arnold L. Raphel Memorial Award for outstanding work in international affairs (1999).

● **Patricia Roberts Harris** (1924–1985) was the first African American woman to be appointed ambassador (1965) and the first black woman cabinet secretary. Her ambassadorship was to Luxembourg. (See individual entry: Harris, Patricia Roberts.)

● **Arlene Render** (1943–) is a three-time ambassador for the United States and a career Foreign Service officer. Born in

International Organizations before World War II

The first international women's organization, the International Council of Women (ICW), was formed in 1888 at the annual meeting of the National Women's Suffrage Association (NWSA). Frances Ellen Watkins Harper gave an address on temperance at that first meeting. In 1893 she spoke at the ICW's Congress of Representative Women at the World's Columbian Exposition. Anna Julia Cooper addressed the same meeting with a speech entitled "The Needs and Status of the Black Woman." Other black women speakers there included Fannie Barrier Williams, Ida B. Wells, Fannie Jackson Coppin, Sarah Jane Early, and Hallie Quinn Brown. Brown, a prominent activist who spoke at the 1895 Third Biennial Convention of the World's Woman's Christian Temperance Union, was the first African American to address an ICW meeting overseas in London in 1899. Margaret Murray Washington attended the same meeting, and it is believed that this spurred her to become involved in international affairs.

Never predominantly a suffrage organization, by 1899 the ICW was concentrating on such issues as equal pay, access to the professions, nursing, women's rights in the workplace, and inclusion in trade unions, among many others. All of these were issues of great importance to African American women, and the ICW proved to be the place where the top African American women's club, the National Association of Colored Women (NACW), focused its most prolonged and avid attention. However, despite their involvement in the organization since its founding, it was not until 1920 that Mary Morris Burnett Talbert became the first official NACW delegate to be seated at an ICW conference. In 1929 Sallie Stewart became a vice president of the U.S. National Council of Women, and therefore a member of the ICW. Not surprisingly, Mary McLeod Bethune was at the forefront of the

Cleveland, Ohio, she attended West Virginia State College (BS, 1965) and the University of Michigan, Ann Arbor (MA, Instruction; MA, Public Health). She joined the Foreign Service in 1970 and has served in Jamaica, the Republic of the Congo, Italy, and Iran. She was named deputy chief of mission for the U.S. Embassy in Ghana in 1986. Four years later she became the ambassador to The Gambia. After she left The Gambia in 1993, she took over the State Department's Office of Central African Affairs. In 1996 she became the ambassador to the Republic of Zambia. She then directed the Office of Southern African Affairs in the Bureau of African Affairs. In 2001 she was named ambassador to the Ivory Coast (Côte d'Ivoire). She has received two State Department Meritorious Honor Awards and one Superior Honor Award.

● **Cynthia Shepard Perry** (1928–) was ambassador to Sierra Leone (1986–1989) and ambassador to Burundi (1990–1993). Born in Terre Haute, Indiana, she attended Indiana State University (BS, 1967) and the University of Massachusetts (EdD, 1972). She was a trainer for the Peace Corps in Kenya (1974–1976), served as the staff development officer for the U.N. Economic Committee for Africa (1976–1978), and was dean of international student affairs at Texas Southern University (1978–1982). In 1982 she was named chief of education and human resources in the African Bureau of the U.S. Agency for International Development. Since her terms as ambassador, she has been the director of International Advisory Services at FCA Corporation Investments (1993). In 2001 she was named director of the Treasury Department's African Development Bank. In 1998 she published her memoir, *All Things Being Equal: One Woman's Journey*. She received the Superior Honor Award from the State Department in 1993 and was named honorary consul to the Republic of Senegal in 1994.

● **Barbara Mae Watson** (1918–1983) was named ambassador to Malaysia in 1980. She was born in New York City and attended Barnard College (BA, 1943) and St. John's University Law School; however, she dropped out of law school before earning her degree. She worked at various jobs, including as a radio broadcaster and running her own charm school and modeling agency, before she returned to law. She graduated from New York Law School in 1962 and began working as an attorney with New York City, eventually becoming the executive director of the New York City Commission to the United Nations. She joined the State Department in 1966, when she became special assistant to the deputy undersecretary of state for administration. Later that year, she was named to the Bureau of Security and Consular Affairs and two years later she was named director of the bureau. In 1977, she was appointed assistant secretary of state for consular affairs, the first black and first woman to achieve this adiplomatic rank. In 1980, Watson became ambassador to Malaysia. She retired in 1981.

activism to end racism within the ICW. For example, through her efforts and those of Hallie Quinn Brown, by 1925 the council began to allow desegregated seating in their meetings.

In 1902 some members of the ICW formed the International Women Suffrage Alliance (IWSA), later renamed the International Alliance of Women. At its first meeting in 1904 in Berlin, Mary Church Terrell, who was the only dark-skinned woman in attendance, gave a speech in fluent German.

Another important international women's organization was the Women's Peace Party, formed in 1915, which became the Women's International League for Peace and Freedom (WILPF) in 1919. Among the many prominent black club women who became involved in the league were Terrell, Talbert, Charlotte Atwood, Dr. Mary Waring, Lucy Diggs Slowe, and Dr. Flemmie Kittrell.

Joyce Blackwell-Johnson has written an excellent examination of black women's involvement in WILPF. In it she delineates two major motivations to join the organization. The first, she writes, was ideological. The second was pragmatic. She quotes Terrell as an example of the ideological member: "In no way can the colored people of this country serve themselves in particular, and humanity on general principles, better than by allying themselves with an organization which is trying to end war and remove friction between the races at one and the same time." One of the resolutions she submitted to the WILPF leadership demanded, in part, "justice and fair play to all the dark races of the world."

Of the pragmatists, Blackwell-Johnson writes,

> Women in this group believed that blacks, men in particular, should be fighting to improve the conditions of African Americans inside the United States. Furthermore, they reasoned that money spent on fighting wars could instead be used to help the underprivileged at home.
>
> (Blackwell-Johnson, p. 469)

Apart from suffrage and temperance, at the turn of the twentieth century international gatherings were organized around the issue of race. For example, both Dr. Susan McKinney Steward and Sarah S. T. Garnet were delegates to the 1911 Universal Races Congress, which met in London to organize the fight against the then predominant "science" of racial inferiority. Steward delivered a paper entitled "Colored American Women." In particular, the growing Pan-African movement provided an avenue for black women to express and explore their universality.

Anna Julia Cooper and Anna Jones were members of the executive committee for the 1900 Pan-African Congress. Both also spoke. Cooper's speech was entitled "The Negro Problem in America" and Jones's was "The Preservation of Race Individuality." Cooper helped draft a message to Queen Victoria that delineated "acts of injustice directed against her Majesty's subjects in South Africa." Charlotta Spears Bass attended the 1919 Pan-African Congress.

One of the most active of the black women internationalists, Addie Waits Hunton, also attended the 1919 Congress and in 1921 was, with Ida Gibbs Hunt, a member of the twelve-person International Committee that worked to organize that year's Pan-African Congress. As part of an unofficial delegation, she observed and wrote about the American occupation in Haiti in 1926. In 1927, through the women's group she founded, the Circle for Peace and Foreign Relations (CPFR), Hunton and other members raised the money for the 1927 Pan-African Congress. In fact, W. E. B. Du Bois acknowledged that without this group there would have been no 1927 congress at all. That congress hosted 208 delegates and had an audience of 5,000. Hunton spoke at the opening session. Other members of the CPFR included Jessie Redmon Fauset and Nina Du Bois.

As Blackwell-Johnson noted with regard to the WILPF, black women had a variety of intentions in international organizations. They were there to prove in an international arena that African American women had the knowledge and ability to belong. While they agitated to change the racism within the women's organizations, they brought women's issues to the Pan-African movement. They used all these organizations to bring international attention to the condition of black women in America. In white organizations in particular, they used their physical presence as a challenge and their unique world view as a catalyst to bring such issues as colonialism and casteism to the attention of these largely Western groups.

Yet even while they recognized the importance of their involvement in the international congresses and councils, black club women in the 1920s realized that no group existed that truly represented them and addressed international policy as it affected black women. As a result several top-level members of the NACW, including Talbert, founded the International Council of Women of the Darker Races (ICWDR) in 1922. Margaret Murray Washington was elected its first president. Later presidents of the ICWDR included Addie Waits Hunton and Addie Dickerson. Washington wrote of the organization's purpose in 1924,

> Our object is the dissemination of knowledge of peoples of color the world over, in order that there may be a larger appreciation of their history and accomplishments and so that they themselves may have a greater degree of race pride for their own achievements and touch a greater pride in themselves.
>
> (Hoyt, pp. 611–612)

The women who ran the ICDWR applied their knowledge from the black women's club movement to the international arena, recognizing that the African American woman's struggles for access to equal and adequate pay, healthcare, and most particularly education were mirrored by women of color around the globe. One of their projects (in cooperation with the Chicago Women's Club) supported the work of Adelaide Casely-Hayford to found a school in Sierra Leone. Their other efforts included the promotion of African American history and literature in public schools, along with studies of Haiti and Cuba. Unfortunately, the ICWDR never achieved its goal of becoming a truly internationally representative organization, and it ceased operations after World War II. However, as Beverly Guy-Sheftall wrote in "Remembering Sojourner Truth: On Black Feminism," "This forward looking organization is reminiscent of recent attempts by contemporary Black feminists to establish linkages with other women of color throughout the world and to struggle for the elimination of sexism on a global level."

Of course, the women of the nationalist movements and the far left were involved internationally by the very nature of the philosophies they espoused. Audley Moore, Louise Thompson Patterson, Claudia Jones, Amy Garvey, and Lucy Parsons all worked and spoke on international issues, as did, more famously, Shirley Graham Du Bois and Eslanda Robeson. While there is not the space here to discuss in detail the international versus local efforts of these women, it should be noted that they frequently participated in the same organizations as their more moderate sisters. At the 1944 Conference on Africa hosted by the Council on African Affairs (founded in 1937), both Garvey and Bethune were in attendance. In addition, Shirley Graham Du Bois, Robeson, and Bass were all members.

The left gained its largest following during the Depression, and many black women joined various political organizations. Also during the Depression, anticolonial movements were building around the world, from India to Africa. In her book *Race Against Empire*, Penny Von Eschen points to the Italian invasion of Ethiopia in 1935 as the time when a broad spectrum of African Americans became aware of and involved in U.S. foreign policy.

Certainly by the end of World War II and the start of the cold war, the role of African Americans in world affairs changed enormously. The cold war and McCarthyism destroyed much of the power of the American left, but it was also an era when a number of new international organizations were formed and anticolonial movements around the world succeeded in gaining their freedom.

United Nations

One of the most important international organizations to be created after World War II was the United Nations. Black women leaders knew from its inception that their presence at the UN was essential to bring to the world's attention the reality of being a black woman in America. In addition, participation in the activities of the UN was a powerful symbol of black women's place at the table of world affairs.

Again at the forefront of the battle was Bethune. Even before the war, Bethune had introduced a more international agenda to the NACW. In 1935, when Bethune called together the top club women of the era to form the National Council of Negro Women (NCNW), most if not all of them had been involved in the ICW and in international affairs, including Brown, Terrell, Dickerson, and Daisy Lampkin. At the 1945 UN Conference on International Organization, which drafted the UN charter, Bethune failed in her attempt to have the NCNW made an official consultant to the U.S. delegation. Not to be stopped, Bethune made sure that her organization was involved, even if unofficially, and asked Eunice Hunton Carter (daughter of Hunton) to be the NCNW observer. Carter went on to become a consultant to the Economic and Social Council of the UN for the ICW in 1947 and chaired its committee of laws. In 1955, at the UN conference in Geneva, she was elected chair of the International Conference of Non-Governmental Organizations.

The UN also provided the first opportunity for an African American woman to officially represent the United States government in an international context when, in 1950, Edith Spurlock was appointed by President Harry Truman to represent the United States at the UN. She spent the next sixteen years working in the international arena with the UN and the North Atlantic Treaty Organization (NATO).

Like her predecessors, Dorothy Height, fourth president of NCNW, made her presence known at the UN. She was a delegate to the United Nations Educational, Scientific, and Cultural Organization (UNESCO) conference on "Woman and Her Rights" held in Jamaica, and, in 1975, she conducted a seminar and participated in the International Women's Year conference in Mexico City. The same year, Height established the NCNW international division to promote relationships with other women's organizations, especially in African countries. By the mid-1980s the NCNW had three international offices: in Dakar, Senegal; in Cairo, Egypt; and in Harare, Zimbabwe. The organization has also developed a collaboration with the Federation of Senegalese Women and the National Union of Togolese Women.

Anna Arnold Hedgeman spent her life working on international affairs through a variety of organizations, including the UN. She worked with the New York City government, hosting visitors to the UN, and served as Mayor Wagner's representative at the tenth-anniversary meeting of the UN in San Francisco in 1955. The following year she participated in a study tour of Israel and the

Middle East through the American Christian Committee on Palestine. She was the keynote speaker at the First Conference of African Women and Women of African Descent held in Accra, Ghana, in 1960 and chaired a panel at the International Conference of Social Work as a representative of the United Seamen's Service. She also worked for a few months with the U.S. State Department. However, she was an exception there.

State Department

Despite all their work and all their advancements, the State Department had still not opened its door to black women by the 1960s. However, black women had become increasingly involved in international organizations and movements outside the government. Like many before them, such women as Fannie Lou Hamer, Angela Davis, and Maida Springer—whose international trade-union work spanned four decades—spoke up about the hypocrisy of a government that fought to extend democracy overseas and denied it at home. In growing numbers they began to ever more vocally challenge American foreign policy in the third world, to link it directly to racist domestic policies, and to ally themselves with women from around the globe. Unfortunately, there is no space here to go into detail about the international aspects of the civil rights, black power, and global women of color movements. The problems and successes within the official foreign policy arm of the U.S. government itself is too large a story.

While other U.S. government agencies do post employees overseas, the State Department is the official U.S. government agency responsible for representing the United States abroad, as well as for developing and pursuing foreign policy. Part of the State Department is the Foreign Service, which is the main interface with foreign governments and people. Foreign Service officers are meant to reflect U.S. policy, whether or not they agree with that policy. At the same time, these employees are the best source for information about what people are thinking and doing outside of our borders. However, from the point of view of other Washington agencies, as well as the Congress, the department and its employees have often been viewed with suspicion if not disdain. Concerns that members of the Foreign Service have "gone native" or do not represent U.S. interests have dogged the department throughout its history. This is ironic because the State Department, and more particularly the Foreign Service, has proved to be the part of the U.S. government most resistant to change.

According to Michael Krenn in his book *Black Diplomacy*, at the beginning of the cold war "Department of State officials slowly came to the conclusion that race would play an important role in the postwar world . . . that

America's domestic racial problem was now a foreign policy problem." However, this realization did not translate into action within the ranks of the department. In 1950, there were only thirty-three blacks in the Foreign Service. Of these, at least twenty-one were posted to Liberia. For the next four decades, the numbers would improve but the problems would still exist.

As late as 1996, the State Department was cited as among the worst government agencies when it came to minority inclusion and promotion. An article that year in *The Nation* by Bruce Shapiro reported that in 1994 W. Lewis Anselem, political counselor in the embassy to Bolivia, sent a telex that called "dark-skinned State Department workers 'unscrupulous race and ethnic jumpers' trying to 'con' their way to the top." While Anselem's language might be extreme even within the ranks of the Foreign Service, its message was not. The State Department and Foreign Service have long had a reputation as "old boy's clubs" of white male Ivy Leaguers who were resistant in the extreme to incursions by outsiders. In fact, a 1989 General Accounting Office study reported that 40 percent of all senior Foreign Service personnel were from Ivy League schools.

That same year, the House Subcommittee on the Civil Service reported that Foreign Service officers who were minorities were denied tenure far more than whites. Even when they were allowed into the Foreign Service, minorities were often given "hardship posts" (that is, Africa and small, "unimportant" countries) and not the "plum" assignments, (that is, Europe and strategically important countries). While many African American Foreign Service officers were and are Africa and Caribbean experts and many Foreign Service officers of all races and both genders are committed to working at so-called "hardship posts" and might even prefer them to the "plum" assignments, there was an undeniable tendency at the State Department to ghettoize its minority employees, whatever their specializations.

In 1986 thirty members of the Foreign Service signed a class action suit on behalf of 359 current and former black Foreign Service officers. The charges included discrimination with regard to employment, assignment, and promotion. These last two charges are particularly important in understanding a Foreign Service officer's ability to advance her career. The Foreign Service is divided into four categories: consular, administrative, political, and economic. The higher-level positions are most frequently given to members of the latter two categories. One of the most important points of the lawsuit was that even when the Foreign Service hired minorities, they were most often given positions in the consular and administrative categories, whether or not that fit with their areas of expertise.

The case was finally settled in 1996. The settlement stated that the State Department would not have to acknowledge its fault in the matter but would have outside supervision of its promotions practices and would pay compensation to some employees. However, while 34 members of the 359 named in the suit wrote to the court supporting the settlement, 55 wrote in opposition to it. As of 2001, three plaintiffs remained, including Mary Cynthia Smoot, and the case was still being appealed in the U.S. District Courts.

There is some reason to be hopeful nonetheless. For example, the number of black women who have achieved the rank of ambassador is steadily increasing. Patricia Roberts Harris became ambassador to Luxembourg in 1965, the first African American woman to be so named. Carol Moseley Braun served as ambassador to New Zealand and Samoa. Other African American women ambassadors include Mabel Murphy Smythe-Haith, ambassador to Cameroon (1977–1980) and the Republic of Equatorial Guinea (1979–1980); Barbara Mae Watson, ambassador to Malaysia (1980–1981); Cynthia Shepard Perry, ambassador to Sierra Leone (1986–1989) and Burundi (1990–1993); and Mosina H. Jordan, ambassador to the Central African Republic (1995–1997).

Among the black women serving as U.S. ambassadors at the beginning of the twenty-first century were Mattie R. Sharpless, the Central African Republic; Robin Renee Sanders, the Republic of the Congo; Dennise Mathieu, Niger; and Wanda L. Nesbitt, Madagascar. Arlene Render is a three-time ambassador: She served in Gambia (1990–1993) and the Republic of Zambia (1996–1999) and then as the ambassador to the Ivory Coast (Côte d'Ivoire) beginning in 2001. Aurelia E. Brazeal has also served as ambassador to three countries: Micronesia, Kenya, and Ethiopia. She is also the first African American woman career Foreign Service officer to be promoted into the senior Foreign Service.

In addition to Brazeal, many of these women are career Foreign Service officers, including Render, Brazeal, Sanders, Nesbitt, and Jordan. Harriet Elam-Thomas is a career minister in the senior Foreign Service and, in 1999, became acting deputy director of the United States Information Agency (USIA). Later that year she was named ambassador to Senegal, a position she held until 2002. Before her appointment to that post, from 1995 to 1997, she was the counselor for public affairs at the American embassy in Brussels.

While it is telling that most of these women have been named ambassador almost exclusively in African countries, one can only hope that in so doing they may be bringing foreign policy with regard to Africa to the forefront of America's international agenda. In addition, their other assignments have included some European posts and increasingly high-level positions in the United States.

A case in point is Ambassador Ruth A. Davis, who served as ambassador to Benin in 1992. She is the first black woman to direct the Foreign Service Institute, and during her tenure there she established the Leadership and Management Institute. More importantly, she is the first black woman to be named a career ambassador. In the Foreign Service, this ranking is equivalent to four-star general. In 2001, Davis was named director general of the Foreign Service and director of human resources. In that position, she almost doubled the staff and instituted the largest minority recruitment drive in the history of the department. She left her position in June 2003 to become an adviser for international affairs. Reportedly, she will hold the position only for a year and will then return to the State Department. If her recruitment drive bears fruit, there may come a time when a black woman will lead U.S. foreign policy in Europe, Asia, and the Middle East, as well as in Africa.

In addition to the ambassadors and career Foreign Service officers, African American women are making their mark in other areas of the State Department, particularly in the U.S. Agency for International Development (USAID). Vivian L. Derryck was sworn in as assistant administrator for Africa of USAID in 1998. After she resigned in 2001, she became the senior vice president and director of public-private partnerships with the Academy for Educational Development. The most highly placed black woman in the department at the beginning of the twenty-first century was Constance Berry Newman, who replaced Derryck as assistant administrator for Africa with USAID before becoming assistant secretary of state for African affairs in 2004.

Susan E. Rice, who has worked both inside and outside the State Department, is one of the brightest stars in foreign policy. The youngest African American woman ever to rise to the level of assistant secretary, at thirty-three she held Newman's former position, assistant secretary of state for African affairs (1997–2001). A Rhodes scholar who studied international relations at Oxford University, she (like Condoleezza Rice—no relation) first lent her international affairs knowledge to the National Security Council (NSC). In 1993 she was named director for international organizations and peacekeeping with the NSC. In 1995 she was named special assistant to the president and senior director for African affairs. She went on to become a senior fellow at the Brookings Institution.

Despite these recent improvements, there is more to be done. As the former Foreign Service officer Ulric Haynes told Bruce Shapiro, "the marginalization of African Americans in the Foreign Service is part and parcel of this country's problems in dealing with dark-skinned people around the world." In addition, the story of how black women have historically fought and surmounted this marginalization is only beginning to be studied in depth. The subject deserves a lengthy and complete treatment, for it is both important and revealing.

See also Left, The.

BIBLIOGRAPHY

"Ambassador Aurelia E. Brazeal" United States Embassy, Addis Ababa, Ethiopia. http://addisababa.usembassy.gov/wwwhambraz.html.

"Ambassador Ruth Davis." The HistoryMakers.com, Political Makers. http://www.thehistorymakers.com/biography/biography.asp?bioindex=710&category=politicalMakers.

Anderson, Carol. *Eyes Off the Prize: The United Nations and the African American Struggle for Human Rights, 1944–1955*. Cambridge, U.K., and New York: Cambridge University Press, 2003.

Bandele, Ramla. "Pan-African Congress in 1927, Black Women Rescue the Movement." Global Mappings: A Political Atlas of the African Diaspora Web site. The Institute of Diasporic Studies at Northwestern University. http://diaspora.northwestern.edu.

Blackwell-Johnson, Joyce. "African American Activists in the Women's International League for Peace and Freedom, 1920s–1950s." *Peace & Change* 23.4 (October 1998): 466–483.

Bureau of Public Affairs, U.S. Department of State. http://www.state.gov/r/pa/ei/biog/c7647.htm.

Chapman, Dan. "Ruth Davis Leads Push for Change in Foreign Service." *Atlanta Journal and Constitution*, 28 August 2002.

Hoytt, Eleanor Hinton. "International Council of Women of the Darker Races." In *Black Women in America: An Historical Encyclopedia*. Brooklyn, NY: Carlson Publishing, 1993.

Krenn, Michael L. *Black Diplomacy: African Americans and the State Department, 1945–1969*. Armonk, NY: M. E. Sharpe, 1999.

Lutz, Christine. "The Horn of Africa and the American Left." Southeastern Regional Seminar in African Studies (SERSAS), Spring 2002 Conference, Georgia State University.

Madison, Alfreda L. "From Capitol Hill: Blacks Can Expect More Positions in Foreign Service." *Washington Informer*, 20 October 1980.

Plummer, Brenda Gayle, ed. *Rising Wind: African Americans and U.S. Foreign Affairs, 1935–1960*. Chapel Hill: University of North Carolina Press, 1996.

Plummer, Brenda Gayle. *Window on Freedom: Race, Civil Rights, and Foreign Affairs, 1945–1988*. Chapel Hill: University of North Carolina Press, 2003.

Rief, Michelle. "Thinking Locally, Acting Globally: The International Agenda of African American Clubwomen, 1880-1940." *The Journal of African American History* 89 (Summer 2004): 203–223.

Shapiro, Bruce. "A House Divided." *The Nation*, 12 February 1996.

Shaw, John. "Ambassador Ruth A. Davis: Diplomatic Pioneer Still Working to Change Face of Foreign Service." *The Washington Diplomat*, February 2004.

Sheftall, Beverly Guy. "Remembering Sojourner Truth: On Black Feminism," *Catalyst* (Fall 1986).

Skinner, Elliott. *African Americans and U.S. Policy toward Africa, 1850–1924*. Washington, DC: Howard University Press, 1992.

"State Department Director General Ruth Davis Assigned to Howard University Post." *Jet*, 30 June 2003.

"Two Black Women Set Diplomatic Records in Europe. (Harriet Elam and Mattie Sharpless Appointed to Rank of Minister Counselors in the US Foreign Service)." *Jet*, 31 March 1997.

Von Eschen, Penny M. *Race against Empire: Black Americans and Anticolonialism 1937–1957*. Ithaca, NY: Cornell University Press, 1997.

The Women's Library. "Administrative/Biographical history; International Alliance of Women; Women's Library, London." http://www.aim25.ac.uk/cgi-bin/search2?coll_id=6701&inst_id=65.

The Women's Library. "Administrative/Biographical history; Records of the International Council of Women; The Women's Library, London." http://www.genesis.ac.uk/archive.jsp?typeofsearch=i&term=notimpl&highlight=1&pk=2202.

—HILARY MAC AUSTIN

ISLAM. Although it is difficult to uncover the early history of black women and Islam in the United States, some scholars have identified African-born Muslim women like "Fatima" and "Samba" as the mothers of the first generation of African American Muslims. Fatima and Samba appeared in East Florida plantation records and local newspapers in 1813, and it is plausible that Samba gave birth to at least one daughter, Saluma, while residing on an Amelia Island plantation. Despite such documented references, much of the early evidence of Muslims in North America cannot be confirmed. Looking at plantation lists, one finds Muslim names and evidence of African-born slaves, but it is difficult to trace the history of these individuals without first understanding the emergence of Islam in Africa.

Islam was introduced into North Africa in the early 1400s by traders traveling along the Mediterranean Sea. Africans in this region were attracted to Islam because it helped unify groups that lived in close proximity to one another but which practiced different indigenous religions. Islam encouraged people to focus on their similarities, and it enabled disparate ethnic and religious groups to enjoy greater political stability and economic security.

Islamic Principles and Belief System

The meaning of Islam is the submission to the will of God, as revealed in the Qur'an, Islam's holy book. God's will is that all members of the Muslim community (*ummah*) are equal. Islam is foundational to political thought because politics and theology are both necessary to legitimize a government and its leader.

The Muslim belief system contends that Allah (God) sent Muhammad as the final Messenger and gave him the Qur'an to share with his followers. Muhammad was a religious and political leader; therefore, Muslims do not believe in separation between the mosque and state—Islam is both a faith and a sociopolitical system. The Book and Prophet provide the fundamental sources for Islamic law (*sharia*); therefore, one should surrender to Islam and Allah's will in order to be his instrument for establishing and spreading Islamic order.

The Islamic faith utilizes five pillars that make up the belief system: profession of faith (*shahada*), daily prayer (*salat*), fasting (*sawam*), almsgiving or charity (*zakat*), and the pilgrimage to Mecca (*hajj*). In addition to following these five pillars, many Muslims rely on the practices

BLACK MUSLIM WOMEN, photographed on 2 December 1970 as they applauded Elijah Muhammad during his annual Savior's Day message in Chicago. (National Archives/John A. Walker; Joe McCary, Photo Response Studio.)

outlined in the Qur'an. The Qur'an consists of *sharia*, which represent Islamic jurisprudence and *hadiths*, which reflect the traditions, reports, and deeds of the Prophet Muhammad and his companions. *Hadiths* provide an extensive roadmap in which the Prophet defines all aspects of life. *Sharia* is based on the Qur'an and is similar to the Ten Commandments in Christianity and Judaism.

Early America

The Moors, who accompanied the Spanish explorers in the fifteenth and sixteenth centuries, were among the first to introduce the Islamic religion to the Americas. Therefore, the Muslim presence in North America predates the arrival of English colonists. Indeed, Muslims populated Spanish Florida and French Louisiana as early as 1565. However, the most significant spread of Islam in North America occurred with the arrival of African Muslims like Fatima and Samba through the transatlantic slave trade. At least thirty thousand Muslim slaves came from Islamic-dominated ethnic groups such as the Mandingo, Fula, Gambians, Senegambians, Senegalese, Cape Verdians, and Sierra Leonians—representing at least 10 percent of all African slaves brought to America between 1711 and 1808.

When Europeans forcibly removed Africans (of whom some were Muslim) and enslaved them on New World plantations, Islamic traditions survived. Within American slave communities of the nineteenth century, for example, some former bondmen and women, as well as their owners, recalled the presence of Muslim slaves who prayed to Allah, wore coverings like turbans and veils (*hajib*), gave their progeny Muslim names, utilized prayer beads, and observed Islamic dietary traditions, all practices consistent with a conscientious pursuit of Islam. Islamic communities developed in early America as slaves emulated Muslim brothers such as Salih Bilali of St. Simons Island, Georgia; Ben Ali of Sapelo Island, Georgia; Abd al-Rahman of New Orleans, Louisiana; and Ayuba b. Sulayman of Maryland.

Likewise, women such as Fatima and Phoebe, the wife (or wives) of Bilali of Sapelo Island, and their daughters Margaret, Hester, Charlotte, Fatima, Nyrrabuh, Medina, and Bintou, were said to be practicing Muslims.

Despite scattered references to Muslim slaves in the seventeenth, eighteenth, and nineteenth centuries, historians use caution when making references to Islam in early America because it is difficult to fully understand its presence. Naming patterns and memories of Islamic slaves did not guarantee the survival of Islam in its pure state. By the late 1880s, the first generation of American Muslims had died, leaving their offspring to interact in a society dominated by Christians.

Modern America and Nontraditional Forms of Islam

Though evidence of traditional Islam appeared as early as the antebellum period of American history, it is clear that the Muslim faith took on other forms in modern America. The scholar Sylviane Diouf argues that "there is no evidence in the United States of any Islamic continuity in the twentieth century." Eventually, some African Americans found their way to nontraditional forms of Islam through the Nation of Islam, activism during the modern civil rights movement, and participation in the Black Panther Party for Self-Defense. Many Islamic movements in the United States emerged at the same time that Marcus Garvey became an important leader of the United Negro Improvement Association and were directly linked to Garvey's Pan-Africanism, Black Nationalism, self-determination, as well as political and economic redemption.

In 1913, for example, Noble Drew Ali founded the Moorish Holy Temple of Science in Newark, New Jersey, and claimed that he was a prophet ordained by Allah; however, this claim was in direct conflict with Orthodox Islam tenets that identify Muhammad as the last prophet. Other nontraditional modern Islamic movements included the Ahmadiyyah Movement of Islam (1930), the Universal Islamic Society (1926), the First Muslim Mosque of Pittsburgh (1928), the Islamic Brotherhood (1929), the Nation of Islam (1930), the Addeynu Allahe Universal Arabic Association (1930s), the African American Mosque (1933), the Islamic Mission Society (1939), the State Street Mosque (1929), Fahamme Temple of Islam and Culture (1930s), the World Community of al-Islam in the West (1976), and the American Muslim Movement (1980).

Although the place of women in modern Islamic movements has received little attention, African American women were in fact active participants. Clara Muhammad (1898–1972), who was born in Georgia and married Elijah Muhammad, the prominent leader of the Nation of Islam, is but one example of an active Muslim woman whose life work was dedicated to educating her family and the Nation of Islam community. Sister Muhammad was the mother of eight children and remembered as a "truly original black woman" among Muslims in the United States for her "modesty, purpose, and total commitment to her husband and her Nation." In the 1930s, Clara Muhammad educated young Muslims from her home and is recognized as one of the pioneers of homeschool education. She taught primary and secondary education in what became the University of Islam Schools. The educational agenda focused on teaching, "poor African Americans that they were members of the tribe of Shabazz who had been separated from their original culture and homeland." When her son Warith Deen Muhammad founded the American Muslim Mission in the late 1970s, he changed the name of the University of Islam schools to the Clara Muhammad Schools in honor of his mother. By 1992, there were thirty-eight Sister Clara Muhammad schools in the United States and one in Bermuda.

Betty Shabazz (1936–1997), the wife of Malcolm X, served the African American community by promoting self-determination, childcare, and health education. The mother of six girls and herself a former member of the Nation of Islam, Shabazz became a registered nurse, received a master's degree in public health administration, and received her doctorate degree in education administration in 1975 from the University of Massachusetts, Amherst. Like Sister Clara Muhammad, her primary focus was the education of her children. Two years after the assassination of her husband in 1967, Shabazz traveled to Mecca to honor his memory. This trip marked a turning point; she knew that she had to move forward and remain strong for her daughters. Upon her return and until her tragic death in 1997, Shabazz served on the boards of the African American Foundation, the Women's Service League, and the Day Care Council of Westchester County, New York, among others. She also served on the faculty at Medgar Evers College in Brooklyn, New York, and later became the school's director of the Department of Communications and Public Relations. Although she preferred to live a private life, Shabazz gave speeches at events like the October 1995 Million Man March, and she established a living memorial in honor of her husband at Columbia University by developing the Malcolm X Medical Scholarship program. Betty Shabazz and Clara Muhammad are just two examples of nontraditional Muslim women who became activists in their respective communities. There are many others. In 2001, the historian Ula Taylor began research on the first book-length study of women in the Nation of Islam, a study that is likely to uncover additional information about women like Shabazz and Muhammad.

Contemporary Women and Orthodox Islam

African American women practicing orthodox Islam at the beginning of the twenty-first century constituted a growing population. For them, Islam represented authentic equality without hypocrisy; therefore, black women felt like a part of a solid community in which relationships and roles were well defined. The role of women is held in high esteem and clearly defined in chapter four of the Qur'an, titled Nissa, which means "for the women." Membership with the Muslim community requires service to Allah, regardless of the worshiper's gender, ethnicity, or class, and Islam provides a spiritual means for black women to reconnect with their African past.

There are myriad reasons why orthodox Islam remains an attractive religion for black women. Some arrived through participation in the Nation of Islam, conversion in prison, desperate circumstances, a search for order, a hunger for knowledge, dissatisfaction with other religions (in particular Christianity), a spiritual growth process, and pressure from their families. Interviewers of African American Muslim women often discover that Islam provides religious empowerment and a clearly defined role in society for those who choose to convert.

Many African American women chose Islam in response to racial discrimination in United States culture as they searched for equality—in social, political, and religious settings. Some black women interpret Islam in a way that allows them to have a greater and more legitimate role both inside and outside of the family. Unlike Christianity, Islam offers equality based on race, which is appealing to African Americans in general, while the Qur'an emphasizes socioeconomic justice and human egalitarianism, which is appealing to African American women in particular. Women and men are considered equal in Islam as annotated in the Qur'an, which specifically commands the God-like treatment of women within society and addresses issues ranging from inheritance rights to the allowance of remarriage after divorce.

Daina Ramey Berry discussed religious faith with a community of African American Muslim women in North Carolina. This group of five women had converted to Islam (at different stages in their lives—some had been practicing Islam for nearly thirty years) because of their dissatisfaction with Christianity. They reported that they found Christianity oppressive in that they could not ask certain questions. One woman, who had been a Muslim for twenty years, was reprimanded when she questioned her parents about why they prayed to Jesus. They said, "Daughter . . . your faith is weak" and provided no other response to her question. Another was chastised for asking what it meant to be saved. However, when these women began to study different religions, they found that Islam had the answers that they had longed for. The youngest member of the group, who had been practicing Islam for four years after having converted at the age of twenty-three, was attracted to the faith because there was "nothing taboo" in terms of the questions she had about Islam. She appreciated the authenticity of the *hadiths* and embraced the principles of Islam because of the clear guidance and consciousness of Allah that "provided order in [her] life." According to these women, Islam is a religion that encourages people to "think and reflect" by studying the Qur'an, and it offers an incredible sense of spirituality.

Other African American Islamic women found their place as community activists—women like Aliyah Abdul-Kareem, who founded Nisa, a national women's organization established in the 1980s. One of the primary goals of Nisa was to promote the concept of "women caring for women," and although the organization eventually disbanded, Abdul-Kareem continued to promote women's activism in New York City. The National Association of Muslim American Women, founded by An-Nisa Abd el Fattah in northern Virginia, was yet another organization open to all Muslim women. Sister An-Nisa was a writer, political science educator, and an editor who focused her considerable energies on restoring Islam in its purist form by educating the community about the lives of Muslim women.

Despite the unity and organizing efforts of Muslim women, the greatest challenge facing African American Islamic women in the United States remained their "triple jeopardy"—being black, female, and Muslim. These women were forced to confront racial, gender, and religious discrimination in the workplace, in public, and sometimes even within their extended families. Despite such challenges, black women Muslims believe in their faith, practice it honorably, and do their best to educate others about the authentic meaning of Islam.

BIBLIOGRAPHY

Anway, Carol Anderson. *Daughters of Another Path: Experiences of American Women Choosing Islam*. Lee's Summit, MO: Yawna, 1996.

Austin, Allan. *African Muslims in Antebellum America*. New York: Garland, 1984.

Blyden, E. W. *Christianity, Islam, and the Negro Race*. Edinburgh: University of Edinburgh Press, 1967.

Clegg, Claude Andrew, III. *An Original Man: The Life and Times of Elijah Muhammad*. New York: St. Martin's, 1997.

Curtis, Edward. *Islam in Black America: Identity, Liberation, and Difference in African-American Islamic Thought*. Albany: State University of New York Press, 2002.

Dannin, Robert. *Black Pilgrimage to Islam*. New York: Oxford University Press, 2002.

Diouf, Sylvianne A. *Servants of Allah: African Muslims Enslaved in the Americas*. New York: New York University Press, 1998.

Gomez, Michael A. "Muslims in Early America." *Journal of Southern History* 60.4 (November 1994): 671–710.

Haddad, Yvonne Yazbeck, and John L. Esposito, eds. *Daughters of Abraham: Feminist Thought in Judaism, Christianity and Islam*. Gainesville: University of Florida Press, 2001.

Haddad, Yvonne Yazbeck, Byron Haines, and Ellison Findly, eds. *The Islamic Impact*. Syracuse, NY: Syracuse University Press, 1984.

Lincoln, C. Eric. *The Black Muslims in America*. Trenton, NJ: Africa World Press, 1994.

Nyang, Sulayman S. *Islam in the United States of America*. Chicago: ABC International, 1999.

Rahman, Fazlur. *Islam and Modernity*. Chicago: University of Chicago Press, 1982.

Rashid, Hakim M., and Zakiyyah Muhammad. "The Sister Clara Muhammad Schools: Pioneers in the Development of Islamic Education in America." *Journal of Negro Education* 61.2 (Spring 1992): 178–185.

Rouse, Carolyn Moxley. *Engaged Surrender: African American Women and Islam*. Berkeley: University of California Press, 2004.

Smith, Jane. *Islam in America*. New York: Columbia University Press, 1999.

Turner, Richard Brent. *Islam in the African-American Experience*. Bloomington: Indiana University Press, 1997.

Walther, Wiebke. *Women in Islam*. Princeton, NJ: Markus Weiner, 1993.

—Lezlee Suzanne Ware
—Daina Ramey Berry

J

JACKET, BARBARA J. (b. 26 December 1935), athlete, coach. In the history of competitive track and field sports, the leadership and athleticism of Barbara J. Jacket are legendary. Barbara Jacket went to Barcelona, Spain, in 1992 as the second African American head coach of an Olympic U.S. women's track and field team. The first was her mentor, Nell Jackson, at the 1956 Olympic games.

Jacket was born in Port Arthur, Texas, and raised along with her two siblings by their mother, Eva Getwood. A track and basketball star before entering college at Tuskegee Institute in Alabama, Jacket was later inducted into the Tuskegee Athletic Hall of Fame. Soon after she left college in 1965, Jacket assumed the job that would be hers for the next three decades. She created and coached a women's track and field team at Prairie View A&M University, a historically black university in Prairie View, Texas. From that time, team championships characterized Jacket's career, distinguishing Jacket as much for her coaching abilities as for her individual athleticism. Jacket's teams claimed eight National Association of Intercollegiate Athletics (NAI) outdoor titles and two indoor titles, several titles in the Association of Intercollegiate Athletics for Women and the U.S. Track and Field Federation, eight Southwestern Athletic Conference (SWAC) cross-country titles, nine indoor SWAC titles, and five outdoor SWAC titles in track and field. In all, Jacket would coach some twenty-three SWAC championship teams and was named the SWAC Coach of the Year twenty-three times. Jacket also tutored fifty-seven All-Americans and claimed the NAIC Coach of the Year five times.

Jacket served as the assistant coach for several U.S. women's Olympic track and field teams. In 1973 Jacket helped coach women's track and field meets in Germany, Poland, and Russia. In 1977 she accompanied the U.S. women's team to track and field meets for the World University Games in Bulgaria. By the time Jacket retired in 1991 as Prairie View's head coach, she had also been head coach of the 1975 World University Games in Japan, an assistant coach in the 1979 Pan-American games, head coach at the 1987 World Championships in Italy, and again in 1991 when the championships were held in England.

Having become the first and only female athletic director in the history of the SWAC when Prairie View named her to that position in 1990, Jacket retired in 1991 to devote more time to her responsibilities as the head coach of the 1992 U.S. Women's Olympic Track Team. In this position, Jacket coached the long-jumper Jackie Joyner-Kersee and the sprinters Gwen Torrance, Gail Devers, and Evelyn Ashford. Jacket's team won four gold medals, three silver medals, and three bronze medals, more awards than any U.S. women's track and field team had garnered since Nell Jackson coached the team in 1956.

After more than half a century as a track and field athlete and coach, Barbara Jacket was honored by the United States Track Coaches Association when in 2001 she became a member of the USTCA Hall of Fame.

BIBLIOGRAPHY

"AIA honors coach Jacket with Hall of Fame Nod." *Jet*, November 1992, 54(1).

"Barbara Jacket." Sports Legends. The Museum of the Gulf Coast. http://museum.lamarpa.edu/bjacket.html.

Pierce, P. J. *"Let Me Tell You What I've Learned": Texas Wisewomen Speak*. Austin: University of Texas Press, 2002.

Prestage, Jewel Limar. "Jacket, Barbara J." In *Black Women in America: An Historical Encyclopedia*, edited by Darlene Clark Hine. Brooklyn: Carlson, 1993: 620.

—LaTrese Evette Adkins

JACKSON, MAHALIA (b. 26 October 1911; d. 27 January 1972), singer. Mahalia Jackson, destined to become one of the greatest gospel singers of all time, was born in poverty in a three-room "shotgun" shack on Water Street between the railroad tracks and the Mississippi River levee in New Orleans. She was the third of six children. Her father, John A. Jackson, was a stevedore, barber, and Baptist preacher. Her mother, Charity Clark, died at twenty-five when Jackson was just a child.

Jackson began to sing at the age of four in the children's choir at Plymouth Rock Baptist. After her mother's death, her mother's sisters, Mahalia "Aunt Duke" Paul, for whom Mahalia was named, and Bessie Kimble, both of New Orleans, raised Mahalia. They lived in the section of the city upriver from Audubon Park that would later be known as Black Pearl.

MAHALIA JACKSON, shown in a publicity photograph from the William Morris Agency, c. 1960s. The great gospel singer became a symbol of the civil rights movement during the famous March on Washington in 1963. (Library of Congress.)

As a young girl growing up in New Orleans, Jackson absorbed the musical sounds of her family's Baptist church, the Sanctified church next door, and local legends-to-be like King Oliver, Kid Ory, and Bunk Johnson. Louis Armstrong was not even in his teens and was already playing trumpet in the New Orleans Waifs' Home Band. Famous brass bands such as the Tuxedos, Eagle, and Eureka rode around town in advertising wagons and played at funerals, picnics, fish fries, lodge parties, and parades of all kinds, including Mardi Gras. The Black Mardi Gras Indians marched on Fat Tuesday, playing their unique sounds. Musicians like Jelly Roll Morton and King Oliver performed in cabarets and cafes, and there was ragtime music on the showboats on the Mississippi River.

Many people were buying gramophones, and everybody had records of blues singers like Bessie Smith and Ma Rainey. Although Jackson grew up among people who were serious about religion, she was an admirer of popular music, and it was difficult not to hear the amalgam of sounds in her community or to notice how Jackson was influenced by the powerful music of the lower Mississippi Delta.

Indeed, Jackson experienced and was influenced by many styles of music; however, the most significant was that of the Sanctified church. A Sanctified church was near her home, and she could hear spirited singing and the drum, the cymbal, the tambourine, and the steel triangle. The church did not have a choir or organ. The whole congregation participated by singing, clapping, and stamping its feet—in essence, utilizing the entire body. Jackson later commented on several occasions that the church literally interpreted the psalmist in the Bible, just as she later would: "Make a joyful noise unto the Lord" and "Praise the Lord with the instruments." Jackson also said that the powerful beat and rhythms of the Sanctified church were holdovers from the antebellum era of slavery, and that the music was so expressive that it brought tears to her eyes. The sacred and secular sounds in her community blended together. When Jackson left New Orleans, she carried this African American musical matrix with her to Chicago.

Making Her Way

In 1927, Jackson moved to Chicago, where she lived with another aunt, Hannah Robinson. She worked as a laundress, a maid in a hotel, and a date packer, and she studied beauty culture at the Chicago branch of Madame C. J. Walker's renowned beauty school. Soon after she arrived in Chicago, Jackson joined the choir of the Greater Salem Baptist Church. After the director heard her sing "Hand Me Down My Silver Trumpet, Gabriel," she immediately became the choir's first soloist.

During the 1930s, Jackson toured the "storefront church circuit," singing to congregations that could not afford conventional places of worship. She married her first husband, Isaac Hockenhull in 1935, and in later years, she married Sigmond Galloway and divorced again. She also became a member of a gospel quintet, the Johnson Singers, at Greater Salem Baptist Church. In addition, she caught the attention of Professor Thomas A. Dorsey, later known as the "Father of Gospel Music." Dorsey was a gospel composer and publisher, who from then on served as Jackson's accompanist, mentor, and publisher. He wrote over four hundred songs and needed singers to sing and popularize them. Jackson, with other singers such as Roberta Martin and Sallie Martin, began performing and demonstrating Dorsey's songs for the Baptist conventions and various churches around the country. Dorsey had been the composer and accompanist for Ma Rainey, the classic blues singer, which explained not only his musical orientation but also why some middle-class congregations initially shunned him and his music. However, by 1947, Mahalia Jackson had become the official soloist for the National Baptist Convention by mostly singing Thomas A. Dorsey and W. Herbert Brewster songs.

Jackson, Dorsey, and the other talented gospel singers and composers helped to revitalize African American religious music by extending the developments that transpired within the Sanctified churches to the more established denominations. They helped bring back into African American church music the sounds and the structure of antebellum street cries and field hollers, folk spirituals and work songs. They borrowed freely from the ragtime, blues, and jazz music of the secular world; they helped keep alive the stylistic and aesthetic continuum that characterized African American music in the United States.

Jackson was criticized for clapping her hands, stomping her feet, moving her body around the stage, and for bringing undignified "jazz into the church." Of course, being the feisty person that she was, she always retaliated, usually with scripture. Jackson liked to invoke the psalms to justify her performance practices, especially, "Oh clap your hands, all ye people! Shout unto the Lord with the voice of triumph!" She said she had to praise God with her whole body, and she did.

Jackson bridged the gap between the sacred and the secular in her performances without compromising her deep-rooted fundamentalist faith. Many of her listeners encouraged her to abandon her commitment to gospel music and switch from the church to the nightclub circuit. After hearing her sing in church, some of her relatives offered to teach her minstrel jazz tunes, and a jazz bandleader offered her $100 per week. Decca Records, based in Chicago, wanted her to sing the blues and offered her $5,000 to play at the Village Vanguard. In addition, she was offered as much as $25,000 per performance in Las Vegas clubs. She turned down all offers. Jackson knew that sacred gospels and secular blues flow from the same bedrock of experience, but she knew that there was a difference, too: "When you sing gospel you have a feeling there is a cure for what's wrong. But when

you are through with the blues, you've got nothing to rest on." Her first recording was through Decca in its Race Division, in 1937. However, the work sold poorly, and Decca did not record her again.

During the years surrounding World War II, Jackson was well known, but after the war, with breakthroughs in communication and another chance to record, she at last became know as a recording and performing artist. In 1946, she recorded four sides on the Apollo label, including "I'm Going to Wait Until My Change Comes," but these recordings sold poorly, too. Her next recording venture on Apollo, which brought gospel singing out of the storefront and basement congregations and onto the world's stage, was "Move On Up a Little Higher." Accompanied by James "Blind" Francis on organ and James Lee on piano, Jackson recorded the song in two parts. A minister and composer from Memphis, Rev. W. Herbert Brewster, composed the song, which was already a musical milestone, but it gained new life as a musical masterpiece after Jackson's recording. The recording, actually released in 1948, became the first gospel record to sell over a million copies (some sources estimate eight million), making gospel history and becoming a transitional landmark record for Jackson. The song made her commercially successful, and her career was launched. African American disc jockeys played her music; African American ministers praised it from their pulpits. When sales passed one million, the African American press hailed Jackson as "the only Negro whom Negroes have made famous." Few Euro-Americans had ever heard her. She had come to fame by singing only in African American communities. From the start, audiences acknowledged her, as did London's *New Statesman*, as "the most majestic voice of faith" of her generation.

The obvious sincerity of Jackson's faith and belief moved audiences even when they could not understand her lyrics. Her warm, uninhibited contralto voice carried a strong emotional message. Jackson's sound depended on the employment of the full range of expression of the human voice—from the rough growls employed by blues singers to the dark and rich sounds of a dramatic contralto; from the shouts and hollers of folk cries to the most lyrical, floating tones of which the voice is capable. This can all be heard in "Move On Up A Little Higher." She utilized to the fullest extent half tones, glissandi, blue notes, humming, and moaning. Her style also made use of a pronunciation that was almost of the academy in one instant and of the broadest southern cotton field dialect the next. Jackson's style employed a broad rhythmic freedom that accented her emotional lyric line to reinforce her musical virtuosity and spiritual genuineness.

Many of these vocal characteristics were exemplified in Jackson's other multimillion sellers such as "Upper

Room," "Didn't It Rain," "Even Me," and "Silent Night." Some of her earliest and best work, recorded originally at 78 rpm, was later reissued on LP and CD. On *Mahalia Jackson* (Grand Award 326), she sings "It's No Secret" and other songs that first gained her popularity in her own community. On *In the Upper Room* (Apollo 474), she performs "His Eye Is on the Sparrow" and, accompanied by a male quartet with a basso profundo, offers an unequaled version of the title song. She had many successes with Apollo Records. When one of her recordings, "I Can Put My Trust in Jesus," won the French Academy Award, Jackson consented to a European tour, though she was not convinced that foreign audiences would understand the sacred music of her people. In Paris, she had twenty-one curtain calls. She doubled the number of her originally scheduled performances when thousands were turned away from her concerts. Before a concert at Albert Hall, greetings came to her from Queen Elizabeth I and Winston Churchill. She gave a command performance before the king and queen of Denmark.

In 1954, Jackson left Apollo and joined the ranks of the highly successful Columbia Records. Signing with Columbia was a giant step for her and a commercially successful career move, launching her name internationally with the label's powerful marketing and distribution avenues. She eventually recorded some thirty albums (mostly for Columbia Records) during her career, a dozen of which went gold. However, in the opinion of many of Jackson's fans, the Columbia recordings were not done in the authentic Mahalia Jackson style. In gaining this international fame, she essentially became a "crossover" recording artist, and much of the criticism involved Jackson's selection of repertoire and musical arrangements. The repertoire featured more and more popular songs, including "You'll Never Walk Alone," "Danny Boy," and "Rusty Old Halo." Large choruses and mixed and male ensembles accompanied the recordings. A number of them even had full orchestras with strings. Though Jackson's voice was still outstanding, many of these Columbia recordings were not in the culturally accepted musical aesthetic vein of gospel music. To remedy the situation, Jackson tried to please both her popular and gospel audiences by creating a double music consciousness: one for her live performances and one for the recording studio sessions. It was important to her to be herself, not only for the sake of her own spirituality and wellbeing but also for her community—the people who had first contributed to her international fame. She had a strong commitment to community and actively worked for its betterment. Still, it was difficult to ignore the economic rewards that came along with not only being a wonderful performer but also being one of the few black women in the field of gospel to be recorded on a major label.

Beyond Music

Mahalia Jackson mobilized against gender and racial discrimination, embracing a wide range of social concerns. A "womanist" consciousness, one concerned with both racial and gender issues, was inherent in Jackson's activities. In fact, other black women in the gospel field, especially in the early and middle years of the twentieth century, had a clear understanding that race and gender issues were inextricably linked. Performers such as Lucie Campbell Williams, Roberta Martin, Sallie Martin, Sister Rosetta Tharpe, and Willie Mae Ford Smith all joined Mahalia Jackson's fight for racial and gender equity in their own ways. These members of the gospel world helped to create an invisible army of black women warriors whose goal it was to alleviate the triple oppression of race, sex, and class prejudice in the gospel world and the larger society.

In the growing racial tensions of the 1940s, 50s, and 60s, Jackson demonstrated a remarkable ability to cross boundaries of color on the sheer strength of her presence and the beauty and power of her voice. Her performances in and out of the church represented potentialities for action, and therefore for change, and had a significant effect on the basic creation and evolution of gospel music.

Despite male domination of one sort or another, Jackson controlled herself and her world through her creative expression, grassroots wit, and management style. In later years, she managed herself after she became suspicious of some managers and promoters and due to some bad experiences. However, several incidents concerning performance fees led some observers to tag her as suspicious of others and sometimes difficult to work with.

Jackson was also an entrepreneur and producer. She had her own CBS radio program and television show, which aired from 1954 to 1955. As host and star of the show, she helped to popularize traditional gospel, making the way for later gospel and soul singers. After attending beauty culture school, Jackson managed her own beauty and florist shop. She also owned a substantial amount of real estate. She appeared in movies such as *Imitation of Life*, *St. Louis Blues*, *The Best Man*, and *I Remember Chicago*. Three books were published about her life, *Movin' On Up* (1966), *Just Mahalia, Baby* (1975), and *Mahalia Jackson, Queen of Gospel* (1992).

For years, a Mahalia Jackson concert assured promoters of sellout crowds at Carnegie Hall in New York, where she was a favorite. In Madison Square Garden, she moved a packed house from tears to thunderous applause. At the 1958 Newport Jazz Festival, the jazz world came to Mahalia on her own terms. Thousands of jazz buffs gave her standing ovations, and when she closed with "The Lord's Prayer," the crowd stood breathless. During two days in 1960, Mahalia taped a show for the Voice of America and gave two sellout concerts at the hall of the Daughters of the American Revolution and one in Constitution Hall. She also appeared on many television shows, most notably the Ed Sullivan Show.

With the advent of the civil rights movement, Jackson yielded to the requests of Dr. Martin Luther King Jr. Alongside King, she supported the fight for equality by traveling and singing at fundraising rallies all over the United States. Mahalia Jackson encouraged the people with songs like "We Shall Overcome" and "If I Can Help Somebody." She also quietly slipped money to leaders who she believed were "for real." She emerged as one of the symbols for the movement when in 1963 millions of television viewers watched as she accompanied King at the famous March on Washington. Immediately before King began his "I Have a Dream" speech at the Lincoln Memorial, Mahalia sang "I Been 'Buked and I Been Scorned." With the lyrics of this traditional spiritual, she summed up the frustrations and aspirations of the entire movement.

An eighth grade dropout, Jackson was especially concerned about educating poor youth. She established the Mahalia Jackson Scholarship Fund and reportedly helped about fifty young adults to obtain college educations. Because of her humanitarian work, she received the Silver Dove Award "for work of quality, doing the most good for international understanding." She received her first Grammy Award in 1962 and received subsequent ones in 1963 and 1976. In 1972, Mahalia Jackson was honored with the Grammy Lifetime Achievement Award.

Jackson died of heart failure at the age of sixty. She was honored with funerals in Chicago and New Orleans and was finally entombed in Providence Memorial Park in Metairie, Louisiana. Jackson believed that she was "ordained to sing the gospel," but she did much more. She was an ambassador of goodwill wherever she traveled. People all over the world were attracted to her. Perhaps it was the simplicity of her ways; she said she was "just a good strong Louisiana woman who can cook rice so every grain stands by itself." Perhaps it was the explicit faith and conviction with which she delivered her messages in song. Jackson brought a wider acceptance and popularity to gospel music in the United States and around the world. Perhaps it was her musical virtuosity that mesmerized her audiences. She also helped make the gospel music industry a multimillion-dollar one and left her imprint on the African American sacred music culture. She achieved universality by living faithfully within the confines of a particular tradition in singing the songs of her people in her own style. Aretha Franklin ended the funeral service by singing for Jackson one of the songs by Thomas A. Dorsey that she loved so well, one that probably epitomized how Jackson had envisioned her transition: "Precious Lord, Take My Hand."

BIBILIOGRAPHY

Boyer, Horace Clarence. *How Sweet the Sound.* Washington, DC: Elliot and Clark, 1995.

Ellison, Ralph. "As the Spirit Moves Mahalia." *Saturday Review,* September 27, 1958.

Goreau, Laurraine. *Just Mahalia, Baby.* Waco, Texas: Word Books, 1975.

Favorites of Mahalia Jackson, the World's Greatest Gospel Singer. New York: Hill and Range Songs, 1955.

Heilbut, Tony. *The Gospel Sound.* New York: Limelight Editions, 1971.

Jackson, Mahalia. "I Can't Stop Singing." *Saturday Evening Post,* December 5, 1959.

Jackson, Mahalia, and Evan McLeod Wylie. *Movin' On Up.* New York: Hawthorne Books, 1966.

Levine, Lawrence W. "Mahalia Jackson." *Notable American Women: The Modern Period.* Cambridge, MA: Harvard University Press, 1980.

Pleasants, Henry, and Horace Boyer. "Mahalia Jackson." In *New Grove Dictionary of American Music.* London: Macmillan, 1986.

Schwerin, Jules. *Got to Tell It: Mahalia Jackson, Queen of Gospel.* New York: Oxford University Press, 1992.

Southern, Aileen. *Biographical Dictionary of Afro-American and African Musicians.* Westport, CT: Greenwood Press, 1982.

Williams-Jones, Pearl. "Mahalia Jackson." In *Notable Black American Women, Book I,* edited by Jessie Carney Smith. New York: Gale Research, 1996.

DISCOGRAPHY

Cooper, David Edwin. *International Bibliography of Discographies.* Littleton, CO: Libraries Unlimited, 1975.

—JOYCE MARIE JACKSON

JACKSON, NELL CECILIA (b. 1 July 1929; d. 1 April 1988), athlete. Nell Cecilia Jackson, one of the pioneers in women's track and field, was born in Athens, Georgia, to Dr. Burnette and Wilhemina Jackson. The second of three children, she spent most of her early life and college days in Tuskegee, Alabama, where her father was a dentist and her mother worked at the Veterans Administration Hospital. By the time Jackson was fourteen, she was a member of the Tuskegee Institute Track and Field Club, an avenue for talented young women in high school and college to gain entry to national meets. From then on, Nell Jackson's life revolved around track.

As a competitor, Jackson was an All-American sprinter and a member of the 1948 U.S. Olympic team. Even though she did not win a medal, she stated that "the Olympics were one of the greatest experience of my life. It's something I never would have traded for anything else." She competed in the first Pan-American games in 1951, placing second in the 200-meter relay and winning a gold medal as a member of the 400-meter relay team. In 1949 she set an American record time of 24.2 seconds for the 200-meter relay, a record that stood for six years.

Jackson received a bachelor's degree from Tuskegee Institute (now Tuskegee University) in 1951, a master's degree from Springfield College in 1953, and a PhD from the University of Iowa in 1962. She taught physical education and coached track at the Tuskegee Institute, Illinois State University, the University of Illinois, and Michigan State University. She was women's athletic director at Michigan State University and, at the time of her death in 1988, professor and director of athletics and physical education at the State University of New York at Binghamton. A renowned scholar, she wrote many track articles for periodicals and books, and she authored a definitive text, *Track and Field for Girls and Women*, published in 1968.

In addition to her collegiate experience, Jackson was coach of the U.S. women's track team at the 1956 Olympic games in Melbourne, Australia, the first black head track coach of an Olympic team and, at twenty-seven years old, one of the youngest head coaches of any sport. Nell Jackson was also head women's track coach at the 1972 Olympic games in Munich, Germany. In 1980 she was one of five Americans selected to attend the International Olympic Academy in Olympia, Greece. In 1987 she was manager of the U.S. women's track team that competed in the Pan-American games. She also conducted innumerable track workshops and clinics all over the United States.

As an official, Jackson served in many capacities. She was the first of two women to serve on the board of directors of the U.S. Olympic Committee, was a vice president and, at the time of her death, secretary of The Athletic Congress (TAC). She also served in varying committee assignments for the American Alliance for Health, Physical Education, Recreation, and Dance; the National Association for Girls and Women in Sports (NAGWS); and the National Collegiate Athletic Association.

Through the years, Nell Jackson received many honors. She was inducted into the Black Athletes Hall of Fame and received the Honor Award twice for her track contributions to NAGWS. Tuskegee Institute honored her three times, the last time with its Outstanding Alumni Award. The University of Iowa also recognized her with its Alumni Merit Award.

Nell Jackson epitomized loyalty, honesty, dedication, and excellence. Her untimely death from the flu at the age of fifty-nine occurred in Binghamton, New York. She was survived by two brothers, Dr. Burnette L. Jackson Jr., and Thomas P. Jackson, both of Philadelphia. Posthumously, on 1 December 1989, Nell Jackson was inducted into TAC's National Track and Field Hall of Fame and was awarded its highest honor, the Robert Giegengack Award, given for outstanding leadership and contributions in track and field.

Since her death, several honors have been awarded in Jackson's name. Beginning in 2000 the National Association of Collegiate Women Athletic Administrators (NACWAA) bestowed the Nell Jackson Award upon "an athletic administrator who exemplifies the personal qualities and professional accomplishments of Dr. Nell Jackson." Each year the National Association for Girls and Women in Sport has given the Nell Jackson Award to an outstanding performer in track and field.

BIBLIOGRAPHY

Ashe, Arthur R. Jr. *A Hard Road to Glory: A History of the African-American Athlete since 1946*. New York: Warner Books, 1988.

Bortstein, Larry. *After Olympic Glory*. New York: Friedrick Warne and Co., 1978.

Davenport, Joanna. "The Lady Was a Sprinter." Conference paper, American Alliance for Health, Physical Education, Recreation, and Dance. Atlanta, GA: 19 April 1985.

Green, Tina Sloan et al. *Black Women in Sports*. Reston, VA: AAHPERD Publications, 1981.

Jackson, Nell C. *Track and Field for Girls and Women*. Minneapolis, MN: Burgess Publishing, 1968.

Funeral program. Tuskegee, Alabama, 9 April 1988.

—JOANNA DAVENPORT

JACKSON, REBECCA COX (b. 1795; d.1871), religious leader and writer. Rebecca Cox Jackson was a charismatic itinerant preacher, the founder of a religious communal family in Philadelphia, and a religious visionary writer. Though an important example of black female religious leadership and spirituality in the nineteenth century, she was virtually unknown after her death until the rediscovery and publication of her manuscript writings in 1981.

Jackson was born into a free black family in Horntown, Pennsylvania, near Philadelphia. She lived at different times in her childhood with her maternal grandmother and with her mother, Jane Cox (who died when Rebecca was thirteen). In 1830 she was married (to Samuel S. Jackson), but apparently childless, and living with her husband in the household of her older brother, Joseph Cox, a tanner and local preacher of the Bethel African Methodist Episcopal (AME) Church in Philadelphia. Jackson cared for her brother's four children while earning her own living as a seamstress.

As a result of the powerful religious awakening experience in a thunderstorm in 1830, the incident that opens her autobiography, Jackson became active in the early Holiness movement. She moved from leadership of praying bands to public preaching, stirring up controversy within AME church circles not only as a woman preacher, but also because she had received the revelation that celibacy was necessary for a holy life. She criticized the churches, including the AME church and its leaders, for "carnality." Jackson insisted on being guided entirely by the dictates of her inner voice, and this ultimately led to her separation from husband, brother, and church.

After a period of itinerant preaching in the later 1830s and early 1840s, Jackson joined the United Society of Believers in Christ's Second Appearing (the Shakers), at Watervliet, New York. She was attracted by the Shakers' religious celibacy, their emphasis on spiritualistic experience, and their dual-gender concept of deity. With her younger disciple and lifelong companion, Rebecca Perot, Rebecca Jackson lived at Watervliet from June 1847 until July 1851. However, she was increasingly disappointed in the predominantly white Shaker community's failure to take the gospel of their founder, Ann Lee, to the African American community.

Jackson left Watervliet in 1851, on an unauthorized mission to Philadelphia, where she and Perot experimented with seance-style spiritualism. In 1857 she and Perot returned to Watervliet for a brief second residence, and at this time Jackson won the right to found and head a new Shaker "outfamily" in Philadelphia. This predominantly black and female Shaker family survived her death in 1871 by at least a quarter of a century.

Rebecca Jackson's major legacy is her remarkable spiritual autobiography, *Gifts of Power*, which describes her spiritual journey as a woman with a divine calling. Jackson records in vivid detail a wide variety of visionary experiences, including mysterious prophetic dreams and supernatural gifts. Her visionary writing has received recognition as spiritual literature of great power. Alice Walker has described Jackson's autobiography as "an extraordinary document" which "tells us much about the spirituality of human beings, especially of the interior spiritual resources of our mothers." In her review of Jackson's writings, however, Walker questioned the editor's speculation that Jackson's relationship with Perot, in the modern age, might have been understood as lesbian. In this context, Walker first coined the term "womanism" to distinguish a specifically black feminist cultural tradition that includes women's love for other women but is not separatist.

BIBLIOGRAPHY

Braxton, Joanne. *Black Women Writing Autobiography: A Tradition within a Tradition*. Philadelphia: Temple University Press, 1989.

Hull, Gloria T. "Rebecca Cox Jackson and the Uses of Power." *Tulsa Studies in Women's Literature* 1.2 (Fall 1982): 203–209.

Humez, Jean McMahon. *Gifts of Power: The Writings of Rebecca Cox Jackson, Black Visionary, Shaker Eldress*. Amherst: University of Massachusetts Press, 1981.

Humez, Jean McMahon. "Visionary Experience and Power: The Career of Rebecca Cox Jackson." In *Black Apostles at Home and Abroad*, edited by David M. Wills and Richard Newman. Boston: G. K. Hall, 1982.

McKay, Nellie Y. "Nineteenth-Century Black Women's Spiritual Autobiographies: Religious Faith and Self-Empowerment." In *Interpreting Women's Lives: Feminist Theory and Personal Narratives*, edited by Personal Narratives Group. Bloomington: Indiana University Press, 1989.

Sanders, Cheryl J., Katie G. Cannon, Emilie M. Townes, M. Shawn Copeland, bell hooks, and Cheryl Townsend Gilkes. "Roundtable Discussion: Christian Ethics and Theology in Womanist Perspective." *Journal of Feminist Studies in Religion* 5.2 (1989): 83–112.

Sasson, Diane. "Life as Vision: The Autobiography of Mother Rebecca Jackson." In *The Shaker Spiritual Narrative*, ed. Sarah D. Sasson. Knoxville: University of Tennessee Press, 1983.

Walker, Alice. "Gifts of Power: The Writings of Rebecca Cox Jackson." In *In Search of Our Mothers' Gardens: Womanist Prose*. San Diego: Harcourt Brace Jovanovich, 1983.

Williams, Richard E. *Called and Chosen: The Story of Mother Rebecca Jackson and the Philadelphia Shakers*. Metuchen, N. J.: Scarecrow Press, 1981.

ARCHIVAL SOURCES

Jackson's manuscripts are in the Shaker collections of the Western Reserve Historical Society, Cleveland, Ohio; the Library of Congress; and the Berkshire Athenaeum, Pittsfield, Massachusetts.

—JEAN MCMAHON HUMEZ

JACKSON, SHIRLEY ANN (b. 5 August 1946), scientist and educator. At the young age of twenty-six, Shirley Ann Jackson became not only the first African American woman to receive a PhD from Massachusetts Institute of Technology (MIT), but also one of the first two women to receive a degree in theoretical physics from any university in the United States. In 1995, Jackson became both the first African American and first woman appointed to head the Nuclear Regulatory Commission, which oversees nuclear power plants in the United States. Additionally, in 1999, Jackson became the first African American president of Rensselaer Polytechnic Institute (RPI) in New York, the oldest university in the United States dedicated to research in science and engineering.

The second daughter of George and Beatrice Jackson, Jackson was born in Washington, DC. She benefited greatly from the strong foundation her parents provided. Her mother Beatrice, a social worker, regularly read to her, often choosing the biography of the African American scientist and mathematician Benjamin Banneker. Jackson's father George, a postal supervisor, eagerly helped her build science fair projects. Her scientific interests found expression in her childhood hobby of collecting live bumblebees, wasps, and hornets in old mayonnaise jars and recording notes on their behavioral changes.

Jackson attended Roosevelt High School, excelling in advanced mathematics, biology, and chemistry classes. She graduated valedictorian of her senior class in 1964, receiving an academic scholarship to MIT to pursue her undergraduate degree. She was one of only fifteen African Americans to enroll and one of forty or so women in an entering class of nine hundred students. As she successfully progressed in her studies, she endured continuous isolation, working through repeated incidents of

SHIRLEY ANN JACKSON was the first African American woman to receive a PhD from Massachusetts Institute of Technology, and one of the first two women to receive a degree in theoretical physics from any university in the United States. (Courtesy of Fermi National Accelerator Laboratory.)

racism. On one occasion she was confronted by a group of white men shouting racial slurs at her, and one of the men spit in her face. A professor felt it necessary to remind her that "colored girls should pursue a trade." Jackson was also excluded from study groups held by her white peers.

Despite working within the boundaries imposed by such harsh racism, she remained committed to her educational success. She received her bachelor of science in Physics from MIT in 1968 and remained at the university to pursue her graduate studies, largely because she felt privileged to work with James Young, MIT's first African American tenured physics professor. In remaining at MIT, she committed herself to drawing more minorities to the school, helping to found the Black Student Union. While still a student, Jackson also demonstrated her commitment to the broader community in which she lived by

volunteering at Boston City Hospital and tutoring at the Roxbury YMCA.

Following completion of her doctorate, Jackson became a research associate at Fermi National Accelerator Laboratory in Illinois. She later expanded her research internationally, serving as a visiting scientist at the European Center for Nuclear Research in Switzerland, where she studied theories of strongly interacting particles. In 1976 Jackson joined the Theoretical Physics Research Lab at AT&T Bell Laboratories, helping to develop new advances in telecommunications. Here she met her husband, a fellow physicist, Morris Washington, with whom she had a son, Alan. After close to sixteen years of intense research, Jackson was appointed professor in the Department of Physics at Rutgers University. During her career she has published close to one hundred scientific papers and abstracts.

Jackson's numerous contributions to the field of physics have resulted in countless awards and honors. In 1986 she was elected as a Fellow of the American Physical Society in recognition of her contribution to scientific research. In 1998 she was inducted into the National Women's Hall of Fame in Seneca Falls, New York, for her contributions as a distinguished scientist as well as a committed advocate of education, science, and public policy.

Jackson was also a staunch supporter of promoting scientific education. She has served on committees for the National Science Foundation, National Academy of Sciences, and the American Association for the Advancement of Science. In 2004 she was a member of the governing board of the American Institute of Physics. She was also a member of the board of trustees at MIT, where, in light of her own struggles and achievements at the school, she played a key role on task forces aimed at promoting science and technology education for minorities and improving science education for all students.

Jackson's accomplishments serve as a testimony to her commitment to education. Having emerged as a success in a field dominated by white males, Jackson remained an inspiration for minorities seeking a career in science.

BIBLIOGRAPHY

"Dr. Shirley Ann Jackson." National Women's History Project. http://www.nwhp.org/tlp/biographies/jackson/jackson_bio.html.

Medea, Andra. "Shirley Ann Jackson." In *Facts on File Encyclopedia of Black Women in America*, edited by Darlene Clark Hine. New York: Facts on File, 1997.

Schrof, Joanie M. "Her Brilliant Career: Shirley Ann Jackson Has Succeeded at Everything She's Ever Tried, but Can She Get RPI Back on Track?" ASEE Prism Online. http://www.asee.org/prism/nov99/html/profile.htm.

"Shirley Ann Jackson." American Association for the Advancement of Science. http://www.aaas.org/ScienceTalk/jackson.shtml.

Sullivan, Otha R., and Jim Haskins, eds. *Black Stars: African American Women Scientists and Inventors*. New York: Wiley, 2002.

—SOWANDE' MUSTAKEEM

JACOBS, HARRIET ANN (b. 1813; d. March 1897), author and abolitionist. Harriet Ann Jacobs is now known as the author of *Incidents in the Life of a Slave Girl: Written by Herself* (1861), the most important slave narrative by an African American woman. Jacobs is also important because of the role she played as a relief worker among black Civil War refugees in Alexandria, Virginia, and Savannah, Georgia. Throughout most of the twentieth century, Jacobs's autobiography was thought to be a novel by a white writer, and her relief work was unknown. With the 1987 publication of an annotated edition of her

INCIDENTS IN THE LIFE OF A SLAVE GIRL, 1861, title page. This work by Harriet Jacobs is among the most important slave narratives of African Americans. She was identified as its author in 1987, when an annotated edition was published. (University of North Carolina.)

INCIDENTS

IN THE

LIFE OF A SLAVE GIRL.

WRITTEN BY HERSELF.

"Northerners know nothing at all about Slavery. They think it is perpetual bondage only. They have no conception of the depth of *degradation* involved in that word, SLAVERY; if they had, they would never cease their efforts until so horrible a system was overthrown."

A WOMAN OF NORTH CAROLINA.

"Rise up, ye women that are at ease! Hear my voice, ye careless daughters! Give ear unto my speech."

ISAIAH xxxii. 9.

EDITED BY L. MARIA CHILD.

BOSTON:
PUBLISHED FOR THE AUTHOR.
1861.

book, however, Jacobs became established as the author of the most comprehensive antebellum autobiography by an African American woman.

Harriet Ann Jacobs was born into slavery in Edenton, North Carolina. Her mother, Delilah, was the daughter of the slave Molly Horniblow and was owned by her mistress Margaret Horniblow; her father, Elijah, a skilled carpenter, was the slave of Dr. Andrew Knox and probably a son of the white Henry Jacobs. *Incidents* is Jacobs's account of a slave woman's sexual oppression and of her struggle for freedom. Written in the first person by Jacobs's pseudonymous narrator "Linda Brent," the book is a remarkably accurate (although incomplete) rendering of Jacobs's life up to her 1852 emancipation. It describes her life as a slave and fugitive in the South and as a fugitive in the North. In this narrative, Jacobs's Linda Brent credits her family, and especially her grandmother (who had gained her freedom and established a bakery in the town), with sustaining her and her younger brother, John S. Jacobs, in their youthful efforts to achieve a sense of selfhood despite their slave status.

When Jacobs was six years old, her mother died, and she was taken into the home of her mistress, who taught her to sew and to read, skills she later used to support herself and to protest against slavery. But when in 1825 Jacobs's mistress died, the slave girl was not freed, as she had expected. Instead, her mistress's will bequeathed her, along with a "bureau & work table & their contents," to a three-year-old niece, and Jacobs was sent to live in the Edenton home of the little girl's father, Dr. James Norcom ("Dr. Flint" in *Incidents*). As the slave girl approached adolescence, the middle-aged Norcom subjected her to unrelenting sexual harassment and, when she was sixteen, threatened her with concubinage. To stop him, Jacobs became sexually involved with a neighboring white attorney, young Samuel Tredwell Sawyer ("Mr. Sands"). Their alliance produced two children: Joseph (c. 1829–?), called "Benny," and Louisa Matilda (1833–1917), called "little Ellen" in the narrative. When Jacobs was twenty-one, Norcom said if she did not agree to become his concubine, he would send her out to one of his plantations. Jacobs again rejected his sexual demands and was sent out out to the country. When she learned that Norcom also planned to make her children plantation slaves, she feared that they would never be free and decided to act.

In June 1835 Jacobs escaped. She reasoned that if she was missing, Norcom would be willing to sell her and the children, and that their father would buy and free them all. Young Joseph and little Louisa were indeed bought by Sawyer, who permitted them to continue living in town with Jacobs's grandmother. Jacobs was hidden by neighbors, both black and white, but with Norcom searching for her, she was unable to escape from Edenton. As the

$100 REWARD

WILL be given for the apprehension and delivery of my Servant Girl HARRIET. She is a light mulatto, 21 years of age, about 5 feet 4 inches high, of a thick and corpulent habit, having on her head a thick covering of black hair that curls naturally, but which can be easily combed straight. She speaks easily and fluently, and has an agreeable carriage and address. Being a good seamstress, she has been accustomed to dress well, has a variety of very fine clothes, made in the prevailing fashion, and will probably appear, if abroad, tricked out in gay and fashionable finery. As this girl absconded from the plantation of my son without any known cause or provocation, it is probable she designs to transport herself to the North.

The above reward, with all reasonable charges, will be given for apprehending her, or securing her in any prison or jail within the U. States.

All persons are hereby forewarned against harboring or entertaining her, or being in any way instrumental in her escape, under the most rigorous penalties of the law.

JAMES NORCOM.

Edenton, N. C. June 30   sva3w

"$100 REWARD." This advertisement for the capture of Harriet Jacobs appeared in a daily newspaper, the *American Beacon* of Norfolk, Virginia, on 4 July 1835. It ran on alternate days for two weeks. (North Carolina State Archives.)

summer wore on, her uncle built her a hiding place in a tiny crawlspace above a porch in her grandmother's home. For almost seven years, Jacobs hid in this space, which, she wrote, measured seven feet wide, nine feet long, and—at its tallest—three feet high.

Finally, in 1842, she escaped and was reunited with her children, who had been sent north. In New York City, Jacobs found work as a domestic in the family of the litterateur Nathaniel Parker Willis. In 1849 she moved to Rochester to join her brother, who had also become a fugitive from slavery. John S. Jacobs was now an antislavery lecturer and activist, and through him, Harriet Jacobs became part of the Rochester abolitionist circle around Frederick Douglass's newspaper, the *North Star*.

After passage of the 1850 Fugitive Slave Law, she left Rochester for New York City, where her North Carolina masters tried to seize her and her children on the streets of Manhattan and Brooklyn. Determined not to be sent back into slavery or to bow to the slave system by permitting herself to be bought, Jacobs fled to Massachusetts. In 1852, however, without her knowledge, Cornelia Grinnell Willis arranged for her and her children to be bought from Norcom's family. Jacobs and her children were free.

Amid conflicting emotions—determination to aid the antislavery cause, humiliation at being purchased, and a deep impulse perhaps prompted by the death of her beloved grandmother in Edenton—Jacobs decided to make public the story of her struggle against her sexual abuse in slavery. A few years earlier, she had whispered her history to Amy Post, her Rochester Quaker abolitionist-feminist friend, and Post had urged her to write a book informing northern women about the sexual abuse of female slaves. Now Jacobs was ready. Harriet Beecher Stowe's newly published *Uncle Tom's Cabin* (1852) had become a runaway best seller, and Jacobs's first thought was to try to enlist Stowe to write her story. When she learned that Stowe wanted to incorporate her life story into *The Key to Uncle Tom's Cabin* (1853), however, Jacobs decided instead to write her life herself. After practicing her writing skills in letters she sent to the *New York Tribune*, she began her book. Five years later, it was finished. Soliciting letters of introduction to British abolitionists from Boston antislavery leaders, Jacobs sailed to England to sell her manuscript to a publisher. She returned home unsuccessful. Finally, with the help of the African American abolitionist William C. Nell and the white abolitionist Lydia Maria Child, Jacobs brought the book out herself. Early in 1861, *Incidents in the Life of a Slave Girl: Written by Herself* was published by the author, with an introduction by L. Maria Child, who was identified as the editor on the title page.

Although Jacobs's authorship was later forgotten, she was from the first identified as "Linda Brent." Reviewed in the abolitionist and African American press, *Incidents* made Jacobs a minor celebrity among its audience of antislavery women. Within months, however, the nation was at war, and in the crisis Jacobs launched a second public career. Using her new celebrity as an author, she approached Northern antislavery women for money and supplies for the "contrabands"—black refugees crowding behind the Union lines in Washington, DC, and Alexandria, Virginia (which had been occupied by the army). With the support of Quaker groups and of the newly formed New England Freedmen's Aid Society, in 1863 Harriet Jacobs and her daughter Louisa went to Alexandria. There they provided emergency health care and established the Jacobs Free School, a black-owned and black-taught institution for the children of the refugees.

Throughout the war years, Jacobs and her daughter functioned as war correspondents, reporting on their Southern relief efforts in the Northern press and in England, where in 1862 her book had been published as *The Deeper Wrong: Incidents in the Life of a Slave Girl, Written by Herself*. In May 1864 Jacobs was named a member of the executive committee of the Women's National Loyal League, an antislavery feminist group mounting a mass petition campaign to urge Congress to pass a constitutional amendment ending chattel slavery. In July 1865 the mother-daughter team left Alexandria, and in 1866 they moved to Savannah, where they again worked to provide educational and medical facilities for the freedpeople. The following year, Jacobs's daughter Louisa joined Susan B. Anthony and Charles Lenox Remond to campaign in upstate New York for the Equal Rights Association—a group of radical feminists and abolitionists who worked for the inclusion of the enfranchisement of African Americans and women in the revised New York State Constitution.

In 1868 Harriet and Louisa Jacobs went to London to raise money for an orphanage and home for the aged in the black Savannah community. Aided by British supporters of Garrisonian abolitionism, they raised £100 sterling for the Savannah project. Despite their success, however, they recommended to their New York Quaker sponsors that the building not be built. The Ku Klux Klan was riding and burning; it would not tolerate the establishment of new black institutions.

In the face of the increasing violence in the South, Jacobs and her daughter retreated to Massachusetts. In Boston, Jacobs was briefly employed as clerk of the fledgling New England Women's Club, perhaps with the patronage of her old employer and friend Cornelia Grinnell Willis and her New England Freedmen's Aid Society colleague Ednah Dow Cheney, both club members. As the new decade began, Jacobs settled in Cambridge, where for several years she ran a boardinghouse for Harvard students and faculty.

When Jacobs, with her daughter Louisa, later moved to Washington, DC, she continued to work among the destitute freedpeople, and Louisa was employed first in the newly established "colored schools," then at Howard University. They did not return south, and in 1892, Jacobs sold her grandmother's house and lot in Edenton, property that her family had managed to arrange for her to inherit despite her earlier status as a fugitive. When in 1896 the National Association of Colored Women held organizing meetings in Washington, DC, Louisa Jacobs apparently attended. The following spring, Harriet Jacobs died at her Washington home. She is buried in the Mount Auburn Cemetery, Cambridge, Massachusetts.

Harriet Jacobs's life spanned her experiences before the Civil War as a slave in the South, as a fugitive in the South and in the North, and as an abolitionist activist and slave narrator in the North. She served as a relief worker among black refugees in the South during the Civil War and Reconstruction and as a war correspondent, commenting on their condition. Later she was involved as an adjunct to the post–Civil War club movement among white women, and she witnessed the birth of the black women's club movement. No other woman is known to have possessed this range of experience and to have written about it.

BIBLIOGRAPHY

Andrews, William L. "The Changing Moral Discourse of Nineteenth-Century African American Women's Autobiography: Harriet Jacobs and Elizabeth Keckley." In *De/Colonizing the Subject: The Politics of Gender in Women's Autobiography*, edited by Sidonie Smith and Julia Watson. Minneapolis: University of Minnesota Press, 1992.

Braxton, Joanne M., and Sharon Zuber, "Silences in Harriet 'Linda Brent' Jacobs's *Incidents in the Life of a Slave Girl*." In *Listening to Silences: New Essays in Feminist Criticism*, edited by Elaine Hedges and Shelley Fisher Fishkin. New York: Oxford University Press, 1994.

Carby, Hazel. *Reconstructing Womanhood: The Emergence of the Afro-American Woman Novelist*. New York: Oxford University Press, 1987.

Doriani, Beth Maclay. "Black Womanhood in Nineteenth-Century America: Subversion and Self-Construction in Two Women's Autobiographies." *American Quarterly* 43.2 (June 1991).

Fleischner, Jennifer. *Mastering Slavery: Memory, Family, and Identity in Women's Slave Narratives*. New York: New York University Press, 1996.

Foreman, P. Gabrielle. "The Spoken and the Silenced in *Incidents in the Life of a Slave Girl* and *Our Nig*." *Callaloo* 13.2 (Spring 1990).

Foster, Frances Smith. *Written by Herself: Literary Productions by African American Women, 1746–1892*. Bloomington: Indiana University Press, 1993.

Garfield, Deborah M., and Rafia Zafar, eds. *Harriet Jacobs and "Incidents in the Life of a Slave Girl": New Critical Essays*. New York: Cambridge University Press, 1996.

Jacobs, Harriet. *Incidents in the Life of a Slave Girl: Written by Herself* (1861). Edited by Jean Fagan Yellin. Cambridge, MA: Harvard University Press, 1987.

Kaplan, Carla. "Recuperating Agents: Narrative Contracts, Emancipatory Readers, and *Incidents in the Life of a Slave Girl*." In *Provoking Agents: Gender and Agency in Theory and Practice*, edited by Judith Kegan Gardiner. Urbana: University of Illinois Press, 1995.

McKay, Nellie Y. "The Girls Who Became the Women: Childhood Memories in the Autobiographies of Harriet Jacobs, Mary Church Terrell, and Anne Moody." In *Tradition and the Talents of Women*, edited by Florence Howe. Urbana: University of Illinois Press, 1991.

Mullen, Harryette, "Runaway Tongue: Resistant Orality in Uncle Tom's Cabin, Our Nig, Incidents in the Life of a Slave Girl, and Beloved." In *The Culture of Sentiment: Race, Gender, and Sentimentality in Nineteenth-Century America*, edited by Shirley Samuels. New York: Oxford University Press, 1992.

Painter, Nell Irvin. "Three Southern Women and Freud: A Non-Exceptionalist Approach to Race, Class, and Gender in the Slave South." In *Feminists Revision History*, edited by Ann-Louise Shapiro. New Brunswick, NJ: Rutgers University Press, 1994.

Smith, Valerie. *Self-Discovery and Authority in Afro-American Narrative*. Cambridge, MA: Harvard University Press, 1987.

Warner, Anne Bradford. "Santa Claus Ain't a Real Man: *Incidents* and Gender." In *Haunted Bodies: Gender and Southern Texts*, edited by Anne Goodwyn Jones and Susan V. Donaldson. Charlottesville: University of Virginia Press, 1997.

Yellin, Jean Fagan. *Harriet Jacobs: A Life*. New York: Basic Civitas, 2004.

MANUSCRIPT COLLECTIONS

Manuscript sources on Harriet Jacobs can be found at the Boston Public Library; the Sydney Howard Gay papers, Rare Book and Manuscript Library, Columbia University Libraries, New York; the Julia Wilbur papers, Quaker Collection, Haverford College Library, Haverford, MA; the Massachusetts Historical Society, Boston; the Norcom Family papers, North Carolina State Archives, Raleigh; the Isaac and Amy Post Family papers, Department of Rare Books and Special Collections, Rush Rhees Library, University of Rochester, Rochester, NY; Schlesinger Library, Radcliffe College, Cambridge, MA; and the Sophia Smith Collection, Smith College, Northampton, MA.

—JEAN FAGAN YELLIN

JAMES, ETTA (b. 25 January 1938), singer. Etta James is one of the most important voices of rhythm and blues music; her life and performances offer insight into unacknowledged traditions and a feminist consciousness among the poor in African American communities long before that political ideology became fashionable.

Etta James was born Jamesetta Hawkins in Los Angeles, California. Her name combined those of her uncle and aunt, James and Cozetta. Her early family life was as rich as it was varied. She herself describes her experience as consisting of "two mothers, two childhoods," "in two different cities." Her mother, Dorothy Hawkins, was African American, and the identity of her father is not clear. In her autobiography *Rage to Survive*, James describes the world that led her to become two people: First Jamesetta, and then Etta. Her early life, by any estimate, was turbulent and troubled. There were mysteries and questions surrounding her birth and the identity of her father, whom some say was the famous pool player "Minnesota Fats." She had a complex relationship with her mother, whom she called Dorothy, or "the Mystery Lady." Dorothy Hawkins was Miss Hip, a jazz chick, a "let the good-times roller." James, as a very young child, faced difficulties that many adults would not have been able to handle. Early on, however, a strong will to survive surfaced as she was forced to develop mechanisms for dealing with the traumatic issues of color, personal pain, disappointment, and loneliness that faced so many African Americans of that era.

In the early 1940s Jamesetta Hawkins was given to Lula and Jesse Rogers, whom she would call Mama and Daddy from then on, and it was Lula Rogers who introduced the young Hawkins to the spiritual community of St. Paul's

Baptist Church on Naomi and Twenty-first Street in Los Angeles. St Paul's Choir, at the time called "The Echoes of Eden," was directed by Professor James Earle Hines, who was to become Hawkins's first musical mentor. During this stage of her life she would hear some of the greatest gospel stars of all time perform at St. Paul's, including Sister Rosetta Tharpe and the Sallie Martin Singers. This was the place that would have the greatest influence on her musical career.

At the age of five, Jamesetta began singing under the tutelage of Professor Hines as a member of "The Echoes of Eden." As she states in her autobiography, she knew immediately that she wanted to develop that "go-tell-it-on-the-mountain, glass shattering force, and a hell-to-heaven vocal range" that was the classic gospel sound of the day. It was this sense of musical clarity that may well have earned her the title of child prodigy. This was also one of the most rewarding periods of her musical life. Recognizing her enormous talent and potential, "Mama" Rogers arranged for Hawkins to begin vocal and piano lessons with Professor Hines every Tuesday. While she has admitted to not practicing as much as she should have, she also acknowledged that she always remembered the confidence that Hines so skillfully instilled in her as a lifelong gift of incalculable value.

By the late 1940s Joe Adams, the deejay know as the "Mayor of Melody," was broadcasting live services from St. Paul's every Sunday morning on KOWL. Through these broadcasts the word got out that there was an extraordinary young girl in the choir whose vocal power and range rivaled those of a grown woman. Jamesetta Hawkins became famous overnight. It is rumored that film stars such as Orson Welles, Lana Turner, and Robert Mitchum would sneak into the back of the church to listen to this young prodigy. As her popularity continued to grow, so too did "Daddy" Rogers's recognition of her economic potential. After several failed attempts to extort more money from the minister and the church, "Daddy" Rogers moved young Hawkins to another church. Bitterly disappointed in having to leave the warm and affirming environment of St. Paul's, Hawkins never sang in church again.

During this period, young Hawkins was listening to the music of the day. For all of its variety, music in the African American community found its richest sustenance in the feelings, experiences, fears, dreams, acquaintances, and idiosyncrasies of its musicians. These experiences would fill the bag of musical materials that Jamesetta Hawkins would use to fashion her career. She began to sing professionally at the age of fifteen, forming a singing group, "The Creolettes," which consisted of Hawkins and two other young women from the projects who imitated the rhythm and blues groups of the time.

ETTA JAMES, onstage with Chuck Berry, 1987. She began her career as a singer at age fourteen and became one of the most important performers of rhythm and blues. (Photofest.)

After hearing them once, Johnny Otis signed the group to a recording contract, changed their name to "The Peaches," and took them on tour with his band. He changed Jamesetta Hawkins's name as well; she would now be known as Etta James.

Fame was not long in coming. James's first recording, "Roll with Me Henry" (1954), was an answer song to Hank Ballard's "Work with Me Annie." It was originally banned by radio stations because of its spicy content. However, the record became a hit and was re-released in 1955 by Modern and King records, who held the publishing rights, under the title "Wallflower." James had no qualms about writing the song. She felt that if Hank Ballad could say "Work with me Annie," she could say "Roll with Me Henry." Even at this young age, her feminist leanings were becoming apparent, before she even knew what a feminist was. But she had her first experience of musical appropriation when the Georgia Gibbs cover of "Dance with Me Henry" sold millions.

In the mid-to-late 1950s, James was one of the most popular singers in rhythm and blues, behind only Dinah Washington and Ruth Brown in her number of hit records. Although she was nominally a blues shouter, her gospel-influenced voice was also by turns sweet, pouting, or gruff. Among her hit records, many of which were recorded for Chicago's Chess Records, were "Good Rockin' Daddy" (1955), "W-O-M-A-N" (1955), "How Big a Fool" (1958), "All I Could Do was Cry" (1960), "Stop the Wedding" (1962), "Pushover" (1963), and "Something's Got a Hold On Me" (1964). James toured with Little Richard, James Brown, Little Willie John, and the man who had a huge impact on her professional career, Johnny Guitar Watson.

Heroin addiction forced James to quit recording in the late 1960s. She eventually entered a rehabilitation program that culminated in a triumphant return to the music industry in 1973 with the album *Etta James*, which earned one of James's six Grammy Award nominations. She then recorded numerous albums, including *Come a Little Closer* (1974), *Etta is Betta than Evvah* (1976), *Deep in the Night* with Eddie "Clean Head" Vinson (1986), *Seven Year Itch* (1988), and *Stickin' to My Guns* (1990). Nonetheless, her pioneering role as a rhythm and blues singer was often overlooked until the 1990s. In 1990 she won the NAACP Image Award and in 1993 she was inducted into the Rock and Roll Hall of Fame.

In spite of her honors, James did not behave like a musician emeritus. In 1990 she recorded *Sticking to My Guns*, following it with both *Mystery Lady: Songs of Billie Holiday*, for which she won a Grammy Award, and *Etta James Live From San Francisco* in 1994. Her autobiography, *Rage to Survive*, was published in 1995. In 1998 she had a huge success with the album *Life, Love and the Blues*. James had to stop touring for a time because of health problems but, after losing two hundred pounds, made a triumphant return tour in 2003. In the meantime, she recorded *Burnin' Down the House* (2002) and *Let's Roll* (2003). She was awarded the Grammy Lifetime Achievement Award in 2003.

From her musical roots in the Black gospel tradition Etta James forged a career that has spanned fifty years. She is as comfortable with the gospel music she used to sing in church choir as she is with rhythm and blues, jazz, rock 'n' roll, ballads, and contemporary sounds. Critics have had a hard time defining her style, but there can be no doubt that the power, honesty, and sexual double entendres of her music evoke reminiscences of Trixie Smith and Victoria Spivey, the great classic blues singers of the 1920s.

BIBLIOGRAPHY

Hess, Norbert. "Living Blues Interview: Etta James." *Living Blues* 54, 1982.

Hoare, Ian, ed. *The Soul Book*. London: E. Methuen, 1975.

James, Etta, and David Ritz. *Rage to Survive: The Etta James Story*. New York: Da Capo Press, 1998.

Kinnon, Joy Bennett. "At Last! Etta James Loses 200 Pounds and Finds a New Zest for Life." *Ebony*, September 2003.

Shaw, Arnold. *The World of Soul*. New York: Cowles Book Co., 1971.

—ROBERT W. STEPHENS

JAMISON, JUDITH (b. 10 May 1943), dancer, choreographer. Judith Jamison has spent most of her life perfecting her craft. As a dancer, choreographer, teacher, and artistic director of the internationally renowned Alvin Ailey American Dance Theater, Jamison has attempted to foster an appreciation for modern American dance and African American cultural expression in both her audiences and her students. She stresses the universality of dance and its ability to promote cross-cultural understanding through the expression of human experiences. "When you come to the theater," Jamison says, "you open your head and your heart and your mind because we are there to transform you. I'm a human being who has seen the world, so I'm giving you that perspective."

Jamison, the younger of two children, was born in Philadelphia. Her parents instilled in her a passion for the arts. As a young child, Jamison studied piano and violin before shifting her focus to dance. At age six, Jamison began her training at Marion Cuyjet's Judimar School of Dance. Here she worked with some of the most respected choreographers in the field, including Anthony Tudor and Maria Swoboda. Although her primary area of concentration was classical ballet, Jamison also studied tap, jazz, Afro-Caribbean dance, and acrobatics. At the age of fifteen, the young dancer made her debut in a production of *Giselle*.

After graduating from high school, Jamison spent a year as a psychology major at Fisk University before deciding to trade in her books for dance shoes. After leaving Fisk, she enrolled in the Philadelphia Dance Academy. In 1964 Jamison made her professional debut with the American Ballet Theatre in Agnes DeMille's *The Four Marys*. One year later, Jamison accepted an offer to join the Alvin Ailey American Dance Theater. She served as principle dancer for the company for fifteen years, during which time she earned a reputation for her passionate

JUDITH JAMISON, artistic director of the Alvin Ailey American Dance Theater. Jamison, a dancer, choreographer, and teacher, also established her own company, the Jamison Project, in 1987. (Dance Theater Foundation, photograph by Andrew Eccles.)

and emotionally charged performances. Although Jamison earned high praise for many of her performances, the fifteen-minute solo "Cry" stands as her most famous piece. Still performed today, "Cry" was originally choreographed for Jamison by Ailey himself as a tribute to African American women.

Although Jamison has always been reluctant to use the terminology (stating "Don't call me a star. Call me a dancer"), her ascent to international stardom was unmistakable in the 1970s. She appeared as a guest artist with the Swedish Royal Ballet (1972), the American Ballet Theatre (1976), the Vienna State Opera (1977), and Bejart's Ballet of the Twentieth Century (1979). In 1980 Jamison left the AAADT to appear on Broadway in *Sophisticated Ladies*. In 1988 she launched her own company, the Jamison Project. However, she decided to table the project in 1989 when her long-time friend and mentor Alvin Ailey passed away and named her artistic director of the AAADT.

As artistic director, Jamison has continued to share her vision and passion for dance with an international audience. Under her direction the AAADT has been expanded and reinvigorated both artistically and economically. Jamison has spent the last fourteen years enhancing the troupe's reputation as a premier dance company committed to promoting "dance as a medium for honoring the past, celebrating the present and fearlessly reaching into the future." Furthermore, as an advocate for education in the arts, Jamison has made a concerted effort to expand the company's educational mission. Initiatives have included a multicultural curriculum at the Ailey School, a joint bachelor of fine arts program with Fordham University, and an outreach and education program designed to bring the arts to the community through summer and after school programs. Jamison has also been part of the Women's Choreography Initiative, perfomed in the 1996 Atlanta Games, appeared in the 2002 Cultural Olympiad, and participated in cross-cultural exchanges with South Africa.

Among Jamison's many awards, some of the most prestigious include the Women of the Arts Award (1992), the Kennedy Center Honors Award (1999), and the Alger H. Meadows Award (2001). In 2001 she received the National Medal of the Arts, the most prestigious American award for achievement in the arts.

Jamison has spent the majority of her career with a dance company known for its commitment to promoting positive images of African Americans on stage. Still, Jamison is quick to point out that her career and her vision are much more than a matter of color. "Maybe it's a generational thing, but I never wanted to be the best black dancer in the world. I just wanted to be the best."

BIBLIOGRAPHY
Asante, Kariamu Welsh. "Judith Jamison." *Facts on File Encyclopedia of Black Women*, edited by Darlene Clark Hine. New York: Facts on File, 1997.
Jamison, Judith, with Howard Kaplan. *Dancing Spirit: An Autobiography*. New York: Doubleday, 1993.
Maynard, Olga. *Judith Jamison: Aspects of a Dancer*. New York: Doubleday, 1982.

ONLINE SOURCES
Alvin Ailey American Dance Theater. "Judith Jamison: Biography." http://www.alvinailey.org/pf/jamisonbio_pf.asp.
DeFrantz, Thomas F. "Judith Jamison." *Free to Dance: Biographies*. PBS. http://www.pbs.org/wnet/freetodance/biographies/jamison.html.
Mackrell, Judith. "I Just Wanted To Be the Best in the World." *Guardian Unlimited*, 6 September 2001. http://www.guardian.co.uk/arts/story/0,3604,547372,00.html.

—JAIME MCLEAN

JAZZ. Betty Carter's 1958 tune proclaims, "Jazz ain't nothing but soul." Jazz, America's art music, was born in the late nineteenth century simultaneously in New Orleans, Atlanta, Biloxi, Mobile, and Memphis. As Mississippi, Missouri, and Ohio River immigrants moved north, so too did jazz. Like most western music, jazz has eastern roots. Its gene pool is filled with blues and spirituals, along with field hollers and the African hand-drumming that slaves imported to the Americas. It is a form in which black women have participated from its inception. At times, they have fought exclusion, but their achievements have been, nonetheless, remarkable.

Origins of Jazz

The immediate predecessor of jazz had no name, unless it could be called "dance music." It was played for family celebrations and in brothels. It was heard from the stages of black vaudeville and minstrel shows. Most of the instruments used during its performances were leftovers from Civil War and other military marching bands. Discharged soldiers brought instruments home with them. Pawn shops doubled as "po' folks' bank" and local music store. Musicians sold and bought instruments at these pawn shops, and pawned marching band instruments were brought indoors to form bands. In these early bands, most of which performed within the community, women were common. There was not yet any significant amount of money to be made or prestige to be garnered from performing this music, and so there was little need for exclusion. That would change, but in the 1880s and 1890s, there were a great many family bands in which mother and daughters played alongside fathers and sons. In fact, jazz great Lester Young was taught the saxophone by his sister Irma who, along with his mother and various female cousins, made up the Young Family band.

Then, in the late nineteenth and early twentieth centuries, Decatur Street in Atlanta, Beale Street in Memphis, and similar districts in other cities saw drunks, prostitutes, shootings, fights, and women playing jazz. Use of the term "jazz" dates back to 1900, when it was first known as "jass." A variety of definitions has been assigned to this colorful word, including "improvised music," "decoration," "jive," "nonsense," "pretentious or braggadocios talk," "lewd copulation," "fecal matter," all in the underground currency of brothels and juke joints. Regardless of its etymology, jazz is the first American art form, and black women were there at its beginnings.

Living in St. Louis in the 1880s, Mama Lou played in a brothel and is credited with either writing or definitively interpreting "Ta-ra-ra-boom-de-ray" and "A Hot Time in the Old Town Tonight," for which songwriter Theodore Metz later took credit. According to Linda Dahl in *Stormy Weather*, she was probably responsible for "Frankie and Johnny" and "The Bully Song" as well. In Storyville, in New Orleans, Mamie Desdoumes played without two middle fingers on her right hand. Miss Antonia Gonzales ran her own brothel, sang, and played the cornet.

Two transitional singers of note in the creation of jazz vocals were Alberta Hunter and Ethel Waters. Both began as blues singers and continued to perform magnificently in that tradition. But they also moved into the jazz form and made major contributions there. Their music illustrates well the movement from blues and vaudeville dance music toward the form that would become jazz.

Alberta Hunter (1895–1984) enjoyed two music careers on four continents. She debuted in rough Chicago joints, and wrote "Down Hearted Blues" for Bessie Smith. Hunter starred in the musical *Showboat* with Paul Robeson at London's Palladium, and sang for the USO. At age sixty-one, Hunter became a nurse in a New York City hospital, but was forced to retire from that work at the age of eighty-two. Then she recorded for *Songs We Taught Your Mother* and *Chicago: the Living Legends*. She sang at New York's Cookery Club till age eighty-nine. Hunter also wrote music for the 1978 film *Remember My Name*. A lesbian, Hunter used aliases—Alberta Prime, Josephine Beatty, and Helen Roberts—to avoid violating so-called morality stipulations in her recording contract.

Philadelphian Ethel Waters (1896–1977) began in vaudeville, sang in clubs, and recorded "Down Home Blues" and many other songs on Black Swan, an African American label. During the 1920s she recorded a string of hits that included both slow, sweet ballads and up-tempo jazz. Beginning in the 1930s, Waters's stage and movie career flourished. She toured with her husband, Eddie Mallory, and appeared in the Broadway production of *Mamba's Daughter*. Waters premiered three hits in the film *Cabin in the Sky* (1943), and won a New York Drama Critic Award for her role in *Pinky* (1949).

By the 1920s, jazz reigned as the popular music of the day. Indeed, the twenties became known as the Jazz Age. But what distinguished jazz from the music that preceded it? What set this music apart, not only from other African American forms, but from all other western musical genres?

Jazz Is

Unlike most western music, jazz musicians don't simply read the composer's music verbatim. Jazz "lead sheets" consist of printed music that may include the "head" or melody, chord symbols in jazz notation, rhythmic patterns, and lyrics. Music is realized when the performer takes the composer's lead or blueprint. Lead sheets are often departure points used to synchronize intros, accents, bridges, cadences, codas, and tags. In its pure form the jazz repertoire is based on three Blues chords: I–IV–V. For example, in the key of F-Major the chords are F, B-flat and C. These chords are expanded via altered notes and substitutions.

Duke Ellington described jazz as "beyond category." Yet genres abound. Among them are traditional, big band, bebop, cool, fusion, avant-garde, crossover, ethnic, and vocal.

New Orleans and Traditional Jazz

New Orleans jazz grew directly out of the dance music of Storyville and the brass bands of street celebrations. Women like New Orleans pianist Olivia Charlot remembered fighting their families and respectable society for the chance to play in clubs in so-called redlight districts. As prejudice against women instrumentalists spread, their best chance for success often rested with becoming strong piano players. These were women such as Sweet Emma Barrett (1898–1983); Billie Pierce (1907–1974); Dolly Adams, who flourished in the 1920s; and Jeanette Salvant Kimball (1906–2001).

Straight ahead, mainstream, or traditional jazz is early 1900s music influenced by ragtime, boogie-woogie and Harlem stride piano, as distinguished from the New Orleans Jazz of the same era. Ragtime, or "ragged time," is a colloquialism for syncopation—playing ahead of or behind the beat, as opposed to playing strict downbeats. Boogie-woogie (also referred to as barrelhouse and honky-tonk, after the joints that featured the style), appeared in the 1928 recording "Pinetop's Boogie-Woogie," by Clarence Pinetop Smith. Boogie-woogie is the art of repeating a left-hand bass pattern in the piano (eighth-note ostinato) while the right-hand plays melodies and countermelodies. The boogie-woogie technique quickly spread from piano to other instruments.

Stride, or Shout, piano playing was popularized at early twentieth-century Chicago and Harlem rent parties. As the name implies, the pianist's left hand establishes stride or jump-bass patterns on beats one and three, with left-hand chords on beats two and four. Meanwhile, the right hand plays chords, or melodies. In more complex settings, the left hand also plays a walking bass line.

Among the black women who excelled at traditional jazz were Ragtime Kate Beckham and Julia Lee in Kansas City and Lil Hardin Armstrong in Chicago. Armstrong met her husband Louis when they both played with famed bandleader Joe "King" Oliver. Lil recorded vocals and piano for Louis's historical *Hot Five* and *Hot Seven* albums. Mother and daughter Dyer Jones and Dolly Jones Hutchinson, in Chicago, were among the first jazz recording artists.

Billie. "Lady Day" Holiday (1915–1959) modeled her untrained voice after her idol, the great blues singer Bessie Smith, and in so doing, she molded a style that is pure jazz. In 1933 Billie Holiday made her recording debut, singing "Your Mother's Son-in-Law" with Benny Goodman. She appeared at the Apollo in a one-reeler with Duke Ellington, and in the film *New Orleans* with Louis Armstrong. Holiday integrated Goodman's and Arte Shaw's bands and sang with Lester Young and Count Basie. Her "Strange Fruit" set the standard for ballads. With its poignant melody and raw, haunting lyrics detailing lynching, it was banned by clubs and radio stations. Thanks to the jukebox, the record and its flip side, "Fine and Mellow," became hits. "God Bless the Child" espouses autonomy. Another notable tune, "Lover Man," was a natural for Holiday, who lived its message a few times. She drank heavily, and smoked opium.

Despite hundreds of records, Holiday was often denied royalties. Two failed marriages and her mother's death sparked heroin use. In 1947 she was imprisoned for possession of illegal substances. As an ex-convict, Holiday was denied the cabaret card she needed to perform in clubs. Successful recordings, tours, and a TV show called *The Sound of Jazz* did not slow Lady Day's downward spiral. She finally succumbed to drug-induced ailments. Hours before her kidneys failed on 17 July 1959, she was arrested on her hospital deathbed for possession. Posthumous tributes include a 1972 movie *Lady Sings the Blues* starring Diana Ross, and reissues of Decca, Columbia, and Verve sides.

Big Bands and Swing. Big bands, also known as dance bands, emerged in the 1930s with ten or more players organized into three sections: reeds, brass, and rhythm. Reeds consist of alto, tenor, and baritone saxophones; some doubling flute or clarinet. Brass instruments include trumpets and trombones. Jazz rhythm sections include guitar, piano, bass, and drums. Pianist Blanche Calloway, Cab's sister, led her own band, the Joy Boys. On occasion, singers "sat in." Sitting in was the practice of having a singer sit on the side of the band. When it was time to sing, she would stand and sing from the sidelines. When her song ended, she returned to her sideline seat.

Big bands of the 1930s and 1940s are classified as "sweet" if they specialized in ballads popularized by vocalists like Ivie Anderson, Pearl Bailey, Kay Davis (Kathryn McDonald Wimp), Maria Ellington (Mrs. Nat "King" Cole), Betty Roche (Mary Elizabeth Roche), Joya Sherrill and Helen Humes. Swing and hot bands *cook*, so to speak, by way of innovative improvisational solos of leaders like Mary Lou Williams, who lived from 1910 to 1981. Such solos were typified by very long lines or phrases. Expansive transitions between swing and bebop typify so-called pre-bop music such as Williams's 1939 *Zodiac Suite*.

Mary Lou Williams. Pianist and composer Mary Lou Williams was born in Atlanta, grew up in Pittsburgh, and later defined the style known as "Kansas City" jazz. Her hit "What's Your Story, Morning Glory?" helped to shape the Andy Kirk Orchestra's distinct sound. Her deftly arranged charts created "the greatest small band" because Williams got a big sound from so few players. "Roll

'Em" was a Benny Goodman chart buster. Williams arranged for such luminaries as Earl Hines, Duke Ellington, and Dizzy Gillespie. She mentored Thelonious Monk, Bud Powell, and other bop, swing, and avant-garde pianists while maintaining her more traditional roots, a feat accomplished by very few.

Zodiac Suite is an example of Williams's diverse repertoire. The Williams Trio recorded seventeen sides, one for each sign of the astrological zodiac and five outtakes at a 1945 Town Hall concert with the New York Philharmonic. The Smithsonian recording label reissued *Zodiac* in 1995. Williams went to Europe in 1952, converted to Catholicism and wrote over one hundred sacred compositions. In 1957 she appeared with Dizzy Gillespie at the Newport Jazz Festival. Among her milestone compositions are *Black Christ in the Andes*, *Mary Lou's Mass*, and *History of Jazz*.

Williams went on to receive fellowships from the NEA and Guggenheim Foundation, as well as five honorary doctorates. In 1996 the Kennedy Center named its Jazz Festival in her honor. In 1977, Williams joined Duke University's faculty, where she remained until 1981.

The Rise of "All-Girl" Bands. The International Sweethearts of Rhythm formed in 1937 at the Piney Woods School for poor and orphaned blacks in Mississippi. After touring to raise funds for the school for several years, band members decided to declare their independence in 1941. Over the years, a handful of white women played with the band, wearing bronze makeup in the Jim Crow South to avoid being arrested. The professional version of the Sweethearts debuted at the Washington, DC, Howard Theatre, where they set 1941 box office records under Anna Mae Winburn's baton. They also broke box office records at Chicago's Regal and New York's Apollo theatres and played jubilee sessions for black soldiers.

International Sweethearts' trumpeters included such notables as Ernestine "Tiny" Davis, Ray Carter, Johnnie Mae Stansbury, and Edna Williams. Marge Pettiford, Amy Garrison, Helen Saine, Grace Bayron, Viola Burnside, Rosaline "Roz" Cron, and Willie Mae Wong played sax. July Bayron, Helen Jones, and Ina Bell Byrd played trombone. The rhythm section included Johnnie Mae Rice on the piano, Lucille Dixon on bass, Pauline Braddy on drums, and Roxanne Lucas on guitar. Evelyn McGee and Anna Mae Winburn provided vocals. The group's ten-year lifespan is documented on Hindsight and Rosetta Records.

Vi Burnside played tenor sax with the International Sweethearts of Rhythm and Vi Burnside & Her All Stars in the 1940s and 1950s. Burnside squared off in a legendary 1945 jam session with Margaret Backstrom, a tenor sax player with the Darlings of Rhythm, another black "all-girl" band. The head-chopping contest is documented in Sherrie Tucker's *Swing Shift: "All-Girl" Bands of the 1940s*.

The International Sweethearts prided themselves on teaching others how it ought to be done. But there are listeners who claimed the Darlings did it better. Many musicians who played with one group also played, at one time or another, with the other, but the Darlings of Rhythm were no school band. They began as professionals and never went in for the glamorous look of the Sweethearts. They weren't "pretty girls," and they didn't wear pretty costumes. They did, however, swing. Backstrom and other Darlings of Rhythm were known for their fast, hot style. Josephine Boyd played alto sax with the Darlings. Boyd and Backstrom were former members of the All-Girl Star Orchestra.

Often dismissed as "ham fats," or inferior musicians, female groups began to thrive as more and more male players were drafted into military service. Among them were the Harlem Playgirls, led by Sylvester Rice, and Bobbie Howell's American Syncopators. The sixteen-piece, "all-girl" band Prairie View Co-Eds began on the Texas A&M campus during WWII, entertaining black servicemen. Despite high-profile gigs at the Apollo and other national venues, the group reverted to its former all-male status after the end of the war.

The Jazz Greats

Anyone near 81st and Golden in 1940s Cleveland heard piano students and a band swinging hit parade tunes. The activity came from the home of pianist Evelyn Freeman, born in 1919. Neighbors sought a court injunction to silence the "racket." It began with a trio of Freeman, her Dad, and brother, Ernie. But Evelyn was the driving force, playing piano, lining up gigs, expanding the group to include an orchestra, and writing a theme song, *Dancing Every Sunday*, subtitled *At Oster's Ballroom for 35 Cents*.

Freeman's debut concert was billed as "Symphony to Swing." By the end of the concert at the Phillis Wheatley Center, the ensemble was swinging so hard, they brought down the house. Some dates were broadcast on WTAM and WHK radio. Freeman protégé Hale Smith was a pianist and composer whose music has been performed by Kathleen Battle, Jessye Norman, and Betty Carter. Ernie Freeman won Grammies for arranging Frank Sinatra's *Strangers in the Night* and Simon & Garfunkel's *Bridge over Troubled Waters*. Freeman moved to Los Angeles to become a recording artist. She married Tommy Roberts, with whom she co-founded The Young Saints, a youth vocal ensemble that sang for President Nixon. Freeman's drummer, James "Chink" McKinley, later played for Dorothy Donegan.

The pianist Dorothy Donegan (1924–1998) was born in Chicago. She cut her chops at DuSable High School and in church. By the age of fourteen, she earned a dollar a night by performing in local clubs. A student of the Chicago Musical College, Donegan recorded blues and boogie-woogie sides for the Bluebird label. At the age of eighteen, Donegan was the first African American to perform at Chicago's Orchestra Hall, an athletic performance that inspired *The New York Times* to dub her "blizzard fingers." Donegan garnered *Time* magazine coverage and a visit from jazz pianist great, Art Tatum, a meeting that sparked a lifelong friendship. As Tatum's protégé, Donegan flaunted virtuoso chops. She kicked her long legs up to her cheeks, sang campy lyrics in parodied voices, put her "hands on her hips and let her backbone slip" without missing a piano lick. Donegan earned $3,000 a week in the United Artists film *Sensations of 1945*. Her career includes albums, tours, and innumerable club dates.

Philadelphian Shirley Scott (1934–2002) began blocking chords behind her brother's sax in the family's basement speakeasy. She studied trumpet but eventually gravitated toward the jazz organ of choice, the famous Hammond B-3. In the early twentieth century, jazz musicians held jam sessions or rent parties and "sang for their supper." Supper could be chicken with spaghetti, coleslaw, and cornbread; or greens, candied yams, crackling bread, and smoked ham hocks, or chitterlings. Among the possible combinations of musicians and instruments on these "Chitlin' Circuit" trios was one known as the "grits-and-gravy group"—guitar, drums, and the Hammond B-3 organ. The Hammond B-3 with its specially designed rotating Leslie speakers was more responsive than a standard-issue pipe organ. Amplified speakers inside the organ cabinet contained rotating horns that sped up or slowed down to alter a note's vibrato. Under Scott's deft fingers and soul-stomping feet, the B-3 hollered aplenty. Scott led a trio with John Coltrane. A gig with Eddie "Lockjaw" Davis led to the so-called *Cookbook* albums. Scott was crowned "Queen of Organ." In the 1950s, she and tenor sax man Stanley Turentine were all the rage. They collaborated for twelve albums, three daughters, and two sons.

Scott recorded twenty–three albums for Prestige, ten for Impulse, three each for Atlantic and Chess, one for Strata East, two on Muse, and three on Candid. Scott was music director for Bill Cosby's revival of the television show *You Bet Your Life*. Memorable albums include three *Cookbooks*, *Great Scott*, and the organ landmark *Have you had Your B-3 Today?*, which featured ten organists. Scott developed heart trouble due to diet pills, for which she filed a lawsuit and won $8 million. Her heart failed in 2002. Scott's legacy includes a professorship at University of Pittsburgh.

Like her friend Shirley Scott, Gloria Coleman married a sax player, George Coleman. Her piano and organ chops ignited clubs in the 1960s and 1970s. She began as a violinist and bassist, playing bass with Sonny Stitt and Sarah McLawler. A composer and poet, Coleman produced work that appeared on the Impulse record label. Organist Sarah McLawler was born in Louisville and attended Fisk University. She founded the All-Star Girl Orchestra in the 1940s, and later the all-female Syncoettes. She formed the McLawler combo with herself on piano, Lula Roberts on sax, Vi Wilson on bass, and Hetty Roberts on drums. She recorded on the Chess, King, and Brunswick labels. Her organ trio, with her violinist husband Richard Otto and drummer Tommy Hunter, is recorded on Vee Jay. Other pianists of note within this highly charged, intense idiomatic B-3 style of jazz include Lovie Austin (1887–1972) and Hazel Dorothy Scott (1920–1981).

"Queen of Trumpet" Valaida Snow (1903–1956) also sang and danced. Four of her CDs were reissued between 1994 and 2001. Ernestine "Tiny" Davis was born 1913 in Memphis and played with the Harlem Playgirls and the International Sweethearts of Rhythm, with whom she also sang. Louis Armstrong offered Tiny ten times her salary to join him. Tiny refused. In the 1950s Tiny led the Hell Divers. Decades later, Tiny and lifetime lover, drummer and singer Ruby Lucas, appeared in a film, *Tiny and Ruby—Hell Divin' Women* (1988).

Bebop

In the 1940s bebop was fathered by Dizzy Gillespie, Charlie "Bird" Parker, Thelonious Monk, and Max Roach. It began as rapid fire playing, heightened syncopation, the compression of countless notes in minute time frames, the use of altered chords, polyrhythms, and polytonality. It is high-energy music, bordering on frenzy. Bop thrives in smaller groups like the trio—piano, bass, and drums—and quintet—piano, bass, drums, saxophone, trumpet—rather than in big band settings. Boppers raised the jazz bar. Musical forms were expanded, and fast riffs were played. Harmonies were altered. The flat 5th/raised 4th was used so often it became known as the "devil's interval." Front beats and backbeats were accented. A few critics feared Jazz was becoming an elitist art form because few musicians could match Bop's breakneck speed, resolve the tension created by non-chord tones within Bop's confines or sustain the high temperature intensity without blinking. Bebop devices included chords progressing in fourths and half-steps, in addition to established motion. Bop was so different that Duke Ellington said, "Playing bebop is like playing scrabble with all the vowels missing."

A variation of bebop, hard Bop is typically louder, more intense, soulful, tinged with funk and gospel elements, and features more interactive drumming. "Drum melodies" become more prevalent, as opposed to the drummer only marking time. Like most labels, this 1950s and 1960s bop label was used more by writers and critics than by musicians.

Featuring Jazz Instrumentalists and Band Leaders

● **Geri Allen** (1959–) created a sound of her own by joining American jazz, funk, gospel, blues, and rhythm and blues with traditional African music. Born in Pontiac, Michigan, and raised in Detroit, Allen began classical piano lessons at the age of seven. While she was studying classical music, she was exposed to the sounds of Charlie Parker and his contemporaries, which her father played at home, and the sounds of Motown, James Brown, and George Clinton, which she played on the radio. During high school she studied composition, arranging, and jazz improvisation at the Jazz Development Workshop, taught by trumpeter Marcus Belgrave and other veteran jazz musicians. She studied jazz at Howard University and did graduate work in ethnomusicology at the University of Pittsburgh.

Allen's first albums included the trio effort, *The Printmakers*, and her solo debut, *Home Grown*. She also performed with Open on All Sides, an octet she formed in the 1970s, and the progressive, African music–oriented ensemble M-BASE. She recorded a second trio album, *Twylight*, in 1989 and worked with bassist Charlie Haden and drummer Paul Motian. Albums she released in the 1990s include *Maroons*, *Gathering*, and another trio outing, *Twenty-One*, with Ron Carter and Tony Williams. *Life of a Song* was released in August 2004.

● **Lillian "Lil" Hardin Armstrong** (1898–1971), a gifted pianist, singer, and songwriter, was instrumental in launching the career of her second husband, Louis Armstrong. She played piano on what are widely considered to be the most important jazz recordings of the twentieth century. (See individual entry: Armstrong, Lillian "Lil" Hardin.)

● **Emma Barrett** (1898–1983), pianist and singer, was an important member of the New Orleans jazz community for more than seventy years. A New Orleans native, Barrett began taking piano lessons at the age of seven and was appearing in dance halls and piano bars by the time she was twelve. She played with many of the most celebrated New Orleans jazz bands, including the Original Tuxedo Orchestra, and the bands of John Robichaux, Sidney Desvigne, and Armand J. Piron. In the 1950s Barrett joined forces with the musicians who eventually formed the nucleus of the Preservation Hall Jazz Band. A constant performer at Preservation Hall, even after the 1967 stroke that cost her the use of her left hand, she had an engaging presence and dynamic keyboard style that were vital elements in the revival of traditional New Orleans–style jazz.

● **Willene Barton** (1930?–) taught herself to play tenor saxophone as a child in Georgia and went on to play alongside musicians such as Ben Webster, Illinois Jacquet, and Gene Ammons. Inspired by the International Sweethearts of Rhythm, the renowned all-women swing band, in the early 1950s she played with bands led by two former members of that group, Anna Mae Winburn and Myrtle Young. In 1955 she formed her own band, the Four Jewels. Later she led an all-male group and played for several years with organist Dayton Selby before joining forces with the great Melba Liston.

Barton worked outside music during the decline of interest in jazz in the 1960s. In the 1970s she was a member of the Jazz Sisters of New York City, led by pianist Jill McManus. In 1979 she played at the Kansas City Women's Jazz Festival, and in 1981 she put together a group that became the first women's jazz band to play at the Newport Jazz Festival. After touring Europe in the 1980s, Barton returned to New York, performing at street festivals and clubs.

● **Cleo Patra Brown** (1909–1995) was a boogie-woogie and stride pianist whose playing influenced Fats Waller and Dave Brubeck. Born in Meridian, Mississippi, she moved with her family to Chicago in 1919. She studied piano as a child and learned boogie-woogie from her older brother Everett, also a pianist. She began her career playing in vaudeville shows at the age of fourteen. For much of the twenties she worked in the Chicago area. In 1935 she took over Fats Waller's New York–based radio show. In 1953 Brown retired from performing and became a nurse. Beginning in the 1970s she played at services and on the radio for her Seventh-Day Adventist church.

● **Clora Bryant** (1927–) shared the spotlight with many of the great jazz players, from Louis Armstrong to Charlie Parker and Dizzy Gillespie, during the course of her long career. Born and raised in Texas, she learned to play her brother's trumpet after he went to fight in World War II. After high school she turned down a full scholarship to Oberlin Conservatory to attend Prairie View College and joined the Co-Eds, the school's professional all-female orchestra. In 1945 Bryant moved with her family to Los Angeles, where she became part of a thriving jazz scene on Central Avenue that included Dexter Gordon, Hampton Hawes, Melba Liston, Frank Morgan, and Sonny Criss. She polished her performing skills working with groups such as the Queens of Swing and accompanying the likes of Josephine Baker and Billie Holiday. She recorded her first album as a leader, *Gal with a Horn*, in 1956. She toured extensively with several bands, including those of Johnny Otis and Jeannie and Jimmy Cheatham and her own group, Swi-Bop. She retired from performing in 1996 but continued to lecture and work on her autobiography.

● **Regina Carter** (1966?–), a classically trained jazz violinist, played with Wynton Marsalis and the Lincoln Center Jazz Orchestra, was a member of the avant-garde chamber jazz group, the String Trio of New York, and backed singers as diverse as Patti LaBelle, Tanya Tucker, and Lauryn Hill. Growing up in Detroit, she began taking piano lessons at the age of two and violin lessons at four. She demonstrated sufficient talent to be admitted to master classes taught by Yehudi Menuhin and Itzhak Perlman.

132

Carter decided to become a jazz musician in high school, inspired by performances by Jean-Luc Ponty, Wes Montgomery, and Stephane Grappelli. After high school she studied music at suburban Detroit's Oakland University and the New England Conservatory of Music. In 1987 she joined the all-female band Straight Ahead. After moving to New York in the early 1990s, she joined the String Trio of New York, with whom she recorded two albums. In 1995 she recorded her first solo album, *Regina Carter*. In the early 2000s she became the first jazz player to perform and record on the legendary instrument of the Italian master violinist Nicolo Paganini.

● **Alice Coltrane** (1937–), pianist, organist, harpist, vibraphonist, and composer, envisioned music as a spiritual and unifying experience, following the ideas she explored and practiced with her husband, the legendary jazz saxophonist, John Coltrane. Born Alice McLeod in Detroit, Michigan, Coltrane took classical piano and organ lessons as a child. She studied jazz piano in Paris with Bud Powell and joined the Terry Gibbs Quartet in New York in 1960. In 1963 she met and married John Coltrane and two years later she joined his band, replacing McCoy Tyner. At the time, John Coltrane was incorporating elements of Eastern spirituality and African, Indian, and Asian music into his work.

After John Coltrane's death in 1967, Alice Coltrane devoted herself to raising her four children and furthering her husband's musical and spiritual ideals. In the 1970s she led several groups and produced and recorded albums of her own compositions. Following a trip to India, she founded the Vedantic Center in Agoura, California, and focused her talents on creating devotional music, appearing only rarely at secular music performances.

● **Dorothy Donegan** (1922–1998) was one of the most accomplished pianists in the history of jazz as well as one of the most flamboyant performers. Born in Chicago, she learned to play piano in the public schools. By the time she was ten, she was playing the organ at church, and at fourteen she was appearing in small clubs on the city's South Side. When she was seventeen she joined Bob Tinsley's jazz band. Her first album of blues and boogie-woogie tunes was recorded in 1942. The following year she appeared at Orchestra Hall, performing Rachmaninoff and Grieg in the first half of the concert and jazz during the second half, becoming the first jazz musician as well as the first African American to grace that stage. Donegan's influences included Earl Hines, Errol Garner, and, more than anyone else, her mentor Art Tatum. She was renowned for her versatility, possessing both the technical mastery and the imagination to shift rapidly from boogie-woogie to stride to contemporary jazz to classical styles all in the course of a single song.

● **Ethel Ennis** (1932–), pianist and singer, appeared with many of the great jazz bands and turned down a chance at stardom in order to retain control of her career and her life. Growing up in Baltimore, Ennis began playing piano at the age of seven. At fifteen she joined a jazz group called Abe Riley's Octet. Although her family was very strict about what kind of music could be played in the home, she was deeply influenced by the rhythm and blues music that she listened to through the floor from the apartment below. After graduating from high school in 1950, Ennis performed with the Jo Jo Jones Ensemble and a rhythm and blues group called the Tilters. Soon she was appearing regularly at nightclubs in Baltimore and New York.

As her reputation grew, Ennis sang with Duke Ellington, Count Basie, Cab Calloway, and Benny Goodman. She sang on Arthur Godfrey's television show for eight years. In the 1960s RCA Victor was ready to sign her to a recording contract and arrange for bookings around the country. Faced with a demand that she move to New York and give up control of her appearances, she opted to remain in Baltimore.

● **Julia Lee** (1902–1958), pianist and singer, was known as "Kansas City's Sweetheart of Swing." Born in Boonville, Missouri, she sang with her father's string trio from the time she was four and began playing piano at the age of ten. From 1920 to 1933 she played with her older brother's band, the George E. Lee Orchestra. She had a steady engagement at Kansas City's Milton's Tap Room from 1933 to 1948, although she occasionally traveled to engagements around the Midwest. Her recording career was most successful between 1944 and 1949 and included hit versions of "Come on Over to My House, Baby" and "Snatch It and Grab It."

● **Melba Liston** (1926–1999), one of the outstanding trombonists of her generation, was the first woman to make a mark in jazz playing a brass instrument. She played with the bands of Gerald Wilson, Dizzy Gillespie, Count Basie, and Duke Ellington. The performers she accompanied included Billie Holiday, Cannonball Adderly, Betty Carter, Jimmy Smith, and Dinah Washington. (See individual entry: Liston, Melba.)

● **Billie Goodson Pierce** (1907–1974) was a pianist and composer whose career began during the classic blues era. She accompanied many of the big blues stars, played with New Orleans–style bands, and ended her career at Preservation Hall in New Orleans. Born in Marianna, Florida, and raised in Pensacola, Pierce was one of seven piano-playing sisters. She was fifteen when she left home to become a touring musician. Throughout the 1920s she appeared with groups such as the Mighty Wiggle Carnival Show, the Nighthawks Orchestra, and Slim Hunter's Orchestra. She frequently accompanied blues singers, including Ma Rainey, Bessie Smith, Ida Cox, and Mary Mack.

In the 1930s she formed her own band with George Lewis and her husband, DeDe Pierce. The Pierces continued to perform together until the late 1950s, when she suffered a debilitating stroke and her husband was blinded by glaucoma. In the 1960s, the couple staged a comeback, becoming two of the principal attractions of the Preservation Hall Jazz Band.

● **Carlene Ray** (c. 1925–), pianist, singer, guitarist, bass player, and educator, had a career ranging through the worlds of jazz, pop, and classical music. Born in New York, she earned degrees at the Juilliard School (1946) and the Manhattan School of Music. After beginning as a singer and pianist, she shifted to rhythm guitar. She joined the International Sweethearts of Rhythm right out of school and then went on to the Erskine Hawkins Orchestra as a singer. In 1956 she changed instruments again, taking up the electric bass, which she taught herself to play in a way that mimicked the sound of a string bass.

Ray toured Europe and the Far East with Melba Liston, played at the Newport Jazz Festival with Sy Oliver's orchestra, and worked with Ruth Brown from 1989 to 1995. As a singer she performed with the Schola Cantorum Camarata Singers and the American Opera Society and sang backup for Della Reese, Patti Page, and Quincy Jones. From 1971 to 1984 she sang in the chorus and played in the orchestra of the Alvin Ailey American Dance Theater. As a teacher she directed the choir at Medgar Evers College, taught guitar at Hunter College, and taught a singing course in the blues at the New School in New York City.

● **Patrice Rushen** (1954–) was a session musician, rhythm and blues star, songwriter, producer, arranger, and composer. Born in Los Angeles, she began studying piano at the age of five. She was in high school when she began doing session work, which helped pay her college tuition. She attended the University of Southern California, majoring in Piano Performance and Music Education. Her first album, *Precision*, was released when she was nineteen. She continued to work sessions for musicians including Sonny Rollins, Jean-Luc Ponty, Stanley Turrentine, and John McLaughlin.

After signing with the Elektra label, Rushen recorded a series of rhythm and blues hits, including "When I Found You," "Haven't You Heard," "Never Gonna Give You Up," "Number One," and "Forget-Me-Nots." During the 1980s, after the hits tapered off, Rushen expanded into film scoring, production, teaching, and serving as tour musical director for Janet Jackson and Sheena Easton. She co-founded and recorded with the fusion group the Meeting and released a new jazz album, *Signature*, in 1997.

Betty "Bebop" Carter (1930–1998) the so-called Queen of Bop, was born Lillie Mae Jones in Flint, Michigan. She studied piano at Detroit's Conservatory of Music and sang in her father's church choir. At sixteen, she sat in as a singer with Bird and other musicians passing through Motown. An amateur contest win led her to Lionel Hampton. Hampton, who fired her seven times, nicknamed her Betty "Bebop" because of her acrobatic vocal abilities. (She remained with Hampton because his wife kept rehiring her.) Her hypnotic blend of clarity, scatting, elastic phrasing, and supersonic up-tempos were executed with harmonic precision. Carter disliked the limitation of being labeled "bebop" and "avant-garde." Among Carter's most successful and diverting performances was her 1976 "Tight," a pithy piece of heaven, and her 1993 live album *Feed the Fire*.

After taking time away from her career to have a child, Carter faced uncompromising record execs. In 1970 she founded Bet-Car Records and produced five albums; two were Grammy nominees. *Look What I Got* won a 1988 Grammy. Her legacy includes innovative compositions, twenty-five albums, and Presidential Medals of Honor. Carter often toured with "young cats," housing them in her Brooklyn home. Ella Fitzgerald, Sarah Vaughan, Carmen McCrae, and Nina Simone lauded Betty's purism. Despite pressures to record pop tunes, Carter remained a Jazz artist, exclusively.

Composer and trombonist Melba Liston (1926–1999) was born in Kansas City and grew up in Los Angeles. She began her career with Gerald Wilson's Orchestra and worked in small combos with Dexter Gordon. She also worked as a big-band section player. In the 1940s, she collaborated with the Count Basie Band and with Billie Holiday. She joined Dizzy Gillespie's bebop big band in 1950. As an arranger, Liston is closely linked to Randy Weston. She tried her hand at acting, taught in Jamaican schools, and arranged for Basie, Dizzy, Johnny Griffin, Milt Jackson, Quincy Jones, and the *Superfly* soundtrack. *Melba and Her Bones* (1958) is her most acclaimed album.

Clora Bryant was active in LA's Central Avenue Jazz community. Her father moved the family to LA to aid her career. Bryant felt compelled to express her femininity lest men treat her like one of the boys. Bryant took her bebop, big band, and Dixieland sound to Russia. In 1957 her *Gal with a Horn* was reissued on CD. Yet another notable player, Barbara Carroll (b. 1925) was called by Leonard Feather "the first girl ever to play bebop piano."

● **Hazel Scott** (1920–1981) was a star of nightclubs, the concert stage, Broadway, radio, movies, and television. Born in Port-of-Spain, Trinidad, she moved with her family to New York when she was four. When she was five she made her American debut as a pianist at Town Hall and at fourteen she joined her mother's band, Alma Long Scott's All Woman Orchestra, playing piano and trumpet. At sixteen she was the star of her own radio show and appeared with Count Basie's Orchestra at the Roseland Dance Hall.

In the late 1930s she made her first appearance in a Broadway musical, *Singing Out the News*. She appeared in five movies in the 1940s and from 1939 to 1945 she performed at Barney Josephson's Café Society Downtown and Uptown. She appeared as a soloist with the New York Philharmonic and the Philadelphia Orchestra. In 1945 she married the preacher and politician Adam Clayton Powell Jr. She was the first black woman to have her own television show, but it was canceled in 1950 after she was accused of being a communist sympathizer. In 1955 she recorded the album *Relaxed Piano Moods* with Charles Mingus and Max Roach.

An outspoken advocate of racial equality, Scott required a clause in her standard contract demanding forfeiture if the audience was racially segregated. She continued to appear on television, perform in clubs, and speak out against racism until her death in 1981.

● **Shirley Scott** (1934–2002) recorded more than fifty albums and was a vibrant presence on the Philadelphia nightclub scene for many years. Born in Philadelphia, Scott attended Cheyney University, earning both bachelor's and master's degrees. She began playing piano in clubs in the 1950s and frequently accompanied the young John Coltrane. At around the same time, the Hammond B-3 organ was becoming a popular jazz instrument because of the work of Jimmy Smith. When a local club owner rented one for Scott, she was intrigued by the instrument and quickly mastered it, becoming one of the leading jazz organists. Most often she worked with a trio, and her sidemen over the years included Eddie "Lockjaw" Davis, Dexter Gordon, and her husband, Stanley Turrentine. In the 1970s Scott formed a bop group and continued to perform and record into the 1990s, when she returned to Cheyney University as member of the faculty.

● **Mary Lou Williams** (1910–1981) was one of the most highly regarded performers, arrangers, and composers of black American music. Her importance in the history of jazz continues to be seen in the homage paid to her by scores of her musical progeny. (See individual entry: Williams, Mary Lou.)

Great Voices of Jazz

In vocal music, too, black women have been dominant figures. Going far beyond the role of "girl singer," they have created a style of singing that has influenced every other popular genre. Vocal jazz is characterized by unique phrasing, bending notes, glissandi (sliding up or down to pitches) and other special effects, tight harmonies, and scatting. Scatting is jazz's signature form of humming, lip buzzing, and vocalizing whereby the performer sings the melody, or improvises on neutral syllables instead of words. While Louis Armstrong is credited as the inventor of scatting, Ella Fitzgerald developed the "vocalese" language that is synonymous with instrumental and vocal jazz improvisation.

Improvisation is the act of spontaneous composition wherein the performer uses jazz vernacular to communicate with her audience by "soloing over chord changes." The performer blows, or performs, a solo using vocabulary with respect to harmonic chord changes, melody, rhythm, and the form of the composition. This improvisation is the performer's discovery and expression of new ideas within a framework or chorus. Many choruses last for an average of thirty-two bars. As the soloist improvises, other band members comp, or accompany the soloist by outlining the composition. Accompanists may play sparse chords. Pianists comp beneath solo instruments to keep the integrity of a composition's form. This "frees" the soloist to express herself. As the saying goes, "Everyone else stays at home while the soloist roams."

Ella. The ultimate "Voice of Jazz" is personified by the inimitable Ella Fitzgerald (1917–1999). Born in Newport News, Virginia, Ella moved to Yonkers when she was fifteen. Early professional success came when Ella won a talent contest at Harlem's Apollo Theater. Though she entered as a dancer, Ella sang "The Object of my Affection" because her legs were paralyzed by stage fright. After many encores Ella won the $25 grand prize and launched her amateur career. Drummer Chic Webb tutored and adopted Ella when her parents died. Ella recorded her debut signature hit, *A-Tisket A-Tasket*, in 1938 with Webb's orchestra. When Webb died in 1939, Ella led his orchestra until the WWII draft depleted the group.

When Ella launched her solo career and toured with Dizzy Gillespie, she honed her bop chops. From 1947 to 1953, Ella was married to bassist Ray Brown and fronted for his trio. Ella changed the voice of Jazz via bell-tone precision as evidenced by the 1956 Verve collaboration with Louis Armstrong, *The Complete Ella & Louis*. Listeners

135

Featuring Jazz Singers

● **Ernestine Anderson** (1928–) sang popular standards with a jazzy feel and was also equally at home with straight jazz and the blues. Born in Houston, Texas, she was exposed to the blues at home through her parents' record collection. She began singing in clubs as a teenager and toured with the rhythm and blues bands of Russell Jacquet, Johnny Otis, and Eddie Heywood before moving over to jazz and joining Lionel Hampton. It was her 1956 album, *Hot Cargo*, that established her reputation in the United States. She retired from music in 1969 but was persuaded to return at the urging of Ray Brown, Benny Carter, and other musicians and by the success of a live appearance in 1976 at the Concord Jazz Festival. Her most recent album, *Isn't It Romantic*, was released in 1998.

● **Betty Carter** (1930–1998) was a musical adventurer, a fearless explorer of the limits of melody, harmony, and rhythm who played her voice the way an instrumentalist plays a horn. Her performances were unpredictable and inspiration-driven, and she paid a heavy price in popularity for that unpredictability, but she weathered the worst times and lived to see younger generations appreciate her. Born Lillie Mae Jones in Flint, Michigan, and raised in Detroit, she studied piano at the Detroit Conservatory of Music. She started appearing in public when she was in high school, sitting in with the likes of Charlie Parker, Dizzy Gillespie, Sarah Vaughan, and Billy Eckstine when they appeared in Detroit.

In 1948 she joined the Lionel Hampton Band, under the name Lorraine Carter. Hampton's traditional sound was not always an easy mix with Carter's more modern style, and the bandleader took to calling her "Betty BeBop." In 1951 she left Hampton's band and began to work the club scene in New York, appearing in several bands and working with Dizzy Gillespie and Max Roach. In 1958 and 1959 she toured with Miles Davis, who brought her to the attention of Ray Charles. It was her duet album with Charles, including their classic version of *Baby, It's Cold Outside*, that made her well known.

Carter spent most of the 1960s raising her two sons. When she returned to recording at the end of the decade, her records attracted few sales. Unable to find a recording contract, she started her own label, Bet-Car, in 1969 and released her own recordings for the next twenty years. Not being beholden to record companies allowed her the experimental freedom to develop her music the way she wanted to. She made a habit of hiring gifted young players in order to keep in touch with current developments, and in the process she nurtured many important new voices, including Jackie Terrason, Jack DeJohnette, and Cyrus Chestnut.

In the late 1980s, the Verve label signed Carter to her first major label contract since the 1960s, reissuing many of her Bet-Car albums to far wider distribution than they had previously received. In the last decade of her life, she received the critical appreciation and acceptance by jazz audiences that had eluded her for much of her life. In addition to recording and performing, she established the Jazz Ahead workshop at the Brooklyn Academy of Music, which provided young musicians the opportunity to work with her. She performed at Lincoln Center in 1993 and at the White House in 1994. In 1997 President Bill Clinton presented her with the National Medal of Arts.

● **Ella Fitzgerald** (1917–1996) was possibly the most admired and technically skilled jazz or popular music vocalist in American history. With an extraordinary vocal range, perfect pitch, incredible enunciation, and an almost surreal sense of timing, Fitzgerald delighted audiences for over fifty years, an amazingly long career in a particularly mercurial business. (See individual entry: Fitzgerald, Ella.)

● **Billie Holiday** (1915–1959) was, in the minds of most jazz critics and historians, the greatest jazz singer ever recorded. Coming into her own a generation after the classic blues singers such as Bessie Smith, Holiday created a place for herself outside the limited confines of the "girl singer" role within the big band, setting standards by which other jazz singers continue to be judged and influencing singers as far-ranging in style as Sarah Vaughan, Frank Sinatra, Carmen McRae, and Lena Horne. (See individual entry: Holiday, Billie.)

● **Helen Humes** (1913–1981) sang blues, ballads, pop songs, and rhythm and blues in a bright, clear voice with a sunny tone that conveyed the joy of singing even in the saddest songs. Born in Louisville, Kentucky, she studied piano, organ, harmonium, and trumpet as a child and first sang in public at church and with a local community center band. She cut her first recordings at age thirteen, singing classic blues numbers for Okeh Records, but her career began formally in the mid-1930s, when she began singing in clubs in the Louisville area. She sang with the Al Sears Band, recorded with Harry James, and sang with the Count Basie Band from 1938 to 1942 before striking out on her own. Beginning in 1944 she was a regular on Norman Granz's Jazz at the Philharmonic tour. She sang mostly ballads with the Basie band, but she was equally at home with blues, pop songs, and jump jazz. Rhythm and blues was a mainstay of her repertoire, including her signature song, "Be-Baba-Leba" (1945) and "Million Dollar Secret" (1950). In the 1950s she toured with vibraphonist Red Norvo and continued to record and perform in clubs. In 1967 Humes returned to Louisville to take care of her ailing mother and found work outside music. In 1973 she staged a memorable comeback at the Newport Jazz Festival and continued to perform and record until her death in 1981.

● **Etta Jones** (1928–2001) was a gifted improviser and interpreter of song who never enjoyed the popularity her music deserved, but she left behind a solid legacy of great recordings.

Born in Aiken, South Carolina, and raised in Harlem, she dreamed of being a singer from childhood on. Her big break came at the age of sixteen, when she won an audition to tour with Buddy Johnson's band while Johnson's sister Ella took time off to have a baby. After the tour she performed with a series of New York–based groups, including the Harlemaires and Barney Bigard's Orchestra, and from 1949 to 1952 she sang with Earl "Fatha" Hines.

Jones had a hard time finding engagements in the 1950s and spent most of the decade working in other fields until she recorded the biggest hit of her career, "Don't Go to Strangers," in 1960. The song sold a million copies, landed on the top forty pop chart, and was nominated for a Grammy Award. She continued to record throughout the 1960s. In 1968 she was appearing in Washington, DC, when she met tenor saxophonist Houston Persons. The two quickly became friends, and for the next thirty years Persons acted as her producer, manager, and musical partner and collaborator. They recorded eighteen albums together for the Muse label. They performed together up to two hundred times a year until her health began to fail. She continued to record even while battling breast cancer. Their final album, *Etta Jones Sings Lady Day*, was released on the day she died in October 2001.

● **Abbey Lincoln/Aminata Moseka** (1930–) was a distinctive jazz singer as well as an activist and a scholar. She was born Anna Marie Wooldridge in Chicago, Illinois, and had a checkered early career, singing in nightclubs in Los Angeles and Honolulu under various names before changing her name to Abbey Lincoln in 1956. That same year, she recorded *Affair: A Story of a Girl in Love*. It was her first album, and she agreed to appear on the cover in a suggestive pose because she simply did not know any better, thus gaining a reputation as a sex kitten. However, with the help of future husband Max Roach, she was able to develop seriously as a musician, recording an album a year until 1962. She appeared in two excellent films in the 1960s, *Nothing but a Man* (1964) with Ivan Dixon and *For Love of Ivy* (1968) with Sidney Poitier. She also became very active in African American politics.

During most of the 1970s, Lincoln traveled and seldom appeared on American stages. In 1972, while on vacation in Africa, she was given her African first and last names—Aminata Moseka—by government officials in Guinea and Zaire. In 1975 she was inducted into the Black Filmmakers Hall of Fame. In 1979 she began recording again with *People in Me*. She recorded three albums in the 1980s and then went into high gear again in the 1990s. By this time she was a prolific and moving songwriter. She continued to be a powerful and exciting performer into the twenty-first century.

● **Carmen McRae** (1920–1994) created her own style and sense of rhythm, although her voice has been consistently compared

to Vaughan and Holiday, her lifelong idol. Reflected in her music is her inclination to tell a story with her lyrics as she forcefully articulates her words through her sharp-edged delivery. (See individual entry: McRae, Carmen.)

● **Mabel Mercer** (1900–1984) was a great singer and an influence on other singers ranging from Frank Sinatra to Leontyne Price. She was born in Burton-on-Trent, Staffordshire, England, the daughter of an American jazz musician and a British actor. She began working as a singer and dancer in Europe when she was a teenager. In the 1930s she performed regularly at Bricktop's in Paris and in 1938 made her successful U.S. debut at the Ruban Bleu in New York City. She was kept out of the country in the early years of World War II but returned in 1941. For the next decade, she appeared in New York's best clubs. In the 1970s, she made several television appearances, including a PBS special entitled *An Evening with Mabel Mercer and Bobby Short and Friends* (1972) and a five-part BBC television series, *Miss Mercer in Mayfair* (1977).

● **Maxine Sullivan** (1911–1987) was a highly respected singer of the 1930s and 1940s. She was born Marietta Williams in Homestead, Pennsylvania. At the urging of pianist Gladys Mosier, she moved to New York in 1936 and auditioned for pianist-arranger Claude Thornhill. She recorded his arrangement of "Loch Lomond," the Scottish folk song, in 1937, with great success. That same year, she married John Kirby, the bassist with the jazz group she appeared with. They recorded together and became co-stars of the NBC radio show *Flow Gently, Sweet Rhythm*. In 1939 Sullivan appeared in *Swingin' the Dream*, a swing version of *A Midsummer Night's Dream*, and two films, *St. Louis Blues* and *Going Places*. After a 1941 divorce from Kirby, Sullivan sang with the Benny Carter Orchestra and then went out on her own. She retired in 1956, appearing from time to time until she came out of retirement in 1970. She toured internationally and performed until her death in 1987.

● **Sarah Vaughan** (1924–1990), with the heart, soul, and mind of a master musician and the voice of a goddess, conquered the worlds of jazz and popular singing and was hailed by her contemporaries as the greatest singer of her time. (See individual entry: Vaughan, Sarah.)

● **Cassandra Wilson** (1955–) was a widely recognized, first-rate, trend-setting jazz vocalist. (See individual entry: Wilson, Cassandra.)

● **Nancy Wilson** (1937–) produced more than sixty albums by the start of the twenty-first century and achieved international recognition for her performances. While some musicians have achieved success in one musical genre, Wilson thrived as a premier "song stylist," successfully singing jazz, pop, and rhythm and blues. (See individual entry: Wilson, Nancy.)

137

enjoyed Ella's impeccable musicianship and innovative, swinging style. Though Ella's years on the Capitol and Reprise labels from 1960 to 1967 were somewhat marred with uncharacteristic pop and R&B tunes, in 1972 she returned to Jazz on the Pablo label. Ella's scatting is flawless Jazz vocalese whose vocabulary was often mimicked, yet never mastered. On *C-Jam Blues* she "trades off" with five icons from Ellington's band. This Santa Monica concert is classic dueling, and shows why Ella reigns as "First Lady of Jazz." Ella enjoyed a sixty-year career, two-and-a-half octave range, Grammy Awards, and a U.S. Presidential Medal.

Lena. Lena Horne was born June 1917 in Brooklyn. She danced in Harlem's Cotton Club and sang with Noble Sissle before being called to Hollywood. With the support of her father, Horne refused roles deemed "appropriate" for blacks and was therefore often relegated to cameo singing spots that could be easily excised from films when they were shown in the South. Her career includes TV and film gigs—many without credit—and roles in *That's Entertainment* (1994), *The Wiz* (1978), *Panama Hattie* (1942), *Cabin in the Sky* (1943), and *Stormy Weather* (1943), for which cosmetics guru Max Factor developed dark makeup to make her look more African. The limitations imposed on Horne as an actor led her to focus on her career as a singer. Here, she modeled her image and repertoire to fulfill her role as a representative of her race. Singing Gershwin and Cole Porter, she became living proof that a black woman could be cool, sophisticated, and above reproach.

Sassy. Sarah "Sassy" Vaughan (1924–1990) was born in Newark. She began as organist and choir member at Mount Zion Baptist Church. In 1942, an amateur night win—for singing *Body and Soul*—fetched $10 and a week at the Apollo Theatre. She was hired as vocalist and second pianist by Earl "Fatha" Hines, and later joined Billy Eckstine's Band. Vaughan's recording of *Lover Man*, with its purring growls, bending notes and elongated phrasing, earned her the nickname "Sassy," and launched her solo career at New York's Café Society. By 1949, she had landed a contract with Columbia Records. Vaughan's theme song, *Misty*, shows why she came to be called the "Divine One" and why *Downbeat* and *Metro-nome* magazine readers voted her top female vocalist from 1947 to 1952. In 1982 she won a Grammy for *Gershwin Live!* Vaughan received a lifetime achievement Grammy in 1989, and was inducted into the Jazz Hall of Fame.

Dinah. Ruth Jones (1924–1963), a native of Tuscaloosa, Alabama, changed her name to Dinah Washington after moving to Chicago. She sang gospel and played piano in Sallie Martin's choir and the DuSable High School band. At the age of fifteen, she won an Amateur Night contest at Chicago's Regal Theatre. Her first hit, "Evil Gal Blues," appeared in 1943. Her 1957 recording of Bessie's least known

CASSANDRA WILSON, contralto, not only is a jazz vocalist but also performs in other genres—including pop, folk, and Hollywood and Broadway musicals. In 2001 *Time* magazine called her the best singer in America. (Courtesy of Cassandra Wilson and Paul Zukoski.)

tunes led critics to label her "defiant." Washington had recorded R&B tunes, but once inspired by Lady Day, she turned exclusively to jazz. Once she made the switch, Washington no longer sang spirituals as she did not believe in mixing the sacred with the secular.

Lionel Hampton is credited with renaming Dinah and helping her select a jazz career. Whatever genre she chose, Washington was queen of drama and diction. She influenced Nancy Wilson and Esther Phillips. Despite a sometimes turbulent personal life, which included seven marriages and struggles with weight, Washington's professional career flourished with recordings on the Verve, Mercury and Roulette labels. At thirty-nine, Washington died of an overdose of diet pills and alcohol.

Abby. Singer, actress, and poet Abbey Lincoln (Aminata Moseka) created art worldwide. She was married to legendary drummer Max Roach and recorded many innovative sides with him. Lincoln's five-decade vocal career is recorded on BMG, Verve, Capitol, and a host of other labels. Lincoln's 1999 *Wholly Earth* CD features an earthy, percussive title track and duets with Maggie Brown, Chicago-based daughter of Oscar Brown Jr.

Black Women in Contemporary Jazz

Cool jazz emerged in the 1950s as a laid-back alternative to the frenzy of bop, accenting jazz's lyrical qualities. Subgenres of cool jazz emerged along geographical lines. West Coast jazz was popular in California and neighboring states. "Dixieland" emerged among musicians on Chicago's Westside, and in St. Louis, not in Dixie per se. By the 1960s, as British invaders and white U.S. pop musicians reached icon status, Jazz was marginalized. This inspired post-bop innovations. Many post-bop categories fall into the progressive camp and take their names from prominent elements. Progressive jazz includes fusion (jazz-rock, soul-jazz, and hybrids that meld electronic and acoustic jazz), avant-garde or 1970s free, crossover or smooth, world, and ethnic jazz.

There are black women in all these genres, and many women transcend them. They include singers Geraldine DeHaas (founder of the Chicago Jazz Festival and member of Andy and the Bey Sisters), Dee Dee Bridgewater, Dianne Reeves, Cassandra Wilson, Nnenna Freelon, Bobbi Wilsyn (founder of the all-female group She), Rachel Farrell, Rita Warford, Cheryl Skinner, Carla Cook, Julia Huff, and Abbey Lincoln. There are pianist and harpist Alice McLeod Coltrane, Renee Rosnes, Gerri Allen, Valerie Capers, Cheryl Skinner, Bethany Pickens (daughter of Willie Pickens), and members of the Association for the Advancement of Creative Musicians (AACM) Ann Ward and Amina Claudine Myers. Founded in 1965, AACM fosters diverse musicianship and experimentation.

Organist Jackie Ivory, an Arkansas native, recorded on the Atlantic and Soul Discovery labels. Bu Pleasant (Frances Chapman) had a heart as big as her home state of Texas, and tragedy to match. Yet she cut several Muse albums and was inducted into the Texas Jazz Archives. Newark native Rhoda Scott spent most of her time in France where she first played the B-3 and its derivatives, the Hammond B-3000, and the Hammond-Suzuki X-B3. Scott and her mentor, Trudy Pitts, were regulars at the annual Jazz Organ Festival.

Philadelphia organist Trudy Pitts was married to drummer Mr. C., alias Bill Carney. Pitts recorded several albums on Prestige label and had a standing gig at Meiji-En, the nation's largest Japanese restaurant.

Bassist Marion Hayden, a Detroit native and member of the all-female group Straight Ahead, composed and taught in Cleveland. Me'shell Ndegeocello is a bassist who also sings Hip-hop. Guitarist and bassist Carline Ray was an active sideman from 1930 to the 2000s. While Deborah Coleman and Shemekia Copeland more often played Blues guitar, they often recorded Jazz.

Drummer Ruby Lucas (Renee Phelan) was a member of the International Sweethearts of Rhythm, and lifelong lover of trumpeter Ernestine "Tiny" Davis. In the 1950s, Lucas and Davis owned Tiny and Ruby's Gay Spot in Chicago. Viola Smith sported stick-twirling showmanship envied by her male peers. A list of later jazz drummers might include Straight Ahead's Gayelynn McKinney, who also played sax.

Terry Lyne Carrington was born in Medford, Massachusetts, in 1965. This child prodigy's mentors included her dad, Sonny, and Jack DeJohnette. At the age of eleven, Carrington won a scholarship to Berklee. She later became an active drum clinician and recording artist, having appeared on a hundred CDs. Accolades included a Grammy nomination for her 1989 *Real Life Story*.

Born in 1959, Cyndi Blackman appeared on several CDs and inside the covers of numerous percussion magazines, and boasts a long list of TV credits. Chicago hand drummer Coco Elysees was a member of AACM and sat in most often on congas. Elysees moved to Los Angeles to pursue a recording career. Vibraphonist and pianist Darlene Hill taught at Chicago State and Roosevelt University, and performed with noted standup comedian Bernie Mack.

Though not much bigger than her baritone sax, Fostina Dixon charmed a mellow sound from the horn. Dixon appeared with the Winds of Change, playing soprano, alto, flute, or clarinet. Diane "Lil' Sax" Ellis emerged from one of Chicago's most prominent Jazz families to become active as an alto sax sideman and leader of her own pickup band. Matana Roberts also played alto sax. Likewise from Chicago, Roberts left her mark on Boston before moving to New York. Her robust sound ignites her solo CD *Gifts*, and also *Sticks and Stones*. Violinist Regina Carter graduated from the New England Conservatory and Oakland University in her native Michigan. Carter appeared with Uptown String Quartet, String Trio of New York, Wynton Marsalis, and Max Roach, and recorded several solo CDs. She appeared on Atlantic Records with Straight Ahead, a quintet that formed in 1987.

Flautist Althea René, also a member of Straight Ahead, was a Howard University graduate who enjoyed a career in France before returning to the United States. AACM member Nikki Mitchell made a home in Chicago where she played flute and founded the Black Earth Ensemble; Mitchell recorded two CDs. Sherry Winston is based in Danbury, Connecticut. Winston's 2002 CD, *For Lovers Only*, is on the Orpheus label. Trumpeter Diane Lyles, a Hampton Institute alumna, taught at Xavier University and lived in Philadelphia.

Early musicians learned jazz by barhopping, attending jam sessions, and copping from masters, but recording devices cut down on pavement beating. Technology and racial integration patterns diffused the jazz community. By the beginning of the twenty-first century, few neighborhood clubs existed where young musicians could sit in and jam with the pros. NEA grants allowed youngsters to study with jazz elders, but artists no longer had direct access to these fellowships. Rather, one had to be directly sponsored by an eligible organization.

It was always difficult for a musician to earn a living unless she lived in an urban area. Night club and theatre gigs were scarce. Jazz musicians were often forced to play commercial music to earn a living. Teaching and other unrelated jobs allowed artists to eat regularly, but did not facilitate recordings. Record companies turned to jazz in their time of need or during those moments when a jazz musician would become popular with somewhat more mainstream audiences, but for them issuing new jazz records regularly was not a top priority. Jazz, however, managed to retain a level of popularity, even when it is not the genre of choice. In 1990 the recording industry, fearing that the ailing Miles Davis would never record again, fostered the new Miles: Wynton Marsalis. Sadly, no such steps were taken when Ella or Betty or Sarah lay dying. Women have had to create their own networks and opportunities.

The first Women's Jazz Festival was held in Kansas City in 1978, followed by the Kennedy Center's festival. New York's Jazz Mobile and Chicago's Jazz Fest are ways for women to get to know others in their own field and to make new professional contacts. However, most festival lineups include recording artists, and since women of color are grossly underrepresented on record labels, they tend to be underrepresented even at these festivals. Still, African American women continue to play and sing in the great traditions of jazz.

See also Armstrong, Lillian "Lil" Hardin; Blues; Fitzgerald, Ella; Holiday, Billie; Horn, Shirley; Horne, Lena; Hunter, Alberta; McRae, Carmen; Simone, Nina; Smith, Bessie; Vaughn, Sarah; Washington, Dinah; Waters, Ethel; Williams, Mary Lou; and Wilson, Nancy.

BIBLIOGRAPHY

Bach, Jean. Great Day in Harlem. Castle Hill Productions, 1995.
Big Bands Database 2002. "Popular Song Vocalists." http://www.nfo.net.
Dahl, Linda. Stormy Weather: The Music and Lives of a Century of Jazzwomen. New York: Proscenium Publishers, 1984.
Fallico, Pete. "Jazz Organ Stories." http://www.doodlinlounge.com.
Gould, Michael. "Comping Exercises and Beyond." Percussive Notes. 18 April 2001.
Handy, D. Antoinette. "Conversations (with M. L. Williams)." Black Perspective, Fall 1980.
Handy, D. Antoinette. Black Women in American Bands & Orchestras. Lanham, Maryland: Scarecrow Press, 1981.
Placksin, Sally. "American Women in Jazz." Downbeat, February 1938.
Taylor, Dr. Billy. What is Jazz? Four lectures. Kennedy Center, Washington, DC, 1994–1995.
Tucker, Sherrie. Swing Shift: "All-Girl" Bands of the 1940s. Durham: Duke University Press, 2000.
Wynn, Ron, editor. All Music Guide. http://www.allmusic.com.

—REGINA HARRIS BAIOCCHI

JEMISON, MAE CAROL (b. 17 October 1956) has accomplished many remarkable feats as a physician, astronaut, teacher, humanitarian, activist, and self-proclaimed womanist. One such feat occurred on 12 September 1992, when she soared to new heights on the space shuttle Endeavor and became the first African American woman to venture into outer space.

The youngest of three children, Jemison was born in Decatur, Alabama, to Charlie and Dorothy Jemison, a maintenance supervisor at United Charities of Chicago and an elementary schoolteacher, respectively. From a young age Jemison dreamed of traveling into outer space, despite the fact that the astronaut corps did not accept American women until 1970. Determined to provide Jemison and her older sister and brother, Ada and Charles, with opportunities not afforded in the South, her family moved to Chicago, Illinois, in search of a better quality of life. At Morgan Park High School she was given the opportunity to explore a variety of areas that captivated her attention. Jemison was academically intrigued and stimulated by the sciences and also took an interest in dance, art, anthropology, and archaeology. Jemison was a well-rounded student, excelling in her academics while still finding time for extracurricular activities such as the modern dance club and the pompom squad. At sixteen she graduated from high school and left Chicago for California to attend Stanford University on a National Achievement Scholarship.

While at Stanford, Jemison was involved in a number of activities, including intramural football, the fine arts, and the Black Student Union, where she served as the first female president. In 1977 she earned a bachelor's degree in chemical engineering and a bachelor of arts degree in African/Afro-American studies. She then enrolled at Cornell University Medical College in New York City. During the summers at Cornell she traveled as a medical volunteer to Cuba, Kenya, and a refugee camp in Thailand, where she helped people suffering from starvation, tuberculosis, and dysentery. In 1981, she earned her MD and went to Los Angeles, where she interned at the Los Angeles County/University of Southern California Medical Center until 1982, when she took a job as a general practitioner. At the age of twenty-six, longing to return to Africa, Jemison joined the Peace Corps for two and a half years. This exploration took her to the West African

MAE C. JEMISON (right) and colleagues at the National Aeronautics and Space Administration. Jemison was NASA's first black female astronaut and on 12 September 1992 became the first black woman in space, aboard the shuttle *Endeavor*. (NASA; Austin/Thompson Collection.)

countries of Sierra Leone and Liberia. During her service, she was a medical officer, which involved not only being a doctor to the volunteers and the embassy staff but also teaching courses, supervising laboratories, writing health manuals, and overseeing general public health and safety in the area.

Jemison's medical career gave her the opportunity to help thousands of people around the world. Although she enjoyed her work, her greatest desire was still set on exploring space. Upon her return to the United States in 1985, she began to take the necessary steps to make her dream a reality. She took a job as a general practitioner at GIGNA Health Plans of California, in Los Angeles, enrolled in engineering courses at UCLA in the evenings, and applied for admission into the NASA space program. However, after the explosion of the space shuttle *Challenger* on 28 January 1986, NASA suspended its shuttle program in order to conduct a full investigation into the tragedy that had taken the lives of all of the astronauts aboard. Later that year, NASA reopened the program, and Jemison renewed her application. Of the two thousand applicants, she was one of fifteen people—and the first African American woman—admitted into NASA's astronaut training program. In August 1988, Jemison became a mission specialist astronaut, the fifth black astronaut and the first black female astronaut in NASA history.

Five years later, she embarked on her first mission: the STS-47 SPACELAB J flight, a cooperative mission between the United States and Japan. On 12 September 1992 Jemison and six other astronauts blasted off for an eight-day voyage on the space shuttle *Endeavor*, making her the first African American woman to explore space. While aboard the *Endeavor*, she conducted experiments in materials processing and life sciences, associated with weightlessness, tissue growth, and the development of semiconductor materials.

In recognition of her many accomplishments, Jemison received a number of distinguished awards, including induction into the National Women's Hall of Fame and several honorary doctorates. She served on several corporate boards of directors, as well as on the Texas Governor's State Council for Science and BioTechnology Development. In addition, the Mae C. Jemison Academy, an alternative public school in Detroit, Michigan, was dedicated in her honor in 1992.

After leaving NASA in 1993, Jemison taught courses on space-age technology and developing countries for five years at Dartmouth College, and later established the Jemison Group Inc., a company devoted to technology advancement. One operation, ALAFIYA, is a satellite-based telecommunications system intended to improve health care delivery in developing nations. In addition, she served as a consultant to the Discovery Channel's *World of Wonders* program and appeared on an episode of *Star Trek: The Next Generation*. She published her autobiography, *Find Where the Wind Goes*, in 2001.

BIBLIOGRAPHY

Black, Sonia. *Mae Jemison*. New York: Mondo, 2000.
Frazer, Jendayi. "Advancing African Health Care Through Space Technology: An Interview with Dr. Mae C. Jemison." *Africa Today*, Summer 1993.
Gelletly, LeeAnne. *Mae Jemison*. Philadelphia: Chelsea House, 2002.
Giovanni, Nikki. "Shooting for the Moon." *Essence*, April 1993, 58–62.
Sykes, Tanisha A. "A Space-Age Idea." *Black Enterprise*, July 2003.
Yannuzzi, Della. *Mae Jemison: A Space Biography*. Springfield, NJ: Enslow, 1998.

—MONIQUE M. CHISM

JESSYE, EVA (b. 20 January 1895; d. 21 February 1992), composer and musical director. In the 1989 book titled *I Dream a World: Portraits of Black Women Who Changed America*, by Brian Lanker, Eva Jessye recollected the difficult experiences she encountered while touring as choral conductor with the Porgy and Bess American Opera: "I wouldn't let anybody get between me and my music. If I belong to anything, I belong to my music . . . Any woman of that time would have had the same trouble I had. They never thought a woman could be as devoted to one idea as a man."

Her artistic talents and dedication to the preservation of African American music set the tone for a remarkable career that would span decades. As a choral director, composer, arranger, writer, poet, actor, and teacher, the multitalented Jessye was a pioneer and a significant figure in American music.

Eva Alberta Jessye was born to Albert and Julia Jessye in Coffeyville, Kansas, and was the only child born from this marriage. Albert Jessye earned a living as a chicken picker in Coffeyville and he separated from his wife, Julia, in 1898, when Eva was still a toddler. After the separation, her mother moved to Seattle to work, and Jessye was left in the care of her grandmother Mollie Buckner. She also spent much of her younger years in the care of her maternal aunts. Jessye recalled her earliest musical influences to be when her great-aunt Harriet and great-grandmother Hill sang Negro spirituals. Jessye always believed that the Negro spirituals were a unique and treasured piece of the African American heritage. She believed that they were written and sung to spread messages of humility, love, and faith. She wrote a book *My Spirituals*, in 1927—a collection she describes as "a priceless heritage of song . . . It is simply a recording of some songs I grew up with." Each spiritual in the book is prefaced with a story that provides the background and inspiration for the song.

EVA JESSYE, musician, composer, and actress, in character for a publicity photograph. In 1935 Jessye was the "guardian of the score" for George Gershwin's folk opera *Porgy and Bess;* and in 1963 the Eva Jessye choir participated in the March on Washington. (Schomburg Center for Research in Black Culture, New York Public Library.)

Jessye attended public schools in Coffeyville and Iola, Kansas, and developed her love for music and poetry at an early age. She took piano lessons while in grade school and began writing poetry as early as age seven. At twelve, she organized a girls' choir among her relatives. In 1908, at thirteen, she was admitted into Western University, where she studied poetry and oratory. Jessye could play the piano by ear. Jessye recollected: "I could read music so easily. The fact is, I didn't have to read the music. The teachers would never let me hear them play 'cause I would just have it. I could always remember. It came naturally to me, not second nature but first nature." While in attendance at Western University, Jessye was a member of the concert choir and became a soloist for spirituals and classical music; she also coached the male quartet and female choral groups.

After graduating from Western University in 1914 with honors in poetry and oratory, Jessye attended Langston University for three consecutive summers, receiving her bachelor's degree and a permanent teaching certificate. From 1914 to 1919, she taught public schools in Taft, Haskell, and Muskegee, Oklahoma. In 1919 she became the director of the Music Department at Morgan College in Baltimore, Maryland. Under her leadership the Morgan College Choir became one of the most notable choral groups in the community. Their repertoire included spirituals, folk songs, and anthems, and they performed choral arrangements for churches and various social events. Jessye would later resign from this position after the president of the college attempted to limit their performances to spirituals alone. Jessye believed that this restriction would suppress their musical versatility while continuing to perpetuate the notion that blacks can only sing spirituals.

After resigning from Morgan State College, Jessye moved back to Oklahoma, where she resumed teaching in public schools. In 1925 she returned to Baltimore and accepted a position as a writer for the Baltimore Afro-American weekly newspaper. In 1926 she moved to New York in search of musical and theatrical opportunities. Jessye became choral director for the Dixie Jubilee Singers, a choral group that performed spirituals, jazz, ballads, and light opera on radio, film, and stage. The group got its first big break after auditioning to perform at the Capitol Theatre on Broadway. The singers became regulars on the "Major Bowes Family Radio Hour." The life of the choir would span more than thirty years. In 1929 Jessye and the Dixie Jubilee singers, which was later renamed the Eva Jessye Choir, provided choral music for King Vidor's film *Hallelujah*, one of the first musicals to feature black actors. Jessye was appointed choral director for *Hallelujah* and was also choral director for the Gertrude Stein and Virgil Thomson opera, *Four Saints in Three Acts* in 1934. It was also during this time that the famed composer and conductor Will Marion Cook became her composition teacher and mentor.

Jessye became nationally recognized for her musical creativity. As choral director, she was able to authenticate many musical scores with the richness of her arrangements of ballads, jazz, ragtime, blues, folk songs in a call-and-response format, and, most importantly, narrative spirituals. She accepted nothing less than excellence from her singers and her choral auditions were rigid, as she demanded rich tonal quality, precise pronunciation and diction, pride in presentation and attire, and complete memorization of the score.

Jessye became known as the unofficial "guardian of the score" for the 1935 George Gershwin folk opera *Porgy and Bess*. She remembered that she had been traveling with her sixteen-member choir in South Carolina, and they returned to New York City to audition for the production: "When we sang, George Gershwin said, 'That's it, that's what I want.' So they were the official choir of the first recorded production, and I was the first choral conductor for *Porgy and Bess*."

Jessye and her choir received favorable reviews both nationally and internationally as they toured with the *Porgy and Bess* opera throughout the United States as well as in Europe, Russia, and Australia. Throughout her career, Jessye remained one of the leading authorities on the *Porgy and Bess* production. The Eva Jessye Choir also performed in a variety of capacities and for different causes, drives, and memorial tributes. In 1963 they were designated as the official choral group for the March on Washington.

Jessye also enjoyed a career as an actress in film as well as on stage. Her stage roles included Strawberry Woman in *Porgy and Bess* during the 1952, 1958, and 1967 productions and Queenie in *Showboat* in 1959. Several of her film appearances included *Black Like Me* in 1964 and *Slaves* in 1969. Jessye was very selective when choosing her stage and film roles; she would not accept roles that she felt were demeaning to the black race.

After the Eva Jessye Choir disbanded in the early 1970s, Jessye returned to academia to continue writing, teaching, composing, and lecturing at many major universities. She moved to Ann Arbor, Michigan, in early 1973 and established the Eva Jessye Collection of Afro-American Music the following year. Jessye donated a collection of her musical memorabilia, which included books, periodicals, musical programs, scores, recordings, and clippings, to the Black Music Students Association and to the University of Michigan School of Music as a cultural contribution to preserve the history of African American life and music. Jessye also established smaller collections of her memorabilia at Taft Junior High School in Taft, Oklahoma, in 1975; Clark University in Atlanta, Georgia, in 1979; and, in 1977, Pittsburg State University in Pittsburg, Kansas, where she was also appointed artist-in-residence. Two of her major folk oratorios, *Paradise Lost and Regained* and *The Chronical of Job*, were performed while she was in residence at Pittsburg State University.

Jessye was the recipient of numerous honors and awards from universities, government agencies, and professional organizations. She held honorary doctorate degrees from Wilberforce University, Allen University, and Eastern Michigan University. She was awarded a Doctor of Determination Certificate from the University of Michigan's Department of African American Studies in

1976. On 1 October 1978, Kansas governor Robert Bennett proclaimed "Eva Jessye Day," and in 1981 Governor John Carlin declared Jessye the Kansas Ambassador for the Arts.

Jessye's career was multidimensional. As a poet, actor, humanitarian, composer and arranger, choral director, teacher, and lecturer, her lifelong goal was to preserve the tradition of African American music and culture. She met her goal with conviction. Jessye married twice but had no children. She died at the age of ninety-seven in Ann Arbor, Michigan.

BIBLIOGRAPHY

Black, Donald Fisher. "The Life and Work of Eva Jessye and Her Contributions to American Music." PhD diss., University of Michigan–Ann Arbor, 1986, University Microfilms International.

"The Eva Jessye Collection." AXE, Special Collections, Eva Jessye. Official Web site of the Leonard H. Axe Library, Pittsburg University. http://library.pittstate.edu/spcoll/ndxjessye.html.

Jessye, Eva. *My Spirituals*. New York: Robbins-Engel, 1927.

Lanker, Brian. *I Dream a World: Portraits of Black Women Who Changed America*. New York: Stewart, Tabori & Chang, 1989.

"Music Motivated Eva Jessye as a Child in Kansas." A Moment in Time. Kansas State Historical Society. http://www.kshs.org/features/feat2976b.htm.

Smith, Jessie Carney, ed. *Notable Black American Women*. Detroit: Gale, 1992.

—ROBBIE CLARK

FIRST MARKET LUNCHROOM, Richmond, Virginia. Its sign, "For Colored," was typical in the south during the Jim Crow period. (Austin/Thompson Collection, by permission of Valentine Richmond History Center.)

JIM CROW ERA.

Jim Crow's scandalous history as a term of opprobrium signifying black/white racial segregation started, then, years before the United States abolished slavery in 1865. The phrase settled as a castelike social description marking African Americans as simultaneously accommodated yet ostracized. Jim Crow cropped up in Louisville, Cincinnati, Philadelphia, and New York City in the 1830s as the name of a song and dance, "Jump Jim Crow." The term quickly became more than a minstrel show title. It appeared in Massachusetts in 1841 to describe railroad cars set apart for blacks, but the name became attached to more than the seating arrangements on railroad cars, as Sarah Roberts's case showed in 1848. When the City of Boston's school board barred five-year-old Sarah from attending her neighborhood public primary school and instead assigned her to one of two "schools appropriate to colored children," her father, the antislavery social reformer Benjamin F. Roberts, sued on her behalf. Sarah lost. In *Roberts v. City of Boston* (1849), the state's highest court, in an opinion by one of its most highly regarded jurists, ruled that Sarah was not "unlawfully excluded from public school." Massachusetts law allowed separate public schools for blacks and whites. As with every aspect of African American experience, the Sarah Roberts suit showed that from the beginning black females were at the front and center of the Jim Crow era.

Civil War and Emancipation

Jim Crow burdened only the small percentage of free blacks before the Civil War (1861–1865). Almost nine in ten (89.2 percent) of the nation's 4,427,294 African Americans in 1860 were slaves and hence subject to more than the strictures of Jim Crow. After the war, patterns shifted. In December 1865 the Thirteenth Amendment to the U.S. Constitution outlawed slavery. In July 1868 the Fourteenth Amendment barred any state from "deny[ing] to any person within its jurisdiction the equal protection of the laws."

The move to emancipate slaves and to articulate civil rights changed black women's positions. It did not, however, reach into the separate spheres that relegated female activity primarily to the shadows. Black women bore the heavy burdens of detailed, day-in-day-out organizing and operating that sustained the institutions of emancipation, but were shunted from the spotlight in the public policy discourse of community representatives and spokespersons.

Beginning with churches, schools, and self-help groups, black women toiled tirelessly to keep black bodies and souls together on the upward climb. They scratched out space to survive and thrive. They sheltered what they could and faced the storm of slavery's demise during Reconstruction (1865–1877) and beyond with determination to vindicate human dignity. They built on their continued tradition of struggle and survival in battling racial oppression and inequality in its sundry insidious guises.

Declaring an end to slavocracy was not to declare an end to patriarchy. Rule by men in male-dominated and male-oriented complexes modeled on a family's deference to the father stood as a matter of fact, as American society announced the end of old-style rule by slaveholders under slavery. Hence Jim Crow attacked postbellum black women on the levels of race, sex, and class.

The new law of emancipation focused on black men, as established American law focused on men. Consistent with its traditional view of females as male appendages, the law cast black women in connection with black men. The legislation creating the primary federal agency handling slaves' transition to emancipation from 1865 to 1870 showed the law's slight to black women. The acts of March 1865 and July 1866 addressed "freedmen." Indeed, they created a Freedmen's Bureau. In providing for rights to the much-spoken-of forty acres (no mule was mentioned), the 1865 act specified that recipients were to be male. The 1866 act shifted the terms to "heads of families of the African race," which allowed black women to qualify. The shift was not to accommodate women's rights, however; it was to privilege men with wives and children over single men.

Freedwomen got little as women from the law. What rights they gained in emancipation arose primarily from race. The gender distinction appeared clearly in the Fifteenth Amendment, adopted in March 1870. It declared "the right of citizens of the United States to vote shall not be denied or abridged by the United States or by any state on account of race, color, or previous condition of servitude." That allowed black men access to the ballot but not black women, who were denied suffrage with other women until the Nineteenth Amendment, adopted in August 1920. They nevertheless proved they could wield significant political and other influence without ballots.

Black Codes

The immediate postwar response to racial readjustment in the defeated South hardly embraced black/white equality. Reactionary Southern legislatures in 1865 and 1866 enacted state Black Codes to legalize paternalistic and otherwise restrictive racial patterns and practices. Mississippi led the way in many respects, from family and labor law to transportation. In November 1865, for example,

the Mississippi legislature enacted a statute to prohibit railroads in the state from permitting blacks to ride in cars reserved for whites. This was Jim Crow in full feather. Justifications for the laws would come later not only from lawyers, judges, and politicians but also from the social science fields and from pseudo-scientific biological studies and experiments in the 1880s and 1890s, as not only white Americans struggled to control the black population, but also as European imperialist powers, especially in Africa and Asia, undertook what the English writer Rudyard Kipling described in his 1899 poem of the same name, "The White Man's Burden."

Black women instantly protested, particularly provisions that abolished or abused the family relations they viewed as essential to emancipation's meaning. They decried the announcement and action of law that, for example, made only black children subject to forced apprenticeships. Authorizing state agents to snatch children away from parents and to give former slaveholders first choice as guardians, as Mississippi's 1865 apprenticeship act did, was something black women refused to tolerate. The emancipation that recognized their right to freedom also meant recognizing their children's rights. Black women demanded justice from the state—and not in the South alone; black women chorused with the black men at an 1865 convention in Xenia, Ohio, in denouncing "laws unjustly making distinction on account of color." They demanded, in the words of the convention, that state laws "be purified, and made to conform to the requirements of Republican justice."

Political power came after Congress in March 1867 demanded that black men be allowed to vote in the South and that states cease racial discrimination, thus staying Jim Crow's sweep—at least momentarily. For example, Louisiana's 1868 Constitution declared:

> All persons shall enjoy equal rights and privileges upon any conveyance of a public character; and all places of business or public resort, or for which a license is required by either State, parish or municipal authority, shall be deemed of a public character, and shall be open to the accommodation and patronage of all persons without distinction or discrimination on account of race or color.

The Transportation Struggle

Josephine DeCuir of Pointe Coupe Parish, Louisiana, became an early champion in the struggle for civil rights. When Capt. John C. Benson of the Mississippi River steamboat *Governor Allen* denied her a berth in the ladies' cabin for a trip upriver from New Orleans in July 1872, DeCuir sued him under Louisiana law. She won. In *DeCuir v. Benson* (1875), Louisiana's Supreme Court upheld her award of $1,000 in damages and upheld, too, the state's power to outlaw racial discrimination in public accommodations.

The discrimination that vexed DeCuir was hardly new to black women, nor was it confined to the South. In 1867, five years before DeCuir's troubles aboard the *Governor Allen*, Mary E. Miles suffered similar treatment—not on a Mississippi steamboat but on a West Chester and Philadelphia Railroad Company streetcar. Boarding the streetcar in the City of Brotherly Love, in an act of defiance that would resonate almost a century later in Montgomery, Alabama, Miles refused the conductor's direction, following Jim Crow rules of the road, to sit toward the rear. When she persisted, Miles was forcibly removed from the car. She sued and won in Philadelphia County's Court of Common Pleas.

Miles's victory proved short-lived. In *West Chester and Philadelphia Railroad Company v. Miles* (1867), Pennsylvania's Supreme Court reversed the lower court, finding fault with a jury instruction. But Justice Daniel Agnew's opinion for the high court majority went beyond ordering a new trial. The court's decision emphasized that the railroad company had a legal right to separate black and white passengers. "The right of the carrier to separate his passengers is founded upon two grounds—his right of private property in the means of conveyance, and the public interest," the court announced. Moreover, it declared that there was a

> natural, legal and customary difference between the white and black races in this state which made their separation as passengers in a public conveyance the subject of a sound regulation to secure order, promote comfort, preserve the peace and maintain the rights both of carriers and passengers.

If their state supreme court's ruling held any solace for Miles and other black Pennsylvanians, it rested in the court's acknowledging that since Miles had brought her case, the legislature had changed Pennsylvania law to declare it an offense for railroads to discriminate between passengers on account of race or color. The court further acknowledged that even before the March 1867 statute, Pennsylvania's common law recognized blacks' right not to be excluded from "a public carrier on account of color . . . or prejudice."

The Pennsylvania court's distinction between being excluded from accommodations and being relegated to Jim Crow accommodations proved crucial. Its decision in Miles's case echoed the lawful-separation note that Massachusetts Chief Justice Lemuel Shaw sounded in his 1849 school decision in Sarah Roberts's case. It also echoed a theme of Michigan Supreme Court in response to blacks' 1858 challenge to Jim Crow treatment on a Great Lakes steamer. In *Day v. Owen* (1858), Michigan's highest court ruled it "reasonable" for a common carrier to separate

black and white passengers. In fact, the Michigan court went so far as to state that while blacks had a right to be passengers, they had no right to any particular accommodations. The carrier decided what blacks got as part of his "control over his own property in his own way," the court said. "The right to be carried is one thing—the privileges of a passenger on board of the boat, what part of it may be occupied by him, or he have the right to use, is another thing. The two rights are very different," the court held.

So DeCuir's troubles in Louisiana were part of a long line of black women's trials and tribulations in the struggle for equal treatment on public transportation. They established the right of blacks not to be excluded as passengers. Whether blacks had rights to the same accommodations for the same fare, however, and whether states could, as did Pennsylvania in 1867 and Louisiana in 1869, dictate equal accommodation on common carriers remained unsettled.

The U.S. Supreme Court Speaks

The U.S. Supreme Court's handling of DeCuir's case on appeal closed some questions and directed attention to the struggle ahead. In *Hall v. DeCuir* (1877), the nation's high court reversed DeCuir's victory. Finding that the *Governor Allen* operated in interstate commerce over which Congress had exclusive power, the Court, in an opinion by Chief Justice Morrison Waite, held Louisiana's 1869 nondiscrimination act to be unconstitutional in its reach to the Mississippi steamer. The Court explicitly declared that its ruling had "nothing whatever to do with [the equal accommodations act] as a regulation of internal commerce, or as affecting anything else than commerce among the States." Yet the ruling limited state law's reach to the most significant modes of transportation. DeCuir thus lost the legal grounds on which she had sued. Her action was nevertheless important: hers and similar cases helped move Congress to pass the Civil Rights Act of 1875, which entitled

> citizens of every race and color, regardless of any previous condition of servitude [to] the full and equal enjoyment of the accommodations, advantages, facilities, and privileges of inns, public conveyances on land or water, theaters, and other places of public amusement.

The public accommodations provisions in the Civil Rights Act of 1875 offered no long-standing shelter to blacks who, like DeCuir, had claims of racial discrimination against common carriers. In a consolidated series of five cases from California, Kansas, Missouri, New York, and Tennessee, the U.S. Supreme Court in 1883 ruled that Congress lacked authority under the Thirteenth or the Fourteenth Amendment to reach private acts of racial discrimination. So if a railway conductor refused to allow a black woman to ride in the ladies' car, as happened in the Tennessee case *Robinson & Wife v. Memphis and Charleston Railroad Company*, it was a private matter, not material for a federal case. Thus did the *Civil Rights Cases* (1883) remove federal protection from the hopes of many African Americans, male and female.

Without recourse in federal courts against individual acts of racial discrimination, black women redoubled their efforts to keep states from sanctioning Jim Crow. Twenty-one-year-old Ida Bell Wells (later Wells-Barnett) exemplified the drive in May 1884 when she challenged Tennessee's separate-but-equal law on a ten-mile trip from Woodstock to Memphis on the Chesapeake, Ohio & Southwestern Railroad. Having paid her fare, she elected to sit in the ladies' car and ignored the conductor's directive that it was reserved for whites only. Reports noted that she was "assisted from the car." She sued and won at trial in Shelby County Circuit Court, but the state supreme court reversed her $500 award. Repeating the line of other cases, the Tennessee high court upheld the railroad's discretion to seat passengers at its direction. In a personal slap at Wells, the court chastised her for being harassing and acting "not in good faith to obtain a comfortable seat for the short ride."

Plessy v. Ferguson

The fact of segregation appeared in custom and practice far beyond the Jim Crow rules that excluded Ida Bell Wells, Mary E. Miles, Josephine DeCuir, and other African American women from the equal accommodations for which they paid. It seeped throughout American society. As in Tennessee in Wells's case and Pennsylvania in Miles's case, state courts deemed it discretionary to separate whites and blacks. Indeed, more than one state court ruled such discrimination "reasonable" decades before the U.S. Supreme Court, in its infamous 1896 decision in *Plessy v. Ferguson*, sanctioned state laws that mandated "equal, but separate, accommodations for the white and colored races."

In upholding Louisiana's 1890 Separate Car Act, the U.S. Supreme Court completed an ugly twist that reached back to DeCuir's case. The Court in *Hall v. DeCuir* denied state power to mandate that "all persons shall enjoy equal rights and privileges upon any conveyance of a public character." Then, in *Plessy*, the Court returned to allow state power to mandate racial separation that insured unequal rights. So states could not enforce equality but could enforce inequality.

The U.S. Supreme Court hardly initiated the segregation that settled into an American version of apartheid; its 1896 sanction in *Plessy* nevertheless allowed Jim Crow to spread after long roosting. Black women had battled the beast from the beginning and they continued to resist at

every turn. I. Wells, for example, did not linger over the Tennessee high court's rebuke of her. She spread the word against Jim Crow, becoming one of the foremost journalists and antisegregation advocates of her era.

Antilynching

Wells made lynching a special target after antiblack rioting swept Memphis in March 1892. As editor of the city's *Free Speech and Headlight*, she turned the weekly newspaper's focus from poor public education for blacks in the Tennessee, Arkansas, and Mississippi Delta region to the near epidemic of brutal attacks on blacks that had become almost commonplace throughout the South. From 1882, when a systematic count began, an average of 100 lynchings had occurred annually by 1892, which proved a record year with 230. Not all the lynchings were of blacks. But the white mobs mostly murdered black victims—and not always males; black women were also lynched.

In a lead editorial in March 1892, Wells lambasted Memphis for tolerating lynching and castigated the practice as a vicious ritual of social control aimed more at intimidation than punishment. In savage response to her outraged words, a white mob wrecked the *Free Speech and Headlight* offices and threatened Wells with death if she were seen again in Tennessee's leading city. Although expelled, Wells was not silenced. Joining the *New York Age*, one of the nation's leading black newspapers, she further exposed lynching as having more to do with white recreation than with black crime. Her October 1892 feature story "Southern Horrors: Lynch Law in All Its Phases" was a classic of investigative journalism and was published as a pamphlet, as was its companion piece, *A Red Record* (1895).

Wells's focus on lynching reflected the lead that black women took in the 1890s in vocally opposing barbarity. Their insistence on exposing the wrong done, often under the pretense of protecting womanhood, contributed later to an interracial women's movement to prevent lynching. It also reflected two broad avenues down which African American women strode in full cry against Jim Crow in all its manifestations at the beginning of the 1900s: journalism and local organizing.

Professionals in Protest

Working in church and local organizations and through the growing club movement, African American women joined together for self-help in bettering their race and racial conditions throughout the nation. The National Association of Colored Women (NACW), organized in 1896 with Mary Church Terrell as president, focused the drive for general reform against Jim Crow and all that oppressed the race. Under the theme "Lifting as We Climb," the NACW promoted black self-development and advances against segregation.

The NACW stalwarts were almost exclusively black professional women and, almost by definition, they were civil rights activists. Reaching a professional position required such activism for black women. At the beginning of the 1900s, as in the Civil War era, Jim Crow closed most economic opportunities to black women. Farm and field or domestic service as maids or washerwomen alone stood open: for most, that was black women's work. A precious few pushed into female-dominated professions such as teaching, nursing, social work, and librarianship.

Not sufficiently noted among black women's tools was the press. Black women worked, as did Wells and her radical antilynching predecessor Lucy Parsons as independent journalists and also for institutional organs such as the *Woman's Era*, which began publishing in Boston in March 1894 as the first monthly magazine owned and edited by black women. At least forty-six black women had made national names for themselves as journalists as the 1900s opened. Most, like Wells and the bulk of the black population, were southerners. They wrote. They edited. They were owners and operators. They made public policy and every aspect of Jim Crow daily fare. They gave voice to rights and wrongs. They tore into stereotypes in battling against the abysmal place of both the Negro and women.

Entrepreneurs in Protest

Black women entrepreneurs also served more than local needs in their shops, stores, and markets. Sarah Breedlove went further than other burgeoning black businesswomen: her Madam C.J. Walker Manufacturing Company, with its door-to-door and mail-order sales of hair straightener, put her in line by 1910 to be the first American, black, woman, self-made millionaire. But as with lesser successes, hers was not merely individual; it resounded in a triumph of advancing community to which Breedlove further contributed as a philanthropist. She gave generously to black educational and social institutions and so staunchly supported the antilynching movement that the U.S. State Department in 1919 labeled her a "race agitator" and denied her a passport. Many other black businesswomen left anonymous by history also contributed significantly to their communities in service and example that stayed Jim Crow's reach and enabled and extended African Americans' expectations.

Black women shouldered the daily burden of racial uplift. Battling prejudice and marginalization, they stitched together the community and countrywide support that allowed and sustained the creation of campaigns such as the League for the Protection of Colored Women (founded in 1906), the Committee for Improving the Industrial Conditions among Negroes in New York (1906), and the Committee on Urban Conditions among Negroes (1910). The three merged in 1911 to form the National League on Urban Conditions among Negroes. They also contributed to the National Association for the Advancement of Colored People (NAACP), organized in 1910 and 1911. They backed local and national assaults on Jim Crow.

Entertainers against Jim Crow

In the 1920s black women moved further into official public roles in combating segregation, thanks in large part to the Nineteenth Amendment's eliminating sex as a bar to voting. In 1927 Minnie Buckingham-Harper became the first black woman legislator in the United States when she was appointed to finish the term of her deceased husband in the West Virginia legislature. In 1936 Mary McLeod Bethune, one-time NACW president (1924–1928) and a founder of the National Council of Negro Women (NCNW), became administrative assistant and then division director for Negro Affairs in President Franklin D. Roosevelt's National Youth Administration—the first black woman to hold so high a federal office, which she used to continue her crusade against Jim Crow.

Also in the public eye, black women entertainers struggled and succeeded against Jim Crow. The travail and triumph of the opera singer and contralto Marian Anderson in 1939 proved particularly telling. Unabashedly, the lily-white Daughters of the American Revolution (DAR) barred Anderson, because she was black, from singing at the DAR's Washington, DC, concert house, Constitution Hall. Outrage moved First Lady Eleanor Roosevelt to resign from the DAR and help arrange for Anderson to sing to an audience of seventy-five thousand at the Lincoln Memorial on Easter Sunday, 1939. The incident spotlighted invidious prejudice for ridicule, but Jim Crow was scarcely affected.

Talented black women such as Anderson fought daily for entry and dignity in the face of segregation and persistent stereotypes on stage and screen, to say nothing of the club circuit. The actress Hattie McDaniel, who won the 1939 Academy Award for best supporting actress for her portrayal of Mammy in the film *Gone with the Wind*, snapped at both segregation and those who criticized her success with the biting comment, "I'd rather play a maid and make $700 a week, than be a maid for $7."

Back to Court

With the NAACP, black women challenged segregation in court, as they had in the post–Civil War era. In 1946 Ada Lois Sipuel challenged Jim Crow admission policies at the University of Oklahoma law school. The state supreme court rejected her claim, but in *Sipuel v. Board of*

Regents (1948), the U.S. Supreme Court directed Oklahoma to admit Sipuel as "concededly qualified to receive the professional legal education offered by the State."

Black female teachers in the Jackson, Mississippi, public schools joined in a class action in March 1948 to challenge the Jim Crow pay schedules that left black teachers like Gladys Noel Bates earning 63 percent of their white colleagues' salaries. Bates and other black teachers received no relief in *Bates v. Batte* (1951). Nor did Vivian Brown receive relief when her father, Julius, in 1948 sued the school board in LaGrange, Texas, on her behalf against unequal public schools—as Benjamin F. Roberts had sued on his daughter Sarah's behalf in 1849. A federal district court in 1951 also denied relief to nine-year-old Linda Carol Brown and other black students in the Topeka, Kansas, public schools when their parents sued the segregated school system. But times were changing.

Brown v. Board of Education

Black students such as Linda Brown and their parents persisted in the more than century-old protest against Jim Crow inequality and discrimination. The NAACP carried Brown's case from Kansas—along with cases from South Carolina, Virginia, and Delaware—to the U.S. Supreme Court. On 17 May 1954, Chief Justice Earl Warren announced the unanimous opinion of the Court that Jim Crow had no place in public education. "Separate educational facilities are inherently unequal," the Court ruled.

Jim Crow had been put to flight. However, the 1954 victory in *Brown* marked not the end. It was another beginning. Jim Crow rules in transportation remained a fixture, and black women continued to fight it as they had since the 1850s. Jim Crow had at least been quelled in interstate transport. In *Mitchell v. United States* (1941), the Supreme Court decided that the Interstate Commerce Act (ICC) of 1887, in outlawing any common carrier's subjecting "any particular person . . . to any undue or unreasonable prejudice or disadvantage in any respect whatsoever," had outlawed racial discrimination on interstate common carriers. The Court reiterated its ruling in *Henderson v. United States* (1950), holding that the ICC ban on segregation included dining cars. In *Morgan v. Virginia* (1946), the Court returned with a twist to Josephine DeCuir's 1875 case and denied state power to require Jim Crow separation of whites and blacks on interstate carriers.

Montgomery Bus Boycott

Intrastate carriers such as that in *Plessy v. Ferguson* remained solidly segregated in the South, so black women localized their efforts. The Baton Rouge bus boycott in 1953 showed their solidarity and organizational resilience. The boycott was called after forty-two-year-old Rosa McCauley Parks followed Mary E. Miles—who in 1867 had refused the conductor's directive to sit toward the rear of a Philadelphia streetcar. On 1 December 1955, Parks refused to yield her seat on a Montgomery, Alabama, municipal bus. After she was arrested for her refusal, the local NAACP secretary and black women and men launched a bus boycott from 5 December 1955 to 20 December 1956. Black ridership on the municipal buses fell from 70 percent to zero. Economics alone appeared to demand the end of Jim Crow. Finally, in *Gayle v. Browder* (1956), the U.S. Supreme Court settled the issue by ruling that "statutes and ordinances requiring segregation of the white and colored races on the motor buses of a common carrier of passengers in the City of Montgomery . . . violate the Constitution of the United States."

Jim Crow increasingly appeared dead, at least as a creature of law. The continuing civil rights movement in the 1950s and 1960s strove to bury it. Black women continued to operate in the forefront. Autherine Lucy in 1956 broke the Jim Crow barrier at the University of Alabama, as did Charlayne Hunter at the University of Georgia in 1961. Ella Baker, Dorothy Height, Constance Baker Motley, Pauli Murray, and Jo Ann Robinson and thousands of others pushed forward the federal law that formally ended Jim Crow: the Civil Rights Act of 1964. It outlawed race and sex discrimination.

BIBLIOGRAPHY

Allen, Zita. *Black Women Leaders of the Civil Rights Movement.* Danbury, CT: Franklin Watts, 1996.

Bundles, A'Lelia. *On Her Own Ground: The Life and Times of Madam C. J. Walker.* New York: Scribners, 2001.

Collier-Thomas, Bettye, and V. P. Franklin, eds. *Sisters in the Struggle: African American Women in the Civil Rights–Black Power Movement.* New York: New York University Press, 2001.

Crawford, Vicki L., Jacqueline Anne Rouse, and Barbara Woods, eds. *Women in the Civil Rights Movement: Trailblazers and Torchbearers, 1941–1965.* Brooklyn, NY: Carlson Publishing, 1990.

Gilmore, Glenda Elizabeth. *Gender & Jim Crow: Women and the Politics of White Supremacy in North Carolina, 1896–1920.* Chapel Hill: University of North Carolina Press, 1996.

Hale, Grace Elizabeth. *Making Whiteness: The Culture of Segregation in the South, 1890–1940.* New York: Pantheon, 1998.

Hunter, Tera W. *To 'Joy My Freedom: Southern Black Women's Lives and Labors after the Civil War.* Cambridge, MA: Harvard University Press, 1997.

Jones, Beverly Washington. *Quest for Equality: The Life and Writings of Mary Eliza Church Terrell, 1863–1954.* Brooklyn, NY: Carlson Publishing, 1990.

Litwack, Leon. *Trouble in Mind: Black Southerners in the Age of Jim Crow.* New York: Knopf, 1998.

Pinkney, Andrea Davis. *Let It Shine: Stories of Black Women Freedom Fighters.* San Diego: Harcourt, 2000.

Ransby, Barbara. *Ella Baker and the Black Freedom Movement: A Radical Democratic Vision.* Chapel Hill: University of North Carolina Press, 2003.

Ross, Rosetta E. *Witnessing and Testifying: Black Women, Religion, and Civil Rights.* Minneapolis, MN: Fortress Press, 2003.

Salem, Dorothy. *To Better Our World: Black Women in Organized Reform, 1890–1920.* Brooklyn, NY: Carlson Publishing, 1990.

Shaw, Stephanie J. *What a Woman Ought to Be and to Do: Black Professional Women Workers during the Jim Crow Era*. Chicago: University of Chicago Press, 1996.

Thompson, Mildred I. *Ida B. Wells-Barnett: An Exploratory Study of an American Black Woman, 1893–1930*. Brooklyn, NY: Carlson Publishing, 1990.

Wesley, Charles H. *The History of the National Association of Colored Women's Clubs: A Legacy of Service*. Washington, DC: Association for the Study of Negro Life and History, 1984.

White, Deborah Gray. *Too Heavy a Load: Black Women in Defense of Themselves, 1894–1994*. New York: W. W. Norton, 1999.

—Thomas J. Davis

JOHNSON, EDDIE BERNICE (b. 3 December 1935), politician. Named by *Ebony* magazine in 2001 as one of the ten most powerful black women in America, Eddie Bernice Johnson became the first African American woman to represent the Dallas, Texas, area in the U.S. Congress in 1992. With a passion for justice and the courage to speak her mind, Johnson has been a leader in championing legislation designed to empower low-income communities. As a member of the House of Representatives, Johnson has taken pride in transcending the actions of the average politician: "The average politician, in my judgment, just wants to get along. Getting along is important, but it's not a number one thing for me. I believe in saying what I mean and meaning what I say."

Eddie Bernice Johnson was born in Waco, Texas, to Edward Johnson and Lillie Mae White Johnson. After finishing high school, she attended St. Mary's at Notre Dame in South Bend, Indiana, where she received a nursing diploma in 1955. In 1967 she earned a bachelor of science degree in nursing at Texas Christian University and in 1976 she completed a master of public administration degree from Southern Methodist University.

Before entering politics Johnson worked as a psychiatric nurse at the Dallas Veterans Administration office for sixteen years. Then, in 1972, she made a successful run for the Texas House of Representatives, making her the first black woman elected from Dallas County since 1935. Johnson established her presence and leadership early in the term. As founder of a Dallas section of the National Council on Negro Women and a member of the Women's Equity Action League she was well aware of the discrimination and lack of opportunity that minority groups experienced. Johnson sponsored bills to guarantee job protection and equal benefits for pregnant teachers, prevent jurors from being fired by their employers for jury service, prevent pregnant women from being denied unemployment compensation, help low-income citizens secure and retain housing, and prevent lending institutions from discriminating in making home loans.

After serving in the statehouse for five years, Johnson left to accept an appointment by President Jimmy Carter as regional director of the Department of Health, Education, and Welfare. Following the presidential election of Ronald Reagan, Johnson left her position to work in the private sector where, in 1980, she opened Eddie Bernice Johnson and Associates, a consulting agency that advised companies who wished to expand or relocate in the Dallas area.

Johnson's return to politics came in 1986 when she won a decisive victory in the Texas state senate race. Among her many accomplishments was getting a resolution passed asking the governor to issue an executive order to raise the number of state agency contracts with minority- and female-owned businesses. Her leadership was also shown in her sponsorship of a bill to allow battered spouses accused of murdering their abusers to enter evidence of abuse in their trials. In 1991 she gained notoriety for her role in redesigning Dallas's Congressional District 30 to secure for herself a congressional seat. This controversial measure engendered severe criticism on the part of some, but others felt Johnson had been underestimated by her colleagues and she had simply outmaneuvered them.

The following year Johnson was elected to represent District 30 in the U.S. Congress. This political victory made her only the second African American to represent the state of Texas in Congress and the first from the Dallas area. Johnson became the ranking Democratic member of the House Committee on Science's Subcommittee on Research and also the Democratic deputy whip. She transferred the same legislative leadership she displayed in the Texas Congress to the national political arena in areas such as aviation and transportation security, and in issues dealing with science and technology. Elected chair of the Congressional Black Caucus for the 107th Congress, she focused on comprehensive election reform, expanding minority capital, improving early healthcare, and getting the administration to provide the same treatment to Africa as it does to its most valuable international allies. In 2002 Johnson also led the way in bringing together leaders of Congress's Asian, African American, and Hispanic Caucuses for a first-of-its-kind meeting on Capitol Hill to address policy issues of mutual concern.

Johnson's leadership has earned her awards and accolades from numerous organizations including honorary doctorates from Bishop College, Jarvis Christian College, Texas College, Paul Quinn College, and Houston-Tillotson College. In an interview in the *Dallas Morning News*, Johnson stated, "I would like to be remembered as somebody who tried to help."

BIBLIOGRAPHY

Baker, Jones, and Ruthe Winegarten. *Capitol Women: Texas Female Legislators, 1923–1999*. Austin: University of Texas, 2000.

Congresswoman Eddie Bernice Johnson. *Welcome to My Office On-line*. http://www.house.gov/ebjohnson.

"Eddie Bernice Johnson." *Notable Black American Women*, vol. 2. Detroit, MI: Gale Group, 1996.

Gill, Lavern. *African American Women in Congress: Forming and Transforming History*. New Brunswick, NJ: Rutgers University Press, 1997.

"Johnson Unites Three Minority Caucuses to Develop New Agenda." *Jet*, 13 May 2002, 4.

Woolley, Bryan. "Eddie Bernice Johnson Is No Ordinary Politician." *Dallas Morning News*, 23 July 2001.

—MONA E. JACKSON

JOHNSON, EUNICE WALKER (b. 1917), magazine publishing executive. With business acumen and a keen aesthetic sense, Eunice Walker Johnson has served as the fashion editor of *Ebony* magazine and the secretary-treasurer of Johnson Publishing Company. In addition she has been producer and director of the Ebony Fashion Fair traveling fashion show for more than forty years. She is also a philanthropist who has donated more than $49 million to the United Negro College Fund (UNCF) and other African American charities.

Eunice Walker Johnson was born in Selma, Alabama, to Nathaniel D. and Ethel Walker. Her family displayed a strong commitment to gaining higher education and to hard work, and it passed those principles down through the generations. Johnson's maternal grandfather, William H. McAlpine, who was born into slavery, was the incorporator and second president of Selma University in Selma, Alabama. He was also one of the founders and the first president of the National Baptist Convention, serving from 1880 to 1882. Her father, a prominent physician in Selma, worked his way through Talladega College and through medical school at Shaw University in Raleigh, North Carolina. Johnson remembers her father telling his children, "If you want to make a difference in this world, you must first get an education." Her mother was a high school principal and also taught education and art at the college level at Selma University. Johnson's sister is a professor at Providence College in Rhode Island and two of her brothers are physicians.

As a self-proclaimed "daddy's girl," Johnson followed in her father's footsteps and attended Talladega College, where she graduated with a bachelor's degree in Sociology. She went on to receive a master's degree in Social Services Administration from Loyola University in Chicago. Johnson also completed some graduate courses in Journalism at Northwestern University. Her interest in interior decorating led her to study at the Ray Vogue School of Interior Design. In the 1950s, she married John Johnson, publisher of *Ebony*. Their daughter, Linda, was born in 1958. As of 2004, she was the president and chief executive officer of Johnson Publishing Company. The couple also had a son, John, who died in 1981 of sickle-cell anemia.

Johnson first began serving as producer and director of Ebony Fashion Fair's traveling fashion show in 1963. Under her direction, it became one of the largest traveling fashion shows in the world and served as a showcase for beautiful black models wearing fashions by the world's top black designers, such as Stephen Burrows, Jeffrey Banks, and the late Patrick Kelly and Willi Smith. Each year Johnson conceives of a theme for the style show, makes the final selection of the garments to be shown, and supervises the models' training.

The Ebony Fashion Fair has played a role in changing the fashion industry both in the United States and Europe. In 1963 Johnson received a phone call from Italian designer Emilio Pucci saying that he had just returned from a trip to Africa. While there, he had been inspired to show his ready-to-wear fashions with fabric that he had designed featuring African masks. He requested two "black models who look like Lena Horne." Johnson had a problem finding the models, who were used at Pucci's show in Florence, Italy, in 1963. The show marked the first time African American models walked down the runways of Europe.

Johnson has also been a leader in championing the cause of higher education for America's children. She has led the way in this effort by overseeing the donation of more than $49 million to the United Negro College Fund and other African American charities from revenue generated by the Ebony Fashion Fair traveling fashion show. In recognition of and gratitude for her generosity, in 2001 Johnson received the UNCF's highest honor, the prestigious Frederick D. Patterson Award, named for the Tuskegee Institute president who helped found the UNCF in 1944. The following year she was awarded the Harold H. Hines Benefactor's Award from the UNCF. While receiving her awards, Johnson expressed her belief that education was the basis for success in life. She credited her grandfather and parents for instilling in her a love for education and a love of the UNCF. "Like those before me, I have a burning desire to educate. . . . I would like to see all young people get the greatest education they can."

BIBLIOGRAPHY

"Eunice Walker Johnson." *Notable Black American Women*, Book 1. Detroit: Gale Research, 1992. An informative biography of Johnson discussing her family background and professional activities.

"Eunice W. Johnson." *Ebony* 32 (August 1977): 74–76. A brief article about Johnson's work as producer-director of the Ebony Fashion Fair traveling style show.

"Eunice W. Johnson Receives UNCF Harold H. Hines Benefactor's Award." *Jet* (1 July 2002). http://articles.findarticles.com/p/articles/mi_m1355/is_2_102/ai_88582499.

Johnson, Eunice. "Ebony Fashion Fair." *Ebony* 45 (November 1990): 185. A brief article discussing how the Ebony Fashion Fair revolutionized the fashion industry.

"Johnson, Eunice Walker." *Who's Who among African Americans.* Farmington Hills, MI: Gale Group, 2002.
"UNCF Honors Ebony Fashion Fair Producer/Director." *Ebony* 59 (June 2001): 94.

—MONA E. JACKSON

JOHNSON, GEORGIA DOUGLAS (b. 10 September 1877; d. 14 May 1966), musician, writer. In 1927 Alice Dunbar-Nelson described her friend Georgia Douglas Johnson as having "as many talents as she has aliases. . . . One is always stumbling upon another nom de plume of hers." Johnson did sometimes publish under various pseudonyms, but the merit of Dunbar-Nelson's comment lies in her recognition of Johnson's many gifts as a musician, poet, playwright, columnist, short-story writer, wife, mother, and friend.

This multitalented woman began her life as Georgia Blanche Douglas Camp on 10 September 1877 in Atlanta,

GEORGIA DOUGLAS JOHNSON, poet, playwright, and teacher, opened her home in Washington, DC, as a salon where writers such as Jean Toomer, Langston Hughes, Angelina Grimké, and Alice Dunbar-Nelson gathered. (Moorland-Spingarn Research Center.)

Georgia, and grew up in Rome, Georgia. Her mother was Laura Jackson, of Indian and African American ancestry, and her father was George Camp, whose wealthy and musical father had moved to Marietta, Georgia, from England. Her mixed ancestry prompted Georgia's lifelong preoccupation with miscegenation.

Camp attended elementary schools in Atlanta, and then entered Atlanta University's Normal School, from which she graduated in 1893. During these years, she was particular about her friends and chose to remain primarily alone, teaching herself to play the violin. Her interest in music took her to Oberlin, Ohio, to train at the Oberlin Conservatory (1902–1903).

On 28 September 1903 Camp married Henry Lincoln Johnson. "Link" had been born to former slaves in 1870 and became a prominent attorney and member of the Republican party. The couple had two children, Henry Lincoln Jr., and Peter Douglas. In 1910 the family moved from Atlanta to Washington, DC, where Link not only established a law practice but also, in 1912, accepted President William Howard Taft's appointment to serve as recorder of deeds for the District of Columbia.

Moving to Washington was the stimulus Georgia Johnson needed to begin her literary career. In 1916 three of her poems appeared in *Crisis*, and in 1918 her first book of poetry, *The Heart of a Woman*, was published. In the introduction, William Stanley Braithwaite praised the work for "lifting the veil" from women. Johnson's musical gifts are evident in the lyrical quality of poems that reveal the difficulties and frustrations faced by women and that echo Johnson's youthful isolation.

Johnson's first book did not explore racial themes, a choice for which she was criticized. During this time of the "New Negro," black writers were expected to address racial issues to expose and overturn prejudice. In 1922 Johnson responded to her critics with a book of poetry titled *Bronze: A Book of Verse*, which addresses miscegenation as well as mothering in a racist world. She was praised by W. E. B. Du Bois and Jessie Redmon Fauset for this work, but Johnson herself admitted in a letter to Arna Bontemps that she preferred not to write on racial themes, saying that "if one can soar, he should soar, leaving his chains behind."

During this productive period, Johnson struggled to balance her roles as housewife and writer. She was an unconventional wife and mother, preferring reading to cooking, and her husband was not always sympathetic to her creative efforts, though he did financially support her in them. After the death of Henry Lincoln Johnson Sr. on 10 September 1925, her difficulties intensified as she divided her day between earning a living and writing, a struggle that would follow her to her death. She put Peter through Williston Seminary, Dartmouth College, and Howard

University's medical school, while Henry Lincoln Jr. went to Asburnham Academy, Bowdoin College, and Howard University's law school.

During this difficult period, Johnson accepted an appointment by President Calvin Coolidge in 1925 to work for the U.S. Department of Labor as Commissioner of Conciliation, requiring her to investigate the living conditions of laborers. Working full-time caused her to feel that she never had enough time to write. However, she did produce a third book of poetry in 1928, *An Autumn Love Cycle*, considered to be her finest. She again avoided racial themes, returning instead to the theme of a woman in love. The best-known poem in this volume is "I Want to Die While You Love Me."

While Johnson refused to limit her poetry to racial themes, she greatly contributed to the New Negro Renaissance by opening her home at 1461 S Street Northwest, Washington, DC, as a salon. Every week, writers such as Jean Toomer, Langston Hughes, Angelina Grimké, and Alice Dunbar-Nelson gathered for a meeting of the Saturday Nighters' Club. She also invited prisoners with whom she had corresponded to the weekly gatherings once they were released. In fact, Johnson named her home "Half-Way Home," in part because she saw herself as halfway between everybody and everything and trying to bring them together, and also because she wanted to make her home a place where anyone who would fight half-way to survive could do so.

Zona Gale—a white writer to whom *An Autumn Love Cycle* was dedicated—encouraged Johnson to try writing plays, which she did with success. In 1926, Johnson received an honorable mention in the *Opportunity* play contest for *Blue Blood*, a drama about miscegenation through rape in the South. Her most famous play, *Plumes*, was awarded *Opportunity*'s first prize in 1927. This drama is a folk tragedy that pits modern medicine against folk customs. Other published plays include *A Sunday Morning in the South* (1974), which was a "lynching play," and the historical dramas *Frederick Douglass* (1935) and *William and Ellen Craft* (1935). While these are the only plays published, Johnson did produce many more dramas about "average Negro life," "brotherhood" between the races, and the intermixture of races. One of her great contributions to drama is the representation of authentic folk speech rather than stereotypical mutilated English.

Life, of course, grew harder for Johnson after the Harlem Renaissance with the onset of the Great Depression. She tried ceaselessly to obtain fellowship money, but with the exception of an honorable mention from the Harmon Foundation in 1928, she never succeeded. Nevertheless, she continued to be productive. She wrote a weekly newspaper column from 1926 to 1932 titled "Homely Philosophy" that was syndicated to twenty newspapers. Though it was somewhat clichéd, Johnson tried to bring cheer into the homes of Americans during economic devastation, with such columns as "A Smile on the Lips" or "Find Pleasure in Common Things." She was listed in the 1932 edition of *Who's Who of Colored America*. She was also asked to join the DC Women's Party, Poets League of Washington, and Poet Laureate League. Losing her position with the U.S. Department of Labor in 1934, Johnson was forced to turn to temporary work, but she continued to write. She won third prize in 1934 in a poetry contest sponsored by the DC Federation of Women's Clubs. Johnson was also a member of several literary social clubs and organizations, such as the American Society of African Culture and the League of American Writers.

During World War II, she continued to publish poetry as well as to read her poems over the radio. She also returned to music during this period and tried her hand at short-story writing. Her three extant stories are "Free," "Gesture," and "Tramp"; the last two were published under the pseudonym "Paul Tremaine," and are derived in large part from the life of Gypsy Drago, a man who did not discover that he was black until the age of thirty. These stories predominantly focus on relationships and not on racial themes, however. Johnson tried in vain to locate a publisher for the biography of her late husband, *The Black Cabinet*, and for her novel, *White Men's Children*. Her last book of poetry, *Share My World*, was published in 1962. One year before her death, in 1965, she was awarded an honorary doctorate from Atlanta University. During these later years, she developed into a local institution, widely known as "the old woman with the headband and the tablet around her neck." The tablet was for her to write down any idea that came to her.

When Johnson died of a stroke on 14 May 1966, she left a multitude of papers that were literally thrown out. Much of what she wrote is lost, but she lived a remarkable and unselfish life.

BIBLIOGRAPHY

Adoff, Arnold, ed. *The Poetry of Black America: An Anthology of the Twentieth Century*. New York: Harper and Row, 1973.

Cullen, Countee, ed. *Caroling Dusk: An Anthology of Verse by Negro Poets*. Secaucus, NJ: Carol Publishing Group, 1993.

Dover, Cedric. "The Importance of Georgia Douglas Johnson." *Crisis*, December 1952.

Fletcher, Winona. "From Genteel Poet to Revolutionary Playwright: Georgia Douglas Johnson as a Symbol of Black Success, Failure, and Fortitude." *Theatre Annual*, February 1985.

Hughes, Langston, and Arna Bontemps, eds. *The Poetry of the Negro, 1746–1970* (1949). Garden City, NY: Doubleday, 1970.

Hull, Gloria T. *Color, Sex, and Poetry: Three Women Writers of the Harlem Renaissance*. Bloomington: Indiana University Press, 1987.

Johnson, James Weldon, ed. *The Book of American Negro Poetry*. San Diego: Harcourt Brace Jovanovich, 1983.

Lewis, David Levering. *When Harlem Was in Vogue*. New York: Penguin Books, 1997.

Shockley, Ann Allen, ed. *Afro-American Women Writers: 1746–1933*. Boston: G. K. Hall, 1988.

—JOCELYN HAZELWOOD DONLON

JOHNSON, HALLE TANNER DILLON (b. 17 October 1864; d. 26 April 1901), physician. "[I] try to keep before [myself] the possibility of failing but unless some harder and more complex [problem] than anything they have given me yet I feel that I can not, but, if they mark me fairly, get thro." With this determination and self-confidence, Halle Tanner Dillon passed the state medical examinations in Alabama in 1891 and became the first woman licensed to practice medicine in the state. Her concern for social justice led her to establish a training school and dispensary at Tuskegee Institute in Alabama, where she became resident physician.

Halle (Hallie) Tanner was born in Pittsburgh, Pennsylvania, to Benjamin Tucker Tanner and Sarah Elizabeth (Miller) Tanner. She was the eldest daughter of nine children, two of whom died in infancy. The Tanners were a prominent family whose home in Philadelphia was a rest haven for travelers and a meeting place for intellectuals, including leading black and white clergy. The parents created a culturally developed and intellectually stimulating atmosphere by introducing their children to the works of prominent African American artists such as Edward Bannister and Edmonia Lewis. The Tanners' son, Henry Ossawa (1859–1937), was guided by the experience; the gifted artist became a celebrated painter of landscape, religious, and genre paintings.

Benjamin Tucker Tanner, a successful minister in the African Methodist Episcopal (AME) Church, edited the *Christian Recorder* beginning in 1868; he was first editor of the *AME Church Review* in 1884, and two years later, he was elected a bishop in the church. He had worked incessantly on the *Review* with daughter Halle as an office staff member. She soon met Charles E. Dillon of Trenton, New Jersey, and after a brief courtship they married in the Tanner home in June 1886. Halle gave birth to the Dillons' only child, Sadie, in 1887. The marriage ended with Charles Dillon's death, although the details and date of death are unknown. Halle Dillon and her daughter returned to the Tanner home on Diamond Street, where they remained for several months.

Determined to put her life back in order, Dillon, then twenty-four years old, enrolled in the Woman's Medical College of Pennsylvania. The only African American student in her class of thirty-six women, she completed the three-year course and graduated with high honors on 7 May 1891. Booker T. Washington, president of Tuskegee

HALLE TANNER JOHNSON, c. 1891, when she passed the state medical examinations in Alabama and became the first woman licensed to practice medicine there. She became the resident physician at Tuskegee Institute, where she established a training school and dispensary. (From the Collections of the University of Pennsylvania Archives.)

Institute, had searched for four years for a black resident physician to provide health care for the local community. He had written for a nomination to the dean of the Woman's Medical College, who apparently mentioned it to Dillon. Dillon was interested in the position and wrote to Washington.

Washington's letters to Halle Dillon introduced her to the social and economic climate in Tuskegee and the responsibilities of the position. Washington preferred a woman, and he offered a salary of $600 a year with board included. The resident physician would teach two classes each day, administer the health department, and compound the medicines needed to serve the sick. Additional compensation was to be derived from the physician's private practice. Much of the work would be missionary in spirit; thus, the physician would need to come for the good of the cause. The physician would need to pass the local or state medical examination and begin work on 1 September 1891.

Halle Dillon found the offer appealing, accepted the challenge, and arrived in Tuskegee in August 1891. Washington had arranged for her to prepare for the strenuous medical board examination through study with Cornelius Nathaniel Dorsett, a practicing physician in Montgomery where the examinations were to be held. Dorsett was the first African American physician to pass the Alabama medical board. Both Bishop Tanner and Halle Dillon were confident of Dillon's ability to pass any reasonable and just examination; however, they were more concerned about the examining board. Halle Dillon's impending appearance before the examiners caused a public stir. Some questioned her daring to sit for the examination. The curious wanted to know what she looked like.

The examination tested her on a different subject on each of the ten days. At the end, the board supervisor was impressed with Halle Dillon's neatness and cleanliness in her work. Three weeks after her return to Tuskegee, she learned that she had passed with an average of 78.81. Confident of her accuracy and completeness in response to the examination questions, Dillon felt that the examiner might have been too critical and too rigid in evaluating her papers. The press took notice of Dillon's success and recognized her as the first woman of any race to become licensed as a medical doctor in Alabama and the first black woman to practice medicine in the state. Dillon's achievement called attention to a double standard regarding the races, for Anna M. Longshore, a white woman who failed the medical examination earlier, had practiced medicine in Alabama without a license before Dillon took the test.

From 1891 to 1894 Halle Dillon was resident physician at Tuskegee. During this time she established a nurses' training school and the Lafayette Dispensary to provide for the health care needs of the local residents and the campus. She also compounded many of her own medicines. In 1894 she married Reverend John Quincy Johnson, who in 1893–1894 was a mathematics teacher at Tuskegee. The next year, John Quincy Johnson became president of Allen University, a private school for African Americans students in Columbia, South Carolina. He received a BD from Hartford Divinity School in Hartford, Connecticut, and the DD from Morris Brown College, Atlanta, Georgia. Halle Johnson joined her husband while he did postgraduate work at Princeton Theological Seminary. They later moved to Nashville, Tennessee, where John Quincy Johnson was pastor of Saint Paul AME Church from 1900 to 1903.

The Johnsons had three sons, who were named after their noted father, grandfather, and uncle—John Quincy Jr., Benjamin T., and Henry Tanner. Complications of childbirth and dysentery led to Halle Johnson's death in her Nashville home on 26 April 1901, when she was thirty-seven years old. She was buried in Nashville's Greenwood Cemetery.

Halle Tanner Dillon Johnson, a member of a noted and highly respected African American family of the nineteenth century, is a notable figure in black and American history and in the racial history of the South. She became an Alabama pioneer when she became the first woman in the state to pass the medical board examination. She withstood the curiosity of a questioning society that had not seen a black woman sit for a medical examination; she opened public discussion of racial discrimination in the medical profession; and she significantly improved the health care of a racially segregated community by providing training for nurses, building a dispensary, and ministering to the needs of the residents.

BIBLIOGRAPHY

Alexander-Minter, Ray. "The Tanner Family." *Henry Ossawa Tanner Exhibition Catalog.* Philadelphia: Philadelphia Museum of Art, 1991.

Brown, Hallie Q. *Homespun Heroine and Other Women of Distinction* (1926). New York: Oxford University Press, 1988.

Harlan, Louis, ed. *The Booker T. Washington Papers.* Urbana: University of Illinois Press, 1972.

Smith, Jessie Carney. "Halle Tanner Dillon Johnson." In *Notable Black American Women*, edited by Jessie Carney Smith. Detroit, MI: Gale Research, 1992.

Wright, R. R., Jr., ed. *Encyclopedia of African Methodism.* Philadelphia: The Book Concern of the AME Church, 1916.

—Jessie Carney Smith

JOHNSON, HAZEL WINIFRED (b. 1927), military officer. Hazel W. Johnson broke through convention, custom, and racial and gender barriers in 1979 when she became the first black woman general in the American military. This accomplishment has guaranteed her a place in African American history, women's history, and military history.

Hazel Johnson was born in 1927 in West Chester, Pennsylvania. Interested in travel and changing her outlook, she entered the army in 1955, five years after completing basic nurses' training at New York's Harlem Hospital. She received a direct commission as a first lieutenant in the U.S. Army Nursing Corps in May 1960. Taking advantage of the educational opportunities provided by the military, she earned a bachelor's degree in Nursing from Villanova University, a master's degree in Nursing Education from

Columbia University, and a PhD in Education Administration through Catholic University.

Johnson was chief of the Army Nurse Corps from 1979 to 1983, the first African American to hold the corps' most powerful position. Her promotion to brigadier general was recommended by a military board and approved by Congress. Nineteen years after she had entered the corps, the one-star insignia representing brigadier general was pinned on her uniform. At age fifty-two then, Hazel Winifred Johnson became the first black woman general in the history of the U.S. military.

In 1983 Johnson retired and rejoined civilian life as director of the government affairs division of the American Nursing Association. She then took a position as assistant professor in the nursing administration program at Georgetown University and, later, assumed a professorship of nursing at George Mason University in Virginia, where she was also director of the Center for Health Policy. During the 1990s, she became part-time faculty and worked as a consultant in health policy and health administration. She has also done considerable touring and speaking.

Her retirement from the army created a void in top female leadership, leaving only two women generals, neither of whom was black. After Hazel Johnson's retirement, two years elapsed before another black woman, in any branch of the military, pinned on the coveted star (Sherian G. Cadoria).

Although Johnson is retired, military mementos adorn the Clifton, Virginia, home of Johnson and her husband, David Brown. The Distinguished Service Medal, the Legion of Merit, the Meritorious Service Medal, and an Army Commendation Medal with an oak leaf cluster are among the general's decorations, awards, and badges.

BIBLIOGRAPHY
Army Records. General Officer Management Office, Headquarters, Department of the Army, Washington, DC.
"Diversification Highlights Upcoming Nursing Symposium." *Stripe*, 12 July 1996.
Reynolds, Barbara A., ed. *Delta Journal* (Winter 1986–1987).

—LINDA ROCHELL LANE

JONES, CLAUDIA (b. 15 February 1915; d. 25 December 1964), activist. Claudia Jones was among a tiny cadre of black women to rise within the ranks of the Communist Party of the United States. Born in Port of Spain, British West Indies (Trinidad), Jones was only nine years old when her family immigrated to Harlem in 1924. Her mother died not long after they came to the U.S., and her father raised Claudia and her two sisters by himself with very few resources. Their poor living conditions resulted in Claudia contracting tuberculosis at the age of seventeen. Despite poor health and poverty, Jones earned a reputation as a promising journalist in high school, but her education was cut short by the Depression, and she was forced to drop out of school in order to work. Like many working-class Harlemites, she was attracted to the Communist Party through the International Labor Defense's campaign to free the Scottsboro Nine, and at eighteen she joined the Young Communist League. Jones rose quickly within the ranks of the Harlem C.P., becoming editor of the YCL *Weekly Review* and the *Spotlight*, and assuming the posts of chairperson of the National Council of the Young Communist League, YCL Education Officer for New York State, and eventually National Director of the YCL.

As one of the preeminent young black Communists in Harlem during the Popular Front, Jones actively supported the National Negro Congress from its inception, serving as a leader of the NNC youth council in Harlem. Although she had been associated with issues pertaining to African American rights and was among the first to criticize Earl Browder's decision to abandon the Party's support for black self-determination in the South, Jones developed a reputation during World War II as a relentless critic of male chauvinism and a leading Party spokesperson for women's rights. After the war she was appointed to the Women's Commission, briefly serving as its secretary.

It was in this capacity that she published her provocative and widely read 1946 article, "An End to the Neglect of the Problems of Negro Women." She argued passionately that "the Negro question in the United States is *prior* to, and not equal to, the woman question; that only to the extent that we fight all chauvinist expressions and actions as regards the Negro people . . . can women as a whole advance their struggle for equal rights." In other words, she insisted that the overthrow of class and gender oppression depended on the abolition of racism. For the women's movement to be successful, antiracism had to be at the forefront of its agenda and black women needed to play leadership roles. The article generated a great deal of debate, earning her respect as a major American Marxist theorist. However, the essay had very little effect on Party policy at the time.

Following a series of arrests and attempted deportations beginning in 1948, Jones was eventually convicted for violating the Smith Act and sentenced to one year in Alderson Federal Reformatory for Women in January 1955. Although her case did not attract as much attention as Angela Davis's two decades later, Jones did become a symbol for a generation of radical black women who had come of age on the eve of the Civil Rights upsurges of the 1960s, many of whom marched and petitioned on her behalf. Her incarceration is one of the few clear-cut examples in history of an African American woman serving time as a political prisoner in the United States.

Despite her deteriorating health, Jones was not released from prison until December 1955, whereupon she was promptly deported to London, where she continued working for radical black causes, including the Caribbean Labour Congress, the West-Indian Workers and Students Association, and the Communist Party. She founded and edited the left-wing *West Indian Gazette* during the late 1950s, initiated the Caribbean Carnival in the wake of the Notting Hill race riots in 1958, and in 1962 formed the Afro-Asian-Caribbean Conference to challenge Britain's Commonwealth Immigration Act. She did not limit her work to England, however; she stayed active in anticolonial and anti-apartheid movements throughout the late 1950s, traveled to the Soviet Union as a delegate to the World Congress of Women in 1963, and attended an international antinuclear conference in Tokyo the following year. As a result of her visit to the USSR, she served as guest editor of *Soviet Women*.

Jones's life came to an end on Christmas Day 1964, when she suffered a stroke brought on by a long-standing heart condition. She was forty-eight years old. Although few histories of the black freedom movement acknowledge Claudia Jones's role, she was celebrated worldwide by the Communist left. Her remains are buried in the Highgate cemetery, right next to Karl Marx.

See also **Left, The.**

BIBLIOGRAPHY

Davis, Angela. *Women, Race, and Class*. New York: Vintage, 1981.

Johnson, Buzz. *"I Think of My Mother": Notes on the Life and Times of Claudia Jones*. London: Karia Press, 1985.

Naison, Mark. *Communists in Harlem During the Depression*. Urbana: University of Illinois Press, 1983.

North, Joe. "Communist Women." *Political Affairs* Vol. 51 No. 3, March 1971.

Sherwood, Marika. *Claudia Jones: A Life in Exile* . London: Lawrence and Wishart, 1999.

—ROBIN D. G. KELLEY

JONES, GAYL (b. 23 November 1949), writer. Born in Lexington, Kentucky, the setting for much of her fiction, Gayl Jones is the daughter of Franklin and Lucille Wilson Jones, a cook and writer respectively. She received her inspiration to write from her mother, grandmother, and a fifth grade school teacher. Her writing interest followed her first to Connecticut College, where she majored in English and received her BA in 1971, and then to Brown University, where she earned the MA in 1973 and the DA in 1975 in creative writing.

When Gayl Jones began publishing in the mid-1970s, her works eschewed the basic tenets of the Black Aesthetic, a 1960s black literary movement spearheaded by Addison Gayle, Hoyt Fuller, and Larry Neal, whose race-based aesthetics prioritized race unity. Jones complicated the racial harmony of black literary aesthetes by engaging black female characters in a resistance to patriarchal status quo and by exposing undercurrents in black male-female relations. Unlike Toni Morrison and Alice Walker, Jones has explored a turbulent psychosexual ambiguity, one that has mixed physical tenderness with sexual violence. The pleasure/pain duality has allowed Jones to invalidate the concept of racial unity while attaching a feminist agenda to a black nationalistic linguistic structure. That is, her black women characters recount their stories of gender violation and resistance in a medium identifiable with the oral black folk tradition.

Corregidora (1975), Jones's first novel, blends the sexual violence of slavery with contemporary black spousal brutality. Ursa Corregidora, the protagonist blues singer and descendant of a Portuguese slave owner, relates in a blues medley the sadist sexual abuse of her great-grandmother and grandmother, sired by the same slave master who subsequently employed them as whores. In an abusive relationship herself, Ursa is unable to pass on to future generations her legacy of female exploitation because Mutt, her husband, throws her when pregnant down the stairs in a violent fit, an act that forces her to have a hysterectomy in order to save her life. Performing fellatio on Mutt years later, Ursa unlocks the secret of how black women can escape the brutalizing sexual ordeals that have burdened them since slavery: They can pleasure or injure the man. Ursa's decision not to injure Mutt grants her power over him.

In *Eva's Man* (1976), Jones's second novel, Eva Medina Canada inflicts pain. She bites off her married lover's penis, and he bleeds to death. Her criminal act, which confines her to a psychiatric prison when she is forty-three years old, may be read as a strike against a history of personal sexual abuse: Her mother's lover propositioned her as a child, her cousin Alfonso made advances to her, a sexual predator whom she stabbed when she was seventeen years of age landed her in a reformatory, and Davis, whom she sexually mutilated, kept her confined for a month as he molested her during her menses. Eva's act of mutilation, however, seems more of a subversive deed, an agent of resistance. She refuses to admit why she committed her crime, thereby impeding authorities in bringing closure to her case. Eva's fragmented blues tale, told through flashbacks, is interwoven with those of other black women, including her mother and her neighbor, who are in conflicted heterosexual relationships.

White Rat (1977), a collection of twelve short stories, explores the irrationality of southern blacks and whites, whose obsession with skin color makes them targets and perpetrators of sexual cruelty. "White Rat," the first story, exposes the stupidity of White Rat, a white-looking black man who hates whites but accepts the white-looking child that his wife delivers but is not his. His irrational abuse of his wife for the child's clubfoot deformity scars her emotionally and causes her to retaliate illogically. Leaving the home with a dark-skinned suitor, she returns and implies that she is pregnant with a dark-skinned child. The husband allows his wife final control, and the story gives a black feminist twist to the problem of color prejudice that has plagued black families for centuries.

"Legend," the tenth story in the collection, offers the flip side of the racial-insanity coin when a white man instigates the rape of his daughter by a black man to satisfy his notion that blacks have no capacity to love. The sexual attack leads to the black man's lynching and the white girl's insanity after she gives birth to a black son. Punctuated by a syncopated, staccato rhythm, the story informs the psychosexual dynamics between the races and questions the white woman's moral ability to nurture a black child.

Song for Anninho (1981), a long narrative poem, revisits the theme of psychosexual violence. Set in 1697 on the Negro maroon settlement of Palmares in Brazil and told from the perspective of Almeyda, the poem details Almeyda's longing for her husband Anninho after rebel soldiers cut off her breasts and leave her to die. Her struggle for mental and physical wholeness takes place while in the care of Zibata, a spiritualist who finds her fevered and delirious. The call-response structure of the poem is punctuated with Almeyda's painful recuperation and her pleasurable memories of her husband.

"Xarque," the first of three poems in *Xarque and Other Poems* (1985), continues the account of the mutilation of enslaved Africans who work at Xarque, a meat slaughtering house, during Brazil's colonial history after the destruction of the second Palmares. Euclida, granddaughter of Almeyda in *Song for Anninho*, listens to the story of her mother, Bonifacia, whose master mutilated her when she tried to escape because she did not want to become his whore. Euclida, who has lost her hand to a snake bite, listens attentively to her mother's tale of pain and desire for her free black lover and wonders what her own future will hold for her.

With the publication of *Liberating Voices: Oral Tradition in African American Literature* (1991), Gayl Jones presented her critical treatise on the oral tradition in black literature. From Paul L. Dunbar's dialect to Langston Hughes's blues to Toni Morrison's folktales, it examines the stylistic effects of African American literature that appropriates black oral forms. Jones believes that in using oral and aural forms, black writers have given new meaning to Western literature and have obtained greater artistic independence for themselves. She views many writers

employing techniques that implicate political, social, and historical vision, but what is important, according to Jones, is that these writers expand and extend the parameters of the original art form to create an ingenious multivoiced and multivalent literary complexity. A landmark in African American literature, *Liberating Voices* outlines a new way of reading black literature at a time when critical studies emphasized theme and content. More important, it gives us an inside perspective on how Jones assessed the oral folk tradition in others' works when she was incorporating that same tradition in her own writings.

For almost twenty years, Gayl Jones published no new novels. Then she asked Beacon Press to cease publishing her earlier work, possibly because she did not want the

THE HEALING, 1999, cover. In this novel Gayl Jones chronicles the life of Harlan Jane Eagleton, a beautician, photojournalist, and traveling faith healer. (Beacon Press, Boston.)

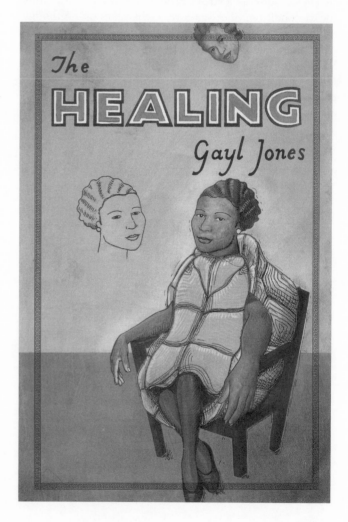

MOSQUITO, 2000, cover. In this novel by Jones, "Mosquito" is the nickname of Sojourner Nadine Jane Johnson, an African American truck driver who becomes involved in a sanctuary movement for Mexican immigrants. (Beacon Press, Boston.)

dark images in the books to be her only representation of African American men. However, editor Helene Atwan persuaded Jones to allow the publication of two novels that she had written in the decades of silence.

Whereas Jones's earlier works examine psychosexual violence in male-female relations, *The Healing* (1998) moves toward restoring the black woman's psyche as a preamble to self-definition. Harlan Jane Eagleton, who leaves her medical anthropologist husband in Africa to chase after a Masai medicine woman, returns to America to pursue her own interests in faith healing and horse betting. Dropping her married name to use her own, she becomes the makeup artist and then business manager to Joan Hermoine Savage, a divorced black rock star who

feigns disinterest in her former husband's affairs with Harlan. Harlan's mental wholeness contrasts with the insecurity of Joan Savage, who stabs Harlan for intruding on her and another man. This novel suggests that with the absence of male betrayal comes a restoration of women's psychological health. Its jazz medium offers contrapuntal stories of women's betrayal told with intricate pacing and harmonic speech ranging from ghettoized slang, to rap, to a cosmopolitan lilt.

The Healing received enormous critical acclaim and was nominated for the National Book Award. It also brought tragedy into Jones's life. Her husband, Bob Higgins, whom she had married in the 1970s while on a writing fellowship at the University of Michigan, had been wanted on an assault charge since 1983, a charge stemming from a political demonstration. When *Newsweek* magazine reported on Jones's triumph, they stated the couple's location, back in Lexington, and police went there seeking Higgins. When a SWAT team entered the house after a five-hour standoff, Higgins took his own life.

Mosquito (1999) continues the saga of self-definition and details the adventures of Sojourner Nadine Jane Johnson, a nominal member of the Perfectibility Baptist Church, and an African American truck driver called Mosquito. Delivering industrial detergent in a south Texas border town, Sojourner helps others to forge new identities as she becomes involved in the new underground railroad movement that grants sanctuary to Mexican immigrants. Her initial involvement in the movement occurs when she finds hidden in her truck a pregnant young Mexican woman, who names her baby Journal, an aural distortion of the name of her benefactor, Sojourner. Defining self, Sojourner challenges descriptions of American beauty and women's work. Her tale is encased in a jazz-like structure with soaring riffs, narrative breaks, and an improvisational telling.

Gayl Jones has published regularly in *Callaloo*. In the early twenty-first century, this African American and African arts journal continues to showcase the latest developments in one of America's most intriguing writers and participates in the expanding vision of her work.

See also Fiction.

BIBLIOGRAPHY

Barksdale, Richard K. "Castration Symbolism in Recent Black American Fiction." *College Language Association Journal* 29.4 (June 1986): 400–413.

Bell, Bernard W. "The Liberating Literary and African American Vernacular Voices of Gayl Jones." *Comparative Literary Studies* 36.3 (1999): 247–257.

Davidson, Carol Margaret. "'Love 'em and Lynch 'em': The Castration Motif in Gayl Jones's *Eva's Man*." *African American Review* 29.3 (Fall 1995): 393–410.

Dubey, Madhu. "Don't You Explain Me: The Unreadability of *Eva's Man*." In *Black Women Novelists and the Nationalistic Aesthetic*, edited by Madhu Dubey Bloomington: Indiana University Press, 1994, 89–105.

"'A New World Song': The Blues Form of Corregidora." In *Black Women's Novelists and the Nationalist Aesthetic*, edited by Madhu Dubey, Bloomington: Indiana University Press, 1994: 72–88.

Robinson, Sally. "*Eva's Man*: Excess as Subversion." In *Engendering the Subject: Gender and Self-Representation in Contemporary Women's Fiction*. Albany: State University of New York Press, 1991: 165–187.

—RITA B. DANDRIDGE

JONES, LOIS MAILOU (b. 3 November 1905; d. 9 June 1998), artist and teacher. An active and acclaimed painter for more than six decades, Lois Mailou Jones enjoyed two impressive careers, one as a professor of art and the other as an artist. Her teaching gave her financial security and served as an inspiration and a challenge.

Lois Jones was born in Boston to Caroline Dorinda Adams and Thomas Vreeland Jones. Her father was superintendent of a large office building and attended night classes at Suffolk Law School, where he received his law degree in 1915 at the age of forty. "I think that much of my drive surely comes from my father," Jones once said, "wanting to be someone, having an ambition." Her mother was a beautician and Jones's first mentor. She filled the Jones home with color and freshly cut flowers, instilling in her daughter a love of beauty.

With the assistance of four annual tuition scholarships, Jones earned a diploma from the High School of Practical Arts (HSPA). During her high school years, she also attended the Boston Museum Vocational Drawing Class, on a scholarship. While at HSPA, she was apprenticed to Grace Ripley, a well-known costume designer and professor at the Rhode Island School of Design. She assisted Ripley in creating costumes for the Ted Shawn School of Dance and a branch of the Bragiotti School in Boston. Working on Saturdays and after school, she designed dance costumes, especially masks. She recalled that "very early I was introduced to Africa through creating the masks with the Ripley studio."

LOIS MAILOU JONES at work, c. 1936–1937. Jones was both an artist and a professor of art, who taught for nearly half a century at Howard University. Her artworks are represented in many American museums and private collections. (National Harmon Foundation; Joe McCary, Photo Response Studio.)

In 1923 Jones was admitted to the Boston Museum of Fine Arts, where each year from 1923 to 1927 she won the coveted Susan Minot Lane Scholarship in Design. Here she studied design concepts, life drawing, and portraiture under such artists as Anson Cross, Phillip Hale, Alice Morse, and Henry Hunt Clark. She graduated from the museum school with honors in 1927. During her last year at the museum school, Jones enrolled in evening classes at the Boston Normal Art School (now the Massachusetts College of Art), receiving a teaching certificate in 1927. That same year she won a scholarship to the Designers Art School of Boston, where she continued graduate study with Ludwig Frank, internationally known designer of textiles. Her studies were extended at Harvard University during the summer of 1928. Jones created a series of designs for cretonne—a strong, unglazed cotton or linen cloth that is used especially for curtains and upholstery—and other fabric and textile patterns.

That year, two eminent educators, Henry Hunt Clark and Charlotte Hawkins Brown, told Jones to "go South" and help her people. Jones had been disappointed by Clark when she applied for a position at the museum school; none was available, and Clark pointed the young designer toward the South and its needs. She balked. Next, she applied to Howard University. She was informed that they had recently hired James A. Porter and had no other positions were available. Then she heard Brown speak in Boston, urging college students to take their talents to the youth of the South. This time she accepted the challenge. Although thought by some to be too young and inexperienced, she was hired by Brown to develop the art department at the Palmer Memorial Institute, one of the nation's first preparatory schools for African Americans, in Sedalia, North Carolina. Jones established the curriculum, served as chairperson of the department, and provided instruction to a small, eager class. In addition to her other duties, Jones also taught dancing, coached a basketball team, and played the piano for Sunday morning worship services.

During the spring of 1930, James Vernon Herring, founder and head of the Department of Art at Howard University, was invited by Jones to lecture at Palmer. He was impressed by the work of her students and recruited her to serve as an instructor of design at Howard. Jones joined the Howard faculty in 1930 and remained there until her retirement in 1977. She, James A. Porter, and James Lesesne Wells constituted the art department and forged a curriculum unique among historically black colleges and universities.

For her first sabbatical, Jones chose the Académie Julian in Paris. During a summer on Martha's Vineyard, she had met the sculptor Meta Warrick Fuller and the composer Harry T. Burleigh. They advised her that, if she wanted to find a niche in the art world, she should travel to Paris for recognition. Also, of course, study in Paris was a tradition for American artists who could manage the expense. With the aid of a General Education Board fellowship, Jones sailed for France on the S.S. *Normandie* on 1 September 1937. Her sojourn there marked a shift in her career from that of designer, illustrator, and teacher to that of painter. The experience allowed her, as Jones said, "to be shackle free, to create and to be myself."

Many of her works from that year were painted on location. It was during one of her painting exercises on the Seine that Jones met Émile Bernard, the father of French Symbolist painting. He encouraged her and critiqued her work. Albert Smith, an African American artist in Paris, also became a friend during Jones's stay and after her return to the United States.

Jones made such progress that, toward the end of the academic year, her friends and instructors urged her to submit paintings to the annual Salon de Printemps of the Société des Artistes Français, one of the most important exhibits of the year. Although her work of this era reveals a commitment to the organizing principles and preferred palette of the impressionists and postimpressionists, her paintings were clearly personal interpretations. As James Porter, author of *Modern Negro Art*, observed: "Thus far her painting has been in the tradition, but not in the imitation of Cezanne.... Miss Jones wishes to confirm Cezanne but at the same time to add an original note of her own.... Sensuous color delicately adjusted to the mood indicates the artistic perceptiveness of this young woman."

Soon after her return to the United States in September 1938, Jones exhibited at the Robert Vose Galleries in Boston. Her work received high praise, and her reputation grew as she exhibited throughout the United States. After her return to Washington, she met Alain Locke, poet laureate of the Harlem Renaissance, or New Negro Movement, and head of the philosophy department at Howard. Telling her of his plans to include one of her Parisian street scenes in his forthcoming book, *The Negro in Art* (1940), Locke strongly encouraged her to reevaluate her subjects and take her own heritage more seriously. An early advocate of African American consciousness, Locke was perhaps the most influential voice on art in the black community at that time. Jones's response to Locke's challenge produced works focused on the African American. The artist refers to the 1940s as her Locke period. Also during this decade, Jones took classes at Howard, receiving an AB in Art Education and graduating magna cum laude in 1945.

When Lois Jones married the noted Haitian graphic artist and designer Louis Vergniaud Pierre-Noel in 1953, both her life and her art were transformed. They took advantage of an invitation from the Haitian government to teach at the Centre d'Art and the Foyer des Arts Plastiques so that they could honeymoon in Haiti. The experience was the beginning of a new way of seeing for Jones, and, from her first visit, she "fell increasingly in love with Haiti and its people." Her early Haitian paintings explored the picturesque elements of the marketplace and its people. Although the essence of Europe was still, at the beginning, very much apparent, the palette and the formal organization of her paintings gradually evolved into a brilliantly spirited style, fresh, energetically fluid, and highly individual. This new style signaled clearly that Europe did not yield the exuberance so vital to expressing the vigor found in this African-oriented culture.

Jones's work in the 1960s drew more upon her knowledge of design techniques and her passion for color while synthesizing the diverse religious and ritualistic elements of Haitian life and culture. It showed a more expressive, colorful, hard-edged style that fused abstraction with decorative patterns and naturalism. These characteristics asserted themselves even more powerfully in the 1970s.

In 1969 Jones received a grant from Howard University to conduct research on contemporary artists in Africa. Between April and July, she compiled biographical material on African artists, photographing their work, conducting interviews, and visiting museums in eleven African countries. More than one thousand slides were given to the Howard University archives upon completion. Jones said her trip "proved to be a revelation and a rich experience." During the 1970s and into the 1980s, she maintained an intense interest in Africa. Undoubtedly this was in part due to the African American quest for cultural identity and the fact that the black cultural movement of these years was even more profound and widespread than that which occurred during the Harlem Renaissance.

In the summer of 1989, Jones returned to France. The works that resulted recall an earlier era. Reminiscent of the impressionist/postimpressionist style she had abandoned more than thirty years earlier, the paintings created during that visit illustrate her continued fascination with nature and her desire to capture the fleeting beauty of place. In 1990 a major retrospective, "The World of Lois Mailou Jones," was sponsored by Meridian House International in Washington, DC. It opened in January and traveled for two years across the United States.

Lois Mailou Jones received numerous awards for her work in competitions, including the National Thayer Prize for excellence in design. She also received honorary degrees from a number of universities, including Howard. In 1954, the government of Haiti awarded her the Diplome and Decoration de l'Ordre Nationale "Honneur et Mérite au Grade de Chevalier." Her work is represented in museums and private collections across the country and the world, including the Metropolitan Museum of Art in New York; the Museum of Fine Arts and the Museum of the National Center of Afro-American Artists in Boston; the National Museum of American Art, the National Museum of Women in the Arts, the National Portrait Gallery, the Hirshhorn Museum and Sculpture Garden, and the Corcoran Gallery of Art in Washington, DC; the Museum of Fine Art in Houston, and the Palais Nationale in Port-au-Prince, Haiti, to name a few notable institutions.

It is difficult to estimate the impact of any given artist during his or her lifetime. About Lois Jones, however, certain things are clear. While teaching and communicating a love of art to generations of students, she has created a body of work characterized by technical virtuosity, consummate skill, versatility, elegance, vitality, structure, design, and clarion color. The last link to the visual artists of the Harlem Renaissance, Jones died in her Washington, DC, home of cardiac arrest in June 1998.

See also **Visual Arts.**

BIBLIOGRAPHY

"Artists of Sunlit Canvases." *Ebony*, November 1968.

Benjamin, Tritobia Hayes. Personal interviews with Lois Mailou Jones (28 September 1986; 29 October 1986; 2 November 1986).

Davis, John P. *American Negro Reference Book*. Yonkers, NY: Educational Heritage, 1966.

Dover, Cedric. *American Negro Art*. Greenwich, CT: New York Graphic Society, 1960.

Driskell, David C. *Hidden Heritage: Afro-American Art, 1800–1950*. San Francisco: The Association, 1985.

Driskell, David C. *Two Centuries of Black American Art*. New York: Knopf, 1976.

Fine, Elsa Honig. *The Afro-American Artist: A Search for Identity*. New York: Holt, Rinehart and Winston, 1973.

Fine, Elsa Honig. *Women and Art: A History of Women Painters and Sculptors from the Renaissance to the Twentieth Century*. Montclair, NJ: Allanheld and Schram/Prior, 1978.

Heller, Nancy G. "Lois Mailou Jones, American Painter." *Museum and Arts Washington Magazine*, July–August 1988.

Heller, Nancy G. *Women Artists: An Illustrated History*. New York: Abbeville Press, 1997.

LaDuke, Betty. "Lois Mailou Jones: The Grand Dame of African-American Art." *Women's Art Journal*, Fall 1986–1987.

Lewis, Samella. *Art: African American*. New York: Harcourt Brace Jovanovich, 1978.

Locke, Alain. *The Negro in Art: A Pictorial Record of the Negro Artist and of the Negro Theme in Art*. New York: Hacker Art Books, 1971.

"One Hundred and Fifty Years of Afro-American Art." Los Angeles: UCLA Art Galleries, Dickson Art Center, 1966.

Porter, James A. Prefatory comments in *Lois Mailou Jones Peintures 1937–1951*. Tourcoing, France: Georges Frére, 1952.

Porter, James A. *Modern Negro Art*, with a new introduction by David C. Driskell. Washington, DC: Howard University Press, 1992.

Robinson, Wilhelmena, ed. *Historical Negro Biographies*. 2nd ed., revised. New York: Publishers Co., 1969.

Rubinstein, Charlotte S. *American Women Artists from Early Indian Times to the Present*. New York: Avon, 1982.

"The World of Lois Mailou Jones." Exhibit at Meridian House International, Washington, DC, 1990.

Wardlaw, Alvia, Barry Gaither, Regina Perry, and Robert Farris Thompson. *Black Arts: Ancestral Legacy: The African Impulse in African-American Art.* New York: Harry N. Abrams, 1999.

—TRITOBIA HAYES BENJAMIN

JONES, SISSIERETTA (b. 5 January 1869; d. 24 June 1933), singer. Discovering Sissieretta Jones is like uncovering a buried treasure. In the twenty-first century, her name may not be a household word, but she was a well-known and respected performer in her time.

Jones was born Matilda Sissieretta Joyner in 1869 in Portsmouth, Virginia, in a middle-class environment. Her father, Malachi Joyner, was a Baptist minister. Her mother, Henrietta Beale Joyner, sang in the church choir and is said to have had a wonderful soprano voice. This appears to be where young Sissieretta inherited her own naturally beautiful voice. It was obvious by the time she was five years old that she had a gift, and her family was instrumental in promoting her talent. To give her a chance for formal music study, the family moved from Virginia to Providence, Rhode Island. She now could study classical voice at Providence Academy of Music. From the Providence Academy, Jones went on to study in Boston, possibly at the New England Conservatory of music. There is, however, some debate about the extent of her studies in Boston and the exact institution. Several accounts state that she studied at the New England Conservatory of Music. While her name does not appear in any school record, she may have been a private student of one or more of the teachers at the conservatory. Jones herself said that she studied with various teachers in different cities, the best being Luisa Cappiani in New York.

Jones began vocal training in earnest when she was about fourteen years old. Not long after, she married David Richard Jones. A compulsive gambler, he squandered most of the money his wife earned singing. Nonetheless, the couple remained married for sixteen years, divorcing in 1899. Little else is known about Jones's early life and marriage.

Jones made her professional debut in Providence in a performance that was so well received it led to a New York concert where she was billed as "the rising soprano from New England." This concert in turn caught the attention of Abbey, Schoffel, and Grau, who were concert managers. Henry Abbey became Jones's manager and sent her on a tour to the West Indies with the Tennessee Jubilee Singers. From there, Jones's career took off.

In 1892, when she was only twenty-three, she played New York's Madison Square Garden, packing the house with a performance that was wildly lauded by critics.

SISSIERETTA JONES was often compared to the great coloratura soprano Adelina Patti (1843–1919) and was known as the "Black Patti." Jones's performing ensemble, the Black Patti Troubadours, had its first season in 1896 and toured successfully for many years. (Moorland-Spingarn Research Center.)

Jones's next major performance was at the 1893 Chicago World's Fair. After this run, she continued to tour in the United States and around the world. In her travels, she sang for United States presidents and foreign royalty. James Weldon Johnson observed that she possessed "the natural voice, the physical figure, the grand air and engaging personality" characteristic of a great singers, and the *Washington Post* described her voice as "a phenomenal attraction . . . the upper notes are clear and bell-like . . . and her low notes are rich and sensuous with a tropical contralto quality. . . . In fact, the compass and quality of her registers surpass the usual limitations."

Early in Jones's career, one enthralled reviewer dubbed her "the Black Patti." This was intended as a compliment, a favorable comparison to the respected Italian opera star Adeline Patti, but Jones disliked it. Unfortunately, she couldn't escape it. When she realized the limitations of her opportunities in white performing venues, particularly in opera, she used the name to launch her own company of singers and musicians. They were known as "Black Patti and Her Troubadours." From 1895 to 1916, Jones toured with her Troubadours throughout the United States and abroad, turning around her rejection by the "white world of classical music" and creating a successful career.

The Troubadours were not totally unlike other shows of the times, vaudeville or minstrel, but some of the differences from the typical shows were significant. For one thing, her chorus was female. The most important change, however, was that whereas minstrel shows usually featured the popular cakewalk, a kind of satirical dance, Jones sang classical arias. The audiences were intrigued and enthusiastic, yet did not know what to make of this strange anomaly, a black woman singing opera in a minstrel show. Despite the peculiar format, she made the show work and gained wide-ranging popularity.

Jones's show became a valuable training ground for many new talents, and over the years, the group included many soon-to-be-independent major stars such as Aida Overton and even Gertrude "Ma" Rainey. In her performances, Jones made numerous breakthroughs for women and African Americans. Singing spirituals and opera gave Jones the chance to do what she wanted, and at the same time gave her exposure to a much broader audience.

Gradually Jones began to move away from the minstrel show structure altogether, and her shows became closer to musical comedy. At the same time, Jones began to appear throughout the entire show, rather than just in her concert-style recitals. The Black Patti company performed shows such as *A Trip to Africa* (1909–1910), *In the Jungles* (1911–1912), *Captain Jasper* (1912–1913), and *Lucky Sam from Alabam'* (1914–1915) in the new black-owned theaters in major cities, but then illness struck Jones, and she was forced to disband her company. She gave farewell performances at the Grand Theater in Chicago and the Lafayette Theater in New York, promising to return. She was not able to. She lived her last years in Providence, taking care of her ailing mother, until she herself died of cancer in Rhode Island Hospital.

See also **Concert Music.**

BIBLIOGRAPHY

Daughtry, Willia E. "Sissieretta Jones." In *Black Women in America: An Historical Encyclopedia*, edited by Darlene Clark Hine. Brooklyn: Carlson Publishing, 1993.

Southern, Eileen. *Biographical Dictionary of Afro-American and African Musicians*. Westport, CT: Greenwood Press, 1982.

Woll, Allen. *A Dictionary of Black Theater: Broadway, Off-Broadway, and Selected Harlem Theater*. Westport, CT: Greenwood Press, 1983.

Woll, Allen. *Black Musical Theater: From Coontown to Dreamgirls*. Baton Rouge, LA: Louisiana State University Press, 1989.

—DIANE EPSTEIN

JONES, VERINA HARRIS MORTON (b. 28 January 1865; d. 1943), physician, club woman, civil rights activist, suffragist. Verina Morton Jones was born in Cleveland, Ohio, and attended State Normal School in Columbia, South Carolina. From 1884 to 1888 she attended the Woman's Medical College of Pennsylvania in Philadelphia—then widely acknowledged to be one of the best medical colleges for women in the country. She received her MD in 1888 and began practice in the African American community at Rust College in Holly Springs, Mississippi. Morton Jones was the first woman, black or white, to practice medicine in the state of Mississippi. She married twice; the first time in 1890 to W. A. Morton, MD, who died in 1895, and the second time in 1901 to Emory Jones, who died in 1927. She had one child from her first marriage, Franklin W., who was born in 1892.

Among the first African American women in the U.S. to receive a degree in medicine, Morton Jones moved to New York to practice in Brooklyn and on Long Island during the Progressive era. She was the first black woman to practice medicine in Nassau County on Long Island, and she played an active role in the largely white, male-dominated Kings County Medical Society. In the 1941–1944 edition of *Who's Who in Colored America*, Morton Jones is described as "the oldest colored physician in Brooklyn in point of practice as well as age." In spite of her long and active career in medicine and healing, Morton Jones also devoted her time to club work, education, suffrage, community "uplift," and civil rights.

Morton Jones headed the Lincoln Settlement House in Brooklyn from its founding in May 1908. Lincoln House began as an extension of the white social reformer and nurse Lillian Wald's Henry Street Settlement House on the Lower East Side of New York City. The primary sponsor of this self-help, community-based program, Morton Jones contributed the down payment on the property for the settlement house and pioneered the first social service organization in Brooklyn that sought to address the needs of the growing black population. Under her directorship, Lincoln House offered a clinic, a day nursery and free kindergarten, a lecture series on health and hygiene, and classes in carpentry, cooking, embroidery, folk dancing, and sewing; it also sponsored choral and debating clubs. It appealed not only to youth but also to the adults of the community. The settlement house incorporated in 1914 and moved from its original quarters at 129 Willoughby Street to 105 Fleet Place, where there was a more spacious building and a nearby lot for a playground.

Morton Jones nurtured diverse social and political commitments. As a club woman, she played an active part in the National Association of Colored Women (NACW, founded in 1896). She was the director of the NACW's Mothers' Club in Brooklyn and was part of the female auxiliary of the radical Niagara Movement in 1905 and 1906. She also participated in the work of the Committee for Improving Industrial Conditions of Negroes in New York City (founded in 1906), which in 1911 merged with two other social reform groups to become the National Urban League. Morton Jones fought to win the vote for all women and fought to protect the right to vote of all African Americans. She rejected the notion that black women had no interest in voting. She assisted in conducting voter education programs, noted instances of race discrimination at the polls, and testified before congressional investigatory committees. Like many other black club women of the Progressive era, Morton Jones drew on the tradition of self-help in the African American community in her tenure as president of the Brooklyn Equal Suffrage League.

Morton Jones was elected to the National Association for the Advancement of Colored People (NAACP) board of directors in 1913 and worked on the executive committee until 1925. Mary White Ovington, a white social reformer and one of the founders of the NAACP, in her 1947 autobiography *The Walls Came Tumbling Down*, reminisced about a typical 1917 board meeting in which Morton Jones was the only "colored woman." Morton Jones was not the only woman of color to have membership in the interracial Cosmopolitan Club, however. This social and political group of New York City and Brooklyn reformers met regularly to discuss racism, civil rights, and reform stratagems. Morton Jones, Ovington, the *Independent* editor Hamilton Holt, the prominent socialist John Spargo, and the *Evening Post*'s Oswald Garrison Villard were among the members of this club. Both black and white reformers active in groups such as the NAACP and the Urban League attended meetings of this club. Morton Jones also held membership in the Association for the Protection of Colored Women and volunteered for the "Phillis Wheatley" chapters of the Young Women's Christian Association (YWCA).

Morton Jones is at once an outstanding and a typical example of the black professional and club women who sought to "uplift" their communities by working within both black and interracial protest groups to combat racism and protect civil rights. Morton Jones, who was an Episcopalian and a Republican, died in 1943.

BIBLIOGRAPHY

Aptheker, Herbert, ed. *The Correspondence of W. E. B. Du Bois*. Amherst, MA: University of Massachusetts Press, 1975.

"Brooklyn's Black Women." *New York Times*, 22 October 1985.

Cash, Floris. "Womanhood and Protest: The Club Movement among Black Women, 1892–1922." PhD diss., SUNY/Stonybrook, 1985.

Connolly, Harry X. *A Ghetto Grows in Brooklyn*. New York: New York University Press, 1977.

Giddings, Paula. *When and Where I Enter: The Impact of Black Women on Race and Sex in America*. New York: Morrow, 1984.

Ovington, Mary White. *The Walls Came Tumbling Down*. New York: Harcourt, Brace, 1947.

"The Role of Black Women in Brooklyn's History." *New York Times*, 19 October 1985.

Salem, Dorothy. *To Better Our World: Black Women in Organized Reform, 1890–1920*. Brooklyn: Carlson, 1990.

Scuggs, Lawson A. *Women of Distinction, 1892*. In *Black Biographical Dictionaries, 1790–1950*. Alexandria, VA: Chadwyck-Healey, 1991.

Sterling, Dorothy, ed. *We Are Your Sisters: Black Women in the Nineteenth Century*. New York: Norton, 1997.

Weiss, Nancy. *The National Urban League, 1910–1940*. New York: Oxford University Press, 1974.

ARCHIVAL SOURCES

Morton Jones's papers are archived at the Moorland-Spingarn Research Center, Howard University, Washington, DC.

—THEA ARNOLD

JONES, VIVIAN MALONE

JONES, VIVIAN MALONE (b. 1942), civil rights activist. On 11 June 1963, at the age of twenty, Vivian Malone Jones challenged more than a century of segregation at the University of Alabama. In a highly publicized confrontation, Jones and fellow African American student James Hood were greeted by Governor George Wallace, who attempted to prohibit their entrance into the University of Alabama's Foster Auditorium by standing in the doorway. The entire incident lasted only fifteen minutes, and Wallace's move proved to be little more than a symbolic gesture. Jones and Hood began classes the next day. Although Hood eventually left the University of Alabama to attend school in Michigan, Jones continued on at the school and in 1965 became the first African American to graduate from the University of Alabama.

Jones began her undergraduate career under much different circumstances. She spent her first two years of college at Alabama Agricultural and Mechanical College, an all-black institution in Normal, Alabama, just outside Huntsville. On the morning Jones transferred to the University of Alabama, she was cognizant of the significance of the moment, both for herself and the larger African American community, but remained focused on the future. Reflecting on the experience later in life, Jones stated, "I went way beyond that day at that point in my mind. . . . My vision was of the future and graduating and going to classes, things like that." Even though she faced incredible hostility and threats of violence from fellow students, community members, and the governor himself, Jones did not want to hide. She said, "I didn't feel I should go around [to] the back door. If [Wallace] were standing in the door, I had every right in the world to face him and to go to school." Jones not only faced Governor Wallace at the schoolhouse doors, she also thrived while attending the university in spite of the negative treatment she sometimes received from white students and faculty members.

Despite the hostile environment at the school, Jones has been quick to point out that not everybody at UA had a negative attitude toward her presence, and she was able to make a few close friends. Although she did not attend dances or date any of the boys at her own school, Jones socialized with boys from Tuscaloosa's Stillman College, where she met her future husband, Mack Jones. In addition to forging a meaningful personal life while at college, Jones thrived academically and managed to achieve excellent grades in her program. Two years after beginning classes at UA, Jones graduated with a bachelor's degree in business management.

Unable to find work in Alabama after graduation, Jones moved to Washington, DC, and began working for the U.S. Department of Justice. In 1969 she moved to Atlanta when her husband was accepted at Emory University's medical school. In Atlanta, Jones raised two children and continued to work for the federal government. She held a position in employee relations as a personal specialist with the Veterans Administration Hospital before accepting a position as Director of Civil Rights and Urban Affairs and later Director of Environmental Justice with the U.S. Environmental Protection Agency. Jones also worked as executive director of the Voter Education Project. In 1996 Jones retired from her thirty-year career with the federal government and began a private-sector career working for Atlanta Associates of MONY Life Insurance Company of America.

In addition to her obvious place in civil rights history, Jones has remained active in civil rights causes throughout her life. She has been part of a number of civic and community organizations, including the NAACP, the Southern Christian Leadership Conference (SCLC), Atlanta's Ben Hill United Methodist Church, and the National Council of Negro Women (NCNW). Over the years Jones has received several awards for her work in civil rights–related efforts, including the Emancipation Day Award from the NAACP and the Drum Major for Justice Award from the SCLC. In 1995 officials in Tuscaloosa, the hometown of Jones's alma mater, dedicated 13 October as "Vivian Malone Jones Day."

In 1996 Jones was chosen by the George Wallace Family Foundation to be the first recipient of the Lurleen B. Wallace Award of Courage. Wallace was not only present at the ceremony, which took place in Montgomery, but he also presented Jones with the award. Unlike their confrontational meeting three decades earlier, this meeting has been described as a moment of reconciliation and forgiveness. Of this second meeting Jones stated, "I forgave George Wallace—as a Christian, that was my responsibility. But I never forgot what he did." Two years later, she would return to Montgomery as one of the thousands present at Wallace's funeral.

The University of Alabama has also honored Jones by endowing a Vivian Malone Jones Scholarship Fund and hanging her portrait in the university's Bidgood Hall, home of the College of Commerce and Business Administration. She received an honorary doctorate of humane letters from the University of Alabama, where she was named one of the most outstanding women in the institution's history. In 2003, on the fortieth anniversary of Jones's courageous stand on the steps of Foster Auditorium, the University of Alabama hosted the Opening Doors Ceremony in honor of her passage through those now-famous portals.

BIBLIOGRAPHY

Bandler, Michael J. "Opening Doors to Equality: Univ. of Alabama Commemorates 40 Years of African-American Enrollment." U.S. Department of State International Information Programs. http://164.109.48.86/usa/civilrights/a061303.htm.

Bandler, Michael J. "The Schoolhouse Door—Forty Years Later." U.S. Department of State International Information Programs. http://164.109.48.86/usa/civilrights/a061103.htm.

"Blocking the Schoolhouse Door: George Wallace Clears His Conscience." *The Journal of Blacks in Higher Education* 14 (Winter 1996–1997): 67–68.

Granger, David M. "Vivian Malone Jones Address Highlights AU's Black History Month." *Auburn University News*, 14 February 2001. http://www.auburn.edu/administration/univrel/news/archive/2_01news/02_01malonejones.html.

"Malone, Vivian Jones." In *Notable Black American Women, Book I*, edited by Jessie Carney Smith. Detroit, MI: Gale Research, 1992.

"Opening Doors." University of Alabama Annual Report 2003. University of Alabama. http://report2003.ua.edu/doors.html.

Scott, Marla. "Vivian Malone Jones: Leading the Way." Opening Doors Opening Minds. DatelineAlabama.com http://www.ccom.ua.edu/od/article_jones.shtml.

—JAIME MCLEAN

JORDAN, BARBARA CHARLINE (b. 21 February 1936; d. 17 January 1996), attorney, politician. Barbara Charline Jordan was the first black woman to sit in the Texas Senate (1967–1973) and the first from the South to be elected to the United States House of Representatives (1973–1979). She was born in the Fifth Ward of Houston, Texas, to a Baptist minister, Benjamin Jordan, and a domestic worker, Arlyne (Patten) Jordan. Her early childhood was spent with her parents, her two older sisters, Bennie and Rose Mary, and her grandfathers, Charles Jordan and John Ed Patten.

BARBARA JORDAN speaking at the National Women's Conference in November 1977. Seated to her left are Bella Abzug (in a characteristic hat) and Rosalynn Carter (who was then the First Lady). (© Bettye Lane.)

Jordan's outlook on life and politics, as well as her strength and determination, can be attributed to the influence of her maternal grandfather, John Ed Patten, the son of Edward A. Patten, one of the forty-two African Americans who sat in the Texas legislature during Reconstruction. As a child, Jordan spent most of her free time with Patten. While working with him in his junk business, she learned how to be self-sufficient, strong-willed and independent. He also instilled in her the value of an education.

Jordan received her early education from Atherton Elementary and Phyllis Wheatley high schools. As a student at Wheatley, Jordan participated in the Honors Society, the debate team, and other extracurricular activities. It

was during her high school years that Jordan was inspired to become a lawyer. She was drawn to the legal profession by a career-day presentation given by a prominent African American attorney Edith Sampson.

In 1952, upon graduation from high school in the top 5 percent of her class, Jordan entered Texas Southern University, where she majored in political science and history and became involved in extracurricular activities such as Delta Sigma Theta sorority and the debate team. An orator in high school, Jordan sharpened her skills even more under the guidance and tutelage of the university's debate coach, Thomas F. Freeman. Freeman taught her how to formulate her words with her tone, which helped her become a great speaker. It was this involvement with the debate team that began for her a series of firsts that became the hallmark of her professional life. Jordan was a member of the first debate team from an historically black university to compete in the forensics tournament held annually at Baylor University in Texas, winning first place in oratory—one of the many first-place trophies in her career in forensics. Freeman not only influenced Jordan's speech pattern, but he also urged her to attend Boston University Law School in 1956. Three years later, Jordan became one of two African American women to receive a law degree from that institution. By 1960 Jordan managed to pass the Massachusetts and Texas bar examinations.

After leaving Boston University, Jordan taught political science for one year at Tuskegee Institute in Alabama. In 1960 she returned to her native Houston to set up private law practice. Unsuccessful in her law practice, Jordan turned to politics. As she put it: "I had a law degree, but no practice, so I went down to Harris County Democratic Headquarters and asked them what I could do. They put me to work [on the John F. Kennedy Campaign] licking stamps and addressing envelopes." While this task seemed mundane, Barbara Jordan's real talents, the power of her voice and the strength of her words, were not underestimated for long. One night while working on the Kennedy campaign, Jordan and some members of the Democratic party "went to a church to enlist voters and the woman who was supposed to speak didn't show up." Jordan volunteered to speak in the woman's place, and the campaign immediately reassigned her from "stamps and envelopes" to speaker bureau. Shortly thereafter, she became intimately involved in politics. For four years, Jordan was very active in local and state Democratic politics and made two unsuccessful runs for the state legislature in 1962 and 1964. Her interest in politics was given a boost in 1965 when she received her first appointive position as administrative assistant to the Harris County Judge, Bill Elliott, and served as project coordinator of a nonprofit corporation to help the unemployed.

In 1966 redistricting and increased voter registration secured Jordan a seat in the Texas Senate, where she became the first African American since 1893 to serve in this august body. As Texas came in compliance with the Supreme Court's decisions in *Baker v. Carr* and *Reynolds v. Sam*, which asserted that the state legislature must redistrict to conform to one man, one vote, Texans saw the beginning of the switch of political power from the rural areas to their larger urban counterparts. The result of this would be the creation of a new Eleventh State Senatorial District in Harris County, made up of wards that Jordan had carried when she ran for the Texas House of Representatives in 1964. She was encouraged to run in that district, and in 1966, Jordan won 65 percent of the Democratic primary vote. She ran unopposed in the general election.

Jordan's six-year record in the Texas Senate showed a sensitivity to issues affecting the working class, the disabled, racial minorities, and women. She championed the cause of each group, although she had to accept compromise to achieve her goal. While in the senate, she was appointed chair of the Labor and Management Committee, vice chair of the Judicial and Legislative Committee, and a member of other committees. Her most noted bill was the Worker's Compensation Act. This bill gave the state its first minimum wage law and increased workers' compensation coverage for on-the-job injuries. When the Texas legislature convened in special session in March 1972, Senator Jordan was unanimously elected president pro tempore. In June of that year, she was honored by being named Governor for a Day.

While completing her term in office at the state level, Jordan achieved another first when she was elected to the United States House of Representatives in 1972. As a result of the 1970 census and redistricting, the 18th Congressional District was established and virtually assured African Americans a seat in Congress. When apportionment occurred in Texas, Lieutenant Governor Ben Barnes named Senator Barbara Jordan vice chair of the redistricting committee, which meant that Jordan took part in drawing the boundaries that guaranteed her own election. When the election was held, she defeated State Representative Curtis Graves in the Democratic primary and, subsequently, Republican Paul Merritt.

As a member of the United States House of Representatives, Jordan's reputation was that of a skilled politician and a forceful, dynamic individual. She left an impressive record in the Ninety-Third Congress when she attached civil rights amendments to legislation authorizing cities to receive direct Law Enforcement Assistance Administration grants, rather than apply to state governments for the money. Jordan also questioned the civil rights record of House Republican leader Gerald Ford when he was nominated for vice president and joined seven other Judiciary Committee members in voting against his confirmation. In 1975 she secured passage of the Consumer Goods Pricing Act, a bill which repealed antitrust exemptions that kept consumer prices artificially high. Jordan also favored a $25 billion extension of the general federal revenue sharing program and worked to toughen its antidiscrimination provisions.

Probably the most important bill that Jordan sponsored as a congresswoman was one to extend the Voting Rights Act of 1965 to Texas and other western states in order to cover individuals with language barriers. In June 1975, the House voted to extend the Voting Rights Act of 1965 for ten years. Jordan sponsored legislation extending the Act to include Spanish-speaking, American Indian, Alaskan Native, and Asian American language minorities, while opposing amendments that would have permitted states and localities covered or partially covered by the act to apply for exemption. This bill was opposed by most Texas officials, as well as President Gerald Ford, but Jordan did not capitulate. Equally important was Jordan's role in convincing the House Judiciary Committee to extend the time allowed by Congress to win state ratification for the Equal Rights Amendment, a statute that would have placed equality of the sexes in the constitution.

Having already caught the attention of Lyndon B. Johnson while she was in the Texas Senate, Jordan sought the former president's advice on the type of committee that she should join when she got to Congress. Subsequently, she became a member of the Judiciary Committee and the Ways and Means Committee. Jordan's membership on the Judiciary Committee gained her notoriety during the 1974 Watergate scandal, when her oratorical brilliance was demonstrated in a speech she made on committee in favor of impeachment of President Richard M. Nixon. In fact, she received national acclaim for her eloquent reaffirmation of faith in the Constitution while voting for all five articles of impeachment. In the deep, resonant voice that was her trademark, Jordan declared: "My faith in the Constitution is whole. It is complete, it is total!" Her televised speech was the center of media attention and critique for days to come.

Barbara Jordan's popularity and eloquence as an oratorical speaker reached its zenith in 1976 when she was asked to serve as the keynote speaker for the Democratic National Convention—the first black woman in the convention's 144-year history to receive such honor. When Jimmy Carter won the presidency, there was a rumor among her supporters that she would become Carter's vice president. Instead, Carter offered her the post of secretary of the Department of Health, Education and Welfare, but she declined; she would have preferred the post of attorney general.

Barbara Jordan retired from public office in 1978 and gave her senatorial and congressional papers and her memorabilia to her alma mater, Texas Southern University. She then went on to become a visiting professor at the Lyndon B. Johnson School of Public Affairs at the University of Texas at Austin. There, she taught courses on intergovernmental relations, political values, and ethics. While teaching, she published her autobiography, *Barbara Jordan: A Self Portrait* (1979) and served as ethics adviser to Texas governor Ann Richards in the early 1990s.

Along with and because of her political accomplishments, Jordan received fifteen honorary doctorate degrees and numerous honors from twenty-five colleges and universities, including Texas Southern University, Tuskegee Institute, Princeton University, and Harvard University. Other honors included the selecting of Jordan as Democratic Woman of the Year in 1975 by the Women's National Democratic Club; Woman of the Year in Politics (1975) by *Ladies Home Journal*; and one of Ten Women of the Year by *Time* magazine (1976). After becoming a member of Texas Women's Hall of Fame, Jordan was inducted into the National Women's Hall of Fame in 1990. In 1992 she was awarded the Spingarn Medal by the NAACP. In 1994 she served as chairwoman of the United States Commission on Immigration Reform and also received a Presidential Medal of Freedom award. Jordan suffered from a number of ailments in her later years, including a form of multiple sclerosis, and was confined to a wheelchair. In 1996 Barbara Jordan succumbed to pneumonia and leukemia in Austin, Texas, in the home she shared with her longtime companion, Nancy Earl. Her funeral was graced by attendance and tributes from dignitaries across the country, including President Bill Clinton. In death, she received yet another honor, as she became the first African American to be buried in the State Cemetery in Austin.

BIBLIOGRAPHY

Bryant, Ira B. *Barbara Charline Jordan: From the Ghetto to the Capitol.* Houston, TX: D. Armstrong, 1979.

Congressional Record (Senate). "Tribute to the Late Barbara Jordan." 22 January 1996, S282.

Jordan, Barbara, and Shelby Hearon. *Barbara Jordan: A Self Portrait.* Garden City, NY: Doubleday, 1979.

Journal of the House of Representatives, Sixtieth, Sixty-first, and Sixty-second Legislature of Texas.

Journal of the United States House of Representatives, Ninety-third, Ninety-fourth, and Ninety-fifth Congress.

Reed, Julia Scott, and Hugh Williams, eds. *Black Texans of Distinction.* Waco, TX: Texian Press, n.d.

—MERLINE PITRE

JORDAN, JUNE (b. 9 July 1936; d. 14 June 2002), poet, essayist. June Jordan was one of America's most widely published African American writers, with a career spanning four decades. Her lifelong friend and former editor,

JUNE JORDAN, writer and teacher, photographed in June 1974. Among her most notable writings are her poetry, her fiction for children and young people, and her essays. (Annenberg Rare Book and Manuscript Library.)

Toni Morrison, called her "our premiere Black woman essayist." The twenty-eight books authored by this activist and scholar contained award-winning poetry and essays. Her most recent works included a memoir, *Soldier: A Poet's Childhood* (2000), and *Some of Us Did Not Die* (2002), a powerful reflection on the events of September 11, 2001, her own battle with breast cancer, and other issues ranging from sexuality to the infamous professional boxer Mike Tyson.

June Jordan was born in Harlem, New York, though her parents were immigrants from Jamaica. Her father was physically and verbally abusive for much of Jordan's childhood. Jordan's family moved when she was five to the Bedford-Stuyvesant area of Brooklyn, and she attended Milwood High School and the Northfield Mount

Hermon School, an exclusive girls school in Massachusetts. In a class with few African Americans, Jordan excelled, graduating in 1953 and enrolling in Barnard College in New York City.

In 1955 Jordan married Michael Meyer, a white Columbia graduate student. They moved to Chicago that same year, and Jordan enrolled in the University of Chicago to continue her studies. She also became active in the civil rights movement, going on the Freedom Rides and working with the outspoken activist Fannie Lou Hamer. Passionately committed, Jordan found that she was beginning to hate all white people after the Harlem riots of 1964. At that moment, she wrote later, "it came to me that this condition, if it lasted, would mean I had lost the point: not to resemble my enemies, not to dwarf my world, not to lose my willingness and ability to love." From that time on, the poet-soldier wrote with love.

Jordan and her husband had one son, Christopher Michael Meyer, born in 1958, but the marriage ended in 1965. Jordan, now a single mother, returned to New York and worked as a production assistant on Shirley Clarke's *The Cool World*, the first commercial film shot in Harlem. Her first teaching position was at City College of New York in 1967. Subsequent positions followed at Connecticut College, Sarah Lawrence, Yale University, and the State University of New York at Stony Brook. In 1989, she taught at the University of California Berkeley, where she founded and directed Poetry for the People, an undergraduate course in which students held poetry readings before large audiences and studied the poetry of many cultures. While Jordan taught in the departments of English, African American studies, and women's studies, she wrote poetry and essays that reflected her personal life and the social and political issues that blacks and women faced. Some of her poems examined her abusive relationship with her father and her distant relationship with her mother. She wrote about her childhood experiences, her mother's suicide, feminism, homosexuality, violence, and world issues.

Jordan's poetic career began in 1969 with her first book of poetry, *Who look at me*, in which she conveys to the reader the many different feelings and conditions of African Americans in a white society. Jordan also wrote the libretto for *I Was Looking at the Ceiling and Then I Saw the Sky* (1995), an opera with music by John Adams, and several children's books, including *Dry Victories* (1972), *Fannie Lou Hamer* (1972), and *New Life: New Room* (1975).

June Jordan was a pluralist in every part of her life and her work. At a time when bisexuality was stigmatized, she refused to deny her own sexuality. Her friend and colleague Samiya A. Bashir wrote after Jordan's death that her bisexuality "extended beyond sexual orientation into a trope for a politics of inclusion, for a love that dare speak the names of many."

Jordan received many honors, including the Rockefeller Grant for Creative Writing (1969–1970), a National Endowment for the Arts fellowship (1982), and the Achievement Award for International Reporting from the National Association of Black Journalists (1984). She also won the Lila Wallace Reader's Digest Writers Award, the Ground Breakers-Dream Makers Award from The Woman's Foundation, the Chancellor's Distinguished Lectureship from the University of California at Berkeley, and the PEN Center USA West Freedom to Write Award (1991). In 1998, she received the Lifetime Achievement Award from the National Black Writers' Conference.

Jordan, a political activist, teacher, writer, and poet, died at the age of sixty-five in Berkeley, California, after suffering from breast cancer.

See also Poetry.

BIBLIOGRAPHY

Ards, Angela. "The Faithful, Fighting, Writing Life of Poet Activist June Jordan 1936–2002." *Black Issues Book Review*, September–October 2002.

Bashir, Samiya A. "Who Do You Love?" *Lambda Book Report*, October 2002.

Bloom, Harold. *Black American Women Fiction Writers*. New York: Chelsea House, 1994.

Jordan, June. *Soldier, A Poet's Childhood*. New York: Basic Civitas Books, 2000.

"'Poetry Is a Political Act': An Interview with June Jordan." *ColorLines*, Winter 1999.

—HATTIE RUTH ROBERTS

JOURNALISM, BROADCAST. In 1968 President Lyndon Johnson's National Advisory Commission on Civil Disorders, in a stinging indictment of the news industry, condemned the broadcast and print media for their exclusion of African Americans in the newsroom and their failure to convey the complexities of black life. "The media report and write from the standpoint of a white man's world," said the report. "The ills of the ghetto, the difficulties of life there, the Negro's burning sense of grievance, are seldom conveyed."

In the year the report was issued, only a handful of black men worked in overwhelmingly white newsrooms and Diahann Carroll made television history by being the first black woman to star in a network television series: surely few in 1968 could have fathomed the day (thirty-some years later) that Oprah Winfrey, a black woman, would be one of the biggest names in the television industry and that another black woman, born in New York's fabled Harlem community, would run NBC's Los Angeles station, KNBC.

Black Women Gain a Voice

By the turn of the twenty-first century black women were making their mark in a variety of positions before and behind the camera. Paula Madison, the president and general manager of KNBC, the number-two market in the country, was among an elite group of black women at or near the top of major broadcasting stations around the country. With more than four hundred employees and a reach of 16 million viewers, Madison was, in 2003, one of the most powerful African Americans or women in television. When she was named to the position in November 2000, she was the first African American woman to become general manager at a network-owned station in a top-five market. In addition, in 2002 Madison was named regional general manager for the two Telemundo television stations in Los Angeles acquired by NBC that year. But she was not alone as an African American woman in a top position in the broadcasting industry; she was joined by, among others, Pamela Thomas Graham, the president and general manager at CNBC, the cable finance and business network. With three degrees from Harvard—the college, law school, and business school—Thomas Graham had already cut her teeth as a pioneer by becoming the first African American partner at the prestigious McKinsey & Co. and as president of CNBC.com.

"I'm not suggesting legions, but when we look at news directors, station managers, there's a pretty significant number," Madison said in a personal interview in 2003. "There are many, many more African American women in the pipeline to ascend to the senior most positions in television." Occupying some of the most coveted positions in television—from Oprah Winfrey's multimedia empire to Star Jones of ABC Television's *The View*; Gwen Ifill, moderator of PBS's *Washington Week in Review*; and Michel McQueen Martin at ABC's *Nightline*—black women have proven themselves a viable commodity.

However, despite these obvious strides by individual African American women in the decades since 1968, African American women, like African Americans as a whole, continue to be underrepresented in broadcasting, particularly in top management. A 2002 survey of the Radio-Television News Directors Association indicated that in that year, whites represented about 70 percent of the nation's population but held nearly 95 percent of television's general management posts. Whites also held 90.8 percent of news director jobs, compared with 2 percent held by African Americans, men and women combined. Even as more African Americans became far more visible in front of the camera—they held about 12 percent of news reporter and anchor positions in 2002—the numbers dropped significantly in decision-making positions such as executive producer, managing editor, and news director. The network nightly newscasts remained the sole province of white men with the exception of the weekend anchor position held by ABC News' Carole Simpson, an African American woman. Simpson made history when, in 1989, she filled in for anchorman Peter Jennings, becoming the first woman of color to anchor the network nightly news during the week. Simpson had

GWEN IFILL moderating a vice-presidential debate between Dick Cheney (at left) and John Edwards, October 2004. The debate was held at Case Western Reserve University in Cleveland, Ohio. (© Jeff Haynes/Pool/Reuters/Corbis.)

Featuring Television Broadcast Journalists

● **Farai Chideya** (1969–) is a political commentator for CNN. Born in New York to a Zimbabwean businessman father and an American journalist mother who also taught high school, she grew up in Baltimore. While attending Harvard University she served an internship at *Newsweek*. She worked in the New York, Chicago, and Washington bureaus of the magazine, and had political articles published in *Time*, the *Village Voice*, and other major publications. Her first book, *Don't Believe the Hype: Fighting Cultural Disinformation about African-Americans* (1995), established her reputation. That same year, she began writing for MTV News and was still there when she began to broadcast on CNN. Soon her appearances on *Inside Politics* led to a position as a full-time panelist. In 1996 she created her own website, *www.popandpolitics.com*, so that she could express her own opinions and ideas in a completely unrestricted way.

● **Gwen Ifill** (1955–) was the first black woman to host a national political talk show. She was born 29 September 1955 in New York City, to the Reverend O. Urcille Ifill, Sr., from Panama, a minister in the African Methodist Episcopal Church, and Eleanor Ifill, from Barbados, a homemaker. She graduated from Simmons College in 1977 with a degree in communication. Having already served an internship at the *Boston Herald-American* (now the *Boston Herald*) she accepted a full-time position as a food writer, the only position available at the time. Soon she was reporting on school board meetings, a job of some significance—and danger—during the "Boston Bussing Crisis" of the 1970s. In 1981 she moved to the *Baltimore Evening Sun* and started covering city hall. She then began to appear on a local news commentary show, and in 1984 took a job at the *Washington Post* and in 1991, at the *New York Times*. She stayed in Washington as a congressional correspondent and then as a White House correspondent.

Upon leaving the *New York Times* Ifill was offered jobs by all three major networks and accepted a position at NBC, appearing on the *Nightly News with Tom Brokaw*, *Meet the Press*, and *Today* on MSNBC. However, after a few years, she grew dissatisfied with the nature of network news reporting. When she was approached by PBS in 1999 to become moderator for *Washington Week* and senior political correspondent for *The Newshour with Jim Lehrer* she did not hesitate to accept. She also serves as managing editor of *Washington Week*.

● **Carol Jenkins** (1944–) was a pioneer black woman in broadcast journalism. She was born in Montgomery, Alabama, but grew up in Jamaica, New York. She earned a bachelor's degree from Boston University (1966) and a master's from New York University in 1968. In 1970 she became a reporter and anchor for New York's WOR-TV and then a moderator for the station's *News Report*. Just two years later, she moved to ABC, serving as a network correspondent with the *Reasoner-Smith Report* and *Eyewitness News*, before moving on to NBC as a general reporter. Soon she became co-anchor of the station's weekend news and guest-anchored news reports for NBC's the *Today Show*. In 1996 Jenkins moved to New York's Fox 5/WNYW as co-anchor of *Fox Midday News*. Shortly thereafter, her daily talk show, *Carol Jenkins Live*, went on the air as the area's first television talk call-in show.

In 1999 Carol Jenkins moved out of broadcast news to become a producer. With feminist publisher Gloria Steinem, she will be making television movies, including a series based on mystery writer Barbara Neely's "Blanche" series. She also co-wrote a biography of black millionaire A. G. Gaston with her daughter, Elizabeth Gardner Hines, which was published in 2003.

● **Vicki Mabrey** (1956–) is best known for her role on *Sixty Minutes II*. She was born in St. Louis, Missouri, to Harold Mabrey, an army officer, and Barbara Mabrey, a teacher. After growing up among racial tensions in a largely white suburb, she went to Howard University, where she earned a bachelor's degree in political science. She was first exposed to the world of journalism during a summer job at the *Washington Post*, selling classified ads. After graduation she took journalism classes at the University of Maryland and then entered an American Federation of Television and Radio Arts (AFTRA) training program. She worked as a production assistant at Baltimore's CBS affiliate before going on the air to read the news in the morning. She was soon noticed by CBS News executives and in 1992 accepted a job in Dallas, Texas. She was just in time to cover the confrontation between David Koresh's Branch Davidians and federal agents. After covering several other major stories, she agreed to move to the CBS London branch in 1995. Her coverage of the bombing of the Atlanta Olympics in 1996 won her two Emmy Awards, and her coverage of Princess Diana's death, and the crash of TWA flight 800, garnered two more. She also worked with Mike Wallace in Baghdad on United Nations arms inspections. In 1999 she achieved her longtime goal of being a regular on *Sixty Minutes* when she was chosen as part of the four-person team to debut *Sixty Minutes II*.

● **Michel McQueen** (1958–) works for ABC's *Nightline*, contributing many reports for the series *America in Black and White*. A native of Brooklyn, New York, she was part of the third class of girls to graduate from St. Paul's School in Concord, New Hampshire, formerly an all-boys school. She received her bachelor's degree from Radcliffe College at Harvard University in 1980. Shortly after graduation, she began covering politics and policy for the *Wall Street Journal* and the *Washington Post*. In 1992 she joined ABC News. She has received one Emmy Award, for a report in the *America in Black and White* series, and has been nominated for two others. For ABC's *Turning Point* she contributed to an hour-long documentary on the Anita Hill–Clarence Thomas case, and a special on AIDS anchored by Barbara Walters. She has also been a regular panelist on the PBS show *Washington Week in Review*.

● **Joan Murray** (1941–) was the first African American woman to report the news on television. She was born in Ithaca, New York, to Isaiah Murray, a Fulbright scholar, and Amanda Pearl Yates Murray. She and her twin sister, June, moved together to New York in the late 1950s with the ambition of breaking into television. She started as a court reporter, was a model and actor, as well as a secretary to *Candid Camera*'s Allen Funt. In 1963 she got a job with NBC, writing for the daytime show, *Women on the Move*, starring Kitty Carlisle. Soon she was doing light news stories on the air for the show, but it was canceled in 1965. At that point Murray decided to pursue an on-air news position aggressively, even though no African American woman had ever held such a position. She wrote a letter to CBS, landed an audition, and was quickly hired. She became a correspondent on the 6 PM and 11 PM newscasts and, for the next six years, contributed to a number of other news programs, including specials. In 1969 she left television news to open an advertising agency.

● **Marquita Pool-Eckert** (1945–) has already won half a dozen Emmy Awards, and was nominated for five more in 2004. She was born in Aurora, Illinois, to Jeanne Boger Jones and Mark E. Jones. She received her bachelor's degree from Boston University (1966) and her master's from Columbia (1969). She tried her hand at writing, producing, and reporting the news but found that producing was her forte. Beginning in 1977, she was field producer for breaking news stories on the *CBS Evening News* working with both Walter Cronkite and Dan Rather. In 1983 she won her first two Emmys for coverage of the war in Beirut, and a news series entitled *The Black Family, A Dream Deferred*. In 1984 she moved up to segment producer and field producer of domestic and foreign news stories and features. In this position she earned Emmys for "The '80s Remembered," "Let It Be," and a segment on the significance for minority Americans of the bicentennial of the Statue of Liberty. She also covered the Jesse Jackson presidential campaign in 1984, produced a series on African famine, and produced coverage of the 1984 and 1988 Republican conventions. In 1990 she became senior producer of the *CBS News Sunday Morning* show. In this capacity she won an Emmy for a broadcast that followed the death of Princess Diana.

● **Norma R. Quarles** (1936–) was the first woman in New York City to co-anchor a 6 PM news program. Born in New York, she was the mixed-race daughter of Trinidadian parents. She attended Hunter College, and at eighteen married and moved to Chicago. After a few years she became a broadcaster at Chicago radio station WSDM. A year later, she moved to television. In 1967 she became a news reporter and then anchor in Cleveland before moving to NBC in New York as a reporter. Soon she was co-anchor of the evening news. She remained with NBC for twenty-one years and received a number of awards for her work, including an Emmy as outstanding reporter for a series she did for the NBC affiliate in Chicago. In 1984 she was a panelist for the vice-presidential debate sponsored by the League of Women Voters. In 1988 she left NBC to join CNN. In 1990 she was inducted into the Hall of Fame of the National Association of Black Journalists.

● **Deborah Roberts** (1960–) was a correspondent for *Dateline NBC* at its inception, and has since moved to ABC's *20/20*. Born in Perry, Georgia, to Ruth and Ben Roberts she received her bachelor's degree from the University of Georgia in 1982. That year she also began working at WTVM-TV in Columbus, Georgia. She worked in Knoxville, Tennessee, and Orlando, Florida, before moving to the NBC News network in Atlanta and Miami. Following the Persian Gulf War, she was a correspondent in Saudi Arabia and Kuwait. She covered the 1992 Summer Olympics in Barcelona, Spain, and then joined *Dateline NBC*. Since joining *20/20* in 1995 she has covered the refugees and orphans of Rwanda, the resignation and subsequent death of a homosexual teacher, child abuse in an Amish community, and dozens of other controversial stories.

● **Robin Roberts** (1960–) is a star among sports broadcasters, the first woman to host an NFL pregame show. She was born in Tuskegee, Alabama, to Lawrence and Lucimarian Roberts. Her father was a member of the Tuskegee Airmen in World War II and became a career Air Force man; her mother was an English teacher. An excellent student and athlete in high school, she went on to become a member of the Lady Lions basketball team at Southeastern Louisiana University. A star at college basketball, she graduated cum laude with a degree in communications in 1983, having worked in the meantime as sports director and broadcaster at a radio station in Hammond, Louisiana. She then went on to work in sports in Mississippi and Tennessee. In 1987 she was named Sportscaster of the Year by *Nashville Scene*. Although she was offered a job by ESPN at that point, she felt she needed to hone her skills, and went to Atlanta. In 1990 she became the first female sportscaster for ESPN. She was soon doing play-by-play announcing for women's basketball. While still at ESPN, she became host of ABC's *Wide World of Sports* in 1995, and began appearing on *Good Morning, America*. She worked on a number of fronts for both networks, and hosted a series entitled *A Passion to Play: The African American Experience*, focusing on black women in sports.

● **Carole Simpson** (1940–) has been widely acclaimed for her work in the broadcasting industry. She has covered some of the most important events in recent memory, including the Senate's impeachment of President Clinton, the Persian Gulf War, the Oklahoma City bombing, and the Clarence Thomas–Anita Hill hearings. (See individual entry: Simpson, Carole.)

already been the first African American woman network anchor as the anchor of ABC's weekend newscast.

Elsewhere on television, African Americans, were, like other racial minorities, woefully underrepresented. In 1999 Kweisi Mfume, president of the NAACP, threatened to boycott the major networks to protest the virtual exclusion of racial minorities in the new fall lineup. While the networks signed an agreement committing to greater diversity, two years later there was little discernible advancement.

Early History of African Americans and Television

Still, the achievements of Madison, Ifill, Winfrey, and others signal progress, particularly if one considers the challenges and roadblocks that paved their path throughout the history of television. As J. Fred MacDonald points out in *Blacks and White Television since 1948*, the early days of television saw no black newscasters, correspondents, or black announcers, even as African American entertainers, particularly comedians and singers, enjoyed high visibility. "On the surface, early television seemed to be almost colorblind," writes MacDonald. "The new industry frequently featured black celebrities. . . . Many felt that TV promised a new and prejudiced-free era in popular entertainment."

In 1950 *Ebony* magazine reported that television offered better roles for blacks than other media venues. That same year, Ed Sullivan, the popular host of CBS's *Toast of the Town*, declared that television played a crucial role in the civil rights movement by taking it "into the living rooms of America's homes where public opinion is formed." The following year NBC published guidelines promoting the equitable portrayal of minorities on television. However, as the profit motive increased, the early promise of equality faded. Television was a $2 billion business by the end of the 1950s, notes MacDonald, and "in light of disastrous financial repercussions that might follow the realization of old expectations, past pledges had to be reconsidered."

With notable exceptions, portrayals of African Americans largely remained stereotypical or limited to comedic roles. And it would take many years for African Americans to gain a foothold in television news. So while Pauline Frederick, a white woman, would in 1953 became the first newswoman to work full time on network news when she was hired by NBC, it would take until 1962 before a black male, Mal Goode, broke the color barrier. Not until the end of the 1960s would a handful of African American women, including Norma Quarles at Cleveland's NBC-owned station and Melba Tolliver at ABC's New York station, follow men and white women into television news.

The Unrest of the 1960s and the Activism of the 1970s

The late Robert Maynard, a prominent African American journalist and editor and publisher of the *Oakland Tribune*, once attributed the progress of all black journalists to the televised images of the Watts riots of 1965 that resulted in millions of dollars in property damage and thousands of casualties. Maynard maintained that the "frightful scene" in the south-central neighborhood of Los Angeles made editors throughout the United States "aware for the first time that there might be an imperative for even the token desegregation of their newsrooms."

The riots in Watts would soon spread to dozens of cities across the country, resulting in President Johnson's commissioning a panel, led by Senator Otto Kerner, to study the nation's racial problems. Among the areas explored was the role the media played in fueling the unrest. While the report did not blame the media for causing the riots, it said that distorted and inadequate coverage of African Americans in both television dramas and news coverage had contributed to black alienation and despair:

> The Commission's major concern with the news media is not in riot reporting as such, but in the failure to report adequately on race relations and ghetto problems and to bring more Negroes into journalism. . . . In defining, explaining and reporting this broader, more complex and ultimately far more fundamental subject, the communications media, ironically, have failed to communicate. (Kerner Commission Report)

The report also criticized as "shockingly backward" the media's record of hiring, training, and promoting African Americans and said the claim that qualified blacks could not be found "rings hollow from an industry where, only yesterday, jobs were scarce and promotion unthinkable for a man whose skin was black." In response, the commission called for "fair and courageous journalism, commitment and coverage that are worthy of one of the crucial domestic stories in America's history."

The commission report garnered headlines from every major news organization, including the *New York Times* and the *Washington Post*. An editorial in the *New York Times* on 2 March 1968 stated:

> It is a warning that transcends all considerations of partisan or group interest—a warning that total national commitment and sacrifice in the cause of genuine racial equality is the price of America's survival as a society built on order and justice.

While the report contributed greatly to the expansion of opportunities for African Americans in the news media, it was not the first or last time that the television industry would come under sharp criticism for its treatment of African Americans. In October 1962 the Committee on Integration of the New York Society for Ethical Culture, a nonsectarian humanitarian group, had found in a two-week study of television programming that of 398 half-hour units of viewing, blacks appeared in only 89 units, the bulk of these being irregular appearances as singers, dancers, or musicians or as the subjects in hard news and documentary programming. Such limited and stereotyped exposure was, it said, "psychologically damaging" to the image of blacks.

Even earlier, in 1947, the Hutchins Commission on Freedom of the Press, a group comprising white academics, had noted the routine stereotypical coverage of African Americans in the media. Its study, "A Free and Responsible Press," recommended the projection of a representative portrait of America and chastised the stereotypical portrayals of racial minorities.

If the Negro appears in the stories published in magazines of national circulation only as a servant, if children figure constantly in radio dramas as impertinent and ungovernable brats—the image of the Negro and the American child is distorted. The plugging of special color and "hate" words in radio and press dispatches, in advertising copy, in news stories—such as "ruthless," "confused," "bureaucratic"—performs the same image-making function.

The report added: "The truth about any social group, though it should not exclude its weaknesses and vices, includes also recognition of its values, its aspirations, and its common humanity."

But while the Hutchins Commission was largely ignored, the National Advisory Panel, commonly called the Kerner Commission, had in its favor the weight of the president who commissioned it. Shortly after its release, the Johnson administration announced a federal policy that would withhold broadcast operating licenses to stations that deliberately practiced employment discrimination. The policy was adopted in 1969 and expanded a year later to require stations to file annual reports detailing their minority recruitment efforts. The data would be used to monitor compliance. In adopting the new policy, the Federal Communications Commission relied on the broad mandate of the Communications Act of 1934 that empowered the agency to protect the public interest by ensuring that stations reflected the viewpoints of the communities they served. Under the new mandate, the percentage of minorities in broadcast news increased to 9.1 percent by 1970, according to the Federal Communications Commission data. A number of measures followed, including one that required licensees with more than fifty full-time employees to file detailed employment profiles. Despite challenges by the National Association of Broadcasters, the policies were upheld in federal court until they were finally struck down in 1998.

In 1974 the National Black Feminist Organization took aim at the portrayals of blacks on prime-time shows, noting that few black women were cast as professionals, paraprofessionals, or working people. Three years later, in August 1977, the United States Civil Rights Commission released its report "Window Dressing on the Set: Women and Minorities in Television," which concluded that the broadcasting industry had hired women and minorities, but had not sufficiently promoted them. It said that while the number of women and minorities had increased between 1971 and 1975, "contrary to the impression one may form from these data, minorities and women have not necessarily made significant employment gains at these stations."

White males continued to hold the overwhelming number of decision-making positions and outnumbered minority and female correspondents by almost nine to one, the report found. It also said that women and minorities rarely covered stories of national significance and that they tended to cover news related to women and minorities. In 1979 the Annenberg School of Communication of the University of Pennsylvania reported the findings of its ten-year study of television programming. It concluded that minorities were routinely stereotyped in network shows. So, even as the number of African Americans and women slowly increased, the impact on coverage appeared minimal. In addition, little attention was paid to the toll integration took on African Americans in the workplace. While the culture clash was significant for all African Americans, African American women would face unique challenges.

Discrimination

Melba Tolliver was a television reporter at New York City's ABC affiliate when, in 1971, she was assigned to cover the wedding of the president's daughter, Tricia Nixon, in the White House Rose Garden. The day before the wedding, Tolliver reported to work with her hair styled in an Afro. Her ethnically unique hairdo caused the producer to call the news director, who told Tolliver her hairstyle was not appropriate for her work. Tolliver proceeded to Washington to cover the wedding, still wearing an Afro. Her scheduled appearance on a local morning show the next morning was canceled and she was summoned to a meeting with the vice president and general manager for news and her news director. For three days, Tolliver was banished from the television broadcast. The deadlock was broken when the situation was leaked to a New York City newspaper. The attention provoked viewers to write the station to support Tolliver's right to wear an Afro. "It proved them wrong," Tolliver later said.

They desperately feared they'd lose part of the audience because people would see me as a Black Pantherette. They were just wrong. They didn't lose ratings. They probably gained.

Nine years later, Dorothy Reed, a television reporter and co-anchor at KGO-TV, the ABC affiliate in San

A BLACK FEMALE TELEVISION REPORTER, the first African American woman hired in this capacity by Channel 11 (owned by the *Daily News*). The photograph was taken in June 1974. (© Bettye Lane.)

Francisco, was suspended for two weeks for appearing on air wearing cornrows. In statements to the press, Reed said her suspension was "a case of white male-dominated management deciding how I should look as an acceptable black woman." She said her hairstyle "gives me a tremendous amount of pride and reflects my heritage." Her suspension resulted in protests outside the station offices and front-page headlines. A settlement was finally reached which required the station to pay her for the two weeks if she dispensed with the colorful beads that adorned her hair. While Reed won the battle, she was, for months, the target of racist hate mail, and when her contract expired, it was not renewed. "When I was let go, I could have demanded a reason," Reed would say later. "I didn't have to let that go but at that point it was so painful I just wanted to get away from it."

Black women broadcasters would face other exceptional challenges. In 1985 Harry Porterfield, an African American anchorman at CBS-owned WBBM in Chicago, was demoted to make way for a returning newsman. The move sparked a boycott of the station spearheaded by Jesse Jackson, the founder of Operation PUSH. While the issue initially appeared to be one of race, it quickly became a gender battle when Henry Hardy, the chief negotiator for Operation Push, was quoted as saying: "White America has always sought to undermine black men and sometimes use black women as a double minority."

Hardy's statement rankled many African American women broadcasters who were, like men, sorely underrepresented in the industry. Max Robinson had been the only African American, male or female, to regularly anchor a network newscast, which he had ceased doing several years earlier. (Although Carole Simpson, at ABC News, had sat in for Peter Jennings, she then returned to her weekend anchor slot.) In 2003 the three anchor chairs at ABC, NBC, and CBS remained white and male. Increasingly, however, black women would be viewed by some as advantageous to stations since they were, in essence, a double minority. But as the numbers would show, both women and African Americans remained underrepresented in the industry.

The 2002 Radio-Television News Directors Association—Ball State University annual survey showed that the percentage of African American men and women in broadcast newsrooms was 9.3 percent, and, as said above, the percentage of news directors was 2 percent, while the percentage of reporters was 12.3 percent. Women as a whole comprised about 40 percent of broadcast news jobs. Meanwhile, a 2002 study of network nightly news showed that in 2001, 92 percent of all U.S. sources interviewed were white and 85 percent were male. Only 7 percent of the sources were black, according to the study commissioned by Fairness and Accuracy in Reporting.

As the NAACP boycott threat indicated, African Americans did not fare much better on television shows in general. In 2000 NBC became the first of the networks to strike a deal with the NAACP to hire more minorities as writers, producers, and directors and to cast more African Americans and other people of color in lead roles. ABC, CBS, and Fox soon thereafter also pledged to diversify their shows. A year later, NAACP president Kweisi Mfume complained that there had only been modest gains. "By any reasonable standard, African Americans and all other races of people are underrepresented in almost every aspect of the television and film industry," Mfume said at a press conference, reported in the *Baltimore Sun* on 19 August 2001. He again raised the prospect of a boycott. Out of thirty-five new shows planned for the fall 2001 lineup, two had African Americans cast in lead roles and both were sitcoms.

Still, there were isolated instances of progress. By the end of 2001 Angela Bassett, an Oscar-nominated actress, had starred in *Ruby's Bucket of Blood*, a television movie broadcast on Showtime, a cable network. Bassett was also executive producer of the movie. In early 2002 Bassett and Cicely Tyson starred in *The Rosa Parks Story*, broadcast on CBS, and black women starred in other television shows, including the Showtime series *Soul Food* and *Girlfriends* on UPN.

Although at the opening of the twenty-first century African American women were more visible and seen in a greater variety of roles in front of and behind the camera, the challenge for greater representation and fair and balanced portrayals of all African Americans remained an elusive goal in broadcasting as it would be in film, newspapers, and magazines.

BIBLIOGRAPHY

MacDonald, J. Fred. *Blacks and White TV: African Americans in Television since 1948.* 2d ed. Chicago: Nelson-Hall, 1992. Perhaps the most definitive work on blacks in the television industry.

Newkirk, Pamela. *Within the Veil: Black Journalists, White Media.* New York: New York University Press, 2000. Examines the plight of black journalists in the news industry, covering both television and print.

"Racial Honesty: Just Another Blurry Screen; Networks and NAACP Have Dropped the Ball on Promises of Diversity." *Baltimore Sun,* August 19, 2001.

Sanders, Marlene, and Marcia Rock. *Waiting for Prime Time: The Women of Television News.* Urbana: University of Illinois Press, 1994. Looks at women in network news.

—PAMELA NEWKIRK

JOURNALISM, EARLY. History was made on 16 March 1827, when the first black newspaper, *Freedom's Journal*, was founded in New York City by the black antislavery spokesmen Samuel Cornish and John Russwurm and became a vehicle to galvanize black communities around the issues of slavery, freedom, and lynching. The newspaper appeared 137 years, or seven generations, after the first colonial American newspaper, *Publick Occurrences*, was published in Boston during 1690. The role played by African American women in the initial creation of the black press is not known because few sources document their journalistic activities as often as they do their male counterparts. The first provable instance of black women's participation in journalism did make a dramatic debut over two decades after the launch of *Freedom's Journal*, when Mary Ann Shadd Cary published a black abolitionist newspaper, the *Provincial Freeman*, in Canada during the 1850s. Still, though the 1850s marked the official entry of African American women into journalism, it is likely they turned to journalistic writing as early as *Freedom's Journal*'s 1827 founding.

Beginnings of the Black Press

To understand and put into context the importance of a newspaper devoted to black issues during the nineteenth century, it is imperative to note certain statistics and information. The advent of the black press did not exist in a vacuum; many factors were directly correlated to why the black press evolved and why some individuals, male and female, felt compelled to start and report for newspapers and magazines. Firstly, it must be understood that the black press was a mechanism used as a survival tool to push "the race" forward. The publications unified communities, disseminated useful and pertinent information, provided economic stimulus for publishers and their families, and encouraged blacks to learn to read. Additionally, religious publications helped churches convey valuable information to their members. Black women were able to use their writing talents to discuss religious issues, as well as social issues within these faith-based periodicals.

By 1860 there were 4,441,830 people of African descent in America. Nearly 500,000 were free. Punitive laws, economic deprivation, and disenfranchisement, however,

JULIA RINGWOOD COSTON, editor and publisher of *Ringwood's Afro-American Journal of Fashion*, which she began issuing in 1891; this was the first illustrated journal for black women. She also published *Ringwood's Home Magazine*, from 1893 to 1895. (Austin/Thompson Collection, by permission of Schomburg Center for Research in Black Culture, New York Public Library.)

often denied enslaved and free access to educational opportunities, contributing to high rates of illiteracy. Most publications founded during the early nineteenth century were clearly intended to assist abolitionists in their efforts to free blacks and to get whites to understand why slavery and its associated atrocities had to be abandoned. Following the Civil War, the number of black newspapers, schools, and churches rose dramatically, and illiteracy experienced a notable decline. Black women played crucial roles in all of these institutions, especially in journalism.

During the antebellum period, black women also contributed their efforts to Frederick Douglass's *North Star* and white-owned abolitionist newspapers, including William Lloyd Garrison's *Liberator*. The masthead for the *North Star*, which first appeared on 3 December 1847,

proclaimed, "Right is of no Sex—Truth is of no-Color—God is the Father of Us All, And All We Are Brethren." Maria Stewart, the first American-born woman to lecture in defense of women's rights, published her essays in the *Liberator*. Other, anonymous, contributions in the antebellum period, conscious of sexual oppression, expressed considerable unhappiness with women's status.

Although some identified themselves simply by bylines such as "a young woman of color," "Zillah, a Young Lady of Color," and "Matilda," their letters to editors provided cultural and psychological insights into the thoughts of literate, free, northern black women. Another insight into how women dealt with their ostracism in the press was by assuming the names of their male relatives. One such occurrence was with C. C. Stumm, the wife of the Reverend C. C. Stumm, who wrote under her husband's name. In 1890, the Stumms together produced the *Christian Banner*, a religious home journal.

Like their brothers in the struggle, black women also recognized the power of newspapers as a vehicle to increase their audience and as a forum to discuss gender and issues important to the black community. They denounced slavery, and addressed political and economic discrimination in the North. Unlike black men, however, African American women's protest extended beyond the horrors of slavery and discussions of race and education to the issues of sex, gender, and class. By introducing the issue of gender into the public domain, black women shifted their symbolic environment significantly by calling attention to the double bind of being both black and female. Some of the men immersed in the publishing and editing of newspapers were quite vocal regarding their opposition to the idea of women working in the press. They were adamant that women were too frail to stand the rigors of meeting deadlines and paid too little attention to detail to work effectively in "hard news."

After the Civil War

In 1891, Irving Garland Penn, a twenty-four-year-old free-born African American, compiled a seminal work titled *The Afro-American Press and Its Editors* that outlined the beginnings of the black press. While Penn apologized profusely for not being able to include every black newspaper and every journalist in the compendium, he did include women. The second, and longest, part of Penn's book gives short profiles and portraits of the leading African American journalists, both male and female, of that period. Of the 140 portraits, nineteen were women. The majority of the women, who were often called "correspondents," appeared to be in their twenties and thirties. They wore formal, dark dresses, and their hair was styled in ways that were fashionable for middle-class black women of that time.

In the introduction to the section on women, Penn wrote, "There is a divine poetry in a life garlanded by the fragrant roses of triumph." All nineteen of the women profiled were selected for their exceptional journalistic abilities, but all had different socioeconomic standings. Some had only completed some college courses, whereas others had earned their degrees. This latter group included Josephine Turpin Washington and A. L. Tilghman, who both graduated from Howard University; C. C. Stumm who attended Berea; Alice McEwen who attended Fisk University; Lucreta Coleman who pursued an education at Lawrence in Canada; and Lavina Sneed, Ione Wood, and Mary V. Cook, who graduated from journalism programs at State University of Louisville, Kentucky.

After the Civil War, black women also utilized the press as a means of creative expression. Frances Ellen Watkins Harper, for example, not only published her poetry and short stories during the 1850s in the black press, but she also published her novel, *Iola Leroy*, in 1892. Harper contributed articles to several prominent black press periodicals including the *Christian Recorder*, the *A.M.E. Review*, and the *Philadelphia Tribune*. Her illustrative career in journalism inspired the historian Garland Penn to refer to her as the "journalistic mother" of the many black women who entered the field after Reconstruction. Following in the footsteps of Harper, other African American women writers showcased their intellectual creative talents in journals and magazines, including the *Repository of Religion and Literature and of Science and the Arts*, a journal of the African Methodist Episcopal Church begun in 1858, and the *Anglo-African* magazine, founded in 1859. Church publications often served as conduits for black women to display their journalistic talents. Lucy Wilmot Smith, who handled the children's column in the *American Baptist*, eventually became head of the women's department at *Our Women and Children* and often contributed to the *Baptist Journal*, the *Boston Advocate* and the *Indianapolis Freeman*.

Scores of other women followed the print tradition, among them, Mary V. Cook, the editor of the education section of *Our Women and Children*, Meta E. Pelham, a reporter for the *Detroit Plain Dealer*, Gertrude Mossell, the correspondent for the *Indianapolis Freeman*, and Lillian A. Lewis, who wrote a fascinating column, "They Say," for the *Boston Advocate* under the pen name Bert Islew. Mary E. Britton wrote under the pen name "Meb" in Lexington, Kentucky, in 1858 and at the age of nineteen she was published in the *Cincinnati Commercial*. Britton, a former teacher, later edited a women's column in the *Lexington Herald*. Before her career ended she had contributed to a number of newspapers in and around the Lexington area.

As the problems faced by freedpeople intensified during post-Reconstruction, black women focused even more vigorously on themes and ideas essential to their uplift—self-reliance, temperance, education, home building, and the creation of social service organizations—as vehicles for mobilizing women. To encourage women's involvement in their communities and to inform them of social service activities in every major city, black women edited several newspapers and journals. Josephine St. Pierre Ruffin, founder of the New Era Club, edited the *Woman's Era*. *National Notes*, founded in 1897 in Tuskegee, Alabama, served as the organ for the National Association of Colored Women, organized in 1896.

Unlike the white press, which often relegated white women to marginalized positions—sob sisters, stunt women, or editing the women's pages—the black press offered more varied opportunities and exposure for the reporting skills of black women. One woman, however, dominated journalism at the end of the nineteenth century: Ida B. Wells-Barnett. Dubbed the "Princess of the Press" by her peers, Wells-Barnett wrote for church

IDA B. WELLS-BARNETT, shown here in a portrait painting, was so prominent in journalism at the end of the nineteenth century that she was called the "Princess of the Press." (© 2004 Corbis.)

Featuring Journalists

● **Charlotta Spears Bass** (1880–1969) was born in South Carolina and spent decades working as a leading African American journalist, civil rights activist, and women's rights advocate. When she transplanted herself to California, she and her husband developed the *California Eagle* newspaper into a top publication. (See individual entry: Bass, Charlotta Spears.)

● **Daisy Lee Gatson Bates** (1920–1999), a powerful journalist, was instrumental in the integration of Central High School in Little Rock, Arkansas. (See individual entry: Bates, Daisy Lee Gatson.)

● **Delilah L. Beasley** (1872–1934) was born in Cincinnati, Ohio, to Daniel and Margaret Beasley. She began her journalism career at the age of twelve writing for the *Cleveland Gazette*. When she was only fifteen, her first column appeared in the Sunday Cincinnati *Enquirer*. As an adult, she moved to California and attended history lectures at the University of California at Berkeley, although she was not registered as a student. She used her research to write and present essays at churches. For almost twenty years she also wrote a weekly Sunday column for the *Oakland Tribune* entitled "Activities among Negroes." Because of her influence, the white press in her area stopped using condescending and derogatory terms to refer to African Americans. In 1919, after eight years of research, she completed her book, *The Negro Trail-Blazers of California*.

● **Carolyn L. Bennett** (1943–) received her PhD from Michigan State University and a subsequent degree in music education. Her writing reflected her wide range of interests: ethics in journalism, the arts, minorities in the media, women's rights, and responsibilities of a free press. In addition to her excellent writing as a reporter, Bennett wrote several books and major magazine articles, including *Talking Back to Today's News*, *An Annotated Bibliography of Mary McLeod Bethune's* Chicago Defender *Columns*, and *America's Human Connection*. Dr. Bennett's essays and features appeared regularly in the *Chicago Defender*. Her award-winning writing expressed a "passion for peace by peaceful means, responsibilities of the free press, education first (priority) . . . and remembrances of the great originals (the writers before her)."

● **Thelma Berlak Boozer** (1906–?) expressed strong feminist views in publications such as *New York Age* long before the feminist era of the 1960s. She was born in Ocala, Florida, and after her parents divorced when she was three, she and her mother moved to New York. After high school she attended New York University, where she received a master's degree in journalism. She began writing professionally while she was earning her degrees. Working as a reporter for many years, she also held a position with the New York City Department of Civil Defense. While working at the *Amsterdam Star News*, she earned the position of assistant editor. In her fifteen years there, she also

developed several columns, including the syndicated society news and another column called "Woman of the Week." In that column she highlighted African American women in all the professions and arts. When she left the New York journalism world, she remained involved in improving the status of journalism, creating a program at the University of Missouri.

● **Mary Ann Shadd Cary** (1823–1893) was the first African American to operate her own newspaper. Her publication was highly political, as was she, working for black freedom and assisting black migration North through the Underground Railroad. (See individual entry: Cary, Mary Ann Shadd.)

● **Marvel Jackson Cooke** (1903–2000) was born in Mankato, Minnesota, the daughter of Amy Wood Jackson and Madison Jackson. Her talents extended beyond writing to art, music, and civil rights activism. Her family moved to Minneapolis, where she graduated from the University of Minnesota before moving to New York. She began her professional life as editorial assistant at *Crisis* and later went to work for the *Amsterdam Star News*. After marriage to Cecil Cooke, an internationally famous athlete, and a job teaching in North Carolina, she returned to New York and became assistant managing editor of *The People's Voice*, a Harlem publication owned by Adam Clayton Powell. In the late 1950s, she immersed herself in political work and emerged as an early civil rights activist. Cooke was the national legal defense secretary of the Angela Davis Defense Committee. In her writing she was devoted to exploring the experiences of African American women in the arts, including writing, music, art, and theater. She believed these aspects of black life were overlooked by the white community.

● **Debra Dickerson** (1959–) was born and raised in the St. Louis ghettos. Her parents, former sharecroppers, had intended for her to become a secretary, but Dickerson had bigger dreams and she joined the Air Force. This allowed her the opportunity to earn bachelor's and master's degrees, and she was offered work as a linguist. She then went on to Harvard to earn a law degree. It was a fluke that she discovered her ability for writing; she sent some ideas to the editors of her hometown newspaper, the *St. Louis Post-Dispatch*, and they liked what they read. One article was all it took, and from then on her work was in demand. Her books include *The End of Blackness* (2004) and an autobiography, *An American Story* (2001).

● **Alice Dunnigan** (1906–1983) was born in rural Russellville, Kentucky, and it would have been difficult to predict that she would be the first African American woman to gain White House press credentials. Although her parents were sharecroppers, she attended Kentucky State College and, while still in school, wrote articles for the local newspapers. After World War II, she became a reporter for the Associated Negro Press in Washington, DC. She was also the Washington correspondent for the *Chicago Defender*. One of the high points of her career was accompanying Harry Truman on his campaign trail from Washington to California. She worked on the Kennedy-Johnson campaign in 1960 and was appointed to the President's Council on Youth Opportunity and other committees. After her retirement in 1971, she wrote her autobiography, *A Black Woman's Experience: From Schoolhouse to White House*.

● **Lillian Parker Thomas Fox** (1866–1917) was a respected journalist and fighter for civil and women's rights. Born in Chicago to AME minister Byrd Parker and Jane Janette Thomas, a teacher, she grew up in Wisconsin. Early in her education she became a contributor to local newspapers, where she expressed her opinions in articles such as "The Rights of Colored People, or a Plea for the Negro." In 1893 she married James Fox and moved to Indianapolis, taking a position as feature writer and correspondent for *The Freeman*, a nationally prominent publication. In 1900 she joined the *Indianapolis News*, becoming the first black journalist to write a news column that appeared regularly in an Indiana newspaper. Although her readership consisted of turn-of-the-century women, her ideas were far ahead of her time. This is clear in the following quote from one of her columns: "We believe that what should most interest women is women; despite the glaring indication that her chief consideration, as well as glorification is man . . . the feminine heart yearns for broader paths wherein to work."

● **Amy Jacques Garvey** (1896–1973), born in Kingston, Jamaica, was a journalist and a pioneer Pan-African emancipator. She joined Marcus Garvey's Universal Negro Improvement Association (UNIA) in 1918, became his private secretary, and married him in 1922. When he was incarcerated, she took the helm of the UNIA, becoming a lifelong fighter for universal African liberation. She was editor of the women's page for the *Negro World* newspaper. In the 1940s she worked for the Peoples National Party of Jamaica, where she and her husband had settled after his release from prison. She wrote and published *Garvey and Garveyism* (1963), followed by her collection of essays *Black Power in America*. Amy Garvey is considered one of the foremost black feminist journalists of the twentieth century. In the last of her writings, *The Role of Women in Liberation Struggles* (1972), she reiterated the key tenets of black feminist philosophy, paying tribute to Sojourner Truth, Harriet Tubman, and Angela Davis.

● **Dorothy Gilliam** (1936–), a respected writer for the *Washington Post*, was born in a housing project in Memphis, Tennessee, to Adee Conklin Butler, an AME minister, and Jessie Mae Norment Butler, a teacher. In 1941, the family moved to Louisville, Kentucky, where she attended Phyllis Wheatley Elementary School and experienced the remarkable dedication of black teachers. Gilliam graduated cum laude from Lincoln University in Missouri with a degree in Journalism. She began work at the *Post* in 1961

as a reporter after having worked as an editor at *Jet* magazine. In 1979 she began writing a Metro column that covered education, politics, race, and related issues. From 1997 she directed the Young Journalist Development Program at the newspaper. She received many honors, including the University of Missouri Medal of Honor in Journalism and the Journalist of the Year Award. She was also president of the National Association of Black Journalists and a member of the group's hall of fame.

● **Charlayne Hunter-Gault** (1942–) was the first African American woman to graduate from the University of Georgia. Starting at the *New York Times* as a metropolitan reporter, she eventually joined the news teams at the Public Broadcasting Service (PBS) and National Public Radio (NPR) and in 2004 was CNN's Johannesburg bureau chief. (See individual entry: Hunter-Gault, Charlayne.)

● **Julianne Malveaux** (1943–), whose work was syndicated in some of the top newspapers in the U.S., was involved at the start of the twenty-first century in researching the labor market, public policy, and the impact of policy on women of color. (See individual entry: Malveaux, Julianne.)

● **Gertrude E. H. Bustill Mossell** (1855–1948) was one of the first African American women to take up a career in journalism, writing columns in the black newspapers of the 1870s. (See individual entry: Mossell, Gertrude E. H. Bustill.)

● **Ethel L. Payne** (1911–1991) was a reporter for the *Chicago Defender* from 1951 until 1978 and then wrote a syndicated column for another decade. She was born in Chicago, where her father worked as a Pullman porter and her mother taught high school Latin. She attended college for a short time and worked at the Chicago Public Library before becoming a hostess at an Army Special Services club in Japan in 1948. When she showed the diary she kept overseas to a *Defender* reporter, he took it to his boss, who ran excerpts from it on the front page of the paper. He also offered Payne a job. Two years later, she became all that existed of the Washington bureau for the paper. Calling herself an "advocacy journalist," Payne represented black interests and points of view at White House press conferences, traveled to Vietnam to report on black soldiers, and stood next to President Lyndon Johnson as he signed both the Civil Rights Act of 1964 and the Voting Rights Act of 1965. She also became the first black woman commentator on a national broadcast network when she appeared on the *Spectrum* program on CBS radio and then on television from 1972 to 1982.

● **Ida B. Wells-Barnett** (1862–1931) was a journalist and an activist who made an indelible mark on the history of the United States and offered a harsh critique of the racial, sexual, and economic exploitation of black people. (See individual entry: Wells-Barnett, Ida B.)

periodicals and later became editor of the *Free Speech and Headlight*, a small weekly in her hometown of Memphis, Tennessee. She used scathing language in her crusading efforts against lynching. In fact, Wells-Barnett, by introducing the idea that white women were culpable in these crimes, redefined lynching, its causes and consequences. At considerable cost, with the burning of the *Free Speech* office and her subsequent exile from Tennessee (induced by letters to editors all over the South that warned she would be torched next if she returned), Wells-Barnett became only the second black female journalist (Cary proceeded her) to focus on issues that were traditionally reserved for black males and to successfully mobilize both black and white readers through print.

In addition to Wells-Barnett's contributions, the post-Reconstruction period also introduced the first periodicals targeting a female audience and featuring the work of black women. In 1887, A. E. Johnson, a woman poet from Baltimore, Maryland, founded a monthly literary journal, *Joy*, perhaps the earliest of these efforts. The magazine was published until 1890 and received complimentary reviews from both black and white contemporaries, a striking testament to the journalistic skills of African American women.

The Twentieth Century

By the close of the nineteenth century an increasing number of African American women were firmly entrenched in the black press. Yet, the writer and activist Gertrude Mossell admonished her female colleagues for remaining "willing captives, chained to the chariot wheels of the sterner element," and she criticized black men for not fully including their female colleagues. Greater opportunities were available to African American women in the twentieth century as the black press evolved into a thriving institution. In the early 1900s, there were close to fifty newspapers and forty magazines and periodicals published by African Americans, and women played a central role in their publication.

In 1900, for example, the *Colored American Magazine* hired the young novelist and writer Pauline Hopkins to edit the women's section of the Boston-based magazine. Three years later Hopkins was literary editor of the magazine, and today she is best known for her four novels serialized in its pages. Despite her efforts to spark a black literary movement, Hopkins was unable to sustain her journalistic career. She supported herself as a stenographer, and although she had achieved such notoriety during her journalistic endeavors, she ultimately died in obscurity. In contrast, Margaret Murray Washington, the wife of Booker T. Washington and the dean of women at Tuskegee Institute, began as editor of *National Notes*. Washington figured prominently in the women's club

movement and African American self-help activities, and she continued as editor of *National Notes* until 1922.

The first decade of the twentieth century witnessed the publication of two black women's periodicals in states west of the Mississippi. *Women's World* was founded in Fort Worth, Texas. *Colored Women's Magazine* began in Topeka, Kansas, in 1907 and was edited by two women, C. M. Hughes and Minnie Thomas, as a monthly family magazine. It was published until at least 1920, and women maintained editorial control throughout its history.

Black women also figured prominently in periodicals targeted to a more general audience. Josephine Silone Yates, a teacher at Lincoln Institute in Missouri and a two-term president of the National Association of Colored Women, served as the associate editor of the *Negro Educational Review*, founded in Vincennes, Indiana, in 1904. Agnes Carroll, a music teacher in Washington, DC, helped edit the *Negro Music Journal*, published in that city during the same period. Amanda Berry Smith, an evangelist, itinerant preacher, and perhaps the most colorful woman journalist of the period, published the *Helper* (1900–1907), a magazine that focused on the issues of child care, temperance, and religion.

The turn of the century brought an era of development and growth for influential African American newspapers, such as the *Baltimore Afro-American*, the *Chicago Defender*, and the *New York Age*. The polemical, romantic writing of nineteenth-century American journalism gradually was replaced with a quest for objective reporting of the news, and powerful black newspapers were part of this developing professionalism. Black women worked at these papers as reporters, columnists, and editors.

Some black women writers of the early 1900s included journalism among their other literary outlets. Alice Dunbar-Nelson, the wife of the poet Paul Laurence Dunbar, is not often identified as a journalist, but she wrote for both black and white newspapers at the beginning of the century, including the *Pittsburgh Courier*, the *Washington Eagle*, the *Chicago Daily News*, the *Chicago Record-Herald*, and the *New York Sun*. She published poetry and short stories in numerous periodicals, and she wrote reviews of other black writers' works, as well as news stories. She also edited the *Wilmington Advocate*, served as an associate editor for the *AME Church Review*, and later tried unsuccessfully to launch her own syndicated newspaper column.

Other contemporaries of Dunbar-Nelson devoted their energies more exclusively to journalism, including Delilah Beasley, who began her career writing for a black newspaper, the *Cleveland Gazette*, and went on to contribute to white-owned papers such as the *Cincinnati Enquirer*. After moving to California, Beasley wrote a regular column for the *Oakland Tribune*—the daily with the largest circulation in the state at that time—from 1915 to 1925.

California was home base for another journalist, Charlotta Bass, who is thought to be the first black woman to own and publish a newspaper in the United States. Bass started her career in 1910 as a writer for the *California Eagle*, a black-owned weekly in Los Angeles, and she purchased the paper two years later. She supported Marcus Garvey's Universal Negro Improvement Association and numerous civil rights organizations on the West Coast. Bass published the *Eagle* for nearly forty years, but she is perhaps best known as the first African American woman to run for vice-president when she joined the Progressive party ticket in 1952.

Political activism frequently became a partner to black women's journalistic work. Marvel Jackson Cooke began her career as an editorial assistant to W. E. B. Du Bois at the *Crisis* in 1926. Two years later Du Bois helped Cooke obtain a position at the *New York Amsterdam News*, where she struggled to improve the newspaper's quality and expand coverage of the African American community. Her efforts to organize a union local and lead a strike against the paper in 1935 prompted a move to the *People's Voice*, founded by Adam Clayton Powell, where she served as assistant managing editor. In 1950, Cooke became the first African American full-time woman reporter for a mainstream newspaper when she joined the staff of the *Daily Compass*, where she worked with the renowned journalist I. F. Stone.

Lucille H. Bluford was an outspoken activist, writer, and editor who began her tenure as a reporter in the early 1930s. As a 1932 graduate of Kansas University, she famously sued the University of Missouri at Columbia in 1939 for denying her admission to its world-renowned journalism school. Although she lost the case, her legal maneuvering did result in the establishment of the journalism school in 1942 at Lincoln University, the black state school. Bluford became managing editor of the *Kansas City Call* during the late 1930s and was cited by Lincoln University for her editing experiences in 1961. She became the only woman enshrined in the Gallery of Distinguished Publishers of the National Newspaper Publisher's Association.

World War II and After

By the 1940s, African American women had seized new challenges within the black press. Hazel Garland broke into the newspaper business as a stringer for the *Pittsburgh Courier*. In 1946, she was hired as a full-time reporter, and she traveled the country to cover crucial issues such as lynching and African Americans' responses to World War II. In one interview she recalled writing an award-winning series titled "The Three I's: Ignorance, Illiteracy, Illegitimacy," based on her travels through poor black communities in the South. During her years at the *Courier*, Garland served as entertainment editor, radio-television editor, women's editor, and finally editor-in-chief. Garland's daughter, Phyllis, also became a journalist, beginning her career at *Ebony* magazine in 1966 and then teaching in Columbia University's Graduate School of Journalism.

Elizabeth Murphy Moss was connected with one of the black newspaper giants at mid-century: her family's paper, the *Baltimore Afro-American*. She began her career at the paper at age eleven and became the first black woman to be certified as a war correspondent from England during World War II. Unfortunately, she became ill and had to return without filing reports. Later Moss became vice-president and treasurer of the Afro-American Company and publisher of the largest black chain of weekly newspapers in the United States, the Baltimore Afro-American Group. Just as Moss had made a name for herself by working with black newspapers, Ariel Perry Strong gained professional stature by working with black magazines. Strong, who began as a proofreader for *Ebony*, *Jet*, and *Tan*, eventually became the first woman to head *Tan* (later *Black Stars*) magazine as managing editor in 1963.

Another woman who gained prominence in the newspaper industry was Daisy Lee Gatson Bates. Bates and her husband settled in Little Rock, Arkansas, and used their savings to launch the *Arkansas State Press* in the early 1940s. After the paper covered the brutal murder of a black soldier by a white police officer, white advertisers withdrew their support. The paper attracted a large following across the state, and Bates became more involved in racial issues. She was eventually elected president of the Arkansas branch of the NAACP. She also was a major figure in the desegregation of schools in Little Rock and a major influence in helping the Little Rock Nine to integrate in 1959. The newspaper, suffering from financial problems, ceased publication in 1959. Following the death of her husband in 1980, Daisy Lee resumed publication of the *Press* in 1984 in his honor. She eventually sold the paper in 1988.

Alice Dunnigan became the first African American woman to cover the White House when she was the Washington correspondent for the *Chicago Defender*. In the mid-1960s, Ethel L. Payne pioneered as a commentator for six years on the CBS network opinion program "Spectrum," the only black woman to have held such a position at that time. She subsequently spent ten weeks in Vietnam covering the war. She traveled extensively throughout Asia and Africa during her career and became one of the first black women in broadcasting when she provided commentary to CBS News. Her most outstanding contribution came from the distinction of being the first black woman war correspondent. For twenty years (1953–1973) she ran the Washington bureau of the Sengstacke newspaper chain.

The death of Philippa Duke Schuyler in Vietnam in May 1967 at the age of thirty-four, as she tried to evacuate Vietnamese children trapped in an orphanage, is a tragic episode among the stories of black women journalists. Schuyler was best known as a child prodigy who performed as a classical pianist when barely in her teens. She began her second career as a journalist in the 1960s, first covering the war in the Congo, and later the Vietnam War, for the Manchester *Union Leader*.

Cynthia Tucker joined the *Atlanta Constitution* in 1976 and served as a reporter, a columnist, and an editorial writer prior to becoming the first black woman to edit a mainstream daily newspaper in 1992.

The diverse and courageous black women who worked as journalists during the mid-1950s and later were women who risked their lives and their families to report and write about the black experience. They served as role models for those who would follow in their footsteps and continue their pioneering legacy. These path-finding women paved the way for the women mentioned above and other individuals like Dorothy Gilliam, the first African American woman columnist for the *Washington Post*; Barbara Reynolds, Washington bureau correspondent for the *Chicago Tribune*, columnist for *USA Today*, and editor of *Dollars and Sense* magazine; and Pamela McAllister Johnson, who became the first black woman publisher of a white-owned daily newspaper, the *Ithaca Journal*, in 1982 (the newspaper was part of one of the largest newspaper chains, Gannett, which later founded the national newspaper *USA Today*). In 1987, Johnson received the Candace Award from the National Coalition of 100 Black Women. She became director of the School of Journalism and Broadcasting at Western Kentucky University in 2003.

Black Women in Broadcast News

Black women also have become increasingly visible in broadcast news; Charlayne Hunter-Gault was the first black woman to anchor a national newscast, public television's *MacNeil/Lehrer NewsHour*. The ABC newscaster Carole Simpson, who was once told by a dean at a journalism program that she would not make it in journalism because she was black, eventually became the first African American female anchor of a national television news broadcast. Simpson's inspiration to succeed may have come from Xernona Clayton, who became the first black woman to host a television program in the South when her show premiered in Atlanta in 1969. Following that, Clayton distinguished herself by becoming the first

black assistant corporate vice president of urban affairs at the Turner Broadcasting System in 1988. Oprah Winfrey became the first black woman to host a nationally syndicated weekday talk show, the *Oprah Winfrey Show*, in 1983. In 1989, Winfrey formed Harpo Productions to develop her own television and movie projects.

Another black woman who made significant strides in the electronic media was Joan Murray. Murray was the first major African American television news correspondent for CBS-TV. In 1969, she co-founded Zebra Associates, the first integrated advertising agency with black principals. There are numerous others who have pioneered in the electronic media, including Norma Quarles, Carol Jenkins, and Renee Poussaint.

Legacy of African American Journalism

Historians have surmised that there have been more than three thousand black newspapers. Due to financial problems, most of them folded within a few years of operation. Fortunately, the journalistic contributions of black women have not been limited to newspapers, and thus, black women have used their writing fortes on the news staff of black-oriented, as well as mainstream, magazines, radio, and television stations. Although the full extent of their writing during the earlier periods of the press are not documented, there is evidence that they were appreciated for the value they brought to the field of journalism.

The *American Baptist* gave an illustrative account of Lucretia Coleman's career in 1884. Articles were featured on Coleman, Kate Chapman, and Gertrude Mossell in the *Indianapolis Freeman*. The *Detroit Plain Dealer* provided a lengthy account of the success of black women working for newspapers during its fifth anniversary issue during May 1888. As another testament to their acceptance, unlike their white female counterparts who were denied acceptance in mainstream trade organizations, black female journalists were allowed to join the Afro-American Press Association. Ida B. Wells-Barnett served as the first assistant secretary, and then later served as secretary of the National Afro-American Press Convention meetings, during 1888 and 1889. Some of the women journalists also wrote about the roles of other black women journalists. One the most comprehensive, *Work of the Afro-American Women*, was written in 1894 by Gertrude Mossell. Another, Lucy W. Smith wrote biographies on black women working in journalism for the *Journalist*.

Today's black women journalists face the challenge of increasing their numbers and visibility in every facet of the news business more so than at any other time in history. Their predecessors demonstrated daily that black women are a vital link in the nation's quest for free expression and social justice.

BIBLIOGRAPHY

Belford, Barbara. *Brilliant Bylines: A Biographical Anthology of Notable Newspaperwomen in America*. New York: Columbia University Press, 1986.

Bullock, Penelope L. *The Afro-American Periodical Press: 1838–1909*. Baton Rouge: Louisiana State University Press, 1981.

Cooper, Anna Julia. *A Voice from the South*. Xenia, OH: Aldine, 1892.

Davis, Marianna W., ed. *Contributions of Black Women to America*. Columbia, SC: Kenday, 1981.

Dunnigan, Alice E. "Early History of Negro Women in Journalism." *Negro History Bulletin*, May 1965.

Duster, Alfreda M., ed. *Crusade for Justice: The Autobiography of Ida B. Wells*. Chicago: University of Chicago Press, 1970.

Giddings, Paula. *When and Where I Enter: The Impact of Black Women on Race and Sex in America*. New York: Morrow, 1996.

Harding, Vincent. *There Is a River: The Black Struggle for Freedom in America*. New York: Vintage, 1983.

Hull, Gloria T. *Color, Sex, and Poetry: Three Women Writers of the Harlem Renaissance*. Bloomington: Indiana University Press, 1987.

Lerner, Gerda, ed. *Black Women in White America: A Documentary History*. New York: Vintage, 1973.

Marzolf, Marion. *Up from the Footnote: A History of Women Journalists*. New York: Hastings House, 1977.

Penn, I. Garland. *The Afro-American Press and Its Editors* (1891). New York: Arno Press, 1969.

Potter, Vilma Raskin. *A Reference Guide to Afro-American Publications and Editors*. Ames: Iowa State University Press, 1983.

Rhodes, Jane. "Mary Ann Shadd Cary and the Legacy of African-American Women Journalists." In *Women Making Meaning: The New Feminist Scholarship in Communication*, edited by Lana Rakow (forthcoming).

Smith, Jessie Carney. *Black Firsts: Two Thousand Years of Extraordinary Achievement*. Detroit: Gale, 1994.

Still, William Grant. *The Underground Railroad*. Philadelphia: Porter & Coates, 1872.

Wilson, Clint C. *Black Journalists in Paradox: Historical Perspectives and Current Dilemmas*. New York: Greenwood Press, 1991.

—Marilyn Kern-Foxworth
—Carolyn Calloway-Thomas

BARBARA REYNOLDS, an award-winning black journalist, created a provocative scenario in one of her columns: the setting is a press conference at the White House during which the president asks, "Why are there so many white faces in here? When is the press going to look like America?" (Courtesy of Dr. Reynolds.)

JOURNALISM, MODERN. In one of her columns, Barbara Reynolds, an award-winning black female journalist, created a scenario during a press conference at the White House in which the president of the United States poses the questions, "Why are there so many white faces in here? When is the press going to look like America?" This was a fictitious event created by Reynolds, but it poses a question that many African American journalists, especially black women, have been asking for over a century.

Black female journalists have long understood that in order to perform their jobs, they must work without regard to the hardships and barriers caused by racial and gender prejudice. Most of these women labored and toiled because they discovered that the images promulgated through the use of mass-mediated vehicles are some of the most influential means of socializing, galvanizing, motivating, dehumanizing, denigrating, and inspiring any group of people. There are some notable African American women who have left indelible impressions upon society and the world-at-large through their journalistic endeavors and for the most part, they used their skills to inspire.

Women of Color Working as Print Journalists

With an influx of immigrants arriving daily from numerous countries and a notable increase in multiracial populations, America has evolved into one of the most diverse republics in the world. According to the 2000 census, there were 281,421,906 citizens residing in the United States. The multicultural demographic breakdown indicated that minority groups represented close to 30 percent of the population. Almost 12.6 percent or 36 million were African Americans and more specifically, 19 million were African American women. According to a report by the Catalyst Organization in 1999, women of color made up 22.6 percent of women in the workplace. During that same period there were more African American women working as journalists than ever before in history.

These guardians of black culture and purveyors of words and language were instrumental in the evolution of the black press and subsequently played pivotal roles in the formation of organizations founded to assist them with their communication aspirations. One of those organizations, the National Association of Black Journalists (NABJ), was founded on 12 December 1975 in Washington, DC. With a mission to create a professional organization for black print and broadcast journalists, it is the largest media organization of people of color in the world. Several African American women were founding members of the organization: Carol Bartel, Congress of Racial Equality (CORE), New York; Maureen Bunyan, WTOP-TV, Washington, DC; Marilyn Darling, WHYY-TV, Wilmington, Delaware; Allison J. Davis, WBEZ-TV, Boston; Sandra Dawson, Wilmington, *Delaware News Journal*; Sandra Dilliard, *Denver Post*; and Sandra Gilliam-Beale, WHIO-TV; Toni Jones, *Detroit Free Press*; Claudia Polley, NBC News; Jennye Thorton, *U.S. News and World Report*; and Norma Wade, *Dallas Morning News*.

It took over eighteen years before the first woman, Dorothy Butler Gilliam, a columnist for the *Washington Post*, became the president of the organization in 1993. By the year 2004, only one other woman, Vanessa Williams, a reporter for the *Washington Post*, had been selected to lead the NABJ, one of the most influential entities in trying to balance the playing field for African Americans working in journalism. Because of the efforts of these two women and other NABJ leaders, more emphasis has been placed on increasing the number of male and female African Americans working as print and broadcast journalists throughout America.

Women Journalists Who Made a Difference

Barbara Reynolds is president of Reynolds News Service: A Think Tank on Race, Religion and Gender, based in Washington, DC, which she founded in 1981. During her illustrious professional career, she became a White House correspondent for the *Chicago Tribune*. In 1976 Reynolds became the second black woman in history to win a Nieman Fellowship at Harvard University. She continued her journalistic pursuits and honed her craft by working for several newspapers and magazines. Her newsroom was the world as she covered the drought and famine in Ethiopia, the rise of the Japanese business class in Tokyo, the women's liberation movement in Italy, and subsequently toured the Middle East, reporting on conflict in the region. Her visibility increased significantly when she became a start-up editor of the op-ed page of the newspaper,

USA Today. The only African American on the newspaper's editorial board, she was one of the most outspoken journalists of her time and wrote scathing columns that addressed racial and gender inequities. An avid civil rights advocate, in 1998 she penned *No, I Won't Shut Up: 30 Years of Telling It Like It Is*, a compilation of some of her most noteworthy columns.

Ethel L. Payne, Washington correspondent of the Sengstacke Newspapers, was the only black newswoman to be assigned to cover the Vietnam War. Payne was one of a group of thirty-five reporters who in 1957 went with then Vice President and Mrs. Richard M. Nixon to various African and European nations. Her newspapers also sent her to write about the Nigerian civil war in 1969 and the World Council of Churches assembly at Uppsala, Sweden, in 1968. Called the "Dean of Black Journalists" by some, she won numerous awards for her work, twice being given

ETHEL L. PAYNE in 1974. Payne was one of the first black women to be accredited to the White House press corps. (© Corbis.)

the Newsman Award of the Capitol Press Club, of which she became president in 1970. The National Association of Black Women named her the Ida B. Wells Media Woman of the Year and she was selected as a Ford Foundation Fellow in Educational Journalism in 1978. Although most of her journalistic career was spent at the *Chicago Defender*, Payne also worked as a national network commentator in radio. Another black female journalist, Cynthia Tucker, has earned distinction as a newspaper columnist and television commentator. After joining the *Atlanta Journal-Constitution* in 1976 as a reporter, she later became a columnist and an editorial writer. In 1992 Tucker became the first black woman to edit a mainstream daily newspaper, the *Atlanta Journal-Constitution*.

Pam McAllister Johnson began her journey in journalism education at the University of Wisconsin, Madison (UW), where she received a bachelor of science degree in Journalism in 1967. While a lecturer at UW, she founded the Students of Color in Mass Communication (SCMC), an organization composed of African American students studying journalism and mass communication. Johnson made history when she became the first African American female publisher of a mainstream newspaper, the *Ithaca Journal*. *Black Enterprise* captured the historical moment by featuring her on its cover. In 2003 she became Director of the School of Journalism and Broadcasting at Western Kentucky. Throughout her career, Johnson established herself as an exemplary academician and industry professional.

In 2003 Sonceria "Sonny" Messiah-Jiles, publisher of the *Houston Defender*, was elected to a two-year term as chairperson of the National Newspaper Publishers Association (NNPA), a federation of more than 200 black-owned newspapers. Prior to purchasing the *Houston Defender* at age twenty-seven, she worked for several radio and television stations including being a news reporter at KYOK-AM, advertising account executive at KMJQ-FM, and being a talk show host on KHOU-TV and KRIV-TV. Messiah-Jiles had previously been selected as the NNPA publisher of the year prior to being named chairperson of the organization.

Dorothy Leavell, one of the most prominent figures in the black press, was born in Pine Bluff, Arkansas, on 23 October 1944. Her first husband, Balm L. Leavell Jr., founded the *Crusader* newspaper in 1940 and twenty years later began publishing a similar newspaper in Gary, Indiana. After her husband's death in 1968, Leavell served as publisher and editor of the *Crusader*, rehabilitating its facilities and modernizing the production process, efforts that have aided tremendously the success of the newspaper. Leavell's contribution to and influence on the black press grew when she became chairperson of Amalgamated Publishers, a company that sells national advertising for

more than two hundred African American papers across the country. As a member of the NNPA, a black newspaper trade organization, for more than twenty-five years, she served in various capacities including president, assistant secretary, and treasurer. Leavell has been featured in both print and television journalism and has received many awards for her contributions to the publishing industry. She tried to change the negative portrayals of blacks in the press by being the cofounder of Heroes in the Hood, a program that celebrates extraordinary accomplishments of young people who have gone unrecognized in the mainstream media.

Karla Garrett Harshaw, a native of Dayton, Ohio, also serves as an example of advancement for black female journalism professionals. The American Society of Newspaper Editors heralded the selection of Harshaw as its new president in its April 2004 newsletter, the *American Editor*. Harshaw began working for Cox Newspaper–owned *Daily News and Journal Herald* (Ohio) while in high school. She worked as assistant city editor, assistance features editor, and executive features editor before turning to the business side of operations and eventually became the newspaper's assistant business manager in 1987. In 1990 Cox Newspapers promoted her to the editorship of the *News-Sun* in Springfield (Ohio) and during 2000 she was given additional responsibilities as senior editor for Cox *Community Newspapers*.

Newspaper officials have attempted novel approaches to entice more people of color to make careers in the journalism business. The introduction of Charleen "Chip" Tracer, a fictionalized Pulitzer Prize–winning cyberjournalist and comic book hero, is one of the innovative strategies that has captured the attention of many. Chip Tracer was originally created by a *Newsday* team. The project, spearheaded by *Newsday*'s Bob Zimmerman, eventually led to a partnership between *Newsday* and the Freedom Forum's Newseum. Tracer serves as an ambassador, bringing educational messages about the newspaper industry to young people. She was created to encourage young people to become more discerning news consumers, to spark interest in how and why news is made, and to give them a better understanding of the role of a free press in our society. Moreover, her inventors sought to create a positive journalistic role model for young people, particularly in girls and young people of color. Chip Tracer uses special electronic equipment built into her cybersuit to travel back and forth in time and to transmit stories back to the newsroom.

Chip Tracer was an extremely positive indicator of the industry's attempt to create a diverse newspaper environment because Chip Tracer garnered enormous visibility among young readers; most important, she is African American. Although a work of fiction, Bill Zimmerman,

Chip Tracer creator, developed an extremely detailed genealogy for the cyberjournalist and gave her roots that began in a village in Ghana, Africa.

Many would agree that journalism education is one area that also should be targeted in order to improve diversity within the ranks of journalism industries. There have been improvements made on that front, as well. Marilyn Kern-Foxworth, the Garth C. Reeves Endowed Chair in the School of Journalism and Graphics Arts at Florida A&M University, was elected the first African American president of the Association for Education in Journalism and Mass Communication (AEJMC) in 2000, an organization founded in 1912. During her presidency, she created and founded the Journalism Leadership Institute in Diversity (JLID) to increase the number of women and people of color in leadership positions in journalism education. The purpose for the Institute, a year-long program funded by the Gannett Foundation, is to identify and select women and multiracial journalism and mass communication faculty who would be trained to occupy leadership positions in all facets of journalism education. In 2004 Jannette Dates was elected president of AEJMC, giving her the distinction of becoming the second African American female to lead the organization.

Black Women Journalists and the Magazine Industry

There has always been a paucity of black females who have held noteworthy positions within general circulation magazines. They were, however, able to find employment in black-oriented periodicals. In 1966, *New Lady*, in California, with an 80 percent black staff, was created as the black counterpart to *Good Housekeeping*. The publisher, Warner Beckett, noted that the magazine was founded to fill a void for black women. Only three issues were printed before the publication was halted due to financial deficits. In 1969 the magazine was reinstated with $70,000 provided by both the Ford Foundation and Opportunity Through Ownership. The magazine was also aided in its efforts by Select Magazines, a distributor that agreed to place it in nearly one hundred communities. The magazine was further assisted by the National Council of Negro Women (NCNW), National Association of Negro Business and Professional Women's Clubs, black sororities, and youth organizations. During the early 1970s magazine executives reported a paid circulation of approximately 100,000.

Essence, the most successful magazine geared toward a black female audience, was founded in 1968. The name *Essence* was selected because black is the essence of all color. Three African American businessmen, Cecil Hollingsworth, Ed Lewis, and Jonathan Blount, launched the magazine after raising $1.5 million in capital; some of the funding came from Playboy Enterprises. The three

men were all in their early twenties at the time. Blount left the publication in 1971.

Ida Lewis, one of the earliest, was a freelance writer for *Life*, *L'Espress*, and several French publications while living in France for five years—all ten years before joining *Essence*. Lewis resigned in 1971. Marcia Gillespie was the next editor in chief. In 1987 the magazine boasted a circulation over 800,000. Gillespie had been a former writer for *Time-Life Books* for four years. She remained editor until 1980, after resigning to take up freelance writing and teaching. In 1988 she was named executive editor of *Ms.*, a white-owned and white-oriented women's magazine. Susan L. Taylor, the fashion and beauty editor at *Essence*, was named editor in chief in 1981, becoming one of the most popular figures in the history of the magazine.

To keep the magazine profitable and increase its visibility, *Essence* entered the competition of fashion catalogs. During the mid-1980s the magazine created a television presence with the debut of *Essence—The Television Program*, a weekly show hosted by editor in chief Taylor. During spring 2004, *Essence* announced plans for another magazine, *Suede*, which debuted during fall 2004. According to company officials, the magazine would be a glossy fashion, beauty, and celebrity-driven publication marketed toward black women ages eighteen to thirty-four. Suzanne Boyd, a Canadian, would take the helm of the publication.

In 1986 Oprah Gail Winfrey began a journey that would establish her as one of the world's most famous and wealthiest women when she became the first black woman to host a nationally syndicated talk show, the *Oprah Winfrey Show*. In April 2000 Winfrey launched a highly successful lifestyle magazine for women, *O, The Oprah Winfrey Magazine*, with a subscription base of 2.5 million readers. The magazine reiterates a mantra that has guided Winfrey through some of her most successful mass media ventures. According to Winfrey's Web site, *O* is designed to meet the needs of confident, intelligent women, delivering the information they need to explore and reach their greatest potential. The magazine offers women an opportunity to express and find their individuality by making the choices that will assist them in leading happier and more fulfilled lives.

Diversity Coverage and Employment in Print Journalism

The black press is greatly responsible for the presentation of positive coverage of African American communities. Additionally, the black press has been a fertile ground for the training and employment of African American journalists as evidenced by a report demonstrating the necessity of the black press. A research study conducted by Linda Williams in 1989 illustrated how the black press supported and published the accomplishments of black female athletes. An in-depth study of the coverage of sportswomen was analyzed in two black newspapers, the *Pittsburgh Courier* and the *Chicago Defender*. The analysis of the *Courier* comprised a period of twenty-five years, from 1924 to 1948, while the analysis of the *Chicago Defender* covered a period of seventeen years, from 1932 to 1948 (884 papers). There were 771 stories relative to black women in sports published by the *Courier* and 1,741 published in the *Defender*. In the *Defender*, approximately 85 percent of the news about black female athletes appeared on the first or second page of the sports section. Photographs composed 23 percent of the 1,741 stories. It is doubtful that coverage of these stories would have survived without the coverage by these two black newspapers and reporters.

The International Women's Media Foundation (IWMF) conducted a national research investigation, a seminal work and the first of its kind, into the monumental trials and tribulations faced by women of color working in all sectors of news media. The project was designed to ascertain the newsroom work experiences of women journalists of color and to provide insights into their job satisfaction. Surveys were sent to 2,986 women journalists of color who were members of the four largest media organizations, including the NABJ. There was a 15 percent rate of return. The largest percentage of respondents was African American at 28 percent. Surveys also were sent to 4,196 newsroom managers, radio, and television stations with a 7 percent rate of return. The majority of the managers who responded were male (57 percent), white, non-Hispanic (79 percent); at 11 percent, black managers made up the second-largest group of respondents. Most of the managers surveyed worked in newspapers (61 percent). Stark differences exist between the predominantly white male managers and women of color, especially regarding the newsroom. The study further observed:

> A majority of women of color working for the media say the progress of their career is hampered by lingering racial stereotypes and subtle discrimination. Women journalists of color still face substantial obstacles to full participation in the newsroom—particularly in terms of promotion opportunities. They still find that their strengths as journalists, and the value that their presence brings, are consistently being ignored and downplayed.

(*Women Journalists of Color*, 1999, p. 4)

Respondents suggested that they are held back by insurmountable prejudices, based on skin color and racial heritage: 61 percent believed they still faced barriers to career advancements that are not faced by their white, male colleagues; 51 percent suspected that discrimination had played a crucial role in circumventing their advancement within the profession. Differences arose between the way the two groups perceived their field. The women journalists of color and managers also disagreed on the correlation of newsroom diversity and diversity reflected in their communities.

Following the publication of the groundbreaking study, *Women Journalists of Color*, the IMWF launched a series of seminars focused on providing women of color working in journalism with the leadership and specialized training needed to advance in their careers. The sessions, offered around the country in places like Atlanta, Los Angeles, and Houston, were attended by African American females, as well as other female journalists of color.

Although the mass media industry has made significant changes regarding the employment and portrayal of African Americans, it also remains one of the most maligned industries by the black community. In 1999, the American Society of Newspaper Editors (ASNE) confessed that its goal established in 1978 of reaching parity in newsrooms with multiethnic populations in the year 2000 would not be met was accepted with consternation, and its promise to meet another self-imposed goal for 2025 was greeted with skepticism.

Because of the goals set by the American Society of Newspaper Editors (ASNE), it is often the barometer used by most scholars, journalists, to determine success or failure of diversity in the media. The organization noted that newsrooms at American daily newspapers increased the number of journalists of color in newsrooms by a half of one percentage point in 2003; at the same time acknowledging, however, that this would not keep them on track to reach their goal for 2025.

More specifically by 2004, the ASNE annual survey indicated that of the 54,200 journalists working in America's newspaper newsrooms, 12.95 percent or 7,000 were journalists of color. More specifically, there were 2,938 African Americans, 2,258 Latinos, 1,507 Asians, and 313 Native Americans. More germane to the focus of this report, there were 1,512 African American males and 1,426 African American females. Although there were increases documented, the diversity percentages in newspaper newsrooms were not proportionate to their representation in the population.

Moreover, the 2004 American Society of Newspaper Editors (ASNE) newsroom employment survey showed 10.5 percent of journalists of color worked in supervisory positions. The most alarming revelation reported by the survey was the fact that 40 percent of daily newspapers employed no journalists of color on their staffs.

Although the actual number of journalists of color employed does not suggest success, one pivotal event has shed a positive light on the situation. As mentioned earlier, in April 2004, Karla Garrett Harshaw, an African American female, became the first person of color to the lead the ASNE.

The Freedom Forum commissioned the Center for Survey Research and Analysis at the University of Connecticut to conduct telephone interviews of members of the four major organizations to which journalists of color belong (NABJ, NAHJ, AAJA, and NAJA) during the summer of 1999. The journalists surveyed worked at newspapers with a circulation of 25,000 or more. Working with ASNE, the Freedom Forum discerned that if newsrooms are to reach parity of journalists of color on par with their representation in the population by 2025, newspapers will need to make half of all journalism hires over the next quarter century from ALANA groups.

More specifically, the study concluded that to achieve the proposed goal of diversity in newsrooms, approximately 625 additional journalists of color would have to join the workforce each year beginning in 2000 and continuing until 2025. Currently, the annual average number is 550. During this twenty-six-year period, an additional 16,000 journalists of color would be added to the estimated 18,000 who would normally be hired through traditional measures.

To increase the number of multiethnic journalists in the pipeline, the Freedom Forum created the Freedom Forum Institute for Newsroom Diversity. Under the leadership of Wanda Lloyd, the founding executive director, the Institute opened in 2002. Participants, identified from nontraditional occupations, are given twelve weeks of intensive journalism training in an effort to fill newsroom vacancies. The state-of-the-art facility is projected to graduate seventy-five to eighty new newspaper journalists of color each year.

A compelling revelation that newsrooms are not reaching diversity parities with population numbers comes annually from *Fortune* magazine. Every year the publication ranks the top fifty companies according to how well they are doing regarding diversity factors. Rarely are media companies listed; however, in the 28 June 2004 issue the second-largest newspaper publisher, Knight Ridder, was ranked thirtieth on the list. At the time of the ranking, the company's workforce was 41 percent female and 29 percent people of color. More important, in 2003 more than 53 percent of the newspaper's new hires were women and 30 percent were people of color. Journalists of color who had been promoted to top editorships had doubled since 2002. Knight Ridder was the only media company selected in 2004. It also made the lists in 1999 and 2002.

The Future for African American Female Journalists

There is a concern regarding the plight and portrayal of black women and the media as evidenced by a forum on the topic that was held at the Kennedy School of Government on the campus of Harvard University on March 1, 2002. Titled "Invisibility to Commodity? Constructions of

 "Where I'm Coming From"

Cartoonist Barbara Brandon was the first black female cartoonist to be syndicated in the mainstream white press. (Jackie Ormes was syndicated in black-owned newspapers beginning in the 1930s.) She was born in 1958 in the Bushwick section of Brooklyn, the youngest of three children of Brumsic Brandon Jr. Her father was the creator of the comic strip "Luther," which first appeared in the late 1960s. The strip, which was about an inner-city black child, ran for seventeen years. Brandon was brought up in New Cassel, Long Island, and attended Syracuse University, where she studied illustration. After graduation, she applied for a job at *Elan*, a magazine for black women. The editor wanted a comic strip to run regularly in the magazine, and Brandon created "Where I'm Coming From." When the magazine went out of business before the strip was published, she took it to *Essence*. They said no to the strip but yes to Brandon, hiring her as a beauty and fashion writer.

In 1988, however, the *Detroit Free Press* asked Brandon's father if he knew of any black cartoonists. Brandon got out her strip. It began appearing in the *Free Press* in 1989 and was acquired by Universal Press Syndicate in 1991. Not thrilled to be the "first black woman" anything in the last decade of the twentieth century, Brandon was nevertheless happy to have a larger audience for her increasingly political cartoons. "Where I'm Coming From" features nine black women with diverse lives and perspectives.

Black Women in Art and Media," its panelists were Carrie Allen McCray, an author; Callie Crossley, a television news producer; and two professors, Evelyn Brooks Higginbotham and Tricia Rose. The discussion focused on the pejorative portrayal of black women in rap videos, as well as the black women anchors and reporters. The panelists concluded that while black women enjoy more visibility in the media and popular culture, the range and scope of that visibility was extremely limited. And in answer to the question posed by the seminar's theme question, the respondents unanimously agreed that although black women are not literally being bought and sold as slaves, they are still being viscerally sold as commodities in a different arena, the television screen.

Various case studies and research reports have suggested that African American women have been hired more frequently than female journalists of other racial groups, but are still underrepresented in the journalism profession. There is growing concern that this disparity makes these industries less effective. Betty Anne Williams, from *USA Today*, asserts that

for the media, turning a blind eye to diversity and gender issues could be a costly mistake in a nation where, census projections show, 87 percent of population growth between now and 2010 will be in minority communities, and where women already make up 51 percent of the population and 45 percent of the workforce.

Newsrooms have often been criticized for not mirroring the diversity represented in the communities they serve. The Census Bureau projects that by the year 2050 the American population will be 47 percent multiracial. Vernon Stone, professor emeritus at the University of Missouri, surmised that if the same average annual percentage of growth occurred in journalism as occurred between 1978 and 1994, by 2050 there will be 15 percent ALANA employment in radio news, 26 percent in television news, and 35 percent at daily newspapers. Using these numbers as a gauge, journalism industries would fall short of their goals by 32 percent in radio news, 21 percent in television news, and 35 percent in daily newspapers.

Not having black women adequately represented as journalists and as supervisors in newsrooms contributes to their being overwhelmingly absent, distorted, and stereotyped in news coverage. In other words, employment and portrayals of African American women are becoming increasingly more important because of the impact that they have relative to the perpetuation of stereotypes. This point was succinctly reinforced by Sandra Evers-Manly in the *Los Angeles Times*:

Our images always seem to be decided upon, judged and court-martialed by an unknown system our community is not supposed to question. The community rarely has a say on the distorted, one-dimensional images that repeatedly find their way into the public consciousness. When they do, the media tend to take honest feedback and make it controversial instead of finding the "root cause" of one's frustration. This is the picture we must focus on and change immediately.

Every negative label, event, and newspaper headline has inadvertently lengthened the life of stereotypes. Moreover, stereotypes of blacks have been accepted by mainstream America and internalized by blacks because of their systematic and methodical repetition. Furthermore, research has shown that stereotypical images impede rising socioeconomic status, employment, and education for African Americans. The mass media is the vehicle that keeps stereotypes alive and flourishing. Thus, racism, bigotry, Jim Crow, segregation, and anti-affirmative action programs have survived based upon the perpetuation of stereotypes within society.

Journalism plays a pivotal factor in lessening the impact of stereotypes. This is why the IWMF, the Freedom Forum, the Center for Integration and Improvement of Journalism, and the ASNE are working in a concerted effort to create programs that will change the dynamics of journalism and increase diversity within journalism professions. These organizations, and others like them, will make sure that the fictitious scenario presented by Barbara Reynolds does not become a reality in 2025. They are keenly aware that employment and coverage of black females in the mass media industry will be the catalyst to neutralizing the detrimental effects of stereotypes.

BIBLIOGRAPHY

"Behind the Scenes Newseum and Newsday Unveil Adventures of Chip Tracer, Cyberjournalist, in Museum and on the Web." http://www.newsday.com/other/education/ny-chip_behind.story or Newsday.com.

"Chip Tracer, Cyberjournalist." *Girl Scout of Suffolk County Happenings*, Winter 2003, 22.

"Cyberjournalist Chip Tracer Is Role Model for Kids." *Annual Report Freedom Forum/Newseum* (Fall 1999): 9.

Evers-Manly, Sandra. "OK, So What's Wrong with This Picture." *Los Angeles Times*, 25 April 1994.

International Women's Media Foundation Annual Report 1999/2000, Washington, DC, 4.

Keels, Crystal L. "Developing Truth Teller: Freedom Forum Institute Sets Out to Help Diversify America's Newsrooms through the Training of Minority Journalists." *Black Issues in Higher Education*, 15 July 2004, 26–29.

Kern-Foxworth, Marilyn. *Aunt Jemima, Uncle Ben, and Rastus: Blacks in Advertising, Yesterday, Today, and Tomorrow*. Westport, CT: Greenwood Press, 1994.

Kern-Foxworth, Marilyn. "Women of Color on the Frontline in the Mass Communication Professions." In *Seeking Equity for Women in Journalism and Mass Communication Education: A 30-Year Update*, edited by Ramona Rush, Carol E. Oukrop, and Pamela J. Creedon. Mahwah, NJ: Erlbaum, 2004.

Kern-Foxworth, Marilyn, and Shirley Biagi. "Minority Newsroom Employment Shows Small Gain." In *Facing Difference: Race, Gender, and Mass Media*, edited by Shirley Biagi and Marilyn Kern-Foxworth. Thousand Oaks, CA: Pine Forge Press, 1997.

McGill, Lawrence. *Newsroom Diversity: Meeting the Challenge*. Arlington, VA: The Freedom Forum, 2000.

Prince, Richard. "Rice's Race: Diversity in Discussing Witness as African American." *Richard Prince's JOURNAL-ISMS*, 9 April 2004. http://www.maynardije.org/columns/dickprince/040409_prince/

Reynolds, Barbara A. *No, I Won't Shut Up: Thirty Years of Telling It Like It Is*. Temple Hills, MD: JFJ, 1998.

Smiles, Robin V. "U.S. Newsrooms: Still a Long Way from Racial Parity." *Black Issues in Higher Education*, 15 July 2004, 24–25.

Stone, Vernon. "Minorities and Women in Television News." *The Diversity Factor*, Spring 1997, 5.

Tucker, Cynthia. "Portrait of the President." *American Editor*, April 2004, 13–15.

Williams, Linda D. "Sportswomen in Black and White: Sports History from an Afro-American Perspective." In *Women, Media, and Sport: Challenging Gender Values*, edited by Pamela Creedon. Thousand Oaks, CA: Sage Publications, 1994.

Wilson, Clint. *Black Journalists in Paradox: Historical Perspectives and Current Dilemmas*. Westport, CT: Greenwood Press, 1991.

Wolseley, Roland E. *The Black Press, U.S.A.* Ames: Iowa State University Press, 1990.

Women Journalists of Color: Present without Power. Washington, DC: International Women's Media Foundation, September 1999.

—MARILYN KERN-FOXWORTH

JOYNER, FLORENCE GRIFFITH

JOYNER, FLORENCE GRIFFITH (b. 21 December 1959; d. 21 September 1998), athlete, businesswoman. Florence Griffith Joyner, or "Flo-Jo," lived her life with all the razzle and dazzle appropriate for a superstar athlete

F<small>LORENCE</small> G<small>RIFFITH</small> J<small>OYNER</small> during the Olympic trials, 1988. That year she was a gold medalist at the games in Seoul, Korea. (© Duomo/Corbis.)

and entrepreneur. As the fastest woman in the world, she demonstrated that beauty, along with athletic speed and strength, could be a winning combination both on and off the track.

Delorez Florence Griffith was born in Los Angeles' Jordan housing projects in 1959, and killed by an epileptic seizure in September 1998. She was the seventh of eleven children of seamstress Florence Griffith. Her parents divorced when she was four years old. Griffith Joyner began running track at the age of seven in a program at the Sugar Ray Robinson Foundation in Los Angeles. At fourteen and fifteen she won the Jesse Owens National Youth Games Award and, while attending Los Angeles' Jordan High School, set records in the sprint and long jump. In 1979 Joyner enrolled at California

State University (CSU), Northridge, but was forced to drop out two years later because of lack of financial support. Fortunately, one of her coaches at CSU helped her get financial aid. When the coach, Bob Kersee, moved to the University of California at Los Angeles (UCLA), he took the talented young athlete with him. Joyner soon confirmed Kersee's evaluation of her athletic ability by winning National Collegiate Athletic Association championships in the 200 meters in 1982 and the 400 meters in 1983. She also validated UCLA's assessment of her academic ability by graduating from UCLA with a major in psychology in 1983.

At the 1984 World Championship Games in Rome, Joyner caused a stir by running the first two rounds in a skintight, leotard-like track suit. She later became well known for her flamboyant clothes and hair, further demonstrating to the world that beauty and strength of will, combined with world-class physical skill, can and should be an option for successful women. From that point forward, into the early twenty-first century, such beautiful physicality became the norm for American fashion and entertainment icons.

At the Twenty-third Olympiad Games in Los Angeles in 1984, Joyner garnered a silver medal in the 200-meter race. Previously, at the Olympic trials in Indianapolis, she had worn an apple-green, one-legged bodysuit, a fluorescent gold bodysuit, and a white lace bodysuit with see-through tights, while coming in first in the 100-meter and 200-meter events and shattering the world record in the 100-meter quarter-final race.

After the 1984 games, Griffith Joyner turned away from athletics for a while, working at a bank and then opening a beauty shop. However, in 1986 she began dating fellow Olympian Al Joyner and in 1987 she married him and went back into serious training with Bob Kersee in preparation for the 1988 Olympics. Wearing the conventional American team jersey at the Seoul Olympic Games, Joyner won the 200-meter event, setting new world records in the semifinal and final races. In addition, she helped establish a new world record in the 100-meter heat and won the gold in the final event. The U.S. team clinched the gold in the 400-meter relay and garnered the silver in the 1600-meter relay. Following her multiple victories in Seoul, Griffith Joyner received the Sullivan Award and the *Track and Field News* New Athlete of the Year Award. She held the world record of 10.54 in the 100 meters as late as the 2000 Olympic Games in Sydney, and the closest track stars could come to her 21.34 Oympic record in the 200 meters was Marion Jones's effort of 21.84.

After the Seoul Games, Griffith Joyner continued to train, asking her husband to replace Kersee as her coach. She also became a fashion entrepreneur, television sports commentator, model, and soap opera and sitcom actress. President Bill Clinton appointed her co-chairperson with Tom McMillen of the President's Council on Physical Fitness in 1993. She had a daughter, Mary Ruth, and remained close friends with her former coach and his wife, Jackie Joyner-Kersee, who was her husband's sister. In November 1995, she was inducted into the National Track and Field Hall of Fame. Through the Florence Griffith Joyner Youth Foundation, she worked with disadvantaged young people.

Her success was not without controversy, however. There were consistent accusations of steroid use before and after her Seoul triumphs, and even her untimely death from an epileptic seizure at her home in 1998 caused lawsuits to be filed against medical professionals and her husband and coach, Al Joyner, regarding her care. None of these accusations has been validated.

Joyner's contributions to track and field continue to be celebrated. In many parts of California there are Florence Griffith Joyner parks, statues, and other memorials. At the Winter Games in Salt Lake in 2002, she was fittingly memorialized in a tribute to selfless athleticism and female heroism in a one-act jazz suite by Judith Jamison of the Alvin Ailey American Dance Theater, performed to the musical score of Wynton Marsalis, at the opening arts component of the Games. It was a fitting tribute to one who dared to be the best.

See also Olympic Games and Amateur Sports, Participation in; Sports; *and* Track and Field.

BIBLIOGRAPHY

Karlsson, Ove. Obituary. *Journal of Olympic History*, no. 2 (Spring 1999).

"Olympic News, Notes." *Journal of Olympic History*, no. 1 (Winter 1999).

Olympic Official Report Los Angeles 1984. Vol. 1, 1984.

Segal, Lewis. "Dance Review." *Los Angeles Times*, February 11, 2002.

Vertinsky, P., and Captain, G. "More Myth than History: American Culture and Representation of the Black Female's Athletic Ability." *Journal of Sports History*, no. 3 (1998).

—D. MARGARET COSTA

JOYNER-KERSEE, JACKIE (b. 3 March 1962), athlete. As she ran a victory lap at the 1992 Summer Olympic games, the tall Illinois native was told by Olympic decathlon champion Bruce Jenner, "You're the greatest athlete in the world." Seven times in the history of the Olympic Games a woman has scored more than 7,000 points in the challenging and grueling heptathlon. Six of those times, the woman was Jackie Joyner-Kersee, who scored 7,291 points in the heptathlon in 1988 and 7,044 points in 1992, earning an Olympic record.

Jacqueline Joyner was born in East St. Louis, Illinois. Joyner's grandmother insisted that the child be named

JACKIE JOYNER-KERSEE wearing her gold medal in Barcelona, Spain, site of the summer Olympics, on 3 August 1992. (© Reuters New Media Inc./Corbis.)

after First Lady Jacqueline Kennedy because "some day this girl will be the first lady of something." Her parents, Alfred and Mary Joyner, were seventeen and nineteen years old and had been married for three years. Life was difficult for the teenaged parents. Mary Joyner worked as a nurse's assistant, and Alfred Joyner traveled to other cities to work in construction before he got a job as a railroad switch operator.

At the age of nine, young Jackie ran in her first track competition. Soon she was bringing home first prizes every time, sometimes four or five of them. When she was fourteen, she won her first National Junior Pentathlon championship. Then she won it three more times. At Lincoln High school, she set a state record for the long jump and played on a basketball team that defeated its opponents by an average of 52.8 points a game. All this time, she excelled in her academic work as well, graduating in the top 10 percent of her class.

The University of California at Los Angeles recruited the remarkable young athlete, offering her scholarships in either basketball or track. She chose basketball and went off to UCLA as star forward. She qualified for the 1982 Olympics and was disappointed when the U.S. boycotted the games. However, a much greater sorrow overshadowed that loss: During Joyner's freshman year, her mother died of meningitis at the age of thirty-eight.

Joyner was concentrating on basketball and the long jump when she was spotted by assistant track coach Bob Kersee. He was stunned by her abilities but dismayed that they were not being encouraged to their fullest. After receiving special permission to coach her, he persuaded Joyner to begin heptathlon training; she set collegiate records in 1982 and 1983. In 1983, she and her older brother, Al, were both chosen to compete in the world track and field championships in Helsinki. There, Joyner discovered that she was not invulnerable. She experienced her first serious injury, a pulled hamstring, and was unable to compete. However, a year later, she qualified for the 1984 Olympics.

Joyner arrived at the Los Angeles stadium with another hamstring injury. In spite of that, and two fouls in her best event—the long jump—she went into the final event of the second day neck-and-neck with Glynnis Nunn of Australia. With her brother running beside her on the final leg of the 800-meter run, urging her on, she came within .06 seconds of winning the gold medal. Al, however, did win a gold, in the triple jump. It was the first time in Olympic history that a sister and brother had won medals on the same day and the first time an American woman had won any multi-event medal. Joyner went home with the silver medal and the recognition by many of her peers that she was someone very special.

In 1986 Joyner and her coach, Bob Kersee, were married. That same year, she gave up basketball to concentrate on the heptathlon and changed her training to avoid hamstring pulls. Her performance immediately improved, peaking at the Goodwill Games in Moscow, where she shattered the 7,000-point mark—the heptathlon equivalent of running the four-minute mile. From that time on, she did it regularly. That same year she won the Sullivan Award for top amateur athlete in the United States. She also received the 1986 Jesse Owens Award.

For the next two years, Joyner-Kersee racked up wins and records. At the 1988 Summer Olympics in Seoul, she won a gold medal in the heptathlon. Then, in 1992, she did the unprecedented: At the age of thirty, after eleven years of competition, she won the gold for the second time. This time, she was ahead after every single event. Her closest competitor, Irinia Belova, finished 199 points behind her. No woman had ever before won back-to-back medals in the heptathlon.

Jackie Joyner-Kersee was not finished, however. "Wouldn't it be great," she said moments after her win, "to complete my career back on American soil, in Atlanta in 1996?" When 1996 came, however, Ghada Shousaa of Syria scored 6,780 points after a teary-eyed Joyner-Kersee was forced by a painful hamstring to withdraw. In 2000 Denise Lewis of Great Britain scored 6,584 points, and in 2004 Carolina Kluft of Sweden scored 6,952. Joyner-Kersee's record, however, remained unbroken.

The disappointing withdrawal was not the end of Joyner-Kersee's 1996 story. She leapt 22 feet, 11.75 inches in the long jump, a bronze medalist by 1.25 inches. Never one to give up, Joyner-Kersee also returned to an earlier love, basketball, in 1996 when she joined the Richmond Rage in the American Basketball League, but she played sparingly. She next came back for a last major victory in the heptathlon at the 1998 Goodwill Games. She then announced her retirement but was soon to change her mind. In 2000 she attempted to make her fifth Olympic team, but finished a disappointing sixth in the long jump. In February 2001, at the age of thirty-eight, she announced her retirement and suggested that this time it was really official.

See also Olympic Games and Amateur Sports, Participation in; Sports; *and* Track and Field.

BIBLIOGRAPHY

Freeman, Patricia. "Is She the Greatest of Them All?" *Women's Sports and Fitness*, January 1987.
Moore, Kenny. "Dash to Glory." *Sports Illustrated*, 10 August 1992.
Moore, Kenny. "The Ties That Bind." *Sports Illustrated*, 27 April 1987.
Olympic Official Report Los Angeles 1984. Vol. 1 1984.
Steffens, Don. "Joyous Junction for Joyners." *Track and Field News*, August 1984.
Vertinsky, P., and Captain, G. "More Myth than History: American Culture and Representation of the Black Female's Athletic Ability." *Journal of Sport History*, no. 3 (1998): 532–561
Willman, Howard. "Track and Field News Interview." *Track and Field News*, September 1986.

—D. Margaret Costa
—Jane D. Adair

K

KECKLEY, ELIZABETH (b. 26 May 1818; d. 1907), seamstress, memoirist. Elizabeth Keckley used her needlework skills to purchase her freedom and went on to have such a flourishing business that she became dressmaker to Mary Todd Lincoln. Fortunately for posterity, she also wrote a book about her life, her sewing work, and her experience as someone closely connected to the Lincoln White House. *Behind the Scenes; or, Thirty Years as a Slave, and Four Years in the White House* (1868) has been a source of historically significant information ever since.

Elizabeth was born Elizabeth Hobbs, the only child of a slave couple, Agnes and George Pleasant Hobbs, in Dinwiddie, Virginia. Her mother was a housemaid and excellent seamstress owned by the Burwells, a prominent family of central Virginia. Her father lived on a neighboring farm and was allowed to visit his family twice a year until he was sold away from them. As a teenager, Elizabeth was repeatedly sexually molested by a white man and, as she wrote in her book, her owners were not helpful in protecting her. Eventually, she gave birth to a son, whom she named after her father and loved dearly, despite the circumstances of his conception. Elizabeth was given to one of the Burwell daughters and her minister husband, Hugh Garland. Garland was not paid well as a minister; he later tried to improve his financial position by moving to St. Louis, and Elizabeth went with them.

During the period of slavery in America, black women were responsible for taking care of the sewing needs of the plantation and, in the city, the general household. They mended and fashioned clothing for the mistress of the house, the family, and household servants. They also used their ingenuity and skills to make and repair clothing for other slaves. A special talent for needlework in a black woman added to her value as a slave. Once the woman became especially competent, her time was spent producing delicate piecework for her owners. Her beautiful quilts and bedspreads were proudly displayed throughout the mansion, and her gowns were the subject of much admiration. The talented seamstress was sometimes hired out to make stylish dresses for the mistresses of other households. In some cases, the slave was able to keep a percentage of the money for her own use.

Elizabeth became just such a seamstress and thus a very valuable asset to her owners. Though the family was socially in the "upper class" in St. Louis, Hugh Garland, now a lawyer, could not bring in the income needed to live as his wife was accustomed, and so they hired out Elizabeth to sew for wealthy women in the area. Elizabeth sewed mostly evening dresses, at a "market rate." The average price of her dresses was from one to two hundred dollars. Those years were hard on Elizabeth, who wrote that she was bringing in enough money from her dressmaking earnings to support seventeen people in the Garland household. While in St. Louis, Elizabeth married James Keckley, who presented himself as a free man. She wrote that she later found out not only that he was a slave but also that he was "dissipated." After eight years, the marriage failed and they separated.

When Keckley was thirty years old, she tried to buy her freedom, but Garland did not want to sell her. Instead, her owner jokingly gave Keckley the choice of staying a slave or taking twenty-five cents from him for the ferry to the free territory of Missouri, telling her that it would be easier for him, and for her, if she joined other fleeing blacks rather going through a purchase process. Keckley refused his offer of ferry fare (although she might have accepted it, since most people in the 1840s felt that slavery would be ending soon), because she did not want to have her life and her business interrupted by bounty hunters.

Nonetheless, Keckley, wanting a legal basis for her freedom, persisted and badgered Garland. Her price, however, had risen because the Garlands had trained and fed Elizabeth for years and because she had taught herself to read and to write. The family thus set the price of Keckley and her son at twelve hundred dollars. Keckley did not have the full amount. She wrote that one of her customers said, "Why don't you visit a friend in New York? No one ever comes back," but she refused. Fortunately, some of her wealthy customers heard of her plight, formed a "syndicate," and lent Keckley the twelve hundred dollars. In 1855 she purchased her freedom and that of her son. Within a year, she had paid off her loan. She kept the purchase paper, which looked much like a mortgage contract, and later published it in her book.

ELIZABETH KECKLEY was Mary Todd Lincoln's dressmaker and friend during Abraham Lincoln's presidency; the friendship ended when Keckley's frank memoir, which revealed some confidential details about the Lincolns, was published in 1868. (By permission of University of North Carolina.)

After Keckley gained her freedom, she moved with her son to Baltimore. Although she had letters of recommendation, she was not able to grow her business to the level she expected, so she moved on to Washington, DC, in early 1860. Soon her business was thriving. She employed twenty young women to sew her designs and attracted a large clientele of wealthy women, including Varina Davis, the wife of Jefferson Davis, who was to become president of the Confederacy. Knowing that secession was imminent, Davis asked Elizabeth Keckley to join her in New Orleans, the city which would be the capital of the newly formed Confederacy. Keckley was tempted with the offer of guaranteed business. She also knew that there were many free blacks in New Orleans, but she had just purchased her freedom and was not sure how other Southerners would treat her. In her book she said that she bade Mrs. Davis a pleasant goodbye, stating she would think over the offer.

Soon after Mary Todd Lincoln arrived in Washington, she asked friends to recommend a good seamstress and was given Keckley's name. Keckley was first to the White House after Lincoln spilled coffee on the dress his wife had chosen for the inauguration, and thereafter made and maintained virtually all Mrs. Lincoln's clothing during her years in the White House. In addition to being Lincoln's dress designer, she also became her "eyes and ears" in Washington and her traveling companion, journeying with Mrs. Lincoln to visit her son Robert at Harvard, to Richmond and St. Petersburg during the war, to New York City, and to Springfield, Illinois, after the assassination. Keckley's own son, George, was killed fighting in the Civil War. The loss seems to have drawn her closer to Mrs. Lincoln, who lost her own young son at about that time.

During the Civil War, Keckley helped out in hospitals and noted how difficult it was for the fleeing slaves to resettle in the nation's capital. She asked various abolitionists to take up collections in Boston, New York, and Washington, DC, to help the former slaves, who were called "contrabands of war." Mrs. Lincoln herself donated two hundred dollars to Keckley's Contraband Relief Association. Keckley's untiring work on behalf of African American soldiers and former slaves continued throughout the war.

The demanding friendship with Mrs. Lincoln was a mixed blessing—it took valuable time away from Elizabeth's business, but it gave her unique access to the private world of the Lincolns. Scholars today are indebted to Keckley's access. She wrote with compassion about Lincoln's troubles with various politicians and generals during the war, and about his love and understanding of his complex, high-strung wife. After the president's assassination, Mary turned to Keckley for comfort, and though she could no longer afford to keep the dressmaker with her, the two remained friends. When Mary Todd Lincoln, believing herself to be in serious financial trouble, decided to sell part of her White House wardrobe, Keckley met her in New York to help her organize the auction. Keckley turned to her own friends to find help for Lincoln, and, at her urging, Frederick Douglass agreed to lecture to raise money for the president's widow.

Scholars have wondered whether Keckley was the actual author of her 1868 book. Keckley explained that she wrote the book in New York City while attending to the selling of Mrs. Lincoln's clothes to various brokers. She worked on the book during the day, and gave the manuscripts to James Redpath, an antislavery newspaper man, each evening. He was, at the least, her editor, but may have done considerable rewriting and also helped to get the book published. However, the words and the observations of the White House, of Lincoln, and of national life during the Civil War in Washington were Keckley's.

Mrs. Lincoln's erratic behavior had created many political and social enemies. Mrs. Keckley tried to explain Mrs. Lincoln to the world in her book, which offers a candid insight into the White House and life in the 1860s.

Although Keckley's intention was to show Mrs. Lincoln in a better light to the world, and to help her pay off her debts, both Mrs. Lincoln and her son Robert, who was a corporate executive at the Chicago Railroad, took offense. The publisher found it hard to distribute the book, and many black people felt that Elizabeth was a traitor to the beloved Lincoln and to the newly formed Republican Party, which had a strong antislavery position. Others felt that Elizabeth was wrong to tell family "secrets." Someone produced a terrible racist parody pamphlet of her book, titled "Behind the Seams, by a Nigger Woman Who Took in Work from Mrs. Lincoln and Mrs. Davis." The sales of her book were almost nonexistent, and it was a terrible failure. Keckley did only one public reading of her book, in Boston, an event arranged by Redpath, and spent most of her time writing letters defending her position and that of Mrs. Lincoln.

Because of the public reaction to her book, Elizabeth lost her customer base. People who had come to her because they knew she designed for and had access to Mrs. Lincoln and the White House shunned her now that she was no longer in favor. She eventually had to close her business, and her income fell. Keckley taught domestic science for one year at Wilberforce University in Ohio, but she lived out her remaining forty years in obscurity. Jennifer Fleischner, in *Mrs. Lincoln and Mrs. Keckly*, states that "one newspaper writer in the late 1800's even wrote that there was no real 'colored seamstress' who did work for Mrs. Lincoln." Various black people proudly wrote letters to the editor saying that Keckley was still alive and active in her church.

Elizabeth Keckley died in Washington, DC, at the Home for Destitute Women, which she had assisted in establishing years earlier with earnings from her business.

BIBLIOGRAPHY

Fleischner, Jennifer. *Mrs. Lincoln and Mrs. Keckly*. New York: Random House, 2003.

Keckley, Elizabeth. *Behind the Scenes; or, Thirty Years as a Slave, and Four Years in the White House* (1868). New York: Oxford University Press with the Schaumburg Library, 1961.

Quarles, Benjamin. "Elizabeth Keckley." In *Notable American Women, 1607–1950*, edited by Edward T. James, Janet Wilson James, and Paul S. Boyer. Cambridge, MA: Belknap Press, Harvard University Press, 1971.

—ROSEMARY REED

KELLY, LEONTINE T. C. (b. 5 March 1920), religious leader. Born Leontine Turpeau in Washington, DC, to Reverend David De Witt Turpeau Sr. and Ila Marshall Turpeau, Leontine Turpeau Current Kelly became, in 1984, the first African American woman to be elected bishop in the United Methodist Church. Her father, a minister in the Methodist Episcopal Church, pastored churches in Pittsburgh, Pennsylvania; Washington, DC; and Baltimore, Maryland, before ending his ministerial career in Cincinnati, Ohio. He also worked for the Anti-Saloon League for three years in the 1910s and served in the administrative position of District Superintendent in the Methodist Episcopal Church's Washington Conference in the 1920s. David D. Turpeau preached and practiced the "Social Gospel," which holds that churches should serve the surrounding community and foster social improvement. With this purpose in mind, he entered politics, winning election as a Republican to five terms in the Ohio State Legislature starting in 1939. Ila Marshall Turpeau was not only a homemaker for her family of eight children but an active supporter of the NAACP and a co-founder of Cincinnati's chapter of the National Urban League in 1948. She was one of several women designated by the *Cincinnati Enquirer* newspaper as "Outstanding Women of the Year" in 1970.

Leontine Turpeau started her public school education in Cincinnati, eventually graduating from Woodward High School. Starting in 1938, she enrolled for three years at West Virginia State College but left her studies to marry a fellow student, Gloster Bryant Current, a 1941 graduate of West Virginia State College. Current was a talented musician and orchestra leader who chose first to work as a career employee for the NAACP and then to become a Christian minister. In the 1930s, Current organized and directed the activities of eight NAACP Youth Councils and sought to integrate restaurants and lunch counters in Detroit. In 1941 he was hired as Executive Secretary to direct the Detroit branch of the NAACP. Under his leadership, efforts were made to reduce housing and job discrimination as well as police brutality. In 1946 Current was called to New York City to serve as Director of Branches for the National Office of the NAACP. Under his direction, branches grew from 800 to over 1700 by 1977. A descendent of Methodist ministers, Current studied and became a Methodist minister, serving first as an assistant pastor and then as pastor of United Methodist Churches in addition to his work as an officer of the NAACP. Gloster and Leontine Current had three children together: Angella Patricia, Gloster Bryant Jr., and John David.

In 1955 Gloster and Leontine divorced and, in 1956, Leontine married Rev. James David Kelly, also a Methodist minister, and moved to live in Knoxville, Tennessee, and then in Richmond, Virginia, as Rev. Kelly's pastoral positions changed. She resumed study for her bachelor's degree, enrolling first at Knoxville College and then completing her undergraduate degree with honors at Virginia Union University in Richmond, Virginia. She was also certified as a lay speaker in the Methodist Church. In 1960, she was hired to teach social studies at Armstrong

BISHOP LEONTINE KELLY of the United Methodist church was the first African American woman to be elected bishop by a major American denomination. She retired in 1988 and then taught at the Pacific School of Religion. (Courtesy of Mike DuBose, United Methodist News Service.)

High School in Richmond and later taught at John Marshall High School. In 1966, Rev. James Kelly became pastor of Galilee United Methodist Church in Edwardsville, Virginia, serving until his death in 1969. Church members asked his wife to take over ministerial duties at Galilee, and she was appointed on a temporary, part-time basis while she continued teaching full-time at Northumberland High School.

By the summer of 1969, Leontine Kelly received the call to become an ordained minister and began formal study for a degree in theology. Receiving a scholarship, Kelly gave up her teaching job to do full-time study and received a Master of Divinity degree in 1976 from Union Theological Seminary, a Presbyterian-affiliated school in Richmond.

Within a nine-year period, from 1975 to 1984, Leontine T. C. Kelly rose from local church pastor to the top office, bishop, in the United Methodist Church. Ending her pastorate of Galilee Church in Edwardsville, Kelly served from 1975 to 1977 as Director of Social Ministries for the United Methodist Virginia Conference Council of Ministries. She then pastored Asbury-Church Hill United Methodist Church in Richmond, from 1977 to 1983, before joining the United Methodist Church's national staff as evangelism executive with the Board of Discipleship, in 1983 and 1984.

Kelly became active with the United Methodist clergywomen's movement in the 1970s. Their objective was to campaign for greater involvement of clergywomen in all levels of church activity, including the top administrative position, the office of bishop. In 1980, the United Methodist Church elected Rev. Marjorie Swank Matthews as its first female bishop. As Bishop Matthews' retirement was approaching in 1984, the clergywomen's movement focused upon Kelly as their preferred choice to be the second woman bishop. Leontine Kelly was elected bishop of the United Methodist Church by the Western Jurisdictional Conference on 19 July 1984 at the age of sixty-four. She became the second female, but the first African American woman, to be bishop of any major religious denomination in the United States. Other African American women became bishops subsequently: Rev. Barbara Harris, suffragan (assistant) bishop in the Episcopal Church in 1989; the Revs. Linda Lee, Beverly Shamana, and Violet Fisher in the United Methodist Church in 2000; and Rev. Vashti Murphy McKenzie in the African Methodist Episcopal Church in 2000.

Kelly was assigned as bishop to administer the Nevada and California Conferences of the United Methodist Church, with four hundred ministers and more than 100,000 members in 386 churches. She worked to increase the church's ministry to women and to a variety of ethnic groups and also to stimulate greater involvement of local churches in the social and economic uplift of their surrounding communities.

KENNEDY, ADRIENNE **199**

A bishop in the United Methodist Church is initially elected to office for a term of four years, renewable until the bishop reaches age sixty-six. Kelly became sixty-six two years into her term and was required to retire in 1988. In her retirement years, she has engaged in a wide range of activities. She taught part-time for one year in the Pacific School of Religion in Berkeley, California. She has been active in campaigns for AIDS awareness and to end the nuclear arms race, in the United Methodist Bishops Initiative on Children and Poverty, and in efforts to gain wider acceptance and ordination of gays and lesbians in the church. She played a significant role in the development of and fund-raising for Africa University in Zimbabwe, a project of the United Methodist Church. A member of the Alpha Kappa Alpha Sorority, she has received numerous honorary doctoral degrees and was inducted into the National Women's Hall of Fame in Seneca Falls, New York, in October of 2000.

BIBLIOGRAPHY

Current, Angella. *Breaking Barriers: An African American Family & The Methodist Story*. Nashville: Abingdon Press, 2001.

Dykes, De Witt S., Jr. "Leontine Kelly." In *Notable Black American Women, Volume I*, edited by Jessie Carney Smith. Detroit: Gale Research, 1992.

Kelly, Leontine T. C. "Preaching in the Black Tradition." In *Women Ministers*, edited by Judith L. Weidman. San Francisco: Harper & Row Publishers, Second Edition, 1985.

Lanker, Brian. *I Dream A World*. New York: Stewart, Tabori and Chang, 1989.

Marshall, Marilyn. "First Black Woman Bishop." *Ebony*, Vol. 40, November 1984.

"Methodists Elect 19 to Leadership." *New York Times*, 29 July 1984.

Reynolds, Barbara. *And Still We Rise: Interviews with 50 Black Role Models*. New York: USA Today Books, 1988.

Who's Who Among African Americans. Detroit: Gale Research, 2003.

—DE WITT S. DYKES JR.

KENNEDY, ADRIENNE (b. 13 September 1931), playwright. In the early 1960s Adrienne Kennedy found a new way to talk about the black experience in America. Rather than describe the outward narrative of the experience of racism she chose to portray the impact of that experience on the consciousness of her characters.

Adrienne Lita Hawkins was born in Pittsburgh, Pennsylvania, and raised in Cleveland, Ohio. Her father, Cornell Wallace Hawkins was a social worker, and her mother, Etta (Haugabook) Hawkins was a teacher. Kennedy starting writing in childhood, keeping diaries on the members of her family. It was also in childhood that she began to collect and store the images, symbols, visions, and dreams that later became a large part of her plays. The most important of these elements is the voice of her mother. In 1987 she told an interviewer that all her writing has the same tone as the stories her mother used to tell about her childhood, and that her writing is an extension of her relationship with her mother.

After graduating from high school, Kennedy attended Ohio State University at Columbus. Columbus was Kennedy's first experience of the sort of overt racism that, at the time, was more characteristic of the Deep South than of her home in northern Ohio. Kennedy was deeply shocked by the behavior of the white girls in the dorm where thirteen black girls lived with nearly six hundred white girls, recalling vividly, decades later, the torment of not being spoken to or acknowledged by her closest neighbors.

A month after her graduation in 1953, she married Joseph Kennedy. While her husband served in the armed forces in Korea, Kennedy lived with her parents and continued the writing she had begun the previous year. By the time her son Joseph Jr. was born in 1955, Kennedy was sending her work to agents, but getting no offers. In 1959, after writing plays, novels, and short stories for seven years to no avail, she became discouraged and stopped.

In 1960, Joseph Kennedy Sr., by now a professor at New York City's Hunter College, won a grant to study in Africa. The young family traveled to Europe and then settled in Ghana. It was this journey that revived Adrienne Kennedy's interest in writing. Moreover, she now found her writing was noticeably different and better than before. She submitted a story to the literary magazine *Black Orpheus* and it was accepted and published. Her next project was the play *Funnyhouse of a Negro*, which she finished in Rome while waiting to give birth to her second son, Adam. It was produced in 1964 by Edward Albee's workshop at New York's Circle in the Square Theatre.

Funnyhouse of a Negro is a one-act play about Sarah, a biracial young woman. In the course of the play she interacts with splintered fragments of her own self, identified as Queen Victoria, the Duchess of Hapsburg, Patrice Lumumba, and a hunchbacked Jesus. Eventually, being unable to reconcile the conflicting parts of herself and unable to accept the black part of her heritage, she hangs herself. Much of the imagery is coarse and violent, and Kennedy seriously considered withdrawing it from production when she realized how much of her inner life she was exposing to the world. Yet, although *Funnyhouse* closed after 46 performances and was hated by many theatergoers and critics, it won an enthusiastic following in the theater community and received an Obie Award from the *Village Voice*.

The opportunity to have her work produced and the sense of having found her own voice gave Kennedy the impetus to write the series of short, surrealistic dramas that followed: *The Owl Answers*, *A Rat's Mass*, and *A Beast's Story*. These plays share the same basic technique: Kennedy's writing

ADRIENNE KENNEDY has won three Obie Awards for her plays and has taught drama and playwriting at Yale, Harvard, Brown, and the University of California at Berkeley. (Courtesy of Signature Theatre Company, New York, by permission of Adrienne Kennedy.)

several roles, but only one character, and abandoning linear narrative in favor of short bursts of emotion that lay bare the inner conflict of her protagonists.

Kennedy's later plays include *An Evening with Dead Essex*, *A Movie Star Has to Star in Black and White*, and *Orestes and Electra*. *People Who Led to My Plays* (1987) is a scrapbook-like memoir of her childhood and early adult life. *Deadly Triplets* (1990) is a juxtaposition of mystery novel and memoir about three years Kennedy spent in London. *The Alexander Plays* depicts a fictional writer recalling and reflecting on her plays and the events of her life.

Adrienne Kennedy has won three Obie Awards, as well as various grants and fellowships, and has taught drama and playwriting at Yale, Harvard, Brown, and the University of California at Berkeley.

BIBLIOGRAPHY

Betsko, Kathleen, and Rachele Koenig. *Interviews with Contemporary Women Playwrights*. New York: Beech Tree Books, 1987. Kennedy speaks extensively about her childhood, early adulthood, and the development of her work.

Feingold, Michael. "Blaxpressionism." *Village Voice*, 3 October 1995, 93. A review of two Kennedy plays and brilliant explication of her technique.

Jones, Lisa. "Beyond the Funnyhouse." *Village Voice*, 19 April 1996, 39–42. An interview in which Kennedy discusses the influences and experiential roots of her work.

Karis, Carolyn. "Adrienne Kennedy." *Notable Women in the American Theatre: A Biographical Dictionary*, edited by Alice M. Robinson, Vera Mowry Roberts and Milly S. Barranger. Westport, CT: Greenwood Press, 1989.

Kennedy, Adrienne. *The Adrienne Kennedy Reader*, with introduction by Werner Sollors. Minneapolis: University of Minnesota Press, 2001. A comprehensive collection of Kennedy's work, with an introduction that provides biographical data, context, and insightful analysis of Kennedy's work.

Kennedy, Adrienne. *People Who Led to My Plays*. New York: Knopf, 1987.

—ROBERT W. LOGAN

KENNEDY, FLORYNCE (b. 11 February 1916; d. 21 December 2000), attorney, activist. In her autobiography *Color Me Flo*, Florynce Rae Kennedy poked fun at herself for having "an acute case of word diarrhea." Not one to hold her tongue, Kennedy built a public career out of this condition, becoming a celebrity activist known for her sardonic political humor and biting social commentary.

Born in Kansas City, Missouri, the second of Wiley and Zella Kennedy's five daughters, "Flo" grew up in a two-parent household. Kennedy's mother was a stay-at-home mom before the Depression, but not the typical maternal figure. Both she and her husband made their children's lives uncommon. The Kennedy children were taught to value themselves and to give authority figures, black or white, only the respect they earned. The Kennedy girls were precious to, and protected by, a father who had no reservations about showing that he would back up what he said. On one occasion he confronted the Ku Klux Klan with his gun on the family's front porch. The Kennedy girls' school principal received similar treatment from their father as he gave the principal a lesson regarding the importance of their safety and sanctity. A former Pullman porter, Wiley Kennedy was a self-employed taxi driver who allowed the girls to drive his car, a rare source of social capital for teens from any working-class family in the 1930s. His indulgence and uncompromising protection characterized the Kennedy girls' socialization, an uncommon childhood which may have set the tone for Flo's societal defiance.

After graduating at the top of her class from Lincoln High School in Kansas City, Kennedy's adult life consisted of various jobs from owning a hat store to singing on the

FLO KENNEDY, feminist attorney and political activist, at a convention of the National Organization for Women (NOW) in New York City, 5 July 1991. Kennedy was a coauthor of *Abortion Rap*, which was published in 1976 and is one of the earliest books on this subject. (© Najlah Feanny/Corbis Saba.)

radio. However, all of Kennedy's stints of employment were a part of what she would later classify as "good times." Kennedy's "good times" had somber moments, as when her mother had a mastectomy in 1938, and Kennedy herself faced serious illness, hospitalization, and a near-death experience. By 1942 Kennedy's mother had died of cancer and Kennedy and her two oldest sisters moved to New York City.

Kennedy held both public and civic assignments during the first few years of her residence in Harlem before pursuing a pre-law major at Columbia University Undergraduate. When she decided to apply to Columbia Law School, Kennedy was refused admission based on her gender, not her race. She nonetheless graduated with a law degree from Columbia in 1951, the dean having been warned that "more cynical" civil rights activists might not have been able to appreciate the differences between race and sex discrimination.

From the beginning of her career as an attorney, similar shrewd and tactical pressures marked Kennedy's practice of negligence law. As a trial lawyer, Kennedy mocked judicious behavior and safe alliances. She represented the civil rights leader H. Rap Brown as well as the estates of the recording artists Billie Holiday and Charlie Parker. She married a Welsh science fiction writer in 1957, but he died not long after. A white colleague embezzled from her and then disappeared. She found it difficult to meet the rent on her law office. Struggling, she began to wonder whether law was really her field.

In 1967, while upstaging the other radicals at a Montreal antiwar convention, Kennedy serendipitously discovered an answer. She had called attention to herself by grabbing the microphone and protesting over Bobby Seale not being allowed to speak out about racism. Kennedy received an invitation to speak in Washington for a fee of $250 plus expenses. So began Kennedy's public career of poking fun at power. During the 1970s, Kennedy's satirical wit and quick tongue convinced her frequent lecture circuit partner, Gloria Steinem, that the latter must always speak first at their college campus engagements. Steinem confessed that she was definitely anticlimactic in the dreaded event that she had to follow Flo.

Kennedy's willingness to be dismissed or criticized because of her outrageous dress (she wore pink sunglasses and a cowboy hat as a sartorial expression of her unconventional personality) and unapologetic vulgarity made her both an easy target and a popular lecture circuit speaker. Her fifty years of political activism benefited poverty, feminist, and civil rights causes. Kennedy was also an advocate for prostitutes, ethnic minorities, and gay rights. Her convictions demonstrated an individual accountability and personal integrity. She lived a rebellious life shaped by doing what she described as "only as much as I was able to do in order to satisfy myself." She died at eighty-four years of age on a Thursday in her Manhattan apartment, 21 December 2000.

BIBLIOGRAPHY

Kennedy, Flo. *Color Me Flo: My Hard Life and Good Times*. Englewood Cliffs, NJ: Prentice-Hall, 1976. Autobiography featuring a personal memoir of her activism in several social revolutions.

Martin, Douglass. "Flo Kennedy, Feminist, Civil Rights Advocate and Flamboyant Gadfly, Dies at 84." *New York Times*, 23 December 2000. Published obituary and career overview.

Thompson, Kathleen. "Kennedy, Flo." In *Black Women in America: An Historical Encyclopedia*, edited by Darlene Clark Hine. Brooklyn: Carlson, 1993: 676–677.

—LaTrese Evette Adkins

KERSEE, JACKIE JOYNER. *See* Joyner-Kersee, Jackie.

KINCAID, JAMAICA (b. 25 May 1949), writer. Born Elaine Cynthia Potter Richardson in St John's, capital of the small Caribbean island of Antigua, Jamaica Kincaid was introduced to the reading public of the *New Yorker* magazine in the early 1970s through a series of short stories that would later be turned into Kincaid's first novel-length work. In fact, this pattern of first publishing each of her novels as magazine short stories was characteristic of her fictional works, as was her preoccupation with the themes of loss, dislocation, and the imbalance of power.

Kincaid grew up in a family of "poor, ordinary people," the oldest and only girl of four siblings. Her mother, Annie Richardson Drew, was a one-time political activist from neighboring Dominica. Taught to read early by a then-doting mother who nourished what became an insatiable passion for books, Kincaid was enrolled in school at age three. Unfortunately, as Kincaid later noted, her mother did not see fit to channel her twelve-year-old daughter's giftedness in more challenging and nurturing ways than by apprenticing her to a local seamstress. By that time, Kincaid's mother had married David Drew, a carpenter and the man from whom most of the father figures of Kincaid's often-autobiographical fiction are derived. Following the birth of her first half brother, Joseph Drew, Kincaid experienced a rather unusual adolescent separation from what she described in her early fiction as idyllic, blissful oneness, "a love affair," with her mother. The births in quick succession of two more half brothers, Dalma and Devon, heightened this estrangement and doomed the mother-daughter relationship for good. Dislike of her mother and her "mother's other children" became the basis for the pervasive mother-hatred in all her works except *A Small Place*.

Jamaica Kincaid speaking at Harvard in November 2001, soon after the terrorist attacks of September 11. The *Harvard University Gazette* quoted her as follows: "We can't handle the truth. . . . The truth is simply too much to bear." (Stephanie Mitchell/Harvard News Office. © President and Fellows of Harvard College.)

Separation and Change

Precociousness, adolescent rebellion, and bitterness at the lack of recognition Kincaid received from teachers and her own mother paved the way for an unusually difficult adolescence. An inner turmoil, held in check only by her passion for reading, gave way to rage at a perceived betraying mother, whose physical and psychological domination were not unlike the indoctrination of the colonial school system that demanded childlike devotion and unquestioning trust. The relentless gaze of an "Anglophile" mother, intent on raising a proper "Afro-Saxon" daughter who would not "behave in the manner of a slut" nor have "ten children by ten different men," merely hardened the adolescent Kincaid's resolve to assert her independence. On the verge of taking her "O levels" of the General Certificate of Education (GCE), which would, in effect, have made her eligible for an Island scholarship to attend university, Kincaid was suddenly pulled out of school by her mother. Vulnerable and powerless and, as she explained in *My Brother*, "always being asked to forego something or other that was essential (her education), to take care of these small children who were not mine," Kincaid agreed to her parents' plan to send her away to America shortly after her sixteenth birthday to work as an *au pair*. Her earnings were to help ease a family financial crisis caused by her stepfather's illness.

In June 1965, Kincaid left Antigua for New York, where she worked as a live-in nanny while studying for her GED. In 1969 she left Manhattan to attend Franconia College in New Hampshire on a full scholarship to study photography, instead of nursing as her now estranged mother had wished. After two unsuccessful years of college studies, Kincaid returned to Manhattan to a string of low-paying, unsatisfying jobs. Turning to freelance writing, she submitted several ideas to *Ingenue* to no avail until the idea to "ask Gloria Steinem what she was like when she was the age of the average reader of the magazine *Seventeen*" landed her an assignment and gave birth to the "When I Was Seventeen" series. From this initial success came assignments with *Ms.*, *Rolling Stone*, and the *Village Voice*.

Becoming Herself

Kincaid's outspokenness, brazen and dismissive to some critics, was rivaled only by her outlandish appearance: short-cropped, bleached blond hair, shaved eyebrows, vibrant red lipstick, gaudy and outmoded fashion, motorcycle boots, white pajamas, seersucker bathrobe and a tam-o'-shanter on a nearly six-foot-tall frame. All this, as she explained in "Putting Myself Together," was the result of her attempt at "the making of a type of person that did not exist in the place where I was born." This desire to invent a character that defied typecasting culminated in a name change in 1973. The pseudonym Jamaica Kincaid, she explained in a *New York Times Sunday Magazine* article, offered her "a way to do things without being the same (Elaine Cynthia Potter Richardson) person who couldn't do them—the same person who had all these weights." More likely, Jamaica Kincaid, a name evocative of the West Indies, offered her a way to keep her parents and a somewhat distant Antiguan community from knowing that she was writing, lest she be "laughed at" and accused of "putting on airs."

Kincaid made her debut on the New York literary scene in 1974 after a friend introduced her to William Shawn,

the *New Yorker* magazine's legendary editor-in-chief. Shawn hired Kincaid to contribute to the "Talk of the Town" column, which evolved into a distinctly Kincaidian specialty, eighty "quaint little stories in themselves," which together made up the collection *Talk Stories* (2002). Kincaid developed a lasting relationship with William Shawn, who hired her as a staff writer in 1976, the same year she met his son, the composer Allen Shawn. Kincaid and the younger Shawn married in 1979.

After the 1978 publication of two short stories, "Girl" and "Antigua Crossing," in the *New Yorker*, Jamaica Kincaid tried her hand at fiction by harvesting the stories she had published in various magazines between 1978 and 1982 into her first novel. *At the Bottom of the River* (1983), with its mélange of complex themes, styles, structure, and voices, represented Kincaid's search for her own voice. The book won the Morton Dauwen Zabel Award of the American Academy and Institute of the Arts and Letters and was nominated for the PEN/Faulkner Award.

Kincaid followed this success with *Annie John* (1983), her fictionalized account of growing up in Antigua. *Annie John* originated as a series of eight short stories in the *New Yorker*. It, too, met with favorable reviews and was one of three finalists for the Ritz Paris Hemingway Award. Although *At the Bottom of the River* launched Kincaid's fiction writing career, it is *Annie John*, with its clear prose and lyrical beauty, that established Kincaid's distinctive narrative voice. Both works are concerned with intense mother-daughter relationships and the precarious balance between power and powerlessness. Kincaid explored this latter theme more fully in *A Small Place*, a book-length essay written after her first visit to Antigua since her departure in 1966, and focused on the vestigial colonialism of the West and the shameless neocolonialism of the Antiguan elite.

If *Annie John* subtly hinted at Kincaid's social and political consciousness, *A Small Place* erupted in an unabashed, in-your-face activism that changed the public's perception of Kincaid as a writer and got her informally banned from the island, albeit temporarily. Although William Shawn had purchased and slated the book-length essay for publication in the *New Yorker*, Robert Gotleib, his successor, rejected it because of its unabated anger. Farrar, Straus and Giroux later published it in 1988, to much pointed criticism. *A Small Place* is not only a scathing indictment of Antigua's postindependence government, but also a vitriolic diatribe against the West—the United States in particular—for its complicity and collusion with the corrupt and oppressive neocolonial Antiguan government.

Two years later, Kincaid followed with yet another fictionalized autobiography, *Lucy* (1990), a sequel, it appears, to *Annie John*, though the innocent, childlike voice of Annie is replaced by that of the bitter but disengaged protagonist Lucy. In *Lucy*, Kincaid explored the theme of voluntary exile and migration. After a three-year hiatus, during which she suffered "something of a breakdown" following a bitter quarrel with her mother during the latter's 1990 visit to Vermont, Kincaid published the first three installments of her third novel, *The Autobiography of My Mother*, in the *New Yorker*. Prior to the book's publication as a novel in 1996, Kincaid resigned from the *New Yorker* after she quarreled with its editor, Tina Brown, for allegedly devaluing the magazine by inviting sitcom actress Roseanne Barr to guest-edit a special issue on women.

The Autobiography of My Mother combines real and imagined experiences from Kincaid's Dominican maternal grandparents with a fictionalized biography of her mother. Although considered her best work by some critics, this narrative of victimization, isolation, and the colonization of the female body is by far Kincaid's most controversial work. It suffered the most scathing criticism from those who wondered if the novel was not merely another outlet for venting the anger first unleashed in *A Small Place*. Despite mixed reviews, the book won the Cleveland Foundation's Anisfield-Wolf Award and the Fisk Fiction Award (*Boston Book Review*). It was a finalist for the PEN/Faulkner Award and was nominated for the National Book Critics Circle Award in fiction.

Disturbed by the illness and subsequent death from AIDS of Devon, her youngest stepbrother, Kincaid came out in 1997 with *My Brother*, another book-length essay of raw and complicated reflections on the difficult and complex relationship with her undisciplined family. *My Brother* chronicled the events and experiences of the frequent trips she had made to Antigua—the first in 1986, when she returned after a twenty-year absence, and several shorter ones to help care for Devon and deliver the supply of AZT, the AIDS drug that helped sustain him until his death in 1996. A tragic portrait of Devon, the book is as much about Kincaid's abiding resentment of her mother and Kincaid's contemplation of a scalded psyche and the life which would have been hers had she remained in Antigua, that "paradise [that] was death." *My Brother*, like *The Autobiography of My Mother*, was nominated for the National Book Award.

Later Work

Kincaid's passion for "growing things" yielded *My Garden Book* in 1999, a collection of previously published articles on gardening. It marked a departure in Kincaid's writing, from the heavily autobiographical to the historical. While the book showcased Kincaid's extensive knowledge of botany and her gardening experiences in her vast Vermont garden, the essays unmistakably form the metaphoric frame for exploring the thematic connections between gardening and conquest, empire, and colonialism.

Another later work, *Mr. Potter* (2002), is a story about a father and a daughter in which Kincaid returned to the pervading themes of alienation, loss, and anger. This could very well be described as a part of a loose autobiographical family series—a companion piece to *Annie*, *Lucy*, *The Autobiography of My Mother*, and *My Brother*. An indifferent, unsentimental, fictive yet vivid genealogy culled from Elaine Cynthia Potter's (alias Jamaica Kincaid's) father's "birth certificate, his death certificate and his father's birth certificate," *Mr. Potter* is an imagined history of Kincaid's biological father, an illiterate chauffeur who played no part in her life and about whom she knew nothing. Like its predecessors full of disillusionment, *Mr. Potter* tells the story of an illegitimate daughter, Elaine, who mourns a lifelong separation from her father but returns to Antigua after he dies to tell his story.

A consummate realist, brazen, and unafraid to "tell the truth," Kincaid fully established herself as one of America's foremost writers and literary stylists, known for her evocative, eloquent prose poetry, and chant-like style, with its lilting, syncopated rhythms, which defy easy categorization. Perhaps no single work charts her maturation as an accomplished writer better than *Talk Stories* (2000), a collection of seventy-seven of her short pieces, published in the *New Yorker* between 1978 and 1983 under the stewardship of William Shawn, her mentor and father-in-law, whom she adored and eulogized as "the perfect reader."

For all the criticism of the pervasive anger running through her *oeuvre*, only Kincaid could articulate what made her the stylist and visionary she became. Simply, in her words: "When I write I don't have any politics. I am political in the sense that I exist. When I write, I am concerned with the human condition as I know it."

BIBLIOGRAPHY

Balutansky, Kathleen M. "On Gardening." *Callaloo* 25.3 (2002): 790–800.

Bernard, Louise. "Countermemory and Return: Reclamation of the (Post-Modern) Self in Jamaica Kincaid's *The Autobiography of My Mother* and *My Brother*." *Modern Fiction Studies* 48.1 (Spring 2002): 113.

Bloom, Harold, ed. *Jamaica Kincaid*. Philadelphia: Chelsea House, 1998.

Covi, Giovanna. "Jamaica Kincaid and the Resistance to Canons." In *Out of the KUMBLA*, edited by Carole Boyce Davis, and Elaine Savory Fido. New Jersey: Africa World Press, 1987: 345–354.

Cudjoe, Selwyn R. "Jamaica Kincaid and the Modernist Project: An Interview." In *Callaloo* 12.2 (1989): 396–411. Also published in *Caribbean Women Writers: Essays from the First International Conference*, edited by Cudjoe Selwyn. Wellesley, MA: Calaloux, 1990.

Garis, Leslie. "Through West Indian Eyes." *New York Times Sunday Magazine*, 7 October 1990: 42.

Gauch, Suzanne. "*A Small Place*: Some Perspectives on the Ordinary." *Callaloo* 25.3 (2002): 910–919.

King, Jane. "A Small Place Writes Back." *Callaloo* 25.3 (2002): 885–910.

Lima, Maria Helena. "Imaginary Homelands in Jamaica Kincaid's Narratives of Development." *Callaloo* 25.3 (2002): 854–865.

Niesen de Abruna, Laura. "Dreams of Leaving: Mother and Mother Country in Jamaica Kincaid's Fiction." In *The Woman, the Writer and Caribbean Society: Essays on Literature and Culture*, edited by Helen Pyne-Timothy. Los Angeles: UCLA Center for American Studies, 1998: 164–175.

Paravisini-Gebert, Lizabeth. *Jamaica Kincaid: A Critical Companion.* Westport, CT: Greenwood Press, 1999.

Scott, Helen. "Dem Tief, Dem A Dam Tief: Jamaica Kincaid's Literature of Protest." *Callaloo* 25.3 (2002): 977–989.

Timothy-Pyne, Helen, ed. *The Woman, the Writer, and Caribbean Society: Essays on Literature and Culture.* Los Angeles: UCLA, 1997.

—PAMELA J. SMITH

KING, CORETTA SCOTT (b. 27 April 1927), activist, civil rights leader. The founding president of the Martin Luther King Jr. Center for Nonviolent Social Change in Atlanta, Georgia, Coretta Scott King emerged as an African American leader of national stature after the death in 1968 of her husband Martin Luther King Jr.

Born in Marion, Alabama, Coretta Scott spent her childhood on a farm owned by her parents, Obie Leonard Scott and Bernice McMurry Scott. By the early 1940s, her father's truck-farming business had become increasingly successful, prompting harassment from white neighbors. The family suspected that resentful whites may have been responsible for a 1942 fire that destroyed the Scott family's home. Hoping for better opportunities for their offspring, Obie and Bernice Scott encouraged their three children to excel in school. Coretta Scott graduated from Lincoln High School, a private black institution with an integrated faculty, and then followed her older sister Edyth to Antioch College in Ohio, where she received a BA in Music and Elementary Education. An accomplished musician and singer, Scott held her concert debut in 1948 in Springfield, Ohio, performing as a soloist with the Second Baptist Church.

Enrolling in 1951 at Boston's New England Conservatory of Music with a grant from the Jessie Smith Noyes Foundation, Scott developed her singing talent and eventually earned a MusB in voice and violin. While there, she also began dating Martin Luther King Jr., a doctoral candidate at Boston University's School of Theology. Despite the initial objections of King's parents, who wanted him to marry a woman from his hometown of Atlanta, the two were married at the Scott family home near Marion on 18 June 1953.

After moving to Montgomery, Alabama, where her husband became pastor of Dexter Avenue Baptist Church,

Coretta Scott King usually remained out of the public spotlight, raising the couple's four children: Yolanda Denise (b. 17 November 1955), Martin Luther III (b. 23 October 1957), Dexter Scott (b. 30 January 1961), and Bernice Albertine (b. 28 March 1963). Nonetheless, she worked closely with her husband and was involved in many of the major civil rights events of the 1950s and 1960s. In 1957, following the successful conclusion of the Montgomery bus boycott movement, she accompanied her husband on a trip to Ghana to mark that country's independence. In 1959, the Kings traveled to India, where Coretta King sang spirituals at events where her husband spoke. In 1960, after the family moved from Montgomery to Atlanta, she helped gain her husband's release from a Georgia prison by appealing to presidential candidate John F. Kennedy for his assistance. Kennedy's willingness

CORETTA SCOTT KING speaking at an antinuclear rally in New York City on 12 June 1982. After the assassination of her husband in 1968, she emerged as a national African American leader. (© Bettye Lane.)

to intervene to help the jailed civil rights leader contributed to the crucial support he received from African American voters in the 1960 election.

In 1962, Coretta King served as a voice instructor in the Music Department of Atlanta's Morris Brown College. During the same year, she also expressed her long-standing interest in disarmament efforts by serving as a Women's Strike for Peace delegate to the seventeen-nation Disarmament Conference held in Geneva, Switzerland. She also attended the 1964 ceremony in Oslo, Norway, where Dr. King was awarded the Nobel Peace Prize. In the mid-1960s, Coretta King's involvement in the civil rights movement increased as she participated in "freedom concerts," which consisted of poetry readings, singing, and lectures demonstrating the history of the civil rights movement. The proceeds from the concerts were donated to the Southern Christian Leadership Conference, headed by her husband. In February 1965, while Martin Luther King was jailed during voting rights protests in Alabama, she met with the black nationalist leader Malcolm X shortly before his assassination. The following year Coretta King participated in antiwar activities during the period before her husband took a public stand opposing the war in Vietnam.

After the assassination of her husband in Memphis on 4 April 1968, Coretta King devoted her life to actively propagating Martin Luther King's philosophy of nonviolence. Just a few days after the assassination, she led a march on behalf of sanitation workers in Memphis, substituting for her husband and, later that same month, she kept his speaking engagement at an anti–Vietnam War rally in New York. In May she also helped launch the Poor People's Campaign March on Washington, and thereafter participated in numerous antipoverty efforts. In addition, during 1969, she published her autobiography, *My Life with Martin Luther King, Jr.*

In 1969, Coretta King began mobilizing support for the Martin Luther King Jr. Center for Nonviolent Social Change (later known as the King Center). Her plans included an exhibition hall, a restoration of the King childhood home, an Institute for Afro-American Studies, a library containing King's papers, and a museum. As the founding president of the center, she guided the construction of its permanent home, located on Auburn Avenue next to Ebenezer Baptist Church, where Dr. King had served as co-pastor with his father. She served as the center's president and chief executive officer until her son Dexter succeeded her in 1995.

By the 1980s, Coretta King had become one of the most visible and influential African American leaders, often delivering speeches and writing nationally syndicated newspaper columns. In 1983, she led an effort that brought more than a half-million demonstrators to Washington, DC, to commemorate the twentieth anniversary of the 1963 March on Washington for Jobs and Freedom where Martin Luther King had delivered his famous "I Have a Dream" speech. She lent her support to various human rights and peace causes, including the campaign against racial barriers that had prevented African Americans from residing in Georgia's Forsyth County.

Also during the 1980s Coretta King reaffirmed her long-standing opposition to the apartheid system in South Africa. In 1985 she and three of her children were arrested during a series of protests at the South African embassy in Washington, DC. The following year, she traveled to South Africa to investigate apartheid. Several black opposition leaders criticized her plans to meet with President P. W. Botha and with Chief Buthelezi, who was viewed by many as an accommodationist. Consequently, King canceled her meetings and instead met with African National Congress leader Winnie Mandela. After her return to the United States, she met with President Ronald Reagan to urge him to support economic sanctions against South Africa. (Congress later overrode Reagan's veto of sanctions legislation.)

Perhaps the most notable achievement of Coretta King's public life was her participation in the successful effort to create a national holiday in honor of Martin Luther King Jr. After Congress passed legislation in 1983 authorizing the holiday, she was elected chairperson of the Martin Luther King Jr. Federal Holiday Commission, established to formalize plans for the annual celebrations that began in 1986. Also notable were Coretta King's speeches at London's St. Paul's Cathedral in 1969 and at Harvard University's Class Day exercises. She was the first woman to speak at each of these events. King has also been involved in various women's organizations such as the National Organization for Women, the Women's International League for Peace and Freedom, and United Church Women.

BIBLIOGRAPHY

Branch, Taylor. *Parting the Waters: America in the King Years: 1954–63.* New York: Simon and Schuster, 1988.

Hampton, Henry, and Steve Fayer. *Voices of Freedom: An Oral History of the Civil Rights Movement from the 1950s through the 1980s.* New York: Bantam, 1990.

King, Coretta Scott. *My Life with Martin Luther King, Jr.* New York: Holt, Rinehart and Winston, 1969.

Reddick, L. D. *Crusader without Violence: A Biography of Martin Luther King, Jr.* New York: Harper, 1959.

Vittoriano, Larry M. "Coretta Scott King: Keeping the Road to Freedom Clear." *Class,* February 1992.

—CLAYBORNE CARSON
—ANGELA D. BROWN

KITT, EARTHA (b. 17 January 1927), singer, dancer, actor, author, cabaret artist. Eartha Kitt began life in an impoverished family that quickly fell apart. By the time she was six she was picking cotton to earn her keep. By the time she was twenty-six, she had grown into the toast of the international nightlife circuit and a star on Broadway. Her stage persona is that of a gold digger, a slinky seductress, a feline presence with a wry sense of humor singing jaded laments about the pursuit of pleasure and wealthy men. There are also sultry interpretations of classic torch songs, ethnic songs from around the world, and a generous supply of comic numbers that poke fun at her image.

Eartha Mae Kitt was born the illegitimate daughter of sharecroppers in North, South Carolina. Her father disappeared when she was just a few years old and she lost her mother when she was six. For the next two years she lived with neighboring families. She was put to work in the cotton fields and cleaning houses until she went to live with an aunt in New York. Living in a Puerto Rican and Italian section of Spanish Harlem, Kitt picked up the languages she heard on the street. Left alone much of the time while her aunt worked as a domestic, she created a dream world centered on her love of singing and dancing.

Kitt excelled at school and won admittance to New York's prestigious Metropolitan High School (later the High School of the Performing Arts). However, she dropped out of school when she was fourteen to work sewing army uniforms in a Brooklyn factory, saving as much money as she could for piano lessons. At the age of sixteen Kitt auditioned for and won a scholarship with Katharine Dunham's dance company. Dunham picked her to join the troupe that toured the United States, Mexico, South America, and Europe. She eventually became one of the group's solo dancers, and when the company returned to the United States in 1949, she elected to stay in Paris.

Performing at Carroll's nightclub, Kitt became a sensation and was dubbed "the rage of Paris." Her success at Carroll's was followed by similar acclaim at the Kervansery in Istanbul and Churchill's in London. In 1951, Orson Welles, who called Kitt "the most exciting woman in the world," cast her as Helen of Troy in his production of *Faust*. Given only two days to learn the role, she crafted a performance that became a critical and popular triumph.

After appearing in two French films, Kitt returned to New York where she appeared at Max Gordon's Village Vanguard in 1952, packing the club for 25 weeks. It was there that she was seen by producer Leonard Sillman, who cast her in his revue *New Faces of 1952*. The show was a hit and established Kitt as a star. Through much of

EARTHA KITT performing in "Val Parnell's Sunday Night at the London Palladium." The singer, dancer, actor, author, and cabaret artist developed—and has sometimes herself poked fun at—a sultry, feline stage persona. (Photofest.)

the run she also appeared at the Blue Angel nightclub on East 54th Street, where she broke the all-time attendance record.

Throughout the 1950s and much of the 1960s, Kitt's life was a whirlwind of television and nightclub engagements, recording sessions, and appearances in movies and on Broadway. In 1954, Kitt starred in the Broadway production of the drama *Mrs. Patterson*, by Charles Sebree and Greer Johnson, with songs written especially for her. She played the fifteen-year-old daughter of a laundress in Kentucky who lives in a dream world based on the lives of white people she observes. In *Shinbone Alley*, the musical dramatization of Don Marquis' *archy and mehitabel*, she played mehitabel, the alley cat who believes that she was Cleopatra in a former life. In films, Kitt starred in *St. Louis Blues*, opposite Nat King Cole and Ruby Dee, and *Anna Lucasta* with Sammy Davis Jr. *Eartha Kitt In Person at the Plaza*, recorded in 1965, documents an exuberant entertainer, singing in English, Tagalog, French, Japanese and Yiddish and obviously enjoying herself as she teases, flirts with, and ultimately conquers her audience.

Kitt had a well-publicized romance with movie theater heir Arthur Loew Jr. and dated Sammy Davis Jr., Charles Revson (the founder of Revlon) and the Dominican diplomat and sportsman, Porfirio Rubirosa. In 1960 she married the real estate dealer, Bill McDonald. The couple had one daughter, Kitt, before they divorced.

In January 1968 Kitt was honored at a White House luncheon for "Women Doers," hosted by the first lady, Lady Bird Johnson. The topic for discussion was juvenile delinquency, but Kitt spoke critically about the war in Vietnam and its effect on black communities, from which a disproportionate number of draftees were drawn. The repercussions were both immediate and long-lasting. The limousine which had brought Kitt to the White House mysteriously disappeared, leaving her to hail a cab, over whose radio she heard a report denouncing her for making Mrs. Johnson cry. It was nearly ten years before she was able to work regularly in this country again. In the meantime she was investigated by the CIA, whose dossier labeled her a "sadistic nymphomaniac."

In 1978 Eartha Kitt returned to the Broadway stage in the musical *Timbuktu!*, based on the 1950s musical *Kismet*. When the show played in Washington, President Jimmy Carter made a point of inviting her to return to the White House. A series of disco recordings, made with producer Jacques Morali, relaunched her recording career.

Well into her sixth decade of performing, Eartha Kitt shows no signs of slowing down. Her 1996 album, *Back in Business*, a collection of thoughtful renditions of standards, finds her in excellent voice. She has become a frequent presence in children's movies, including *Harriet the Spy* (1996), *The Emperor's New Groove* (2000), and *Holes* (2003). In 2001 she played the Fairy Godmother in the national tour of the musical *Cinderella*, and she appeared on Broadway in the musical *Nine* in 2003. She is the author of three autobiographies and *Rejuvenate! It's Never Too Late* (2001), a book about staying healthy at any age. Her career is managed by her daughter Kit Shapiro.

BIBLIOGRAPHY

Bogle, Donald. *Brown Sugar: Eighty Years of America's Black Female Superstars*. New York: Harmony Books, 1980.

Brennan, Carol. "Eartha Kitt." *Contemporary Black Biography: Profiles from the International Black Community, Volume 16*, edited by Shirelle Phelps. Detroit: Gale Research, 1998.

Candee, Marjorie Dent, ed. *Current Biography Yearbook 1955*. New York: The H. W. Wilson Company, 1955.

Gill, Glenda E. "Eartha Kitt." *Notable Black American Women*, edited by Jessie Carney Smith. Detroit: Gale Research, Inc., 1992.

Internet Broadway Database (http://www.ibdb.com).

Kitt, Eartha. *Alone With Me*. Chicago: Henry Regnery Company, 1976.

Kitt, Eartha. *Confessions of a Sex Kitten*. London: Sidgwick & Jackson, Limited, 1989.

Patner, Andrew. "Whatever Audience Wants . . ." *Chicago Sun-Times*, 4 April 1999.

Ranaldo, Ronald M. "Eartha Kitt." *Black Women in America: An Historical Encyclopedia*, edited by Darlene Clark Hine, Elsa Barkley Brown, and Rosalyn Terborg-Penn. Brooklyn, NY: Carlson Publishing Company, 1993.

—ROBERT W. LOGAN

KITTRELL, FLEMMIE PANSY (b. 25 December 1904; d. 1980), home economics pioneer. Dr. Flemmie Kittrell was the first African American woman to receive high honors in the general field of home economics and science, a term which she put into use and which encompasses nutrition, child development, and related sciences. She was the first African American to receive a doctorate from Cornell University; she accomplished this in the 1920s, when few black women went on to receive advanced degrees. She received her PhD with honors, and there is a home sciences building on the Cornell campus named for her. Her accomplishments were noted not just because of her academic excellence, but because she was instrumental in the actual building of the structure. Further, her ideas added to the development of the new home sciences curriculum. Kittrell traveled down paths that even few white women would have considered at the time. More than just her scholarship distinguished her; she had the daring to travel to many underdeveloped countries. Indeed, a significant portion of her life was devoted to teaching and research programs in these countries.

Kittrell came from a family that emphasized learning, creativity, and perseverance. All of these factors were keys to her ability to accomplish her dreams. She was born into a large family, the seventh of nine children. Her family lived in North Carolina, and from all accounts they were a close-knit group. Both of her parents were descendants of Cherokee Indians and African Americans. According to Kittrell, it was her family that praised her efforts, encouraged her to act on her ideas, and challenged her to set high goals.

Flemmie Kittrell attended public schools in Vance County, North Carolina. After high school graduation, she attended Hampton Institute. She received a BA in science in 1928. Although she was at first reluctant, her instructors convinced her that her abilities warranted further education. She enrolled at Cornell University and received an MA in 1930 and PhD in 1938. Kittrell's positive experiences in college motivated her to become a strong advocate of higher education for all black women.

Kittrell began her career as a home economics instructor in 1928 at Bennett College in North Carolina. She taught for several years while working on her doctoral degree. In both teaching and curriculum development, she instituted many innovative additions to the Bennett program. Her ideas transcended the traditional home economics model and natural and social sciences, emphasizing research. Eventually, at the personal invitation of the school's president, Kittrell was offered the position of head of the home economics program at Howard University.

As Kittrell's reputation spread, her travel and research increased. In 1947, she went to Liberia to conduct research on nutrition and its relationship to general living conditions. The results were published in a booklet, "Preliminary Food and Nutrition Survey of Liberia," which exposed the deleterious effect of what she called "hidden hunger." She made short- and long-range proposals to the Liberian government to remedy these nutritional deficiencies and was honored by the country for her work.

As a result of her work in Liberia, Kittrell was invited in 1950 to do nutritional research in India. She worked primarily with Baroda University and helped develop a food and nutritional research program. Kittrell returned to India in 1953 to conduct seminars in food and nutrition, meal planning, child feeding, and to give home economics lectures.

In 1957, under the auspices of the Department of State, Kittrell traveled to Japan and Hawaii to do similar studies in home economics. Following these educational excursions, she made three tours of West and Central Africa, always learning while she taught and stretching her knowledge. Back in the United States, she was instrumental in the promotion of a child development program within the home economics curriculum. She had a special interest in children and was convinced of the importance of enhancing the home environment for their maximum development. Kittrell officially retired from teaching in 1972. However, she continued to work as a fellow on numerous projects.

Kittrell was a visionary in her field, and as such she received numerous awards and distinctions. Hampton University selected her as the outstanding alumna of 1955; the National Council of Negro Women presented her with a scroll of honor; the University of North Carolina conferred on her an honorary degree, and the American Home Economics Association established an international scholarship in her honor. Over the years, Kittrell was also the recipient of several Fulbright awards for study and lecturing.

Flemmie Kittrell was a strong but modest person. She attributed much of her success to the influence of early family experiences, to the attention, love, and encouragement of her family. In her lifetime, she laid the groundwork for other black women to work toward the highest level they could achieve.

BIBLIOGRAPHY

Kessler, James H., et al. *Distinguished African American Scientists of the 20th Century*. Phoenix, AZ: Oryx Press, 1996.

Krapp, Kristin, ed. *Notable Black American Scientists*. Detroit, MI: Gale Group, 1999.

Newsome, Virginia J. "Flemmie Kittrell." *Notable Black American Women*, Vol. 1, edited by Jessie Carney Smith. Detroit, MI: Gale Research, 1992.

Warren, Wini. *Black Women Scientists in the United States*. Bloomington: Indiana University Press, 2000.

—DIANE EPSTEIN

KNIGHT, GLADYS (b. 28 May 1944), rhythm and blues singer. Gladys Knight, widely recognized as a legendary R&B singer, has received numerous noteworthy awards. She was inducted into the Rock and Roll Hall of Fame in 1996 and the Vocal Group Hall of Fame in 2001. She has six gold singles, a gold album, and a platinum album. She has won five Grammy awards, including two in 1973. Other awards she earned include the Clio Award in 1972 and 1982, the Society of Arts Academy Honor for musical distinction, the Soul Train Heritage Award in 1988, the NAACP Image Award, the Rhythm and Blues Foundation Lifetime Achievement Award, and the American Music Award (with the Pips) in 1984 and 1988. She has also received a Congress of Racial Equality Creative Achievement Award, an honorary doctorate degree from Shaw University, and the B'nai B'rith International Humanitarian Award. She is an honorary member of the Alpha Kappa Alpha sorority.

Knight entered the mainstream soul music culture with her 1967 hit with the Pips, "I Heard It through the Grapevine." By the early twenty-first century, she had produced twenty-eight albums with the Pips, thirteen compilation albums, and six as a solo artist. Her life and contributions have been featured in magazines such as *Jet, Ebony, Essence, Rolling Stone*, and *Billboard*. The most detailed account of her life comes from her autobiography, *Between Each Line of Pain and Glory: My Life Story*, published in 1997.

Gladys Maria Knight was born in Atlanta, Georgia, to Merald Knight Sr. and Sarah Elizabeth Woods Knight. Her father was one of Atlanta's first black post office employees. During the era of Jim Crow segregation, being a postal worker was a well-respected vocation in the African American community. Her mother was a nurse's aide who instilled religious values in her children. Her parents, singers in the Wings over Jordan gospel group, valued education, and gospel music was at the center of their family life. Knight explained her upbringing: "We were expected to develop our gifts and to follow our dreams, as many of us strived to live up to those expectations," which came from not only her parents but also the people in her community. In 1948 Knight began singing in her church choir at Mount Moriah Baptist Church and had her first recital there at the age of four. As a youngster, from 1950 until 1953, she also

GLADYS KNIGHT AND THE PIPS. Knight, who is recognized as a legendary rhythm and blues singer, was inducted into the Rock and Roll Hall of Fame in 1996 and into the Vocal Group Hall of Fame in 2001. (Photofest.)

toured with the Morris Brown Choir. In 1952 she gained national exposure by winning first place on the popular television show *Ted Mack's Original Amateur Hour*. Though she was gaining exposure, she remained grounded in her community, often singing at church and social functions with her brother Merald "Bubba," her sister Brenda, and her cousins Eleanor and William Guest. In 1957 they turned professional and another cousin, James "Pip" Wood, became their manager and gave his nickname to the entire group. The group changed form in 1959 when

Eleanor and Brenda left the group to get married. They were replaced by cousins Edward Patten and Langston George, who left the group in 1962.

Gladys Knight recounted in her autobiography, "My sixteenth year was a major one. All sorts of firsts occurred: my first record, my first song on the charts, and my first romance." She graduated from Archer High School in 1960 and married James "Jimmy" Newman. She had two children by Newman, James in 1962 and Kenya in 1963. In 1961 Gladys Knight and the Pips produced their first rhythm and blues Top-20 hit with a version of Johnny Otis's "Every Beat of My Heart." During the latter part of the 1960s, several of their singles would reach the Top 40. Her group signed with Motown's subsidiary, Soul, in 1965. The group teamed up with the songwriter-producer Norman Whitfield in the spring of 1967. They had several hits, including "I Heard It through the Grapevine" (1967), "The

Nitty Gritty" (1968), "Friendship Train" (1969), and "If I Were Your Woman," which became one of Motown's biggest-selling releases in 1970. "Neither One of Us (Wants to Be the First to Say Good-bye)" would follow in 1973. That same year, they changed labels. Knight believed Motown gave preferential treatment to Detroit-based acts and limited the Pips' potential for mainstream success by promoting them as an R&B group.

Their first album released with Buddah Records was *Imagination*, their biggest-selling album to that point. Not only did the album go gold, but it also produced three gold singles: "Midnight Train to Georgia" (number 1 in 1973), "I've Got to Use My Imagination" (number 4 in 1974), and "Best Thing That Ever Happened to Me" (number 3 in 1974). Knight eventually divorced Newman and married Barry Hankerson in October 1974. Awards and three more Top-10 singles followed, and in 1975 the group had its own TV variety show. However, Knight's film debut, *Pipe Dreams*, was a disappointment at the box office in 1976.

By 1979 she and Hankerson had divorced but had one son, Shanga Ali, from their marriage. In 1986 she produced and starred in *Sisters in the Name of Love*, an HBO special costarring Patti LaBelle and Dionne Warwick, which received a Cable Ace Award. That same year, she proved her acting ability when she costarred with Flip Wilson in the CBS comedy *Charlie & Co*. Still, Gladys Knight and the Pips kept working as a group, and "Love Overboard" took them into the Top 20 again in 1988. In 1989 Knight debuted as a solo artist and recorded the theme song for the James Bond movie *License to Kill*.

Knight was still disturbed about the segregation of pop and R&B music on radio. "I take it as an insult to my intelligence when anyone tries to tell me that race is not a factor in the music business," she said. "I have been performing for fifty years, yet my records still have to go through the R&B Top 10 in order for it to cross over to pop radio and even be heard."

In 1991 the Pips agreed to disband, but Knight had no intention of stepping out of the spotlight. Three years later, her album *Just for You* earned two Grammy nominations.

Other acting roles followed on *Benson*, *The Jeffersons*, in addition to a recurring role in *New York Undercover*, and in such films as *An Enemy among Us* and *Desperado*. In 1995 Knight earned a star on the Hollywood Walk of Fame. She married Les Brown in 1995, and they were divorced in 1997. Gladys Knight and the Pips were inducted into the Rock and Roll Hall of Fame in a ceremony on 17 January 1996. Knight reminded the audience that she had spent forty-three years with the Pips and had worked closely with nine different record companies. In 1998 her mother died of type 2 diabetes. The following year, her son and manager, Jimmy, died. Her daughter, Kenya, became her new manager and was still performing the role in the early twenty-first century. In 1999 Gladys Knight completed a starring run on Broadway in the musical hit *Smokey Joe's Cafe*.

Gladys Knight is co-owner of the popular Gladys Knight and Ron Winan's Chicken & Waffles restaurant in Atlanta, Georgia, of which her youngest son, Shanga Ali, is manager. Knight, with Abe Ogden, wrote a cookbook in 2001 for diabetics, *At Home with Gladys Knight: Her Personal Recipe for Living Well, Eating Right, and Loving Life*. On 12 April 2001 Gladys Knight married William McDowell, a business executive. In 2004 she was the headliner for the Flamingo Hotel in Las Vegas. Gladys Knight's emotionally powerful, soulful singing voice has continued to earn her fans well into the early twenty-first century.

See also **Rock and Roll**.

BIBLIOGRAPHY

"Cover Story: Gladys Knight." *Jet*, 3 March 2003, 58–64.
"Gladys Knight Talks about *At Last*, Her First Album in Six Years, and Why She's Not a 'Diva.'" *Jet*, 5 March 2001, 58–63.
Grammy Awards. "Gladys Knight." http://www.grammy.com/awards/search/index.aspx.
Kinnon, Joy Bennett. "Top Weddings of the Year." *Ebony*, February 2002, 104–111.
Knight, Gladys. *Between Each Line of Pain and Glory: My Life Story*. New York: Hyperion, 1997.
Mazur, Marcia Levine. "Gladys Knight: Lessons from My Mother." *Diabetes Forecast*, August 2001, 78–83.
Rock and Roll Hall of Fame. "Gladys Knight and the Pips." http://www.rockhall.com/hof/inductee.asp?id=139.

—MARSHANDA SMITH

L

LABELLE, PATTI (b. 24 May 1944), singer, author, and actor. Patti LaBelle, Grammy-winner, best-selling author, women's shoe and fragrance designer, and self-help guru is a bona fide diva. Her five-octave voice is passionate and compelling, and, after more than forty years in the business, shows no signs of becoming tame.

Patti LaBelle was born Patricia (Patsy) Louise Holte in Philadelphia, Pennsylvania. Her parents were Bertha Lee Robinson and Henry Holte Jr. LaBelle's mother had two children by a previous relationship: her brother Thomas and her sister Vivian were fourteen and twelve years, respectively, her senior. In addition to Patti, Bertha and Henry had two other daughters, Barbara (two years older than Patti) and Jackie (one year younger).

A very shy young girl (so shy, in fact, that she once wet her pants in elementary school rather than raise her hand to ask for permission to go to the bathroom), she first began singing in front of the mirror and later in the Young Adults Choir at Beulah Baptist Church in Philadelphia under the direction and encouragement of Harriett Chapman, the church organist and choir director. LaBelle's older brother Thomas introduced her to the music of Gloria Lynne, Dakota Staton, Dinah Washington, and Sarah Vaughan, music that made a tremendous impression on her. She was hooked on the music by junior high school and knew she wanted to be a singer.

LaBelle was raised in the Elmwood neighborhood of Philadelphia; hence the first singing group she was a part of was called the Elmtones, which after a period of practicing had but one public performance. The next singing group she belonged to was the Ordettes, a name closely resembling that of the group's first performance venue, the Orchid Ballroom. LaBelle was still attending John Bartram High School when the group formed. She withdrew from high school one semester shy of graduating to focus instead on the rigorous, disciplined, and frequent practice sessions and performances of the musical group. The decision to drop out of school haunted LaBelle for years, so much so that twenty years later she returned to Bartram High School to complete her work and receive her high school diploma.

The demanding rehearsal and practice schedule took its toll on the original Ordettes, who were managed by Bernard Montague with support from his wife Mary. One by one, the three other members fell away, leaving only LaBelle. They were eventually replaced by three young women from New Jersey: Nona Hendryx, Sarah Dash, and Cindy Birdsong (who later joined the Supremes in 1967). On 8 April 1962, the group signed its first recording contract with the Bluebelle Record Company. As a result, the group changed its name to the Bluebelles. A short while later, at the age of eighteen, Patsy Holte became known as Patti LaBelle. For most of the next decade, Patti LaBelle and the Bluebelles were a popular and hit-making singing

PATTI LABELLE, singer, author, and actress, is a genuine diva with a passionate, compelling voice and a five-octave range. Her career has spanned more than forty years. (Photofest; photograph by Marc Raboy.)

group, performing all over the country. By the end of the 1960s, however, the group's popularity had begun to wane. The music scene in America had radically changed as a result of the influence of the Beatles, the impact of the civil rights movement, and social unrest due principally to the opposition to the Vietnam War.

The decade of the 1970s brought dramatic changes for the group. Their new manager, Vicki Wickham, a British television producer, insisted that the group embrace the times and perform a more politically charged and radical style of music. The group changed its name to LaBelle in 1970 and burst on the scene provocatively dressed in leather, feathers, and glitter, singing disco anthems of progressive funk and rock. "Lady Marmalade," a widely played song, was a number-one hit for LaBelle in 1974. That same year, they performed at the Metropolitan Opera on 6 October—the first time a black vocal group had appeared in that venue. The group disbanded in 1976, however, as a result of artistic and personal differences.

In the early twenty-first century, Patti LaBelle continued to successfully record and perform before enthusiastic full houses as a solo artist. She was nominated for eight Grammy Awards and won a Grammy in 1992 for Best Rhythm and Blues Vocal Performance/Female for the album *Burnin.* She also is an accomplished actor with three Emmy nominations, having appeared in film (*A Soldier's Story, Beverly Hills Cop*), on Broadway (*Your Arms Too Short to Box with God* and *Patti LaBelle on Broadway*), and on television (*A Different World*). She also has had her own television special and starred in the television series *Out All Night* (NBC). In addition, she received seven NAACP Image Awards and was awarded an honorary doctorate in 1996 from the Berklee College of Music in Boston.

LaBelle wrote four books, all with Laura B. Randolph. The first, a *New York Times* best-seller, *Don't Block the Blessings: Revelations of a Lifetime,* is her autobiography. The others are *LaBelle Cuisine: Recipes to Sing About; Patti's Pearls: Lessons in Living Genuinely, Joyfully, Generously;* and finally *Patti LaBelle's Lite Cuisine.* In 1995, LaBelle had a Flory Roberts cosmetic line on the market. She also had a shoe collection for Sears in 2001.

In 1969, LaBelle married Armstead Edwards, a man she had known since her school days. They have one son, Zuri, born on 17 July 1973. In addition, they unofficially adopted two other boys, Dodd and Stanley Stocker-Edwards. The marriage ended after thirty-one years. Patti LaBelle has had a long and distinguished career, yet she never believed that she would live to be fifty years old. Each of her three sisters died from cancer at a young age, with only one reaching the age of forty-four. However, after five decades in the public eye, Patti LaBelle is more than a survivor; she is an inspiration.

BIBLIOGRAPHY

Byrd, Kenya N. "Patti Drops Her Pearls." *Black Issues Book Review,* November 2001.

Clarke, Donald, ed. *The Penguin Encyclopedia of Popular Music.* New York: Penguin, 1990.

Clifford, Mike, consultant. *The Illustrated Encyclopedia of Black Music.* New York: Harmony, 1982.

Ebert, Alan. "Girlfriend: A Down-Home Diva!" *Essence,* March 1991.

Edwards, Audrey, and Karen Thomas. "Patti LaBelle." *Essence,* May 1998.

LaBelle, Patti, and Laura Randolph-Lancaster. *Patti LaBelle's Lite Cuisine.* New York: Gotham, 2003.

LaBelle, Patti, with Laura B. Randolph. *LaBelle Cuisine: Recipes to Sing About.* New York: Broadway, 1999.

LaBelle, Patti, with Laura Randolph. *Don't Block the Blessings: Revelations of a Lifetime.* New York: Riverhead, 1996.

LaBelle, Patti, with Laura Randolph-Lancaster. *Patti's Pearls: Lessons in Living Genuinely, Joyfully, Generously.* New York: Warner, 2001.

Moritz, Charles, ed. *Current Biography Yearbook 1986.* New York: Wilson, 1986.

Reynolds, J. R. "Patti LaBelle Sparks a Flame." *Billboard,* May 1997.

Smart-Grosvenor, Vertamae. "Patti!" *Essence,* October 1985.

                                                            —LAWRENCE J. SIMPSON

LABOR MOVEMENT. Since their first arrival aboard a Dutch ship at the shores of Jamestown in 1619, African American women have resisted exploitation even as they have struggled to control the terms and conditions of their labor. While indentured servants and slaves, black women engaged in work slowdowns to protest their treatment; once emancipated, freedwomen employed strikes and boycotts to assert their demands. Yet although already doubly exploited by gender and racial discrimination, African American women in the United States have also faced bias from an organized labor movement dominated by white men focused on organizing the industrial sector. Shut out of better-paying industrial jobs until the mid-twentieth century, most black women were forced to work as domestics and agricultural laborers. Thus, until recently, the history of black women and the labor movement has been a story of resistance that was organized and supported as often by short-lived black-led collective actions as it was by integrated national unions.

Early History

While the first black women came to America as indentured servants, by the mid-seventeenth century slavery had replaced indentured servitude in the colonies. In the North, where with few exceptions the small slave population was urban, both slave and free black women worked as domestics, with a limited number of free women working in such trades as spinning and dressmaking. Unlike the industrializing North, however, slave labor was not incidental but rather integral to the South's agricultural economy. Therefore, slave women in the South worked

LABOR PICKETERS, c. 1979–1980. These black workers were striking the Memphis Furniture Company, which tried to break their union. The photograph—by Larry Coyne for *Press-Scimitar*—appears in Michael Keith Honey's oral history *Black Workers Remember*, published in 2000. (University of Memphis, Mississippi Valley Collection.)

not only in city households and on small farms, but also on plantations with slave populations numbering in the hundreds. Plantation work included such domestic labor as cooking, housekeeping, and childcare. Most often, however, women labored in the fields, working alongside men planting and harvesting tobacco, rice, and cotton.

Even while working within an inhumane labor system, slaves attempted to control their labor. One way slave women shaped the terms of their work was through task labor. Unlike the gang system where slaves worked from sunup to sundown, the task system, most often used in the cultivation of rice, assigned work by chore or task. With a daily task completed, slave women worked within their own homes, permitting them a limited measure of autonomy. Both field laborers and house workers sought to control their labor by other means as well. Resisting their bondage through collective actions such as work slowdowns and individual acts such as sabotage of crops and theft of equipment, slaves contested their exploitation, even when such protests yielded limited results.

While the vast majority of antebellum African American women performed agricultural or domestic work, a pattern that would continue long after emancipation, a small number of slaves were rented out by their owners to southern industries. The treatment of slaves in industry, where they were frequently used as strike breakers, mirrored the brutality of plantation farming. Cotton and wool mills, food and tobacco processors, and even canal and railroad builders relied on female slaves who were often underfed, poorly clothed, and forced to work twelve- to sixteen-hour days, sometimes seven days a week. Slaves were viewed as chattel by business owners at the same time that white workers in both the North and the South viewed them as a threat to their wages and job security. This was a sentiment black women would encounter time and again from organized labor as they attempted to establish themselves in American industry following emancipation.

The value of slave women's labor was not limited to their productive capacity in the field, plantation household, and factory. Indeed, enslaved women were, as Adrienne Davis points out, "both a mode of production and a mode of reproduction." Owners looked to slave women to reproduce the labor force, both increasing their profits and perpetuating the institution of slavery. Sexual availability of slaves was taken for granted by many owners and overseers and sanctioned by laws that gave slaveholders full authority over the bodies of their property. Such beliefs about the availability of black women's bodies followed them into the workplace after their legal emancipation. By the eve of emancipation, assumptions about the role of African American women in the labor market had been firmly established.

Free Labor

Upon emancipation, expectations about the labor of freedwomen became a battleground between southern black families and both northern and southern white society. While the Victorian middle-class ideal placed white women in the private sphere of the home, freedwomen's attempts to engage in full-time domesticity laboring for their own families were met with considerable hostility. Eager to reunite the nation and its markets, northern leaders saw in freed black women a cheap labor source whose work in southern fields supported northern manufacturers such as textile mills. Southern leaders also expected freedwomen to labor outside their homes to help to rebuild the southern agricultural economy. Just as important, many southerners looked to African American women's labor to maintain a social barrier between black and white women. With freedmen earning far less than white laborers, often for the same work, African American women were forced into the wage labor market to support their families. Therefore, following emancipation black married women established a precedent of working outside their homes in larger percentages than their white working-class counterparts, a pattern that continued until the 1990s.

Choices for employment for African American women remained largely limited to physically demanding agricultural and domestic work. In both of these occupations,

workers encountered difficult barriers to organizing. Black women performing domestic work in private homes as cooks, maids, child-nurses, and laundresses remained isolated from one another, making union organizing nearly impossible. Long hours, including twelve- to sixteen-hour days, and close supervision by their employers further discouraged unionizing efforts. Yet poor pay and long hours were not the only workplace issues facing domestics. The threat of physical abuse by employers, including sexual assault, remained a concern of freedwomen and their families. Efforts to escape the close scrutiny of white employers led African American domestics to seek work in hotels and as laundresses working from their own homes.

"Taking in" laundry allowed black women to work within the autonomy of their homes while building and maintaining community networks. It also allowed for association with other workers in the community, the first step in organizing collective actions. As Tera Hunter writes, between 1866 and 1881 southern washerwomen organized mass labor protests in an attempt to set the terms of their labor. Workers in Jackson, Galveston, and Atlanta struck for the right to determine their wage rates. Parading through the cities, the striking women not only withheld their labor but also attempted to prevent nonstriking white laundresses from undermining their efforts by crossing picket lines. The most dramatic of these uprisings was the Atlanta strike, where on 19 July 1881, the city's newly formed Washing Society demanded the right to set their prices at a uniform rate. Eventually numbering several thousand striking women and supporters, the strike encouraged laundresses, cooks, maids, and nurses to join in what threatened to become a general strike. Newspaper coverage of the strike suggests African American workingwomen in the Reconstruction South recognized the importance of organizing, even if their actions were short-lived and local. Machine-run steam laundries eventually replaced southern washerwomen, forcing African American women into industrial settings. Yet, these strikes proved the first of many attempts by black workers to organize their ranks and improve their wages and working conditions.

Like domestics, agricultural workers in the Reconstruction-era South struggled to establish control of their labor; and like domestic work, the isolation experienced in tenant farming hindered collective action. Under the sharecropping system, freedmen and women worked on former plantations, farming the land in return for a percentage of its yield. Landowners supplied the tools and seed needed for cultivation, subtracting their costs along with housing expenses at the end of the growing season. Many owners took advantage of the system, keeping farmers in debt by overcharging them for basic needs and claiming nearly all of their production. By keeping land ownership in the hands of whites, and allowing them to set housing rental rates as well as the rates paid for crops, sharecropping significantly limited the opportunity for black families to achieve self-sufficiency.

Yet, as Jacqueline Jones writes, sharecropping also offered black women's opportunities and protections not enjoyed by domestics living in the homes of their employers. By living on the land they worked, mothers of sharecropping families were better able to balance the demands of field and housework. Sharecropping also kept African American women out of the homes of whites, eliminating black families' fears about physical and sexual exploitation. Finally, the ability of black families to labor away from the close scrutiny of white supervision helped to blunt the effects of the often harsh and unfair labor practices of white landowners. Only with the passage of New Deal labor legislation did southern tenant farmers find the government and community support necessary to establish unions to fight the exploitative practices of white southern landowners.

By the late nineteenth century, black workers were still largely excluded from the labor movement in spite of notable attempts at both integrating white industrial unions and at forming their own unions. Organizations such as the Colored National Labor Union, founded in 1869 by workers not included in the all-white National Labor Union, proved no match for the forces arrayed against them. Although the small northern black population faced discrimination in the labor market, it could not compare with the violent southern hostility to the labor movement. Attempts by both northern and southern Blacks to integrate such organizations as the Knights of Labor also failed when, despite its rhetorical commitment to integration, the Knights continued to segregate many of its local chapters. The decline of the Knights in the late 1890s and the rise of the American Federation of Labor (AFL), which had little interest in either black or female workers, presaged continued struggles for African American women laborers as they entered the twentieth century.

The Great Migration and World War I

Black women's desire to escape the social and economic oppression of the Jim Crow South led them to migrate first to southern cities, and then to join their fathers, brothers, and husbands in the Great Migration northward. Between 1916 and 1930, over one million African Americans moved North, with between fifty and seventy-five thousand settling in Chicago alone. Washington, DC, proved another popular destination for migrants, especially young women seeking jobs as domestics, as did Philadelphia and New York City. With the entry of the United States into the First World War, the lives of many

black women working in both the North and South changed dramatically.

During the war black men and women found employment for the first time in industry in significant numbers, filling vacancies left by young men serving in the military. It was even more common, however, for black women to fill the jobs of white immigrant domestics moving into industrial jobs in northern cities. Still, one manufacturing industry that opened to black workers in both the North and South during the war was the textile industry. War-induced labor shortages not only forced southern mills to employ more African American women, but also forced northern mills to recruit them as well. Although black women already worked in the southern textile industry, they had most often been consigned to low-paid janitorial work; labor demands of the war allowed them access to more lucrative jobs running machines. In other industries, such as munitions, meatpacking, metalworking, and food processing, newfound access to skilled and semiskilled jobs did not change black women's relegation to the most physically demanding and low paying jobs available. As in prewar days, even those performing the same work as white women took home significantly lower wages. Efforts to integrate unions during the war made little headway. Even the AFL-affiliated Women's Trade Union League (WTUL) largely failed at their attempts to fill positions opened by the promotion of white women with black workers.

Demobilization at the end of World War I reversed many of the temporary gains made by both black and white women during the war. Returning servicemen reclaimed the industrial jobs held by both black and white women. In 1920, 80 percent of employed black women still worked as agricultural or domestic workers. Whites' resistance to working beside blacks continued the prewar segregation of the work force. Following a now-familiar pattern, racism impeded attempts at building worker solidarity.

Nonetheless, the labor shortage produced by World War I also provided opportunities for black women outside of industry to organize themselves. Under the guidance of middle-class activists including Mary Church Terell, in 1917 the Women Wage-Earners' Association headquartered in Washington, DC, led the domestics, waitresses, nurses, and tobacco stemmers of Norfolk, Virginia, in a strike for increased wages and improved working conditions. Like the washerwomen strike in Atlanta over thirty-five years earlier, working black women stood poised to disrupt white society by withholding their labor. White unions refused to support the strike, however, and many in the community attacked its timing as unpatriotic. Accusations of interference with the war effort led to the strike's failure and ultimately to the demise of the Norfolk union. While black women had failed to

win their immediate demands, they had proven their resolve to fight for economic justice.

Throughout the 1920s, black working women continued to organize. Though most domestics still worked not
in hotels and restaurants but in private homes, domestic
workers affiliated with the AFL's Hotel and Restaurant
Employees Union and established ten locals in the South.
The International Ladies Garment Workers' Union's ill-
fated attempt to organize blacks in the late 1920s alongside the discriminatory practices of most AFL unions,
however, left African American women more comfortable
with black-led organizations.

The founding of the Brotherhood of Sleeping Car
Porters (BSCP) by A. Phillip Randolph in 1925 proved
a far more successful vehicle for organizing black women.
Believing the backing of porters' wives would influence the
success of his organization, Randolph relied on women to
help build the union into the most influential black labor
organization of its time. In spite of the reality that most
African American married women had to work to support
their families, BSCP leaders held the middle-class view
that women hired by the railroads were temporary workers, only employed until they married. Thus, the BSCP
leadership looked to the wives of workers rather than
women laborers to organize. Women's auxiliaries were integral to the success of the union, as women lectured on
the importance of union membership and collected union
dues. They worked not only for economic equality but social and political equality as well, uniting the goals of the
nascent civil rights and labor movements. In the process,
they helped to establish a black middle class at a time
when occupations considered middle-class gateways, such
as clerical and sales jobs, as well as nursing, remained all
but closed to black women. The economic crisis of the
next decade, however, would limit the opportunities of
black families struggling to work their way out of poverty.

The Great Depression

The competition for jobs created by the Great Depression
meant the further marginalization of black women workers, as employment that white men and women hesitated
to take in better economic times became far more desirable to whites. Moreover, New Deal legislation intended to
ameliorate the effects of the economic crisis, such as the
Fair Labor Standards Act, did not extend coverage to those
occupations dominated by black workers, such as agricultural and service work. Even those working in occupations
covered by New Deal legislation suffered from discriminatory implementation of the laws. Despite their exclusion
from most labor, entitlement, and welfare programs, black
working women found inspiration in a revitalized labor
movement attributable to the Roosevelt administration's
support for the right of workers to organize.

The impracticality of government regulation of work
performed in private homes hindered attempts at setting
labor standards for domestic workers. Still, black women
lobbied to include their work in the Fair Standards Act
that set maximum work hours and minimum wage requirements. With between 30 and 40 percent of African
American adults unemployed in some areas of the country,
intense competition for jobs meant that attempts by the
white-led National Committee on Household Employment
and the black-led Domestic Worker's Union of New York
City enjoyed limited success. The popularity of New York
City's "slave markets" possibly best reveals the desperation
of domestic workers in the depths of the Depression. In
street-corner markets, domestics stood on sidewalks waiting for middle-class housewives to drive by and negotiate
wages for a day's work. Such conditions left black women
vulnerable to exploitation by white employers who could
easily replace workers with daily trips to the market.

With the founding of the Congress of Industrial Organizations (CIO) in 1935, black women employed in industry
enjoyed far more success at organizing. Unlike the AFL,
which organized by trades, the CIO organized workers,
both skilled and unskilled, by industry. Recognizing that
business had often used black women as strikebreakers,
the CIO set out to forge worker solidarity by integrating
such unions as the newly affiliated International Garment
Workers Union (IGWU) and the Amalgamated Clothing
Workers of America (ACWA), the latter of which helped to
establish the United Laundry Workers (ULW). With a significant number of its leaders influenced by the racially
egalitarian ideology of the American Communist Party,
the CIO not only encouraged integrated unions but also
brought black women like Mary Sweet of the ILGWU and
Evelyn Macon of the ULW into leadership positions.

In the mid-1930s, the CIO took its organizing strength
South to agricultural producers such as the tobacco
industry, a leading employer of black women. Since the
late nineteenth century, the weak AFL-affiliated Tobacco
Workers International Union (TWIU) had organized the
industry, but virtually ignored the needs of its black members. By the late 1930s, such CIO unions as the Food, Tobacco, and Allied Workers of America (FTA) competed
with the TWIU to represent black women, who since slavery had labored in gender and race segregated factories
performing the dirty and physically demanding work of
stripping tobacco leaves of their stems. Like other CIO
unions, the FTA offered organizers such as Moranda
Smith the opportunity to lead unionization efforts.

Attempts to organize African American workers in
integrated unions during the Depression were perhaps
nowhere more dramatic than among sharecroppers in the
South, where the Socialist and Communist parties dominated organizing. In the Socialist-led Southern Tenant

Farmers' Union (STFU), founded in Arkansas in the mid-1930s, black women like Carrie Dilworth led strikes protesting sharecropper evictions, common during the Depression, and demanded federal legislation to aid tenant farmers. The STFU is probably best remembered for leading nearly two thousand black and white members in a 1939 sit-down strike on Missouri public highways to protest farmer evictions. During World War II the union sent southern black women to northern farms to fill food-processing jobs, and following the war affiliated with the AFL, changing its name to the National Farmer Labor Union.

Depression-era Alabamans fought tenant evictions through the racially integrated, Communist-led Share-croppers' Union (SCU), organized largely through the efforts of black women. Robin D. G. Kelley writes that SCU women's auxiliaries, known as "sewing clubs," were the foundation for the union as women fought to provide for their families in the midst of severe economic circumstances. Yet while the STFU and SCU shared similar goals, long-standing political differences between socialists and communists prevented the unions from uniting in their struggles.

World War II

With the United States's entry into World War II, the job shortages of the Depression abated, and black women were once again called on to fill vacancies created by men entering the military. As white middle- and working-class women moved into defense work, the number of black private household workers rose 13 percent. This meant that in cities like Baltimore, where large numbers of white women worked in the defense industry, the wages and working conditions of black domestics improved as the demand for their work grew. In Baltimore, the CIO-affiliated United Domestic Workers' Local Industrial Union 1283 helped to establish a nine-hour day along with a uniform wage rate for its workers. By the end of the war the union had added paid sick leave and vacation pay to its members' benefits. Demobilization following the war, however, lessened the labor shortage and with it the power of unions like the United Domestic Workers to negotiate favorable contracts.

As in the First World War, during World War II southern black men and women migrated to northern cities like Detroit in hopes of gaining entry to jobs in industries previously closed to them. Yet surveys show that while black males found employment in industrial job classifications during the war, many industries hired black women to fill low-paying janitorial positions. Karen Anderson writes that even a year after the United States entered the war, only 1,000 of the 96,000 war industry jobs in Detroit held by women were held by nonwhites. While service-type jobs in industry paid far better than domestic work, they did not represent significant occupational advancement for African American women.

Management pointed to "hate strikes" conducted during the war by white workers as one reason for denying blacks well-paying jobs. When attempts to integrate the shop floor resulted in white worker walkouts in factories like Detroit's U.S. Rubber plant, managers cited the demands of wartime production as reason to avoid the disruptions precipitated by hiring black workers. Even appeals to the Fair Employment Practices Committee (FEPC), established by President Roosevelt in 1941 to combat discrimination in defense and government employment, proved ineffective in bringing about significant changes in hiring practices in many of these industries. As black women were treated like men, given the hard and dirty work rather than the production jobs reserved for white women, they united to challenge the discriminatory practices of defense industries. Besides filing complaints with the FEPC, black steelworkers sought support from the United Steel Workers union. When these efforts failed, they engaged in wildcat strikes. Only after considerable pressure from the FEPC did companies like American Telephone and Telegraph Company (AT&T) hire African American women, and even then their employment was concentrated in service work such as elevator operators and cafeteria employees. Although AT&T did employ black women as clerks, only 2 percent of all its clerical workers at the time were black.

Nursing represents one of the few bright spots for long-term gains by black women in the 1940s, with many of the gains attributable to their labor organizing. Since 1908, the National Association of Colored Graduate Nurses (NACGN) had fought for parity between black and white nurses. Theirs was a hard-fought battle, however, as black nurses were excluded from employment in white hospitals and from military service during World War I. Yet with the support of white progressives like Eleanor Roosevelt, black nurses gained the right to serve during World War II, and the government's Cadet Nurse Corps trained more than five hundred African American women during the war. These gains led to the NACGN's dissolution and the integration of the white-led American Nursing Association in 1950.

Ultimately, the Second World War ended with mixed results for black women active in the labor movement. While job shortages gave them increased bargaining power in domestic work and limited access to better-paying industrial jobs, these gains for the most part proved temporary. Even CIO-affiliated unions like the United Auto Workers that sought to build integrated memberships had difficulty matching their rhetoric to their deeds, as white members engaged in hate strikes in an effort to maintain the racial status quo. Soon after the war, black women were, in the words of Jacqueline Jones, "demobilized and redomesticated" as they returned to service jobs of the prewar years.

"You Have to Fight for Freedom"

Changes in the American economy following the war left fewer African American women employed as agricultural workers. Mechanization of cotton growing in the South resulted in less than 10 percent of employed black women working in the fields. At the same time factory automation reduced the number of manufacturing jobs available. The introduction of machinery to remove tobacco stems in the late 1940s, for example, led to the unemployment of one thousand black women workers in the American Tobacco Company alone. Thus, low-paying domestic work again provided employment for black women pushed out of defense factories, cotton fields and tobacco processing plants. In an effort to ensure that postwar wages would not slide back to Depression-era levels, domestics continued to organize. Nationally, the Women's Bureau's Household Employment Committees, which had integrated leadership, attempted to mediate uniform standards for domestics. Locally, community organizations in cities like Atlanta established services to oversee the placement and fair treatment of domestics.

The CIO's "Operation Dixie" provided the single largest effort to organize black workers in the postwar era. While both the AFL and the CIO conducted campaigns to bolster membership in the South following the war, it was the latter that attempted to unite industrial unionism with a civil rights agenda. Launched in 1946, Operation Dixie represented the CIO's acknowledgment that it could not compete with the larger AFL without the support of black workers. Despite its early promise, the campaign fell victim to cold war tensions. Passage of the anti-Communist, anti-labor Taft-Hartley Act in 1947 served to create a split between the left-wing faction of the union that was against compliance with the act and the right-wing faction willing to accede. Also undermining solidarity in Operation Dixie was its leadership's reluctance to fully incorporate black and women members by actively recruiting them for leadership positions. The conservative tenor of the cold war, combined with a historic inability of labor to overcome race and gender issues, hampered the CIO's efforts to challenge the status quo through a combined civil rights and labor movement. Seeing the writing on the wall, in 1951 black leaders founded the short-lived National Negro Labor Council, giving women a valuable role in its leadership. The domestic and service workers' boycott of Montgomery buses in 1955 illustrates that, despite setbacks in the union movement, black women continued their fight for social and economic equality, playing an instrumental role in organizing the civil rights movement of the 1950s and 1960s.

Dennis Deslippe writes that "the fifteen years preceding the arrival of federal equal employment opportunity measures in the mid-1960s marked a slow but definitive advance for African-American workers." Often, however, these advances were attributable to the civil rights movement as much as to the labor movement. Title VII of the Civil Rights Act of 1964 prohibited discrimination in hiring based on race, color, religion, sex, or national origin, and established the Equal Employment Opportunity Commission (EEOC) to address worker grievances, cementing the relationship between civil and labor rights. Black women, however, often turned to the National Association for the Advancement of Colored People (NAACP) and not to labor organizations to guide them in their dealings with the EEOC. Nonetheless, commitment to both movements is evident in the work of women like Maida Springer-Kemp, who, in the decade following the merger of the AFL and CIO in 1955, worked to organize laborers in the American South and in Africa as part of the union's international efforts.

While the period between 1930 and 1960 saw a significant growth in domestic work for African American women, following the passage of Title VII, there was a dramatic drop in their employment in private household work, as blacks made sizable inroads into clerical and sales jobs. In the 1970s, black women increasingly entered the clerical field as employees of the U.S. government, where they joined the powerful American Federation of State, County, and Municipal Employees (AFSCME). Not surprisingly, these advances were fueled by increases in the level of education among black workers. And although they were still overrepresented in low-paying jobs, by the 1970s the median income of African American women was nearly equivalent to that of white women.

The 1974 founding of the Coalition of Labor Union Women (CLUW) represented a significant attempt by working-class women to bridge long-established racial divides. CLUW's agenda includes the promotion of affirmative action policies, increased membership and participation of women in labor unions, and the passage of family-centered legislation such as family leave bills. Estelle Freedman writes that "by the 1980s about half of the members in CLUW's seventy-five chapters were women of color," revealing the organization's commitment to integrated unionism.

Although not a steady road to improvement, throughout the twentieth century African American women gained hard-earned economic advancement through the labor movement, as they organized locally and nationally, in integrated and in all-black associations, with black men and on their own. Despite innumerable setbacks they have not turned away from labor organizing as part of a comprehensive program for securing their democratic rights. As the U.S. economy's base shifted from manufacturing to the service industry in the latter part of the twentieth century, black women were still underrepresented in the well-paying unionized skilled trades and overrepresented in traditionally nonunion service jobs. Yet they entered the twenty-first century with an impressive history of organized resistance to labor exploitation that had taught them, in the words of UAW official Sylvia Woods, how to "fight for freedom."

BIBLIOGRAPHY

Anderson, Karen. "Last Hired, First Fired: Black Women Workers during World War II." *Journal of American History*, June 1982.

Chateauvert, Melinda. *Marching Together: Women of the Brotherhood of Sleeping Car Porters*. Urbana: University of Illinois Press, 1998.

Clark-Lewis Elizabeth. *Living In, Living Out: African American Domestics in Washington, D.C., 1910–1940*. Washington: Smithsonian Institution Press, 1994.

Davis, Adrienne. "'Don't let Nobody Bother Yo' Principle': The Sexual Economy of American Slavery." In *Sister Circle: Black Women and Work*. New Brunswick, NJ: Rutgers University Press, 2002.

Dusinberre, William. *Them Dark Days: Slavery in the American Rice Swamps*. New York: Oxford University Press, 1996.

Freeman, Estelle. *No Turning Back: The History of Feminism and the Future of Women*. New York: Ballantine, 2002.

Foner, Philip S. *Organized Labor and the Black Worker, 1619–1973*. New York: New Praeger, 1974.

Foner, Philip S. *Women and the American Labor Movement, From the First Trade Unions to the Present*. New York: Free Press, 1982.

Gabin, Nancy F. *Feminism in the Labor Movement: Women and the United Auto Workers, 1935–1975*. Ithaca: Cornell University Press, 1990.

Gordon, Lynn D. "Education and the Professions." In *Blackwell's Companion to American Women's History*, edited by Nancy Hewitt. Malden, MA: Blackwell, 2002.

Harley, Sharon. "When Your Work Is Not Who You Are: The Development of a Working-Class Consciousness among Afro-American Women." In *Gender, Class, Race, and Reform in the Progressive Era*. Lexington: University Press of Kentucky, 1991.

Honey, Michael K. *Southern Labor and Black Civil Rights: Organizing Memphis Workers*. Urbana: University of Illinois Press, 1993.

Hunter, Tera W. *To 'Joy My Freedom: Southern Black Women's Lives and Labors after the Civil War*. Cambridge, MA: Harvard University Press, 1997.

Janiewski, Dolores E. "'Seeking a New Day and a New Way': Black Women and the Unions in the Southern Tobacco Industry." In *"To Toil the Livelong Day": America's Women at Work, 1780–1980*, edited by Carol Groneman and Mary Beth Norton. Ithaca, NY: Cornell University Press, 1987.

Jones, Jacqueline. *Labor of Love, Labor of Sorrow: Black Women, Work and the Family from Slavery to the Present*. New York: Vintage Books, 1985.

Kelley, Robin D. G. *Hammer and Hoe: Alabama Communists during the Great Depression*. Chapel Hill: University of North Carolina Press, 1990.

Kessler-Harris, Alice. *Out to Work: A History of Wage-Earning Women in the United States*. New York: Oxford University Press, 1982.

Korstad, Robert, and Nelson Lichtenstein. "Opportunities Found and Lost: Labor, Radicals and the Early Civil Rights Movement." *Journal of American History*, December 1988.

Lerner, Gerda, ed. *Black Women in White America: A Documentary History*. New York: Vintage, 1972.

Lynd, Alice, and Staughton Lynd, eds. *Rank and File: Personal Histories by Working-Class Organizers*. Boston: Beacon Press, 1973.

Mitchell, H. L. *Roll the Union On: A Pictorial History of the Southern Tenant Farmer's Union*. Chicago: Charles H. Kerr, 1987.

Naison, Mark. *Communists in Harlem during the Depression*. New York: Grove Press, 1983.

Palmer, Phyllis. "Housewife and Household Worker: Employer-Employee Relationships in the Home, 1928–1941." In *"To Toil the Livelong Day": America's Women at Work, 1780–1980*, edited by Carol Groneman and Mary Beth Norton. Ithaca, NY: Cornell University Press, 1987.

Schneider, Dorothy, and Carl F. Schneider. *The ABC-CLIO Companion to Women in the Workplace*. Santa Barbara, CA: ABC-CLIO, 1993.

Terborg-Penn, Rosalyn. "Survival Strategies among African-American Women Workers: A Continuing Process." In *Women, Work, and Protest: A Century of U.S. Women's Labor History*, edited by Ruth Milkman. Boston: Routledge & Kegan Paul, 1985.

U.S. Department of Labor Employment Standards Administration, Women's Bureau. *1975 Handbook on Women Workers*. Washington, DC: U.S. Department of Labor, 1975.

U.S. Department of Labor, Women's Bureau. *Time of Change: 1983 Handbook on Women Workers*. Washington, DC: U.S. Department of Labor, Women's Bureau, 1983.

U.S. Department of Labor, Women's Bureau. *1993 Handbook on Women Workers: Trends and Issues*. Washington, DC: U.S. Department of Labor, Women's Bureau, 1994.

Wertheimer, Barbara Mayer. *We Were There: The Story of Working Women in America*. New York: Pantheon, 1977.

White, Deborah Gray. *Ar'n't I a Woman?: Female Slaves in the Plantation South*. New York: Norton, 1999.

—JACQUELINE CASTLEDINE

LADNER, JOYCE A. (b. 12 October 1943), sociologist. Joyce Ladner has been one of the leading proponents of the racial uplift tradition that bore close ties to the activities of black clubwomen at the turn of the twentieth century. Ladner's many years of activism and academic pursuits have focused on advancing a tradition that adheres to the core values of self-help, self-respect, honesty, strong families, religious faith, and education as the means to social uplift. Her steadfast commitment to these values, reflected in her numerous books and articles on subjects such as black families, higher education, poverty, parenting, and children, was born out of her experiences in the segregated South and the civil rights movement. These experiences also played a key role in the making of Ladner the activist, scholar, and community leader.

Joyce A. Ladner was born in a hamlet on the outskirts of Hattiesburg, Mississippi. Ladner credited her stepfather and especially her mother, Anne Ruth Perryman, with the success of her early development. They furnished each of their children with the necessary tools needed to meet and overcome the challenge of living in a segregated society by imparting the virtues of perseverance, self-confidence, respect for others, integrity, resourcefulness, faith, hard

JOYCE LADNER produced an impressive body of literature while teaching at schools in Illinois, New York, Washington, DC, and Tanzania; serving as vice president of academic affairs and interim president at Howard University; and working as a senior fellow at the Brookings Institution. (Day Walters Photography; courtesy of the Brookings Institution, Washington, DC.)

Ladner's involvement in the civil rights movement began in high school when she and her sister Dorie joined the Hattiesburg NAACP youth council. The two sisters later enrolled in Jackson State College, but their links to Medgar Evers and civil rights activities led administrators to expel them from this institution. Undaunted by the experience, the sisters restarted their undergraduate careers at Tougaloo College. At Tougaloo, the encouragement of John R. Salter Jr. and a few other progressive professors accelerated Ladner's transformation from a young woman dabbling in civil rights activities into an ironclad scholar and activist. This transformation was fostered by her membership in one of the most potent organizational arms of the movement, the Student Nonviolent Coordinating Committee (SNCC). Never really severing their ties to the NACCP, the Ladner sisters went on to organize a protest campaign to force the release of their former youth group leader, Clyde Kennard, from prison. They raised money, mobilized black Mississippians to attend the August 1963 March on Washington, and joined the Mississippi Freedom Democratic Party. They also engaged in the painstaking SNCC mission of voter registration in apartheid Mississippi.

Ladner's work in the civil rights movement had a lasting effect on the ideas she expressed in many publications during the last three decades of the twentieth century. This body of work, ranging from studies on poor black women in St. Louis to the against-all-odds struggles of black leaders in contemporary American cities, was an outgrowth of one of her central ideas: that the history of black individuals and their families was a testament to creativity and adaptability in a "pathological society" obsessed with constructing and implementing racist ideas. Ladner therefore argued that previous sociological models that used the behavior of middle-class whites as a norm for other racial or ethnic groups to follow, if only for the sake of tasting the fruits of progress in their lives, should be abandoned, because they often sidestep the socioeconomic salience of racism in the making of American culture. Ladner produced this impressive body of literature while teaching at schools in Illinois, New York, Washington, DC, and Tanzania; serving as vice president of academic affairs and interim president at Howard University; and working as a senior fellow at the Brookings Institution in Washington, DC. Never complacent, Ladner remained on the cutting edge of sociological research and public activism, while speaking frequently on issues such as high rates of teen pregnancy, affirmative action, and the need for a "a new civil rights agenda."

BIBLIOGRAPHY
Dittmer, John. *Local People: The Struggle for Civil Rights in Mississippi.* Urbana: University of Illinois Press, 1995.

work, taking responsibility, and recognizing education as means to social improvement. Ladner drew most of her inspiration from a hard-working mother who received only a third-grade education but managed to raise a daughter who graduated from high school at sixteen and Tougaloo College at twenty, and earned a doctorate in sociology from Washington University by the age of twenty-four. Overlapping the young Joyce Ladner's fast-track educational experiences was a steady diet of civil rights activism that helped produce one of the most influential public intellectuals in the latter half of the twentieth century.

Gaines, Kevin. *Uplifting the Race: Black Leadership, Politics, and Culture in the Twentieth Century*. Chapel Hill: University of North Carolina Press, 1996.

Hine, Darlene Clark. *Black Women in United States History*. Brooklyn, NY: Carlson, 1990.

Vise, David A. "Out Front in the DC School Debate." *Washington Post*, 29 October 1996.

—JOHN WESS GRANT

LAFONTANT-MANKARIOUS, JEWEL STRADFORD ROGERS

(b. 28 April 1922; d. 31 May 1997), activist, lawyer. Jewel LaFontant-Mankarious expanded the parameters of tokenism to produce tangible effects for women and African Americans. Often the first woman or African American to hold leadership positions in several arenas, LaFontant-Mankarious challenged discrimination as an activist and lawyer and used her legal acumen and negotiating skills to broker deals in corporate America and the world of Republican politics, all while balancing the often difficult responsibilities of career and family.

Born in Chicago, Illinois, to Cornelius Francis and Aida Carter Stradford, Jewel Carter Stradford was the daughter of an attorney father and artist mother who raised

JEWEL LAFONTANT-MANKARIOUS, shown here during an interview, had an impressive career in law, business, and government. In several fields, she was often the first woman or the first African American to hold a leadership position. (The History Makers.)

their daughter to believe that unlimited possibilities were available to her. Both her grandfather and her father graduated from Oberlin College in Ohio and entered the legal profession. In 1943 Stradford continued the family tradition when she received a BA from Oberlin, and in 1946 she became the first black woman to earn a JD from the University of Chicago. As one of the founding members of the Congress of Racial Equality (CORE), she participated in sit-ins during the early 1940s.

In 1946 Stradford married a fellow law student, John Rogers. Despite her admission to the Illinois state bar in 1947, major Chicago law firms refused to offer her a position, and she could not obtain any office space for her own practice. Undeterred, she worked as a volunteer, becoming the first black trial attorney for the Legal Aid Bureau of the United Charities of Chicago from 1947 to 1953. From 1952 to 1954 she also worked as a partner in her husband's law firm—Rogers, Rogers, and Strayhorn—and served as precinct captain for the sixth ward of Chicago. A lifelong Republican, Rogers believed African Americans should have a voice in both parties and often disagreed with Chicago's local Democratic leadership. In 1955 Illinois Senator Everett Dirksen recommended her appointment as an assistant U.S. attorney for the Northern District of Illinois, where she worked on immigration issues. She thus became the first black woman to serve in this capacity, but left in 1958 after the birth of her son John. As an alternate delegate to the Republican National Convention, she seconded the nomination of Richard M. Nixon for president in 1960. After divorcing John Rogers in 1961, she married the Haitian-born attorney Ernest LaFontant later that year. The LaFontants then joined the law firm of Jewel's father. In 1963 Jewel LaFontant argued and won *State of Illinois v. Beatrice Lynum* before the Supreme Court. The Court's ruling, that a confession made by Lynum was inadmissible because the police threatened to take her children away, served as the foundation for the landmark Supreme Court 1966 *Miranda* decision, which established the rights of the accused upon their arrest.

From September to December 1972 LaFontant served as U.S. representative to the United Nations. President Nixon also appointed her deputy solicitor general of the United States in 1973. Serving from 1973 to 1975, she was chairperson of federal women's programs for the Department of Justice, where she represented the United States before the Supreme Court on numerous occasions. After Ernest LaFontant's death in 1976, she continued to practice with her father and later became president of the law firm of LaFontant, Wilkins, Jones, and Ware. LaFontant acted as commissioner of the Martin Luther King Jr. Federal Holiday Commission and chair of the Illinois

Advisory Committee to the U.S. Civil Rights Commission. She also served on numerous corporate and nonprofit boards of such companies and universities as Jewel Companies, Mobil, Oberlin College, and Howard University. In 1983 she joined the law firm of Vedder, Price, Kaufman, Kammholz, and Day.

President George H. W. Bush, a personal friend, appointed LaFontant ambassador at large and U.S. coordinator for refugee affairs in 1989. She aided in the negotiations and development of U.S. refugee policy with foreign governments and international organizations. In December of the same year, she married Naguib Mankarious, an Egyptian business consultant. In 1993 she returned to Chicago and joined the law firm of Holleb and Coff. Jewel La-Fontant-Mankarious died of breast cancer in her Chicago home at the age of seventy-five.

BIBLIOGRAPHY

"Biography of Jewel LaFontant-Mankarious." Jewel LaFontant-Mankarious Papers in the Oberlin College Archives, Oberlin, Ohio.

LaFontant-Mankarious, Jewel. *An Autobiography of Black Chicago*. Chicago: Urban Publishers, 1982.

Pace, Eric. "Jewel LaFontant-Mankarious, Lawyer and U.S. Official Dies." *New York Times*, 3 June 1997.

Thomas, Jerry. "LaFontant Is Remembered as a Multifaceted Gem." *Chicago Tribune*, 6 June 1997.

—SONYA RAMSEY

LAMPKIN, DAISY ELIZABETH ADAMS (b. c. 1884; d. 10 March 1965), activist. When Daisy Elizabeth Adams Lampkin died at her Pittsburgh home, the whole nation took note. An editorial in the *Pittsburgh Post-Gazette* stated that "Americans owe a debt to Mrs. Daisy Lampkin" and that Lampkin had been "instrumental in advancing the cause of the National Association for the Advancement of Colored People, and indirectly, the case which led to legally enforced desegregation of public schools." The *New York Times* characterized her as a "Negro leader," calling attention to her contributions to civil rights, to her thirty-six years as vice president of the once-powerful *Pittsburgh Courier*, and to her work with the National Council of Negro Women (NCNW) and the National Association of Colored Women (NACW). On 9 August 1983, the Pennsylvania Historical and Museum Commission dedicated an official historical marker bearing the state insignia in front of Lampkin's home, a mecca for African American activists for half a century. Lampkin was the first black woman to be so honored by the Commonwealth of Pennsylvania. Then-governor Dick Thornburgh wrote in a statement issued for the ceremony, "Daisy Lampkin courageously sought full equality for Blacks and women throughout the country. Today her work stands as an inspiration for countless citizens." The former Pennsylvania house speaker K. Leroy Irvis recalled

DAISY ELIZABETH ADAMS LAMPKIN was perhaps best known as national field secretary of the NAACP; she was also vice president of the *Pittsburgh Courier* for three decades, and she did notable work with the National Council of Negro Women and the National Association of Colored Women. (Austin/Thompson Collection, by permission of Moorland-Spingarn Research Center.)

how Lampkin had guided young men like himself and Supreme Court justice Thurgood Marshall in their public careers. Officials of city and county government, the Urban League, the NCNW, Delta Sigma Theta sorority, the Links, the Lucy Stone Civic League, and church and neighborhood groups all gave testimony of Lampkin's numerous humanitarian achievements.

Daisy Elizabeth Adams was born in the District of Columbia, according to the 1900 census for Reading, Berks County, Pennsylvania, which lists her as the stepdaughter of John Temple and his wife, Rosa. Daisy completed high school in Reading and was an active member of the Presbyterian Church.

In 1909, Adams moved to Pittsburgh, where, in 1912, she married William Lampkin, a native of Rome, Georgia.

That December, the *Pittsburgh Courier* ran an article to commend her for promoting a successful woman's suffrage event. In 1913, Lampkin began her lifelong association with the noted publisher and politician attorney Robert L. Vann. She won a cash award for selling the most new subscriptions to the *Courier* and traded it in for stock in the publishing company, continually augmenting her investment until she was named vice president of the corporation in 1929, a post she held for the rest of her life.

Lampkin was best known for her work as national field secretary for the National Association for the Advancement of Colored People (NAACP), but she established herself as a prominent national figure long before Walter White recruited her for the civil rights association. She gained recognition for her leadership ability in liberty bond drives during World War I, when the black community of Allegheny County raised more than $2 million. She started her political career in 1915, as president of the Negro Women's Franchise League, affiliated early with the National Suffrage League, and held top positions in the women's division of the Republican party. She was elected president of the National Negro Republican Convention in Atlantic City, New Jersey, in July of 1924, when, according to the *New York Times*, the assembly passed a strong antilynching resolution. In 1926, Lampkin was elected delegate-at-large to the Republican National Convention in Cleveland, Ohio.

Before she joined the NAACP staff, Lampkin served as national organizer and chair of the executive board of the NACW. When James Weldon Johnson organized a group of African American leaders to meet with President Calvin Coolidge at the White House in 1924 in an attempt to secure justice for the black soldiers accused in the 1917 Houston riot, he summoned Lampkin, the only woman among the twelve or more national leaders. Lampkin also was a delegate, with Mary McLeod Bethune, Nannie Burroughs, Alice Dunbar-Nelson, and Addie Dickerson, all noted clubwomen, when Sallie Stewart, NACW president, was elected a vice president of the National Council of Women of the United States, whose membership extended to the International Council of Women. This November 1929 meeting marked the first formal recognition of African American women as official participants in world affairs.

When the January 1930 edition of the *Crisis* announced the appointment of Lampkin as NAACP regional field secretary, the periodical noted, "The name of Daisy Lampkin will be known wherever colored women meet together. Her achievements have been so unusual that they have long been the subject of public knowledge and comment." Significantly, Lampkin had been named vice president of the Pittsburgh Courier Publishing Company just a few months earlier and had worked closely with Walter White,

then acting NAACP executive secretary, before she was hired by the board of directors.

Lampkin was able to use the connecting forces of the NAACP and the *Courier*—the two most effective civil rights institutions of the era—to ensure success in a number of important campaigns. In fact, records indicate that Lampkin mediated numerous bitter fights among the men, fights that threatened the viability of a united African American front in the battle against Jim Crow. Her devotion to the cause of black progress earned Lampkin the respect of rivals and opponents throughout the community. Lampkin plunged into membership and fund-raising drives, using the NAACP's role in the defeat of Supreme Court nominee Judge John J. Parker of North Carolina as a rallying cry.

The NAACP announced that its staff and members would do everything possible to defeat senators who had voted for Judge Parker, whom they considered to be an archenemy of the race, and in 1930 Lampkin played a major role in the defeat of Senator Roscoe McCullough of Ohio. Even before she was hired, she had begun to reorganize the Ohio State NAACP Conference by working in twenty-three towns and cities, speaking two and three times a day, using her superb oratorical skills. At the same time, Roy Wilkins, editor of the Kansas City *Call*, was out in front in the battle to bring down Senator Henry J. Allen of Kansas. His resounding victory brought Wilkins into the NAACP fold as assistant secretary to White. Lampkin, Wilkins, and White formed a dynamic triumvirate whose relentless efforts laid the foundation for civil rights triumphs on battlefronts all over the nation.

Named national field secretary in 1935, Lampkin embarked on an astonishing fund-raising membership campaign schedule, often attending more than forty meetings in one month. Throughout her tenure as field secretary, Lampkin remained active with the NACW and NCNW, serving as a vice president of the former and on the board of directors and education foundation chair of the latter. In 1945 she headed the drive to establish an NCNW headquarters and turned over a check for $49,000 at the Washington, DC, annual workshop. She also chaired the 1952 campaign to raise funds for Delta Sigma Theta's national home, sharing her triumph in a letter to her lifelong friend Nannie Burroughs.

Lampkin joined the Democratic Party with Robert L. Vann and the *Courier* during the New Deal era of President Franklin Delano Roosevelt, skillfully skirting NAACP nonpartisan directives to staff members. She asserted her right to speak for women, telling White, "The public knows that I have many other interests in addition to the NAACP." However, in 1947, Lampkin invoked the NAACP's nonpartisan stance to decline repeated efforts by Congressman William Dawson to recruit her for the committee to elect Harry Truman.

It is true that Lampkin's fund-raising ability was unmatched, but some observers underestimated her worth to the civil rights movement by focusing only on this facet of her work. Fatigued, Lampkin finally resigned her field position in 1947, despite fervent pleas from White, Wilkins, and Marshall that she hold on. To their great satisfaction, she immediately accepted an assignment with the board of directors and continued to conduct membership drives in branches where leaders made it clear that they wanted no other person.

Lampkin began her job at $50 a week in 1930, and her salary never was higher than a meager $5,200 annually. During all those years, she gave herself totally to what she always referred to as "the cause," the elevation of black people all over the world. C. L. R. James, the noted author, recognized her great influence when, in 1956, he wrote to her requesting that she make sure the Negrophobic pamphlet "Ordeal of the South" by England's Alistair Cooke was refuted. James described the articles as sneers and slanders, harmful to international race relations. The NAACP's Henry Moon was joined by black journalists everywhere in voicing scathing rebuttals of Cooke's stories published by the *Manchester Guardian*.

Keeping her finger on the political pulse of the nation, Lampkin switched back to the Republican party in 1952 when the Democrats ran a segregationist, John J. Sparkman of Alabama, for vice president.

Still campaigning for the NAACP in October 1964, Lampkin collapsed on the stage of a Camden, New Jersey, auditorium moments after delivering a stirring appeal. Lampkin was too feeble to attend the elaborate ceremony in New York's Waldorf-Astoria Hotel when the NCNW presented her its first Eleanor Roosevelt–Mary McLeod Bethune Award the following 22 December. Lena Horne, who had formed a close friendship with Lampkin when the young singer lived in the same Pittsburgh neighborhood, accepted the tribute for her.

During the remaining few months of her life, Lampkin was cared for by her adopted family, Dr. and Mrs. Earl Childs and their son, Earl Douglas Childs, who lived with her in her apartment building, the home that was later a historic site.

BIBLIOGRAPHY

McKenzie, Edna B. "Daisy Lampkin: A Life of Love and Service." *Pennsylvania Heritage*, Summer 1983.

Levin, Steve. "Daisy Lampkin Was a Dynamo for Change." *Pittsburgh Post-Gazette*, 2 February 1998. http://www.post-gazette.com/black-historymonth/19980202lampkin.asp.

NAACP papers, Library of Congress, Washington, DC. Guide and descriptions available at: http://www.lexisnexis.com/academic/2upa/Aaas/PapersNAACP.asp.

Twelfth Census of the United States. Schedule No. I, Population, Berks County, Pennsylvania.

—EDNA CHAPPELL MCKENZIE

LANEY, LUCY CRAFT (b. 13 April 1864; d. 24 October 1933), educator. Born in Macon, Georgia, Lucy Craft Laney was the seventh of ten children of David and Louisa Laney. Her father, who had succeeded in purchasing his freedom and that of his wife during slavery, was a carpenter by trade. A deeply religious man, David Laney co-founded the John Knox Presbytery, the first all-black Presbyterian Synod in the United States, which was received into the Northern Assembly in 1868.

Lucy C. Laney received her first formal education at the Lewis School, an institution opened by missionary teachers in 1865, and from which she graduated in 1869. One of the brightest students at Lewis, Laney was among the first eighty-nine students admitted to Atlanta University in 1869. She graduated four years later, becoming one of the first students to receive a degree from Atlanta University.

Laney began her teaching career in Milledgeville, Georgia, and later taught at schools in Macon and Savannah. When illness necessitated a more healthful climate, she moved to Augusta, where she secured a position as a grammar school teacher in the public school system. There, Laney played a major role in the successful fight for Georgia's first black public high school and was instrumental in the selection of Richard R. Wright as the institution's first principal.

Concerned over the increasing number of young black "children out of school without the care of parents, left to grow up idle and ignorant," Laney made it her short-term goal to establish a boarding school for girls. Her long-range vision was to create a training school for teachers. On 6 January 1886, in a rented hall at Christ Presbyterian Church, Laney greeted her first class of students: four girls and two poor boys whom she did not have the heart to turn away. Although boys were admitted to the school from its inception, the institution remained predominantly female throughout its history. The school, later named Haines Normal and Industrial Institute, was chartered by the state of Georgia the same year, giving Laney the distinction of being the only black woman at the head of a major school affiliated with the Presbyterian Church.

After the first month of operation the school was already overcrowded. Consequently, in February 1886, Laney rented a house from the president of the Augusta Board of Education. Overcrowding remained a problem as the number of students in attendance went from 75 at the end of the 1886 school year to 362 in 1887. In just that year, the primary, grammar, and elementary normal departments were established. In addition, an industrial course had begun, an effort was under way to secure a foot-press, and plans for a class in printing had been finalized. To accommodate the school's growth, Laney rented a two-story frame house with a barn in the rear, structures that constituted the campus of Haines Institute until 1889 when the Presbyterian board purchased a permanent site for Haines and erected the institution's first building, Marshall Hall. The following year, Laney organized a well-equipped kindergarten; over the course of the next several years, she created a strong literary department and a well-planned, scientific normal program. In 1892, in conjunction with the city hospital she had helped to create, Laney began a training program for nurses. In 1906 the school grew further with the construction of McGregor Hall. The last major new building on the Haines campus was Cauley-Wheeler Hall, in 1924.

Although the school was sanctioned by the Presbyterian board, Laney was left to her own devices and what she could collect for its support. She received no salary and was forced to live on the food provided by the parents of her students and to maintain the school on contributions from the community. During the school's first year, Laney was the only teacher, and she worked around the clock, personally overseeing each student as well as managing the affairs of the institution.

Although Lucy Laney never married or had a family of her own, she loved children, and devoted her career to improving their chances in life. Through self-sacrifice, devotion, faith, and hard work, Laney developed Haines Institute into one of the best secondary schools in the South. In the course of accomplishing this feat, she earned the title "mother of the children of the people." With boundless zeal for the elevation of her race and a keen sense of the welfare of women and of the larger society, Laney did not confine her activities to her school. She was a member of the National Association of Colored Women, the Southeastern Federation of Women's Clubs, the Georgia State Teachers Association, and the National YWCA, and she chaired the Colored Section of the Interracial Commission of Augusta. Laney was the first woman to be awarded honorary degrees from Atlanta University (1898) and Lincoln University (1904). She was similarly honored by South Carolina State College (1925) and Howard University (1930). Although she was never its recipient, Laney was nominated for the prestigious William E. Harmon Award for Distinguished Achievement among Negroes in 1928, 1929, and 1930.

After a lingering illness, Lucy Laney died of nephritis and hypertension. Two days later, funeral services were held in the chapel of Haines Institute, and she was buried on the campus of the school.

BIBLIOGRAPHY

Brawley, Benjamin. *Negro Builders and Heroes* (1937). Chapel Hill: University of North Carolina Press, 1965.
Daniel, Sadie Iola. *Women Builders*. Washington, DC: The Associated Publishers, Inc., 1931.
Gibson, J. W., and W. H. Crogman. *Progress of a Race* (1902). New York: Arno Press, 1969.
Griggs, A. C. "Lucy Craft Laney." *Journal of Negro History*, January 1934.
Laney, Lucy C. "The Burden of the Educated Colored Women." In *Black Women in Nineteenth-Century American Life*, edited by Bert James Loewenberg and Ruth Bogin. University Park: Pennsylvania State University Press, 1976.
McCrorey, Mary Jackson. "Lucy Laney." *Crisis*, June 1934.
Ovington, Mary White. *Portraits in Color*. New York: Viking Press, 1927.
—JUNE O. PATTON

LARSEN, NELLA (b. 13 April 1891; d. 30 March 1964), novelist and short story writer. Nella Larsen was born in Chicago to a West Indian father and a Danish mother. Larsen's father died when she was two years old, and her mother later married a white man with whom she had a second daughter. Growing up in a family of European descent was uncomfortable for Larsen, who rarely spoke of her family except to recall that she attended a private school in Chicago with her white half-sister.

After attending high school in Chicago, Larsen studied science at Fisk University in Nashville, Tennessee. From the all-black world of Fisk, Larsen attended the University of Copenhagen from 1910 to 1912. Larsen's odyssey next found her in New York City, where she studied nursing at Lincoln Hospital from 1912 to 1915 before serving as assistant superintendent of nurses at Tuskegee Institute in Alabama from 1915 to 1916. Returning to New York City, Larsen worked at Lincoln Hospital from 1916 to 1918 and for the New York City Department of Health from 1918 to 1921.

Never feeling connected to her mother and half-sister and a stepfather who viewed her as an embarrassment, Larsen found solace in her relationship with the physicist Elmer S. Imes, whom she married on 3 May 1919. She worked as a library assistant and children's librarian from 1921 to 1926, a career that inspired her to read voluminously and write. Her favorite authors included James Joyce, John Galsworthy, the eighteenth-century playwright Carlo Goldoni, Marmaduke Pickthall, Taylor Gordon, Rudolph Fisher, Walter White, and Carl Van Vechten, who was instrumental in securing a contract for Larsen's novels from Alfred A. Knopf.

As a socialite wife, Larsen became acquainted with a cadre of black authors in New York City, including James Weldon Johnson, Jessie Fauset, Jean Toomer, and Langston Hughes. With strong support from the black author Walter White and the leading white patron of New Negro authors, Carl Van Vechten, Larsen published her first novel, *Quicksand*, in 1928.

Substantially autobiographical, *Quicksand* focuses on a mulatto of Danish and West African parentage, named Helga Crane, whose quest in search of self takes her from Naxos, a southern black college, to Chicago to seek white relatives, to Harlem to mingle with African Americans, to Copenhagen to live with white relatives, to Harlem again,

NELLA LARSEN at the Zion Church during a Harmon Award ceremony. The others include Miss Harmon (at left), Channing H. Tobins, James Weldon Johnson (accepting an award for Claude McKay), and Dr. George Haynes (secretary of a commission on race relations). (© Bettmann/Corbis.)

and finally to rural Alabama, where she marries the arrogant, despicable, and unkempt Reverend Pleasant Green. Her husband minimally fulfills her spiritual as well as sexual needs, which she has repressed because of Victorian notions of womanhood. The novel concludes with Helga, still weak and bedridden from the birth of her fourth child, preparing to give birth to a fifth.

Larsen's novel skillfully captured the lives of many northern middle-class African Americans at the turn of the twentieth century, who, because they were formally educated, cultured, and of mixed parentage, found themselves alienated from white Americans and from the masses of black Americans, many of whom had rural southern roots. In addition to exploring race and class-related conflicts,

Larsen also treats gender issues in *Quicksand*. The delicate, fickle, and passionate Helga seems not only to be running from her divided racial self but also from her own sexuality. When Helga has an opportunity to take a lover, something that happens on several occasions, she bolts. Larsen's novel showed the limitations of black bourgeois women in the 1920s, forced to choose marriage at any cost as the only way to express their sexuality. The ending of *Quicksand* is less than satisfying because Helga, who has progressively become stronger and more self-assured, reverts to self-doubt. She becomes a pathetically helpless woman whose destiny will be determined by a man she does not love and with whom she has little in common.

With the publication of Larsen's second novel, *Passing*, in 1929, just thirteen months after the national acclaim of *Quicksand*, Larsen, age thirty-eight, was hailed as a major New Negro author. *Passing* centers on women's friendship, women's sexuality, mixed ancestry, and the preoccupation with respectability and materialism. *Passing* illustrates that African Americans who pass for white often yearn to be part of the black community. Born in poverty and raised by her white aunts, Clare Kendry risks losing her wealthy white husband, daughter, and social standing for the chance to socialize with her Harlem friends. Irene Redfield, Clare's friend who passes for white when it is expedient, ruins her marriage because she fears change and because of her obsession with maintaining middle-class standing. Like *Quicksand*, *Passing* has a weak ending. Larsen leaves unresolved whether Clare has fallen, jumped, or been pushed out of a window by Irene, who suspects her friend of having had an affair with her husband. In spite of the less-than-satisfying ending, *Passing* depicts the dilemmas and complexities of a growing black middle class.

Following the success of her two novels, Nella Larsen, in 1930, became the first black woman to win a creative writing award from the Guggenheim Foundation. Shortly before Larsen was to leave for Europe to do research in Spain and France for her third novel, she was accused of plagiarizing one of her short stories published in *Forum*. Though she responded to the attack with an essay in *Forum* and was supported by her editor, Larsen's public humiliation stifled her writing, and she never completed another novel. A marriage that had begun to show signs of deterioration in 1930 ended in divorce in 1933 when rumors spread that Larsen's husband was having an affair with a white woman and that Larsen had tried to kill herself by jumping out of a window. This second public humiliation apparently weakened Larsen's self-confidence and diminished her productivity as a writer.

From 1941 on, Larsen worked as a nurse at several hospitals on the East Side of Manhattan. She later died in New York City. Larsen made a significant contribution to black history and culture by capturing in impressive detail the mannerisms, values, concerns, and emotional conflicts of the black bourgeoisie, underscoring that even members of this class were victimized by racism. Especially important is Larsen's exploration of the lives of the black women of her time. Her legacy is a map of the complex lives of America's black nouveau riche during the New Negro movement.

BIBLIOGRAPHY

McDowell, Deborah E. "Introduction." In *Quicksand and Passing*. New Brunswick, NJ: Rutgers University Press, 1986.

Perry, Margaret. *Silence to the Drums: A Survey of the Literature of the Harlem Renaissance*. Westport, CT: Greenwood Press, 1976.

Soto, Hiroko. "Under the Harlem Shadow: A Study of Jessie Fauset and Nella Larsen." In *Harlem Renaissance Remembered*, edited by Arna Bontemps. New York: Dodd, Mead, 1984.

Tate, Claudia. "Nella Larsen's *Passing*: A Problem of Interpretation." *Black American Literature Forum*, Winter 1980.

Washington, Mary Helen, ed. *Invented Lives: Narratives of Black Women 1860–1960*. Garden City, NY: Anchor Press, 1987.

—ELIZABETH BROWN-GUILLORY

LAUNDRESSES. A laundress worked for an elite family as an adjunct to a full-time, live-in staff made up of cooks, maids, butlers, gardeners, and chauffeurs. As an independent contractor, a laundress was a stable, regularly employed, younger woman, responsible for doing her employer's washing and ironing on a weekly basis. She did the laundry work on the premises of her employer's home and incurred few out of pocket expenses. Also, because a laundress did not live in her employer's household, she often served as a confidante to other household workers and learned the problems confronting live-in servants, including their private feelings about employers or future employment plans. Above all, the laundress profession allowed women to return home at the end of the workday, so that the line dividing the personal and the professional was more clearly defined than in other occupations in the domestic service sector during the late nineteenth and early twentieth centuries.

Laundresses had more control over their working conditions than live-in servants, who usually worked seven

WOMAN AT WASHTUB. She may be a washerwoman, holding a status quite different from that of a laundress. A laundress worked in the employer's household, like the full-time staff, whereas washerwomen worked off the premises—for example, in a backyard, as this woman seems to be doing. (Austin/Thompson Collection.)

days a week, from sunup to sundown, and who typically had vague job descriptions and lacked power to bargain for better wages and hours. Cooks, maids, nurses, and waitresses tended to work under the gaze of their employer and could be confined to one area of the house during the day. When in the presence of their employer, or if caught in the middle of verbal exchanges between members of the employer's family, they were expected to make themselves invisible. Domestic servants might also fall prey to unwanted sexual advances from their employers.

Although laundresses and washerwomen both worked in the domestic service sector, a laundress held a status very different from that of a washerwoman. A laundress worked on the premises of her employer's household and commanded the same respect as a full-time staff member. Washerwomen worked in backyards or at common wells with other women in the neighborhood. These work arrangements offered African American women the opportunity for personal autonomy, allowing them to participate in social networks virtually shut off for cooks, maids, and butlers. For black women who needed time at home to care for their young children, washing and

ironing were an alternative to full-time domestic work. A washerwoman's workday was long and arduous. Water had to be carried from wells and hydrants for the different wash cycles. A washerwoman would pick up the dirty piles of clothes from her clients and deliver the clothing, and collect her money later in the week. Yet, a client's complaint about a lost or stolen item could result in the customer's refusal to pay for her services for the week, which generally amounted to a few dollars.

African American women were adamant about the distinction between laundresses and washerwomen. In urban areas such as New York; Washington, DC; Atlanta; and Charlotte, North Carolina, the laundress profession was one of the most coveted occupations among African Americans in the domestic service sector. In her study of domestic workers in Washington, DC, the historian Elizabeth

WOMAN WITH LAUNDRY. Since she is evidently carrying laundry to or from a client's home, she too may have been a washerwoman. The photographer was Marion Post Walcott. (Austin/Thompson Collection; Odum Photo Study, by permission of University of North Carolina.)

Clark-Lewis found that African American women who were employed as domestics ranked the laundress profession as one of the most desirable. Clark-Lewis also found that the laundress profession was one of the few house-to-house positions that was not considered precarious work among African American women.

African American women in the domestic service sector experienced a profound transformation when they made the full transition to day work. In doing so, they were able to control their work hours and conditions, gain more privacy, and participate more fully in the African American community. For black women who made the transition from the independent laundress to commercial laundry work, the mechanization of the industry had dire consequences in different regional economies. For example in 1877, African American washerwomen went on strike in Galveston, Texas, over depressed wages and increased competition from steam laundries and Chinese laundrymen. Around the same time similar struggles manifested in California, where black women reportedly confronted storeowners and picketed in the streets.

The historian Tera Hunter noted that one of the main advantages of laundry work was that whites were not employers as much as they were clients. As independent contractors, laundresses typically worked on the staff at five to six households. But, as with most other laundry workers, their wages were typically low. A laundress might increase her earnings by adding clients to her work roster. According to a study conducted by the Women's Bureau during the Great Depression, black women outnumbered white women in commercial laundries, took shorter lunch hours, and received about one-half the pay of white women industrial workers in general. As late as 1935, black women did housework and laundry for three dollars per week, and washerwomen did a week's wash for seventy-five cents.

The laundress profession has been a source of economic opportunity, status, and personal autonomy for black women in the United States since the colonial era. The transition to free labor and industrial expansion had little impact on African American women's ability to move out of the domestic service sector of the economy until the early twentieth century. In their pursuit of autonomy, dignity, and decent wages, black women have used the laundress profession to circumvent race, class, and gender subordination in different regional economies.

BIBLIOGRAPHY

Clark-Lewis, Elizabeth. *Living In, Living Out: African American Domestics and the Great Migration.* New York: Kodansha International, 1996.

Hunter, Tera. *To 'Joy My Freedom: Southern Black Women's Lives and Labors after the Civil War.* Cambridge, MA: Harvard University Press, 1997.

Jones, Jacqueline. *Labor of Love, Labor of Sorrow: Black Women, Work, and the Black Family.* New York: Basic Books, 1985.

—BRANDI C. BRIMMER

LAURIE, EUNICE RIVERS (b. 12 November 1899; d. 28 August 1986); nurse, public health advocate. Eunice Rivers Laurie may have been America's most controversial and frequently discussed black public health nurse. In l958 she was given the U.S. Department of Health, Education and Welfare's highest honor, the Oveta Culp Hobby Award, for her "notable service covering 25 years during which through selfless devotion and skillful human relations she has sustained the interest and cooperation of the subjects of a venereal disease control program in Macon County, Alabama."

Fourteen years later, media coverage revealed that the control program was in reality what would be considered the United States' longest-running unethical medical experiment. Nurse Rivers, as she was called in her community, had been crucial in sustaining the Tuskegee Syphilis Study. It was a forty-year "study" (1932–1972) by the U.S. Public Health Service of late-stage syphilis in 399 African American men (and 201 others as controls) that kept its subjects ignorant of their disease and their experimental status while working to deny them treatment. When African Americans express their concerns and fears of treatment at the hands of health care practitioners and scientists, "Tuskegee" becomes the one-word symbol for centuries of abuse. Nurse Rivers's role in the study would remain a subject of debate among the public, media, artists, and scholars for generations.

Eunice Verdell Rivers was born in Early County, Georgia, the oldest child of three in the family of Albert and Henrietta Rivers. Rivers's mother died when she was fifteen, and her father gained a modicum of independence by working a small farm as well as toiling in a sawmill. This kind of independence could be dangerous. A Ku Klux Klan bullet whizzed into their home after Albert Rivers was wrongly accused of aiding the escape of a black man wanted for the murder of a white policeman. To save the family, Albert Rivers moved them away and stayed to protect his house.

Eunice Rivers's father also took a stand for her education. He sent her off to a school under the tutelage of a cousin in Fort Gaines, Georgia, and then to a mission boarding school in Thomasville. When Albert Rivers discovered that the mission school had only white teachers in the upper grades, he pulled his daughter out (one year shy of high school graduation) and sent her on to the black-run Tuskegee Institute in Alabama in 1918.

Eunice Rivers spent her first year at Tuskegee learning handicrafts, in keeping with the school's philosophy of vocational education. But Albert Rivers wanted more for his daughter, and he encouraged her to switch to nursing. Graduating in 1922, Rivers did some private nursing and was subsequently hired to travel with Tuskegee Institute's Moveable School, a truck that carried an agricultural extension and home demonstration agents, a public health nurse, and their equipment into Alabama's countryside. Rivers focused primarily on the health needs of black women and children, teaching basic health education, simple sanitation methods, and childcare. She also demonstrated cleanliness techniques to Alabama's extensive network of midwives. At the time, she was one of only four black public health nurses in the entire state. She also worked for the state's Bureau of Vital Statistics and devised techniques for midwives to report births accurately.

Rivers's great skill was her nonjudgmental understanding of the medical beliefs of rural African Americans and her support of their dignity and individual needs in medical encounters. By 1931, however, the state had to cut its workforce, and Rivers lost her position. She was then hired as a night supervisor at Tuskegee's John A. Andrew Hospital.

Eight months and many sleepless nights later, Rivers was offered a new half-time day position as a scientific assistant to what was referred to in the medical literature as a "study of untreated syphilis in the male Negro." Rivers's job for the next forty years was to find men for the study, follow up on their condition; assist in their examinations, which included painful spinal taps; provide aspirins and tonics; gain agreement from many of their families for autopsies; and modify the primarily white physicians' behaviors toward their "subjects." She also helped the men's families in numerous ways, providing referrals to doctors and food for the hungry.

Rivers was integral to community life in Tuskegee. While working on the "study," she was also employed in the maternal and child health clinics at the Institute's hospital and taught in its nursing school. She was also active in the Red Cross and the Greater St. Mark Missionary Baptist Church in Tuskegee. Numerous awards testified to her nursing skills. In 1952, she married Julius Laurie, an orderly at the hospital.

When the story of the "study" broke on the Associated Press wire on 26 July 1972, it caused an uproar across the country. Charges of racism, genocidal medicine, and paternalism gone awry were among the outraged criticisms of the health care system's notorious willingness to use poor people, especially African Americans, for experimentation without any kind of consent. Edward Kennedy convened hearings in the United States Senate, a federal investigation condemned the study, the institutions and governmental units involved offered varying justifications, and a class-action civil suit filed by the prominent

civil rights attorney Fred Gray ended in a $10 million out-of-court settlement for survivors and their families. The outcry was instrumental in the creation of institutional review boards (IRBs) to monitor human subject research. Nurse Rivers, however, was never called before the Senate hearings or named in the lawsuit.

Different interpretations of Nurse Rivers's role were put forward. The attorney Fred Gray argued that she was as much a victim as were the male subjects. In *Miss Evers' Boys*, a widely produced play and television movie that is a fictionalization of the story, the playwright and physician David Feldshuh showed Rivers torn between her devotion to the men and the black and white physicians' assurances that what she was doing was proper. Nursing ethicists have pointed to her lack of power. Historians found evidence that Rivers may have helped some of the men to get treatment and leave the study.

Eunice Rivers Laurie died in Tuskegee. More than a decade later, in May 1997, President Bill Clinton apologized to the remaining survivors and the nation for the federal government's role in the study. Nurse Rivers never had the chance to tell the public what she really thought.

BIBLIOGRAPHY

David Feldshuh. "Miss Evers' Boys." *American Theatre* 7, no. 8 (November 1, 1990): special supplement following page 35.

Fred D. Gray. *The Tuskegee Syphilis Study*. Montgomery, AL: Black Belt Press, 1998.

"Interview with Eunice Rivers Laurie, October 10, 1977." Black Women's Oral History Project: From the Arthur and Elizabeth Schlesinger Library on the History of Women in America, Radcliffe College, volume 7. Edited by Ruth Hill. Westport: Meckler, 1991.

James H. Jones. *Bad Blood: The Tuskegee Syphilis Experiment*. New York: Free Press, 1993.

Susan M. Reverby, ed. *Tuskegee's Truths: Rethinking the Tuskegee Syphilis Study*. Chapel Hill: University of North Carolina Press, 2000.

—SUSAN M. REVERBY

LAVEAU, MARIE (b. 10 September 1801; d. 16 June 1881) and **MARIE LAVEAU** (b. 2 February 1827; d. c. 1890), mystics, Voodoo priestesses. Marie Laveau and her daughter of the same name were free women of color living in a slave society. They founded and led the interracial societies of Voodoo in New Orleans from the 1820s to the 1880s. The Laveaus were descended from and related to many prominent Catholic families of all colors and conditions of life in colonial Louisiana; they had ancestors from France, Spain, Senegal and the kingdom of Kongo in West Africa, and among the Native American nations living by the Mississippi River. Both women spoke French and had been baptized at the altar of St. Louis Cathedral by Père Antoine, a famous and saintly "priest of the people." In their own time and in the decades that followed their deaths, the two practitioners were often mistaken for one other. Eight women in their extended families

<small>TOMB OF MARIE LAVEAU THE FIRST in St. Louis Cemetery, New Orleans, 1995. Laveau, called a "Voodoo queen," had remarkable power and influence during the nineteenth century. The plaque notes, in part, that she was "the most widely known of many practitioners of the cult." (© Robert Holmes/Corbis.)</small>

used variations of the same name, often with different spellings. Historical evidence, archival documents, eyewitness accounts, newspaper articles, and the intense gossip that still circulates disagree on details, interpretations, sources, and most matters of importance about the women's lives. Moreover, in the atmosphere of racial and religious prejudice in nineteenth-century New Orleans, Protestant Anglo-Americans promoted the accusations that the priestesses were witches and evildoers who worshiped snakes and conducted grisly ceremonies in graveyards at midnight.

The Marie Laveaus, mother and daughter, were Creoles, born and bred in the New World and more culturally attached to the unique society of South Louisiana than to that of Africa or Europe. Creoles were French-speaking Catholics with complex family structures adapted to the racial and sexual mores of French, Spanish, and American administrations. With lavish public ceremonials, distinctive cuisine, clothing, burial customs, and drinking habits, Creole was much more a culture than a color.

Scholarly Views

The most accessible sources on the Laveaus are by the anthropologists Zora Neale Hurston writing in the 1930s and Martha Ward seventy years later. Hurston, an African American novelist and folklorist, was initiated into the Laveau spiritual lineage and New Orleans Hoodoo-Voodoo at least six times, the last time at the hands of the grandnephew of Marie the Second. She wrote a scholarly report that took up an entire issue of the *Journal of American Folklore* in 1931, and later a brilliant personal mythological and poetic account, the last part of *Mules and Men*. Until Ward's book on the Voodoo queens (2004), few scholars paid attention to Hurston's groundbreaking New Orleans fieldwork. Ward centered her biography of the two women on the suffering that slavery, segregation, Jim Crow, illness, and poverty created in their community.

Most scholars accept that the Laveaus had careers founded on service to the Creole community of New Orleans; they belonged to a number of social aid and benevolent societies that helped to bury the dead and care for the sick, unemployed, or orphaned. It is known that both women wore *tignons*, the Creole turbans that were the symbol of resistance to the punitive racial rules of Spanish, French, and American administrations and a proud marker of their status as free women of color. Both Laveaus were famous for their performances of spirit theater—Marie the First in Congo Square in Tremé, the largest and most assertive antebellum community of color in the United States—and Marie the Second at the lakefront beaches, where racial restrictions were discarded during the celebrations that foreshadowed the New Orleans Jazz and Heritage Festival.

Marie Laveau the First was buried in an aboveground or "high tomb" in St. Louis Cemetery One, New Orleans' oldest and most famous "city of the dead." Holding at least nine members of her family, Laveau's tomb is one of the most visited in America. The bronze plaque that cemetery preservationists placed on the front suggests that the "real" Marie is not buried there. It labels her spiritual activities as "cultic" and "mysterious," and says that Voodoo itself came from Haiti. These are common misconceptions or stereotypes about the priestesses' spiritual activities.

The tomb, probably built in the late 1830s, reads in translation from French, "Family of the Widow Paris born Laveau." Working from documents in church and civil archives, scholars reconstructed some of the trajectories and tragedies of the women's personal lives. In 1819, a month before her eighteenth birthday, Marie the First wed a free man of color named Jacques Paris who came from the island of St. Domingue, later called Haiti. Her father, Charles Laveaux (his spelling), a free man of color and prominent land owner, legally acknowledged Marie by giving his "natural" daughter a piece of property on Love Street, renamed Rampart.

But a few years after they wed, Jacques Paris disappeared forever. Persistent rumors in New Orleans claimed, using the language of Voodoo, that he crossed his young wife and she fixed him. Gossip also suggested that Marie the First helped other women to find a mate, keep him faithful and employed, or, failing that, to obtain a Voodoo divorce in a Catholic city. On her tomb and in reliable historic documents signed after her husband's disappearance, Marie Laveau identified herself as "the Widow Paris," although no other evidence of Jacques's fate survives.

Marie Laveau the First was a prominent member of St. Louis Cathedral, and in her career as a fever nurse probably tended British and American soldiers after the Battle of New Orleans in 1815, both Confederate and Union wounded during the Civil War, and many Creoles through the annual summer seasons of cholera, yellow fever, and other deadly epidemics.

A few years after Jacques Paris disappeared, the young and beautiful Widow Paris met a Creole veteran of the Battle of New Orleans named Christophe Glapion. But Marie the First could not marry him—he was white and the racial laws of the new American administration forbade their union. So Christophe, in order to live with and, from all accounts, to love the queen of the Voodoos, changed his race. For the rest of his life, he apparently passed as a free man of color. The major account of this period in the Widow Paris's life is the obituary that her younger daughter, Philomene, gave to the *New Orleans Picayune* on 16 June 1881.

Although civil and church records do not agree, evidence suggests that Marie, the alleged Widow Paris, and Christophe, a white man posing as a free man of color, had five children together. Their first, born on 2 February 1827, was baptized Marie Eucharist Heloise Glapion. As an adult, she adopted her mother's ceremonial name, Marie Laveau. Only she and another daughter, Philomène, survived childhood. Each sister had five children, and it appears they lived together in their grandmother's house on St. Ann Street in the French Quarter. The three women of the Laveau-Paris-Glapion household buried half of the fifteen children they bore between them. The Laveaus paid regular visits to their family graves. Elaborate Catholic and Creole mourning customs revolved around funerals, mourning rituals, and the annual observances of death. These habits and the city's inability to bury its dead during the summer epidemics created images of open coffins or skeletal remains and fueled vivid, often vicious speculation about the Voodoos.

The Practice

The Voodoos were then, as now, accused of the worst crimes of the human imagination. Voodoo practitioners knew how to curse and kill; they trafficked in evil spirits—or so it was said. Their primary transgressions, however, were their challenges to the slave system of the United States. Marie Laveau the First and her husband Christophe Glapion forged documents that freed enslaved people; Marie the Second developed charms, spells, and magical manipulations that offered enslaved people power and control over masters and mistresses. Both hid escaped slaves and lied to authorities. These Voodoo-inspired projects were a salve on the great wound of slavery.

Both Maries challenged the legal system in other ways, often in protection of poor, even guilty, citizens of New Orleans. The enemies of Marie the First claim that, after one particularly gruesome double hanging at Parish Prison, she compelled the state of Louisiana to ban public executions as spectator sport. Her friends said that she spared condemned men on Death Row the humiliation and shame of the gallows by poisoning them first. Marie the Second hypnotized policemen sent to arrest her and caused them to bark like dogs, circle three times, and fall asleep on the doorstep of the priestesses' St. Ann Street home. Songs about fixing someone who has crossed us, Love Potion No. 9, or that old black magic pay tribute to the skills of Voodoo women, community social workers who helped friends and neighbors manipulate the contrary fortunes of love, luck, and the law.

In the decade before the Civil War, Anglos complained about loud music, lewd dances, sexy Voodoo rituals, and the explosive potential of free and enslaved black people. They congregated by the hundreds, sometimes thousands, at Congo Square, the old parade ground outside the original city walls, the epicenter of African American dance, music, and cultural life, and the only place in America where free blacks, whites, and enslaved people could gather as equals. So, anxious authorities built a fence around Congo Square and stationed a policeman at each of its four gates. Marie Laveau the First, the most prominent practitioner in town, hypnotized the guards and walked into the plaza like the queen she was. There she picked up a large snake and danced in the embodiment of freedom—or so the few surviving eyewitness accounts claimed.

Such rituals and revels were slaps in the face of the systems of segregation and racial apartheid then developing in New Orleans. In the summer of 1850, police raided Voodoo gatherings in New Orleans on the pretext of breaking up illegal assemblies. The next morning, newspapers carried shocked stories of the white women who danced with black men at the gatherings; they used phrases like "promiscuous," "panting and raving," or "frothing at the mouth." Local magistrates turned the nameless white women over to the authority of their husbands or fathers; they remanded enslaved women to the mercies of masters or mistresses. Women of color, though fined and harassed, went free. Although there is no evidence that either of the Laveaus was arrested and charged, these stories testify to the number of women of all races who worked with them, trained with them, or followed similar spiritual paths. Hundreds of newspaper stories throughout the nineteenth century criticized the Voodoos in general and the Laveaus in particular. The press of their day favored words like "mystical," "sensuous," "primitive," "fantastic," "evil," "naked orgies," "lascivious," "voluptuous," "throbbing," "sweaty," and "entirely nude."

Changing Times

Marie the Second, who led Voodoo organizations after the Civil War, faced a different set of challenges from those of her mother and grandmothers. At the end of the war, Marie the Second celebrated in the Voodoo manner. She threw red-hot interracial parties on the beaches of Lake Pontchartrain, the largest one at Midsummer, 23 June, in honor of St. John the Baptist and High John the Conqueror. She invited the entire city to partake of "nearly nude" bathing and dancing, funky jazz, polyrhythmic drumming, and flowing spirits of rum, beer, and champagne. The jazz composer and Creole Jelly Roll Morton wrote a song called *Milenberg Joys* in honor of the "shimmie queens," or Voodoo leaders, like Marie the Second and her colleague, Eliza of the Dance.

Eucharist Glapion, Marie the Second, born in 1827, also loved a man she could never marry. Her lover Pierre Crocker, a well-to-do Creole stockbroker, a free man of color, was already married. Marie the Second contrived, successfully, to hide their connection and five children from the journalists who stalked her relentlessly and from neighbors who suspected her of leaving magical charms on their brick-scoured doorsteps. Marie the Second, intent as it were on hiding in plain sight, seems to have disappeared by the time her aged mother died in 1881. Despite extensive oral and written claims to knowledge about what happened to her, no reliable or verifiable date of death, cause of death, or gravesite exists.

With the death of the elder Laveau and the disappearance of the younger, the civil authorities of New Orleans, still obsessed with the imagined vices of Voodoo, passed laws that forbade "fortune-tellers" like Marie the Second to

> settle lovers' quarrels, bring together the separated, locate buried treasures, jewels, wills, bonds, or other valuables, effect marriages, heal sickness, reveal secrets, give luck or foretell the results of lawsuits, business transactions or investments, and to bring together bitterest enemies, converting them into staunchest friends.

The authorities of the period stalked, harassed, and sent hundreds of women into exile across the Mississippi River; they vilified the names of all the post-Laveau practitioners and made their spiritual lives a synonym for evil.

Although there are no historically reliable images of either Marie Laveau, people continued to claim to have seen her in trances, visions, dreams, and possession states, and to have received favors or blessings from her. The high tomb in St. Louis Cemetery One was the site of thousands of tourist visits and spiritual pilgrimages each year. They left gifts to her—fresh or silk flowers, candy, wine or other alcohol, gum, salt, money, baked goods, Mardi Gras beads, or offerings with personal meanings like the bride and groom statue from a wedding cake.

The stucco sides and marble front of the famous grave of the Widow Paris were covered with û marks. Despite frequent cleaning, the signs, often in groups of three, appeared as if by magic. Although no one knows what they mean, most have theories. Tour guides said that the marks represented wishes or requests to ask the Voodoo queen to grant special favors. Scholars pointed to the universal symbolism and spiritual meaning of two lines crossing. Another interpretation for the recurring û marks may be found in documents at the New Orleans Notarial Archives that Marie the Widow Paris signed. Sometimes her signature appears to be an intricate strategy to trick American authorities and secure freedom from bondage for a woman of color and her children. Others are bold lies that protected her children, property, and illegal marital arrangements with Christophe Glapion. It is clear from the persistent appearance of the marks on the tomb that both Marie Laveaus, later merged as one spiritual practitioner in the popular mind, still rule the imagination of New Orleans.

BIBLIOGRAPHY

Domínguez, Virginia R. *White by Definition: Social Classification in Creole Louisiana.* New Brunswick, NJ: Rutgers University Press, 1994.

Hirsch, Arnold R., and Joseph Logsdon, eds. *Creole New Orleans: Race and Americanization.* Baton Rouge: Louisiana State University Press, 1992.

Hurston, Zora Neale. "Hoodoo in America." *Journal of American Folklore* 44, no. 174 (1931): 317–417.

Hurston, Zora Neale. *Mules and Men* (1935). New York: Harper-Perennial, 1990.

Kein, Sybil, ed. *Creole: The History and Legacy of Louisiana's Free People of Color.* Baton Rouge: Louisiana State University Press, 2000.

Ward, Martha. *Voodoo Queen: The Spirited Lives of Marie Laveau.* Jackson: University Press of Mississippi, 2004.

—MARTHA WARD

LEE, JARENA (b. 11 February 1783; d. unknown), preacher. Jarena Lee was the first woman known to petition the African Methodist Episcopal (AME) Church for authority to preach. She was born in Cape May, New Jersey, and is recorded to have made a first request to preach in 1809 at Bethel African Methodist Church of Philadelphia. The

JARENA LEE, the first African American woman preacher. This portrait was the frontispiece to *Religious Experience and Journal of Mrs. Jarena Lee*, published in 1836. (Austin/Thompson Collection, from the Library of Congress.)

denial of this request did not stop Lee from preaching, and neither did her family life.

She married Reverend Joseph Lee, an AME pastor, in 1811 and moved to Snow Hill, New Jersey. In the sixth year of marriage, Joseph Lee died, and Lee was left with two children and a commitment "to preach his gospel to the fallen sons and daughters of Adam's race."

Jarena Lee returned to Philadelphia and renewed her request to preach. Reverend Richard Allen, who at Lee's first request could find no precedent in Methodist discipline for women preaching, had become bishop of the newly organized African Methodist Episcopal Church. Lee asked "to be permitted the liberty of holding prayer meetings in my own hired house, and of exhorting as I found liberty." Bishop Allen granted the request and was affirmed in the decision when Lee was moved to speak when Reverend Richard Williams, the assigned preacher for Bethel Church, appeared to lose the spirit. She spoke so well and so connected the text to her life that Bishop Allen publicly proclaimed her gifts.

Lee went on to preach throughout the northeastern region. Although she often traveled alone, her autobiography reports constant companionship among African American evangelical women. Because Lee was an itinerant preacher and because she carried out her ministry with and among other "sisters in Christ," she was a pathfinder for future preaching women, particularly women of the AME Church. The constant and successful preaching efforts of AME women eventually forced the denomination to create gender-specific positions where no organizational authority for women had previously existed.

BIBLIOGRAPHY

Collier-Thomas, Bettye. *Daughters of Thunder: Black Women Preachers and Their Sermons, 1850–1979.* San Francisco: Jossey-Bass Publishers, 1998.

Lee, Jarena. *Life and Religious Experience of Jarena Lee, A Coloured Lady, Giving an Account of Her Call to Preach.* Philadelphia, printed and published for the author, 1836. One copy is in the special collection of Wilberforce University and another at Atlanta University's Negro Collection. Electronic version available at http://digilib.nypl.org/dynaweb/digs/wwm9716/.

Lee, Jarena. *Religious Experience and Journal of Mrs. Jarena Lee, Giving an Account of Her Call to Preach the Gospel* (1849). Nashville: AMEC Sunday School Union/Legacy, 1991.

—JUALYNNE E. DODSON

LEE, SHEILA JACKSON (b. 12 January 1950), congresswoman and civil rights advocate. Congresswoman Sheila Jackson Lee represented the Eighteenth Congressional District of Houston, Texas, filling the seat once held by the trailblazer Barbara Jordan. In the tradition of her distinguished predecessor, Lee served as a leader on civil rights and a forceful and articulate advocate of the physical and economic health of her constituents and the welfare of children, the poor, and the elderly.

Sheila Jackson Lee was born in Jamaica, New York. She earned a BA degree, with honors, at Yale in 1972 and a JD degree from the University of Virginia Law School in 1975. Before entering politics Lee was an attorney in the Houston area and served as staff counsel to the U.S. Select Committee on Assassinations in 1977 and 1978. She was a corporate attorney for several years before becoming an associate judge of the Houston Municipal Court in 1987. She served two terms as an at-large member of the Houston City Council from 1990 to 1994.

In 1994 she defeated incumbent Congressman Craig Washington in the Democratic primary for the Eighteenth District and easily won the general election. The Eighteenth Congressional District was indirectly created by the Voting Rights Act in 1965 and was first represented by Barbara Jordan, a gifted politician and dynamic orator who was the first black Texan to join the U.S. Congress.

The class of freshman Democrats of the 104th Congress named Lee their president, and she was appointed to the House Democratic Steering and Policy Committee. During the 105th Congress, Lee founded the bipartisan Congressional Children's Caucus and then introduced legislation that strengthened criminal laws against child sexual predators, created greater access to mental health services for children, and provided funding for international child nutrition programs.

Lee was a member of the House Science Committee's subcommittee on Space and Aeronautics. Representing a district that is a home to the aerospace industry and the Johnson Space Center, she was a champion of funding for NASA and a promoter of the space program's contributions to science and medical research. In 1998, as a member of the House Judiciary Committee, Sheila Jackson Lee took part in the presidential impeachment hearings that eventually led to President Bill Clinton's trial in the Senate. The hearings were bitterly partisan, with Lee and Representative Maxine Waters of California sparring with Bob Barr, Chairman Henry Hyde, and other conservative committee members. Lee and three other committee Democrats wrote a resolution that would have provided for censure of the president rather than impeachment, but it lost in a vote of 22 to 16. In the wake of the collapse of Houston's Enron Corporation in 2002, Lee introduced the Omnibus Corporate Reform and Restoration Act to protect the retirement investments of workers, punish corporate officers for destroying records, and prohibit corporate loans to company officers and directors.

Early in 2003 Lee became a prominent opponent of President George W. Bush's plan to invade Iraq, sponsoring a resolution to repeal the Authorization for the Use of Military Force against Iraq resolution that had been signed into law the previous October. As an alternative course of action, she advocated trying Saddam Hussein as a war criminal in the International Criminal Court. When the resolution failed, she joined five other representatives in asking a federal judge to issue an injunction barring the invasion, but the judge rejected the lawsuit.

Lee sponsored legislation to offer benefits to families of soldiers who receive posthumous citizenship through death on active duty during military hostilities and to provide stiffer penalties for smugglers of illegal aliens. She also traveled to Nigeria to witness the inauguration of President Olusegun Obasanjo, visited Norway to participate in a conference focused on adding the voices of women to the partnership for peace in the Middle East, and joined other Democratic representatives on a ten-day tour of the Middle East to promote the Bush administration's so-called Roadmap for Peace. Sheila Jackson Lee was a member of the House Select Committee on Homeland Security and the House Judiciary and Science Committees, as well as six subcommittees. She was the first vice chair of the Congressional Black Caucus, a member of the Human Rights Caucus, and a delegate to the United Nations Special Session on Children.

She married Elwyn C. Lee, vice-chancellor for student affairs at and special assistant to the chancellor of the University of Houston. They had two children.

BIBLIOGRAPHY

"Congresswoman Sheila Jackson Lee." http://www.jacksonlee.house.gov.

Lawrence, J. M. "Bush Urges Court to Nix Antiwar Lawsuit." *Boston Herald*, 23 February 2003.

Masterson, Karen. "Houston Lawmakers Plan to Counter DeLay's Speech." *Houston Chronicle*, 1 August 2003.

Medea, Andra. "Sheila Jackson Lee." In *Facts on File Encyclopedia of Black Women in America*, edited by Darlene Clark Hine. New York: Facts on File, 1997.

"Sheila Jackson Lee." In *Notable Black American Women Book 3*. Farmington Hills, MI: Gale Group, 2002. Reproduced in Biography Resource Center. http://galenet.galegroup.com/servlet/BioRC.

—ROBERT W. LOGAN

LEFT, THE. In much of the history and historiography of the American Left, African American women have largely been invisible, lost in the cracks somewhere between the "Negro question" and the "woman question." Most white and black male Communists, Socialists, and even New Leftists of the 1960s have tended to view African American struggles through the lenses of race, saving the category of gender (when it was applied) to white women. Not surprisingly, in most left-wing movements where African Americans as a whole and women of various ethnic groups have struggled to remain visible and find an authoritative voice, black women radicals were probably the most invisible of all.

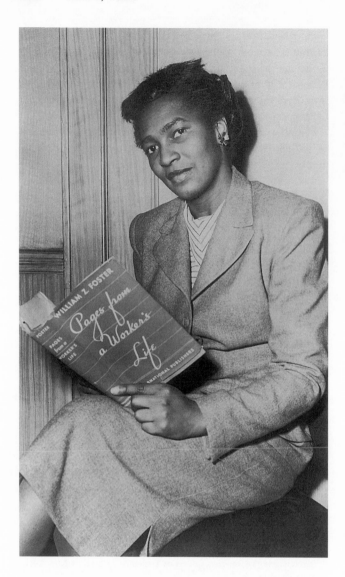

CLAUDIA JONES in the 1940s, when she was facing deportation. The book she holds is William Z. Foster's *Pages from a Worker's Life*, published in 1939. Foster was a union organizer and a leader of the American Communist Party. (Schomburg Center for Research in Black Culture, New York Public Library.)

Early Socialism

From the rise of the U.S. branch of the First International Workingmen's Association in 1864 to the collapse of its successor—the Second International—in the aftermath of World War I, the U.S. Left did not take an interest in the specific struggles of African American women, nor did black women figure prominently in left-wing movements. The best-known black woman radical of the late nineteenth and early twentieth century was Lucy Parsons, although it

was only later in her life that the fair-skinned Parsons even claimed her African heritage. Indeed, although she would eventually become an avid fighter for the rights of all women and actively protest racist attacks, during the height of her popularity she regarded issues of race and sex secondary to the class struggle.

By the first two decades of the twentieth century, there was some limited Socialist activity among African American women in Harlem, and to a lesser degree in parts of the Midwest, especially in Oklahoma, where a large number of independent black towns were located. A handful of Harlem women, including housewives, schoolteachers, and full-time domestics, listened to street corner lectures by the black Socialists Hubert Harrison, A. Philip Randolph, Chandler Owen, and Frank Crosswaith, as well as by black women such as Anna Jones, Elizabeth Hendrickson, Helen Holman, and Grace P. Campbell. Holman and Campbell emerged as significant leaders in the Socialist Party. Campbell, a popular social worker who maintained a home for young single mothers, ran for the state assembly in New York on the Socialist ticket and garnered 25 percent of the Harlem vote. However, Holman and Campbell were exceptions; black women held no substantive leadership positions in the Socialist Party.

The Socialist Party failed to attract many black working-class women or men to its ranks for several reasons. First, Socialists' official doctrine considered race and gender issues secondary to the class struggle. Second, leading black male Socialists, despite their support for women's suffrage, directed their attention to the condition of male industrial workers, the relationship between African Americans and the labor movement, and southern lynching. Third, white women Socialists showed little, if any, interest in the specific problems of black working women. Although the publication of August Bebel's *Women under Socialism* in 1879 had provided a theoretical framework with which white women within the Socialist Party could discuss the "woman question" in a Marxist context, there was no effort to examine the disproportionate numbers of African American women engaged in wage work, the racist character of the early birth control and suffrage movements, the ways in which race hinders the possibility of a radical sisterhood, or the dominant, racist views of black women's sexuality and the unequal treatment they received in courts of law in incidents of rape and other cases. Moreover, there was no serious attempt to challenge the tendency among many white Socialist women to employ black female domestic workers.

African American women became slightly more visible with the founding of the African Blood Brotherhood (ABB) in 1918 by the West Indian migrant Cyril Briggs. Under Briggs's editorship, the ABB published a radical newspaper called the *Crusader*, in which Bertha De Basco edited a short-lived women's column. Leading black female activists in the ABB included Gertrude Hall and Grace Campbell, both of whom joined the Communist Party in 1924, after Brotherhood leaders decided to liquidate the ABB. Although we know little about the role black women played within the ABB, the public rhetoric of the Brotherhood couched the struggle in terms of black male redemption. A secret, underground organization of radical black nationalists, the ABB advocated armed defense against lynching, the right to vote in the South, the right to organize, equal rights for blacks, and the abolition of Jim Crow laws. While it is plausible that black women ABB members might have carved out autonomous spaces for themselves within the organization, much like Garveyite women had done within the Universal Negro Improvement Association, the ABB left little documentation. By 1922 most of its leadership had joined the Communist Party of the United States (CPUSA), effectively liquidating the ABB within two years.

Early Communism

Initially, the CPUSA's official position on the "Negro question" hardly differed from that of the Socialists', and throughout most of the 1920s the "woman question" was almost nonexistent. Before 1928, the party's discussion of women's problems centered primarily on their role as wage laborers, although the Communist platform included a list of demands unique to working mothers (maternity leave, nurseries, and feeding time at factories). By the onset of the Great Depression, the Communists, with some nudging from the Comintern, began to pay more attention to both the "Negro question" and the "woman question." However, the party's position on black liberation after 1928—namely, its insistence on self-determination for African Americans in the southern black belt—essentially precluded a serious theoretical framework combining the "Negro" and "woman" questions. The party's advocacy of black self-determination conjured up masculine historical figures such as Toussaint-Louverture, Denmark Vesey, and Nat Turner, and writers such as Eugene Gordon and V. J. Jerome portrayed the movement as a struggle for "manhood."

While it never occurred to most leading Communists that there could be a "Negro woman question" distinct from other categories, the party's shift in the way it conceived of class struggle opened up at least a few free spaces in which African American working-class women could pursue their own agenda. Although the party's early forays into labor organizing via the Trade Union Unity League ignored the majority of African American women because they were concentrated in domestic work and agriculture, black women joined the Communist-led Unemployed Councils, neighborhood relief committees, and

a variety of housewife organizations and auxiliaries. In cities such as Chicago, Birmingham, Los Angeles, Detroit, and especially Harlem, black working women participated in relief demonstrations, resisted eviction efforts, confronted condescending social workers, and fought utilities shutoffs. Working through a variety of Communist-led mass organizations, from the Housewives League and the International Labor Defense to the Hands-Off Ethiopia Campaign, the Harlem Communist Party produced a significant group of black women leaders, including Louise Thompson Patterson, Claudia Jones, Audley Moore, and Bonita Williams. African American women also participated in Communist-led strikes, the most famous of the period being the St. Louis nutpickers' strike of 1933, which involved at least twelve hundred black women.

The Communist Party was not the only option for black women on the Left. The activist and future attorney Pauli Murray became active in the Communist opposition led by Jay Lovestone—a group of renegade Communists who split from the Communist International over their understanding of capitalism in the United States. In the late 1920s, the Lovestoneites believed that capitalism was more resilient in the United States than elsewhere and thus the country was not on the brink of revolution. Following her tutelage with the Lovestoneites, Murray ended up in the Socialist Party camp and led the SP-sponsored Workers Defense League's efforts to save Odell Waller (a black Virginia sharecropper who had killed his landlord in self-defense) from execution.

For committed black women in the CPUSA, the Marxist education they received nurtured an incipient, though somewhat muted, feminist consciousness. The Communists not only encouraged working-class women's participation as activists but also offered black women an empowering language with which to define and critique gender oppression. On both a personal and collective level, black women activists appropriated from the party's tabloid, *Working Woman*, such phrases as "the woman question" and "male chauvinism" as weapons with which to negotiate relationships, the sexual division of labor, and their participation in the movement. It was out of such discussions and actions that black working-class women developed an incipient class-conscious black feminist or, more appropriately, "womanist" perspective.

This unique form of militant class-conscious black "womanism" that emerged within the CP found its strongest voice in the South. The party gained its largest black female following in rural Alabama, where upward of five thousand women joined the Communist-led Share Croppers Union (SCU), the Young Communist League (YCL), or the Communist Party during the first half of the Depression decade. Founded in 1931 by African American tenant farmers and sharecroppers in Tallapoosa County,

Alabama, the SCU attracted a substantial number of rural women, many of whom had been radicalized by the deterioration of the rural economy and its effects on their proscribed roles in the division of labor. Women were not only burdened with fieldwork and housework but were also responsible for providing meals for their families with whatever food was available. When planters cut back on food and cash advances, and New Deal agricultural policies resulted in mass evictions of thousands of tenant and sharecropper families, black families were threatened with starvation. The crisis prompted a group of black women SCU activists to form a "Committee of Action," which marched down to the Tallapoosa County Civil Works Administration office in Camp Hill and won some of its demands for relief.

The success and direction of the SCU depended to a large degree on women's participation. Women's social and cultural networks served as conduits for radical organization; women activists possessed indispensable organizing skills (they tended to have higher rates of literacy); and women's religious and social organizations were prototypes for the women's auxiliaries. Frequently called "Sewing Clubs," the women's auxiliaries exercised considerable power within the union. Although they met separately to divert the suspicions of local authorities and divide childcare responsibilities, the Sewing Clubs provided forums for women to discuss conditions and formulate strategy. Black women also emerged as leaders: nineteen-year-old Eula Gray assumed leadership of the union for nearly a year after it had been driven underground in 1931. Although she was replaced by a black male comrade in 1932, she continued her union work and led the Young Communist League in Alabama, serving as a delegate to the party's Eighth National Convention in April of 1934.

Ironically, the party's shift to Popular Front politics after 1935—a period known for emphasizing the "woman question"—spelled disaster for rural Alabama women. The Central Committee disbanded the SCU in 1937 and divided its twelve thousand members between the all-white Alabama Farmers' Union and an AFL-led farm laborers union, the latter becoming a section of the United Cannery, Agricultural, Packing, and Allied Workers of America, which was a Congress of Industrial Organizations (CIO) affiliate. Although the old SCU kept most of its locals intact, it now had to conform to the standards of the Farmers' Union or the CIO. The social movement reflecting women's concerns gave way to simple trade unionism, and women's critical role as decision makers was replaced by unfamiliar, white male bureaucracies.

SNYC and CRC Activism

Just as the SCU collapsed, the Southern Negro Youth Congress (SNYC) emerged as an important site for the elaboration of a class-conscious black womanist perspective. Founded in 1937, the Communist-led SNYC attracted a number of black women activists, many of whom were young middle-class intellectuals who came of age in the South during the New Deal era. Although SNYC chapters were located throughout the South, its organizational centers were located in Richmond, Atlanta, New Orleans, and Birmingham—the latter serving as the SNYC's national headquarters from 1939 until its demise in 1948.

From the time of its founding, the SNYC's Communist and non-Communist leadership adopted a program that proved more radical than most other civil rights organizations of the period. Despite its rather traditional slogan of "Freedom, Equality and Opportunity," the SNYC's program emphasized the right to vote, job security, the right of black workers to organize, and general improvement in the health, education, and welfare of black citizens. The Youth Congress also opposed regional wage differentials, police brutality, and segregation in public spaces. And although socialism was rarely mentioned in SNYC literature, it remained a point of discussion within Congress circles throughout its eleven-year history.

Women also held more substantial leadership positions in the SNYC than any other non–gender specific civil rights organization of the day. The most important national leaders in the SNYC were Communist women such as Esther Cooper, who rose to the position of executive secretary during the war; Augusta Jackson, editor of the SNYC newspaper *Cavalcade*; and executive board members Grace Tillman, Dorothy Burnham, and Thelma Dale. Ethel Lee Goodman, CP member and former organizer of relief workers in Birmingham, assumed leadership of SNYC's Rural Committees, whose members consisted of many former SCU members. Non-Communist women also held critical leadership roles; the most prominent being Bertha Boozer, the primary strength in the Atlanta chapter who attempted to organize black domestic workers, assisted a strike of garbage collectors, and led a boycott of department stores that refused to hire African Americans. Mildred McAdory led a group of five SNYC activists to protest segregation on public transportation in Fairfield (a suburb of Birmingham), for which she was beaten and arrested. Sallye Davis, a young schoolteacher in Birmingham whose daughter, Angela, would become the most celebrated black Communist in history, was also a vital force in the Birmingham SNYC local.

The Youth Congress was founded at an auspicious time with respect to the Communist position on the "woman question." During the Popular Front (1935–1939), party leadership encouraged more debate on women's oppression and its publications placed greater emphasis on women's rights and the sexual division of labor in working-class households. These issues were brought to the forefront within the party by Communists such as Margaret Cowl, director of the CPUSA Women's Commission during the period, and Mary Inman, whose influential book *In Woman's Defense* (1939) still stands out as a pioneering effort to wed Marxism and feminism. The newfound importance of the "woman question" during the Popular Front prompted challenges to traditional gender relations within the party as well as Communist-led organizations. Men were criticized more frequently for male chauvinism and efforts to recruit and involve women were more pronounced. Within the Youth Congress, in particular, some black women and men strove to eradicate sexist relations in their personal life; black Communist couples who led the SNYC during the 1940s recalled sharing household duties and childcare.

It is possible that the prominent roles black women played in leadership positions partly account for the SNYC's tendency to focus its legal defense activities on cases involving black women. This marked a substantial shift in left-wing legal defense work on behalf of African Americans, which had grown out of the Communists' defense of black men falsely accused of rape (for example, the Scottsboro case and the Willie Peterson case). During and after the war, the SNYC's most important cases were its defense of Nora Wilson, a black Alabama domestic worker convicted of assaulting her boss with intent to kill, and Recy Taylor, a young black woman who had been kidnapped and raped by six white men in Abbeville, Alabama.

The Youth Congress's emphasis on legal justice for black women also had an impact on the actions of the Civil Rights Congress (CRC), a left-wing legal defense organization founded in 1946, just two years before the SNYC's demise. One of CRC's better-known campaigns centered on Rosa Lee Ingram, a black Georgia tenant farmer and widowed mother of twelve who, along with two of her sons, was convicted and sentenced for the murder of a neighboring white tenant farmer, John Stratford. Stratford, who initiated the altercation on Ingram's property in November 1947, assaulted Rosa Lee with the butt of a rifle and, by some accounts, sexually harassed her. Her son intervened, wrested the gun from Stratford, and struck a blow to his head that proved to be fatal. Throughout the country, African Americans, white liberals, and radicals rallied in defense of Rosa Lee Ingram and her sons, angered especially by the speedy and unconstitutional trial which resulted in their conviction, the racist application of the death sentence in a clear-cut case of self-defense, and the conviction of all three defendants when the responsibility of Stratford's death lay with only one of Rosa Lee's sons. Black women, in particular, viewed the case as proof that the courts did not recognize their right to defend themselves against physical assault or sexual violence. The case spurred the creation of a number of radical women's organizations linked to the CRC campaign, founded primarily by black women who had some association with the Communist Party. One of the most important organizations was the Sojourners for Truth and Justice. Launched by Louise Thompson Patterson and Beulah Richardson (an actress and poet known later as Bea Richards), the Sojourners attracted most of the leading radical black women intellectuals and activists, including the *California Eagle*'s editor Charlotta Bass, Dorothy Hunton, Shirley Graham Du Bois, Alice Childress, and Rosalie McGee (the wife of Willie McGee, who was on death row in Mississippi on false charges of raping a white woman).

Post–World War II Activism

Despite these breakthroughs in Communist-led movements during and after World War II, African American women and issues affecting them still remained the most invisible component of party work. In 1949, for example, the black CP leader Claudia Jones published a scathing critique titled "An End to the Neglect of the Problems of Negro Women!" in the party's theoretical journal, *Political Affairs*. Indeed, Jones's essay stands out as one of the clearest articulations of a class-conscious womanist perspective emerging out of the Communist Party. She insisted that black women's struggles should be foremost on the Communists' agenda because black women were the most exploited segment of the American working class. Not only did black women earn less than all men and white women, she argued, but postwar economic restructuring had the effect of forcing large numbers of black women into domestic work for white families. She railed against left-wing labor organizers for refusing to organize domestic workers and noted with disgust that "many progressives, and even some Communists, are still guilty of exploiting Negro domestic workers." Jones was especially critical of the casual, allegedly unconscious racist and sexist remarks directed at black women within the party, and demanded that African American women hold more substantial leadership positions. The latter demand was crucial to Jones's argument, for she suggested that black women's position in the hierarchies of race, gender, and class uniquely situated them to push the party in the most progressive direction.

Nevertheless, just as in the early 1930s, radical black working-class women found free spaces within certain left-wing trade unions in which to resist multiple forms of oppression. For example, the Food, Tobacco, Agricultural, and Allied Workers (FTA), especially Local 22 rooted in R. J. Reynolds Tobacco Company in Winston-Salem, was one of the most important unions in the postwar period. Led by a number of militant black women closely associated with the Communist Party, including Miranda Smith, Velma Hopkins, Theodosia Simpkins, and Viola Brown, FTA's Local 22 waged strikes, resisted sexual harassment at the workplace, taught worker education classes, set up a library stocked with volumes on African American history and Marxist literature, registered black voters, refused to sign anti-Communist affidavits required by the Taft-Hartley Act after the war, and supported the Progressive Party's presidential candidate in 1948, Henry Wallace. As a radical union in the age of the cold war, FTA was eventually expelled from the CIO in 1950.

Another important union in the postwar era was Local 1199 of the Drug, Hospital, and Health Care Employees Union in New York City. While FTA's Local 22 grew out of a predominantly black female work environment, New York's Local 1199 was initially made up of white male pharmacists, clerks, soda men, and black porters and retail hospital workers in Harlem. Founded in the 1930s by Jewish Communists active in the CPUSA Trade Union Unity League, its composition changed dramatically by the late 1950s when a left-wing breakaway group within the union began organizing black and Latino hospital service workers and waged a partially successful strike in 1959. Although the union eventually abandoned its ties to the CP, it retained a left-wing political culture, struggled against racial and gender inequality at the workplace and beyond, opposed the Vietnam War, actively supported the civil rights movement, and pledged solidarity with democratic movements in Central America and South Africa solidarity committees. Local 1199 was also the first union to support Jesse Jackson's presidential candidacy in 1988.

In the aftermath of the Communist Party's decline in the 1950s, due largely to postwar repression and general disillusionment with the Soviet Union after Stalin's crimes were revealed in 1956, there were few Marxist organizations in which African American women figured prominently. Nevertheless, a handful of radical black female intellectuals, artists, and organizers continued to work relatively autonomously. Among this group were Esther Cooper Jackson, a former SNYC activist and cofounder of *Freedomways* magazine; Elizabeth Catlett, one of the most important visual artists of the postwar period; and the extraordinary poet and playwright Lorraine Hansberry. Hansberry had been a supporter of left-wing causes ever since she was a teenager. She protested the House Un-American Activities Committee's hearings, studied at the CP's Jefferson School of Social Science, and joined the editorial staff of Paul Robeson's short-lived magazine *Freedom*, which carried articles by several radical black women involved in Sojourners for Truth and Justice. She eventually married Robert Nemiroff, who was then director of the left-wing Camp Unity in upstate New York. In addition to writing, she participated in a number of progressive political campaigns until her untimely death in 1965.

Civil Rights Organizations

Finally, left-leaning African American women also participated in, and at times influenced, mainstream civil rights organizations. The former Communist Mae Mallory, for instance, provided critical support for Robert Williams during his armed self-defense campaign in Monroe, North Carolina, in 1957. Marvel Cooke, a former CRC activist, continued to offer her talents to various civil rights movements during the 1960s. Perhaps the most powerful radical female voice within both the Student Nonviolent Coordinating Committee (SNCC) and the Southern Christian Leadership Conference (SCLC) was that of Ella Baker, whose experience with left-wing politics began in Harlem during the 1930s. By example she prompted a number of young militants in SNCC to pay closer attention to the struggles of the poor and working-class, to challenge male chauvinism within the movement, and to erect a fully democratic organization where decisions are made collectively and in the context of struggle.

Although the activities of radical black women in particular, and Communist-led movements in general, had the potential of inspiring the new generation of militants in the 1960s and 1970s, the lessons of the past were largely (though not entirely) lost to black New Leftists. In an age when the metaphors for black liberation were increasingly masculinized and black movement leaders insisted on privileging race over class and gender oppression, even the most Marxist of the black nationalist movements of the time—the Black Panther Party (BPP)—initially ignored or belittled the "woman question." Yet, in spite of these adverse circumstances, when it was possible, radical black women sustained the tradition of carving out free spaces within existing male-dominated organizations in order to articulate a class-conscious womanist perspective and to challenge the multiple forms of exploitation black working-class women and men faced daily. Whether it was the Panther's free breakfast and educational programs or various black nationalist organizations such as the Congress of Afrikan People, African American women radicals devised strategies that, in varying degrees, challenged capitalism, racism, and patriarchy. And in some instances, African American women radicals rose to positions of prominence and, sometimes by sheer example, contributed toward developing a militant, class-conscious black feminist perspective. The most important figures in this respect include Kathleen Cleaver, Erica Huggins, and Assata Shakur (formerly JoAnne Chesimard) of the Black Panther Party and the Communist leader Angela Davis.

Black Womanist Organizations

On the other hand, when it was not possible to build progressive class-conscious womanist movements within radical nationalist organizations, a number of leading black women activists collectively organized autonomous black feminist organizations. Between 1966 and 1970, black women formed several autonomous organizations, including the Black Women's Liberation Committee of SNCC and its offspring, the Third World Women's Alliance; the Harlem-based Black Women Enraged; and the Oakland-based Black Women Organizing for Action. One group based in Mount Vernon, New York, led by Patricia Haden, Donna Middleton, and a radical social worker named Pat Robinson, put forward the argument that a revolutionary black movement without an understanding of class struggle is worthless, and a class movement without a consideration of gender and sexuality is equally worthless. In 1973, they, along with many anonymous black community people, published a remarkable little book, *Lessons from the Damned*, which offered an analysis of the forces arrayed against the black poor—especially poor women. In a section titled "The Revolt of Poor Black Women," they write eloquently of how their own families contribute to the exploitation of black women and youth. They insisted that revolution must take place on three levels: overthrowing capitalism, eliminating male supremacy, and transforming the self. Suspicious of cultural nationalist injunctions to return to "African traditions," these women insisted that revolution is supposed to usher in a new beginning; it is driven by the power of a freed imagination, not the dead weight of the past.

The National Black Feminist Organization (NBFO) founded in 1973 represented the most visible national organizing effort during this period. The NBFO provided a forum to challenge racist and gender oppression but tended to ignore the specific struggles of poor and working-class women and limited their discussions to the problems of heterosexual women. Within a year, the left-wing of the NBFO abandoned the movement and sought to build something more radical and inclusive. In 1974, a group of radical black feminists in Boston who had broken with the NBFO formed the Combahee River Collective. The women who formed the collective came from different movements in the Boston area, including the Committee to End Sterilization Abuse and the campaign to free Ella Ellison—a black woman inmate who, like Joan Little in North Carolina, was convicted of murder for killing a prison guard in self-defense. Nearly all the women had worked together to bring attention to a series of unsolved murders of black women in Boston.

In 1977, three members of the collective—Barbara Smith, Beverly Smith, and Demita Frazier—issued "A Black Feminist Statement." It was the clearest articulation of black socialist feminism ever produced. The authors understood the racial and sexual dimensions of domination, arguing that the history of white men raping black women was "a weapon of political repression." At the same time, they rejected the idea that all men are oppressors by virtue of biology and broke with lesbian separatists who advocated a politics based on sexuality. In their view, such an analysis "completely denies any but the sexual sources of women's oppression, negating the facts of class and race." And while they did not see black men as enemies and called for broad solidarity to fight racism, they did acknowledge patriarchy within black communities as an evil in need of eradication. Black people as a whole, they argued, cannot be truly free as long as black women are subordinate to black men. As socialists, the collective believed that a nonracist, nonsexist society could not be created under capitalism, but at the same time they did not believe socialism was enough to dismantle the structures of racial, gender, and sexual domination. Their vision was manifest in their political practice. Combahee members saw connections between class, race, and gender issues and worked in support of "Third World women" workers, challenging healthcare facilities that provided inadequate or unequal care, and organizing around welfare or day care issues. And like Ella Baker before them, they knew that the very process of struggle, in a democratic organization, invariably produces new tactics, new strategies, and new analyses. "We believe in collective process and a nonhierarchical distribution of power within our own group and in our vision of a revolutionary society. We are committed to a continual examination of our politics as they develop through criticism and self-criticism as an essential aspect of our practice."

By the 1980s there really was no single, identifiable black socialist-feminist movement to speak of. While groups like the Combahee River Collective ceased to exist, radical black women worked within an endless number of left-wing groups, welfare rights campaigns, regional organizations such as the Southern Organizing Committee for Economic Justice, the predominantly white feminist movements, militant trade unions, as well as a variety of Marxist and left-leaning black nationalist organizations ranging from the Republic of New Africa, the African People's Party, the Patrice Lumumba Coalition, the All-African People's Revolutionary Party, and the National Black Independent Political Party (whose steering committee included the former Harlem Communist Audley "Queen Mother" Moore). Radical black women such as Angela Davis and Charlene Mitchell played major leadership roles in the Communist Party, and later the Committees of Correspondence, throughout the 1980s, 1990s, and into the new millennium. More recently, black women such as Barbara Ransby and Frances Beal have played a key role in the Black Radical Congress (BRC), a national umbrella organization founded in 1997. The Feminist Caucus within the BRC continues to be one of the most vibrant and active sections of the Congress.

Although black women continue to participate in a variety of different movements and articulate a wide range of radical positions, both within and outside the U.S. Left, today's black women radicals share with their predecessors a commitment to simultaneously challenging racism, capitalism, and patriarchy, and to rendering visible the unique struggles of African American working-class women. They continue to insist that to fight for black women's freedom is to fight for freedom for humanity. The most recent and perhaps clearest articulation of this vision comes from the "Statement of Purpose" (available online) issued in June 2000 by the BRC's Feminist Caucus:

We recognize that if we eliminate just imperialism and capitalist exploitation, we will not be free; if we only eliminate white supremacy, we will not be free; if we eliminate only patriarchy and heterosexism, we will not be free. Our vision is to forge a radical Black feminist movement which battles on each of these fronts simultaneously. We unite with our sisters across the globe who are fighting to eliminate the same systems of oppression. A radical Black feminist vision challenges us to root out injustices at every level and in every crevice of our lives, communities, organizations and societies.

BIBLIOGRAPHY

Black Feminist Caucus. "Statement of Purpose, June 22, 2000." www.blackradicalcongress.org/organizing/committees/bfc.htm

Collier-Thomas, Bettye, and V. P. Franklin, eds. *Sisters in the Struggle: African American Women in the Civil Rights–Black Power Movement*. New York: New York University Press, 2001.

Davis, Angela Y. *Angela Davis: An Autobiography*. New York: Random House, 1974.

Davis, Angela Y. *Women, Race, and Class*. New York: Random House, 1981.

Dawson, Michael C. *Black Visions: The Roots of Contemporary African American Political Ideologies*. Chicago: University of Chicago Press, 2001.

Echols, Alice. *Daring to Be Bad: Radical Feminism in America, 1967–1975*. Minneapolis: University of Minnesota Press, 1989.

Foner, Philip. *American Socialism and Black Americans: From the Age of Jackson to World War II*. Westport, CT: Greenwood Press, 1977.

Giddings, Paula. *When and Where I Enter: The Impact of Black Women on Race and Sex in America*. New York: Morrow, 1984.

Gore, Dayo. " 'A Candle in a Gale Wind': Black Women Activists and Post–World War II U.S. Politics, 1940–1960." PhD diss., New York University, 2003.

Guy-Sheftall, Beverly, ed. *Words of Fire: An Anthology of African-American Feminist Thought*. New York: New Press, 1995.

Horne, Gerald. *Communist Front? The Civil Rights Congress, 1946–1956*. Rutherford, NJ: Fairleigh Dickinson University Press, 1988.

Horne, Gerald. *Race Woman: The Lives of Shirley Graham Du Bois*. New York: New York University Press, 2000.

Inman, Mary. *In Woman's Defense*. Los Angeles: Committee to Organize the Advancement of Women, 1941.

James, Joy. *Shadowboxing: Representations of Black Feminist Politics*. New York: St. Martin's, 1999.

James, Winston. *Holding Aloft the Banner of Ethiopia: Caribbean Radicalism in Early Twentieth-Century America*. New York: Verso, 1998.

Jones, Claudia. "An End to the Neglect of the Problems of Negro Women!" (1949). Reprint, *Political Affairs* 53.3 (March 1974).

Kelley, Robin D. G. *Freedom Dreams: The Black Radical Imagination*. Boston: Beacon Press, 2002.

Kelley, Robin D. G. *Hammer and Hoe: Alabama Communists during the Great Depression*. Chapel Hill: University of North Carolina Press, 1990.

King, Deborah. "Multiple Jeopardy, Multiple Consciousness: The Context of Black Feminist Ideology." *Signs* 14 (Autumn 1988): 42–72.

Matthews, Tracye. " 'No One Ever Asks What a Man's Role in Revolution Is': Gender and the Politics of the Black Panther Party." In *The Black Panther Party Reconsidered*, edited by Charles Jones. Baltimore: Black Classic Press, 1998.

McDuffie, Erik. "Long Journeys: Four Black Women and the Communist Party, 1930–1956." PhD diss., New York University, 2003.

Nekola, Charlotte, and Paula Rabinowitz, eds. *Writing Red: An Anthology of American Women Writers, 1930–1940*. New York: Feminist Press at the City University of New York, 1987.

Ransby, Barbara. *Ella Baker and the Black Freedom Movement: A Radical Democratic Vision*. Chapel Hill: University of North Carolina Press, 2003.

Schaffer, Robert. "Women and the Communist Party, USA, 1930–1940," *Socialist Review* 45 (May–June 1979).

Smith, Barbara. *The Truth That Never Hurts: Writings on Race, Gender and Freedom*. New Brunswick, NJ: Rutgers University Press, 1998.

Springer, Kimberly, ed. *Still Lifting, Still Climbing: Contemporary African American Women's Activism*. New York: New York University Press, 1999.

Washington, Mary Helen. "Alice Childress, Lorraine Hansberry, and Claudia Jones: Black Women Write the Popular Front." In *Left of the Color Line: Race, Radicalism, and Twentieth-Century Literature of the United States*, edited by Bill V. Mullen and James Smethurst. Chapel Hill: University of North Carolina Press, 2003.

Weigand, Kate. *Red Feminism: American Communism and the Making of Women's Liberation*. Baltimore: Johns Hopkins University Press, 2001.

—Robin D. G. Kelley

LEGAL PROFESSION.

LEGAL PROFESSION. Now visible at almost every level of the legal profession, African American women lawyers in the twenty-first century have finally made significant inroads in their struggle to study and practice the law. Being doubly marginalized by both race and gender prejudices has meant that they have made such inroads in spite of great obstacles. From preparation to practice, the legal profession proved to be rough terrain for African American women. Yet, black women lawyers have distinguished themselves in private practice and government agencies, as law professors and as judges. Their personal and professional lives tell a story of hard work, commitment, and service to the bar, the black community, and the nation as a whole.

Early Pioneers

Black women were among the first women of any race to practice law. In 1796, a black woman named Lucy Terry Prince, although not a lawyer, became the first woman to argue a case before the United States Supreme Court. The first generation of African American women lawyers, however, did not emerge until the late nineteenth century. In 1872, almost three decades after Macon B. Allen became the first African American lawyer, and three years after Arabella Mansfield became the first American woman to practice law, Charlotte E. Ray (1850–1911) became the first black woman lawyer in the United States, and the first woman lawyer in the District of Columbia, when she graduated from Howard University Law School and was admitted to practice law. She remained the nation's only black woman lawyer for eleven years. In 1883 Mary Ann Shadd Cary (1823–1893), who began law school at Howard a year before Charlotte Ray, became the nation's second black woman lawyer. Since Cary was admitted to Howard's first law class in 1869, she has the distinction of being one of the first women admitted to an American law school. Eliza Chambers graduated from Howard in 1888 and practiced in Washington, DC, in the general areas of equity, patents, pensions, and land claims. Ida G. Platt, who graduated from the Chicago Law School (now the Chicago-Kent Law School) with high honors in 1892, was admitted to practice law in Illinois in 1894. Lutie Lytle, the last in this generation of black women lawyers, graduated from Central Tennessee Law School in 1897 and was admitted to the Tennessee bar in the same year.

Howard Law School and other black law schools, such as Central Tennessee Law School, trained this first cohort of African American women lawyers. Whereas black men, whether self-taught or tutored by lawyers or judges, first entered the legal profession by reading the law, black women entered the legal profession only after being formally trained in law schools. However, during the nineteenth century most of the nation's law schools excluded blacks, and those that admitted a token number were seldom open to women. For example, Harvard Law School, which admitted its first black student, George Lewis Ruffin, in 1868 and graduated black men such as Raymond Pace Alexander, William Henry Hastie, and Charles Hamilton Houston, routinely denied admission to women, both black and white, until 1950. Pauli Murray, a black woman law graduate of Howard Law School, was told upon application to pursue a graduate law program at Harvard in the early 1940s that she was not of the sex entitled to be admitted to Harvard Law School.

Other white male schools were not quite so intransigent, but they were sufficiently backward to retard the progress of women, and especially black women, for the greater part of the nation's history. Yale Law School lifted its restrictive policy against women in 1918, two years before women finally achieved the right to vote, and in 1928 Jane Matilda Bolin, America's first African American

woman judge, became the first black female law student at the law school. Although the University of Michigan was one of the first publicly supported law schools to admit and graduate African Americans, the first black woman to attend the university's law school left after three months. The second, Lucia Theodosia Thomas, who entered in 1936, was told by the admissions officer that she would be better off pursuing a career in medicine since the law school's mission was to train judges and legislators, roles in which he did not foresee a black woman.

Clearly, the establishment of black law schools was critical to the training of the first generation of black women lawyers. Several law schools were established in the late nineteenth century to train black lawyers. They usually adhered to a nondiscriminatory policy of admission, and a few, such as Howard Law School, opened their doors with a racially integrated faculty, a practice unheard of in other American law schools. Howard Law School is the nation's first black law school. It was established in 1869 under the leadership of John Mercer Langston, who was one of the first black lawyers in the nation admitted to practice law but was also the first known African American in the nation denied admission to a law school. From its inception, Howard Law School was committed to training both men and women, irrespective of race, ethnicity, or religion. It had a higher enrollment of women students than most American law schools. Between 1882 and 1904, the law school graduated at least seven white women who were denied admission to white law schools. Between 1896 and 1944, it graduated twenty-eight black women. Central Tennessee Law School was one of ten black law schools established between 1870 and 1896. It was the second black law school in the South when it opened in 1879.

The nineteenth-century African American woman lawyer had few prospects for law-related employment. The government did not hire black lawyers, and black communities were an insufficient source of potential clients. Charlotte E. Ray maintained a small practice in Washington, DC, and became the first black woman lawyer to try a case when she served as attorney for the plaintiff in a divorce case heard before the Supreme Court of the District of Columbia in 1875. But by 1879 she had given up all hope of a successful practice and returned to her hometown of New York to become a teacher in the Brooklyn public schools. Mary Ann Shadd Cary, author of an 1870 corporation law thesis that was commented upon favorably by Howard University's president, General O. O. Howard, practiced for four years in Washington, DC. Cary also utilized her training and years in the abolitionist movement in her advocacy of women's suffrage. In testimony before the United States Senate Judiciary Committee in the late nineteenth century, Cary demanded that as a citizen and taxpayer she have the right to vote and the right to be governed by her own consent the same as men.

Lutie Lytle, who was admitted to the bar of Tennessee and Kansas, intended to begin private practice immediately following her graduation. However, she escaped the disappointment of trying to obtain sufficient legal business when she joined the law faculty at Central Tennessee Law School in 1897, where she taught domestic relations, evidence, and criminal procedure for four years. She was the first black female lawyer in the South and the first female law professor of a chartered law school in the world. Ida Platt was the only one from this first generation of black women lawyers to establish a successful practice. Platt, who probably passed for white, established a partnership with a white lawyer following her admission to the Illinois bar and practiced away from Chicago's African American community. Platt's ability to exploit society's racial code to her professional advantage reveals the distance between the experiences of black and white women in the legal profession.

LUTIE LYTLE, the first black female lawyer in the South, graduated from Central Tennessee Law School in 1897 and was admitted to the Tennessee bar in the same year. (Kansas State Historical Society.)

By 1900 eighteen of the nineteen law schools that had been established to train black lawyers were closed, mainly because of the standards of legal education established by the American Bar Association (ABA). This is one of many situations in which the "professionalization" of a field forced out African Americans and their institutions. Howard survived and, under the leadership of Charles Hamilton Houston, gained full ABA and Association of American Law Schools (AALS) accreditation in 1930 and 1931 respectively. But the possibilities for legal training for black women were greatly diminished. As late as 1910 there were reportedly only two practicing black women lawyers in the nation.

As nineteenth-century legal professionals, Charlotte E. Ray, Mary Shadd Cary, Lutie Lytle, and Ida B. Platt were members of a profession that considered women unsuited for the practice of law. Their chances for truly active practice were therefore severely limited. However, as early pioneers these women set a precedent of what was possible for generations of African American women. Black women had always worked outside the home, but they were disproportionately represented as domestic servants well into the twentieth century. They tended to enter the professions as teachers, either because of a desire to avoid domestic service or because they were motivated by the serious need for teachers in the black community. However, although most of the more than thirty thousand black women professionals in the early twentieth century were teachers, Ray, Cary, Lytle, and Platt represent a small cadre of black women who sidestepped teaching and dared to become lawyers. Understanding what was possible, the next wave of black women lawyers became twentieth-century pioneers who carved out their own niche and constructed their own professional identity as they made inroads in a profession that still considered them outsiders.

Inroads in the Legal Profession, 1920–1960

The passage of the Nineteenth Amendment and women's new political status broadened their opportunities in the legal profession. Having secured the right to practice law in every state by the 1920s, women in general and black women in particular began to make significant inroads in the legal profession. African American women established themselves in noticeable numbers, and several even distinguished themselves in the legal profession in the 1920s and 1930s. The Great Migration had brought many African Americans from the rural South to the urban North, to major cities like Chicago and New York, and provided a black clientele for this second generation of black women lawyers. By 1935, there were black women lawyers in California, Illinois, Indiana, Iowa, Kansas, Massachusetts, Michigan, Minnesota, Missouri, Nebraska, New York, North Carolina, Ohio, Pennsylvania, Virginia, and the District of Columbia, with Illinois leading in the number of black women lawyers. Still, the black woman lawyer's experience at the early-twentieth-century bar was defined largely by discrimination and exclusion.

Among the African American women admitted to practice law in Illinois in the 1920s were Violet Neatly Anderson Johnson, who graduated from the Chicago Law School in 1920; Sophia Boaz Pitts, who graduated from Kent College of Law in Chicago in 1923; Edith Spurlock Sampson and Georgia Jones-Ellis, who both graduated from John Marshall Law School in Chicago in 1925; Anna Crisp, who graduated from the Chicago Law School in

VIOLETTE ANDERSON. During the 1920s, she was the first African American woman to practice law in Illinois. She was also the first to argue a case before the United States Supreme Court. (General Research and Reference Division, Schomburg Center for Research in Black Culture, New York Public Library, Astor, Lenox, and Tilden Foundations.)

1926; and Alice Huggins, who graduated from John Marshall Law School in 1929. By the 1920s, several of the nation's law schools had begun admitting a token number of black women, but Howard University Law School again took the lead in training black women. Among the black women lawyers licensed to practice law in the 1920s, several had graduated from Howard Law School, including Ollie M. Cooper and Isadora A. Letcher, who were both 1921 graduates; Zephyr Moore Ramsey, a 1922 graduate; and L. Marian Poe, a 1925 graduate.

By the 1920s, the number of black female law students was sufficiently large at black law schools to support legal sororities to further their professional development. In 1921, black female law students at Howard founded Epsilon Sigma Iota, the nation's first black legal sorority. It was incorporated by Ollie May Cooper, Bertha C. McNeill, and Gladys E. Tignor, who were upper-level students at the law school. The sorority functioned as the only social and legal association for black women law students and lawyers for almost two decades. There were even pledges from black women who were law students at the Robert H. Terrell Law School to establish a chapter of Epsilon Sigma Iota at their law school, or to be considered for membership in the Howard Chapter. However, before a decision could be made about whether Epsilon Sigma Iota should admit non-Howard students, Gamma Delta Epsilon was formed in 1937 at Terrell Law School, with the commitment to forge bonds among all black women lawyers. Ollie May Cooper, one of the founding members of Epsilon Sigma Iota, was a leader in both legal sororities.

Epsilon Sigma Iota and a growing number of local black professional associations, such as the John M. Harlan Law Club of Ohio and the Cook County Bar Association of Illinois, predated the founding in 1925 of the National Bar Association, which became a beacon for this second wave of African American women lawyers. Before 1943, the American Bar Association and local bar associations generally excluded African Americans from membership and therefore limited their access to professional opportunities and social networks. The National Bar Association, which was cofounded by Gertrude Durden Rush, a black woman lawyer who was admitted to practice in Iowa in 1918, was specifically committed to organizing black lawyers nationally and providing them with the networks necessary for professional development and advancement.

In addition to producing African American women lawyers, black law schools were also instrumental in black women's advancement in the legal profession. Ollie May Cooper, who graduated from Howard Law School in 1921, was a member of Howard's law faculty from 1925 to 1930. Before joining the law faculty she served as secretary to the dean of Howard's law school. Jane M. Lucas

Featuring Early Judges

● **Jane Bolin** (1908–) became the first black woman judge in the United States upon her appointment to the Domestic Relations Court of New York City in 1939. (See individual entry: Bolin, Jane.)

● **Edith J. Ingram** (1942–) was the first black judge in Georgia. Born near Sparta, Georgia, she attended Fort Valley State College (BA, Education, 1963) and then became a schoolteacher. In 1969 she was appointed Judge of the Court Ordinary of Hancock County. Four years later she became a judge of the Hancock County Probate Court. In addition to ruling on probate cases, she heard cases on issues such as guardianship, insanity, and estate administration. She also performed marriages, was an election supervisor, and issued writs of habeas corpus. Her many memberships included the National and International Association of Probate Judges and the County Officers' Association of Georgia. She also served on the boards of the Georgia Democratic Executive Committee and the Georgia Council on Human Relations. In the 1970s she was president of the Ogeechee-Lakeview Management Company. The recipient of a number of honors, in 1969 she was awarded the Outstanding Courage in Southern Political Arena Plaque by the NAACP. After thirty-five years on the bench, Ingram retired in 2004.

● **Norma Holloway Johnson** (1932–) was the first black woman to be appointed to the federal bench in Washington, DC. Born in Lake Charles, Louisiana, she attended Miner Teachers College, and in 1962 she became the first black woman to graduate from Georgetown University Law School. After working in private practice for a year, she joined the civil division of the Justice Department. In 1967 she became the assistant counsel for the Office of the Corporation Counsel for the District of Columbia. President Richard Nixon appointed her to the District's Superior Court three years later. After she had served on the Superior Court for a decade, in 1980 President Jimmy Carter appointed her to the U.S. District Court for the District of Columbia (her appointment was approved by the Senate). In 1997 she was named chief judge for that court. The following year she was the presiding judge on Kenneth Starr's case against President Bill Clinton in the Monica Lewinsky scandal. A founding member of the National Association of Black Women Attorneys and a member of the National Association of Women Judges, she also cofounded the Court Appointed Special Advocates, a group that provides legal help for abused children.

● **Amalya L. Kearse** (1937–) was the first woman judge appointed to the Second Circuit Appeals Court in New York. Born in Vauxhall, New Jersey, she attended Wellesley College (BA, Philosophy, 1959) and the University of Michigan Law School (JD cum laude, 1962). She was editor of the *Law Review* and won the Jason L. Honigman Prize for her work on the editorial board. After she passed the bar, she became a trial lawyer for Hughes, Hubbard, and Reed. When she was made partner, she became

the first black woman to reach that level in a top Wall Street firm. In 1979 President Jimmy Carter appointed her to serve on the U.S. Court of Appeals. In addition to her work on the bench, she was on the executive committee of the Lawyers Committee for Civil Rights under Law (1970–1979), on the board of directors of the NAACP's Legal Defense and Educational Fund, Inc. (1977–1979), and on the board of the National Urban League (1978–1979). She was so highly respected that her name came up for a Supreme Court appointment in three different presidential administrations (Reagan, Bush, and Clinton). At the beginning of his first term, President Bill Clinton also considered her for the position of attorney general.

● **Marjorie McKenzie Lawson** (1912–2002) was the first black woman judge appointed by a president. Born in Pittsburgh, Pennsylvania, she attended the University of Michigan in Ann Arbor (BA, Sociology, 1933; MS, Social Work, 1934). In 1939, after attending night school at the Terrell Law School in Washington, DC, she earned her first law degree. Her second came from Columbia School of Law in 1950. Throughout much of her career she practiced with her husband, concentrating on real estate and administrative law. In 1962, President John F. Kennedy appointed her to the Washington, DC, Juvenile Court. However, her work with presidents and presidential administrations did not start there. During the Roosevelt and Truman administrations, she was first assistant director and later director of the Division of Review and Analysis of the President's Commission on Fair Employment Practices. Starting in the mid-1950s, Lawson advised and campaigned for Kennedy. She won a Supreme Court case in 1950 when *Henderson v. United States* ended segregation in train dining cars. In addition, she was a *Pittsburgh Courier* columnist for over fifteen years and served the National Council of Negro Women as both vice president and general counsel. In 1965, she was named by President Lyndon B. Johnson to the Social Commission of the United Nations Economic and Social Council.

● **Mary Johnson Lowe** (1924–1999) was the second black woman appointed to the federal court; like the first one, Constance Baker Motley, she served the Southern District of New York. Born in New York City and raised in Harlem, she attended Hunter College (BA, 1952), Brooklyn Law School (LLB, 1954), and Columbia Law School (LLM, 1955). After passing the bar, she went into practice with two friends. Later she became a criminal defense attorney. In 1971 she became a judge in the New York City Criminal Court for the City of New York. Two years later she was appointed Acting State Supreme Court Justice for Manhattan Supreme Court's Centralized Narcotics Team. In 1975 she was transferred to the Supreme Court in Bronx County and in 1977 she was elected to the State Supreme Court. She was there for only a year before President Jimmy Carter appointed her federal judge in the Southern District of New York. In 1991 she became the senior judge for that court and in 1994 she retired from the bench. She was given the award for outstanding service to the criminal justice system from the Bronx County Criminal Courts Bar Association (1974) as well as the first Elizabeth Cady Stanton Award from the National Organization for Women (1984).

● **Consuelo B. Marshall** (1936–) was the first black woman judge of the U.S. District Court for the Central District of California. Born in Knoxville, Tennessee, and raised in Los Angeles, she attended Howard University (BA, 1958) and Howard University School of Law (LLB, 1961). Upon passing the bar, she became the first woman deputy city attorney for Los Angeles, a position she held until 1967. While with the city attorney's office, she served as an advisor to numerous city departments and the Civil Service Commission. She then spent two years in private practice before being appointed commissioner of the California Superior Court in 1972. In 1976 she was named municipal county judge in Inglewood, California, and the following year she was appointed to the California Superior Court, Criminal Division. Her colleagues on the court elected her to the court's executive committee within a year of her appointment. In 1980 President Jimmy Carter named her to the U.S. District Court, Central District of California. As of 2004 she was the chief judge of that court. Among many awards, she has received the Bernard S. Jefferson Jurist of the Year Award, the Judicial Excellence Award, and the Criminal Court Judge of the Year. In addition she has served on the Drug Violence Task Force sponsored by the United States Sentencing Commission.

● **Gabrielle Kirk McDonald** (1942–) was a president of the United Nations International Criminal Tribunal for the former Yugoslavia (ICTY) and the third black woman appointed to the federal bench. Born in St. Paul, Minnesota, she attended Boston University and Hunter College but did not receive an undergraduate degree. Despite this she moved on to graduate at the top of her class from Howard University Law School (LLB, 1966). From 1966 through 1969 she was a staff lawyer with the NAACP Legal Defense and Education Fund. She then moved to Texas, began a private practice, and taught at Texas Southern University and the University of Texas at Houston. In 1979 she was appointed to the U.S. District Court, Southern District of Texas, Houston Division, where she remained for nine years. In 1988 she became a partner with the firm of Matthews and Branscomb, opening its Austin office. However she stayed with the firm only two years before moving over to the firm of Walker, Bright, and Whittenton. In 1993, she was nominated (and won the highest number of votes for) a judgeship with the UN General Assembly's War Crime Tribunal. Two years later, the World Court–ICTY, held at the Hague in the Netherlands, finally began hearing cases. She was named president of the tribunal in 1998. While working for the ICTY, McDonald also served as appellate judge for the International Criminal Tribunal for Rwanda. In 1999 McDonald resigned. In 2000 she

was presiding judge of a four-judge panel of the Women's International War Crimes Tribunal during a mock trial against the Japanese military and government. The trial was based on charges that hundreds of women were made sexual slaves by the Japanese during World War II. The panel of judges found the late Emperor Hirohito guilty of crimes against humanity.

A member of the board of Freeport-McMoRan Copper and Gold Inc., McDonald is special counsel to the chairman on human rights of McMoRan Exploration Co. In 2001 she received the Margaret Brent Women Lawyers of Achievement Award from the American Bar Association's Commission on Women in the Profession.

● **Constance Baker Motley** (1921–) was a prominent civil rights attorney, state senator, and the first black woman to sit on the federal bench when she was chosen to serve the Southern District of New York. (See individual entry: Motley, Constance Baker.)

● **Velvalea (Vel) Rogers Phillips** (1924–) has a long list of firsts attached to her biography, including being the first African American member of the Wisconsin judiciary. Born in Milwaukee, Wisconsin, she attended Howard University (BS, 1946) and the University of Wisconsin Law School (LLB, 1951). She was the first black woman to graduate from the latter. In 1956 she became the first African American and the first woman elected to Milwaukee's Common Council. In 1971, after sixteen years as an alderman, she attended the University of Nevada Summer College for juvenile court judges and was elected to the Wisconsin bench. From 1972 through 1974 she served as a judge for the Milwaukee children's court. In 1978 she was elected secretary of state of Wisconsin, the first woman to hold that post and the first African American to be elected to statewide office in Wisconsin. In addition to her involvement in local and state politics, in 1954 Phillips became the first African American on the Democratic National Convention's Committee on Rules and Order of Business and in 1960 she was made cochair. She has also been a visiting lecturer in the department of African American Studies at the University of Wisconsin–Madison, and a visiting professor at the law school there. A civil rights leader in Wisconsin, she has served as a member of the Women's International League for Peace and Freedom and of the Day Care and Child Development Council at the John F. Kennedy School of Government at Harvard University, among many other positions.

● **Elreta Alexander-Ralston** (1919–1998) was the first African American woman and the second African American person, male or female, to become a judge by popular election. Born in Smithfield, North Carolina, she attended North Carolina Agricultural and Technical College (now University) and graduated with a BA in 1937. She was a schoolteacher for four years before she decided to continue her education at Columbia University Law School. In 1945 she graduated with an LLB degree, making her the first black woman to do so. After two years clerking in New York, she returned to her home state and became the first black woman to practice law there. In addition, she was the first black woman to argue a case before the State Supreme Court. By 1965 she had become a senior partner in her law firm, which was North Carolina's first integrated one. A longtime Democrat, in 1968 she switched parties and ran for district judge as a Republican. She remained on the bench for thirteen years before returning to private practice. In addition to her many awards and honors, Ralston published two books, *When Is a Man Free?* and *Vital Speeches of Today.*

● **Leah Ward Sears (Sears-Collins)** (1955–) was the first African American woman and the youngest person to sit on the Georgia Supreme Court. Born into a military family in Heidelberg, Germany, she attended Cornell University (BS, 1976) and Emory University Law School (JD, 1980). Only two years later, after a short period at a prominent Atlanta firm, she became a municipal traffic court judge. In 1988, she was elected to the Fulton County Superior Court, becoming the first black woman in the state's Supreme Court system, and its youngest. Four years later, the governor named her to the Georgia Supreme Court, becoming the first woman, as well as the youngest person in history, to achieve the position. She did not stop her education once she had attained that position. In 1995 she received her LLM degree from the University of Virginia School of Law and also studied at the National Judicial College. While most Supreme Court judges are not challenged, Sears-Collins had to fight three election battles to retain her seat. She won the first in 1992, shortly after she was appointed, the second in 1998, and the third in July 2004. Involved in a large variety of legal and civic associations, she established and was the first president of the Georgia Association of Black Women Attorneys. Among her many awards and honors, she received the Distinguished Leadership Award for Outstanding Service in the Judiciary (1988) and the American Bar Association's Margaret Brent Women Lawyers of Achievement Award (1992).

● **Juanita Kidd Stout** (1919–1998) was the first black woman to be elected to a judgeship when she won a place on the Philadelphia County Court in 1959. She was also the first to serve on a

began teaching at Howard in 1946, making her its second black woman law faculty member. She taught contracts, bills and notes, and legal bibliography until she resigned in 1951. She was followed in 1956 by Cynthia Starker, who taught legal bibliography and insurance and was also a law librarian. The Robert H. Terrell Law School, a black law school named after one of the first African American judges in the District of Columbia, the husband of the club woman Mary Church Terrell, was founded in the District of Columbia in 1931. It was in direct competition with Howard Law School and, like Howard, did not exclude women as students or as members of its faculty. Indeed, Helen Elsie Austin, who was a 1939 graduate of the University of Cincinnati Law School, became the third black woman in the nation to teach law when she was appointed to the Robert H. Terrell Law School faculty in 1941. She was followed by Marjorie Lawson, who taught labor law for one year in 1943, and Margaret A. Haywood, who taught personal property, wills and administration, and insurance law before the law school closed its doors in 1945.

Black women lawyers of this generation had more opportunities for practice than their sisters in the late nineteenth century. Some were fortunate enough to have had fathers or husbands whose firms they could join. Many black women lawyers of this generation secured early opportunities for active practice through a professional association with their fathers or husbands who were lawyers. In the 1930s and 1940s, many lawyer wives, such as Marjorie MacKenzie Lawson of Washington; Elizabeth F. Allen of South Bend, Indiana; Margaret B. Wilson of St. Louis; Alice Huggins of Chicago; Sadie Tanner Alexander of Philadelphia; Edith Sampson Clayton; and Jane Matilda Bolin formed legal partnerships with their lawyer husbands. However, most of the black firms formed during the first half of the twentieth century were financially precarious and short-lived.

Sadie Tanner Mossell Alexander and Jane Matilda Bolin are two distinguished practitioners who secured early opportunities for active practice with their husbands. Sadie Alexander, who was born in 1898 into one of Philadelphia's old elite black families, became the first African American woman to graduate from the University of Pennsylvania Law School in 1927. Her father, Aaron Mossell, was the law school's first black graduate, but Alexander obtained her early legal practice through her professional association with her lawyer husband, Raymond Pace Alexander, in whose firm she practiced for thirty-two years beginning in 1927. She specialized in trusts and estate, which was typical of the kind of work accessible to women lawyers. Although her opportunities for court practice were limited, Alexander established a successful practice among Philadelphia's black residents and built a reputation for professionalism and effectively

State Supreme Court when she was appointed to the Pennsylvania Supreme Court in 1988. (See individual entry: Stout, Juanita Kidd.)

● **Anna Diggs Taylor** (1932–) was a chief judge in the U.S. District Court, a federal judicial position. Born in Washington, DC, she attended Barnard College, Columbia University (BA, Economics, 1954), and Yale Law School (LLB, 1957). Upon graduating, she was immediately hired by the solicitor's office in the U.S. Department of Labor. In 1961 she moved to Michigan and worked as an assistant prosecutor for Wayne County for a year. In 1964, during "Freedom Summer," she was a volunteer legal counsel for National Lawyers Guild cases in Mississippi. In 1966 and 1967 she was an assistant attorney with the U.S. Attorney's Office for Michigan's Eastern District. She then reentered private practice until 1975, when she became supervising assistant corporation counsel for the Detroit Law Department. In 1979, President Jimmy Carter appointed her to the U.S. District Court, Eastern District of Michigan. In 1997, she became the chief judge of that court, a position she still held at the start of the twenty-first century.

● **Anne E. Thompson** (1934–) was the first black and the first woman to become a federal judge for the New Jersey District. Born in Philadelphia, Pennsylvania, she attended Howard University (BA, 1955), Temple University (MA, 1957), and Howard University Law School (LLB, 1964). Upon graduating, she joined the office of the solicitor of the U.S. Department of Labor and in 1966 moved on to become a staff attorney for the Legal Aid Society of Mercer County, New Jersey. A year later she became an assistant public defender in Trenton, New Jersey, and by 1970 had become a prosecutor for Lawrence Township. In 1975 she became the first woman and the first African American county prosecutor in New Jersey history when she was named Mercer County Prosecutor. She repeated these firsts when, in 1979, President Jimmy Carter named her to the federal bench as a judge for the District of New Jersey. In 1994 she became chief judge, a position that is obtained by seniority and that is held for seven years. She reached senior status in 2001. Among many awards and honors, she received the Outstanding Leadership Award from the New Jersey County Prosecutors Association and the Gene Carte Memorial Award from the American Criminal Justice Association (both in 1980).

practicing law. Like Sadie Alexander, Jane Matilda Bolin was born into an upper-middle-class professional black family in Poughkeepsie, New York, in 1908, where her father, Gaius Charles Bolin, was a successful lawyer in the mostly white town. She practiced with him for a year immediately following her graduation from Yale Law School in 1931, and she later practiced with her husband, Ralph Mizelle, in New York City for five years before the firm of Bolin and Mizelle dissolved. There were a few black women lawyers, such as Ruth Whitehead Whaley, who were successful sole practitioners. Whaley obtained her law degree from Fordham University School of Law in 1924, and between the late 1940s and early 1950s had established such a successful practice that when she ended her practice in New York City she referred an impressive caseload to Pauli Murray.

For many black women lawyers of this generation, jobs in government offered greater opportunities for legal practice. The exodus of men from the civilian labor force during World War II opened up short-lived opportunities for more women to attend law schools and to secure employment in private practice as well as with the government. In 1947 over 50 percent of black women lawyers worked in government agencies, social service, or civil liberties organizations. When race and gender prejudices made actual practice too precarious, these jobs offered greater security. Many served as assistant attorneys general, while others established successful careers in the offices of the solicitors general, the corporation counsel, and the district attorney. Violette Neatly Anderson, who graduated from the Chicago Law School in 1920 and was admitted to practice law in Illinois, became the first woman of any race to serve as assistant city prosecutor in Chicago from 1922 to 1923. She later served as vice-president of the Cook County Bar Association and became the first black woman admitted to practice before the United States Supreme Court. Eunice Hunton Carter, a 1932 graduate of Fordham Law School, was an assistant district attorney in New York City who was instrumental in the successful investigation and prosecution of the biggest organized crime case in the nation's history. Working with New York County District Attorney William C. Dodge, then with Special Prosecutor Thomas E. Dewey, Carter exposed the racketeering that flourished in New York City and the corruption of the magistrate's court to which she was assigned. In recognition, she was appointed the assistant district attorney in charge of the Court of Special Sessions, where she supervised more than fourteen thousand criminal cases each year. Jane Bolin, who first practiced with her husband, sought government employment after their law practice faltered. She was appointed in 1937 to the Office of the Corporation Counsel of New York Law Department with an assignment to the City's Domestic Relations Court, where she served for two years.

Featuring Women in Law Enforcement

According to a 1999 report by the National Center for Women and Policing entitled "Equality Denied: The Status of Women in Policing," 6.8 percent of local, county, and state law enforcement officers were women of color. They made up 1.1 percent of the top command and 2.8 percent of supervisors. Of lower-paid civilian jobs, 25.7 percent were held by women of color, who comprised only 6.4 percent of management. In the area of corrections, women of color fared a little better; they held 14 percent of all corrections positions. However, only 1.6 percent of the top command posts in corrections were held by women of color. The Federal Bureau of Investigation (FBI) opened the doors to minorities and women after the death of J. Edgar Hoover in 1972. As of 1999 there were a total of 10,497 agents working for the FBI, and 118 of these were black woman, according to Jack Owens, "Don't Call Us: Why the FBI Isn't Hiring Black Women," in the March 2001 issue of *Atlantic Monthly*. Though there is still far to go, throughout law enforcement black women are breaking down the barriers and moving up in the ranks.

● **Saundra Brown Armstrong** (1947–) was the first black woman to join the Oakland, California, Police Department and the first black woman prosecutor in Alameda County. Born in Oakland, she attended California State University, Fresno (BA, 1969), and the University of San Francisco (JD, magna cum laude, 1977). Three years after she joined the force, she began working toward establishing equal hiring rules in the department. At the time, only seven spots were allotted for women in the force. In addition, women were required to have college degrees, and men were not. Finally, women were not allowed to seek advancement. Armstrong was a policewoman until 1977, when she graduated from law school. She then joined the Alameda County district attorney's office (1978–1979 and 1980–1982). In 1982, she joined the Department of Justice and became the commissioner and vice chair of the Consumer Products Safety Commission in 1983. Three years later she was named commissioner of the Parole Commission before becoming a judge of the Alameda County Superior Court. In 1991 she became a federal judge and was named to the United States District Court for the Northern District of California.

● **Jacquelyn H. Barrett** (1950–) was the first black woman sheriff in the United States. She was born and raised in Charlotte, North Carolina, and attended Beaver College (BA, criminal justice) and Clark-Atlanta University (MA, sociology). She worked at the Georgia Peace Officer Standards and Training Council (1976–1986) and was director of the Fulton County Public Safety Training Center (1987–1992). In 1992 she was elected sheriff of Fulton County, Georgia, and was reelected in both 1996 and 2000. She was president of the National Organization of Black Law Enforcement Executives from 1997 to 1998 and received the Trumpet Award from Turner Broadcasting System in the latter year. With only a few months left in her third term and no plans

to seek reelection, she came under investigation for reportedly losing $2 million in public money to bad investments. Barrett denied the charge, saying she was the victim of fraud.

● **Pamela Carter** (1949–) was the first woman and the first African American in the United States to be elected a state attorney general. She was born in South Haven, Michigan, and raised in Indianapolis, Indiana. She attended the University of Detroit (BA, 1971), as well as the University of Michigan, Ann Arbor (MA, social work, 1973), and Indiana University's School of Law (JD, 1984). She went to work for Indiana governor Evan Bayh in 1988, serving as the executive assistant for health and human services before becoming his deputy chief of staff. She became attorney general in 1992. During her tenure, she succeeded in getting passed the Victims of Crime constitutional amendment, and her office recovered close to $4 million in Medicare overpayments. She was also the first African American and second woman chosen as vice president of the National Association of Attorneys General. In 1997 Carter returned to the private sector. A year later, she became vice president–general counsel of Cummins, Inc., a Fortune 500 company. In 2000 she was the cochair of the Indiana Democratic Party's state convention and in 2002 she was named vice president of Fleetguard, Inc., a subsidiary of Cummins.

● **Cassandra McWilliams Chandler** (1958–) was the highest-level black woman in the FBI, serving as an assistant director and national spokesperson. Raised in Compton, California, and Geismar, Louisiana, she attended Louisiana State University (BA, English) and the Loyola University Law School in New Orleans (LLD). She joined the FBI in 1985. Recruited while still in school, Chandler graduated and then passed the FBI's rigorous physical, psychological, and background checks. She spent four years in the New Orleans office before transferring to Washington, DC. In 1991 she became a supervisory special agent and moved again, this time to the San Diego office, receiving a promotion to acting special agent in charge. In 1997, Chandler became the agent in charge of the San Francisco white-collar crime unit. In 2002 she became the head of training for the entire agency. At the start of the twenty-first century, she was the agency's top black woman agent.

● **Charlotte Ann Council** (c. 1955–) was a deputy commissioner with the Philadelphia Police Department. Born and raised in Philadelphia, she attended LaSalle University (BA and MA, both in education). Before she joined the police force in 1982, she taught in the Philadelphia public schools. After moving up through the department and holding the ranks of sergeant, lieutenant, and captain, in 2003 Council was put in charge of the Internal Affairs Bureau, the first black woman to hold that position. Among her many awards, she was honored with the American Legion Certificate of Commendations and the Shirley

Chisholm Award. She was a member of the National Organization of Black Law Enforcement Executives and the National Organization of Black Women in Law Enforcement.

● **Gwendolyn (Gwen) J. Elliott** (c. 1946–) was a commander of the Pittsburgh Police Force. Prior to joining the force, she served with the U.S. Air Force (1964–1969) and the Air National Guard (1969–1973). After she left active duty, she served in the Army Reserves (1974–1979). She then became a crisis intervention and mental health counselor until, in 1976, she became one of the first female police officers in Pittsburgh. Eight years later she was the first woman on the force to be promoted to sergeant. In 1986, she became the first black woman commander of the force. Her first position at that rank was as night watch commander overseeing five precincts. In 1990 she was commander in charge of the Office of Family Violence, Youth, and Missing Persons. In addition, from 1994 to 1996, she was assistant to the mayor for youth policy. Before her retirement she was commander in charge of the Zone 3 Station. After she retired in 2002, she founded Gwen's Girls, an organization devoted to empowering girls. Elliott was a member of a variety of organizations, including the National Center for Women and Policing of the Feminist Majority Foundation and the National Organization of Black Women in Law Enforcement. Among her many awards, she received the Athena Award in 2003.

● **Beverly Harvard** (1950–) was the first black woman in the United States to serve as chief of police of a major city (Atlanta, Georgia). Born in Macon, Georgia, she attended Morris Brown College in Atlanta (BA, sociology) and Georgia State University (MS, urban government and administration). She joined the police force as a patrol officer in 1973. The first woman in the Atlanta Police Department to graduate from the FBI National Academy (1983), she also attended the FBI's National Executive Institute. Among her jobs in the department, she was the first woman to serve as an executive protection officer, was director of public affairs (1980–1982), and served as deputy chief of police (1982–1994). Chief of police from 1994, she was a board member of the Executive Committee of the International Association of Chiefs of Police and the U.S. Attorney General's Working Group on Reducing Violence in America, among many others positions. Her many awards included the Turner Broadcasting Trumpet Award (1998).

● **Rosie Mason** (1918–2001) was one of the first black policewomen in the United States and was the first black policewoman in Kansas City, Missouri. She began working for the department in 1944, not as a police officer but in the maintenance department. Three years later she became an elevator operator at the department and in 1956 was promoted to senior clerk. In 1960 she was made an acting policewoman assigned to the youth unit. Finally, in 1967, she was officially made a police officer, still with the Youth Division. She remained with the department for the next sixteen years, retiring in 1982. She was president of the International Association of Women Police and inducted into the knighthood of Michael the Archangel Police and Fire Legion.

● **Carolyn Morris** (1939–) was the first black woman to reach the rank of assistant director with the FBI. Born in Jackson, North Carolina, she attended North Carolina Central University (BS, mathematics, summa cum laude, 1960) and Harvard University (MS, mathematics, 1963). She continued her education with postgraduate work in applied mathematics, computer science and artificial intelligence at Virginia Tech, the University of Michigan, and George Washington University. She also worked for the Defense Department, winning the Army PACE Award, the highest award given to a civilian. She joined the FBI in 1980 as chief of the Systems Development Section. In 1995, she joined the Information Resources Division as assistant director in charge and took responsibility for developing the National Crime Information Center. She retired from the FBI in 2000 and became president of Innovative Management and Technology Approaches, Inc., in the same year.

● **Elsie L. Scott** (c. 1946–) spent much of her career overseeing training programs in a variety of police forces. She attended Southern University (BA, 1968), the University of Iowa (MA, 1970), and Atlanta University (PhD, political science, 1980). She became an assistant professor at Howard University in 1981 and moved on to serve as the program executive with the National Organization of Black Law Enforcement Executives (1983–1985) before being named executive director (1985–1991). In 1991 she was appointed deputy commissioner of training of the New York Police Department. Six years later she joined the Washington, DC, police force, ultimately becoming head of the Police Training Standards Board. She moved on to direct the training bureau of the Detroit Police Department before resigning in 2004. An expert on community policing and training, she also served as the president of the National Conference of Black Political Scientists (1980–1981) and on the advisory board of the National Institute Against Prejudice and Violence (1987–1993). Among her many awards was the Achievement Award from 100 Black Women in 1988.

● **Joyce Stephen** (c. 1958–) was the first black woman female to be named captain and deputy inspector with the New York City Police Department (NYPD). Born in Sumter, South Carolina, she attended John Jay College of Criminal Justice in New York, where she received a bachelor's of science degree in Criminal Justice. In 1981 she joined the NYPD as a patrol woman in the Bronx (Forty-sixth Precinct). She ultimately rose to the position of commanding officer (Twenty-eighth Precinct, Manhattan) before being named deputy commissioner of training. Named captain and deputy chief in 2003, Stephen was in charge of the Employee Relations Section as well as the Office of Community Affairs.

A number of black women pursued advanced degrees in the law. This route was an alternative to immediate practice after law school, or maybe an investment in securing an edge in the job market. Edith Spurlock Sampson returned in 1927 for her master of laws degree at Loyola Law School after graduating from John Marshall Law School in 1925. Sampson quickly moved into a series of positions in the juvenile court, serving first as a probation officer and then as referee—a quasi-judicial post where she heard preliminary evidence in pending cases. In the 1930s, she opened her own office and practiced there part-time, specializing in divorce work. By 1943, she had resigned her juvenile court post for full-time private practice. She returned to the government as a salaried trial lawyer in 1947 and secured a position as an assistant state's attorney. In the mid-1950s, Sampson moved on to a post in the Chicago Corporation Counsel's Office, and she rounded out her career by winning elections for municipal court judge, and later for circuit judge, in the 1960s. Pauli Murray, a 1944 graduate of Howard Law School and one of the first black women to apply to and be rejected by the Harvard Law School graduate program, obtained a master of laws degree from Boalt Hall, and years later, in 1965, a doctor of juridical science from Yale Law School. In 1946, Murray worked as an assistant attorney general of the state of California before establishing a private practice in New York City in the 1950s. She would turn in her shingle for a robe in 1977 and become one of three women first ordained as priest in the Episcopal Church. Goler Teal Butcher received a master of laws in international law in 1958 from the University of Pennsylvania, and became the first black woman to clerk in the federal system when she clerked for Circuit Court Judge William Henry Hastie Sr. Following her clerkship with Hastie, she established a successful private practice.

For many black women lawyers of this generation, a law degree was often a ticket to high-level staff positions in the domestic relations and juvenile courts, which brought increased prestige and professional contacts that allowed them to move into private practice or government positions, which in turn opened up further opportunities for professional advancement. This circuitous route to the black woman lawyer's active practice of law shows the serious impediments to her full equality within the profession. Despite their more than fifty years at the bar, black women lawyers had gained only a tenuous foothold in the legal profession, but nonetheless a foothold that would be strengthened by succeeding generations.

Post–Civil Rights Years, 1965–Present

With the civil rights movement it became increasingly clear that this post-1965 generation of African American women lawyers would not take so circuitous a route to full practice in the profession. In the 1950s, many black women lawyers were actively involved in the civil rights movement. Constance Baker Motley, who later became the first black woman to sit on the U.S. District Court for the Southern District of New York, joined the NAACP Legal Defense and Educational Fund in 1946 right after graduation from Columbia Law School, and years later became its principal trial lawyer in its fight to end segregation. She argued ten cases before the U.S. Supreme Court and won nine of them, helping to lay the foundation for the NAACP's successful dismantling of the 1896 *Plessy v. Ferguson* doctrine of "separate but equal." Althea Simmons, a 1956 graduate of Howard Law School, dedicated her life to civil rights. She organized voting rights drives and became the chief lobbyist for the NAACP in 1979, testifying before Congress on issues of civil rights. Other black women lawyers, such as Ruth Harvey Charity, a graduate of Howard Law School and former president of the National Association of Black Women Attorneys, incorporated activism into their practice. Ruth Harvey Charity filed suits and organized sit-ins against the segregation of libraries and other public places in Danville, Virginia. She also defended civil rights marchers and protesters, and in 1963 successfully defended 1,300 civil rights demonstrators in Danville.

There were black women lawyers such as Eleanor Holmes Norton, Marian Wright Edelman, Mary Frances Berry, and Frankie Muse Freeman, who became professional legal advocates in the African American fight for civil rights. A 1964 Yale Law School graduate, Eleanor Holmes Norton, began as a lawyer for the American Civil Liberties Union in 1965 after clerking for Judge A. Leon Higginbotham of the U.S. District Court in Philadelphia. Norton then became the first woman to head the New York City Commission of Human Rights in 1970 before being appointed chair of the Federal Equal Employment Opportunities Commission by President Jimmy Carter in 1977. Marian Wright Edelman, who graduated from Yale Law School a year before Norton in 1963, began her legal career as a staff attorney with the NAACP Legal Defense and Educational Fund, which she later directed for several years before she became president of the Children's Legal Defense Fund in 1973. Much like Norton and Edelman, Mary Frances Berry concentrated on public service areas. A 1970 University of Michigan law graduate, Berry served as assistant secretary of education under President Carter and in 1980 became a member of the U.S. Commission of Civil Rights, a post first held by a woman in 1964 when President Lyndon Johnson nominated Frankie Muse Freeman. Ever vigilant in the fight to protect the constitutional rights of all American citizens, Berry became actively involved in the commission to investigate allegations of black disfranchisement in Florida during the 2000 presidential election.

The careers of Ambassador Patricia Roberts Harris and the former congresswoman from Texas Barbara Jordan broke a number of barriers in the early 1970s and painted an impressive picture of the African American woman lawyer in politics. Patricia Roberts Harris, who graduated first in her class at George Washington University Law School, was appointed ambassador to Luxembourg by President Johnson and U.S. Secretary of Housing and Urban Development by President Carter in 1977, and served as U.S. Secretary of Health, Education, and Welfare until 1982. Barbara Jordan, a native of Houston, graduated from Boston University Law School in 1959 and returned to Houston, where her first political appointment was as an administrative assistant to the county judge of Harris County. She was then elected to the state senate in 1966 and to the U.S. House of Representatives in 1972. As a congresswoman, Jordan was an advocate for the poor and disadvantaged of the nation, promoting bills such as the Workman's Compensation Act to maximize benefits to injured workers. But Jordan is best remembered for the position she took and the eloquent speech she made during the impeachment hearing of President Richard Nixon in 1974 while she served on the House Judiciary Committee. She captured the nation's respect and went on to be the keynote speaker for the Democratic National Convention in 1976 and 1992.

Opportunities for black women to teach at white law schools remained almost nonexistent in the 1970s. Jean Camper Cahn, who taught at Howard for a year, became the first black woman to teach at a white law school, when she joined the faculty of George Washington University School of Law in 1968. She was a visiting professor during the time she spent at the law school and director of the Urban Law Institute at George Washington's law school from 1968 to 1971. She taught law and poverty, jurisprudence, international law, federal programs, police and community, and community organization, but she was never offered a teaching position on tenure track at George Washington's law school, which led to her resignation. At the time that she left, she was the only black professor on the law school faculty. This was typical for most black women teaching at white law schools, but in 1971, Joyce Anne Hughes became the first black woman to teach on tenure track at a white law school when she joined the law faculty at the University of Minnesota's law school after spending her early career clerking for U.S. District Judge Earl R. Larson and working in a major law firm in Minneapolis. She was also the first African American woman to graduate from and to instruct at the University

of Minnesota's law school, where she taught practice, modern real estate, and the legal profession. She continued teaching at the University of Minnesota until 1975, when she joined the law faculty at Northwestern University, where she taught banking, evidence, immigration, and real estate transactions. In 1988, Lani Guinier, who graduated from Yale Law School in 1974, joined the law faculty at the University of Pennsylvania Law School, and in 1998 when she joined the faculty of Harvard Law School she became the law school's first black tenured professor.

The Judiciary

Black women's legacy in the judiciary spans fifty-five years, and began with Jane Matilda Bolin, a 1931 Yale Law School graduate, who became the nation's first black woman judge in 1939 when Mayor Fiorello La Guardia appointed her to New York's Domestic Relations Court for a ten-year term. She was reappointed for consecutive ten-year terms by mayors O'Dwyer, Wagner, and Lindsay, but remained the sole black woman judge in the nation for twenty years. In 1950, Hannah Elizabeth Byrd of Philadelphia, though not a lawyer, served in the judiciary as a magistrate. Byrd had established an enviable reputation for herself, working with community organizations and professional women's groups, when Governor James Duff appointed her to complete her deceased husband's term as a magistrate. The first black woman magistrate in Pennsylvania, Byrd served with distinction for two years, but it was not until 1959 that the nation had its second African American woman on the bench. Juanita Kidd Stout, a 1948 graduate of Indiana University Law School, was first appointed to finish the term of a deceased judge in 1959. When the term ended in two months, Stout was elected as a Philadelphia county court judge in 1960 to a ten-year term and became the first African American woman elected to a court in the United States. Stout was reelected for consecutive terms and was appointed to the state supreme court in 1988, making her the first black woman to serve on a state supreme court. She retired in 1989, but subsequently served as a senior judge in the Court of Common Pleas in Philadelphia. These early judicial pioneers entered the judiciary by appointment, whether mayoral or gubernatorial. Prior to their judicial appointments they served in government positions in the office of the corporation counsel or district attorney. Judge Bolin had been an assistant corporation counsel in the Domestic Relations Court for two years when she was appointed a judge in that court. A few years before her 1959 judicial appointment, Judge Stout had served in the district attorney's office.

Many female African American judges were appointed, and many more were elected, as the 1960s and 1970s ushered in a more enfranchised black community in the United States. By 1972 there were twenty-three black women judges in the United States, with four in New York City; three each in Chicago and Washington, DC; two each in Atlanta, Cleveland, and Philadelphia; and one each in Detroit, Greensboro (North Carolina), Los Angeles, Milwaukee, Omaha, Portland (Oregon), and Sparta (Georgia).

In 1961, Vaino Hassen Spencer, a 1952 law graduate of Southwestern School of Law, was appointed as a municipal court judge in Los Angeles, the first such appointment in Los Angeles. Marjorie McKenzie Lawson's appointment to the DC Juvenile Court by President John F. Kennedy in 1962 made her the first black woman ever appointed to a judicial post by a United States president and approved by the Senate for a statutory appointment. She had earned law degrees from Terrell Law School and Columbia University and was engaged in private practice with her husband, Belford Lawson, prior to her judicial appointment. Edith Spurlock Sampson, who was elected an associate judge of Chicago's Municipal Court in 1962 and a judge of the Circuit Court of Cook County in Chicago, was a 1925 graduate of John Marshall Law School. She had been a referee of the Cook County Juvenile Court from 1930 to 1947 when she was appointed an assistant state's attorney, and in 1950 she was made an alternate delegate to the United Nations General Assembly by President Harry S. Truman. From 1955 to her election to the Municipal Court in 1962, she worked as an assistant corporation counsel for the City of Chicago. Of singular judicial achievement during this period was Constance Baker Motley, who became the first black woman in the federal judiciary when President Johnson appointed her to the U.S. District Court of the Southern District of New York in 1966. A 1946 Columbia University Law School graduate, she had had a very impressive legal and political career before her judgeship, serving with the NAACP Legal Defense Fund from 1946 to 1963 and serving in the New York Senate and as Manhattan borough president.

Whereas some African American women chose to remain in the court of first appointment, Consuelo Bland Marshall, a 1961 Howard Law School graduate, served in a variety of jurisdictions over a ten-year period. She first became a judge in 1971 after working as a city attorney in Los Angeles from 1962 to 1967. She first served as a judge in the Juvenile Court in Los Angeles, before serving as a judge on the Inglewood Municipal Court, Los Angeles County, and on the Criminal Court, for the Superior Court of California, Los Angeles County. But the plum position came in 1980 when President Carter appointed Judge Marshall to the United States District Court, where she became one of the few black women serving on this court in the nation. Black women's presence in the local, state, and federal judiciary was first secured by political appointments, which later combined with elections to gradually increase their numbers, which were never in keeping with the gains made by their black male and white female counterparts.

Closing Statements

Black women first entered the legal profession in 1872 with few prospects for law-related employment. The generations that followed benefited from an African American community that was ushered in by the Great Migration and by salaried positions in government. Half a century later, in 1939, black women lawyers entered the judiciary by appointment. After more than a century at the bar black women lawyers continue to achieve many firsts in a profession defined by a culture of exclusion. The president of the National Bar Association in 1996, Keith Waters, declared that affirmative action has failed black women in the legal profession and added that the percentage of lawyers in the United States who are black women has remained the same since the 1960s. Although African American women lawyers are no longer an anomaly in the profession, they continue to struggle against prejudices and discrimination that aim to relegate them to the bottom rungs of the professional hierarchy.

BIBLIOGRAPHY

Crenshaw, Kimberle. "Demarginalizing the Intersection of Race and Sex: A Black Feminist Critique of Antidiscrimination Doctrine, Feminist Theory, and Antiracist Politics." *University of Chicago Legal Forum* 139 (1989). Addresses the experiences of black women lawyers and the intersection of race, gender, and class.

Epstein, Cynthia Fuchs. *Women in Law*. New York: Basic Books, 1981. A general examination of women in the legal profession.

Mack, Kenneth W. "A Social History of Everyday Practice: Sadie T. M. Alexander and the Incorporation of Black Women into the American Legal Profession, 1925–1960." *Cornell Law Review* 87 (September 2002): 1405–1474. An analytical examination of black women's transformation of their status in the legal profession through the life of Alexander.

Morello, Karen Berger. *The Invisible Bar: The Woman Lawyer in America 1638 to the Present*. New York: Random House, 1986. The "Double Impairment" chapter addresses the particular experiences of black women.

Motley, Constance Baker. *Equal Justice under the Law: An Autobiography*. New York: Farrar, Straus and Giroux, 1998.

McNeil, Genna Rae. "To Meet the Group Needs: The Transformation of Howard University School of Law, 1920–1935." In *New Perspectives in Black Educational History*, edited by Vincent P. Franklin and James D. Anderson. Boston: G. K. Hall, 1979. An examination of the importance of Howard University in the making of the black lawyer.

Prestage, Jewel L. "Black Women Judges: An Examination of Their Socio-Economic, Educational, and Political Backgrounds and Judicial Placement." In *Readings in American Political Issues*, edited by Franklin D. Jones and Michael O. Adams. Dubuque, IA: Kendall, 1987.

Segal, G. R. *Blacks in the Law: Philadelphia and the Nation*. Philadelphia: University of Pennsylvania Press, 1983.

Smith, J. Clay, Jr., ed. *Emancipation: The Making of the Black Lawyer, 1844–1944*. Philadelphia: University of Pennsylvania Press, 1993. A comprehensive study of black lawyers.

Smith, J. Clay, Jr., ed. *Rebels in Law: Voices in History of Black Women Lawyers*. Ann Arbor: University of Michigan Press, 1998. An anthology of the works of black women lawyers on a variety of topics.

Tollett, Kenneth S. "Black Lawyers: Their Education and the Black Community." *Howard Law Review* 17 (1972): 326–357.

"Why Black Women Lawyers Have a Difficult Climb to Success." *Jet*, 12 February 1996.

Wilkins, David B., and G. Mitu Gulati. "Why Are There So Few Black Lawyers in Corporate Law Firms? An Institutional Analysis." *California Law Review* 84 (1996): 493–618.

—JACQUELINE A. McLEOD

LEGAL RESISTANCE. Black women in America have been uniquely oppressed. Not surprisingly, the form, substance, and successes of their methods of resistance to such oppression have been marked by a singularly complex history, a history which continues to unfold and has variously found black women's lives affected by the actions and attitudes of white men and black men, of white women, and of themselves. Cast in a tangled web of human experience, socioeconomic history, politics, and evolving cultural "norms" directing every conceivable aspect of life, it is a remarkable story, and the law lies at its very core. For the fundamental sociological truth is that law is both the embodiment and dynamic reflection of the prevailing and dominant social code. Law is about life. And, thus, the law as applied to and resisted by black women, is very much a part of their life stories.

The story of black women's oppression by and resistance to American law has its genesis in the legal status of black women as they were first brought by force from Africa in the early 1600s. Slavery as a formal, legal entity did not exist at the time in the Americas. However, slavery flourished in various forms with various names until it did indeed acquire formal status. One by one, the original thirteen colonies—Georgia being the lone exception—legalized the practice in the years between 1641 to 1717. Georgia actually enacted a law banning the importation and use of persons as slaves in 1735. But laws are formalistic shells, which do not necessarily affect life as it is lived, and so the Georgia ban on slavery was repealed in 1749. A mere year thereafter, Georgia followed its colonial neighbors, legalizing slavery. The legal status of black women in America could hardly have been derived from a bleaker place, and their oppression under slavery was both greater and more complex than that suffered by black men.

To further complicate the matter, the law, and black women's status within it, cannot be fully understood without reference to law within the shadow of the law, as various laws interact to create discriminatory effects. This phenomenon exists because of the interplay between laws that explicitly oppress persons, including black women, and those that appear on their face to have nothing whatsoever to do with them and the conduct of their lives.

The legal story of black women begins with enslaved people's designation as living property or chattel. Laws sprang up in the wake of slavery's legalization that were designed to enforce a social order that was fundamentally inconsistent with the nature of America's emerging political structure. The colonists had to conceive of laws to regulate behavior by and toward slaves. An elaborate and oppressive system of legal fictions was brought into being, chief among them the bright-line axiom that slaves simply were not, nor could they be, citizens.

From the mid-1600s to approximately 1800, literally hundreds of laws were enacted throughout all thirteen colonial territories in an attempt to define every nuance of a slave's status and life: where a slave could go, what a slave could do, how a slave could be treated. The volume and complexity of these regulations reflect both the inherent difficulty and the moral and intellectual dishonesty of stripping people of that which makes them human by means of nonparticipatory legislation.

Since the slaves brought to America were black, the "solution" was to build the assumption into the law that white people could not be slaves. In a bit of tidy semantics with fully intended legal ramifications, white persons could be indentured servants, but not slaves. An indentured servant was essentially a limited-term slave going by another moniker. Thus, the relative degrees of restrictiveness under the law that attached to slaves, indentured servants, and citizens formed the basic social order.

But the most salient and oppressive feature of this system of social constructs was that it was created by what was, under the norms of the day, democratic vote. Among the colonists, only white men could vote, a direct recreation of one aspect of the culture from which the colonists came. The laws enacted by social contract by and among white men permitted a minority to control the lives and fates of the majority: black men and women, white women, Native American men and women, and, notably, a growing population of persons of mixed heritage. This majority population had no voice in the decisions that determined their status and rights, or, rather, the absolute lack of rights. And so the stage was set for the struggle to follow.

Forms of Legal Resistance

Three distinct threads emerge in the history of black women's resistance to oppression by legal means. First, there is the direct and purposeful invocation of legal processes by black women. Second, there is the "use" of the law by black women as a form of protest. Finally, there

HARRIET SCOTT. Around 1846 she and her husband, Dred Scott, who were slaves, undertook a legal struggle for emancipation on the ground that they had resided in free territory. The U.S. Supreme Court ruled against them, and this decision was a factor leading ultimately to the Civil War. (William Loren Katz Collection.)

The second thread involves breaking laws, rather than making them. Legal action took place as a direct result of black women's refusal to obey the harsh and unjust laws that oppressed them. Instead of going to the law in these cases, they acted in such a way that the law came to them, most notably in the direct-action strategies of the civil rights movement, but often before and after that era.

These forms of legal resistance shared a common complication, a difficulty germane most particularly to the plight of black women in America. It was widely observed that black women suffered from discrimination on the basis of race and discrimination on the basis of gender. But prejudice against black women is not one of simplistic additive effect: race plus gender equals twice the hardship. Rather, race is frequently multiplied by gender to create a discriminatory environment that is exponentially more difficult to understand and remedy, for "solutions" to prejudice against women help but do not address all patterns particular to black women any more than "solutions" to prejudice against black men solve all patterns of repression affecting black women. As a consequence, black women have been forced time and again to see that, while alliances are often demanded of them, they must often work for and by themselves.

Litigation in the Antebellum South

Direct and active reliance on the legal system and processes represents the oldest and most continuous thread in the history of black women's resistance to the law. It is difficult to know how many, much less catalog them all, but numerous black women sued for their freedom in the colonial, state, and federal courts in the period stretching from the mid-eighteenth to the mid-nineteenth centuries. In what is perhaps the earliest traceable example, Elizabeth Key, the daughter of a black enslaved woman and a free white father, initiated a suit for her freedom in the Virginia courts in 1655, advancing a series of sophisticated theories, chief among them that her station in life ought to be determined by that of her father. Key's cause was advanced not by her directly, but by her lawyer, a free white man, William Greensted, who later married her. Eventually, Key prevailed and was freed.

The Virginia legislature responded to this and similar cases in 1662 by closing the loophole, passing a law which decreed that a child's legal status would be determined by the mother's legal status. Victories in the courts by the oppressed led predictably to reactive legislation designed to reinstate the pre-litigation state of inequality.

Jenny Slew represents the tack that the disenfranchised and disempowered black woman took after 1662. Like Key, Slew was a biracial woman, but unlike Key's, her mother was white. In 1762, when she was forty-three years old, Slew was kidnapped from her home in Massachusetts and

is cultural infiltration of the legal establishment, a thread that did not emerge until late in the nineteenth century.

The first of these threads is actually formed by two strands inextricably twisted together. Black women actively pursued change and reform as prosecuting litigants—pressing for rights as varied and crucial to their humanity as the right to inherit property from their husbands, the right to vote, the right to receive parity in opportunity in everything from education to employment options and conditions to the day-to-day decencies of public accommodation. They also participated as voters, legislators, and lobbyists, having a direct voice and hand in shaping new laws and changing old ones. The actions of black women in this regard effected profound changes for themselves, and for black men, as well as for other victims of prejudice and racism.

The Case of Jenny Slew

A little more than a decade before the American Revolution, an African American woman sued for her freedom in a Massachusetts court. Unlikely as it seems to us today, her suit was only one of many.

Jenny Slew was born in about 1719. Although she was African American, she was born a free woman. Her mother was white and her father was of African descent, probably a slave. In the colonies at that time, the condition of the child was determined by the mother, so Slew was free. Over the course of her life she was married several times, each time to an enslaved man. Then, in 1762, she was kidnapped and forced into slavery by "Gentleman" John Whipple Jr. She went to court. She pleaded for her freedom before the Inferior Court of Common Pleas, which arbitrarily dismissed her case. In 1765 she filed a civil suit against Whipple. In most states she would not have been able to do so, but Massachusetts recognized the right of enslaved people to bring civil actions, even though they were technically property and not persons. Slew asked for a jury trial.

The defendant's lawyers argued that her marriages to enslaved men nullified her status as a free person. They insisted that, like all other women, she had no legal status separate from her husband. But Jenny Slew was saved by a law that had been intended for quite a different purpose. In 1706 a law had been passed in the state of Massachusetts outlawing marriage between the races. Each of Jenny Slew's marriages to enslaved men was illegal, the court decided, and so she was a spinster. As a spinster, she was legally her own person. Moreover, as the daughter of a white woman, she was free. She was awarded court costs and four pounds.

For more information, see Godfrey D. Lehman, *We the Jury: The Impact of Jurors on Our Basic Freedoms* (Amherst, NY: Prometheus Books, 1997).

enslaved. She obtained counsel and sued her master for her freedom on the ground that her legal status followed that of her mother, who was white and therefore free. She lost at the trial level but ultimately prevailed on appeal.

Slew's master had fashioned a new argument to invoke the status quo. He argued that Slew had no right or standing to sue him, for she was married, and a married woman was universally treated under the law at the time as having no identity distinct from that of her husband. All legal rights collapsed into his person, and she ceased to exist as a legal person capable of possessing and pursuing rights on her own. Thus, ironically, Slew had more rights as a slave than as a married woman. However, Slew was a "spinster" at the time she brought suit, because although she had been married several times, each husband was an enslaved man. Massachusetts law, like the law everywhere in the colonies, did not confer legal legitimacy upon marriages in which one or both parties were slaves. Thus, the Superior Court determined that Slew

was single and could sue, and that under the law of the time, her mother's race determined her legal status as a free woman.

In 1781, some sixteen years after Jenny Slew's victory and also in Massachusetts, Elizabeth Freeman, a black woman, brought suit for her freedom, together with a black male slave named Brom, invoking the newly minted Bill of Rights to the Massachusetts Constitution, adopted in 1780, which declared that all persons within its purview were free and equal. Freeman had been born into slavery and sold as an infant of six months, together with her sister, to a Massachusetts farmer and landowner, Colonel John Ashley. When she was nearly forty, Freeman, who was then known as Mum Bett, ran away from her master's house in a fury, after intervening and taking a blow from a fireplace-heated shovel intended for her sister by the mistress of the house. Colonel Ashley petitioned the courts for her return, and she resisted. She was joined in her resistance by Brom in the case known as *Brom & Freeman v. Ashley*, in what was the equivalent of a municipal court jurisdiction.

Freeman could neither read nor write, but was bright, spirited, and perceptive. She had listened to the talk of the well-to-do colonial landowners who were frequent guests in her master's house, discussing and debating the Bill of Rights in its formative stages. Displaying strategic shrewdness, she enlisted the assistance of Theodore Sedgewick, a lawyer with known antislavery sentiments. Freeman and Brom prevailed, to a jury no less, and Freeman lived out her life a free woman, as Sedgewick's valued housekeeper and a much-revered midwife and nurse. The arguments made by Sedgewick were later upheld in the Quock Walker case, which led ultimately to the formal abolition of slavery in Massachusetts. Notably, Freeman's family followed in her distinguished footsteps as freedom fighters and intellectuals. W. E. B. Du Bois was her great-grandson.

Black women were quick and persistent in pressing for further equities bearing on all aspects of life's operations. Lucy Terry Prince was such a woman. She wound up in the U.S. Supreme Court not only as a litigant but also as orator for her cause. The underlying issue was not her own legal status, but the status of land owned by her family. Terry had come to America as an infant, having been stolen and sold into slavery from her native Africa sometime around 1730. She was purchased by a childless couple in Massachusetts and continued in servitude until she was twenty years old. She married a free black man, Abijah Prince, who was prosperous and able to purchase her freedom. They moved to Vermont in the 1760s, where they farmed with their family of five children. A neighboring white farmer, Colonel Eli Bronson, attempted to steal, by annexation, some of the Terrys' land, and they brought suit. Lucy Terry was well equipped for this endeavor, having earned a reputation as a skillful orator in matters ranging from threats against her family by another neighboring white family to a petition to Williams College to admit one of her sons. She was unsuccessful in the latter cause, despite what was noted as "an earnest and eloquent speech of three hours." Terry's claim against Colonel Bronson wound its way through the legal system to the U.S. Supreme Court, where she herself argued and won. One of her defeated opponents in that forum later became chief justice of the Vermont Supreme Court, and Samuel Chase Smith, the U.S. Chief Justice presiding over the argument, paid a lavish compliment to Prince, observing that her argument was far better than any he had heard from any Vermont lawyer.

The debate over slavery, laced as it was with moral, ethical, political, economic, practical, and religious elements, came to a North versus South divide when the Dred and Harriet Scott decision in the U.S. Supreme Court put the relative powers of the states and the federal government squarely on display. Ultimately, it would take the Civil War to settle the matter, but it is perhaps singularly appropriate that a black man and a black woman triggered the most elemental power struggle in American history with the simple act of suing for their freedom based on the irony that their white master had taken them with him into free states.

Lawbreaking in the Antebellum South

As wonderful as these stories of courage and wits are, they remained the exception to the iron rule of the slave system, both in the South, where basic human rights hinged on the genetic serendipity of parentage and legally recognized marital relations, and in the relatively free North, where prejudice likewise was rooted in genetics but practiced in covert fashion. Still, if the law in the form of formal litigation offered a spotty record of success and reactive legislation, black women refused to give up, taking whatever actions were available to them. And that, given the state of law, shrank to the non–window of opportunity of breaking and defying the law. In the United States prior to the Civil War, free African Americans and enslaved people faced different sets of laws, but both resisted the limitations on their lives and freedom by breaking the laws that bound them.

For slaves, the ultimate resistance was breaking the law of slavery itself, in effect stealing themselves from their owners by running away. Slaves ran away by the hundreds, poignant evidence of the desperation of their condition in life. They were tracked with particular vehemence and cruelty. The inhumanity of their stories in turn further inflamed the volatile political environment, moving the nation toward the ultimate schism. It is against this terrible backdrop that a familiar story appears—one of the few black women, indeed black Americans, who most Americans, black or white, male or female, later recognized and correctly linked with her achievements.

Harriet Tubman broke the laws of slavery in the first place by running away from bondage, attaining freedom in the North by means of the Underground Railroad. She then went back into the South and helped others to do the same. On trip after trip, she flouted the laws of the land by helping enslaved people to escape. And she was far from the only black woman to do so. Anna Murray Douglass, for example, maintained a station on the Underground Railroad while her husband, Frederick Douglass, toured to speak against slavery.

Free black women resisted the laws that limited their freedom outside slavery. Elizabeth Jennings was one such woman. She refused to leave a bus (i.e., a streetcar) in New York City and was forcibly removed, and subsequently sued for damages. In New York in the mid-1800s, bus transportation existed on a limited basis, and African Americans had scant access to it, able to board only those vehicles marked "Colored Persons Allowed." New York was not so hostile in its racial laws to black as the states of the Deep South, but day-to-day living presented plenty of opportunity for racial unease.

On a terribly hot July Sunday in 1855, Jennings, a young schoolteacher, boarded a bus to take her to church services. The conductor tried to remove her, at first alleging that the car was full and then that the other passengers were objecting to her presence. She resisted, and he removed her by force, assaulting her before a crowd on the boarding platform. She resisted throughout, and the fracas was broken up only when a police officer removed her.

Jennings was the daughter of a powerful black businessman and religious leader. Well-connected and with excellent resources for legal redress, she sued the bus company, the driver, and the conductor. Her legal advocates included the then twenty-one-year-old Chester A. Arthur, later to become president of the United States. Jennings prevailed in the Brooklyn Circuit Court in 1855. The judge awarded her $225 in damages, a hefty sum at the time, and declared that "[c]olored persons if sober, well behaved and free from disease, had the same rights as others and could neither be excluded by any rules of the Company, nor by force or violence." Other black commuters followed her example, suing for refusals of service with success. As the Civil War broke out, discriminatory practices in the New York transportation system subsided altogether.

Postbellum Resistance through Legislation and Election

The Thirteenth Amendment to the U.S. Constitution was the codification of the Emancipation Proclamation, with no less than Abraham Lincoln pressing for its passage with all his formidable political currency. It declared in sweeping language that

> [n]either slavery nor involuntary servitude, except as a punishment for crime whereof the party shall have been duly convicted, shall exist within the United States, or any place subject to their jurisdiction.

The Fourteenth Amendment was an attempt to remedy the way in which the Dred Scott issue—that of the competing sovereignty of the states, territories, and federal union—had divided the nation and led ultimately to the Civil War. The Amendment does a number of things, including clarification of who could be an elected governmental figure and on what conditions, but more importantly, it provided that anyone born in the United States, including those formerly enslaved, was a citizen. The signature provision went still further, providing that

> No State shall make or enforce any law which shall abridge the privileges or immunities of citizens of the United States; nor shall any State deprive any person of life, liberty, or property, without due process of law; nor deny to any person within its jurisdiction the equal protection of the laws.

The source of some of the most celebrated constitutional litigation, the so-called due process and equal protection clauses of this amendment have provided the backbone of American culture and parity as it has evolved. Stripped to its essentials, this amendment makes every guarantee and protection under the federal law directly and unavoidably applicable to every American citizen, regardless of state of residence. In turn, the states can grant citizens greater freedoms than those afforded by the federation, but none less or essentially different in character. The Constitution was a floor, not a ceiling, and the elastic tendons of the union were formally inaugurated. But it was the Fifteenth Amendment that would provide the crucial element for African American leverage. The Fifteenth Amendment proposed that the right to vote could not be denied to citizens of the United States or of "any state on account of race, color, or previous condition of servitude." But this sweeping grant was to apply to men only. Women, of any color, remained disenfranchised.

Black women were split in their feelings about the proposed amendment, with some viewing the right to vote, if flawed and incomplete in its exclusion of women, as beneficial for blacks generally. These women tended to view the vote as akin to a family asset or property, in essence. Elsa Barkley Brown makes the point that African American women were an integral part of the decision as to how a family's vote would be used. They organized political groups to discuss the issues and lobby for their concerns. They took an active part in the political meetings held before each southern state's constitutional convention. With black men, they took time off work to discuss what would and would not be demanded at those conventions. One family, one vote, in their view, was far preferable to one family, no vote.

On the other hand, many black women, among them the legendary Sojourner Truth, saw things differently, in part because of the reality of many of the relationships between black men and women coming out of slavery. Truth and those of her philosophical bent believed that increased power in the hands of black men without a corresponding grant of power to black women would lead to the continued and further oppression of black women, this time primarily at the hands of black men. They saw partial loosening of the cultural rules to be worse than none at all and so advocated defeat of the amendment.

The split opinions of African American women were enmeshed in the complexities of the women's suffrage movement generally. At first, an all-woman alliance seemed natural and prudent, especially as many of the white women in the suffrage movement were at least sympathetic to, if not openly and actively supportive of, the abolitionist movement. But when the currents of political opinion, not to mention the attention and contributions of white men to the white women's cause, became clear, a fundamental split occurred.

The Fifteenth Amendment was approved by Congress in 1869, and ratified in 1870, as a matter of brilliant political duress. In passing the amendment, Congress provided that the states of the defeated Confederacy had to accept the Fourteenth and Fifteenth Amendments to be readmitted to the Union and restored to statehood. The sweeping guarantees of the Thirteenth, Fourteenth, and Fifteenth Amendments were deliberately sabotaged by a host of reactionary and clever, though apparently neutral, laws and practices, which were clearly motivated by extreme resistance to the full citizenship of blacks.

Black women may not have had the vote, but they actively influenced, and often determined, the votes of black men. When Andrew Johnson, the successor of the assassinated Abraham Lincoln, ran for a new term against Ulysses S. Grant, black women wielded their influence to squelch Johnson's chances, for he was the much-hated architect of numerous antiblack policies and political appointments with sway over the day-to-day administration of frontline postwar policies affecting black lives and fortunes. One witness to the electoral process observed that black wives accompanying their husbands to the polls carried hickory sticks, some with nails driven in them in the shape of the cross, daring, in effect, their spouses to vote any way but Republican.

Jim Crow

Ulysses Grant's presidential victory made black men players in politics, in the South in particular, and so was born the Jim Crow era, with its systemic practice of treating blacks as inferiors, and all under the tacit support of the law. Separate "but equal" facilities and opportunities were anywhere and everywhere: "colored only" drinking fountains, seating sections of buses, waiting rooms, restaurants, trains, theaters—virtually every venue of life. The most mundane events, such as getting to and from work or getting something to eat, became an exercise in humiliation.

In this atmosphere, another black woman "sat down on the bus," metaphorically speaking. Ida B. Wells-Barnett was a young woman in 1884 who was forcibly removed from her routinely occupied commuter's seat in the "ladies" car of a Memphis-bound train, to the "smoking car," a huge sociopolitical demotion, if not humiliation. Wells-Barnett struggled, biting her would-be evictor and eventually engaging in a physical tussle with three other white conductors, all to the enthusiastic cheers of the white passengers. Enraged, Wells-Barnett hired the lone black lawyer in Memphis to bring an action on her behalf. When his performance suggested to her he had been bribed by white establishment figures to make her case languish, she fired him, hiring a white lawyer and former Union soldier, who prevailed. Her victory was overturned on appeal, and an outraged Wells-Barnett became an even more visible figure and revolutionary, with her searing columns and essays, most notably in Memphis's black newspaper, *Free Speech*, of which she was a co-owner and editor.

But Jim Crow also rose up in an infinitely more sinister fashion. Early on in the postbellum period, lynching more and more became the manifestation of white discontent, extra-political and extra-judicial expressions of rage and frustration, targeting blacks for affronts as varied as crimes against whites assumed upon innuendo, rumor, and fabrication without due process of law, to simply being successful and the subject of unbridled envy. It was mob behavior in the classic sense. Terrorist organizations such as the Ku Klux Klan sprang up and began to murder blacks with systematic design.

The bloody tide began to turn, if slowly, when black women began to lobby for antilynching legislation. Ida B. Wells-Barnett and Mary Church Terrell were touched and motivated by the same tragic event. Three black men, Thomas Moss, Calvin McDowell, and Henry Stewart, were friends who went into business together in the spirit of the new nation, opening and operating a general store just outside Memphis, Tennessee. The "People's Grocery" became a popular gathering place for blacks, a fact that upset local whites on behalf of a nearby white grocer, who was accustomed to his entrenched monopoly on trade.

Moss was a postman, in fact the first black person in Memphis ever to hold a federal job. It was his salary that made the store possible. He staffed the store in the evenings. His partners McDowell and Stewart worked days. The white grocer, whose business suffered as a result of their success, incited an escalating series of anti-competitive "events," culminating in an assault on the business by a gang of white insurgents whose aim was nothing less than to destroy the business, down to the building itself. This attack came on a Saturday night, when the store was packed with armed black men. The black patrons held off their assailants, but three white men were shot and wounded in the fray. Moss, McDowell, and Stewart were rewarded for their defense of their business with arrest, along with one hundred other area blacks, for supposed conspiracy with the People's proprietors. Press coverage and editorializing was intense and virulent. Tensions abated somewhat as the three white men recovered from their wounds, and a protective black vigil outside the jail where Thomas, McDowell, and Stewart were held dissipated. To have done so turned out to be naive and premature. In a predawn raid, the three men were taken from jail by an angry white mob and lynched. The People's Grocery was looted, gutted, and reduced to ruins. The white grocery owner arose again as the sole proprietor in the area. It was 1892, some thirty years after the end of the Civil War.

The People's Grocery matter, as tragic as it was, would have languished as yet another statistic in an escalating cycle of violence, were it not for the energy and vision of black women such as Ida B. Wells-Barnett and Mary Church Terrell.

Ida B. Wells-Barnett was a good friend of Moss and his wife, Betty. She was a contemporary of Terrell's, and their interest and actions intersected in powerful witness against the lawless savagery of lynching. Wells-Barnett, the driving force of the antilynching movement, wrote against the crime in the *New York Age* and the book *Southern Horrors: Lynch Law in All Its Phases* and lectured in the West, as well as the North. She went to England in 1893 and helped to form the British Anti-Lynching Society.

Back in the United States, Wells-Barnett drew the deep and unremitting support of black women in the cause. *Southern Horrors* was published because of funds raised by an event in Lyric Hall in New York by black clubwomen. Slanders against Wells-Barnett and, by extension, all black women, from a pro-lynching journalist were the catalyst for the creation of the National Association of Colored Women (NACW), headed by Mary Church Terrell.

Terrell and Thomas Moss had been friends since childhood. Terrell was well traveled and educated; she received a degree in education from Oberlin College. Moss had followed his own trajectory of mainstream success, but the two remained in contact. Moss's death had an enormous effect on Terrell. Transformed by her friend's death, she contacted another friend, the powerful black abolitionist, publisher, and activist Frederick Douglass, and they embarked on an antilynching campaign, which would get them an audience with President Benjamin Harrison, who declined to take a public stance against the practice, despite Douglass's eloquent plea.

Terrell continued to advocate, write, and speak out against lynching and discrimination in every form in a remarkable public career that lasted some sixty-two years following her historic audience with the president. She served on the governing and founding boards for many notable black activist organizations in Washington, DC, and was a primary figure in the black women's club movement. She was also one of the charter members of the National Association for the Advancement of Colored People (NAACP). Terrell made headlines again when in 1950 she headed a picket line and subsequent lawsuit to desegregate a District of Columbia eatery, Thompson's Restaurant.

The legal resistance of these two women spans the time from 1884, when the twenty-two-year-old Wells-Barnett refused to give up her seat on the train, through the years of battle to get an antilynching law passed in the U.S. Congress, to 1950, when eighty-nine-year-old Terrell paced the sidewalk in front of Thompson's Restaurant with the aid of a cane.

Jim Crow Is the Law of the Land

Jim Crow became institutionalized, in essence, in 1896, when the U.S. Supreme Court rendered its decision in *Plessy v. Ferguson*. In that case, the Court coined one of the most famous phrases in American jurisprudence, the "separate but equal" doctrine, a philosophical approach taken directly from the lawsuit Benjamin Roberts brought in the Massachusetts court system on behalf of his daughter Sarah.

The *Plessy* court was not unanimous. Justice John Marshall Harlan cast the lone dissenting vote. Justice Harlan understood the fallacy of the majority's approach. He wrote: "[E]very one knows that the statute in question had its origin in the purpose, not so much to exclude white persons from railroad cars occupied by blacks, as to exclude colored people from coaches occupied by or assigned to white persons." His opinion handed black activists the raw material of profound change. Opinions, which are the formal, written explanations for the vote choices of the judges, are a form of law, called the common law, and every bit as controlling as statutes enacted by legislatures. Their language and logic are often revisited later by judges in new cases and used to support a different result. So when Harlan exposed the logical flaw in the majority's opinion, he fashioned the underpinnings for some of the most powerful advances black Americans have achieved via legal resistance.

Still, sheltered by the *Plessy* decision, the Jim Crow era held sway for nearly fifty years to come, with black women and men slowly creating the superstructure for ultimate change and challenge as the 1900s unfolded. Especially through the club movement, first the NACW and then the National Council of Negro Women, black women quietly and determinedly pursued every angle they could for education and ownership, for inroads on voting rights strictures, for political and religious and media connections. Their gains would form a network and financial base from which lasting change could be crafted.

Cultural Infiltration

Black women understood that the trappings of law as a profession—to practice, and later to frame, study, and teach—formed a power center for lasting change and reform, not only setting an agenda, but also establishing inclusive and reasoned cultural norms. Women of color, and others, faced a stronger challenge in the pursuit of legal careers than in virtually any other. The law was created by white men and has largely been interpreted by white men, establishing a virtual monopoly of the social order.

The first black women lawyers, unlike many of their white counterparts, aggressively sought to establish practices. When Charlotte Ray graduated from Howard University Law School in 1872, she did so with honors, despite studying the law in the evenings while supporting herself teaching days in Howard's Preparatory and Normal School. She launched her solo practice in the shadow of Howard and its connections, where she tried to target a black constituency. She advertised her practice, for example, in Frederick Douglass's weekly paper the *New National Era and Citizen*, and quickly gained a reputation as one of the best minds on the subject of mercantile law in the country. And yet, despite her credentials and connections, she was obliged to close her office just five years later, in 1879: prejudice cost her sufficient business to sustain herself as a lawyer. She returned to New York, where she worked as a teacher for the remainder of her professional life.

Over time, matters changed as black women increasingly adopted and adapted the very norms of the profession to their own distinctive use. Sadie Tanner Mossell Alexander was Pennsylvania's first and only black woman lawyer in 1939, the year in which she began corresponding with several dozen African American women attorneys practicing throughout the United States. Alexander had impressive credentials, including a thriving practice with her attorney husband, Raymond Pace Alexander, but still chose to go beyond, gathering basic information about the experiences of black women in the profession. She sent out form letters to every black woman lawyer she could identify, seeking information on their practices and experiences.

The result was the first network of black women professionals in the law. They knew little about one another, but found much in each other, and gave Alexander much to share with the world. Alexander published the results of her original survey in 1941, finding just fifty-seven African American women admitted to active practice of law, and clustered predictably in the country's major urban centers. Few of Alexander's generation practiced law as a full-time occupation, encountering essentially the same obstacles as Charlotte Ray had years before. Early black women lawyers encountered hostility from every quarter, as the profession's white, male, native-born elite scurried to change the standards for legal education and professional certification in ways that were calculated to exclude both black women and the growing tide of ethnic immigrants to the United States.

In the two decades following Alexander's survey and networking project, black women finally started to practice law as a full-time occupation in appreciable numbers. The issues then, as later, were thorny and involved not only basic ability but also the struggles of black women for the coexistence of family and professional life, as well as parity with their male colleagues in everything from pay to basic acceptance by everyone, including persons of their own race. Notably, Alexander and her husband understood the power of networks and alliances and were among the early members of the National Bar Association, the professional association of African American lawyers. Such affiliations would prove central to improvements in the lives of African Americans

In 1938, a young woman named Pauli Murray applied for admission to the graduate school at the University of North Carolina and was rejected because she was black. She went to Howard University Law School instead and earned an LLB. She was first in her class. She applied then to Harvard University Law School for an advanced degree and was rejected because she was a woman. So she went to the Boalt Hall of Law at the University of California and got an LLM. That was 1945. Twenty years later, in 1965, Murray became the first African American to earn the doctor of juridical science from the Yale University Law School.

In the meantime, Murray was admitted to practice in California, in New York, and before the U.S. Supreme Court. She fought for civil rights with the Commission on Law and Social Action, an agency of the American Jewish Congress, and then went into private practice. Even in the early 1940s, she was "sitting down on the bus," protesting segregated seating on interstate buses. She served as student adviser to a direct-action assault on Washington, DC, restaurants in 1941, starting the campaign that would end in Mary Church Terrell's act of courage at Thompson's Restaurant. In the years to come, Murray would help found the National Organization for Women and, later, become an Episcopal minister.

Most prominent in the civil rights struggle of the middle of the twentieth century was Constance Baker Motley, the first black woman attorney to argue in front of the Supreme Court. She was a clerk for Thurgood Marshall in her last year at Columbia Law School in 1945 and remained on the NAACP legal defense team until 1964, when she became a New York state senator. She was the first woman on the team and years later became its principal trial lawyer in the fight to end segregation. She argued ten cases before the U. S. Supreme Court and won nine of them, including *Meredith v. Fair*, which got James Meredith admitted to the University of Mississippi. She represented Charlayne Hunter-Gault and Hamilton Holmes in their successful attempt to integrate the University of Georgia and Harvey Gantt, who integrated Clemson College and went on to become mayor of Charlotte, South Carolina. All of these cases were part of the preparation for the NAACP's successful battle against *Plessy v. Ferguson* in the case of *Brown v. Board of Education*.

Motley accompanied Marshall to virtually every case he argued from the time she joined the team. In 1952, he moved for her admission to the Supreme Court Bar so that she could work on the school desegregation cases.

The Battle Is Joined

Linda Brown had a tremendous and treacherous journey to and from school each day. She was in the third grade, an eight-year-old at the time. She would depart from her home, walk one mile, alone, and through a route that obliged her to navigate the dangers of a railroad switchyard, and then only to a point where a bus would pick her up and transport her still farther away, and then to an all-black and disparately staffed and equipped school. She would repeat the long trek at the end of her school day, only to have to get up and do it all again the next day and the next. All the while, a white elementary school, forbidden to her courtesy of *Plessy's* rationalizations, was located just seven blocks from her home. Her father, Oliver Brown, beseeched the school system to admit her to the closer, "white" school, and was turned down. Brown then tapped into the black activist culture, which now had the NAACP, the nation's premier civil rights organization, at the helm. Linda Brown, and the other claimants whose cases were joined with hers, gave Marshall and his team what they had been looking for.

By 1954, "separate but equal" had been discredited once and for all. Besides Constance Baker Motley, Marshall had also relied on a black woman psychologist for the most telling evidence in his case. Mamie Phipps Clark had begun landmark work in graduate school at Howard University.

LINDA BROWN SMITH with Ethel Louise Belton Brown, Harry Briggs Jr., and Spottswood Bolling Jr., at a press conference at the Hotel Americana on 9 June 1964, ten years after *Brown v. Board of Education*. (Library of Congress, New York World-Telegram and Sun Collection; Sun photo by Al Ravenna.)

Her master's thesis, "The Development of Consciousness of Self in Negro Pre-School Children," explored the development of racial identity in young children. With her husband, Kenneth Clark, she published the fact that black children had a sense of their "blackness" when they were no more than three years old and that it negatively affected their self-image. She later went on to show that segregation was a major factor in that negativity. Thurgood Marshall used her results to show that "separate" was inherently unequal.

That Supreme Court decision was, in effect, the beginning of the modern civil rights movement. Legal resistance to discriminatory laws and customs moved into high gear. "The Law," with a capital "L" is far larger and more diverse in form than the text of the U.S. Constitution, the constitutions of the fifty states, and the statutes enacted by the federal and state and municipal governing bodies of the country. In addition to legislation, there is so-called judge-made law, the common law, which is set over time as litigation pursuant to constitutions and statutes leads to questions of interpretation and application, and at times manipulation, unanswered by legislation. Also, there are administrative regulations and practices promulgated in furtherance of constitutional and statutory edicts, as well as the directives in the growing body of the common law. Then there is the law in its most frontline sense, as it is applied and enforced, and many times manipulated, at the discretion of persons charged with its day-to-day dispensation, at the hands of governmental administrators and agents of every stripe, from police officers to customs inspectors, social workers, and soldiers. There is, in addition, the whole course of human dealings, as people rent apartments, purchase appliances, apply for jobs, eat in restaurants, ride on buses, and on and on. Virtually all transactions in American life involve persons obliged, in theory, to obey the law as it may direct the mode and manner in which the law says such activities are to be conducted.

If litigation and legislation have achieved success in protecting and expanding civil rights, it has been in no small part due to the manner in which political resistance set the stage, creating an atmosphere of righteous pressure, in which the ugliness and emptiness of biases were exposed and bravely and skillfully exploited. Political resistance created the emotional currency and climate that allowed successful litigation and legislation, and successful penetration of the legal culture as a profession. Black women played highly visible roles here, and the irony is that much of their influence is perhaps attributable to the fact that they were and are women, a group historically both pushed down and protected, most often because of immutable traits.

For the present purposes, political resistance can be seen as the deliberate and studied "use" of the law by black women against the law as a form of protest. These are the stories in which legal action was a result of black women's planned resistance to the harsh and unjust operation of the laws that oppressed them. Black women were leaders in the direct assault against all these facets of the law. The quintessential example of this form of resistance is, of course, Rosa Parks and her refusal to surrender her bus seat to a white man upon demand. In one sense, Parks was exactly what she looked like—a soft-spoken woman of dignity and quiet, inoffensive self-possession. She was also an active member of the NAACP who had attended workshops in political resistance at the Highlander Folk School led by Septima Clark, an experienced union organizer and voter registration and rights educator. Parks was far from naive and, if she was tired that day, it was a weariness that was mixed with outrage and political savvy. The path had been prepared for her act of resistance by the Women's Political

Not at the Back of the Bus

Private Sarah Louise Keys was in the first generation of members of the Women's Army Corps to serve in an officially integrated military. In August 1952 she was an information clerk and receptionist at the Army hospital at Fort Dix, New Jersey, when she received a furlough to go home to North Carolina. She was wearing her uniform when she stepped on the bus and took her seat near the front of the bus. At Roanoke Rapids, North Carolina, a new driver came onto the bus to replace the one who had been driving since New Jersey. He asked her to change seats with a white Marine who was sitting near the back of the bus. Private Keys refused.

That was the beginning of one of the most important cases in civil rights history. The bus driver had all his other passengers move to a second bus, provided by the bus company, refusing to allow Keys to board. She was forcibly removed to the police station, where she was charged with disorderly conduct and jailed overnight, with no phone call allowed. She was released the following afternoon after paying a twenty-five dollar fine.

Sarah Keys's family was outraged and persuaded her to go to court, but she lost. Then a friend suggested that the Keys family hire Dovey Johnson, another black military woman. After fighting to be admitted to the Women's Army Auxiliary Corps (WAAC), Johnson had become one of thirty-seven black women in the first class of commissioned officers in the WAAC in 1942. After World War II she attended Howard University Law School and practiced in Washington, DC. Sarah Keys hired Dovey Johnson to represent her, and the two military women, working together, began to fight for equality and dignity on a legal battlefield.

The U.S. District Court for the District of Columbia refused to hear the suit, stating that it was out of its jurisdiction. Keys and Johnson, along with her law partner Julius Robertson, then went to the Interstate Commerce Commission (ICC) and filed a suit alleging unjust discrimination, undue and unreasonable prejudice, false arrest, and imprisonment on the basis of race and color. At first, the ICC refused to review the case, in spite of the Supreme Court's *Brown v. Board of Education* ruling. The reviewing commissioner claimed that precedent did not apply in the matter of a private business. But Keys's lawyers kept fighting until they were able to get a review by the full commission. The decision of that commission, handed down in November of 1955, reversed the "separate but equal" policy established in 1896. Black passengers who paid the same amount for their fares must be given the same service.

For more information, see Judith Bellafaire, "Challenging the System: Two Army Women Fight for Equality." Women in Military Service for America Memorial Foundation, Inc. http://www.womensmemorial.org/Education/BHMSys.html.

seem less than suitable. Claudette Colvin, for example, was fifteen and pregnant. However, upon hearing of Parks's arrest, the WPC mobilized and, over the course of a weekend, had organized the boycott.

What is particularly interesting in looking at the legal resistance of black women is that this case is one in a series that stretches back a century. Starting with Elizabeth Jennings in 1855, black women repeatedly chose public transportation as a site of protest against law and its interpretation. Black women used buses daily and therefore were subjected to discomfort and humiliation on a regular basis. Riding the bus was a necessity, especially for the working women who made up the vast majority of the black female population. Also, riding the bus was public, and therefore the humiliation was public.

Diane Nash, one of the most important members of the Student Nonviolent Coordinating Committee (SNCC), would take Rosa Parks's act of defiance to the next level and turn civil disobedience into an enormously powerful form of legal resistance for African Americans. Nash was a young woman from a middle-class black family in Chicago who encountered new depths of racism as a college student at Fisk University in Nashville, Tennessee, in 1959. Appalled, she began attending workshops on nonviolent resistance to Jim Crow. In doing so, Nash met and learned from a number of prominent resisters, including the strategist James Lawson, who had recently been to India. With other students, she began doing sit-ins at lunch counters, a tactic that had been originated some time before by Clara Luper in Oklahoma City.

Students staged lunch-counter sit-ins in the Nashville area in the late winter and spring of 1960, most notably at Woolworth's and other similarly well-known stores; such businesses were good tactical targets because of their mainstream nature and the fact that their lunch counters were strictly segregated. The sit-ins received a great deal of attention, with mob violence finally boiling over against the students, who, true to their training, remained nonviolent and were rewarded with arrest and incarceration for disorderly conduct. Outraged, area blacks boycotted lunch counters targeted by the students, and fearful whites avoided shopping downtown. Commercial activity was greatly affected. The attractive and articulate Nash became a highly sought-after press interview.

On 19 April 1960, events took a tragic and galvanizing turn. The home of Z. Alexander Looby, a conservative black city councilman, a far cry from the image of a radical or outside agitator, was bombed, presumably as retribution for the boycott and sit-ins. The bombing infuriated the black community and a sector of the increasingly frightened and frustrated white community as well. Some twenty-five hundred people marched that same afternoon on city hall, at first singing, and then finally in silence, a

Council (WPC) of Montgomery, led by Jo Ann Robinson, which had threatened a bus boycott a year earlier. Working with the NAACP, the WPC had passed over two other black women as test cases because of factors that made them

S<small>IT-IN AT A LUNCH COUNTER</small>, Nashville, Tennessee, 1960. Lunch counters at Woolworth's and other well-known stores were a good target for civil rights activism because of their mainstream nature and because they were strictly segregated. (Library of Congress, New York World-Telegram and Sun Collection.)

powerful statement. They were met by Nashville's mayor, Ben West, who attempted to engage in a calming dialogue. He found himself responding to level-headed and pointed questions from Nash that forced him to examine the unfairness and immorality of selling merchandise to blacks only to refuse them service within the same store. West ended the encounter by asking all present, "How about we pray together?" The quick-witted Nash reportedly countered, "What about eating together?" to which West, impressed, responded that they should try to arrange just that. West came to champion the abolishment of segregation in venues of public accommodation and entertainment in Nashville.

With similar student activities going on in a number of areas, the legendary Ella Baker, who was at that time working with the Southern Christian Leadership Conference, organized a conference in Raleigh, North Carolina. The result was the formation of SNCC, under Baker's guidance. Nash became heavily involved with the organization, leaving school to become one of the organization's fieldworkers. When a difference of opinion about goals and tactics caused a split in SNCC, she became head of the direct-action half of the organization. Her election to this position was a stunning victory for black women, who were kept out of most leadership positions in the movement.

Nash was a brilliant strategist, as was the man she soon married, James Bevel. They created the "jail-no-bail" policy of the direct action wing, using arrest and incarceration as a powerful form of resistance. It was dangerous for African Americans to go to jail in the South, but it made a strong statement to the rest of the United States and to the world. Nash coordinated the Freedom Rides that became so much a part of the American consciousness about race. Together with Bevel, she organized the Selma, Alabama, demonstrations that were a response to the church bombings that killed four black girls. Those demonstrations became the pivotal moment when the rest of the country turned its attention and outrage toward the South and demanded justice.

At that point, Diane Nash was twenty-five years old, and she had used the legal system in the United States perhaps better than anyone else ever had in the cause of freedom and equality.

Some Landmark Cases

It is not possible to give a short summary of the avalanche of litigation that followed the Civil Rights Act of 1964, which made history and increasingly formed an enduring protective net of guarantees to black Americans, among others. Title VII of the Act, which prohibited discrimination in employment practices, has a particularly rich history and is crucial to black progress. Because Africans were brought to the United States for commercial exploitation, and all aspects of their fates have flowed from that tainted source ever since, it can be fairly said that being black in America was always about work.

Slack v. Havens was a garden-variety case that did not make headlines, much less elicit Supreme Court attention, but represents a necessary element of proof—what constitutes direct evidence of discriminatory intent by an employer. Isabell Slack and three black female co-workers brought suit under Title VII for their dismissal from a large industrial manufacturing enterprise. At the end of three of the plaintiffs' work day on 31 January 1968, their immediate supervisor informed them that they were not to report to their regular stations on the production line the next day, but to engage instead in a general cleanup of the entire department's environs. The work was to include washing walls and windows, all of which had sills twelve to fifteen feet above the floor, the cleaning of lighting fixtures, and the scraping and washing of the floor, which was caked and layered with the hardened residue of plastic resins from the plant's manufacturing processes. The women objected because they had not been hired with any expectation of janitorial duties, but the company insisted. They were three of just four women in the department; the fourth was a white woman. The three black women were compelled to engage in the general cleaning while their white coworker was reassigned to another department for the day. The supervisor drafted a fourth black woman from yet another department to assist the first three. They protested and were fired.

This case says nearly everything about the black woman's work experience. They were in a minority of a minority in doing the type of work they did. They were asked and expected to be willing to scrape petrified gunk from the floor of a factory, in front of, or rather beneath the feet of, their overwhelmingly male co-workers, both white and black. Their interactions with their supervisors indicate a high degree of savvy, as their alert protests flushed out the very material that would lead to their victory, direct evidence of discriminatory intent on the part of their employer.

One of the most profound signals of progress in attitudes and living conditions for African Americans, and black women in particular, could be seen in changes to statutes banning legally sanctioned marriage between blacks and whites, antimiscegenation laws, and laws creating harsher penalties for adultery, fornication, and marriages between partners of different races as opposed to partners of the same race. Frustratingly, laws providing for disparate penalties for adultery and fornication were generally upheld upon challenge, as they tended to be worded in such a way that if the partners were of different races, the penalties applied equally to both persons. Application and enforcement were a different matter, however, and this practice held sway until miscegenation laws were successfully challenged and explicitly overruled by the Supreme Court in the 1964 case of *McLaughlin v. Florida*.

In 1967 the Supreme Court took up the case of *Loving v. Virginia*, which squarely posed Virginia's ban on interracial marriage for review. Richard and Mildred Loving were married in Washington, DC; Richard was white and Mildred was black. A Virginia judge sentenced them harshly under the state's "Racial Integrity Act," employing reasoning devoid of logic. Richard was sentenced to spend a year in prison, but the sentence was suspended on the condition that the couple leave the state and not return for at least twenty-five years. The Supreme Court overturned the Virginia statute on equal protection grounds. In so doing, it employed strong and sweeping language which made clear that no ban on interracial marriages could pass constitutional muster. Terming all such bans "invidious racial discrimination," which is to say calculated to give offense and motivated by hatred, the Court ruled such laws unjustifiably deprived the Lovings of one of the basic civil rights. Bigotry and mistrust are, of course, not subject to the Court's purview. But significantly, polls taken after the *Loving* decision showed a gradual change in attitudes toward interracial couples, as well as less negative attitudes toward children of mixed racial heritage.

Attitudes about violent sexual conduct toward black women began to show change in this period as well, and the effect of direct official address of the terribly controversial subject of interracial sexual behavior generally cannot be underestimated. Joan Little was an inmate in a North Carolina women's prison in the 1970s when she was raped by a white, male guard in her cell. Little was missing, an escapee from the prison, after the guard was found stabbed to death in her cell. Little was caught and charged with his murder, in a case that provoked national attention, outrage, and debate for months. Prominent persons became vocal in their support for her; Angela Davis in particular generated and kept sympathies for Little in the fore. That Little, a black woman and a felon, in one of the most conservative jurisdictions in the country, was ultimately acquitted in 1975 of a particularly violent crime says much about a definite change in the political and social climate. Sexual exploitation of black women, especially involving imbalance of power, was on the landscape not just as an issue but also as a matter of clear prohibition.

Legal Resistance at the Turn of a New Century

The history of racial justice in America follows a familiar pattern of change and opposition, followed by more change and more opposition. The enormous advances of the 1960s and the 1970s were followed by an extended period of conservative backlash in law and government, and

BLACK STUDENTS IN CIRCUIT COURT, Tallahassee, Florida, 1963. These students and others, numbering 220 in all, were facing charges of contempt for picketing a segregated movie theater after a judge had ordered their demonstrations halted pending a hearing. (Florida State Archives; Florida Memory Project: Florida Photographic Collection.)

black women, indeed women and minority groups of every sort, were left battling to hold on to ground gained. The very language and approach taken in *Brown*, the language of equal protection, was manipulated by whites, and largely white men, as the concept of "reverse discrimination" was created and injected into the debate over the extent of rights and the means of their establishment. This, of course, led to the question of where the responsibility of white Americans lay with regard to centuries of oppression of black Americans. Discussion of that question was later cast in terms of reparations.

Reparations, as a legal concept, refers to the movement seeking to compensate the present descendants of African slaves for sustained economic losses to their families over time as the result of the practical injustices of the slave economy and the ensuing history of inferior access to work, wages, and opportunities, relative to that of whites. There are some formally enacted state statutes dealing with reparations. Though these cases were not successful, the matter grew in attention and study. The reparations movement was predictably controversial, not just because of the potential amounts of money involved but also because of the perceived remoteness in time and history of black women and men nearly 150 years removed from slavery and the resulting culpability of potential payers for their predecessors' actions. Supporters view it as

appropriate, for the slaves were brought to the Americas against their will, victims of a crime against humanity, and their descendants never had unfettered, meaningful choice over their economic fortunes.

Legacy

Black women have, over the centuries in the United States, put a realistic human face upon their plight, affecting profound change, while creating and accumulating power, leverage, and efficacy. Although not what it could and ought to be, this is nonetheless an ongoing dynamic process. But the most salient aspect of this phenomenon is that it has come about with and through the very legal system that was used to oppress black women. It would take a long and painful history to reach a critical mass of situation and sentiment that could clear the path for real and systematic change—from the barbarous history of slavery and the Civil War to the Emancipation Proclamation to the women's suffrage movement to pressures for voting rights and land ownership and beyond. But black women have worked through, with, and even against the law to gain their freedom. Infiltrating the culture of the law, black women have become lawyers and judges, legislators and administrators, commentators, critics, scholars, and teachers of the law. In so doing, they make and shape the law itself and thus the culture in which it arises and is applied. They have inserted themselves and their unique voices and experiences into the fabric of the law as social order and ordering.

See also Antilynching Movement; Civil Rights Movement; Civil Rights Organization; Jim Crow Era; *and* Political Resistance.

BIBLIOGRAPHY

Appiah, Kwame A., and Henry Louis Gates Jr. *Africana*. Philadelphia: Running Press, 1999.

Bell, Derrick. *Race, Racism, and American Law*. New York: Aspen, 2000.

Bell, Derrick. *Silent Covenants: Brown v. Board of Education and the Unfulfilled Hopes for Racial Reform*. New York: Oxford University Press, 2004.

Davis, Ronald L. F. "Creating Jim Crow: In Depth Essay." www.jim-crowhistory.org/history/creating2.htm

Drachman, Virginia G. *Sisters in Law: Women Lawyers in Modern American History*. Cambridge, MA: Harvard University Press. 2001.

Hine, Darlene Clark, and Kathleen Thompson. *A Shining Thread of Hope*. New York: Broadway Books, 1999.

Giddings, Paula. *Where and When I Enter*. New York: HarperCollins, 1984.

Matsuda, Mari. "When the First Quail Calls: Multiple Consciousness as Jurisprudential Method." 14 *Women's Rights Law Reporter* 297 (1988).

Nowak, John E., Ronald D. Rotunda, J. Nelson Young. *Constitutional Law*. St. Paul, MN: West, 1986.

Osborne, Tonya Michelle. "Charlotte E. Ray: A Black Woman Lawyer." Women in the Legal Profession Web site. Stanford Law School, 2001. http://www.law.stanford.edu/library/wlhbp/papers/ CharlotteRay.pdf

Spelman, Elizabeth V. "Theories of Race and Gender: The Erasure of Black Women." *Quest* 5.4 (1982): 109–131.

Sterling, Dorothy. *We Are Your Sisters*. New York: Norton, 1997.

Still, William. *The Underground Railroad*. Philadelphia: Porter and Coates, 1872.

Toll, Robert C. *Blacking Up: The Minstrel Show in Nineteenth-Century America*. New York: Oxford University Press, 1974.

Williamson, Joel. *The Crucible of Race: Black-White Relations in the American South since Emancipation*. New York: Oxford University Press, 1970.

Winbush, Raymond A. *Should America Pay? Slavery and the Raging Debate on Reparation*. New York: Amistad, 2003.

Wormser, Richard. *The Rise and Fall of Jim Crow*. New York: St. Martin's Griffin, 2004.

—SARA VAN WINKLE

LEGISLATORS.

The experiences of black women legislators, the circumstances that have motivated them to serve, and the issues they have championed, have been both similar to and different from the experiences of their black and white male peers. Until recently, studies of legislative leadership have primarily focused on white men and women, and to a lesser extent, African American men. The predominant body of literature has often failed to stress the extent to which white women legislators have sacrificed women's solidarity and racial equality at the altar of white privilege. Likewise, most histories of black legislative leadership have analyzed black men's efforts to secure political influence, and socio-economic capital for beleaguered African American communities. Yet, from Shirley Chisholm and Carol Moseley Braun to contemporary leaders such as Sheila Jackson-Lee and Maxine Waters, black women legislators have consistently fought for the rights of all Americans to exist on an equal basis, consistently supporting legislation that advances social, economic, and political equality across race lines. Studies have shown that black women legislators, like their white women counterparts, have demonstrated interest in health care, education, families, and economic equality. Until recently, their contributions and experiences have received little attention. Many historians, by focusing primarily on their white, male peers, and through the overemphasis of the "manhood" metaphor in black legislative leadership, which seeks to recover allegedly usurped black male authority and autonomy through language and action, have failed to assess the impact of black women legislators and have silenced some of the most progressive, powerful, and effective voices in American history.

Earliest African American Women Legislators

Reconstruction (1863–1877) ushered in the election of the first African American to local, state, and federal lawmaking bodies. During this period there were two black male senators in Congress (Hiram Revels and Blanche K. Bruce, both Mississippi natives who had been educated in the

SHEILA JACKSON-LEE speaking in 1998 at a hearing held by the House Judiciary Committee regarding the impeachment of President Bill Clinton. (© Wally McNamee/Corbis.)

North) and fourteen black members of the House. It would take roughly one hundred years for the first African American women to be elected to Congress. The first black woman to be elected to the U.S. House of Representatives was Shirley Chisholm. Born Shirley Anita Saint Hill, in the Bedford-Stuyvesant section of Brooklyn, New York in 1924, Chisholm made history when she ran against James Farmer for the seat in the newly formed Twelfth Congressional District of Brooklyn in 1968. Farmer was the former leader of the Congress of Racial Equality (CORE). No matter who won the race, when the final votes were tallied, Brooklyn would have its first black member of Congress. Chisholm won by a landslide, however, and became the first black woman to be elected to the

U.S. House of Representatives. She served in the House for fourteen years, was known as a champion of civil rights and women's rights, and was an early member of the National Organization of Women (NOW), a founder of the National Women's Political Caucus (NWPC), and a leading advocate for the National Abortion Rights Action League (NARAL). In 1972, attempting to capitalize on her experience and the electoral power of her diverse constituencies, Chisholm made history again when she became the first African American, and the first woman, to launch a serious bid for the presidential nomination.

An Increasing Voice

Although their numbers were growing, in 1969, blacks in Congress still represented a small yet vocal minority. To offset their small numbers, a group of influential and outspoken black Congressional leaders formed an organization that would allow them to pool their resources and speak with one voice. On 2 January 1969, Shirley Chisholm rallied the support of Louis Stokes of Ohio, Bill Clay of Missouri, William Dawson of Chicago, Adam Clayton Powell Jr. of New York, Charles Diggs of Detroit, Robert Nix of Philadelphia, Augustus Hawkins of Los Angeles, and John Conyers Jr. of Detroit. The group met initially as the Democratic Select Committee under the leadership of Charles Diggs. On 2 February 1971 the group agreed to be known as the Congressional Black Caucus (CBC). The Caucus is officially nonpartisan, but in practice it has been almost exclusively composed of Democrats, and tends to function as a lobbying group with the wider Congressional Democratic Party. Only three black Republicans have been elected to Congress since the Caucus was founded: Senator Edward W. Brooke of Massachusetts and Representatives Gary Franks of Connecticut and J. C. Watts of Oklahoma. Unlike Brooke and Franks, Watts refused to join the Caucus.

The goals of the CBC have been to "positively influence the course of events pertinent to African Americans and others of similar experience and situation, and to achieve greater equity for persons of African descent in the design and content of domestic and international programs and services." The Caucus has not only been at the forefront of issues affecting African Americans, but has garnered international acclaim for advancing agendas aimed at protecting human rights and civil rights for all people. The vast majority of black people elected to Congress have become members of the CBC. Black women have played a critical role in advancing the CBC's agenda. One of the earliest leaders of the CBC was Cardiss Robertson Collins, widow of U.S. Representative George Collins from Illinois. Collins had been politically active before her husband's death, working on her husband's campaigns, and representing the Democratic Party as a committeewoman.

When George Collins was killed in an airplane crash in a residential area of Chicago, Cardiss Robertson Collins launched a bid for her husband's vacant seat in Congress. She won the election on 5 June 1973.

In 1979 Collins became chair of the CBC, the first woman to occupy that position. Her primary goal was to unify the seventeen members of the CBC, and to expand their power and influence. She possessed tremendous leadership skills and was known for aggressiveness and diplomacy, qualities she used to deal with the many personalities in the CBC. As the nation and Congress began to embrace conservatism in the 1980s, and retreat from the more progressive agenda of the 1960s and 1970s, black women legislators such as Collins fought to ensure that gains in civil rights were not completely reversed. She led the way in thwarting an antibusing amendment to the Constitution, and called for economic sanctions against the apartheid regime in South Africa. She also criticized the Reagan administration for its lack of attention to issues affecting African Americans, minorities, women, and the poor, and logged serious opposition to discrimination in the private sector.

Most black women legislators began their political careers at the local and state levels. One of the most famous of these leaders was Barbara Jordan. Jordan began her political career as administrative assistant to the county judge of Harris County, Texas. Not long after that, she was elected to the Texas state senate in 1996, the first black Texan to be elected to that body since 1883. In 1967 she became the first African American resident of Texas to preside over the state's senate. Then, in 1972, the same year that Shirley Chisholm ran for president, Jordan was elected to the U.S. House of Representatives by Houston's Eighteenth Congressional District. As a state senator and a U.S. congresswoman, Jordan sponsored bills that supported the poor, disadvantaged people, and racial minorities, sponsoring the Workman's Compensation Act and working to expand the Voting Rights Act of 1965 to protect Mexican Americans throughout the Southwest and other disenfranchised people across the nation.

In 1982 Katie Beatrice Green Hall was elected to the U.S. House of Representatives. Like Collins and Jordan, Hall began her career in local and state lawmaking bodies, serving as an Indiana state representative (1974–1976), a state senator (1976–1982), and a charter member of the Democratic Party. By 1982 Hall was primed for service at the national level. Like Chisholm, Collins, and Jordan, Hall was an ardent supporter of equality, tolerance, and the legacy of the civil rights movement. She is best known for her unyielding efforts to create a federal Martin Luther King Jr. holiday. Hall primarily sponsored and supported legislation that sought jobs for the unemployed. She drafted the Fair Trade in Steel Act, which was designed to stimulate the lagging steel industry, backed the Humphrey-Hawkins

 "We the People"

Mr. Chairman:

I join in thanking you for giving the junior members of this committee the glorious opportunity of sharing the pain of this inquiry. Mr. Chairman, you are a strong man and it has not been easy but we have tried as best we can to give you as much assistance as possible.

Earlier today, we heard the beginning of the Preamble to the Constitution of the United States, "We, the people." It is a very eloquent beginning. But when the document was completed on the seventeenth of September 1987 I was not included in that "We, the people." I felt somehow for many years that George Washington and Alexander Hamilton just left me out by mistake. But through the process of amendment, interpretation and court decision I have finally been included in "We, the people."

Today, I am an inquisitor; I believe hyperbole would not be fictional and would not overstate the solemnness that I feel right now. My faith in the Constitution is whole, it is complete, it is total. I am not going to sit here and be an idle spectator to the diminution, the subversion, the destruction of the Constitution.

. . .

The Constitution charges the President with the task of taking care that the laws be faithfully executed, and yet the President has counseled his aides to commit perjury, willfully disregarded the secrecy of grand jury proceedings, concealed surreptitious entry, attempted to compromise a federal judge while publicly displaying his cooperation with the process of criminal justice. "A President is impeachable if he attempts to subvert the Constitution."

If the impeachment provision in the Constitution of the United States will not reach the offenses charged here, then perhaps that eighteenth century Constitution should be abandoned to a twentieth century paper shredder.

Has the President committed offenses and planned and directed and acquiesced in a course of conduct which the Constitution will not tolerate? This is the question. We know that. We know the question.

We should now forthwith proceed to answer the question. It is reason, and not passion, which must guide our deliberations, guide our debate, and guide our decision.

Statement made by Representative Barbara Jordan (D-TX) explaining the constitutional basis for impeachment, Washington, DC, 25 July 1974.

bill to prevent domestic violence and child abuse, and supported the Equal Rights Amendment.

Hall's service in the House marked the growing influence black women wielded in the national legislative process. Yet by the end of the 1980s, there were no African Americans in the Senate, and no black woman had ever served in the entire history of that legislative body. Carol Moseley Braun made history in 1992 when she became the first black woman, and only the second

African American since Reconstruction, to be nominated and elected to the U.S. Senate by a major political party.

When she ran for the Democratic nomination from Illinois, she was relatively unknown to most Americans and had only a relatively small amount of money to fund her campaign. Her trailblazing victory in the primary threw her almost immediately into the national spotlight. Mosley Braun was a part of growing class of women who won elections across the country and who were motivated and supported, in part, by resolute groups of women and minorities who wanted legislators who would represent their interests. She also capitalized on the fact that a growing number of Americans had become very dissatisfied with a slumping economy, egregious national debt, the erosion of civil rights protections, and rising social unrest.

Mosley Braun, like Collins, Jordan, and Hall, had begun her legislative career in a state legislature. In 1978 she was elected to the Illinois House of Representatives. She soon developed a reputation as an adept coalition builder and an effective politician. Between 1980 and 1987, she sponsored every school-funding bill that influenced the city of Chicago. In 1985 she helped draft the Urban School Improvement Act, which created parents' councils in Chicago schools. She supported programs that assisted the indigent and would-be college students, and sponsored bills to eliminate discrimination in housing and private clubs. During her tenure in the U.S. Senate (1992–1998), Mosley Braun continued to draft and support legislation that paid particular attention to inequalities in education. In addition to serving as a U.S. Senator, she served as the U.S. Ambassador to New Zealand (1998–2002). In 2003 Mosley Braun's commitment to positive change, her political ambitions, and her "sense of duty to the nation," led her to launch a campaign for the office of the President of the United States.

Leadership Styles

Mosley Braun, like most women legislators, particularly black women lawmakers, excelled in her role because of her ability to practice a more fluid kind of leadership than her male counterparts. Scholars have argued that women's leadership style, in general, has differed from that of men. Legislative leadership has traditionally been viewed as "transactional," a kind of aggressive negotiating method to mediate specific interests in a predominantly male legislative political arena. As Cindy Simon Rosenthal and Lucinda Simon Rosenthal argue in *When Women Lead: Integrative Leadership in State Legislatures*, however, women leaders generally bring with them an integrative and inclusive leadership style that brings to light the important contributions that women as legislative agents make to the institutions in which they operate. Black women legislators such as Chisholm, Collins, Hall, and Mosley Braun, in particular, have demonstrated that

by encouraging collaboration, shared problem-solving, and consensus, leaders can build broad-based coalitions that address the specific needs of African Americans, while also addressing some of the basic needs of people regardless of race, ethnicity, and gender.

Generally women legislators, particularly those who chair important committees, come to their roles from different life experiences, and as a result are uniquely motivated and adopt strategies and visions of leadership that differ in important ways from those of their male counterparts. Black women's experiences in America have placed them among those most attuned to oppression and inequality in our country. Black in a racist society, female in a sexist culture, and invariably connected to poorer constituents in a nation that stigmatizes poverty, black women legislators have been keenly aware of our most pressing socioeconomic problems, and uniquely equipped by virtue of their background and constituencies to devise effective ways to solve them. Black women, like women in general, tend to see political leadership as something more than the act of satisfying particular interests. Many have endeavored to alter the ways in which the legislative process works, because they believe it *is* the process that has played a critical role in oppressing many of the people they represent. They have done so by employing a more flexible style of leadership that reflects the diversity of their experience.

The hallmark of black women's legislative leadership has been the efforts to mobilize black women against the interwoven race, class, and sex exploitation and discrimination that they face in everything from employment to housing. Most black women legislators learned early on that to ensure the advancement of their constituents, especially black people, they had to champion a process that encouraged other African Americans, and all of the people that they serve, to take responsibility for their own futures while simultaneously becoming agents of social, economic, and political change. This process has produced some influential and effective black women legislators, and it has had a serious impact on individuals and communities throughout America.

One of the more pronounced aspects of black women's style of leadership, from the grassroots level to the halls of Congress, is that inside it is a legitimate critique of sexism that is not rooted in intellectual discourse cultivated by obscure white feminist theory, but rather derived from the historical, intimate, real-word experiences of everyday black women. Black women's comprehension of the intersection of race, class, and gender has prompted them to dismiss relations of power and privilege based on male concepts of rank and status. Most black women, particularly legislators, unlike most men, have believed that leadership should be multilateral, heterogeneous, and not centered on one individual or a chosen few.

Featuring Legislators

● **Hannah Diggs Atkins** (1923–) was elected to the Oklahoma state legislature in 1969 and served there until 1980. She was born in Winston-Salem, North Carolina, in 1923 and received her BA from Saint Augustine's College (1943), her BLS from the University of Chicago (1949), and her MPA from the University of Oklahoma (1989). Among a large variety of jobs, she worked as a news reporter, teacher, biochemical researcher, and librarian. She was the assistant director of Human Services for Oklahoma (1983–1987) and both secretary of Human Resources and secretary of state (1987–1991). In these capacities she was the highest-ranking woman in Oklahoma state government. In 1980 she became a delegate to the United Nations. In 1990 she received the award for Distinguished Service to State Government from the National Governors' Association.

● **Corinne Brown** (1946–) was a congresswoman for Florida's Third District. She was born in Jacksonville, Florida, and attended Florida A&M University (BS, 1969) and the University of Florida (EdS, 1974). She taught at Florida Community College of Jacksonville, the University of Florida, and Edward Waters College. She became a member of the Florida House of Representatives in 1982 and ten years later became one of the first African Americans to represent Florida in the U.S. Congress since Reconstruction. She was a member of various congressional committees including the Committee on Transportation and Infrastructure and the Committee on Veteran's Affairs.

● **Carol Moseley Braun** (1947–) was the first African American women elected to the U.S. Senate. (See individual entry: Moseley Braun, Carol.)

● **Yvonne Braithwaite Burke** (1932–) was the first woman to chair a Democratic National Convention and the first African American woman from California elected to the U.S. Congress. She was born in Los Angeles and attended the University of Southern California (JD, 1956). In 1966 she was elected to the California State Assembly. In 1972, she was named co-chair of the Democratic Convention in Miami. In the same year she was elected to Congress and, while there, was a member of the Appropriations Committee and chair of the Congressional Black Caucus. In 1973 she became the first person to give birth while a sitting member of Congress. She resigned in 1978 and returned to local politics, winning a seat on the Los Angeles County Board of Supervisors for the Fourth District. After a year in that position, she reentered private practice. In 1992 she was elected to the Los Angeles County Board of Supervisors again, this time for the Second District. She became the first African American chair of the Board of Supervisors the following year. She again served as chair from 1997 to 1998 and from 2002 to 2003.

● **Julia Carson** (1938–) was the first woman and the first African American ever elected to the U.S. Congress from Indianapolis. She was born in Louisville, Kentucky, and grew up in Indianapolis. Her mother was an unmarried teenager who found work as a housekeeper. She completed three years of college, attending Indiana Central Business College, Indiana University-Purdue University at Indianapolis, and St. Mary of the Woods external degree program. In 1965, a single mother herself, Carson became a legislative assistant to Congressman Andy Jacobs. In 1972 she was elected to the Indiana House of Representatives and in 1990 to the state senate. At the same time as she filled her house seat (1972–1982), she was also manager of the Public Affairs Department of Cummins Engine Company. In 1990, she became Center Township Trustee, a position she held for six years before winning her seat in 1996 to the U.S. Congress. In Congress she was a member of the Committee on Financial Services and the Committee on Transportation and Infrastructure.

● **Shirley Chisholm** (1924–2005) was the first black woman ever elected to the U.S. Congress and the first woman to seek the nomination of a major party for president of the United States. (See individual entry: Chisholm, Shirley.)

● **Eva Clayton** (1934–) was the first black woman to be sent to the U.S. Congress from North Carolina. (See individual entry: Clayton, Eva.)

● **Barbara-Rose Collins** (1939–) served as the congressional representative for Michigan's Thirteenth District. (See individual entry: Collins, Barbara Rose.)

● **Cardiss Robertson Collins** (1931–) was the first African American woman to represent a congressional district in the Midwest and the first woman and African American to serve as the Democratic Whip at Large. (See individual entry: Collins, Cardiss Robertson.)

● **Crystal Dreda Bird Fauset** (1894–1965) was the first African American woman to be elected to a state House of Representatives (Pennsylvania). (See individual entry: Fauset, Crystal Dreda Bird.)

● **Grace Towns Hamilton** (1907–1992) is best known for being the first African American woman to serve in the Georgia legislature. (See individual entry: Hamilton, Grace Towns.)

● **Eddie Bernice Johnson** (1935–) became in 1992 the first African American woman to represent the Dallas, Texas, area in the U.S. Congress. (See individual entry: Johnson, Eddie Bernice.)

● **Stephanie Tubbs Jones** (1949–) was the first African American woman elected to the United States House of Representatives from Ohio. She was born and grew up in Cleveland, Ohio, and attended Case Western Reserve University (BA, 1971) as well as its School of Law (JD, 1974). She was elected to a judgeship in Cleveland's municipal court in 1981. Two years later she became the first black woman to serve as a judge with Cuyahoga County's Court of Common Pleas. She was the first black and the first woman to be county prosecutor, a job she held from 1991 to 1998, after which she was elected to the U.S. Congress. In the House of Representatives, Jones was the first African American woman to be a member of the Ways and Means Committee. She was also a member of the Committee on Standards of Official Conduct (Ethics) and the Congressional Black Caucus. She was co-chair of the 2004 Democratic Convention.

● **Barbara Charline Jordan** (1936–1996) was the first black woman to sit in the Texas Senate and the first from the South to be elected to the U.S. Congress. (See individual entry: Jordan, Barbara Charline.)

● **Carolyn Cheeks Kilpatrick** (1945–) represented Michigan's Thirteenth Congressional District in the U.S. House of Representatives. Born in Detroit, Michigan, she received her BS from Western Michigan University (1972), and her MS from the University of Michigan, Ann Arbor (1977). She was a public schoolteacher for two years and then became a member of the Michigan House of Representatives. During her eighteen years in the Michigan house, Kilpatrick was the first black woman to serve on its Appropriations Committee. In 1996, she won election to the U.S. Congress, where she sat on its House Appropriations Committee as well as the Transportation, Treasury, and Independent Agencies Committees. She was the first woman to chair the Congressional Black Caucus's Political Action Committee. She was also a member of the U.S. Air Force Academy Board.

● **Barbara Lee** (1946–) was the representative for the Ninth Congressional District in California, which includes Oakland, Berkeley, and Alameda. She was born in El Paso, Texas, and moved to California in 1960. She attended Mills College (1973) and the University of California, Berkeley (MA, Social Welfare, 1975). While at the university, she founded a community mental health center in Berkeley. She became chief of staff for Ninth District congressman Ron Dellum, whom she would later replace. She was elected to the California State Assembly in 1990 and to the state senate from 1996. In 1998, Dellum retired, and Lee won a special election to become the Ninth District's representative. She was the whip for the Congressional Black Caucus and chaired its Task Force on Global HIV/AIDS. She was also the co-chair of the Haiti Task Force of the Congressional Black Caucus. She was the assistant Democratic whip and co-chair of the Progressive Caucus and was on the International Relations Committee and the Financial Services Committee. She was perhaps most famous for being the sole member of Congress (both the Senate and the House of Representatives) to vote against a resolution authorizing President George W. Bush's use of military force in response to the 11 September 2001 terrorist attacks.

● **Sheila Jackson Lee** (1950–) was the Congressional Representative for the Eighteenth District in Houston, Texas. (See individual entry: Lee, Sheila Jackson.)

● **Cynthia McKinney** (1955–) was an outspoken congressional representative for Georgia from 1992 through 2002. (See individual entry: McKinney, Cynthia.)

● **Carrie Meek** (1926–) became the first African American from Florida elected to the U.S. Congress since the era of Reconstruction. She served from 1992 to 2002. (See individual entry: Meek, Carrie.)

● **Juanita Millender-McDonald** (1938–) was elected to represent California's Thirty-Seventh District in Congress in 1996. Born in Birmingham, Alabama, she attended the University of Redlands (BS, Business Administration, 1981); California State University, Los Angeles (MEd, Educational Administration, 1987); and the University of Southern California (MA/PhD, Public Administration). After working as a public school teacher, she became a city council member (1990) and mayor pro tempore (1991) for the City of Carson. Two years later, she was elected to the California State Assembly. Entering the U.S. Congress in 1996, she was a Democratic whip, vice chair of the Congressional Women's Caucus, and vice chair of the International Task Force on HIV/AIDS. A member of the Transportation Committee, the Small Business Committee, and the Committee on House Administration, she was also the Democratic chair of the Congressional Caucus for Women's Issues and was deeply involved in international women's issues.

● **Eleanor Holmes Norton** (1937–) was the sole representative for the District of Columbia in the Congress from 1990 into the start of the twenty-first century. It is a nonvoting position. (See individual entry: Norton, Eleanor Holmes.)

● **Maxine Waters** (1938–) represented her congressional district in California from 1990 into the start of the twenty-first century. (See individual entry: Waters, Maxine.)

● **Diane E. Watson** (1933–) was the congressional representative for the Thirty-Second District in California, which encompasses much of Los Angeles. Born and raised in Los Angeles, she attended the University of California, Los Angeles (BA, Education, 1955); California State University (MA, School Psychology, 1958); and Claremont Graduate School (PhD, Educational Administration, 1987). She also attended the Kennedy School of Government at Harvard University. She was an elementary school teacher and school psychologist and in 1975 was elected to the Los Angeles Unified School District Board of Education. Three years later, she was elected to the California State Senate. While there, she served as chair of the Health and Human Services Committee and of the Judiciary Committee. In 1998 she left the state senate to become the U.S. Ambassador to the Federated States of Micronesia. In 2001 she became a U.S. representative after a special election was called after the death of Congressman Julian Dixon. She served on the International Relations and Government Reform Committees.

Most black women legislators began their careers in state lawmaking bodies. Prominent black women legislators who have served at the national level—such as Shirley Chisholm, Barbara Jordan, Katie Beatrice Hall, Carol Moseley Braun, and Maxine Waters—all served in state legislatures prior to running for House and Senate seats. The number of black state legislators, like the number of blacks who have served at the national level, has always been small. Although their numbers began to grow by 1970, they, like their counterparts at the national level, were still a small yet outspoken minority. To pool their resources and network with black lawmakers in other states, a group of black state legislative leaders formed the National Black Caucus of State Legislators (NBCSL) in 1977. Currently NBCSL consists of more than 600 legislators from 46 states, and it represents more than 20 million voters. Although the majority of the group's members are black men, the organization boasts a number of powerful and highly productive black women leaders such as Leah Landrum-Taylor (AZ), Rosemary Marshall (CO), Gloria Butler (GA), Shirley Jones (IL), Mary Waters (MI), and Ruth Hassell-Thomson (NY). While each of these black women legislators, and their peers, have various issues that they champion, the NBCSL serves as a clearinghouse of information and works with these women on a number of policy issues. They, like their peers at the national level, have been strong defenders of civil rights, women's rights, juvenile justice, affordable healthcare, diversity, economic equality, and international human rights. In 2002, for example, Vice President Milagros Ortiz Bosch of the Dominican Republic in her capacity as Secretary of Education of the Dominican Republic, signed an agreement with NBCSL to establish the NBCSL International Technical Assistance Center (ITAC) in Santo Domingo. The agreement will provide minority students an opportunity to study abroad.

Into the Twenty-First Century

By 2003 the CBC boasted thirty-eight members. At least fifteen of them were black women, all Democrats. They included Rep. Corrine Brown, Florida, Rep. Julia Carson,

REPRESENTATIVE STEPHANIE TUBBS JONES at a commemorative event at Ground Zero held in September 2002 to mark the first anniversary of the terrorist attack on the World Trade Center. (© Reuters/Corbis.)

called the Valiant Women, she ran for the state House of Delegates in 1958. In 1962 she was elected to the state senate, where she continued to fight for civil rights for the next twenty years. Her legislative successes included desegregating public accommodations and the repeal of a miscegenation law. She was also instrumental in passing gun control, voter registration, and equal pay legislation. She survived a 1964 attempted assassination and died in 1990.

Indiana, Del. Donna Christian-Christensen, Virgin Islands, Rep. Eva Clayton, North Carolina, Rep. Sheila Jackson-Lee, Texas, Rep. Eddie Bernice Johnson, Texas, Rep. Stephanie Tubbs Jones, Ohio, Rep. Carolyn Kilpatrick, Michigan, Rep. Barbara Lee, California, Rep. Cynthia McKinney, Georgia, Rep. Carrie Meek, Florida, Rep. Juanita Millender-McDonald, California, Del. Eleanor Holmes Norton, District of Columbia, Rep. Maxine Waters, California, and Rep. Diane E. Watson, California.

In 2003 Eddie Bernice Johnson was selected to chair the CBC. Upon her election as Chair, she expounded on the history and hope of the CBC:

The Congressional Black Caucus is one of the world's most esteemed bodies, with a history of positive activism unparalleled in our nation's history. Whether the issue is popular or unpopular, simple or complex, the CBC has fought for thirty years to protect the fundamentals of democracy. Its impact is recognized throughout the world. The nation will face serious challenges over the next two years. At the same time, it will be blessed with unprecedented opportunities. Over the past eight years, the progress that minorities have fought for through centuries of struggle finally began to be realized. The Caucus is committed to ensuring that the standard of living for minorities in America does not retrogress, but instead rises to meet the expectations of both our ancestors and our children. Our diversity makes us stronger, and the expertise of all of our members has helped us be effective beyond our numbers.

("Congressional Black Caucus")

One of the most powerful legislators in America at the end of the twentieth century, and the dawn of the twenty-first, has been Maxine Waters. Elected in November 2000 to her sixth term in the House of Representatives with an overwhelming 87 percent of the votes, she represents a large part of South Central Los Angeles. Formerly the Chair of the CBC, Waters has held the influential leadership position of Chief Deputy Whip of the Democratic Party since the 106th Congress. Throughout her twenty-five years of public service, Waters has confronted difficult and controversial issues. Following the Los Angeles riot in 1992, she clearly articulated the hopelessness and despair in urban areas throughout America. She also made headlines when she accused the CIA of involvement in the Contra cocaine trafficking of drugs in South Central Los Angeles in the mid-1980s.

Prior to her election to the House of Representatives in 1990, Waters served for fourteen years in the California State Assembly, where she rose to the powerful position of Democratic Caucus chair. She was responsible for some of the boldest legislation in California history. She spearheaded the largest divestment of state pension funds from South Africa, landmark affirmative action legislation, the nation's first statewide child abuse prevention training program, and the prohibition of police strip searches for nonviolent misdemeanors. She has used her skill to shape public policy and deliver billions of dollars to minorities and the poor. She helped expand U.S. debt relief for Africa and other developing nations, and helped create the Center for Women Veterans. As an advocate for human rights, Congresswoman Waters was a leader in the movement to end apartheid and ensure one-person, one-vote democracy in South Africa. She founded the Los Angeles Free South Africa Movement and continues to be an adviser to the TransAfrica Forum. In 1994 she was on the official U.S. delegation to Nelson Mandela's inauguration as president of a free South Africa. Waters was a key figure in Congressional efforts to restore to power Haiti's democratically elected president, Jean-Bertrand Aristide.

On 25 October 1997 Waters spoke to a crowd of between six hundred thousand and 2.5 million, according to various estimates, at the Million Woman March in Philadelphia. Black women from across the country and beyond gathered on that day to engage in what the historian, Ernestine Jenkins, described as a "very public revolutionary act of resistance." As Waters argued, they gathered to "put America on notice," that the issues and problems that black women faced would no longer be marginalized by an indifferent power structure, and that black women, and their representatives, would continue to fight for themselves and their communities. "We are driven," she proclaimed, "by our commitment to ourselves, our children and our families to live in a fair and just society that respects us and our role in this nation and in this world." Waters continues to serve, and as she confronts the present Republican-controlled Congress on issues such as poverty, economic development, equal justice under the law, and other issues of concern to people of color, women, children, and poor people, she enjoys a broad cross section of support from diverse communities across the nation.

Black women legislators such as Jackson-Lee, Johnson, Norton, and Waters, are participants in a dynamic legacy of black female activism. African American women have been involved in non-violent and violent resistance to slavery, the abolitionist movement, the anti-lynching crusade, the civil rights and black power movements, and the women's movement. These examples illuminate one of the notable attributes of African American women's historical activism, and its dual nature. Indeed, as Jenkins indicates, "the majority of black women are participants, whether they are conscious or not, in the everyday political activism described as group survival." When black women such as Jackson-Lee, Johnson, Norton, and Waters "add participation in overt, public, political activism to their arsenal of weapons against race and class oppression, then they are utilizing their activist heritage in ways unique to black women."

Black women legislators have used their diverse backgrounds to become influential leaders and champions for access and opportunity. They continue to be active legislators at the local, state, and national levels, pursuing and successfully achieving a number of legislative objectives. They have distinguished themselves as staunch defenders of the Constitution, civil rights, quality and affordable healthcare, juvenile justice, gun safety and responsibility, diversity, women's rights, child safety, and economic empowerment for low and middle income America. In addition, black Congresswomen have been outspoken on domestic and global human rights issues. They have been strong advocates for historically black colleges and universities, and have been consistent supporters of affirmative action. Through their dynamic, fluid, shared leadership style, rooted in a legacy of black women's activism, black women legislators continue to fight for a more equal and just America. As Waters has declared, African American women and their representatives "are not powerless," and they will continue to "call on government and elected officials to rethink what they do and how they do it. We continue to call for a new politic of integrity and principled leadership. We will continue to fight against racism and marginalization."

BIBLIOGRAPHY

"Congressional Black Caucus." Wikipedia Encyclopedia. http://en.wikipedia.org/wiki/Congressional_Black_Caucus, Wikimedia Foundation, Inc., 2003.

Fenno, Richard F. *Going Home: Black Representatives and Their Constituents.* Chicago: University of Chicago Press, 2003.

Jenkins, Ernestine. "The Historical Dimensions of the Million Woman March: A Gendered Perspective." In *Million Woman March, Philadelphia, PA, October 25, 1997: A Commemoration,* edited by Darlene Clark Hine. East Lansing: Michigan State University, 1997, 3.

Rosenthal, Cindy Simon, and Lucinda Simon Rosenthal. *When Women Lead: Integrative Leadership in State Legislatures.* New York: Oxford University Press, 1998.

Shaw, Stephanie. *What A Woman Ought to Be and to Do: Black Professional Women Workers during the Jim Crow Era.* Chicago: University of Chicago Press, 1996.

Waters, Maxine. "Statement by Rep. Maxine Waters, Million Woman March." Speech given at the Million Woman March, Philadelphia, PA, 27 October 1997.

—Matthew C. Whitaker

LESBIANISM. Lesbian sexuality has always existed among women of the African diaspora. Lesbianism is not a new phenomenon, nor is it wholly a result of interaction with Europeans, as many blacks claim. White anthropologists in Africa perpetuated this notion, failing to acknowledge in their reports the preexistence of homosexuality or, when acknowledging it, attributing it to the influence of aberrations of Western behavior. In turn, this morality, often steeped in Christianity, became the morality of the first generation of postcolonial Africans. There is even a persistent school of thought within the black community that gays and lesbians simply do not exist. In truth, homosexuality and same-sex relationships have always been a natural part of African communities, whereas homophobia was largely an import from the West. A prevailing perception is that black people as a whole are intolerant of homosexuality within their community, often attributing it to the negative influence and practices of white people, but statistics have shown that homophobia is no greater in the black community than in society at large.

Most anthropological studies of African sexualities have focused on male relationships; however, occasionally female same-sex relationships are examined. "Woman-woman" marriages, or "female husbands," have been identified in more than thirty African populations. In these arrangements, a woman (often childless) marries another woman in much the same way as she would marry a man, by paying the brideprice in cattle. She would then enlist a male relative, neighbor, or friend to inseminate the wife, and offspring born to the wife were regarded as the children of the female husband. Sexual practices between the women in these marriages, however, remain unclear, although the "husband" was expected not to engage in intercourse with men or women, in part for fear of conception and the complications of inheritance that that would introduce. These types of marriages migrated to the Americas, where such unions, or *mati* (probably derived from the Hausa words *mata* or *mace*, meaning woman or wife), were commonly found in Suriname. They were surely present in some form in North America as well,

RALLY IN NEW YORK CITY, 14 August 1980, during the final session of the Democratic National Convention. The woman at center, Gwenn Craig of San Francisco, was supporting Ted Kennedy's candidacy. (©Bettmann/Corbis.)

though specific research has not yet been done. Likewise, erotic relationships existed, but between women they were often not regarded as sexual, even when they involved genital contact.

The idea that gender is a social role rather than a biological determination was also prevalent in African cultures. Gender was commonly regarded as situational and symbolic, based on gender-coded dress and lifestyle. One relatively early example of this type of gender fluidity in the United States is the story of Annie Lee Grant, who successfully "passed" for fifteen years as "Jim McHarris" working as a short-order cook, cabdriver, gas station attendant, preacher, and shipyard worker in order to receive higher-paying "men's work." Her secret life was only

discovered when she was stopped for a traffic violation in 1954 and her driver's license identified her as female.

Defining Terms

The etymology of "lesbian" derives from the Greek isle of Lesbos, where the poet Sappho lived. In antiquity natives of Lesbos were known as "lesbians." Its contemporary usage dates to the late nineteenth century, when Sappho's love poems written to women gained popularity. There has not always been agreement as to what constitutes lesbianism. In the nineteenth century, the designation did not exist, and intimacies that are now regarded as sexual, such as kissing, may or may not have been regarded as such at the time. For some the definition is biological: a lesbian is a woman who is sexually oriented toward other women. Some fix this definition narrowly, refusing to accept as lesbian any woman who has ever been attracted to or had a sexual relationship with a man. For others, including the pioneering black lesbian writer and activist Audre Lorde (1934–1992), lesbianism is defined as a woman determining her primarily relationships, both sexual and nonsexual, with women and identifying primarily with women. Useful alternatives to "lesbian" are "woman-identified woman" or "same-gender-loving."

Because of enduring racism and a need to distance themselves from noninclusive liberation movements, black lesbians have often struggled with self-identifying as "black lesbians." Within the women's movement, white feminists and lesbians were not always inclusive of race and class. Lisa Collins, in her 1979 essay for *Sepia* magazine, "Black Feminists and the Equal Rights Amendment," made the assertion that most black feminists considered lesbianism a "gay issue," not a feminist one. Further, within the black community the attitude persists that racism is a bigger issue than homophobia. Many contemporary women prefer the more inclusive and political designation "queer."

The term "bisexual" has been preferred by some black women, as it acknowledges the fluidity of sexuality as well as the reality that many black women have both male and female sexual partners at different times in their lives. Among the most well-known self-identified bisexual black women are Angela Y. Davis, June Jordan, Alice Walker, Rebecca Walker, and Meshell Ndegéocello.

Nineteenth Century: Private Lives

Prior to the nineteenth century, little documentation exists on black lesbians in the United States. Oral histories and personal narratives are therefore of utmost importance and primacy in constructing a black lesbian history. In the late twentieth century, black lesbian filmmakers, artists, and activists have revived the life stories of many early lesbians, thus making a connection and preserving a legacy.

The correspondence from 1854 until 1868 between a schoolteacher, Rebecca Primus, then twenty-three, in Royal Oak, Maryland, and an eighteen-year-old domestic worker, Addie Brown, in Hartford, Farmington, and Waterbury, Connecticut, and New York City, reveals their intimate friendship. It is significant in that Primus and Brown were not published authors but two ordinary black women who maintained a romantic relationship that they expressed through writing. Brown's letters to Primus comprise the whole of their extant correspondence; the historian Farah Jasmine Griffin has yet to uncover Primus's responses. Brown's correspondence is fairly explicit in her expressions of love, and in one letter she tells Primus, "No kisses is like yours." While it is clear that their relationship was romantic, and Brown writes of sleeping with women, the sexual nature of their relationship is unknown.

One early documented life is that of the western pioneer Mary Fields. Six feet tall, short-tempered, mean-spirited, and strong, Fields, who had been born into slavery in Tennessee, reputedly packed a pair of six-shooters or a shotgun that she did not hesitate to use. After Emancipation, Fields worked as a heavy laborer in an Ursuline nuns' mission near Cascade, Montana. Legend has it that Fields single-handedly held off a pack of wolves after being attacked at night out on the prairie. She later became a mail carrier, and her tenacity and reliability earned her the nickname "Stagecoach Mary." Though there is no evidence of Fields's sexual relationships, she is significant for her gender-bending lifestyle.

In the late nineteenth century, a group of American women sculptors, including Mary Edmonia Lewis and the white lesbians Harriet Hosmer, Anne Whitney, and Emma Stebbins, went to Rome in order to pursue their work more freely. Lewis, the only daughter of an Ojibwa (Chippewa) Indian mother and African American father, was born in upstate New York and orphaned at an early age. She attended Oberlin College in Ohio, but her years there were marred by a bizarre incident in which Lewis was accused of poisoning her two white housemates with an aphrodisiac. Although charges against her were eventually dismissed, she was taken by a lynch mob and badly beaten. It is this incident that some historians believe indicates the first signs of Lewis's alleged homosexuality—that the women, who were out on dates with male companions when the poison took effect, had been targeted because of romantic jealousy.

Lewis's studio in Rome near the Spanish Steps was a popular destination for tourists and a gathering place for other expatriate artists and intellectuals, many of them women. Although there has never been any explicit "proof" of Lewis's homosexuality, her decision to enter into what many considered a male profession in part

determined assumptions about her sexual preferences. Furthermore, she never married, she had no male companions and no children, and she wore so-called mannish attire (somewhat evident in the only known photographic portraits made of her, on a visit to Chicago).

In the literary world of the nineteenth century, two figures stand out for their unprecedented openness in their expressions of love for other women. Angelina Weld Grimké, a poet and writer, was born into a Boston abolitionist family. Grimké began writing love letters to women when she was around fourteen; at sixteen, a letter she wrote to Mamie Burrill included the unequivocal, oft-cited lines, "I know you are too young now to become my wife, but I hope, darling, that in a few years you will come to me and be my love, my wife! How my brain whirls how my pulse leaps with joy and madness when I think of these two words, 'my wife.' "

Highly educated, Grimké started her teaching career as a gym teacher in 1902 and later taught English. One of Grimké's plays, the lynching-themed *Rachel* (1916), is credited as the first drama by a black woman to be professionally produced. Grimké frequently published her poems and essays in journals, newspapers, and anthologies, including Alain Locke's *The New Negro* in 1925. Although she sometimes assumed a white male persona as the protagonist of her poems, perhaps in order to skirt the issue of lesbianism, at other times she explicitly did not. Among her poems expressing lesbian desire are "Rosalie," "If," "To Her of the Cruel Lips," "El Beso," "Autumn," "Give Me Your Eyes," "My Shrine," "Another Heart Is Broken," "Naughty Nan," and "Caprichosa," which includes these words of longing:

> Little lady coyly shy
> With deep shadows in each eye
> Cast by lashes soft and long,
> Tender lips just bowed for song,
> And I oft have dreamed the bliss
> Of the nectar in one kiss.

> (quoted in Herron, 1991)

But desire may have been the extent of it—aside from the correspondence with Burrill there are no records of any requited relationships between Grimké and other women.

The New Orleans–born author, educator, club woman, and feminist Alice Ruth Moore Dunbar-Nelson was an accomplished author of fiction, poetry, and drama and a widely published journalist who regularly addressed issues of race in her work. Unlike Grimké, Dunbar-Nelson had relationships with several prominent women and men. She married three times, including a brief union with the celebrated poet Paul Laurence Dunbar. "You! Inez!" is one of her few public works that is explicitly lesbian-themed, although the literary historian Gloria T. Hull suggests that Dunbar-Nelson's unpublished novel *This Lofty Oak* focuses on the life of her lover Edwina B. Kruse. Her full-length diary, which she began in 1921 and kept during the most productive period of her career, in the 1920s and 1930s, has become one of her most important works, documenting her relationships with other women, including an extensive network of other black lesbians. This sonnet from her diary is believed to have been written for her lover, the journalist Fay Jackson Robinson, with whom she had a relationship from 1930 to 1931:

> You did not need to creep into my heart
> The way you did. You could have smiled
> And knowing what you did, have kept apart
> From all my inner soul. But you beguiled
> Deliberately.
>
> (quoted in Hull, 1985)

Dunbar-Nelson's poem "Little Roads" also contains a reference to Robinson.

Apart from the evidence of woman-identification in private lives, the issue of lesbianism came up in the stereotypes of black women prevalent in the culture and the media. In the late nineteenth century, scientific discourses on race and sexuality were frequently linked, with black female sexuality often being associated with lesbianism. For example, black women and lesbians were both thought to have abnormally large clitorises. As the historian Sander Gilman has noted, the physical development of black female genitalia was related to that of the lesbian because of the so-called excesses of sexuality related to both.

1900–1930s: The Blues

As in the nineteenth century, lesbian history of the early twentieth century is dominated by a handful of personal narratives. The entertainment world provided a welcoming community for many lesbians, and some of the best-known lesbians of the era were entertainers, especially blues singers. The theme of lesbianism and the terms associated with it often made their way into the lyrics of blues songs, particularly those performed by women, especially Gertrude "Ma" Rainey's "Prove It on Me Blues" and Lucille Bogan's "B.D. [Bull Dyke] Woman's Blues." Of the terms most associated with "butch," or masculine-looking lesbian women, "bull-dyker," "bull-dagger," "bull-dyke," or simply "dyke" were originated in black communities to refer to lesbians or bisexual women. Sexually explicit material was commonplace in early blues songs, and many early blues performers, including Bessie Smith, Rainey, and Alberta Hunter, were either openly bisexual or lesbian. Smith and Bogan explicitly stated their preferences in songs, creating arguably the only moment in American history when the black lesbian voice and image was popular within the dominant culture.

In 1928 Rainey wrote "Prove It on Me Blues," which contained the lyrics:

> They said I do it, ain't nobody caught me
> Sure got to prove it on me
> Went out last night with a crowd of my friends
> They must've been women, 'cause I don't like no men
> It's true I wear a collar and a tie.
> Talk to the gals just like any old man.

The married Rainey lived it as she wrote it: in 1925 she was arrested for indecency, caught naked with a group of women at a private party. Smith bailed her out, and they would often joke about the humorous yet awkward incident afterward—the still-undressed Rainey fell down the stairs trying to get away. Smith, though also married, likewise made no secret of her numerous affairs with women. Other renowned blues singers of the era included Ethel Waters, called "Sweet Mama Stringbean," who, according to Alberta Hunter, flaunted her girlfriends in public.

After Mamie Smith's 1920 hit "Crazy Blues" ushered in the era of "race records"—records targeted expressly at black consumers—publishers rushed to capitalize on this previously unconsidered market, quickly employing popular club singers such as Hunter to make recordings. Hunter, born and raised in Memphis, Tennessee, left home at age fifteen for Chicago, where, lying about her age, she launched her singing career in the city's nascent saloon and club scene. Molested as a child, Hunter was largely disdainful of men, particularly those who would control and manipulate her. In part because she was fiercely independent, which in those days was especially unusual for a woman, rumors began to circulate regarding Hunter's sexuality. In 1919—perhaps, in part, to quell the stories about her—Hunter briefly married Willard Townsend, but they never slept together; after the wedding the couple moved in with Hunter's mother, Miss Laura, and Hunter slept with her instead. But even this degree of marriage closeness was not for her, and Hunter left two months later, though they did not obtain a divorce until 1923. And although Hunter never discussed her lesbianism, she also did not keep her lesbian relationships hidden.

"Empress of the blues" was the regal title rightly bestowed on Bessie Smith, whose history has been filled with persistent, colorful legends. Born in severe poverty in Chattanooga, Tennessee, Smith was gifted with a powerful voice that would make her the undisputed favorite blues singer of ticket and record buyers alike throughout the 1920s and 1930s. She started out singing on Chattanooga street corners at age nine and by the time she was a teenager had joined "Ma" Rainey in the Moses Stokes traveling show, which operated in tent shows throughout the South. Even though she was born a black woman in the Jim Crow South, Smith managed to conduct her life by her own set of rules; by nearly all accounts she was violent, foul-mouthed, a heavy drinker, promiscuous, and notoriously cheap and often preferred the company of women. Interestingly, Smith's most explicit lyrical reference to homosexuality, in her composition "Foolish Man Blues," is rather condemning: "There's two things got me puzzled, there's two things I can't understand/That's a mannish actin' woman and skippin', twistin' woman acting man."

House Parties and the Harlem Renaissance

Private house parties at which lesbians socialized seem to have been common across the country. From approximately 1920 until 1936, New York's Harlem became a mecca for black gays and lesbians who sought an atmosphere of tolerance and freedom to express their same-gender loving impulses. Private parties—rent parties, buffet flats—were the most popular sites of socialization for black women, although lesbians also occasionally gathered in clubs and speakeasies. A'Lelia Walker, heir to the Madam C. J. Walker hair-care fortune and arts patron, threw frequent and lavish soirees at which gays and lesbians freely mingled.

Gladys Bentley, born in Philadelphia, was the most flamboyantly out lesbian of the Harlem Renaissance era. She performed at rent parties and in clubs in Harlem, revamping popular songs of the day with bawdier lyrics she had written. She is most associated with Harry Hansberry's Clam House on 133rd Street in Jungle Alley, the

Gladys Bentley

The lesbian entertainer Gladys Bentley was one of many popular gay artists during the Harlem Renaissance. Born in 1907, she left home at sixteen and traveled to New York to find an atmosphere in which she could live her life openly. Performing at rent parties and at speakeasies along "Jungle Alley" (133rd Street between Lenox and Seventh Avenues), she wore a tuxedo and top hat, put cleverly raunchy lyrics to tunes of the day, flirted with female audience members, and flaunted a "marriage" with her white female lover. She began recording at the age of twenty-one. Successful enough to live in a Park Avenue apartment, she became the model for a number of fictional characters in writings of the time. Her popularity continued some years into the Great Depression, but eventually she moved to California to live with her mother and look for work. During World War II she performed in gay bars that catered to the military. In the 1950s, however, an increasingly repressive society forced her to repudiate her homosexuality in order to work. She died of complications of flu at the age of fifty-two.

Rosetta Records, a small feminist label, has reissued some Bentley songs on the "Women in Jazz" compilation series.

well-known gay club where Bentley was an early "drag king," performing in a signature white tuxedo with top hat and openly flirting with women. Ahead of her time, Bentley placed a newspaper announcement for her "marriage" in New Jersey to her white female lover. When the high life of the Renaissance period ended in the Great Depression, Bentley moved to Los Angeles to live with her mother, where she met with sporadic success as an entertainer. In San Francisco she performed at Mona's Club 440, the first lesbian bar opened there, in the 1930s.

Mabel Hampton, from Winston-Salem, North Carolina, moved to New York at age eight to live with her aunt. After her uncle raped her, she ran away and was adopted; she remained with her adoptive family until she was seventeen. Because lesbians were often the targets of police raids, Hampton was arrested on trumped up prostitution charges and spent two years in Bedford Hills Reformatory. After her release Hampton became a dancer in Harlem clubs, where she met Waters, Hunter, Bentley, and Jackie "Moms" Mabley. Hampton later was employed as a domestic worker and hospital matron. Late in life she became an activist and worked at the Lesbian Herstory Archives (founded in 1973) in New York, where she recorded oral histories and donated much valuable material about her own life, including documentation of her forty-five-year marriage to Lillian Foster.

The remarkable life of Ruth C. Ellis attests to the importance of these communities for one black lesbian whose experiences spanned the entire twentieth century. Ellis came out in 1915. In 1936 she met Ceciline "Babe" Franklin, her partner of thirty-four years. From 1946 to 1971, their home in Detroit, "the Gay Spot," became the place for generations of black lesbians to party and socialize. Ellis, the first woman in northwestern Detroit to own her own printing business, also took up photography, chronicling her long and active life as an out lesbian. "Tell your story. Let everyone know," Ellis advised in an interview late in her life. The black lesbian mediamaker Yvonne Welbon chronicled Ellis's life in the 1999 documentary *Living with Pride: Ruth Ellis @ 100*.

1950s and 1960s

The conservatism of the 1950s proved very destructive to black lesbians. Gladys Bentley was one of those who suffered. Harassed by police for her cross-dressing and eager to distance herself from public persecution in the increasingly repressive McCarthy era, Bentley took to wearing dresses. In August 1952 Bentley published a supposed autobiographical essay in *Ebony* magazine, "I Am a Woman Again," in which she characterizes her homosexuality as a "malignant growth" and a "hell as terrible as dope addiction" from which she was cured with female hormone injections. Historians have speculated, however, that it was a desperate desire to revive her career and fear of persecution that led Bentley to publish this piece. This also makes sense in light of the historian Gregory Conerly's research, published in *Ebony* and *Jet* magazines in the 1950s, on the treatment of gays, lesbians, and bisexuals. *Ebony* and *Jet* were the leading national magazines for the black community, and they frequently reported on homosexuals, especially drag balls. What Conerly discovered is that gay male relationships were occasionally tolerated but lesbian relationships virtually never were. Lesbianism was routinely treated as a behavior that needed to be overcome and that was a threat to the black family, and Bentley's article played directly into this notion. In response to the article, *Ebony* published only positive responses from readers, including one from a presumed lesbian who praised Bentley for "telling the world that we hate ourselves too."

Nevertheless, lesbians continued to make inroads in mainstream society in the 1950s. Big Mama Thornton was a powerful performer who frequently dressed in masculine clothing and who released the classic "Hound Dog" in 1953, three years before Elvis Presley. Another drag performer—or, as she preferred, male impersonator—was Stormé DeLarverie. During the 1950s and 1960s DeLarverie worked the black theater circuit as a mistress of ceremonies and the sole male impersonator of the legendary *Jewel Box Revue*, America's first integrated female impersonation show. Michelle Parkerson's 1987 film *Stormé: The Lady of the Jewel Box*, chronicled her life. In the 1950s the trumpeter and vocalist Ernestine "Tiny" Davis and her partner of more than forty years, the drummer Ruby Lucas, owned Tiny and Ruby's Gay Spot in Chicago. Davis gained renown as a trumpeter in the 1940s, performing with an interracial all-women jazz band called the International Sweethearts of Rhythm. The 1988 film *Tiny and Ruby: Hell Divin' Women* was a tribute to their lives.

Outside of Harlem and the entertainment world, black lesbians had to negotiate more difficult terrain. In a recorded oral history, "Debra," an African American lesbian who had her first sexual affair with a white woman in Virginia in 1934, tells the reality of having to hide the relationship from both women's families. Audre Lorde's 1982 book *Zami: A New Spelling of My Name* discussed her experiences in lesbian New York in the 1950s and the difficulty of identifying and acknowledging other black lesbians on the street. Her poetry collections of the 1960s and 1970s openly addressed her lesbianism as well. The need for gays and lesbians to socialize with one another was essential to the community. In 1964 the Big Glass opened on Fillmore Avenue in San Francisco, California— the first black-owned and African American–oriented gay bar in the city.

In 1959, at age twenty-nine, the playwright Lorraine Hansberry won the New York Drama Critics Circle Award for "Best Play of the Year" for her first complete play, *A Raisin in the Sun*. It was the first time a black woman playwright's work appeared on Broadway. Hansberry, from a well-off Chicago family, was also a committed political activist who supported the emerging lesbian rights movement. In 1953 she married Robert Nemiroff, but by 1957 she had come out privately as a lesbian, writing two letters of support, published anonymously, to the lesbian journal the *Ladder* in August of that year. She and Nemiroff separated and later divorced, though they remained close until her early death. Hansberry believed that homophobia and antifeminism were inextricably linked. Although her second play, 1964's *The Sign in Sidney Brustein's Window*, includes a gay male character, and she addressed female homosexuality in her unfinished 1961 play *Toussaint*, Hansberry did not include any lesbian characters in her best-known works.

As previously mentioned, the black press routinely covered stories about homosexuals, but they were often sensationalistic and critical. Nevertheless, ordinary black women's voices began to emerge in the gay and lesbian press, painting a fuller picture of lesbianism at midcentury. In August 1959, "Mrs. M.A.," a domestic worker from New Jersey, wrote to the gay publication *Mattachine Review* seeking a lesbian partner. In June 1966, Ernestine Eckstein (a pseudonym), an African American civil rights activist and chapter president of the first American lesbian organization, Daughters of Bilitis (DOB), was interviewed for and put on the cover of the *Ladder*, DOB's national publication. In the interview she expresses the belief that black lesbians were not quite at a stage in which they were free to explore. Significantly, before joining DOB Eckstein had never heard or used the terms "homosexual" or "lesbian."

As the civil rights movement reached its apex in the 1950s and 1960s, gays and lesbians emerged to test their own voices and demand that their presence be recognized and their right to love be honored. The Supreme Court's decision in *Brown v. Board of Education* (1954) and Rosa Parks's refusal to give up her seat on a Montgomery, Alabama, bus the following year were watershed events in the movement. The leadership of the Black Panther Party became the first explicitly to include gay and lesbian rights in its platform. Although the party minister Eldridge Cleaver had referred in his autobiography to homosexuality as "a sickness," in 1970 the party leader Huey P. Newton wrote in the party's platform of the need to unite with homosexuals, whom he identified as "the most oppressed people in the society."

The most significant event of the decade for gays and lesbians of all colors, however, was the Stonewall uprising on 27 June 1969 at the Stonewall Inn, a tiny dive bar in New York's Greenwich Village. On this particular summer night, the "queens"—especially the black and Latino queens—fought back against police harassment, sparking a revolution for gay and lesbian rights.

1970s: Visibility and Change

The 1970s marked a slowly but steadily increasing lesbian visibility. In October 1970 *Jet* magazine reported the "marriage" of two women in Chicago. Then, in 1971 two black women in Milwaukee, Wisconsin—Manonia Evans and Donna Burkett—filed a class-action suit against the Milwaukee county clerk for refusing to issue them a marriage license. Although they did not win their suit, they brought to the fore the need to legitimize same-sex marriages, a debate that continued in the early twenty-first century. In 1975 the African American lesbian and psychologist E. Kitch Childs was instrumental in getting the American Psychological Association no longer to regard homosexuality as a disease.

In the literary world, lesbian voices began to emerge. The Houston-born poet Pat Parker began publishing her lesbian-themed poetry in 1969, when *Movement in Black* appeared. Ann Allen Shockley's 1974 novel *Loving Her* broke new ground when it featured a black lesbian protagonist; Rosa Guy's young adult novel *Ruby* followed two years later. The staunchly feminist journalist Anita Cornwell collected articles and autobiographical portraits from the 1960s and 1970s in her 1983 publication *Black Lesbian in White America*. In February 1978 the first Annual Third World Lesbian Writers Conference was held in New York. Around that same time the Jemima Writers Group, a black lesbian writers group, was formed.

If the history of lesbianism in the nineteenth and early twentieth centuries was one of personal narratives, the history of the 1970s was one of organizing and collective change. The establishment of several significant journals, groups, and organizations for black lesbians occurred in the 1970s. In 1973 approximately thirty black women feminists who did not feel at home within the predominantly white women's movement founded the National Black Feminist Organization (NBFO). Michele Wallace, writing in 1975 about meeting in the spring of 1973 to establish NBFO, recalled the reaction to the black lesbian feminist Margaret Sloan, an editor at *Ms.* magazine, who was voted chairman. "It was probably our first mistake," Wallace wrote of that vote:

> because the only thing my grandmother and thousands of other black women knew about Margaret Sloan was that she had sung a love song to her white female lover locally on television, strumming her guitar, her child at her feet. Margaret Sloan as chairman ruled out the possibility of NBFO having a mass appeal   (p. 174).

The unwillingness or inability within NBFO to engage fully the rights and concerns of lesbians led to the formation in 1974 in Boston of the Combahee River Collective (CRC), which took its name from the South Carolina river site of the Harriet Tubman–led military action that freed 750 slaves. Barbara Smith, Demita Frazier, and Beverly Smith were among the cofounders of the group, which focused on African American women's issues. In 1978 the collective published its "Combahee River Collective Statement on Feminism." For six years CRC worked on such issues as violence against women, racism, sexism, heterosexism, and reproductive rights. Barbara Smith became an influential and important writer, editor, and publisher. Her groundbreaking 1977 essay, "Toward a Black Feminist Criticism," questioned the absence of black women's writing from the literary canon. In 1983 she published *Home Girls: A Black Feminist Anthology*, which contained contributions from black lesbians.

More independent lesbian organizations began to form. In 1974 Reverend Dolores Jackson, Harriet Austin, Sonia Bailey, Luvenia Pinson, Yvonne Flowers, and others cofounded the Salsa Soul Sisters (now the African Ancestral Lesbians United for Societal Change [AALUSC]) in New York. Two years later the group began publishing a newsletter, *Third World Women's Gay-zette*, the first such periodical for lesbians of color. *Azalea: A Magazine for Third World Lesbians* followed in 1977. AALUSC is now the oldest American organization for black lesbians.

In 1978 A. Billy S. Jones and Reverend Delores P. Berry cofounded the National Coalition of Black Gays (renamed the National Coalition of Black Lesbians and Gays [NCBLG] in 1985 explicitly to include lesbians). The following year NCBLG became one of the organizers of the Third World Conference for gays and lesbians of color, which took place in conjunction with the first March on Washington for Lesbian and Gay Rights. In August 1979, *Blacklight*, NCBLG's newsletter, debuted, featuring news, articles, and book reviews.

By the end of the decade, the diversity of the black lesbian community had begun to be reflected in its organizations. In 1979 Caryn Williams founded Sapphire Sapphos, a social organization for Third World gay women in Washington, DC. That same year the mainstream black women's magazine *Essence* published its first article on a black lesbian; in April 1980 it did a feature on the lesbian Lea Hopkins, a former Playboy bunny turned civil rights activist. In 1980 the black lesbian group Gentle Waves was founded in Chicago.

1980s to the Present: Invisible No More

If personal narratives and group organizing and identification marked the way in which previous decades of black lesbian life were defined, then the 1980s and 1990s were distinguished by increased media presence and visibility. In literature there was an explosion of books published by black lesbians. *Black Lesbians: An Annotated Bibliography* (1981) became the first book of its kind on the subject. That same year brought Barbara Smith's *Home Girls* and *This Bridge Called My Back: Writings by Radical Women of Color*, which included the writings of several black lesbians. In 1982 a Berkeley, California, African American lesbian collective began publishing *Onyx*, a black lesbian newsletter, which lasted for approximately two years, and in 1989 two black lesbians in Albany, California, founded the journal *Aché*, "a project for lesbians of African descent." Major writings by Audre Lorde, Alice Walker, Cheryl Clarke, Alexis DeVeaux, S. Diane Bogus, Becky Birtha, and June Jordan, among others, were published in the 1980s, and in the 1990s books by Jewelle Gomez, Nikky Finney, Sapphire, Helen Elaine Lee, April Sinclair, Shay Youngblood, Jacqueline Woodson, and others appeared.

Nowhere was the increased presence more evident than in film. The 1984 documentary *Before Stonewall: The Making of a Gay and Lesbian Community* includes footage of Bessie Smith and interviews with Mabel Hampton and Audre Lorde. The following year it was Stephen Spielberg's Oscar-nominated film version of Alice Walker's Pulitzer Prize–winning 1982 novel *The Color Purple* that sparked what was perhaps the biggest mainstream discussion of black lesbianism in American culture. The film, which depicts the intimate friendship between Celie (Whoopi Goldberg) and Shug Avery (Margaret Avery), was loudly criticized as being anti-male, thus perpetuating the stereotype of man-hating lesbians. Gays and lesbians, however, praised the film for its sensitive portrayal of the relationship between two women. The 1989 television adaptation of Gloria Naylor's 1982 novel *The Women of Brewster Place* included the lesbian characters Theresa and Lorraine (Paula Kelly and Lonette McKee). Homophobic violence directed against them is the backdrop for the drama's finale. As with *The Color Purple*, groups, including the NAACP, expressed concern prior to filming about the way in which black men would be portrayed.

The portrayal of black lesbian characters occurred intermittently and with varying degrees of authenticity and complexity in film and television. Positive portrayals include the 1994 film *Go Fish*, which features Kia (T. Wendy McMillan), a somewhat butch black lesbian professor, in a committed relationship with Evy (Migdalia Melendez), her Latina girlfriend. Whoopi Goldberg also played the lesbians Jane Deluca in *Boys on the Side* (1995) and Candy Bliss in *The Deep End of the Ocean* (1999), Queen Latifah played the butch lesbian bank robber Cleopatra "Cleo" Sims in *Set It Off* (1996), Nia Long played Karen in *If These Walls Could Talk 2* (2000) and

Leslie in *The Broken Hearts Club* (2000), and LaTanya Richardson played Judge Atallah Sims on the television show *100 Centre Street* (2001).

Out characters are one thing; real-life out lesbians remain far less common. The out comedian, actress, and playwright Danitra Vance became the first African American woman to join the cast of the television comedy program *Saturday Night Live*, in 1985, but was so frustrated with being typecast as maids and hookers that she quit after only one season. The slam poet Staceyann Chin is a regular on HBO television's *Def Jam Poetry* and performs her work throughout the world. Linda Villarosa's essay "Coming Out," written with her mother and published in *Essence* magazine's Mother's Day issue in May 1991, received the most reader mail in the history of the publication. The issue also received an award from the Gay and Lesbian Alliance Against Defamation (GLAAD).

Cheryl Dunye's breakthrough 1996 film, *The Watermelon Woman*, addresses lesbian life at both ends of the twentieth century. The semiautobiographical film stars Dunye as a lesbian filmmaker who sets out to make a film about an obscure black actress from the age of 1930s Hollywood cinema, who initially was credited only as "the Watermelon Woman." The film is fiction, but Dunye's "discovery" of the character's lesbianism and her attempts to reconstruct the woman's history speak both of the dearth of documentation of black lesbian lives from the first half of the twentieth century and of the profound need on the part of contemporary black lesbians to uncover nonetheless their histories. The filmmaker, performance artist, and activist Jocelyn Taylor and the writer Cheryl Clarke have small parts in the film; the singer-songwriter Toshi Reagon has an uncredited cameo as a street performer. Other important black lesbian filmmakers include Aishah Shahidah Simmons, Shari Frilot, and Debra Wilson, whose award-winning 2003 film *Butch Mystique*, which aired on Showtime television's *Black Filmmaker Showcase* in 2004, featured the emerging lesbian flutist Kymberly Jackson.

The increased visibility of black lesbians is evident not only in filmmaking but also in the performing arts and music. Winifred R. Harris is the artistic director and choreographer of Between Lines dance company. Vicki Randle is the popular bass player in the *Tonight Show* television band, seen nightly in millions of American homes. The vocalist, percussionist, and historian Linda Tillery explores the roots of African American music and storytelling; in 1992 she formed the Cultural Heritage Choir to preserve this history and to perform traditional folk music, such as slave field "hollers," work and play songs, and spirituals. Queen Pen became the first female rapper to address lesbianism, in her song "Girlfriend" (from her 1997 album *My Melody*), which sampled the bisexual singer-songwriter Meshell Ndegéocello's 1993 song "If That's Your Boyfriend (He Wasn't Last Night)."

Activism remains a priority for many black lesbians as homophobia, discrimination, and acts of violence continue to plague the community. The writer and activist Jacquie Bishop, whose work focuses on HIV/AIDS prevention and LGBT people of color communities, has written about Sakia Gunn, a fifteen-year-old black lesbian murdered in May 2003 in New Jersey after identifying herself as homosexual. The National Black Justice Coalition (NBJ) is an alliance of community leaders, public figures, and activists united to fight discrimination in their communities. The organization's mission is to break down the barriers of prejudice through education, visibility, and other activity. As of 2004 the NBJ planned to conduct a nationwide campaign to generate black support for marriage equality and to fight against the proposed Federal Marriage Amendment.

Significantly, there are more out black lesbians of the past two decades than can be chronicled here. On the other hand, many black lesbians, famous and unknown, remain closeted for fear of retribution or rejection. For example, there are no out black lesbian athletes, and Sakia Gunn's murder remains a sobering cautionary tale for all black lesbians. As of the early 2000s, no systematic history of lesbianism in the black community has been written. However, scholars and historians continue to uncover previously hidden or suppressed stories, documents, and histories of the lives of black women who love women. Likewise, the women themselves are now telling their stories.

See also Civil Rights Movement; Davis, Angela; Dunbar-Nelson, Alice Ruth; Feminism; Fields, Stagecoach Mary; Goldberg, Whoopi; Hansberry, Lorraine Vivian; Hunter, Alberta; Jordan, June; Lewis, Mary Edmonia "Wildfire"; Lorde, Audre; Naylor, Gloria; Parks, Rosa; Queen Latifah; Rainey, Ma (Gertrude Pridgett); Smith, Bessie; Walker, A'Lelia; Walker, Alice; Wallace, Michele; *and* Waters, Ethel.

BIBLIOGRAPHY

Carbado, Devon W., Dwight A. McBride, and Donald Weise, eds. *Black Like Us: A Century of Lesbian, Gay, and Bisexual African American Fiction*. San Francisco: Cleis, 2002.

Cornwell, Anita. *Black Lesbian in White America*. Tallahassee, FL: Naiad, 1983.

Davis, Angela Y. *Blues Legacies and Black Feminism: Gertrude "Ma" Rainey, Bessie Smith, and Billie Holiday*. New York: Pantheon, 1998.

Delroy Constantine-Simms, ed. *The Greatest Taboo: Homosexuality in Black Communities*. Los Angeles and New York: Alyson, 2000.

Griffin, Farah Jasmine, ed. *Beloved Sisters and Loving Friends: Letters from Rebecca Primus of Royal Oak, Maryland, and Addie Brown of Hartford, Connecticut, 1854–1868*. New York: Knopf, 1999.

Harrison, Daphne Duval. *Black Pearls: Blues Queens of the 1920s*. New Brunswick, NJ: Rutgers University Press, 1988.

Herron, Carolivia, ed. Introduction to *Selected Works of Angelina Weld Grimké*. Oxford and New York: Oxford University Press, 1991. Cited at http://www.english.uiuc.edu/maps/poets/g_l/grimke/herron.htm.

Hull, Gloria T., ed. *Give Us Each Day: The Diary of Alice Moore Dunbar-Nelson*. New York: Norton, 1985.

Hull, Gloria T., Patricia Bell Scott, and Barbara Smith, eds. *All the Women Are White, All the Blacks Are Men, but Some of Us Are Brave: Black Women's Studies*. New York: Feminist Press, 1982.

McKinley, Catherine, and L. Joyce DeLaney, eds. *Afrekete: An Anthology of Black Lesbian Writing*. New York: Anchor, 1995.

Moore, Lisa C., ed. *Does Your Mama Know? Black Lesbian Coming Out Stories*. Washington, DC: Redbone, 1997.

Murray, Stephen O., and Will Roscoe. *Boy-Wives and Female Husbands: Studies of African Homosexualities*, New York: St. Martin's, 1998.

Nestle, Joan. "I Lift My Eyes to the Hill: The Life of Mabel Hampton as Told by a White Woman." In *Queer Representations: Reading Lives, Reading Cultures*, edited by Martin Duberman. New York and London: New York University Press, 1997: 258–275.

Rainey, Gertrude "Ma." "Prove it On Me Blues" (1928). Cited at http://www.lambda.net/~maximum/rainey.html.

Roberts, J. R. *Black Lesbians: An Annotated Bibliography*. Tallahassee, FL: Naiad, 1981.

Ruff, Shawn Stewart, ed. *Go the Way Your Blood Beats: An Anthology of Lesbian and Gay Fiction by African American Writers*. New York: Henry Holt, 1996.

Somerville, Siobhan B. *Queering the Color Line: Race and the Invention of Homosexuality in American Culture*. Durham and London: Duke University Press, 2000.

Taylor, Frank C., with Gerald Cook. *Alberta Hunter: A Celebration in Blues*. New York: MacGraw-Hill, 1987.

Wallace, Michele. "On the National Black Feminist Organization." In *Feminist Revolution*. New York: Random House, 1978.

Watson, Steven. *The Harlem Renaissance: Hub of African-American Culture, 1920–1930*. Circles of the Twentieth Century series, no 1. New York: Pantheon, 1996.

—CARLA WILLIAMS

LEWIS, MARY EDMONIA "WILDFIRE" (b. 4 or 14 July 1845?; d. c. 1911), sculptress. Edmonia Lewis was the first major sculptress of African American and Native American heritage. Her early biographical circumstances are sketchily known at best. Although Lewis claimed 1854 as her birth date, it is more likely that she was born in 1843 or 1845. Various sources, including the artist herself, claimed Greenhigh, Ohio, and Greenbush, New York, as well as the vicinity of Albany, New York, as her birthplace, but none can be verified.

Lewis's father, employed as a gentleman's servant, was African American; her mother was a Chippewa Indian who may have been born near Albany. It was she who presumably named her daughter "Wildfire." Lewis appears to have spent little if any time with her father and instead lived with her mother's tribe. Orphaned before she was five, Lewis remained with the Chippewa until she was about twelve years old. As Wildfire, she learned to fish, swim, make baskets, and embroider moccasins. She often sold her crafts as the nomadic tribe made its way through New York State.

During the 1850s, Lewis left the Chippewa because her brother, Sunrise, a California gold miner, had arranged for her schooling near Albany. Adapting to her new circumstances proved difficult, but her brother persisted

MARY EDMONIA LEWIS, photographed c. 1870 by Henry Rocher. During this period she was at the height of her popularity as a sculptor, and her studio in Rome was often visited by Americans traveling abroad. (National Portrait Gallery, Smithsonian Institution.)

pursuing the college department's liberal arts program. Her only extant drawing, *The Muse Urania*, later held in the Oberlin College Archive, was done in 1862 as a wedding present for her classmate, Clara Steele Norton. She may have been inspired by optional drawing courses offered by the Young Ladies' Course. Later in life, Lewis recalled, "I had always wanted to make the form of things; and while I was at school I tried to make drawings of people and things."

Although Oberlin College and its namesake village actively promoted racial harmony, Lewis became the focus of a racially motivated controversy in 1862 when two white female students accused her of poisoning them. Lewis subsequently was beaten by vigilantes. John Mercer Langston—a prominent lawyer also of African American and Native American heritage—came to her defense, and she was exonerated because of insufficient evidence. A year later, she was accused of stealing art supplies. Despite her second acquittal, the college refused to allow her to graduate.

Shortly thereafter, Lewis moved to Boston, in part because her brother believed that the city's resources could support her interest in becoming a sculptor. Upon her arrival, she was greatly inspired by seeing Richard Greenough's life-size statue of Benjamin Franklin at City Hall. With letters of introduction from Oberlin College, Lewis met William Lloyd Garrison, the abolitionist writer, who introduced her to Edward Brackett, a well-known portrait sculptor of the time. Brackett lent Lewis fragments of sculptures to copy in clay and critiqued her early efforts, then a customary alternative to academic training. Equipped only with this limited preparation, Lewis began to establish herself in Boston as a sculptor and was listed as such in the city's directories in 1864 and 1865. According to these same directories, she worked in the Studio Building, where the African American painter Edward Mitchell Bannister and other artists maintained work spaces during the 1860s. To date, however, the extent of her interaction with this artistic community and specifically with Bannister has not been established.

Exposure to Edward Brackett's sculpture and the effect of the Civil War combined to determine Lewis's first sculptures—medallion portraits of white antislavery leaders and Civil War heroes, which she modeled in plaster and clay. She also attempted her first portrait bust during this period. Its subject was Colonel Robert Gould Shaw, the young Boston Brahmin who was killed as he led his all-black battalion against Confederate forces. Lewis's bust of Shaw and most of her early efforts were later lost, despite the fact that she made numerous plaster copies to help finance her move to Europe in 1865.

Lewis initially considered living in England because of its active abolitionist community. Following visits to London, Paris, and Florence, however, she instead established

in efforts to educate her. Thus, in 1859, Lewis entered Oberlin College in Oberlin, Ohio, with his financial assistance. This event triggered her name change, and the school's records indicate that she assumed the name Mary Edmonia Lewis. Throughout her career, however, she seldom used her new first name, as reflected in her correspondence as well as the signatures on her sculptures.

Lewis was a moderately successful student, completing the preparatory department's high-school courses and her studio in Rome during the winter of 1865–1866. She was barely twenty years old at the time. Her interest in Italy and the decision to settle in Rome were not unique. Since the 1820s, American sculptors, led by Hiram Powers, had been attracted by Italy's venerable artistic traditions, classical sculpture, abundant marble, and inexpensive artisan labor. Moreover, American women artists and writers considered Rome particularly congenial because it disregarded the sexist restrictions of their Anglo-American world.

Settled into a large studio near the Piazza Barberini, Lewis quickly began learning to carve in marble, experimenting with the challenge of creating full-length figures. To increase her skills, she followed the common practice of copying classical sculptures in public collections. Proving adept at this, Lewis made copies of classical statuary, which she regularly sold to Americans who visited artists' studios in Italy as part of their European tours.

Lewis, however, shunned other customs of the art community. She avoided instruction or criticism from her peers and refused to hire native artisans to enlarge her small clay and plaster models and to carve the final marbles. Fierce pride in her heritage and the desire to achieve legitimacy as a sculptor persuaded her that her sculptures would not be considered original if she did not execute them. This attitude limited her production, making the loss of much of Lewis's original work all the more significant.

Commissions for small portrait busts in terra-cotta and marble became Lewis's most reliable means of support. Patrons in Boston, especially prominent white male abolitionists and social reformers, were her most regular clients. She also recognized the American market for "conceits" or "fancy pieces"—sculptures that used mythological children to convey human, often sentimental themes. *Poor Cupid* (or *Love Ensnared*) of 1876 was probably her best-known effort in this vein.

Messages Trapped in Stone

Financial security, however, was not Lewis's principal concern. Slavery and racial oppression were the central issues of her sculptures, a focus greatly facilitated by her distance from America. It also distinguished Lewis from her fellow sculptors in Italy, who derived their ideas and images from classical literature, history, and art. Between 1866 and 1883, Lewis created at least six major figurative groups featuring either African Americans or Native Americans. *The Freed Woman and Her Child* of 1866 and *Forever Free* of 1867, for example, both captured the powerful emotion of emancipation. The latter's title was taken from the Emancipation Proclamation.

Lewis's exploration of the black figure reached as far as the African continent, when in 1868 she made *Hagar*, a marble also known as *Hagar in the Wilderness* (National Museum of American Art collection). Egyptians such as Hagar, the biblical maidservant to Abraham, were considered black by the nineteenth-century western world, and in this sculpture, Lewis included the issues of gender and women's rights in her interpretation of oppression.

Lewis also reacted against the period's negative stereotypes of Native Americans as murderous savages or a dying primitive race. Eschewing the direct social commentary and ethnographic accuracy of her black figures, however, Lewis took a more literary, sentimental approach when carving her small-scale Indian groups such as *Old Arrow Maker* of 1872, also known as *The Old Arrow Maker and His Daughter* (National Museum of American Art). Lewis was greatly influenced by the narrative poem, "The Song of Hiawatha" (1855) by Henry Wadsworth Longfellow. He posed for his portrait bust, which she began carving in Rome in 1869 and finished in 1871 (Harvard University portrait collection, Cambridge, Massachusetts).

Lewis's career in Rome coincided with those of other American women artists and writers who gathered around the neoclassical sculptor Harriet Hosmer and actress Charlotte Cushman. Both women welcomed Lewis to Rome, and their influential circle greatly benefited her. Social reformer Lydia Maria Child, one of Lewis's longtime patrons in Boston, nonetheless wondered if American artists abroad would free themselves of "American prejudice" and come to Lewis's aid when she fell deeply into debt. By 1865, it was evident that Cushman and others would not.

During the height of her popularity in the late 1860s and 1870s, Lewis's studio was a frequent stop for those who visited American artists abroad. She was also well-received during her several return visits to the United States between 1870 and 1876 when she exhibited works in Chicago, California, Boston, and Philadelphia. Perhaps the American highpoint of her career came in 1876 when her ambitious sculpture *The Death of Cleopatra* (Forest Park Historical Society, Forest Park, Illinois) was exhibited and awarded a medal at the Centennial Exposition in Philadelphia.

From the outset, however, Lewis was considered "an interesting novelty . . . in a city [Rome] where all our surroundings are of the olden time." Dressed in her rakish red cap and mannish costumes, Lewis captivated both Europeans and Americans, who regularly described her as childlike, charming, and picturesque. In 1863 she had already recognized the pitfalls of her triple heritage as a black Indian woman when she asked that her sculpture not be praised solely because of her background. Unfortunately, Lewis represented a tempting opportunity to those in Boston and Rome eager to demonstrate their support of human rights, and the encouragement she subsequently received ranged from sincere belief in her talents to well-meant but misguided indulgence.

MINNEHAHA AND HIAWATHA, two sculptures by Mary Edmonia Lewis. Her depictions of Native Americans were a reaction against the prevailing stereotypical images of her time. (Moorland-Spingarn Research Center.)

Equally diverse, if not confused, were the interpretations of Lewis's appearance. Some described her hair as black and straight like an Indian's and associated her complexion and willfully proud character with her mother's ancestry, while others believed that her facial features and hair reflected her father's background. Lewis herself was amused by a Bostonian's observation that "as her father had been a 'man of color' it would have seemed as though she ought to have been a painter, had it not been that her mother was a 'Chippe-e-way' Indian, and that made it natural for her to be a sculptor."

In 1883 Lewis received her last major commission, *Adoration of the Magi*, for a church in Baltimore, no doubt a reflection of her conversion to Catholicism in Rome in 1868. After 1883, demand for her work declined, as it did for neoclassical sculpture in general. Her presence in Rome was reported in 1911, but the activities of her final decades are barely documented and the date and place of her death are unknown.

Following a visit to Lewis's studio, an anonymous American writer wondered in 1867 if "the youthful Indian girl" would create a "distinctive if not original style in sculpture." Lewis indeed represented a fresh approach to the neoclassical sculpture tradition, injecting into it timely yet universal human rights issues and developing a more emotional, naturalistic style than had her contemporaries.

BIBLIOGRAPHY

Blodgett, Geoffrey. "John Mercer Langston and the Case of Edmonia Lewis: Oberlin, 1862." *Journal of Negro History*, July 1968.

Gerdts, William H. *American Neo-Classic Sculpture: The Marble Resurrection*. New York: Viking Press, 1973.

Goldberg, Marcia. "A Drawing by Edmonia Lewis." *American Art Journal*, November 1977.

Hartigan, Lynda Roscoe. *Sharing Traditions: Five Black Artists in Nineteenth-Century America*. Washington, DC: Smithsonian Institution Press, 1985.

James, Henry. *William Wetmore Story and His Friends* (1903). New York: Kennedy Galleries, 1969.

Leach, Joseph. *Bright Particular Star: The Life and Times of Charlotte Cushman*. New Haven, CT: Yale University Press, 1970.

Locke, Alain. *The Negro in Art*. New York: Hacker Art Books, 1940.

Sterling, Dorothy, ed. *We Are Your Sisters: Black Women in the Nineteenth Century*. New York: W.W. Norton, 1984.

Tuckerman, Henry T. *Book of the Artists: American Artist Life, Comprising the Biographical and Critical Sketches of American Artists* (1867). New York: J. F. Carr, 1966.

Wolf, Rinna Evelyn. *Edmonia Lewis: Wildfire in Marble*. Parsippany, NJ: Dillon Press, 1998.

ARCHIVAL RESOURCES

The James Thomas Fields collection, F1650, Huntington Library, San Marino, California; Oberlin College archives, Oberlin, Ohio;

Robie-Sewall papers, Massachusetts Historical Society, Boston, Massachusetts; and Anne Whitney papers, Wellesley College archives, Wellesley, Massachusetts.

—LYNDA ROSCOE HARTIGAN

LIBRARIANSHIP.

LIBRARIANSHIP. African American women librarians and others on library staffs have strived to provide excellence in assistance and quality information resources to the communities they have served. Black women librarians have attempted to counter the negative attitudes found outside and within libraries by creating places to locate information on terms shaped by black library workers. In doing so, these women have made great contributions to the library and information literacy of the race.

Early History

The early tradition of library service by black women may have begun with school materials, Sunday school collections, and the work of early female literary societies. The

SCENE AT THE DENVER PUBLIC LIBRARY, Cosmopolitan Branch, c. 1930s. The librarian is showing the card catalog to the children; the sign on the shelf reads "Young People's Collection." (Denver Public Library.)

Sunday schools were the only schools for black children and provided secular as well as religious education. New York City's Sunday schools were inaugurated in 1803 for the poorest residents, white and black girls. In 1816, Quakers in Wilmington, Delaware, founded a school and library for the education of free African Americans.

African Americans were prohibited from using local public libraries; therefore, they formed their own cultural and educational societies. Free black women and men organized and maintained circulating collections of books, periodicals, and newspapers for intellectual and moral improvement. Among the organizations fulfilling that purpose were the Reading Room Society, established in Philadelphia in 1828; the New York African Clarkson Society, founded in 1829; and the New York Philomathean Society, founded in 1830. Similarly, the Philadelphia Library Company of Colored Persons was established in 1832 as a literary society and incorporated in 1836. By 1838, the library contained six hundred volumes.

Free black women in Philadelphia organized the Female Literary Association in 1831 and Minerva Literary Association in 1834. The Female Literary Association's membership consisted of black women who believed they had to overcome the general prejudice against their people through self-education with the assistance of a librarian. The eighth article of the Association's constitution stated, "The librarian shall have charge of all books belonging to the Association, and after each meeting, take care that they be placed in the Library."

Professional Education and Contributions

Jessie Carney Smith's historical survey, *Black Academic Libraries and Research Collections*, notes that "the early history of black academic libraries is frequently unavailable because early record-keeping practices were poor or because records were destroyed during the passing years." Smith asserts that the oldest of these libraries was founded at Virginia Union University in 1865, the year in which the university was established.

More than fifty years later, Thomas Fountain Blue, Kentucky's first black librarian, began to train blacks at the Western Colored Branch of the Louisville Free Public Library. During its operation from 1912 to 1931, forty-one women completed the program. The American Library Association (ALA) used Blue's school as a model for the first ALA accredited library science school for African Americans, which opened at Hampton Institute (Virginia), later Hampton University, in 1925. Florence Rising Curtis served as director of the Hampton school that graduated 183 librarians with bachelor of science degrees during the fourteen years of its operation.

The North Carolina College for Negroes, later North Carolina Central University, began offering courses in school librarianship in 1935, and Eloise Ward Phelps became the first full-time teacher of Library Science in 1938. The following year, Mary Peacock Douglas, library supervisor for the North Carolina State Department of Public Instruction, organized a program for school librarians. The School of Library Science began as a professional program in 1941 and was accredited by the ALA in 1975.

The Atlanta University School of Library Service opened in 1941 with Eliza Atkins Gleason as dean. The school held a six-day conference for ninety-seven black public librarians in 1947, and that began a tradition of convening black librarians. From its beginning until the announcement of its closing in 2003, Virginia Lacy Jones (1912–1984) was responsible for the education of more African American librarians than was any other individual during her tenure as dean of the Library School at Atlanta University.

A later degree program in librarianship began in 1969 when Alabama A&M University initiated its program for African Americans in the School of Library Media.

Black Women Professionals

Belle da Costa Greener (1870–1950), a librarian and confidante of the financier J. P. Morgan, was director of the famed Pierpont Morgan Library in New York City from 1905 to 1948. Trained at Princeton University Library, she headed one of the world's finest research collections.

The publications *The Black Librarian in America, The Black Librarian in America Revisited, The Black Librarian in the Southeast,* and *The Handbook of Black Librarianship* provide details about the achievements and contributions of hundreds of black women librarians who ensured access to library resources across geographical regions.

Among the earliest librarians to receive professional training was Virginia Proctor Powell Florence, who earned a degree from Pittsburgh's Carnegie Library School in 1923.

Dorothy B. Porter Wesley (1905–1995) was also a pioneer, in that she was the first African American woman to receive a master's degree in Library Science from Columbia University, in 1932. Wesley began work as curator of the Moorland Foundation and later the Moorland-Spingarn Collection at Howard University in 1930. During a career at Howard that spanned forty-three years, she attracted numerous donors, developed the library and manuscript collections, and authored numerous books.

Eliza Atkins Gleason was the first African American to earn a PhD in librarianship from the University of Chicago. In 1940, she completed her dissertation, "The Government and Administration of Public Library Service to Negroes in the South." Virginia Lacy Jones followed Gleason and became the second African American to earn a doctorate in librarianship from the University of Chicago.

No less committed to library service than Gleason and Jones was Susan Dart Butler (1888–1959), who provided library assistance to blacks in Charleston, South Carolina. Trained in library science at Hampton Institute in the summer of 1932, she housed her family's library in the Charleston Industrial Normal Institute, founded by her father, John L. Dart, a distinguished educator and leading minister in the city. Butler facilitated grants from the Rosenwald Fund and the Carnegie Corporation to finance library service while serving as librarian of the Dart Hall Branch Library for twenty-six years.

Several well-known librarians worked and made their homes in New York City. Among them was Sadie Peterson Delaney (1889–1959), who received library training at the New York Public Library. In 1919, she began work at the 135th Street Branch, a focal point of the Harlem Renaissance. Delaney built a Negroana Collection that was enhanced by the collections of Arthur Schomburg. In 1923, Delaney organized the library at the Veterans Hospital in Tuskegee, Alabama. Active in professional associations, she helped to advance the field of bibliotherapy, a great contribution to the profession.

Catherine Allen Latimer, hired by the New York Public Library in 1920, also worked at the 135th Street Branch. Latimer conscientiously kept a file of clippings on black history and set up a small collection of books dealing with the subject. Soon, other black librarians were assigned to the branch. Among them was Roberta Bosely, a cousin of the poet Countee Cullen, who was in charge of children's services, while Regina Anderson, whose apartment was a frequent meeting place for Harlem Renaissance writers and artists, set aside a small work area for them in the library. Langston Hughes, Eric Walrond, and Claude McKay were among its users.

Jean Blackwell Hutson (1914–1998), another librarian in the New York Public Library system, attended the University of Michigan, Barnard College, the New School for Social Research and in 1936 received a Master of Library Science degree from Columbia University. Between 1949 and 1980, she served as curator and chief of New York's Schomburg Center for Research in Black Culture, where she helped build the premiere collection on black life and culture.

Black women librarians distinguished themselves in a number of midwestern and western metropolitan areas as well. In 1927, Mariam Matthews became the first black professional librarian in the Los Angeles Library System, and Vivian Harsh (1890–1960), who began working for the Chicago Public Library in 1909, became its first black librarian in 1924, and the first black woman to head a Chicago Public Library branch in 1932. With a Rosenwald grant, Harsh built an outstanding collection, later named in her honor, by and about blacks. She also instituted

Featuring Librarians

● **Hallie Brooks** (1907–1985) worked as a librarian and educator for almost fifty years. She was a native of West Baden, Indiana, and her academic credentials included an AB from Butler University, a BLS from Columbia University, and a master's degree from the University of Chicago. In 1930 Brooks was a public librarian in Indianapolis when she was tapped by John Hope, the president of Atlanta University, to organize library services for the university's experimental, progressive, Laboratory High School. In 1941 Brooks joined the faculty of the university's School of Library Service, where she taught until 1977. Brooks also held offices or committee memberships in a number of professional organizations, including the Association for Library and Information Science Education, the Southern Library Association, the Georgia Library Association, and the Metropolitan Atlanta Association. Brooks was an expert on the art of bookmaking and the author of *A Panoramic Chart of the Manuscript Period in Bookmaking*, a standard text in graduate library schools.

● **Sara "Sadie" Marie Johnson Delaney** (1889–1958) was the founding chief librarian of the U.S. Veterans Administration (VA) Hospital in Tuskegee, Alabama. Born in Rochester, New York, she attended the City College of New York. In 1920 she joined the staff of the 135th Street Branch of the New York Public Library, where she worked with children and the blind and booked numerous cultural events. In December of 1923, Delaney was appointed chief librarian of the VA hospital in Tuskegee and opened the library in January 1924 with one table and two hundred books. A year later she had moved the library to a larger space, introduced photographs and plants, and acquired four thousand books. She founded a literary society, promoted book discussion groups, instituted a separate library for the medical staff, and became a pioneering practitioner of bibliotherapy, which she described as "the treatment of a patient through selected reading." During her thirty-four years at the VA hospital, Delaney was the recipient of many awards and honors, including an honorary doctorate from Atlanta University.

● **Virginia Florence** (1903–1991) was the first African American woman to be professionally trained in librarianship. Born in Wilkinsburg, Pennsylvania, Florence earned a bachelor's degree in English from Oberlin College in 1919. Frustrated in her ambition to teach school in Pittsburgh by the school system's refusal to hire African Americans, she attended the Carnegie Library School. Florence worked for the New York Public Library system from 1923 until 1927, when she became the librarian at Seward High School in Brooklyn. In 1931 she moved to Jefferson City, Missouri, where her husband was the president of Lincoln University. She returned to librarianship at Cardoza High School in Washington, DC, in 1938. From 1950 until her retirement in 1965, she was the librarian at the Maggie L. Walker Senior High School in Richmond, Virginia.

● **Eliza Atkins Gleason** (1909–) was the first dean of Atlanta University's School of Library Service, which has educated more than half of the African American librarians in the United States. After graduating from Fisk University, she earned a BS from the University of Illinois in 1936 and a master's degree from the University of California at Berkeley. In 1940, at the University of Chicago, she became the first African American to receive a doctorate in Library Science. Dr. Gleason began her professional career at Louisville Municipal College and Fisk University. It was during her term as director of college libraries at Talledega (Alabama) College from 1936 to 1937 that her attention was drawn to the lack of public library services available to African Americans throughout the South. She responded by opening the college libraries to black citizens of the region and addressed the problem in her doctoral dissertation, "The Southern Negro and the Public Library."

After serving as dean of the School of Library Service at Atlanta University from 1940 to 1946, Gleason moved to Chicago, where she worked in the library at Wilson Junior College and taught library science at the Illinois Teacher's College. In the 1960s and 1970s she was assistant librarian at the John Crerar Library and taught at the Illinois Institute of Technology and Northern Illinois University.

● **Jean Blackwell Hutson** (1914–1998) was a working librarian for nearly fifty years, as well as an author, educator, and curator of the most extensive collection of artifacts of black culture and history in the world. An eager student, she graduated from high school at the age of fifteen and studied at the University of Michigan before receiving a BA from Barnard College in 1935 and a BS from Columbia University in 1936. After working as a high school librarian in Baltimore, Hutson joined the New York Public Library system in 1936. While working in the Bronx, she ordered Spanish-language resources for her branch, making the library accessible to many neighborhood residents who lacked fluency in English. From 1939 until 1943 Hutson was a high school librarian and English teacher in Baltimore before returning to the New York Public Library. In 1948 she became the curator of what is now the Schomburg Center for Research in Black Culture. For more than thirty years she worked to organize, preserve, and expand the collection into what is now the world's largest collection of art and artifacts by and about people of African descent. Hutson also taught history at the City College of New York, wrote numerous short stories, and was assistant librarian at the University of Ghana from 1964 to 1965.

● **Clara Stanton Jones** (1913–) had a distinguished career capped by the leadership of both the American Library Association and the Detroit Public Library, the fifth largest library in the United States. Born in St. Louis, Missouri, Jones graduated with a BA from Spelman College and earned an AB from the University of Michigan. After working at Dillard University in New Orleans, she taught library science and was associate librarian at Southern University in Baton Rouge, Louisiana. Her career at the Detroit Public Library began with the position of children's librarian in 1944. By the late 1960s she had become a neighborhood library consultant and in 1970 she was appointed the library's director. From 1976 to 1977 she served as the first African American president of the American Library Association.

● **Virginia Lacy Jones** (1912–1984), librarian, scholar, educator, and author, was the dean of Atlanta University's School of Library Service for thirty-five years. Born Virginia Lacy in Cincinnati, Ohio, she was a high school student in St. Louis, Missouri, when she encountered the public reference librarian whose competence and commitment inspired her to pursue a library career. After graduating from Virginia's Hampton Institute in 1933, she worked in the libraries at Hampton and Louisville Municipal College before earning a master's degree at the University of Illinois in 1938. In 1939 she joined the staff of Atlanta University's Trevor Arnett Library, and when the university opened its School of Library Service, she was appointed to the faculty, teaching Cataloging and Classification, School Library Service, and Children's Literature. In 1945, at the University of Illinois, Jones became the second African American to earn a doctorate in Library Science. In 1946 she was named dean of the School of Library Service, a position she held until 1981.

● **Catherine Allen Latimer** (1895?–1948), the first black professional librarian in the New York Public Library system, was a reference librarian who was treasured by writers and historians and was instrumental in laying the foundation for what is now the Schomburg Center for Research in Black Culture. A native of Nashville, Tennessee, she studied at Howard and Columbia Universities and served as assistant librarian at the Tuskegee Institute in Alabama.

In 1920 she joined the staff of the New York Public Library's 135th Street Branch, which housed the Division of Negro Literature, History, and Prints. Latimer merged Arthur Schomburg's personal library into the library's collection. She also created and developed a clipping file of articles on all aspects of the African American experience that is still an important reference source. She wrote for publications that included *Crisis, Looking Forward*, and the *Negro History Bulletin*.

● **Miriam Matthews** (1905–2003) was a librarian, administrator, activist, and a historian of African American life in California. Born in Pensacola, Florida, she grew up in Los Angeles and earned an AB from the University of California and an MA from the University of Chicago. In 1927 she became the first black professional librarian hired by the Los Angeles Public Library system. She was a branch librarian from 1929 to 1949 and a regional librarian, supervising twelve branch libraries, from 1949 to 1960.

Always interested in the history of black people, Matthews helped organize the observance of Negro History Week in 1929 and over the years became a leading authority on the history of African Americans in California. Her collection of historic documents, photographs, and art has been an important resource to museums and researchers. In June 2004, the Los Angeles Public Library voted to rename the new Hyde Park Branch Library in her honor.

● **Alethia Phinazee** (1920–1983) was a librarian, educator, administrator, and the first African American president of the North Carolina branch of the American Library Association. She earned a bachelor's degree from Fisk University, a bachelor's and a master's degree from the University of Illinois, and a doctorate in Library Science from Columbia University. She taught at the Atlanta University School of Library Service from 1961 until 1969, when she founded the Cooperative College Library Center, the first national association of black academic libraries. In 1970 she was named dean of the School of Library Science at North Carolina Central University, where she was instrumental in gaining accreditation from the ALA. She also created the school's program in early childhood librarianship. Phinazee was active in both the state and national ALA and was nominated to run for president of the national association in 1980.

● **Charlemae Hill Rollins** (1897–1979), a children's author and librarian, an activist, lecturer, and educator, was also a crusader against stereotyped depictions of black people in children's literature. Born in Yazoo City, Missouri, she attended Howard University and received her library education at the University of Chicago and Columbia University. Rollins was hired by the Chicago Public Library in 1926. In 1932 she was assigned to run the children's room of the new George C. Hall branch, where she became renowned for her storytelling. Rollins was a vocal critic of the lack of print resources about the lives of prominent African Americans and the racist depictions of black characters in children's books. Her criticisms and searches for better alternatives led to the creation of *We Build Together*, a bibliography of children's literature featuring realistic depictions of black people. Rollins was a lecturer on intercultural relations and children's literature, taught Children's Literature at Roosevelt University, led storytelling workshops, and contributed to professional journals. She wrote several books for children and young people, including *Black Troubadour: Langston Hughes.*

public forums featuring noted black authors. Doris E. Saunders began her career in the Chicago Public Library System in 1942 and seven years later became the first librarian at Johnson Publishing Company. She established the Johnson Publishing Company Book Division in 1961. Clara Stanton Jones was the first black and the first woman appointed director of the Detroit Public Library. In 1976 she was elected president of ALA, the first black librarian to win the office. By 1984 Mary F. Lennox had become the first black dean of the library school at the University of Missouri-Columbia, and in 1986 Monteria Hightower was named Missouri's first black state librarian.

Black women across the South also moved into leadership positions within their field. For example, Jessie Carney Smith, recipient of a PhD in Library Science at the University of Illinois, was university librarian and professor at Fisk University in the 1960s. She lectured widely on the process of developing black collections, collecting black memorabilia, and studying genealogy. Carney's publications include *Black Academic Libraries and Research Collections: An Historical Survey*, *Ethnic Genealogy*, *Images of Blacks in American Culture*, and *Notable Black American Women*. Carney's colleague at Fisk University, Ann Allen Shockley, organized the school's Black Oral History program in 1970. Shockley was a noted author, journalist, librarian, feminist, and political activist. In the meantime, Doris Hargrett Clack (1928–1995), professor at Florida State University's library school, advocated improvements in the vocabulary and classification schemes used to access information on the black experience. Finally, Ella Gaines Yates was the first black director of the Atlanta Public Library (1976) and the first black appointed Virginia state librarian and archivist (1986).

Other librarians with a special expertise in children's libraries included Augusta Baker, New York Public Library; Mollie Houston Lee, Raleigh, North Carolina, Public Library; Effie Lee Morris, San Francisco Public Library; and Charlemae Rollins, Chicago Public Library. These women removed books that negatively depicted African American characters. Baker, New York's first black administrator, built a landmark collection of children's literature. Her 1957 bibliography of the collection, *Books about Negro Life for Children*, was well used by the profession. Lee, the first black to receive a scholarship to Columbia's library school, forged Raleigh's first library for blacks in 1935. Morris was the first coordinator of children's services for the San Francisco Public Library. Rollins, a specialist in children's literature, lectured and wrote many children's books.

Achievements and Honors

Librarians who were the first black women elected to preside over state, regional, or national library associations included Rebecca Bingham (Kentucky, 1971), Estelle M. Black (Illinois, 1990), Alma Jacobs (Pacific Northwest, 1957; Montana, 1960), Barbara Williams Jenkins (South Carolina, 1986), Gleniece Robinson (Texas, 1998), and Lucille C. Thomas (New York, 1977). Rebecca Bingham served on the 1979 White House Conference on Library and Information Services, and in 1998 she was named to the National Commission on Libraries and Information Science.

Effie Lee Morris was the first black president of the Public Library Association (1971), and in 1975, Louise Giles became the first black president of the Association of College and Research Libraries (ACRL). The following year, Jessie Carney Smith was elected the first black president of Beta Phi Mu, the international library science honor society. In 1976 Virginia Lacy Jones was the first black elected president of the Association of American Library Schools, and in 1973, she was the first black woman to receive the Melville Dewey Medal. Additionally, in 1978, Vivian Davidson Hewitt became the Special Libraries Association's first black elected president. Althea Jenkins was appointed the first black director of ACRL in 1991. ALA bestowed its highest accolade, Honorary Memberships, upon Charlemae Rollins (1972), Augusta Baker (1975), Virginia Lacy Jones (1976), Clara Stanton Jones (1983), and Lucille Cole Thomas (2003).

This discussion of African American women who are school, public, academic, and special librarians and who have served as administrators, association leaders, archivists, authors, bibliographers, catalogers, curators, deans, information technology specialists, library educators, and advocates for black librarianship ends during the term of ALA president Carla D. Hayden, director of the Enoch Pratt Free Library in Baltimore. Hayden was the second black woman elected to lead the world's largest professional library organization. Hayden's presidential platform, with its focus on equity of access to library and information services, continued in the long tradition of black librarianship.

BIBLIOGRAPHY

Battle, Thomas C., ed. *Black Bibliophiles and Collectors: Preservers of Black History*. Washington, DC: Howard University Press, 1990.

Dawson, Alma. "Celebrating African-American Librarians and Librarianship." *Library Trends* 49.1 (Summer 2000): 49–87.

DeLoach, Marva, and E. J. Josey, eds. *Handbook of Black Librarianship*. Lanham, MD: Scarecrow Press, 2000.

Jones, Reinette. *Library Service to African Americans in Kentucky: From the Reconstruction Era to the 1960s*. Jefferson, KY: McFarland, 2001.

Josey, E. J., ed. *The Black Librarian in America*. Metuchen, NJ: Scarecrow Press, 1970.

Josey, E. J., ed. *The Black Librarian in America Revisited*. Metuchen, NJ: Scarecrow Press, 1994.

Josey, E. J. *What Black Librarians Are Saying*. Metuchen, NJ: Scarecrow Press, 1972.

McPheeters, Annie L. *Library Service in Black and White: Some Personal Recollections, 1921–1980*. Metuchen, NJ: Scarecrow Press, 1988.

Phinazee, Annette L., ed. *The Black Librarian in the Southeast: Reminiscences, Activities, Challenges: Papers Presented for a Colloquium*. Durham, NC: The School, 1980.

Sinnette, Elinor Des Verney. *Arthur Alfonso Schomburg: Black Bibliophile and Collector*. Detroit: New York Public Library and Wayne State University Press, 1989.

Smith, Jessie Carney. *Black Academic Libraries and Research Collections: An Historical Survey*. Westport, CT: Greenwood Press, 1977.

Speller, Benjamin F., ed. *Educating Black Librarians: Papers from the Fiftieth Anniversary Celebration of the School of Library and Information Sciences, North Carolina Central University*. Jefferson, NC: McFarland, 1991.

Tucker, John Mark, ed. *Untold Stories: Civil Rights, Libraries, and Black Librarianship*. Champaign: University of Illinois at Urbana-Champaign, Graduate School of Library and Information Science, 1998.

—KATHLEEN BETHEL

LISTON, MELBA (b. 13 January 1926; d. 23 April 1999), jazz trombonist, composer, and arranger. Music came to Liston when she was seven years old, enchanted by the gleaming brass face of a trombone. Her arms were barely long enough to reach some of the standard positions, but once she picked up that instrument, she remained with music for the rest of her life. One of the outstanding trombonists of her generation, Liston was the first woman to make a mark in jazz playing a brass instrument. She played with the bands of Gerald Wilson, Dizzy Gillespie, Count Basie, and Duke Ellington. The performers she accompanied include Billie Holiday, Cannonball Adderly, Betty Carter, Jimmy Smith, and Dinah Washington. Her instrumental skills were matched by her talent for arranging music, which led to collaborations with many of the leading jazz and pop musicians of her time. Later in life she became an educator, working in Jamaica, New York, and Los Angeles to pass along her passion and experience to younger generations. Liston paid a very high price to live the life of a traveling musician, including intimidation and physical assaults. There were times when she walked away from performing and decided to pursue a more ordinary kind of life, but her trombone and piano and charts kept calling her back to music, and when she died she left behind recordings of exciting performances, a library of exquisite arrangements and compositions, and the memory of an indomitable spirit.

Liston was born in Kansas City, Missouri, to Lucile and Frank Liston. For the first eleven years of her life, she divided her time between her hometown and the Kansas City, Kansas, home of her grandparents. Her father was a lawyer and musician. When she was seven, Liston decided to join the band at her school. She chose the trombone as her instrument, based on the beauty of its physical appearance. On the day she got her first trombone, she and her grandfather sat outside, late into the night, as she sounded out all of the tunes that she knew. By the time she was eight, she was playing solos on the radio.

When Liston was eleven, the family moved to Los Angeles. There she joined a youth band sponsored by the parks and recreations department that was conducted by Alma Hightower. The band practiced in a playground, where Hightower taught the members various aspects of show business and the performing arts as well as harmony and music theory. The band played on street corners and at dances at the local churches, the YMCA, and the state fair in Sacramento.

Liston studied trombone and harmony at the Los Angeles Polytechnic High School. Her most important influences were trombonists Lawrence Brown, of Duke Ellington's band, and Tommy Dorsey. Liston's high school teachers were impressed with her ability to read and write music and urged her to consider a career as an arranger. Her assigned classwork included writing charts for ensembles and orchestras. By this time Liston had moved her piano into her bedroom, where she wrote and arranged for long stretches of time, emerging only for meals. Immediately after graduation, at age sixteen, she joined the musicians' union. Her first job was in the pit band at Lincoln Theatre. Here she acquired her first experience in professional performance, and she wrote some of her earliest arrangements for visiting acts who did not bring their own music.

The Lincoln Theatre closed in 1943 and Liston and the rest of the band joined trumpeter, arranger, and composer Gerald Wilson's big band. In addition to performing, Liston wrote charts and copied music for the band, and Wilson tutored her in the fine points of arranging. Working with Wilson's band brought her into contact with many of the best jazz players of the day and it was during this time that she first made the acquaintance of Dizzy Gillespie, Count Basie, Duke Ellington, and Charlie Parker.

Liston's earliest recordings were made with the Wilson band, and in 1947 she played in sessions with Dexter Gordon, a friend from school. In 1948 Liston and Wilson joined Dizzy Gillespie's progressive big band, which included John Coltrane, Paul Gonsalves, and John Lewis. When Gillespie's band broke up in 1949, Billie Holiday, preparing for a tour of the South, hired Wilson as the director and Liston as the assistant director and arranger of her band. The tour was a financial disaster, and the band found itself stranded on the bus for days in Charleston, South Carolina, before it could raise the funds to return home.

After returning to Los Angeles, Liston worked for several years as an administrator for the board of education. She continued to arrange and compose, but retired temporarily from performing. In 1956 Liston left the board of education to join the band Dizzy Gillespie was forming to tour the Middle East and Asia for the U.S. State Department. Although her arranging assignments were limited to standards, ballads, and vocal backgrounds, she distinguished herself with her arrangements of "Stella by Starlight," "Annie's Dance," and "My Reverie" by Debussy.

Female vocalists frequently traveled with jazz bands during the 1940s and 1950s, but women instrumentalists were rarely seen. Regarded as unwelcome competition by many of her male colleagues, Liston was faced with verbal and physical harassment on the road. Decades later she would talk to interviewers about overhearing herself being referred to as the "bitch trombonist," of being threatened on the bandstand and forced offstage after taking solos, and of being raped and suffering other forms of physical assault at the hands of some of her fellow musicians.

In 1958 Liston formed her first band, an all-woman jazz quintet. Later that year she recorded a solo album, *And Her Bones*. That same year she began a lifelong musical collaboration writing arrangements for the pianist and composer Randy Weston. This partnership freed her from the ballad assignments she had been relegated to in other bands and gave her a chance to work with African rhythms, jazz for orchestra, and other challenging forms. She worked with Weston on six albums: *Blues to Africa*, *Little Niles*, *The Spirits of Our Ancestors*, *Tanjah*, *Music from the New African Nations*, and *Volcano Blues*. In 1959 Liston joined the Quincy Jones orchestra and toured Europe with them in the musical *Free and Easy*.

In the 1960s Liston's career as an arranger blossomed. As a veteran instrumentalist who had grown weary of standard arrangements that treated each band section as one big instrument playing the same line, she strove to make each musician's line distinctive and beautiful. Her decades of education and experience, her facility in handling multiple styles, and the uniquely personal quality of her scores made her one of the most sought-after arrangers of the decade.

Working as the house arranger for the distinguished jazz label Riverside Records, and arranging for Motown and Bluenote Records, she wrote charts for Gloria Lynne, Billy Eckstine, Milt Jackson, the Supremes, Marvin Gaye, Tony Bennett, Abbey Lincoln, and the bands of Count Basie and Duke Ellington, among many others. She wrote symphonic arrangements for Randy Weston and the Boston Pops, the trumpeter Clark Terry and the Buffalo Symphony Orchestra, and the Brooklyn Philharmonic. For a short time, she co-led a big band with Clark Terry. She arranged for Charles Mingus and appeared with him in his Town Hall Concert in 1962. Later in the 1960s she returned to Los Angeles, where she worked with youth orchestras, following the example of her early mentor, Alma Hightower.

In the early 1970s Liston traveled to Jamaica, where she taught at the University of West Indies and founded and directed the African American division of the Jamaica School of Music. After more than five years in Jamaica, Liston was persuaded to return to the United States for the Kansas City Women's Jazz Festival in 1979. The festival was followed by successful engagements in New York and Boston, after which she moved to New York and formed an all-woman band, Melba Liston and Company. The band worked and toured in various incarnations until 1983.

In 1985 Liston suffered a stroke that confined her to a wheelchair and brought an end to her performing career. After an extended convalescence, she returned to writing and arranging music with the help of newly developed computer programs, which took the rote copying factor out of composing and arranging. In 1991 she wrote the charts for a New York City tribute to Dexter Gordon and scored the arrangements of the Randy Weston African Rhythms Orchestra concert, "Blues to Africa," which led off the first season of Jazz at the Lincoln Center. Her own compositions include "Just Waiting," "Deliberate Speed," and "Melba's Blues."

A recipient of numerous awards and honors, Liston was named an American Jazz Master by the National Endowment for the Arts in 1987. Many of her lead sheets and scores are preserved in the archives of the Center for Black Music Research in Chicago. She died in Inglewood, California, following a series of strokes.

BIBLIOGRAPHY

Bryant, Clora, et al., eds. *Central Avenue Sounds: Jazz in Los Angeles*. Berkeley: University of California Press, 1998. An abridged transcription of an oral history project in which Liston speaks about her music, career, and some of the hardships she endured.

Feather, Leonard, and Ira Gitler. *The Encyclopedia of Jazz in the Seventies*. New York: Horizon Press, 1976.

Larkin, Colin, ed. *The Guinness Encyclopedia of Popular Music*. Enfield, Middlesex, U.K.: Guinness, 1992.

Placksin, Sally. *American Women in Jazz, 1900 to the Present: Their Words, Lives, and Music*. New York: Windview Books, 1982. A fascinating history of American women jazz musicians, featuring a personal interview with Liston.

Placksin, Sally. "Melba Liston." In *Black Women in America: An Historical Encyclopedia*, edited by Darlene Clark Hine. Brooklyn, NY: Carlson, 1993.

Woolley, Stan, and Barry Kernfeld. "Melba (Doretta) Liston." In *The New Grove Dictionary of Jazz*, edited by Barry Kernfeld. 2d ed. London: Macmillan, 2002.

—ROBERT W. LOGAN

LITTLE ROCK NINE. The battle to desegregate the public schools in Little Rock, Arkansas, and the crisis that erupted when nine African American students attempted to desegregate Little Rock's Central High School are well known in the history of the civil rights movement. Daisy Bates, co-owner of the *Arkansas State Press*, and

The Little Rock Nine with Daisy Bates, photographed by Cecil Layne c. 1957–1960. The crisis that ensued when the nine African American students attempted to desegregate Little Rock's Central High School was an important episode in the civil rights movement. (Library of Congress.)

state president of the Arkansas National Association for the Advancement of Colored People (NAACP), coordinated the efforts of the nine children selected and advocated for their protection throughout their time at Central High.

Efforts to desegregate the school system began soon after the Supreme Court's May 1954 *Brown v. Board of Education* decision. Soon thereafter, the Little Rock School Board publicized its integration plan, which tentatively scheduled the desegregation of senior high schools in the fall of 1957. Since the *Brown* decision, Bates had campaigned for desegregation in Arkansas schools. She frequently accompanied African American students who attempted to enroll in white schools and made certain those efforts were publicized in the state's newspapers. As a result of the ambiguity of the school board's integration plan, thirty-three African American parents contacted officers of the Arkansas NAACP, including Bates, to organize a suit against the Little Rock School District in the spring of 1956.

When this case failed to win a decisive order, NAACP lawyers appealed the case. In September 1957, a judge from the Eighth Circuit Court of Appeals ordered the school board to implement its desegregation plan. Although the Arkansas State Legislature passed four bills aimed at preserving segregation and an organized segregationist group called the Mothers League of Little Rock Central High School filed an injunction against school integration, the NAACP attorneys succeeded in obtaining a decision that overruled the injunction.

Over the previous months, Daisy Bates had handselected Minnijean Brown, Elizabeth Eckford, Ernest Green, Thelma Mothershed, Melba Pattillo, Gloria Ray, Terrance Roberts, Jefferson Thomas, and Carlotta Walls from a large pool of students who hoped to desegregate Central High. All nine students were members of Bates's NAACP Youth Council. She tried to prepare them for the open hostility they would undoubtedly encounter. The night before the teens were to enter Central High, Governor Orval Faubus ordered the Arkansas National Guard to surround the school and prevent any of the African American students from entering. Quickly, Bates changed the plan for the next morning and informed all but the parents of Elizabeth Eckford, whose family had no telephone. Bates decided to find her early the next morning. The next morning, however, Bates did not contact Eckford and her parents, and the girl arrived at Central High School alone. Photos of the young African American girl, engulfed in a white mob that threatened to lynch her, appeared in the newspaper headlines across the nation. Like later events in the civil rights movement, the national publicity that resulted from the crisis helped ensure support from citizens nationwide and, indeed, even from the federal government.

Eckford and the other eight students waited until the attorneys for the NAACP could ask the United States District Federal Court on 20 September for an injunction against the interference of the desegregation of Little Rock High School. The judge granted the injunction, and on 23 September, Daisy Bates accompanied all nine children to Central High School, where police escorted them through a side entrance. That night, police prevented a white mob armed with dynamite, guns, and clubs from attacking Bates's home.

The next day, President Dwight D. Eisenhower federalized the Arkansas National Guard and authorized the secretary of defense to send in one thousand paratroopers from Fort Campbell, Kentucky. On 25 September, paratroopers escorted the nine students into Central High School. Throughout the remainder of the year, white students continually harassed the nine students. At the graduation ceremonies in the spring of 1958, over one hundred national guardsmen were in attendance to handle any protest that may have arisen from Ernest Green's graduation.

During the summer of 1958, Governor Faubus announced that the four high schools in Little Rock, three white and one African American, would close for the 1958–1959 school year. His actions were representative of the retaliatory measures some white politicians implemented as a means to discourage those who supported desegregation. Although the battle to achieve integration in the public schools in Arkansas was not without great controversy, the experiences of the Little Rock Nine were invaluable to the modern civil rights movement. They paved the way for thousands of schools across the South to admit African American students.

The legacy of the Little Rock crisis is an important one. A resulting court case, *Cooper v. Aaron*, mandated that state governments must enforce the Supreme Court's *Brown* decision. In addition, the Civil Rights Act of 1957, passed after the events in Little Rock, served as a precursor to the Civil Rights Act of 1964. Most importantly, however, President Eisenhower's use of army paratroopers and national guardsmen revealed the federal government's willingness to enforce federal mandates above state segregation laws, a component essential to future successes of the civil rights movement.

BIBLIOGRAPHY

Bates, Daisy. *The Long Shadow of Little Rock: A Memoir*. New York: David McKay, 1962.

Huckaby, Elizabeth. *Crisis at Central High: Little Rock, 1957–58*. Olympic Marketing Corporation, 1980.

Kirk, John A. *Redefining the Color Line: Black Activism in Little Rock, Arkansas, 1940–1970*. Gainesville: University of Florida Press, 2002.

—Courtney L. Tollison

LOGAN, ADELLA HUNT

LOGAN, ADELLA HUNT (b. 1863; d. 12 December 1915), educator. Born in Sparta, Georgia, Hunt was the daughter of a free mulatto woman and a white planter—the fourth of eight children. During her childhood, she

ADELLA HUNT LOGAN (third from left) in a family photograph taken by Arthur Bedou in Tuskegee, Alabama, in 1913. The others are her husband Warren and six of their nine children. (Austin/Thompson Collection and Collection of Adele Logan Alexander.)

lived on Hunt's Hill, an enclave where the town's more comfortably situated African American population resided.

Hunt attended Bass Academy in her hometown and became a certified teacher at sixteen. She acquired a scholarship to Atlanta University, and in 1881, she completed the normal course there, since four-year programs were closed to women. The school later awarded her an honorary MA for her continuing work in education.

Hunt taught for several years in an American Missionary School and in 1883 declined a teaching opportunity at her alma mater, choosing instead to go to Alabama's new Tuskegee Institute. During the early years at Tuskegee, Hunt filled a number of positions. She taught English and social sciences, became the institute's first librarian, and was "Lady Principal" for a short time. She also met Warren Logan, a schoolmate and old friend of Booker T. Washington.

These two educators married in 1888. The impoverished new school could not support two-salary families, however, and since Logan's work was considered less critical, she subordinated her career to her husband's. In 1890 she gave birth to the first of nine children.

Adella Hunt Logan taught only intermittently between difficult pregnancies and was limited as well by domestic demands and official responsibilities as the wife of Tuskegee's second-ranking official. Teaching remained her greatest passion, however, and she was the creative force behind Tuskegee's model school and teachers' training facility.

Logan immersed herself in activities of the Tuskegee Women's Club, a chapter of the National Association of Colored Women (NACW), as well. Logan's most important work centered around the club's efforts on behalf of local farm women and their children. She advocated health care for all and education for every child.

Logan's other major interest was women's suffrage. At the turn of the century, most white Alabamans vehemently opposed the franchise for women, but Logan led regular forums about suffrage at Tuskegee and encouraged students to debate and participate in demonstrations of participatory democracy. She lectured at NACW conferences as well and served briefly as that group's national director of both suffrage and rural affairs. She also wrote about suffrage in the *Colored American* and the *Crisis*.

Because of her predominantly white ancestry, Adella Hunt Logan looked white. When the National American Woman Suffrage Association (NAWSA) held conventions in the segregated South, she attended without identifying herself as "colored." Subsequently, she brought back information from those meetings to share with colleagues in the African American community. For a decade, she was the only Life Member of the NAWSA from the state of Alabama. She also contributed articles about NACW activities to that organization's newspaper.

Though Logan became swept up in the ideological feud between Booker T. Washington and W. E. B. Du Bois over the direction of the black community, she managed to maintain her philosophical alliance with Du Bois even while remaining a personal friend, professional associate, and next-door neighbor to Washington.

A combination of events, including defeats for the suffrage movement and tensions in her marriage, led to an emotional collapse in September 1915, at which time Adella Hunt Logan was sent to a Michigan sanitarium. A few weeks later, however, news of Booker T. Washington's precipitously declining health summoned her home. After her friend's death, Logan never recovered. As visiting dignitaries assembled at Tuskegee to attend a memorial service for Washington, Logan jumped to her death from the top floor of one of the school's buildings.

BIBLIOGRAPHY

Alexander, Adele Logan. *Ambiguous Lives: Free Women of Color in Rural Georgia, 1789–1879.* Fayetteville: University of Arkansas Press, 1991.

Culp, D. W., ed. *Twentieth Century Negro Literature* (1902). New York: Arno Press, 1969.

Work for the Colored Woman of the South, comp. Mrs. Booker T. Washington (1984). Booker T. Washington papers, Manuscript Division, Library of Congress.

—ADELE LOGAN ALEXANDER

LORDE, AUDRE GERALDINE (b. 18 February 1934; d. 17 November 1992), poet, writer. Among mid- to late-twentieth-century writers, few so completely challenged attempts at facile categorization as did Audre Lorde. Her challenge took the interesting and powerful form of embracing all the categories into which she herself fit or could be made to fit. "I am a Black lesbian feminist poet," she said, "and I *am* your sister."

Audre Lorde was born in Harlem. Her parents, Frederic Byron and Linda Bellmar Lord, had come to New York from their home country of Grenada and for many years firmly believed that they would one day go home. When, during the Great Depression, they realized that they would probably never go back, a permanent sorrow entered their household. Their nostalgia for the country of their birth provided the background of Lorde's childhood. For this young New York girl, there was an island in the West Indies—an island she had never seen—that she was expected to think of as home.

One of Lorde's books, *Zami: A New Spelling of My Name* (1982), presents a clear picture of her early life. A fictionalized biography—or biomythography, as she calls it—the work graphically retells racist incidents the author suffered as a child. It also describes with wonder her discovery of language and its power. At an early age, she began to use the latter as a tool to resist and even manipulate racist attitudes.

The strictness of her parents' home, along with her own sense of herself as an outsider, led Lorde into rebellion as a teenager. She sought out others who felt as she did, and she found them at Hunter College High School. One such companion, later so important, was the poet Diane Di Prima. After graduation from high school, Lorde moved to her own apartment and began to support herself. The jobs she was able to find were low-paying and unsatisfying. She endured great loneliness because of her inability to find a world in which she felt at home. It was during

AUDRE LORDE. "I am a black lesbian feminist poet," Lorde once said, "and I *am* your sister." (© Salimah Ali. All rights reserved.)

this time that she had her first lesbian affair, in Connecticut, while she was working in a factory.

Another affair with a woman, in Mexico in 1954, led Lorde into the Greenwich Village "gay-girl" scene. It was the closest she had come to a sense of belonging, and she found it in a sea of almost entirely white faces. This irony, and the conflict it aroused in her, provoked years of thinking, writing, and feeling. At this time, she also went to college and began to work as a librarian, and she wrote poetry.

The poetry led Lorde, for a time, to involvement with the Harlem Writers Guild. Its members, including Langston Hughes, were the vanguard of a growing movement in African American literature. Here was another possible home for the aspiring young writer. Hughes him-

self showed an interest in her work. Yet, according to Lorde, the homophobia of the Guild members alienated her once again.

In 1959 Lorde received her BA from Hunter College. In 1960, she was awarded an MLS from Columbia University's School of Library Service. For a number of years, Lorde wrote poetry and worked as a librarian, eventually becoming head librarian at the Town School in New York. She also married and had two children. The marriage and its circumstances are not recorded in Lorde's writing and therefore little is known of it. Then, in 1968, the Poet's Press scheduled *The First Cities*, her first book of poetry, for publication. Her old high school friend, Diane Di Prima, was instrumental in its publication. At about the same time, Lorde was invited to Tougaloo College, in Mississippi, to be poet-in-residence.

Lorde was at Tougaloo for only six weeks, but during that time her life changed suddenly and radically. The public had begun to recognize her work; she was teaching poetry at a historically black institution, an empowering experience she later described with great emotion in her poem "Blackstudies"; and she had met and initiated a romance with Frances Clayton, the woman with whom she would share the rest of her life.

Upon her return to New York City, Lorde continued teaching. She gave courses in writing at City College and on racism at Lehman College and John Jay College. Her second book of poetry, *Cables to Rage*, was published in 1970. In 1971, she read publicly for the first time a lesbian love poem. The same poem was published later in *Ms*. It was not, however, included in her next volume of poetry, *From a Land Where Other People Live*, having been rejected by the editor of that volume. In 1974, the book was nominated for a National Book Award, bringing Lorde greater recognition for her work and, after two more publications with small presses, a contract with W. W. Norton.

Norton brought out *Coal* (1976), a collection of new poems and poems selected from her first two, hard-to-find books, and emblazoned with a jacket blurb written by Adrienne Rich, at that time one of Norton's most prominent poets. The association between Lorde and Rich continued over the years. *The Black Unicorn*, widely considered Lorde's most important work, appeared in 1978. In the summer of 1981, Rich published an interview with Lorde in *Signs: Journal of Women in Culture and Society*, thereby introducing her to a large white readership.

The Black Unicorn was probably Lorde's most successful poetic attempt to merge her different worlds. In it she used the image of the unicorn (which she believed Europeans took from the African agricultural goddess Chi-Wara, a one-horned antelope) to explore the influences of European and African cultures upon each other. She plumed the sexual significances of the symbol, pointing out how the European myth divides meaning into the masculine, the phallic horn, and the feminine, the pale virgin who alone can tame the animal. In contrast, African culture combines those meanings to emphasize the power of growth.

With the appearance of *The Black Unicorn*, Lorde became an acknowledged, widely reviewed poet. Critical articles began to be written about her work. Her prose, too, though published by small presses, began to command attention and respect. Published in 1982, *Zami: A New Spelling of My Name* was reviewed in the *New York Times*. A different audience grew out of the publication of a collection of essays titled *Sister Outsider* (1984). It was widely adopted in Women's Studies courses and quickly achieved the status of a feminist classic.

During the 1970s, Lorde traveled in Africa, the Caribbean, Europe, and Russia. In 1980, her autobiographical work *The Cancer Journals* was published. In it, she described her feelings during and after her affliction with breast cancer. The experience had added yet one more identity to her long list. In another prose work, *A Burst of Light* (1988), she recounted her decision not to undergo further surgery after a return of the disease and her experience with alternative methods of treatment. Despite her illness, Lorde traveled extensively, teaching and giving readings. She died in 1992.

The stubborn reality of her own experiences and her own feelings served as the basis of Lorde's worldview. When political oversimplifications collided with her personal affections and loyalties, she saw a reason to challenge the politics, as in her essay "Man Child: A Black Lesbian Feminist's Response." In that work, she explores, among other issues, the meaning of being a lesbian and a mother in a culture that often refuses to accept that combination.

Lorde's focus as a writer and a person was to strive for unity by embracing diversity. She challenged all political and social actions that arbitrarily separate one individual from another, that exclude and ostracize. She did this by fervently defending the individual's right to define herself and her possibilities. In her poetry, she created a world of eroticism, sensuality, and symbolism that, ultimately, aspired to the same goal.

BIBLIOGRAPHY

Annas, Pamela. "A Poetry of Survival: Unnaming and Renaming in the Poetry of Audre Lorde, Pat Parker, Sylvia Plath, and Adrienne Rich." *Colby Library Quarterly* 18 (March 1982): 9–25.

Avi-ram, Amitai F. "*Apo Koinou* in Audre Lorde and the Moderns: Defining the Differences." *Callaloo* 26 (Winter 1986): 193–208.

Bowles, Juliette, ed. *In the Memory and Spirit of Frances, Zora, and Lorraine: Essays and Interviews on Black Women and Writing*. Washington, DC: Institute for the Arts and Humanities, Howard University, 1979.

Brooks, Jerome. "In the Name of the Father: The Poetry of Audre Lorde." In *Black Women Writers (1950–1980): A Critical Evaluation*, edited by Mari Evans. Garden City, NY: Anchor Press/Doubleday, 1984.

Carruthers, Mary J. "The Re-Vision of the Muse: Adrienne Rich, Audre Lorde, Judy Grahn, Olga Broumas." *Hudson Review* 36 (Summer 1983): 293–322.

Chinosole. "Audre Lorde and Matrilineal Diaspora: 'Moving History beyond Nightmare into Structures for the Future . . .' " In *Wild Women in the Whirlwind: Afra-American Culture and the Contemporary Literary Renaissance*, edited by Joanne M. Braxton and Andrée Nicola McLaughlin. New Brunswick, NJ: Rutgers University Press, 1990.

Christian, Barbara. "The Dynamics of Difference: Review of Audre Lorde's *Sister Outsider*." In her *Black Feminist Criticism: Perspectives on Black Women Writers*. New York: Pergamon Press, 1985.

Hammond, Karla. "Audre Lorde: Interview." *Denver Quarterly* 16.1 (Spring 1981): 10–27.

Hull, Gloria T. "Living on the Line: Audre Lorde and Our Dead behind Us." In *Changing Our Own Words: Essays on Criticism, Theory, and Writings by Black Women*, edited by Cheryl A. Wall. New Brunswick, NJ: Rutgers University Press, 1989.

Martin, Joan. "The Unicorn Is Black: Audre Lorde in Retrospect." In *Black Women Writers (1950–1980): A Critical Evaluation*, edited by Mari Evans. Garden City, NY: Anchor Press/Doubleday, 1984.

Perreault, Jeanne. " 'That the Pain Not Be Wasted': Audre Lorde and the Written Self." *A/B: Auto/Biography Studies* 4.1 (Fall 1988): 1–16.

Stepto, Robert. "The Phenomenal Woman and the Severed Daughter." *Parnassus* 8.1 (1979): 312–320.

Tate, Claudia, ed. *Black Women Writers at Work*. New York: Continuum, 1983.

Winter, Nina. "On Audre Lorde" and "Audre Lorde." In *Interview with the Muse: Remarkable Women Speak on Creativity and Power*. New York: Random House, 1978.

—Margaret Homans

LUPER, CLARA

LUPER, CLARA (b. 3 May 1923), civil rights activist. The daughter of Ezell and Isabell Shepard, Clara was born in rural Okfuskee County, Oklahoma. Clara Shepard grew up in the small community of Hoffman in Okmulgee County, Oklahoma. Her father was a laborer who did farm work, drove buses, moved houses, chopped cotton on contract, and picked pecans. Her mother took in laundry.

Shepard went to a segregated school and wrote about the experience in her autobiography, *Behold the Walls* (1979):

The books . . . had been mainly discarded from the white elementary school. We were separate and we possessed through Education Calculated Manipulation an overabundance of *promises* for better books, equipment, and supplies that never came. We were Separate and Unequal.

She attended a segregated high school five miles away at Grayson. The microscope had no lenses; pages were missing from the handed-down history books and dictionaries; the outdated encyclopedia sets were missing some letters of the alphabet. After graduating with five other black seniors, Shepard went on to Langston University, then a segregated institution in central Oklahoma. It also had inferior equipment, books, and supplies compared to those at the white universities in the state. In 1944 Shepard earned her BA in mathematics with a minor in history. When she went to the University of Oklahoma, where she completed her master's degree in secondary education and history in 1951, Shepard encountered separate restrooms and separate sections in the cafeteria. The classrooms had bars to segregate black and white students.

Shepard's first marriage, to Bert Luper, an electrician, ended in divorce after thirteen years. In 1977 she married Charles P. Wilson, a truck driver.

When she described her experiences, Luper told of the twenty-six times she was jailed for her part in nonviolent demonstrations to end segregation. Her civil rights work began in earnest on 19 August 1958, when she and the local National Association for the Advancement of Colored People (NAACP) Youth Council carried out their first sit-in at the Katz Drug Store in Oklahoma City. When the group was refused service at the lunch counter and, in turn, refused to leave, the police were called, and the media came. Two days later, Katz announced that its thirty-eight outlets in Oklahoma, Missouri, Kansas, and Iowa would serve all people, regardless of race.

The sit-ins grew to involve hundreds of young black Americans and some white supporters. Participants set out on foot from Calvary Baptist Church for various downtown establishments. Often, they were jailed for trespassing, but they always kept coming back. Starting in August 1960, general boycotts were a commonly used tactic to force the end of segregation. Luper helped spread the word and build support with her regular radio broadcast. Sit-in demonstrations continued off and on for almost six years until the Oklahoma City Council enacted a public accommodations ordinance on 2 June 1964 to resolve problems with those establishments still resisting integration.

Luper continued her efforts in other areas, working for a fair housing ordinance and establishing a Freedom Center for Youth Council activities—and rebuilding it after it was firebombed on 10 September 1968. At their insistence, Luper led the predominantly black sanitation workers in their strike in 1969 for better pay and working conditions. Though she had no lack of causes in Oklahoma, she joined the danger-filled civil rights march from Selma to Montgomery, Alabama, in 1965, among many other national activities. In 1972 Luper ran for the U.S. Senate from Oklahoma, but lost the election.

Throughout her many years of civil rights involvement, Luper taught in public schools and often drew criticism for her outside activities. For seventeen years, she taught at Dunjee High School, a black school in Oklahoma City. She spent two years at Northwest Classen High School and then taught at John Marshall High School, both in Oklahoma City. In spring 1989, she was honored with a retirement dinner after forty-one years in education. Clara Luper received the NAACP Youth Council Advisor of the Year national award several times. Other honors include the Langston University Alumni Award, 1969; the Zeta Phi Beta, Chi Zeta Chapter Woman of the Year, 1970; and the Sigma Gamma Rho Service to Mankind Award, 1980. Clara Luper continued to address audiences around Oklahoma about her experiences and to raise funds for the Freedom Center of Oklahoma City, of which she was a founder.

In June 1961 Luper wrote down her thoughts during the height of her sit-ins:

> As I see it, Blacks must become the active conscience of America, but conscience is a drowsy thing. It stirs, turns over, takes another nap and falls into a deep, dead sleep. "Leave me alone," conscience cries. "Let me sleep, let me sleep," conscience cries. "Let time take care of it—time, time is the answer. Maybe ten years or maybe another hundred years." Oh, no, America, your conscience, like old Pharaoh's of old, will not rest or sleep until we can eat here at John A. Brown's. We will arouse your conscience and will not let you rest until we can eat.

Clara Luper did not rest, and Oklahoma was different for it ever after.

BIBLIOGRAPHY

Graves, Carl R. "The Right to Be Served: Oklahoma City's Lunch Counter Sit-ins, 1958–1964." In *We Shall Overcome: The Civil Rights Movement in the United States in the 1950s and 1960s*, edited by David J. Garrow. Brooklyn: Carlson Publishing, 1989.

Luper, Clara. *Behold the Walls*. Oklahoma City, OK: Jim Wire, 1979.

Rice, Darrell. Telephone interview with Clara Luper, 18 July 1992.

—DARRELL RICE

M

MABLEY, JACKIE "MOMS" (b. 19 March 1897?; d. 23 May 1975), entertainer. A young girl in a small town facing an uncertain future, Jackie "Moms" Mabley ran off with a minstrel show when she was thirteen and never looked back. Her six-decade career encompassed black vaudeville, the chitlin circuit, the Harlem Renaissance, off-Broadway revues, Broadway musicals, records, television, nightclubs and movies. She was a path-breaking comedienne and social satirist who nurtured the careers of younger performers and anticipated the day when no subject matter would be considered out of bounds for standup comedy.

Born Loretta Mary Aiken in 1897 in Brevard, North Carolina, Mabley was one of twelve children of Jim Aiken, a businessman and grocer, and a mother whose name is not known. Her ancestry was mixed African American, Cherokee, and Irish. She was especially close to her grandmother (some sources say her great-grandmother), a former slave, who lived to be 104 years old. She credited her grandmother for encouraging her to stay close to God and for advising her to leave Brevard, see the world, and make something of herself.

Life in Brevard was hard on young Loretta. By the time she was thirteen, she had been raped twice; both rapes resulted in children who were given up for adoption. Around this time her father died and her mother married a man with whom she did not get along. Acting on her grandmother's advice, Loretta added three years to her age and joined a minstrel show, becoming a performer on the black vaudeville circuit, TOBA (Theater Owners Booking Association). She changed her name to Jackie Mabley after a brief engagement to a Canadian performer named Jack Mabley. Throughout the 1910s, she made the rounds of the TOBA circuit and appeared in revues such as *Look Who's Here*. At first her act consisted of singing and dancing with a little comedy. While appearing in Texas in 1921, she caught the attention of the comic song and dance team of "Butterbeans and Susie" (Jody and Susan Edwards), who brought her into their act. They also introduced her to their agent and helped her get better bookings. By 1923 Mabley was appearing regularly in New York at the theaters associated with the Harlem Renaissance, including Connie's Inn, the Cotton Club, and

JACKIE "MOMS" MABLEY. Her six-decade career encompassed black vaudeville, the chitlin circuit, the Harlem Renaissance, off-Broadway revues, Broadway musicals, recordings, television, nightclubs, and movies. (Library of Congress.)

the Savoy Ballroom. Here she shared the stage with Pigmeat Markham, Tim "Kingfish" Moore, Bill "Bojangles" Robinson, and the bands of Louis Armstrong, Duke Ellington, Count Basie, Cab Calloway and Benny Goodman.

Like most black comics of the time, Mabley began by performing skits with other comedians, but in the late 1920s in New York she began developing monologues, with the help of black comedienne Bonnie Belle Drew.

Mabley was beginning to build the character for whom she would become known, a sharp-tongued, street-smart elderly woman, based largely on her memories of her grandmother in Brevard. At the same time she performed in revues and musical comedies, including *Bowman's Cotton Blossoms* (1923), *Miss Bandanna* (1927), and the Broadway plays *Fast and Furious: A Colored Revue in 37 Scenes* (1931) and *Blackberries of 1932*. In *Fast and Furious* she appeared in skits that she co-authored with Zora Neale Hurston; Mabley and Hurston performed together in one scene as cheerleaders.

The Depression closed many black entertainment venues, and Mabley scrambled to find work at rent parties, church socials, and movie houses, sometimes working as many as fifteen performances in one day. In 1933 she appeared in the movie version of Eugene O'Neill's *The Emperor Jones*, starring Paul Robeson. In 1939 she appeared with Louis Armstrong and Butterfly McQueen in *Swingin' the Dream*, a jazz adaptation of *A Midsummer Night's Dream*.

In 1939 Jackie Mabley became the first black comedienne to appear as a solo act at the Apollo Theater in Harlem. She quickly established herself as a regular, appearing for as many as fifteen sold-out weeks at a time. Langston Hughes saw her there and became a fan. It was in this era that many of the comedy acts at the Apollo recall seeing many of the established white comedians sitting in the front row with secretaries copying the material in shorthand. In later years Mabley told interviewers that Jack Benny was the only comedian who never stole from her.

Mabley also developed a reputation for taking a maternal interest in the careers of younger performers, who gave her the nickname "Moms," a name that also suited her stage persona. Among the younger performers she encouraged were Pearl Bailey, who was strictly a singer until Mabley urged her to develop her comedic talent, Slappy White, and Redd Foxx.

In the 1940s, Mabley continued to tour the country's black clubs and theaters and appeared in three movies that were showcases for established black vaudeville acts: *Big Timers* (1945), *Killer Diller* (1948), and *Boarding House Blues* (1948). By now her "Moms" character was well defined. She shuffled on stage wearing a shapeless, worn dress, sagging argyle socks, oversized shoes and a funny looking hat, greeting the crowd with a toothless grin. Speaking loudly and slowly in a southern drawl accentuated by an exaggerated nasal twang, she told jokes, sang parodies of popular songs, dispensed advice and talked about the desirability of young men and the undesirability of old men. The eternal quest for a young man became a defining aspect of the character.

Addressing the audience as her children, she presented herself to them as a family member or neighbor, not a performer looking down from a stage, but someone who would be welcome in their living rooms, bringing around the latest gossip, jokes, and news of the community. Her timing was brilliant and she could veer from grandmotherly sagacity to leering sexual innuendo in an instant. As Donald Bogle pointed out in *Brown Sugar: Eighty Years of America's Black Female Superstars*, Mabley offered men the same kind of rough treatment in her comedy that Bessie Smith afforded them in her songs.

Using her voice like an instrument, she would alter the volume and pitch, add syllables to words or completely re-invent them on the spot in order to convey her meaning. What started as a scripted act gradually became a constant improvisation. Modulating a comedy monologue according to audience response, on the fly, can be a risky business, but most of the chances Moms Mabley took paid off, and when they didn't, she was adept at circling back to illuminate her point from another perspective. If that didn't work there was always the next funny story, one liner, song or impression. Her vocal impersonation of Louis Armstrong was particularly accurate.

Mabley was a pioneer of comedy as social satire and commentary, foreshadowing the subject matter that would become the focus of sharp, edgy comedy in the 1960s. Long before Lenny Bruce, Dick Gregory, and Richard Pryor, she was using her wit to scalding effect in her portrayals of southern racism, race relations throughout the country, and the smug hypocrisy of politicians. By the 1950s purported conversations with presidents, first ladies, and world leaders at the United Nations were a staple of her act. According to her accounts these national and international leaders relied on her for the advice she dispensed in an offhand manner, referring to them by first names and nicknames, while they deferentially addressed her as "Mrs. Mabley."

In 1960 Moms Mabley recorded her first album, *The Funniest Woman Alive*, for Chess Records. It sold a million copies and was the first of twenty-five albums for Chess and other record labels, including *Moms Mabley at the UN*, *Moms Mabley Breaks It Up* and *Now Hear This*. It was on these records that Mabley began to be heard by the white American public for the first time, fifty years into her career. She was invited to the White House by Presidents John F. Kennedy and Lyndon B. Johnson. By the late 1960s she was commanding ten thousand dollars a week for her appearances at the Apollo.

In 1967, at the age of seventy, Mabley made her television debut on *A Time for Laughter*, an all-black comedy special produced by Harry Belafonte. Mabley portrayed the maid of a middle-class black couple, played by Godfrey Cambridge and Diana Sands, who are trying to escape their blackness, only to be rudely dragged back to reality by Mabley's maid character every time. Her success on the Belafonte special opened the doors of television to Moms Mabley, and she appeared on shows hosted by the Smothers Brothers, Merv Griffin, Mike Douglas, Flip Wilson, and Bill Cosby, among others. In the last years of her life she achieved a level of recognition commensurate with her talent, appearing at the Copacabana, Carnegie Hall, and the Kennedy Center in Washington, DC.

In 1974 Mabley played her first starring role in a feature film, *Amazing Grace*. Filming was suspended for three weeks after Mabley suffered a heart attack and was fitted with a pacemaker. *Amazing Grace* was a commercial success, but touring to promote the movie weakened Moms Mabley's health and she died on 23 May 1975 in White Plains Hospital in New York.

BIBLIOGRAPHY

Bogle, Donald. *Brown Sugar: Eighty Years of America's Black Female Superstars*. New York: Harmony Books, 1980.

Curl, Richelle B. "Jackie 'Moms' Mabley." In *Notable Black American Women*, edited by Jessie Carney Smith. Detroit, MI: Gale Research, Inc., 1992.

Escamilla, Brian. "Jackie 'Moms' Mabley." In *Contemporary Black Biography: Profiles from the International Black Community, Volume 15*, edited by Shirelle Phelps. Detroit, MI: Gale Research, 1997.

Fox, Ted. *Showtime at the Apollo*. New York: Da Capo Press, 1993.

Moritz, Charles, ed. *Current Biography Yearbook 1975*. New York: The H. W. Wilson Company, 1975.

Nassour, Ellis. "Mabley, Moms." *American National Biography Online. American Council of Learned Societies*, February 2000. http://www.anb.org/articles/18/18-00763.html.

Watkins, Mel. *On the Real Side: Laughing, Lying, and Signifying: the Underground Tradition of African-American Humor*. New York: Simon & Schuster, 1994.

Williams, Elsie Arrington. "Jackie 'Moms' Mabley." In *Black Women in America: An Historical Encyclopedia*, edited by Darlene Clark Hine. Brooklyn, NY: Carlson Publishing Company, 1993.

Williams, Elsie A. *The Humor of Moms Mabley: An African American Comedic Tradition*. New York: Garland Publishing, Inc., 1995.

—ROBERT W. LOGAN

McCLAIN, LEANITA

McCLAIN, LEANITA (b. 1951; d. 1984), journalist, editor. Leanita McClain, the first black member of the *Chicago Tribune* editorial board, was born in 1952. McClain grew up in a public housing project fittingly named for the pioneering black woman journalist Ida B. Wells-Barnett. McClain was a high achiever in the public schools, and while a student at Chicago State University, she decided to pursue a career in journalism. McClain received a full scholarship to the Medill School of Journalism at Northwestern University, completed her master's degree in 1973, and went to work as a general assignment reporter at the *Chicago Tribune*, where she met and married Clarence Page. The marriage ended in divorce.

McClain's superior journalistic abilities earned her frequent promotion. She moved from general assignment reporter to the copy desk, to the picture desk, and then to the perspective department. Soon she was a weekly columnist, the second black person to become a staff columnist in the 137-year history of the newspaper. In fewer than ten years after joining the *Tribune*, she became a member of the editorial board. McClain was barely thirty years old.

Her writings and professional accomplishments were honored outside the *Chicago Tribune*. She received the Chicago chapter of Sigma Delta Chi's Peter Lisagor Award, the 1983 Kizzy Award for an outstanding black female role model, and the Chicago Association of Black Journalists' top award for commentary, as well as being listed by *Glamour* magazine as one of the country's ten most outstanding career women.

After accomplishing so much so quickly, she painfully asked of herself and her friends, "I have made it, but where?" In an article that was an important catalyst to her career, she answered quite clearly by saying, "I have overcome the problems of food, clothing, and shelter, but I have not overcome my old nemesis, prejudice. *Life is easier, being black is not.*" An accomplished black professional woman from the housing projects of Chicago's South Side, McClain was caught with one foot in each world. "Whites won't believe I remain culturally different. . . . Blacks won't believe I remain culturally the same." Leanita McClain committed suicide at the age of thirty-two, and though she left a stack of suicide notes, including one labeled "generic suicide note," it is possible that her publications reveal some of the conditions of her life that led her to choose that end.

McClain began her professional career just after the pressures of the civil rights movement opened some doors for talented young African Americans, and she was conscious of the privileges that the movement enabled her to enjoy. Her first major article, published in *Newsweek* in 1980, about the responsibilities and burdens of the black middle class, addressed the frustration that black professionals felt over being unfairly accused of having forgotten where they came from. McClain was committed to her race as well as to her professional position. She was optimistic about her ability to bridge these two worlds, but she was not a romantic. She noted in that article that,

> I am burdened daily with showing whites that blacks are people. I am, in the old vernacular, a credit to my race. I am my brothers' keeper, and my sisters', though many of them have abandoned me because they think that I have abandoned them. I run a gauntlet between two worlds, and I am cursed and blessed by both. I travel, observe and take part in both; I can also be used by both. I am a rope in a tug of war. If I am a token in my downtown office, so am I at my cousin's church tea. I assuage white guilt. I disprove black inadequacy and prove to my parents' generation that their patience was indeed a virtue. I have a foot in each world, but I cannot fool myself about either
>
> (*Newsweek*, 13 October 1980, p. 2).

McClain also achieved prominence just before Chicago politics turned its ugliest—when Harold Washington won the 1983 Democratic primary in the mayoral contest. She was appalled and apparently shocked by the incessant virulent racist attacks, and the equally persistent efforts, following Washington's election, to prevent his governing effectively.

Ultimately, her anger led her to write an article that was published in the *Washington Post* under the headline "How Chicago Taught Me to Hate Whites" (so titled by *Post* headline writers). McClain's point was that, until the 1983 campaign, she had always believed that race relations were improving and that racism and bigotry would be eradicated, but the campaign and its aftermath were so vile that she had to acknowledge that "an evilness still possesses this town, and it continues to weight down my heart"; the constant mean-spiritedness confounded her and led her to "begin that morning [after the election] to build my defenses brick by brick." She realized she could never trust even her own judgment as easily as she had before. Worse still, the campaign and its aftermath made her realize that she had the capacity to hate. McClain worked to reclaim her old working relationships and to shed her hate, but many Chicagoans never forgave her for exposing them in the national press.

In her essays for *Newsweek* and *The Washington Post*, as well as in her weekly and then twice weekly columns for the *Tribune*, it is clear that Leanita McClain was a crusader, and she was a responsible one. She fought for better government, better schools, better housing. She worked to convince people that politics and race were inseparable, that privilege came with responsibility, that public schools could work, that public housing did not have to be a scourge, and that racism, sexism, and bigotry could and would destroy us all.

BIBLIOGRAPHY

Klose, Kevin. "A Tormented Black Rising Star Dead by Her Own Hand," *Washington Post*, 5 August 1984.

McClain, Leanita. "How Chicago Taught Me to Hate Whites." *Washington Post*, 24 July 1983.

McClain, Leanita. "The Middle-Class Black's Burden." *Newsweek*, 13 October 1980, 21.

Page, Clarence, ed. *A Foot in Each World: Essays and Articles by Leanita McClain*. Evanston, IL: Northwestern University Press, 1986.

—STEPHANIE J. SHAW

McCLENDON, ROSE (b. 27 August 1884; d. 12 July 1936), actor. Born in Greenville, South Carolina, Rosalie Virginia Scott was the daughter of Sandy and Lena Jenkins Scott. Around 1890 the family moved to New York, where Rosalie attended Public School 40. In 1904 she married Henry Pruden McClendon, a licensed chiropractor and Pullman porter. During the early years of their

ROSE MCCLENDON AS MEDEA, photographed by Carl Van Vechten in 1935. She was a distinguished actress and director, was one of the organizers of the Negro People's Theater, and (with John Houseman) headed the sixteen "Negro Units" of the Federal Theater Project during the Depression. (Library of Congress; gift, Carl Van Vechten Estate, 1966.)

marriage, Rose McClendon directed and acted in church plays and cantatas at Saint Mark's African Methodist Episcopal (AME) Church, but it was not until she received a scholarship to the American Academy of Dramatic Arts in 1916 that she devoted her life to theater. Her first professional role was in the play *Justice* (1919), by John Galsworthy.

The Harlem Renaissance helped to open up opportunities for black actors in dramatic roles for the first time. Because of the interest in African American life and cultures, McClendon was able to appear regularly on the New York stage. Hailed by the *Afro-American* as the "Negro first lady of the dramatic stage," she appeared in such shows as *Roseanne* (1926) with Charles Gilpin and Paul Robeson; *Deep River* (1926) with Jules Bledsoe; *In Abraham's Bosom* (1926), Paul Green's Pulitzer Prize–winning drama for which she received the Morning Telegraph Acting Award the following year, along with Ethel Barrymore and Lynn Fontanne. She played the role of Serena in the premiere production of Dorothy and DuBose Heyward's *Porgy* (1927), touring in the United States and Canada. She also appeared in *House of Connelly* (1931); *Black Soul* and *Never No More* (1932); *Brainsweat* and *Roll Sweet Chariot* (1934); and *Panic*. Her last appearance was as Cora in *Mulatto* (1935), a role Langston Hughes created for her. The play ran on Broadway for 375 shows, becoming the second-longest-running play by a black playwright to that time. In large part, the critics said, the success was a result of McClendon's performance.

In the late 1920s McClendon was a director for the Negro (Harlem) Experimental Theatre, located in the basement of the 135th Street branch of the New York Public Library, later the Schomburg Center for Research in Black Culture. In the 1930s President Franklin Delano Roosevelt's New Deal created the Federal Theatre Project. Rose McClendon suggested that separate Negro units be established to ensure that resources from the project would support the production of plays that dramatized black themes and showcased black talent. She and the white director John Houseman were put in charge of the Negro People's Theatre, based in Harlem's Lafayette Theatre. Among its productions was Shakespeare's *Macbeth*, adapted by Houseman and Orson Welles to a location in the West Indies and featuring Rose McClendon.

McClendon envisioned the establishment of a permanent "Negro Theatre" that produced plays dealing "with Negro problems, with phases of Negro life, faithfully presented and accurately delineated"—a theater that would not merely develop "an isolated Paul Robeson, or an occasional Bledsoe or Gilpin, but a long line of first-rate actors." Toward this end, she and Dick Campbell founded the Negro People's Theatre in Harlem in 1935. Unfortunately, a year later, Rose McClendon died of pneumonia. To keep her dreams alive, Dick Campbell and his wife, Muriel Rahn, organized the Rose McClendon Players. Later, in 1946, the philanthropist Carl Van Vechten established the Rose McClendon Memorial Collection of Photographs of Distinguished Negroes at Yale and Harvard universities.

BIBLIOGRAPHY

Anderson, Jervis. *This Was Harlem: A Cultural Portrait, 1900–1950.* New York: Farrar, Straus, and Giroux, 1982.
Bordman, Gerald. *The Oxford Companion to the American Theatre.* New York: Oxford University Press, 1992.
Logan, Rayford W., and Michael R. Winston, eds. *Dictionary of American Negro Biography.* New York: Norton, 1982.
Johnson, James Weldon. *Black Manhattan* (1930). New York: Da Capo, 1991.
Kellner, Bruce. *The Harlem Renaissance: A Historical Dictionary for the Era.* New York: Methuen, 1987.
Mitchell, Lofton. *Black Drama: The Story of the American Negro in the Theatre.* New York: Hawthorn Books, 1967.
Plum, Jay. "Rose Mcclendon and the Black Units of the Federal Theatre Project: A Lost Contribution." *Theatre Survey,* November 1992.
Ross, Ronald. "The Role of Blacks in the Federal Theatre, 1935–1939." In *The Theatre of Black Americans*, edited by Errol Hill. New York: Applause, 1987.
Woll, Allen. *Black Musical Theatre: From Coontown to Dreamgirls.* New York: Da Capo, 1991.

ARCHIVAL SOURCES

Documents concerning Rose McClendon may be found in the James Weldon Johnson Collection at the Beinecke Rare Book and Manuscript Library at Yale University in New Haven, Connecticut.

—ANNETTA GOMEZ-JEFFERSON

McDANIEL, HATTIE (b. 10 June 1895; d. 26 October 1952), actress. A woman of strong character, committed to the uplift of the black community, and willing to fight for the causes she believed in, Hattie McDaniel is best remembered for her Academy Award–winning performance as Mammy in the 1939 production of *Gone With the Wind.* McDaniel was the first African American to win this distinguished honor; in fact, her career included many notable firsts in vaudeville, radio, and film. In many respects, her life exemplified the burden an individual is faced with when called upon to represent an entire race of people. While McDaniel was celebrated for her Hollywood success, she was just as often criticized for taking roles that perpetuated racist stereotypes of African Americans. Although her portrayal as subservient maids may have infuriated some black activists, she knew how to pick her battles and contributed to the fight for equal rights on many fronts, often without public recognition.

Early Life and Career

McDaniel was born in Wichita, Kansas, the youngest of thirteen children. While McDaniel loved both of her parents, she particularly admired her father, Henry McDaniel, and his work ethic, and wanted to fulfill his wish that none of his children work as domestics. Also, through her father, once a performer in minstrel shows, McDaniel was exposed to "show business." She loved every aspect of performing—it connected her to her family, her creativity, and in a sense was all that she knew.

Despite the racial climate of the United States, coming of age during this time was also filled with hope and belief in new opportunity. Although there were still forms of discrimination in Denver, where the McDaniels made their home, social conditions were much different than those in the South. Though McDaniel was one of two black children to attend the predominately white elementary and high school, she was loved by her teachers and classmates. In fact, her teacher, Louise Poirson, often

HATTIE McDANIEL,
c. 1940s. At the left is Walter
Francis White, a leader of
the NAACP. (Library of
Congress.)

permitted her to sing and recite poetry to the class. Throughout high school, she continued to work on her theatrical skills. As early as 1908, when she was only thirteen, she was billed in J. M. Johnson's "Mighty Modern Minstrels," a minstrel show that included her sister Etta and brothers Otis and Samuel. At fifteen, McDaniel competed in the Woman's Christian Temperance Union oratorical competition. Her recitation of "Convict Joe," a story about a wayward drunk, earned her the gold medal.

Around 1910 McDaniel's father formed the "Henry McDaniel Minstrel Show," which performed all over Colorado. At first, her mother did not allow her to travel with the group because of the risks involved. Determined to pursue her heart's desire, McDaniel left school her sophomore year and convinced her mother to let her travel. During this time, she toured with a number of minstrel groups, often writing many of the songs. When Hattie's brother Otis died in 1916 at the age of thirty-five, the family show experienced some difficulty, forcing McDaniel to take domestic work to help pay the bills. In 1920 she joined Professor George Morrison and his "Melody Hounds." Morrison was a well-known musician in Denver and offered McDaniel the exposure and opportunities she needed to advance her career. While traveling with the Morrison Orchestra, she was billed as the female Bert Williams, an internationally known vaudeville performer. In 1922, just as her career was flourishing, McDaniel experienced two great losses: her father died at the age of eighty-two and her husband, George Langford, to whom she had been married for only three months, was shot and killed.

The beginning of the 1920s also marked the great broadcasting boom throughout the nation. The necessity of advanced technology during World War I had improved radio capabilities and stations were popping up all over the nation. On 15 December 1924, the radio station KOA in Denver aired its first broadcast, marking the beginning of McDaniel's extended radio career. McDaniel was the first black person to sing at the station, making her one of the first, if not the first, black person to sing on radio in the nation. Her radio successes led to extensive travel on the black entertainment circuit. McDaniel was booked as a blues singer, primarily through the Theater Owners Booking Association (TOBA), which helped launch the careers of Bessie Smith, Ethel Waters, Ma Rainey, and many others. The organization was also well known for cheating their entertainers out of their earnings, which meant that McDaniel often had little money and was not guaranteed housing.

The TOBA run ended, as did the roaring twenties, in 1929, when the stock market crashed. McDaniel was stuck in Chicago with no job and decided to head for Milwaukee on the chance that she might find work at Sam Pick's Club Madrid. Indeed, she was hired, but only as a ladies room attendant. She earned one dollar per week plus tips. However, during one slow night and at the encouragement of patrons who had heard her sing in the ladies room, McDaniel was given the opportunity to sing at the establishment, which booked only white performers. Her show-stopping performance, singing "St. Louis Blues," earned her $90.36 in tips, as well as a regular booking.

However, the Depression brought an end to the club's prosperity. In 1931, with twenty dollars in her pocket, McDaniel joined her sister Etta and brother Sam in Los Angeles. Her brother was able to get her a part on KNX's *The Optimistic Do-Nut Hour*, where McDaniel had immediate success and soon became known as "Hi-Hat Hattie," a name given to her when she showed up for the first broadcast in formal evening wear. In 1932 McDaniel made her first movie appearance in Fox's *The Golden West*, in which she played a house servant. This was the first of over three hundred film appearances, for which in the beginning she earned just five dollars per film.

African Americans first began appearing on screen around 1898; however, the depictions mostly fell in line with the racial stereotypes of the day. Blacks were portrayed as chicken thieves, venal preachers, and savages to be feared. Most memorable, perhaps, was D. W. Griffith's *The Birth of a Nation*, in which the black men were presented as murderous tormenters out to defile white southern womanhood. It was, in part, as an effort to curtail the negative images coming out of Hollywood that the black cinema emerged. There were several noble production attempts early on, but things did not take off until after World War I. The films gave their audiences success stories, adventures, and dramas illustrating a variety of issues within the black community. While independent black artists persisted, blacks in mainstream Hollywood were still mostly restricted to playing servants.

In 1935 McDaniel appeared in Fox's *The Little Colonel* as Mom Beck. The movie starred Shirley Temple and Lionel Barrymore and was criticized for implying that blacks wanted to return to the "comforts of slavery," where they were supposedly happier and economically stable. For McDaniel, the film marked the beginning of tension between her and black activists, critical of Hollywood for its inaccurate, stereotypical, and racist depictions of black people. That same year, McDaniel appeared in RKO's *Alice Adams*, in which she played Malena Burns, a sassy servant. This portrayal produced a great deal of resistance from white southerners who were more accustomed to seeing black domestics as docile and submissive. White southern patrons pressured filmmakers to conform to these stereotypical portrayals of blacks and threatened to boycott any film that did not comply with their expectation.

The conversations around the characters McDaniel portrayed were much bigger than the roles she took; she was caught in the middle of an ideological and political debate that would not soon end. In this climate of racial unrest, she was charged with the challenge of mending race relations in America, a daunting task for anyone, let alone one who was just beginning to make a name for herself as an actress. McDaniel defended her right to choose her roles, noting that many of her characters had shown themselves equal to their white employers. She often responded to criticisms by saying "I would rather play a maid and make $700 a week than be a maid for $7."

Gone with the Wind

McDaniel's big break came when she was cast in David O. Selznick's *Gone with the Wind*, an adaptation of Margaret Mitchell's best-selling novel. From the beginning, there was no doubt that the movie would be a success. McDaniel won the role over several other talented actresses, signing a contract with Selznick for $450.00 per week. Arguments ensued immediately about the depiction of blacks in the upcoming movie. McDaniel was direct with Selznick and joined others in voicing her concern about racist language in the script. Selznick decided to leave in "darkie" but compromised by removing the word "nigger." This was a major accomplishment for McDaniel and the others, given the situation. On the set, McDaniel personified her character, and her performances often overwhelmed her fellow cast members. Everyone speculated that she would be a sure candidate for an Academy Award. The Academy of Motion Picture Arts and Sciences agreed. She was nominated for and won an Oscar for best supporting actress for her portrayal of Mammy in 1940, beating her co-star Olivia de Havilland. McDaniel's win made her the first black person ever to receive an award from the academy since its inception in 1916.

Despite her popularity and newfound celebrity status, McDaniel was unable to escape the perils of a racist society. In fact, she had a double burden to bear. She faced a daily battle for respect, fair housing, equal pay, and equality, which mirrored the experiences of black Americans all over the nation. In addition, she faced the emotionally trying challenge of fighting off criticism from leaders in the black community, who asserted that her work hindered the progress of black Americans by perpetuating racist stereotypes. Her strongest critic was Walter White, executive secretary of the National Association for the Advancement of Colored People (NAACP). McDaniel and other actors under attack formed their own group, the Fair Play Committee (FPC), which focused on the battles they had won in Hollywood. Nevertheless, McDaniel took the criticism to heart and was often perplexed by the complexity of the issue.

Activities During World War I and Later

Although one would not readily identify her as a social activist, McDaniel led quietly by example. During World War II, she was a captain in the American Women's Volunteer Service, and she headed a black subcommittee of the Hollywood Victory Committee, which raised funds so that black soldiers could enjoy performances. In addition, she sold war bonds to help raise money for the war effort. Perhaps more importantly, McDaniel was involved with a court case that had a substantial affect on fair housing policies for black Americans. In 1942 McDaniel moved into a thirty-two-room mansion in a predominantly white West Adams neighborhood known as "Sugar Hill." In 1945, an association of white property owners sought to enforce a code of restrictive covenants, a residential deed that designated neighborhoods as "white only" or limited the number of houses that could be sold to minorities. Enforcement of such a statute would have meant that McDaniel could be evicted from her home. A total of fifty defendants, including neighbors Ethel Waters and Louise Beavers, fought the action, and on 6 December 1945 the judge ruled in favor of the defendants, citing the rights of full citizenship guaranteed by the Fourteenth Amendment. This important ruling set the precedent for the 1948 U.S. Supreme Court case, *Shelly v. Kraemer*, which declared restrictive covenants unconstitutional.

On 24 November 1947, McDaniel made history again when she was named star of the CBS radio production of *The Beulah Show*, which was about a black maid and the white family she worked for. The show had been on the air for a number of years, but white male actors had played Beulah. McDaniel became the first black person to star in a radio program intended for a general audience. However, before she signed the contract, she insisted on being allowed to alter any script that she did not like and refused to speak in dialect. Producers readily agreed to her conditions. Ratings soared, and it is estimated that over seven million listeners heard the show each weeknight. This number grew to approximately fifteen million by the time the program ended its run. In 1950, the show continued to air on radio and also ventured into the realm of television. While McDaniel continued starring in the radio version, Ethel Waters was cast for the television show. However, in 1951, by popular demand, McDaniel starred in the radio version and filmed six episodes for television. When a health condition forced her to stop,

Louise Beavers replaced her, followed by Lillian Randolph. The six shows she filmed were never broadcast.

While McDaniel's career soared, her personal life was plagued with disappointment and failed relationships. Beleaguered by the stresses of Hollywood, criticism from leaders in the black community, court cases, and four failed marriages, McDaniel was constantly in search of happiness and unconditional love. Thus, in 1944, while still married to Lloyd Crawford, her third husband, she was ecstatic to find out that she was pregnant, and publicly declared her excitement, only to find out that doctors had misread her condition. The news sent her into a deep depression that culminated in 1949, when she tried to end her life with a bottle of sleeping pills. Only a timely visit from a friend saved her life.

Soon thereafter McDaniel's physical health began to deteriorate after she suffered a series of strokes and heart attacks and to further complicate matters, in 1952, doctors diagnosed her with breast cancer. Perhaps sensing that the end was near, with the help of her friend and secretary Ruby Goodwin, she began to sell her belongings, donating memorabilia such as her Oscar to Howard University. After she sold her house, she moved into the Motion Picture Home and Hospital, a building she had helped dedicate just a year earlier. She was the first black resident.

At the age of fifty-seven, McDaniel passed away. Her funeral six days later was a spectacular Hollywood homecoming. More than five thousand people arrived for the service, and the procession included 125 limousines. In her will, McDaniel asked to be buried at the Hollywood Memorial Park Cemetery, but her request was not honored because the cemetery did not accept blacks. Despite protest by some, she was buried in the Angelus-Rosedale Cemetery, another facility that had previously been reserved for whites. Fifty years after her death, the new owner of the Hollywood cemetery, renamed Hollywood Forever, installed a memorial to recognize her.

Throughout McDaniel's forty-five-year span as an entertainer, she bridged many gaps and opened a number of doors for black performers that came after her. She started from humble beginnings, with a natural talent and drive to achieve her dream. The road to stardom was difficult; however, after she gained her due respect from the industry, she was able to voice her concerns and help change the negative stereotypes that permeated the film and radio industry.

BIBLIOGRAPHY

Bogle, Donald. *Brown Sugar: Eighty Years of America's Black Female Superstars*. New York: Harmony Books, 1980.

Bogle, Donald. *Toms, Coons, Mulattoes, Mammies, and Bucks: An Interpretive History of Blacks in American Films*. New York: Continuum, 1994.

Brown, Charlotte. *Mammy: An Appeal to the Heart of the South*. New York: Prentice Hall, 1995.

Evans, Augusta. *Beulah*. Baton Rouge, LA: Louisiana State University Press, 1992.

Jackson, Carlton. *Hattie: The Life of Hattie McDaniel*. Lanham, MD: Madison Books, 1990.

Jewell, K. Sue. *From Mammy to Miss America and Beyond: Cultural Images and the Shaping of the U.S. Social Policy*. New York: Routledge, 1992.

Kelleher, Terry. "Beyond Tara: the Extraordinary Life Of Hattie McDaniel." *People Weekly*, 6 August 2001, 30.

"Life of Oscar-Winning Actress Hattie McDaniel Recounted in American Movie Classics Original Film Hosted by Whoopi Goldberg." *Jet*, 20 July 2001, 20.

"Oscar Winner Hattie McDaniel Memorialized at Hollywood Cemetery Which Had Refused to Bury Her." *Jet*, 15 November 1999, 20–22.

Yearwood, Gladstone Lloyd. *Black Film as a Signifying Practice: Cinema, Narration, and the African American Aesthetic Tradition*. Trenton, NJ: Africa World Press, 2000.

—MONIQUE M. CHISM

McKENZIE, VASHTI (b. 28 May 1947), pastor. Vashti McKenzie worked as a model as a teenager, later became a newspaper reporter, hosted radio and television shows, and served as vice president of a television station before entering the Christian ministry. After becoming pastor of two small African Methodist Episcopal (AME) churches, she was appointed pastor of Payne Memorial AME Church in Baltimore, Maryland. At the end of ten years of this pastorate, she was the first woman elected as a Bishop of the African Methodist Episcopal Church denomination.

Vashti Murphy Smith was born in Baltimore, Maryland, to Edward Smith and Ida Murphy Smith Peters. Her mother was the daughter of Vashti Turley Murphy, one of the twenty-two cofounders of the national African American sorority, Delta Sigma Theta. Ida Murphy Smith worked from a young age for the *Baltimore Afro-American*, serving as reporter for several decades and managing the marketing and advertising departments. Edward Smith was a high school teacher and track coach. Vashti was the youngest of three children born to the Smith family, two daughters and a son.

Vashti Murphy Smith attended school in Baltimore. As a member of the high school track team coached by her father, she participated in the high jump. Her father set the bar higher for her in practice to show there was no favoritism. This extra effort resulted in Vashti winning the high jump in a citywide track meet. Throughout her life, she accepted the challenge to aim higher and to achieve more than her peers.

Murphy Smith attended Morgan State University in Baltimore but left in her junior year to marry Stanley McKenzie, then a professional basketball player with the Baltimore Bullets. Stan McKenzie earned a bachelor's degree from New York University and played guard with National Basketball Association teams in Baltimore, Phoenix, Portland, and Houston from 1966 to 1973. While in Phoenix, Vashti McKenzie worked as a reporter for the *Arizona Republic* newspaper.

When the McKenzies returned to Baltimore, Vashti McKenzie worked as a reporter for the newspaper owned and managed by her grandfather, Carl J. Murphy, writing a column, "The McKenzie Report." She later worked for two Baltimore gospel radio stations, WEBB and WYBC, and hosted a television show before becoming program director and, later, Corporate Vice President of Programming for WJZ-TV in Baltimore. She resumed college studies, receiving a bachelor's degree in journalism from the University of Maryland in 1978.

During that year, McKenzie received a call to become a Christian minister and entered the School of Theology at Howard University in Washington, DC. After receiving a master of divinity degree from Howard, she enrolled in the doctoral program at the United Theological Seminary in Dayton, Ohio, later receiving a doctor of ministry degree. After graduation, McKenzie was assigned to small circuit churches in Maryland. She moved on to pastor Oak Street AME Church in midtown Baltimore. In December 1990, she was appointed to one of the larger and historically significant churches of the AME denomination, Baltimore's Payne Memorial AME Church.

McKenzie was pastor of Payne until 2000. During that ten-year period, she was considered a highly inspirational preacher, a builder of church membership, and a developer of innovative church-based community outreach programs. Under her leadership, membership rose from approximately three hundred to over seventeen hundred. Practicing the social gospel of developing church programs to benefit the larger community, Payne acquired buildings as well as property and instituted numerous programs. The value of the church's buildings and property rose from $1.6 million to $5.6 million, including a thirty thousand-square foot office building and a five-story apartment complex. Emphasizing social uplift and empowerment, Payne's programs included job training and placement for six hundred former welfare recipients, a food pantry for the needy, a boy scout ministry, rites of passage for both girls and boys, and a seven-to-nine week summer camp program for over one hundred children. Payne also managed a public school for the Baltimore Public School System.

McKenzie was selected for an Honor Roll of Great African-American Preachers in the November 1993 issue of *Ebony* and as one of the magazine's fifteen greatest African American female preachers in November of 1997. Union Theological Seminary in New York awarded her its prestigious Union Medal in 2003, recognizing her as a trailblazer for women in ministry.

McKenzie authored three books: *Not Without A Struggle, Strength in the Struggle,* and *Journey to the Well.*

BIBLIOGRAPHY

"After Reluctant 'Yes' to Ministry, Confident Climb to Top." *New York Times,* 15 July 2000.

"After 213 Years, A.M.E. Church Elects First Woman as a Bishop." *New York Times,* 12 July 2000.

"A.M.E. Church May Elect Its First Woman as Bishop." *New York Times,* 9 July 2000.

"First AME Female Bishop in 213 Years." *Ebony,* September 2000.

Official Website of the Eighteenth Episcopal District, African Methodist Episcopal Church. http://www.18thame.org.

"The Rev. Vashti Murphy McKenzie: A Bishop for the New Millennium." *Crisis,* November/December 2000.

—De Witt S. Dykes Jr.

McKINNEY, CYNTHIA ANN (b. 17 March 1955), legislator. When Cynthia McKinney walked into the halls of Congress in her gold tennis shoes, no one there was ready for her. She carried herself with confidence and spoke with a frankness that took aback the older, whiter, and mostly male members of the United States House of Representatives. Fortunately, her intelligence and her passionate concern for issues of equality and justice backed up her brashness. Still, the congressional gadfly was to find herself in hot water more than once in the next decade.

Cynthia McKinney was born in Atlanta, Georgia, the daughter of James Edward "Billy" McKinney, a police officer, and Leola Christion McKinney, a nurse and homemaker. Her father was a lifelong activist. After his return from serving in the military during World War II, he was arrested for using the "Whites Only" drinking fountain in his hometown. While he was one of the first black police officers in Atlanta, he also picketed the force for racist policies and practices. He passed his hatred for injustice on to his daughter, who went with him to civil rights demonstrations and challenged a nun in her Catholic school for using racist language in class. When those in authority didn't believe her, she secretly tape-recorded the teacher.

After high school, McKinney went on to the University of Southern California, majoring in international relations and graduating in 1978. The following year, she and her father were at a Southern Christian Leadership Conference demonstration in Alabama to protest the rape conviction of a mentally retarded black man. When Klansman in full costume appeared, the National Guard was forced to restore order, but McKinney was never the same. She later said that it was her day of awakening, the day she learned firsthand that there were people who hated her without even knowing her. She also said that it was the day she knew politics was something she would do.

McKinney entered Tufts University to work on her PhD, married Jamaican politician Coy Grandison, and moved to Jamaica. There, she received a startling message from her father. Billy McKinney had been elected in 1973 to the Georgia state legislature. One day in 1986, he became intensely frustrated with one of his colleagues and decided his daughter should run against her. Without consulting Cynthia, he registered her to run for the state legislature. Without campaigning, McKinney won 20 percent of the vote. The next time around, in 1988, she launched a serious campaign and won. By this time, she had divorced Grandison and returned to Georgia.

While in the legislature, McKinney helped design a redistricting plan to remedy inequities in minority representation in the United States Congress, in accordance with the guidelines of the Voting Rights Act of 1982. In 1992, she ran from one of the redrawn districts and won with 75 percent of the vote. In her first term, she supported President Bill Clinton on most issues, a notable exception being the North American Free Trade Agreement. In this case, she lined up with organized labor. She engaged in a debate with Illinois Republican Henry Hyde, who was fierce in his opposition to abortion. She sponsored a bill to prohibit the United States from selling arms to countries with a history of human rights violations. At one point, a budget fight threatened to shut down the federal government, and McKinney was one of a tiny group of representatives who demanded that Congress forego their own pay until government employees could be paid.

McKinney was re-elected in 1994 and immediately began a campaign of criticism against the Republican majority's so-called "Contract with America." She opposed welfare "reform" and attacked the ethics of the House Speaker, Newt Gingrich.

McKinney's 1996 election was from a newly redrawn district. In spite of the white majority that composed her new constituency, she won the primary handily and went on to defeat her Republican opponent in a negative campaign fight. Although she continued to support the Clinton administration, she was as quick to point out racism in that camp as in the Republican legislature. At one point, she protested in writing to the President about her treatment at a welcoming ceremony in the White House for the Prime Minister of Italy. Of her reception at the gate she wrote, "I had a White female staff person with me. The guard did not address his question to me nor did he acknowledge my presence. The guard assumed that my 23-year-old staff person was the Member of Congress." When she got to the West Wing, she was again stopped by a security guard. Representative James Moran vouched for her and she was allowed to continue. She then saw several white guests enter without being stopped or questioned. She received an apology.

When the administration changed, McKinney became a vocal critic of George W. Bush. The gadfly became ever angrier and more frustrated as she saw what she thought to be the chances for justice, equality, and the rights of the individual diminishing. Then, after the World Trade Center disaster on 11 September 2001, she stood up to question the administration's responsibility for the tragedy. "What did this administration know and when did it know it, about the events of September 11?" she asked in April 2002 in a radio interview on Berkeley, California's KPFA. "Who else knew, and why did they not warn the innocent people of New York who were needlessly murdered?"

That statement was incendiary in itself, although it also turned out to be a question that others would raise later. But McKinney went on. In a press release dated 12 April 2002 she said,

I am not aware of any evidence showing that President Bush or members of his administration have personally profited from the attacks of 9-11. A complete investigation might reveal that to be the case. For example, it is known that President Bush's father, through the Carlyle Group had—at the time of the attacks—joint business interests with the bin Laden construction company and many defense industry holdings, the stocks of which have soared since September 11. On the other hand, what is undeniable is that corporations close to the Administration, have directly benefited from the increased defense spending arising from the aftermath of September 11.

In the months that followed, conservatives called McKinney everything from "loony" to "a traitor." Her words were interpreted as an accusation that the president had allowed the attacks to occur, deliberately, in order that his business cronies might profit. On the other side, liberals tried to ignore the extremes of the statement, focusing on the questions she raised and insisting she was vindicated, while ignoring her suggestion of profit from the attacks on the part of the Bushes.

It seemed that McKinney had gone too far and that her re-election would be imperiled. She might have lost on that issue, but that will never be known. She was opposed in the 2002 Democratic primary by a conservative black woman judge, Denise Majette, but it was not her opponent who defeated her. Because of McKinney's stand on the Middle East, more than $1.1 million flowed into Majette's campaign from pro-Israeli donors outside the state of Georgia. McKinney herself received considerable financial support from Arab-Americans. The woman who had worked so well for her constituency on issues vital to them and their lives was defeated in a contest between opposing foreign policies.

In August 2003, McKinney accepted an appointment at Cornell University.

BIBLIOGRAPHY

"Congresswoman McKinney Presses for Investigation of Bush Administration Links to 9–11." KPFA, Flashpoints News Radio, 12 April 2002.

Glanton, Dahleen. "Low Turnout of Black Voters Costly for McKinney." *Chicago Tribune*, 21 August 2002. K36–39.

Jones, Ricky L. " 'Black Hawk' Down: Cynthia McKinney, America's War on Terror, and the Rise of Bushism." *The Black Scholar*. San Francisco: Fall 2002.

McKinney, Cynthia. Press Release, 12 April 2002. Congresswoman Cynthia McKinney, GA's 4th District. http://www.ratical.org/co-globalize/CynthiaMcKinney/news/pr020412.htm.

Medea, Andra. "Cynthia McKinney." In *Facts on File Encyclopedia of Black Women in America: Law and Government*, edited by Darlene Clark Hine. New York: Facts on File, Inc., 1997.

Nichols, John. "McKinney Redux." *The Nation*, 10 June 2002.

"White House Apologizes to Black Woman Lawmaker Denied Admission to White House Ceremony." *Jet*, 25 May 1998.

—HILARY MAC AUSTIN

McMILLAN, ENOLIA PETTIGEN (b. 20 October 1904), activist, educator. In 1985 Enolia Pettigen McMillan became the first woman elected President of the National Association for the Advancement of Colored People (NAACP). By that time, she had experienced several "firsts" in her lifetime. She earned the first scholarship offered by the Epsilon Chapter of Alpha Kappa Sorority, Incorporated, to finance her undergraduate degree at Howard University in Washington, DC. She was the first woman elected President of the Maryland Colored Teachers' Association, the first woman chair of the Morgan State College Trustee Board, and the first black trustee for the executive committee of the Public School Teachers Association.

Enolia Pettigen McMillan was born to Elizabeth and John Pettigen in Willow Grove, Pennsylvania. The Pettigens's strong belief in self-improvement through education helped lay a strong foundation for McMillan's lifelong commitment to black youth, education, and equal access to resources. When McMillan was three years old, the Pettigens moved to Maryland.

Enolia Pettigen McMillan graduated from the segregated public school system. She eagerly searched for Maryland colleges open to black students, but to no avail. She was forced to commute to attend Howard University in Washington, DC, since the family could not afford the cost of room and board. The combination of hard work, sacrifice, and scholarship allowed McMillan to graduate with a bachelor of arts in education in 1926.

McMillan's commitment to education and self-improvement carried over into her first classroom. She used her own car to transport students to and from school when the school's second-hand bus was in disrepair. McMillan fully understood her students' need for parental and

ENOLIA PETTIGEN McMILLAN (right), with Irma Jones (left) and Leah Patterson in May 1970, during a spring renewal membership drive by the Baltimore branch of the NAACP. McMillan was the president of that branch. (Library of Congress.)

teacher encouragement for a successful academic career. She coordinated annual May Fair days as teacher and principal of Pomonkey High School, the first school for blacks in Charles County, Maryland.

McMillan wanted to pursue an advanced degree but soon discovered that no local graduate schools accepted black applicants. Enrolled in Columbia University, McMillan again commuted and continued to actively research disparities in Maryland's public education system. She chose as the topic for her master's thesis the unequal access to resources in public funding, maintenance, and staff salaries in Maryland's public schools. The thesis, entitled "Factors Affecting Secondary Education in the Counties in Maryland," garnered so much attention that McMillan was denied promotions in the Baltimore City School System. Undaunted, she was elected president of the Maryland Colored Teachers' Association and regional vice-president of the National Association of Colored Teachers, and worked closely with Thurgood Marshall to promote equality in school systems nationwide.

McMillan's involvement with the NAACP began in 1935. As an active member, she continued to educate and assist black youth in Baltimore. In 1938, she was awarded the NAACP Merit Medal. She was elected Baltimore Chapter President in 1969, the same year she retired from the public school system. During her tenure, the Baltimore branch increased its membership and effectively worked with the surrounding community on issues related to education, voter registration, job opportunities, civil rights, and other social issues. With McMillan as president, the NAACP moved its national headquarters to Baltimore in 1986.

Enolia Pettigen McMillan maintained her commitment to social equality throughout her life as an educator, school administrator, community leader, and president of two major organizations working toward social change, the Maryland State Colored Teachers' Association and the NAACP. McMillan's numerous achievements and dedication to forge a better future for black youth through education and legislation brought her much acclaim. Among the honors bestowed upon McMillan were induction into the Douglass High School Hall of Fame in 1972, the Distinguished Citizen Award from the Democratic Ladies Guild in 1984, Top 100 Black Business and Professional Women in 1986, induction into the Maryland Women's Hall of Fame in 1990, and a 1999 Nation Builder Award by the National Black Caucus of State Legislatures. In 2000, the Baltimore branch office of the NAACP was renamed the Enolia P. McMillan Building. Perhaps most fittingly, a scholarship for low-income Baltimore students was named for her.

BIBLIOGRAPHY

"Inside Our School World: African American Schools during a Century of Segregation, Charles County, Maryland." College of

Southern Maryland, 2001. http://www.csmd.edu/Library/SMSC/ccschools/activities.

Lee, Vicki. "The Baltimore Local Today." *Baltimore Afro-American* 108.47 (14 July 2000): C25.

Maryland Archives Online. http://www.mdarchives.state.md.us/msa/educ/exhibits/womenshall/html.

Schatzman, Dennis. "Gibson's Die Was Cast by 90-Year-Old National Board Member." *Los Angeles Sentinel*, 60.47 (1 March 1995): A16.

—VALERIE L. RUFFIN

McMILLAN, TERRY (b.18 October 1951), novelist, writer. Terry McMillan was born in Port Huron, Michigan. The eldest of five children, McMillan was raised in a single-parent household by her mother, Madeline Washington Tilman. Her father, Edward McMillan, died three years after a divorce that left McMillan's mother with the difficult task of supporting five children on the salaries provided by a series of low-paying jobs. Beset, the McMillan household was not a fertile environment for the development of literary interests. McMillan recalled that she was not interested in reading as a child until she accepted a job shelving books at a local Port Huron library at the age of sixteen. There she discovered that African Americans could, and did, write books, often the same books that she was hired to shelve. This was the beginning of a lifelong interest in reading and creating fiction.

TERRY MCMILLAN, shown in a still from an interview. Her novel *Waiting to Exhale*, published in 1992, spent four months on the *New York Times* best-seller list and sold more than 4 million copies. (The History Makers.)

In 1979 McMillan graduated with a bachelor's degree in Journalism from the University of California at Berkeley, where she published her first short story, "The End." She then moved to New York, where she supported herself and her son Solomon, born in 1984, as a word processor while earning an MFA at Columbia University and pursuing her craft at a writing workshop operated by the Harlem Writers Guild. In 1988, McMillan was appointed associate professor at the University of Arizona.

In 1987 McMillan, discouraged by the lack of support given new black authors by white publishing houses, promoted her first book, *Mama*, by directly contacting black organizations and tirelessly giving readings in black bookstores nationwide. The book was a success, in part, because of McMillan's self-promotion and because of word-of-mouth praise for its realistic portrayal of contemporary black women's lives. Based on the struggles of many black single mothers, not unlike her own, who struggled against overwhelming odds, abusive husbands, the welfare system, and low-paying jobs to raise their families with wit, love, and dignity, *Mama* resonated with millions of black readers not served by white publishers.

With her second novel, *Disappearing Acts* (1989), McMillan established herself as a distinctive voice in contemporary black fiction by capturing contemporary urban black male and female relationships. The two main characters, Zora and Franklin, find love by overcoming obstacles with humor, warmth, and a growing respect for each other as individuals. The novel proved to be a success as McMillan's growing number of fans recognized the kind of love story that they could not find elsewhere, one that reflected the strength, tenderness, and love of black relationships.

Waiting to Exhale (1992) exceeded all expectations for contemporary black fiction to "cross over" to the notice of a wider white readership. The novel spent four months on the *New York Times* best-seller list, and sales exceeded four million copies. Continuing her exploration of black male and female relationships, *Waiting to Exhale* is arguably McMillan's most popular, and controversial, book to date. Black men accused the novel of "male bashing." However, McMillan's work tapped into a growing demographic of highly educated, intelligent black career women who put their commitment to family and to each other above unfulfilling romantic attachments. The novel was hailed for its depictions of black female friendship and was translated to the screen in 1995 by McMillan, as screenwriter, to wide acclaim and grosses of over $66 million.

How Stella Got Her Groove Back (1996) continued McMillan's use of autobiographical material as Stella, modeled on McMillan herself, finds love and her groove in Jamaica with a man twenty years her junior after personal loss leaves her emotionally adrift. Again, McMillan hit a nerve with her public in exploring the relationship between an older woman and a younger man within a black context. *A Day Late and A Dollar Short* (2001), a family saga of old hurts, love, and redemption, returned to McMillan's themes concerning the challenges facing the wholeness of black family life. The novel also continued her vibrant depictions of black female bonding and, perhaps in response to criticism of her earlier work, includes strong black male characters.

Although some critics have frowned on McMillan's "unconventional" writing style, it is a style, McMillan counters, that gives her the freedom to accurately portray the diversity of the black community and the African American vernacular in written form. This style has won her critical acclaim from scholars of African American writing and from a growing and very loyal fan base.

McMillan's success has changed life for black women novelists. As *Waiting to Exhale* climbed the best-seller lists in 1992, publishers began signing contracts. A couple of years later, the books started hitting the stands. The results were dramatic. African Americans showed conclusively that they would buy books if offered what they wanted. In 1991, African Americans bought $181 million worth of books, according to the research firm Target Market News. In 1996, they bought $296 million. Terry McMillan can take a great deal of credit for that.

BIBLIOGRAPHY

Leland, John. "How Terry Got Her Groove." *Newsweek*, 29 April 1996.

Martin, Norma. "The 'Exhale' Effect." *Austin American Statesman*, 9 February 1997.

Patrick, Diane. *Terry McMillan: The Unauthorized Biography*. New York: St. Martin's, 1999.

Richards, Paulette. *Terry McMillan: A Critical Companion*. New York: Greenwood, 1999.

—DOLORES V. SISCO

CLAUDIA MCNEIL as Mamie in *Simply Heavenly* by Langston Hughes. The photograph was taken by Carl Van Vechten on 10 June 1957. (Library of Congress.)

McNEIL, CLAUDIA (b. 13 August 1917; d. 25 November 1993), actor. Claudia McNeil had a long and distinguished career in American theater; however, the critically acclaimed actor was perhaps best known for her portrayal of the powerful matriarch in Lorraine Hansberry's award-winning play *A Raisin in the Sun*. McNeil's interpretation of Lena Younger helped make Hansberry's play one of the longest-running Broadway productions by a black playwright.

McNeil was born in Baltimore, Maryland, to Marvin Spencer McNeil and Annie Mae Anderson McNeil. However, marital difficulties led to her parents' divorce just two months before she was born. Her mother, an Apache Indian, decided to move the family to New York where she established herself as a grocery store owner. McNeil revered and admired her mother despite their often-contentious relationship, and credited her mother as the inspiration for her acting career.

When McNeil was twelve years old, her mother became ill and McNeil was put up for adoption. While working for the Heckscher Foundation as a mother's helper, she met the Toppers, a Jewish family who later adopted her and taught her to speak Yiddish. She attended Wadley High School in New York City and, upon graduation, became a licensed librarian. However, she was drawn to singing and had her debut at a Greenwich Village Supper Club, The Black Cat, when she was just sixteen years old.

McNeil married her first husband when she was nineteen, and they had two sons. Her husband and both sons died fighting for the United States in World War II and the Korean War, respectively. Later in life, McNeil remarried, but the union was short-lived, ending in divorce after only two years.

At the age of twenty, with five hundred dollars from the Toppers, McNeil set out to pursue her singing career. She performed at a variety of nightclubs, such as Famous Door, the Onyx, and the Greenwich Village Inn, with her act centering on the works of legendary singer Ethel Waters. McNeil did both radio and vaudeville for a short time. Eventually she toured as a vocalist in *Hot from Harlem* with Bill Bojangles Robinson and the Katherine Dunham dance troupe. After a twenty-five-year singing career, she decided to pursue acting after receiving some encouragement from Ethel Waters. Her first Broadway appearance, at the age of thirty-six, was in 1953, as a replacement in Arthur Miller's *The Crucible*. In 1957, she achieved celebrity status when she played Mamie in Langston Hughes's stage production of *Simply Heavenly*, based on Hughes's *Simple Takes a Wife* and other Simple stories. The following year McNeil played Mary in *Winesburg, Ohio* and made several television appearances. She was featured in an NBC Dupont Show of the Month as Bernice Sadie Brown in Carson McCullers's *Member of the Wedding*.

McNeil was best remembered, however, for her powerful portrayal of Lena Younger in *A Raisin in the Sun*. The play opened in 1959, and was hailed as a watershed in American drama. Set in Chicago, *A Raisin in the Sun* centers on the aspirations of an African American family whose dreams never seem to materialize. Lena Younger, the matriarch, parlays her husband's unfortunate death into an opportunity when she uses his life insurance money to move the family out of the inner city ghettos and into white suburbia. However, the dream is almost shattered by her imprudent son, Walter Lee, when he recklessly loses the money. The play posed important questions about racism, identity, justice, and moral responsibility. McNeil gave 531 show-stopping performances and was applauded for her portrayal of the God-fearing, powerful matriarch. The original cast, including Sidney Poitier, Ruby Dee, and Diana Sands, went on to do the film version of the play, which was directed by Daniel Petrie. The film led to McNeil's Golden Globe nomination in 1961 for best actress in a leading role.

In 1962 McNeil played the role of Mama in Peter S. Feibleman's *Tiger, Tiger Burning Bright*, for which she received a Tony nomination. In 1963, she received an Emmy nomination for her role in an episode of *The Nurses*, "Express Stop from Lenox Avenue." McNeil's career successfully continued on both stage and screen and took her overseas. In England, she received the London Critics Poll Award for best actress for her part in James Baldwin's *The Amen Corner* (1965). During the late 1960s and 1970s, she appeared in numerous plays and films, including *Roll of Thunder, Hear My Cry* (1978), which was based on Mildred Taylor's classic children's book

In 1973 *A Raisin in the Sun* was adapted as a musical, entitled *Raisin*. That musical was revived in 1981 when McNeil agreed to re-create her role. At sixty-six, she retired, and in 1985, she moved into the Actors' Fund Nursing Home in Englewood, New Jersey, where she lived for nine years. At the age of seventy-seven, this star of stage and screen died of complications from diabetes.

BIBLIOGRAPHY

Mapp, Edward. "Claudia McNeil." In *Directory of Blacks in the Performing Arts*. Metuchen, NJ: Scarecrow Press, 1990.

Morton, Carol. "Claudia McNeil-136 Pounds Lighter." *Ebony*, September 1975, 70–75.

Pace, Eric. "Claudia McNeil, 77, an Actress Best Known for 'A Raisin in the Sun.'" *New York Times*, 29 November 1993.

—MONIQUE M. CHISM

McRAE, CARMEN (b. 8 April 1922; d. 10 November 1994), jazz singer. Carmen McRae was one of the leading jazz singers of the twentieth century, taking her rightful place among such acclaimed artists as Billie Holiday, Sarah Vaughan, and Ella Fitzgerald. Although her voice has been consistently compared to Vaughan's and Holiday's, McRae created her own style and sense of rhythm. Reflected in her music was her inclination to tell a story with her lyrics as she forcefully articulated her words through a sharp-edged delivery. She once stated "Every word is important to me, the lyrics of a song I might decide to sing must have something that I can convince you with." In the early years of her career, McRae's voice was higher, softer, and prettier. As years passed, her voice began to mature and become lower and coarser. Critics have described her voice and musical style as seductive and sexy, with the ability to blend tones that ranged from the nasal to the guttural as she produced phrases that seemed effortless.

Carmen McRae was born to Oscar McRae of Costa Rica and Evadne McRae of Jamaica. She grew up in Harlem, where she studied piano as a child. Her parents encouraged her to study classical music but her love for modern pop music was stronger. She told the *New York Post* in 1966 "I'd keep sheet music for pop tunes in among the classical stuff on the piano, as soon as everyone was out of earshot, I let go with the pops." In her late teens McRae met composer and songwriter Irene Kitchings, the former wife of pianist Teddy Wilson. As their friendship developed, Kitchings introduced McRae to the Harlem jazz scene and to some of the most prominent musicians of that time, including bandleader Count Basie, Nat King Cole, Benny Carter, Duke Ellington, and her lifetime idol Billie Holiday, who recorded one of McRae's first songs, "Dream of Life," in 1939.

In the early 1940s McRae became more familiar with the Harlem jazz clubs and ballrooms, frequenting such clubs as Clark Monroe's Uptown House, the Cotton Club, and the

CARMEN MCRAE, one of the leading jazz singers of the twentieth century, created her own style and sense of rhythm and was renowned especially for her eloquent articulation of lyrics. She once remarked, "Every word is important to me." (Photofest.)

most popular, Minton's Playhouse. McRae met jazz drummer Kenny Clarke, who often performed with trumpeter Joe Guy, bassist Nick Finto, and pianist Thelonius Monk at Minton's Playhouse. Clarke and McRae married in Gadsden, Alabama, where Clarke was stationed in the U.S. Army as a technical sergeant, but the marriage ended in divorce.

Unhappy with the restrictions of segregation in the South, McRae decided to leave Alabama. She lived briefly in Washington, DC, where she performed a variety of government jobs, but soon realized that she missed the excitement of the jazz music scene and returned to New York. She worked during the day and performed at night, singing as Carmen Clarke with Benny Carter's band in 1944 and later with Count Basie's band. She also toured and played piano with Mercer Ellington's band, recording her first song, "Pass Me By," in 1946. Ellington's band reportedly dissolved in Chicago while on tour.

McRae remained in Chicago and performed in several night clubs and lounges before returning to New York in the early 1950s. In 1953 she worked as an intermission pianist and singer at Minton's Playhouse in Harlem.

It was not until the mid-1950s that McRae's career began to evolve beyond the New York night club gigs and after-hour joints. The influences of Billie Holiday and Sarah Vaughan became apparent in her style as she began recording as a lead singer for the Decca label. This relationship with the label produced a series of albums that gained national recognition, including some of McRae's most popular works, especially "Torchy" (1955) and "Blue Moon" (1956). McRae was ecstatic when she was voted "best new female singer" in 1954 by *Down Beat* magazine and tied with Ella Fitzgerald for *Metronome* magazine's Singer of the Year Award.

During the next three decades of her career, McRae recorded dozens of albums for various record labels, touring nationally and abroad and earning as much as $20,000 in one week. She toured Canada, Japan, Sweden, and Brazil and performed countless gigs in concert halls and prestigious jazz clubs and at festivals in Las Vegas, Chicago, New York, and other cities. She played at the Newport Jazz Festival in 1965 with Dizzie Gillespie, as well as the Monterey Jazz Festival in 1971. Considered some of her finest pieces of work were her tributes to Billie Holiday (1983), pianist Thelonius Monk (1988), and Sarah Vaughan (1991). In January 1994 McRae was the recipient of the National Endowment of the Arts "American Jazz Masters" award for her contributions to the jazz tradition.

Barry Kernfeld described her musical style best when he stated that she had "an actress's commanding stage presence . . . and a jazz instrumentalist's talent for phrasing. Her cutting, mocking vocal timbre was inimitable, conveying a sound that was, as writer Jack Batten described it, lazy, sexy, kind of autumnal and a little bittersweet."

McRae smoked for many years and suffered respiratory problems, including asthma and bronchitis. She had a stroke in October 1994, lapsed into a coma a month later, and died on 10 November 1994. Her secretary, Jan March, quoted her as saying "I don't want a memorial. I don't want a funeral. I don't want flowers. All I want to be remembered for is my music."

BIBLIOGRAPHY

"Carmen McRae." National Endowment for the Arts American Jazz Masters. http://www.iaje.org/bio.asp?ArtistID=24.

"Carmen McRae Dies—Jazz Singer Was 74." *San Francisco Chronicle*, 12 November 1994.

Gourse, Leslie. *Carmen McRae—Miss Jazz*. New York: Billboard Books, 2001.

Kernfeld, Barry. "Carmen McRae." American National Biography. American National Biography Online. http://www.anb.org/articles/18/18-03454-article.html.

Sachs, Lloyd. "Carmen McRae's Death at 74 Leaves Void in Jazz World." *Chicago Sun Times*, 13 November 1994.

—ROBBIE CLARK

MAHONEY, MARY ELIZA (b. 7 May 1845; d. 4 January 1926), nurse. Mary Eliza Mahoney was born in Dorchester, Massachusetts, to Charles and Mary Jane Stewart Mahoney. On 1 August 1879, she completed a sixteen-month diploma program in nursing at the New England Hospital for Women and Children in Boston, at a time when the institution's charter stipulated that each class include only one black student and one Jewish student.

Mahoney registered with the Nurses Directory at the Massachusetts Medical Library in Boston upon receipt of her diploma. Like the vast majority of new nurses, she entered private-duty nursing. Not until after World War II would the majority of nurses secure staff employment in hospitals, and black nurses would wait even longer for hospital staff appointments.

MARY ELIZA MAHONEY, the first African American professional nurse, c. 1860s. In 1976 she was named to the nursing Hall of Fame. (Schomburg Center for Research in Black Culture, New York Public Library.)

Mahoney was able to secure membership in the Nurses Associated Alumnae of the United States and Canada, organized in 1896 and later renamed the American Nurses' Association (ANA). By the turn of the century, few black nurses were allowed to become members of the ANA. Nurses were required to become members of state nursing associations before they were granted membership in the national organization, and southern associations refused to admit black women.

In 1908 black nurses organized the National Association of Colored Graduate Nurses (NACGN). Mahoney delivered the welcoming address at its first convention in Boston in August 1909. Two years later, the membership honored Mahoney by awarding her life membership in the NACGN and electing her national chaplain, a position that bore the responsibility for the induction of new officers.

In 1911 Mahoney became supervisor of the Howard Orphan Asylum for Black Children in Kings Park, Long Island. She retired in 1922, but continued to participate in and observe the activities of the NACGN until her death.

As a lasting tribute, the NACGN established in 1936 an award in her name to honor distinguished black nurses. When the NACGN merged with the ANA in 1951, the practice of giving the Mary Mahoney Award was preserved. In 1976 Mahoney was named to nursing's Hall of Fame.

See also Nursing.

BIBLIOGRAPHY

Davis, Althea T. *Early Black American Leaders in Nursing: Architects for Integration and Equality*. Boston: Jones and Barlett Publishers, 1999.

Miller, Helen S. *Mary Eliza Mahoney, 1845–1926: America's First Black Professional Nurse*. Atlanta: Wright Publishing Company, 1997.

National Association of Colored Graduate Nurses, Minutes, 1908–1917, 1917–1937, Schomburg Center for Research in Black Culture, New York Public Library.

—DARLENE CLARK HINE

MALONE, ANNIE TURNBO (b. 9 August 1869; d. 10 May 1957), black beauty businesswoman. The dawn of the twentieth century witnessed the materialization of the black beauty culture industry and the emergence of the black female beauty industry mogul. Annie Turnbo Malone, while not as well known as her contemporary, Madam C. J. Walker, pioneered many of the methods and goals of this global enterprise and transformed the role of African American women in business.

Annie Turnbo Malone was a child of the Reconstruction Era. Her father, Robert Turnbo, fought for the Union in the Civil War while her mother, Isabella Cook Turnbo, fled their native Kentucky with their two children. Eventually,

ANNIE TURNBO MALONE. This photograph, dating from 1927, was captioned "A. E. Malone, Manufacturer of Toilet Articles." The practices she implemented became a model for combining business enterprises with racial responsibility. (Moorland-Spingarn Research Center.)

the family reunited in Metropolis, Illinois, and the couple had nine more children. Annie was second youngest. Robert and Isabella Turnbo died while Annie was young, and her elder sisters raised her. After moving to Peoria, Illinois, Annie attended high school, where she acquired a fondness for chemistry, which, combined with her penchant for grooming and styling her sisters' hair, provided the inspiration and ingenuity for her successful journey into the black beauty industry.

In 1900 Malone and her sisters moved to the all-black town of Lovejoy, Illinois, where they rented a building and began marketing their hair and scalp treatments to the local women. It is difficult to determine the exact ingredients Malone used in her preparations; what is certain is that she quickly gained a reputation for rejuvenating and restoring African American women's hair. Malone was so adept that she soon set her sights on a city with a larger black population, St. Louis.

Malone's move to St. Louis was planned to coincide with the excitement and attention surrounding the World's Fair of 1904. Shortly after arriving in the city, she rented a four-room apartment and began making hair and scalp preparations and selling them door-to-door. Malone's presence in St. Louis also coincided with the arrival of Sarah Breedlove, a former washerwoman who had recently migrated to the city from Vicksburg, Mississippi. How Breedlove and Malone first became acquainted is not certain; Malone claims to have given Sarah Breedlove a hair treatment, something that Breedlove never confirmed. What is undeniable is that Breedlove eventually became one of Malone's first sales agents during 1903. In subsequent years, Breedlove, who became known as Madam C. J. Walker, became Malone's primary business rival. Walker began creating her own hair and scalp treatments while working for Malone, and by 1905 realized that St. Louis was not big enough for both of their ambitions. Walker moved to Denver to embark on her own enterprise, which eventually became the successful Walker Manufacturing Company. Based in part on her experience with Walker and to further protect her products from imitation, Malone copyrighted her company in 1906 under the name Poro, the name of a West African spiritual society.

As Malone's company became more successful and expanded to include beauty colleges, her arm reached out to extend the benefits of her enterprise to the members of her race. In 1918 Malone built a massive complex for the Poro Company's headquarters in St. Louis. Heralded as "one of the most unique and most complete institutions in the World," the building was worth more than half-a-million dollars. Malone envisioned the building as more than a testament to the furtherance of her beauty empire and declared, "Poro College is consecrated to the uplift of humanity—Race women in particular." She connected her enterprise not for the promotion of white beauty standards—a marketing strategy used by white-owned beauty companies—but for racial betterment and economic opportunity. At the height of her success, Malone's company had trained more than seventy-five thousand women in the United States, Africa, the Caribbean, and South America. For black women normally relegated to the low pay and drudgery of domestic labor, a job as a Poro sales agent or beauty operator provided a unique opportunity for social and economic advancement.

An avid philanthropist, Malone supported orphanages and religious, social, and civic organizations, and gave generously to educational institutions. In fact, her contribution of $25,000 to the Howard University School of Medicine in the early 1920s was the largest gift given by an African American to an institution of higher learning at that time.

Poor management as well as the failure of Malone's marriage to Aaron Malone led to the downfall of the Poro Company. As early as 1921, the Malones's marriage was souring and with it their business relationship. Named as the president of the Poro Company, Aaron Malone eventually tried to take complete control of Poro by publicly defaming his wife in the black press. After a lengthy legal battle, Annie Malone maintained her company and was granted a divorce in 1927. However, irreparable damage had been inflicted on the company and on Malone's image as a businesswoman. Poro College continued educating women in beauty culture throughout the 1930s and 1940s. But in 1951, due to Malone's inability to pay real estate taxes, the company was seized, and all of its properties and assets were sold.

Though Malone died of a stroke in May 1957 with very little wealth, her philanthropic and entrepreneurial legacy has continued into the early twenty-first century. In St. Louis, an orphanage that she helped to build has been renamed in her honor. Perhaps more significantly, the business practices she implemented have become a model for combining business efforts with racial responsibility.

BIBLIOGRAPHY

Bundles, A'Lelia. *On Her Own Ground: The Life and Times of Madam C.J. Walker.* New York: Scribner Books, 2001.

Peiss, Kathy. *Hope in a Jar: The Making of America's Beauty Culture.* New York: Metropolitan Books, 1998.

Rooks, Noliwe. *Hair Raising: Beauty, Culture, and African American Women.* New Brunswick, NJ: Rutgers University Press, 1996.

—TIFFANY M. GILL

MALONE, VIVIAN. *See* Jones, Vivan Malone.

MALVEAUX, JULIANNE (b. 22 September 1953), economist. Julianne Malveaux refers to herself as the "Mad Economist" because, she says, "you've got to be either angry or crazy . . . to interpret economic data and keep a level head. Some days I want to scream at the bifurcation and trifurcation in this country, the double standards and triple meanings, the way that the rich get richer, the poor, poorer and the rest of us more complacent."

Recognized for her witty, insightful, and passionate commentary on economic and political issues, Malveaux is known as one of the nation's most intellectually progressive economists, authors, lecturers, syndicated columnists, and civic leaders. Her voice demands attention as she argues some of America's most complex social and economic issues with fierceness, conviction and humor. Cornel West described her as "the most provocative, progressive and iconoclastic public intellectual in the country."

JULIANNE MALVEAUX is recognized as an intellectually progressive economist, author, lecturer, syndicated columnist, and civic leader. She is shown here in a still from a video interview. (The History Makers.)

The oldest of five children, Malveaux was born in San Francisco, California, to Warren Malveaux and Proteone Marie Malveaux, a feminist who often encouraged her daughter to take risks, listen to her inner voice, and embrace history and context. Malveaux began writing at an early age; she published her first poem at sixteen in the *Journal of Black Poetry* and in 1973 became *Essence* magazine's first college editor. After studying economics, she earned a bachelor's degree and an MA in 1974 and 1975, respectively, from Boston College and her doctorate in 1980 from MIT. Malveaux worked as an assistant professor of economics from 1980 to 1981 for the New School for Social Research and later joined the staff of San Francisco State University from 1981 to 1985. She continued in academia, teaching Public Policy, Economics, and African American Studies as a visiting scholar and professor from 1985 to 1992 at the University of California at Berkeley.

Malveaux began writing a column for the *San Francisco Sun Reporter* in 1981. Her articles appeared in more than twenty newspapers and magazines nationwide. In 1986, Malveaux co-edited *Slipping through the Cracks: The Status of Black Women.* She was the author of two collections: *Sex, Lies and Stereotypes: Perspectives of a Mad*

Economist (1994) and *Wall Street, Main Street, and the Side Street: A Mad Economist Takes a Stroll* (1999). These works explored issues ranging from poverty, affirmative action, misconstrued images, and untold stories of African American women to welfare reform, black consumerism, and the distorted notion of economic equality. Each column conveyed her opinions and criticism on such issues as affirmative action in the workplace and higher education, where she defended the policy, stating that "affirmative action merely asks employers to look at the applicant pool for workers, to diversify as if by casting a net broader and wider, and to hire equally qualified people from underrepresented groups where possible." She also argues that black economic activity is important, pointing out that $400 billion in the American economy is generated by black consumers, and she says African Americans should use their dollars to influence corporations through collective or selective buying. "I'm a fan of boycotts," she says, as a way "to make sure folks understand that black dollars matter."

In *Unfinished Business: A Democrat and a Republican Take on the Ten Most Important Issues Women Face* (2002), Malveaux and her co-author Deborah Perry describe a 2000 forum that allowed women to come together to discuss economic and political issues. The authors collaborated on this book to share their viewpoints with millions of women who struggled to understand the political and decision-making process. They debated issues of equal pay, education, reproductive rights, and work and welfare reform. In the book, Malveaux criticized the George W. Bush administration's proposal to spend $300 million of public assistance dollars to promote marriage to welfare recipients. She stated, "The fact that children in married households 'on average' do better than those who are not in married households does not mean you can sprinkle magic dust on unmarried parents, hook them up, and expect poverty to magically disappear."

In 2002 Malveaux also co-edited *The Paradox of Loyalty: An African American Response to the War on Terrorism*, a collection of essays written by a talented group of professionals who shared their insights on war, terrorism, and the catastrophe of 11 September 2001. While the attacks on 11 September were horrific and unimaginable, in the book Malveaux criticizes the federal government for funding homeland security and the war on terrorism but neglecting to fund areas such as education and health care. She states, "A war on terrorism abroad is also a war on poor people at home. We're allowing ourselves to use this war to push away from other priorities."

Malveaux has appeared on numerous radio and television programs and has served on the boards of several civic, political, and women's organizations. She was founder, president, and CEO of Last Word Productions, a multimedia company that developed diversity training programs and educational seminars for Fortune 500 companies. Malveaux has inspired, educated, and challenged her audiences with sheer brilliance to think about relevant economic issues.

BIBLIOGRAPHY

"Julianne Malveaux: Biography." Business Makers 1900. The History Makers. http://www.thehistorymakers.com/biography/biography.asp?bioindex=131&category=businessmakers.

Malveaux, Julianne. Biographical information. At http://www.juliannemalveaux.com.

Victor, Dionne. "Economist Explores Roles of Women." *Daily Cougar*, 21 March 2002.

Sanchez, Brenna. "Julianne Malveaux." *Contemporary Black Biography: Profiles from the International Black Community*. Vol. 32. Detroit: Gale, 2002.

"The Latest on Dr. Julianne Malveaux." Hannaian News Community Notes. Hannaian.com, 18 January 2000. http://www.hannaian.com/cblack/malveaux.html.

—ROBBIE CLARK

MARRIAGE. Sociologically speaking, marriage is the cornerstone of the traditional nuclear family. It is the basis for the formation of the family as an institution and as a group that contains both individuals and relationships: husband-wife, parent-child, and sibling-sibling. These relationships indicate bonds, connections, attachments, and obligations between individuals. The bonds and attachments are conjugal and consanguine, with the former based on husband-wife relationships and the latter on blood ties. But both relationships are intrinsically connected. Therefore, many of the responsibilities of the conjugal relationship are connected to the family.

Marriage in the United States is highly valued. More than 90 percent of Americans express a desire to marry at some point in their lives. This reflects the country's Judeo-Christian ethic, which emphasizes marriage as a requirement for heterosexual sex and childbearing. But because of changing attitudes about sexuality and intimate relationships, neither sexuality nor childbearing is confined to marriage.

Black marriage in the United States may be better understood by a historical overview of its African roots, which explains how African marriages were transformed by slavery. An examination of traditional West African marriages forms the basis for understanding the African roots since we are unable to pinpoint the particular countries or tribes from which the slaves came. However, it is commonly agreed by historians and other scholars that the majority of the slaves came from the regions of West Africa that included the Gold Coast, Guinea, and Nigeria. The slaves were from diverse tribes, and marriage was the norm.

African Background

The evidence from historical and ethnographic studies has shown that African slaves came from cultural backgrounds that were diverse, complex, and highly civilized. Contrary to the belief that African slaves were rescued from savagery and the uncivilized, they were forcibly uprooted from long-standing, strong communities and family life that were as viable as that of their European captors. Thus, marriage and family life of West African countries were highly integrated in cultures that had an enduring history, unified by customs, traditions, laws, and rituals. This is implied when the historian John Hope Franklin wrote, "When the Arabs went through West and North Africa in the Seventh Century, they found a civilization that was already thousands of years old." Hence, several African family patterns survived the American experience. They were transformed and modified but never destroyed.

Marriage in Africa was an affair that united not only two people but also two families, which resulted in a network of extended kin. Both the kinship network and the community had a significant influence on the family and a responsibility for its development and well-being. To enter or dissolve marriage required community support. A second feature was the primacy given to consanguine relations (blood ties) over conjugal relations (married pair). A third characteristic was the importance placed on children. Societies were child centered, meaning that children were the responsibility not only of the biological parents but also of the extended family and community. A fourth important feature was role flexibility. Even though roles were gendered, they were interchanged without stigma. Therefore, these men and women came from cultures of well-established family systems, but the marital and family patterns transmitted from those systems were transformed when Africans became slaves in a society in which they had no legal rights. Yet extralegal marriages were consummated through affectionate bonds and procreations that were characteristic of their African cultures. For slaves to have pursued such marital relationships attests to their tenacity, perseverance, and commitment to sustain a black family system.

Marriage and Slavery

A historical, contextual examination and analysis of African American marriages in the United States provides some insight into what Niara Sudarkasa describes as the transformation of African American family structure from Africa to America. This transformational process began in colonial America and is still evident in the United States in the early twenty-first century.

Since the beginning of slavery, marriage has been a challenging experience for black people, especially for women. Slave marriages were extralegal rather than legal unions, meaning that those who entered into these relationships had no legal rights or protection under the law. These marriages were sometimes sanctioned by the slave masters, who would arrange the wedding, but even the most elaborate, solemn, and dignified slave weddings reeked of trouble in the omission of what was the essential Christian message given during the exchange of vows: "Till death do you part." Slaves were aware that this statement was the climax of a wedding ceremony. So instead of this message, the white minister who performed the ceremony would offer a modified statement: "Until death or distance do you part." As one slave explained, slaves knew that these words were not binding. He explained this awareness by the following: "Don't mean nothing lessen you say, 'What God has joined, caint no man pull asunder.' But dey never would say dat. Jus say, 'Now you married.'" On some plantations the slaves did not seek approval for marriage from their masters. Instead, as told by one former slave, those on his plantation who wanted to get married would consult a respected elder in the community, usually a woman who was called *Ant*. These weddings were voluntary and were a mixture of folk traditions and Christian beliefs. However, the ceremony was tendered with the knowledge that any marital bonds created by slaves could be broken by the master. Slaves also voluntarily entered interplantation marriages that were agreed to by slave masters. The slave masters did not like these marriages because this meant time off on Saturdays and Sundays for husbands to visit spouses and children. Despite the tenuous nature of slave marriages, as indicated by the ease with which they could be broken as well as by the physical and sexual brutality imposed by slave masters or overseers, slaves still got married.

Many slaves preferred interplantation marriages because spouses, especially men, could escape witnessing any brutal treatment of their wives and children. They knew they had no authority to protect them. It was painful to observe the cruel treatment of those they loved. However, Eugene Genovese reports that more than a few "Black men braved their wrath by interposing themselves between their wives and the white man who sought to harm them." Black women even fell victim to white lust, but many were able to escape it, because white men knew the women had men who would rather die than stand idly by while their wives were sexually exploited. In some cases men who protected their women got off with a whipping, but in other cases they lost their lives. In view of the risks for protecting their women against white male predators, whether slave masters, overseers, or sons of slave masters, it is amazing that so many black men defended their women. Black women had to caution

"THE BROOMSTICK WEDDING." Mary Ashton Rice Livermore, in *The Story of My Life*, published in 1897, describes how the slave couple jumped over the broomstick into married life. This was a frequent marriage ritual among slaves, whose owners condoned it and might even take part in the ceremony. (University of Virginia, Alderman Library.)

self-control in black men or have them risk their lives. Hence, slaves were able to strengthen each other by recognizing and sometimes accepting the reality that the prevention of such outrages against women carried too high a price. If, for some, submission to such outrages sometimes revealed cowardice, for others it revealed a strength that was greater than most men and women should ever be asked to display.

Such fortitude shown by slave men in the protection of slave women demonstrates commitment to marriage and the community of slave women. Furthermore, this shows the willingness of slave men to sacrifice their lives to stop the sexual exploitation and physical abuse of their women. Marital bonds developed between husbands and wives, despite the tenuous nature of slave marriages.

The affective ties that bound married slaves together were noted everywhere by whites. For example, in the Yamaasee War, fought against the Native Americans, the Virginia Colony offered to send slave men to South Carolina to help suppress the Indians in exchange for a monetary payment and a "Negro woman . . . to be sent in lieu of each man." South Carolina whites rejected the offer because they feared that to take slave wives from their husbands would cause discontent, which might have occasioned a slave revolt. Also, according to Herbert Gutman, in North Carolina slaves were "allowed to plant a sufficient quantity

Letter by Jane Giles

Jane Giles, slave of Margaret Wickliffe Preston of Lexington, ran away while they were on a trip to New York. This letter of 8 February 1854 gives her reasons.

Mrs William Preston

Madam. I take this oppertunity to wright you these few lines to inform you that I am well at this time and I hope you are the same. Dear madam I sopose you wonder why that I left you. Well I will tell you the Reason one Reason was because you Parted me and my housbond as tho we had no feeling and the Next Reason was because you accused me of stealing Money and I was not gilty of it but because I am coulard You sopose that I have not got any feelings I have feelings thank god as well as you and I sopose you feel the Loss of me as much as I do the loss of you. I worked for you when I was with you and dear madam I am working for my Sealf and let me inform you that I Loved my housbond as well as you do yours if I never see him again in this world but I am in hopes to meet him in Haven

I sopose you will call this impedance But I do not I have nothing Against Mr. Preston he treated me well he would not have sent my husbound away had it not been for you and I would have been yet with you. But Never mind Every boddy must have trubble

I Remane Yours

Jane Giles

From the University of Kentucky Special Collections—Preston Papers, Box 49.

of tobacco for their own use and they sold some and purchased linen, bracelets, ribbons, and several toys for their wives and mistresses." Other examples are of wives who lived on different plantations than their husbands, who they saw only periodically. But whenever they were moving away and visitations were no longer possible, wives lamented parting with their husbands, not knowing whether they would ever see them again.

A transformation of the traditional African family had taken place by the 1830s. However, white churches reinforced the African tradition of marital fidelity in the slave quarters by widespread emphasis on the biblical pronouncements against adultery and fornication, while urging submission of wives to husbands. Despite this urging, slave men could no longer exercise the same authority over their slave families as they did in Africa. But even in West African societies, women's independence was recognized. According to John Blassingame, while a man ruled his household, he had to listen to his mate: "If you want peace, give ear to your wife's proposal." The creation and transformation of African familial roles led to "the creation of America's first democratic family in the quarters, where men and women shared authority and responsibility."

Many slaves had masters who did not interfere in family affairs. In such cases, men struggled to gain and retain status in their family and in the slave community. There were several avenues opened to these men in their efforts to gain status. Many of these men assumed roles that were indicative of the traditional husband. For example, some men hunted game to add delicacies to the monotonous diet of cornmeal, fat pork, and molasses. Husbands could also demonstrate their importance by making furniture for their cabins and by building partitions within cabins that housed more than one family. Sometimes with extra money, slave men purchased clothing for their wives and children when adequate clothing was not provided by slave masters. Men also led their wives in undertaking the cultivation of garden plots when masters permitted it.

Through the review of black marriages during slavery, several facts are evident: (1) marriages were extralegal, resulting in insecurity and fragmentation; (2) despite the extralegal nature of the marriages, substantial numbers of slaves lived in intact, stable marriages; (3) slave wives experienced sexual and physical brutality at the hands of or with the approval of slave masters; and (4) blacks already had a tradition, despite its frailty, of marriage and family living at the time of Emancipation. By examining the historical evidence of black marriages after the Emancipation of slaves, there is some understanding of how slavery affected African American marriage and family life from the standpoint of sustaining and changing it.

Marriage after Emancipation

Accounts of marriage after slavery vary. Some observers reported that marriage involved sexual laxity, while others reported that the unions were based on commitment, mutual attraction, love, and faithfulness. When slavery was over, none of the marriages were legal; hence, many of the couples took the necessary steps to legalize them. A legislative approach to legalize marriage was to declare that the relationship formed under slavery was binding. The couples showed evidence of love and affection, and this was sufficient to certify the marriage. However, because a number of men had been separated from one spouse and remarried, some were liable for charges of bigamy and adultery. But if a former slave had more than one partner, he or she had to select one. Even though multiple partners were allowed for slaves, now the free men and women had to conform to the monogamous legal rule, one partner at a time. Those who did not comply with the law were rendered violators and were liable for charges of adultery. In some cases, concessions were given to common-law marriages. But many whites were accustomed to polygamous relationships among slaves; therefore, they ignored violators and refused to investigate reported violations. However, most married couples conformed to the law. The idea of marriage dignified by a minister was appealing to many recently freed slaves, for it implied equality with whites. The desire to legalize marriage was indicated by the efforts to do so and by sentiments expressed.

The number of former slaves who registered marriages shows that the desire was widespread. In Virginia, early fall 1866 was the legal deadline for registering marriages. By the deadline more than 50 percent of former slaves had registered, and 47 percent were registered in North Carolina. A similar pattern of registering marriages occurred in the lower South, such as in Mississippi where the legislature, in November 1865, approved all slave marriages and declared their offspring "legitimate for all purposes." To register a marriage required a fee of twenty-five cents in North Carolina and three dollars in Mississippi. Registering marriages was a conscious decision, but living in a cash-shortage economy resulted in a significant monetary cost to the freedmen.

Some individuals, particularly women, because of a strong desire to register their marriages, used their creative genius to raise the twenty-five cents that was required to buy a "ticket" for registering a marriage. Some people presented commodities for the purchase of the tickets and expressed sentiments that demonstrated their desire. One woman wanted to buy a ticket with six eggs that she brought plus a promise to bring a chicken toward the fall because all " 'spectable folks is to be married, and we's 'spectable." Another woman brought a quart of strawberries to buy the ticket and said, "Me and my old man has lived more than twenty years together; I's proud the children's all had the same father." Still, a third woman brought an empty basket and complained, "Everybody's getting married, and my old man can't get the money." The legalization of black marriages was the first step in the institutionalization of monogamous marriages, which meant a lifelong commitment and birth of children in wedlock.

In addition to difficulties encountered in legalizing slave marriages, former slaves faced other challenges related to social structural realities of the time. Most black marriages were between persons who were poor and had limited education, and most workers were unskilled and nonprofessional. Hence, rural men worked as cash tenants, farm laborers, or sharecroppers, and women were mostly field laborers. This resulted in a majority of husbands and wives having to do physical labor. Those who were tenants or sharecroppers were not far removed from slave status. They were still under the domination of plantation owners, who were often former slave masters. But there were those blacks who sought to completely sever their relationship with former slave owners by moving to urban areas in the South or by making an exodus to the North.

In the urban South, black men were unskilled laborers or service workers, and women were servants or washerwomen. Black men and women, after Emancipation, could exercise some authority over their marriage and family life, but this required human agency in making the transition from slavery to freedom. And their values and survival strategies that were transformed from Africa to slavery helped them to adapt to the new transition, which presented many challenges of socioeconomic status and race.

Many freed blacks went to New York City between 1905 and 1925. Here, marriages and men as heads of households were as important as in the South. This was true despite migration and the changing composition of the African American household, as was reflected in the relative decline of the nuclear household in comparison to the South. More households in New York City than in the South contained subfamilies, augmented by kin other than the nuclear (immediate) family. Additionally, most families took in one or two lodgers. Yet there is no evidence that husbands and fathers were more prevalent in these families than in the South in 1880 and 1900.

Gutman points to historical evidence showing that slaves created and sustained important family and kin sensibilities and ties. The behavioral choices that many made immediately after Emancipation, but before having gained substantive legal rights, were not based on ideas and beliefs learned from owners or in freedom. Such behavior originated from the ways in which African and African American descendants adapted to enslavement, a capacity that was enhanced by the African cultural heritage.

Black Marriages in the Late Twentieth Century

African Americans continued to sustain a monogamous marriage pattern after Emancipation, yet there was a steady decline in the marriage rate from the 1970s through the 1990s. A decline in marriage rates occurred in the general population, but it was more dramatic in the black population. This drop-off is observed from the standpoint of the "ever married" and the "currently married." Moreover, many individuals delayed marriage until their late twenties.

The proportion of women and men "ever married" between 1890 and 1980 began to decline in 1950. A pattern of decline was also noted for the "currently married," but that decrease began a decade earlier in 1950. For black women the highest proportion of "ever married" reached its zenith in 1950 (80.5 percent), and the highest proportion of "currently married" was reached in 1960 (62.5 percent). For men the respective proportions "ever married" and "currently married" were 70.3 percent in 1960 and 64.8 percent in 1950, according to Henry Walker. The proportion of men and women "ever married" showed the sharpest decline from 1970 to 1980 (72.7 percent to 65.5 percent and 66 percent to 58.6 percent, respectively). A corresponding decline was also evident in the same year for the "currently married" men and women (from 53.4 percent in 1970 to 43.5 percent in 1980 and from 57.8 percent to 47.5 percent, respectively).

In 1998 41.8 percent of African Americans were married, compared with 64 percent in 1970 and 51.4 percent in 1980, a decline of 22.2 and 12.6 percent, respectively. In 1991, 44.4 percent of men had never married, and 38.5 percent were "currently married." In the same year, 39.3 percent of women had never married, and 30.9 percent were "currently married." Additionally, census data shows that few African Americans were marrying, and even fewer were staying together after marriage. The latter is reflected in divorce and separation rates. In 1991 8.3 percent of males were divorced and 5.5 percent were separated, whereas 11.4 percent of women were divorced and 7.5 percent were separated. The divorce rates for African Americans in 1980 and 1998 were 8.4 and 17.7 percent, respectively.

African American women have had fewer opportunities for marriage than African American men. In fact, demographers estimate that 25 percent of African American women still never marry, which is three times the rate for white women. There are several possible reasons for this projection. One is an unbalanced sex ratio, caused by several factors: black male death rate (both natural and homicidal), incarcerated males, homosexual males, and interracial marriages of black males. Both of the latter factors represent a small percentage of the imbalanced sex ratio. However, every factor that reduces the available African American male pool further undermines African American women's chances to marry. After examining black marriage trends, it is clear that marriage for African Americans was more difficult in the early part of the twenty-first century, especially for women. However, while opportunities for marriage have declined, African Americans, like the general population, still desire to marry, and for those who marry, research evidence shows that they derive benefits.

Black family research that has given most attention to primary relations or expressive functions has investigated primary/affective relations, which include marital interaction patterns, decision making, marital happiness, and marital disagreement. The results generally show husbands and wives to have relationships that could be classified as "normal" or "healthy" Research investigating husband-wife relations shows that African American spouses, the same as white spouses, seek "primary relations" or expressive gratification from marriage: someone to do things with (companionship), someone to love (physical affection), and someone to talk to (empathy). These primary relations can also be labeled "affiliative," "cathectic," and "cognitive gratifications."

Husbands and wives considered marital interaction goals "highly important." The goal most highly valued was to be a good spouse. It was slightly more important for wives (94.9 percent) than for husbands (92.1 percent). There was consistency between the marital interaction goals and chances and successes in achieving them. Even where there were inconsistencies, most of them were in a positive direction, meaning chances and successes for achieving goals exceeded the value placed on them. Only a small proportion of the inconsistency was negative, meaning that the women's chances and successes for achieving the goals were less than the value they placed on them.

When husbands and wives were asked to evaluate companionship, physical affection, and empathy, a majority of them replied "very good." The pattern for all three primary husband-wife interactions among blacks was consistent from the standpoint of husbands perceiving the gratifications in more positive terms than wives. Although black men and women reported a significant level of marital happiness, when married men and women were compared, men reported more happiness or satisfaction than women.

As another component of marital relations, disagreements about money, leisure (companionship), and sex were reported most frequently, but the most reported disagreement was over leisure. Disagreement or discord is inevitable and is not necessarily dysfunctional. In fact, arguments or disagreements have a functional nature; they serve to "clear the air" and to release tensions and emotions that might otherwise remain dangerously suppressed. Moreover, disagreement for some married couples can be stimulating and enjoyable. The primary or expressive gratifications are what black women seek in marriage; however, when compared with husbands, wives perceive these gratifications in less positive terms. Differences in these perceptions can be explained by differences in gender socialization. Traditionally, females have invested more in marriage than males. They have been socialized to focus on marriage as their central life interest, especially in terms of expressive gratifications. Men, on the other hand, desire these goals, but their central life interest is not as much the family as production, as in employment.

Assessment

It is evident that the conjugal relationship has a long-standing history among African Americans that began in

Africa and has been sustained to the early twenty-first century. However, marriage has become more difficult to achieve. The decline of available mates for African American women has had a critical effect on African American families. Traditionally, marriage was the cornerstone for the formation of two-parent families. In the beginning of the twenty-first century and beyond, society can expect increasing numbers of female-headed families with concomitant consequences. Hence, more resources will be needed to supplement these families, many of which live in poverty.

BIBLIOGRAPHY

Baca Zinn, Maxine, and D. Stanley Eitzen. *Diversity in Families*. 6th ed. Boston: Allyn and Bacon, 2002. A text that treats family diversity as the norm by showing how race, class, gender, and sexuality produce a variety of familial structures and relationships. The text analyzes families as social forces within societies, rather than as "building blocks" of societies. The authors' main goal is to demystify and demythologize the family. This is done through exposing long-standing myths, stereotypes, and dogmas.

Berlin, Ira, Marc Favreau, and Steven F. Miller, eds. *Remembering Slavery: African Americans Talk about Their Personal Experiences of Slavery and Freedom*. New York: New Press, 1998. A compilation of personal experiences of slavery and freedom. It brings together the diversity and commonalities as told by former slaves and their descendants. The narratives provide knowledge that for many years was ignored and disdained by many white scholars and historians. The former slaves described the conditions they faced, their oppressions, and their resistance alongside the day-to-day violence inflicted on the young and old.

Billingsley, Andrew. *Black Families in White America*. New York: Simon and Schuster, 1968. A rational analysis of the history, structure, aspirations, and problems of black families. It is a refutation of the long-standing pathological image of black families. The author examines the diversity of black family structure by employing a social system approach and shows how family structure, other than the two-parent family, functions in nonpathological ways.

Billingsley, Andrew. *Climbing Jacob's Ladder: The Enduring Legacy of African-American Families*. New York: Simon and Schuster, 1992. A study of black families that expands our knowledge about the challenges and successes that they have endured historically and face in the future. It sheds light on the strengths and vitality of black families.

Blassingame, John W. *The Slave Community: Plantation Life in the Antebellum South*. rev. and enlarged ed. New York: Oxford University Press, 1979. A history of the slave community that describes slavery as it must have been for the insiders. It provides a good account of the human realities of slavery, including the struggles and resiliency of black families in sustaining family life, even though it was protracted.

Blood, Robert O., Jr., and Donald M. Wolfe. *Husbands and Wives: The Dynamics of Married Living*. Westport, CT: Greenwood Press, 1978. A study of husband-and-wife relationships, including marital satisfaction, disagreement, and decision making. It compares black and white spouses and shows what variables are associated with the outcomes of these relationships.

Broman, Clifford. "Satisfaction among Blacks: The Significance of Marriage and Parenthood." *Journal of Marriage and Family* 30 (February 1988): 45–51. A study based on data from a national representative survey that finds both marital and parental status have important effects on life satisfaction of blacks. Marital status was found to interact with age, education, and rural residence to predict life satisfaction.

Dornbusch, Sanford M., and Myra H. Stober, eds. *Feminism, Children, and the New Families*. New York: Guilford Press, 1988. A compendium of insights for understanding the realities of the changing American family as reflected in the expanding roles of women, which shows that women's goals are in harmony with the interests of children and are seldom in conflict with men.

Genovese, Eugene D. *Roll, Jordan, Roll: The World the Slaves Made*. New York: Vintage Books, 1976. An historical examination of the slave life of African Americans as they struggled to survive spiritually as well as physically "to make a livable world for themselves and their children" under the most limited living space and under the harshest adverse conditions. The author makes note of the fact that even though the slaves laid a foundation for a separate black national culture, they greatly enriched the American culture as a whole. The study reveals a lot about family and married life that enhances our present understanding of black families.

Gutman, Herbert G. *The Black Family in Slavery and Freedom, 1750–1925*. New York: Vintage, 1977. Traces the black family from slavery through freedom, challenging the traditional view that slavery destroyed it. He argues persuasively that neither the savagery of slavery nor the chaos of Reconstruction could sever the relationships between husbands and wives or parents and children. Gutman found that two-parent households were the norm during slavery and even after Emancipation, a finding that dispels a long-standing myth.

McAdoo, Harriette. "African American Families." In *Ethnic Families in America: Patterns and Variations*, edited by Charles H. Mindel, Robert W. Habenstein, and Roosevelt Wright Jr. Upper Saddle River, NJ: Prentice Hall, 1998. An overview of the history, culture, and diverse family life of African Americans. It focuses on the tragedies of history, the achievements, and the problems that persist. Many of the families are resilient, having overcome many life-threatening and often overwhelming barriers, yet the author explains that many African American families are in trouble.

Myers, Lena Wright. *Black Women: Do They Cope Better?* Englewood Cliffs, NJ: Prentice Hall, 1980. A study of four hundred black women, showing how they maintain positive self-images while coping with obstacles of race and gender. It describes the effective coping strategies the women may have developed in these regards.

Rutledge, Essie Manuel. "Husband and Wife Relationships of Black Men and Women." In *Black Marriage and Family Therapy*, edited by Constance E. Obudho. Westport, CT: Greenwood Press, 1983. A comparative, descriptive study of the marital relations of black men (252) and women (256). The analysis is an examination of three categorical variables—marital interaction, marital happiness, and marital disagreement—resulting in insights into the attitudes and perceptions that these women and men have about their marriages.

Rutledge, Essie Manuel. "Marital and Family Relations of Black Women." PhD diss., University of Michigan, Ann Arbor, 1974. A descriptive and analytical study of 256 black women, married and living with their spouses. Various aspects of marital and family (parent-child) relations of black women are examined. Some of these include marital happiness, marital interaction goals, marital disagreement and instability, affective relations toward spouse and children, traditional and modern attitudes toward child-rearing goals, and parental satisfaction.

Rutledge, Essie Manuel. "Marital Interaction Goals of Black Women: Strengths and Effects." In *The Black Woman*, edited by LaFrances Rodgers-Rose. Beverly Hills, CA: Sage, 1980. A study of 256 black women that analyzes "strengths" on the basis of marital interaction goals and examines factors that seem to have the greatest impact or influence on these goals. These include extrafamilial activities, degree of general happiness, and education.

Scanzoni, John H. *The Black Family in Modern Society*. Boston: Allyn and Bacon, 1971. A pioneering work that concerns the majority of black families in which fathers are present, children are "legitimate," and middle-class stability was achieved. The author makes clear the inseparable link between economic resources and family structure.

Sudarkasa, Niara. "African American Families and Family Values." In *Black Families*, 3rd ed., edited by Harriette Pipes McAdoo. Thousand Oaks, CA: Sage, 1997. Examines African family structures, values, and historical and socioeconomic influences on African American families. The author shows that survival of African culture has persisted in African American families.

Zollar, Creighton, Ann Williams, and J. Sherwood Williams. "The Contribution of Marriage to the Life Satisfaction of Black Adults." *Journal of Marriage and Family* 49 (February 1987): 87–92. From combined data based on two national surveys, an examination of the effect of marital status on general or global happiness of black adults. The authors report that levels of happiness are higher among married than nonmarried persons and that marital happiness and age are significant predictors of general or global happiness.

—ESSIE MANUEL RUTLEDGE

MARSHALL, PAULE (b. 9 April 1929), writer. From the beginning of her literary career, Paule Marshall consistently addressed issues created by the cultural divergence and convergence of West Indians and African Americans. Her thematic range, however, gradually expanded to include all peoples of African descent. What is perhaps most impressive, in her novels especially, is her reconstruction of history through myth. Myth is used to identify and analyze the sociopolitical, economic, and psychological effect of colonization on both the powerless and the powerful. Marshall's work not only provides discursive models of resistance and change, but also augurs possibilities for a future world that honors cultural differences and celebrates the human capacity to triumph.

A Portrait of the Artist

Marshall, nee Valenza Pauline Burke, was born to Ada and Samuel Burke, emigrants from Barbados. She grew up in Bedford-Stuyvesant, a tightly structured West Indian-American community in Brooklyn, New York, listening to stories about a home she had never seen. Her visit to the island when she was nine years old may have made her understand the value of her Barbadian ethnicity as different from her African American identity. But it was not until she began to write serious fiction that a distinct cultural pattern began to emerge. She also began to focus on black female characters as subjects and preservers of cultural practices, the origins of which can be traced to Central and Western Africa.

A student of social work at Hunter College, Marshall married psychologist Kenneth Marshall in 1950. She then transferred to Brooklyn College, where she changed her

PAULE MARSHALL, photographed by Edmund Edwards. Her writing explores many aspects of the African diaspora. (Austin/Thompson Collection, by permission of Schomburg Center for Research in Black Culture, New York Public Library.)

major to English literature and graduated Phi Beta Kappa in 1953. In 1959, she gave birth to her only child, Evan-Keith Marshall. Divorced in 1963, she wed Nourry Menard, a Haitian businessman, in 1970.

Marshall's initial forays into fiction writing came with a number of short vignettes, usually composed at the end of her day as a staff writer and researcher for *Our World*, a small black magazine published in New York City. From these exercises came her first published short story, "The Valley Between" (1954). Her subsequent work included *Brown Girl, Brownstones* (1959), *Soul Clap Hands and Sing* (1961), "Reena" (1962), "Some Get Wasted" (1964), "To Da-duh: In Memoriam" (1967), *The Chosen Place, the Timeless People* (1969), *Praisesong for the Widow* (1983), *Daughters* (1991), and *The Fisher King* (2000). Her early short stories, along with the novella, "Merle," were reprinted in her collection *Reena and Other Stories* (1983). This collection included Marshall's seminal essay, "The

Making of a Writer: From the Poet's in the Kitchen." Originally appearing in the *New York Times Book Review* in 1983, this important essay paid tribute to Marshall's West Indian mother and female kinfolk who passed on to her the power of the spoken word, thus laying the foundation for the artist's unique literary voice. Another, earlier essay on her craft, "Shaping the World of My Art," appeared in *New Letters* in 1973.

Marshall was also a teacher. Having taught at a number of noteworthy institutions within the United States, she later divided her time as a professor of English and creative writing at Virginia Commonwealth University and New York University. She received several important awards, including the Guggenheim Fellowship, the Rosenthal Award, an American Book Award, the New York State Governor's Award for Literature, the John Dos Passos Award for Literature, and the John D. and Catherine T. MacArthur Fellowship.

Marshall's emphasis on female characters and the inextricable link between race and gender began as early as 1954 with the publication of "The Valley Between." Her only short story to feature white characters exclusively, this piece not only describes the nature of gender oppression in marriage, but also the woman's compliance, albeit with submerged anger and resentment. In this way, the story suggests the development of female consciousness, a subject which nearly a quarter of a century later would dominate critical thought. It also represented the artist's challenge to American norms and values as the first step toward exploring the distinction between ethnicity and culture.

"Reena," "Some Get Wasted," and "To Da-duh: In Memoriam"—all written during the 1960s—are reflections of the political and cultural fervor of the period. Through the various settings of these stories, however, and with her masterful use of West Indian and African American dialects, Marshall created a panoramic view of her multicultural society. From the worlds of urban, West Indian-American women who gather at a wake to discuss what it means to be a black woman in America, to the underground scenes of African American teenage boys engaged in gang warfare, to the island of Barbados where the narrator reminisces about a childhood visit with her grandmother, Marshall focuses on themes of loss and dislocation. These short stories reflect the author's search for reconciliation between her various identities. Marshall increasingly relied on African images to suggest that, in spite of cultural differences, a value system originating in the Motherland remained a daunting influence.

The Novels

Brown Girl, Brownstones explores the coming of age of a young girl as her family struggles for survival in a black immigrant community. In this highly acclaimed first novel, Marshall paid tribute to her West Indian heritage, particularly in her treatment of women as oral transmitters of a distinctive culture. But through her compassionate portrayal of several complex male and female characters, Marshall showed how individual development is inseparable from the development of the collective body.

As its title suggests, architectural imagery cements this novel together. Beyond the coveted brownstones in Brooklyn, New York, is the "glitter and tumult" of city life. But Marshall also engaged her artistic imagination with the island of Barbados. In both locales, we experience fluctuating tensions that underscore problems associated with the "American Dream" and the "Dream of the Return." As one critic has said, the question becomes not where to live, but how. Divided between love for her father and respect for her mother, the protagonist resolves to journey to Barbados in the hope of defining herself more clearly within a culturally diverse population.

Soul Clap Hands and Sing is, in fact, a collection of four novellas, the titles of which indicate their settings: "Brooklyn," Barbados," "British Guiana," and "Brazil." With the exception of "Brooklyn," whose major character is Jewish, Marshall focused primarily on elderly, black male characters whose colonized status brings about confusion and alienation from indigenous customs and beliefs. Contributing to their long and unhappy lives are the psychic and social forces that lead to their selfish quests for money and prestige. At a moment of truth, they all reach out for love, only to find that their conversion comes too late. Marshall suggested in this collection that, in order to transform human suffering into compassion and responsible behavior, one must first take the difficult step of honestly confronting one's values.

The Chosen Place, the Timeless People, an epic novel, considers the development and perpetuation of colonialism on a fictive Caribbean island. Bringing together the Jew, the West Indian, and the White Anglo Protestant—all with their separate and complicated histories—Marshall illustrated how particularized historical and social limitations influence human relationships and national economies. Contemporary world politics play an important role in a plot that involves American assistance to an underdeveloped country. Within this plot, however, is a series of other considerations, including the celebration of Carnival, hetero-homosexual relationships, conflict between black and white women, and more. Judeo-Christian imagery, as well as the multiple significations of the sea, come to symbolize cleansing and renewal. In this masterful novel, Marshall evoked a global consideration of the two themes central to her artistic vision: "the importance of truly confronting the past, both in personal and historical terms, and the necessity of reversing the present order."

Praisesong for the Widow refers to a traditional heroic poem recited or sung at various celebrations in Africa, as well as to religious songs commonly used by African American congregations. In Marshall's hands, it further announced special tribute to an elderly, African American, middle-class widow who, having escaped poverty, undertakes a yearly vacation cruise. Suddenly she is barraged with dreams and memories of her past as she undergoes a harrowing odyssey. It becomes, in short, a subconscious then conscious search to regain her lost identity. Marshall interspersed cultural parallels between the Gullah people of South Carolina and the peoples of Haiti, Martinique, Grenada, and Carriacou. She included lyrics and lines from African American songs and poems to specify the widow's particular cultural identity. But Marshall was equally concerned with ways in which upwardly mobile blacks could fend off the debilitating effects of American materialism, cautioning that people of African descent must revere and nurture their cultural groundings and instill that lesson in the generations to come.

In *Daughters*, Marshall went beyond the biological connections between mother and child to include sisters and friends, "other mothers," and the "other woman." Primarily the compelling story of a father-daughter relationship, the novel also concerns the spread of Western imperialism in impoverished nations, as well as the devastating effects of capitalism on America's poor and disenfranchised. A product of both the Caribbean and American worlds, the major character struggles with political and familial allegiances, even as she attempts to understand the choices that the women in her life have made. This immensely complex novel ultimately reveals the transformation of conventional female identities that, while culturally focused, become self-defined and ever-evolving.

Both stylistically and thematically, jazz music resounds throughout the short, dense novel *The Fisher King*. Female characters continue to be important to the development of the storyline, as do adult men, but it is an eight-year-old boy who shapes our final response to this fascinating tale. Marshall allowed only glimpses of the West Indian dialect she so lovingly illustrated in *Brown Girl, Brownstones*. In this novel, she made use of French phrases to create the backdrop for the story of a jazz pianist who, because of his mother's disapproval and the racial prejudice in America, expatriates to Paris. Marshall moved her people from Brooklyn to the antebellum American South to the Paris of the 1940s and back again to Brooklyn to create variations on a single motif: the understandable but misguided efforts of transplanted black families who, in striving to achieve the American Dream, destroy family bonds and thwart individual ambitions.

The story at hand stretches across four generations to reveal the several intertwining relationships that lead to the life of the child who, with his "surrogate" mother, has lived in Paris under impoverished conditions. With a trip financed by an estranged uncle, the boy and his mother travel to Brooklyn to attend a memorial concert honoring the musical genius of his grandfather. A product of the still feuding families, the boy is in a position to intervene as only an innocent child might. We are left with the hope for the healing of frictions between families, disparate cultures, and future generations. Through the boy, especially, we see the redemptive power of love. Just as importantly, we acknowledge an opportunity for those who remain to support the creative artist the child promises to become.

See also Fiction.

BIBLIOGRAPHY

Busia, Abena P. A. "What Is Your Nation? Reconnecting Africa and Her Diaspora through Paule Marshall's *Praisesong for the Widow*." In *Changing Our Own Words: Essays On Criticism, Theory and Writing by Black Women*, edited by Cheryl A. Wall. New Brunswick, NJ: Rutgers University Press, 1989: 196–211.

Christian, Barbara. *Black Feminist Criticism: Perspectives on Black Women Writers*. New York: Pergamon Press, 1985.

Christian, Barbara. *Black Women Novelists: The Development of a Tradition 1892–1976*. Westport, CT: Greenwood Press, 1980.

DeLamotte, Eugenia C. *Places of Silence, Journeys of Freedom: The Fiction of Paule Marshall*. Philadelphia: University of Pennsylvania Press, 1998.

Denniston, Dorothy Hamer. *The Fiction of Paule Marshall: Reconstructions of History, Culture and Gender*. Knoxville: University of Tennessee Press, 1995. Knoxville: University of Tennessee Press, 1995.

Pettis, Joyce. *Toward Wholeness in Paule Marshall's Fiction*. Charlottesville: University of Virginia Press, 1995.

Spillers, Hortense J. "Chosen Place, Timeless People: Some Figurations on the New World." In *Conjuring: Black Women, Fiction and Literary Tradition*, edited by Marjorie Pryse and Hortense J. Spillers. Bloomington: Indiana University Press, 1985: 151–175.

—DOROTHY HAMER DENNISTON

MARTIN, ROBERTA EVELYN

MARTIN, ROBERTA EVELYN (b. 12 February 1907; d. 18 January 1969), gospel singer, pianist, composer, and publisher. Roberta Evelyn Martin was one of six children born to William and Anna Winston in Helena, Arkansas. She began taking piano lessons from her oldest brother's wife at the age of six, at which time she played the piano for the local Sunday school. When she was eight, the family moved to Cairo, Illinois, and later to Chicago. Roberta graduated from Wendell Phillips High School, where she studied piano with the choral director, Mildred Bryant Jones. While preparing for a career as a concert pianist, she accepted her first church position as pianist for the Young People's Choir at Ebenezer Baptist Church.

Martin initially was not attracted to the new gospel music being sung in Sanctified churches. In 1932, when

Thomas Dorsey and Theodore R. Frye organized one of the first gospel choirs at Chicago's Pilgrim Baptist Church, Martin was recruited as pianist. However, in 1933, after she heard the Bertha Wise Singers of Georgia, she adopted the Wise gospel piano style and, with the help of Frye, organized a group of male singers, first called the Martin-Frye Singers. The members were Willie Webb, Robert Anderson, Eugene Smith, and Narsalus McKissick. In 1935 she severed her relationship with Frye and renamed the group the Roberta Martin Singers. In the 1940s Martin added female singers Delois Barrett Campbell and Bessie Folk and refined the "Roberta Martin gospel style," one marked more by the potential of gospel than by its tradition, since she cultivated the well-modulated voice, as opposed to the encumbered, raspy tone so often associated with gospel. Martin eschewed the low bass voice, instead creating a vocal harmony of soprano, alto, tenor, and high baritone. She favored the aggressive rather than the passive lead, supported by background voices that more often hummed a response than repeated the lyrics of the lead, thereby placing more emphasis on the lyrics and the leader, and she created a gospel piano style marked more by nuance and refinement than by virtuosity and flamboyance.

In 1939 Martin opened her publishing firm, the Roberta Martin Studio of Music, and one of her first successes came in 1941 with the publication of "He Knows How Much We Can Bear" by Phyllis Hall. She composed her first gospel song, "Try Jesus, He Satisfies," in 1943. Before her death she had composed over one hundred songs under her own name and that of Fay Brown. Among her best-known compositions, in addition to "Try Jesus," are "God Is Still on the Throne" (1959), "No Other Help I Know" (1961), "Let It Be" (1959), and "Teach Me Lord" (1963). Less concerned with publishing her own compositions than those of other composers, her firm published compositions by James Cleveland, Alex Bradford, Lucy Matthews, Sammy Lewis, Kenneth Woods, and Dorothy Norwood. Her most famous publication was her theme song, "Only a Look" by Anna Shepherd.

Martin began recording in the late 1930s, and during her career earned six gold records for selling a million copies of a song or an album. She received gold records for the songs "Only a Look" and "Old Ship of Zion" on the Apollo label and "Grace," "God Specializes," "God Is Still on the Throne," and "I'm So Grateful" on the Savoy label. Adamant that her name never appear on a marquee, she refused engagements at New York's Apollo Theatre and Las Vegas night clubs, though the Roberta Martin Singers appeared in almost every other gospel venue. From the huge tents of New York's Reverend A. A. Childs, to the small churches of Cocoa, Florida, to the elegant auditoriums of Los Angeles, to the domed cathedrals of Italy, where they were invited to perform at the Spoleto Festival by its creator, Gian Carlo Menotti, in 1963, the Roberta Martin Singers carried their gospel message throughout the world for over thirty-five years. Other singers associated with the group include Archie Dennis, Sadie Durrah, Gloria Griffin, Myrtle Jackson, Romance Watson, Louise McCord, Myrtle Scott, Delores Taliaferro (Della Reese), and James Lawrence. Roberta Martin was honored by a colloquium and concert at the Smithsonian Institution in 1982. In 1997, along with Mahalia Jackson, Clara Ward, and Sister Rosetta Tharpe, Martin was given a postage stamp by the United States Postal Service in a series commemorating African American gospel artists.

BIBLIOGRAPHY

Boyer, Horace Clarence. "Black Gospel Music." In *The New Grove Dictionary of American Music*, edited by H. Wiley Hitchcock and Stanley Sadie. New York: Grove's Dictionaries of Music, 1986.

Heilbut, Anthony. *The Gospel Sound—Good News and Bad Times*. New York: Limelight Editions, 1985.

Jackson, Irene V. "Afro-American Gospel Music and Its Social Setting with Special Attention to Roberta Martin." PhD diss., Wesleyan University, Middletown, CT, 1974.

Williams-Jones, Pearl. "Roberta Martin: Spirit of an Era." In *Roberta Martin and the Roberta Martin Singers: The Legacy and the Music*, edited by Bernice Johnson Reagon and Linn Shapiro. Washington, DC: Smithsonian Institution Press, 1982.

—HORACE CLARENCE BOYER

MARYLAND FREEDOM UNION.

On 9 February 1966, some twenty black women, working as nurses' aides, housekeepers, and kitchen staff, walked off their jobs at Lincoln Nursing Home in Baltimore, Maryland. They called field secretaries from the Congress of Racial Equality (CORE) with whom they had met the previous week, and told them that Lincoln was "on strike," that the workers had named their union "Maryland Freedom Local No. 1," and that the CORE organizers had better come down to Lincoln Nursing Home immediately to show the workers how to "run a proper picket line." The workers, who made as little as twenty-five cents an hour and worked up to seventy-two hours a week, became the nucleus of what they called a "new kind of union," the Maryland Freedom Union (MFU).

The concept of a "freedom union" of poverty-wage workers had been advanced by CORE staff frustrated with failed efforts to assist black workers in struggles for union rights and benefits. Convinced that the American Federation of Labor and Congress of Industrial Organizations (AFL-CIO) unions were not interested in organizing such workers, and exhilarated by the success of the Student Nonviolent Coordinating Committee's (SNCC) 1965 Mississippi Freedom Labor Union project, CORE selected Baltimore as the site of its own freedom union experiment.

Black women workers at two other nursing homes soon joined the Lincoln Nursing Home strikers. Meeting jointly, they elected Vivian Jones, a nurses' aide at Bolton Hill Nursing Home, as MFU president, and Ola Mae Johnson, an aide at Lincoln, as secretary. The union members, with no prior public speaking experience, spoke to church groups, student meetings, and outdoor rallies to explain the strike and to appeal for funds.

Together with CORE members and supporters from local churches and schools, they picketed the suburban homes of nursing home owners and marched on city hall. By March 1966, they created a union study group on black and labor history, reading a history of black struggles, *American Civilization on Trial* (1963), and inviting its author, political philosopher Raya Dunayevskaya, to lecture at the MFU's Freedom House. Dunayevskaya's suggestion that the workers view themselves as "self-developing thinkers" made an impact.

After completing a covert study of retail stores along the mall shopping streets of the West and East Baltimore ghettos, the MFU opened an organizing drive among retail workers there. For the campaign, MFU President Vivian Jones designed a large button showing two black hands breaking a chain and the union slogan, "Breaking Free at Last." Thousands of the buttons, distributed in the black community, helped garner support for an MFU plan that any store they picketed was to be boycotted by black shoppers. The boycotts proved effective, and MFU strikers succeeded in winning union contracts at three of the largest retail chain stores in the ghettos by August 1966.

The campaigns aroused opposition from both merchants' associations and AFL-CIO unions. The unions accused the MFU of organizing in direct competition with them. Walter Reuther, then head of the AFL-CIO's Industrial Union Department, complained to Floyd McKissick, national director of CORE, about CORE becoming a union. McKissick, citing CORE's deep financial crisis, soon severed formal ties with the MFU.

Later MFU campaigns included food stores, hospitals, and a print shop, but its momentum slowed under the impact of tight finances and the ideological crises afflicting civil rights organizations in the late 1960s. The inner-city stores and nursing homes organized by the MFU closed in the early 1970s, victims of economic decline or neighborhood gentrification.

While it flourished, the MFU's membership, nearly all black and 90 percent women, and many of them recently arrived from the rural South, created a union quite different from the typical AFL-CIO affiliate. What drew so many of these workers to the MFU was not only that it was a union willing to accept them as members. It was that this organization called itself a *freedom* union and sought to organize low-wage workplaces as an integral part of a movement to transform the whole of American society. As a forerunner of both the black caucuses within established unions and black feminist critiques of civil rights organizations, the Maryland Freedom Union was a unique learning experience.

BIBLIOGRAPHY

Congress of Racial Equality papers, 1941–1967. State Historical Society of Wisconsin, Madison.

Flug, Michael. "Organized Labor and the Civil Rights Movement of the 1960s: The Case of the Maryland Freedom Union." *Labor History* (Summer 1990).

Johnson, Ola. "Low-Paid Workers Win Fight for Union." *News and Letters* (August–September 1966).

Meier, August, and Elliott Rudwick. *CORE: A Study in the Civil Rights Movement, 1942–1967.* Urbana: University of Illinois Press, 1973.

Raya Dunayevskaya Collection. Archives of Labor and Urban Affairs, Wayne State University, Detroit, MI, 1969.

—MICHAEL FLUG

MASON, VIVIAN CARTER (b. 10 February 1900; d. 10 May 1982), activist, clubwoman. In her many roles as a clubwoman, social worker, and social activist, Vivian Carter Mason lived up to her words. The daughter of a Methodist minister, George Cook Carter, and Florence Williams Carter, a music teacher, she credited her parents with instilling values that inspired her social concerns.

Born in Wilkes-Barre, Pennsylvania, Vivian Carter received her early education in the public schools of Auburn, New York, and graduated from the University of Chicago, where she studied political economy and social welfare. She later pursued graduate course work at Fordham University and at New York University.

While a student at the University of Chicago, Vivian Carter met her future husband, William T. Mason, a native of Trinidad, West Indies. They married in Brooklyn, New York, where Vivian Carter Mason worked as a Young Women's Christian Association (YWCA) program director. Their only child, William T. Mason Jr., was born in 1926 in Norfolk, Virginia, where his father established a lucrative real estate and insurance business.

Unwilling to place her son in poorly equipped schools in segregated Norfolk, Mason moved with her son to New York City in 1931. In New York, she worked her way through the ranks to establish herself professionally as the first black woman administrator in the city's Department of Welfare. She also gained prominence in a number of local and national organizations. A member of the National Association for the Advancement of Colored People (NAACP), Mason sat on the national board of the YWCA and on the executive board of the National Council of Negro Women (NCNW). She also founded the Committee of 100 Women, an organization that sent poor New York City children to summer camp.

VIVIAN CARTER MASON fulfilled many roles as a club woman, social worker, and social activist. She is shown here (second row, left) with Mary McLeod Bethune (first row, center), Dorothy Height (second row, third from left), and others at Bethune-Cookman College in Daytona Beach, Florida, c. 1950s. (National Park Service, Mary McLeod Bethune Council House National Historic Site. Beach Photo Service, photographer.)

In the mid-1940s, Mason returned to Norfolk, where she continued to devote herself to social and political reform. She represented the NCNW at the inaugural meeting of the International Women's Democratic Federation (IWDF) in Paris in 1945. She served on the executive board of the IWDF and as vice president of its American affiliate, the Congress of American Women. From 1949 to 1953, Mason served as president of the Norfolk chapter of the NCNW and founded the Norfolk Women's Council for Interracial Cooperation. In 1953, she was elected to the first of two terms as president of the NCNW. During her term of office, she steered the council through the tumultuous years following the Supreme Court's historic ruling in *Brown v. Board of Education*. As the organization's leader, Mason emphasized interracial coalition building and support for grassroots efforts to bring about racial justice.

Following her tenure as NCNW president, Mason turned her attention again to local politics. She urged women to become involved. "We have to educate women to realize that they have a right to share in the legislative process," she said. She challenged women not only to vote but also to run for office themselves. As she put it, "any governing body is better for having women on it." She led the way. In 1968, she was the only black woman on Virginia's Democratic central committee.

Long an outspoken critic of local school administration, Mason was nonetheless appointed to the Norfolk City School Board in 1971, becoming the first black woman to serve on the board. In 1971, Virginia Press Women named Mason "Newsmaker of 1971," citing "her work with black and white women to achieve equality" and "her demonstrated belief in the American political system." Yet Mason saw perhaps more clearly than those who honored her that, although black and white women might find common cause, the agenda of black women sometimes differed from that of white women: "Black women realize that to get ahead they have to work with the Black man because he has been so beaten down it would be a form of self-destruction to do otherwise." Still, she believed, "Black women have unique capabilities, tempered by decades of oppression and indignities. . . . they have the qualities of endurance, determination, and foresight."

Her own involvement in conventional party politics toward the end of her life did not prevent Mason from supporting the more radical choices other black women made. In 1972, for example, Mason risked her reputation and political standing to defend the rights of the Communist party member Angela Davis. It also did not alter her course, one that always sought new avenues for social change and social justice. In 1978, Mason resigned from the Norfolk school board to focus attention on founding a local chapter of the National Urban League, feeling that the need for direct support to black economic enterprise was pressing. Vivian Carter Mason died in Norfolk, Virginia.

BIBLIOGRAPHY

Collier-Thomas, Bettye, ed. *NCNW, 1935–1981*. Records of the National Council of Negro Women, 1981.

Gagliardi, Martha. "Vivian Mason Never Gives Up." *Virginia Pilot*, 24 September 1971.

Lake, Marvin Leon. "Mrs. Mason, Rights Crusader, Dies at 82." *Virginia Pilot*, 12 May 1982.

"Newsmaker of Year Award to Mrs. Mason." *Journal and Guide*, 4 October 1971.

"Black Women Work with Men." *Virginia Pilot*, 28 August 1974.

ARCHIVAL SOURCES

Papers of Vivian C. Mason are in the files of the National Council of Negro Women and Women's Interracial Council, Norfolk Public Library, Norfolk, Virginia; and National Council of Negro Women, records in the Bethune Museum archives, Washington, DC.

—V. A. SHADRON

MATTHEWS, VICTORIA EARLE (b. 27 May 1861; d. 10 March 1907), journalist, settlement house founder, club woman.

Matthews was born in Fort Valley, Georgia, one of nine children of Caroline Smith. Her mother, a native of Virginia, escaped from slavery to New York during

VICTORIA EARLE MATTHEWS, born into slavery, went on to become a writer, an editor, and an activist in settlement work, social welfare, and club organizations. In 1895 she gave a notable speech, "The Value of Race Literature," at the first national conference of black women. (Austin/Thompson Collection, by permission of Schomburg Center for Research in Black Culture, New York Public Library.)

the Civil War but returned to Georgia for her children after emancipation. Victoria, her mother, and the rest of the family arrived in New York City around 1873, after spending three years in Richmond and Norfolk.

Matthews received little formal education. She attended Grammar School 48 in New York City until poverty and the illness of a family member forced her to leave. She began working as a domestic but continued to read and attend lectures. In 1879, at the age of eighteen, she married William Matthews, a coachman and native of Petersburg, Virginia. During the early years of her marriage, Matthews wrote short stories and essays for *Waverly* magazine and other publications.

In 1893, under the pen name "Victoria Earle," Mathews published *Aunt Lindy*, in the genre of family oral history and southern history. Matthews did freelance writing for the *New York Times*, the *New York Herald*, and the *Brooklyn Eagle* and wrote articles for the nation's leading African American newspapers: the *Boston Advocate*, *Washington Bee*, *Richmond Planet*, and *Cleveland Gazette*. She also edited *Black Speeches, Addresses, and Talks of Booker T. Washington* (1898).

A journalist for the *New York Age*, Matthews was sympathetic to the antilynching crusader and writer Ida B. Wells-Barnett. A testimonial she organized for Wells-Barnett on 5 October 1892 at Lyric Hall in New York City brought together African American women from Boston, Philadelphia, and New York. This event inspired the founding of the Woman's Loyal Union of New York City and Brooklyn two months later. Matthews was also a founder and the first president of the women's club and its auxiliary Black Protection and Women's Rights Society.

At the first national conference of African American women in July 1895, Matthews presented a stunning address on "The Value of Race Literature," in praise of the creative ability of African American men and women and their contributions to race literature and race building. The national conference sparked the founding of the National Federation of Afro-American Women (NFAAW), and Matthews was appointed to the executive board and to the editorial staff of the *Woman's Era*, the official journal of the NFAAW.

In July 1896 the National Colored Women's League of Washington and the Federation of Afro-American Women held their conventions in Washington, DC. Seven women from the two national organizations, including Matthews, formed a joint committee to consider uniting. Their recommendations led the two women's organizations to join as the National Association of Colored Women (NACW). Mary Church Terrell was elected president of the NACW, and Matthews became its first national organizer, as well as the New York State organizer for the Northeastern Federation of Women's Clubs.

In December 1895 Matthews attended the Congress of Colored Women of the United States in Atlanta, which comprised black clubwomen from twenty-five states. Immediately after the congress, she toured the South and was appalled at the red-light districts in New Orleans and other southern cities. Following her investigations, Matthews returned to New York determined to continue her "uplift" and improvement work.

Victoria Matthews's concern for social welfare work in the black community increased after the death of her son and only child, Lamartine, at the age of sixteen. She began to focus on issues related to the well being of children and young women. She visited local families and held mothers' meetings in various homes.

The White Rose Mission, established by Matthews, opened on 11 February 1897. Founded with the purpose of "establishing and maintaining a Christian, non-sectarian Home for Colored Girls and Women, where they may be trained in the Principles of practical self-help and right living," it offered a social center for community women and children as well as shelter and protection to young women coming from the South in search of employment. Matthews organized a group of women from different religious denominations to assist in operating her program.

At about this time, Matthews also began to lecture. With a talent for dramatic and forceful speeches, she spoke before black audiences on the political and social responsibilities of self-improvement. She encouraged respect for African American women, their work, and accomplishments. Aware of race and gender connections in sexuality as shaped by racism, Victoria Matthews raised her voice in defense of black women. In her address at the 1897 San Francisco convention of the Society of Christian Endeavor, "The Awakening of the Afro-American Woman," Matthews stated that it was the responsibility of the Christian womanhood of the country to join in "elevating the head, the heart, and the soul of Afro-American womanhood." Despite the real cultural differences between middle-class white Americans and African Americans, Victoria Matthews realized that the dominant sexual values emanating from the white middle class strongly affected the ways other groups were seen and how they saw themselves.

Matthews expressed concern about African American women who came north in search of employment. Black and white employment agents went into the rural districts of the South with convincing stories of the North and of New York. Young women, often victimized by procurers disguised as legitimate labor agents, were pressured into signing contracts. These unfortunate young women were then at the mercy of agencies that had financed the trip to the North. A skilled journalist, Matthews discovered that employment agencies in New York received large fees to send African American women seeking employment as domestic servants to houses of ill repute. Matthews was convinced that such exploitation of women's sexuality would affect the reputations of all African American women seeking employment.

A pioneer in travelers' aid work, Matthews met the boats at the Old Dominion pier and, with her assistants, helped the inexperienced young women from the South. As superintendent of the White Rose Mission, she established a series of social services from Norfolk to New York. In 1905 she organized the White Rose Travelers' Aid Society. White Rose agents watched the docks to prevent African American women from becoming victimized. The appointed agents were Dorothy Boyd in New York and Hattie Proctor in Norfolk.

Matthews established a special library of books by and about African Americans at the White Rose Home and Industrial Association for Working Girls. Many of the books were used in her teachings on "Race History." As her health gradually failed, her duties were assumed by her assistants, including Frances Reynolds Keyser. Matthews maintained her Brooklyn residence at 33 Poplar Street and her membership at St. Philips Episcopal Church. A plaque outside distinguished the brownstone as "The White Rose Home," and a large photograph which dominated the entry hall memorialized her inspiring and dedicated service. Victoria Earle Matthews died of tuberculosis at the age of forty-five and was buried in the Maple Grove Cemetery, New York City.

BIBLIOGRAPHY

Brown, Hallie Q. *Homespun Heroine and Other Women of Distinction* (1926). New York: Oxford University Press, 1988.

Davis, Elizabeth. *Lifting As They Climb: An Historical Record of the National Associaton of Colored Women* (1933). New York: G. K. Hall, 1996.

Hutson, Jean Blackwell. "Victoria Earle Matthews." In *Notable American Women*, edited by James, Edward T., Janet Wilson James, and Paul S. Boyer. Cambridge, MA: Belknap Press, Harvard University Press, 1971.

Logan, Rayford W., and Michael R. Winston, eds. *Dictionary of American Negro Biography*. New York: W.W. Norton, 1982.

Meier, August. *Negro Thought in America, 1880–1915: Racial Ideologies in the Age of Booker T. Washington* (1963). Ann Arbor: University of Michigan Press, 1988.

Obituary: *New York Age*, 14 March 1907.

Richings, G. F. *Evidence of Progress among Colored People* (1897). Chicago: Afro-Am Press, 1969.

Scruggs, Lawson A. *Women of Distinction: Remarkable in Works and Invincible in Character*. Raleigh, NC: L. A. Scruggs, 1893.

Wesley, Charles Harris. *The History of the National Association of Colored Women's Clubs: A Legacy of Service*. Washington, DC: NACWC, 1984.

—FLORIS BARNETT CASH

MAYORS. Taking her place as mayor of Atlanta, Georgia, one of the largest cities in the United States, Shirley Clark Franklin said, "I proudly represent all of the women who have toiled in the fields, worked in the kitchens, fought for our rights, and challenged our society." Elected in November 2001, Mayor Franklin joined "the great sisterhood" of over 125 black women heading cities and towns in the United States. Their ranks have grown in unprecedented number since the 1972 election of Ellen Walker Craig-Jones, of Urbancrest, Ohio, as the first black woman mayor. The election in Urbancrest came more than 350 years after the first African woman set foot on these shores, 100 years after the Emancipation Proclamation, 100 years after the election of the first black man as mayor of an American town, and almost 50 years after the election of the first white woman mayor.

SHARON SAYLES BELTON, former mayor of Minneapolis. She was elected in 1994 and was the first African American and the first woman to hold the office. (Courtesy of City of Minneapolis Department of Communications.)

From having numbers "too small for reliable analysis," and "not being a viable force," at the start of the twenty-first century black women constituted a fourth of the 451 black mayors of America's cities and towns. They led cities ranging in population from 56 citizens in tiny Neylandville, Texas, to 428,000 in rapidly growing Atlanta, Georgia. The states of Mississippi (13), Oklahoma (12), and South Carolina (8) had the highest numbers of black women mayors. While it is true that these women mayors served at the local level (sometimes viewed as less prestigious), devolution at the national level, in particular, makes their leadership of greater importance to the quality of life of their citizens.

Sharon Pratt Kelly was elected mayor of Washington, DC, in 1990, becoming the first African-American woman to be mayor of a major city. Before that, she served for thirteen years as the District of Columbia's representative to the Democratic National Committee. (Reuters/Bettmann, from the Austin/Thompson Collection.)

Perhaps it is the nature of mayorship itself that makes it attractive to black women. Murphy explains that the political process is distinctly more personalized for the mayor. Local policies have a more immediate and tangible impact on constituents, and constituents have more personal knowledge of the mayor's performance. In terms of relationships with citizens, women mayors may benefit from the perception of women as more caring and concerned than their male counterparts. Further, Burns suggests that women are more likely to be transforming leaders than men are, meaning that they tend more often to pursue goals aimed at changing the situation for the better rather than maintaining the status quo.

Where They Serve

As Darling and others note, black women's chances of being elected have been best for municipal positions in small towns in the South and Midwest. Nearly three-fourths of them are mayors of towns with populations under three thousand. However, the elections of Doris Ann Lewis Davis as mayor of Compton, California (1980), Loretta Thompson Glickman as mayor of Pasadena, California (1982), and Carrie Saxon Perry as mayor of Hartford, Connecticut (1987), showed that black women could win in larger cities and in cities outside the South. In 2002, thirteen black women were elected to lead cities with populations over thirty thousand. According to Census Bureau data, nearly one-fourth of black women mayors represented majority white cities and more than one-third served in cities and towns outside the South. Darling suggests that the increasing numbers reflect the interests, training, and leadership strengths of African American women elected to public office in the South since 1969, when they first began to break into the system.

Black women seeking public office benefited from the Voting Rights Act of 1965, as did black male politicians. Morrison notes that in Mississippi, for example, just prior to the Voting Rights Act of 1965, a mere 6 percent of the black population was even registered to vote. By 1966, the state had only one African American elected official. But in the following decades, African American men and women expanded their participation as voters and as officeholders in the South. Census 2000 data suggest that an important factor in the increase may be the return migration of African Americans to the South, with six of the top growth states being in the South.

If the election of Shirley Franklin as mayor of Atlanta is indicative, black women voters are often key to the elections of black women mayors. Walton and Smith assert that the emerging significance of black women voters is an important part of Franklin's story. They note that from October 2000 to October 2001, Atlanta's black (and white) women registered to vote in high numbers. Oral accounts from other black women mayors note the centrality of the support by black women as campaign workers and as voters.

Survey of Black Women Mayors

Face-to-face interviews of twelve women mayors in December 2002 and a national mail survey of 125 black women mayors yielded the following profile.

Background. The majority of black women mayors interviewed grew up in rural areas (69 percent), most in the same cities where they served as mayor (or nearby). While most of the respondents grew up in large families (average of seven siblings), they had fewer children themselves, with two children being the average. By and large, these women are the children of working-class parents; only 17 percent of their fathers and 15 percent of their mothers had professional jobs. A third describes their mother's occupation as housewife. One woman mayor surveyed wrote, "Our parents were not educated. They instilled values that shaped our lives and helped make us who we are. I taught my mother to read and write."

Marital Status. Only 30 percent of the respondents were married at the time of interview, 23 percent were widows, and 23 percent were divorced. This finding is consistent with patterns observed by Carroll and Strimling that compared with white women politicians, black women officeholders are much less likely to be married and more likely to be divorced or separated.

In terms of age, the women mayors in the survey averaged fifty-seven years of age, ranging from thirty-four to seventy-seven; 70 percent of them are over the age of fifty. Murphy argues that older mayors have fewer years to advance their careers and are less likely to use city hall as a stepping stone to higher office. In a reversal of the stepping-stone model, Dayton, Ohio, mayor Rhine McLin ran for the mayor's seat after a successful tenure in the Ohio state legislature. While not yet a trend, it is worth noting that younger black women may begin challenging older black women incumbents. For example, seventy-one-year-old Unita Blackwell, longtime mayor of Mayersville, Mississippi, was defeated in 2001 by the thirty-four-year-old Linda Williams Short, who said she ran against Mrs. Blackwell as the candidate who communicates better with the town's young people.

Education and Income. At least half of the respondents had a bachelor's degree, another finding consistent with Carroll and Strimling's survey results. About a third of the women were teachers before entering politics. The husbands of the married women were less likely to be college graduates and more likely to hold skilled jobs such as electrician, dye setter, and truck driver. Few of the women were married to teachers or preachers. The median income of the respondents was $41,000, with 42 percent of the women contributing at least half of the family income.

Religion. Respondents emphasized the centrality of religion in their lives. Eighty percent identify themselves as Baptists. Two described being mayor as their "ministry." Yet one woman pointed to the traditional gender roles sometimes seen in the African American community. She wrote, "the men in my community don't believe in women as leaders in church. They think women should be seen and not heard. I believe you can be what you desire to be and do." Their religion was described as a "source of strength," and they said that decisions were made, and difficult situations handled, with prayer.

Mayoral Campaign and Duties. For just under half of the women (43 percent), being mayor was their first public office, although the most recent election was the first election for only one of the women. In general, the women had a five-year average of service; only 10 percent had been mayor for ten years or more. Of those who had held prior public office, nearly half (48 percent) had served on the city council before being elected mayor. Not surprisingly, more than 63 percent of the black women mayors said they ran at the urging of their citizens. In general, these women relied on family and friends for campaign support, although three of the women identified young voters as being especially helpful in the last election, and one mentioned the white community as being very supportive. Among national organizations that helped them in their campaign for mayor, the women cited the National Conference of Black Mayors (20 percent) and the NAACP (15 percent).

The majority of the towns they served were described as strong mayor jurisdictions (68 percent); that is, the mayor can hire and fire workers. About 69 percent believed they had the power, if not the resources, they needed to accomplish things. The number of council members ranged from a low of three to a high of nine, with an average of five members. Among council members, men dominated, holding 57 percent of the total council seats (black men, 39 percent, and white men, 18 percent). Black women held 36 percent of the seats, and white women, 7 percent.

Over half of the women mayors defeated male candidates to win their seats, 34 percent of whom were white men and 23 percent black men. In most cases (80 percent), the elections could be said to be landslides (defined as winning 60 percent or more of the votes).

Leadership Style and Motivations. Asked to characterize their leadership style, the majority of black women mayors described themselves as process-oriented, predictable, task-oriented, loyal, assertive, attractive, frank, and team-oriented. Their motivations for running for mayor included service, responsibility, and challenge, in that order. Similar to the black women in the study by Geiger and colleagues, service was the highest scoring factor for 66 percent of the black women mayors. The comments of Emma Gresham, mayor of Keyesville, Georgia, are typical: "Anybody who knows me knows I wasn't doing it to get money or my name in the paper. I was doing it to improve the quality of life."

In addition to the economic and social challenges of their communities, black women mayors also faced problems related to attitudes about race and gender. A mayor from the South noted that the local media criticized her for saying that minorities and women are held to a higher standard than white men when elected or appointed to positions of authority. In an editorial she was accused of playing the race card. As to white women, the relationship

Featuring Mayors

● **Sharon Sayles Belton** (1951–) was the first woman and first African American mayor of Minneapolis, Minnesota. Born in St. Paul, Minnesota, she attended Macalester College from 1969 to 1973. She dropped out before she graduated, and gave birth to a daughter who was mentally retarded. She immediately found work as a parole officer and raised her daughter while fighting to obtain the resources she needed to do so. In 1983, she left the department of corrections and became the assistant director for the Minnesota Program for Victims of Sexual Assault. The following year she was elected to the Minneapolis City Council. While remaining a council member, she returned to school in 1986, entering the program for senior executives at the John F. Kennedy School of Government at Harvard University. She served as president of the city council from 1989 to 1993. In 1994, Belton was elected mayor of Minneapolis. She was re-elected in 1997 but was defeated in 2001. In addition to her political work, she was a member of a wide variety of organizations and co-founded the Harriet Tubman Shelter for Battered Women, the Minnesota Minority Education Program, and Success By Six.

● **Unita Blackwell** (1933–) was the first black woman elected mayor in the state of Mississippi in 1976. (See individual entry: Blackwell, Unita.)

● **Lelia Smith (Foley) Davis** (1941–) became the first black woman mayor in the United States when she was elected to that position in the black town of Taft, Oklahoma. Before she decided to run for mayor, Davis was a single mother of five and on welfare, but her run for mayor was not the first time she had become involved in local politics. She had run for the local school board and lost, and then ran for a seat on the local council and won. In the town of Taft, the mayor is elected through the town's board of directors. Davis won the board of director's vote in 1973 and became mayor. She soon became known outside her small town of fewer than five hundred people. She was named one of the Ten Outstanding Young Women of America in 1974 and met with President Gerald Ford. She remained mayor until 1989; while in office, she brought water service to Taft, created a volunteer fire department, and had twenty-four rental units built for low-income residents. After Davis lost her post in 1989, she did not leave politics; she was re-elected to the town council in the 1990s and in 1999 once again became the mayor of Taft, though she served only a short time. She also ran for state representative once and state Senator twice, but lost each time. Davis intended to run for mayor again in April 2005.

● **Gwendolyn A. Faison** (c. 1925–) was the mayor of Camden, New Jersey, an industrial city of close to eighty thousand people with a population that is 53.3 percent African American. Born and raised in Clinton, North Carolina, she received her postsecondary education at Shaw, Temple, and Rutgers universities. She became a member of the Camden City Council in the early 1980s, holding her seat until 1995, when she retired. In 1997 she came out of retirement and was elected to the council again and became the city council president. In 2000, she was appointed acting mayor and won the mayoral election the following year. As mayor she took the helm of the poorest city in New Jersey, where three of the past five mayors had been convicted of corruption. In addition to her involvement in a variety of local charities and programs, Faison was a member of the National Political Congress of Black Women and the National Hook-up of Black Women.

● **Shirley Franklin** (1945–) was the first woman to be elected mayor of Atlanta, Georgia, a city of over 400,000 people, 61.4 percent of whom are African American. She was also the first black woman elected mayor of a major southern city. Born in Philadelphia, Pennsylvania, she attended Howard University (BA, Sociology, 1968) and the University of Pennsylvania (MA, Sociology, 1969). Before moving to Atlanta in 1972, she was a member of the faculty at Talladega College, teaching political science. In 1978 she was appointed Atlanta's commissioner of cultural affairs. In 1982 she became chief administrative officer/city manager, the first American woman to be named to such a position. In 1990 she moved from her city manager role to become the city's executive officer for operations, a position she held until 1991, when she became senior vice president for external relations for the Atlanta Committee for the Olympic Games, Inc. In 1997, she founded the firm Shirley Clarke Franklin and Associates, a management and consulting firm for public and community affairs. The following year she joined Urban Environmental Solutions, LLC, as a majority partner and was appointed to Governor Roy Barnes's transition team. In 1999 she became vice chair of the Georgia Regional Transportation Authority. After a two-year campaign, Franklin was elected mayor of Atlanta in 2001. It was her first run for public office.

● **Wilmer Jones-Ham** (1950–) was the mayor of Saginaw, Michigan, a city of 61,799 that is 43.3 percent African American. Born and raised in Saginaw, she attended Delta College (AD, Arts, 1975) and Saginaw Valley State University (BA, Elementary Education, 1978; MA, Supervision and Administration, 1982). After completing school, she returned to her hometown and became a teacher. She taught middle school for over twenty years. In 1994 she was elected to the Saginaw City Council and in 2001 she was elected mayor as well. Among many other community roles, she was a board member of the Boys and Girls Clubs and the 2004 honorary chair of Habitat for Humanity.

● **Rhine McLin** (1948–) was the mayor of Dayton, Ohio, a city of 166,179 people, 19.9 percent of whom are African American. Born and raised in Dayton, she attended Parsons College (BA, Sociology and Secondary Education) and Xavier University (MEd, Guidance Counseling). After attending Cincinnati College of Mortuary Science, she received her associate's degree in Mortuary Science. She was a licensed funeral director and embalmer and worked at the family funeral home, the McLin Funeral Home in Dayton. In addition, from 1982 to 1997 she was a teacher of Criminology, Juvenile Delinquency, and Race Relations at Central State University West. She was elected to the Ohio House of Representatives in 1988, taking over her father's seat, which he had held for twenty-two years. In 1994, she left her house seat when she was elected to the state senate, the first black woman to become a member of that body. Four years later she became the minority whip and in 2000, minority leader. In 2002, she became the first woman mayor of Dayton.

● **Lorraine H. Morton** (c. 1920–) was mayor of Evanston, Illinois (a city of close to 75,000 people that is 22 percent black), from 1993 and at the start of the twenty-first century was in her third term. She was born and raised in Winston-Salem, North Carolina, and attended Winston-Salem State University (BS, Education) and Northwestern University (MS, Education), where she also did post-master's work. She moved to Evanston to attend Northwestern in 1953 and later worked in the city's public schools. Her first job came when the school system was still segregated, and she was the first African American to teach an academic subject. In 1977 she became principal of the Haven Middle School. She served on Evanston's city council from 1982 through 1991. In 1993, she was the first African American and the first Democrat to be elected mayor of the city since its founding. She was a member of the U.S. Conference of Mayors and chair of its Humanities Committee, was on the Legislative Committee of the Northwestern Municipal Conference, and was a member of the Workforce Development Council of Northern Cook County.

● **Carrie Saxon Perry** (1931–) was the first African American woman elected mayor of a capital city when she became the leader of Hartford, Connecticut. Raised in poverty in Hartford during the Depression, she went to Howard University, where she studied political science and law. After leaving Howard, she became a social worker and was named administrator for the Community Renewal Team of Greater Hartford. Later she became the executive director of Amistad House. She was elected to the Connecticut State General Assembly in 1980 and served there until 1987, when she was elected mayor. She served until 1993. After leaving the mayor's office, Perry returned to social work and pursued a master's degree in Criminology. A lifetime member of the NAACP, she was also a member of the National Organization of 100 Black Women and was president of the Hartford chapter.

● **Sharon Pratt (Dixon) (Kelly)** (1944–) was the first black woman mayor of a major U.S. city. Born in Washington, DC, she attended Howard University (BA, Political Science, 1965) and the Howard University School of Law (JD, 1968). She became house counsel for the Joint Center for Political Studies in Washington, DC, in 1970. In the following year she joined the law firm of Pratt and Queen. In 1976 she joined the general counsel's office of the Potomac Electric Power Company. She quickly moved up the ladder at that company, becoming director of consumer affairs (1979), vice president of consumer affairs (1983), and finally, vice president of public policy (1986). From 1985 through 1989, she served as national treasurer of the Democratic Party, the first woman to hold that position. She was also the Democratic national committeewoman representing Washington, DC. (1977–1980). When Pratt was elected mayor of Washington in 1990, she was the first woman to hold that position as well as the first DC native. (She was elected as Sharon Pratt Dixon, then became Kelly after her marriage, and in 2004, went by Pratt again.) She was not reelected. After returning to the private sector, she became a consultant on homeland security and health care.

● **Lottie Shackelford** (1941–) was the first woman elected mayor of Little Rock, Arkansas. Born and raised there, she attended Philander Smith College (BA, Business Administration, cum laude, 1979) and was a senior fellow at the Arkansas Institute of Politics (1975) and at the John F. Kennedy School of Government at Harvard University (1983). In 1978 she was elected to the board of directors of Little Rock, a position she held for four terms. In 1987 she was elected mayor, a position she held until 1991. In 1992 she served as a deputy campaign manager for the Clinton/Gore presidential campaign and was co-director for intergovernmental affairs for the president's transition team. In 1993, she was appointed to the board of directors of the Overseas Private Investment Corporation by President Clinton. Long involved with the Democratic Party, she has served as chair of the Arkansas Democratic State Committee and as co-chair of the Democratic National Convention in 1988 and is currently a vice chair of the Democratic National Committee. She is a member of the Little Rock Airport Commission and the Southern Regional Council in Atlanta, Georgia. She also serves on the corporate boards of Chapman Funds, Inc. and Medicis Pharmaceutical Corp. and is an executive vice president of Global USA, Inc., a government relations firm.

is mixed. One woman noted the support of white women for the candidacy of Atlanta mayor Shirley Franklin. Another stated that in her experience, black women with education appear to be a threat to white women politicians.

One mayor said, "The only real problem I have experienced is locally from the men on my council. When I became mayor, the attitudes changed." Another commented that "We fight more with our black males." Similarly, some black women mayors said that problems were experienced in cities that have always been controlled by white males and the "good ole' boy" network. Another noted that "Caucasian males are the biggest problem. I have had to work extremely hard to prove that I was capable of getting things accomplished. Change has been hard for this group to accept." Nearly all the women cited black male politicians at the state level as having been most helpful.

Challenges and Hopes. Like mayors elsewhere, the black women mayors had a long list of concerns. Their top three problems were: lack of money, crime, and declining economic development and jobs. The majority of black women mayors served in small (three thousand to thirty thousand) and very small (under three thousand) cities. In the rural South in particular, the black women mayors were moving into leadership positions in communities once dominated by white males (cotton-planter elites). One observer asserts that more blacks in City Hall means the South is slowly but surely changing.

More realistically, Morrison argues that black elected officials often attempted to reverse years of neglect of African American concerns. In the past, federal funds, in particular, strengthened the hand of the earlier cohort of African American mayors in the South. As those resources diminished under a succession of national administrations intent on cutting the federal role in local government, these towns were hard hit. In the past, many of these jurisdictions could seek federal assistance for infrastructure and social-program support. Budget shortfalls at the federal and state levels exacerbate the problems of many cities, including those headed by black women mayors. They are responding to the challenges in creative ways, seeking funding wherever they can get it, partnering with other black mayors, especially through the National Conference of Black Mayors, and asking citizens to help produce the changes needed in their communities. In spite of the challenges, one black woman mayor urged more black women to get involved with public office and "show the world that we are a force to be reckoned with."

BIBLIOGRAPHY

Bennefield, Robin M. "Generations of Power." *Essence*, May 2000. http://www.findarticles.com.

Burns, James M. *Leadership*. New York: Harper and Row, 1978.

Bryce, Herrington J., and Alan E. Warrick. "Black Women in Electoral Politics." In *A Portrait of Marginality: The Political Behavior of the American Woman*, edited by Marianne Githens and Jewel L. Prestage. New York: David McKay, 1977.

Carroll, Susan J., and Wendy S. Strimling. "Black Women's Routes to Elective Office: An Exploratory Essay." In *Women's Routes to Elective Office: A Comparison with Men's*. Rutgers, Center for the American Woman and Politics, New Brunswick, NJ: Rutgers University, 1983.

Chenault, Julie. "Her Honor, the Mayor." *Essence*, July 1983, 14–17.

Colburn, David, and Jeffrey S. Adler. *Race, Politics, and the American City*. Urbana: University of Illinois Press, 2001.

Darling, Marsha. "Black Women and Elected Political Office," in *Women and Elective Office: Past, Present, and Future*, edited by Sue Thomas and Clyde Thomas. New York: Oxford University Press, 1998.

Geiger, Shirley, Anne McCulloch, and Belinda Gergel. "Motivations and Behavioral Styles of Women Leaders." *The Leadership Journal* 1.1 (July 1996): 51–64.

Geiger, Shirley. Interviews with black women mayors, Miami Beach, Florida, December 15–16, 2002, and written survey completed in January 2003. Thirty-five women mayors responded to the written survey (30 percent response rate). From the responses, the author has attempted to sketch a profile of a black woman mayor. Respondents represent all of the kinds of cities in the survey and may be assumed to be fairly typical of all black women mayors in the United States.

Graves, Earl G. "Black Mayors Make a Difference." *Black Enterprise* 31.12 (July 2001): 13.

Morrison, K. C. "Federal Aid and Afro-American Political Power in the Rural South," *Publius* 17.4 (Fall 1997).

Murphy, Russell D. "Whither the Mayor." *Journal of Politics* 42 (1980): 277–290.

Rich, Wilbur. *Coleman Young and Detroit Politics*. Detroit: Wayne State University Press, 1989.

Thomas, Sue, and Clyde Wilcox, eds. *Women and Elective Office: Past, Present, and Future*. New York: Oxford University Press, 1998.

Tremaine, Marianne. "Women Mayors Say What It Takes to Lead: Setting Theory against Lived Experience." *Women in Management Review* 15.5/6 (2000): 246–252.

Walker, Clarissa. *Augusta Chronicle*, 14 April 2001, A01.

Walton, Jr., Hanes, and Robert C. Smith. "New South Heroine." First published 10 January 2002. http://www.africana.com/articles/oped/bl_views_84.asp.

—SHIRLEY M. GEIGER

MEEK, CARRIE (b. 29 April 1926), congresswoman. When the Democratic congresswoman Carrie Meek stepped down from her position in the House of Representatives in 2002, she did so with the knowledge that she had served her district with distinction. In 1992 Meek became the first African American elected to the United States Congress from Florida since Reconstruction. Meek is most often remembered for her key role in securing $100 million in relief after Hurricane Andrew wreaked havoc on southern Florida in 1992. However, during her stay in office, Meek also established a solid reputation as a loyal representative of her constituents, a supporter of cooperation across party lines, and a sympathetic voice for Haitian refugees.

The granddaughter of a slave, Carrie Meek was born in Tallahassee, Florida, the last of the twelve children of Carrie and Willie Pittman. The Meek family lived in one of the poorest sections of Tallahassee, known as Black Bottom. Despite early obstacles, strict segregation, and having to work as a domestic to pay for her college tuition, Meek became a top scholar and athlete at Florida A&M University. In 1946 she earned a BS in Biology and Physical Education. Because of southern segregationist policies, Meek was forced to leave the South and head north for graduate school. She attended the University of Michigan, where she earned an MS in public health and physical education in 1948.

After graduation, Meek moved back to Florida and secured a position teaching biology and physical education and coaching women's basketball at Bethune-Cookman College in Daytona. She also taught these subjects at her alma mater, Florida A&M. In 1961 Meek accepted a position as the special assistant to the vice president of Miami-Dade Community College. She used her position to push for the desegregation of Miami-Dade, which was finally integrated in 1963.

Meek continued to work in the field of education for almost fifteen more years. However, in 1978 she shifted careers and entered politics at the age of fifty-two. Her first political position was in the Florida State House of Representatives. Just three years later she became the first black woman ever to be elected to the Florida State Senate, where she remained until her election to the U.S. House of Representatives in 1992.

Meek had a distinguished career as a Florida state representative. During her tenure, she passed bills that made home ownership more attainable and established one thousand new affordable rental units for Florida residents. Meek also left her mark on Florida's educational policies. She chaired the education subcommittee of the Florida State Senate Appropriations Committee. While holding this position, Meek was responsible for budgeting over $10 billion for the education of all Florida residents, from kindergarteners to graduate students.

Meek's strong record at the state government level was only a small indication of her political capabilities; she was even more effective at the national level. In 1993, shortly after she arrived at her new position in the U.S. House of Representatives, she wasted no time in aiding her south Florida constituents in the wake of Hurricane Andrew. She also made waves early in her national career by being the only incoming Democrat to be appointed to the House Appropriations Committee.

Throughout her nine-year career, Meek demonstrated that she was a skilled politician. She was known for her disarming charm and candor. In matters of Congress she proved that her "strong intuition about people" was often correct. Despite left-wing tendencies in Meek's political platform, she remained strategically shrewd during her stay in the House of Representatives. She was willing to cross party lines when necessary but remained true to the Democrats on important close votes.

Although Meek's influence on the national political stage extended far beyond the residents of her home state, she is most proud of what she was able to accomplish for the people of south Florida during her time in office. She secured funds for a variety of initiatives, including veterans' centers, college programs, and an economic development package for Overtown. Meek was not only diligent in improving conditions in south Florida but also keen in pointing out injustice in U.S. foreign policy. She was essential in the campaign to promote equal treatment for Haitian refugees by successfully sponsoring the Haitian Refugee Immigration Fairness Improvement Act in 1998. Through her attention to politics at home and to foreign policy, Meek demonstrated that she was both a formidable politician and a strong advocate for the people of south Florida.

BIBLIOGRAPHY

American Civil Liberties Union Freedom Network. "Rep. Carrie Meek (D-FL-17th)."

Bridges, Tyler. "Meek's Heartfelt Speech Touches Congregation." Racematters.org. http://www.racematters.org/meeksspeechtoucheschurch.htm.

"Charm Made Carrie Meek Effective Even When Outnumbered." *Miami Herald*, 1 December 2002.

Florida Commission on the Status of Women. "Carrie P. Meek." Hall of Fame. http://www.fcsw.net/halloffame/WHOFbios/carrie_p.htm.

The HistoryMakers. "Carrie Meek." *PoliticalMakers*. http://www.the-historymakers.com/biography/biography.asp?bioindex=132&category=politicalMakers.

Houston, Gary. "Meek, Carrie P." *Facts on File Encyclopedia of Black Women*, edited by Darlene Clark Hine. New York: Facts on File, 1997.

—DANIEL DALRYMPLE

MERIWETHER, LOUISE (b. 8 May 1923), author. Louise Jenkins Meriwether is a versatile writer of essays, juvenile fiction, short stories, and novels who has consistently used her talents as a writer to redress omissions in American history.

Meriwether was born in Haverstraw, New York. She was the third of five children born to Marion Lloyd Jenkins and Julia Jenkins and their only daughter. Originally migrants from South Carolina, the Jenkins family moved from Haverstraw to Brooklyn, and subsequently to Harlem, New York. Lloyd Jenkins, a bricklayer by trade, became a numbers runner during the Great Depression as a means of providing for his family. Meriwether attended P.S. 81 and later graduated from Central Commercial High School. She earned a BA in English from New

York University and an MA in journalism from the University of California in Los Angeles in 1965. She married and divorced Angelo Meriwether; she later married and divorced Earl Howe.

As a journalist in the early 1960s, Meriwether contributed articles to the *Los Angeles Sentinel* on little-known but successful African Americans, such as the singers Grace Bumbry and Leontyne Price, the attorney Audrey Boswell, the judge Vaino Spencer, and the explorer Matthew Henson. In the early years of the next decade, Meriwether shifted from short articles to longer biographies, publishing three books for children on African American pioneers: *The Freedom Ship of Robert Smalls* (1971), *The Heart Man: Dr. Daniel Hale Williams* (1972), and *Don't Ride the Bus on Monday: The Rosa Parks Story* (1973). As a fiction writer, Meriwether revisited 1930s Harlem in her first novel, *Daddy Was a Number Runner* (1970), and the Civil War in her second novel, *Fragments of the Ark* (1994). Both novels move the African American experience to the forefront of the historical moment.

In the late 1960s, Meriwether joined the Watts Writers' Workshop and began making her name as a fiction writer. "Daddy Was a Number Runner" appeared as a short story in the fall 1967 issue of *Antioch Review*. "A Happening in Barbados" was published in the same journal the next year, and "The Thick End Is for Whipping" appeared in *Negro Digest* in 1969. In 1970, Prentice-Hall published *Daddy Was a Number Runner*, the first novel to come out of the Watts Writers' Workshop. The Feminist Press reissued the novel in 1986, and it remains Meriwether's best-known work.

Daddy Was a Number Runner is a masterful blend of autobiographical and historical elements. The novel recreates the Harlem of Meriwether's childhood and is peopled by such historical figures as Adam Clayton Powell Jr. and Father Divine, as well as street speakers, prostitutes, and numbers runners. The coming-of-age story documents thirteen-year-old Francie Coffin's maturation in a world of rent parties and relief applications. Through the eyes of a young black girl, readers witness the disintegration of a Harlem family in the face of insurmountable economic pressure. In its foreword, James Baldwin praised the novel's veracity and affective power.

In her second and long-delayed novel, Meriwether reached further back into history to reimagine events during the Civil War. *Fragments of the Ark* (1994) revisited the story of Robert Smalls, the Sea Island slave who stole a Confederate transport vessel to sail his friends and family to Union headquarters and freedom. Meriwether retained historical accuracy in the extensively researched book while taking creative liberties with the characters and their personal histories. She changed Robert Smalls's name to Peter Mango and developed an extensive cast of characters to form Mango's network of family and friends. The novel illuminates a pivotal moment in black history and explores the relationships in a community of people who suffered enslavement, daringly seized their liberty, and struggled with the scars of their experiences.

Meriwether's third novel, *Shadow Dancing* (2000), deals with much more recent history. The setting is the post–civil rights era, and the characters are well-educated black professionals. Although the setting and approach distinguish this novel from her earlier work, Meriwether's exploration of the dynamics between black men and women is a consistent thread that runs through her novels. In *Shadow Dancing*, a successful writer, Glenda Jackson, becomes involved with a theater director, Mark Abbitt. Their personal histories create obstacles in a relationship that is set squarely in the black professional class. The novel illustrates Meriwether's continued endeavor to offer honest and complex representations of black people in American culture.

Meriwether's concern with issues of representation appears in her activism as well as her writing. This link is seen perhaps most directly in her campaign to block the film adaptation of William Styron's *The Confessions of Nat Turner* (1967). Styron's distortions of both historical and psychological truths about the insurrectionist hero were denounced by the black intellectual community. When Hollywood director Norman Jewison and Twentieth Century–Fox producer David L. Wolper wanted to make a movie based on Styron's novel, Meriwether and Vantile Whitfield, founder of Performing Arts Society of Los Angeles (PASLA), formed the Black Anti-Defamation Association. The historian John Henrick Clark joined the fight and edited a volume of essays, *William Styron's Nat Turner: Ten Black Writers Respond* (1968). The protest was successful and the film project was abandoned. At the heart of the controversy was the black community's demand for accurate and responsible representations of black historical figures. Meriwether was an active participant in these critical conversations of the 1960s and 1970s about black experience, cultural authority, and historical truths.

As a professional writer, Meriwether has earned awards, honors, and support for her work. After the publication of *Daddy Was a Number Runner*, Meriwether received grants from the National Endowment for the Arts and the Creative Arts Service Program, an auxiliary of the New York State Council on the Arts. While writing *Fragments of the Ark*, she received a grant from the Mellon Foundation to assist her historical research. In 2001, Meriwether received a Gold Pen Lifetime Achievement Award from the Black Writers Alliance.

Meriwether's life work—literary, political, and cultural—has been dominated by her concern with representations of African Americans and the material consequences of those representations. Her activism confronts injustice directly while her writing offers correctives to the omissions and distortions in American history. Meriwether continues to merge her interests in history, young people, and social justice.

In April 2003, Meriwether met with students at the Young Women's Leadership School in Harlem to talk with young women about the historic community. The Feminist Press cosponsored the event, distributing copies of *Daddy Was a Number Runner* to the participants. To their benefit and delight, a new generation of readers was introduced to both the novel and its remarkable author. As of 2004, Meriwether was living and writing in New York City.

BIBLIOGRAPHY

Collins, Janelle. "'Poor and Black and Apt to Stay that Way': Gambling on a Sure Thing in Louise Meriwether's *Daddy Was a Number Runner*." *Midwest Quarterly* 45.1 (2003): 49–58. An analysis of numbers running as a metaphor for the economic instability and overwhelming odds against success that black families faced in Depression-era Harlem.

Dandridge, Rita. *Dictionary of Literary Biography. Afro-American Fiction Writers after 1955*, edited by Thadious Davis and Trudier Harris, vol. 33. Detroit: Gale Research, 1984. Excellent and extensive discussion of Meriwether's life and work through the early 1980s.

Dandridge, Rita. "From Economic Insecurity to Disintegration: A Study of Character in Louise Meriwether's *Daddy Was a Number Runner*." *Negro American Literature Forum* 9.3 (1975): 82–85. An early and still significant reading of the novel's disintegration motif.

Duboin, Corinne. "Race, Gender, and Space: Louise Meriwether's Harlem in *Daddy Was a Number Runner*." *College Language Association Journal* (2001): 26–40. Analyzes the public and private spaces in Francie's Harlem community and their relation to gender restrictions.

Walker, Melissa. *Down from the Mountaintop: Black Women's Novels in the Wake of the Civil Rights Movement, 1966–1989*. New Haven, CT: Yale University Press, 1991. Places *Daddy Was a Number Runner* in the historical and cultural context of black women's fiction post–civil rights movement. Walker suggests that the ending of the novel would be read as hopeful rather than despairing because it would be filtered through readers' consciousness of the gains made by the movement.

—JANELLE COLLINS

MIDWIVES. When asked to state their occupation, the majority of African American midwives who were active in the 1940s in Talladega County, Alabama, said they were midwives and agricultural laborers, or midwives and domestic workers. From the period of slavery until well into the twentieth century, lay midwifery was an occupation that offered African American women of the South an alternative to the drudgery of agricultural and domestic labor. It was also an occupation that was absolutely indispensable. Since segregation and discrimination had put rural black women beyond the reach of doctors and medical institutions, African Americans were critically dependent on their midwives to bring each new generation into the world.

Indeed, rural southern communities considered the work of the midwife to be sacred. Midwives believed they were called by God to assist women in labor. The position of midwife is one that was handed down through the generations, often from mother to daughter or niece. Because of their link to the ancestors of the community, their knowledge of healing, and their ties to the spirit world, midwives were highly respected members of southern agricultural communities.

Midwife Work during Slavery and Before Supervision

From the period of slavery through the first decades of the twentieth century, the African American midwife of the South practiced with little to no interference from

SYBIL HARBER was a prominent midwife in Lakeview, Oregon, in the late nineteenth century. (Oregon Historical Society, Portland.)

white or black medical authorities. Midwifery was part of the wide range of health work practiced by enslaved African American women. The plantation midwife was often an elderly woman who had an extensive knowledge of herbal and ritualistic healing. She was called upon by the plantation owner to attend white as well as enslaved women in labor. She was often the most trusted health provider within the plantation community.

After the Civil War, African American freedwomen continued to work as healers and childbirth attendants in southern rural communities. Around the turn of the twentieth century, they were known to work in apprentice-type relationships with a local white physician and were sometimes called to assist the doctor in the homes of white families. It was in this setting that they acquired new skills and learned medical techniques. Midwives incorporated these practices into their existing body of knowledge in traditional healing methods.

Physicians relied upon midwives to cover cases they could not attend to and to assist them on cases they did cover. In return, midwives relied on the physician for medical training, access to new methods of healing, and medical supplies. This mutually beneficial arrangement came to an end in 1921 with the passage of the Sheppard-Towner Act.

Midwife Supervision and the Sheppard-Towner Act

White doctors who sought to elevate the status of the growing field of obstetrics launched a campaign against traditional, mostly female midwives in the first decade of the twentieth century. Photographs of elderly midwives from various ethnic groups were used to promote the idea that these women were diseased, ignorant, and superstitious. African American midwives were especially targeted. Referred to as the "granny" midwife, and associated with folk methods of healing and "voodoo practices" that were considered dangerous and backward by medical professionals, black midwives were represented as threats to the health of mothers and their babies. Even though a National Children's Bureau study concluded that low family income was the most common denominator in infant and maternal deaths, medical authorities nevertheless concluded that the lack of "skilled care" during labor and birth was the primary cause of high death rates, and recommended that the federal government assume responsibility for prenatal care among rural and low-income families in the United States. This conclusion, which led in part to the passage of the Sheppard-Towner Act, precipitated the nationwide decline of midwifery, a circumstance that hit black midwives and the African American community hard.

The 1921 Sheppard-Towner Act made available funds that were to be used for education and training of midwives in each state that requested them. A program for midwife registration and education was one of the most prominent programs funded by the Act. Since African American midwives of the South were the largest group of unregulated childbirth attendants at this time, these programs had a profound effect upon African American midwives.

Mississippi was the first state to act. In 1921, Laurie Jean Reid, a chief nurse of the United States Public Health Service, presented her proposed plan for the supervision of midwives to the Mississippi State Medical Association. Reid found it troubling that the state required its seventeen hundred practicing physicians to meet certain medical qualifications to practice, while the estimated three to four thousand active midwives in Mississippi practiced independently and according to their own standards. Although she recognized that black midwives, whom she described as illiterate, ignorant, and unclean, performed indispensable services by serving a population that the medical establishment had abandoned, she nevertheless considered black midwives undesirable. Since newly minted young white obstetricians were unlikely to attend to the large population of poor black agricultural workers, the Mississippi State Board of Health, under the advisement of Reid, decided that midwives would continue to cover the majority of pregnancy cases, but would do so under the supervision of the state and local health departments.

From the passage of the Sheppard-Towner Act in 1921 through the Great Depression of the 1930s, there was intense investigation into the work of the traditional African American midwife. Each southern state where traditional midwives were active established a system of midwife education, regulation, and gradual elimination, similar to the plan devised in Mississippi. A public health nurse often carried out the first step in midwife regulation programs by investigating the personal qualifications of each midwife. In each state, women who were active in the practice of midwifery were asked to meet in small groups at their local churches in order to be registered by the public health nurse assigned to that region. The initial meetings were held in the mid 1920s. Training sessions, licensing, and organization into smaller midwife clubs followed. Those who were found to be fit for practice by the nurse were issued a health department permit to practice midwifery and assigned to a midwife club to meet regularly for further training and inspection by the health department. The remaining women were instructed to discontinue their practices.

African American midwives initially welcomed the opportunity to be recognized and licensed by the medical authorities in their state. Many of them had worked in apprentice-like relationships with a local physician and considered themselves to be health officials to their communities. The prospect of further training by the health department and official recognition seemed appealing and beneficial to their practice. They were unaware that the state health officials planned to eventually eliminate the services of the midwife. They did not know they were considered a necessary and temporary evil.

Rituals of Childbirth

Although state health officials considered black midwives a menace, pregnant women were comforted by the services provided by the traditional African American midwife. These services included a wide array of rituals and healing practices that had deep roots in southern black culture—some even dated back to the period of enslavement. Although nurses and doctors involved in midwife regulation work forbade the use of traditional healing methods, such as the use of herbal teas, successful midwives combined the spiritual belief system that was at the heart of traditional healing practices with medical training received from the health department.

A case in point involved the treatment of pain. Midwives had to treat pain differently than did doctors because during the period of midwife regulation they had little or no access to such modern medical techniques as anesthesiology. It was common, therefore, for a midwife to use herbal teas in an effort to relieve the physical pain of labor. Midwives were known to prepare a tea from Dirt Dauber or to place a pair of shoes upside down under the patient's bed to help her "carry" the pain. A midwife might also place an ax under the bed or pillow to "cut" the pain of labor, or tie a piece of cord around her patient's leg to keep the pain localized. Throwing hot coals on hen feathers and putting the ashes under the bed of the woman in labor was also thought to assist in the process of birth.

Whereas doctors relied heavily on medical books, African American midwives were known to refer to the Bible for inspiration and reassurance before, during, and after a birth. The Bible was as important in their practice as the medical equipment they carried. In order to mentally and spiritually prepare for a birth, midwives used prayer and readings from scripture. Certain verses were read and interpreted during difficult moments of a birth. One southern midwife recounted that when she was attending a woman who was at risk of hemorrhaging, she would elevate the woman's feet and read the Bible. In this case, as in so many others, religious belief had to stand in for medical technology.

The Bible was also read at midwife club meetings in order to set the tone for a discussion of childbirth practices. Although midwives had been organized into local clubs by the health department in order to assist the process of regulation, they were still able to orchestrate the content and tone of most of their meetings. So intertwined were the clubs with the spiritual belief systems of southern women that their singing and Bible reading resembled a religious gathering rather than a secular meeting about medical matters. Despite the interference of medical authorities, midwives managed to maintain some control over this aspect of their work.

The power of childbirth rituals lay in their continuity of practice. Traditional healing methods had been handed down through the generations and were associated with the ancestors of the community. Older midwives were considered wise women. It was their connection to the past and their association with the divine that gave them validity with laboring women. Much of their authority was derived from their close association with the spirit world.

In fact, many women felt unprepared and reluctant to embark on the journey of midwife training and work because of this connection. Midwife work was often referred to as "the burden." However, once a woman received the calling to be a midwife or was chosen by an elder to take over her practice, it was difficult for her to ignore it. Those who chose to follow "the call" were believed to derive their medical knowledge from a divine source as much as from the medical training they received. According to the traditional midwives of the South, a woman was not qualified to work as a birth attendant unless she was familiar with the spiritual aspects of the work.

And it was these traditional healing methods, the spiritualism of them, that kept expectant mothers returning to midwives. Toward the middle of the twentieth century, when most midwives had gone through many years of training and inspection from the health department, some began to question the effectiveness of herbs and other ritual practices. They continued to use them, however, because their patients requested them and found them comforting. The power of the traditional midwife lay in her access to the rituals of childbirth.

From 1921 on, health departments throughout the South attempted to replace elder midwives who were expert in traditional healing methods with younger women who were considered more adaptable to health department ways. In fact, the majority of women who were denied permits were older midwives. Childbearing women, however, often preferred the elder, more traditional childbirth attendant to one who had been chosen by the health department. The most successful midwives were those who combined folk and ritualistic healing methods with modern ways. In the privacy of the birth room, they maintained only the appearance of complete compliance to health department regulations.

"AUNT" NANCY PHILLIPS was a nurse and midwife in remote gold towns in Wyoming. According to the obituary published in the *Wyoming Star* when she died in 1904, she had been born into slavery in 1834. The reporter remarked, "Many a kind act has been performed by the kind hands of Auntie during her long residence in Green River," where residents often "looked upon her advice as they would that of their family physician." (From the collection of the Sweetwater County Historical Museum, Wyoming.)

Midwives as Health Workers

Throughout the 1930s and 1940s, African American midwives extended the type of health work they performed in their communities. Midwives utilized their status as spiritual leaders to spread a broad range of health care information. Midwives, who had worked under strict guidelines and close surveillance, had, by the 1930s, created ways to utilize the medically acceptable aspects of

their faith to do effective health work. They utilized their position in local churches to spread health care information. Midwives, for example, led prayers and made announcements during services telling congregants where to go to receive medical care. African American midwives held vaccination clinics at churches all over the rural South. Midwives were also active in venereal disease treatment and prevention and used their churches as a base to spread information and provide care to people who had contracted any number of diseases.

Midwives also encouraged their ministers to participate in their health campaigns. Ministers gave health sermons from their pulpits at the urging of midwives and spoke at midwife club meetings. Lillie Bell Hill, secretary of her midwife club in Lee County, Mississippi, reported that the lecture given by her minister inspired the midwives to think differently about their work and to get more understanding out of their midwife manuals.

Contribution

Although the numbers of active midwives declined throughout the course of the twentieth century, those who persevered had a significant effect on the experience of childbirth among southern rural women. The training they received by health department–sponsored programs was often rudimentary and redundant. However, they continued to do effective health work, despite the constant surveillance of the local health department. By the 1950s, African American midwives of the South were known to hold prenatal care clinics in their homes and to accompany their patients to be examined by a physician. They were active in health programs, such as dental hygiene and family nutrition, that spread beyond the scope of labor and birth.

In both the public and private arena, their voices were heard. In the public space of midwife club meetings and health department activities, they emphasized their position within the Christian church. Within the private arena of the birth room, they used modern methods while they preserved the traditional healing methods and rituals of childbirth that were preferred by mothers. They responded to health department supervision with creativity and determination.

Modern health workers, hospitals, and maternity wards could not compete with the creative, dynamic, spirit-based approach that traditional African American midwives of the South were known to offer. Despite the plans to eliminate them, traditional midwives continued to practice in some southern states until the 1970s. Their numbers decreased over the years, but their influence over the experience of childbirth was lasting and strong.

See also **Childbirth; Motherhood;** *and* **Nursing.**

BIBLIOGRAPHY

Beardsley, Edward. *A History of Neglect: Health Care for Blacks and Mill Workers in the Twentieth-Century South*. Knoxville: University of Tennessee Press, 1987.

Campbell, Marie. *Folks Do Get Born*. New York: Garland, 1984.

Dougherty, Molly. "Southern Midwives as Ritual Specialists." In *Women in Ritual and Symbolic Roles*, edited by Judith Hoch-Smith and Anita Spring. New York: Plenum Press, 1978.

Fett, Sharla. *Working Cures: Healing, Health, and Power on Southern Slave Plantations*. Chapel Hill: University of North Carolina Press, 2002.

Fraser, Gertrude Jacinta. *African American Midwifery in the South: Dialogues of Birth, Race, and Memory*. Cambridge, MA: Harvard University Press 1998.

Holmes, Linda Janet. "African American Midwives of the South." In *The American Way of Birth*, edited by Pamela Sue Eakins. Philadelphia: Temple University Press, 1986.

Leavitt, Judith Walzer. *Brought to Bed: Childbearing in America, 1750–1950*. New York: Oxford University Press, 1986.

Litoff, Judy Barrett. *American Midwives 1860 to the Present*. Westport, CT: Greenwood Press, 1978.

Logan, Onnie Lee. *Motherwit: An Alabama Midwife's Story*. New York: Dutton, 1989.

Mongeau, Beatrice, Harvey Smith, and Ann Maney. "The Granny Midwife: Changing Roles and Functions of a Folk Practitioner." *American Journal of Sociology* 66 (1961).

Smith, Margaret Charles, and Linda Janet Holmes. *Listen to Me Good: The Life Story of an Alabama Midwife*. Columbus: Ohio State University Press, 1996.

Smith, Susan L. *Sick and Tired of Being Sick and Tired: Black Women's Health Activism in America, 1890–1950*. Philadelphia: University of Pennsylvania Press, 1995.

Susie, Debra Ann. *In the Way of Our Grandmothers: A Cultural View of Twentieth Century Midwifery in Florida*. Athens: University of Georgia Press, 1988.

Wertz, Richard, and Dorothy Wertz. *Lying-In: A History of Childbirth in America*. New Haven, CT: Yale University Press, 1977.

—KELENA REID MAXWELL

MIGRATION. In May 1879 black delegates from fourteen states met at a convention in Nashville, Tennessee. Congressman John R. Lynd of Mississippi presided. The delegates supported a migration resolution declaring "the colored people should emigrate to those states and territories where they can enjoy all the rights which are guaranteed by the laws and the Constitution of the United States." The convention asked for $500,000 from Congress for this purpose. Given the past history of this segment of the population, it was a modest request. It was one that was never honored.

The internal migration of African Americans within the United States has occurred over several centuries and reflects nothing so much as the peculiar incorporation of these unwanted but necessary citizens. Four mass migrations in particular serve to highlight the hopes and fears of the people and the designs and manipulations of the states. The first and perhaps the largest migration was the westward movement of blacks, still slaves, into what was the western rim of the United States at that time. An involuntary migration, brought on by the collapse of the system of slave labor in the Chesapeake, it separated families in an often wrenching fashion. The second exodus was the movement to Kansas during Reconstruction, a more traditional migration where populations left settled areas for a frontier in hopes of a better life. The Great Migration was the third, starting during World War I, a labor migration in search of employment and opportunity. The second part of this migration began during World War II, when once again labor needs and war combined to encourage yet another generation to search for opportunity in the North. The fourth migration, still in progress as of the early twenty-first century, represents a return to the South. In the approximately two hundred years between the first and the fourth migrations, the nation had industrialized, fought a Civil War, ended slavery, conferred official rights of citizenship, and ended the highest stages of white supremacy. What the nation had not done was find a permanent place for this expelled population. Almost from the beginning, African Americans struggled to achieve this goal for themselves.

Migration from Chesapeake

Chesapeake slavery was one of the oldest slave societies in America. Beginning with the first slave settlements in the early 1600s, the institution evolved and consolidated over a period of nearly one hundred years. The first African laborers were hardly distinguishable from the European indentured servants brought to labor in the same fields. According to Philip Morgan, "Not only did many blacks and whites work alongside one another, but they ate, caroused, smoked, ran away, stole, and made love together."

In the mid-1600s the supply of English indentured servants bound for the colonies was in sharp decline. Landowners were forced to turn to the expensive African slave trade for a more reliable source of labor. Over time, as the slave system matured "colonists were permitted to buy and hold enslaved Africans for a lifetime, and to 'own' the lifetime rights to their children, and children's children, as well."

In the late 1700s the Chesapeake experienced another economic transformation as soil depletion forced slave owners to diversify out of tobacco and into other crops. Tobacco represented 90 percent of the area's agricultural production in 1747. By 1849 it had fallen to 14 percent. Diversification often meant the elimination of the need for slaves, as shifts into wheat production, rye, and barley required fewer laborers or more temporary ones. In wheat production, for example, a large work force was required only at harvest. As Barbara Fields observes, "Once wheat became the predominant or sole cash crop, it made

THE "COLORED WAITING ROOM" AT A TRAIN TERMINAL, c. 1920s, during the Great Migration of African Americans from the south to the north in search of employment and opportunity. (Austin/Thompson Collection, from Florida State Archives.)

little sense to maintain a large slave force that could not be productively employed much of the time."

Slave owners adopted several strategies to offset the decline in the demand. For many, slaves represented the only real capital they had, so they entered into an elaborate mortgage system using the slaves as collateral. When times were good, slaves lived as before. When bad, the slaves, who had greatly increased in value, were sold off.

This precipitated the first internal migration. According to Peter Kolchin, about 1 million slaves moved west between 1790 and 1860. Most of the departures were from Maryland, Virginia, and the Carolinas. They moved to Georgia, Alabama, Mississippi, Louisiana, and Texas. Between 1810 and 1860, according to Kolchin, 100,000 migrants per decade were moved. Sometimes they moved en masse with their owners, who left in search of a better life in the "frontier." The more prevalent option for owners was to sell their slaves. Preference was given to children and young adults who, it was believed, could be apprenticed and trained. In 1820 children living in the upper South had a 30 percent chance of being sold, especially to markets in New Orleans, Louisiana, Natchez, Mississippi, and Montgomery, Alabama. Because so many were children, family reunification was difficult. Harriet Tubman's mother recalled with horror the tear-stained faces of her young daughters sold away from her and never seen again.

Kansas Exodus

The second migration was the Kansas exodus. It is estimated that between 1870 and 1880, nearly thirty thousand black people left the Deep South to start a colony in Kansas. They were initially led by Benjamin "Pap" Singleton, an escaped slave turned entrepreneur from Nashville, Tennessee, who had a vision that landownership and economic independence were keys to African American advancement. In 1874 Singleton and his associates formed the Edgefield Real Estate and Homestead Association. His idea was to seek out and establish all-black settlements, attempting to capitalize on the federal Homestead Act of 1862, which guaranteed "160 acres to any settler who paid a filing fee and improved the land within five years." Black settlers were encouraged by some of the local press to settle in Kansas: "Come West, Come to Kansas. . . . This is a great state for the industrious." Railroads induced migration by offering reduced fares. But land prices soared as a result of the influx and quickly outpaced the resources of most migrants. Singleton withdrew from the project by 1879. Some "exodusters," as they became known, returned to the South. Many stayed and eked out a life, but not a good life.

Great Migration

The Great Migration began in the spring of 1916 with little fanfare. The press had focused public attention on President Wilson, who was preparing for reelection, on women who were demonstrating for a suffrage amendment, and to the early start of what would be an unusually warm summer in the East. A nation with a passion for peace was also cautiously discussing "preparedness" for war. Hardly noticed, at first, was the tiny stream of workers that the Pennsylvania Railroad Company brought north to work on the rail lines. Yet the company's experiment precipitated one of the largest population shifts in the country's history. From beginning to end, nearly one-tenth of the African American population of the United States would move from the South to the North. As James Weldon Johnson, poet, statesman, and executive officer of the NAACP, wrote, "Migrants came north in thousands . . . they came, until the number, by conservative estimate, went well over the million and a half mark. I witnessed the sending North from a southern city in one day a crowd estimated at twenty-five hundred." Simply stated, it was a journey into freedom.

Over 400,000 left in a two-year period, 1916 to 1918, leaving at an average rate of 16,000 per month, 500 per day. The migration was a major watershed in the history of African Americans. First, it was the beginning of regular urban industrial employment with higher wages and fixed hours. Second, the exodus diminished the overwhelming southern concentration of the population. As late as 1910, 7 million blacks resided in the South while less than 1 million lived in all other regions of the country combined. And, most notably, third, with the extension of the right to vote, migration was a significant move toward citizenship itself.

One of the leading stimulants for migration was the boll weevil. The tiny insect invaded Texas in 1898 and ate its way across the South from west to east. In its path, thousands of agricultural laborers were thrown off the land, and the South's dependency on a single crop, cotton, ended.

A second, concurrent stimulant was World War I. The war in 1914 encompassed most of Europe but not the United States. It also halted the massive immigration of European industrial workers that had taken place since the 1850s. Secession of immigration created a labor shortage. Though not involved in the fighting until 1917, the United States was almost immediately called upon to furnish munitions and supplies. The war produced a booming economy. A huge demand and an acute labor shortage necessitated a search for an alternate supply. Where better to look than the South, an area still struggling with the ravages of the boll weevil invasion and an economy overflowing with labor made unemployed by the combination of agricultural disaster and underdevelopment?

Nascent industrialization had begun in the South as early as the 1880s, when campaigns for economic development brought investment and mechanization to a variety of industries. When compared with workers in the Northeast and Midwest, however, southern workers were grossly underpaid. Earnings in the South represented only about two-thirds of those paid elsewhere. The South's separation from the rest of the country was caused in part by unique historical factors: its institution of slavery, its slow recovery from the devastating Civil War, and its over-reliance on cotton. Behind the rest of the country at the start of Reconstruction, the South saw its disadvantage increase over time. In comparison with the rest of the country, it had fewer schools, lower levels of literacy, and fewer basic services. Rural areas were also disadvantaged by slow and inadequate communication with the outside world.

Mechanisms that would have facilitated the normal movement of labor from one region to the next were all but absent. Indeed, the South represented more of a colony merely exporting raw material than an equal trading partner to the more economically advanced North. It depended on the North for both financing and manufacturing. Indigenous industries like tobacco, furniture making, and ore mining were small scale and made little profit. Its local products were undercut by cheaper ones made outside the South. In the absence of a market exchange of workers and products, the information channels crucial for employment were inadequate. Large numbers of skilled workers, white and black, traditionally the first labor sector to leave for better wages, were trapped.

Boosterism. Reports were spread that opportunities existed in the North. Sophisticated campaigns of boosterism were structured to entice the novice with fantastic promises. Migrants were touched by these appeals but cautious. They awaited reports from "pioneers" who went north "to test the waters." Said one, "Of course everything they say about the North ain't true, but there's so much of it true don't mind the other."

Once the market was tapped, every means possible was used to attract the black labor supply. Labor agents from northern companies were sent to stand on street corners in the South and offer train passes to workers who fit a profile—young, male, and strong. Job advertisements touting the good wages and other advantages of living in the North were placed in black newspapers. Newspapers also published success stories about people who had recently migrated and were already making more money than they had ever dreamed possible. Letters were read aloud in local churches, barbershops, and meeting halls, bringing information and confirmation. And southern blacks wanted all the information they could get on this effort. Was it real? Would they pay? What was it like in the North?

Still, not everybody went north. As the historian Gavin Wright explained, 50 percent or more of the migrant population was urban and "had long since left agricultural work. The great majority of departures from the Alabama steel town of Birmingham and Bessemer were experienced miners heading for the coal fields of Kentucky, West Virginia and Pennsylvania."

Selectivity went beyond work experience. Migration streams of young and old, parent and child, able-bodied and dependent were rare. It was too expensive to take everyone at once. Young men were usually the first to go. Between the ages of eighteen and thirty-five, they had worked as unskilled laborers at one or two industrial enterprises in the South. About one-quarter of the migrants were from the agricultural sector, according to surveys done in Pittsburgh and Chicago. Many were married and had children. They left expecting to reunite with their families as soon as they had "made their way."

Reasons given for leaving varied among the migrating population. Some talked of "freedom and independence" as their primary motives. Some said simply "to increase wages." Others wanted better educational opportunities for their children. Still others intended to stay long enough to make a little savings and return. Maggie, mother of the educator James Comer, said of her husband, "He first planned to work and go back, like so many others. So many of the people that came here back in those days didn't come here to stay. They didn't like it here. They didn't like the weather. It was so different to their way of life at home." But Maggie's husband never went back.

Journey to a New Life. Migrants, journeying thousands of miles in some cases, headed to the large industrial centers—Detroit, Pittsburgh, New York, and, most of all, Chicago. Leaving home was hard. Left behind were family and friends, familiar places, and ways of life. But it was also exhilarating as hope for the future in some instances drowned out the accustomed sounds of the past. A migrant from Gulfport reported from Chicago, "I'm tickled to death over this place. Sorry I was not here years ago."

Though influenced by a host of agents, migrants made decisions about the timing of their moves, location, specific employment, and even the nature of that employment. The historian Peter Gottlieb notes that a woman who eventually migrated to Pittsburgh reported that her husband had first found a job in Cincinnati, where he wrote to her to come join him. But she was resistant to her husband's urgings, citing that she would like to be with her sister in Pittsburgh. In response to her husband's request to join him, she stated, "And I wrote him back and said, 'I don't want to stay in Cincinnati. I want to go to Pittsburgh.' Next letter I got, he got a job in Pittsburgh and sent for me." Migrants constantly attempted to control the world around them by negotiation, bargaining, and compromise. As Joe Trotter concludes, "In fundamental ways, they actively shaped and directed their own experience."

The South in 1916 was isolated. Yet, in a matter of months, over 400,000 blacks were mobilized and transported from the farthest corners of the region. At face value, it would seem impossible. How does one get from Laurel, Mississippi, to Cottage Grove Avenue on the South Side of Chicago?

The journey itself was often difficult. Segregated waiting rooms and train cars, limited facilities for food and drink, unfamiliar procedures, and unfriendly conductors—these were the norm for migrants. And it could take days, weeks, even years. Transportation costs alone precluded many from making the trip. A relatively short trip of six hundred miles, Norfolk to Pittsburgh, would have cost eight dollars per adult or forty-eight dollars for a family of six. It was not an easy task for anyone to get to "The Promised Land."

Many who did work for a wage found that they had to make the journey north in stages, stopping off and working in several intermediate points in the South before arriving in the North. This step migration, as it is called, could take a long time. "It took Sara Brooks," points out the historian Darlene Clark Hine, "almost fifteen years to reconstitute her family, to retrieve her three sons left behind in Orchard, Alabama."

At first, help was provided by northern employers. One of the first industries to recruit employees was the railroad industry. Gathering workers to transport war-related goods and maintain rail lines was a central component of the war economy. In the summer of 1916, the Pennsylvania

Railroad imported twelve thousand blacks from the South to do unskilled labor. The Illinois Central Railroad issued passes through labor agents to bring workers to Chicago. War-related industries like the steel mills, with contracts backing up and labor tight, made great promises to dig into this new labor pool. It did not take long for the migration fever to spread.

Agents were so successful in spreading the word that employers soon cut back their travel passes. So many came without waiting for agents that it was unnecessary to advance the tickets. Agent activity was also severely curtailed by local authorities. Fearing that these outsiders were up to no good, they tried to prevent access to the black community. In some cases, local officials refused to honor the passes. In others, they pulled travelers off trains to prevent them from going north. Migrants were left on their own.

More influential than agents in the long run were family and friends. Tickets to the North were purchased by selling all that was owned. When funds were insufficient, family members pooled their resources and sent a single member. The researcher Abraham Epstein's study of five hundred migrants to Pittsburgh, for example, suggests that 89 percent of them paid for the trip through the use of savings and the sale of property and household goods.

With the migrant absent from the family, other family members had to support themselves until the migrant made good. Many women took jobs, particularly as domestics, to support the family and save up for the fare. As one commented in a letter, "So many women here are wanting to go. They are all working women and we can't get work here so much now, the white women tell us we just want to make money to go North and we do." Women would also negotiate labor contracts through domestic agencies, in which northern employers would agree to pay transportation north in exchange for their labor. They also sold household items and moved in with other family members to keep costs down. In some families, both parents went north and grandparents or some other family member cared for the children.

Family branches or friends in the North also had to be relied upon to help with finding a job and providing initial shelter. Some migrants did, of course, board trains in the South and arrive in a northern city without a job or knowledge of how to get one. But a majority arrived with a name and an address of someone, often previously contacted, who would be used to cushion the shock of the move.

Letters Encouraged Those Back Home. Letters written to those back home about the migration experience were instrumental in encouraging the journey for others. Specific accounts of jobs and housing from trusted informants were, of course, key to persuasion as was a little money included in the envelope to give further truth to

the claims. Sara Brooks, encouraged by her brother to move to Cleveland, saved for the trip. Brooks states, "I saved what I could, and when my sister-in-law came down for me, I had only eighteen dollars to my name, and that was maybe a few dollars over enough to come up here. If I'm not mistaken it was about a dollar and fifteen cents over."

Letters from the North were often read in churches on Sunday mornings, and some worshipers started thinking that maybe the Lord had a hand in this. For many, the Great Migration was like a religious revival. Some churches formed migration clubs to exchange information and facilitate passage to the North. Leaders were chosen who corresponded with northern industries, newspapers, and placement services on behalf of the entire group. Letters brought comfort and gave assurance. This is real, they said. "Home ain't nothing like this." Service organizations, voluntary associations in northern cities, flourished during this time to provide further aid and support to migrants. In Chicago, the Chicago Urban League was founded in 1917 to help migrants settle in the city. As many as fifty-five thousand sought jobs and dwellings from the organization. Its Industrial Department in 1920 reported that it "placed more than 15,000 migrants in positions, made industrial investigations in sixteen plants, provided lectures for working men in plants, for foremen over black workers, investigated worker complaints and assisted in other ways." The league in Chicago and the NAACP in New York and similar organizations in other cities collected information on jobs and housing, provided clothing for those inadequately prepared for the northern climate, and granted any other social services that they could handle.

Newspapers provided the last essential link, offering information and representing an important vehicle for the articulation of the goals of migration. They often fanned the migration spark. "Allow me to congratulate you on your wonderful paper," a migrant wrote from the South, "it is a help to a lot of the people of our race it shows us the difference between north and south."

Several southern cities tried to halt distribution of papers like the *Chicago Defender* by confiscating copies. Vendors responded by smuggling them in from rural areas. Some copies were sent through the U.S. mail in disguised packaging. One Mississippi county declared that the *Defender* was really German propaganda and had it banned. All of the intrigue, of course, made the paper even more exciting.

The *Defender* did more than simply editorialize about the benefits of leaving. It published advertisements of employers, and those seeking work were instructed to apply. These ads stressed opportunities for young males "able to take charge of their positions." It was these announcements to which migrants responded. "Your advertisement appearing in the *Chicago Defender* have influenced me to write to you with no delay," wrote one. "In reading a copy of the *Chicago Defender* note that if I get in touch with you you would assist me in getting imployment," wrote another.

Migrants flowed into northern cities. Between 1910 and 1920, for example, New York experienced a 66 percent increase in its black population; Chicago, a 148 percent increase; Detroit, a 611 percent increase; and Philadelphia, a 500 percent increase. Once settled, migrants worked hard to achieve their version of the American Dream. Long hours and several jobs were not unusual. One migrant told the Chicago Race Commission that after coming to Chicago he worked in a foundry as a molder's helper until he learned the trade. "I can quit any time I want to, but the longer I work the more money it is for me, so I usually work eight or nine hours a day. I am planning to educate my girl with the best of them, buy a home before I'm too old, and make life comfortable for my family."

Migrants Moved Toward Success. Yet even in the face of discrimination and exclusion, migrants strove to move forward. Their success can be documented. In 1890, 63 percent of all black male laborers worked in agriculture. By 1930, only 42 percent did so. At the same time, the number of black schoolteachers more than doubled, the number of black-owned businesses tripled, and black literacy rose from 39 percent to 85 percent. Allen Ballard suggests that in Philadelphia "Black building and loan associations flourished during the 1920s—some thirty-six by 1923—under the aegis of the churches." Joe Trotter indicates that in Milwaukee there was a 120 percent increase in the number of blacks engaged in professional, business, and clerical occupations between 1920 and 1930.

The critical mass of the migration also permitted new institutions. Darlene Clark Hine suggests that the forces of white racism, black self-help initiatives, and white philanthropic largesse combined at the turn of the century to produce a black hospital movement to improve the system of healthcare delivery for blacks. By the mid-1920s, there were over two hundred black hospitals and over twenty-five black nursing schools in the country.

Under the banner of black self-help, several social service organizations were founded to specifically aid migrants and in general to uplift the community from the inside. As Trotter concludes, "Afro-Americans established all of their larger and most profitable businesses in the wake of migration." Most migrants paid dearly, in some coin or other, for the chance to participate. The Great Migration was about migrants starting over and making sacrifices for future generations that they would probably never see. As W. E. B. Du Bois concluded, the journey north represented not the end of a struggle but only its beginning.

Second Wave

Part two of the Great Migration began in 1941 when war industries once again went south to recruit able-bodied and cheap labor. It is estimated that over 700,000 left during the war; after the war, 300,000 moved to the North by the end of the decade. This migration was larger than part one, and its impact on economic, political, and social advancement was obvious. Blacks participated in the dramatic post-war expansion of the economy. "This spectacular rate of economic growth made possible an increasing income for Blacks, their entry into industries and labor unions . . . and a gain in occupational status as the constant shortage of workers necessitated a slackening of restrictive promotion policies."

Black migrants not only entered northern cities, they transformed them. Working from a critical mass, blacks were elected to municipal offices, to state legislatures and, in increasing numbers, to the U.S. House of Representatives. No longer dependent on white political patronage, they demanded a voice in civic affairs. Pressure applied by blacks during and after the war created employment in the government sector. Some 2 million blacks worked in defense plants and another 200,000 entered the federal civil service. Progress was made in opening educational institutions at all levels. The 1954 Supreme Court decision signaled, for the first time, protection in the courts. A civil rights revolution fought in the South to topple the most egregious forms of white supremacy was won in part by a newly emboldened second generation.

Start of Fourth Migration

But the seeds of the fourth migration, a return migration, were already forming at this time. The North had been no promised land for Great Migration migrants. Even as the victories in the South were celebrated in Selma, Alabama, northern cities were beginning to burn. In 1967 the President's Commission on Civil Disorders concluded, "Our nation is moving toward two societies, one black, one white—separate and unequal. . . . To pursue our present course will involve the continuing polarization of the American community and, ultimately, the destruction of basic democratic values." Even as gains were made in the urban North in the 1950s, profound social and economic changes were also apparent, including "a deepening division between the relatively secure middle and working classes and an increasingly vulnerable and isolated segment of the minority poor." In Chicago, for example, in 1954 there were over 10,000 manufacturing establishments and over 500,000 blue collar jobs. By 1984, the number of firms had been cut in half and employment was down 63 percent. As William Julius Wilson observes, the urban core lost much of its economic and social resources when the stably employed left. As joblessness rose, problems abounded. Schools declined, churches left. The relatively stable middle and working classes moved to the outskirts of cities and to the suburbs. The proportion of African Americans living in suburbs doubled between 1970 and 1990 and approached 40 percent in the early twenty-first century. They moved for better housing and better schools, but many worried about the higher prices and lower quality of housing and the incorporation of their children into single class, segregated communities. The affluent who were able to move to predominately white areas often expressed similar concerns.

Beginning in 1970 to 1980, black migration from the South began to wane. As William Frey notes, "The long standing trend of Black migration loss from the South reversed." States like Alabama, Arkansas, Mississippi, and South Carolina, which had lost population in the decade 1960–1970, gained population in the decade 1970–1980. Following a net loss of almost 300,000 blacks in the second half of the 1960s, the South had a small net gain in 1970–1975 of 100,000 and almost 200,000 in 1985–1990. While the immediate factors of the South's booming economy, reduction of restrictions, lower cost of living, and milder climate were all factors in the return migration, it is also likely that these second, third, and fourth generation sojourners, free at last, wanted to go home.

BIBLIOGRAPHY

Ballard, Allen B. *One More Day's Journey: The Making of Black Philadelphia*. Philadelphia: Institute for the Study of Human Issues, 1987.

Comer, James P. *Maggie's American Dream: The Life and Times of a Black Family*. New York: New American Library, 1988.

Fields, Barbara Jeanne. *Slavery and Freedom on the Middle Ground: Maryland during the Nineteenth Century*. New Haven, CT: Yale University Press, 1985.

Frey, William. "Migration to the South Brings U.S. Blacks Full Circle." *Population Today* (May–June 2001).

Gottlieb, Peter. *Making Their Own Way: Southern Blacks' Migration to Pittsburgh, 1916–1930*. Urbana: University of Illinois Press, 1997.

Henri, Florette. *Black Migration: Movement North*. Garden City, NY: Anchor Press, 1975.

Hine, Darlene Clark. *Hine Sight: Black Women and the Re-Construction of American History*. Bloomington: Indiana University Press, 1997.

Kolchin, Peter. *American Slavery, 1619–1877*. 1st rev. ed. New York: Hill and Wang, 2003.

Lacquant, Loic. "The Ghetto, the State, and the New Capitalist Economy." *Dissent* (Fall 1989).

Marks, Carole. *Farewell—We're Good and Gone: The Great Black Migration*. Bloomington: Indiana University Press, 1989.

Morgan, Philip D. *Slave Counterpoint: Black Culture in Eighteenth-Century Chesapeake and Lowcountry*. Chapel Hill: University of North Carolina Press, 1998.

Painter, Nell Irvin. *Exodusters: Black Migration to Kansas after Reconstruction* (1977). Lawrence: University Press of Kansas, 1986.

Scott, Emmett J. *Negro Migration during the War* (1920). New York: Arno Press, 1969.

Sitkoff, Harvard. *The Struggle for Black Equality, 1954–1992*. rev. ed. New York: Hill and Wang, 1993.

Spear, Allan H. *Black Chicago: The Making of a Negro Ghetto, 1890–1920*. Chicago: University of Chicago Press, 1967.

Trotter, Joe William, Jr. *The African American Experience*. Boston: Houghton Mifflin, 2001.

Trotter, Joe William, Jr., ed. *The Great Migration in Historical Perspective: New Dimensions of Race, Class, and Gender*. Bloomington: Indiana University Press, 1991.

Wilson, William J. *The Truly Disadvantaged: The Inner City, the Underclass, and Public Policy*. Chicago: University of Chicago Press, 1987.

—CAROLE MARKS

MILITARY, BLACK WOMEN IN THE.

While serving one's country is widely held to be an honor and an act of patriotism, historically most governments have been reluctant to enlist women into their armed services. Combat in particular has been considered unnatural for women. Yet some women have defied traditional norms and become soldiers in various parts of the world.

Becoming a soldier in the United States has been a long and arduous process for women. Black women have had an especially difficult time entering the armed forces and have been forced to go through several stages in the quest to serve their country. The first phase consisted of individual acts of heroism and displays of patriotism. Next came the spirited efforts of individuals and groups to provide organized support. From these efforts sprang a number of support organizations in which serving the soldier and his family were primary objectives. A major turning point for black women and the military occurred during World War II, when black and white women finally donned the military uniform. At the next major juncture black women successfully tackled double integration: that of integration into white female units and then integration into all-male forces. Some even lived in coed facilities, which was a first for the military. While serving in an increased number of combat support roles and technical specialties, an ever-increasing number of women have found themselves on the battlefield. For women as a group, the 1991 Persian Gulf War was the point at which these increases and changes became truly significant. Today, black women contribute to most aspects of the United States military.

Although there were a number of conflicts during the colonial period, the American Revolution was the first war waged by the nation. The fighting that began in 1775 became a war with the 1776 signing of the Declaration of Independence. Like their white counterparts, black Americans were torn between supporting Great Britain or siding with the United States. Indecisiveness in black men and women, however, arose out of their political status and not their political affiliations or loyalties. Most were slaves, and free black Americans were treated as quasi Americans. Moreover, it was unclear whether the

WOMEN IN THE U.S. ARMY, 1985. They were photographed on 11 November—Armistice Day, later Veterans Day. (© Bettye Lane.)

British—who promised freedom to all black soldiers supporting the crown—or the Americans espousing ideals like "liberty and justice for all" offered the greatest opportunity for racial change. As a result, thousands of black men fought on both sides during the American Revolutionary War.

Though black men were able to enlist in the militia, black women were relegated to support roles. Little is known of their activities. One nameless free black maid contributed a large portion of her meager monthly wage to the war effort. Another unnamed free black woman gave soup and bread to hungry, incarcerated patriots. Phillis Wheatley composed an inspirational poem for General George Washington while he was stranded that dreadful winter at Valley Forge. Some black women were likely among the camp followers providing services such

as cooking, washing, and caring for the sick, but existing records show no evidence of this. The records recall the names of only a few women who actually took up arms and fought during the Revolution. These include Nancy Hart, a six-feet tall Georgian; Margaret Corbin, known as Captain Molly, who was wounded in the 1776 attack on Fort Washington; and Deborah Sampson Gannett. Some historians have identified Gannett as a black heroine.

After the Revolutionary War ended, some escaped black slaves took shelter in Florida at a fort abandoned by the British during the war. General Andrew Jackson considered the fort a threat to United States security and ordered its destruction. At "Fort Negro," as it was known, as many as three hundred black men, women, and children were killed. The fort was completely destroyed.

Wars of Emancipation and Empire

Black women played more varied military support roles in the Civil War (1861–1865), the bloodiest war in U.S. history. Slave women in the South sustained plantations by tending the cotton, which the Confederate government relied on to finance the war. The Union army utilized

Mary Elizabeth Bowser, a slave girl, to spy on the Confederate president, Jefferson Davis. The most noted black woman spy of the period is Harriet Tubman. She served in South Carolina, gathering information from informants behind Confederate lines. Besides being a legendary leader of the Underground Railroad, Tubman was also a nurse and a scout who led Union soldiers during several expeditions to the South. She is likely the first black woman in U.S. history to lead men to war. Tubman was buried with full military honors, though she was a civilian employed by the U.S. military.

The fiery abolitionist speaker Sojourner Truth participated in the Civil War. Truth organized fundraisers for black troops and nursed wounded soldiers confined to Freedmen's Hospital in Washington, DC. She worked with Clara Barton, the white nurse who organized the American Red Cross. "Aunt" Daphney Whitlow, a former slave from Virginia later employed by the Freedmen's Hospital, also served as a Civil War nurse.

Susie King Taylor, a native of Georgia, worked for the Union Army as a nurse and teacher to black soldiers. Charlotte Forten was another who taught black soldiers during the Civil War. Two others, Mary Chase and Mary Peake, opened schools for the freedmen, who were considered contrabands of war, in Alexander and Hampton, Virginia, respectively. Elizabeth Keckley supported the war effort in a slightly different way. Keckley, seamstress for the president's wife, Mary Todd Lincoln, organized the Contraband Relief Association of Washington, DC, during the summer of 1862 to assist black Americans displaced by the war. Starting with forty members, the highly successful organization quickly expanded as it attracted the attention of black churches across the North. Keckley's Contraband Relief Association was the forerunner to twentieth-century black women's organizations designed to serve the military. Some of these organizations were the Negro War Relief, Women's Committee of the Council of National Defense, and women's auxiliaries to various military units. Modern research indicates that over 250 women actively served in the Civil War disguised as men. One such soldier was a black woman, Maria Lewis, who for eighteen months masqueraded as a white male with the Eighth New York Cavalry Regiment.

Evidence of black women's participation in military events in the West is sketchy, but there are at least two accounts of black women being present in confrontations with Native Americans. In the colonial period, Lucy Terry wrote a poem describing a battle between white settlers and Native Americans. The poem, "A Slave Report in Rhyme on the Indian Attack on Old Deerfield, August 25, 1746," helped to establish Terry as the first published black woman in the United States. Over 125 years later, a black woman known as "Aunt Sally" Campbell traveled

with George Custer before his defeat and death at the Battle of Little Big Horn (1876). She probably served as his cook and washerwoman. When Custer left the Dakota Territory to search for the Sioux in Montana, Campbell remained in South Dakota, where she became the first non-Indian woman to reside in the territory.

Much of the Spanish-American War (1898) took place in Cuba and in the Philippines. As Teddy Roosevelt made his famous charge up San Juan Hill, the Twenty-fourth Infantry, an all-black unit, provided cover. Additionally, the Ninth and Tenth Cavalry and the Twenty-fifth Infantry were all-black units that participated in combat during the ten-week war. Though the United States won the war, thousands of black and white soldiers contracted a number of tropical diseases. In July 1898, the Surgeon General asked that a corps of black women be organized to nurse infirm black soldiers. Thirty-two black women were sent to care for black troops located at Camp Thomas, Georgia. These trailblazers were so well received Congress created a permanent Army Nurse Corps in 1901. The Navy Nurse Corps was established in 1908. Women had finally become an official part of the military, but ironically, black women were barred from both corps for another four decades.

However, black nurses were accepted into the Red Cross. The opportunities for black nurses to serve the military directly and through the Red Cross were important during the era of Jim Crow because there were very few black health care facilities and black nurses were rarely permitted employment in white hospitals.

The World Wars

During World War I, 650,000 black men served in the U.S. military, with approximately a third of these stationed in France. Nationwide hundreds of black nurses registered with the American Red Cross. In June 1918 the secretary of war issued a call for black nurses who were affiliated with the Red Cross to volunteer for overseas duty as well as for service at home. Among those who responded was Adah B. Thoms, the president of the National Association of Colored Graduate Nurses. Many others served the more than 38,000 black troops confined to base hospitals in Kansas, Illinois, Iowa, Kentucky, Ohio, and New Jersey. Elizabeth Miller was even assigned to a government military hospital in Alabama. Blacks had to fight for an official Red Cross charter just as they fought other racial oppression. In 1918 Tuskegee Institute in Alabama received the first Red Cross chapter awarded to African Americans. Bess Bolden Walcott, known as "the Red Cross Lady" was the executive secretary of the chapter from 1918–1951, leading the group during World War I, World War II, and the Korean War as the Red Cross aided soldiers and their families in time of war and peace, assisted with disaster relief, provided health care to rural inhabitants, fed the needy, initiated blood and milk banks, and raised funds for war causes.

Black women were mobilized on the home front in various capacities. They took advantage of employment opportunities in the war industries, working at factories and plants in Detroit, St. Louis, Louisville (Kentucky), Baltimore, Philadelphia, and Washington, DC. More significantly, they were active leaders in volunteer work to support the war. Black clubwomen organized Hostess Houses in states with military bases and services. Under the leadership of the National Association of Colored Women (NACW), founded in 1896, African American clubwomen had provided considerable support to their men and the nation in the Spanish-American War. During the short war, the group had investigated the conditions under which black soldiers served and made recommendations for improvement. In World War I their contributions were more significant as state and local club affiliates became involved to a greater extent in the war effort than ever before allowed. Martha F. White, who headed the state effort for black clubwomen in Iowa during World War I utilized the media, black churches, and her club to solicit aid that manifested itself mostly in canning jelly for black servicemen confined to hospitals, knitting various items of clothing, making flags, and serving as camp mothers to the 366th Infantry at Camp Dodge, Iowa. Statewide the group raised more than six thousand dollars in Liberty War Bonds. Mary McLeod Bethune, a later NACW president, worked with the Emergency Circle, Negro War Relief in Florida.

Black women in Colorado formed the Negro Women's Auxiliary War Council, a Negro Women's League for Service, and a Red Cross auxiliary. Alice Dugged Carey headed war relief work in Georgia under the umbrella of the Georgia State Federation of Colored Women's Clubs. Marion B. Wilkerson coordinated war work through the South Carolina Federation of Colored Women's Clubs in her state, where the Phyllis Wheatley Club was already very active in war relief activities. The Circle of Negro War Relief and the Crispus Attucks Circle were organized in Philadelphia. Detroit had a Josephine Gray Colored Lady Knitters Club. Black women in New York formed a woman's auxiliary to the Fifteenth Regiment, an all-black unit that became the first New York State Guard. These and numerous other clubs knitted for soldiers, provided comfort kits, organized letter writing campaigns, cooked food, provided entertainment, and raised large sums of money. One of the most successful fundraisers by black women during World War I was staged in Savannah, Georgia, where 250,000 dollars was raised. Nationally, black women raised five million dollars for the war effort.

The United States entered World War II in December 1941. During the war and throughout the 1940s a number of developments improved opportunities for black women to participate in the armed forces. Pressure from civil rights activists such as A. Philip Randolph, Mary McLeod Bethune, the National Association for the Advancement of Colored People (NAACP), the black press, and Franklin D. Roosevelt's "Black Cabinet," combined with the military's changing needs to create opportunities for black women to serve their country. Perhaps the most important development was the creation of the Women's Army Auxiliary Corps (WAAC) in May 1942. The WAAC was incorporated into the regular U.S. Army in 1943 when it became the Women's Army Corps (WAC). Black and white women were accepted into both but segregation and discrimination prevailed. By the end of World

WILLA BEATRICE BROWN c. 1941–1945, when she was in her thirties and was training pilots for the U.S. Army Air Force. She was the first woman commissioned as a lieutenant in the Civil Air Patrol. (National Archives; Joe McCary, Photo Response Studio.)

War II more than four thousand black women had joined the WAC.

The first black woman in U.S. history to be commissioned as an officer was a WAC, Charity Adams. Attaining the rank of major she was the highest-ranking black woman throughout World War II. Adams described her military experience in the book *One Woman's Army: A Black Officer Remembers the WAC* (1989). The second highest ranking woman during World War II was an Alabama native with a degree in Home Economics Education, Abbie Noel Campbell. Campbell was the Executive Officer to Company B of the Third Training Regiment. This company was the first all-black WAAC training unit in the U.S. military. Company B later was incorporated as part of the WAC Training Center at Ft. Des Moines. With Charity Adams serving as commander, Adams and Campbell were responsible for running the company. All WAAC and later WAC recruits came into this company for their basic training. In 1945 the company, along with eight hundred other black women went to Birmingham, England, to form the 6888th Central Postal Battalion. They were the first all-black female unit to deploy overseas.

There were thirty-four women beside Adams and Campbell in that first group of black women commissioned as military officers in the WAAC at Ft. Des Moines. Forty black women with college degrees were invited to join the six-week course but only thirty-nine showed up. While all four hundred white women invited to take the course completed it, only thirty-six black women received commissions as Second Lieutenants in the United States Army. This first graduating class included Charity Adams, Frances Alexander, Myrtle Anderson, Violet Askens, Varaneal Austin, Mary Bordeaux, Geraldine Bright, Annie Brown, Harriet Buhile, Abbie Campbell, Mildred Carter, Irma Cayton, Natalie Donaldson, Sarah Emmert, Geneva Ferguson, Ruth Freeman, Evelyn Green, Elizabeth Hampton, Vera Harrison, Dovey Johnson, Alice Jones, Mary Kearney, Mary Lewis, Ruth Lucas, Charline Mary, Ina McFadden, Mary Miller, Glendora Moore, Sarah Murphy, Doris Norrel, Mildred Osby, Gertrude Peebles, Corris Sherard, Jessie Ward, and Harriet West. The WAC also had a renowned black band. The 404th Army Service Band sang and performed nationwide at black and white military, civilian, and church functions.

The navy opened its doors to black women during World War II with a plan to raise black recruitment to 10 percent of the navy's total personnel and to form the Women's Reserve of the United States Navy, also called WAVES (Women Accepted for Volunteer Emergency Service). In 1944 Bessie Garret became the first black woman accepted. Two black women, Frances Wills and Harriet Pickens, were among the first WAVES officers from Smith College. The Coast Guard admitted five black women during World War II. Among them were Olivia J. Hooker, who later became a clinical psychologist. The first black WAVES to enter the Hospital Corps were Ruth C. Issacs, Katherine Horton, and Inez Patterson.

The navy's plan fell short of its goals. The 10 percent black quota was never achieved during World War II and as of 1945 there were only fifty-six black WAVES. However, the navy became the first of the armed services to incorporate women into its active-duty force, where they worked alongside men. The WAC, in contrast, did not become part of the regular army until 1978. With the elimination of these separate auxiliaries, the navy and the army actually increased the total number of commissioned and enlisted women in active service.

Both the army and navy, however, continued to maintain a separate nurse corps. While both branches formed their nurse corps at the beginning of the twentieth century, black nurses were not admitted until World War II, due largely to the efforts of Nurse Mabel Keaton Staupers and Mary McLeod Bethune. The first black women to serve on active duty in the armed forces, in fact, were members of the Army Nurse Corps. The first group included fifty-six nurses, among them Lt. Della Raney and Lt. Susan Elizabeth Freeman who entered in 1941. Phyllis Mae Daley became the first black inducted into the Navy Nurse Corps in 1945. Considerably more black females served in the army Nurse Corps than the navy. Black nurses served in all-black military hospitals as well as in four general hospitals, regional hospitals, and at least nine station hospitals. Additionally, black women nurses served in Africa and in Europe during World War II.

Out of the Cold War and into the Twenty-first Century

The United States led the United Nations war in Korea during the early 1950s. Women who went to Korea were nurses with the Red Cross, the Army Nurse Corps, or the Navy Nurse Corps. Small numbers of other women served during the Korean War in Tokyo, Japan, and other places in the Far East Command far from the battle zone. When the Korean War began, there were about 29,000 total women in all branches of the military services. The numbers increased to nearly 100,000 by 1956. It is not known how many of these were black, but the great majority were white. One black soldier, I. C. Rochell, was on duty in Korea for more than seventeen months and reported seeing only one black woman, a nurse with the Red Cross. One of the lasting achievements of women during the Korean War was the formation of the Defense Advisory Committee on Women in the Armed Services (DACOWITS), a group that still functions today in the interest of women in the military. One black woman who later served on this powerful committee was Clara Adams-Ender, a general in the Army Nurse Corps.

Featuring Women in the Military

● **Clara Leach Adams-Ender** (1939–) was the second black woman to achieve the rank of brigadier general in the U.S. Army, but that feat was preceded by a number of amazing firsts. Raised in Wake County, North Carolina, she attended North Carolina A&T State University (BS, Nursing, 1961) and joined the army right after she graduated. She was the first woman awarded the Expert Field Medical Badge (1967) and the master of military art and science degree from the Command and General Staff College (1976). She was the first black woman to graduate from the U.S. Army War College (1982) and to become chief of the Department of Nursing at Walter Reed Army Medical Center (1984). Only three years later she was made chief of the Army Nurses Corps, and a month after that, brigadier general. In 1991, she became the first nurse to serve as commanding general of a major military base (Fort Belvoir, Virginia). She retired in 1993. In addition to her other duties, Adams-Ender served as a member of the Defense Advisory Committee on Women in the Services and was also a member of the National Council of Negro Women and the National Association for Female Executives. Among her many awards, she received the military's Distinguished Service Award and Meritorious Service Medal with three oak-leaf clusters. Her autobiography, *My Rise to the Stars: How a Sharecropper's Daughter Became an Army General*, was published in 2002.

● **Vernice Armour** (1973–) was the first black woman combat pilot. Born in Memphis, Tennessee, she attended Middle Tennessee State University (BA, Exercise Science, 1997). While there she joined the Army Reserve Officers' Training Corps and the Reserves. She became a police officer in Nashville, Tennessee, and was the first woman on its motorcycle squad, before moving to the Tempe, Arizona, force. In 1998 she joined the Marine Corps and attended Officer Candidate School. When she received her wings in 2001, she was the top-ranked soldier in her class of two hundred. As a result, she was awarded the Naval Air Station's academic achievement award. A Super Cobra helicopter pilot, Armour was assigned to the Marine Light Attack Helicopter Squadron 169 and served in the Iraq War in 2003. The same year she was named one of the "50 Women Who Are Shaping the World" by *Essence* magazine. In 2004, Armour was promoted to captain and returned to Camp Pendleton. An athlete as well as a pilot, she won the Marine Corps Community Services Female Athlete of the Year Award (2001) and was a two-time winner of the Camp Pendleton Strongest Warrior competition. She also played running back for the San Diego Sunfire women's professional football team. She returned from Iraq in 2004.

● **Margaret E. Bailey** (1915–) was the first black nurse in the U.S. Army to become a lieutenant colonel (1964) and the first to hold the rank of full colonel (1970). Born in Selma, Alabama, she attended the Fraternal Hospital School of Nursing in Montgomery and San Francisco State College. She joined the U.S. Army in 1944 and served at Fort Huachuca, Arizona. A specialist in medical and surgical nursing, she later continued her education by studying psychiatric nursing at Fort Sam Houston, Texas. In addition, she headed the Nightingale nursing program (named for Florence Nightingale) at Fitzsimmons General Hospital in Denver, Colorado. Throughout her career, she not only recruited nurses for the Army, but fought segregation and inequality within its ranks. When she retired in 1971, she was awarded the Legion of Merit for Exceptionally Meritorious Conduct. In 1999 she published her autobiography, *The Challenge: Autobiography of Colonel Margaret E. Bailey—First Black Nurse Promoted to Colonel in the U.S. Army Nurse Corps* (1999).

● **Sherian Grace Cadoria** (1940–) was the first black woman in the regular U.S. Army to achieve the rank of brigadier general and the second black woman in history to earn the honor. (See individual entry: Cadoria, Sherian Grace.)

● **Julia Cleckley** (?–) was the first black woman in the Army National Guard to achieve the rank of brigadier general. Raised in Aliquippa, Pennsylvania, she attended Hunter College (BA, Psychology and Education) and Golden Gate University (MA, Human Resource Management). She first enlisted in the Women's Army Corps as soon as she graduated from high school and served for three years. She then became a schoolteacher and in 1976 joined the National Guard and was commissioned with New York's 42nd Infantry Division. In 1987 she became a full-time member of the Guard and began climbing the ranks. In order to advance her career, she attended the U.S. Army War College and received a senior service fellowship to the Fletcher School of Law and Diplomacy at Tufts University. In 2002, she was promoted to one-star general. Her other firsts include becoming the first woman of color to become a branch chief with the National Guard, the first black woman colonel in the Army National Guard Active Reserve, and the first woman and black to serve on the Army National Guard director's special staff as chief of Human Resources. She also taught military science at Hampton University. In 2003 she was named Special Assistant for Military Women for Federally Employed Women. Among her many awards and honors, in 1998 she received the NAACP Roy Wilkins Renowned Service Award.

● **Charity Adams Earley** (1918–2002) was an officer in the Women's Army Auxiliary Corps. She trained women to become soldiers, fought segregation in the army, and left the military with the rank of lieutenant colonel. (See individual entry: Earley, Charity Adams.)

● **Rhonda Fleming-Makell** (1962–) was the first black woman in the U.S. Coast Guard to retire as a commissioned officer. Born in Morgantown, North Carolina, she attended South Carolina State

University (BS, Psychology). She joined the Coast Guard in 1984 and graduated from Coast Guard Officer Candidate School in 1986. She also earned a master's degree in business administration from the University of Phoenix in Arizona. While working her way up the ranks in the Coast Guard, Fleming-Makell was operations officer at the Coast Guard Command Center, chief of district personnel, and law enforcement specialist at the Coast Guard's Office of Law Enforcement. When she retired in 2004 after twenty years in the service, she had earned the rank of lieutenant commander.

● **Lillian Elaine Fishburne** (1949–) was the first black woman rear admiral in the U.S. Navy. She was born into a career naval family and raised in Rockville, Maryland. After receiving her BA in Sociology from Lincoln University (1971), she joined the U.S. Navy and graduated from the Women Officer's School (1973). In the late 1970s she returned to school and received a master's in Management from Webster College (1980) and another in Telecommunications Systems Management from the Naval Postgraduate School (1982). For the next two years, she served as assistant head in the Joint Allied Command and Control Matters Branch of the Command, Control, Communications Directorate, Chief of Naval Operations. She also served as executive officer at the Naval Communication Station, Yokosuka, Japan (1984–1987), and as commanding officer at the Naval Computer and Telecommunications Station, Key West, Florida (1990–1992). She spent 1993 studying at the Industrial College of the Armed Forces and then became chief of the Command and Control Systems Support Division of the Joint Staff. In 1995, she became the commander of the Naval Computer and Telecommunications Area Master Station for the Eastern Pacific. She was promoted to navy flag officer and rear admiral in 1998 and then became director of the Information Transfer Division for the Space, Information Warfare, Command and Control Directorate, Chief of Naval Operations. Rear Admiral Fishburne retired in 2001. Over the course of her long career she received numerous medals and awards, including the Defense Superior Service Medal and the Legion of Merit.

● **Marcelite Jordon Harris** (1943–) was the first and only black woman to earn the rank of major general in the U.S. Air Force. At her retirement in 1997, she was the highest-ranking female officer in the Air Force. (See individual entry: Harris, Marcelite Jordon.)

● **Hazel Winifred Johnson-Brown** (1927–) broke through convention, custom, and racial and gender barriers in 1979 when she became the leader of the U.S. Army Nurses Corps and the first black woman general in the American military. (See individual entry: Johnson, Hazel Winifred.)

● **Mabel Keaton Staupers** (1890–1989) was best known for her role in implementing the desegregation of the U.S. Army Nurse Corps during World War II. (See individual entry: Staupers, Mabel Keaton.)

● **Harriet Ross Tubman** (c. 1821–1913) earned distinction as the only woman in American military history to plan and execute an armed expedition against enemy forces. Serving in numerous capacities, Tubman was a spy, scout, and nurse for the Union Army stationed in the Carolinas and Florida. For thirty years, Tubman fought to receive a pension from the U.S. government for her military services and eventually won a $20-per-month stipend. (See individual entry: Tubman, Harriet Ross.)

● **Cathy Williams** (c. 1844–?) was a buffalo soldier serving on the frontier. Information about her life is sketchy at best; however, according to Williams's own testimony she was born near Independence, Missouri, the daughter of a free man and an enslaved woman. She became a contraband (a slave who during the Civil War escaped to or was brought within the Union lines) during the Civil War and worked as a cook and laundress for various army officers. She enlisted in the army under the name William Cathay or Cathey on 15 November 1866. Army medical exams during this period were superficial at best, and no one questioned Williams's gender. At the time she was recorded as being 5 feet, 9 inches tall and twenty-two years old. (She may have lied about her age.) She served with the Thirty-Eighth U.S. Infantry until 1868. Although she was frequently ill during her time in the army, her gender was never discovered. When she was not ill, she seems to have served her unit adequately. On 14 October 1868, William Cathay was discharged from the army because of disability. She went back to being Cathy Williams and became a cook and laundress working in various towns in New Mexico and Colorado. In 1891, she applied for an invalid pension from the army. Living in Trinidad, Colorado, her story was finally told. The army, however, refused her pension after an examiner determined that her disabilities were not related to her time in service.

● **Matice Wright** (c. 1965–) was the Navy's first black female naval flight officer. She attended the United States Naval Academy, where she received a BS in Physical Sciences and Engineering in 1988. After becoming a flight officer, she was assigned to Fleet Air Reconnaissance Squadron 3 in 1993. After leaving the Navy, she worked for Sikorsky Aircraft Corporation, SRA International, Booz Allen Hamilton, Inc., and United Technologies Corporation. She also continued her education, receiving a master's degree in Public Administration from the John F. Kennedy School of Government at Harvard University. In addition, she was a White House Fellow with the U.S. Treasury Department and a member of both the Council for Emerging National Security Affairs (CENSA) and the Council on Foreign Relations.

President Truman's executive order banning segregation in the armed forces in the late 1940s and the 1954 *Brown v. Board of Education* Supreme Court ruling against school segregation began the long process of eliminating racial separation in the United States. In the military, by 1973, toward the end of the Vietnam War, almost 10 percent of the American troops who served in Vietnam were black, including thousands of black women. From this point on, a series of new firsts signaled the gains made by black women. The Reverend Alice Henderson became the first woman chaplain in the country in 1974. During the same year, Jill Brown became the first black woman in U.S. military history to qualify as a pilot. In 1975 the Naval Medical Corps appointed its first black female physician, Donna P. Davis. Black women were being admitted to all military academies by 1976 when entrance requirements were the same for both sexes, except weight and height. During the 1970s the Reserved Officer Training Corp (ROTC) also opened its doors to women and in 1973 Linda Rochell and Mary Hudson became the first black women admitted to the ROTC program in the University of Missouri system. In March 1980 Hazel W. Johnson-Brown became the first black woman in U.S. history to hold the rank of general. Johnson, who also had a PhD, was Chief of the U.S. Army Nurse Corps. Two other black women generals promoted during the 1980s were General Sherian Cadoria in the army and General Clara Adams-Ender of the Army Nurse Corps. General Marcelite J. Harris, in the air force, received her rank in 1990. Mary Saunders of Texas also became an air force general.

Today, black women are allowed to join all areas of the U.S. armed services, except combat arms units (infantry, armor, artillery, and combat engineers). Women are attached to combat arms units, however, in support capacities. During operations Desert Shield and Desert Storm, Captain Cynthia Mosley commanded Alpha Company of the 24th Forward Support Battalion, 24th Infantry Division, while Captain Greta Garrett was the Headquarters Company Commander in an infantry unit at Fort Benning, Georgia. Mosley's company was responsible for refueling vehicles and resupplying troops located in the war zone. Moreover, a black woman, Lieutenant Phoebe Jeter, was instrumental in shooting down the first Scud missile in the Gulf War. As many as 40 percent of the thirty-five thousand female soldiers involved in the Gulf War were black, and three black women lost their lives.

September 11, 2001, will live in infamy for twenty-first-century Americans after the terrorist attacks that struck the Pentagon in Washington, DC, and destroyed the World Trade Center in New York City left U.S. citizens in shock from traumatic scenes of victims jumping from the towering infernos, twin symbols of architectural superiority and

 Black Women Killed in the September 11, 2001, Attack on the Pentagon

Samantha L. Allen, civilian budget analyst with the U.S. Army.

Carrie Blagburn, 48, civilian budget analyst with the U.S. Army.

Angelene Carter, 51, civilian accountant with the U.S. Army.

Sharon Ann Carver, 38, civilian accountant with the U.S. Army.

Sarah M. Clark, 65, sixth-grade teacher at Backus Middle School, American Airlines Flight 77.

Asia Cottom, 11, sixth grader at Backus Middle School, American Airlines Flight 77.

Ada Marie Davis, 57, civilian accountant with the U.S. Army.

Amelia V. Fields, 36, civilian secretary with the U.S. Army.

Sandra Nadine Foster, 41, civilian senior management officer for the Defense Intelligence Agency, Defense Department.

Brenda Colbert Gibson, 59, civilian budget analyst with the U.S. Army.

Diane M. Hale-McKinzy, 38, civilian employee with the U.S. Army.

Carolyn Halmon, 49, civilian budget analyst with the U.S. Army.

Peggie Hurt, 36, civilian accountant for the U.S. Army.

Brenda Kegler, 49, civilian budget analyst with the U.S. Army.

Ada Wilson Mason, 50, civilian budget analyst with the U.S. Army.

Odessa V. Morris, 54, civilian budget analyst with the U.S. Army.

Marsha D. Ratchford, 34, information technician for the U.S. Navy.

Cecelia E. Richard, 41, accounting technician with the U.S. Army.

Judy Rowlett, 44, civilian employee with the U.S. Army.

Janice Scott, 46, civilian budget officer with the U.S. Army.

Antoinette "Toni" Sherman, 35, civilian budget analyst with the U.S. Army.

Edna Lee Stephens, 53, civilian budget analyst with the U.S. Army.

Hilda E. Taylor, sixth-grade teacher at M. V. Leckie Elementary School, American Airlines Flight 77.

Sgt. Tamara Thurman, 25, assistant in the office of the deputy chief of staff for personnel, U.S. Army.

Lt. Col. Karen Wagner, 40, medical personnel officer, deputy chief of staff for personnel, office of the Army surgeon general.

Meta Fuller Waller, 60, civilian special programs manager with the U.S. Army.

Staff Sgt. Maudlyn A. White, 38, U.S. Army.

Sandra Leticia White, civilian budget analyst with the U.S. Army.

Lisa Young, 36, civilian personnel assistant with the U.S. Army.

industrial might tumbling to the ground. In response, President George W. Bush declared a war on terrorism, which in the ensuing years placed a number of African American men and women in the Middle East in a war zone, fighting Islamic and Arab peoples and cultures that are foreign to most Americans. In 2004 Rep. Charles Rangel (D-NY) introduced a bill to reinstate the draft. The chief of the Selective Service System also proposed that women register for the military draft. The director of the

Selective Service further recommended the extension of the proposed draft age from twenty-five to thirty-four in order to bring in the critical skills, education, and experience required by a U.S. military that in all aspects and at all levels relies to a great extent on technology—from fighter planes to submarines to Army infantry and Marine footsoldiers, from supply and medical services to the combat arms. While the proposed draft was still under discussion as of early 2005, another gender-based military policy enforced by Defense Secretary Donald Rumsfeld caused a furor among women when those stationed in Saudi Arabia and other Islamic countries were ordered to wear Muslim religious attire—long black cloaks called *abayas*—when off base, even though the majority of U.S. women in the armed forces are Christian. A white colonel, Martha McSally of the air force, successfully challenged this policy.

While thousands of black women have served in the Middle East as part of a war on terror that in 2004 looked to have no end, few stories are more poignant than that of Shoshana Johnson. A native of Panama who resided in El Paso, Texas, Johnson was a member of the 507th Maintenance Company from Ft. Bliss and is considered the first African American woman soldier to be a prisoner of war. She was held twenty-two days in captivity in Iraq after her military convoy of supply vehicles was ambushed. In the ambush, eleven American soldiers were killed and five taken prisoner, Shoshana Johnson and Jessica Lynch among them. Johnson was shot and suffered beatings along with her male comrades, but after the Iraqis realized Johnson was female, the beatings stopped and she began to get slightly better treatment. Johnson and the male captives were rescued 13 April 2003 by the U.S. Marines.

See also Civil War; Revolutionary War; Vietnam; World War I; *and* World War II.

BIBLIOGRAPHY

Blanton, DeAnne and Cook, Lauren M. *They Fought Like Demons: Women Soldiers in the American Civil War*. Baton Rouge, LA: Louisiana State University Press, 2002.
Earley, Charity Adams. *One Woman's Army: A Black Officer Remembers the WAC*. College Station, TX: Texas A&M University Press, 1989.
Holm, Jeanne. *Women in the Military: An Unfinished Revolution*. New York: Ballantine Books, Inc., 1982.
MacGregor, Morris J. and Bernard C. Nalty, eds. *Blacks in the United States Armed Forces: Basic Documents*. Wilmington, DE: Scholarly Resources, Inc., 1977.
Moore, Brenda L. *To Serve My Country, To Serve My Race: The Story of the Only African American WACs*. New York: New York University Press, 1996.
Moore, Brenda L. *Serving Our Country: Japanese American Women in the Military During World War II*. Camden, NJ: Rutgers University Press, 2004.
Moskos, C. and Butler, J. *All That We Can Be: Black Leadership and Racial Integration the Army Way*. New York: HarperCollins Publishers, 1996.
Putney, Martha S. *When The Nation Was In Need: Blacks in the Women's Army Corps During World War II*. Chicago: Rowman & Littlefield Publishers, Inc., 1992.
Putney, Marcha S. *Blacks in the United States Army: Portraits Through History*. Jefferson, NC: McFarland & Company, Incorporated Publishers, 2003.
Wallace, Terry. *Bloods: An Oral History of the Vietnam War by Black Veterans*. New York: Random House Publishing Group, 1984.

—Linda Rochell Lane

MILLER, CHERYL (b. 3 January 1964), basketball player, coach, and sports broadcaster. Cheryl Miller is one of the best known figures, male or female, in American basketball. Her successes as a player, coach, and broadcaster secured her place in basketball lore. Along the way, she helped raise the level of and respect for women in the sports as few others have. On the court, she showed that "women have game, too." Behind the microphone, she has shown that a woman can bring the knowledge and insight of a player to the profession of sports broadcasting.

Cheryl Miller, who led the United States to a gold medal in the Olympics of 1984, was elected to the Basketball Hall of Fame in 1995. (Basketball Hall of Fame, Springfield, Massachusetts.)

Cheryl De Ann Miller (also known as Cheryl DeAnne Miller) was born in Riverside, California. She is the third child and oldest daughter of Saul Miller, who worked on computers in both the military and civilian sectors, and Carrie Miller, a nurse. Growing up with two older brothers, Saul Jr. and Darrel, a younger brother, Reggie, and a younger sister, Tammy, Cheryl had plenty of company and competition to hone her athletic skills. Through pickup games on her backyard and neighborhood basketball courts as well as on organized youth teams, she first developed the game and attitude that would eventually lead her to stardom. Often, she played with and against boys (her brother Reggie was also a great player who would go on to professional stardom). She remembers that in many of these games, some of the boys initially questioned her abilities. Yet, after seeing her play, the same boys who had doubted her gave her their respect.

With the encouragement of her family, Miller first gained national prominence as a high school player at Riverside Polytechnic High School from 1979 to 1982. There, she achieved unprecedented success and acclaim. While she set numerous records in high school, some of her most astounding achievements included scoring 105 points in one game, making the first two dunks recorded in women's competition, and leading the Riverside Polytechnic basketball team to four consecutive California state championships with a cumulative record of 132 wins and 4 losses. By the end of her high school career, she was a four-time *Parade* magazine all-American, an accomplishment never before achieved by any male or female athlete. Named *Street and Smith's* national High School Player of the Year in 1981 and 1982, she received more than 250 college scholarship offers.

Miller eventually chose to attend and play for the University of Southern California (USC). In her four years at the university, Miller continued her string of athletic successes. She led her teams to back-to-back National Collegiate Athletic Association (NCAA) championships in 1983 and 1984, which solidified the Trojans as one of the first dynasties in women's college basketball. While still in college, Miller simultaneously began her climb toward international prominence as a member of the gold medal–winning U.S. national teams at the Pan American, Olympic, and Goodwill Games. By the end of her college career, Miller held a multitude of university and NCAA records, was named to numerous all-American teams, and won several national player of the year awards. In addition, she became the first USC athlete, male or female, to have her jersey retired, an astonishing feat given the storied athletic tradition of that university.

After her stellar college career, Miller decided not to play professional women's basketball, which at that time was essentially limited to European leagues. This decision, along with a knee injury, combined to end her playing days. As a result, she decided to put her degree in broadcast journalism to use. Gaining a position with ABC Sports, she became a successful sports broadcaster for college basketball and football.

After a few years, Miller returned to a more active role in basketball as a coach. Beginning as a part-time assistant coach at USC, she eventually became head coach at her alma mater in 1993. Despite a tumultuous work environment that was caused by an extensive legal battle between the university and former head coach Marianne Stanley, Miller led the Trojans back to national prominence by winning the 1994 Pac-10 title in her first season and taking her team into the NCAA tournament in 1994 and 1995. After the 1995 season, she resigned as coach of the Trojans, despite what was deemed a successful run, to become a National Basketball Association (NBA) analyst for Turner Sports.

Miller's coaching career was not over. By 1997 she was back, this time as head coach and general manager for the Phoenix Mercury, part of the new Women's National Basketball Association (WNBA). Her presence undoubtedly gave the league added interest and credibility during its early years. In her first season, she coached the Mercury to the WNBA finals, but she was unable to repeat that success in the following years. In 2000 Miller retired from coaching again and returned to her career as a sports broadcaster. As of 2004, she was once again working for Turner Sports as an NBA analyst.

Miller remains one of the most celebrated basketball players in history. She won more than 1,140 trophies and was inducted into both the Basketball Hall of Fame (1995) and the National Women's Hall of Fame (1999). She maintains that one of her remaining goals is to become a head coach in the NBA. Already well respected as a studio analyst by players and fans, and the first female broadcaster to call a nationally televised NBA game, she is one of the leading candidates to become the first female coach in the NBA. If she does, it will be a crowning achievement to an already stellar career.

BIBLIOGRAPHY

Barrington, Deborah. "Miller Rises in Phoenix: WNBA Attracts 80s Star, TV Analyst Adds Roles as GM, Coach." *USA Today*, 18 June 1997.

Boeck, Greg. "Cheryl Miller Confident She Will Coach in the NBA." *USA Today*, 8 June 2000.

"Cheryl Miller." The Official Site of the Naismith Memorial Basketball Hall of Fame. http://www.hoophall.com/halloffamers/MillerC.htm.

Medea, Andra. "Cheryl Miller." In *Facts on File Encyclopedia of Black Women in America*, edited by Darlene Clark Hine. New York: Facts on File, 1997.

Martzke, Rudy. "Turner's Miller Earns Respect around the NBA." *USA Today*, 26 April 1996.

Smith, Jessie Carney, ed. *Notable Black American Women*. Book 3. Detroit, MI: Gale Group, 2002.

Who's Who among African Americans. 15th ed. New York: Gale Group, 2002.

Who's Who in America 2003. New Providence, NJ: Marquis Who's Who, 2003.

—ERIC D. DUKE

MILLINERY. A skilled needle trade of the nineteenth and twentieth centuries, millinery required that a woman not only know the techniques of hat making but also have some natural artistic talent of her own. Millinery required a great deal of expert handwork. Once she envisioned the hat, the milliner molded, shaped, and manipulated the materials to achieve the desired silhouette. All of this creativity expressed itself through skilled handwork and intimate knowledge of the materials.

Artisans at Work

Millinery was a well-respected occupation for women; however, it was never an occupation dominated by black women. Some black women worked as assistants to well-established milliners, while others owned their own shops. Of this latter group, some worked out of their homes in a "parlor trade," or private clientele. A parlor trade required less capital than a millinery shop. Black women milliners who conducted their professions in business establishments or shops rather than at home had to have greater funds for both custom-made and retail stock, yet the millinery shop generated a larger

MILLINERS' CLASS AT TUSKEGEE. Tuskegee, Wilberforce, Hampton, and other schools gave at least one course in millinery. If a woman did not master this craft in school, she might learn it from a relative or through an apprenticeship, or in on-the job training. (Austin/Thompson Collection, from the National Archives.)

HAT SHOP. A clerk (left) and the manager (right) at Cecilia's Specialty Hat Shop, 454 East 47th Street, Chicago, in April 1942. (Library of Congress.)

customer base. Most shops included a milliner who designed the hats and several assistant milliners who constructed the hats. All had to be experts at their profession in order to have a successful business.

Millinery, an occupation for women that paid better than others, was a skilled profession. However, it was also an unstable one. Millinery held women to seasonal work (usually eight to ten months a year), demanded loyal customers, and required expertise of its milliners. Add to these facts the need for resources to buy the materials required to create hats, and one can understand why fewer black women worked in millinery than in the other needle trades.

Milliners were considered artists who worked in a variety of mediums (straw, felt, silk, fur, wire, and buckram)

that were then embellished with feathers, flowers, sequins, ribbons, bows, and other trims. Hats were as important as the dress or suit—the object was to impress the beholder. Successful milliners studied a woman's features as well as the prospective outfit to create a hat that harmonized with the ensemble. A milliner's skill included the ability to make a hat that was not only becoming but also up to date. Successful black milliners possessed these traits and were continuous students of the fine art of fashion change. Every season brought new styles of hats made of innovative materials or made of traditional textiles with a unique twist. Black milliners reinvented old hat styles, copied Parisian models illustrated in *Vogue* and other fashion publications, and created innovative shapes. Successful milliners were noted for their skills as designers and talent at creating the hat itself. Designing a successful hat included the knowledge of color and harmony. The milliner, like the dressmaker, had to understand how the shape and color of a hat worked with the shape of the head and the complexion of the client. In addition, a hat also had to work well with the client's wardrobe.

Changing Styles

During the late nineteenth century, women's hat styles changed as often as their dress and skirt styles. Both bonnets and hats were worn, depending on the fashion period. Some had high crowns with narrow brims, others had low crowns with wide brims. Felt, velvet, beaver, and plush constituted winter hats, while straw, felt, velvet, and wire supported summer hats. Hat styles in the early twentieth century ranged from the wide-brimmed picture hats of the early years of the century to the brimless toques, accentuated with one tall feather in the 1910s, to the molded felt dome-shaped cloches of the 1920s. The artistry of a milliner expressed itself not only through the hat's style but also in its decorations. In the early twentieth century, milliners used some of the same materials from the nineteenth century: feathers, flowers, ribbons, and bows.

Hats remained an important component of a woman's overall appearance in early-twentieth-century America. Milliners continued to supply the desires of their communities, towns, and cities. In the South, Jim Crow policies forced black women to establish businesses to serve the needs of their communities. Poor treatment in white-owned businesses motivated black women to establish millinery businesses in their own neighborhoods. Newspaper advertisements provide evidence of millinery companies located in black communities throughout the United States. The Mays Millinery company in Atlanta was one such company. Perhaps most large southern cities had at least one black-owned and -operated millinery company.

Historical evidence also indicates that in the early twentieth century the number of black women milliners working in the United States increased. Although the numbers were small and not comparable to the number of women working as dressmakers and seamstresses, black women continued in millinery as a profession. In fact, millinery was one of the artisan occupations listed and discussed in W. E. B. Du Bois's published study "The Negro American Artisan." According to the study, in 1900 there were 180 black women working as milliners nationwide, compared with 11,538 working as seamstresses and 12,572 as dressmakers. Such schools as Tuskegee, Wilberforce, and Hampton taught at least one course in millinery. If a woman did not master the craft in school, she learned it from a relative, by means of on-the-job training, or through an apprenticeship that lasted two to three years. Starting out, the apprentice was little more than an errand girl. As time went on, she learned not only the specific techniques of molding felt, braiding straw, or pleating silk but also important business skills that might lead to the ownership of her own establishment.

Industry Decline and Revival

Millinery continued as a trade for black women throughout the twentieth century. But as the century progressed, wearing a hat with every outfit and for every occasion became less popular. Millinery declined as an occupation in the 1930s as women gave up making their own hats or going to milliners for special orders. Women began reserving hats for church and special occasions. By the 1930s a store-bought hat usually looked better than a homemade one and was less expensive than a custom-designed hat. At this time the mass-production of hats, the millinery section of retailers, and the number of milliners also decreased. During World War II women wore hats of straw and felt in wide- and narrow-brimmed styles; in addition, it became fashionable to don a turban or a scarf to cover the head or protect the hair from machinery while working in factories. In the 1950s hats became immensely fashionable again as the industry of millinery revived, but hats were small feather, felt, and straw creations that generally fit close to the head.

Magazines, such as *Ebony*, documented in its pages some of the leading black milliners of the 1950s. They included Arti-Bell, Mildred Blount, Juanita Chapman, Evelyn Killings, Nancy Lockhart, Juanita Scott, Juliet Stewart, Ruth Toles, Artie Williams, and Ellie Williams. All of the women achieved fame and respect for their

 The Hats of Mildred Blount

Actors Hattie McDaniel and Butterfly McQueen were not the only African American women involved in the film *Gone with the Wind*. Behind the scenes, milliner Mildred Blount worked to design hats for the period drama. Born in North Carolina in 1907, Blount grew up with relatives in Philadelphia as well as other northern cities. While working as an errand girl in a New York City shop, she became interested in millinery and soon opened a dress and hat shop with her sister Clara. Later, Blount was hired by John-Frederics Millinery of New York. At the 1939 World's Fair, a collection of period-inspired hats she had designed was exhibited, leading to her hiring for *Gone with the Wind*. She later designed for a number of films, but seldom received credit. Blount also designed for individual clients and, in 1942, had a hat on the cover of *Ladies' Home Journal*. She also received a Rosenwald Fellowship to do historical research on millinery design in American.

—KATHY A. PERKINS

Additional information about Mildred Blount can be found in the Fisk University Special Collection Archives in Nashville, Tennessee.

expertise and their stylish creations. Two of this group, Nancy Lockhart of Cleveland, Ohio, and Ellie Williams of St. Louis, Missouri, gained success not only as milliners but also as operators of millinery schools in their cities.

By the late 1960s the fashion industry lost interest in hats altogether. As a result, the millinery industry again declined. At this same time, black Americans looked to Africa for inspiration in apparel and headwear. In the late twentieth century, both black men and women were again showing an interest in hats, some African-inspired. Others wore the traditional American baseball cap but embellished it with an X to celebrate Malcolm X or with a portrait of Martin Luther King Jr. to honor his message. In addition, designers used West African fabrics like adinkra, kente, and bogolanfini to create a variety of hat styles. Rasta hats from Jamaica, produced in yellow, green, black, and red, became popular. By the 1990s McCall's Pattern Company printed patterns for making headwraps, tams, and other headwear of African-inspired fabrics. So as the passion for hats in the fashion industry declined, black Americans continued wearing hats but in newly inspired modes. Moreover, many black women continue to wear hats to church. As Michael Cunningham and Craig Marberry documented in their book *Crowns: Portraits of Black Women in Church Hats*, hats continue to adorn the head as well as to express one's connection to the past. This tradition of millinery continues into the early twenty-first century as black women create headwraps of varying styles and of multitudes of fabric to adorn their heads. These headwraps serve as a form of creative expression and as a means of connecting to the past—to the headwraps of Africa and the tignons of African slaves and free black women in America. Perhaps millinery's modes, materials, and functions have changed, but the essence of creating has not.

BIBLIOGRAPHY

Arnoldi, Mary Jo, and Christine Mullen Kreamer. *Crowning Achievements: African Arts of Dressing the Head*. Los Angeles: Fowler Museum of Cultural History, 1995.

Butler, Elizabeth Beardsley. *Women and the Trades: Pittsburgh, 1907–1908*. New York: Charities Publication Committee, 1909.

Cunningham, Michael, and Craig Marberry. *Crowns: Portraits of Black Women in Church Hats*. New York: Doubleday, 2000.

Du Bois, W. E. B., and Augustus Granville Dill, eds. *The Negro American Artisan*. Atlanta, GA: Atlanta University Press, 1912.

"Easter Bonnet Designers." *Ebony*, May 1950, 92–97.

Gamber, Wendy. *The Female Economy: The Millinery and Dressmaking Trades, 1860–1930*. Urbana: University of Illinois Press, 1997.

Hunter, Tera W. *To 'Joy My Freedom: Southern Black Women's Lives and Labors after the Civil War*. Cambridge, MA: Harvard University Press, 1997.

Jensen, Joan M. "Needlework as Art, Craft, and Livelihood before 1900." In *A Needle, a Bobbin, a Strike: Women Needleworkers in America*, edited by Joan M. Jensen and Sue Davidson. Philadelphia: Temple University Press, 1984: 3–19.

—PATRICIA HUNT-HURST

MILLION WOMAN MARCH. The gods seemed to have been against black women on 25 October 1997, the day of the Million Woman March. The rain kept up a steady drizzle, and the sound system failed. But the hundreds of thousands of women who flocked to Philadelphia's Benjamin Franklin Parkway would not be deterred. With heads covered in an array of beautiful head wraps, hats, and even plastic bags, they gathered on the Parkway to celebrate African American womanhood.

The Million Woman March was an unprecedented event. Black women had, in the past, celebrated black womanhood, organized in defense of black people and black women, and marched for black rights. But never had black women stood consciously separate from black men to voice their needs to the world. Never had so many women from different walks of life gathered to discuss, celebrate, defend, commiserate, strategize, and commune. That day, 25 October 1997, marked a watershed in black women's history.

MILLION WOMAN MARCH, 25 October 1997. This demonstration was a watershed in black women's history and underscored many issues that black women historically confronted. (© Salimah Ali. All rights reserved.)

It also painfully accentuated the many historical dilemmas black women had confronted. Throughout history, the ties that bound—race and sex—have always mixed with those that divided—class, color, sexuality, age, religion, and politics. In each other's company, black women had too often become confused over the meaning of "sisterhood," the value of "unity," and the place of black women's solidarity in race struggles. So it had been throughout the century, so it was in October 1997. The Million Woman March was, therefore, a window onto the black woman's past, present, and future.

Origin of a Movement

Phili Chionesu and Asia Coney, the march's organizers, would hardly have called themselves exceptional. Unaffiliated with any major national organization and proud of their grassroots outsider credentials, Coney and Chionesu reveled in their ordinariness. At the time of the march, Chionesu was the owner of a local African clothing and craft store and mother of a nine-year-old daughter. Coney, who had once lived in a one-bedroom apartment with her mother, stepfather, grandmother, and five siblings, had survived welfare and the murder of her twenty-three-year-old son, and had organized her fellow tenants at the Tasker Homes housing project to save it from demolition. Together, they seemed the most unlikely organizers of a march that, depending on who was counting, (the police, the press, the organizers, or attendees) brought anywhere from 500,000 to 1.5 million women to Philadelphia.

The march, however, bore Chionesu and Coney's imprint. Although some critics thought that they were trying to rival the Million Man March that had been held two years earlier, with much brouhaha over the exclusion of black women, Chionesu and Coney insisted that the Million Woman March was not conceived in the spirit of revenge or competition with black men. It was, rather, a way to address the relationships among black women. "Sisters," said Coney, "needed and wanted to get together, just as men did, to show a force of unity and support for each other."

Many, however, opposed the march. A Baltimore woman thought it an affront to African American men who needed black women to allow men "to do what they need to do to get to the point where they can honestly and respectfully stand proud as our mates and not be jealous or competitive when they finally decide to make a positive effort on behalf of the betterment of us all in the long run."

June Jordan, the late sociologist of the African American experience, also opposed the march, though for different reasons. Three months after the march, Jordan chastised black women for "standing, unified, 300,000 plus, in one place" with "no political purpose." Given the disproportionate number of women of color on welfare, women forced into already saturated low income areas of the labor market, women who were unheralded victims of urban and domestic violence, Jordan thought it tragic that so many black women would gather with no "outcry for rescue funds for public education, and rescue funds for public or subsidized housing, and rescue funds for job training and retraining, and rescue funds to establish acceptable, attainable, child care." "Not one petition," lamented Jordan.

Obviously Asia Coney, Phili Chionesu, and many others disagreed with Jordan. Their march did have a political purpose because to them "the personal was political." For them, the march was a way to get black women's attention, to remind them that racism and sexism were the source of most of their woes, and that each and every black woman was and would always be connected to all others in this way. The key to the future was to get black women to work together to address individual concerns. Power was their ultimate goal. Congresswoman Maxine Waters agreed: "We know what kind of power we have. We will act on that power." The march was just a beginning.

If Chionesu and Coney had learned anything from the Million Man March, it was that togetherness had to be cultivated, nurtured, and even learned. Hence, they emphasized their Mission Statement and Organization Purpose Issues more than they did their Platform Issues. The latter included the investigation of the drug problem in many black communities and the development of independent schools, health facilities, and support mechanisms for teenage girls, women seeking professional careers, released female prison inmates, and the homeless. The Platform Issues also expressed concern over human rights violations in the African diaspora, gentrification of black neighborhoods, aid to the elderly, and the fostering of an environment conducive to the progress of black youth.

It was the spiritually inspired Mission Statement and Organization Purpose Issues, however, that took center stage. These called for "Repentance, Restoration, and Resurrection." "Repentance" so that class divisions decreased; "Restoration" so that black women could help each other heal; and "Resurrection" in order to connect with black men and family. If black women could realize these objectives then individual and familial peace would be renewed and black women and the black community would be reborn. As the Mission Statement so eloquently put it, "The Million Woman March will revive life as we once exemplified it."

In fact, the march had the feel and flavor of a revival. "We sisters need to become family again," pined a fifty-year-old secretary from Baltimore County. Another marcher claimed, "We can be so rude to each other. . . . You see . . . a lot of black women who think, 'I can take stuff out on you because you're as low as I am.' " Like so many others, the leader of the Detroit contingent embraced the theme of healing: "Once we heal ourselves and each other, then we can heal our families, our community."

Part of this healing involved affirming black womanhood. Marchers were pained by their history. The Howard University psychologist Audrey Chapman said "black women have been assigned by society the role of 'universal mammy.' . . . [We] suckle everybody and get sucked dry. When there's nothing left to feed ourselves, we get angry. . . . There are so many angry, overwhelmed, emotionally depleted sisters." Black women wanted to see different media representations of themselves: "What I usually see in the media are black women being put down—as welfare cheats or sexually active teens," mourned a former maid whose great-grandmother had wet-nursed white babies. "I feel betrayed when I see black women portrayed as lazy and no-account." Many women saw the Million Woman March as a chance to "challenge stereotypes of black women as 'Sapphires, matriarchs and welfare queens who make babies and little else.' " As one marcher put it, "the march is . . . an independence day; Independence from poverty, from discrimination, independence from abuse." "This March is a way to show it's not a negative thing to be a woman and black. . . . Or woman, period," said a twenty-seven-year-old records manager. The march was the signal for change.

Such was the hope, a hope that stood as a phenomenal commentary on turn-of-the-century black womanhood. The need to feel a spiritual connectedness that would fill a present void was pressing. There was a profound sense of loss of communion with the only people who could possibly know how terrible racism and sexism really was. The loneliness and feeling of betrayal was so palpable that the hard "political" agenda—the platform issues mentioned here above—were hardly referred to. The deepest wounds seemed not to be those inflicted by the government, or by racists and sexists, but rather by black women themselves. Regrettably or not, Million Woman Marchers took responsibility for their own marginality and resolved to do something about it, to look inward, with people whose identity was their own.

A Look Back

This was not the first time black women had chosen such a course. At the turn of the twentieth century and through the first quarter of it, many black women, indeed most middle- and working-class black people, accommodated the period's virulent racism by adopting the introspective strategy of "uplift." Instead of prioritizing civil and political rights and vigorously protesting the role the state

played in disfranchisement, segregation, sexual exploitation, and wholesale terror against African Americans, much of black America turned inward and focused on community and individual self-improvement. Women came together in associations in which they combined their resources and helped each other. Women's groups established mutual aid societies to perform banking, funeral, and everyday support services for their members; and middle- and upper-class women established settlement houses, kindergartens, employment centers, libraries, hospitals, and schools for themselves and the lower classes.

On some levels, "uplift" succeeded, even if, paradoxically, it separated the black middle and upper classes from the masses and made them overseers of lower class progress. It was they who delineated the desirable qualities of morality and industry and decided just who did or did not measure up. Thus, in addition to the institutions they built to help black people, middle-class women issued a litany of advice and criticism on how black women could uplift themselves. The National Association of Colored Women, an organization founded in 1896, counseled black women to keep themselves and their homes clean, bathe their children regularly, and provide them with music, games, and books to keep them usefully occupied. Working- and lower-class women were told to stop sitting on stoops and talking and laughing loudly in public. Girls were counseled to stick close to home, boys to stop wandering. Families were urged to live within their means, domestic workers to stop buying clothes they could not afford. Above all, women had to lead, and teach their daughters to lead, virtuous lives. That discrimination and exploitation impeded adherence to these strictures seemed to have mattered less than adherence at any cost. This kind of living was thought to be the key to a better life, to race progress, and to breaking down racist and sexist barriers for entry into the American mainstream. However well intentioned, middle-class black women had made their less fortunate sisters unduly responsible for their own sexual exploitation, for their own exclusion from lucrative areas of the labor market, for stereotypical media portrayals, and for the familial dysfunction that flowed from wholesale discrimination and prejudice. "Uplift" unintentionally blamed the victim. As the historian Kevin Gaines noted, the effects of oppression were mistaken for its causes.

Million Woman Marchers could have learned a lot from this era of black history, for though much of the historical malaise, distrust, and frustration in black female America was seen as a direct and indirect product of institutionalized racism and sexism, marchers, like their forebears, seemed to accept responsibility for their own oppression. Marchers needed to understand that much of their alienation from each other was a consequence, not a cause, of their historic and contemporary marginalization in America; that African American women were not solely responsible for the stereotypes that haunt them, nor the poverty they need to overcome, nor the limitations on their aspirations, nor the anxiety that flowed from all of these. They were not even solely responsible for the lack of unity that brought them to Philadelphia. It was a complex historic process that pitted light- against dark-skinned black women, the straight-haired against the kinky-haired, the middle class against the working class and the welfare class.

This history, however, lay buried under the image of an idealized past cherished by many marchers. Although marchers wished to rekindle the unity they believed black women once enjoyed, the sad truth was that black women had never gotten along in the way marchers believed. Race and sex sameness had always provided the impetus for organizing, but it had not been a guarantee of sisterhood. As the problems of "uplift" demonstrated, class had been a stumbling block. Middle- and upper-class black women had reached down to aid their less fortunate sisters but had seldom reached across class lines. Moreover, black women had always lamented the discord between themselves. "Keep us, oh God, from pettiness. . . . May we strive to touch and know the great common woman heart of us all, and O Lord God let us not forget to be kind," were lines from the prayer of the National Association of Colored Women. Historically, black women had also divided over gender in race politics. Most black women had kept their distance from white women's movements because white women excluded them and had seldom understood how race changed the black woman's female experience. But black women had also disagreed among themselves over the place of gender in their own movements. Could black women support black women's issues and not divide the race? Where should the emphasis be in black women's activism—on race or sex? Could black women work on both at the same time, and if so, how? And what about sexual preference? Just as religion, ethnicity, and geography had divided black women, black female heterosexuals and lesbians had seldom made common cause. Like class issues, these seeds of division had been present in black women's thought and activism for most of the twentieth century. Unfortunately, they were present, too, on that rainy October day in 1997.

Dividing Lines

Ironically, divisiveness was embedded in the march's organizing strategies. Coney and Chionesu wanted nothing to get in the way of the sisterhood, and they eschewed everything they felt might. That included corporate sponsors and mainstream media, local churches, and high-profile

civil rights and service organizations, including black women's sororities and organizations like 100 Black Women and the National Council of Negro Women.

Judging from the turnout, this approach worked not only for Coney and Chionesu but also for the hundreds of thousands who lined Benjamin Franklin Parkway. That there was no dominating female counterpart to Minister Louis Farrakhan, the organizer of the Million Man March, seemed to suit marchers as much as did the absence of nationally recognized black women. C. Delores Tucker, the chair of the National Political Congress of Black Women, professed not to mind that her organization was excluded from the organizing. "These community workers felt that they were not sometimes invited to the other marches and that the platforms of other marches didn't necessarily speak to their concerns. So I understand how they feel." Tucker, in fact, thought it refreshing "to see a march like this come up from the grass root."

Grassroots aside, some women clearly felt left out and put down. The Reverend Jeffrey Leath, pastor at one of Philadelphia's largest black churches, felt that many women in his congregation did not attend because churches had not been in on the planning. A *Philadelphia Daily News* editor did not attend because she had heard that "professional women weren't welcome at the march." Although her friend told her that that was just a rumor, "part of the misinformation flying around," Frances Walker, a veteran civil rights worker in Philadelphia and one of the original thirteen members of the march's organizing committee, confirmed what to some was the march's narrow pitch. In fact, she and eight others broke away from the organizing committee over what she called a "difference in philosophy and organizing styles." Said Walker, organizers were "not as inclusive as we felt they should have been. Their focus was on grassroots; we felt they needed more women who were pioneers."

Two pioneers, Rosa Parks and Coretta Scott King, declined invitations to speak. Although organizers were pleased that they had pulled hundreds of thousands to Philadelphia without the lure of these women, or other high-profile mainstream personalities, some took their absence as an indication that middle-class women with mainstream ideas were not welcome. Others took the fact that the sound system was inadequate for a march of such proportions as proof that "untried activists had no business planning a march."

It was probably best that most marchers could not see or hear the speakers gathered on the dais. The gospel group, the Winans Sisters, for example, was well-received, but their homophobic, anti-gay song, "Not Natural," was a turn-off for many black women. Winnie Mandela was there, but for some she had lost her halo when she was accused of sanctioning the kidnapping and torturing of four South African boys and the killing of one. Few felt a connection with, or even knew, Ramona Africa, a radical left-wing leader of MOVE, a group some felt had for years preyed on one of Philadelphia's viable working-class black neighborhoods. Sister Souljah was there too, but her speech seemed aimed at anything but sisterhood. "If there is one thing I can't stand," she railed, "it's a phony. . . . Some of you who are cheering today will be buck naked in a club tomorrow. . . . Some of y'all don't understand the definition of what it means to be an African Woman." And although many women were sympathetic to Congresswoman Maxine Waters's call for investigation of the CIA's role in disseminating crack in black neighborhoods, and her attention to other platform issues, most marchers had come with some other personal concerns they wanted addressed.

Indeed, since each marcher went to Philadelphia with her own idea about the meaning of black womanhood, each had her own idea about what needed to be accomplished. Healing and unity were the ultimate goals, but each woman brought to this generic goal a personal experience that individualized her need for healing and unity with black women. For example, like so many others, forty-three-year-old Yolanda Lee went because she thought black women needed "something positive." This need grew out of her experience as a single professional woman. Lee was in Philadelphia to "support women's rights." A junior at the University of Oklahoma needed a "source of renewal" because her "community on campus" was "breaking down." Another woman thought black women needed to "come together in prayer and unity" so they could "bring back the family unit that has been lost." And yet another, an entrepreneur, went to "experience sisterhood" and "encourage black women to go into business for themselves." In other words, there were as many reasons behind the need for healing as there were marchers.

Since the march could not meet everyone's needs, dissatisfaction was inevitable. Like June Jordan, many marchers wanted a more concrete agenda. Personal introspection, spiritual renewal, unity, and healing were, for some, not nearly enough. Some wanted leaders to be "harder on the federal government," especially its new welfare policy. Others wondered why the march did not address more "everyday Black woman concerns," such as daycare, domestic violence, and strained relationships with black men. To some, the march seemed more like a "food fair"; one woman likened it to "a Million Woman Expo." For a college senior from Atlanta, Georgia, the march signified weakness rather than strength. "We don't need marches to save our community," she complained, "We marched throughout the 60's, and that had its place. . . . It's like our leaders have run out of ideas."

She was only partly right. African American women had marched in the past, but the Million Woman March, while it repeated so much of the past—the class, color, and political conflicts—also marked a significant departure. For better or worse, this was the first time in history that black women had marched without black men. It was the first time that black women had publicly professed their personal feelings of aloneness and vulnerability. Thirty years before, black women had marched for civil and voting rights; now they were marching for their own well-being. Obviously, things had changed. The Million Woman March was testimony that they had not stayed the same.

BIBLIOGRAPHY

Brand-Williams, Oralandear. "Congresswoman Maxine Waters 'Million Woman March: Black Women Vow to Act on Power.'" *Detroit News*, 26 October 1997, Section A–1.

Britt, Donna. "Black Women's Dilemma: Do We also March." *Washington Post*, 24 October 1997, Section B–1.

Britt, Donna. "Desperately Seeking Sisterhood." *Essence*, January 1998.

Brown, DeNeen L. "Away From Home, Marchers Find Mix of Kinship, Disappointment." *Washington Post*, 26 October 1997.

Campbell, Douglass A., Anneter John-Hall, and Karen E. Quinones Miller. "Thousand Join Here, as One." *Philadelphia Inquirer*, 26 October 1997.

Dennis, Yvonne. "To March Or Not To March? Many Are Still Undecided." *New York Daily News*, 24 October 1997.

Editorial. From the Afro Website. *Baltimore Afro-American*, 8 November 1997.

Editorial. "Sisters Challenging the Stereotypes." *Philadelphia Daily News*, 24 October 1997. Philadelphia Online, http://www.philly.com/packages/wmill/Opin/DNS1EDIT24.asp.

Fletcher, Michael A., and DeNeen L. Brown. "Anticipation, Hopes Build for Million Woman March." *Washington Post*, 24 October 1997.

Foege, Alec, and Karen E. Quinones Miller. "Philadelphia Story." *People Weekly*, 10 November 1997.

Gaines, Kevin K. *Uplifting the Race: Black Leadership, Politics, and Culture in the Twentieth Century*. Chapel Hill: University of North Carolina Press, 1996.

Giddings, Paula. *When and Where I Enter: The Impact of Black Women on Race and Sex in America*. New York: Bantam Books, 1984.

Higginbotham, Evelyn. *Righteous Discontent: The Women's Movement in the Black Baptist Church, 1880–1920*. Cambridge, MA: Harvard University Press, 1993.

Janofsky, Michael. "At Million Woman March, Focus Is on Family" *New York Times*, 26 October 1997.

Janofsky, Michael. "When a Rally's Strength Is Seen as Its Weakness." *New York Times*, 25 October 1997, Section A7.

Jordan, June. "A Gathering Purpose." *The Progressive*, January 1998.

Kee, Lorraine. "To Be Like an Independence Day for Many." *St. Louis Post-Dispatch*, 19 October 1997.

Kee, Lorraine. "Black Women Get On Their Own Bus." *St. Louis Post Dispatch*, 7 November 1997, Section C–11.

Lee, Felicia. "Thousands of Women Share Wounds, and Celebrate." *New York Times*, 26 October 1997.

Milloy, Courtland. "For One Woman, a Million Fond Memories." *Washington Post*, 29 October 1997, Sec. D, B1.

Reyes, Damaso. "Beyond the Million Woman March." *New York Amsterdam News*, 24 December 1997.

Towns, Hollis R. "Potential Marchers reluctant to Sign On." *Atlanta Journal–Constitution*, 18 October 1997.

White, Deborah Gray. *Too Heavy a Load: Black Women in Defense of Themselves, 1894–1994*. New York: W. W. Norton, 1999.

—DEBORAH GRAY WHITE

MILLS, FLORENCE (b. 25 January 1896; d. 1 November 1927), performer. Florence Mills was arguably the first black female superstar. According to her contemporaries, she was idolized by a generation of African Americans, particularly in Harlem, and represented for them success, fame, and happiness. A lifelong performer, Mills was born in Washington, DC, the youngest of three sisters. Her parents were John and Nellie Simons Winfrey, both born in slavery. They had migrated from Lynchburg, Virginia, to escape a depression in the tobacco industry. John worked as a day laborer, and Nellie took in laundry.

The family lived in one of Washington's poorest slums, Goat Alley.

Early Performances

As "Baby Florence," Mills began to enter and win local amateur contests at the age of four. She performed for Washington diplomats, including the British ambassador Lord Pauncefote and his wife. Her first formal stage appearance was in 1903, when she was a special act added to a road production of Bert Williams's and George Walker's *Sons of Ham* singing "Miss Hannah From Savannah." Mills soon became a major source of income for her family. Her next known employment was as a "pick"—or "pickaninny"—in a white vaudeville show. In 1910, she formed the Mills Sisters vaudeville act with her sisters, Maude and Olivia, and successfully toured the East Coast. After her sisters left the act, Mills toured with Kinky Caldwell, later Clark, and traveled as far west as Chicago.

FLORENCE MILLS dancing the Charleston with a seal named Charlie, 28 October 1925. Mills, a celebrated entertainer whose signature song was "I'm a Little Blackbird Looking for a Bluebird," also spoke out on racial issues and was active in charitable work. (© Bettmann/Corbis.)

Touring the vaudeville circuit was tough work for anyone in the early years of the twentieth century, but particularly for African American performers and children. The black TOBA circuit—Theatre Owners and Bookers Association, or as it was more commonly spelled out, Tough On Black Asses—was notorious for its exploitation of black performers. The schedule was relentless, the pay was low, and the living conditions squalid.

In Chicago at the beginning of the Chicago Renaissance and tired of touring, Mills began to work at the infamous Panama Café, where she formed the Panama Trio with Ada "Bricktop" Smith and Cora Green. She met Bill "Bojangles" Robinson there, too, and he gave her dancing lessons and became a life-long friend. However, Mills's time in Chicago did not last long. The Panama Club, long a source of complaints as a "center of vice," was closed down after a shooting incident only a few years after Mills arrived, and she was forced to go back to touring.

For a short time, the Panama Trio toured on the white Pantages circuit. After the group split up, Mills joined The Tennessee Ten, where she met dance man Ulysses "Slow Kid" Thompson. The two fell in love and were married. For the rest of Mills's life, they were devoted to each other and frequently performed together. For a time, Thompson, a legendary dancer in his own right, served as Mills's manager.

Up to this point Mills's life was similar to those of many talented vaudeville or nightclub performers. She had paid her dues and become a well-respected trouper by her fellow performers. Her next opportunity, however, shot her into the history books. In 1921, while she performing at Baron Wilkins's Club in Harlem, she was asked to replace Gertrude Saunders in the famed musical *Shuffle Along* by Noble Sissle and Eubie Blake. Mills made her name with the song "I'm Craving for That Kind of Love," which she performed so well that Saunders's rendition was completely outshone.

One member of the appreciative audience was a young white producer named Lew Leslie. When he created an all-black cabaret, the *Plantation Revue*, he asked Mills to be its star. Initially performed late at night, after *Shuffle Along* was over, the revue was so popular that Leslie renovated the club just for the show and Mills went to work for him full-time. While the club's decor was wildly racist, with a log cabin and a chandelier shaped like a watermelon, it was the first time that there was a "high class" cabaret on Broadway featuring only black performers. On 22 July 1922, the show began a successful run on Broadway, and Mills's fame grew. It was during this period that Mills became known as "Little Twinks."

Although she might have played the naif, Mills was not an innocent. She knew where she came from and what she had gone through. Throughout the rest of her successful career, she used her position to champion the rights of African Americans. In addition, she never left her first audience behind and, according to the biographer Bill Egan, always found time to make sure her shows played for black audiences at cheaper prices in Harlem and other parts of the country. She once said, "For years before I became a success and the white people smiled on me, I struggled against adversity and prejudice. When I was born I was just a poor pickaninny, with no prospects but a whole legacy of sorrow."

International Fame

In 1923 Mills became an international star when Leslie was asked to bring the *Plantation Revue* to England by the producer Sir Charles Cochran. However, there was an uproar over African American performers taking British jobs. Cochran came up with a compromise: *From Dover to Dixie*. The first half, "Dover," was performed by white English actors and the second half, "Dixie," was performed by Mills and the Plantation Revue cast. The story of the opening night is a classic. During the first act, "Dover," the audience was tense and totally silent—never a good omen for musical comedy. When the "Dixie" section of the show began, the first two pieces were so loud that anyone intending to cause trouble couldn't be heard. And then Florence Mills entered. Her song was a ballad. According to Cochran,

> She controlled the emotions of the audience as only a true artist can. . . . And the audience applauded as any audience applauds an artist in whom it detects genius. That night, and every night she appeared at the London Pavilion, Florence Mills received an ovation each time she came on stage—before every song she sang. This is a tribute which in my experience I have never known to be offered to any other artist.
>
> (Cochran, p. 414–415.)

Mills not only moved the British music hall audiences but she also profoundly affected many among the literati of London society, including the composer Constant Lambert, whose *Rio Grande* was inspired by Mills's performance and whose *Elegiac Blues* was a tribute to her. *Dixie to Dover* traveled to Paris after London, where it met with equal success. When Mills returned to New York, her fame preceded her, and she was asked to perform in *The Greenwich Village Follies*, even though the white cast threatened to walk out. She was the first black woman to star in a mainstream white production.

Shortly after, Mills was asked by the leading impresario of the day, Florenz Ziegfeld, to join his *Follies*. To his amazement, she turned him down and was explicit as to her reasons. She noted that Bert Williams had moved the position of black performers forward by working with Ziegfeld, and that with Leslie, she had a similar opportunity. Rather than promote her own career by joining with the most famous showman of the day, Mills chose to help advance the careers of other black performers.

In late 1924, the all-black version of *From Dixie to Dover* opened as *From Dixie to Broadway*. Mills's hit song from the show was "I'm a Little Blackbird Looking for a Bluebird," which became her signature tune and gave her yet another nickname, "The Little Blackbird." Like all of the other revues before it, *Dixie to Broadway* contained stereotypical and racist material. The critic Theophilus Lewis wrote that the show was demeaning. Yet even he could not seem to criticize Mills. "When she sings her song 'I'm a Little Blackbird' she lets herself out, and—My God! Man, I've never seen anything like it! Not only that, I never imagined such a tempestuous blend of passion and humour could be poured into the singing of a song."

After *Dixie to Broadway*, Mills was the unchallenged toast of New York. She went on to the Palace Theatre, where she was the first African American woman to headline at the country's premiere vaudeville venue. In 1926, she took an enormous artistic risk when she performed the work of the great African American classical composer William Grant Still. Performing four of his songs at the Aeolian Hall in New York, Mills brought a new audience under her spell. George Gershwin and Arturo Toscanini were in attendance.

Mills returned to Broadway later that year as the lead in the enormously successful Leslie production *Blackbirds of 1926*, which was written specifically for her. It opened at the Alhambra Theatre in Harlem before it traveled to Paris and London, where, reportedly, the Prince of Wales was so enamored of the show and its star that he attended at least six, if not as many as sixteen, performances. True to her reputation for generosity, while in England, according to the London *Times*, Mills gave a special performance for "about 1,000 disabled soldiers, who are still undergoing treatment in the various hospitals." According to another newspaper, "It was her custom . . . to entertain the poor children and carry flowers to the hospitals."

Premature Death

However, Mills had been driving herself for twenty-five years and the toll was beginning to tell. Her health was failing. She was suffering from either acute appendicitis and peritonitis or from a form of tuberculosis that mimicked the symptoms of peritonitis. Whatever the cause, by 1927, she was overworked and dangerously ill. Finally, at the insistence of her doctors, Mills left the show, and she and Thompson spent two weeks in Baden-Baden, Germany. In September 1927, the two headed back to the United States.

Even after her return, Mills delayed a necessary operation for over a month because she did not want to upset her mother, who was also not well. Finally on 25 October she entered the hospital. For a week after the operation, Mills's condition deteriorated, yet her care of others continued. She is said to have sung to both Lewis Leslie and her nurse in an effort to cheer them up. She was operated on again, but the effort to save her life failed, and in the early morning hours, Florence Mills died.

No one was prepared for the star's premature death. Up to fifty-seven thousand mourners reportedly came to see her lying in state. Five thousand people attended her funeral, while 150,000 lined the streets. It was the largest funeral Harlem had ever seen. But this came as no surprise. As James Weldon Johnson noted, "She was more their idol than any other artist of the race."

In the decades after her death Florence Mills accomplishments began to be forgotten. Since the mid-1980s, however, interest in her began once again to grow. Biographies were written about the late "Little Blackbird." A motion picture about her and Bricktop in Paris was planned. The Flo-Bert Award, named for Mills and Bert Williams, was been created to honor lifetime achievement in tap.

Mills left behind few photographs and no decent audio or film recording of her work. Based on contemporary reports she had incredible talent and energy combined with powerful technical skills. Described variously as an elf, pixy, or gamine, she was small, five-feet, four-inches tall and less than a hundred pounds. Her voice was high and sometimes described as soft. She specialized in ballads. She danced superbly, and nobody could do comedy better. She improvised and responded brilliantly to each audience she faced. Perhaps it was this skill combined with amazing charisma that made the audience—black and white—fall in love with her. And the superlatives flowed in. The English ballet critic, Arnold Haskell wrote, "I would put the late Florence Mills . . . on a par with any of the admittedly great artists of the dance." Cochran wrote, "Florence Mills is one of the greatest artists of our time." Theophilus Lewis wrote that she was "incomparable."

She was also smart, courageous, generous, and loyal. An early member of the NAACP, she never tried to deny who she was, and she never forgot where she came from. Apart from perhaps Aida Overton Walker, no other black female popular performer opened as many doors for black women on the national and international stage as this young, hardworking woman. But this thin summary cannot encapsulate Mills. Perhaps her own words explain her best.

> I belong to a race that sings and dances as it breathes. I don't care where I am, so long as I can sing and dance. The wide world is my stage and I am my audience. . . . Our singing and

our music is part of our history and tradition. . . . It is our laughter and our tears; it is our home and our exile (undated clipping, *Florence Mills file*, Theater Collection, Philadelphia Free Library).

BIBLIOGRAPHY

Cochran, C. B. *Secrets of a Showman*. London: William Heinemann, 1925.

Hughes, Langston, and Milton Meltzer. *Black Magic: A Pictorial History of the African-American in the Performing Arts* (1967). New York: Da Capo Press, 1990.

Johnson, James Weldon. *Black Manhattan* (1969). New York: Da Capo Press, 1991.

Kellner, Bruce, ed. *The Harlem Renaissance: An Historical Dictionary for the Era*. New York: Methuen, 1987.

Newman, Richard. "East of Broadway: Florence Mills at Aeolian Hall." *Sonneck Society for American Music Bulletin*, 20.3 (1994): 9–10.

Newman, Richard. "Florence Mills." In *Notable Women in American Theatre: A Biographical Dictionary*, edited by Alice M. Robinson, Vera Mowry Roberts, and Milly S. Barranger. Westport, CT: Greenwood Press, 1989.

Woll, Allen. *Black Musical Theatre*. New York: Da Capo Press, 1991.

—HILARY MAC AUSTIN

MITCHELL, JUANITA JACKSON (b. 2 January 1913; d. 7 July 1992), civil rights activist. Juanita Jackson Mitchell was the first national youth director of the National Association for the Advancement of Colored People (NAACP) and, later, the first African American woman to be admitted to practice law in Maryland. Although these distinctions marked her transition from one career to another, Mitchell's prominence is primarily a consequence of her civil rights advocacy for more than half a century.

Strong Values

Jackson was born in Hot Springs, Arkansas, to Lillie M. Carroll Jackson, a schoolteacher and property owner, and Keiffer Albert Jackson, a traveling promoter and exhibitor of religious films. Lillie and Keiffer Jackson consistently emphasized core African American cultural values—freedom, black self-determination, resistance, and education. During the era of segregation, the parents' values and occupations placed the Jacksons within a black middle class committed to racial "uplift." Accordingly, priority was given not only to that which was designed to provide a degree of economic independence and security, but also that which would enable the family and the black community to overcome black subordination, inclusion within the citizenry, and greater freedom.

Jackson was reared in Baltimore with her two sisters, Virginia and Marion, and her brother, Bowen Keiffer. In the Jackson home, none of the children experienced affirmation of the dominant society's notion of the home as the sphere of the "true" woman, its idealization of motherhood, or a neat partition between male dominance and female dependence. Whereas family life for Jackson and her siblings included an assertion of the significance of a male head of household, home life was also built upon more of an egalitarian partnership that would facilitate the education of the children and the improvement of conditions for the larger black community. For Keiffer and Lillie Jackson, the economic well-being of the family rested upon the work and investment of both husband and wife.

In the Jackson home, giving priority to education was axiomatic to an affirmation of racial uplift. The Jacksons expected all their children to excel in high school and college. Jackson graduated from the Frederick Douglass High School with honors in 1927. For two years she attended Morgan State College in Baltimore but then transferred to the University of Pennsylvania in Philadelphia. She graduated in 1931 with a BS in education.

Three forces in Jackson's life motivated her to return home during the Great Depression to work toward improving the conditions of African Americans living in Baltimore: racial consciousness nurtured by her parents and her sorority, Alpha Kappa Alpha; an anti-elitist stance required by her mother ("You're not to come back and separate yourselves into an intelligent few, but to give back so our people can be free"); and her leadership in the interracial national Methodist youth movement. Jackson saw the crisis of the economic depression, with its massive unemployment, racial segregation, other forms of racist discrimination, and continued lynching as fundamental challenges. Her mother's activities with the African American community of Baltimore and the NAACP offered an example of an approach to facilitating racial uplift and fighting a system characterized by racial inequality.

Influences outside of the African American community were also important in Jackson's development. When she returned from the University of Pennsylvania, she became acquainted with the socialist Elisabeth Coit Gilman, the daughter of the first president of Johns Hopkins University. Jackson and Clarence M. Mitchell Jr., a Lincoln University (Pennsylvania) graduate, attended Gilman's radical "town hall" meetings. Hosted at Gilman's home, the group customarily discussed political and structural changes required to improve conditions in Baltimore and the nation. These meetings also served as a catalyst for Jackson's ideas concerning an effective approach to fostering change in her hometown.

Youth Leader

Implementing her idea to hold a forum to address challenges facing African Americans, women, youth, the working class, and the unemployed during the Great Depression, Jackson, Clarence Mitchell, and approximately a dozen other African American youth founded the

City-Wide Young People's Forum of Baltimore. Jackson's mother served as one of the advisors. In Jackson's promotion of the forum and acceptance of its presidency, Jackson transgressed traditional boundaries associated not only with race and gender but also with age.

As the first president of the Baltimore City-Wide Young People's Forum, Jackson helped develop programs and projects with other officers, older advisers, and many of Baltimore's African American citizens. Jackson led the forum through 1934, even after she had found employment as a secondary schoolteacher in the public schools. As Jackson had hoped, the forum proved to be a boon to the African American community throughout its existence from 1931 until 1940. The forum held well-attended weekly public meetings, featuring black leaders and prominent educators. The forum also sponsored anti-lynching petition drives, demonstrations, and employment campaigns for African Americans in Baltimore. Although her mother tended to stress what was "palatable," Jackson and the other young people organized to empower African Americans for greater political participation as well as for direct action.

In 1935 Walter White, the executive secretary of the NAACP, invited Jackson to assume the leadership of the NAACP's first nationwide youth program. Despite White's patriarchal tendencies, his appointments of women (among them Daisy Lampkin, Juanita Jackson, and by 1940 Ella Baker) to leadership positions not only reflected an understanding of the organizing skills and experience of African American women, but also acknowledged their "culture of resistance." The NAACP could not succeed without continued growth in its rank-and-file membership. It could not conduct protracted struggle for first-class citizenship without building a base of young people to continue the struggle. White had observed the success of Baltimore's forum in mobilizing youth as well as adults and had been impressed by Jackson (she had earned an MA in sociology).

From 1935 to 1938 Jackson served as national youth director and special assistant to Walter White. She wrote a constitution, organized youth councils, revived junior NAACP branches, and established a national network. She also worked with youth primarily on four problems—education, jobs, civil rights, and lynching—doing for youth what Ella Baker had done for the NAACP's branches. Support from other women for this youth work came as a result of Jackson's participation with Mary McLeod Bethune in the founding conference of the National Council of Negro Women (NCNW) and its subsequent activities.

Jackson's August 1938 marriage to Clarence M. Mitchell Jr. (then the National Youth Administration's Maryland director of the Division of Negro Affairs, but later the NAACP's chief lobbyist until 1978) interrupted her employment with the NAACP but did not end her association with that organization or her political activism. As a new wife and mother in the early 1940s, Mitchell coordinated a civil rights march of two thousand citizens on the state capital, participated in a White House conference on children, and directed the first NAACP citywide voter registration campaign in Baltimore. After giving birth to four sons—Clarence III, Keiffer, Michael, and George—and desiring to be better armed for the civil rights struggle, she decided to change vocations. She studied law at the University of Maryland, served on the *Law Review*'s staff, and earned her law degree by 1950.

Lawyer and NAACP Leader

When Mitchell became the first African American woman admitted to practice law in Maryland, she had one objective in mind: to litigate on behalf of African Americans seeking an end to racial discrimination. Her legal achievements were notable throughout the 1950s and 1960s. She was counsel in Maryland litigation initiated in 1950 to eliminate the racial segregation of state and municipal beaches and swimming pools, which she won in November 1955. A secondary-school desegregation case filed in 1953 and handled successfully by Mitchell resulted in Baltimore becoming the first southern city to desegregate public schools after *Brown v. Board of Education*. During the 1960s she served as counsel for students engaged in sit-ins to desegregate Maryland restaurants and litigated *Robert Mack Bell v. Maryland*. On appeal in 1964, the students represented by Mitchell and the NAACP Legal Defense Fund prevailed in the U.S. Supreme Court. Viewing the Baltimore police commissioner's authorization of mass searches of private homes without warrants (known as the Veney raid) as a affront to African Americans and a gross violation of civil liberties affecting all citizens, Mitchell represented several homeowners in proceedings to enjoin further such mass searches. As counsel for the homeowners she won the Veney raid cases on appeal from the U.S. District Court for Maryland to the U.S. Court of Appeals, Fourth Circuit, in September 1966.

Although Mitchell devoted considerable time and energy to the family law firm (both her husband and her son Michael earned law degrees) during the late 1950s through the 1980s, public advocacy of civil rights continued to be a priority. Recognition of Mitchell's particular talents and expertise resulted in her holding several important positions with the NAACP and other organizations. She directed, both in 1957 to 1958 and in 1960, two major voter registration campaigns that placed more than fifty thousand new voters on the books. She presided over the Baltimore NAACP branch, later served as the legal redress chairperson of the Maryland state conference, and, in the 1970s, succeeded her mother as president of the state conference of NAACP branches. A life member of NCNW, she also chaired for a time that organization's legal committee.

Throughout her adulthood, Mitchell resisted race-based inequalities and exclusion of African Americans and women from the full exercise of rights and privileges. Significantly, consistent with a theme of "black women's community work," identified by Patricia Hill Collins and Darlene Hine, Mitchell worked within the church and other African American community organizations while, as quoted in the *Maryland Law Review*, retaining an overarching commitment to "ethical principles . . . and ideas more broadly based than explicitly anti-racist or feminist." When she recalled in 1972 her life of struggle, Jackson's assessment of her careers was a contextual evaluation of sources of power for women's resistance to authority: "I've done a lot of living and a lot of fighting. I've found that the best ways to fight are with the ballot, through educating public opinion and through the courts."

Legacy

Mitchell slowed her pace after her husband's death in 1984 and her subsequent illness, but she continued to maintain a lively interest in protecting the rights of African Americans. Her distinguished careers and activism of more than fifty years resulted in her being the recipient of such honors as the NCNW's award for Special Distinction in Law, the Outstanding Service Award of the Youth/College Division of the NAACP, and the Bicentennial Award of the University of Maryland's Black American Law Studies Association. In recognition of achievements as a state citizen and woman, Juanita Jackson Mitchell joined her mother when she was inducted into Maryland Women's Hall of Fame in 1985.

At the age of seventy-nine, Mitchell, who had been in poor health for some time, succumbed to a heart attack and stroke. Benjamin Hooks, the executive director of the NAACP, praised her as "one of the greatest freedom fighters in the history of Maryland and the nation," and Maryland Governor William Donald Shaefer paid tribute to Mitchell as "an inspiration, a fighter [who] never deviated from her principles." A memorial service attended by many admirers and friends was held at the Sharpe Street Memorial Methodist Episcopal Church, where she had so often worshipped and met with others to further civil rights causes. Her principle legacy was a life of courageous and consistent struggle for civil rights.

BIBLIOGRAPHY

Chateauvert, Melinda. *Marching Together: Women of the Brotherhood of Sleeping Car Porters*. Urbana: University of Illinois Press, 1998.

Collier-Thomas, Bettye, and V. P. Franklin, eds. *Sisters in the Struggle: African American Women in the Civil Rights–Black Power Movement*. New York: New York University Press, 2001.

Collins, Patricia Hill. *Black Feminist Thought: Knowledge, Consciousness, and the Politics of Empowerment*. rev. ed. New York: Routledge, 2000.

Collins, Patricia Hill. *Fighting Words: Black Women and the Search for Justice*. Minneapolis: University of Minnesota Press, 1998.

Franklin, V. P. *Black Self-Determination: A Cultural History of African-American Resistance*. Brooklyn, NY: Lawrence Hill Books, 1992.

Gaines, Kevin K. *Uplifting the Race: Black Leadership, Politics, and Culture in the Twentieth Century*. Chapel Hill: University of North Carolina Press, 1996.

Giddings, Paula. *When and Where I Enter: The Impact of Black Women on Race and Sex in America*. New York: W. Morrow, 1984.

Hine, Darlene Clark, and Kathleen Thompson. *A Shining Thread of Hope: The History of Black Women in America*. New York: Broadway Books, 1998.

McNeil, Genna Rae. *Groundwork: Charles Hamilton Houston and the Struggle for Civil Rights*. Philadelphia: University of Pennsylvania Press, 1983.

McNeil, Genna Rae. "Youth Initiative in the African American Struggle for Racial Justice and Constitutional Rights." In *African Americans and the Living Constitution*, edited by John Hope Franklin and Genna Rae McNeil. Washington, DC: Smithsonian Institution Press, 1995.

Mullings, Leith. *On Our Own Terms: Race, Class, and Gender in the Lives of African American Women*. New York: Routledge, 1997.

Perkins, Linda. "The Impact of the 'Cult of True Womanhood' on the Education of Black Women." *Journal of Social Issues* 39:3 (1983).

Ransby, Barbara. *Ella Baker and the Black Freedom Movement: A Radical Democratic Vision*. Chapel Hill: University of North Carolina Press, 2003.

Wagandt, Charles. Interviews with Juanita Jackson Mitchell. *Washington Post*, 8 July 1992.

Watson, Denton L. *Lion in the Lobby: Clarence Mitchell Jr.'s Struggle for the Passage of Civil Rights Laws*. New York: Morrow, 1990.

White, Deborah Grey. *Too Heavy a Load: Black Women in Defense of Themselves, 1894–1994*. New York: W.W. Norton, 1999.

—GENNA RAE MCNEIL

MIXED-RACE WOMEN. Black/white mixed-race women have been alternately praised and defiled in American racial discourse, literature, and film. For centuries in the United States, black people were classified according to the amount of their "black blood." This "one-drop rule" emerged from the South, constructing social and legal definitions of who was black. *Quadroon* and *octoroon* described someone who was one-fourth black and one-eighth black, respectively. The term *mulatto* (*mulatta*, feminine) originates from the Latin word *mulus*, meaning "mule," and from the Spanish word for "young mule." The word was originally used for someone who was the offspring of a "pure negro" and a "pure white." During and after slavery, most whites thought that mulattoes were intellectually superior to and more attractive than "pure" blacks, while simultaneously classifying them as hopelessly confused and psychologically unstable.

So-called scientists compared mulattoes to mules, claiming that mixed-race people could not procreate. At slave auctions, slaveholders sold light-skinned female slaves, often as domestic servants, at a higher price than dark-skinned slaves. Walter Johnson suggests in *Soul by Soul: Life inside the Antebellum Slave Market*, "Those buying household slaves associated lightness with feminine domesticity." Though not all light-skinned slaves were domestic servants, slaveholders often viewed them as more delicate and refined.

After Reconstruction, a significant number of white writers and "scientists" regarded mulattoes as immoral, criminal, and violent. For example, in *Anthropology for the People: A Refutation of the Theory of the Adamic Origin of All Races* (1891), William H. Campbell contended that mulattoes received no morality from their whiteness, instead suggesting that they had a natural propensity for mischief. While whites branded mixed-race men rapists and murderers, they labeled mixed-race women licentious and over-sexual. These stereotypes were not unlike the white racist propaganda circulated about all blacks. The contradiction lies in mixedness being subsumed into blackness (by both whites and blacks) while sometimes also remaining a distinctive racial "other."

During the late nineteenth century, white men in New Orleans and Charleston viewed mulatta women as sexual objects and bid on them at "quadroon balls." In New Orleans, well-to-do white men would choose from a select group of mulatto women to court as prospective mistresses and often participated in a system known as *placage* (placement). After meeting with the woman's parents, a man would set up his mulatto mistress in her own home, taking care of her financial responsibilities. The "woman" in these arrangements was often a girl of thirteen or fourteen. Contemporary novels such as Lalita Tademy's *Cane River* (2001) and Anne Rice's *The Feast of All Saints* (1979) depict such supposedly sinful arrangements. Although all black women were victims of sexual exploitation and rape, mixed-race women were often a prime target for sexual abuse because of white constructions of beauty.

In the 1920s the introduction of Madam C. J. Walker's hair-straightening products and the plethora of skin lightening treatments encouraged many black people to believe mulattas represented the black female physical ideal. Yet, at the same time, mulatto women also represented sin, sexual promiscuity, and illegitimacy, particularly in the eyes of the black elite. As demonstrated in Nella Larsen's *Quicksand* (1928), many upper-class blacks disapproved of race mingling and miscegenation. These bourgeois beliefs placed mulattas in a precarious situation: though they were admired for their more white-washed beauty, they also represented black/white sexual relations that many blacks deemed perilous.

Contradictory images of mixed-race women persisted in the 1930s, 1940s, and 1950s, up until the Black Power movement. The 1960s ushered in black pride and black power as well as fashion trends and hairstyles that reflected those emerging social and political movements. Whereas mixed-race women may have been long admired for their physical proximity to whiteness, Afro hairstyles and "black is beautiful" sentiments popularized a new physical beauty. Many mixed-race (and lighter-skinned) women felt pressured to "prove" their blackness, particularly when they lacked traditionally "black" physical signifiers.

Since the 1990s images of mixed-race women have permeated the media in advertisements and magazines. America's taboo on interracial relationships has prompted a fascination with mixed race, especially mixed-race women. In "The Hazards of Visibility: 'Biracial' Women, Media Images, and Narratives of Identity," Caroline Streeter warns that an increase of mixed-race women in advertising (or, more generally, the media) does not necessarily point to more progressive thinking about race. Instead, these advertisements tend to romanticize mixed-race identity and exoticize multiracial models. Many would argue that contemporary biracial celebrities, such as the singer Mariah Carey, continue to project a seductive image associated with stereotypes of mixed-race women.

Representations of the Tragic Mulatto in Literature

In *Neither Black nor White Yet Both: Thematic Explorations of Interracial Literature*, Werner Sollors credited the poet and critic Sterling A. Brown for first using the term "tragic mulatto" in a literary sense. According to Brown, several different elements define the tragic mulatto: the character is clichéd, her or his presence eschews important issues, the character's gender makes her or him distinctly doomed (female) or militant (male), the character represents a supposed biological division, and white prejudice prompts the stereotype. In addition, Brown claimed that white writers used the archetype more frequently than black writers. Since the mid-twentieth century, the term has come to more generally represent a mixed-race character whose racial confusion and marginalization cause her or him personal despair and inner turmoil. Tragic mulattas are often characterized as exceedingly beautiful but destined to live tragic lives. Late-nineteenth-century and turn-of-the-century writers have used the tragic mulatto archetype for multiple ends: to denounce slavery, to critique the paradox of race, to condemn miscegenation through disturbing characterizations, or simply to foster an already destructive stereotype. Early-twenty-first-century criticism has attempted to reclaim late-nineteenth-century and early-twentieth-century mixed-race characters as biracial feminists and boundary-challenging women.

Lydia Maria Child, a white writer and radical abolitionist, first employed the tragic mulatto characterization in "The Quadroons" (1842). In this short story, Edward, a white man, and Rosalie, his quadroon mistress, fall in love and have one daughter, Xarifa. Shortly after Edward marries a white woman, Rosalie dies. Edward's death soon follows, and Xarifa learns her mother was the daughter of a slave. This discovery forces Xarifa on the auction block and on a miserable path of self-destruction. After her white lover dies trying to rescue her, Xarifa goes insane and commits suicide. "The Quadroons" established a familiar character type found in many abolitionist novels: the beautiful white-looking slave. Novels such as Harriet Beecher Stowe's *Uncle Tom's Cabin* (1852), William Wells Brown's *Clotel; or, The President's Daughter: A Narrative of Slave Life in the United States* (1853), and Frances Ellen Watkins Harper's *Iola Leroy* (1892) portray similar characterizations. These texts described quadroons and mulattoes as fragile and exceedingly attractive, with pale white skin; long, flowing hair; and one subtle feature that almost "betrays" blackness. Writers commonly used these near-white characters to demonstrate the cruelties of slavery using a character with whom whites might more easily identify. Harriet Beecher Stowe, a white abolitionist, created characters who would prove slavery as unchristian, immoral, and unjust. Brown and Harper, both black writers, employed similar melodramatic literary techniques.

Late-nineteenth and early-twentieth-century mulatta characters shared sad, pitiable, and unfortunate endings. In *Clotel*, for example, both Clotel and her niece commit suicide; her other niece dies of a broken heart. This melodrama follows three generations of mixed-race women who face the auction block because of their black blood. Each of these women dies tragically. Similarly, in Charles Chesnutt's *The House behind the Cedars* (1900), Rena Walden dies from illness and heartache. Rena decides to pass for white and falls in love with a rich white southerner. Her lover rejects her when he finds out her secret, and Rena's deep anguish over his rejection prompts her failing health. Like tragic mulattas before and after, Rena cannot deal with her own duality.

During the Harlem Renaissance, passing continued to be a popular theme in literature, featuring mixed-race women entangled in the complex world of racial masquerade. In Nella Larsen's *Passing* (1929), Clare Kendry accidentally runs into an old friend, Irene, while both are passing for white in a hotel. After seeing Irene (who only occasionally passes), Clare regrets her life decision to pass as white and begins a kind of reverse "racial slumming," passing for white at home but cavorting with

blacks at dinners, dances, and teas. In the novel's dramatic end, Clare's white husband unexpectedly shows up at a black party Clare secretly attends. Though the novel left it ambiguous whether Clare jumps to her death or is pushed, one thing is clear: the mixed-race character is unable to live in her "white" body.

Although mixed-race characters continue to embody mulatto stereotypes, many contemporary novels offer less constricting characterizations. Fran Ross's *Oreo* (1974), Michelle Cliff's *Abeng* (1984), Elaine Perry's *Another Present Era* (1990), and Lucinda Roy's *Lady Moses* (1998) are just a few novels that feature "un-tragic" biracial female characters. Danzy Senna, for example, also rewrites the tragic mulatta character in her 1998 debut novel, *Caucasia*. In *Caucasia*, Birdie Lee's white activist mother decides to go on the run to evade the FBI during the 1970s civil rights movement. In order to the hide from the police, Birdie escapes with her mother while her darker-skinned sister, Cole, goes with her black father. Birdie passes for white as she and her mother attempt to start a new life. Though Birdie struggles with her white-looking body, her racial identity does not render her hopelessly confused or tragic. Birdie represents mixed-race characters who are not entrapped by their racial backgrounds.

Images of Mixed-Race Women in Television and Film

One of the earliest images of the tragic mulatta on film is in *The Debt* (1912), a film about a mulatta girl who falls in love with a white man she learns is her half brother. This film followed a commonly repeated literary motif: a mulatta whose "one drop" of black blood ruins her life. D. W. Griffith's infamous and racist *The Birth of a Nation* (1915) portrayed a mulatta character, Lydia, as a manipulative seductress. The film rewrote the history of Reconstruction and the emergence of the Ku Klux Klan by creating offensive caricatures of black people as animalistic, savage, and incapable of taking care of themselves. Lydia's sexual aggressiveness may have laid the foundation for later representations of mulattas as lustful temptresses.

In the 1930s motion pictures began to employ the theme of racial passing to captivate audiences. *Imitation of Life* (1934), *Show Boat* (1936), *God's Step Children* (1937), and *Pinky* (1949) all exposed the multiple dilemmas associated with trying to pass for white. In many ways, the lives of these mulatta characters epitomized the sad fate of the tragic mulatto; each character's trace of black blood somehow dooms the mulatta's happiness. Based on Fannie Hurst's best-selling novel, *Imitation of Life* relates the story of Peola, the daughter of a black cook, played by Louise Beavers, who passes in order to escape the hardships of a black life. Peola, played by Fredi Washington, returns for her mother's funeral and feels regretful and ashamed of her actions. The movie suggested that passing can have no happy ending and that one cannot escape blackness. When *Imitation of Life* was remade in 1959, a white actress played the part of Peola, now renamed Sara Jane. Despite changes in plot, the story maintained the idea that mixed blood causes anguish and heartbreak. Some reviews of the first *Imitation of Life* remarked on the film's suggestion that attempts to cross the color line will be futile. Perhaps a warning for blacks and whites not to socialize or a cautionary tale to blacks to "keep their place," films like *Imitation of Life* were not subtle in their admonitions about black/white mixing.

In *Pinky*, the mulatta, again played by a white actress, also returns to her black childhood home after passing in the North. Pinky returns to a miserable life and runs into numerous misfortunes during her stay. Still, Pinky has an epiphany regarding her racial affiliation, deciding that she will never again deny her black heritage by passing. She breaks up with her white fiancé and resolves to take care of her people. The tragedy of Pinky is her personal life. Though she perhaps makes an admirable decision, she sacrifices her own happiness to do so. In many ways, films such as *Pinky* had a Hollywood moralistic tone, blaming mulatto characters for their attempts to pass as white. Some films cast white actresses as mulattas in order to make white audiences more sympathetic to the plight of mixed-race characters like Pinky, played by the white actress Jeanne Crain.

Up until the 1960s, dark-skinned black actresses were often given only mammy or Aunt Jemima roles. Donald Bogle wrote that D. W. Griffith's division of black women according to skin color set a precedent for films that followed. Lighter-skinned actresses with "café au lait" complexions like Dorothy Dandridge, Lena Horne, and Eartha Kitt often continued the image of the mulatta as sex object in films throughout the 1940s and 1950s. Dorothy Dandridge, for example, embodied the tragic mulatta both in her films and in her personal life. In films such as *Carmen Jones* (1954), *Tamango* (1957), and *Island in the Sun* (1957), Dandridge played sexually exotic yet vulnerable and self-destructive characters. The last seven years of Dandridge's real life were particularly difficult and tragic. She divorced her husband, the white restaurateur Jack Denison, declared bankruptcy, and began to abuse alcohol. Dandridge died at the age of forty-two after overdosing on antidepressants.

Eartha Kitt, the daughter of a black woman and a white farmer, and Lena Horne, known for her copper-colored skin, both epitomized exotic sex appeal. Horne was often given roles that perpetuated the stereotype of sexually available mulattas. For example, in *Cabin in the Sky* (1943), Horne played the bad-girl seductress. Though these actresses had options other than mammy roles, they were often restricted to playing sex objects.

By the late 1950s and early 1960s, the mulatta film archetype lost its popularity. Yet, *Devil in a Blue Dress* (1995) continues a familiar theme with its mixed-race character, Daphne Monet. Based on Walter Mosley's novel, *Devil in a Blue Dress* uncovers a mystery regarding the enigmatic girlfriend of a white politician. Though written in the 1990s, the narrative takes place in the 1940s and reflects the same clichéd themes of the mulatta character. Audiences soon learn that Daphne, played by the mixed-race actress Jennifer Beals, is a black woman passing for white. Again, the movie ends with a sad and teary-eyed mixed-race female character whose life seems full of misfortune.

Mixed-Race Women and Identity, 1975–2003

Images of mixed-race women since 1975 are more diverse, although many still rely on racist or outdated stereotypes. Consider Aaron McGruder's comic strip, *The Boondocks*, which features a biracial girl, Jazmine DuBois, who is described as confused but cute. Though this comic representation may seem harmless, it follows a cultural tendency to assume that mixed-race individuals, particularly women, may be beautiful but are unstable. America remains fascinated with multiracial identity, and print media continue to emphasize the sexual availability of mixed-race women. The use of a large number of racially ambiguous models in advertisements intimates a continued valorizing of "mixed-race beauty." Companies such as Benetton and Calvin Klein have taken advantage of this image, often using racially ambiguous or exotic models—women whose "look" intimates the merging of two racially distinct backgrounds—in their advertisements.

In the late 1990s, MTV's *The Real World* commodified biracialism by seemingly choosing mixed-race "twenty-somethings" over "non-mixed" black participants in this reality show that throws seven strangers in a house to see how they live and interact with each other. Especially beginning with season 9, located in New Orleans, *The Real World* spotlighted lives of a noticeably high number of mixed-race women, suggesting that the public's voyeuristic fascination with mixed-race female bodies has not diminished. In a show that depended upon controversy, stereotypes, and drama, mixed-race housemates were expected to bring an exotic (and often erotic) alternative to the jock, cheerleader, naive country person, gay person, or black token.

Efforts at showing mixed-race women as other than confused or promiscuous emerged in television in the 1970s. In 1975 *The Jeffersons* debuted, showing a recently upper-class black family who are friends with one of the first interracial couples on television, Helen and Tom Willis. The couple's biracial daughter, Jenny Willis (Jefferson), experiences difficulties due to her mixed parentage (such as her resentment toward her lighter-skinned brother), but overcomes her issues and eventually marries Lionel Jefferson. *A Different World* premiered in 1987, showcasing a number of black college students, including Winifred "Freddie" Brooks, a biracial college student who is defined by her leftist, multicultural approach to the world. UPN's show *Girlfriends*, which debuted in fall 2000, features a biracial character named Lynn. Although a white family adopts Lynn, her biological mother is white and her biological father is black. Lynn, like Freddie, is marked by her "otherness"; her "artsy," hippie style; and biracial background. Though her character is sex-crazed and promiscuous, she does not appear drastically different from her three other black female friends, who consider themselves independent women of the new millennium. Characters like Freddie and Lynn break out of the mulatta stereotype and are not tragically marked by their racial backgrounds.

A growing mixed-race movement has prompted debate over racial identification choices, particularly on governmental forms like the U.S. Census. Miss America 2003, Erika Harold, proudly proclaimed a mixed-race identity along with other mixed-race female celebrities like Mariah Carey. Numerous other biracial celebrities such as Halle Berry, Jasmine Guy, and Alicia Keys seem to acknowledge a mixed-race background but assert a black identity. Yet the tragic mulatta stereotype still remains in Hollywood. Halle Berry and Mariah Carey are frequently referenced as modern-day tragic mulattoes, both in their personal lives and their careers. For example, the biting and humorous *Ego Trip's Big Book of Racism* (2002) names Carey and Berry as two of the "Top Ten Tragic Mulattoes" (also included are Lisa Bonet from *The Cosby Show* and the singer-actress Vanessa Williams). Halle Berry's 2001 Academy Award for Best Actress in a Leading Role for *Monster's Ball* (2001), for example, upset many viewers who felt that her role perpetuated negative images of black and mixed-race women as sexual objects. Mariah Carey has been similarly judged for her provocative dress in videos, magazines, and celebrity events. Rightly or wrongly, both women are criticized for their career choices that seem to continue stereotypical images of mixed-race women.

Images of mixed-race women have both revised and regurgitated representations of mulattoes as unhappy, racially confused, immoral, and unchaste. Women writers with multiracial backgrounds often critique and challenge conventional notions of race in works such as *Miscegenation Blues: Voices of Mixed-Race Women*, edited by Carol Camper (1994); Lisa Jones's *Bulletproof Diva: Tales of Race, Sex, and Hair* (1994); Shirlee Taylor Haizlip's *The Sweeter the Juice: A Family Memoir in Black and White*

(1994); Judy Scales-Trent's *Notes of a White Black Woman: Race Color, and Community* (1995); and Rebecca Walker's *Black, White, and Jewish: Autobiography of a Shifting Self* (2001). The late 1990s witnessed a growth in biracial organizations, literature, and theory. Critical discussions of race and identity will perhaps also prompt changes regarding the ways in which mixed-race women are represented in public discourses of mixed-race identity.

See also **Berry, Halle; Cliff, Michelle; Dandridge, Dorothy; Harper, Frances Ellen Watkins; Horne, Lena; Kitt, Eartha; Larsen, Nella;** *and* **Walker, Madam C. J.**

BIBLIOGRAPHY

Berzon, Judith R. *Neither White nor Black: The Mulatto Character in American Fiction.* New York: New York University Press, 1978.

Bogle, Donald. *Toms, Coons, Mulattoes, Mammies, and Bucks: An Interpretive History of Blacks in American Films.* 4th ed. New York: Continuum, 2001.

Bost, Suzanne. *Mulattas and Mestizas: Representing Mixed Identities in the Americas, 1850–2000.* Athens: University of Georgia Press, 2003.

Davis, F. James. *Who Is Black?: One Nation's Definition.* University Park: Pennsylvania State University Press, 1991.

Hutchinson, George. "Nella Larsen and the Veil of Race." *American Literary History* 9.2 (Summer 1987): 329–349.

Johnson, Walter. *Soul by Soul: Life inside the Antebellum Slave Market.* Cambridge, MA: Harvard University Press, 1999.

Mencke, John G. *Mulattoes and Race Mixture: American Attitudes and Images, 1865–1918.* Ann Arbor, MI: UMI Research Press, 1979.

Russell, Kathy, Midge Wilson, and Ronald Hall. *The Color Complex: The Politics of Skin Color among African Americans.* New York: Harcourt Brace Jovanovich, 1992.

Smalls, Stephen. "Black People of Mixed Origins and the Politics of Identity." In *Black Identity in the Twentieth Century: Expressions of the US and UK African Diaspora*, edited by Mark Christian. London: Hansib, 2002.

Sollors, Werner. *Neither Black nor White Yet Both: Thematic Explorations of Interracial Literature.* New York: Oxford University Press, 1997.

Streeter, Caroline A. "The Hazards of Visibility: 'Biracial' Women, Media Images, and Narratives of Identity." In *New Faces in a Changing America: Multiracial Identity in the Twenty-first Century*, edited by Loretta I. Winters and Herman L. DeBose. Thousand Oaks, CA: Sage Publications, 2003: 301–322.

Williamson, Joel. *New People: Miscegenation and Mulattoes in the United States.* Baton Rouge: Louisiana State University Press, 1995.

—SIKA ALAINE DAGBOVIE

MONTGOMERY BUS BOYCOTT. Tired after an arduous day of sewing at the Montgomery Fair Department Store, Rosa Parks sank into the nearest available bus seat in the first row of the black section and gazed out of the window. Her thoughts were interrupted by the driver's harsh voice, ordering her to move out of her seat to accommodate a white passenger. She refused and was arrested for disorderly conduct.

Many narratives retell Rosa Parks's experiences on Friday, 1 December 1955; and the resulting nonviolent direct action, the Montgomery bus boycott, is cited as one of the opening events of the modern civil rights movement. It catapulted the Reverend Martin Luther King Jr. into the national and international spotlight and prompted the organization of the Southern Christian Leadership Conference. The organization and execution of the boycott exemplified the active and vital role of black women as leaders in their community and organizers of grassroots activities.

Earlier that year, the arrest of fifteen-year-old Claudette Colvin for refusing to surrender her seat spurred the Women's Political Council (WPC)—a group of black women primarily concerned with voter registration—to meet with city officials about the city's segregation ordinances. Despite this intervention, Colvin, an NAACP Youth Council member, was convicted in juvenile court on all charges. An appeal resulted in a reduced sentence of indefinite unsupervised probation. Because she was unwed, pregnant, and part of the working class, leaders weighed the risk of using Colvin's conviction as a test case against the system and finally decided that her circumstances would pose too great a liability. But her case laid the foundations of future protest.

Rosa Parks was the model plaintiff. She was married, God-fearing, nurse to her sick mother, and an industrious seamstress; African Americans as well as segregationists and defense lawyers would have a hard time finding character flaws. The prosecution was able, with absolute honesty, to present a picture of dignified black womanhood persecuted by an unjust system. Parks was also well equipped to play the role through her service as secretary of the local NAACP branch and youth director, and her training at the Highlander Folk School in July 1955.

Pushed by WPC torchbearers such as Johnnie Carr and Alabama State College professors Jo Ann Robinson and Mary Fair Burks, who produced thousands of flyers overnight, the male leadership agreed to promote a boycott. Scheduled to begin on Monday 5 December, it was to coincide with Parks's trial. The women began to mobilize.

Montgomery was home to many black women's clubs whose members dedicated their time to improving their people's welfare. Operating in the background and on the periphery of public meetings and discussions, they rendered themselves invisible to accolades and acknowledgements. Many members had attended the Montgomery Industrial School, where black girls received a good education and mentoring not often found in the region, thus producing politically aware and socially active women equipped to fight for their children's futures.

A gathering that first afternoon on 5 December established the Montgomery Improvement Association (MIA) to take care of the boycott's direct needs. The following mass meeting elected Rev. Martin Luther King Jr. as president. Initial demands to the city commissioners called for equitable seating, with blacks starting at the rear and moving forward and whites starting from the front and moving back on a first-come, first-served basis. Though desegregated seating was not discussed during the first month, the homes of both King and E. D. Nixon were attacked. Most of the city leaders, including the mayor, publicly announced their membership in the pro-segregationist White Citizens' Council.

With negotiations halted, litigation sought to end the crisis. The MIA filed *Browder v. Gayle* in federal court on 1 February 1956, challenging bus segregation. By the end of February, leaders of the boycott were indicted under Alabama's antiboycott law. In June, the federal district court found bus segregation unconstitutional and the city appeal went to the U.S. Supreme Court. On 21 December 1956, one year and three weeks after Rosa Parks's arrest, the Supreme Court decision officially concurred with the federal court.

Throughout this year, amid the public drama played out in the courts, boardrooms, and mass meetings, ordinary black men and mostly women struggled to support the boycott and get to work. Women, after full days working in the homes and businesses of the very men who sought to keep them segregated, walked long distances in all kinds of weather, or car-pooled, returning home exhausted and late to their own children and domestic duties. Women from all walks of life managed the upkeep of the boycott from its inception, keeping track of the details, the finances, and the needs of the protesters. If men represented the faces and public voices of the boycott, women were its backbone and organs. Women, particularly of the WPC, passed on many of the practical ideas to the men, who articulated and managed the execution of plans. Their resolve was bolstered by the city's stubbornness and refusal to give an inch and the violence perpetuated on protesters' bodies and homes. Their courage and perseverance stirred a nation and African Americans elsewhere who were yearning to shed the shackles of segregation.

See also Civil Rights Movements; Civil Rights Organizations; Parks, Rosa; Political Resistance; *and* Robinson, Jo Ann.

BIBLIOGRAPHY

Burns, Stewart, ed. *Daybreak of Freedom: The Montgomery Bus Boycott*. Chapel Hill: University of North Carolina Press, 1997.

Crawford, Vicki L., et al., eds. *Women in the Civil Rights Movement: Trailblazers and Torchbearers, 1941–1965*. Bloomington: Indiana University Press, 1993.

Garrow, David J., ed. *The Walking City: The Montgomery Bus Boycott, 1955–1956*. New York: Carlson, 1989.

King, Martin Luther, Jr. *Stride Toward Freedom: The Montgomery Story*. New York: Harper and Row, 1958.

Leventhal, Willy S., ed. *The Children Coming On: A Retrospective of the Montgomery Bus Boycott*. Montgomery, AL: Black Belt Press, 1998.

Morris, Aldon D. *The Origins of the Civil Rights Movement: Black Communities Organizing for Change.* New York: Free Press, 1984.

Robinson, Jo Ann Gibson. *The Montgomery Bus Boycott and the Women Who Started It: The Memoir of Jo Ann Gibson Robinson.* Knoxville: University of Tennessee Press, 1987.

—FRANÇOISE N. HAMLIN

MOORE, AUDLEY "QUEEN MOTHER" (b. 27 July 1898; d. 2 May 1997), political activist. In recalling the events of her life, "Queen Mother" Moore stated its theme: "there wasn't nothing to do but get into the struggle." A powerful street speaker and adept political organizer, Moore was involved for almost a century in a host of crucial campaigns in support of Garveyism, the Harlem boycott and renters' rights movements, the Republican and Communist parties, the Scottsboro defense, Pan-Africanism, and the reparations movement.

Born in New Iberia, Louisiana, Moore had experiences growing up in the South that profoundly influenced her political vision. Her parents' lives had been shaped by white violence, and her own memories included lynchings, manhunts, and overt discrimination. Moore's father, St. Cyr Moore, born as a result of his mother's rape by a white man, ran a livery stable. Moore's mother, Ella Henry, was raised in a middle-class French Creole household after her father was lynched by whites and her mother driven from their property. Both parents died by the time Moore was in the fourth grade, ending her formal schooling. Moore trained in the Poro hairdressing system and at age fifteen became the primary supporter of herself and her two younger sisters, Eloise and Lorita.

Moore worked as a volunteer nurse during the 1918 influenza epidemic. She and Eloise lived in Alabama during World War I and organized support services for black soldiers, which were denied by the Red Cross. Moore joined the Universal Negro Improvement Association in New Orleans and embraced its tenets. She was attracted by Marcus Garvey's oratory and the beauty and self-fulfillment she found in his talk of the grandeur of ancient African civilization and pride in African culture and heritage. Moore often described an incident in New Orleans when she and other audience members defied white authorities by mounting benches and waving weapons while chanting for Garvey to speak. She remembered this as a victorious experience that contributed to the militancy of the grassroots methods she used in later struggles.

Moore moved to Harlem, New York, in the 1920s. She organized domestic workers in the Bronx labor market and helped black tenants to defy evictions by white landlords. Arrested repeatedly for her activities, she used her jail sentences to organize fellow inmates. In the 1930s, she joined the International Labor Defense and the Communist Party, becoming one of the leading black Communist women organizers in New York. An extraordinary and persuasive speaker, she agitated on such issues as the Scottsboro defense, the Italo-Ethiopian war, economic boycotts, black political representation, racial prejudice in film, and a myriad of other causes. She was a Communist Party candidate for the New York State Assembly in 1938 and for alderman in 1940, and she was campaign manager for Benjamin Davis's successful bid for the New York City Council in 1943.

Moore left the Communist Party in 1950. She and Eloise joined Mother Langley and Dara Collins in founding the Universal Association of Ethiopian Women, which worked on welfare rights, prisoners' rights, antilynching, and interracial rape issues. She increasingly embraced cultural nationalism and identification with Africa, including the wearing of African dress. In 1962 she formed the Reparations Committee of Descendants of U.S. Slaves, Incorporated, demanding federal reparations to blacks as partial compensation for the gross exploitations of slavery and its aftermath, and she continued in the forefront of the reparations movement for the rest of her life.

In 1972 Moore traveled to Africa to attend Kwame Nkrumah's funeral. During the trip she was honored with the title of "Queen Mother" and spoke at the All African Women's Conference in Dar es Salaam. Her tours of African farms and industries inspired her to found the Queen Mother Moore Research Institute and the Eloise Moore College of African Studies and Vocational and Industrial School in the Catskill Mountains (destroyed by fire in 1978).

Moore was a member of the National Association of Colored Women and a founding member of the National Council of Negro Women. Her view of the women's movement in the 1970s was negative, however, and she has described feminism as an "alien ideology emanating from the white woman," whereas the black woman's fight is "alongside of her man." She never relented in her activism. In 1995 she was among the revered elders invited to speak at the Million Man March in Washington, DC.

Moore's long career of political activism merged black nationalism, Pan-Africanism, and the Left. Her simultaneous support of black women's organizations and alienation from the white feminist agenda speaks to the racial bifurcation of the women's movement.

See also **Black Nationalism** *and* **Left, The.**

BIBLIOGRAPHY

Ahmad, Muhammed. "Queen Mother Moore." In *Encyclopedia of the American Left*, edited by Mari Jo Buhle, Paul Buhle, and Dan Georgakas. Urbana: University of Illinois Press, 1992.

"Black Scholar Interviews: Queen Mother Moore." *Black Scholar* March–April 1973.

Gilkes, Cheryl Townsend. "Audley Moore." Interview 6 and 8 August 1978. Black Woman Oral History Project, Schlesinger Library, Radcliffe College.

Lanker, Brian. "Queen Mother Audley Moore." In *I Dream a World: Portraits of Black Women Who Changed America*. New York: Stewart, Tabori, and Chang, 1989.

Naison, Mark. *Communists in Harlem during the Depression*. Urbana: University of Illinois Press, 1983.

Obituary. *New York Times*, 7 May 1997.

"Queen Mother Moore." *New Afrikan*, 18 December 1983.

"Queen Mother Moore Receives Garvey Award." *Burning Spear*, January–March 1987.

—Barbara Bair

MORRISON, TONI (b. 18 February 1931), writer. Born Chloe Anthony Wofford in Lorain, Ohio, a steel-mill town on the shore of Lake Erie, Morrison was the second of four children. Her father was a welder in the steel mills, and her mother was a homemaker. Morrison's parents and maternal grandparents migrated to Lorain from the South in the early 1900s. Her maternal grandparents were sharecroppers in Greenville, Alabama, who had lost

Toni Morrison was awarded the Nobel Prize for Literature on 7 October 1993. The Swedish Academy, in bestowing the award, described her work as "characterized by visionary force and poetic import." (Photograph by Timothy Greenfield-Sanders.)

their land in the late 1890s and were never able to get out of debt. Her father's family had been sharecroppers in Cartersville, Georgia, and his painful memoirs of racial strife left him with a bitter attitude toward whites. Morrison was thus brought up with a strong distrust of whites and an understanding that the only tangible or emotional aid on which she could depend would come from her own community. Group loyalty was among the earliest values she was taught as a child. It was, her parents believed, one of the most important lessons that she could learn in order to survive the harsh racial environment of the 1930s and 1940s.

Morrison's growing years were filled with the jokes, lore, music, language, and myths of African American culture. Her mother sang to the children, her father told them folktales, and they both, she recalled, "told thrillingly terrifying ghost stories." It was at their knees that she heard the tales of Brer Rabbit and of Africans who could fly; heard the names, the imagery, the rhythm of the language; and observed the naming rituals that would become a significant part of her later work as a novelist. Her grandmother played the numbers by decoding dream symbols, and she had an abiding belief in "signs, visitation, and ways of knowing beyond the five senses: We were intimate with the supernatural." This rich variety of songs, stories, beliefs, and history would later give Morrison's fiction its wonder, humor, and depth of understanding of the cultural life of African Americans.

By their own example, Morrison's parents set a model for the shared role that men and women could play in a family. While her father often worked at three jobs to provide for his family, role division in the household was not enforced on the basis of gender. The possibility held out to her by the example of her parents—the absence of typecasting, the desire for individual excellence, an appreciation for literature, and an abiding belief in the viability of her own culture—would mark Morrison's personality and her success as an artist.

The small midwestern community where Morrison grew up was important in developing her sensitivity to the cultural ways of black life that would later become the subject of her novels. The black community of Lorain was composed mostly of migrants who found jobs there when they fled the South in the early 1900s. Having left Georgia and Alabama during the Great Migration of blacks out of the South, her family had a strong sense of community, camaraderie, and defiance. Also, in the 1920s and 1930s, when blacks had not begun to assimilate the ways of the larger culture or forgotten the sustaining cultural values taught in separate cohesive black communities, there was a stronger connection to tradition. Because Lorain was a small, midwestern, working-class community made up of people from various ethnic backgrounds—Greeks,

Italians, Irish—the young Morrison became sensitive to the integrity of cultural differences.

The people of Morrison's community formed a cast of rich personalities. "People were more interesting then than they are now," she told Thomas LeClair in an interview. She noted more excesses in women and men, and these were accepted at that time. "In the community where I grew up there was eccentricity and freedom, less conformity in individual habits—but close conformity in terms of the survival of the village of the tribe." Thus, in all of Morrison's novels, the eccentrics—the rejected, the orphaned, the deformed, the mentally ill, the evil, the wayward—share center stage with the stable and responsible. In her writing, Morrison probed their separate lives and the roles they served in their communities. As she would tell Colette Dowling in a 1977 interview, Morrison wanted to find out "who those people were and why they lived the way they did—to see the stuff out of which they were made."

Young Chloe, as she was called by her family, attended the public schools in Lorain. An intelligent child, Morrison made an early distinctive impression on her teachers. In first grade, she was the only black child in her class. As the only child who could read, she was often asked to help others who were having trouble. Her superiority in reading, however, did not exempt her from rejection on the basis of race. One student, a recent Italian immigrant, was assigned to sit next to her so that she could help with his reading. They read together, Morrison recalled, and were becoming good friends. After a few weeks, however, he suddenly stopping sitting next to or speaking to her. Once he had assimilated and learned the American hierarchy of race, Morrison concluded, he was willing to give up his friendship and his tutoring assistance in order to distance himself and thus feel superior to the little girl who was black.

Understanding racism as a fact of life, Morrison continued to read on her own. As an adolescent, she eagerly read the works of Dostoevsky, Tolstoy, and Austen. Reading these writers taught Morrison how the specificity of one's group culture could be captured in a novel. As she explained to Jean Strouse in a 1981 interview, after noting that those novels were not written for a black girl in Ohio, "they spoke directly to me out of their own specificity. . . . When I wrote my first novel years later, I wanted to capture that same specificity about the culture I grew up in."

At Lorain High School, Morrison was an honor student and participated in many school activities. She was a member of the yearbook staff, the National Honor Society, and the chorus. She was also a library helper and treasurer of the senior class. Her success in writing and journalism classes impressed her teachers so much that her English teacher sent a special note home to her mother. "You and your husband would be remiss if you didn't send this child to college." Her mother never forgot those words and would later take a job outside the home in order to send her daughter to college, the first in her family to go.

After graduating from Lorain High School in 1949, Morrison entered Howard University in Washington, DC. The years at Howard were important years for her later development as a writer and her deeper understanding of black life that extended beyond small towns in the Midwest. Always an avid reader, Morrison majored in English and minored in Classics. She studied dance, joined Alpha Kappa Alpha Sorority, and was a member of the Howard Repertory Theater. With the theater company, she took memorable trips to the South, where she got a firsthand look at Southern black life. What she saw there echoed the stories her father had told her about the poverty and racism he had known as a young man. During these trips, Morrison was also able to see that within the community of blacks there were many similarities between those Southern black communities she visited and her own in the Midwest. Thus, early in her life she confirmed something about the shared nature of the cultural life of blacks despite regional differences. It was a commonality she learned to trust and would rely on later to write her novels.

At Howard, Morrison stopped using her first name and used "Toni" instead, a shortened version of her middle name, because students at Howard had difficulty pronouncing "Chloe." She graduated from Howard in 1953 with a BA in English. In 1955 she received her master's degree in English from Cornell University. Morrison wrote her master's thesis on William Faulkner and Virginia Woolf. From 1955 to 1957, she taught at Texas Southern University in Houston. She returned to Howard in the fall of 1957 as an instructor of English.

While teaching at Howard, she met and married Harold Morrison, a Jamaican architect. The couple had two sons, Slade Kevin and Harold Ford. In 1964, after the marriage ended in divorce, Morrison returned to Lorain. A year and a half later, in 1965, she moved to Syracuse, New York, to work as a textbook editor for a subsidiary of Random House. Always sustained by community and family, Morrison had written only for her own pleasure as a teenager and as a member of her writing group at Howard. In Syracuse, away from a nourishing community, she began to approach her writing seriously as a way to connect to the way of life she had left behind.

Alone in the evenings after the children had gone to bed, she wrote as a way of keeping in touch with her community and combating her loneliness at a time when she had no one to talk to. Morrison worked on a story that she had begun in her writing group at Howard about a little black girl who wants blue eyes. And while the issue of Anglo-Saxon standards of physical beauty and the problems of growing up black and poor in a society that holds whiteness and middle-class values up as the norms were the major conflicts in the novel, these conflicts, as those in future novels would be, were unraveled against the backdrop of a black community largely sustained by its own cultural values.

Told by a young narrator, the nine-year-old protagonist who prays for blue eyes, *The Bluest Eye* offered an insider view of what happens to a family trapped by standards of beauty and success that exclude them. Recent migrants from the South, the Breedloves cast their hopes on an urban, material, Anglo-Saxon culture that ultimately destroys them. This oppressive and abiding standard renders them ugly and worthless. It leads the father and mother to low self-esteem and mutual hatred and the little girl to madness and victimization by her community and her family. Morrison explored the Breedlove family through the eyes of another little black girl, Claudia McTeer, who is buoyed by the love of her family, though subject to the same demeaning standards. Through Claudia's eyes, we see how self-destruction comes to one black family and how questions and assumptions about black reality can prevent this destruction in another black family. Morrison finished *The Bluest Eye*, her first novel, in 1969, and after several early rejections, it was finally published in 1970. Although criticized by some reviewers for its episodic development, most reviewers praised Morrison's deft use of language and her sensitive probing of a problematic issue, not often discussed, in the black community.

By the time *The Bluest Eye* was published in 1970, Morrison had moved from the textbook subsidiary of Random House located in Syracuse to the textbook and later the trade book division at Random House in New York City. She would remain at Random House for nearly twenty years and become a major voice in the publishing industry. As senior editor, Morrison was committed to publishing works by black authors, and she was successful in encouraging the publication of works by Gayle Jones, Toni Cade Bambara, Muhammad Ali, Andrew Young, and many others. She was also committed to continuing the cultivation of her own writing. "I would write," she said, "even if there were no publishers." Six months after she completed *The Bluest Eye*, she began work on her second novel. In 1973, *Sula* was published by Alfred A. Knopf, was met with largely favorable reviews, and was nominated for the 1973 American Book Award. The *Time* magazine reviewer Peter Prescott called it an "exemplary fable . . . its brevity belied by its surprising scope and depth." Margo Jefferson called its language passionate and precise, and Barbara Smith declared it "beautiful, needed, mysterious." The *New York Times* reviewer Sara

Blackburn, however, caused a stir when she criticized Morrison in her review of *Sula* by saying that she was "too talented a writer to remain only a marvelous recorder of the Black side of provincial American life." Her review set off a wave of letters from readers and writers to the *New York Times* chastising Blackburn for her biased remarks. It was a controversy that would be a pivot point for debates about the merits and drawbacks of fiction by African American writers for years to come.

Sula, like *The Bluest Eye*, was another growing-up story focusing on young black girls. It is the tragic story of two young childhood friends and the separate ways that they approach womanhood. Nel Wright and Sula Peace grow up in opposite households. Nel's house is neat and traditional, and Sula's wayward and filled with a cast of community stragglers. The traditional, safe personality of Nel versus the more innovative and daring personality of Sula become a way for Morrison to talk about what she saw as the dual desire and ability of black women to be both of these kinds of women and about how the black community often demanded the former and punished the latter. The real value of the friendship of Nel and Sula is in their ability to accept and accentuate the differences in one another. "Together," says Morrison, "they would have been a perfect, marvelous human being." Written at the height of the women's movement and at the beginning of what would become a renaissance of literary production for black women writers, *Sula* became a celebrated text. Like *The Bluest Eye*, however, *Sula* was also written with a look back at life in the black community as it had once been. The challenges and complexities of that life as well as its sustenance would become a hallmark of Morrison's fiction.

An Expanded Vision

In 1973, after the publication of *Sula*, Morrison began an in-house editing project that would enlarge her understanding and knowledge of the range of black history and culture. The project was called *The Black Book* (1974). Though Morrison's name appeared nowhere in the book, she was both the originator of the idea and the book's in-house editor. She was so involved in the project that she collected materials from her friends and family to add to the enormous collections of the official editors, Middleton Harrison, Morris Levitt, Roger Furman, and Ernest Smith. The book was filled with information about the struggles and the triumphs of African Americans. In explaining her desire to do this kind of book, Morrison said that she was tired of histories of black life that focused only on leaders, leaving the everyday heroes to the lumps of statistics. She wanted to bring the lives of those who always got lost in the statistics to the forefront—to create a genuine black history book that simply recollected life as lived. Loosely chronological, moving from slavery to roughly the 1940s, the book contained newspaper clippings, bills of sale, sheet music, announcements, dream books, definitions, letters, patents, crafts, photographs, sports files, and other memorabilia taken largely from the collections of its editors, but it also included an array of contributions from the attics, scrapbooks, and trunks of other supporters of the project. *The Black Book* became a major resource for Morrison's later novels. It provided rich historical background and informed her sense of the magnitude of the struggle and of the persistent heroism of blacks in America. Here were the stories from African American culture of slavery, root-working, dream interpretations, Father Divine, and Harlem, including accounts of the Middle Passage and, most significantly for Morrison, the story of Margaret Garner, the slave who killed her child rather than have her returned to slavery— the story that became the genesis of her Pulitzer Prize–winning novel, *Beloved*.

After the publication of *The Black Book*, the range of historical connection in Morrison's novels became more expansive. In *The Bluest Eye* and *Sula*, Morrison depended mostly on the history of her own life in Ohio. After *The Black Book*, she traveled places in her novels where she had not gone before. She recorded black life from Ohio to Florida, from New York to Kentucky and the Caribbean and, later, to Oklahoma; her inclusion of black history, myths, songs, folktales, and ways of life was greater and more expansive than it had been in the earlier novels. From the myths of first-generation Africans in the New World and the details of the Middle Passage to the Harlem of the 1920s and the all-black townships of Oklahoma in the 1890s, Morrison's voice became larger, her historical depth greater, her awareness of the mythical possibilities of her fiction more revealing. Perhaps no experience had greater influence on the cultural and historical depth of her later novels than editing *The Black Book*.

In 1977, Morrison published *Song of Solomon*, her third novel and the first since her work on *The Black Book*. *Song of Solomon* was a triumphant endorsement of knowing and accepting ancestral heritage. All of the knowledge of *The Black Book*, all of the sensitivity to the needs of ancestral connection for a contemporary generation moving rapidly toward a materialist, upwardly mobile culture, was used by Morrison to create a rich and powerful novel. Moving away from her focus on women in her first two novels, Morrison wrote *Song of Solomon* as a tribute to her father and grandfather. Her father had been a fiercely proud man, unequivocal in his hatred and distrust of whites. John Solomon Willis, her great-grandfather, though not as angry as Morrison's father, was just as hopeless about the potential for coexistence with whites. His family history was particularly implicated in

Song of Solomon. Willis was a musician, and his father, like the title character in the novel, had married an Indian woman and had had his land stolen by whites. *Song of Solomon* was a way for her to assume the perspective of black men like her father and grandfather, who suffered the physical and psychic wounds of racism, and to better understand the love of danger and adventure, and the desire for flight held by her sons.

It is the story of a black middle-class Michigan family in the 1950s and 60s, whose patriarch, Macon Dead, steadily loses touch with the sustaining values of family and culture as he struggles to maintain black middle-class power and position. In the process, he mistreats his wife, rejects his sister, holds his daughters up as emotionless trophies, and ultimately has nothing to pass on to his son but schemes for how to make more money. Everyone, including Macon, is emotionally bereft in the Dead household, and what finally saves the son, Milkman, is his relationship with his Aunt Pilate, the sister his father rejects because of her total disregard for money and power and the trappings of middle-class influence. The story is the tale of Milkman Dead who, in a quest to find gold, inadvertently at first and then intentionally and with great triumph finds the story of his ancestry, of his great-grandfather, a native-born African, who could fly.

In *Song of Solomon*, Morrison also considered the limitations of two political options available to blacks in the wake of the civil rights movement: rapid financial advancement by blacks and violent retaliation against whites. She attacks both materialism, represented by Milkman's father, and vigilantism, represented by Milkman's friend, Guitar. Morrison showed the emptiness of self-definition in economic terms, the shortsightedness of the willful violence of revenge, and the healing growth possible in individuals when they know and are nourished by the history and culture of their ancestry. The heroes and heroines in the novel are not financial kings or outlaws, but rather those who find their solace, their wealth, their sense of joy in community and ancestry.

Heralded for its language, its cultural richness in song, its folklore, and its myths, *Song of Solomon* was a triumphant endorsement of the possibility of renewal and transcendence through ancestral reconnection. It became the most celebrated novel by a black writer since Ralph Ellison's *Invisible Man* (1952). In 1977, *Song of Solomon* was chosen as the Book-of-the-Month Club main selection, a recognition no novel by a black writer had received since Richard Wright's *Native Son* (1940). By 1979, more than 570,000 copies had been sold. In addition to the National Book Critics' Circle Award for fiction, *Song of Solomon* brought Morrison an American Academy and Institute of Arts and Letters Award and inclusion in the widely respected public television series *Writers in*

America. The novel was printed in five languages and sold over three million copies through 1990. When it was chosen as an Oprah Book Club selection in 1997, twenty years after its first publication, its sales rose again, to phenomenal levels. Many critics, despite the Pulitzer Prize for her later work, *Beloved*, considered *Song of Solomon* to be Morrison's best work.

Still concerned with the challenges of contemporary postintegration society, and more comfortable now than she had ever been in her role as writer, Morrison completed her fourth novel, *Tar Baby*, in 1981. In *Song of Solomon*, Morrison had been concerned with the effect of materialism on a young black man. This time, her concern was its effects on a young black woman. In *Tar Baby*, as in *Song of Solomon*, Morrison relied on myth to validate the need for her protagonist to remain connected with the African past.

Coming after the celebrated publication of *Song of Solomon*, *Tar Baby* was received with great fanfare. The novel appeared on the *New York Times* bestseller list less than a month after its publication. Morrison appeared on the 30 March 1981 cover of *Newsweek* magazine. It was the first time a black woman had been on the cover of a national news magazine since Zora Neale Hurston had been so in the 1940s. By 1981, Morrison was fast becoming a literary icon on the American scene.

Though thematically similar to *Song of Solomon*, *Tar Baby* was a more stylistically innovative novel, wherein Morrison mythologized the landscape as well as the history of the Isle de Chevaliers: "Clouds looked at each other, then broke apart in confusion. Fish heard their hooves as they raced off to carry the news of scatterbrained river to the peaks of hills and the tops of the champion daisy trees." The novel was not as well received by critics as had been the earlier novels. Susan Lardner of the *New Yorker* called the prose labored; Wilfred Sheed of the *Atlantic* called it "heavy handed." "We have experienced Morrison," Sheed concluded, "half at her very best, and the other half presumably having fun." Valerie Smith, in a more serious assessment of the novel, while noting the excesses of the descriptions of the landscape, concluded that "the deft characterization, flawless ear for dialogue, and free play of imagination that one expects from Morrison are as evident here as they are [in her other novels]." *Tar Baby* stretched Morrison's geographical range beyond the United States—from Paris to the Caribbean. It also differed in the contemporary nature of its conflict: a successful black woman of the postintegration 1970s struggles with whether to wrap herself in the trappings of European success, which will necessarily distance her from the black community, or to abandon success, stay close to her community, and choose the "culture-bearing role" expected of women in traditional black communities. Despite its less auspicious reception, the novel sold well and firmly established Morrison as a major American novelist. The *Newsweek* cover story and a stunning lineup of promotional tours increased sales and catapulted Morrison into enduring fame. She was, one reviewer claimed after the publication of *Tar Baby*, "the toast of the literary world." Both *Song of Solomon* and *Tar Baby* were widely read in college courses and were translated into several languages.

After the publication of *Tar Baby*, Morrison became comfortable saying that she was a writer. She had been a major force in the publishing world as an editor, overseeing the works of many black writers. With four novels to her credit, visiting lectureships at Yale, Bard College, Rutgers, and Stanford, and with a growing number of literary awards, Morrison became highly sought-after in the literary world beyond Random House. Considered by 1984 to be a major American writer in her own right, Morrison left her job as senior editor at Random House and accepted an appointment to the Albert Schweitzer Chair in the Humanities at the State University of New York (SUNY) at Albany.

There, Morrison began work on a commissioned play for the first anniversary celebration of the Martin Luther King Jr. holiday. The play, *Dreaming Emmett*, was performed at the Capitol Repertory Theater of Albany on 4 January 1986. It was a dream reenactment of the murder of Emmett Till and the incident leading up to it. Reviewers praised the language and the innovative stage production. The play won the New York Governors Award in the arts.

Beloved

While at SUNY, Morrison also began work on her fifth, and perhaps most famous, novel, the story of a slave woman who escapes slavery with her four children from Kentucky to Ohio. She appears to have taken a more expansive look at her novelistic work and begun work on what she conceived of as a trilogy of African American history. The first of this three-part work, *Beloved*, was a major work based on the life of Margaret Garner, the slave woman who tried to kill her children rather than have them returned to slavery. The artistic and textual complexity of *Beloved*, with its embedded time shifts, its recall of the horror, machinery, and degradation of slavery, its brave movement into a ghost-world consciousness, and the great moral depth and complexity of the story, was a major literary achievement. *Beloved* won the 1988 Pulitzer Prize for fiction, and Morrison was recognized in many literary and academic arenas for what was considered the most grand and riveting of all of her novels. For it, she received the Ainsfield Wolf Award in Race Relations (1987), the Elmer Holmes Bobst Award for Fiction (1988), the Melcher Book Award (1988), the Robert

Kennedy Book Award (1988), the Modern Language Association of America Commonwealth Award in Literature (1989), the Sara Lee Corporation Front Runner Award in the Arts (1989), and, from Italy, the Chianti Ruffino Antico Fattore International Literary Prize (1990). *Beloved* was also chosen as a Book-of-the-Month Club selection upon its publication.

Morrison's first four novels had dealt with issues of growing up and identity in a world negotiated by race and how that negotiation affected individual relationships within families and between men and women. With *Beloved*, Morrison began a more expansive project. It was clear that Morrison wanted to write the narratives that would give metaphorical import to all of African American history. She had outlined just such a project for herself, and *Beloved* was to be the beginning of an historic trilogy that would move from the era of slavery to the 1970s. The novel engaged literary critics like no other novel had done in recent memory. Over one hundred dissertations in the next ten years would include *Beloved* as a subject. Books and hundreds of essays were devoted to the implications of its meaning. Motherhood, slavery, the Middle Passage, the supernatural, the afterlife, and the artistic challenge of its creation all became the subjects of literary analysis. In 1988, Oprah Winfrey, television mogul, actor, and avid reader of literature by African American women, bought the film rights to *Beloved*. It was a novel as stunning in its artistry as in its thematic and interpretive import. Its publication heralded a transforming moment in American literature and in Morrison's stature as a great American writer.

In 1989, Morrison accepted the Robert Goheen Chair in the Humanities at Princeton University, where she taught literature and creative writing. While at Princeton, Morrison also began work on her sixth novel, *Jazz* (1992), and she would also assume a more prominent role as literary and cultural scholar. In 1989, she delivered the Robert O. Tanner Lectures at the University of Michigan; in 1990, the Massey Lectures at Harvard University. She would later publish the Massey lectures, a reflective collection of essays on the African presence in canonical American literature, as *Playing in the Dark: Whiteness and the Literary Imagination* (1992). *Playing in the Dark* became a much-used text in American literary criticism, as much for the exemplary rigor of its analysis as for the subject of its critical gaze. After Morrison's analysis, the covert uses of race in American literature by white writers became a growing subject of critical inquiry in American literary scholarship. Morrison also edited scholarly responses to two major political trials in the 1990s that had important implications for race and gender in American society. The first was a response to the Clarence Thomas–Anita Hill hearings, which had captured the

imagination of the American people in 1991: *Race-ing Justice, En-gendering Power* (1992). The other was a scholarly response to the implications of the O. J. Simpson trial in 1996: *Birth of a Nation'hood* (1997). Morrison also wrote important scholarly articles on African American literature that became theoretical touchstones for literary critics; among them were "Unspeakable Things Unspoken: The African American Presence in American Literature" (1989) and "Rootedness: The Ancestor as Foundation" (1984).

During the early 1990s, Morrison also published *Jazz* (1992), her sixth novel and the second in the historic trilogy she began with *Beloved*. She began *Jazz* in much the same way she began *Beloved*. *Jazz* evolved from a piece of history that Morrison had seen while working on *The Black Book* in 1974. James Van der Zee, an important historical photographer in Harlem during the 1920s, took pictures of everyday life in Harlem—from dapper young men strolling on Lenox Avenue to children at play, to city policemen, and to young women who had died love-sick deaths laid out in their coffins. One such photo from the latter scenario, collected in Camille Billops's manuscript *The Harlem Book of the Dead*, was accompanied by a story that recounted that the woman in the photograph, who had been shot by her boyfriend, told friends, when they asked who had shot her, "I'll tell you tomorrow. I'll tell you tomorrow." The boyfriend got away and the young girl died. "Who loves *that* intensely any more?" Morrison asked rhetorically in an interview in 1973 with Paula Giddings.

Nearly twenty years later, Morrison was able to take the kernel of the passion and write the story of the working, loving, dying, and displaced black folks outside of the literary circles of the Harlem Renaissance. Understanding those Harlemites would require long looks at the psyches of the migrants who had come to New York in the 1920s to escape a lifetime of emotional pain, who had come to the city hoping to be lifted emotionally just by the size and tempo of the city itself. The story of how the city both fails and succeeds in this effort is the story of *Jazz*. The central characters are migrants from the South, Joe and Violet Trace, both motherless runaways whose bizarre behavior in the North can only be explained by taking the winding road back to the South to see what sent them running and what they were hoping to find. There are also other characters, though, who have arrived in New York hoping to forget past wrongs and move on with their lives: Alice Manfred and her niece Dorcas, who dies at Joe Trace's hand and who lost her family in a fire in the East St. Louis riots in 1917; Malvone and Felice, more at ease than the other characters with the city and the catalysts, finally, for helping Joe and Violet find their way.

In the novel, Joe Trace, a recent migrant, chauffeur, and door-to-door salesman of Cleopatra cosmetics products, kills Dorcas, a dreamy-eyed eighteen-year-old who was his lover three months before she breaks off the relationship. At the funeral, Violet, Joe's wife, who is "given to stumbling into dark mental cracks," tries to cut the dead girl's face with a knife. The real story in *Jazz*, however, as in all of Morrison's novels, is not about who shot whom but why. The novel, mimicking the riffs and improvisational form and meaning of jazz music, is a tour de force of rhythm, voice, and upbeat and layered revelations of the past and present and how the two combine to give a real-life story of the pain, the spontaneity, the improvisational quality of human desire represented by the music. *Jazz* was praised for its vision of a metaphorical connection between the inherent pain and joy in the music and the life of blacks who actually lived day to day in that celebrated period of history referred to as the Jazz Age.

With a narrator who questions his or her own reliability and admits what he does not know and what he needs to know in order to figure the characters out, *Jazz* gave literary and cultural critics the complete package: a work that is technically advanced and written in a way that is representative of the cultural, social, and psychological changes that occur within a society.

After a twenty-year career that had included eighteen years as senior editor at Random House, six novels, one Pulitzer Prize, and an established preeminence as one of the most distinguished novelists and intellectuals of the twentieth century, Morrison was awarded the Nobel Prize for Literature on 7 October 1993. The Swedish Academy, in naming Morrison, praised her for a body of work "characterized by visionary force and poetic import [that] gives life to an essential aspect of American reality." Morrison became the eighth woman, the fourth American, and the first African American to win the Nobel Prize for Literature. Morrison was understandably effervescent, and she was thrilled that she could represent so many areas, women, and her race. "I know it seems like I'm spreading like algae when I put it this way, but I'd like to think of the prize being distributed to these regions and nations and races."

In a celebrated event in Stockholm, Sweden, in December of that year, Morrison accepted the prize and gave a stirring Nobel Lecture on the power of language. "Word work is sublime," she concluded in her speech. "We die. That may be the meaning of life. But we do language. That may be the measure of our lives." As if she had been given too much good news in the space of the fall and winter, Morrison's house burned to the ground later in December of 1993. It was a devastating emotional and professional loss. Many of her early manuscripts were lost in the fire. She began the process of retrieval and recovery, and what original manuscripts she could save

were preserved in a special collection at Princeton University.

By 1994, Morrison had already began to expand her range as an artist when she was commissioned by Carnegie Hall in 1992 to collaborate with composer André Previn to write the lyrics for *Honey and Rue*, a six-song cycle for the opera singer Kathleen Battle. After her own experience with artistic collaboration, she established in 1994 the Princeton Atelier, a creative workshop that brought together guest artists from different media to create works of art that involved both the creators and the students. Though each Atelier project culminated in a public performance of a new work, the focus of the Atelier was on the process of creating a work of art rather than on the finished product. Morrison directed the highly regarded Atelier program at Princeton, and she brought together a stunning group of guest artists to participate in the program with students and Princeton faculty, including Jacques d'Amboise, director of the National Dance Institute; the novelists A. S. Byatt and Gabriel Garcia Marques; the musicians Yo Yo Ma and Edgar Meyer; the composers André Previn and Richard Danielpour; and the filmmaker Louis Massiah. Morrison also continued her own artistic collaborations, including writing the lyrics for song cycles for Jessye Norman with Richard Danielpour—*Sweet Talk* (1997)—and with Judith Wier—*Woman. Mind. Song* (2000). Morrison also composed lyrics for Sylvia McNair with Andre Previn—*Four Songs* (1997)—and she wrote the lyrics for the production of *Margaret* (2005), an opera based on the life of Margaret Garner with music by Richard Danielpour.

The publication of the novel *Paradise* in 1998 was a much-heralded achievement, with Morrison garnering the cover of the January issue of *Time* magazine. *Paradise* was an immediate bestseller and was widely reviewed. It was also chosen as an Oprah Book Club selection, a choice guaranteeing an even wider readership. It would be safe to say that, by April of 1998, there was hardly an individual in the United States who listened or read even a trickle of news who did not know who Toni Morrison was and the title, if not the story line, of her seventh novel. As she had done in *Beloved* and *Jazz*, Morrison seized an important historical moment as the pivotal point in *Paradise*. In the 1890s, after the disappointments and lawlessness of Reconstruction, many blacks, mostly from Mississippi, Arkansas, and Louisiana, migrated west to Oklahoma. All-black towns were one of the results of this migration. After reading a newspaper invitation for homesteaders while doing archival research, Morrison noticed the phrase "come prepared or don't come at all." The lack of charity and the haughtiness in that statement coming from blacks seemed shocking for a group or people who themselves had just recently fled the oppression of others in the South.

"I suppose being a novelist, I was interested in what on earth it must have felt like to have come all that way and look at some other Black people who said you couldn't come in." Morrison felt that such behavior was symbolic of what can happen when those who have been oppressed begin to use power in the same way as their oppressor. And so *Paradise* became the story of a group of dark-skinned black Oklahoma homesteaders who seek to keep their town all black and, on the surface at least, pure. The conflict, complexities, hypocrisy, and violence that erupt from that effort become the story of *Paradise*. In this case, the scapegoat for all the fears of the town guardians was a reckless group of wayward women, who have also taken refuge just outside their town. *Paradise* was Morrison's most feminist text. It made the most scathing indictment on the ill uses of power and the particular way in which black men use it against women. The novel also engages a post-civil-rights debate among blacks about whether or not affirmative action programs should continue.

In 1998 the film adaptation of *Beloved* was released. The film received mixed reviews and did not attract the viewer base that Winfrey had expected. A period piece with the riveting story of slavery and infanticide proved to be too much for popular audiences. Morrison's popular readership did increase tremendously during the 1990s, however, after four of her novels were selected for the Oprah Book Club. Thanks to the Book Club selections and the televised discussion of her novels, Morrison enjoyed the rare combination, for a novelist, of both a popular and critical audience.

In 1999, Morrison began to write children's books. She was the co-author of *The Big Box* (1999), in which she gave a rhythmic and rhyming homily for freeing the independent spirit of young children; *The Book of Mean People* (2002) in which, from the point of view of a child, the character names a surprising list of mean people in his family and community. The last three works were part of an eight-book series that revised and updated the Aesop fables, called *Who's Got Game?* The books in that series included *Who's Got Game?: The Ant or the Grasshopper?*; *Who's Got Game: The Lion or the Mouse?*; and *Who's Got Game?: Poppy or the Snake?* In the midst of collaborating on operas, lecturing, and co-writing children's books with her son, Morrison published her eighth novel, *Love*, in October 2003.

While *Paradise* had had early mixed reviews, *Love* enjoyed unreserved acclaim. A concise novel, *Love* was called Morrison's most tightly woven tale. Her editor, Richard Gottlieb, said of the novel, "It knows the story it wants to tell and it's found the language to tell it. Nothing is there that shouldn't be, and everything that should be there is there." Another reviewer said, "Morrison is at the top of her game." Adam Langer of *Book* magazine called the novel "a powerhouse."

Reminiscent of *Sula*, *Love* looks back at a pre-1960s, preintegration black community, the resort town of Silk, New Jersey, where a prominent black businessman, Bill Cosey, had once owned a resort hotel. The story revolves around the many women who have a place in Cosey's life: Julia, his first wife; Heed, his twelve-year-old second wife; May, his daughter-in-law; Christine, his granddaughter and a close friend of Heed's; L and Vida, his former employees; and Celestial, the true love of his life. The narrative, with many revelatory flashbacks, details what's left of Silk and the resort after Cosey dies. His widow, whom he married when she was eleven and he fifty-two, and his granddaughter, once his wife's best friend, are determined to get what they both believe is rightfully theirs from the Cosey estate. As in other Morrison novels, most notably *Tar Baby*, what they're searching for is not what they find.

In the course of the novel, many of the emotionally damaging secrets—sexual, financial, criminal, familial—that the community has kept close in order to survive are revealed. Unraveling the secrets and understanding what they have meant in the moral world of this community is the challenge of reading *Love*. Morrison again calls upon her reader to explore the love-driven, in-group dimensions of the black community lived on their own terms for survival. *Love* is, like *Sula*, a novel about women's friendships. With Heed and Christine, as she did with Nel and Sula, Morrison cautions women against the ability of self-absorbed men to create a wedge of distraction within the often lifesaving friendships of women. "We could have been living our lives hand in hand instead of looking for Big Daddy everywhere." And she once again heralds the defiant "sporting woman" who rejects the demands of the community and breaks its rules, but who also serves as a model—albeit risqué—of hope and survival for black women.

With *Love*, Morrison also reminded contemporary readers of the rich complexity of the life of all-black communities in a preintegration period when they had the wisdom, the restraint, and the fortitude to know how and when to keep community secrets. "Nowadays silence is looked on as odd and most of my race has forgotten the beauty of meaning much by saying little." In all of these levels of meaning, Morrison concluded, as evident in the novel's title, the cause and the solution for most of the conflicts in the novel, those told and those kept secret, is love—too much, not enough, ill begotten, or carelessly used.

For her remarkable literary corpus, Morrison received honor and critical acclaim from around the world. In addition to the Nobel Prize for Literature in 1993, Morrison was recognized for her long career of literary achievements by receiving the Condorcet Medal and the

Commander of the Order of Arts and Letters from France in 1994; the National Book Foundation Medal for Distinguished Contribution to American Letters in 1996; the Medal of Honor for Literature from the National Arts Club in 1998; the 2000 National Humanities Medal from the President of the United States; and, all in 2001, the Jean Kennedy Smith Creative Writing Award from New York University; the Pell Award for Lifetime Achievement; the Cavore Prize, Tureen, Italy; the Fete du Livre, Cite du Livre, Les Ecritures Croisees, from France; and the Enoch Pratt Free Library Lifetime Achievement Award.

Since beginning to write in 1970, Toni Morrison achieved an esteemed and commanding place in the American literary canon. Her works are anthologized in every literary history of major American writers. The Toni Morrison Society enjoyed a growing international presence as an intellectual and archival base for Morrison scholars. More than three hundred dissertations and thirty books have been published about her work. Her works are taught in nearly every college course on major American writers, women writers, or African American literature. Toni Morrison came a long way from the culture-rich nurturing of her family in Lorain, Ohio, but, cognitively and emotionally, she took that culture with her to all the places she traveled and used it as a lens through which she and her readers could imagine a new literary world. Morrison holds a firm, revered, and revolutionary place in the annals of American letters.

See also Children's Literature *and* Fiction.

BIBLIOGRAPHY

Andrews, William L., and Nellie Y. McKay. *Toni Morrison*. Oxford University Press: New York, 1999.

Beaulieu, Elizabeth Ann. *The Toni Morrison Encyclopedia*. Westport, CT: Greenwood Press, 2003.

Bjork, Patrick Bryce. *The Novels of Toni Morrison: The Search for Self and Place within the Community*. New York: P. Lang, 1994.

Bloom, Harold. *Toni Morrison: Modern Critical Views*. New York: Chelsea House Press, 1990.

Bouson, J. Brooks. *Quiet as It's Kept: Shame, Trauma, and Race in the Novels of Toni Morrison*. Albany: State University of New York Press, 2000.

Carmean, Karen. *Toni Morrison's World of Fiction*. Troy, NY: Whitson Publishing Company, 1993.

Century, Douglas. *Toni Morrison*. New York: Chelsea House, 1994.

David, Ron. *Toni Morrison Explained: A Reader's Road Map to the Novels*. New York: Random House, 2000.

Denard, Carolyn. "Blacks, Modernism, and the American South: An Interview with Toni Morrison." In *Studies in the Literary Imagination*, Fall 1998.

Denard, Carolyn. "Toni Morrison: A Biographical and Critical Essay." In *Modern American Women Writers*, edited by Elaine Showalter. New York: Scribner's, 1991.

Fultz, Lucille. *Toni Morrison: Playing with Difference*. Urbana: University of Illinois Press, 2003.

Furman, Marva Jannett. *Toni Morrison's Fiction*. Columbia: University of South Carolina Press, 1996.

Gates, Henry Louis, Jr., and K. A. Appiah, eds. *Toni Morrison: Critical Perspectives Past and Present*. New York: Amistad, 1993.

Giddings, Paula. "The Triumphant Song of Toni Morrison." In *Encore*, 12 December 1977.

Grewal, Gurleen. *Circles of Sorrow, Lines of Struggle: The Novels of Toni Morrison*. Baton Rouge: Louisiana State University Press, 1998.

Harding, Wendy, and Jacky Martin. *A World of Difference: An Intercultural Study of Toni Morrison's Novels*. Westport, CT: Greenwood Press, 1994.

Harris, Trudier. *Fiction and Folklore: The Novels of Toni Morrison*. Knoxville: University of Tennessee Press, 1991.

Holloway, Karla F. C., and Stephanie Demetera Kopoulos. *New Dimensions of Spirituality: A Biracial and Bicultural Reading of the Novels of Toni Morrison*. Westport, CT: Greenwood Press, 1987.

Jones, Bessie W., and Audrey L. Vinson. *The World of Toni Morrison: Explorations in Literary Criticism*. Dubuque, IA: Kendall/Hunt, 1985.

Kubitschek, Missy Dehn. *Toni Morrison: A Critical Companion*. Westport, CT: Greenwood Press, 1998.

Mbalia, Doreatha Drummond. *Toni Morrison's Developing Class Consciousness*. Selingsgrove, PA: Susquehanna University Press, 1991.

McKay, Nellie Y., and Kathryn Earle, eds. *Approaches to Teaching the Novels of Toni Morrison*. New York: MLA of America, 1997.

McKay, Nellie Y. *Critical Essays on Toni Morrison*. Boston: G. K. Hall, 1988.

Middleton, David L., ed. *Toni Morrison's Fiction: Contemporary Criticism*. New York: Garland, 1997.

Middleton, David L. *Toni Morrison: An Annotated Bibliography*. New York: Garland, 1987.

Page, Philip. *Dangerous Freedom: Fusion and Fragmentation in Toni Morrison's Novels*. Jackson: University Press of Mississippi, 1996.

Peach, Linden, ed. *Toni Morrison*. New York: St. Martin's Press, 1998.

Peterson, Nancy J. *Toni Morrison: Critical and Theoretical Approaches*. Baltimore: John Hopkins University Press, 1997.

Ranveer, Kashinath. *Black Feminist Consciousness*. Jaipur, India: Printwell, 1995.

Reyes-Conner, Marc Cameron, ed. *The Aesthetics of Toni Morrison: Speaking the Unspeakable*. Jackson: University Press of Mississippi, 2000.

Rice, Herbert William. *Toni Morrison and the American Tradition*. New York: Peter Lang, 1996.

Rigney, Barbara Hill. *The Voices of Toni Morrison*. Columbus: Ohio State University Press, 1991.

Roberson, Gloria Grant. *The World of Toni Morrison: A Guide to Places and Characters in Her Novels*. Westport, CT: Greenwood Press, 2003.

Samuels, Robert. *Writing Prejudices: The Psychoanalysis and Pedagogy of Discrimination from Shakespeare to Toni Morrison*. Albany: State University of New York Press, 2001.

Samuels, Wilfred D., and Clenora Hudson-Weems. *Toni Morrison*. Boston: Twayne Publishers, 1990.

Sumana, K. *The Novels of Toni Morrison: A Study in Race, Gender, and Class*. New Delhi, India: Prestige, 1998.

Taylor-Guthrie, Danille. *Conversations with Toni Morrison*. Jackson: University Press of Mississippi, 1994.

—CAROLYN C. DENARD

MORTON JONES, VERINA HARRIS. *See* Jones, Verina Harris Morton.

MOSELEY BRAUN, CAROL (b. 16 August 1947), first African American woman senator. Moseley Braun made history in 1992 when she became the first African American woman—and first African American Democrat—elected to the U.S. Senate. With her election to the nation's top legislative body, she instantaneously became a symbol of both racial and gender diversity. However, Moseley Braun's career as a U.S. Senator was only one highlight in her successful career as both a lawyer and public official. With a résumé composed of service at the local, state, and federal levels, Moseley Braun proved to be more than simply a "symbol." She established herself as one of the premier public officials in the United States, for any race or gender.

Born to Public Service

Carol Moseley was born in Chicago to Joseph J. Moseley, a law-enforcement official, and Edna W. Davie Moseley, a medical technician. Carol spent her early childhood in a middle-class neighborhood in Chicago. Her father (who

CAROL MOSELEY BRAUN made history in 1992, when she became the first African American woman and first African American Democrat elected to the United States Senate. (Austin/Thompson Collection.)

she remembered as a follower of W. E. B. Du Bois's ideal of the "Talented Tenth") and her mother (who embraced Booker T. Washington's pragmatic emphasis on the ability to earn a living) combined to create an atmosphere of racial pride and commitment to the broader black community. However, she also remembers the family home as a "United Nations of 41st Street," often filled with people of diverse ethnic and racial backgrounds, which added an integrated and multiracial component to her world. In this environment, which did not present either race or gender as an obstacle to success, her idealism and sense of duty were forged.

With her parents' divorce in 1963, Moseley Braun's world began to change. She and her other brothers and sisters moved with their mother to her grandmother's Chicago neighborhood, nicknamed the "Bucket of Blood." Here Moseley Braun was introduced to the world of poverty and despair that, unfortunately, was familiar to many African Americans. This experience further fueled Moseley Braun's sense of duty to help the downtrodden and economically disadvantaged. During her high school years, Moseley Braun showed early signs of political inclinations. She staged a one-person sit-in at a restaurant that refused her service and also marched in an open-housing demonstration led by Martin Luther King Jr.

After her graduation from the Chicago Public Schools system, Moseley Braun entered the University of Illinois at Chicago. There she majored in political science and began to create more formal ties to the world of politics through her efforts as a campaign worker for future Chicago mayor Harold Washington's state representative campaign. Upon completion of her bachelor of arts degree in 1968, Moseley Braun entered the University of Chicago Law School, where she earned her juris doctorate in 1972. During her time at Chicago, she also met Michael Braun, a fellow law student, whom she married in 1973.

After working briefly in a private firm, Moseley Braun joined the U.S. Attorney's Office in Chicago in 1973. As an assistant U.S. attorney in the Northern District of Illinois, she worked primarily on civil and appellate law, eventually winning the Attorney General's Special Achievement Award in recognition of her work in housing, health policy, and environmental law. In 1977, Moseley Braun left the U.S. Attorney's Office to start her family, giving birth to son Matthew the same year.

While busy as a new mother, Moseley Braun also volunteered her time on local environmental issues. After seeing her in action, friends encouraged Moseley Braun to run for the position of state representative for her diverse Hyde Park neighborhood. Running as a Democrat, she won election to the Illinois General Assembly in 1978, and began a ten-year career as an Illinois state representative. Moseley Braun proved to be a quick study in the world of politics, earning the respect and admiration of her constituents and colleagues for her work on such issues as education and health care. She also continually worked against various forms of discrimination, particularly in the fight for redistricting—an issue that eventually led her to sue her own Democratic Party and the state of Illinois, seeking fair reapportionment for African Americans and Latinos. Her work as a state representative won her two Best Legislator Awards (1980 and 1982) from the Independent Voters of Illinois and awards from various other professional organizations in Illinois. Recognition from within the political community included her appointment as assistant majority leader in the general assembly (the first African American to hold that position), as well as floor leader for then-Chicago mayor Harold Washington. She was even mentioned as a possible candidate for lieutenant governor in 1986. That opportunity never materialized, purportedly due to the veto of Harold Washington, who may have been displeased with Moseley Braun's independent nature.

The year 1986 proved to be a trying one in Moseley Braun's personal life. During this year, Moseley Braun divorced her husband, lost her brother Johnny to drugs and alcohol addiction, and her mother suffered a serious stroke. Despite these personal devastations, Moseley Braun continued to work as a state representative until 1988. At that time, she left the general assembly and won election as the recorder of deeds and registrar of titles for Cook County. Though this city-level position may have seemed a step backward to some onlookers, Moseley Braun had once again made history, becoming the first African American elected to an executive position in Cook County. During her tenure in this position, Moseley Braun was credited with leading the reorganization and streamlining of her agency, including the establishment of a code of ethics for employees.

In 1991 Moseley Braun, like many women (especially African American women), watched the Senate confirmation hearing of the Supreme Court nominee Clarence Thomas in disbelief. The whole country watched as the almost exclusively male Senate appeared to close ranks behind Thomas and treat the Oklahoma law professor Anita Hill, who charged that Thomas had sexually harassed her, with both contempt and disrespect. One of the senators who voted to confirm Thomas was longtime Illinois politician Al "The Pal" Dixon. Angered by what she witnessed, and further fueled by others with similar outrage, Moseley Braun launched an improbable bid for the U.S. Senate in 1992.

Elected into History

Moseley Braun's campaign for the Senate drew little attention at first, but by the time the general election

occurred in 1992 she had made history. In a three-way race for the Democratic nomination, Moseley Braun ran a grassroots campaign alongside the incumbent, Al Dixon, and Alfred Hofeld, a free-spending, multimillionaire personal-injury lawyer. While the two men waged a high-profile campaign against each other, Moseley Braun maintained her grassroots appeal to the wide array of Illinois voters—men and women, rural and urban—who were tired of politics as usual. When the dust settled from the March primary, Moseley Braun had won the Democratic nomination and became the first African American woman nominated to the U.S. Senate by a major political party. Some political pundits sought to explain her nomination as the result of the three-way race in which the other two candidates' campaigns against each other supposedly opened the door for Moseley Braun to slide into the nomination. However, such explanations ignored Moseley Braun's political appeal to the broad coalition of voters who supported her.

Whereas her campaign had once been low profile and largely ignored by state and national media outlets, Moseley Braun took on an almost celebrity status after her primary victory. The former city and state official was almost instantaneously launched into political stardom as national media outlets celebrated, and scrutinized, her campaign. While the months leading to the general election were marked with some internal campaign turmoil, Moseley Braun rode her coalition of voters to a general election victory over the conservative Republican nominee, Richard S. Williamson.

Many deemed the 1992 national elections the "Year of the Woman" and saw Moseley Braun's election to the U.S. Senate as the crowning achievement. Her election was historic for many reasons. Moseley Braun was the first African American woman and the first African American Democrat elected to the U.S. Senate. In addition, she was the first female senator from Illinois and the sole African American member of the Senate at the time.

In making history, Moseley Braun, in addition to her political duties to Illinois, carried the extra responsibilities of a symbol. She was, for many, the "women's senator" and the "African Americans' senator." Moseley Braun admits that she sometimes felt overwhelmed in her role as both symbol and senator, receiving up to five hundred requests a week for her participation in various events, far more than any other senator. Nevertheless, Moseley Braun worked hard in the Senate to be more than a symbolic presence and proved to be more capable than many expected a freshman senator to be. In a particularly poignant episode in 1993, Moseley Braun made a stand to block the Senate's renewal of a federal patent for the logo of the United Daughters of the Confederacy, which included the flag of the Confederacy. Backed by the support of the powerful senator Jesse Helms, and discreetly attached as an amendment to a national service bill, the renewal initially passed a test vote 52 to 48. However, outraged by what she believed would be the U.S. Senate's approval of a symbol of slavery, Moseley Braun gave an impassioned speech against the motion. While recognizing that the women of the organization had a right to celebrate their history, she argued that a symbol of slavery must not be "underwritten, underscored, adopted, approved by this United State Senate." After hearing Moseley Braun's compelling and convincing argument, numerous senators were convinced to change their votes and the measure was soundly defeated.

This proved to be only the beginning of Moseley Braun's distinguished career as a senator. Moseley Braun worked as an ardent advocate of numerous education, health care, and civil rights measures. She went on to serve on such committees as the Senate Judiciary Committee; the Senate Banking, Housing, and Urban Affairs Committee; and the Senate Finance Committee. Moseley Braun continued to work as both a senator for the state of Illinois and a symbol to the broader African American community. The latter was not always an easy task, as she sometimes received the ire of other black leaders if she did not side on a subject the way some believed she should have. Nevertheless, she remained liked and admired by most within the black community and was acknowledged for her work on numerous issues, including her advocacy of the Underground Railroad Act to preserve historic sites associated with the escape routes of former slaves.

While many people originally believed Moseley Braun would be reelected easily at the end of her term, by 1998 she faced an increasing amount of opposition. Plagued by inquiries into her personal and campaign finances, as well as controversy surrounding her questionable trip to Nigeria (where she visited the family of the military dictator General Sani Abacha), Moseley Braun's reelection proved a harder task than originally assumed. Though exonerated of financial misdoings, she failed in her reelection bid, losing to the Republican Peter Fitzgerald in 1998.

Though Moseley Braun's political star appeared to dim briefly, she was not ready to resign from political life. In 1999, Moseley Braun accepted a consulting position with the U.S. Department of Education. Later that year, she was also appointed the ambassador to New Zealand and Samoa. After her ambassadorship ended, Moseley Braun took on various consulting jobs and briefly worked as a professor at Morris Brown College and DePaul University.

In 2003, Moseley Braun surprisingly reentered the political arena when she announced her candidacy for the president of the United States. Assuring voters that her résumé was "second to none" and that she was more qualified than many other candidates, Moseley Braun presented herself as the antithesis of the then-current president, George W. Bush. Her campaign called for increased spending on education, the protection of civil liberties (which she felt were eroded by such post-September 11 legislation as the Patriot Act), and an end to U.S. military action in Iraq. Moseley Braun withdrew from the presidential race in January 2004. However, her political future remained uncertain in mid-2004. Regardless of a return to national politics, Moseley Braun's astonishing and history-making career made her one of the most important African American women in American government

See also Legislators.

BIBLIOGRAPHY

"Carol Moseley Braun for President." http://www.carolforpresident. com.

"Carol Moseley Braun OK'd as U.S. Ambassador to New Zealand." *Jet*, 29 November 1999.

Clymer, Adam. "Daughter of Slavery Hushes Senate." *New York Times*, July 23, 1993.

Haynes, Karima A. "Will Carol Moseley Braun Be the First Black Woman Senator?" *Ebony*, June 1992.

Krol, Eric. "Moseley Braun Battles Odds in Bid for a Political Comeback." *Chicago Daily Herald*, 22 September 2003.

Marks, Alexandra. "The Quest of Carol Moseley Braun." *Christian Science Monitor*, 20 November 2003.

Merida, Kevin. "Senator, Symbol, Self; with Three Big Roles to Juggle, Carol Moseley Braun Always Has Her Hands Full." *Washington Post*, 15 August 1994.

Moseley-Braun, Carol. "Between W. E. B. Du Bois and B. T. Washington." *Ebony*, November 1995.

"Moseley-Braun Takes Consulting Post with U.S. Education Department." *Jet*, 25 January 1999.

"President Clinton Signs Underground Railroad Act to Preserve Sites of Historic Slave Escape Route." *Jet*, 10 August 1998.

"Sen. Carol Moseley-Braun's Recent Trip to Nigeria Causes Foreign Policy Uproar." *Jet*, 9 September 1996.

Thompson, Kathleen. "Carol Moseley-Braun." *Facts on File Encyclopedia of Black Women in America*, edited by Darlene Clark Hine and Kathleen Thompson. New York: Facts on File, 1997.

Walsh, Edward. "Carol Braun's Rocky Road to History; After the Upset, It's Still a Long Way to the Senate." *Washington Post*, 28 April 1992.

Wilkerson, Isabel. "Black Woman's Senate Race Is Acquiring a Celebrity Aura." *New York Times*, 29 July 1992.

Wilkerson, Isabel. "Milestone for Black Woman in Gaining U.S. Senate Seat." *New York Times*, 4 November 1992.

Wilkerson, Isabel. "Storming the Senate 'Club.'" *New York Times*, 19 March 1992

—ERIC D. DUKE

MOSSELL, GERTRUDE E. H. BUSTILL (b. 3 July 1855; d. 21 January 1948), social reformer, author, and educator. Through her books, articles, and newspaper columns, Mossell wrote about her political and social ideology, reflecting the views of a feminist and social

GERTRUDE MOSSELL, frontispiece portrait with two children, from the second edition of her book *The Work of the Afro-American Woman*, published in Philadelphia in 1908. (Manuscripts, Archives, and Rare Books Division, Schomburg Center for Research in Black Culture.)

reformer in the late nineteenth and early twentieth centuries. She encouraged women to go into such professions as medicine and journalism, and she dismissed the notion that a woman had to choose to have either a family or a career. Mossell and other black women leaders of her era combined roles as activist and professional with those of wife and mother. Taken together, her views would not be seriously considered by most African Americans for at least another generation.

Gertrude E. H. Bustill Mossell was born in Philadelphia, Pennsylvania. Her parents, Charles H. and Emily (Robinson) Bustill, were among the free-black elite of nineteenth-century Philadelphia. The prominent Bustill family included generations of achievers, including Mossell's great-grandfather, the former slave Cyril Bustill (1732–1806), who earned his freedom and served on George Washington's staff as a baker during the American Revolution. One of Cyril's daughters, Grace Bustill Douglass (1782–1842), was an abolitionist and a member and officer of the Philadelphia Female Anti-Slavery Society, as was her daughter, Sarah Mapps Douglass (1806–1882), who also married a Douglass. Sarah was not only an abolitionist but a feminist and noted educator. Perhaps the most illustrious member of the Bustill family was Mossell's cousin, Paul Bustill Robeson (1898–1976), who became a Rhodes scholar after graduating from Rutgers University and went on to become a prominent actor, singer, and political activist.

Gertrude Bustill and her elder sister, who later became Mrs. William D. Robertson, were raised as Quakers, as were many of the Bustills. Both women later followed the lead of several family members and joined the Presbyterian church. They were educated in Philadelphia "colored" schools.

After completing Roberts Vaux Grammar School, Gertrude Bustill taught school for seven years at various places, including Camden, New Jersey, and Frankford, Delaware. As was the custom, her marriage to physician Nathan F. Mossell of Lockport, Pennsylvania, probably in the early 1880s, ended her formal teaching career. She returned to live in Philadelphia, where she reared two daughters, Mazie and Florence. A few years after her marriage, however, Mossell resumed her writing and developed a career as a journalist, educating the public about women's rights and social reform movements.

Mossell's career goal emerged from her exceptional ability as a writer who came from a family of political activists and feminists. The Reverend Benjamin Tucker Tanner discovered Mossell's writing potential, probably in the late 1860s, when he was a guest at the closing exercises of the Roberts Vaux Grammar School, where he heard her read her essay "Influence." He invited her to submit it for publication to the periodical he edited, the *Christian Recorder*. As a result of this first literary success, Mossell began an outstanding literary career, writing essays and columns for numerous newspapers and periodicals and eventually writing two books, *The Work of the Afro-American Woman* (1894) and *Little Dansie's One Day at Sabbath School* (1902).

Mossell developed a national reputation as a journalist writing for African American newspapers. Her articles and columns appeared in the *AME Church Review*, the (New York) *Freeman*, and the (Indianapolis) *World*. In Philadelphia, she wrote for leading papers with syndicated columns in the *Echo*, the Philadelphia *Times*, the *Independent*, and the *Press Republican*. In addition, Mossell assisted in editing the *Lincoln Alumni Magazine*, the journal of her husband's alma mater.

African American women journalists were few and far between during the 1880s when Mossell wrote the column "Our Woman's Department," which appeared in the first issue of T. Thomas Fortune's New York *Freeman*, in December 1885. Mossell introduced her column by titling the first one "Woman Suffrage." She wrote that her column would "be devoted to the interest of women" and that she would "promote true womanhood, especially that of the African race." Mossell encouraged readers ignorant about the issues of woman suffrage to read books and periodicals to educate themselves. She hoped that with new awareness those who thought unfavorably about votes for women would be convinced to change their opinions. Married women, Mossell argued, supported woman suffrage. Her words indicated a significant political awareness and sophistication shared by only a few outspoken black woman suffragists in the 1880s.

Mossell's column appeared every other week throughout 1886, and in it she promoted career development in business and the professions. She called for the training of women in skills that would prepare them for businesses, such as the restaurant industry. As for literary and journalistic careers, Mossell introduced her readers to such role models as Frances Ellen Watkins Harper, Josephine Turpin, and Charlotte Ray; to such essayists as Mary Ann Shadd Cary; and to such journalists as Ida B. Wells-Barnett, Clarissa Thompson, and Mattie Horton, using her column to promote women and to encourage them to seek their rights.

Mossell died at the age of ninety-two at Frederick Douglass Memorial Hospital in Philadelphia, the city where she spent most of her life. She had been ill for about three months.

Mossell believed that all types of African American women needed to ally themselves in order to help one another in a process that she and others of her era called "racial uplift." Although she was known as a product of Philadelphia's black elite, Mossell looked beyond the lines of status when she called for women of color to come together to work on behalf of their race.

BIBLIOGRAPHY

Logan, Rayford W., and Michael R. Winston, eds. *Dictionary of American Negro Biography*. New York: Norton, 1982.

Majors, Monroe, ed. *Noted Negro Women: Their Triumphs and Activities* (1893). Freeport, NY: Books for Libraries Press, 1971.

Mossell, Mrs. N. F. *The Work of the Afro-American Woman* (1894). New York: Oxford University Press, 1988.

Penn, I. Garland, ed. *The Afro-American Press and Its Editors* (1891). New York: Arno Press, 1969.

—ROSALYN TERBORG-PENN

MOTHERHOOD.

Black and white American motherhood have always differed. Unlike white motherhood, black mothering has always existed in tandem with productive labor, and it has seldom been an isolated, individual undertaking. Where white motherhood has always been revered, black mothers have been maligned through the centuries. Though their hardships have been great, at times overwhelming, African American mothers made themselves a bulwark against American racism. Indeed, the history of African American motherhood proves beyond doubt that motherhood is powerful.

Enslavement Era

For close to two hundred and fifty years, enslavement defined African American motherhood. Women who, in Africa, were guided by the tradition of their people in everything from choosing a husband to child spacing and child rearing, in America had their reproduction controlled and manipulated by Europeans with a foreign culture and motivations that had nothing to do with the African woman's needs and wishes.

In the early years of the American colonies, the heavy labor done by African women kept their fertility low. In fact, at times during the sixteenth and seventeenth centuries there was little price differential between male and female slaves because owners figured that women would perform the same arduous labor as men. In most colonies, women, like men, cleared the land and also planted and harvested the crop, be it rice, hemp, indigo, sugar, or tobacco.

Even though women were put to work downing trees, digging ditches, and plowing dirt, this heavy productive labor did not exempt them from the responsibilities of childbearing. Despite low fertility, slaveholders focused on African reproduction. When they bequeathed a woman's progeny, both born and *yet to be born*, they showed just how much their calculations of current and future wealth were based on African women's ability to have children. Not only did they buy equal numbers of men and women, and in that way try to keep ratios fairly even, where possible they willed males and females in couples—whether or not there was an emotional connection—all in the attempt to keep reproduction constant.

From the colonial period to the Civil War, enslavers never ceased pressuring black women to have children. In fact, in the one hundred years after 1750, the American

Louisiana Royalty

Mention the name Marie Therese or Marie Thereze to people in the Cane River region of southern Louisiana and it is a good bet that all of them will be able to tell stories about her that they learned in childhood. Many will also be descendants of this woman, called Coincoin, a slave who created a veritable empire of color that is still celebrated today in history and folklore for its emphasis on hard work, mutual assistance, and loyalty.

The story starts in Natchitoches in the Louisiana Territory, a confluence of French, Spanish, and Indian cultures, where the child baptized as Marie Thérèse was born in 1742 to imported slave parents. She would be known by the African name Coincoin, given to her by her parents. Her family was owned by Luis Juchereau de St. Denis, who founded the post on the Red River and later became its commandant. Coincoin was passed from St. Denis to his widow, their son, and, in a stroke of good fortune, their daughter, Marie de Nieges de St. Denis. A woman with a reputation for being "spirited and unconventional," de Nieges rented her slave—in defiance of the church and local custom—to the French merchant Claude Thomas Pierre Metoyer. They produced ten children in their twenty years together, in addition to five that Coincoin had borne before her relationship with him.

Around 1778, under pressure to end his "scandalous alliance" and fearing that she might be sold, Metoyer purchased Coincoin, granting her and her infant child freedom. The previous six children she had borne him, as well as the other five, remained in slavery. They parted ways in 1786, when Metoyer chose to marry in order to produce legitimate offspring, giving his mistress sixty-eight acres of land plus a yearly stipend. She started her new life at the age of forty-six with a clear goal: to procure the freedom of her children and grandchildren. Her industry showed in the way she raised crops and cattle, qualified for a Spanish land grant, and continued to acquire property, eventually including slaves. With the same industry, she tracked down her children, traveling from outpost to outpost to negotiate for their release. At sixty-two she even renegotiated her annuity agreement with Metoyer, who had remained close to the family, in order to see all of her children by him finally freed.

These same children begat generations of people of color who became an agricultural and business dynasty, at one time owning 20,000 acres of land and 500 slaves, making them the largest slaveholding family of color in the United States. Coincoin's son Louis founded the Melrose Plantation, which became an arts colony and eventually a National Historic Landmark. Many Cane River citizens trace their roots to "Grandpere," her son Augustin.

For more information, see Gary B. Mills, *The Forgotten People: Cane River's Creoles of Color* (Baton Rouge: Louisiana State University Press, 1977).

black population, 90 percent of which was enslaved, was notable for its fertility. In most other places in the Western Hemisphere, families were scarce because slave owners increased their enslaved population primarily by purchasing slaves from Africa. By contrast, in the United States, there was far more community development among slaves. Although slave "marriages" were not legally binding, and enslavers were not bound to recognize relationships made between slave men and women, in the United States enslavers encouraged family formation and procreative sexual relations.

This aspect of American slavery was especially important after the foreign slave trade ended in 1807. Once slave owners could no longer legally purchase slaves from Africa, they became more dependent on their enslaved women to reproduce the labor force. Remarkably, in each year between 1800 and the Civil War, more than one-fifth of the black women between the ages of fifteen and forty-four bore a child. On average, enslaved women had their first child at age nineteen, two years before the average southern white woman had hers, and continued to have children at two-and-a-half-year intervals until they reached the age of thirty-nine or forty.

Enslavers achieved this high rate of fertility through the use of verbal encouragement, subtle manipulation, and overt coercion. They wanted adolescent girls to have children, and to this end they practiced an insidious kind of breeding. While it was not unheard of for a planter to put a male and female together and demand that they "replenish the earth," it was more likely that an enslaver would use his or her authority to encourage young slaves to make binding and permanent the relationships they themselves had initiated. Some did this by granting visitation privileges to a young man of a neighboring plantation who had taken an interest in a particular young woman. If the man and woman married, these visitations continued throughout the marriage. Occasionally, arrangements were made whereby a slave owner purchased a slave so that a man and woman could be together.

Beyond this were the more subtle practices that were built into the plantation system. For example, most, though by no means all, pregnant and nursing women did less work and received more food than nonpregnant women. Frances Kemble reported that on her husband's Georgia and South Carolina rice plantations, when children were born, "certain additions of clothing and an additional weekly ration were bestowed upon the family." If inducements such as these were not sufficient to secure the cooperation of a woman of childbearing age, the slave owner always had recourse to punishment or sale. According to the ex-slave Berry Clay, "a barren woman was separated from her husband and usually sold." And it was not uncommon for slaveholders to demand their money back for female slaves they had purchased who later proved incapable of giving birth.

Enslavers ensured their wealth when they forced relationships, sold nonprolific women, and gave all sorts of incentives for women to have children, but these actions also unwittingly promoted and sanctioned slave families and made motherhood central to African American survival. Slaveholders did not mean to, but when they encouraged family creation they gave enslaved men and women a point of reference that did not begin and end with the master. The family gave bonded men and women the role of parent. It gave their children the sibling role, which evolved into the roles of aunt and uncle. With the family, slaves became providers and protectors for their spouses and their children. If parent and child were lucky enough to survive into old age without being separated, and usually it was a mother surviving with a daughter, then the mother could count on caretaking from her daughter. Clearly, family life happened within the constraints of slavery, but the little room left by the master's dependence on the slave allowed it to happen nevertheless.

Similarly, what was simply reproduction for the master became motherhood for the enslaved woman, and motherhood was the centerpiece of African American survival as well as the enslaved woman's most important rite of passage—more important even than "marriage." Crucial is the fact that since nonprolific women were usually sold, childbearing was a way to anchor oneself to a given plantation for an extended period of time and thus maintain enduring relationships with family and friends. Childbirth, therefore, somewhat secured the nuclear family against breakup by sale, and the slave woman's ability to bear many children and to nurture them through infancy was often the crucial element in the length and stability of a slave "marriage." Beyond this, mothers made the African American community possible. They gave it the ability to say collectively what one slave woman once said of her offspring: "My child him is mine."

But motherhood was a mixed blessing. Although we know that only a few black mothers killed their infants, even in the face of the auction block, and that there was little self-imposed sterility and few self-induced miscarriages, we can only imagine the ambivalence, and anguish, that accompanied pregnancy and childbirth in slavery. It was only in the last months of pregnancy that an expectant mother had her work decreased, and then she was still expected to do "light" hoeing or other kinds of fieldwork. Excessive workload, combined with less-than-adequate nutrition, resulted in high rates of miscarriages and maternal mortality. Mothers also had a tiring day, since nursing and child care did not relieve a slave woman of the burdens of heavy fieldwork. If women were not tired from their work, and from nursing, and from running back and forth between their children and the field, they were worried sick with fear that the child who had been left under a tree to care for itself would be bitten by a snake or otherwise harmed. Besides knowing that a master or mistress could, at any time, for any reason, beat or otherwise abuse one's child, every slave mother and slave family had hanging over them like the sword of Damocles the fear of separation. An unexpected expense on the part of an owner, a turn in the economy, a death, or a needed wedding gift could result in the sale or separation of mother and child. And always there was the threat of death. By 1850 black infant mortality was twice that of whites.

On the other hand, motherhood gave many women a reason for living. Runaway statistics tell an important story. Women ran away less frequently than men because they more often than not refused to run without their children. Writing about female runaways, William Still, an operator of the Underground Railroad, observed that "females undertook three times the risk of failure that males are liable to." Speaking of two female runaways, both of whom had two children, he noted: "none of these can walk so far or so fast as scores of men that are constantly leaving."

There is no doubt that fugitive men loved their children, but mothers had a special connection. Unlike the runaway male, the enslaved woman who left her children behind could not be certain that they would be given the best possible care. A father could not provide for a nursing infant because "in dem days no bottle was given to no baby under a year old." Moreover, since women and small children were often sold as a group, a father was more likely to be sold away from his children. Runaway advertisements are clear: mothers either escaped with their children or did not try to escape at all. Most were in the latter group.

In addition, most women helped other women with the tasks of motherhood. Slave women had an intensive workday before child care was added. Few could satisfy the demands made by the master on the one hand and children on the other. Enslaved women had to have help if they were to survive the dual responsibilities of laborer and mother. Slavery, thus, made African American motherhood a cooperative undertaking. In depending on elderly women who did not work in the fields, on slave midwives and nurses who combined folk and contemporary medical techniques to treat illnesses, and on other female relatives and friends to provide food, clothing, and supervision, enslaved women shared child-rearing responsibilities. Most importantly, communal motherhood helped the enslaved hurdle one of the most difficult of predicaments—the care of children whose mother had died or had been sold. In the absence of a female relative, nonkin women assumed the fictive kin-mother role. On southern plantations, the female community made sure that no child was truly motherless.

After Enslavement

Cooperative motherhood, like many of the patterns established during enslavement, continued after slavery's end primarily because African American women continued to have to combine the responsibilities of motherhood and work, and because white prejudice continued unabated. In fact, in the years immediately following the Civil War, a reign of white terror made black motherhood perilous beyond belief. Defeated in war, former slaveholders resolved to win the peace by thwarting African American citizenship at every turn. Through the use of laws called black codes, the courts, labor contracts, the penal system, and most of all, raw violence, white southerners pinioned black freedom in a near-successful effort to reimpose slavery.

Having survived slavery, however, black women were not about to succumb to freedom. They fought for the rights of citizenship and the right to raise their children as they saw fit. First among their many struggles was the right to claim their children as their own. In many cases this proved difficult because masters and mistresses refused to relinquish children to their parents. Such was the case with Sarah Debro, whose mistress had taken Sarah as a house servant. When Sarah's mother came to get her after the war, she had to fight for her child. Tearing her daughter from the mistress's arms, she reminded the white woman of her cruelty: "You took her away from me an' didn' pay no mind to my cryin', so now I'se takin' her back home. We's free now, Mis' Polly, we ain't gwine be slaves no more to nobody." In what amounted to legal reenslavement, apprenticeship laws allowed the Ms. Pollys of the world to keep and employ black children under the age of twenty-one whose parents or relatives were deemed by a court to be either unfit or unable to keep them off the public dole. As often as did men, women fought for custody of their children and other kin.

They also had to make some difficult decisions about the hard lives ahead of them. In the immediate aftermath of the Civil War, many women had to find the husbands they had been separated from during slavery, and many black women separated from husbands they had been forced to take. Discrimination against black men, however, kept men from being able to make enough money to support black families alone. Therefore, black women had to work. Whether a woman raised children as a single parent or in a two-parent household, motherhood was always coupled with work—work for the landowner as a sharecropper or tenant, work as a maid in the homes of white people, work in the few industries that dotted the southern landscape, and always, always, work in her own family plot for subsistence and work for her family's day-to-day welfare. Single women with children had it the hardest. Responsible for their own survival, they had to feed, shelter, and clothe children who were regarded by landowners as a liability and who were not allowed to accompany mothers who worked as maids. The discrimination single mothers faced forced them to work for pitiful wages and left them vulnerable to being run off the land before they got paid and to other forms of sexual and economic exploitation.

Whether single or married, black women did as they had done during slavery and looked to other women to share the responsibilities of motherhood. In the period after slavery, and even after black people began migrating North in the 1930s, black women depended on their female kin to provide help with child care. Starting as early as age eight, daughters began looking after their younger siblings. Aunts and female cousins pitched in when they could, and grandmothers became a staple in many an African American household. In fact, migration for women often began with child care—a young girl or young woman was sent North to look after the children of a woman who needed help juggling work and her children.

Although most rural and urban black women relied on female relatives for help with small children, women in cities had greater access to child-care facilities. Not because the government or local agencies stepped in to help—government-sponsored social service did not begin until the New Deal era, and local agencies concentrated their aid on the white needy—but because black, middle-class clubwomen established kindergartens to help their less-fortunate sisters. Along with kindergartens, clubwomen established mother's clubs, which, true to the tradition of the all-encompassing definition of black motherhood, established community-watch programs, taught women how to buy land and build houses, and served as a distribution center for health care and child-raising information.

The most significant changes in black motherhood between the end of the Civil War and the years of mass migration were the decrease in black fertility and the switch from live-in to live-out domestic work. Across the board, black women began having fewer children. To be sure, middle-class black women had fewer children than the average black woman and rural women had more children than those who lived in urban areas. In general, however, black fertility declined by one-third between 1880 and 1910. A combination of disease, poor nutrition, and unhealthful living conditions, as well as the voluntary use of birth control, led to this decline. Combined with the tragically high incidence of child mortality, decreased fertility made black households smaller, even as it made motherhood potentially more distressing.

Just as important to black motherhood was the self-conscious and deliberate way that black women transformed domestic work. By 1920 black women comprised 40 percent of all domestics and 73 percent of all laundresses outside of commercial laundries. As long as black women lived in, white employers had unlimited control over their time and labor. Not only did they work very long hours, but, as one domestic complained, "I am allowed to go home to my own children . . . only once in two weeks, every other Sunday afternoon." For the pitiful sum of ten dollars a month, she was, she anguished, "the slave, body and soul, of this [the white] family." Throughout the course of the early twentieth century, black female domestics changed this situation. Using the example of laundresses who usually did their work in their own homes, domestic workers stopped working for employers who would not let them live at their own home and work on a daily basis. Day work, or living out, not only gave black women control over their own lives, it also gave them more time to be with their children and families.

Demonization of Black Motherhood

Although black mothers worked hard to protect their children and families from white violence and economic injustice, they nevertheless were the target of continuous criticism. White America had always demonized black motherhood. Enslavers, for example, had not blamed their own heartless practices for infant slave deaths, but faulted black women for their supposed lack of maternal instincts. After slavery, whites liked to think that black women were more promiscuous than motherly, and that they were too diseased and mentally deficient to be good mothers. Most black men and families knew better, but that knowledge was not enough to keep black mothers from being maligned and victimized by both blacks and whites.

Victimization came in the form of sterilization. Early in the twentieth century birth-control advocates joined forces with eugenics proponents in arguing that black women were largely socially inadequate and that they threatened the nation's future by having too many inferior children who were unfit for citizenship. As the century progressed, the limitation of black fertility became an answer to black teenage pregnancy, poverty, and crime in the inner cities, and to spiraling welfare costs. Although black women and families had their own reasons for using family planning, throughout the century, first surgical sterilization, then drugs like Depo-Provera and then Norplant became the means by which disproportionate numbers of black women were involuntarily sterilized by doctors acting on behalf of white-controlled social-service agencies and state governments.

Another disturbing development was the increased acceptance, by both whites and blacks, of the idea that black women dominated their husbands and emasculated their sons. The stereotype of the "black matriarch" gained currency in the late 1930s when social scientists identified the "disorganized family" as a source of black dysfunction and located the cause of supposed black male failure in the paralyzing relationships that developed between black sons and their working mothers. According to the black sociologist E. Franklin Frazier and the white psychologist Erik Erickson, among others, white racism did indeed spawn conditions that kept black Americans from flourishing, but it was black mothers who bore equal if not greater blame because they failed to equip their sons with the means to resist racism. The economically self-sufficient black mother, they all argued, instilled dependency, rather than a healthy aggressiveness, and hostility, rather than self-esteem. In 1965, these ideas made their way into the notorious Moynihan Report and became the basis for national social-service programs that prioritized the needs of black men, who, it was argued, had lost economic and social ground to black females.

Contemporary Black Motherhood

African American mothers persevered through the tyranny of these reports. Despite the 1970s black nationalist call for black women to retire from the workforce, submit to men, and "have babies for the revolution," African American women continued to nurture and provide economic support for their families. From slavery through Jim Crow violence, black women had combined work with nurturance. The late twentieth century was no different, particularly in light of the rise of single motherhood.

The end of the twentieth century found African American women heading one half of all black families, a most significant development since, as difficult as life had always been for black men and women, the single parent rate had, before the 1970s, never gone above 25 percent. Yet, at the dawn of the new millennium, a single parent headed 65 percent of African American families with 50 percent headed by women. Some of this increase was accounted for by widowhood, but mostly it was due to singleness. By 1993, 61 percent of black women and 58 percent of black men were not married. This compared with 38 percent for white men and 41 percent for white women. In 1950 only one-third of black adults were not married. In 2004, a majority were not.

The consequences for children and mothers have been dire. A mother and a father do not raise most African American children; most are raised only by their mothers. Although some of these children fare well, especially those raised in households where their mothers have a college degree, 40 percent of families headed by African American single mothers lived in poverty in 2002, meaning that nearly half of all children living in female-headed households live below the poverty line.

LABOR DAY RALLY in New York City, 1981. These women demonstrated, with their children, to emphasize the need for day care. (© Bettye Lane.)

women, being a mother is a major source of positive identity. Most still believe that motherhood is powerful.

See also Childbirth; Marriage; *and* Midwives.

BIBLIOGRAPHY

Clark-Lewis, Elizabeth. *Living In, Living Out: African American Domestics in Washington, DC, 1910–1940*. Washington, DC: Smithsonian Institution Press, 1994.

Feldstein, Ruth. "Antiracism and Maternal Failure in the 1940's and 1950's." In *"Bad" Mothers: The Politics of Blame in Twentieth-Century America*, edited by Molly Ladd-Taylor and Lauri Umansky. New York: New York University Press, 1998.

Guy-Sheftall, Beverly. *Daughters of Sorrow: Attitudes toward Black Women, 1880–1920*. Brooklyn, NY: Carlson, 1990.

Jones, Jacqueline. *Labor of Love, Labor of Sorrow: Black Women, Work, and the Family from Slavery to the Present*. New York: Vintage, 1995.

Morgan, Jennifer Lyle. *Laboring Women: Reproduction and Gender in New World Slavery*. Philadelphia: University of Pennsylvania Press, 2004.

Polatnick, Rivka, M. "Diversity in Women's Liberation Ideology: How a Black and a White Group of the 1960s Viewed Motherhood." *Signs: Journal of Women in Culture and Society* 21 (1996): 679–706.

Roberts, Dorothy. *Killing the Black Body: Race, Reproduction, and the Meaning of Liberty*. New York: Pantheon, 1997.

"Single Mothers and Their Children Suffered the Most in the Last Year with Persistently High Poverty; Gender Wage Gap Stagnant." *U.S. Newswire*, 26 September 2003.

White, Deborah Gray. *Ar'n't I a Woman?: Female Slaves in the Plantation South*. New York: Norton, 1999.

White, Deborah Gray. *Too Heavy a Load: Black Women in Defense of Themselves, 1894–1994*. New York: Norton, 1999.

—DEBORAH GRAY WHITE

These developments have had a profound effect on the nature of black motherhood. They have deepened the tradition of communal mothering but also have increased women's burdens, which, in turn, have had a detrimental effect on every aspect of life, from health care to education, from economic to psychological well-being. Black male and female relationships have suffered as well. As more black women find themselves mothering alone, they are increasingly bitter toward those they once believed were their natural allies.

Despite these travails, studies show that on average black women still maintain an optimistic attitude toward motherhood, if not marriage. Because so many black women are trapped in exploitive, low-paying, unsatisfying labor, mothering remains the most meaningful work available to them. For both single and married black

MOTLEY, CONSTANCE BAKER (b. 14 September 1921), attorney, judge, and senator. As a leading figure of the era, Motley was on the ground floor of the civil rights revolution. Not only did she help to ensure the legal incorporation of African Americans, but she also was instrumental in laying the foundation for the women's movement and the continued protection of civil liberties for other marginalized groups. As a pioneer in her profession, Motley repeatedly broke gender and racial barriers. She was the first black woman attorney to argue before the United States Supreme Court, first black woman to serve in the New York State Senate, first woman elected as president of the Manhattan Borough, and first African American woman on the federal bench.

Motley was born in New Haven, Connecticut. Her West Indian parents, Willoughby Alva and Rachel Huggins Baker, migrated to the United States from the Caribbean island of Nevis. Constance was the ninth child in a family of twelve; however, three of her siblings died in infancy before she was born. Her father worked as a chef for the Yale fraternity, Skull and Bones, an elite social club.

At an early age, Constance was exposed to black history and culture. The ministers at the Episcopal Church her

CONSTANCE BAKER MOTLEY being sworn in as Manhattan borough president by Mayor Robert Wagner. Her husband, Joel Wilson Motley Jr., and her son, Joel Wilson Motley III, are at right. New York City, 24 February 1965. (Schomburg Center for Research in Black Culture; photograph by New York Courier.)

family attended introduced her to the works of James Weldon Johnson and W. E. B. Du Bois, scholars who poignantly addressed the black experience in America. Constance took on leadership roles in such organizations as the New Haven Youth Council and the New Haven Adult Community Council, both of which focused on the elimination of racial discrimination. She even served for a short time as president of the local youth division of the National Association for the Advancement of Colored People (NAACP), an organization to which she would later devote twenty years of her life as a lawyer.

Constance Baker graduated from high school with honors and dreamed of going on to college. However, she knew this was impossible because her family could not afford to send her. For a short time, she took work as a domestic and then settled into a job at the New Haven branch of the National Youth Administration. One night, while delivering a speech encouraging the members of the Dixwell Community House, a black social organization, to fight for greater control over the facility's operation, she caught the eye of Clarence Blakeslee, a wealthy white contractor and philanthropist who had built the center. Blakeslee was so struck by Baker's intelligence and disposition that he offered to pay for her education. In February 1941 at the age of twenty, Baker enrolled at Fisk University, a prominent black institution in Nashville, Tennessee. A year and a half later she transferred to New York University and graduated from its Washington Square College in 1943 with a degree in economics.

The following academic year, she was one of the few women admitted to Columbia Law School. During her last year, she began clerking for Thurgood Marshall, chief counsel for the NAACP legal defense team and future Supreme Court justice. In 1946 Baker graduated from law school and also married Joel Wilson Motley Jr., a real estate and insurance broker. The couple had one child, Joel Wilson Motley III, who eventually graduated from Harvard University, becoming a lawyer and investment banker.

In 1948 Motley was involved with the preparations for the *Sweatt v. Painter* restrictive covenant case, which the NAACP legal defense team tried and won in the Supreme Court. In 1950 Motley joined the team, becoming an associate lawyer and the first black woman to work on the defense team. Her cases focused on issues of school desegregation, transportation, housing, recreation, and public accommodations. She was an instrumental part of the *Brown v. Board of Education* case, which outlawed school segregation. Between 1961 and 1964 Motley tried ten civil-rights cases before the Supreme Court and won all except one. All of these cases made important progress toward dismantling Jim Crow laws throughout the South and helped win civil liberties for blacks throughout the nation. One such example is the case of *Meredith v. Fair*, in which Motley argued that the University of Mississippi had engaged in racial discrimination by not admitting James Meredith, a black man, to the school. The Supreme Court ruled in Meredith's favor and ordered the university to admit him. This decision set a precedent that would lead to the eventual desegregation of other universities.

In 1964 a Democratic candidate for the New York State Senate was taken off the ballot due to a technicality. Motley was offered the nomination and won the election, making her the first black woman to hold the office. Her political career continued, and during a 1965 special election of the New York City Council, Motley was asked to fill a one-year vacancy as the president of the Borough of Manhattan. After the term expired, she was reelected for a full four-year term. She was the first woman and third black person ever to hold the office. Then, at the suggestion of New York Senator Robert F. Kennedy, Lyndon B. Johnson nominated Motley for a federal district court judgeship for the southern district of New York. Despite opposition to her appointment, she was confirmed in August 1966. At the time of her nomination, there were only two other female federal district judges. She was the first black woman to hold this position, and it made her one of the highest-paid black women in government. On 1 June 1982, she became chief justice, a position she held until 1986 when she became a senior U.S. district judge.

Motley has been awarded more than twenty honorary degrees from various universities and has received widespread recognition for her accomplishments and commitment to civil rights. In 1993 she was inducted into the National Women's Hall of Fame in Seneca Falls, New York, and in 2003 she received the NAACP's Spingarn Award, the organization's highest honor for distinguished achievement. Motley has written extensively for legal and professional journals and published two books, *Equal Justice Under Law: An Autobiography*, and *Perspectives on Justice*, which she coauthored with Telford Taylor and James K. Feibleman. Motley's hard work and tenacious spirit have left an enduring mark on the jurisprudence that shapes and governs the United States.

BIBLIOGRAPHY

Cosby, Camille O., and Renee Poussaint, eds. *A Wealth of Wisdom: Legendary African American Elders Speak*. New York: Atria Books, 2004.

MacLean, Nancy. "Using the Law for Social Change: Judge Constance Baker Motley." *Journal of Women's History* (1 July 2002).

Motley, Constance Baker. *Equal Justice Under Law: An Autobiography*. New York: Farrar, Straus and Giroux, 1998.

Washington, Linn. *Black Judges on Justice: Perspectives from the Bench*. New York: New Press, 1994.

—MONIQUE CHISM

MURRAY, PAULI (b. 20 November 1910; d. 1 July 1985), lawyer, writer, professor, priest, and activist. Anna Pauline Murray led and contributed to the most important social movements transforming American life in the middle third of the twentieth century. She was born in

PAULI MURRAY in 1946, when she won a Mademoiselle Merit Award for signal achievement in law. She was not only a lawyer but also a teacher, poet, minister, and advocate of women's rights. (Library of Congress.)

Baltimore, Maryland, the fourth of six children of Agnes Fitzgerald, a graduate of the Hampton Training School for Nurses, and William H. Murray, a Howard University graduate and teacher and principal in Baltimore's segregated schools. Murray's light skin reflected the mixed racial heritage of both parents. Her mother's death when she was three and her father's ill health caused her to be sent to Durham, North Carolina, in 1914. There she was adopted by her aunt Pauline Fitzgerald Dame, a schoolteacher, and grew up in the modestly middle-class household of her maternal grandparents and another aunt. After graduating from high school, determined to attend an integrated college, she moved to New York City in 1928 and enrolled in Hunter College. Her brief marriage in 1930 was later annulled.

As a young person, Murray began a lifelong love of writing, publishing short stories and essays in her high school newspaper and in the Hunter student magazine. Later, she wrote a memoir of her grandparents, *Proud Shoes: The Story of an American Family* (1956), a collection of poetry in 1970, and her own autobiography, *Song in a Weary Throat: An American Pilgrimage*, published posthumously in 1987. In addition, she authored a study of state laws on race, a study of Ghana's laws and government, and articles for legal and political journals and black newspapers, including her classic essay on "Jane Crow."

Working for social justice, however, claimed her greatest energies. After graduating from Hunter in 1933, Murray survived the Depression years by patching together various social-justice-oriented jobs and study with progressive organizations, including *Opportunity*, the journal of the National Urban League; a Works Progress Administration worker education project; the union-sponsored Brookwood Labor College; and the Workers Defense League. In 1938, she launched her first challenge to racial discrimination, applying for graduate work in sociology at the all-white University of North Carolina. Although her appeals to the university's president, the student body, and President Franklin D. Roosevelt were in vain, she gained courage, "a new sense of self-respect," and a lifelong friendship with Eleanor Roosevelt.

Murray needed that confidence as she served jail time for challenging segregation on interstate buses in Virginia and then entered Howard Law School in 1941, only to find that, where she was welcomed because of her race, she faced discrimination because of her sex. Refusing to be broken by the sexism expressed by students and professors alike, she piloted student sit-ins at segregated restaurants in the District of Columbia, while leading her class academically and winning a postgraduate fellowship.

Rejected for graduate work by Harvard's law school because of her sex, Murray completed a master's degree in law at the University of California in 1945, while she also challenged housing segregation and the Red Cross's segregation of blood. She returned to New York, gained admission to the state bar, and maintained her involvement in interracial liberal politics and civil-rights activism while struggling to support herself as a single lawyer, never sure whether sex or race was the greater obstacle. From 1956 to 1959 she worked as an associate with the liberal firm Paul, Weiss, Rifkind, Wharton, and Garrison. There she met Irene Barlow, a white office manager who shared her Episcopalian commitment and who became Murray's housemate and closest companion until Barlow's death in 1973.

In 1960 Murray's perspective on human rights took an international turn when she accepted an invitation to teach at Ghana's School of Law; during her sixteen months in Ghana she wrote a textbook on that nation's constitution and government. Returning to the United States, she entered Yale University's law school, earning a doctorate in 1965. It was during those years that Murray became a figure of central importance to the emerging second-wave feminism.

Inclined to feminism from her education at the all-female Hunter College and with her consciousness of sex discrimination honed by her experiences at Howard, her rejection by Harvard, and her struggles as a female lawyer, Murray had spoken out against "Jane Crow" as early as the 1940s. When John F. Kennedy appointed his President's Commission on the Status of Women (PCSW) in 1961, her connections with Eleanor Roosevelt and others involved in the commission won her a place on its Committee on Political and Civil Rights. There she orchestrated a compromise in the decades-long conflict between feminists who advocated an equal rights amendment to the Constitution and opponents who believed that such an amendment would invalidate state laws protecting women workers. Murray's compromise relied on a litigation strategy that could persuade the Supreme Court to apply the equal protection clause of the Fourteenth Amendment to women and thereby vitiate the need for a constitutional amendment. As a member of the executive board of the American Civil Liberties Union, Murray played a central role in committing the organization to that strategy and establishing a Women's Rights Project—led by Ruth Bader Ginsburg—that became the most active litigator for gender equality before the Supreme Court.

Murray's passionate concern for black women and her understanding of the complicated intersections of race and gender in their lives put her at odds with black leaders and liberal feminists when Congress considered an amendment to add sex discrimination to Title VII of the Civil Rights Act of 1964, banning discrimination in employment. While opponents worried that including women could jeopardize the entire bill or invalidate protective laws, Murray insisted that without the amendment only half the black population would be protected. After the bill passed, the enforcement agency's failure to take sex discrimination seriously mobilized Murray and other feminists to found the National Organization of Women (NOW) in 1966.

While never ceasing to align herself with feminist causes, in 1967 Murray left the national board of NOW, dismayed at its failure to represent all women and to embrace a universal commitment to the struggles of all oppressed groups. After a year of administering projects for black students at Benedict College in Columbia, South Carolina, in 1968 Murray moved to Boston where she taught at Brandeis University for the next five years. Her steadfast integrationist position brought painful conflicts with militant black students and the Afro-American Studies department, yet she initiated curriculum innovations with her courses in legal studies, women's studies, and African American studies and led campus efforts to improve the status of women.

A lifelong Episcopalian who had worked with several religious women's organizations and challenged the church's discrimination against women, Murray decided at the age of sixty-two to enter General Theological Seminary in New York City. Shortly after her denomination reversed its ban on female priests, she was ordained in 1977 at the Washington National Cathedral, one of the first women to join the Episcopalian ministry. She served as pastor in several churches in Washington, DC; Baltimore; and Pittsburgh until her death.

BIBLIOGRAPHY

Edenfield, Paul L. "The American Heartbreak: A Biographical Sketch of Pauli Murray," 2000. http://www.stanford.edu/group/WLHP/-papers/paulimurray.pdf. Although based only on printed sources, this sixty-page essay offers thoughtful analysis of the forces that informed her multifaceted commitments.

Hartmann, Susan M. *The Other Feminists: Activists in the Liberal Establishment.* New Haven, CT: Yale University Press, 1998. Chapters 3 and 6 provide information on Murray's contributions to second-wave feminism and efforts to bridge gaps between women's rights and civil rights.

Kerber, Linda K. *No Constitutional Right To Be Ladies: Women and the Obligations of Citizenship.* New York: Hill and Wang, 1998. An incisive discussion of Murray's contributions to the legal death of Jane Crow can be found on pp. 185–206.

Murray, Pauli. *Dark Testament and Other Poems.* Norwalk, CT: Silvermine, 1970.

Murray, Pauli. *Proud Shoes: The Story of an American Family* (1956). Boston, MA: Beacon Press, 1999.

Murray, Pauli. *Song in a Weary Throat: An American Pilgrimage.* New York: Harper and Row, 1987. Reissued as *Pauli Murray: The Autobiography of a Black Activist, Feminist, Lawyer, Priest, and Poet.* Knoxville: University of Tennessee Press, 1989. Murray was working on the final revisions of this detailed and reflective autobiography when she died.

Ware, Susan, et al. "Dialogue: Pauli Murray's Notable Connections." *Journal of Women's History* 14 (Summer 2002): 54–87. Seven essays reflecting on civil rights, feminism, literature, law, religion, and sexuality in Murray's life.

—SUSAN M. HARTMANN

MUSEUMS. *See* Black Museums.

MUSICAL THEATER. Women were involved in the creation of black musical theater since the second half of the nineteenth century, a surprising fact given that what we call musical theater did not really exist until about 1920. Throughout the nineteenth century, there were no available roles for African Americans except in minstrel show, which began as all-male and all-white and dominated American entertainment for almost ninety years, until nearly the end of the century. Consisting of white interpretations of black music and dance and racist stereotypes of black life, minstrelsy thrived on and perpetuated the country's obsession with race while it

DIXIE TO BROADWAY. WPA poster—with a chorus girl, band members, and a cotton motif—for the Federal Theatre Project presentation in Decatur, Illinois, 1937. (Library of Congress.)

enforced gender limitations. Still, black women, through their own agency, were onstage and making musical theater as early as 1870.

Nineteenth Century

The first black women to make musical theater their profession were the operatically trained Hyers sisters, Anna Madan and Emma Louise. These two prodigies made their debut when they were in their early teens and then returned to their studies until their parents felt they were ready to perform professionally. After a brilliant performance at the World Peace Jubilee in Boston in 1872, they faced the usual dead end for classically trained black musicians. In response, the Hyers sisters formed a professional black repertory company and began to produce musical plays about the black experience, and this at a time when other black performers felt themselves lucky to be allowed to play the fool. Their first, *Out of Bondage*, was described as the story of a black man's journey from slavery to "education and refinement." Under their own management most of the time, the Hyers produced musical theater until 1893. Among their actors was Sam Lucas, who usually worked in minstrelsy but took time away from that higher-paying venue to work with the Hyers.

The next step in the development of the black musical theater was *The Creole Show* in 1890, starring the same Sam Lucas. Its most important departures from the minstrel show were that it had a female chorus, a female interlocutor or emcee, and an urban setting. *The Octoroons*, produced by John W. Isham in 1895, followed the same pattern and went further by casting female leads, including Anna Hyers. Isham's next show, *Oriental America*, actually made it to Broadway for a short run.

It was another opera singer who made the next major step forward for black women in the field. Sissieretta Jones was an outstanding operatic soprano and was recognized as such by critics and peers. Probably the first black performer to appear at Carnegie Hall, she sang with Antonín Dvořák and the National Conservatory of Music and appeared at both the Wintergarten in Berlin and Covent Garden in London. She auditioned for and won roles at the Metropolitan opera in 1892, but the contracts were never signed, and Jones never appeared. By this time in her career she had been dubbed "Black Patti," after the white singer Adelina Patti, and under that name she toured the country. The Black Patti Troubadours were a variation on the minstrel show, with two important differences. There were black women performers, unheard of in minstrelsy. And the second act, usually a cakewalk, was instead a presentation of operatic arias by Jones.

The Troubadours were an important training ground for both women and men, who would be instrumental in the creation of the black musical. The great dancer and choreographer Aida Overton Walker got her start with Jones's company. Jones hired Bob Cole to write the show, and he was inspired to begin experimenting with "mini-musicals." One, "At Jolly Coon-ey Island," starred performer Billy Johnson and Cole's wife, Stella Wiley, and later was the core for Cole's *A Trip to Coontown*.

In 1898, *A Trip to Coontown* became the first all-black musical comedy. It was created, managed, and directed by African Americans. Though not far from the traditions of the minstrel show, even though it had a bit of a plot tying the musical acts together, the show did, however, feature female performers, something that distinguished it from its predecessors.

A few months later, Will Marion Cook opened *Clorindy, the Origin of the Cakewalk*. *Clorindy* was originally intended to be a vehicle for the popular vaudeville team of George Walker and Bert Williams, but they had to pull out at the last minute because of scheduling. Ernest Hogan emerged from Black Patti's Troubadours to take the male lead, but when the show went on tour, Walker and Williams took over, with George's wife, Aida Overton Walker, dancing the title role.

The New Century

George Walker, Bert Williams, and Aida Overton Walker became one of the most important teams in the new black musical theater. The two men were a highly successful comedy team in vaudeville, and, in 1900, they decided to create their own Broadway musical. Fortunately, they had Aida Overton to choreograph and dance in it. *The Policy Players* was so successful that they opened *The Sons of Ham* the same year. *In Dahomey* followed in 1903, with Hattie McIntosh coming to the cast from Black Patti's Troubadours. *In Dahomey* was the first black show produced in a major Broadway theater. The final Williams and Walker show was *Bandanna Land*, in 1908. During the run of the show, George Walker became too ill to perform, and Aida Overton Walker took over his role. She was startlingly successful wearing her husband's costumes, dancing his dances, and performing his comedy. George Walker died in 1911, never having taken back his role.

The Williams and Walker shows, important as they were, were not the only black musical theater on Broadway at the time. Bob Cole continued to write, direct, perform, and produce, teaming up with two brothers from Florida, John Rosamond Johnson and James Weldon Johnson. First successful as songwriters, Cole and Rosamond Johnson went on to produce and star in *The Shoo-Fly Regiment*, notable as the first black musical to feature a serious love scene. Though this was an important step forward, especially for women, the prohibition against romance in black theater continued into the 1920s. Aida Overton Walker appeared in the second Cole-Johnson musical, *Red Moon* (1909), as did Abbie Mitchell, who would go on to a long and illustrious career on Broadway. The Smart Set Company produced *His Honor the Barber* (1911), in which Aida Overton Walker drew rave reviews.

Black musicals were popular, successful, and increasingly sophisticated. Then, in the early teens of the century, it all stopped. Many explanations for this have been proffered. George Walker and Bob Cole were dead by 1911 and Aida Overton Walker by 1914. Bert Williams, after his partner's death, had joined the *Ziegfeld Follies*. Many of the great stars were gone. Other observers blamed the rising hysteria of Jim Crow racism. In *On with the Show*, Robert C. Toll stated that, in this atmosphere, the success of black musicals was incendiary. But, he also says, "Violence did not drive Negroes off Broadway. . . . Bias, insidious invisible bias and middle-class financiers and producers did."

It was perhaps for many of these reasons that black theater left Broadway and reappeared in a very different place—Harlem.

Off Broadway

Once again, a black woman was in the forefront of the new wave of black theater. Anita Bush was the daughter of a tailor who catered to performers. She talked her parents into letting her join the chorus of the Walker and Williams company when she was sixteen, even though she couldn't really sing or dance. Later, she tried unsuccessfully to find straight dramatic work. Finally, she decided to form her own company. In 1915, the Anita Bush Players opened at the Lincoln Theatre in Harlem with a show called *The Girl at the Fort*. The company soon moved to the Lafayette Theatre and became the Lafayette Players.

The Lafayette Players had an enormous advantage over earlier black performers. Their audience wasn't white. They were not compelled to act stereotypical characters in order to sell tickets and avoid offending white audiences and backers, so they did the kind of acting they wanted to do. They did *Macbeth* and *Madame X*. They did straight drama and musicals. They kept an entire generation of black performers working during the drought on Broadway and trained another generation. After a few years, Anita Bush went to Chicago to form another troupe of Lafayette Players. Eventually there were four, including two touring companies.

In essence, this group changed the situation of black women in the American theater. To this point, black women had seen the stage only as singers and dancers, usually in the chorus or in tiny parts. They had no place to learn the skills needed to be successful in the theater, even if there had been any chance for them to use them. Soon, the women of the Lafayette Players—Evelyn Ellis, Evelyn Preer, Edna Thomas, Laura Bowman, Inez Clough, and many others—would give the theater a new perspective. There would be few roles, and many of them would be stereotypical, but these black women would find their way.

Other companies began to perform in Harlem, as did several musical shows. Black women and men would be ready for the renaissance of black musical theater that occurred in the 1920s.

Shuffle Along

The 1920s saw the advent of the Harlem Renaissance. One all-black musical played a part in kicking off that explosion when it took the theatergoing public by storm. *Shuffle Along* was written by Noble Sissle and Eubie Blake and opened on Broadway in 1921. Not so heavily laden with racist stereotypes, this show had a book with a plot and featured a new music called ragtime.

Although men, in the person of Aubrey Lyles and Flournoy Miller, were the stars, there were opportunities for women, including the original players, Lottie Gee—who received rave reviews for her rendition of "I'm Just Wild about Harry" and the duet "Love Will Find a Way"—and Gertrude Saunders. Florence Mills replaced Gertrude Saunders and went on to become the first black woman superstar. Josephine Baker mugged her way out of the chorus before going off to a remarkable career in Paris. Adelaide Hall moved from the chorus in *Shuffle Along* to an important role in the next Miller and Lyles musical, *Runnin' Wild*. Moreover, *Shuffle Along* inspired a rash of other black musicals. Though none was as successful as the original, nine musicals were written and performed by African Americans in the next three years. These

FLORENCE MILLS posing as a hobo. The phenomenally talented Mills had a triumph in *Shuffle Along* and was the first black headliner at the legendary Palace Theatre. (Beinecke Rare Book and Manuscript Library, Yale University.)

shows introduced a number of black women performers. The most important of these was probably Florence Mills, but among the others were such remarkable women as Adelaide Hall and Ethel Waters.

The *Plantation Revue* (1922) was built around the enormously talented Mills after her triumph in *Shuffle Along*. The show became *Dixie to Dover* when it traveled to London, where Mills inspired the critics to ecstasies. Back in the states, Mills turned down an offer from Flo Ziegfeld because she believed she could do more for the race by taking the re-transformed, all-black show to Broadway as *Dixie to Broadway*. Her success surpassed virtually anything the black musical had yet seen, and she went on to become the first black headliner at the legendary Palace Theatre. But she was soon back on Broadway in *Blackbirds of 1926*, which then toured to London and Paris. A year later, she was dead, having worked through a serious illness. It is reported that 150,000 people lined the streets of Harlem to say good-bye.

Adelaide Hall is not well known now, but after her appearance in the chorus of *Shuffle Along*, she played feature roles in *Runnin' Wild* (1923) and *Chocolate Kiddies* (1925), followed by *Brown Buddies* (1928) at the Liberty Theatre in London. She replaced Florence Mills in the *Blackbirds of 1928*, after Mills's death. She moved to London in 1938

RUBY ELZY, soprano, c. 1942. She was chosen for the role of Serena in *Porgy and Bess* after one hearing and played this part more than 800 times in her career. The photograph is inscribed to John Springer. (© John Springer Collection/Corbis.)

 In Her Own Words: The Magic of Florence Mills

I never know what I'm going to do. Perhaps I'm the black Eva Tanguay: I don't know. And I don't care. I just go crazy when the music starts and I like to give the audience all it craves. I make up the dances to the songs beforehand, but then something happens, like one of the orchestra talking to me, and I answer back and watch the audience without appearing to do so. It's great fun. Something different at every performance. It keeps me fresh. Once in New York I fell down, literally. Did the split. The audience thought I was hurt. I heard some sympathetic expressions. So I got up and started to limp comically. It got a burst of applause. Then I winked and that got another hand. So the producer ran backstage and asked me to keep it in. I did for several nights but other things happened and I forgot. I never remember just what to do. I'm the despair of stage managers who want a player to act in a groove. No groove for me. The stage isn't large enough for me at times. But it is during the midnight performances that I "let out" the most. We all do. Not that we overstep the conventions, you understand. But it's just the feeling that it's after hours, I suppose. And we whoop it up.

For more information, see Allen Woll, *Black Musical Theatre* (Baton Rouge: Louisiana State University Press, 1989).

but came back to Broadway for a number of shows and continued to do club work and recording.

Another extraordinary voice from this era was Ethel Waters. Coming from poverty, like many of her peers, she became one of the most successful women in Broadway history. After performing with great success in white vaudeville and in clubs, Waters was an obvious choice for Broadway. Scheduled to appear in *Oh, Joy!* in 1922, she left the show because the producers could not find a theater and expected her to perform in a tent. She eventually arrived on Broadway in 1927, starring in Earl Dancer and Donald Heyward's all-black revue, *Africana*, and then in Lew Leslie's *Blackbirds of 1928*. After making her debut in movies, she returned to Broadway in *Blackbirds of 1930*. The next year, she was in *Rhapsody in Black*.

Waters made a hugely important transition for black women when songwriter Irving Berlin heard her singing "Stormy Weather" at Harlem's Cotton Club and offered her a role in *As Thousands Cheer* (1933). The only black woman in a white cast, she sang four songs, one of which was "Suppertime," the lament of a woman preparing dinner for her family on the day that her husband has been lynched. That year, 1933, she became the highest paid woman on Broadway.

However, while Waters thrived, the black musical was having problems. In the early 1930s, the Depression had seriously crippled Broadway production. Still, there were a number of black musicals on Broadway because black performers were willing to work for almost nothing to keep their families alive. In addition, the long-running hit *The Green Pastures* opened. Adapted by a white man, Marc Connelly, from a novel by a white man, Roark Bradford, it had an all-black cast. Although it was not a musical, it did have music, and it was important to the development of the black musical because it provided work, and a training ground, for another generation of black performers. Its success also persuaded producers to do more black shows.

Brown Buddies (1930) brought back Adelaide Hall, starring with the great Bill Robinson. *Singin' the Blues* (1931) introduced Isabell and Fredi Washington, two highly talented sisters. There were dozens of others. And then there was *Porgy and Bess*.

Bess and Beyond

The historian Allen Woll put it well when he said that *Porgy and Bess*, sometimes thought of as the zenith of the black musical, "actually symbolizes the end of the black musical tradition that flourished in the early part of the century." At the beginning, black musicals were created by black artists, onstage and backstage. *Porgy and Bess* was entirely white, except for its performers. Its story was written by white people, as was its music. It was produced, directed, designed, and choreographed by white people. Still, it showcased the highly talented Anne Wiggins Brown. Indeed, based on a novel and a straight play called *Porgy*, it became *Porgy and Bess* as a result of her talent and influence. It also featured such significant performers as Abbie Mitchell and Georgette Harvey. Eva Jessye, the great choral director, provided the chorus and directed it.

The next step in the black musical was unexpected. One of the New Deal's social programs, administered under the Works Progress Administration, was the Federal Theatre Project (FTP), designed to provide theatrical work to unemployed artists. As were many Depression-era social programs, the FTP was segregated. The Negro Unit was headed by the dramatic actor Rose McClendon, who worked in tandem with white director John Houseman until she died of cancer a few months into the program. Many of the plays presented by the Negro Unit were straight dramas written by black playwrights. There were only a few musicals, but one of them stands out. It was a swing version of Gilbert and Sullivan's *The Mikado*, and it started a trend toward black interpretations of white classics that would include *Swingin' the Dream* (1939) and *Carmen Jones* (1943). The latter introduced Muriel Smith and Muriel Rahn and would later be made into a film starring Dorothy Dandridge. *Memphis Bound!* (1945) was a jive version of *H. M. S. Pinafore*, which featured Edith Wilson alongside Bill Robinson.

One exception to this trend was *Cabin in the Sky* (1940), which was an original story, but it was still one written by white authors. It stood out in black musical history for introducing the luminous Katherine Dunham. She played the femme fatale who tries to steal the husband of Petunia. She may have been the only performer who ever played on Broadway between getting a Guggenheim fellowship for anthropological research and writing a PhD dissertation on the dances of Haiti. Her own ballet company also appeared in *Cabin in the Sky*, and she worked with George Balanchine on the choreography. The musical would become a film vehicle for Lena Horne.

In the period following World War II, there were a few all-black musicals, including *St. Louis Woman*, notable for having introduced Pearl Bailey to Broadway. It was also notable for being the first time that a black cast refused to perform the stereotypes in a show written by whites. They objected in particular to one moment in the show and refused to rehearse until it was changed. Bailey acted as liaison for the cast, and the moment was indeed changed. Another show, *Jamaica*, written by Harold Arlen and Yip Harburg, was Lena Horne's first starring role on Broadway and featured Ricardo Montalban as her leading man, which made the show somewhat controversial.

Some opportunities were open for black performers in mostly white shows. Juanita Hall, formerly a member of the Hall Johnson Choir, played Bloody Mary in *South Pacific*, for example. Soon, however, it became clear that the decline of the all-black show meant a decline in employment for black performers. The problem only got worse throughout the 1950s. Once, African American women were cast in white shows only as maids. Now, for fear of offending, directors no longer filled even those roles with black actors.

During the 1950s and early 1960s, the black musical was kept alive by Langston Hughes. *Simply Heavenly* (1957), based on his Jesse Simple stories, started off-off-Broadway and went to Broadway, where it baffled white audiences and delighted black ones. It starred the legendary Claudia McNeil. *Black Nativity* (1961) was an African American version of the Christmas story and starred the gospel music great Marion Williams. Hughes used gospel music again in *Tambourines to Glory* (1963).

The cast included Micki Grant, Helen Ferguson, Rosetta Lenoire, Hilda Simms, and Clara Ward, who also acted as choral director. *Jerico-Jim Crow* (1964) showed the effects of Jim Crow discrimination on black Americans. Hilda Harris and Rosalie King were in the cast.

One of the few black women to emerge into stardom during the 1950s was Eartha Kitt, who grew up in Harlem, attended the High School for the Performing Arts, and then became a solo performer for Katherine Dunham. She reached a turning point in her career with her Broadway debut in the musical *New Faces of 1952*. She went on to *Mrs. Patterson*, in which she played a poor teenager who wanted to grow up to be like the white woman who employs her mother. Her last Broadway musical was *Shinbone Alley* (1957), a largely white show in which she played a cat.

The New Black Musical

As the civil rights movement evolved, those who fought for meaningful black theater and black audiences again went to Harlem and other off-Broadway venues. The director Vinette Carroll offered *Trumpets of the Lord* (1963), a musical she adapted from James Weldon Johnson's *God's Trombones*, written in 1927. Both Theresa Merritt and Cicely Tyson starred, alongside Al Freeman Jr. Carroll followed this with a Hughes one-act, *The Prodigal Son*, featuring Glory Van Scott and Dorothy Drake.

Again, a long-running play written by a white man helped to facilitate the blossoming of a new black theater. In addition to showing producers that there was an audience for black plays, Jean Genet's *The Blacks* (1961) had, in effect, a revolving cast, so that dozens of black performers were able to act in that show intermittently while developing other projects. Charles Gordone was one of those performers and later won a Pulitzer Prize for *No Place To Be Somebody*. Micki Grant was one of those performers. In 1970, having done everything from Genet to soap opera, she began to work with Carroll, who had founded New York's Urban Art Corps (UAC). With Carroll's encouragement, Grant wrote *Don't Bother Me, I Can't Cope*. Carroll directed it, first in Greenwich Village. Then, after touring small theaters in New York and Washington, DC, the show went to Broadway, where it ran for more than a thousand performances. The two women worked together on a number of projects and were on Broadway again with *Your Arm's Too Short to Box with God*, written by Carroll with some music by Grant. That show was a gospel version of the biblical Book of Matthew and won great praise and a Tony for gospel singer Dolores Hall.

The UAC was only one of several small black production companies. The Negro Ensemble Company (NEC), whose creation was sponsored by the Ford Foundation, was foremost among them. However, the NEC did not produce musicals. *The Believers* (1968), by Josephine Jackson and Joseph A. Walker, came out of this off-Broadway black theater movement and surveyed African American history.

Two of the most successful black musicals on Broadway at the time were based on dramatic plays by black writers of some years before. *Purlie* (1970) was based on Ossie Davis's play *Purlie Victorious*, produced in 1961. It starred Melba Moore. The child of two musically gifted parents—a jazz singer and a saxophonist—Moore was brought up in Harlem and later Newark, where she attended the Arts High School. She made her stage debut in the original, multiracial cast of *Hair* before appearing in and winning a Tony for *Purlie*. Novella Nelson and Linda Hopkins were also in the cast. *Raisin* (1973) was a musical adaptation of Lorraine Hansberry's *Raisin in the Sun*. It was successful and won a Tony for Virginia Capers as best actress in a musical.

Two other Broadway musicals were written by Marvin Van Peebles. The first, *Ain't Supposed to Die a Natural Death* (1972), was dark and angry and managed to run for 325 performances because of the extraordinary efforts of black celebrities to keep it alive. For example, Shirley Chisholm announced her intention to run for president from the stage one night during a post-show discussion. That same season, Van Peebles presented a much different play, *Don't Play Us Cheap!*, which portrayed a loud, joyous Harlem rent party and was greeted with raves from black and white critics alike. It starred Esther Rolle and Rhetta Hughes alongside Avon Long.

The Wiz (1975) was a throwback to the "black versions" of classic works. After a rough start, it became a box office success and won seven Tony awards, setting the stage for a rash of "light-hearted" black musicals, including *Me and Bessie* (1976), starring Linda Hopkins, and *Bubbling Brown Sugar* (1976). The latter, honoring the music of Eubie Blake and Fats Waller, was developed at Rosetta Lenoire's AMAS repertory theater and directed by Lenoire. It went on to the ANTA Theatre and was highly successful.

In 1978, Eartha Kitt returned to Broadway in *Timbuktu!* and was well received critically, as was the rest of the cast, and *Ain't Misbehavin'* introduced the talented Nell Carter. Again, the music of Fats Waller was featured. After *Eubie!* also struck critical and box office gold, three more musicals dealing with black musical history were produced. *One Mo' Time* (1979) visited black vaudeville and *Black Broadway* brought back some of the stars of the early part of the century, including Edith Wilson from *Put and Take* (1921), Elisabeth Welch from *Runnin' Wild* and Adelaide Hall, who returned from London for the occasion. Nell Carter also starred. Finally, *Sophisticated Ladies* (1981) paid homage to the music of Duke Ellington and starred dancer Judith Jamison alongside Gregory Hines.

LENA HORNE receiving applause and flowers after her last performance in *Lena Horne: The Lady and Her Music* at the Nederlander Theater, 1 July 1982. She was preparing to take the show on the road a few days later. (© Bettmann/Corbis; photographer, Ezio Petersen.)

For the next two decades, with few exceptions, black musicals on Broadway would follow the two basic patterns of success set in the 1960s and 1970s. They would draw their music either from black musical history or from gospel. *Jelly's Last Jam* (1992), *It Ain't Nothing but the Blues* (1999), and, earlier, *Dreamgirls* (1981) followed the former pattern. *The Gospel at Colonus* (1988) followed the latter and introduced the radiantly talented Isabell Monk.

Dreamgirls, conceived and created by white men, was probably for black women the most significant musical of the day. A fictionalized story of the career of the singing group the Supremes, it starred Jennifer Holiday as the lead singer who is replaced by a slimmer backup singer in both the group and the heart of their manager. Holiday stunned audiences and critics. The show also featured the very talented Loretta Devine and Sheryl Lee Ralph.

But perhaps the show that most paid tribute to the history of the black musical theater was *Lena Horne: The Lady and Her Music*. At the age of sixty-three, this veteran performer revived her own hits and created a remarkable, critically and popularly successful evening of entertainment that had a long run on Broadway before touring and being featured on PBS' *Great Performances* series. There is something wonderfully satisfying about this closing of the circle.

See also **Horne, Lena; Mills, Florence; Walker, Aida Overton;** *and* **Waters, Ethyl.**

BIBLIOGRAPHY

Bogle, Donald. *Brown Sugar: Eighty Years of America's Black Female Superstars* (1980). New York: Da Capo Press, 1990.

Fletcher, Thomas. *100 Years of Negro Show Business*. New York: Da Capo Press, 1995.

Hine, Darlene Clark, and Kathleen Thompson. *A Shining Thread of Hope: The History of Black Women in America*. New York: Broadway Books, 1998.

Hughes, Langston, and Milton Meltzer. *Black Magic: A Pictorial History of the Negro in American Theater* (1967). New York: Da Capo Press, 1990.

Krasner, David. *Resistance, Parody and Double Consciousness in African American Theatre, 1895–1910*. New York: St. Martin's Press, 1998.

Morgan, Thomas L., and William Barlow. *From Cakewalks to Concert Halls: An Illustrated History of African American Popular Music from 1895 to 1930*. Washington, DC: Elliott & Clark: 1992.

Riis, Thomas. *Just before Jazz: Black Musical Theater in New York, 1890–1915*. Washington: Smithsonian Institute Press, 1994.

Southern, Eileen. *The Music of Black Americans: A History*. 3d ed. New York: W. W. Norton, 1997.

Toll, Robert C. *Blacking Up: The Minstrel Show in Nineteenth-Century America*. New York: Oxford University Press, 1974.

Toll, Robert C. *On with the Show*. New York: Oxford University Press, 1976.

Waters, Ethel, with Charles Samuels. *His Eye Is on the Sparrow*. New York: Da Capo Press: 1992.

Woll, Allen. *Black Musical Theatre: From Coontown to Dreamgirls*. Baton Rouge: Louisiana State University Press, 1989.

—Diane Epstein

—Kathleen Thompson

MUSIC INDUSTRY. The story of black women in the American music industry reflects all the issues of gender, class, and race that have bedeviled Americans throughout their history. Still, black women have been involved in making music in America, and in the making of American music, since they first stepped ashore in 1619. From churches to slave festivals, cotton fields to smokehouses, middle-class parlors to the greatest concert halls of the world—black women were there. They faced the same restrictions as did white women and all of the prejudices that hindered black men, but they persevered.

An industry connected to music did not develop until the late nineteenth century and cannot be divorced from the development of the entertainment industry. Because of issues of money and control, women, and especially black women, in both industries were frequently in the background, when they found a place at all. It was only at the end of the twentieth century and the beginning of the twenty-first that black women finally began to gain entry into the highest positions of power. However, behind the power and off the beaten track, black women have been tremendously important in the various phases and forms of the music and entertainment industries.

The Birth of an Industry

Until the late nineteenth century, both popular and classical music in the United States was published as broadside ballads or as sheet music. There was no system in place to give the creators and publishers (much less the performers) of music any rights or payment for their product. It took the Industrial Revolution to create the fertile ground from which the twin industries of music and entertainment would grow. Newly middle class households wanted to emulate the wealthy. Their goal was for women to stay at home and learn the "finer arts," as befitted their new class status. Only one instrument, the piano, was deemed

acceptable for a woman to play. By the 1880s, relatively cheap, mass-produced, upright pianos were gracing parlors all over America. It could even be argued that the American music industry owes its birth to thousands of women in cities all over America who wanted something to play on their new pianos.

These women needed music that was easier to play, more familiar, and more inclusive than was European classical music. As much as they wanted to emulate the wealthy, they also wanted some entertainment for their newfound leisure time. They needed something the entire family could enjoy, songs everyone could sing. Tin Pan Alley came to the rescue. An area of New York City named for the cacophonous sound of many upright pianos pounding out new song compositions, Tin Pan Alley created a mass-produced music product for the American people. By 1895, sales of sheet music were such that Tin Pan Alley music publishers were able to influence publishing and copyright laws. In that year, they formed the Music Publishers Association of the United States. The American music industry was under way.

It is now generally accepted that the music of Tin Pan Alley owed an enormous debt to African Americans, both men and women. However, there were only a few black music publishing companies, most notably Gotham Attucks and Pace-Handy, and none were started or managed by women. In fact, few black women can be directly connected to the business of Tin Pan Alley, and those who can be were performers whose link to the industry was through advertising. At Tin Pan Alley's height, only a few black women were popular enough to be used on sheet music covers to advertise the music. One was Aida Overton Walker, who was pictured on the cover of the sheet music for "I'd Like to Be a Lady" as well as on "Build a Nest for Birdie." Two others were Hattie Payton of The Paytons and Estelle Johnson.

This same absence from the new industry can be seen in the development of one of its most important organizations: the American Society of Composers, Authors, and Publishers (ASCAP). Founded in 1914 by the publishers and composers of Tin Pan Alley, ASCAP soon had a virtual monopoly over the American music industry. Yet even by 1925 there were only six black members, in part because ASCAP excluded the "vernacular forms" such as blues and country, then known as race and hillbilly music. According to Reebee Garofalo in the article "Music Publishing to MP3":

> Copyright laws kept artistic expression firmly anchored to the European cultural tradition of notated music, in that the claim for royalties was based on the registration of melodies and lyrics, the aspects of music that most readily lend themselves to notation. Artists or countries with musical traditions based on rhythm rather than melody or those that valued improvisation

over notation were excluded from the full benefit of copyright protection right from the start.

However, it was these marginalized vernacular forms that would turn the music industry on its head.

From the days of Tin Pan Alley through the era of rock and roll, the place to find powerful African American women was on the edges of the mainstream or at the beginning of a musical movement. Once a musical form became mainstream, black women often lost out to the national corporations that had no place for them. One of the first such examples, and one of black women's often unacknowledged American music industry influences, was about burst into American music.

God and the Devil: Blues, Jazz, and Gospel

Tin Pan Alley may have started the American music industry, but the record revolutionized it. Once recorded music entered the scene, the distinction between the recording industry and the music industry was largely erased. The development of blues and jazz coincided with this technological change. Blues and jazz were harder to notate than was popular music, so the development of the recording industry was essential to spreading their popularity. At the start of it all were black women and the "race record."

According to Donald Bogle in *Brown Sugar*, the race record "arrived in the hands of a black woman." Mamie Smith recorded "Crazy Blues" in 1920 for Perry Bradford, and the record sold 200,000 copies in the first year alone. The popularity of the race record spawned an entire industry. In addition, for the first time a positive image of the proud, strong, unapologetic, lower- or working-class African American woman was presented to the white public. No doubt to the horror of some, the blues diva altered white America's perceptions of African Americans. Bogle notes that, "By the mid-twenties the blues sisters had had such an extraordinary effect on popular culture that even so mainstream a publication as *Vanity Fair* ran an article about the blues performers Ethel Waters, Bessie Smith, and Clara Smith." These same women created the foundations of rhythm and blues and rock and roll as well as the auxiliary styles those forms spawned.

Many of these women had an unusual amount of control over their lives and careers. Gertrude "Ma" Rainey, the "Mother of the Blues," created and managed her own traveling company, the Georgia Jazz Band. Ma Rainey was not only an artist of extraordinary talent and presence but was also a stylist credited with altering the basic nature of the minstrel and vaudeville circuit. The "Uncrowned Queen of the Blues," Ida Cox also had her own revue, wrote her own music, and hired the musicians. Bessie Smith, "the Empress of the Blues," brought the blues to white as well as to black audiences. She managed her own road band and traveled with an entourage. She circumvented segregated accommodations by traveling in her own railroad car, which would be detached when it arrived at the town for a performance. By 1924 Bessie Smith had become the highest-paid black performer in America, earning $2,000 per week.

Another blues queen, Ethel Waters opened a number of doors in the music and entertainment industries that other African Americans were later able to walk through. In the 1920s, while she was the highest-paid woman on Broadway, she was also being paid $2,500 per week to sing in a nightclub and at the same time sang on the radio with the Jack Denny Orchestra. It is no coincidence that the control these women maintained over their business lives is reflected in the freedom expressed in their music.

Still, while some black women made money for themselves, most black women musicians made a lot more money for other people. During the 1920s Ma Rainey made so much money for the new recording company Paramount that she turned it into one of the major record labels of the era. Similarly, Smith played a direct role in the rescue of financially troubled Columbia Records, even though she didn't earn royalties on her recordings. According to at least one source, Clarence Williams, who brought Smith to Columbia Records, attempted to defraud her and take half her earnings. Smith was both savvy and powerful enough to put an end to this. Unfortunately, many women were not.

The Swing/Big Band era created another type of singer in the jazz/blues idiom, the "girl singer," but these women generally enjoyed even less control. The bands of this era were managed and led by men, even when the women had top billing. The most famous of these women was Billie Holiday, who made hundreds of recordings but received royalties on only a few. An exception to the rule, at least for a time, was Ella Fitzgerald, who served as the singer but also led Chick Webb's big band for a few years after he died.

If the blues queens were exploited, they at least had a period of stunning success. If the girl singers had less control, they at least had some measure of fame and acceptance. For the women instrumentalists of jazz, however, financial success and fame were rarely attainable. The February 1938 article, "Why Women Musicians Are Inferior" in *Down Beat* magazine was just one example of the lack of respect for women's abilities in jazz playing. However inferior women were considered as instrumentalists, they were thought to be completely incapable of running the business behind the music. Though World War II provided opportunities for a number of all-girl jazz bands such as the International Sweethearts of Rhythm, Vi Burnside & Her All Stars, the Darlings of Rhythm, the Harlem Playgirls, the American Syncopators, and the

Bleaching the Blues

Bessie Smith and many other black women introduced the blues to the white community. Once the form had been established as profitable, record companies brought in white women such as Sophie Tucker, Ruth Etting, and Helen Morgan to provide a white audience with a more "acceptable" version of what it wanted. Later, white women such as Peggy Lee, Dinah Shore, and Doris Day had huge successes singing what came to be known as "torch songs." In the meantime, many of the blues women who had made their record companies rich were left behind, poor and largely forgotten. Others simply never got the credit for their achievements.

A case in point: the authors of Bessie Smith's first hit, "Downhearted Blues." Not only did Lovie Austin and Alberta Hunter frequently go unmentioned in reports of the song's success, but there was also no proof that they received royalties for their work. When Bessie Smith recorded the song, it sold over 750,000 copies within the first six months of its release. Well known was that Smith was paid only $125 and received no royalties. Less often mentioned was the fact that Austin and Hunter, who actually wrote the song, probably didn't receive royalties. The two women were not members of ASCAP and therefore were not protected by that powerful organization.

Willie Mae "Big Mama" Thornton did not write the song "Hound Dog." It was created by the white Brill Building team of Jerry Lieber and Mike Stoller. However, although it was later covered by Elvis Presley and became a hit, Thornton herself sold as many as two million copies of the song, and said that she only ever received one check for $500 for her recording. She also wrote "Ball and Chain," which was later covered by Janis Joplin and became an enormous hit. Yet Thornton, who was signed with Baytone Records when she wrote the song, never received any royalties from Joplin's version because Baytone held the copyright. Of course, Joplin became a rock and roll legend by singing in the style created by the great black women blues singers.

Etta James, like Thornton, experienced the frustration of seeing a song she co-wrote and recorded sell well but be far outstripped when it was covered by a white artist. Her recording of "Wallflower" sold 400,000 copies and made it to number two on the R&B charts. When Georgia Gibbs covered the song as "Dance with Me Henry," it sold more than a million copies.

Prairie View Co-Eds, most of these groups were unable to continue after the men returned from the war.

Singers aside, most women musicians succeeded on the only instrument deemed acceptable for women at the time, the piano. Despite hardship, the pianist Lovie Austin composed, performed, and worked as a bandleader on the Theater Owners Booking Association (TOBA) circuit. Lil Hardin Armstrong composed, played the piano, and was the "woman behind the man" in teaching and managing her famed husband, Louis. Particularly early in their careers, Hardin Armstrong ran the business side of their affairs. The pianist Blanche Calloway, Cab's sister, led her own band, the Joy Boys, and later in her career managed the rhythm and blues great Ruth Brown.

Both Hardin Armstrong and Austin bring up another point about the development of American music. They were both trained musicians. Austin received musical training from Roger Williams University and Knoxville College. Hardin Armstrong received a postgraduate degree from the New York College of Music. Black women musicians were frequently the only musically educated members of a band. As a result, it was the women who made the notations, preserved an arrangement for posterity, and provided the publishers of the industry with scores. However, it was in another genre of music, gospel, that black women had real power in the music publishing industry.

As it did not with the nightclub venues of blues and jazz, society often accepted women's creativity if it was expressed in the church, but even gospel music was radical at first. In the 1920s and 1930s, gospel was not allowed in many churches, much less published, recorded, or played on the radio. Decades later, the gospel music industry would sell tens of millions of records and generate hundreds of millions of dollars in sales, and it could be fairly stated that black women were at the forefront of making gospel a commercial form, both as artists and entrepreneurs.

Gospel took longer to become a successful recorded form of music than did jazz or blues. It did, however, become a well-published form right away. It is stunning to see the list of women who published gospel music, especially compared to the dearth of female names in other music forms. While some of these women are virtually unknown, others are rightly credited with making gospel music internationally renowned.

Sallie Martin, "the mother of gospel music," helped popularize the form, not only composing classic gospel songs and forming legendary choirs but also organizing "the gospel highway circuit" of venues where the music was accepted. She worked with "the father of gospel," Thomas Dorsey, and helped turn his music store into a profit-making enterprise. In 1933, she and Dorsey, along with Beatrice Brown and others, organized the National Convention of Gospel Choirs and Choruses. Perhaps most importantly, certainly from an industry point of view, Martin was the co-founder of the Martin and Morris Publishing Company, later the largest black gospel publishing house in the United States. Founded in 1940, the company stayed in business until the 1980s. Martin served as the company's "song-plugger," taking the music on the road to publicize it. In its heyday, the Martin and Morris

Publishing Company made Sallie Martin the country's wealthiest gospel artist. She sold her share to co-founder Kenneth Morris in 1973.

Among the other female pioneers of the gospel music industry was Willie Mae Ford Smith, who helped found the National Convention of Gospel Choirs and Choruses (NCGC) and put together that organization's Soloist's Bureau. Roberta Martin founded the Roberta Martin Music Studios and is often credited not only for her artistry but also for the ways in which she linked spirituality, music making, and commerce. With Sallie Martin, she arranged one of the first Gospel concerts that charged admission, at DuSable High School in Chicago. Clara Ward not only revolutionized the sound of gospel but she also brought it everywhere, even to nightclubs, but it was Ward's mother, Gertrude, who ran the business end of the show. Gertrude Ward founded the Clara Ward House of Music publishing company. A shrewd businesswoman, she often double-billed concerts with The Ward Singers and The Clara Ward Specials and received a percentage for both as the booking agent.

Lillian Bowles was an early gospel music publisher who ran the Bowles Music House out of Chicago. Margaret Aikens, Lucille Campbell Bowles, Dorothy Akers, and Beatrice Seay all published gospel. The pioneering names in early gospel, Sallie Martin, Roberta Martin, and Clara Ward, all published their own music as well as that of others.

One later company that published gospel was Conrad Music. During the 1950s and 1960s, the recording arm of the company, Vee Jay Records, produced some of the nation's most popular gospel records. But it was Vee Jay Records's involvement with recording a new kind of music called rhythm and blues that would make the company important in the history of the music industry.

Rhythm and Blues to Disco and Soul

Vivian Bracken founded Vee Jay Records in 1953 with her husband and brother, and for the next decade they recorded some of the most important gospel groups in the country. But Vee Jay is best known as an early independent producer of blues, rhythm and blues, and rock and roll records. Almost a decade before Motown hit the charts, Vee Jay Records was churning out recordings of these newer musical styles. In fact, Vee Jay first brought the Beatles' music to American audiences. Among the many other stars and groups who recorded with Vee Jay were the Four Seasons, John Lee Hooker, Jerry Butler, and Betty Everett and the Dells. Though the company went into bankruptcy in 1966, it was the first major black-owned record label in the United States and was instrumental in making R & B and rock and roll the new musical phenomenon.

Motown was the second major black-owned record label in the country. Ramona Gordy—wife of the founder, Berry Gordy—claimed to have been a co-founder of the company but says she was asked to remove her name from the papers by her husband. Though not co-owned by a black woman, the company had more women working in prominent positions behind the scenes than did any other recording company of the time. Prior to Motown's founding, Berry Gordy's sisters, Gwen and Anna, owned their own recording company, Anna Records. In addition, Gwen founded Tri-Phi Records with her husband, Harvey Fuqua. A renowned producer and composer, she later started Gwen Glenn Productions, Der-Glenn Publishing Company, and Old Brompton Road Publishing Company. She and her sisters Anna and Esther all became vice presidents at Motown, and Gwen is credited with founding the company's famed Artist Development Department. In addition, Maxine Powell ran the finishing school of the department, which taught etiquette to Motown performers.

Suzanne de Passe, however, is the best-known Motown woman. Perhaps the most successful black woman film and television producer in Hollywood, she was hired by Motown in 1968. De Passe discovered Michael Jackson and the Jackson 5 and went on to develop Lionel Richie and the Commodores, the Four Seasons, Thelma Houston, and the Temptations before she moved into the film and television divisions of the company.

Unfortunately, Vee Jay and Motown did not signal the beginning of a run of record labels owned or even well staffed by black women. For the majority of black women, the advent of rhythm and blues meant "business as usual," even though they yet again changed the face of American music. One R & B pioneer, Ruth Brown, made so much money for Atlantic Records, an independent record company, that it was dubbed "the House that Ruth Built." Yet she did not see most of the royalties due her until decades later.

The famed girl groups of the late 1950s and 1960s faced the same sorts of difficulties. They earned millions of dollars for their record companies, yet were only rarely paid the money they deserved. For example, in 1961 the Shirelles were the first all-female group to top the singles charts, with "Will You Love Me Tomorrow?" Over the next two years, ten more of the group's songs made it into the Top 40 charts. Yet despite their success, they discovered that the money that had been put in trust for them by their record company, run by Florence Greenberg, had allegedly been spent on promotion, touring, and recording costs. The Shirelles were hardly alone. Many of the girl groups of the era experienced the same thing.

Considering that taking advantage of artists, white or black, male or female, seemed to be the overarching credo of the recording industry, it is stunning that some of these young women had the courage to challenge the status quo. The Shirelles sued Greenberg. The Crystals, who recorded with Phil Spector, also sued for unpaid royalties. They lost but ultimately did regain the right to use the group's name, as did the Blue Belles, who also took their record company to court. Control of the group's name was vital to the success of any girl group, as the individual members were less known, or entirely unknown. Nona Hendryx, a member of the Blue Belles, said that though they lost a great deal of money due them for the success of their records, gaining control of the group's name allowed them to work without limitations that otherwise would likely have spoiled their continued success.

The Supremes, of course, are the ultimate girl group of the era. They, along with Mary Wells and others, can be credited with turning Motown into one of the most successful black businesses in the country. The Supremes in particular crossed the color line and were the first black group to achieve enough fame to be merchandised, a process that would soon become as much a part of the recording industry as the songs. By the end of the 1960s, the Supremes were recording commercials and were among the first black performers to have marketing tie-ins associated with their name: the Supremes White Bread.

However, despite the success female performers brought to Motown and the number of women on the staff, the company was not free of the exploitative practices typically associated with record companies. For example, when Florence Ballard, one of the founders of the Supremes, split from the group, she signed a settlement that gave her only $2,500 per year for six years and no more royalties on the songs she recorded as a member. She found a lawyer and renegotiated, but her lawyer absconded with the money. Even though he was found and disbarred, only $50,000 ever came to Ballard. Diana Ross, on the other hand, parlayed her growing prominence in the Supremes into an enormously successful solo career. In 1989 she bought 2 percent of Motown.

Other performers at Motown tried to take control of their careers and their money. Martha Reeves of the Vandellas challenged Motown when she asked for an accounting of her group's earnings. Mary Wells sued to be released from her contract, arguing that she had signed it as a minor. Perhaps not surprisingly, Mary Wells had a female personal manager, her childhood friend Maye James. James moved on to work as vice president of promotions for a variety of labels, including Scepter Records and Roadshow Records. In so doing, she became one of the first black women to hold such a position.

The blues singer Victoria Spivey took advantage of the blues revival to start her own record label in the early 1960s. An enormous success in the 1920s, Spivey continued to perform and record through the 1950s when she retired. She came out of retirement a short ten years later to create Spivey Records in around 1962. Spivey recorded her own work as well as that of legends such as Memphis Slim, Alberta Hunter, Lonnie Johnson, Otis Spann, the Muddy Waters Band, Big Joe Williams, Roosevelt Sykes, and Koko Taylor. A young Bob Dylan was featured as an accompanist on one of Spivey's first records, *Kings and the Queen, Volume 2*. In 1970 the jazz singer Betty Carter founded her own label, Bet-Car Records, and produced five albums. Two of those albums received Grammy nominations, and *Look What I Got* won in 1988.

An early music industry entrepreneur who did not get her start as an artist was Ruth Bowen, the founder and president of the Queen Booking Corporation. She was introduced to the music industry through her husband, Bill Bowen, one of the original Ink Spots, and in 1946 became Dinah Washington's press secretary. She founded her first company, Queen Artists, in 1959. This company had expanded to become the Queen Booking Corporation by 1969 and was the largest black-owned entertainment agency in the world. Among the most famous performers handled by the company were Sammy Davis Jr., Aretha Franklin, Ray Charles, Patti LaBelle and the Blue Belles, the Drifters, and Curtis Mayfield.

In the 1980s, new economics and new music forms yet again challenged black women in American music. MTV became the ultimate arbiter of success, and it took many years for a black person, much less a black woman, to get aired on the music video channel. The new white music forms of Punk and New Wave were garnering all the attention. Disco, Glam Rock, and Soul, despite the best efforts of Donna Summers, Patti LaBelle, and Aretha Franklin, were losing popularity. However, one album was soon to change the relationship between black women and the mainstream music industry.

Whitney Houston and Beyond

On Valentine's Day 1985, Whitney Houston released her first album. It immediately went to the top of the charts, making Houston the first female solo artist to have an album debut at number one. Her stunning success opened doors at MTV through which a new breed of black women artists followed, among them Janet Jackson. Jackson took over her career when she became her own manager, deposing her father. In 1991, she moved to Virgin Records for somewhere between $32 and $60 million. By the end of the twentieth century, she was co-writing some of her music and was credited as a co-producer on many of her songs. However, even as Houston and Jackson were changing the role of and respect for black women performers in the pop music industry, it was again on the fringes of a new culture and musical form where black women could find the openness to build their own empires: rap and hiphop.

The perception of the business end of rap and hiphop is that a few "bad boy" music moguls changed the music industry as well as America. While true, this simplification ignores, yet again, the influence of the women. Ironically, rap—a form frequently criticized as misogynist—has produced some of the most independent and powerful black women in the history of the American music industry. In fact, a black woman named Sylvia Robinson helped to start it all.

Robinson was a mid-level music industry pioneer who owned several record labels, including All-Platinum, Stang, Turbo, and Vibration, as well as the rights to Chess Records. In the late 1970s, she recognized the business possibilities behind rap music and created her own rap group, the Sugarhill Gang. The group recorded "Rappers Delight," which reached 36 in the Top 40 charts and became the first crossover rap hit. As a result of her success with "Rapper's Delight," Robinson founded Sugarhill Records, which recorded some of the classic rappers, including Grandmaster Flash and the Sequence.

Maye James is credited with bringing rap music to mainstream radio through the radio personality "Mr. Majic!" when she was music director of New York's WBLS. Because the show was so successful, other New York stations added rap to their format, and the genre ultimately caught on throughout the country. James returned to the recording side of the industry when she became the General Manager of Black Music for SBK Records. She later became the president of Unique Artistry and Hampton Marketing.

Twenty-first century music superstars were a far cry from the exploited pawns of the past. Though unscrupulous activities certainly still existed, the young women who made it to the top of the charts in the first years of the new millennium expected to control both their financial and creative destinies, an expectation that existed because of the hard-fought battles of their musical forebears.

The Mainstream Music Industry in the New Millennium

In terms of black women's involvement in the American music industry, management of the major labels is the highest level of achievement. For all of the money black women made for record labels in the twentieth century, none were allowed to ascend to the level of top management. This finally and slowly began to change as a result of empowerment by the civil rights movement and the women's movement, as well as changes in the industry itself. By the 1990s, black women had spent twenty years working their way to the top.

As of 1995, there were six major labels and distribution companies in the United States: Warner Elektra Atlantic (WEA), PolyGram Group Distribution, MCA Music Entertainment, BMG Distribution, Sony Music Entertainment, and CEMA/UNI. (By 2003, the names and alliances had changed only slightly.) These companies, either through distribution contracts with independent labels or through their own divisions and sub-labels, made up 90 percent of the U.S. market, totaling $12 billion in domestic sales alone. At the time, black music in the forms of urban contemporary, hip hop, jazz, gospel, and pop music accounted for over 25 percent of all record sales and brought in $3 billion in U.S. sales each year.

In 1991, when Sylvia Rhone was named CEO of East West Records, she was at the top of the heap in terms of black women in the corporate music industry. The first black woman to serve as CEO of a major record label, Rhone soon became the chair of the Elektra Entertainment Group, a subsidiary of Warner-Elektra-Atlantic with gross revenues of at least $400 million annually. She held this position until 2004.

Often overshadowed in the press by her husband, Kenny "Babyface" Edmonds, Tracey Edmonds also became a powerhouse in the music industry. As co-owner, president,

SYLVIA RHONE was the first black woman to become CEO of a major recording company. (Austin/Thompson Collection, courtesy of Eastwest Records America.)

and CEO of Edmonds Entertainment Group, in 2004 Edmonds was responsible for a budget of $5 million and a staff of sixty. Edmonds Entertainment grew to include Edmonds Music Publishing, Edmonds Management, and Edmonds Record Group, as well as a film company, e² Filmworks, and a recording studio, Tracken Place.

Strong prejudices remained, however. Most women found their place or at least their start at the major labels as salespeople or promoters, and by the beginning of the twenty-first century the number of black women who had served as vice presidents of promotion was quite stunning and impossible to list here. They include LaVerne Perry-Kennedy, senior vice president of publicity with Columbia/Epic Records/Sony Music; Lisa Ellis, senior vice president in charge of R & B and crossover promotion at Columbia/Epic Records; Michelle Madison, vice president of R & B promotion for Elektra Entertainment Group; Ornetta Barber Dickerson, vice president of marketing in the Black Music Division of Warner-Elektra-Atlantic; Cynthia Johnson-Harris, a senior vice president of Urban Promotion for Columbia Records; Gwen E. Franklin, a former vice president of marketing for Mercury Records, among others; and Juanita Stephens, a former vice president of publicity for Bad Boy/Arista Records before she started her own company JKS Media Relations. Johnnie Walker, founder of the National Association of Black Female Executives in Music and Entertainment (NABFEME), became a senior vice president of R & B promotion for Russell Simmons's Island Def Jam Music Group.

Other women, though fewer of them, managed to move into the Artist and Repertoire (A & R) Divisions of the major labels or actually ran a sub-label. Jean Riggins became an executive vice president and general manager at Universal Records. Riggins worked her way up through several key positions among the major industry labels. She was president of Black Music for Universal and before that vice president and general manager of Black Music at Capitol Records. In 1985, Vivian Scott Chew became the first African American woman to become a membership representative at ASCAP. Among many positions at the major labels, she served as the head of A & R and Urban Music Division for Epic Records before founding her own entertainment company, Chew Entertainment, and a marketing and promotions firm, TimeZone International.

Black women outside the mainstream were able to find their expression in the music industry by starting up smaller labels as well, particularly in the gospel genre. Vicki Mack Lataillade, the CEO of Gospo Centric Record Label, the company that first signed gospel superstar Kirk Franklin. Another leader in the gospel recording field, Raina Bundy worked on her own and among the major labels. She was the head of Lection Records, the gospel music division of Polygram before starting her own gospel label, Fixit Records. In 1993, her company won a Best Gospel Album Grammy for Edwin Hawkins's *Music and Arts Seminar*. While running her own label, Bundy also worked at Columbia Records as a vice president of A & R and Marketing. In 1997, she was chosen to head, as vice president and general manager, Sony Music's gospel label, Harmony Records.

In the modern world, the auxiliaries to the recording industry, such as music videos and entertainment law, were essential. In these areas as well as at the labels, black women made enormous strides. For example, Christina Norman was named the General Manager of the music television station VH1. Sharon Heyward became a senior vice president with the Trawick Group, an artist management and entertainment company, and Denise Brown-Noel founded her own firm, which specialized in entertainment law.

What the future holds for the music industry in America is anyone's guess. The Internet and MP3 technology are changing the rules yet again, and the major labels are struggling to keep up. Wherever American music goes, however, black women will not be left behind. As they have throughout history, they will help define the art. And if today's black women are any indication, they will finally also be paid for it.

See also **Blues; Gospel Music; Hip Hop (Rap) Music; Jazz;** *and* **Rock and Roll.**

BIBLIOGRAPHY

Alexander, Scott. "Lovie Austin." *A History of Jazz before 1930*. The Red Hot Jazz Archive. http://www.redhotjazz.com/austin.html.

Bogle, Donald. *Brown Sugar: Eighty Years of America's Black Female Superstars*. New York: Harmony Books, 1980.

Boyer, Horace Clarence. *The Story of Gospel Music: The Men and Women Behind the Music, Part II: A New Sophistication—Brewster, Martin, and Morris*. Great Performances. London: British Broadcasting Corporation and Boston: Educational Broadcasting Corporation, Thirteen/WNET, 1996. http://www.pbs.org/wnet/gperf/feature10/html/body_behind.html.

Crawford, Richard. *America's Musical Life: A History*. New York: Norton, 2001.

Dahl, Linda. *Stormy Weather: The Music and Lives of a Century of Jazzwomen*. New York: Limelight Edition, Proscenium Publishers, 1989.

Daniels, Cora. "The Most Powerful Black Executives in America." *Fortune Magazine*, 22 July 2002.

Fox, Roberta. *Martin & Morris Gospel Sheet Music Collection*. Chicago Public Library Online. http://www.chipublib.org/008subject/001artmusic/gospel/martinmorris.html.

Gaar, Gillian G. *She's a Rebel: The History of Women in Rock & Roll*. Seattle, WA: Seal Press, 1992.

Garofalo, Reebee. "From Music Publishing to MP3: Music and Industry in the Twentieth Century." *American Music*, Fall 1999.

Hughes, Langston, and Milton Meltzer. *Black Magic: A Pictorial History of the African American in the Performing Arts*. New York: Da Capo Press, 1990.

Jasen, David A., and Gene Jones. *Spreadin' Rhythm Around: Black Popular Songwriters, 1880–1930*. New York: Schirmer, 1998.

Morgan, Thomas L. "Lonesome Blues, 1918." *Jazz Roots. Early Jazz Essentials*. 1999. http://www.jass.com/lonesome.html.

National Association of Black Female Executives in Music and Entertainment (NABFEME) home page. http://www.womenet.org/.

Nations, Opal Louis, and Lin-Woods. "Chapter and Verse: The Stories Behind the Songs." Liner notes to *Testify! The Gospel Box*. Rhino Records Online. http://www.rhino.com/features/liners/75734lin5.html.

Norment, Lynn. "Top Black Executives in the Music Industry." *Ebony*, July 1997.

Petrie, Phil W. "Making a Joyful Noise: Music or Ministry?" *Crisis (The New)*. September/October 2000.

Richardson, Deborra. "Biographical/Historical Note." *Martin and Morris Music Company Records, ca. 1930–1985, #492*. Washington, DC: The Archives Center, Smithsonian Institution, March 1996. http://americanhistory.si.edu/archives/d5492b.htm.

Sellman, James Clyde. "Bessie Smith." *Encarta Africana*. http://www.africana.com/research/encarta/tt_493.asp.

Smith, Shawnee. "Artists Take Control with Own Labels." *Billboard*, 5 December 1998.

"The 10 Most Powerful Black Women." *Ebony*, March 2001.

Vaughn, Christopher. "Pumping Up the Jam for Profits." *Black Enterprise Magazine*, December 1991.

"Vee Jay Records." The History of Rock 'n' Roll. http://www.history-of-rock.com/veejay.htm.

—HILARY MAC AUSTIN

MUTUAL BENEFIT SOCIETIES.

Mutual beneficence, traceable to the African tradition of collectivity, has a long and rich history among African Americans. It revealed itself in the lives of enslaved Africans in America who used their heritage of mutual aid to support each other throughout slavery, Reconstruction, and beyond. Through mutual aid, the slave community and later the emancipated freedwomen and -men engaged in their greatest form of resistance, that of survival. Mutual beneficence is an essential part of the Afrocentric perspective which reorganizes the frame of reference so that African culture, history, and worldview become the context for understanding Africans and African Americans. The Afrocentric approach recognizes the interconnectedness of all things, the oneness of mind, body, and spirit, and the development of collective rather than individual identity. The work of mutual benefit societies that proliferated from the mid-1800s into the early 1900s was enmeshed in the sentiment of collective identity and consciousness and reflected African patterns of problem-solving and service.

Mutual benefit societies included an array of organizations, clubs, and sporadic needs-based group meetings. Literary, temperance, maternal, and moral reform organizations designed to serve the social welfare needs of the African American community all made up the assemblage of organizations referred to as mutual benefit societies. Whether isolated to poor rural women who stole a little time when possible to come together for mutual beneficence or more formally identified through the church or on the society pages of African American newspapers, women's mutual benefit societies existed in large number. The exact number, however, is impossible to determine because some were short-lived, isolated, or left no record of the existence of their legacy of service, while others were well publicized, had large middle-class memberships, and left copious documents. Regardless of the ability to identify each group, it is known that African American women worked to protect, serve, and inspire each other, their families, and their communities through mutual benefit societies. W. E. B. Du Bois described the business of mutual benefit societies as extremely safe and simple. This simple process involved a group of mutually known people who were neighbors or members of the same church who organized and agreed to pay a fee into a common treasury. Funds from the treasury were paid to members who become ill. Upon the death of a member, others were assessed a small amount beyond the regular fee in order to defray burial expenses. Membership also required that individuals agree to give their services in caring for the sick.

A variety of other services were also included in the work of mutual benefit societies, such as the education of African American children. The Woolman Benevolent Society, the Phoenix Society, and the Resolute Beneficial Society all sponsored schools in New York and Washington, DC, respectively. Some of the earliest and most popular mutual benefit societies were the Free African Society (1778), the Brown Fellowship Society (1790), the New York African Society for Mutual Relief (1808), the Female Benezet (1818), and the Female Lundy Society (1833).

Guiding Values

Specific values and principles guided the establishment and operation of African American women's mutual benefit societies. These values reflected the fundamental ethics of African American women during the nineteenth and early twentieth centuries and epitomized the "black helping tradition," a largely independent struggle of African Americans to collectively promote survival and advancement. The values and ethics that these women embraced stemmed from their mutual experiences of race, class, gender, sexual, and economic exploitation. As mutual benefit societies evolved, the common values that they demonstrated included the importance of sisterhood, women's work or domesticity, standards of behavior and moral correctness, economic development, cultural improvement, and race uplift.

In many ways the mutual benefit societies emulated the communalism displayed in the traditional African village.

LUGENIA BURNS HOPE (right) and members of the Neighborhood Union, which was the first women's agency in Atlanta to address black residents' educational, medical, social, and recreational needs. (Neighborhood Union Collection, Atlanta University Center, Robert W. Woodruff Library.)

W. E. B. Du Bois wrote that the African village socialized individuals completely but also allowed individuality to survival. For Du Bois, being a part of that village tradition was essential, otherwise African American people risked becoming soulless, divisive, and antagonistic. Essentially the mutual benefit societies allowed African American women to eschew individualism and extol the sense of communalism.

The notion of sisterhood celebrated that sense of communalism among African American women. Institutionalized in the church, the practice of embracing each other as sisters reflected commonly shared experiences and mutual understanding. Women of esteem in the African American church were routinely addressed as "sister." Since the church was the center of networking and activism among African American women, reaching a position of prominence and having the title of sister suggested that a woman was indeed worthy, had some modicum of power, and stood as a role model for younger church women.

Through formal institutions like the church, and various clubs and organizations, African American women have nurtured relationships that have led to powerful African American communities simultaneously reinforcing strong sisterhoods. Informally and in the comfort of private conversations, sister or "Sis" were terms that younger women used as "handles" or titles when addressing older women. These handles were used as expressions of respect and deference. Women's mutual benefit societies built on the existence of this powerful African American sisterhood.

Among African American women, a sense of shared standards of behavior also existed. These shared standards included ideals of women's work or domesticity and moral correctness. Coming together to form mutual benefit societies reflected a need to value African American womanhood, to strengthen women's roles and domesticity along with an emphasis on moral uprightness that was deemed essential to respectability. For these women, the mutual benefit societies codified these standards of behavior. They also deemphasized the notion of the African American woman as "wench" and accorded her a sense of power and self-efficacy. For example, the Colored Female Religious and Moral Society of Salem (Massachusetts), founded in 1818, constitutionally mandated that its members set aside four quarterly days in the year in January, April, July, and October for solemn fasting and prayer. Such a requirement suggests that the society recognized the importance of purity of body and soul as prerequisite for both membership and useful service.

African American women were the keepers of the hearth. Their uprightness was essential for respectability and for adequate family and community development. Women were seen as responsible for the welfare of their own children and ultimately of society's children. Women were also believed to possess a heightened moral sensitivity that could best be used in caring for society's unfortunates. Moreover, good moral character was a requirement for membership in most mutual benefit societies.

Moral uprightness was a pervasive theme among African American women. Armed with a strict set of guiding principles and explicit rules, mutual benefit societies maintained a gatekeeper function. They allowed admission or membership only to those women who proved to be worthy upon entry and who maintained that worthiness throughout. Once a woman expressed interest in joining a society, club members discussed her character at great length before membership was offered. Worthiness versus unworthiness was a central factor, and deviation from correct moral behavior, neglect of personal health, or lack of frugality rendered women unworthy of group acceptance and service. Consequently, many services through mutual benefit societies were not universal. Instead they were residual and means-tested. That is, they were given only to those who maintained dues-paying status, were in need, were able to demonstrate need, and were not personally responsible for their state of need. According to the constitution of the Afric-American Female Intelligence Society of Boston, any member in good standing who became sick was entitled to both aid and sympathy as long as she had not rashly sacrificed her own health.

Purposes

Mutual benefit societies were also interested in protecting women from sexual victimization and from exploitation in general. The Afric-American Female Intelligence Society specified that one of its purposes was the suppression of vice and immorality. Having strict rules to guide behavior and sanctions against inappropriate conduct was believed to be strategic in helping members and nonmembers alike to conduct themselves in ways that demonstrated irreproachable character. Constitutions sometimes specified that if members committed any scandalous sin or "walked unruly," they risked being excluded from the society until they provided evidence of repentance. This also demonstrated that mutual benefit societies served as mechanisms of social control. Most stipulated a resolve to watch "charitably" over each other and to advise, caution, and admonish when the society deemed it necessary. The member had to agree to receive the advice or reproof without resentment. Further controls were levied, including meeting attendance policies. Members who missed regular meetings were sometimes required to pay a fine or offer a satisfactory apology to the society.

Even though poverty was pervasive, economic independence was recognized as essential to women's well-being. While the cult of true womanhood embraced the notion of women and families being cared for by breadwinner husbands, it was an unrealistic expectation; given the impoverished conditions of most African Americans and the employment opportunities that eluded many poorly educated men and women, lower-class African American women felt that they were ultimately responsible for their own economic well-being.

Seeking and achieving economic independence was a pervasive message from the elite to working-class women. During the early 1860s, Fanny Jackson Coppin, educator and club woman, argued for women's economic independence. Similarly, during the early 1900s, the sociologist and political activist Elizabeth Ross Haynes encouraged women to seek job training and to fight against restricted job opportunities in favor of economic independence. Ross Haynes further cautioned girls against hasty marriages that, she believed, would ensure a life of poverty and want. Supporting employment opportunities for African American women, the hair care mogul Madam C. J. Walker taught women how to be astute and successful business owners while simultaneously providing employment options beyond the boundaries of personal and domestic service. Moreover, Ross Haynes's seminal research study of African American domestics encouraged women to join mutual benefit societies in lieu of spending their free time in the dance halls and saloons.

Mutual benefit societies similarly embraced the call for women's economic independence. Like many other institutions at that time, mutual benefit societies wanted to inculcate thrift and saving among the poor. These organizations provided some sense of economic security for African American women through life insurance policies, medical care, and burial policies and services. Among domestic workers, membership in benevolent societies bolstered their ability to leave oppressive employment situations and provided a covert mechanism for cohering unscrupulous employers to behave more justly. Essentially the goal of economic independence was not selfish but was attentive to the needs of the entire African American community. For example, the historian Jacqueline Jones indicates that a spirit of cooperation beyond economic self-interest discouraged men and women in some towns from accepting jobs from which neighbors had been fired. Through mutual benefit societies these mutual bonds were developed and nurtured among both poor and middle-class African Americans alike.

In 1905 a prominent Chicago clubwomen, Fannie Barrier Williams, described benefit societies as mechanisms for creating social bonds in Chicago's Black Belt. Second only to the church, Williams observed, these societies were run with efficiency and without scandal or money mismanagement. With thousands of dollars paid monthly into these societies in Chicago alone, mutual benefit societies represented the epitome of communal obligation and mutual respect. Williams described mutual benefit societies as more prompt, sympathetic, and faithful in their care for the sick and burial of the dead than any other form of society at that time.

Rise of Mutual Benefit Societies

Philadelphia was the leading city for mutual benefit societies, with women making up the majority of the societies' membership. W. E. B. Du Bois's lauded empirical sociological study of African Americans in Philadelphia during the late 1800s revealed a large number of mutual benefit societies. Free African American men preceded women in organizing self-help and mutual aid societies. The Female Benevolent Society of St. Thomas Protestant Episcopal Church organized in Philadelphia in 1793 was the first such organization established by African American women. In 1821, the Daughters of Africa was founded to provide for the sick, bury the dead, and distribute other social welfare services. The African Educational and Benevolent Society was established in 1828 in Providence, Rhode Island, and a similar group was organized in New Haven, Connecticut, in 1829. The groups focused on supporting public schools for African American children. The Female Lundy Society was established in Albany in 1833 and later in Cincinnati. These societies focused on antislavery and social welfare needs. Among the numerous other societies formed between 1822 and 1828 in Pennsylvania were the Daughters of Wesley, the Female Methodist Assistant Society, the Benevolent Daughters of Zion, the Daughters of Noah Bethel Church, and the Female Beneficial Philanthropic Society of Zoar.

Mutual benefit societies were in their heyday throughout the 1880s. Baltimore, for example, boasted thirty-five benevolent societies by 1853. Even a medium-sized place like Petersburg, Virginia, had at least twenty-two different benevolent societies by 1898; about half of these were exclusively for women. Taking on biblical names that also reflected a sense of family and sisterhood, societies included the Sisters of Friendship, Young Sisters of Charity, Daughters of Bethlehem, Loving Sisters, Sisters of David, Daughters of Zion, and Sisters of Rebeccah. Signifying a simultaneous commitment to work and service, some clubs took on names like Working Club or Willing Workers Club. For example, the Willing Workers Club of Stamford, Connecticut, was organized in 1901 to give aid to churches and to outdoor poor. Focusing on protecting poor young girls and women, the Willing Workers Club planned to establish a rescue home for this population.

With such a large number of societies in such proximity, it was not unusual for the women to exhibit some of the usual behaviors peculiar to groups that compete for scarce resources. In response, it was not uncommon for leaders of the organizations to encourage members to avoid allowing petty jealousy and competition to interfere with their mission. As further assurance, harmonious behavior was often mandated through the societies' constitutions. Because these societies were also concerned about their image and reputation, they placed specific and exacting requirements on their members.

Mutual benefit societies sought every mechanism possible to enhance their image and to project their goals. The names that they selected for themselves sometimes described their purpose, desired membership, and religious affiliation. For example, the name of the Abyssinian Benevolent Daughters of Esther Association of New York (1839), which was founded for moral and relief purposes, suggests that the organization was for women who were affiliated with a prominent local church and identified themselves as strong and courageous like the Old Testament image of Esther. An overwhelming number of mutual benefit societies were quasi-religious or church-related. Another gender-conscious, church-related group, the African Dorcas Society (ADS), founded in New York in 1827, also identified itself as an organization for women who were committed to doing good deeds in the way that Dorcas served. This society's name also indicated that it served women of African ancestry; however, the term "African" was eventually replaced with "Colored" as a second generation of free women matured in the mutual benefit societies. The women of the Dorcas societies met in sewing circles to mend or make suitable clothing for children as a way to encourage their regular school attendance. Noted as supporting an ideal role for women's domestic inclinations and for their natural feelings for the welfare of their friends, these mutual benefit societies modeled desired behavior within their community. In Philadelphia, many of the women's groups providing food to the needy were Dorcas societies. While the women did the work of the Dorcas societies, as they believed was gender-appropriate, an advisory committee of New York's African American male ministers arranged for the ADS's first meeting, penned its constitution, and kept its records.

The Independent Order of St. Luke of Richmond, Virginia, originally founded in 1867 in Baltimore, epitomized the mutual benefit society and demonstrated its evolution. Through the work of the charismatic leader Maggie Lena Walker, the Independent Order of St. Luke became an institution and model for community development. Walker, highly skilled and focused, took over the floundering organization around 1900 and was able to build it through impassioned public speaking and massive membership drives. She urged African Americans to seek economic independence from the white community and encouraged women to enter the business world in search of economic independence from men.

The Order of St. Luke became a successful diversified business organization with a bank, real estate association, paint plant, department store, and newspaper. The newspaper, the *St. Luke Herald*, was a literary organ capable of vehement protest with regard to issues such as lynching, and women's rights. The *St. Luke Herald* regularly railed against unfair treatment of African Americans, simultaneously encouraging racial unity and cooperative work. Reflecting an Afrocentric perspective, the Order of St. Luke engaged in an array of activities to meet the varied needs present in the African American community. While some were concerned that the Order of St. Luke and others of Richmond's many institutions for social betterment were too preoccupied with and engrossed in moneymaking, St. Luke continued to thrive. The Independent Order of St. Luke could boast more than 100,000 members in twenty-eight states by 1920. Men were also active with the Order of St. Luke; however, Walker emphasized women in the organization's work. Insurance became the Order of St. Luke's primary business, and it was reputed to have faithfully made every death benefit payment during Walker's lifetime.

As the South Carolina educator and community activist Mamie Garvin Fields noted in *Lemon Swamp and Other Places* (1983), dying was the reason some of Charleston's early organizations emerged; the need for proper burial and the lack of burial insurance prompted the development of what she called "parlor societies." Like other mutual benefit societies, Fields recalled, the parlor societies carried such names as "the Lily" and "the Esther." Fields described the parlor societies as small intimate groups that met regularly, each starting the meeting with its own special song and prayer followed by dues collections, payments to sick members, and burial insurance payments.

Essentially, membership in mutual benefit societies signified fundamental habits of thrift, good judgment, moral uprightness, and piety. It also represented the spirit of cooperation, mutual respect, and group identity. Moreover, these societies were strict in the enforcement of right living, charity, and truthfulness. They were unique, yet each shared a common mission and adhered to similar values and principles.

Mutual Aid Tradition

The mutual benefit societies were eventually replaced by modern, secular organizations that provided similar services, albeit on a larger, more comprehensive scale. Settlement houses, with their array of specifically tailored clubs and programs, insurance companies, savings banks, hospitals, and eventually governmental organizations began to take on the work of mutual benefit societies during the early 1900s. However, these large, formally organized groups did not completely supersede mutual benefit societies.

As African American women left the agrarian South and migrated to cities in large numbers during the Great Migration, they embraced the ideal of mutual support and continued to form mutual benefit societies, sometimes under the name of "savings clubs." For example, the Jonquil Savings Club, formed by twelve young working-class women in East Baltimore, met monthly to socialize, provide support for each other, and raise and save money. They shared their southern roots, the need for economic security that the city promised, and a longing for the closeness that they had left in their rural face-to-face communities. The Jonquil Savings Club became a social support group, informally nurturing and caring for sisters in the close city blocks of East Baltimore. Eventually, the club expanded its services, giving small scholarships to club members' children and sponsoring educational and recreational bus trips to neighboring states and local fairs. Like many similar organizations, the Jonquil Savings Club did not have an agenda of elaborate civic programs. The women have left no records of their club's existence, save the oral testimony of a few elders who have continued to inhabit that now-dilapidated city block in East Baltimore. Yet this small group of African American clubwomen, descendants of the mutual aid tradition, thrived. They set beautification standards for their city block, with uniform flower boxes flanking the white marble steps that lined the street, served each other during times of illness and death with food, visits, and prayer, and rejoiced with each other during times of celebration. The Jonquil Savings Club's mutual benefit activities mimicked the organizations that preceded it and continued a legacy of women serving communities, families, and each other with compassion, warmth, fidelity, and sisterhood.

Essentially, the mutual benefit societies' legacy was not simply direct service to those in need; it also reflected a perception of mutual obligation, social support, interdependence, and interconnectedness among African American women within their communities.

See also Independent Order of St. Luke *and* Walker, Maggie Lena.

BIBLIOGRAPHY

Cash, Floris. *African American Women and Social Action*. Westport, CT: Greenwood Press, 2001. Discusses clubwomen and volunteerism from Jim Crow to the New Deal.

Du Bois, W. E. B. *The Philadelphia Negro: A Social Study*. New York: Lippincott, 1899. A reputable pioneer's scientific study of the lives of African Americans in Philadelphia.

Du Bois, W. E. B. *Some Efforts of American Negroes for Their Own Social Betterment*. Atlanta, GA: Atlanta University Press, 1898. This is a report of an investigation under the direction of Atlanta University and includes the proceeds of the Third Conference for the Study of the Negro Problem.

Fields, Mamie. *Lemon Swamp and Other Places*. New York: Free Press, 1983. A memoir of Fields's life as a community activist in South Carolina.

Genius of Universal Emancipation. *The Afric-American Female Intelligence Society of Boston*, 1832. An example of the constitution that governed benevolent societies.

Harley, Sharon. "Northern Black Female Workers: Jacksonian Era." In *The Afro-American Woman: Struggles and Images*, edited by Sharon Harley and Rosalyn Terborg-Penn. Baltimore, MD: Black Classic Press, 1997: 5–16.

Jones, Jacqueline. *Labor of Love, Labor of Sorrow*. New York: Vintage, 1985. An excellent chronicle and discussion of African American women's labor involvement.

Marlowe, Gertude. "Maggie Lena Walker (c. 1867–1934)." In *Black Women in America: An Historical Encyclopedia*, edited by Darlene Clark Hine, Elsa Barkley Brown, and Rosalyn Terborg-Penn. Bloomington: Indiana University Press, 1994: 1214–1219.

Martin, Elmer, and Joanne Martin. *Social Work and the Black Experience*. Washington, DC: National Association of Social Workers Press, 1995. This book offers a heuristic framework for social work practice in the black community that the authors call black experience-based social work.

Quarles, Benjamin. *The Negro in the Making of America*. New York: Collier Books, 1969. This book is designed not for the history scholar but for the general reader who wants to better understand the history of African Americans in the United States.

Sterling, Dorothy. *We Are Your Sisters*. New York: Norton, 1984. This book is a documentary portrayal of African American women who lived between 1800 and the 1880s, including oral histories and other primary documents.

Turner, Roberta. "Affirming Consciousness: The Africentric Perspective." In *Child Welfare*, edited by Joyce Everett, Sandra Chipungu, and Bogart Leashore. New Brunswick, NJ: Rutgers University Press, 1991: 36–57.

Weare, Walter. "Mutual Benefit Societies." In *Black Women in America: An Historical Encyclopedia*, edited by Darlene Clark Hine, Elsa Barkley Brown, and Rosalyn Terborg-Penn. Bloomington: Indiana University Press, 1994: 829–831.

Yee, Shirley. *Black Women Abolitionists: A Study in Activism, 1828–1860*. Knoxville: University of Tennessee Press, 1992. Documents black women's involvement in freeing and serving enslaved Africans in America.

—IRIS CARLTON-LaNEY

N

NASH, DIANE (b. 15 May 1938), civil rights activist. Diane Nash was a nonviolent strategist and tactician, one of the most underrated leaders of the civil rights movement. From spearheading the early student activists to strategizing the victory at Selma, Alabama, Nash put her body and her brain behind the movement, even as the movement gave much of the credit to the men around her. Modest and unassuming but with steely determination, Nash has emerged to receive full recognition as a crucial figure.

Born on the south side of Chicago, Diane Nash grew up Catholic with her mother, Dorothy, and her stepfather, John Baker. She attended a parochial grade school, then Hyde Park High School, before going on to college at Howard University. After one year she transferred to Fisk University in Nashville, Tennessee. Intelligent and attractive, Nash was a runner-up in the Chicago trials of the Miss America Pageant. She could have been a shining social success, but Nash chose social justice.

Nonviolence Training Sessions

In Nashville she first encountered hard-core segregation at the same time the civil rights movement was beginning to gather momentum. Nash attended training sessions given by James Lawson, who had recently returned from India where he had studied Gandhian nonviolence, but she was a reluctant convert. She studied with Lawson because she wanted to fight racism and there was no other movement. After a while, though, she began to see that nonviolence could actually work. Articulate and personable, Nash was elected chair of the activist group, known "the Nashville students," and they began their first campaign to desegregate local lunch counters.

While she was working support at one sit-in, a gang of young whites pointed her out, saying, "That's Diane Nash! She's the one to get!" She got away from them, then sat down on a curb to pull herself together. She was frightened, but she forced herself to face her fears. She realized that, as a leader, she could not ask people to do things that she would not do herself, so she got up and went back to the sit-in.

The existing power structure did all it could to stop the Nashville students, but it served only to strengthen the group. For instance, a lawyer who represented the students had his house bombed, a blast so powerful it also damaged nearby houses and Meharry Medical College. After the bombing, a massive crowd of protestors marched downtown. They had requested the mayor to meet with them on the capitol steps. The mayor asked the blacks and whites to pray together, but after prayer the mayor dodged more substantive questions. Nash listened to the exchange and thought that this was not getting them any closer to desegregating lunch counters. Nash asked the mayor if he would appeal to the town to stop racial discrimination. The mayor did, but only in general terms. Nash asked, "Do you mean that to include lunch counters?" Pinned before the crowd, the mayor realized that the only decent answer was yes. It made headlines in Nashville and turned the disaster around.

The Nashville movement continued to grow, picking up more allies. Not everyone was willing to sit in and be arrested, but adults stopped shopping at the stores in question. The resulting economic slowdown had a serious impact on white businesses, and the tactic spread to other cities.

Meanwhile, similar student groups sprang up around the country. Unlike the more formal organization of Martin Luther King Jr.'s Southern Christian Leadership Conference (SCLC), the students preferred fewer speeches, more daring direct action, and joint leadership. Under the guidance of Ella Baker, they came together to form the Student Nonviolent Coordinating Committee (SNCC) in mid-April 1960 at Shaw University in Raleigh, North Carolina. The Nashville students were one of the largest contingents and the first to have successfully desegregated their lunch counters. Many expected Nash to become head of the national group, but she arrived late to the election after working all night and another Nashville student was elected instead.

Freedom Riders Campaign

Nash soon played a pivotal role with the Freedom Riders, a group of students from the Congress of Racial Equality (CORE) who rode a Greyhound bus across the South to oppose segregation. When the first group of Freedom Riders was mobbed and beaten outside of Birmingham,

Alabama, Nash asked CORE if the Nashville students could step in, then called a meeting to ask for volunteer replacements. People understood they might be killed on this project. The group decided Nash was too valuable to risk, so she was named co-coordinator. She led, strategized, kept the press informed, and served as liaison with the U.S. Justice Department, while at the same time forcing the country to face its racial violence.

The Freedom Riders were beaten, mobbed, run out of the state, laid siege to within a church—and still continued. In fact, the Freedom Rides were so dangerous that they forced an unlikely dialogue between adults, both black and white, who wanted the participants to stop. Yet even as Nash and the students forced the issue, they were cut out of the actual negotiations. By the summer of 1961 the students had to decide whether to continue with direct action tactics, such as the Freedom Rides, or concentrate on winning the vote. Nash, at first, was the leader of the direct action strategy, but she soon realized that gaining the vote required direct action of the most daring kind. She moved to Mississippi with James Bevel to organize voter registration. At this time she married Bevel, who was often her co-strategist.

Bevel was recruited by King's SCLC, while Nash worked on various projects and had the first of her two children. That first child was nearly born in jail, as she returned to face old charges relating to the Freedom Riders, and she preferred prison to paying the fine. Not wanting scandal, the authorities thought it better to release her.

Nash and Bevel were in North Carolina in 1963 when they learned of the church bombing that killed four little girls in Birmingham. They believed that they had to do something and knew they could probably find out who was responsible and arrange to have them killed. The decision went to the core of the nonviolent system. In a conflict, someone is going to change, but who? Will the peaceful people change to become violent, or will the violent people change to learn tolerance? That afternoon, Nash and Bevel decided that the other side was going to change. The most powerful change they could think of was to shut down the state of Alabama until black people there had the vote.

While the students of SNCC thought this was feasible, the adults of the SCLC dismissed Nash's plan or were noncommittal at best. When Nash approached King with the plan, he simply said no. Finally, she and Bevel agreed that he would go ahead to Alabama anyway to start setting the groundwork. This was disobeying orders, but they decided that, if local people in Alabama asked for the SCLC to intervene, the leadership could not refuse. Ultimately, they did not shut down the state; they created the confrontation in Selma, Alabama, which so jarred the nation that the rest was unnecessary.

America was fighting the cold war at the time, and around the world, the pictures of white troopers beating black children in Selma called into question American democracy. Stung by international criticism, President Lyndon Johnson forced through the Voting Rights Act of 1965. This overturned voting bans throughout the South, not just in Alabama. Their success in Selma brought Nash and Bevel the Rosa Parks Award, the highest award of the movement. They were nominated by Andrew Young, one of the people who initially refused to consider the Alabama campaign.

Legacy of Nonviolence

By the mid-1960s, Nash's marriage with Bevel was coming apart, and she left Alabama. She had two small children to raise and so started a new life for herself in Chicago. She then realized that much of her work and her credentials were not under her name but her husband's. Still, she found work as a copywriter, proofreader, and photo librarian for publications with Nation of Islam; later she was involved in the antiwar movement. The rise of the Black Power movement shook Nash's faith in nonviolence, and for a while she believed that violence was the more powerful choice, but she came back to nonviolence after a number of years. She compared what she had accomplished using nonviolence with what she had accomplished using violence, and decided that nonviolence was her better choice. She lectures widely to pass that lesson on.

Nash has spoken at college campuses such as UCLA, the University of Virginia, and even the University of Alabama. She spoke at Charlotte, North Carolina, near Rock Hill, where she was threatened with jail. The city council of Rock Hill passed a resolution thanking the demonstrators who went to jail. In an indication that her true value to the movement has at last been recognized, in 2003 she was awarded the Distinguished American Award from the John F. Kennedy Library and Foundation.

Nash had that rare gift, the ability to turn defeat into victory. This was a gift the movement needed in those years. When the Nashville allies were bombed, when Freedom Riders were beaten and dispersed, when the little girls were killed in the Birmingham church bombing, Nash was instrumental in turning the situation around. Though the icons of the movement might have hesitated, she decided what to do and went ahead and did it, often over their objections. In the middle of a crisis she could think of a plan and get it done, and nothing more can be asked of any leader.

BIBLIOGRAPHY

Branch, Taylor. *Parting the Waters: America in the King Years, 1954–63*. New York: Simon and Schuster, 1989.

Branch, Taylor. *Pillar of Fire: America in the King Years, 1963–65*. New York: Simon and Schuster, 1998.

Halberstam, David. *The Children*. New York: Random House, 1998.

Nash, Diane, personal interview, 9 April 2004.

Olson, Lynne. *Freedom's Daughters: The Unsung Heroines of the Civil Rights Movement from 1830 to 1970*. New York: Scribners, 2001.

Powledge, Fred. *Free at Last?: The Civil Rights Movement and the People Who Made It*. Boston: Little, Brown, 1991.

—ANDRA MEDEA

NATIONAL ASSOCIATION OF COLORED WOMEN.

The national club movement developed as a response to increasingly complicated social welfare demands on community resources, a reaction to the growing racism of the late nineteenth century, a need to build a national reform network, and a mission to demonstrate the abilities of black women. Reflecting the spirit of progressive reform, black women subordinated denominational, regional, and ideological identities to forge a national club movement dedicated to racial betterment. The northeastern urban areas dominated the early years of national organization, influencing the direction and leadership during the formative years. As a result of these efforts, the National Association of Colored Women (NACW), through its regional, state, and city federations, developed institutions to serve the race for generations to come.

The groundwork for successful club work emerged from beneficial, church, and literary societies in the urban North, where black women used their relative freedom to develop social organizations for serving the race. By 1890, Philadelphia, the city with the largest nineteenth-century black population in the North, was home to many mutual aid societies. Church-related missionary societies, often called Dorcas societies after the biblical woman who dedicated her life to good deeds, maintained several organizations to provide aid to ill and dependent women and children. The African Dorcas Association in New York City provided clothing, hats, and shoes for children who attended the African Free School. Other women held fairs in New York City to support the Colored Orphan Asylum.

Literary societies, primarily social improvement associations meeting in a member's home, provided a structure through which women became informed about issues and skilled in effecting change. Literary societies offered poetry readings and musical performances, experience with parliamentary procedures, opportunities to develop leadership skills unhampered by either male or white dominance, and increased educational awareness of racial issues, which included segregation in transportation, lynching, debt peonage, and voting rights. Such literary societies often adopted projects to benefit the race. Their fund-raising skills supported local homes for the aged, colored schools, and orphanages.

JOSEPHINE SILONE YATES (1859–1912) was the second president of the NACW, from 1901 to 1906. (Library of Congress.)

Responding to specific community needs, these early club efforts were narrow in scope, limited to a particular denomination or social clique, and short-lived due to lack of administrative knowledge or finances. The post-Reconstruction retrenchment in the South created problems of social injustice, and so black women were called to take on a more active role in helping the less fortunate of their race. By the late nineteenth century, the potential for organized action increased as the black population gained education, settled in urban areas, developed organizations to respond to local needs, and faced intensified racial discrimination and violence. During the last decade of the nineteenth century, all these preconditions came together and resulted in the national club movement to improve life for black Americans.

Birth of a Movement

The national club movement emerged from three centers of club life in the North and East: Washington, DC, New York, and Boston. Washington, DC, a center of the black elite, attracted a national audience through conventions, conferences, and a forum, the Bethel Literary and Historical Association, founded in 1881. This public platform engaged the intellectual elite, including Mary Ann Shadd Cary, the first black female editor of *Provincial Freeman*; Hallie Q. Brown, lecturer for the British and American temperance movements; Mary Church Terrell, daughter of the first black millionaire; Fannie Barrier Williams, Chicago community leader, and Anna Cooper, leader in black secondary education. Most of the Washington women were teachers, aware of children's problems and of educational reforms. Many were volunteers at the Home for Friendless Girls, founded in 1886 by Caroline Taylor. Leaders in education, benevolence, and literary societies, these women joined together during the summer of 1892 to form the Colored Woman's League of Washington, DC.

Black women in New York City were likewise involved in a variety of activities. On 5 October 1892, the black female leadership from the New York-Brooklyn community held a testimonial dinner to honor the antilynching crusader, Ida B. Wells-Barnett. Organized by Victoria Earle Matthews (a contributor to several New York dailies), Maritcha Lyons (a public school teacher), Sarah Smith Garnet (principal of a Manhattan grammar school), Susan Smith McKinney (a Brooklyn physician), and others, the testimonial dinner recognized Wells for her courage in researching, writing, and lecturing about lynching. This dinner stimulated the formation of two important women's clubs: the Woman's Loyal Union, organized by Mathews and Lyons later that month, and the Woman's Era Club of Boston, founded by Josephine St. Pierre Ruffin in January 1893.

The Boston women reflected the town's educational and community activism. Ruffin had served on the Sanitary Commission and in the Kansas Relief Association, Women's Industrial and Educational Union, and Moral Education Society. With her daughter, Florida Ridley, and Maria Baldwin, principal of Agassiz School, one of the most prestigious white schools in Cambridge, Ruffin met to collect data, publish and disseminate tracts and leaflets, and develop any other service to improve the image of black women through example.

While these three centers were developing services for their communities, several events soon drew these women together in a national effort. In preparation for the Columbian Exposition in Chicago, a Board of Lady Managers encouraged women from other countries to participate in an international demonstration of progress commemorating the discovery of America. When black women's groups from Washington, DC, and Chicago petitioned for inclusion in the planning process, they were rejected since they had no national organization to represent them. The Colored Woman's League of Washington, DC, attempted to organize a convention to become a national group, but lack of cooperation from other centers resulted in failure to gain exposition participation. Soon after, the Washington League invited women in all parts of the country to affiliate for racial advancement. Women's clubs from Kansas City, Denver, Norfolk, Philadelphia, and South Carolina responded. Black women in Chicago also responded to the rejection from the Columbian Exposition. In September 1893, the Chicago Women's Club was formed to take leadership in civic and community reform.

The move to develop a national representative body quickened. In January 1894, the Colored Woman's League incorporated with affiliated leagues. Two months later, the Boston Woman's Era Club launched the first monthly magazine published by black women, *The Woman's Era*, which informed subscribers about fashion, health, family life, and legislation. Women from Chicago, Kansas City, Washington, Denver, New Orleans, and New York contributed to the magazine and served as heads of the magazine's departments. In October 1894, the National Council of Women invited the Colored Woman's League to become a member and send delegates to the spring 1895 convention. Eligibility required the Colored Woman's League to call itself a national organization. Through the columns of *The Woman's Era*, the league requested delegates from other clubs, but only a few accepted. Even though the announcement appeared in *The Woman's Era*, the Woman's Era Club sent no delegates since the Boston leadership was seeking a similar national role. Although the league behaved as a national organization at this 1895 National Council of Women's convention, no national convention of black women had yet taken place.

The catalyst for calling a national convention was a slanderous letter sent by the Southern white journalist James W. Jacks. He wrote an open letter to the English reformer, Florence Belgarnie, to discount the charges made by Ida B. Wells-Barnett in her speeches about lynching in the United States. He accused all black women of being "prostitutes, thieves, and liars" with "no sense of virtue" or character. Belgarnie sent the letter to Josephine Ruffin, editor of *The Woman's Era*, who included a copy in a communication to subscribers. The black elite reacted with moral outrage, leading to Ruffin's call for a national conference in Boston. The newly elected leaders of the First National Conference of Colored Women of America represented an alliance of competing groups: Ruffin (Boston) as president, Helen Cook (Washington, DC) and Margaret Murray Washington of the newly formed Tuskegee Woman's Club as vice presidents, and Elizabeth Carter (New Bedford, Massachusetts) as secretary. Before leaving the conference, the delegates voted to form a permanent organization, the National

Federation of Afro-American Women (NFAAW) to correct the image of black women using example to counter the charges of immorality. The conference's 104 delegates and 54 clubs represented 14 states and the District of Columbia and reflected the focus on female benevolence stressing middle class interest in home life and racial uplift. The women sought to lead the masses to social righteousness. They discriminated against no race or gender and welcomed the support of similarly concerned white women and African American men.

As a result of this meeting, NFAAW accepted an invitation to participate in the Women's Congress at the 1895 Cotton States and International Exposition in Atlanta, Georgia. Prominent black women from twenty-five states attended to demonstrate the race's skills, culture, and talents. The separate black exhibition provoked conflict among the women. Josephine St. Pierre Ruffin expressed the northern integrationist opinion when she declined the invitation due to the racial segregation of contributions. Yet she did not speak for all northern women. Victoria Matthews attended and gathered information for the New York women. The group declared itself the Colored Women's Congress of the United States. The group met once more in Nashville during the Tennessee centennial in 1897, during which time they disbanded to strengthen the national aspirations of black women, aspirations threatened by the proliferation of so-called national organizations.

To strengthen these aspirations the National League of Colored Women and the National Federation of Afro-American Women had to clarify their interrelationships as national organizations. The women realized that competition for members, financial resources, and the attention of the white press could endanger the emerging club movement. Both groups held their national conventions in Washington, DC, during July 1896, a duplication of effort that left their organizational quest open to ridicule. The leadership of both groups sought unity. Therefore, a representative body of seven women from each organization deliberated together to overcome the factionalism and conflicts that historically had constrained the effectiveness of these black women's clubs. The joint committee elected Mary Church Terrell as chair and recommended the two organizations merge to form the National Association of Colored Women (NACW). For self-protection, self-advancement, and social interaction, the NACW gradually lessened the city and class divisions that had historically prevented national unity.

Mary Church Terrell became the first president of the NACW, aided by vice presidents from Boston, Philadelphia, Kansas City, and New Orleans. The strength of the NACW remained in the Northeast with Washington, DC, and the Boston area predominating. These women valued

 Scribe of the Club Movement

Much of what is currently known about the early club work of African American women is due to the commitment of Elizabeth Lindsay Davis, who documented the history of black women's clubs. The eldest daughter of Thomas and Sophia Lindsay, she was born in Peoria County, Illinois, in 1855, and grew up to be a teacher. When she married William H. Davis of Frederick, Maryland, in 1885, she retired from teaching to do club work.

Davis ardently believed in reform and social uplift. She believed that elite black women should be at the forefront of the reform movement. Thus, she organized the Chicago Phyllis Wheatley Women's Club in 1896 and served as president for twenty-eight years. This club, in 1908, opened the Phyllis Wheatley Home for young black females who needed a safe place to live. The home provided living accommodations, recreation, and an employment bureau. It also operated a club program and classes in domestic arts. The home and its activities were solely managed and supported by the black community.

Davis was also a member of the Ida B. Wells Club, the Woman's City Club, the Chicago Forum League of Women Voters, the Woman's Aid, the Giles Charity Club, the E. L. D. Study Club, and the Service Club. In 1918 the Elizabeth Lindsay Charity Club was organized in her honor. The club provided legal counsel, educational facilities, medical aid, food, and clothing to the thousands of southern black migrants seeking economic opportunity in Chicago.

Davis's long involvement in the National Association of Colored Women—she was national organizer from 1901 to 1906 and from 1912 to 1916—led to her success as state organizer and president (1910–1912) of the Illinois Federation of Colored Women's Clubs. Under her presidency, the federation endorsed the National Association for the Advancement of Colored People (NAACP) and pushed for the ballot for women.

Davis's documentation of the women's club movement in *The Story of the Illinois Federation of Colored Women's Clubs* (1922) is the first record of women's clubs in the state. Her *Lifting as They Climb* (1933) is the first national history of the club movement. A committed reformer and active club woman, Davis helped build and document the reform agenda for black Americans throughout the last decade of the nineteenth century and the first decades of the twentieth century.

For more information, see Sylvia G. L. Dannett, *Profiles of Negro Womanhood* (Yonkers, NY: Educational Heritage, 1964).

—WANDA A. HENDRICKS

self-help, protection of women, honesty, and justice. They honored the past and present black leadership with organizations named the Sojourner Truth Club, Phyllis Wheatley Club, Lucy Thurman WCTU Club, Ada Sweet Club, and Ida B. Wells Club. The religious roots appeared in clubs such as the Calvary Circle and Christian League. Joining heroines of the past with younger, ambitious women filled with hopes for the future, merging old traditions with new scientific methods of social organization, the NACW became a major vehicle through which black women attempted reform during the next four decades.

After founding the NACW, the women responded to the general reform context. As educated, elite women, they actively supported the major women's reform movements seeking moral purity, temperance, self-improvement, and suffrage. Their racial identity, however, complicated participation in national women's organizations that included the National Congress of Mothers, the Women's Christian Temperance Union, the National Council of Women, the General Federation of Women's Clubs, the National American Woman Suffrage Association, and the Young Women's Christian Association. Black women had different perspectives on the women's issues; they possessed a triple consciousness because they were American, black, and women.

They reassembled in Nashville to formalize the organizational structure of the NACW and to demonstrate black female worth and capabilities. Held during the Nashville centennial, the first annual conference (the first biennial was in Chicago in 1899) became a platform for racial self-defense. Unlike their failure to win recognition as a national organization for the Chicago Exposition, the NACW won recognition from the Nashville Centennial's Woman's Department as a national organization representing about five thousand members.

The focus was on women and children. The NACW sought kindergartens to educate young children and improved care within the home. The leadership wanted to protect women. Mothers' meetings became a means for racial uplift. Reflecting the optimistic spirit of progressivism, the women wanted less criticism and more emphasis on the progress of the race. Themes of self-help and racial solidarity appeared in every speech. The defensive character of the NACW mission appeared in evidence of the moral, mental, and material progress made by people of color. The status of the race required black women's leadership in self-help beginning in the home and carrying through mothers' congresses, kindergartens, and schools to develop the intellect and to prepare for jobs. The elite leaders were duty bound to protect and sympathize with their fallen sisters, not only by preaching, but also by practicing race unity and race pride. By the end of the Nashville meeting, the NACW had gained both a formal structure and a communications network in the publication of the *National Notes*, a means through which local, reform-minded black women could disseminate information, discuss issues, and stimulate further organization.

Conflict Resolution

The strength of the North in leadership, conference locations, and issues appeared in the biennials of the NACW during the pre–World War I period, a time when 90 percent of the black population lived in the South. During these early years, regional, personal, and ideological conflicts threatened to halt the precarious unity of the national club movement. At the first biennial in Chicago (1899), all three types of conflict were present. Mary Church Terrell had to rely on the local Chicago women for assistance in planning and executing this meeting. The Chicago club women warned Terrell that the participation of Ida B. Wells-Barnett would lead them to resist. Since Terrell relied on these local women for the planning and program, she decided to omit Wells-Barnett during these early stages. Wells-Barnett, offended by the exclusion, charged that Terrell feared losing her position to Wells-Barnett. Terrell, however, was more a practical politician than a jealous competitor. Terrell did not include Wells-Barnett in the planning stages for many reasons. First, since the convention took place in Chicago, Terrell could not offend the leading club women, who disliked working with Wells-Barnett. Second, Wells-Barnett, as the secretary to the Afro-American Council, which was holding its annual meeting in Chicago during the same week, would be involved in other activities. Third, Wells-Barnett's reputation for being outspoken and for creating controversy was not a desirable trait for an organization attempting to unite factions of black women and to provide a positive public image of reserved, ladylike leadership. Terrell personally admired Wells-Barnett's courage and direct approach to many issues, but that very style of interaction could threaten the loosely organized, infant federation. Terrell was an excellent judge of the politically expedient. She understood the need to build a structure through which black women could effectively attack racial injustices.

A second conflict emphasized regional jealousies over the recognition of credentials, selection of officers, and parliamentary procedures. Some of the delegates arrived with no credentials. To avoid setting a negative precedent for the NACW, Mary Church Terrell ruled that those delegates lacking proper credentials could not take part in the proceedings. When Josephine St. Pierre Ruffin attempted to speak on a subject, Terrell ruled her out of order. The past rivalry of the Boston-Washington clubs was reinforced by the credential and parliamentary procedure difficulties.

The regional rivalries erupted again during the election process. The NACW constitution prevented a president from serving more than two consecutive terms. Since Terrell had served as the head of the joint committee and as president of the NACW when formally organized at Nashville in 1897, many delegates thought Terrell ineligible. The NACW did not count Terrell's leadership before the adoption of the constitution in 1897. With the constitutional issue resolved, Terrell won reelection. The position of first vice-president had Ruffin, Libby Anthony, and Josephine Bruce in competition. Ruffin and Anthony withdrew, giving that office to Bruce. The position of recording secretary, too, produced conflict between Chicago's Connie A. Curl, New Bedford's Elizabeth C. Carter, and Pittsburgh's Mary Sutton. Even though the South had won only three of the eleven offices, Carter withdrew, charging the NACW with playing power politics by using her Northeastern Federation for money and influence to help expand the NACW.

These conflicts in parliamentary procedure and selection of officers led to negative publicity. Carter announced the withdrawal of the Northeast Federation, the only regional federation. The Woman's Era Club of Boston and Northeast Federation took their complaints to the press. The NACW responded with public refutations of the charges and persuaded the northern women to remain for the sake of unity.

The next seven biennials deliberately attempted to balance the centers of club activity in biennial location and leadership to lessen the regional conflicts. Hence, the northern interests received four biennials: 1901 Buffalo, 1906 Detroit, 1908 Brooklyn, and 1914 Wilberforce. Centers of club activity received recognition in the election of their leaders to the presidency: Josephine Silone Yates (1901–1906) of the Kansas City League, Lucy Thurman (1906–1908) of the Michigan State Federation, Elizabeth Carter (1908–1912) of the Northeast Federation, and Margaret Murray Washington (1912–1916) of the Tuskegee Women's Club and the National Federation of Afro-American Women. The clubs of the North were satisfied, but conflict did not cease. The election of the darkest-skinned candidate, Lucy Thurman, demonstrated the color consciousness of the black female network. By choosing a dark-skinned sister, the women sought to counter white opinion that light-skinned elites proved the relationship between leadership skills and the percentage of white blood. The publication of *National Notes* at Tuskegee provoked charges of "Tuskegee machine" censorship from Ida B. Wells-Barnett at the Louisville meeting. More a personal than ideological conflict, the charges failed to gain adherents and Tuskegee continued publishing the newsletter through 1922.

Contributions and Advancements

The club women shared more in common as the decades progressed. During the pre–World War I years, the NACW expanded in numbers, regions, and interests. Only one regional and six state federations existed in 1901, yet by 1909, the southern federation and twenty state federations had developed. By 1916 three hundred new clubs had joined the NACW since the last biennial. The departments within the NACW grew and changed from social science, domestic science, juvenile court, humane and rescue work, religion, temperance, music, literature, and publication to include mothers' clubs, kindergartens, and business and professional women. The expansion and increased specificity of interests responded to the participation of educated women in business, social work, and the professions while still showing interest in women's issues and the family. The club women stressed the responsibility of the privileged to help their social inferiors, since white Americans increasingly judged the race by its lowest elements. By training the lower classes to adopt attitudes, manners, and other behavior acceptable to the middle class, these "missionaries" hoped to improve the perceptions held by whites about the race. The self-help method fit the careers of the overwhelming majority of the NACW leaders and was the most acceptable path to advancement supported by white reformers and philanthropists alike.

These self-help efforts to uplift and serve the community were best seen in the local club activities in the North. Typically, care for the race's aged was the first type of organized reform initiated by club women. Lack of programs to care for aging former slaves mobilized groups of women to organize, charge membership fees, hold socials, and solicit county funds. They raised money to cover services, purchase facilities, and hire qualified personnel to manage these homes for the aged. The Alpha Home in Indianapolis, the Cleveland Home for Aged Colored People, and similar services in Chicago, Brooklyn, New Bedford, Newark, and Philadelphia emerged from the efforts of individual women joined by organized clubs adopting the projects. For example, Gabrella Smith of Chicago founded the Home for Aged and Infirm Colored People by taking homeless elderly into her house. She interested other women in her project. Soon, Anna Hudlin organized a club for the placement of aged in the home. The club raised funds, obtained other properties, provided furnishings, and managed an endowment for the home's operation. The club women assumed many of the daily responsibilities by developing a network of volunteers. The Woman's Loyal Union established a Home for Aged Colored People. The same group provided the support for a venture started by club woman Elizabeth Carter, whose New Bedford Home for the Aged received recognition from the NACW as the greatest such enterprise established by the race. Clubs accepted responsibility for the aged in their communities. New Haven's Twentieth Century Club assumed the financial obligations for the Hannah Gray Home. Detroit club women developed the Phyllis Wheatley Home for Aged Colored Women under the leadership of Mary E. McCoy, wife of the inventor Elijah McCoy and founder of the Detroit club.

Closely related to care for the aged were the local programs to aid the infirm and dependent populations.

Women's clubs aided the colored departments or wards in hospitals, created medical facilities for black communities, and developed specialized medical services. The New York club women contributed food, clothing, and services in the form of lectures and performances to the Lincoln Hospital and Home. New Jersey women formed the Charity Club to assist Christ Hospital in Jersey City. Berean Church club women helped Dr. Caroline Still Anderson establish a dispensary in Philadelphia, while the Yates Women's Club supported a small black hospital in Cairo, Illinois. The need for health care for tuberculosis patients led the Indianapolis Woman's Improvement Club to establish the Oak Hill Tuberculosis Camp, the first of its kind in the nation. Gradually, these health care efforts emerged from their charity roots to reflect the general trends in progressive reform calling for investigation, planning, and alteration of the environment rather than merely treating the patient.

Mixtures of charity and social welfare approaches were also evident in the club women's efforts for youth. As with the homes for the aged, many of the orphanages started out with one woman's concern for dependent children. Amanda Smith, international evangelist and temperance lecturer, used her own money to start a children's home in Harvey, Illinois. Joined by the Illinois club women and aided by the State of Illinois, the home expanded to care for over sixty children by 1908. Smith was over sixty at the time she began the effort, but her dream prospered and continued after her death through the organized efforts of the club women. Chicago club women aided the Louise Children's Home and Home for Dependent Children. The New Bedford Women's Club supported a children's home founded in 1904. As with the homes for the aged, the segregated facilities did not provoke conflict due to their charitable nature and to the belief that the race could better care for its own.

Black club women thought that the most efficient way to reform society was to care for and instruct the young. As a result of that belief, club women developed day nurseries and kindergartens that required little expenditure for facilities or staff. Provided in a church basement, a club woman's home, or a rented house, day nurseries needed only to rely on the women as volunteers. Kindergartens, a concept imported from German liberals, were usually established by the educated leaders in clubs. In many kindergartens, the club women instructed mothers in child care, health, and hygiene. The Chicago club women helped Wells-Barnett establish a kindergarten at Bethel Church in 1897. The Women's Christian, Social and Literary Club of Peoria, plus several others in the Illinois Federation, supported similar kindergarten and day nursery projects. Due to the integration of social services in Boston, the club women of Boston supported a

kindergarten for black children in Atlanta through the Georgia Educational League. Before the Great Migration of black Americans came from the South to these northern cities, women had developed self-help services for the aged, infirm, and dependent populations from New York to Chicago to Detroit.

The seeds for the development of urban multi-service centers grew out of the homes or missions for the protection of young black women coming to the northern population centers. The travelers' aid services could not or did not meet the expanding needs of black women migrating in search of better wages, working conditions, or opportunities. Victoria Earle Matthews, president of the Brooklyn Women's Club and Woman's Loyal Union, had been concerned about young women since her trip to attend the Atlanta Exposition. Upon her return, she gathered club women together to develop a social service for young working girls: the White Rose Home. These club women served as founders, administrators, teachers, and volunteers in kindergartens and in industrial training programs in cooking, laundry, sewing, chair caning, and wood burnishing. The White Rose Home in New York City became a model settlement house for other institutions in the North. The National League for the Protection of Colored Women, one of the three organizations that merged to form the National Urban League, was directly influenced by the White Rose Home. Soon, such homes for working women as the Phyllis Wheatley Home in Evanston and Chicago, Lincoln Settlement in Brooklyn, and the Phillis Wheatley Association in Cleveland (some clubs used the normative Phyllis spelling, others the actual Phillis form) expanded as community needs increased with the Great Migration.

As jobs opened during World War I, black Americans left the South for northern opportunities. Between the 1910 and 1920 census, Detroit's black population had expanded by 623 percent, Cleveland's by 308 percent, and Gary, Indiana's by 1,284 percent. New York gained the highest urban black population, while Chicago went from eighth place to fourth place in similar population growth. By 1920, 85 percent of black Americans outside the South were urban residents. Such growth exacerbated the conditions that black women had been trying to improve through their self-help efforts. These multi-service centers filled the needs for lodging, job placement, night classes, industrial training, day nurseries, kindergartens, libraries, boys and girls clubs, savings clubs, choir and music programs, and social gatherings. They became the training ground for black visiting nurses and social workers graduating from nascent educational programs in social work. These multi-service community centers cooperated with the National Urban League through affiliation and laid the foundation for major social services in black communities for generations. As these services changed, so too did the women.

The biennials of the NACW demonstrated the growth of competence and confidence among club workers. The 1916 Baltimore biennial highlighted trends toward racial pride and inter-organizational cooperation. By the time the women reconvened, the NACW had passed formal resolutions to support the woman suffrage amendment, to cooperate with the Young Women's Christian Association, National Urban League, and the National Association for the Advancement of Colored People, and to support federal antilynching legislation. The newly elected president, Buffalo club woman Mary B. Talbert, directed the NACW to assume financial obligations for the redemption and restoration of the Frederick Douglass home. Organized groups of black men had failed to redeem the Douglass Home. It was time for black women to demonstrate their abilities. Talbert's creative fund-raising and participation techniques appealed to racial identity, to female pride, and to an individual's need for recognition. All ages, regions, and institutions assisted. The campaign was so successful that the 1918 Denver biennial held a ceremonial burning of the mortgage on the Frederick Douglass home, which came to symbolize the success of one black man and the triumph of organized black club women.

While rescuing the Douglass home, international conflict influenced the American home front. World War I created the occasion for club women to prove their patriotism, their abilities, and their solidarity. The war meant an end to laissez-faire social policy as the government guided national health campaigns, mobilized housing and urban development, and encouraged reforms such as industrial education, social insurance, and community activism. This surge in organizational activity created a growth in confidence and self-image because women felt needed. They proved their abilities, performed nontraditional jobs, and increased their expectations for postwar progress. The club women raised money through Liberty Loans, War Savings Stamps, and United War Work campaigns. Many club leaders served in the six black base hospitals and hostess houses. The Circle for Negro War Relief called on the national club movement for help. The club women used the war years to garner services for their communities and to demonstrate racial pride.

As the war ended, demobilization produced thousands of returning soldiers, unemployment caused by reversion to peacetime economy, and readjustment to civilian life. Economic and social tensions exploded in the Red Summer of 1919, when twenty-six cities suffered race riots that left hundreds dead. By year's end, seventy-seven people had been lynched, including eleven soldiers. The postwar period provided the context in which rising expectations collided with reality. Black club women, armed with better training, inter-organizational connections, and confidence, sought less charity and more justice. They embodied both the New Negro and the New Woman as they attacked the chronic injustice of lynching.

Mary Talbert built on wartime networks to mobilize women against lynching. She utilized women's imagination, money, and volunteer time to spread the information and raise the funds to cooperate with the NAACP in the national campaign against lynching. Talbert formed an ad hoc group for fund-raising and publicity that became known in 1922 as the Anti-Lynching Crusaders. Broader based than the NAACP, the Crusaders directed religious fervor into their attempt to unite one million women to suppress lynching and to pass the Dyer Anti-Lynching Bill. Although federal legislation was never achieved, the public and political awareness of injustices changed and lynching declined. Talbert completed her term of office with the NACW and became a board member of the NAACP. The club women approached the 1920s as activists in the NACW, NAACP, and National Urban League. These multi-layered commitments modified the club women and the NACW.

The change in the NACW was gradual at first. The biennials of 1920 and 1922 were held in Tuskegee and Richmond under the leadership of a northern club woman, Hallie Q. Brown, of Wilberforce, Ohio. With the NAACP fighting the legal and political battles and the National Urban League negotiating and investigating social and economic problems in the communities, the NACW had to carve out a niche for itself. Brown's leadership began to shape that role in education through what came to be known as the Hallie Quinn Brown Scholarship Loan Fund. Ohio club women honored Brown by leading the states in contributions to the fund. The letters NACW came to mean: National pride, Achievement, Cooperation, and Willingness to serve. The publication of *National Notes* was turned over to Myrtle Foster Cook of Kansas City, Missouri, who developed the newsletter into a magazine with reports, comments, and items of interest to club women. The departments of the NACW had changed to include the Frederick Douglass Memorial and Historical Association, Education, Child Welfare, Health and Hygiene, Social Service, Legislation and Law Enforcement, Big Sisters Movement, Fine Arts, Business, and Interracial Cooperation.

The biennial attempts to balance location of meeting and national presidency continued under the leadership of the Southeast Federation's leader, Mary McLeod Bethune, president of the NACW from 1924 to 1928. The biennials during her leadership took place in Chicago and in Oakland, a recognition of the regional and numerical expansion of the NACW, which in 1924 included over

100,000 members. The NACW, now in the consolidation phase of its growth, gave Bethune authority to establish a national headquarters in the nation's capital and to compile the first official directory.

A generational transition was also in progress. With the founding leaders of the NACW either dead or aging, the organization initiated plans to attract younger women through a junior division. The younger generation had its own interests that reflected the social life of the 1920s. The NACW adapted to these changes.

When the club women came to the fifteenth biennial in Washington, DC (1928), the NACW dedicated the national headquarters at Twelfth and O Streets and the caretaker's cottage at the Frederick Douglass home, both physical examples of their achievements. The new president, Sallie W. Stewart of the Indiana Federation, reported that the junior division work was growing rapidly. The women memorialized past leaders and looked to the future, not knowing that this would be their last, great celebration of club work.

Shift in Focus

The Great Depression modified their optimism. The women met for the next biennial in Hot Springs, Arkansas (1930). Two days of executive sessions focused on the financial problems confronting the organization. As if to escape the unpleasant realities surrounding them, the club women toured a model house, viewed exhibits of beautiful homes and fine art, and expressed optimism about the scholarship fund, expansion, and the nation's future. The departments merged to form the Board of Control (a financial monitor), a National Association of Colored Girls, and Women in Industry, and Mother, Home, and Child.

The NACW did not meet again in biennial until 1933, when club women came to celebrate the Chicago Exposition. Dr. Mary Waring, one of the original club women in Chicago, became president. The discussions, although permeated with references to the causes of and solutions to the Depression, focused on traditional women's goals to standardize the home; create a good environment for the child; train girls to be industrious, artistic and gracious; improve working conditions for women and girls; and increase community service. At the 1935 Cleveland biennial, Waring informed members about threatened court action against the NACW for the printing costs of the official history compiled by Elizabeth L. Davis. Past president Mary McLeod Bethune, director of the National Youth Administration's Division of Negro Affairs, reported on the financial condition of the NACW headquarters.

Bethune's position in the administration of Franklin D. Roosevelt had demonstrated to her a need for a united coalition of all black women's organizations to pressure the political system into action to help the race. Criticized by many of the older leaders of the NACW for attempting to weaken or destroy the national club movement, Bethune nevertheless organized the National Council of Negro Women (NCNW) in 1935. With this united coalition, Bethune continued to influence the national direction of black women through national political structures. Her efforts in the National Youth Administration provided work experience for over 400,000 blacks and utilized over 700 to administer these programs. Self-help could make no such claims. Just as some years earlier, local club women united to form a national club movement, now Bethune saw a need to influence national politics through a united coalition of black women's groups.

With the creation of the NCNW in 1935, the NACW declined in its original importance. With the NACW's cooperation and support, other organizations had taken over responsibilities for the black community by specializing in goals and tactics. City, state, and private organizations provided institutional support for many of the services started by the club women. The Depression brought economic devastation to black communities and a changing political context through which reform was directed. The younger generation joined the NACW more as a social outlet than as a means to serve the community. They sought means to affect their personal mobility, not to uplift their downtrodden sisters.

As the political and ideological contexts changed, the NACW persisted with fewer members and a different direction after 1935. It was during the period of the club movement's greatest growth, the 1890s through the 1920s, that the NACW achieved its legacy—shaping the leadership, the institutions, and the identity of a people through its women.

See also Bethune Museum and Archive; Bethune, Mary McLeod; Brown, Charlotte Hawkins; Height, Dorothy Irene; Hope, Lugenia Burns; Hunton, Addie Waits; Matthews, Victoria Earle; Stewart, Sallie Wyatt; Talbert, Mary Morris Burnett; Terrell, Mary Eliza Church; Washington, Margaret Murray; Wells-Barnett, Ida B.; Williams, Fannie Barrier; World's Columbian Exposition; *and* Young Women's Christian Association.

BIBLIOGRAPHY

Brawley, Benjamin. *Women of Achievement*. Chicago: Woman's American Baptist Home Mission Society, 1919.

Brown, Hallie. *Homespun Heroines*. Xenia, OH: Aldine, 1926.

Cash, Floris. "Womanhood and Protest: The Club Movement among Black Women, 1892–1922." PhD diss., SUNY/Stony Brook, 1986.

Culp, D. W., ed. *Twentieth Century Negro Literature: Or, a Cyclopedia of Thought on the Vital Topics Relating to the American Negro*. Naperville, IL: J. L. Nichols, 1902.

Dannett, Sylvia. *Profiles of Negro Womanhood*. Chicago: Educational Heritage, 1964.

Davis, Elizabeth. *Lifting as They Climb*. Washington, DC: NACW, 1933.

Du Bois, W. E. B., ed. *Social and Physical Conditions of Negroes in Cities*. Atlanta, GA: Atlanta University, 1897.

Duster, Alfreda, ed. *Crusade for Justice*. Chicago: University of Chicago Press, 1970.

Field, Emma. "The Women's Club Movement in the United States." MA thesis, Howard University, 1948.

Hamilton, Tullia. "The National Association of Colored Women, 1896–1920." PhD diss., Emory University, 1978.

Harley, Sharon, and Rosalyn Terborg-Penn, eds. *The Afro-American Woman: Struggles and Images*. Port Washington, NY: Kennikat, 1978.

Loewenberg, Bert, and Ruth Bogin, eds. *Women in Nineteenth-Century American Life*. University Park: Pennsylvania State University Press, 1976.

MacBrady, J. E., ed. *A New Negro for a New Century* (1900). Miami, FL: Mnemosyne, 1969.

Majors, Monroe. *Noted Negro Women*. Chicago: Donohue and Henneberry, 1893.

Mossell, Gertrude. *The Work of the Afro-American Women* (1908). Freeport, NY: Books for Libraries Press, 1971.

Salem, Dorothy. *To Better Our World: Black Women in Organized Reform, 1890–1920*. Brooklyn, NY: Carlson, 1990.

Terrell, Mary. *Colored Woman in a White World*. Washington, DC: Ransdell, 1940.

Wesley, Charles H. *The History of the National Association of Colored Women's Clubs: A Legacy of Service*. Washington, DC: NACW, 1984.

White, Deborah Gray. *Too Heavy a Load: Black Women in Defense of Themselves, 1894–1994*. New York: Norton, 1998.

—DOROTHY SALEM

NAYLOR, GLORIA

NAYLOR, GLORIA (b. 25 January 1958), novelist, essayist, columnist. Gloria Naylor was born to working-class parents, Roosevelt and Alberta Naylor, in New York City. Her passion for reading was nurtured by her mother, who remembered her own experiences with her native Mississippi's segregated public libraries. Unable to borrow books, Alberta Naylor had been forced to earn money to buy them. Her daughter was more fortunate and as a high school student began to write, an activity that earned high praise for her budding talent. In 1963, the family moved to the borough of Queens, where the shy and introverted Naylor became increasingly aware of racism. In 1968, Naylor's mother introduced her to Jehovah's Witness members who gave her the opportunity to trust the power of words and provided shelter from a racist outside world.

However, in 1975 Naylor left the religion when she realized that the group also sheltered her from the heady days of black political consciousness and a new flowering of black cultural movements. During her college years (1975–1981), Naylor attended Medgar Evers and Brooklyn Colleges where she discovered feminism and Toni Morrison. Deeply influenced by Morrison's novel *The Bluest Eye* (1970), Naylor made her own foray into fiction writing in 1979 when she submitted a short story to *Essence* magazine. Encouraged by the magazine, Naylor received a

GLORIA NAYLOR, whose novels include *The Women of Brewster Place* (1982) and *Linden Hills* (1985), won a Guggenheim Fellowship in 1988. (Austin/Thompson Collection, by permission of New York Public Library.)

publishing contract for her first novel *The Women of Brewster Place* (1982), graduated with a bachelor of arts from Brooklyn College, and began graduate work at Yale (in African American Studies) in 1981, where her second novel, *Linden Hills* (1985), began as a master's thesis.

In 1983 Naylor received a master's degree from Yale, won the American Book Award for Best First Novel, and the Distinguished Writer Award from the Mid-Atlantic Writers Association for *The Women of Brewster Place*. Naylor's creative prowess was also recognized when she was appointed writer-in-residence at Cummington Community of the Arts and visiting lecturer at George Washington University. Further recognition followed with a fellowship from the National Endowment for the Arts in 1985 and recognition as an important black writer in 1986 when she received the Candace Award from the National Coalition of One Hundred Black Women.

As a visiting professor at Boston University, Naylor began work on *Mama Day* (1988), received a prestigious Guggenheim Fellowship, and became a member of the selection committee for the Book-of-the-Month Club. Naylor received the Lillian Smith Award in 1989 and began work on her fourth novel, *Bailey's Café* (1992). In 1990, she expanded her creative interests by establishing her own multimedia production company, One Way Productions, as a vehicle for promoting positive black images. In 1992, Naylor was a visiting writer, sponsored by the British Arts Council, at the University of Kent. She has traveled and lectured extensively throughout Europe and Africa.

Naylor's creative work was hailed by literary critics for the richness of her language and the depth and variety of her characters. Her themes of hope, survival, and personal redemption, articulated in a series of novels and essays, won her popular acclaim. Furthermore, Naylor unflinchingly took the black community to task for its homophobia and color bias, and the sometimes destructive nature of black male and female relationships. Her first novel, *The Women of Brewster Place*, recounts the experiences of seven representative black women brought together in a run-down urban apartment building, a building that in Naylor's skillful hands becomes an important character in its own way.

Critics and readers have observed Naylor's penchant for linking her novels with recurring characters and thematic situations. *Linden Hills* (1985) established this pattern as characters and places appeared, or are referred to in other works. *Linden Hills* was also hailed for Naylor's adaptation of Dante Alighieri's *Inferno* as an organizational plan for allegorical warnings aimed at recovering the spiritual morality of the black community. *Mama Day* (1988) was influenced by the rich, rural black culture of Naylor's Mississippi-born parents, the otherworldy "magic" of black folk customs, and the strength of female bonding. The novel also experimented with narrative structure, the way "truth" and "reality" are constructed, and the unstable nature of personal and collective memory. *Bailey's Café* (1992) continued the themes and concerns of Naylor's previous books, which featured a diversity of black female characters, the conscious privileging of black supernatural folk customs, and the experimental narrative strategies which contributed to her wondrous and intricate art.

BIBLIOGRAPHY

Felton, Sharon, and Michelle Loris, eds. *Naylor: The Critical Response to Gloria Naylor*. Westport, CT: Greenwood Press, 1997.

Fowler, Virginia. *Gloria Naylor: In Search of Sanctuary*. New York: Twayne, 1996.

Gates, Henry Louis, Jr., and K. A. Appiah, eds. *Gloria Naylor: Critical Perspectives Past and Present*. New York: Amistad Press, 1993.

Kelley, Margot Anne, ed. *Gloria Naylor's Early Novels*. Gainesville: University Press of Florida, 1999.

Whitt, Margaret Earley. *Understanding Gloria Naylor*. Columbia: University of South Carolina Press, 1999.

—DOLORES V. SISCO

NORMAN, JESSYE (b. 15 September 1945), opera singer. The voice of Jessye Norman is a wonderful thing. Renowned for its prodigious size and the warmth and sumptuous beauty of its sound, it is capable of soaring over Wagnerian waves of orchestral crescendo or delineating the subtleties of a Schubert lied. For more than thirty years Jessye Norman has shared this gift with the world as one of the great divas of the operatic stage and a nonpareil interpreter of art songs and spirituals.

Jessye Norman was born in Augusta, Georgia, to Silas Norman, an insurance broker, and Janie King Norman. Both parents were musically inclined. Her father sang in the choir at Augusta's Mount Calvary Baptist Church, and her mother was an amateur pianist. Norman and her four siblings took piano lessons during childhood, and she won third place in a church singing contest at the age of seven.

Although her talent was widely recognized from an early age, Norman did not consider music as a career or study singing formally until she went to Howard University to study under Carolyn Grant. After graduating cum laude from Howard, she studied with Alice Duschak at the Peabody Conservatory in Baltimore and with Elizabeth Mannion and Pierre Bernac at the University of Michigan, where she was awarded an MA degree in 1968. The French tenor Bernac was an expert in the interpretation of the art song, and under his tutelage Norman learned to perform the songs and lieder of a broad spectrum of composers.

In 1968 Norman took first prize in the International Music Competition in Munich. This showing brought invitations to sing at a number of German venues. In 1969 she moved to West Berlin and signed a three-year contract with the Deutsche Opera. She made her operatic debut there, singing Elisabeth in Wagner's *Tannhäuser*. Elisabeth was followed by Verdi's Ethiopian princess, Aida, and Elsa in Wagner's *Lohengrin*.

Norman's voice defies description as either a strict mezzo or soprano instrument, and it is also a felicitous match with certain works from the contralto repertoire. From 1975 to 1980, she withdrew from performing opera in order to develop her voice, limiting her performances to concerts and recitals.

Norman's first appearance on the American opera stage took place in Philadelphia in 1982, and she made her Metropolitan Opera debut in 1983, singing the part of Cassandre in Berlioz's *Les Troyens*. The many other roles she has recorded or performed include Donna Elvira in Mozart's

Don Giovanni, Countess Almaviva in Mozart's *Le nozze di Figaro*, Idamante in Mozart's *Idomeneo*, Leonore in Beethoven's *Fidelio*, and the title role in Bizet's *Carmen*. Many of her recitals have featured Wagner's *Wesendonck-Lieder*, and she has also performed and recorded songs by Mahler, Schubert, Schumann, Poulenc, Brahms, Ravel, Satie, Duparc, Gounod, Franck, and Wolf, among others. Some of her most memorable characterizations have been preserved on video and DVD, including Cassandre in *Les Troyens*, Sieglinde in Wagner's *Die Walküre*, and Ariadne and the Prima Donna in Strauss's *Ariadne auf Naxos*.

In the late 1990s, as her voice darkened, Norman moved away from staged opera and concentrated on recitals and collaborations with contemporary composers and artists in other disciplines. In May 1998 she premiered *Spirits in the Well*, a song cycle composed for her by Richard Danielpour and set to texts by the novelist Toni Morrison. Ten days later her collaboration with the choreographer Bill T. Jones, *How! Do! We! Do!*, opened in New York as part of Lincoln Center's Great Performers New Visions series. In 2000 she premiered the song cycle *woman.life.song* composed by Judith Weir to texts by Morrison, Maya Angelou, and Clarissa Pinkola Estés. In July 2003 she provided a musical complement to the film *7th November* by the artist Steve McQueen at the Tate Gallery in London as part of the performance series Tate and Egg Live. Her recordings include *Mythodea* by Vangelis and *I Was Born in Love with You*, a collection of songs by Michel Legrand.

Jessye Norman sang at the Olympic Games in Atlanta in 1996 and the inauguration of President Bill Clinton in 1997 and performed "La Marseillaise" at France's bicentennial celebration in 1989. She became the youngest recipient of the Kennedy Center award in 1997 and was made a Commander of the Order of Arts and Letters and awarded the Legion of Honor by the government of France. She has been involved in numerous nonprofit social and arts organizations, including service as the national spokesperson for both the National Lupus Foundation and The Partnership for the Homeless.

BIBLIOGRAPHY

de Lerma, Dominique-René. "Jessye Norman." In *Black Women in America: An Historical Encyclopedia*, edited by Darlene Clark Hine, Elsa Barkley Brown, and Rosalyn Terborg-Penn. Bloomington: Indiana University Press, 1994.

Moritz, Charles, ed. *Current Biography Yearbook 1976*. New York: H.W. Wilson, 1976.

Mueller, Michael E. "Jessye Norman." In *Contemporary Black Biography: Profiles from the International Black Community*, edited by Barbara Carlisle Bigelow, vol. 5. Detroit, MI: Gale Research, 1996.

Stephens, Robert W. "Jessye Norman." In *Notable Black American Women*, edited by Jessie Carney Smith. Detroit, MI: Gale Research, 1992.

—ROBERT W. LOGAN

NORTON, ELEANOR HOLMES (b. 13 June 1937), congresswoman, law professor, and civil rights activist. Eleanor Holmes Norton has established a stellar career as one of the most influential black women in politics in the United States. A tenured professor of law at Georgetown University, she serves in the U.S. House of Representatives as the congressional representative for the District of Columbia. Combining a quest for social justice with a belief in the principles of American democracy, Norton has actively worked to further the struggle for freedom and equality for all Americans.

Born in Washington, DC, to Vela Lynch, a schoolteacher, and Coleman Holmes, a government worker, Eleanor Holmes Norton could never have imagined as a child that one day she would represent her birthplace in national politics. During Norton's early years, Washington was one of the most vibrant centers of the early civil rights legal campaign, which was led by Howard University–trained lawyers, including Thurgood Marshall. Growing up there shaped Norton in two important ways. First, she developed a profound sense of race consciousness that would follow her throughout her life. Second, she learned to value education as a tool for racial uplift and progress.

From Medicine to Law

After graduating from Dunbar High School in 1955, Norton attended Antioch College in Yellow Springs, Ohio. Originally, she worked toward a career in medicine, but after participating in Encampment for Citizenship, a summer public affairs program in New York for college students, she decided to focus on law. During her years at Antioch, Norton took an active role in political organizing for the campus and the larger community. She served as a student representative for the Antioch Community Council and Civil Liberties Committee. In addition, she was named president of the campus chapter of the NAACP. Her involvement in these organizations facilitated important moments in Norton's evolution as a civil rights activist. Influenced by the burgeoning student-led civil rights movement of the 1960s, Norton organized and participated in a number of local protests and boycotts that focused on black civil rights and integration of public facilities.

Upon graduating from Antioch in 1960, Norton returned to Washington and was active in the local chapter of the Student Nonviolent Coordinating Committee (SNCC) before beginning law school at Yale University. There she pursued a dual degree program in Law and American Studies and channeled her activism into forming a local chapter of the Congress of Racial Equality, which provided another important northern-based branch of support for the national civil rights movement.

ELEANOR HOLMES NORTON, delegate from the District of Columbia, addressing the Democratic National Convention in Los Angeles on 15 August 2000. (© Reuters/ Corbis.)

During the summer of 1963, Norton traveled to Mississippi, worked with SNCC, and helped in organizing the landmark March on Washington. In 1964 she became a lobbyist for the seating of black delegates of the Mississippi Freedom Democratic Party, led by Fannie Lou Hamer, at the Democratic National Convention. Norton's involvement in the civil rights movement not only allowed her an avenue to seek social justice for black America but, more important, strengthened her commitment to making the United States a place where all persons could reap the benefits of equality and freedom.

After completing her advanced degrees at Yale, Norton began working for the American Civil Liberties Union (ACLU) in New York. There she represented a range of clients, including Julian Bond and George Wallace, and interests pertaining to the right of freedom of speech. The exposure and legal experience that Norton gained from her early work with the ACLU challenged her ability to respect and remain committed to the cause of individual freedom of expression even when a person's views did not reflect her own. Learning this lesson became an important tool that allowed Norton to foster broad political coalitions based on a shared belief in the preservation and extension of democracy.

Work at the National Level

Norton married Edward Norton in 1965 and became the mother of Katherine Felicia in 1970 and John Holmes in 1972. Marriage and motherhood, however, did not

sidetrack her career. In 1970 Norton was appointed to serve as chair of the Commission on Human Rights in New York City. In this position Norton drew local and national attention to the rights of minorities and women, particularly in the employment sector. Working in this capacity was the perfect prelude to her appointment as chair of the Equal Employment Opportunity Commission (EEOC) under President Jimmy Carter in 1977. The first black woman to occupy this role, Norton was responsible for overseeing the major government organization designed to enforce many of the legal gains made from the civil rights movement, including the Civil Rights Act of 1964 and affirmative action. During her tenure, Norton instituted new guidelines for affirmative action compliance, defined procedures for sexual harassment claims, and persuaded a number of large companies (including AT&T and Ford) to adopt hiring practices that created greater job opportunities for women and minorities.

When Ronald Reagan was elected president, Norton resigned as head of the EEOC, trading the political scene for the academic community. In 1982 Norton was appointed a full professor at the Georgetown University Law Center. There she established the Women's Law and Public Policy Fellowship Program, designed to increase the presence of female legal scholars at the institution. Academia offered Norton another route to channel her ideas about equitable employment opportunities, civil rights, and public policy. Even so, she continued to travel extensively in public support of issues pertaining to welfare rights, the economic marginalization of people of color, and the defeat of apartheid in South Africa.

The year 1990 represented a turning point in Norton's personal and professional life. In that year Norton was elected congresswoman for the District of Columbia. Her marriage did not survive the transition, and she divorced Edward Norton when evidence of his financial mismanagement threatened to taint her political appeal. Since that time, Norton has championed a number of causes to benefit her constituency, including greater federal funding for city programs; home buyer tax credits, which have increased home ownership; and educational credits for DC residents who attend public colleges and universities nationwide. In 2003 she served on the Committee on Government Reform, the Select Committee on Homeland Security, and the Committee on Transportation and Infrastructure.

One of the most pressing concerns shaping Norton's political agenda has been full congressional representation for Washington, DC, citizens. Her constituents are responsible for federal taxes, but as their representative Norton does not have voting privileges in either the House or the Senate. For Norton, this represents erosion of the democratic principles that have shaped her involvement in American politics and continue to motivate her quest to attain equality and social justice for all Americans.

BIBLIOGRAPHY

"Biography of Congresswoman Eleanor Holmes Norton." United States House of Representatives. http://www.norton.house.gov/display2.cfm?id=1832&type=News.

Lester, Joan Steinau, as authorized by Eleanor Holmes Norton. *Eleanor Holmes Norton: Fire in My Soul.* New York: Atria Books, 2003.

Norton, Eleanor Holmes, and Jamie Raskin. "Eleanor Holmes Norton and Jamie Raskin Discuss Their Attempts to Have the District of Columbia Fully Represented in Congress." Interviewed by Lisa Simone. *Weekend All Things Considered.* Washington, DC, NPR, 22 October 2000.

Office of the Clerk: U.S. House of Representatives. "Member Information: Eleanor Holmes Norton." http://clerk.house.gov/members/inter_mem_list.html?statdis=DC00.

Smith, Jessie Carney, ed. *Notable Black American Women.* Detroit: Gale, 1992.

Hardy, Gayle J. *American Women Civil Rights Activists: Bibliographies of Sixty-eight Leaders, 1825–1992.* Jefferson, NC: McFarland, 1993.

—KENNETTA HAMMOND PERRY

NURSING. The history of the development of the nursing profession is the story of the struggle of a group of women to overcome social and economic adversities. Within this history, however, is another, almost parallel chronicle of the effort of black women to acquire nursing education, to end economic discrimination, and to win professional acceptance from their white counterparts.

GOOD SAMARITAN HOSPITAL NURSE TRAINING SCHOOL. A graduating class, probably in the late 1920s. (Richard S. Roberts Collection.)

The Professionalization of Nursing

During the formative phases of the nursing profession in America, a plethora of concerns riveted the attention of most white nurse leaders: the exploitation of student nurses in hospital training schools, limited employment opportunities for graduate nurses exacerbated by competition from untrained women, the absence of certification or licensing boards, and the need to develop collegiate nursing programs while raising the low social status and esteem accorded to nurses.

The first three American nurse training schools were established in 1873. These early schools operated within hospitals, but in keeping with traditions initiated in Florence Nightingale's movement in 1850s Britain to establish an organized system for training nurses, they were characterized by a degree of faculty autonomy, a separate funding apparatus, and the use of women as nurse supervisors. However, insufficient capital and endowment and

Featuring Nurses

● **Anna De Costa Banks** (1869–1930) was head nurse and then superintendent of the Hospital and School for Nurses in Charleston, South Carolina. Banks was also a visiting nurse with the Ladies Benevolent Society. (See individual entry: Banks, Anna De Costa.)

● **Hattie Bessent** (1926–) was born in Jacksonville, Florida, and held a BS in Nursing Education from Florida A&M University (1959), an MS in Psychiatric Nursing from Indiana University (1962), and an EdD in the Psychological Foundations of Education from the University of Florida (1972). She was the first black nurse in Florida to earn such an advanced degree. She was also the first black nurse to head a psychiatric unit in Jacksonville and the first African American dean of Vanderbilt University's Graduate School of Nursing. For more than twenty years she served as the program director for the Ethnic Minority Fellowship Program of the American Nurses Association, which provides fellowships for nurses to earn advanced degrees in Psychiatric and Mental Health Nursing. In 2002, Bessent became the project director of the American Nurses Foundation's minority nurses leadership enhancement and development project. She is also the author of *Minority Nurses in the New Century*. She received an honorary doctorate of science degree from Hunter College in 2002 and held a lifetime membership in the National Black Nurses Association.

● **Carrie E. Bullock** (d. 1961) was born in Laurens, South Carolina. She graduated from the Scotia Seminary Normal Department in Concord, North Carolina, in 1904. She received her nurses training at Dixie Hospital in Hampton, Virginia, and then at Provident Hospital in Chicago. After graduating from Provident in 1909, she continued to work there. She also worked for the Chicago Visiting Nurse Association, where she served first as an assistant supervisor and then, in 1929, was named supervisor of black nurses. Deeply involved in the National Association of Colored Graduate Nurses (NACGN), in 1923 she succeeded in bringing that group's annual meeting to Chicago; at that meeting, she became the NACGN vice president. Four years later she was elected president of that association, a position she held until 1930. During her tenure, she founded and edited the monthly publication *National News Bulletin*. She also lobbied the Julius Rosenwald Fund to inaugurate a fellowship program for black graduate nurses. She was awarded the NACGN's Mary Mahoney Award in 1938.

● **Maude Callen** (c. 1898–1990), nurse-midwife, served as the main health care provider for ten thousand poor people in Berkeley County, South Carolina, and was profiled in *Life* magazine in 1951. (See individual entry: Callen, Maude.)

● **Mary Elizabeth Lancaster Carnegie** (1916–) was born in Baltimore, Maryland, on 19 April 1916. She received her nurse's training from Lincoln Hospital School for Nurses and, in 1942, a BA in Sociology from West Virginia State College. The following year she became the assistant director of nursing at Hampton University and founded Virginia's first black baccalaureate program in Nursing. In 1945, she left Hampton to take the post as first dean of the School of Nursing at Florida A&M University in Tallahassee. Joining the fight for blacks to be admitted to the Florida State Nurses' Association, she ultimately won a seat on its board, becoming the first African American to achieve that distinction not only in Florida but in any state nursing association. She did not become a legitimate member of the board (as opposed to a courtesy member) until 1949. Carnegie left Florida A&M in 1953 to begin working at the American Journal of Nursing Company. In 1978 she retired and became editor emeritus of *Nursing Research*. In the same year she was elected president of the American Academy of Nursing (AAN). In addition to all her other achievements, in 1972 she received a doctorate in Public Administration from New York University. She was the author of three editions of her book, the latest being *The Path We Tread: Blacks in Nursing 1854–1994*. In 2000, she was inducted into the ANA's Hall of Fame.

● **Frances Elliott Davis** (1882–1965) was the first black nurse with the Red Cross. Born in Knoxville, Tennessee, in 1882, she obtained her Nursing degree from Freedmen's Hospital Training School (now Howard University) in 1912. In 1915 she decided to join the Red Cross, even though that organization did not employ black nurses. Two years later, the organization finally agreed to accept Davis if she got some advanced training. In order to accomplish this, she took a course in rural nursing at Columbia University's Teachers College. In 1917 she began her work with the Red Cross in Jackson, Tennessee. Her Red Cross nurse's pin had an "A" on it to signify that she was black. The organization did not change this practice for black nurses until 1949. After World War I, Davis became the director of Nurses Training at the John A. Andrews Hospital in Detroit. She also organized the first training school for African American nurses in Michigan at Dunbar Hospital and, in 1927, became the first black nurse to work for the Detroit Department of Health. She died in May 1965, just a few months prior to being honored by the American Red Cross.

● **Sara Iredell Fleetwood** (1849–1908) was born in April 1849; she attended Oberlin College and was a member of the first class of the Freedmen's Hospital Nurse Training School. She graduated in 1896 and became a private-duty nurse. In 1901 Fleetwood returned to Freedmen's as the first black superintendent of the Nurse Training School. Shortly thereafter she was named directress of nurses. However, a conflict with the surgeon-in-chief, William Warfield, led to her resignation in 1904. She was an active advocate for nursing and health care in the black community. She founded the Freedmen's Nurses Association and in 1907 became the first and only African American member of the District of Columbia's Nurses Examining Board. She was also a founder of the Colored Women's League and was a delegate to the 1895 meeting of the National Council of Women (a predominantly white organization). She was married to Christian A. Fleetwood and had one daughter, Edith. She died on 1 February 1908, when she was only fifty-eight years old.

● **Martha Minerva Franklin** (1870–1968) was the founder and first president of the National Association of Colored Graduate Nurses. (See individual entry: Franklin, Martha Minerva.)

● **Mamie Odessa Hale** (1911–c. 1968), nurse-midwife, attended the Tuskegee School of Nurse-Midwifery in Alabama and later served as the only black nurse-midwife for the State Board of Health in Arkansas. (See individual entry: Hale, Mamie Odessa.)

● **Jane Edna Hunter** (1882–1971) was born on 13 December 1882, on a plantation near Pendleton, South Carolina. She attended Ferguson-Williams College in Abbeville, South Carolina, and then the Canon Street Hospital and Training School for Nurses in Charleston, South Carolina. She finished her training at Dixie Hospital and Training School at Hampton Institute. After moving to Cleveland, Ohio, in 1905, she discovered that nursing opportunities were few and far between for black women. Accessible housing was equally problematic. Hunter decided to address the issue and approached the Young Women's Christian Association for help in creating a separate home for black women. The association agreed, and Hunter founded and became executive director of the Phillis Wheatley Association in 1913. With the success of the Cleveland association, Hunter went on to create the Phillis Wheatley Department of the National Association of Colored Women. She also served as a state president and national vice president of that organization and was a member of the board of the Colored Welfare Association of Cleveland, the Empire Savings and Loan Association, and the International Council of Women of the Darker Races, among many others. Hunter retired in 1946. She later founded a scholarship fund, the Phillis Wheatley Foundation. When she died on 19 January 1971, her estate was valued at close to $500,000, most of which was given to the foundation.

● **Eunice Rivers Laurie** (1899–1986) is best known for her participation in the U.S. Public Health Service's forty-year study

of late-stage syphilis. The "Tuskegee Experiment" involved nearly four hundred black men who were kept ignorant of their disease and denied treatment. (See individual entry: Laurie, Eunice Rivers.)

● **Mary Eliza Mahoney** (1845–1926) became the first trained black nurse in the United States when she received her diploma from the New England Hospital for Women and Children in Boston. (See individual entry: Mahoney, Mary Eliza.)

● **Estelle Massey Riddle Osborne** (1901–1981) was born in Palestine, Texas, on 3 May 1901. She attended Prairie View State College before entering, in 1920, the first nursing class at St. Louis's City Hospital No. 2 (later the Homer G. Phillips Hospital Training School). Following her graduation, she became that hospital's first black director of nursing. After earning a BS in Nursing from Teachers College, she was hired by Harlem Hospital's School of Nursing, becoming its first black teacher. She soon returned to Teachers College and in 1931 became the first black woman in the United States to earn a master's degree in Nursing. She was then hired by Freedmen's Hospital Nurse Training School as its first educational director of nursing. In 1934, Osborne was elected president of the National Association of Colored Graduate Nurses and served for five years. During the same period she became the first black superintendent of the Homer G. Phillips Nurse Training School. In 1942, she joined the National Nursing Council for War Service as a consultant, becoming that group's first black appointee. In 1946, she moved to the nursing faculty at New York University, again becoming the first black to do so. From 1948 through 1952, she served on the board of directors of the American Nurses Association (ANA) and was associate general director of the National League for Nursing. She retired in 1967 and died in 1981. In 1984 she was inducted into the ANA Hall of Fame.

● **Mabel Keaton Staupers** (1890–1989) was perhaps the woman most responsible for the desegregation of the U.S. Army Nurse Corps during World War II. (See individual entry: Staupers, Mabel Keaton.)

● **Adah Belle Samuels Thoms** (c. 1870–1943) was active in many different areas in the nursing profession. She was the assistant superintendent of nurses at the Lincoln Hospital and Home in New York, served as president of the National Association of Colored Graduate Nurses from 1916 to 1923, agitated during World War I to get black nurses accepted into the American National Red Cross Nursing Service, and wrote the first history of black nurses. (See individual entry: Thoms, Adah Belle Samuels.)

the demand for more scientific-based instruction determined that this type of relatively autonomous nurse training school was soon eclipsed by hospitals, which came to dominate nursing education.

There were fifteen hospital nurse training schools in 1880 and 431 schools twenty years later. The number of graduates increased from 157 to 3,456 within this time. The proliferation of nurse training schools continued as hospitals garnered increased respectability from the public, which began to accept them as places of good care, not dens of death. By 1926 there were 2,150 schools with 17,000 graduates, virtually all of which excluded black women.

As hospital nurse training schools mushroomed on the educational landscape, nurse leaders questioned the instructional quality and low admission standards. The inadequate, random instruction provided at the hospitals, the exploitation of student nurses, and the general low status accorded to even trained nurses motivated nurse leaders to organize what would be renamed, in 1911, the American Nurses' Association (ANA). Its official organ, the *American Journal of Nursing*, had commenced publication in 1901. The National League of Nursing Education, the ANA, and the many other emergent national societies struggled to upgrade the status of and to professionalize nursing.

Training for Black Nurses

The professionalization of nursing had a negative effect on black nurses. Black women had long worked as nurses on slave plantations and, after emancipation, in the homes of white southerners. However, as the number of nurse training schools grew and nursing became another way out of domestic service for thousands of European immigrant and poor white women, black women were increasingly denied the opportunity to acquire this training. Mary Eliza Mahoney, a black 1879 graduate of the New England Hospital for Women and Children in Boston, was an exception to this rule of exclusion. Left with little alternative, African Americans founded their own network of nursing schools and hospitals.

In 1886, John D. Rockefeller contributed the funds for the establishment of a school of nursing at the Atlanta Baptist Seminary, later Spelman College, a school for black women. This was the first school of nursing established within an academic institution in the country. The earliest black hospital nursing schools came into existence in the 1890s, established mostly by black physicians and black women's clubs. In 1891, Daniel Hale Williams, the famed open-heart surgeon, founded Provident Hospital and Nurse Training School in Chicago. He was also instrumental, in 1894, in creating the Freedmen's Hospital and Nurse Training School in Washington, DC. Under the

aegis of Booker T. Washington, the Tuskegee Institute School of Nurse Training in Alabama came into existence in 1892. In the same year, the Hampton Nurse Training School at Dixie Hospital in Hampton, Virginia, began accepting students. In October 1896, the black women of the Phillis Wheatley Club founded the only black hospital and nurse training school in New Orleans. The Phillis Wheatley Sanitarium and Training School for Nurses began rather inauspiciously in a private residence consisting of seven beds and five patients. This institution was later renamed the Flint Goodridge Hospital and Nurse Training School. Finally, on 4 October 1897, Alonzo Clifton McClennan, an 1880 graduate of the Howard University Medical School, founded the Hospital and Nursing Training School in Charleston, South Carolina. Anna De Costa Banks, one of the first graduates of the Dixie Hospital School of Nursing, became the first head nurse of the South Carolina institution. By 1920 there were thirty-six black nurse training schools.

The impetus leading to the founding of black schools of nursing was an effort to respond to an array of perceived and real needs of black Americans. Providing adequate training and educational opportunities for black women was only one of many motivational factors. McClennan, for example, was angered by the stubborn refusal of the white municipal hospital administrators in Charleston to allow black physicians to attend their patients, even in segregated wards. He and his black colleagues initially created their hospital in order to advance their practices and to care for their patients. They added the nursing school in order to acquire help in the delivery of medical care to the hordes of poor, superstitious African Americans of Charleston and surrounding counties who sought their services. The black women of the Phillis Wheatley Club were inspired to establish a nursing school after observing the poor quality of health and the high mortality rates of African Americans in New Orleans. Between 1890 and 1900, the overall death rate in New Orleans dropped from 25.4 to 23.8 per thousand, while that of the city's black population increased from 36.6 to 42.4 per thousand. These conditions were similar in cities both above and below the Mason-Dixon line. The lack of adequate hospital facilities and black health care professionals lessened the already slim chances of survival for African Americans. The establishment of the Phillis Wheatley Sanitarium and Nurse Training School marked the first attempt by African Americans to improve black health care in the city.

Other founders and heads of black nursing schools articulated different reasons for their actions. Alice Bacon, the white founder of the Hampton Nurse Training School at Dixie Hospital, justified the establishment of the school as a means to retain "in the hands of trained colored women a profession for which, even without training, the

Negro women have always shown themselves especially adapted." She declared that black women had "to take up the work laid down by the home trained women of the old days, and to hold for their race throughout the South a profession that has always been theirs." Likewise, Booker T. Washington declared, "Colored women have always made good nurses. They have, I believe, a natural aptitude for that sort of work."

These early black nursing schools were, for the most part, as deficient in quality and standards as were many of their white counterparts. In keeping with prevailing practices, student nurses were exploited as an unpaid labor force. In every institution, they performed the domestic and maintenance drudgery, attended the patients, and dispensed medicine. Many student nurses at Tuskegee Institute required extended leaves of absence to recover from damage done to their health while working in the hospital. It was not inconsequential that one of the early Tuskegee catalogs noted that the major admission requirement into the nursing program consisted of a strong physique and stamina to endure hardship.

The most oppressive aspect of black nursing training at some of these early schools, notably at Tuskegee and Charleston's Nursing Training School, involved the hiring out of student nurses to supplement a hospital's income. In the Charleston school, the student nurses were required to turn over to the hospital the dollar a day they earned on private cases. These nurses also managed the hospital's poultry operation, tended the vegetable gardens, and organized public fund-raising activities. In spite of the attendant hardship and the mediocre instruction, hundreds of black women graduated from these segregated hospital nursing programs and went on to render invaluable service to black patients.

World War I

A little-noted aspect of America's involvement in World War I was the struggle of black women nurses to serve in the U.S. Army Nurse Corps. Although this particular quest for unfettered access to professional opportunities proved futile, it is nevertheless a revealing case study in both the military history of America and in the history of black women. An examination of the nature and extent of the U.S. government's staunch resistance to the inclusion of black women nurses in "the fight to make the world safe for democracy" illuminates some of the implications of armed forces interracial relations and policies.

More than 367,000 black men were called into service during World War I, and, following an effective black protest campaign and lobbying effort, the U.S. Congress authorized the establishment of a separate reserve officers' training camp for black soldiers. Though African Americans were barred altogether from the marines and the pilot section of the aviation corps, they were permitted to serve in almost every branch of the army and in menial jobs in the navy. Yet black women who fervently desired to use their professional talents and expertise to aid their country were consistently denied the right to serve in the Nurse Corps.

Black Americans had been understandably cautious when, in 1914, Woodrow Wilson, a southerner, became president of the United States. However, in spite of their already low expectations of his administration insofar as black rights were concerned, even the most cynical African Americans were shocked by the depth of Wilson's apparent commitment to racial segregation and discrimination. Wilson had not been in office long, for instance, before he issued an executive order establishing separate eating and restroom facilities in government buildings; other laws segregated and eliminated large numbers of African Americans from civil service jobs. With Wilson's reelection to the presidency came America's plunge into World War I. Black Americans immediately offered their services in the armed forces. Even radicals such as W. E. B. Du Bois and several leaders of the National Association for the Advancement of Colored People urged black men to volunteer for the army. Ironically, confronted with the warm response of African Americans to the draft, the U.S. Congress continued to debate legislation for the drafting and training of African Americans in separate military units.

Of all black professionals, women nurses needed no special persuasion to volunteer their services to aid and care for their wounded countrymen. The advent of World War I helped to raise their expectations and excite their professional dreams. Black women nurses had long despaired over their status as professional outcasts. They could not attend the better-equipped and -managed nurse training schools, were denied individual membership in the American Nurses' Association (ANA), and were denied supervisory or administrative positions in hospitals, nurse training schools, and public health agencies and bureaus. At every level of employment, they earned lower salaries than white nurses. Furthermore, the general low regard and esteem they possessed in the public mind exacerbated their unfair treatment.

In the prewar years, black women nurses had engaged in a number of largely unsuccessful activities designed to improve their position within the ranks of organized nursing. In 1908, they had founded their own professional body, the National Association of Colored Graduate Nurses, to better structure and intensify their struggle to win membership and integration into the ANA. Yet professional equality eluded them. Thus, black women nurses desired to seize the opportunity created by the war emergency to accomplish these objectives.

Although the first wave of black women nurses who attempted to enlist in the U.S. Army Nurse Corps expected to encounter racism, they were not prepared for the total rejection of their services during one of America's greatest crises. Disillusioned and hurt, black women nurses focused their anger initially on the American Red Cross, reorganized and incorporated by an act of Congress on 5 January 1905. The Red Cross, an auxiliary of the U.S. Army Nurse Corps, recruited and enrolled nurses, then classified them as First Reserve nurses or Second Reserve nurses. The First Reserve was composed of nurses with the educational, moral, and professional qualifications required by the military Nurse Corps. The Second Reserve consisted of nurses available for critical civilian nursing who, because of some technicality, such as being over forty years old, were not eligible for the First Reserve. In effect, the American Red Cross enjoyed quasi-governmental status, particularly within the Army nursing group. Indeed, the second superintendent of the Nurse Corps, Jane Delano, served simultaneously as head of the Red Cross Nursing Service.

Black nurses demanded to know why so few of them were called or enrolled into either the First or Second Reserve. Delano's response to their inquiries was both evasive and defensive: "We are enrolling colored nurses at the present time," she explained, "and shall continue to do so in order that they may be available if at any time there is an opportunity to assign them to duty in military hospitals." That time and opportunity never seemed to come, and most black nurses waited in vain for the call. Later, criticized for their failure to enroll black nurses, Red Cross leaders shifted blame to the office of the surgeon general, who, they insisted, had simply not called for black nurses. Red Cross officials further asserted that many black nurses had not met the Red Cross prerequisite of graduation from a fifty-bed-hospital nurse training school. The Red Cross also steadfastly insisted that it had given black nurses who lacked the necessary credentials a provisional enrollment until they registered or acquired additional training.

Unconvinced by these rationalizations and evasions, black nurses in particular and black Americans in general felt the injustice deeply. Black criticism of the Red Cross increased as the war continued. The army was markedly reluctant to tap the nursing services of black women, and the navy refused even to consider the matter. As black pressure and anger mounted, the Red Cross belatedly prepared a list of black nurses to serve in a proposed segregated hospital to be established in Des Moines, Iowa. The signing of the armistice on 11 November 1918, and the end of the war, however, aborted the proposed installation. A month before the war's end, though, two dozen black nurses were called for service at Camp Sherman,

Ohio; Camp Grant, Illinois; and Camp Sevier, South Carolina. This number represented only a fraction of the 21,000 white women who had been given the opportunity to serve their country as nurses. Commensurately, as the status of the white nursing profession skyrocketed in the aftermath of the war emergency, that of black nurses plummeted. Because black nurses had not served their country, they apparently bore no claim to a share of nursing's newly earned public esteem.

Black educators and leaders such as Robert R. Moton, successor to Booker T. Washington as president of Tuskegee Institute, and Emmett J. Scott, special assistant for Negro Affairs in the War Department, had joined the chorus of protests against the exclusion of black women nurses from service in the Nurse Corps. Moton and Scott informed the secretary of war and the surgeon general of the widespread dissatisfaction of African Americans with the war effort, emphasizing that they were particularly disillusioned with the American Red Cross. Moton wrote, "The Red Cross's exclusion of colored nurses . . . results in a certain sort of indifference on the part of colored people which ought not to be when the country needs every ounce of effort along every available line." In the face of the war emergency, some African Americans had accommodated themselves to the exclusion and segregation practiced by the U.S. War Department, convinced that it was temporarily important to do so given the worldwide threat to democracy. The discrimination practiced by the Red Cross was a different matter, however, because that institution symbolized humanitarianism in its most pure form. Black nurses especially believed that the Red Cross had not vigorously pushed for their entry into the Nurse Corps and had failed to uphold its democratic principles.

The intransigence of the Nurse Corps and the inertia of the Red Cross had motivated some black nurse leaders and liberal white allies to take matters into their own hands. In a fashion reminiscent of Booker T. Washington's emphasis on racial solidarity and self-help, an interracial group of some of New York City's most prominent, wealthy, and influential citizens met on 2 November 1917, to launch the black or, more precisely, the interracial counterpart of the American Red Cross. The new organization, incorporated as the Circle for Negro War Relief, was structured similarly to the Red Cross. Officers of the Circle were Emilie Bigelow Hapgood, president; George Foster Peabody, treasurer; and Grace Neil (Mrs. James Weldon) Johnson, secretary. The vice presidents were former governor Charles S. Whitman, W. E. B. Du Bois, Robert R. Moton, Charles Young, and Ray Stannard Baker. Other members of the board of directors included Gertrude Pinchot, Arthur B. Spingarn, Edward Sheldon, R. J. Coady, and Russell Janney.

The primary objectives of the Circle included the promotion of the interests and improvement in the conditions of black soldiers and sailors at home and abroad. Beyond this, Circle members pledged to aid those people related to or dependent upon black servicemen. Within two years, the Circle had fifty-three local chapters in seventeen states and boasted a membership of more than three thousand. Circle committees on the local levels initiated many activities designed to help black servicemen and their families. Committee members sewed, knitted, baked, and collected supplies to send to servicemen via channels established by the American Red Cross. This sharing of Red Cross information and a transfer network was the extent of the cooperation between the Circle and the Red Cross throughout the war years. The Circle also raised money for black soldiers who returned from the war penniless and for those discharged from hospitals without money. In such cases, government funds were, more often than not, both late and inadequate.

The successful execution of all Circle work depended largely on Blue Circle nurses. Through arrangements similar to those of Red Cross nurses, Blue Circle nurses provided relief to needy black families. Furthermore, they instructed many poor rural African Americans on the importance of sanitation, proper diet, and adequate clothing. The nurses also maintained necessary contact with city, county, and state health officials, often alerting them to serious community health problems.

After the war ended, the board of directors voted to continue a revised program of the Circle's work. On 19 May 1919, the board changed the name of the organization to the Circle for Negro Relief, dropping "War" from its title. Circle leaders then turned their attention to seeking funds and developing a new peacetime program. In an effort to raise money, Circle leaders submitted grant proposals to the heads of the major white philanthropic foundations, but with discouraging results. Edwin Embree of the Rockefeller Foundation assured the Circle of the foundation's sympathy and commitment to improving the health of black people but denied its request for funds. In a private memorandum, Embree observed that as far as he could determine, most of the Circle's meager resources were used to cover overhead expenses. More important, however, he maintained that it was against the Rockefeller Foundation's policy to contribute to private voluntary health agencies.

Circle leaders thus drafted a new program, this time with more success. They attempted to construct a national plan that included raising scholarship funds to train and pay part of the salaries of black visiting Circle nurses in southern communities. Their new peacetime program also called for the creation of day nurseries and kindergartens and for providing financial assistance to small community hospitals. Under the new Circle program, each local Circle committee was instructed to organize a County Health Club and to appeal to its respective county Board of Health for financial support to pay half of the salary of a Blue Circle public health nurse. Will W. Alexander of the Commission on Interracial Cooperation in Atlanta attested to the feasibility of the county health plan in a wire to Circle headquarters on 15 January 1921. He enthusiastically claimed that the Board of Health of South Carolina was "greatly interested" in public health nursing for African Americans and would look upon the Circle's plan with favor. Circle leaders justified their plan by noting that the white nursing services such as the Red Cross devoted little attention and meager resources to addressing the health needs of African Americans, especially in the South. They argued that the new Circle plan would improve general black health care, help the families of poor black servicemen, and provide more employment for black women nurses. The Circle for Negro Relief continued throughout the 1920s until the Great Depression.

Black women nurses had looked to the war crisis and the peacetime need for trained nurses to allow them a chance to serve their country, demonstrate their usefulness and value, and enhance their image in the American mind. But they soon discovered that not even a war could give them that stature. Although they were able to provide some service in the Circle, American racism emerged from World War I unscathed and more entrenched than ever. The integration of black women into the Army and Navy Nurse Corps would have to await another crisis: the coming of World War II.

Graduate Nurses

Although, with financial assistance from wealthy philanthropists, African Americans had, by 1928, fashioned an extensive nursing training school network, the process of becoming a respected member of the nursing profession involved more than the acquisition of basic training and a diploma. Access to specialized training or graduate education was of equal importance. Black women desiring to secure graduate education or specialized training, however, were consistently denied admission into many of the country's leading graduate nursing programs.

At every juncture in their quest for professional acceptance and advancement, black nurses encountered entrenched racist attitudes. Challenging career opportunities such as employment in hospitals, visiting nurse associations, and municipal departments of health proved to be as elusive as sympathetic work environments that held out possibilities for promotion to supervisory or administrative positions. In fact, the vast majority of black graduate nurses, like their untrained predecessors, worked in private-duty jobs, where they frequently were expected to perform domestic chores in addition to providing nursing care. When asked about the absence of black women in supervisory positions at her hospital, the white superintendent of nurses at the Lincoln Hospital in New York asserted that "colored" head nurses did not have the capacity to fill positions that entailed heavy responsibility and that discipline could not be maintained unless there was firm, competent white direction. As bleak as the situation was in the North, the advancement opportunities for black graduate nurses were even more limited in the South. Almost all black graduate nurses in the South worked for lower wages than their white colleagues.

Besides the injustice of unequal pay, black women graduate nurses considered the denial of membership in the American Nurses' Association the most visible and demeaning manifestation of professional ostracism. Barred from membership in local and state ANA affiliates, the majority of black women nurses could not participate in the largest professional association of nurses. The only significant number of black women in the ANA had become members when the Alumnae Association of the Freedmen's Hospital in Washington, DC, had merged with the ANA in 1911.

The ANA's exclusionary practices motivated Martha Franklin, a black graduate of the Women's Hospital in Philadelphia, to launch a separate black nursing organization. Beginning in 1906–1907, Franklin mailed over two thousand inquiries to black graduate nurses, superintendents of nursing schools, and nursing organizations to determine whether interest existed for a separate black society. Her letters struck a responsive chord among the members and leadership of the Lincoln Hospital nursing school. Adah Belle Thoms, president of the Lincoln School of Nursing Alumnae Association, arranged a meeting. In August 1908, fifty-two nurses convened at St. Mark's Episcopal Church in New York City to found the National Association of Colored Graduate Nurses (NACGN). In 1912, the NACGN members numbered 125, and by 1920 it boasted a membership of 500.

Under the leadership of two of its more forceful presidents, Adah B. Thoms (1915–1920) and Carrie E. Bullock (1927–1930), the NACGN accomplished much. It secured a temporary headquarters in 1918, which consisted of a room in New York City's Young Women's Christian Association's 137th Street Branch. In 1920, Thoms filed the NACGN incorporation papers and established a national registry of black graduate nurses to assist them in finding employment. Bullock, a 1909 graduate of the Provident Hospital School of Nursing, was supervisor of black nurses at the Chicago Visiting Nurses Association during her presidency. She focused on two key issues during her tenure. In 1928, to facilitate communication and to foster a greater sense of professional involvement among black

nurses, Bullock founded and edited the organization's official organ, the *National News Bulletin*. Second, to encourage black women nurses to pursue postgraduate education, Bullock secured the support of managers of the Julius Rosenwald Fund for the establishment of a Rosenwald fellowship program for black graduate nurses.

In spite of these accomplishments, problems remained. Salary inequities in hospitals and public health agencies persisted; the multiplication of unaccredited black hospital nurse training schools that grossly exploited their students and produced poorly trained nurses continued; and white nurses remained unresponsive to the entreaties of black women for recognition and acceptance within the nursing profession. Under the auspices of the Hospital Library and Service Bureau, Donelda Hamlin, in 1925, conducted a survey of state board of health officials and visiting nurse association heads to determine their evaluation and perceptions of black women public health nurses. In her subsequent report, Hamlin emphasized, as representative of the overall response, the comments of the superintendent of the Public Health Nursing Association in the Louisville, Kentucky. The respondent reported that the type of training the average colored nurse received in the Louisville area was far inferior to white nurses' training and that the best training for colored nurses barely equated to the poorest training given to white nurses. The respondent added, "From another standpoint, their educational background is not so good. Therefore I think the type of service rendered would necessarily be of lower grade than under other circumstances."

In late 1925, the Rockefeller Foundation employed Ethel Johns to examine the status of black women in the nursing profession. Johns visited twenty-three hospitals and nurse training schools for black women during a four-month period. In Chicago, Johns interviewed the chief nurse of the city's health department, which employed ten black graduate nurses and 154 white nurses. She asserted that black nurses' "technique is inferior to that of the white nurses, they are not punctual, and are incapable of analyzing a social situation." She maintained that there was a marked tendency among them "to organize against authority" and "to engage in political intrigue." Not surprisingly, Johns ended her report on a discouraging if understated note. She wrote, "Negro nurses in every part of the country feel very keenly that they are debarred from qualifying themselves for leadership and it is true that most doors are closed to them."

Black graduate nurses and the NACGN made the opening of doors to their profession a top priority. It would take twenty years, the emergence of a cadre of resourceful black nurse leaders, and a world war crisis for them to break through the negative attitudinal barriers, gain entry into the ANA, and win acceptance as full members in the profession of nursing. In the mid-1930s the NACGN's situation improved when grants from the General Education Board of the Rockefeller Foundation and from the Julius Rosenwald Fund made it possible for the NACGN to employ Mabel K. Staupers as executive secretary and to move into permanent headquarters at Rockefeller Center in New York City, where all the major national nursing organizations had offices. Following a long and relentless struggle, Staupers and the NACGN president Estelle Massey Osborne succeeded in winning recognition and acceptance for black nurses.

Staupers's fight to eliminate quotas established by the U.S. Army Nurse Corps constitutes one of the finest periods in NACGN history. Although many black nurses volunteered their services during World War II, they were refused admittance into the navy, and the army allowed only a limited number to serve. In 1943, although the navy had notified Staupers that it had decided to place the induction of black nurses under consideration and the army had raised its quota of black nurses to 160, the situation had not greatly improved. In an effort to draw attention to the unfairness of quotas, Staupers requested a meeting with Eleanor Roosevelt. In November 1944, the First Lady and Staupers met, and Staupers described in detail black nurses' troubled relationship with the armed forces. In January 1945, when Norman T. Kirk announced the possibility of a draft to remedy a nursing shortage within the armed forces, Staupers made a well-publicized response, "If nurses are needed so desperately why isn't the Army using colored nurses?" Afterward she encouraged nursing groups of all races to write letters and send telegrams protesting the discrimination against black nurses in the Army and Navy Nurse Corps. The groundswell of public support for the removal of quotas on the number of black nurses in the Nurse Corps proved effective.

Buried beneath an avalanche of telegrams from an inflamed public, Kirk, Rear Admiral W. J. C. Agnew, and the War Department declared an end to quotas and exclusion. On 20 January 1945, Kirk stated that nurses would be accepted into the Army Nurse Corps without regard to race, and five days later Agnew announced that the Navy Nurse Corps was open to black women. Within a few weeks, Phyllis Daley became the first black woman to break the color barrier and receive induction into the corps.

The end of discriminatory practices by a key American institution helped to erode entrenched beliefs about the alleged inferiority of black health care professionals and paved the way for the integration of the American Nurses'

Association. In 1948, the ANA opened the gates to black membership, appointed a black nurse as assistant executive secretary in its national headquarters, and elected Estelle Osborne to the board of directors. The decision to grant individual memberships to black nurses barred from state associations in Georgia, Louisiana, South Carolina, Texas, Virginia, Arkansas, Alabama, and the District of Columbia was followed by the adoption of a resolution to establish biracial committees in district and state associations to implement educational programs and promote development of harmonious intergroup relations.

With the removal of the overtly discriminatory barriers to membership in the ANA, members of the NACGN recognized that their needs would now be served by the ANA, which agreed to take over the functions of the NACGN and to continue to award the Mary Mahoney Medal honoring individuals for their contributions to interracial understanding. Thus, during the NACGN's 1949 convention, the members voted the organization out of existence, and the following year, Staupers, then president, presided over its formal dissolution.

See also Health; Staupers, Mabel Keaton; World War I; *and* World War II.

BIBLIOGRAPHY

Bullough, Bonnie, and Vern L. Bullough. *The Emergence of Modern Nursing* (1964). New York: Macmillan, 1978.

Du Bois, W. E. B. *The Autobiography of W. E. B. Du Bois*. New York: International Publishers, 1968.

Elmore, Joyce Ann. "Black Nurses: Their Service and Their Struggle." *American Journal of Nursing*, March 1936.

Flikke, Julia O. *Nurses in Action: The Story of the Army Nurse Corps*. Philadelphia, New York: Lippincott, 1943.

Franklin, John Hope. *From Slavery to Freedom* (1947). Boston: McGraw-Hill, 2000.

Hine, Darlene Clark. *Black Women in White: Racial Conflict and Cooperation in the Nursing Profession, 1890–1950*. Bloomington: Indiana University Press, 1989.

Staupers, Mabel Keaton. *No Time for Prejudice: A Story of the Integration of Negroes in Nursing in the United States*. New York: Macmillan, 1961.

Staupers, Mabel Keaton. "Story of the National Association of Colored Graduate Nurses." *American Journal of Nursing*, April 1961.

Thoms, Adah B. *Pathfinders: A History of the Progress of Colored Graduate Nurses*. New York: Garland, 1929.

Wilkins, Roy. "Nurses Go to War." *Crisis*, February 1943.

ARCHIVAL SOURCES

The American Red Cross Papers are in the National Archives, Washington, DC; Rockefeller Foundation Papers, Rockefeller Archive and Research Center, Pocantico Hills, New York; Arthur B. Spingarn papers, Manuscript Division, Library of Congress, Washington, DC.

—DARLENE CLARK HINE

O

OBERLIN COLLEGE. Founded in 1833 in Oberlin, Ohio, on the principle of educating Americans regardless of race, gender, or class, Oberlin College was one of the few institutions of higher learning that extended educational opportunities to black women. African American women faced discrimination on two fronts. Not only were they forced to battle sexist assumptions, but also racist ones. Traditionally, women were thought incapable of withstanding the rigors of competing academically with men. Blacks were considered inherently mentally inferior. Many whites thought the education of blacks, especially women, was folly at best and dangerous at worst.

Backed financially by abolitionists, Oberlin became an outpost in the nineteenth century for African Americans wishing to pursue a higher education. White students committed to abolition pressured the school to admit African American students in 1835. As a coeducational institution, Oberlin College presented African American women the opportunity to obtain a college education. Initially, there was a great deal of resistance from white trustees. It was feared the school would become a den of miscegenation, with African American men dating white women and African American women seducing white men. However, the promise of donations from wealthy abolitionists persuaded the school to proceed with its integration plan.

Oberlin's educational philosophy was to grant access to African American applicants who met the same qualifications required of whites. To gain admittance, one had to possess the requisite academic training, Christian moral character, and financial wherewithal to pay tuition. Rooted in an abolitionist ideology, the mission of the school was not necessarily to educate African Americans, but instead to prove that blacks were intellectually the equals of whites. Therefore, little financial aid was offered to students and academic standards were strictly enforced.

Throughout the country, African Americans faced circumscribed educational opportunities. In the South, educating African Americans was illegal, while in the North common schools were scarce. Enrolling in college would therefore require a good deal of remedial preparation. Prior to the Civil War, 141 African American women

attended Oberlin College. Many of them enrolled in the school's Preparatory Department. Sarah Watson, the first African American woman to register at Oberlin, enrolled in the Preparatory Department for one year from 1842 to 1843.

Though the doors of higher education were open, not many were qualified to enter. Because of the admission requirements, Oberlin admitted African Americans of a similar background to both the Preparatory Department and college. With few exceptions, nearly all students were born free, their parents having claimed freedom a generation earlier. Most of the students came from a privileged background. Parents were artisans such as barbers, carpenters, or brick masons. Additionally, anecdotal evidence suggests that many young ladies were mulattoes. The mixed heritage of some students created an ironic twist of events. White southern planters paid for their African American daughters to attend a school openly supporting the cause of abolition.

During the antebellum period, one hundred African American students, male and female, matriculated through Oberlin's collegiate curriculum. Of that group, thirty-two graduated with college degrees. Fifteen of those were women. A vast majority of the antebellum women pursued what was known as the Ladies Course. Although committed to coeducation, Oberlin clung to misperceptions of women's mental acuity. Essentially, the Ladies Course was a bachelor's degree devoid of the institution's more rigorous coursework, focusing instead on religion, morality, and ethics. Lucy Stanton Day, who completed the Ladies Course in 1850, was the first African American woman to attain a degree in higher education from Oberlin. Twelve years later, Mary Jane Patterson became the first African American to graduate from Oberlin with a bachelor's degree.

Oberlin's social climate during the antebellum period and Reconstruction was a reflection of its abolitionist foundation. However, by the late nineteenth century, it would more closely reflect America's hardening conceptions of race relations. Fanny Jackson Coppin graduated from Oberlin in 1865. Progressive racial attitudes afforded Coppin the chance to teach white students in the Preparatory Department. Mary Church Terrell, a student

OBERLIN COLLEGE, women graduates of 1855. Ann Hazle is third from left in the middle row. (Oberlin College Archives.)

at Oberlin in the 1880s, recalls the campus as an oasis in the racially charged America of the nineteenth century. White women hoping to prove their liberal credentials jockeyed to sit next to her in the dining hall. Throughout her college experience, she recalled being treated as an equal to any white student.

By the late nineteenth century, Oberlin's abolitionist heritage was being slowly replaced with America's new racial doctrine—Jim Crow. Beginning in the 1880s, white women refused to dine with African American women. Admonishments from the administration, encouraging equitable treatment for African American students, did little to curb the segregationist tide. Literary societies

banned African American women from joining. Campus housing enforced restrictions limiting the number of African Americans residing in dormitories. When Terrell returned in the early twentieth century to enroll her daughter at Oberlin, she was dismayed to find the school had abandoned its progressive legacy.

Despite the degrading and debilitating effects of segregation, African American women refused to bow to racist policies. They rejected a plan to build a separate dormitory for them and protested a segregated local bowling alley. They championed the Scottsboro Boys and supported an antilynching campaign. As the country entered the era of the civil rights movement, the school evolved with the times. An egalitarian atmosphere replaced the vestiges of Jim Crow.

For much of the nineteenth and early twentieth century, African American enrollment at Oberlin never exceeded 5 percent. Yet the school's impact was immense. The vast majority of the women educated at the school

Lawson, Ellen N., and Marlene Merrill. "The Antebellum 'Talented Thousandth'—Black College Students at Oberlin Before the Civil War." *Journal of Negro Education* 52 (Spring 1983): 142–155.

Waite, Cally. "The Segregation of Black Students at Oberlin College after Reconstruction." *History of Education Quarterly* 41:3 (2001): 344–364.

—BARRY F. MALONE

FANNY JACKSON COPPIN (1837–1913), who graduated from Oberlin in 1865 and went on to a distinguished career as an educator. (Oberlin College Archives.)

became teachers. They left Oberlin with a zealous belief in the power of education to liberate and uplift the race. Their very accomplishment proved that blacks were intellectually astute. Additionally, a ripple effect occurred that ultimately created an African American middle class. These teachers molded young minds, challenging them to become teachers, doctors, lawyers, and military officers. As a result, Oberlin College directly and indirectly supplied America with many future generations of black professionals and scholars.

BIBLIOGRAPHY

Bigglestone, William. "Oberlin College and the Negro Student." *Journal of Negro Education* 56 (July 1971): 198–219.

Diepenbrock, David. "Black Women and Oberlin College in the Age of Jim Crow." *UCLA Historical Journal* 13 (1993): 27–59.

Fletcher, Juanita D. "Against the Consensus: Oberlin College and the Education of American Negroes, 1835–1865." PhD diss., American University, 1974.

Horton, James Oliver. "Black Education at Oberlin College: A Controversial Commitment." *Journal of Negro Education* 54:4 (1985): 477–499.

ODETTA (b. 31 December 1930), American folk and blues singer. Odetta was a forerunner of the folk revival movement that began in the late 1950s. Her enormous and powerful voice—in a class with those of Bessie Smith and Mahalia Jackson—her deeply felt interpretations of carefully chosen material, her distinctive guitar accompaniments, and her commitment to social justice exerted a powerful influence on upcoming generations of singers from that day to this.

Odetta Holmes was born in Birmingham, Alabama. Her father, Reuben Holmes, was a steelworker, and her mother, Flora (Sanders) Holmes, worked as a domestic. Her father died shortly after her birth, and her mother married Zadock Felious. When she was six, the Felious family, including Odetta and her stepbrother and stepsister, moved to Los Angeles.

Odetta's earliest explorations of music took the form of picking out tunes on the piano in her grandmother's house. In junior high school she joined the glee club and took voice lessons. She graduated from Belmont High School in 1947 with an academic record that earned her the Bank of America's high school achievement award.

After high school Odetta worked as a housekeeper by day and studied classical music at Los Angeles City College at night. In 1949 she joined the chorus of a local production of *Finian's Rainbow*. In 1950 a summer stock production of *Guys and Dolls* took her to San Francisco. It was there that folk music first attracted her interest, during a song-swapping session at a party in the city's bohemian North Beach District. She was especially taken with prison work songs, with their depictions of blatant racism. In them she found a release for the frustration, fury, and hatred felt by a black woman coming of age in a Jim Crow society. After that party, Odetta borrowed a guitar, learned three chords, and started to sing at parties.

Within a few years she was appearing at small folk music clubs. She auditioned for a job at the hungry i club in San Francisco and was hired after just one song, but objections from the featured artist caused that offer to be withdrawn. Soon afterward she began a year-long engagement at the Tin Angel, which established her reputation as a singer of work songs, spirituals, and the blues. Her next job was at the Blue Angel in New York, which brought her to the attention of prominent folk singers, including Harry Belafonte and Pete Seeger.

ODETTA, photographed in 1964. Her artistry has expressed the soul of the folk revival movement. (Library of Congress.)

A two-year run at the Turnabout Theatre in Los Angeles and a hit appearance at Chicago's Gate of Horn were followed by the recording of her first two albums for the Tradition Label: *Odetta Sings Ballads and Blues* (1956) and *Odetta at the Gate of Horn* (1957).

One of the first African American women to appear as a public figure without straightening her hair, she presented a striking appearance that accentuated her distinctive musical presence. Unlike some folk traditionalists who went to great lengths to re-create original performance conditions, Odetta strove to present the songs she treasured in a way that made them her own. This personal touch, combined with guitar accompaniments designed to support and complement her voice, lent her interpretations an air of authenticity that characterized her work and transcended the cultural and historical gap between the original songwriters and the contemporary singer.

Through her concerts, recordings, and tours of the United States and Canada—and later the world—Odetta carried the seeds of the folk music revival wherever she or her music went. She was one of the foremost interpreters of the songs of Huddie Ledbetter ("Leadbelly"), and her recordings and performances of his songs kept them in the public eye in the years following his death. Bob

Dylan, Janis Joplin, and Joan Baez all credited Odetta as an inspiration, and her influence can be heard in the more recent works of Joan Armatrading, Tracy Chapman, and Nanci Griffith.

Odetta became a familiar figure in the civil rights movement, singing for 250,000 people at the March on Washington in 1963 and taking part in the March on Selma, Alabama, in 1965. She sang for President John F. Kennedy on the civil rights television program "Dinner with the President."

Odetta has continued to tour, record, and perform into the early twenty-first century, releasing *Blues Everywhere I Go* in 1999 and *Lookin' for a Home*, a collection of Leadbelly songs, in 2001. Those albums displayed a voice that had aged but retained the power and intensity that it first revealed nearly fifty years ago.

BIBLIOGRAPHY

Boehm, Mike. "Dylan to Chapman, They All Owe Odetta." *Los Angeles Times*, 20 June 1991.

Edgers, Geoff. "Working toward Righteousness: Odetta, Queen of '60s Folk Is Still Singing with Hope." *Boston Globe*, 6 December 2002.

Moritz, Charles, ed. *Current Biography Yearbook 1960*. New York: H. W. Wilson, 1960.

Stambler, Irwin, and Lyndon Stambler. *Folk and Blues: The Encyclopedia*. New York: Thomas Dunne, 2001.

Taylor, Lewis. "Odetta's Music Touches Many Genres." *Eugene* (Oregon) *Register-Guard*, 13 December 2002.

Thompson, M. Dion. "The Magic's in Her Music". *Baltimore Sun*, 8 January 1998.

—ROBERT W. LOGAN

O'LEARY, HAZEL R. (b. 17 May 1937), former secretary of energy. In one unprecedented moment, President Bill Clinton altered the face of the United States government. He named four African Americans to his cabinet—Hazel O'Leary, Ronald Brown, Jesse Brown, and Alphonso Michael Espy. This was the first time in U.S. history that four African Americans had served in a presidential cabinet. Furthermore, Hazel O'Leary became the first woman to serve as secretary of energy. Clinton appointed O'Leary to the problem-plagued Department of Energy based on her twenty years of experience in both the private and public sectors of fuel and energy industries. In control of an $18 billion budget, O'Leary soon emerged as one of the most influential and powerful women in not only Washington, DC, but throughout the world.

Hazel Rollins Reid was born to two physicians. The couple divorced when Hazel was eighteen months old and the responsibility of her upbringing fell upon her father, Russell E. Reid, and stepmother, Hazel (Mattie) Palleman Reid, who raised Hazel and her older sister, Edna Reid McCollum, in the segregated community of

HAZEL O'LEARY, the first woman and the first African American to hold the office of secretary of energy. (U.S. Department of Energy.)

Newport News, Virginia. Hazel and Edna lived a sheltered youth, with their father driving them everywhere and providing all of the material advantages that were allowed in a segregated town. Although the Reid girls had many middle-class advantages, they still faced the brutal ugliness of discrimination. Because of this reality, their family repeatedly stressed the importance of inclusion and helping others.

Lessons at School and Home

O'Leary's life-defining moral lessons occurred in school as well as in her own home. O'Leary described how her grandmother kept various boxes of different-sized clothes on the porch year round to help families in need. O'Leary stated, "So I grew up in a family and an environment where opening doors for others and literally opening your front door to others was not only expected but was a practice." O'Leary's grandmother organized and established the first African American library in Newport News, Virginia.

The Reid girls attended public schools in Newport News for eight years. Hoping for a better life, their parents decided to send their daughters north to Essex County, New Jersey. While living with their aunt, the girls attended integrated Arts High School for artistically gifted youth. Along with her regular course of study, O'Leary also displayed her musical talent by studying voice and the alto horn. In 1959 O'Leary graduated cum laude and earned a BA degree from Fisk University in Nashville, Tennessee. In 1966 she received a JD degree from Rutgers University School of Law. In 1980 Fisk University's Phi Beta Kappa chapter elected O'Leary as an alumni member. To further honor her various achievements, Fisk University awarded her an honorary JD degree on 30 April 1994.

O'Leary has had wide and varied work experiences. Her first public service job was as the assistant prosecutor in Essex County, New Jersey, in 1967. She continued practicing law as the state's assistant attorney general before moving to Washington, DC, to become partner in the accounting firm of Coopers and Lybrand. Under the Ford administration, O'Leary served as general council to the Community Services Administration, which regulated many antipoverty programs that had been initiated during the Great Society of the 1960s. During this time, O'Leary acquired a reputation as an advocate for the poor. From 1974 to 1976 O'Leary served as the director of the Office of Consumer Affairs for the Federal Energy Administration (FEA). Her advocacy work and negotiation skills came to light as she competently balanced the demands of the wealthy and high-powered representatives of the energy industry and those citizens, including Native Americans, who were on the margins of society fighting over energy-producing land. In 1977 O'Leary was serving as the assistant administrator for conservation and environment for the FEA when it became part of the newly created Department of Energy (DOE) under the Carter administration.

At the Department of Energy from 1978 to 1980, O'Leary served as chief of the Economic Regulatory Administration. O'Leary supervised a staff of more than two thousand that was responsible for regulating price controls on energy sources and also directed the federal government programs for conservation and the environment. As the head of this organization, O'Leary received both praise for her innovative conservation programs—including underwriting the cost of insulating homes of lower-income families—and criticism for the Fuel Use Act, which critics argued encouraged the use of cleaner natural gas to the exclusion of the energy-industry-friendly power sources of coal, oil, and nuclear fuel.

O'Leary left the DOE to start an international energy, economics, and strategic planning firm in Washington, DC, with her husband, John E. O'Leary. Hazel O'Leary served as general counsel and vice president from 1981 to 1989. Soon, the O'Learys became respected voices and in demand as domestic and international consultants, attributable in part to the chaotic shifts in energy policies. In 1989, two years after John O'Leary's death, Hazel O'Leary dissolved the firm and joined Northern States Power Company in Minneapolis, one of the largest energy utilities in the Midwest. As executive vice president for environmental and public affairs and as vice president for human resources, O'Leary successfully helped develop Northern States Power Company into a leading and progressive utilities company. However, O'Leary's handling of radioactive fuel near a Shakopee Mdewakanton Sioux reservation brought questions and critiques from concerned environmentalists. Despite the highly charged atmosphere of energy policies, O'Leary employed her keen intellect, fairness, and honesty to deal with tenuous issues such as the safe disposal of atomic waste and conservation.

New Direction for Department

O'Leary's extensive work experiences paved the way for President Bill Clinton's nomination of her as secretary of energy in 1993. O'Leary undertook the immense problems of the Department of Energy by forging a new direction for the department. O'Leary implemented Clinton's new mandates, with innovative and creative solutions gleaned from her past experiences. These mandates included the safe cleanup and disposal of years of nuclear waste generated during the Cold War, transformation of U.S. reliance on oil and coal, exploration of all alternative energy sources and technologies, and the creation of new jobs in the environment sector. While giving the president's mandates for the Department of Energy top priority, O'Leary also identified lack of diversity and overwhelming silences and secrets as two key problems within the department. O'Leary's first order of business was to create diversity at all levels of the Department of Energy that represented a cross section of the U.S. population. In addition, upon learning of human radiation tests in the 1940s and 1950s, O'Leary began to declassify documents and accept responsibility for the DOE's past actions. In creating a culture of openness, O'Leary also met with whistle-blowers in attempts to learn from past mistakes and change the DOE from within. O'Leary resigned from her post in 1997.

Throughout her career, O'Leary has been active in numerous organizations and committees. She also works with the Colorado-based think tank, the Keystone Center, and is active with various black organizations that promote education and the sciences.

O'Leary has been married three times. The first marriage was to a physician, Carl Rollins. This union produced O'Leary's only child, Carl G. Rollins III, who is now a practicing attorney in Washington, DC. She was briefly married to the late news anchor Max Robinson. She married John E. O'Leary in 1980. He was a former deputy energy assistant in the Carter administration and her partner in their international energy consulting firm, O'Leary Associates, Inc.

Throughout her life, Hazel O'Leary has stayed true to her firm moral commitments of diversity and inclusion. Despite controversy and criticism, she won the support of many who questioned her commitment to the environment. O'Leary earned this respect by making difficult political decisions based on her own practical experience and knowledge and on her firm convictions. As the first woman and African American to hold the office of secretary of energy, O'Leary demonstrated not only her skillful ability as an administrator but also her compassion and concern for the welfare of all citizens.

BIBLIOGRAPHY

African American Biography. Vol. 3. Detroit: UXL, 1994.

"Black Clout in the Clinton Administration." *Ebony*, May 1993, 60–64.

Elliott, Joan C. "Hazel O'Leary." In *Notable Black American Women*, edited by Jessie Carney Smith. Detroit: Gale, 1996.

Haywood, Richette L. "Secretary Hazel O'Leary: Bright, Charming, Tough." *Ebony*, February 1995, 94–100.

Rosen, Isaac. "Hazel O'Leary." In *Contemporary Black Biography: Profiles from the International Black Community*, edited by Barbara Carlisle Bigelow, vol. 6. Detroit: Gale, 1994.

Thompson, Garland L. "Four Black Cabinet Secretaries: Will It Make the Difference?" *Crisis: A Record of the Darker Races*, March 1993, 17–18.

Wald, Matthew L. "Interview with Sec. Hazel O'Leary." *New York Times*, 20 January 1997.

—ANNE M. HEUTSCHE

OLYMPIC GAMES AND AMATEUR SPORTS, PARTICIPATION IN.

The history of black women's participation in the modern Olympics is one of struggle and discrimination. The founders of the modern Olympics in 1896 had no intention of women—white or black—being full participants in the games. Following societal norms at the time, a woman's role was to be supportive of men, not to compete alongside them.

White Women's Participation in the Olympic Games

The first Olympics in 1896 had no women competitors, even though one woman, Melpomene, tried to enter the marathon. She was refused but ran unofficially and finished the last lap outside the stadium by herself. The 1900 Olympics had nineteen women participants in three events—golf, lawn tennis, and croquet. Margaret Abbott became the first woman to win an Olympic gold medal when she won the golf competition. An art student in Paris, Abbott won with a score of forty-seven over nine holes.

BARBARA JONES won an Olympic gold medal at age fifteen, in the games of 1952 at Helsinki. She was on a relay team led by Mae Faggs. (Courtesy of Tennessee State University.)

In 1904, at the third Olympic Games, women were allowed to compete in archery. By 1908 the number of female athletes increased to 36, compared to 1,999 male competitors. Madge Syers became the first woman figure skater to win the gold medal in the 1908 games. Two additional sports, swimming and diving, became Olympic events in 1912, and 57 women from 11 nations competed.

In a move that set back the efforts of American sportswomen, the United States Olympic Committee voted in 1914 to formally oppose women's athletic participation in the Olympic Games. The floor exercise portion of the gymnastics competition was the only exception, and women were required to wear long skirts. At the same time, the Amateur Athletic Union (AAU), in contrast to the United States Olympic Committee, sponsored its first swimming championships and allowed women to register and compete.

The 1916 Olympics were cancelled due to World War I. At that time, no African Americans—male or female—had ever competed in the Olympic Games. It would take societal change to open the doors for blacks—especially black women—to compete in sports at the highest levels.

During the war, the United States government found that too many American soldiers were not physically fit. To address the issue, the government began to sponsor sports programs for the general population and created organizations such as the National Amateur Athletic Foundation (NAAF). The NAAF established various divisions with different missions for men and women. The Women's Division emphasized fitness while denouncing competition for women. With more and more women interested in fitness, facilities intended for women's use were needed. To meet that need, the Young Women's Christian Association (YWCA) emerged to establish facilities for women across the United States in public parks and schools.

Black Women's Participation in the Olympic Games

Despite disparities in Olympic competition caused by World War I and the U.S. ban on female participation, women's events were added to the 1920 Olympics, and American women gained full status. However, it was not until the 1924 Olympics that African American men went to the games. The first African American women did not compete until 1932. Tidye Pickett and Louise Stokes were the first African American women to qualify for the United States Olympic team. While they qualified as members of the 400-meter relay team, they were replaced in the race with white runners whom they had beaten in previous competition. Undaunted, Pickett qualified again in 1936 but was once again replaced in the race by a white woman.

In the early decades of the twentieth century, black women were able to make their greatest progress in track and field due to support from the Amateur Athletic Union and black colleges such as Tuskegee Institute and Tennessee State University. Major Cleveland Abbott was the coach of Tuskegee's program and the primary reason for its success. He provided training for black women athletes at the collegiate level that was unique for the time. Abbott did not subscribe to the notion that women were the "weaker sex"; instead he believed that women should be physically active. Major Abbot's daughter Jessie left Tuskegee and became the track coach at Tennessee State. Using her father's ideas, she turned the Tigerbelles into one of the most successful programs ever.

In 1939 Alice Coachman (who was trained at Tuskegee) won the first of her ten national high jump titles. In 1946 she became the first African American woman to become a member of the United States All-American Track and Field Team. By 1948 nine of the twelve members of the women's Olympic track team were black. As a member of that team, Coachman became the first African American female to win an Olympic medal and the first to win an Olympic gold medal when she won the high jump.

Additionally, Audrey Patterson (who trained at Tennessee State) won a bronze medal in the 200 meters. Though segregation was still an instrumental part of American society, President Harry Truman invited Coachman to the White House when the games were over. In 1956, Nell Jackson, a 1948 Olympian, became the first woman and first African American woman to be named an Olympic track and field coach.

After the 1948 and 1952 Olympics, in which African American women showcased their skills, determination, and grace, female African American athletes began to set new standards of excellence within amateur sports. Wilma Rudolph first participated in the 1956 Olympics. However, it was not until the 1960 games that she attained legendary status by becoming the first American woman to win three gold medals in a single Olympics. Earlene Brown, Mae Faggs, Willye White, and Mildred McDaniel also earned Olympic fame with medal performances that year. In 1961 Rudolph received the Amateur Athletic Union's James Sullivan Award as the most outstanding amateur athlete in the United States.

At the 1964 Tokyo and 1968 Mexico City Olympics, Wyomia Tyus and Willye White excelled in track and field. White became the first American woman to compete on five Olympic track and field teams. She was also a member of thirty-nine international teams and held the American record in the long jump for sixteen years. Tyus left her mark on the Tokyo and Mexico City Games when she became the first woman to win two consecutive Olympic gold medals in the 100-meter dash.

In the years following Mexico City, black women athletes continued to compete in—and succeed in—the Olympic Games. Track and field continued to draw top athletes, including such standouts as Evelyn Ashford, Jackie Joyner-Kersee, Gail Devers, and Marian Jones. However, black women also established themselves in other Olympic sports. Women such as Cheryl Miller and Cynthia Cooper, Ruthie Bolton, Brianna Scurry, and Venus and Serena Williams won Olympic medals in their sports.

Title IX's Impact

Participation expanded greatly over the last three decades of the twentieth century for black women—and women in general—due to Title IX, federal legislation that required equal opportunity for women at the high school, collegiate, and Olympic levels. Congress passed Title IX as a part of the Education Amendments of 1972. This legislation stated that, "No person in the United States, shall on the basis of sex, be excluded from participation in, be denied the benefits of, or be subject to discrimination under any education program or activities receiving federal financial assistance."

When President Richard Nixon signed the act, 31,000 women were involved in collegiate sports; spending for athletic scholarships was less than $100 thousand, and the average number of sports offered by colleges for women was 2.1. There were a total of 817,073 girls participating in high school sports. The landmark legislation, combined with Billie Jean King's win over Bobby Riggs in the widely viewed "Battle of the Sexes" tennis match in 1973, connected women's sports to the women's rights movement. The two historic events led to more women demanding equal opportunity, equal treatment, and equal pay in the sports world.

The 1980s saw tremendous growth in the total number of girls and women participating in all levels of sport. By 1999, 7.5 million girls were playing soccer in the United States. Not surprisingly, the 2000 Olympics added sixteen women's sports and had the highest number of female participants ever. In fact, women composed 42 percent of the total competitors at the Sydney Summer Games in 2000 and 50 percent at the Salt Lake City Winter Games in 2002. In Sydney, women competed in the same number of team sports as men for the first time in Olympic history. By 2001, there were 2,784,154 girls participating in high school sports, while college participation grew to 150,916.

Title IX unequivocally increased opportunities for black girls and women. The increased number of athletic grants-in-aid (athletic scholarships) awarded to women also allowed more to attend college and reach their academic and athletic potential. Title IX created these new opportunities; unless the law is diminished by congressional or presidential action, the number of black women taking advantage of those opportunities will continue to increase.

See also **Sports** *and* **Track and Field.**

BIBLIOGRAPHY

Ashe, Arthur R., Jr. *A Hard Road to Glory: A History of the African-American Athlete, 1919–1945.* New York: Warner Books, 1988.

Ashe, Arthur R., Jr. *A Hard Road to Glory: A History of the African-American Athlete, 1946–1986.* New York: Warner Books, 1988.

Page, James A. *Black Olympian Medalists.* Englewood, CO: Libraries Unlimited, 1991.

Porter, David L. ed. *African-American Sports Greats: A Biographical Dictionary.* Westport, CT: Greenwood Press, 1995.

—PAM GILL-FISHER

OPERA. *See* **Concert Music.**

ORAL HISTORIES. An essential tool for researchers and historians, oral histories are powerful instruments that preserve the past and give voice to marginalized groups, among them African American women. As a methodological process, oral history transcends academic disciplines and constitutes a multifaceted approach not only to preserving an individual's spoken recollections but also to providing an enduring and lively memory of the past. While written records have traditionally afforded only the most educated and affluent an opportunity to shape their own histories, the uneducated and the poor are often denied that chance. Oral records reshape and redefine the methodological approach, blurring class lines and equalizing the contributions and influences of even the most marginalized.

Preserving Voices

Black women's voices are an indispensable element in the narratives of the Federal Writers' Oral History Project—created under the auspices of the Depression-era Works Progress Administration—and Radcliffe Institute's Schlesinger Library's Black Women Oral History Project. Slave Narratives include the life histories of former slaves that capture their recollected experiences. As historical documents, they contribute dimension and texture as well as compelling stories of survival.

From 1936 to 1938, over 2,300 former female slaves from across the American South were interviewed under the auspices of the Works Progress Administration. These former slaves provided firsthand accounts of their experiences on plantations, small farms, and in urban areas. These oral accounts capture the very voice of American slavery, revealing the texture of life as it was experienced and remembered, tales of labor, flight, family life, relationships, and religion.

The scholarly use of these narratives has not, however, been without controversy. Some scholars find them unreliable sources while others like Stephanie J. Shaw argue that slave narratives should be seen as valuable, inasmuch as they preserve for posterity the life histories of thousands of ordinary people. These interviews with former slaves make it possible to reconstruct the multiple meanings and identities of southern ante- and postbellum history from the perspective of the slave. Shaw stipulates that although the "new" histories of slavery represented a breakthrough in African American, southern, and American history, historians have not agreed about how and whether to use the WPA slave narratives as source material. Indeed, some historians have called into question the process by which the interviews were collected, the competence and objectivity of the interviewers themselves, as well as the reliability of subjects of such advanced age, and the geographic distribution of the subject pool. However, Donna Spindel charges historians to embrace the richness of the narratives, arguing that their inherent value overshadows any weaknesses. Overall, slave narratives offer insights into the oral traditions of African American women and highlight the gendered and racialized constructs of black women's lives.

Spreading the Word

The Arthur and Elizabeth Schlesinger Library on the History of Women in America was founded in 1943 as the

BILL AND ELLEN THOMAS, former slaves, photographed on 22 May 1937 in Hondo, Texas. (Library of Congress.)

Women's Archives at Radcliffe College and has maintained a purpose of documenting women's lives and achievements. Long considered the country's foremost library of women's history, the Library's Black Women Oral History Project began by collecting memories of selected African American women aged seventy and over who had been important in their communities. Their oral histories speak candidly of growing up during the early years of the struggle for racial equality, prior to the civil rights movement. The respondents recalled their childhood religious experiences and educational and cultural opportunities. Many offered family genealogies, including stories passed from generation to generation about slave and Native American forebears. Several were social, political, and labor activists. They made substantial contributions to the improvement of their lives as well as the lives of others. From 1976 to 1981, seventy-two women from throughout the United States were interviewed. The women were born within fifteen years before or after 1900, and came from rural and urban areas representing a broad cross-section of the country. The respondent's educational levels ranged from little formal education to advanced college degrees. The women discussed topics such as childhood, significant life influences, the effect of skin color on life, their most important achievement, awards, and honors. These women were pioneers in business, social work, medicine, government, trade unions, athletics, and education. Their stories emphasized the effect of race and gender on their individual success and offered insights into the professional opportunities created by World War II for women and blacks. Also important were extensive discussions about organizations that broadened the public awareness of black culture, such as the YWCA, Urban League, NAACP, and the National Council for Negro Women. The Schlesinger Library holds the original tapes, transcripts, and photographs of the project. Complete sets of transcripts have been deposited at thirteen college and university libraries and oral history offices throughout the country. By 2004, sixty-eight of the seventy-two transcripts had been published in a ten-volume set, *The Black Women Oral History Project*.

African American women's oral history collections online further expanded and transformed research opportunities. Numerous manuscript sources, special collections, and online retrieval systems were housed at universities and other institutions across the United States. Available online, the Civil Rights Oral History interviews were one of the few civil rights oral history projects organized around the remembrances and memories of persons from a particular geographic locale. This collection of eight oral history interviews, conducted by Rebecca Nappi, was created in part by the Washington State University library in collaboration with the Spokane *Spokesman-Review*. This collection is both a regional study and a history of racial prejudice.

Another important research project was Beverly A. Bunch-Lyons's oral histories of African American women in Cincinnati, Ohio, which examines the migration of southern African American women to that midwestern city. Most poignant are the memories detailing the factors that pushed them out of the south and the opportunities that pulled them to the Midwest. As long as Jim Crow laws circumscribed their social, political, and economic lives in the South, most could only find employment as domestic servants. By contrast, the North was a geographic space where better-paying jobs and easier access to educational facilities awaited African American women and their families. Built of authentic accounts from the African American women who lived in these regions, oral histories provide a more vivid and didactic picture of life in the South and the North.

The Search for Work

Elizabeth Clark-Lewis's scholarship analyzes the black migration from the South to the North. Citing statistical data on African American female employment in the District of Columbia from 1900 to 1940, Clark-Lewis argues that the black female experience during the black migration was influenced by the narrow employment options open to black women. For many African American women living in the South, servant and domestic work in the homes of whites provided an alternative to the hard labor of the cotton fields. With the onset of the industrial era in the North, many African Americans opted to migrate to northern cities in hopes of a better life and more employment opportunities. Nonetheless, domestic service awaited African American women in the North as well. Clark-Lewis relies on more than one hundred oral interviews with African American women who left their homes and sharecropper existence in the rural South to live and work as domestic servants in Washington, DC, in a period when American society in general and the African American population in particular were undergoing a profound socioeconomic transformation.

The real strength of Clark-Lewis's work is its focus and reliance on the oral histories of elderly black working class women whom she calls the "pioneers of African American labor." Oral histories in this sense bring into sharp focus the often-neglected gender dimension of the Great Migration by explaining in vivid detail the factors involved in the migration from the rural South and revealing the implications the transition had not only for the economic autonomy of African American female domestic workers but also for their personal, political, social, and cultural growth as well. Clark-Lewis argues that the "new path of their work did raise their collective consciousness about the personal and social change and about their right to effect such change."

Oral histories focusing on African American women in the workplace augment the social history of the working class black woman—by focusing on workers, workplaces, racial and ethnic groups, social movements and communities. One oral history that provides such a rich array is Richard Halpern's and Roger Horowitz's 1999 case study of black packinghouse workers, *Meatpackers: An Oral History of Black Packinghouse Workers and Their Struggle for Racial and Economic Equality*. In the 1980s, Halpern and Horowitz interviewed members of the United Packinghouse Workers of America (UPWA), covering the years

Mary Crane, a former slave, photographed c. 1937–1938 in Mitchell, Indiana, when she was eighty-two years old. (Library of Congress.)

from the establishment of the union in the late 1930s to the closing of the major meatpacking centers in the 1960s. The authors focused on interviews most concerned with civil rights issues in the plant and the nearby communities of Chicago, Kansas City, Forth Worth, and Waterloo, Iowa. By the 1930s, black workers were an integral part of the meatpacking processes. Black workers recognized that a unified front was needed to change their working environment. The collection of their interviews includes stories told by African American women of their attempts to gain equality and the equal protection of the law both on the job and off. One central theme is the importance of activism, and how activism within the labor movement often paralleled activism within the broader struggle of African American women to achieve social justice. One such instance is Rowena Moore, an African American woman meatpacker from Omaha who catapulted to labor activism from her involvement within the city's African American women's clubs and the local chapter of the National Association for the Advancement of Colored People (NAACP). Moore became a symbol of her

African American sisters' calls for industrial equity and was a leader in their struggle to achieve both racial and gender fairness in the workplace.

The labor of black workers has been crucial to the economic development of America. Yet because of racism and segregation, their voices remain largely unknown. Michael Keith Honey's *Black Workers Remember: An Oral History of Segregation, Unionism, and the Freedom Struggle* tells the history of African American workers in their own words. It relates striking firsthand accounts of the experiences of black southerners living under segregation in Memphis, Tennessee. Eloquent and personal, these oral histories compose a unique primary source and a new way of understanding the black labor experience during the industrial era—underscoring the active role of black working people in history. They examine how black workers constructed their day-to-day struggle against racism and segregation. It also shows how black workers transferred the lessons of how they were treated on the job and in society at large to joining and organizing unions to improve working and overall economic conditions. Collectively, these oral histories are testaments to the struggles for dignity, respect, and basic civil and labor rights.

Oral narratives often function as a chronicle of the labor and employment patterns of black women. For example, the New York University Web site features an online link to historical documents concerning United States women and labor. These documents and oral histories by and about working women tell of their experiences and their activism. Racism and sexism determined African American women's status in the workforce. Subjected to different standards for production and wages, they were often the last hired and the first fired. Expected to work longer hours, black women were relegated to the most menial jobs and received the least pay. In spite of the hardship and because of the inequity, many found their activist voices by joining local labor unions. For instance, in the meatpacking industry, black women like Rowena Moore of Omaha, Nebraska, and Mary Salinas of Forth Worth, Texas, coordinated efforts with other women to defend themselves against unfair labor practices.

African American women who sought employment in professional fields had to endure the rigors and "chilly climate" of higher education. The University Archives of Virginia Tech has the Black Women at Virginia Tech Oral History Project. This project involves identification of the first black women students, staff, and faculty. The collection includes interviews with some of the first African American women students at Virginia Tech, among them Jacquelyn Butler Blackwell, Marguerite Harper Scott, and Linda Edmonds Turner; Marva Felder Davis, first African American homecoming queen; and Cheryl Butler McDonald, first African American woman in the Corps of Cadets. It includes oral history narratives and interviews that focus on their entry experience and their perceptions on race and gender for the African American woman's entrée to the academy. Included is the voice of Elaine Carter, founder of the project and, at the time, doctoral candidate. Nell Sigmon told a Southern Oral History Program interviewer in 1979 that, "you don't have to be famous for your life to be history." This profound statement of the extraordinary significance of ordinary lives has guided continuing efforts to seek out and record personal memories of past events.

The end of segregated education challenged and altered the professional lives of black teachers. Michele Foster in *Black Teachers on Teaching* conducted twenty "life history" interviews with black teachers between 1988 and 1996. *Black Teachers on Teaching* gives firsthand reactions to school integration and its results for teachers and students, as well as an overview of blacks in education over much of the twentieth century. For many of these teachers, integration was a failure, not only depriving black children of the dedicated instruction of black female teachers but also resulting in the firing or displacement of many black female teachers and school staff. Foster juxtaposes the voices, perspectives, values, and pedagogical insights of a group of excellent African American teachers from diverse communities across America. Lisa Delpit notes in the foreword that the teachers represented include those who have retired from the classroom, veteran teachers still practicing, and novice teachers. African American teachers' perspectives on difficult situations and circumstances in the teaching force depicted a struggle against racial oppression, and in the end the creation of a sense of connection between students and their communities. This intersection of oral histories, professional employment, and African American women in a specific place and time provides a context and a lens for viewing the past for African American women in America and their struggles for equality.

Education is not the only professional field in which African American women have overcome barriers. The University of Michigan Medical School Oral History Project highlights the hardships and successes of many black women in the health care industry. The project evokes the historical context of black female professional employment and connects that history to the ongoing struggle in health care. The life of Mary Eliza Mahoney, the first African American woman to receive a nursing school degree and to be certified as a registered nurse, is examined, as are the experiences of Adah Belle Samuel Thoms, who crusaded for equal opportunities for blacks in nursing. Thoms was among the first to recognize a new field of nursing, public health. The University of Michigan Medical School Oral History Project also emphasizes a regional state history by exploring the experiences of African American women and the long-term effects of segregated health care in southeast Michigan. Ellen S. More shares historical voices of African American female physicians in her 1999 work *Restoring the Balance: Women Physicians and the Profession of Medicine*. Another important book, *In Her Own Words: Oral Histories of Women Physicians* includes interviews with African American women physicians across America. In *Balm in Gilead: Journey of a Healer*, Sara Lawrence Lightfoot shares the life history of her mother, Margaret Morgan Lawrence, an African American woman pioneer in pediatric psychiatry. These represent only a few voices among many unknown voices in the realm of African American women and the health professions.

African American women have a long history of struggle and survival. To cope, they have developed, according to Cornel West, cultural spheres and structures of meaning and feeling that created and sustained communities. It is imperative that their stories of struggle, as well as their values of service, sacrifice, love, care, discipline, and excellence, be woven into the very fabric of American history. Active participation in the African American community's religious, social, and educational realm fostered almost total intimacy between African American women and their communities. Black women's narratives often demonstrate the myriad ways their lives are connected to their community's history. The oral tradition's influence before, during, and after slavery has been a powerful weapon of resistance. As a scholarly resource, oral narratives remove black women from the margins and place them at the center of the ongoing historical discourse.

BIBLIOGRAPHY

Bunch-Lyons, Beverly. "No Promised Land: Oral Histories of African-American Women in Cincinnati, Ohio." *OAH Magazine of History*, 11.3 (1997): 9–14.

Clark-Lewis, Elizabeth. *Living In, Living Out: African American Domestics in Washington, D.C., 1910–1940*. Washington, DC: Smithsonian, 1994.

Foster, Michele, ed. *Black Teachers on Teaching*. New York: New Press, 1997.

Gluck, Sherna, and Daphne Patai, eds. *Women's Words: The Feminist Practice of Oral History*. New York: Routledge, 1991.

Halpern, Richard, and Roger Horowitz. *Meatpackers: An Oral History of Black Packinghouse Workers and Their Struggle for Racial and Economic Equality*. New York: Monthly Review Press, 1999.

Hill, Ruth, ed. *The Black Women Oral History Project: From the Arthur and Elizabeth Schlesinger Library on the History of Women in America, Radcliffe College*. Westport, CT: Meckler, 1991.

Hill, Ruth, and Patricia King, eds. *The Black Women Oral History Project: A Guide to the Transcripts*. Cambridge, MA: Schlesinger Library on the History of Women in America, Radcliffe College, 1987.

Hine, Darlene Clark. *Black Women in the Nursing Profession: A Documentary History*. New York: Garland, 1985.

Hine, Darlene Clark. *The Black Women in the Middle West Project: A Comprehensive Resource Guide, Illinois and Indiana: Historical Essays, Oral Histories, Biographical Profiles, and Document Collections*. Indianapolis: Indiana Historical Bureau, 1986.

Hine, Darlene Clark. *Black Women in White: Racial Conflict and Cooperation in the Nursing Profession, 1890–1950*. Bloomington: Indiana University Press, 1989.

Hine, Darlene Clark, ed. *Black Women in America: An Historical Encyclopedia*. Brooklyn: Carlson, 1993.

Hine, Darlene Clark, and McLeod, Jacqueline, eds. *Crossing Boundaries: Comparative History of Black People in Diaspora*. Bloomington: Indiana University Press, 1999.

Honey, Michael. *Black Workers Remember: An Oral History of Segregation, Unionism, and the Freedom Struggle*. Berkeley: University of California Press, 2000.

Lightfoot, Sara. *Balm in Gilead: Journey of a Healer*. Reading, MA: Addison-Wesley, 1988.

Littlefield, Valinda. "A Yearly Contract with Everybody and His Brother: Durham County, North Carolina Black Female Public School Teachers 1885–1927." *Journal of Negro History*, 79.1 (1994): 37–53.

McAdoo, Harriette. "Oral History as a Primary Resource in Educational Research." *Journal of Negro Education*, 49.4 (1980): 414–422.

Ruiz, Vicki. "Situating Stories: The Surprising Consequence of Oral History (Practice And Pedagogy: Oral History in the Classroom)." *Oral History Review*, 25.1–2 (1998): 71–80.

Shaw, Stephanie. "Using the WPA Ex-Slave Narratives to Study the Impact of the Great Depression." *Journal of Southern History*, 69.3 (2003): 623–658.

Shopes, Linda. "What Is Oral History?" The Making Sense of Evidence Series on *History Matters: The U.S. Survey on the Web*. http://historymatters.gmu.edu.

Thompson, Paul. *The Voice of the Past: Oral History*. New York: Oxford University Press, 1978.

Wendling, Laura. "Oral History: Capturing the Past in the Present." *Social Studies Review*, 39.2 (2000): 47–50.

ORAL HISTORY ON THE WEB

Activist Women's Voices: Oral History Project. City University of New York. http://web.gc.cuny.edu/womencenter/CSWS_ActivistWomens Voices.htm.

African American and Race Relations. Sophia Smith Collection and College Archives, Smith College. http://www.smith.edu/librariesssc/subjafrican.html.

African American History and Culture. Smithsonian Institution. http://www.si.edu/resource/faq/nmah/afroam.htm.

African-American Women Online Archival Collections. Special Collections Library, Duke University. http://scriptorium.lib.duke.edu/collections/african-american-women.html. http://scriptorium.lib.duke.edu/women/afroamer.html.

American Life Histories, Manuscripts from the Federal Writers' Project, 1936–1940. Library of Congress, American Memory. http://memory.loc.gov/ammem/wpaintro/wpahome.html.

American Women's History: A Research Guide. African-American Women. http://frank.mtsu.edu/~kmiddlet/history/women/wh-afam.html.

Archives of American Art, Oral History Collections. Smithsonian Institution, Archives of American Art. http://www.archivesofamericanart.si.edu/oralhist/oralhist.htm.

The Black Women at Virginia Tech Oral History Project. http://spec.lib.vt.edu/archives/blackwomen/.

Born in Slavery: Slave Narratives from the Federal Writers' Project, 1936–1938. Library of Congress, American Memory Project. http://lcweb2.loc.gov/ammem/snhtml/snhome.html.

Center for the Historical Study of Women and Gender. Binghamton University (SUNY). http://chswg.binghamton.edu/living.htm.

Civil Rights in Mississippi Digital Archive. McCain Library and Archive, University of Southern Mississippi. http://www.lib.usm.edu/~spcol/crda/index.html.

Guide to African-American Workers. Martin P. Catherwood Library, Cornell University. http://www.ilr.cornell.edu/library/kheel/collections/topicalGuides/africanAmericaLabor/default.html.

Oral History Online!, Regional Oral History Office (ROHO). Bancroft Library, University of California, Berkeley. http://www.lib.berkeley.edu/BANC/ROHO/ohonline/.

Papers of African American Women. Iowa Women's Archives, University of Iowa Libraries. http://www.lib.uiowa.edu/iwa/Topical_holdings_lists\Aahold.htm.

Pioneer African American Women Nurses. http://www.nurses.info/history_womans_african_american.htm.

Schomburg Center for Research in Black Culture. New York Public Library. http://www.nypl.org/research/sc/sc.html.

Southern Oral History Program (SOHP). University of North Carolina, Chapel Hill, Southern Historical Collection. http://www.sohp.org.

The University of Michigan Medical School Oral History Project. http://www.med.umich.edu/haahc/aboutpro.htm.

US Women and Labor. Published Documents and Oral Histories. http://www.nyu.edu/library/bobst/research/tam/women/doccolls.html.

Women's History. Esther Raushenbaush Library, Sarah Lawrence College. http://www.sarahlawrence.edu/library/web_resources/selected sub/humanities/womehist.htm.

—ANTHONY EDWARDS

OSBORNE, ESTELLE MASSEY (b. 3 May 1901; d. c. 1981), nurse and nursing advocate. Estelle Massey Osborne devoted her life to nursing—as a practitioner and as an advocate for improved training and better job opportunities for black nurses. Estelle Massey was born in Palestine, Texas, the eighth of eleven children of Hall and Bettye Estelle Massey, a remarkable couple with strong opinions about child rearing. The Massey children raised and sold vegetables for spending money. The Massey daughters were not allowed to work for white employers because their mother did not want them exposed to racism. The Masseys brought up their children to be strong, confident, and proud.

Estelle Massey attended Prairie View State College. After graduation, she taught, became a nurse, and then taught nursing. At that point, she decided that she needed more education. While attending Teachers College at Columbia University in New York, Osborne taught at Lincoln Hospital School for Nurses in the Bronx. Later, she was hired by Harlem Hospital School of Nursing and became the first black nursing instructor there. After receiving her bachelor's degree at Columbia in 1931, she became the first educational director of nursing at Freedmen's Hospital School of Nursing (later Howard University College of Nursing). Her goal while at Freedmen's was to provide black student nurses with the same quality education that white students were receiving at the best nursing schools, but Osborne had another goal. She wanted to change the quality of education for black nurses across the country.

Working through the National Association of Colored Graduate Nurses (NACGN), as well as on her own, Osborne organized conferences, gave seminars, and conducted workshops all over the country. For five years, she was president of the NACGN.

In 1936, Osborne became the first black director of nursing at City Hospital No. 2 (later the Homer G. Phillips Hospital Training School). In 1943, she served as a consultant to the National Nursing Council for War Service. As the first black consultant on the staff of any national nursing organization, she helped to increase the number of training schools that would admit black students from fourteen to thirty-eight in just two years. She also fought to lift the color ban on black nurses who wished to enlist in the army and navy nurse corps and, in the case of the army, she was successful.

In 1946, Osborne received her MA degree and became the first black member of the nursing faculty at New York University in New York City. This position brought Osborne a great deal of visibility and prestige and allowed her to make even greater strides in her fight for the advancement of black nurses. In 1948, she won a position on the board of directors of the American Nurses Association.

In the years that followed, Osborne served in an executive position with most of the important nursing organizations in the country. When she retired in 1967, she was associate general director of the National League for Nursing.

BIBLIOGRAPHY

Dannett, Sylvia G. L. *Profiles of Negro Womanhood*. Yonkers, NY: Educational Heritage, 1966.

Safier, Gwendolyn. *Contemporary American Leaders in Nursing: An Oral History*. New York: McGraw-Hill, 1977.

—MARIE MOSLEY

P–Q

PARKS, ROSA (b. 4 February 1913), civil rights activist. From the moment her photograph was first published in newspapers across America, Parks, with her quiet dignity, has been a symbol for the civil rights movement in this country. Those who orchestrated the Montgomery bus boycott bypassed several other women to choose Parks as a representative of all the black women and men who were forced to live with Jim Crow laws and customs in the South, and she lived up to their expectations.

Early Life and Activism

Rosa Louise McCauley was born in Tuskegee, Alabama, the daughter of James McCauley, a carpenter, and Leona Edwards, a teacher. Her father migrated north to find work when Rosa was two years old and did not often communicate with the family after that. Her mother moved Rosa and a younger brother to Pine Level, Alabama, to be nearer her own parents and siblings. In Pine Level, Parks worked as a field hand, in addition to taking care of her grandparents while her mother worked, often as a teacher. Parks's mother homeschooled her until she was eleven, then sent her to live with her aunt in Montgomery so that she could go to school. While attending the Montgomery Industrial School for Girls, she did household chores for her aunt and also went out to do domestic work outside the home. She attended the Booker T. Washington High School but left before graduation to take care of her mother. Her experience in all these situations left her angry about the injustices in the world, and, when she was nineteen, she met Raymond Parks, a barber who was involved in the civil rights movement. On 19 December 1932 they were married.

The couple did not have children. With her husband's encouragement, Parks completed her high school education, receiving a diploma in 1934. From the beginning of their marriage, both were social activists. They worked to secure the release of the Scottsboro Boys, nine black youths accused of raping two white girls. Parks joined the Montgomery Voters League and worked to enfranchise African Americans in the community. During the 1940s she joined the Montgomery chapter of the NAACP and served as secretary of the branch from 1943 until 1956. Edgar Daniel Nixon Jr., organizer of the Black Brotherhood of Sleeping Car Porters Union in Montgomery and head of the Progressive Democrats, was president of the local NAACP chapter.

Particularly good at working with young people, Parks helped train a group of NAACP youths to protest segregation in the Montgomery Public Library, and she participated in voter-registration drives. In 1945 Parks became one of just a few African Americans in the city who were registered to vote. The registrar had failed her the first two times she took the literacy text, but she remained determined, a foreshadowing of her determination in choosing to be arrested rather than to continue to suffer segregation on Montgomery's buses. She took classes and attended seminars in civil rights tactics. In June 1955 Parks attended a summer workshop at the Highlander Folk School founded by Myles Horton in Monteagle, Tennessee, long a training ground for labor organizers and social activists. In 1959 the state of Tennessee would label the Highlander Folk School a subversive organization. Still, at Highlander, Parks, like her fellow activists Ella Baker and Septima Clark, acquired a deeper appreciation of and skills for community organizing, use of direct-action tactics, and administration of citizenship schools. Their preparation and long involvement in community affairs placed black women at the center of the civil rights movement. Parks's grounding in the organizational and institutional infrastructure of the Montgomery black community was essential to her ability to inspire the modern civil rights movement.

The Montgomery Bus Boycott

On 1 December 1955, Parks took the bus home. She had often walked rather than deal with Jim Crow segregation on the buses. The city's complex segregation laws dictated that African Americans pay their fares, exit the bus, and reenter through the rear door. Whites enjoyed the privilege of sitting in the front of the bus, and blacks occupied reserved seats in the rear. If the white section filled up and more white passengers boarded the bus, the black passengers were required to move. On this day, Parks decided to ride the bus anyway. And on this day, she refused to comply with the bus driver James F. Blake's order that she give the bus seat she occupied in the first row of the

ROSA PARKS on her way to jail in Montgomery, Alabama, December 1955. Her attorney Charles D. Langford is at the right; a deputy police officer is at the left. (Library of Congress.)

black section to a white male passenger. Three other African Americans vacated their seats, but Parks refused to move.

Parks had not planned to disobey the law on that fateful day, but her thirty-year commitment to social justice prepared her to do so. For her defiance of the segregation ordinance, the Montgomery police took Parks to jail. Montgomery's police lieutenant, Drue Lackey (who served as police chief from 1965 to1970), took her fingerprints. Responding to a call from Nixon, the white attorney Clifford Durr took her case, but Nixon posted her bail. The court found Parks guilty of disorderly conduct and fined her ten dollars and another four dollars in court costs.

Parks was not the first black woman to have suffered arrest for refusal to countenance bus segregation. In 1941 an angry mob beat Hannah Cofield before she was arrested for refusing to yield her seat to a white passenger. In 1944 Viola White met a similar fate. In March 1955, a

few months before Parks's arrest, Claudette Colvin, an unmarried, pregnant fifteen-year-old girl, had objected to vacating her seat and was jailed.

The local black leadership had long debated challenging bus segregation, but decided to wait for an incident involving someone who embodied the politics of respectability and whose private life could withstand relentless scrutiny. Thus, although Cofield, White, Colvin, and later, Mary Louise Smith, protested bus segregation, their resistance failed to ignite a larger social protest movement. Propitiously, in July 1955, the U.S. Court of Appeals in Richmond, Virginia, declared in *Flemming v. South Carolina Electric and Gas Company* that bus segregation, even on buses that operated within one state, was unconstitutional.

When the police arrested Parks, diverse factions within the Montgomery black community swung into nonviolent direct action. On 2 December 1955 the Women's Political Council (WPC), under the leadership of Jo Ann Robinson, an English professor at Alabama State College, mimeographed and, with two hundred volunteers, distributed more than thirty thousand handbills imploring black citizens to stay off the buses. The flyer declared,

Another Negro woman has been arrested and thrown into jail, because she refused to get up out of her seat on the bus for a white person to sit down. . . . Negroes have rights, too, for if Negroes did not ride the buses, they could not operate. . . . The next time it may be you, or your daughter, or mother.

(Robinson, 45–46)

Actually, the WPC had long prepared to declare a boycott. Black leaders called a mass meeting at Holt Street Baptist Church and voted to continue the boycott under the aegis of the newly formed Montgomery Improvement Association (MIA). A number of women served on the MIA executive committee, including Robinson and Parks and Erna Dungee Allen, who served as financial secretary. A young minister of Dexter Avenue Baptist Church, the Reverend Martin Luther King Jr., accepted the presidency of the MIA and led the discussions and negotiations with white authorities. Parks's arrest sparked the bus boycott movement that began on 5 December 1955 and lasted 381 days, ending on 20 December 1956. The black attorney Fred D. Gray, on behalf of the MIA, filed a lawsuit against segregation in federal court on 1 February 1956. On 2 June 1956, in a two to one decision, the federal court found the Montgomery bus segregation ordinances to be unconstitutional. On appeal, on 13 November 1956, the U.S. Supreme Court concurred with the federal court, ruling that racial segregation on public transportation in Montgomery and throughout the South was unconstitutional.

Later Life and Legacy

Parks's successful challenge to racial segregation attracted threats of violence and harassment and resulted in the loss of her job as a seamstress at Montgomery Fair Department Store. In 1957 Raymond and Rosa Parks and Rosa's mother joined her younger brother, Sylvester, in Detroit to seek jobs and personal security. For several years, Parks worked as a seamstress. In 1965 she accepted a special assistant position on the staff in the Detroit office of Representative John Conyers Jr. She remained in his employ for nearly twenty years, during which time she assisted Conyers in his efforts to make Martin Luther King Jr.'s birthday a national holiday. In 1977 Parks's husband and brother died. Ten years later she and a friend, Elaine Eason Steele, founded a nonprofit organization, the Raymond and Rosa Parks Institute for Self-Development, to honor her husband's memory and commitment to the struggle for social justice and human rights.

In the last decades of the twentieth century Parks received national recognition for her role in the civil rights movement. The NAACP gave her its highest honor, the Spingarn Award, in 1977. She also received the Presidential Medal of Freedom, the nation's highest civilian honor. On 15 June 1999, Parks was awarded the Congressional Gold Medal. In introducing the bill authorizing the award, Representative Julia Carson of Indiana declared, "Rosa Parks is the Mother of America's Civil Rights Movement. Her quiet courage that day in Montgomery, Alabama, launched a new American revolution that opened new doors of opportunity and brought equality for all Americans close to a reality." In 2003, the home Parks was living in at the time of the bus boycott, 620–28 Cleveland Court, was placed on the National Register of Historic Places.

See also Civil Rights Movement; Montgomery Bus Boycott; *and* Robinson, Jo Ann Gibson.

BIBLIOGRAPHY

Brinkley, Douglas. *Rosa Parks*. New York: Viking, 2000.

King, Martin Luther, Jr. *Stride toward Freedom: The Montgomery Story*. New York: Harper, 1964.

Parks, Rosa, with Jim Haskins. *Rosa Parks: My Story*. New York: Dial, 1992.

Robinson, Jo Ann Gibson. *The Montgomery Bus Boycott and the Women Who Started It: The Memoir of Jo Ann Gibson Robinson*. Knoxville: University of Tennessee Press, 1987.

Thornton, J. Mills, III. *Dividing Lines: Municipal Politics and the Struggle for Civil Rights in Montgomery, Birmingham, and Selma*. Tuscaloosa: University of Alabama Press, 2002.

United States House of Representatives Press Release, "Carson Calls for Cosponsers for Bill to Award Congressional Gold Medal to Rosa Parks," February 24, 1999.

—Darlene Clark Hine

PARKS, SUZAN-LORI (b. 10 May 1964), playwright. Parks was the first African American woman to win the Pulitzer Prize for drama, one of only a handful of black women playwrights to make it to the Broadway stage, and one of the only African American avant-garde playwrights in history. Her plays were nonlinear, nonrealistic, poetic, challenging, and often controversial.

Born in Fort Knox, Kentucky, Parks began writing stories almost as soon as she could hold a pencil. An "army brat" whose father was a colonel in the U.S. Army, she had lived in six different states by the time she was a teenager. When the family was posted to Germany, Parks experienced for the first time life outside of America's prism of race. In Germany, she was regarded as an American—a foreigner—first and a black person second. Because her parents decided to place their daughter in the local German school rather than in the American school for military and diplomatic personnel, Parks had a great deal of contact with German society. In addition, she learned to speak German fluently. This gave her a different perspective on language and influenced her later, brilliant explorations into spoken and written English.

Upon returning to the United States, Parks attended Mount Holyoke College, where she participated in a master writing class taught by James Baldwin. Baldwin's reaction to Parks's animated reading of her work was to tell

SUZAN-LORI PARKS, 19 June 2003. She was the first African American woman to win a Pulitzer Prize for drama; it was awarded for *Topdog/Underdog*. (© Jamie Painter Young/Corbis.)

her to write plays. She took his advice. Shawn-Marie Garrett, who wrote one of the most in-depth articles on Parks for *American Theatre*, quotes Baldwin as saying that Parks was "an utterly astounding and beautiful creature who may become one of the most valuable artists of our time." It was after this class that Parks wrote her first play, *The Sinner's Place*. The play won an honors citation from the English department but was too radical to be produced by the drama department. Parks graduated Phi Beta Kappa and cum laude from Mount Holyoke in 1985 with a BA in English and German literature.

Following her graduation from college, Parks attended the Drama Studio, London, for an intensive one-year course in theater. By 1987, she was back in New York

and writing her first off, off, off-Broadway show. Like many young, passionate theater artists, Parks ensured that *Betting on the Dust Commander* would come to life by contributing not only the words but also part of the production budget: she spent her own money to buy the six folding chairs required for the set.

Two years later, the story would be very different. In 1989, Parks's *Imperceptible Mutabilities in the Third Kingdom* opened at the Brooklyn Arts Council Association (BACA) Downtown. The play won the 1990 Obie Award for Best Off-Broadway Play. At the same time, the *New York Times* named Parks the "Year's Most Promising Playwright." *Imperceptible Mutabilities* was the first of what are called Parks's "history plays." Her next play, the provocatively titled *The Death of the Last Black Man in the Whole Entire World* was also presented, in 1990, at BACA Downtown. In 1992, Parks was commissioned by the Actors Theatre of Louisville's Humana Festival to write *Devotees in the Garden of Love*. The following year, Theatre for a New Audience commissioned *The America Play*, which opened at the Yale Repertory Theatre before moving to off-Broadway under the auspices of the New York Shakespeare Festival. In 1996, *Venus*, commissioned by the Women's Theatre Project, premiered at the Public Theatre under the direction of the famed avant-garde writer and director Richard Foreman. *Venus* won Parks her second Obie Award for Best New American Play. The same year, Parks wrote the screenplay for Spike Lee's movie *Girl 6*, which received generally negative reviews and disappeared quickly.

Parks broke away from the history plays after *Venus*, writing *In the Blood* (1999), *Fucking A* (2000), and *Topdog/Underdog* (2001), which won the 2002 Pulitzer Prize for Drama. Parks was quoted after hearing the news: "As the first African-American woman to win the Pulitzer Prize [for theater], I have to say I wish I was the 101st." The day before the prize was announced, *Topdog/Underdog* made history in another way: It opened on Broadway.

While Whoopi Goldberg and Anna Deavere Smith had both performed one-woman shows on Broadway, the last multicharacter play written by a black woman to make it to the "Great White Way" was *for colored girls who have considered suicide/when the rainbow is enuf* by Ntozake Shange, which opened more than twenty years before, in 1976.

In addition to her plays, Parks wrote the screen adaptation of the novel *Gal* and rewrote *God's Country* for Jodie Foster. She taught and lectured all over the country. She was a playwriting professor at both Eugene Lang College and Yale University, an associate artist at Yale School of Drama, and a member artist of New Dramatists. As of 2004, she was chair of the Dramatic Writing Program at CalArts. Her many grants, fellowships, and awards include two National Endowment for the Arts Playwriting Fellowships (1990 and 1991), a Rockefeller Foundation grant (1990), and a Guggenheim Fellowship (2000). In addition, Parks received the PEN-Laura Pels Award for Drama (2000) and the John T. and Catherine D. MacArthur Foundation "genius grant" (2001). Her plays can be found in *The Bedford Introduction to Drama*, *The Best of Off-Broadway*, and *Moon Marked and Touched by Sun*. Theatre Communications Group also published *The America Play and Other Works*. In 2003, Parks published her first novel, *Getting Mother's Body*.

Describing Parks's work can be tremendously difficult, if not impossible. In terms of her style and language, Parks certainly owes a debt to her favorite novelists, James Joyce, Virginia Woolf, and William Faulkner. The structure of her plays and use of language also seem to be influenced by the avant-garde German playwrights Bertolt Brecht and Heiner Muller. However, Ntozake Shange and Adrienne Kennedy, author of the groundbreaking work *Funnyhouse of a Negro*, are perhaps the most important writers in Parks's past. Through their daring and skill, both of these earlier playwrights showed Parks that experimenting with—even creating—language and abstract situations was possible for a black woman in the American theater.

The actress Pamela Tyson described performing Parks: "[She] does incredible things with language. She does the same thing with her work that Shakespeare does with his text. You can't have a lazy tongue. You have to open your mouth, you have to articulate . . . you have to be melodic, you have to have colors and levels and intonations, and she allows you to use your entire instrument." Garrett wrote that "like Ntozake Shange . . . she crafts a theatrical poetry that bears the same relation to black dialectical forms that, for example, Joyce's language bears to the speech of the Dubliners he heard and remembered." Garrett goes further to say that Parks "indisputably altered the landscape of American drama and enriched the vocabulary of contemporary playwriting and theater practice." However, despite her critical success, Parks was not often produced by black theater companies. Garrett points out in her article that while many African American critics "admired Parks's talent, they objected, in essence, to her politics." This seemed to change somewhat with the success of *Topdog/Underdog*, however.

Whatever anyone thinks of her style, language, or politics, Parks made history. She was part of a tiny revolutionary vanguard exploring the human experience through the theater. As she herself said, "My plays are much larger and more intelligent than I am. The knowledge that is inside my plays can reach miles, hundreds of thousands of miles."

See also **Playwriting** *and* **Theater.**

BIBLIOGRAPHY

Garrett, Shawn-Marie. "The Possession of Suzan-Lori Parks." *American Theatre* 17 (October 2000). New York: Theatre Communications Group, 2000.

Hannaham, James. "Funnyhouse of a Negro." *The Village Voice*, 3–9 November 1999. http://villagevoice.com/issues/9944/hannaham.php.

Rasbury, Angeli R. "Pulitzer Winner Parks Talks about Being a First." Women's Enews. 04/11/02. http://www.womensenews.org/article.cfm/dyn/aid/874.

"Suzan-Lori Parks." In *Contemporary Black Biography*, vol. 34, edited by Ashyia Henderson. Detroit, MI: Gale, 2002.

"Suzan-Lori Parks." *Newsmakers*, Issue 2. Detroit, MI: Gale, 2003. Reproduced in Biography Resource Center.

—HILARY MAC AUSTIN

PARSONS, LUCY (b. 16 March 1853; d. 7 March 1942), radical leftist revolutionary. A veteran of the anarchist, socialist, and communist movements in Chicago during the late nineteenth and early twentieth centuries, Parsons was the first black woman to play a prominent role in the American Left. A committed revolutionary, Parsons devoted sixty years of her life to improving the situation of the poor, the jobless, the homeless, women, children, and people of color.

LUCY PARSONS, a committed revolutionary, was the first black woman to play a prominent role in the American Left. Here, she is addressing a rally of the Farm Equipment Union, c. 1930. (Walter P. Reuther Library, Wayne State University.)

Born in Waco, Texas, of African, Indian, and Mexican ancestry, she met and subsequently married Albert Parsons, a former Confederate army scout turned radical. Because of their mixed marriage, the couple was forced to flee Texas in 1873. They ultimately ended up in Chicago, where they both joined the socialist-oriented Workingmen's Party in 1876. Within three years, Parsons began contributing articles to the *Socialist* and became a primary speaker on behalf of the Working Women's Union. The Parsonses were eventually drawn to anarchism, which emphasized cooperative organization of production, the abolition of the state, and the free exchange of products without profit or market intervention. Along with her husband and several other white Chicago radicals, Parsons helped form the International Working People's Association (IWPA) in 1883. She continued to develop as a talented propagandist and radical intellectual, publishing a popular article in *Alarm* (a revolutionary socialist newspaper) in 1884 that called on the jobless to "learn to use explosives!"

Less known, however, are her early writings on lynchings and racist violence in the South, which were published several years before Ida B. Wells-Barnett's famous pronouncements on the subject. She viewed racial oppression as primarily a class question and suggested that African American working people adopt violent strategies of self-defense. Commenting on a multiple lynching that had occurred in Carrollton, Mississippi, in 1886, Parsons insisted that race had nothing to do with the brutal murders. "It is because [the black man] is *poor*. It is because he is dependent. Because he is poorer as a class than his white wage-slave brother of the North." Her tendency to focus on economic causes and de-emphasize the role of racism might be linked to her own denial of her black heritage. Her complexion and features not only enabled her to pass as Spanish but also her social world consisted almost entirely of white leftists. Because racism was not something she had to endure all her life, it was difficult for her to see how it could have shaped the lives of African Americans.

Like so many other anarchists and radical labor leaders, Parsons helped organize the famous attempted general strike on May 1886, demanding a general eight-hour workday. Three days into the strike, Albert Parsons and eight other IWPA members were arrested for allegedly throwing a bomb at police during a demonstration at Chicago's Haymarket Square. Parsons led a campaign to free her husband and the other seven political prisoners, but her efforts were to no avail: Albert Parsons and three other defendants were executed in 1887. Just two years later she lost her youngest of two children, eight-year-old Lulu, to lymphadenoma.

Despite these tragedies, Parsons continued her work on behalf of anarchist and socialist causes, addressing radical gatherings throughout the United States as well as England. In 1891, she published and edited a short-lived newspaper called *Freedom: A Revolutionary Anarchist-Communist Monthly*, in which she began dealing with the woman question much more rigorously, publishing essays on rape, divorce, marriage, and the role of women's oppression as a function of capitalism. Like her views on racism, Parsons believed that sexism would automatically disappear with the construction of a socialist society.

By the turn of the century, Parsons had become somewhat of a legend of the Left. She was one of two women in attendance at the founding convention of the Industrial Workers of the World (IWW) in 1905; she gained some notoriety for leading mass demonstrations of homeless and unemployed people in San Francisco in 1914 and Chicago in 1915; and she was a vocal opponent of World War I. In 1927 Parsons joined the International Labor Defense, a Communist-led organization devoted to defending "class war prisoners," notably incarcerated labor organizers such as Tom Mooney, and African Americans unjustly accused of crimes such as the Scottsboro Nine and Angelo Herndon. After working closely with the Communists for more than a decade, the eighty-six-year-old Parsons joined the party in 1939. Three years later her life came to an end when a fire engulfed her home.

See also The Left.

BIBLIOGRAPHY

Ashbaugh, Carolyn. *Lucy Parsons: American Revolutionary*. Chicago: Charles H. Kerr Publishing Company for the Illinois Labor History Society, 1976.

Davis, Angela. *Women, Race, and Class*. New York: Random House, 1981.

Parsons, Lucy E. *The Life of Albert R. Parsons, with Brief History of the Labor Movement in America*. Chicago: L. E. Parsons, 1889.

—Robin D. G. Kelley

PATTERSON, LOUISE THOMPSON (b. 9 September 1901; d. 27 August 1999), educator, cultural critic, early civil rights activist, and pioneering advocate of black women's rights in Harlem. Thompson brought to the Communist Party an unusually sophisticated understanding of the complexities of race and gender oppression—a unique perspective for an organization that emphasized class exploitation above all else. Born in Chicago, but raised in several predominantly white, often racist communities in the West, she eventually settled with her family in Oakland, California, in 1919. She earned a degree in economics from the University of California, Berkeley, in 1923, but racism limited her career opportunities. She chose to go back to the Midwest and work toward a graduate degree at the University of Chicago, but she abandoned the idea soon thereafter. Giving up school, as well as a lucrative position at a black-owned Chicago firm, Thompson headed south to accept a teaching job in Pine Bluff, Arkansas, in 1925, and a year later accepted a faculty position at Hampton Institute in Virginia. Because of her open support of a student strike in 1927, Hampton's administration pressured Thompson to resign, after which she headed to New York to accept an Urban League Fellowship to study at the New York School for Social Work.

Unimpressed with social work paternalism as a means to improve the lives of poor blacks, she discontinued her education in 1930 and turned to New York's Congregational Educational Society (CES), a liberal organization interested in the problems of race relations and labor. Simultaneously, she became a prominent figure in black cultural circles, serving as editorial secretary for Langston Hughes and Zora Neale Hurston and offering her spacious apartment as a meeting place for black artists and intellectuals. The combination of social work and cultural politics, compounded by the Depression, the Scottsboro case, and the growing strength of the Communist Party in Harlem, radicalized Thompson. She and the artist Augusta Savage formed a left-wing social club called the Vanguard, out of which developed a branch of the Friends of the Soviet Union (FOSU). Soon thereafter, Thompson attended classes at the Workers' School, moving deeper into the Party's inner circle.

As secretary of the Harlem chapter of FOSU, she became principal organizer of a group of black artists invited to the Soviet Union in 1932 to make a film about African American life. Although the project was abandoned, she returned to New York with a deeper appreciation of socialism and a greater affinity for Communist politics. In 1933 she left CES and served as assistant national secretary of the National Committee for the Defense of Political Prisoners (NCDPP), through which she was officially asked to join the Communist Party. A year later she accepted a full-time position in the International Workers' Order (IWO) and continued to organize cultural and political events on behalf of the Communist Party in Harlem and elsewhere (including Alabama, where in 1934 she spent a night in a Birmingham jail). As black artists joined the WPA in the late 1930s, Thompson was a critical liaison linking black popular culture and Harlem's literati with Communist popular front politics. In 1938, for example, she and Langston Hughes organized the IWO-sponsored "Harlem Suitcase Theatre," which performed a number of works by black playwrights.

In 1940 Thompson married her longtime friend the veteran Party leader William L. Patterson, who more than a decade earlier had suggested she read Marx and look seriously at events in the USSR. Soon afterward she joined "Patt" in Chicago and continued her work nationally and locally. Among other things, she served as national recording secretary of the IWO and helped establish a black community center on Chicago's South Side. She also gave birth to her only child, Mary Louise. Following World War II, Patterson was among the founders and leading activists of the Civil Rights Congress (CRC) and in the 1950s joined such luminaries as Charlotta Bass, Shirley Graham, and Alice Childress in forming the Sojourners for Truth and Justice, a black woman's auxiliary of the CRC.

For the remainder of her life, she remained active in movements for social justice and began working on a memoir that as of 2004 was still unpublished. Patterson died at the age of ninety-seven at the Amsterdam Nursing Home in New York City.

See also The Left.

BIBLIOGRAPHY

Horne, Gerald. *Communist Front?: The Civil Rights Congress, 1946–1956*. Rutherford, NJ: Fairleigh Dickinson University Press, 1988.

McDuffie, Erik. "Long Journeys: Four Black Women and the Communist Party, 1930–1956." PhD diss., New York University, 2003.

Naison, Mark. *Communists in Harlem during the Depression*. Urbana: University of Illinois Press, 1983.

Patterson, Louise. Interview by Ruth Prago, Oral History of the American Left, Tamiment Institute, New York University, 16 November 1981.

—ROBIN D. G. KELLEY

PETIONI, MURIEL MARJORIE (b. 1 January 1914), physician, pioneer in substance abuse treatment. The long and distinguished career of the Trinidadian-born Harlem physician Muriel Marjorie Petioni exemplifies the multiplicity of influences on a generation of talented Afro-Caribbean immigrant women who emerged in the mid-twentieth century. Petioni, the daughter of the prominent anticolonial activist and physician Charles Augustin Petioni, grew up in African American as well as Caribbean communities and began a career typical of black female professionals during the era of Jim Crow. In the 1940s she held a series of positions as a physician in historically black colleges in the midwestern and southern United States. After her father's death in 1950, Petioni returned to Harlem and established her community and holistic-oriented practice in his office at 114 West 131st Street. While she drew on family influence and contacts, Petioni pursued her own approach to medical services in Harlem. Among her notable contributions are her pioneering work in substance abuse treatment and the organization of black women physicians. In 2004, at the age of ninety, Petioni remained active as head of a $1 million endowment fund she established for Harlem Hospital.

The daughter of Rose Alling and Charles Petioni, Muriel Marjorie Petioni immigrated to New York with her family in 1919. She attended New York public schools 68 and 136 and Wadleigh High School. After two years at New York University, she entered an accelerated program at Howard

University, where she graduated with a BS in 1934 and was the only black woman in her medical class in 1937. In 1939 she completed her internship at Harlem Hospital, one of the few hospitals admitting black interns to its training program, and then completed her residency at the black-operated Homer Phillips Hospital in St. Louis, Missouri. In 1942 Petioni married Mallalieu S. Woolfolk, a lawyer, and they had one son, Charles M. Woolfolk, a New York business executive. Petioni's marriage broke up in the 1970s, but for much of her career she balanced the roles of physician, wife, mother, daughter, and community leader.

Petioni grew up helping her father in his medical office and listening to political discussions and debates in the family brownstone, which doubled as her father's office. Harlem intellectuals and radical thinkers were frequent guests. Before immigrating to New York, Petioni's father had been fired from his job as a newspaper reporter in Port-of-Spain, Trinidad, for criticizing the colonial government. Petioni recalled that her father vowed to establish his own independent occupation so that he would always be in a position to express his political views without fear of losing his job. Charles Petioni worked as an elevator operator, a porter, and a stock clerk while attending college and medical school. Petioni's mother, who had been a department store clerk in Trinidad, organized the family's resources while employed as a garment worker in a New York sweatshop. Although they both experienced temporary downward mobility, the family eventually joined the African American professional class while maintaining vast networks in the Caribbean immigrant community in New York and Trinidad. From the vantage point of their own struggle to gain economic independence, they encouraged their daughter's entry into the relatively small black female professional class and fostered a commitment to social change and activism. Acknowledging her family's influence, Petioni said in a 1993 interview, "My whole orientation was fighting for the rights of black people in Harlem."

Petioni's more than fifty-year medical career bridges the era of Jim Crow medical training and the period of desegregation in the 1960s and 1970s. When Petioni entered medical school in the 1930s, black female representation in the profession had already declined from a generation before. The census identified only sixty-five black practicing physicians in 1920. The historian Darlene Clark Hine suggests that instead of entering the medical profession as physicians, many career-aspiring black women found nursing a more feasible alternative career in the health field at that time. Like most black men, the women who were in practice were excluded from medical and surgical specialties. Years of segregated and male-dominated medicine in the North as well as the South meant women faced severe obstacles in both training and practice.

Petioni held a series of appointments in historically black colleges and universities at Wilberforce University in Ohio, Alabama Teachers College, Bennett College, and Hampton University in Virginia before she began her practice. Hine points out that many women found the cost and emotional strain of establishing a successful private practice prohibitive at first. The college appointments "provided small but steady stipends and much-needed experience at working in an institutional setting." In addition, the appointments assured some professional autonomy, status, and visibility in the profession. Petioni credited her southern and midwestern experience as important to her understanding of the politics of segregation and as contributing to her expanding political consciousness.

After a decade as a college physician, Petioni returned to New York in 1950 and set up her practice in her father's office. She recalled in those days "many black patients did not want to come to a black physician. People still felt white physicians were better physicians." Regarding such these matters, Hine wrote, "The newly minted black woman doctor frequently spent considerable effort persuading, cajoling, and winning confidence before being allowed to treat physical illness." She cited May Chinn, the first black woman graduate of the University of Bellevue Medical Center in New York in 1892, who recalled both the skepticism of black patients and "support" of black male colleagues who "sent me their night calls after midnight."

In the face of these and other challenges, Petioni nevertheless provided direct outreach to the most disadvantaged members of her community and attempted to address the specific concerns of black female physicians. In her Harlem practice, she soon saw the necessity of integrating medical treatment with the social and economic realities that affected her patients. Many could not afford the two or three dollars she charged for an office visit or a house call, and so they sometimes paid her with food. In the 1960s she began an innovative drug treatment program, and at the end of the decade she became the first medical director of Harlem Drug Fighters, a short-term community-operated detoxification unit based at Harlem Hospital. She also performed free medical screening for addicts as part of a program sponsored by the New York Council of Small Churches. The city of New York honored her for her work in the treatment of drug addiction in 1983. Petioni also became an activist for children's health while serving as school physician in the Department of Health between 1950 and 1980.

During the 1970s, Petioni earned a national reputation as a pioneer activist for black women physicians. In 1974 she started one of the first organizations of black women doctors, the New York–area Susan Smith McKinney Steward Medical Society, named for the prominent nineteenth-century Brooklyn physician. She continued as its first president until 1984. The organization functioned as a support network for area women physicians, organized medical seminars for its members, established a mentoring program for young women interested in medicine, and documented medical contributions of black doctors. In 1977 Petioni organized black women physicians nationally in Medical Women of the National Medical Association. It was the first female physicians' group admitted officially as a component of the Black National Medical Association formed in 1895. In 1988 Petioni established Friends of Harlem Hospital, a philanthropic organization, for which she developed a $1.7 million endowment fund. The fund enabled the hospital to purchase critical equipment, expand treatment facilities, and provide needed services for patients. Although she retired as a practicing physician in 1990, Petioni kept up a five-day-a-week schedule for sixteen years at her small Harlem Hospital office.

In many ways, Dr. Petioni's career is characteristic of black women physicians of her generation, whose approach to medical practice brought them into direct contact with community and family concerns. These medical women were the organizers within local and national medical societies and were more often leaders in the social service arena than their male colleagues were. An examination of Petioni's career reveals the links between the work of an earlier generation of female physicians, such as Susan Smith McKinney Steward, and those trained in the post–civil rights era. Her initiation of a formal organization for black women physicians in the 1970s reflected new-wave feminist concerns among black professional women who were encouraged by their expanding numbers and the need to organize the support they could receive only from other women. Significantly, Petioni's Caribbean background also represented an opportunity to examine the critical historical relationship and linkages among a generation of women in the black diaspora.

See also **Chinn, May Edward; Physicians;** *and* **Steward, Susan McKinney.**

BIBLIOGRAPHY

Hine, Darlene Clark. *Hine Sight: Black Women and the Re-Construction of American History*. Brooklyn, NY: Carlson, 1994.

Petioni, Muriel Marjorie. Interview with Irma Watkins-Owens. 23 December 1993.

Shaw, Stephanie J. *What a Woman Ought to Be and to Do: Black Professional Women Workers during the Jim Crow Era*. Chicago: University of Chicago Press, 1996.

Watkins-Owens, Irma. *Blood Relations: Caribbean Immigrants and the Harlem Community, 1900–1930*. Bloomington: Indiana University Press, 1996.

Watkins-Owens, Irma. "An Introduction to the History of Black Physicians, Dentists, and Pharmacists in Brooklyn, 1850–1985." In Brooklyn Collection of the Central Branch, Brooklyn Public Library, Brooklyn, New York.

—IRMA WATKINS-OWENS

PETRY, ANN LANE (b. 12 October 1908; d. 28 April 1997), writer. Ann Lane Petry was the first African American woman to write a best-selling novel, one that eventually sold more than two million copies. *The Street*, first published in 1946, demonstrates the power of Petry's vivid characters and realistic portrayal of life in Harlem in the 1940s. Throughout her life, Petry explored the humanity of individuals through her novels, essays, poetry, and children's stories.

Ann Lane was born in Old Saybrook, Connecticut. The Lane family was one of a handful of African American families in this small New England town. Her father, Peter C. Lane, was one of the first registered African American pharmacists in Connecticut and the only one in Old Saybrook. Lane came from a long line of pharmacists; her grandfather was a chemist, and an aunt and uncle, both pharmacists, helped her father run the family-owned pharmacy. In spite of several racist threats, the Lane family's business prospered. Bertha James Lane,

ANN LANE PETRY, author of fiction, essays, and poetry, was the first African American woman to write a best-selling novel: *The Street*, published in 1946. A realistic portrayal of life in Harlem, it eventually sold more than 2 million copies. (Austin/Thompson Collection.)

Ann's mother, worked in various occupations, at times a chiropodist, a barber, and owner of a linen business.

Though Ann Lane started to write promising short stories in high school, she decided to follow in her family's footsteps. After her graduation from high school in 1920, she enrolled at the University of Connecticut and, in 1934, graduated with her doctorate in pharmacy. She returned home and worked in the family-owned businesses, both in Old Saybrook and Lyme, as a pharmacist. However, she still spent her spare time reading and writing short stories. Her dream of becoming a writer became a reality after her marriage to George Petry, himself a writer, in February 1938. Shortly after their marriage, the couple moved to New York City.

From 1939 to 1941, Petry worked at the *Amsterdam News*, a prominent African American newspaper, in the advertisement department and as a copywriter. During World War II, she moved to the *People's Voice*, a newspaper based in Harlem, where she worked as a general news reporter and the editor of the women's page. Petry's work at the newspaper exposed immense poverty, high unemployment rates, unsafe and expensive housing, police brutality, segregation, and sexual harassment. This harsh and racist reality encouraged her to become active in the Harlem community, working with an experimental after-school program in Harlem to help lessen and alleviate the effects of segregation, starting a legislative group that encouraged the active involvement of African American women, and teaching business classes for the Young Women's Christian Association. She also explored creative outlets by taking painting lessons, enrolling in creative writing courses at Columbia University, writing short stories, and participating in the American Negro Theatre.

In 1942, Petry's first published story, "On Saturday the Siren Sounds at Noon," appeared in *Crisis* magazine. *Crisis* rejected her second short story, "In Darkness and Confusion," which dealt with the Harlem riots, because of its length, but published "Olaf and His Girl Friend" and "Like a Winding Sheet" in 1945 and 1946, respectively. "Like a Winding Sheet" earned the best American short story award in 1946. "On Saturday the Siren Sounds at Noon" gained the attention of an editor at Houghton Mifflin, who inquired whether Petry was working on a novel. With this professional encouragement, Petry finished the first five chapters and a detailed outline within a year. Impressed with the chapters, Houghton Mifflin awarded Petry the Houghton Mifflin Literary Fellowship in 1945. The $2,400 award permitted Petry to work for ten months without interruption. In January 1946, *The Street* was published.

The novel was an overnight sensation. Based in Harlem, *The Street* vividly captures daily life through the eyes of its female protagonist, Luti Johnson, who tries to provide a better life for herself and her son, Bub. Despite her hard work, honesty, and strict morality, Lutti watches as the insidious effects of poverty corrupt her neighborhood and her son. Petry was one of the first women to examine contemporary social ills and problems that black women faced on a daily basis. Numerous reviewers, noting the realism of her portrayal of life in Harlem, compared her work to that of Richard Wright.

The celebrity that accompanied the success of her first novel made Petry uncomfortable, and in 1948, with the financial security the book's sales gave them, Petry and her husband moved back to Old Saybrook. She soon demonstrated that her work could not be pigeonholed. Her next two novels, *Country Place* (1947) and *The Narrows* (1953), were set in New England. *Country Place* focused on white characters and explored the aftereffects of World War II, specifically the gender dynamics caused by the breakdown of conventional codes of behavior. *The Narrows* examined the inner workings of an interracial relationship.

Petry also wrote children's books and poetry. Most of her children's books concentrate on African American life and culture. They include *The Drugstore Cat* (1949), *Harriet Tubman: Conductor on the Underground Railroad* (1955), *Tituba of Salem Village* (1964), and *Legends of the Saints* (1970). Her poetry, while not bearing her name, is included in several poetry anthologies. The poems are "Noo York City 1," "Noo York City 2," "Noo York City 3," "A Purely Black Stone," and "A Real Boss Black Cat." Petry's final work of fiction, *Miss Muriel and Other Stories*, was published in 1971.

The Street was reissued in 1985, reviving critical and popular interest in Petry's work, and she received honorary degrees from the University of Connecticut (1988) and Mount Holyoke College (1989). Ann Lane Petry died in a convalescent home in Old Saybrook.

See also Fiction.

BIBLIOGRAPHY

Chambers, Veronica. "Ann Lane Petry, 1909–97: The Passing of a Sister Griot." *Essence*, August 1997, 148.

Davis, Arthur. *From the Dark Tower: Afro-American Writers, 1900 to 1960*. Washington, DC: Howard University Press, 1974: 193–197.

Ervin, Hazel Arnett. "Petry, Ann." In *The Concise Oxford Companion to African American Literature*, edited by William L. Andrews, Frances Smith Foster, and Trudier Harris. New York: Oxford University Press, 2001: 323–325.

O'Brien, John, ed. *Interviews with Black Writers*. New York: Liveright, 1973: 152–163.

Reynolds, Clarence V. "Ann Lane Petry." *Black Issues Book Review* (July/August 2002).

—ANNE HEUTSCHE

PHILANTHROPY. African American women have always been at the forefront of philanthropic work for their local communities and fund-raising for national campaigns against racial oppression. Black women raised millions of dollars for charitable causes through early church-based charity work in the eighteenth and nineteenth centuries, through fund-raising for social reform and race uplift at the turn of the twentieth century, and through donations by wealthy individual black women in the late twentieth century. Whether they raised money through soliciting donations from white donors and white foundations or through bake sales, fairs, and other community activities, African American women created and sustained many of the charitable and reform institutions aiding their communities. While their primary focus was the social welfare needs of blacks in their community, they also aided causes of particular interest to the race, such as the movement to abolish slavery or the campaign to end lynching.

The most striking aspect of black women's philanthropic work was perhaps its ability to raise the money needed for a variety of programs and institutions, despite a relative lack of wealth within the community. Through a range of fund-raising techniques, black women did the "wholly impossible." As members of organizations led by men, ladies' auxiliaries to men's groups, women's clubs and other female-led organizations, they were central to the success of much of the social welfare work for African Americans.

Early Efforts

For many years, black women's philanthropy tended to take the form of local charity work, where women knew the individuals they assisted. African American women provided service as well as funds, rather than large-scale anonymous financial contributions. While some women's organizations limited their membership to the most educated or wealthy, many groups, especially church groups, had poor and working-class women alongside their wealthier sisters. These organizations believed that the work they did serviced the entire community as it uplifted the race.

In the eighteenth and nineteenth centuries, most black women's philanthropic work was done through women's church groups, lodges, and mutual improvement or benevolent associations, primarily in the North. Local benevolent groups composed of free blacks, such as the African Benevolent Society of Newport, Rhode Island, founded in 1808, and the African Marine Fund of New York City, had both male and female members. Women were most often included in societies dedicated to education or literary associations and usually were excluded from mutual aid groups that provided funeral assistance and aid to widows and orphans. One of the earliest women's benevolent societies, the African Dorcas Society, was founded in 1828 in New York City for the benefit of needy black schoolchildren in want of clothing and shoes to wear to school. Meeting in sewing circles, society members made and mended clothing for poor children.

ANITA STROUD devoted herself to caring for the children in the housing project where she lived in Charlotte, North Carolina. A park in Charlotte is named after her. (Public Library of Charlotte-Mecklenburg County, by permission of the *Charlotte Observer*.)

Women's church associations were the most popular vehicles for women's philanthropic work in the nineteenth century. As women and as mothers, they followed their Christian duty to minister to those in need, particularly other women and children. Members of Philadelphia's St. Thomas Methodist Episcopal Church, for example, formed two women's groups, the Female Benevolent Society in 1796 and the Daughters of St. Thomas in 1822 with separate treasuries. Like white women, black women raised funds through a variety of fairs and sales. New York City's African Methodist Episcopal Church women, held a fair in 1837, where they sold "a general assortment of Fancy Articles, Dry Goods, Toys, Confectionery, &c." The funds were usually used to purchase or build church property or to pay off debts.

Black women also played an integral role in the abolitionist movement, often raising funds as well as organizing public events that promoted the cause. They belonged both to interracial organizations such as the Boston Female Anti-Slavery Society and to exclusively black societies such as the Female Colored Union Society of Nantucket, Massachusetts.

While men often applauded women's efforts, they sometimes disapproved of work that took women away from their homes. The debate over what roles women should play became a particularly thorny source of discord in the abolitionist movement. However, black women remained committed to the cause and their varied courses of action in its behalf. They published abolitionist-themed articles and poetry, signed petitions, and gave public speeches supporting not just abolition but also immediate abolition with an extension of full rights for former slaves and free people of color. Not only did they give their time and talent to abolition but also their earnings and inheritances. They realized that financing a national reform movement was a costly affair that needed every donation possible. With this in mind, they sponsored sales of baked goods, handmade cloth goods, and more eclectic bazaars—donating the proceeds from such sales to the abolitionist cause. The importance of the money these abolitionist women raised became evident in a rift among the Boston Female Anti-Slavery Society members, which resulted in the two factions holding competing fund-raising fairs in 1839.

Post–Civil War

After the Civil War, black women continued to have among their ranks some of the most important fund-raisers for their communities. A primary goal for all communities was the provision of schools for their children.

Featuring Early Philanthropists

● **Clara Brown** (c.1800–1885) was one of Colorado's first important philanthropists. Born into slavery in Virginia, she lived most of her early life in Kentucky. In 1856 her latest owner died, freeing her in his will and leaving her $300. She went first to Kansas and then, in 1859, accompanied some prospectors to Denver in exchange for cooking and washing. After two years she bought a miner's cabin in Central City and opened a laundry. In addition to serving as the Methodist church, her house became, according to a local paper, "a hospital, a hotel and a general refuge for those who were sick or in poverty." That included whites, blacks, and Native Americans.

Brown expanded her business and began buying real estate. By 1864 she owned seven houses in Central City and sixteen lots in Denver, as well as property in Boulder and Georgetown. If she had held onto her business and property, she might have become one of Colorado's wealthiest women. Instead, when 1865 brought emancipation, she went back to Kentucky to find her children, who had been sold away from her. She returned to Denver with a large group of former slaves (estimates range from sixteen to thirty-four), for whom she found homes and jobs. She also helped pay for their education. She spent a year in Kansas, helping the Exodusters, who were trying to start a new life. Eventually she sold off almost all of her property in order to support churches, friends, family members, and the needy. Then, in 1882, Clara Brown found one of her daughters, Eliza Jane, in Council Bluffs, Iowa. The eighty-year-old mother went to Iowa and brought back her fifty-year-old widowed daughter. A year later, the Colorado Pioneers Association changed its by-laws so that it could vote Clara Brown its first woman member.

● **Mary Ann Akins Shire Campbell** (1817–after 1902) was born in Philadelphia into a very strict religious home. She had four children with her first husband, Joseph Shire, and was widowed shortly after the birth of their last child. Her second marriage was to a bishop of the African Methodist Episcopal (AME) church, Jabez Campbell. Mary Campbell co-founded the Women's Parent Mite Missionary Society and became active in other missionary organizations. She was a life member of the Home for the Aged and Infirm Colored Persons and one of the founders of the Frederick Douglass Hospital in Philadelphia. She made outright financial contributions to numerous charities. However, the recipients of her largest gifts were the Home for the Aged in Philadelphia, the Mite Missionary Society, and two AME schools—Wilberforce University and Jabez Pitt Campbell College in Jackson, Mississippi.

● **Elizabeth Denison Forth** (c. 1787–1866), also known as Lisette, was born a slave in Michigan to Peter and Hannah Denison. After the Northwest Ordinance of 1787 was passed, Lisette and her siblings became involved in a legal battle for their freedom. After a court defeat, they escaped to Canada but were back in Michigan by 1820. Forth worked as a domestic for the Sibley family and invested her savings in several lots in Pontiac, Michigan. She married but was widowed within three years. In 1836 she went to work for the Biddle family, where she remained for thirty years,

Black women, like black men, emptied their pockets to help finance school buildings and to pay teachers and school administrators. Some black women, like Mary Peake and Maria Stewart, opened and operated schools for recently freed black children.

Much of the black community-based philanthropy after the Civil War was centered in black churches, as it had been before the war. It was through these churches that women made their primary financial impact. As the majority members in almost every African American church, black women of every region and class were the backbone of black philanthropic endeavors. Indeed, African American churches could not have provided the social services that families and communities needed—from food and clothing for the needy, to building schools, orphanages, and homes for the elderly—without the funds raised by women. Women in the National Baptist Convention were exemplary in their efforts. They exhibited and sold needlework. They instituted Stamp Day, an annual drive to save stamps and donate them to be used by their national women's convention for much-needed mass mailings, as well as solicited funds from nonmembers.

Driven by the need to support ongoing self-improvement efforts, black Baptist women began to organize themselves in statewide organizations in the 1880s. In Kentucky, for example, the first statewide convention of black Baptist women took place specifically to raise money for the State University at Louisville (later Simmons University), a private university owned by black Baptists. Between 1883 and 1900, they raised $12,000, erected a dormitory for female students, retired the school's debt, and successfully raised a matching grant from the all-white American Baptist Home Mission Society. At the national level, they formed the Women's

continuing to invest her earnings; they began to pay significant dividends. She saved enough to travel to Europe and buy herself a home. She did not otherwise live extravagantly. When she died in 1866, her will provided for the building of a church. It stated, "Having long felt the inadequacies of the provisions made for the poor in the houses of worship, I wish to do all in my power as far as God has given me means to offer to the poor man and stranger 'wine and milk without price and without cost.'" The church, St. James, was built in Grosse Ile, Michigan, where the doors to the old chapel bear an inscription to her memory.

● **Frances Joseph-Gaudet** (1861–1934) founded and gave considerable financial support to the Gaudet Normal and Industrial School for black youth in New Orleans, in 1902. She was born in Holmesville, Pike County, Mississippi, and became a seamstress, a vocation common among black women in the nineteenth century. She was married at twenty-three and divorced ten years later. In 1894 she began to work for prison reform, founding the city's first juvenile court. After a speaking tour of England and Europe in 1900, she returned to New Orleans and bought 105 acres of farmland. Her goal was to build a school for destitute black children that would prepare them to support themselves. The first secretary of the board of the school was Adolphe P. Gaudet, whom Frances Joseph later married.

● **Nettie Langston Napier** (1861–1938) was a prominent philanthropist, dedicated to improving the lives of all members of the black community. She was born in Oberlin, Ohio, to a prominent lawyer and founder of the Howard University Law School. After an education at Howard and Oberlin, she married James Napier and settled in Washington, DC. When James Napier resigned from his post in the Register of the Treasury in protest of Woodrow Wilson's segregationist policies, the couple moved to Nashville, where Nettie Napier formed the Day Homes Club in 1907 and became its president, making generous financial contributions to its support. She was also active in the National Association of Colored Women, the New Idea Club, and the City Federation, and worked with the Red Cross during World War I through the Committee of Colored Women.

● **Mary Ellen Pleasant** (1814–1904) worked as cook, accountant, abolitionist, and entrepreneur in San Francisco. She gave John Brown financial support for his activities and was generous in other political and charitable causes. (See individual entry: Pleasant, Mary Ellen.)

● **Madam C. J. (Sarah Breedlove) Walker** (1867–1919) was one of the first self-made woman millionaires in the United States and gave large sums to black causes. (See individual entry: Walker, Madam C. J. [Sarah Breedlove].)

● **Fannie Barrier Williams** (1855–1944) was a consultant and fund-raiser for a training school for black nurses at Provident Hospital, established in 1891. She and her husband helped fund the Frederick Douglass Center, a settlement project opened in 1905, and many other projects supporting the black community. (See individual entry: Williams, Fannie Barrier.)

Featuring Philanthropists

● **Tyra Banks** (1973–) is a successful model, actor, and television celebrity, and a philanthropist with an interest in increasing the self-esteem of young women. She grew up in Los Angeles, California, an avid reader and became a model while she was a teenager. She lived for a year in Paris modeling on the runways for such designers as Chanel and Ralph Lauren, and then she returned to the United States to become a major print and television model. She was the first black model on the cover of *Sports Illustrated* and the first black woman and first model to be featured on the cover of *GQ*. Eventually, she parlayed her modeling into an acting career. In 2000 she established the Tyra Banks Foundation to support T-Zone, a weeklong summer camp she created in response to letters she received from girls who were insecure as they approached adulthood.

● **C. Sylvia Brown** (1940?–), a noted philanthropist, with her husband gave $5 million to create the Turning the Corner Achievement Program, a scholarship program to assist African American students in two of the poorest neighborhoods in Baltimore, Maryland. Born C. Sylvia Thurston in rural King William County, Virginia, she was valedictorian of her high school class. She earned a bachelor's degree from Howard University and a master's from Indiana University. She married Eddie C. Brown, a financial adviser who founded Brown Capital Management, Inc., one of the country's leading African American investment management firms. C. Sylvia Brown taught middle school in Red Bank, New Jersey, and in Hyde Park, New York. She also taught at Baltimore City Community College, and for five years she was assistant director of Admissions and Registration. In recent years she has managed the family's real estate holdings in Baltimore. The Browns have made large donations to many different causes, including $6 million to the Maryland Institute College of Art. They established the Brown Capital Management Fund and the Brown Capital Lecture Series, with a $250,000 endowment at the Howard University School of Business.

● **Mariah Carey** (1970–), one of the most popular singers of the last two decades, is also a generous and involved philanthropist. She was born on Long Island, New York, to a black Venezuelan engineer, Alfred Roy Carey, and an Irish opera singer, Patricia Hickey Carey. She broke on to the popular music scene in June 1990 with a debut album called *Mariah*, which had several singles that rose to the top of the charts. From that time on she has dominated popular music and given regularly and freely to causes she cares about. All proceeds from her hit single *Hero*, for example, went to the families of the six victims of the 7 December 1993 Long Island Railroad shooting. She donated $1 million to establish Camp Mariah for the Fresh Air Fund, of which she is a director. The camp is located in Fishkill, New York. She also established the Mariah Carey Scholarships at the Usdan Center, a summer school for the arts, and among other worthy causes has made large contributions to the Make-A-Wish Foundation.

● **Camille O. Cosby** (1944–) is a film producer, speaker, and, along with her husband, the comedian Bill Cosby, is one of America's foremost philanthropists. She was born in Washington, DC, to Guy and Catherine Hanks. She attended the University of Maryland and married Bill Cosby in 1964. Later she returned to school and earned an EdD from the University of Massachusetts in 1992. Involvement in philanthropic work is second nature to both Cosbys. Their special interest areas are education and the impact of racial prejudice. They have the personal experience of losing a son in what appeared to be a botched robbery, but which may have been a racially motivated shooting, and have established a foundation in his name.

Camille Cosby initiated the National Visionary Leadership project, a long-term endeavor to collect oral histories of older African Americans. She is working with the writer and journalist Renee Poussaint to interview at least sixty notable African Americans seventy-two years of age or older. Students are involved in the rest of the project. When asked why she is making this investment of time and money, she responded, "We must become critical thinkers. And the only way is to know the truth about our history." At a Temple University commencement, Camille Cosby was the special guest speaker. She was awarded an honorary doctorate of human letters for innovative philanthropic work and public projects. The remaining speakers included men and woman who benefited from Cosby Scholarships at Temple University.

● **Sarah L. Delany and A. Elizabeth Delany** The sisters, Sarah (1889–1999) and Elizabeth Delany (1891–1995), made a $1 million bequest to create a scholarship fund at St. Augustine's College in North Carolina in honor of their father, Bishop Henry B. Delany, a former vice principal at the college. The Delany sisters, who graduated from the college in 1910 and 1911, were co-authors with Amy Hill Hearth of *Having Our Say: The Delany Sisters' First 100 Years*. (See individual entry: Delany Sarah Louise, and Annie Elizabeth Delany.)

● **Jean Fairfax** (1920–) has established an outstanding profile of accomplishments in both civil rights and philanthropy. She was born in Cleveland, Ohio. Both of her parents had university educations and stressed the importance of learning. She earned her BA from the University of Michigan and MA from Union Theological Seminary and Columbia University. She did postgraduate work at Harvard and was a visiting scholar at Radcliffe.

World War II sparked Fairfax's interest in greater involvement in community and charity work. After the war she directed Quaker relief efforts in Austria. In 1965 she began working for the NAACP. She worked for more than thirty years for racial and gender justice in supporting the American Friends Service Committee and the NAACP's Legal Defense and Educational Fund. She and her sister, Betty Fairfax, drew considerable attention in 1987 when they adopted the eighth-grade class at Phoenix's

Mary McLeod Bethune School. They promised scholarships to all ninety-two students at the inner-city school who finished high school and went to college. Fairfax has been active in philanthropy for the past thirty-five years, serving as a trustee of numerous foundations. In 1995 she began working as a consultant on issues of black philanthropy.

● **Whoopi Goldberg** (1949–) has had a stunningly successful career as an actor and comedian. She is also an advocate for children, the homeless, and the human rights movement. Active in the battle against AIDS and substance abuse, she is Goodwill Ambassador for the American Health Foundation. (See individual entry: Goldberg, Whoopi.)

● **Ruth Wright Hayre** (1911–1989) believed in the value of education. She was born in Atlanta, Georgia, and grew up in West Philadelphia. After entering the University of Pennsylvania at the age of fifteen and getting her degree, she fought for ten years to be allowed to teach in the Philadelphia public schools. She was the first black woman secondary school teacher, secondary school principal, and superintendent in Philadelphia. She was also the first woman to head the city's school board. Ruth Wright Hayre lived by the words from a poem by John Greenleaf Whittier, "Tell them we are rising." These words form the title of her autobiography and provide the name of a program instituted by Hayre in a Philadelphia school. She created a program of hope for 116 sixth-grade students when she promised that, if they stayed in school the next six years and received grades acceptable to attend college, she would provide them with scholarships. She also created the Wings of Excellence Program to motivate and encourage young urban black girls.

● **Whitney Houston** (1963–) is one of the most successful pop singers of all time. She is also a philanthropist on a large scale. A grant from her foundation led to the creation of The Whitney Houston Pediatric Special Care Unit at the University of Medicine and Dentistry of New Jersey University Hospital in Newark. A gift from Houston enabled Hale House to start the "Time Out for Moms" program, which provides a physical and emotional haven for women worn out by parenting and from living in drug- and crime-infested neighborhoods. She has also given to Rainbow House, the families of military personnel who served in the Gulf War, a number of South African children's charities, and other organizations devoted to the welfare of children. (See individual entry: Houston, Whitney.)

● **Janet Jackson** (1966–), the popular music icon, is also a philanthropist who has quietly made a difference in the lives of others. Born in Gary, Indiana, into the famously musical Jackson family, she first caught the attention of the public through her acting when she was eleven. The role of Penny on *Good Times* led to other television appearances. Then, at the age of sixteen, Jackson made her recording debut, but she did not make an impression on the pop music world until her third album, *Control*, which sold 8 million copies. After her world tour in 1990 she donated almost half a million dollars to the United Negro College Fund, and she has been making generous contributions ever since to a variety of causes. She donated the proceeds from a two-day concert at New York's Radio City Music Hall to the Rwandan relief effort. A portion of the proceeds from her smash hit single "Together Again" was donated to AIDS activism. She also supports charities such as the Make-A-Wish Foundation.

● **Eunice Walker Johnson** (1917–) has served as the fashion editor of *Ebony* magazine and the secretary-treasurer of Johnson Publishing Company. In addition, she has been producer and director of the Ebony Fashion Fair traveling fashion show for more than forty years. She is also a philanthropist who has donated more than $49 million to the United Negro College Fund and other African American charities. (See individual entry: Johnson, Eunice Walker.)

● **Sheila C. Johnson** (1949–) is a rare individual whose generosity is as wide-ranging as her talent. She grew up outside Chicago, the daughter of a neurosurgeon, and became interested in music early in life. After marrying Robert L. Johnson in 1969 she taught violin, founded and ran a 140-member children's orchestra, and established a music conservatory. She was also executive vice president of the company her husband cofounded, Black Entertainment Television, and began her philanthropic career. After their divorce in 2002 she stepped up her philanthropic work considerably. In particular she has made major contributions to art and musical education, including $7 million to the Parsons School of Design in New York. She also founded the Sheila C. Johnson Performing Arts Center at Hill School in Middleburg, Virginia.

As of 2005, Johnson was reaching out even further in her position as CEO of Salamander Development. This project resulted from her involvement with the Christopher Reeve Paralysis Institute, established to build quality-of-life programs for the physically challenged. Another accomplishment is the financial support and formation of "Young Strings in Action," an ensemble for students between the ages of three and eighteen.

● **Alicia Keys** (1981–), five-time Grammy winner, is a committed spokesperson for Keep A Child Alive, which supports HIV/AIDS clinics in Africa. Born in New York City, she was the child of an African American father and an Italian-Irish mother. She trained as a classical pianist, and at fourteen developed an interest in jazz. She majored in choir at New York's Professional Performance Arts School while she pursued her music career. Her debut solo album, *Songs in A Minor*, sold more than 50,000 copies its first day in the stores. In 2002, while in Africa for an MTV concert to support World AIDS Day, she began to take a serious interest in the tragic situation there. She began working with Keep A Child Alive and sent out a call to other young people to support its work.

● **Oseola McCarty** (1908–1999), a woman who lived simply and put away her pennies to buy candy for a neighborhood child, caught everyone by surprise when she contributed $150,000 to Southern Mississippi University in Hattiesburg. The humble washerwoman became the University of Southern Mississippi's most famous benefactor. McCarty was born in Wayne County, Mississippi, into a very poor family and, at a very early age, started earning money by doing ironing when she came home from school. Unfortunately, she was forced to leave school by the sixth grade in order to care for an ailing aunt. She worked for much of the social register of Hattiesburg. In some cases she took in laundry from three generations of their families. McCarty said, "After the war when I started making ten dollar a bundle I started saving." She put her savings in an account that drew compound interest. At eighty-seven years of age, and having no family, she felt that the money she had scraped together over a lifetime "should help some child go to college." The president of the university found her generosity so extraordinary that she commented that she had never been so touched by a gift. After her contribution to the school her life was filled with all kinds of new experiences—travel to Washington, DC, interviews on all the major television networks, and an honorary doctorate from Harvard University. Her philosophy for living, working, and self-pride are expressed in her autobiography, *Simple Wisdom for Rich Living*.

● **Melba Moore** (1945–) is a Tony Award–winning, Grammy-nominated singer and actor. She was born Beatrice Hill in New York City to Melba (Bonnie) Smith, a singer, and Teddy Hill, a jazz saxophonist. She was raised by her mother and stepfather, pianist Clement Moorman, and attended Arts High School in Newark before enrolling in Montclair State Teacher's College for a bachelor's degree. She taught in the Newark public schools for a year and performed with a vocal group. She then began to do backup vocals, sing commercial jingles, and perform in the Catskills resort area. In 1967 she was asked to audition for *Hair*, the revolutionary musical about sex, drugs, and rock and roll. She remained with the production for eighteen months, eventually taking over the female lead from Diane Keaton. It was the first time a black woman had moved into a female lead previously played by a white woman on Broadway. Moore's star rose steadily from that time through the show *Purlie* (1969), for which she won a Tony, and on to several films and her own television variety show. She continued to have good times and bad throughout the 1970s and 1980s but began to flounder in the early 1990s. She was divorced from her manager-husband, Charles Huggins, and left broke. Her struggles during this time probably inspired the work she began to do in philanthropy when her star began to rise again a few years later. With a thoroughly rehabilitated career Moore founded the Melba Moore Foundation for Abused and Neglected Children, which provides funding for a variety of organizations devoted to the welfare of children.

Convention, whose first project was to raise money for a missionary, Emma Delaney, to go to Africa. They also supported Nannie Helen Burrough's National Training School for Women and Girls, giving it 59 percent of the money donated to the Women's Convention between 1900 and 1920.

Black female philanthropists also sustained their fight against racial oppression in more direct and radical ways. Of primary concern to African Americans at the end of the nineteenth century, for example, was the growing problem of lynching taking place in the South. Ida B. Wells-Barnett was a leading crusader in the antilynching movement. She owed much of her success in this effort to the fund-raising work and support of other black women. In 1892 Maritcha Lyons and Victoria Earle Matthews, active in community work in Brooklyn, wanted to rally New York women's clubs behind Wells-Barnett. They held a testimonial dinner that raised $200 to fund the printing of Wells-Barnett's best-known antilynching pamphlet, "Southern Horrors: Lynch Law in All Its Phases." Not to be outdone by New York women, African American

women gathered in the following year at the Metropolitan African Methodist Episcopal Church in Washington, DC, to raise funds and hear Wells-Barnett speak.

Church Groups and Federated Women's Clubs

Black women's clubs began to flourish at the end of the nineteenth century. They were, however, the natural descendants of literary- and reform-oriented clubs that elite black women had founded in the earlier decades of the century. Now free to openly agitate their causes nationally, black club women felt a keen need to create an umbrella organization under which they could coordinate and support their broadly based efforts. In 1896 they formed the National Association of Colored Women (NACW). Thousands of black club women in local clubs across the country joined. Through both their local clubs and the national federation, club women raised thousands of dollars for a variety of causes, particularly education, health, and the protection of young black women. The protection of young girls was central to their mission of uplifting the race by defending black women's morality and promoting

● **Phylicia Rashad** (1948–) works with and donates to the Diabetes Association; PRASAD (Philanthropic Relief, Altruistic Service And Development); the Children's Hospital of Washington, DC; and the Educational Teachers Association. After the death of her close friend Madeline Kahn she also became active in the Ovarian Cancer National Alliance. (See individual entry: Rashad, Phylicia.)

● **Jada Pinkett Smith** (1971–) has established with her husband the Will and Jada Pinkett Smith Family Foundation, which funds charitable organizations in several cities, focusing on youth education and urban family welfare. She was reared by her grandmother, a social worker, and her mother in Baltimore, Maryland, where she attended the Baltimore School of the Arts before spending year at North Carolina School of the Arts. Her formal education ended in 1991 when she was cast in the *Cosby Show* spin-off, *A Different World*. That exposure led to film roles, and she has been very busy acting ever since. In 1997 she married fellow actor Will Smith, and together they formed their foundation. Pinkett Smith's aunt, Karen Banfield Evans, is the executive director of the foundation.

● **Velma R. Speight-Buford** (1932–) donated $1.1 million in land and other assets to North Carolina A&T State University. Born in Snow Hill, North Carolina, she received a bachelor's degree from the university in 1953, and then went on to earn a master's degree and a doctorate from the University of Maryland. She had a distinguished career in teaching at both the high school and university levels and was former director of alumni affairs at the university.

● **Mary Eliza Church Terrell** (1863–1954), founder and first president of the National Association of Colored Women (NACW), was one of thousands of black women's club members whose charitable donations supported social services for the black community for decades. (See individual entry: Terrell, Mary Eliza Church.)

● **Dionne Warwick** (1940–) has used her star power to raise awareness and support for an array of social causes, particularly the fight against AIDS. She collaborated with the producer Burt Bacharach and the singers Gladys Knight, Stevie Wonder, and Elton John in 1985 to record "That's What Friends Are For," with profits donated to the American Foundation for AIDS Research, and she teamed up with other artists in 1990 to raise more than $2.5 million for AIDS organizations at a benefit at New York City's Radio City Music Hall. In 2004 she received the American Citizen Honor Award from the U.S. government in recognition of her humanitarian efforts. (See individual entry: Warwick, Dionne.)

● **Oprah Winfrey** (1954–), television star and entrepreneur, is one of the richest women in the world and a philanthropist on a major scale. It is estimated that she gives about 10 percent of her income to charitable and philanthropic ventures. In 2003, for example, she donated $2.5 million to fund the Oprah Winfrey Scholars Program for African women at New York University's Robert F. Wagner School of Public Service and she donated $5 million to the historically black Morehouse College. (See individual entry: Winfrey, Oprah.)

the home and respectability. Led by Janie Porter Barrett in 1915, the Virginia State Federation of Colored Women's Clubs raised over $6000 while soliciting state funding to purchase a farm on which to build the Industrial Home School for Wayward Colored Girls.

Club and church women recognized the need to protect young women migrants. Whether from rural southern communities or cities, they were in need of skills and connections to acquire work, safe housing, and the support of a community. In Detroit, local women feared that unsuspecting or desperate female migrants would be lured into prostitution or unsavory living arrangements, and they were determined to protect them from such a life. In 1919 one hundred women at the city's Second Baptist Church formed the Big Sister Auxiliary. The original group quickly recruited three hundred more members, and within four years they had raised $5000 and purchased a building, creating a home for young women.

Because fund-raising for the institutions they built was so difficult, many black women eventually turned to the state to solicit support for their programs. It was a way not

only to get additional funding for efforts they believed were worthy, but it also signaled the state's recognition of the rights of African Americans to solicit and receive funds to assist their protection and improvement. These kinds of fund-raising efforts often paid off—Virginia gave $6000 to support a girls' home. Yet, these grants rarely were enough to sustain an institution or program. States and municipalities sometimes were willing to fund an institution entirely, but that meant the women had to relinquish control.

Given the spotty and uncertain state support for their efforts, black women philanthropists continued to work in innovative ways in their fund-raising. The South Carolina Federation of Colored Women's Clubs used a number of fund-raising techniques to support the Fairwold Home for Colored Girls, which included pledging their own salaries, appealing to local congregations for donations, and "planting" Fairwold Christmas Trees that had to be "decorated" with money. In 1925 they raised $235 on the tree in only twelve minutes. The Culture Club of Columbia raised money through admission receipts from an annual play, a turkey raffle, a baby contest, and a baseball game for the benefit of Fairwold and numerous other causes, including the Good Samaritan Hospital. Another club planted and picked an acre of cotton and donated the receipts from its sale. South Carolina club women raised money for kindergartens through the sale of a pamphlet, "The Progress of Colored Women," authored by the NACW president Mary Church Terrell. Clubs with an elite urban membership held charity balls. Chicago's Silver Leaf Charity Club, for example, sponsored grand charity balls that were attended by the best families, with women dressed in their finest to raise money for their less-advantaged neighbors.

African American philanthropists not only helped to support the needy and to create necessary community institutions like schools, hospitals, and orphanages but they also helped to preserve historic and cultural sites that documented the unique contributions of African Americans to American society. One of the NACW's largest early twentieth century fund-raising efforts allowed them to purchase and restore Frederick Douglass's home. Under President Mary Talbert, the NACW formed a Douglass Home Committee, started a fund drive, and paid off the mortgage in only two years, by 1918.

African American women kept up their philanthropic endeavors as much as possible during tough economic times like the Great Depression. One solution was to solicit funds from white donors and foundations. This was the manner in which Charlotte Hawkins Brown was able to finance the creation of a normal school for black women in North Carolina, the Palmer Memorial Institute in Sedalia, named for one of her white patrons, the Wellesley College president Alice Freeman Palmer. Accepting financial assistance from whites sometimes meant political compromise. Jane Edna Hunter, who established the Phillis Wheatley Association and home for working class young women in Cleveland, Ohio, understood that many whites donors hoped that its existence would help ensure that the local Young Women's Christian Association remained all-white. Furthermore, many local whites who hired black domestic servants assumed that the Association would train them to be better servants.

It was a constant struggle for economic survival for Brown, Hunter, and other African American women who founded schools and other institutions. Black women supported one another both financially and morally. Hunter and Nannie Burroughs sent each other contributions from their own salaries and helped each other raise funds by lecturing on behalf of each other's institutions. Their correspondence with each other underscores the moral support and inspiration each drew from the other.

Other Avenues

African American women provided philanthropy through a variety of organizations in addition to church groups and federated women's clubs. Selena Sloan Butler organized the first African American Parent Teacher Association (PTA) in Atlanta, Georgia, in 1919, branches of which aided schools all over the nation. By 1927 there were 770 local associations in North Carolina alone, which raised more than $65,000 for local black schools. Black branches of the Woman's Christian Temperance Union (WCTU) not only fought for temperance but also assumed much of the charitable work in African American communities. Greek-letter sororities for black women also contributed significantly. Alpha Kappa Alpha began donating grants-in-aid in the 1950s, beginning with a $6,000 grant to the Howard University College of Medicine for research in child development. With its focus on education, AKA gave $25,000 to Central State University to restore a rare book collection, $500,000 to the United Negro College Fund, and by the 1990s, annual awards of up to $300,000 for scholarly pursuits through its Educational Advancement Foundation. Women in Jack and Jill of America, Inc., created a foundation that routinely donated thousands of dollars to various community groups that serve black youth. The Links, Inc., also promoted educational, cultural, and civic activities through its Grants-in-Aid program. These women contributed over $10 million to various causes, including pledges of $1 million each to the United Negro College Fund and the NAACP Legal Defense and Education Fund.

The Links, Jack and Jill, and black sororities represented groups of elite female philanthropists. Still, working-class women gave consistently through the years, especially within their various church organizations. While most confined themselves to aiding children, distressed families, and various church-driven charitable initiatives, some also used their funds for political purposes. Pullman maids and the wives of Pullman porters, through the Ladies' Auxiliary of the Brotherhood of Sleeping Car Porters, raised much of the money used to organize African American Pullman porters into one of the most successful black unions of the early twentieth century. The Ladies' Auxiliary was particularly important because the nature of their husbands' work kept the men on the railroad, forcing their wives to sustain the union at times.

Individual Philanthropists

Most black female philanthropy was traditionally a group effort. There were, however, significant numbers of wealthy black women who gave generously as individuals to various causes. Madam C. J. Walker, for example, was the first black woman to amass a significant fortune and make a name for herself as a philanthropist. She gave willingly to the NAACP's antilynching fund, the YWCA, and homes for the aged. Walker was active in the NACW and made substantial contributions to several educational institutions for women established by NACW members, including Charlotte Hawkins Brown's Palmer Memorial Institute, Mary McLeod Bethune's Daytona Normal and Industrial Institute for Negro Girls in Florida, and Lucy Laney's Haines Institute in Augusta, Georgia. Walker also contributed money for women to attend Booker T. Washington's Tuskegee Institute and made a significant gift to the fund to secure the Frederick Douglass home.

As the twentieth century progressed, more black women—principally artists, entertainers, athletes, real estate magnates, and successful professionals in various fields—gained popular and financial success. The gains of these African American women allowed them to continue the legacy of groups and individuals who gave in the past. Women like Oprah Winfrey, Whitney Houston, Janet Jackson, and Venus and Serena Williams made donations to many causes, including organizations dedicated to aiding African Americans in particular, such as the NAACP and the United Negro College Fund.

As individuals and as members of organizations, African American women raised and donated tens of millions of dollars, along with their skills and service, to a number of charities, institutions, and causes. Even with little state support, publicity, financial resources, and political power, for centuries they provided assistance to other African Americans.

See also National Association of Colored Women; Protestant Churches, Black; Sororities Movement; *and* Walker, Madam C. J.

BIBLIOGRAPHY

Bundles, A'Leila P. *Madam C. J. Walker: Entrepreneur.* New York: Chelsea House, 1991.

Bundles, A'Leila P. "Sharing the Wealth: Madam Walker's Philanthropy." *Radcliffe Quarterly* (December 1991).

Giddings, Paula. *In Search of Sisterhood: Delta Sigma Theta and the Challenge of the Black Sorority Movement.* New York: Morrow, 1988.

Harris, Robert L., Jr. "Early Black Benevolent Societies, 1780–1830." *Massachusetts Review* (Autumn 1979): 603–625.

Hendricks, Wanda. *Gender, Race, and Politics in the Midwest: Black Club Women in Illinois.* Bloomington: Indiana University Press, 1988.

Higginbotham, Evelyn Brooks. *Righteous Discontent: The Women's Movement in the Black Baptist Church, 1880–1920.* Cambridge, MA: Harvard University Press, 1993.

Hine, Darlene Clark, "'We Specialize in the Wholly Impossible': The Philanthropic Work of Black Women." In *Lady Bountiful Revisited: Women, Philanthropy, and Power,* edited by Kathleen D. McCarthy. New Brunswick, NJ: Rutgers University Press, 1990.

Johnson, Joan Marie. "The Colors of Social Welfare in the New South: Black and White Clubwomen in South Carolina, 1900–1930." In *Before the New Deal: Social Welfare in the South, 1830–1930,* edited Elna C. Green. Athens: University of Georgia Press, 1999.

Knupfer, Anne Meis. *"Toward a Tenderer Humanity and a Nobler Womanhood": African-American Women's Clubs in Turn-of-the-Century Chicago.* New York: New York University Press, 1996.

Parker, Marjorie. *A History of The Links, Incorporated.* Washington, DC: National Headquarters of the Links, 1982.

Parker, Marjorie. *Alpha Kappa Alpha Through the Years 1908–1988.* Chicago: Mobium Press, 1990.

Wadelington, Charles W., and Richard F. Knapp. *Charlotte Hawkins Brown and Palmer Memorial Institute: What One Young African American Woman Could Do.* Chapel Hill: University of North Carolina Press, 1999.

Wolcott, Victoria W. *Remaking Respectability: African American Women in Interwar Detroit.* Chapel Hill: University of North Carolina Press, 2001.

Yee, Shirley J. *Black Women Abolitionists: A Study in Activism, 1828–1860.* Knoxville: University of Tennessee Press, 1992.

—JOAN MARIE JOHNSON

PHOTOGRAPHY. As subjects, photographers, and workers in the photographic field, black women have participated in the medium of photography since its introduction in 1839. Immediately after the announcement of this democratic new medium, photography gained a particular stronghold in the United States, a young nation eager to see itself pictured. To date, scant evidence of black women photographers in the nineteenth century has been uncovered, although one can reasonably hypothesize that black women occupied some of the same roles that white women did in early photographic endeavors—as studio attendant, the person who would prepare subjects for their sittings; as darkroom assistant, helping the photographer to prepare and process his plates; or as photo finisher, adding hand coloring and other enhanced effects to the finished plate or print.

As photographic subjects, however, black women were very savvy about the new medium and its powers of communication. Probably the most famous relationship in the nineteenth century of a black woman to her photographic image is that of Sojourner Truth (1797–1883), a former slave turned abolitionist and feminist. After initially earning money to support her abolitionist activities through selling the narrative of her life as a slave, Truth sold *cartes-de-visite* and cabinet card portraits for thirty-three and fifty cents each to support herself. "I am living on my shadow," she wrote, and eventually the images were distributed with the now famous caption "I Sell the Shadow to Support the Substance."

Black women were frequently the subject of the photographer's lens both as hired models and paying customers. During the New Negro Movement in the early twentieth century, black women became frequent patrons of photographic studios as they consciously sought to create a new, positive identity for themselves and by extension their larger communities. Although their collaborative contributions have gone largely uncredited, black women who worked as models for artistic photographers advanced radical new definitions of black beauty that celebrated and claimed agency over their bodies.

The first black photography historians were, arguably, the women who compiled the family photo albums. These mothers, daughters, and aunts assumed the task of constructing their families' visual histories in ways that were highly personal, subjective, and creative. Subsequent generations of artists have drawn directly from that legacy, using the family album as a starting point for addressing and rewriting personal histories through image and text. The academic discipline of black photographic history came into existence with the pioneering work of Deborah Willis (b. 1948). Willis was the first historian to research and publish scholarship on black photographers, male and female. Her groundbreaking *Black Photographers 1840–1940: An Illustrated Bio-Bibliography* from 1985 and its companion *An Illustrated Bio-Bibliography of Black Photographers 1940–1988* from 1989 permanently changed the history of photography as it had been studied. Jeanne Moutoussamy-Ashe's definitive 1986 publication, *Viewfinders: Black Women Photographers,* is the only publication to date exclusively devoted to black women photographers. Both Moutoussamy-Ashe (b. 1951), and Willis are practicing photographers, simultaneously creating and writing this history. Likewise, the 1992 essay, "Olympia's Maid: Reclaiming Black Female Subjectivity," by the artist Lorraine O'Grady (b. 1940) has influenced the work of many second-generation photo historians.

For the first hundred years or so after photography's invention, black women photographers worked almost entirely in commercial endeavors; consequently their ties to the communities they photographed were strong. With a groundswell of creative activity that began during the Black Arts Movement of the 1960s, black women have increasingly used photography to articulate their diverse and powerful artistic voices. In the 1980s an unprecedented number of black women photographers burst onto the photographic scene. Largely college-trained, these artists built on the past, and their tremendous contributions have reshaped not only the history of black photography but of the medium itself.

Working the Medium

Although little information is known about early black women practitioners of the medium and there are no extant examples of their work, their efforts (and their names) must be acknowledged. As Moutoussamy-Ashe noted in *Viewfinders,* an 1866 business directory from the city of Houston, Texas, lists a Mary E. Warren, "colored," as a "photograph printer." An 1886 note in the *Cleveland Gazette,* a black newspaper, remarked that one Fanny Thompson of Memphis, Tennessee, was planning to "devote her school vacation to the study of photography,"

while the following year Hattie Baker placed an ad in the *Gazette* advertising her services as someone who made photographic enlargements. According to Moutoussamy-Ashe, black women's occupations were not even recorded until the 1890 census, yet that census listed six black women with the profession of photography. Within ten years, there were seventeen; ten years later it had doubled, and it would continue to do so each decade.

In 1904, Mary E. Flenoy, an active photographer from 1893 to 1909 from Danville, Illinois, was the first black woman photographer in attendance at Booker T. Washington's Fifth Annual National Negro Business League Convention. She was first listed in the Danville city directories as a photographer in 1899. While James VanDerZee is an acknowledged early black master of photography, virtually no recognition has been given his sister, Jennie Louise Welcome, born in 1885 and active from 1910 through the 1920s; she operated a New York studio under her married name, Mme. E. Toussaint Welcome. Welcome offered art courses in all media, including "Photo Enlarging in Crayon," which was probably some kind of hand coloring applied to photographic prints.

Defining a Community

During the New Negro Movement in the early twentieth century, a conscious effort was made on the part of photographers and subjects to create a positive image of black people. Black women assumed a central role in the projection of an image of progress and success within their communities. Black women photographers played a crucial role in examining and reinterpreting the dreams and ideals of the working class by making socially relevant and class-conscious images of the African American community. Their images document a vibrant family life and a growing middle class. Elise Forrest Harleston, who lived from 1891 to 1970; Wilhelmina Roberts, who died in 1976 in South Carolina; Elnora Teal, who was active from 1919 to the 1960s in Texas; and Adine Williams, who was active from 1936 to the 1980s in New Orleans all partnered with their husbands in commercial photographic endeavors. Beginning around 1920 Elise Harleston and her husband, Edwin, ran the Harleston Studio in Charleston; he operated the painting studio and she operated the photography studio. Harleston had studied photography in New York, where she was the only female student and only one of two blacks. She completed her study in 1921 at Tuskegee Institute in Alabama with the noted black photographer C. M. Battey. Harleston made sensitive portraits of her clients that her husband would use as the bases for his paintings. She also photographed the elderly men and women of Charleston.

Wilhelmina Pearl Selena Roberts also paired with her husband, Richard Samuel Roberts, in Roberts' Art Studio in Columbia, South Carolina, where 95 percent of their clientele was black. An expert seamstress, Roberts often crafted different styles of clothing for her sitters. Though she primarily assisted her husband, Roberts became a photographer herself, specializing in portraits of children. Elnora Teal and her husband, Arthur Chester Teal, ran the Teal Portrait Studio in Houston, Texas, from 1919 until 1965. Initially learning the process from her husband, Teal maintained the couple's original Milam Street studio as her own when her husband branched out to a second location. Elnora Teal's subjects included everyone from local people to the famed tenor Roland Hayes. Significantly, Arthur's assistant in the second studio was also a woman, Lucille Moore, who worked for him from 1925 until 1946 and who fulfilled the studio work while Arthur traveled around the state photographing.

Beginning in the 1940s, Adine Mitchell Williams operated four successful photography studios in Louisiana and California. With her first husband she ran the McLain Studio in New Orleans. After their divorce she ran her own studio, Camera Masters, before marrying Eddie Williams and opening a new studio in New Orleans and then relocating Camera Masters to Monterey, California. In the 1980s the Williamses operated the Picture Place in Baton Rouge. Williams's three children all became professional photographers, including her daughter Leah Ann Washington, who became the first black woman graduate of Brooks Institute of Photography in California.

Florestine Perrault Collins (1895–1988) owned and operated a studio in New Orleans from 1920 until 1949. Starting out photographing her own family, Collins opened her first studio in her living room. Working as a photographer's assistant gave her the exposure and skills that she needed to perfect her craft. As a "creole of color," Collins was mistaken for white. As she later recalled, she would not have gotten her job—and the chance to hone her skills—if her employer had realized she was black.

Opportunities for black women photographers remained consistently strong throughout the early to mid-twentieth century. In Wilmington, North Carolina, Lydia Mayo and Carol Augustus were co-owners of the Vanderbilt Studio, and Alberta H. Brown and her husband, George O. Brown, ran the Browns' Studio in Richmond, Virginia. Winifred Hall Allen, originally from Jamaica, managed a Harlem studio for twenty years. Hall had apprenticed at William and Emma King Woodard's studio before taking it over and renaming it the Winifred Hall Photo Studio. She documented the Harlem community, particularly the women-owned businesses. Allen taught photography to her husband, Fred Allen, before giving up the practice in 1950 to devote herself to nursing.

Defining the Self

Black women also actively participated in photography during this period as photographers' models. Virtually every artistic photographer included at least one study of a black woman in his or her oeuvre. Unfortunately, most of these models' names were not recorded and are now unknown, but there are some that stand out because they maintained separate artistic careers in other disciplines. The dancer Edna Guy worked as both an artist's model and as a photographer for *Our World* magazine in the 1940s. During the 1930s and 1940s the most prolific and successful of these models was Maudelle Bass (1908–1989), a California- and later New York–based dancer who posed for some of the most renowned photographers of the day, including Edward Weston and Manuel Alvarez Bravo. Bass maintained a successful, long-term artistic career in her own right, and she was exceptional in that she is the only black female model who appears as herself with such frequency in the work of so many well-known artists from this period.

In the mid-twentieth century some black women began to use photography for their own artistic ends. Louise E. Jefferson's career as photographer and illustrator spanned more than thirty years. In 1973 she published *The Decorative Arts of Africa*, which included photographs she made over a ten-year period in five visits to the continent. Inge Hardison (b. 1914) studied photography in the 1930s in New York at the Art Students' League. She quickly found her niche photographing children, and her work was reproduced frequently in *Color* magazine. In 1969 Hardison became the only female founding member of the Black Academy of Arts and Letters. Although Hardison is better known as a sculptor, her photographic work of the 1940s and 1950s is important.

Eslanda "Essie" Cardoza Goode Robeson (1896–1965), the wife of Paul Robeson, was a chemist who took up photography while living in London. Applying her scientific training to attain mastery of the medium, Robeson photographed in the Soviet Union, South Africa, and China, often in conjunction with her anthropological studies and political work. Billie Louise Barbour Davis (1906–1955), wife of the professor Collis Davis, was teaching dance at Hampton Institute in Virginia when she became interested in photography. Her main interest was portraiture, though she also photographed Hampton events. Beginning in the late 1940s, Davis began to experiment with the more artistic and abstract possibilities of the medium, making cloud studies and experimental photograms and manipulations. Her work is significant, perhaps marking the first photographic work by a black woman to consciously explore the formal artistic possibilities of the medium.

The Cultural Landscape

Wartime directed several black women into the fields of journalistic and applied photography. The Women's Army Corps, established during World War II, introduced a new group of black women to the medium. Among them was Elizabeth "Tex" Williams, born in 1924, who had worked as an assistant in a Houston studio learning the basics of photography. Stationed at Fort Huachuca, Arizona, she became an official army photographer for the Public Information Office, doing everything from ID photos to medical photography. Williams later became the first black woman to attend and graduate with honors, first in her class, from Photo Division School.

In Los Angeles, the destination of many black migrants from the South, several black women photographers found their niches as businesswomen and photojournalists. Ruth Washington ran the successful Avalon Photography Studio specializing in school photographs and portraits. Her studio assistant, the photographer Dora Miller (d. 1952), eventually took over the business. During that same period in the mid-1940s, the Los Angeles nightclub owner Charles Williams employed the wildly popular "Camera Girls" to walk around and photograph the clientele in his establishments. Vera Jackson, born in 1912, covered the glamorous Hollywood beat for the society page of the *California Eagle* newspaper. Among the famous women whom Jackson photographed were the actor Dorothy Dandridge and the educator Mary McLeod Bethune.

As the civil rights movement gained momentum and black people began to gain social and political access across the country, black women continued to make small yet crucial inroads in the field of photography. The photojournalist Elaine Tomlin, active in the 1960s through the 1980s, became the official photographer for the Southern Christian Leadership Conference, documenting the marches, demonstrations, and ordinary participants in the struggle for equality. Also an educator, Tomlin taught photography in the 1970s and was named Photographer of the Year by the Atlanta Media Women. Louise Ozell Martin (1911–1995), wanted to be a photographer from the moment her mother bought her a Kodak box camera when she was a child in Texas. Martin later studied photography at the Art Institute of Chicago and the University of Denver, where she earned money photographing soldiers stationed nearby at army camps. In 1946 she opened her own studio in Houston, the Louise Martin Art Studio, and earned a reputation as Houston's society photographer. An active chronicler of the black community, Martin was among the photographers present at Martin Luther King Jr.'s funeral in 1968. From 1973 until 1976 she operated the Louise Martin School of Photography in Houston.

After studying photography as the only woman in her class at the Art Institute of Chicago, Valeria "Mikki" Ferrill (b. 1937) worked in Mexico as a freelance foreign correspondent. Upon her return to the United States, Ferrill's work appeared in *Jet*, *Ebony*, and *Time* magazines, among others. Among her early subjects, Ferrill chronicled gang life on Chicago's South Side. She has also worked as a curator, organizing exhibitions of photography, but she continues to photograph. Her recent work includes series on black women bodybuilders and black cowboys. The photojournalist Marilyn Nance (b. 1953) focuses on African American spiritual life, Collette Fournier (b. 1952) has documented the activities of women in the Caribbean and United States, and Chandra McCormick (b. 1957) photographs black cultural rituals in New Orleans.

Salimah Ali (b. 1954) also focuses on black women's lives, specifically Muslim women. A graduate of the Fashion Institute of Technology in New York City, Ali has photographed such black celebrities as Eartha Kitt, Patty LaBelle, Grace Jones, Earth Wind and Fire, Bob Marley, and Stevie Wonder. Her work has appeared in *Essence*, *Ms.*, *Black Enterprise*, *USA Today*, *Newsday*, the *New York Times*, the *Los Angeles Times*, and the *Washington Post*, among others. Carroll Parrott Blue, born in 1943, now primarily a filmmaker, has photographed African American icons such as Angela Davis and Fannie Lou Hamer. Other photojournalists have used their cameras to focus on underrepresented groups within the black community. In 1979 the photographers Leigh Mosley (b. 1945) and Sharon Farmer, active in the 1980s, documented the historic Third World Lesbian and Gay Conference in Washington, DC, and *Blacklight* magazine published a special photo edition on the conference with their images. In the 1990s, during President Bill Clinton's tenure, Farmer became the first black woman White House staff photographer and the first black chief photographer. She was also given the Exposure Group's Photographer of the Year Award.

Many black women photographers have located their practice between documentary and artistic work that focuses on their communities and the human condition. Cheryl Miller (b. 1953) and Linda Day Clark (b. 1963) photograph the worlds at their doorsteps in New York and Baltimore, respectively. Susan J. Ross, a photographer who also focuses her lens on the African American community, is a founding member of Sistagraphy, an Atlanta-based collective of black women photographers organized in 1993. The Bay Area photographer Jean Weisinger (b. 1954) has traveled the world photographing people of color. Weisinger is perhaps best known for her self-portraits and for her candid, intimate portraits of writers and lesbians, including Audre Lorde and Alice Walker, which she published as a weekly calendar, *Imagery: Women Writers*, in 1996. Fern Logan (b. 1945), an Illinois-based, largely self-taught photographer, began photographing African American artists in the early 1980s. In 2001 she published those portraits in *The Artist Portrait Series: Images of Contemporary African American Artists*.

An Art of Their Own

The late 1960s and early 1970s witnessed a conscious move toward photography not necessarily as a practical vocation but as an artistic expression, as a growing awareness developed among black photographers of their own aesthetic. Although the debate had been waged since its invention, in the 1970s photography began to gain mainstream acceptance as a fine art medium and one that could successfully compete in the art marketplace. In the midst of this moment and the burgeoning Black Arts Movement, Ming Smith, active beginning in the 1970s, became the only female member of Kamoinge, a black photographer's workshop founded in New York in 1963 by Roy DeCarava and others in order to foster an exchange among black photographers. A former model, in 1992 Smith self-published a monograph of her images entitled *A Ming Breakfast: Grits and Scrambled Moments*.

The latter part of the twentieth century witnessed a dramatic increase in photographic images produced by black women. The atmosphere of support and cultural pride born of the movements of the 1960s gave rise to more personal expressions by photographers beginning in the late 1970s. The late 1980s saw an explosion of exhibitions and publications devoted to the work of black women photographers in the United States. Photography and the history of photography had fully entered the academy; academic opportunities for artists had increased and the emphasis on photography as a fine art medium had entered the marketplace. An increasing number of black women photographers have used self-portraiture to locate and define themselves in contemporary society. Some write an autobiography of the body, using their own likenesses and those of other black women. The diversity of imagery in self-portraiture reflects the range of interests, concerns, and experiences of women photographers. This type of work tends to be less representative and more interpretive than documentary photography.

In 1979, while in labor, the photographer Cary Beth Cryor (1947–1997), photographed the birth of her child in the series "Rites of Passage" and later photographed her aging grandmother as she transitioned through the final cycles of her life. Cryor's fearless work anticipated the highly personal, family-based imagery of artists like Clarissa Sligh (b. 1939), emerging in the 1980s with work that incorporated family photographs and personal history, including *Reading Dick and Jane with Me* and *What's Happening with Momma?* which are both artist's books. As the keeper of her family's photo album, Sligh used the opportunity to incorporate those images in her prints and reconstruct an alternative family album that addresses such painful issues as childhood sexual abuse and incest. Sligh has also tackled larger cultural issues such as civil rights, African burial grounds, and explorations of masculinity.

Cynthia Wiggins, active in the 1980s, Mfon (Mmekutmfon) Essien (d. 2002), and Renée Cox (b. 1960) are three photographers who have expressly used the self-portrait to explore issues of beauty, strength, desire, and identity. Wiggins responds to the influence of popular culture, while Essien, in the series "The Amazon's New Clothes," unflinchingly documented her body, which had been altered by mastectomy, forcing the viewer to examine how we define femininity and strength. The Jamaican-born, New York–based photographer Cox met then-mayor Rudolph Giuliani head-to-head when he attempted to censor her version of *The Last Supper* in which she appears, nude, as the figure of Christ. This controversy occurred during the Brooklyn Museum's 2001 exhibition Committed to the Image, which, along with Deborah Willis's traveling exhibition Reflections in Black, brought younger photographers' work to a national audience.

Equally personal but not utilizing self-portraits is the work of Lynn Marshall-Linnemeier (b. 1954), a painter, writer, and photographer who rephotographs or restages images from our collective history, as in her "Snapshot and Topsy" series. Marshall-Linnemeier's exuberantly painted photographs incorporate history and folklore in an informed retelling of the past. H. Lenn Keller (b. 1951) created the 1993 mixed media series "Dark Adventure" using selective cropping of heavily coded black women's bodies to address racial objectification and fetishism of African American lesbians within the lesbian community.

Photographic artists who emerged in the 1980s and 1990s found many more opportunities for exhibition, publication, and sale of their work. Championed by historians such as Kellie Jones and Deborah Willis who curated, exhibited, and wrote about their work, black women photographers found an audience that had previously not existed. In exhibitions including 1989's Constructed Images: New Photography and Black Photographer's Bear Witness: One Hundred Years of Social Protest, 1990's Convergence: Eight Photographers, and 1994's Imagining Families: Images and Voices, Willis introduced the work of Pat Ward Williams (b. 1948), Lorna Simpson (b. 1960), Coreen Simpson (b. 1942), Elisabeth Sunday (b. 1958), Clarissa Sligh, and others who have gone on to achieve hitherto unprecedented success. Personal Narratives: Women Photographers of Color, a 1993 exhibition organized by the Southeastern Center for Contemporary Art in Winston-Salem, North Carolina, included the work of seven black women artists: Lorraine O'Grady, Coreen

Simpson, Lorna Simpson, Sligh, Carrie Mae Weems, Williams, and Willis. Both Lorna Simpson's conceptual image/text pieces from the 1980s and the folklore-influenced photographs of Weems (b. 1953) have gained widespread recognition within the art world, and each has been the focus of numerous publications, solo exhibitions, and awards. Weems's 1995–1996 image/text installation commissioned by the J. Paul Getty Museum in Los Angeles, *From Here I Saw What Happened and I Cried*, is considered to be one of that most important artworks of that decade.

In the late 1990s and the first years of the twenty-first century, younger artists, curators, and historians have emerged to continue the dialogue begun by those pioneering women. Contemporary photo historians, including Lisa Henry, Carla Williams, Lisa Gail Collins, and Camara Holloway, were expanding the curatorial and historical work that Willis and Moutoussamy-Ashe began twenty years before them. These younger artists who have just begun to exhibit and publish their work include Sheila Pree (b. 1967), Myra B. Greene (b. 1975), Deborah Jack (b. 1970), Delphine A. Fawundu (b. 1971), Andrea Davis Kronlund (b. 1965), Keisha Scarville (b. 1975), and Lauri Lyons (b. 1971). With the new technical possibilities of digital photography, black women photographers of the new century have limitless potential for expression.

Figurative, representative work still dominates black women's photographic production. Pree's series "Recontextualizing the Black Female Body" directly addresses the historical precedents of representation and reclaims black female sexuality through the bodies of her subjects. Greene's mixed media work has incorporated hair, antique jewelry, and other loaded signifiers to investigate memory, popular culture, and beauty. In 2002's "The Beautiful Ones," Greene juxtaposes magazine images and family photographs of her mother and herself, rephotographed and manipulated to suggest erasure and loss, in order to examine the ways in which her personal notions of beauty have been constructed. In a more straightforward style, Kronlund's portraits also explore the complicated relationship between black women, beauty, and hair. Scarville's delicate still-life "portraits" of ordinary objects position memory as both personal and universal. At the beginning of the twenty-first century, the wealth and breadth of black women's photography was staggering. As photographic artists, black women had fully come into their own.

See also Willis-Kennedy, Deborah.

BIBLIOGRAPHY

Isaak, Jo Anna. "Essay." In *Renée Cox: American Family*, by Renée Cox. New York: Robert Miller Gallery, 2001.

Jones, Kellie, et al. *Lorna Simpson (Contemporary Artists)*. London: Phaidon, 2002.

Kirsh, Andrea, and Susan Fisher Sterling. *Carrie Mae Weems*. Washington, DC: National Museum of Women in the Arts, 1993.

Logan, Fern. *The Artist Portrait Series: Images of Contemporary African American Artists*. Carbondale: Southern Illinois University Press, 2001.

Millstein, Barbara Head, ed. *Committed to the Image: Contemporary Black Photographers*. New York: Brooklyn Museum of Art, 2001.

Moutoussamy-Ashe, Jeanne. *Viewfinders: Black Women Photographers*. New York: Dodd Mead, 1986.

Piché, Thomas, Jr. "Essay." In *Carrie Mae Weems: Recent Work, 1992–1998*, by Carrie Mae Weems. New York: Braziller, 1998.

Rony, Fatimah Tobing, et al. *Personal Narratives: Women Photographers of Color*. Exhibition catalog. Winston-Salem, NC: Southeastern Center for Contemporary Art, 1993.

Smith, Ming. *A Ming Breakfast: Grits and Scrambled Moments*. New York: de Ming Dynasty, 1992.

Thompson, Kathleen, and Hilary Mac Austin, eds. *The Face of Our Past: Images of Black Women from Colonial America to the Present*. Bloomington: Indiana University Press, 1999.

Weems, Carrie Mae. *Carrie Mae Weems: The Hampton Project*. New York: Aperture, 2000. Includes essays by Vivian Patterson and others.

Weisinger, Jean. *Imagery: Women Writers. Portraits by Jean Weisinger (Aunt Lute's Weekly Planner 1996–1997)*. San Francisco: Aunt Lute Books, 1996.

Williams, Carla. *Carlagirl Photo*. http://www.carlagirl.net. Includes an extensive annotated research library related to black women artists and images of black women, plus extensive links to other sites related to black women artists.

Williams, Pat Ward. *Pat Ward Williams: Probable Cause*. Philadelphia: Goldie Paley Gallery, Moore College of Art and Design, 1992. Includes essays by Kellie Jones and others.

Willis, Deborah. *Lorna Simpson*. San Francisco: Friends of Photography, 1992.

Willis, Deborah. *Reflections in Black: A History of Black Photographers 1840 to the Present*. New York: Norton, 2000.

Willis, Deborah, and Carla Williams. *The Black Female Body: A Photographic History*. Philadelphia: Temple University Press, 2002.

Willis-Thomas, Deborah. *An Illustrated Bio-Bibliography of Black Photographers 1940–1988*. New York: Garland, 1989.

Willis-Thomas, Deborah. *Black Photographers 1840–1940: An Illustrated Bio-Bibliography*. New York: Garland, 1985.

Wright, Beryl, and Saidiya Hartman. *Lorna Simpson: For the Sake of the Viewer*. Chicago: Museum of Contemporary Art, 1992.

—CARLA WILLIAMS

PHYSICIANS. The 140-year history of black women physicians began during the Civil War, on 1 March 1864, when thirty-two-year-old Mrs. Rebecca Davis Lee (1831–1895), a former nurse, graduated from Boston's New England Female Medical College. Lee's pioneering accomplishment occurred seventeen years after the first black man, David John Peck, and fifteen years after the first white woman, Elizabeth Blackwell, had received their degrees. The minutes of the faculty meeting that voted to award Lee's "doctress of medicine" degree noted that she was "colored." The need to identify her racially and the conferral of a gender-specific degree underscored the fact that she was just not a physician, let alone a woman

DR. JUSTINA FORD, who graduated in 1899 from Hering Medical College in Chicago, was the first black woman licensed to practice medicine in Colorado. (Denver Public Library.)

physician, but a black woman physician. Such a distinction would also by made for those women who followed in Lee's professional footsteps. As was the case when Justina Ford, an 1899 graduate of Chicago's Hering Medical College and the first black woman licensed to practice in Colorado, applied for her medical license in 1902, the clerk was reluctant to accept the fee because he said that she had two strikes against her—she was a woman and she was black.

The history of black women physicians illuminates the difficulty of trying to advance in a prestigious profession when one has to face obstacles based on race and gender. Black women physicians were forced to battle not only sexism, including that of black men, but also racism, including that of white women. They also had to confront stereotypes about black women and about the contours of black women's work. Yet the history of black women physicians also reveals that despite these obstacles, black women physicians advanced in their profession and made significant contributions to medicine and the black community.

The Trailblazers

Rebecca Lee began her journey to become the first black woman physician on 8 February 1831 when she was born at an unknown location in Delaware to Matilda (Webber) and Absolum Davis. Not much is known about Lee's early life except that she was raised in Pennsylvania by an aunt. By 1852, she had moved to Charlestown, Massachusetts, where she worked as a nurse for various physicians. At some unknown point, she married a man surnamed Lee. In 1860, with letters of support from her physician-employers, Lee sought and gained admission to the New England Female Medical College.

Lee's accomplishment was trailblazing. In 1860, of the 54,543 physicians in the United States, only 300 were women. Most physicians of the time did not attend medical school, but received their training through apprenticeships with practicing physicians. Most medical schools denied admission to African Americans and women. The first black medical school, Howard University, did not open until 1869. The historical record is silent on Lee's medical school experiences. However, it is clear that she encountered difficulties graduating. On 24 February 1864, Lee and her two white classmates came before the faculty for their final oral examinations. Each candidate had fulfilled the other requirements for graduation. At the conclusion of the oral exam, the faculty recommended degrees for all three students, but registered concerns about Lee's academic deficiencies. Despite these reservations, she shortly became the school's first and only black alumna.

After her graduation from medical school, Lee practiced in Boston, specializing in the care of women and children. For a time, she sought additional training in an unspecified location in the "British Dominion." For a few months in 1866, she worked for the Freedmen's Bureau in Richmond, doing missionary work and providing medical care to recently emancipated slaves. At the end of her Freedmen's Bureau service, Lee returned to Boston where she married Arthur Crumpler, a native Virginian. By 1880, she had stopped actively practicing medicine. The 1880 census listed her occupation as keeping house and that of her husband as porter. However, Crumpler had not completely severed her ties to the world of medicine. In 1883, she published *A Book of Medical Discourses*, a manual to advise women on medical care for themselves and their children. On 9 March 1895, Rebecca Crumpler died at the age of sixty-four. In *A Book of Medical Discourses*, Crumpler discussed her motivation for entering medicine: "I [had] early conceived a liking for and sought every opportunity to be in a position to relieve the suffering of others." Her comments underscore the fact that Crumpler was following the long tradition of black women who provided care as midwives, herbalists, and folk healers, while at the same time forging a new path for black women to provide care as physicians.

Three years after Crumpler received her medical degree, Philadelphian Rebecca Cole (1846–1922) became the second black woman physician when in 1867 she graduated from the Woman's Medical College of Pennsylvania. Afterward, Cole worked as a resident physician and a so-called sanitary visitor with Elizabeth Blackwell at the New York Infirmary for Women and Children. Her responsibilities consisted of visiting poor women in their homes and instructing them in the basics of hygiene.

After completing her training, Cole forged a career that foreshadowed those of black women who followed in her professional footsteps—she combined medicine, public health, and activism. During her fifty-year career, she worked for a variety of medical and social agencies that provided services to poor African Americans. She provided care at the Home for Aged and Infirmed Colored People and the Woman's Directory, a social welfare agency that she co-founded in 1873 to provide medical and legal aid to poor women. Cole also spoke out against racial discrimination and segregation. She wrote letters to Philadelphia newspapers, protesting the establishment of racially separate women's committees to celebrate the nation's centennial. Cole also emerged as a vocal critic of medical and social theories that attributed the poor health status of African Americans to immoral lifestyles and inherent susceptibilities. She instead called attention to social and economic conditions such as racism, poor health care, and poverty. In addition to her public health work, Cole maintained a private practice in Philadelphia where she died in 1922.

The third black woman physician, Susan Smith McKinney Steward (1847–1918), was born Susan Maria Smith in 1847 in Brooklyn to a successful pig farmer and his wife. She taught school in Washington, DC, for two years before she entered New York Medical College for Women, a homeopathic institution. (Homeopathy was a popular and accepted medical practice then). Smith graduated as the valedictorian of the 1870 class. At a time when postgraduate training was not rare for the average practitioner, she went on to complete such training.

Eventually, Steward established a successful medical career. In 1881, she helped establish Brooklyn's Woman's and Children's Hospital and served on its staff and that of other institutions such as the Brooklyn Home for Aged Colored People. Steward also maintained a prosperous private practice that catered to both black and white patients.

Steward was involved in political and community activities. She served as the organist and choir director at her church. She helped found the Woman's Loyal Union, a black women's club, and the Equal Suffrage League of Brooklyn. She served as a member of the U.S. delegation to the 1911 World Congress of Races, convened in London to refute theories of racial inferiority.

Steward married twice. After her second marriage, she closed her New York offices. She later practiced on army posts in Montana and Nebraska and worked as the resident physician at Wilberforce University where she died on 7 March 1918.

Following in the Steps of the Pioneers

According to the Census Bureau, in 1890, 104,805 physicians practiced in the United States, including 115 black women and 909 black men. By 1920, the number of physicians nationwide had grown to 144,977, and the number of black male physicians had increased to 3,495, but the number of black females had declined to 65. The decline was due in large part to a growing resistance to women practicing medicine (the number of white female physicians had also declined).

Many of the black women physicians who practiced in the late nineteenth and early twentieth centuries came from elite, prosperous families who supported their professional aspirations. In addition, many of these women combined their medical careers with work in a wide variety of civic, charitable, and religious organizations.

Sarah Loguen Fraser (1850–1933) was the daughter of Jermain Loguen, a bishop in the African Methodist Episcopal Zion Church and a wealthy landowner in Syracuse. Bishop Loguen, a former slave, and his wife, Caroline, ran one of the most active stations of the Underground Railroad. Their daughter Sarah entered Syracuse Medical College in 1873 and graduated three years later. She then interned at the Woman's Hospital in Philadelphia and Boston's New England Hospital for Women. In 1880, she became the first African American woman with a medical degree to practice in Washington. In the ceremony that opened her office, Frederick Douglass, her sister's father-in-law, hung her office shingle.

Caroline Still Wiley Anderson (1848–1919) also hailed from a prosperous and politically active family. Her parents, William and Letitia Still, founded the Underground Railroad in her native Philadelphia. In 1868, Anderson graduated from Oberlin College, the only black woman in a class of forty-four. The following year, she married Edward Wiley, a former slave. After his untimely death, Anderson moved to Washington, DC, with

SARAH LOGUEN FRASER, one of the earliest black women doctors in the United States, with her graduating class at Syracuse Medical College, 1876. She was the only Negro member in the class of eleven men and four women. (Austin/Thompson Collection, by permission of Moorland-Spingarn Research Center.)

her young daughter, where she taught music, drawing, and elocution at Howard University. In 1875, she began her medical studies at the Howard University Medical Department. She completed one year before she transferred to the Woman's Medical College of Philadelphia, from which she graduated in 1878. She was one of two black women in her graduating class of seventeen; the other was Georgiana E. Patterson Young (1845–1887) of New York.

Anderson also did her internship at the New England Hospital for Women. Initially, she had been denied a position because of her race. In 1879, she returned to Philadelphia, and the following year she married the Reverend Matthew Anderson, a prominent Presbyterian minister and educator. She practiced medicine for more than thirty years, and much of her medical work was centered at the clinic that she operated at her husband's church, the Berean Presbyterian Church. In 1889, she helped her husband establish the Berean Manual Training and Industrial School, a facility that helped to train African Americans. She served as the school's assistant principal for thirty-two years. Anderson also helped found the Philadelphia YWCA for black women and the Berean Women's Christian Temperance Union.

Ionia Rollin Whipper (1872–1953), a 1903 graduate of the Medical Department at Howard University, was the daughter of William J. and Frances A. Rollin Whipper. Her father was a prominent Republican politician, lawyer, and municipal judge in South Carolina. Her mother was an

Featuring Black Women Physicians

● **Caroline Virginia Still Wiley Anderson** (1848–1919) was one of the first black women to graduate from a medical school in the United States. Born in Philadelphia, she attended Oberlin College before enrolling in Howard Medical School. She transferred to the Woman's Medical College, graduating in 1878, and then interned at the New England Hospital for Women and Children. After completing her education, she returned to Philadelphia and established a private practice. She also ran a clinic and dispensary out of her second husband's (Matthew Anderson) church, Berean Presbyterian. With him she established the Berean Manual Training and Industrial School in 1899. She taught elocution, physiology, and hygiene and served as assistant principal there until 1914. In addition to her medical and educational work, Anderson helped found the first black YWCA in Philadelphia. She was a member of the Women's Medical Society and the president of the Berean Women's Christian Temperance Union.

● **Dorothy Lavinia Brown** (1919–2004) was the first African American woman surgeon in the South, the first African American woman to serve in the Tennessee state legislature (1966), and the first single woman to adopt a child in Tennessee (1956). Born in Philadelphia, Brown grew up first in an orphanage in Troy, New York, then with her biological mother, and finally in foster care. She attended Bennett College (BA, 1941) and Meharry Medical College (MD, 1948), and interned at Harlem Hospital. Her residency in surgery was at Meharry and Hubbard Hospital. In 1957 she was named chief of surgery at Nashville's Riverside Hospital, a position she held until 1983. She became a fellow of the American College of Surgeons in 1959. She was a clinical professor of surgery at Meharry Medical College; educational director for the Riverside-Meharry Clinical Rotation Program; and a consultant on health, education, and welfare for the National Institutes of Health (NIH). She received numerous awards in her lifetime, including the humanitarian award from the Carnegie Foundation in 1993 and the Horatio Alger Award in 1994.

● **Helen Octavia Dickens** (1909–2001) was the first black woman to be admitted as a fellow of the American College of Surgeons. Born in Dayton, Ohio, she attended the University of Illinois (BS, 1932; and MD, 1934). Both her internship and obstetrics residencies were at Chicago's famed Provident Hospital. She continued her education with a master's of medical science degree from the University of Pennsylvania (1945). She was certified by the American Board of Obstetrics and Gynecology (OB-GYN) in 1946 and became a fellow of the American College of Surgeons in 1950. She was the director of the OB-GYN department of Mercy Douglass Hospital (no longer in existence) (1948–1967) and chief of the department of obstetrics at the

Woman's Hospital (1956–1964). She was also an educator, serving on the faculty of the Medical College of Pennsylvania (1954–1965) and the University of Pennsylvania (1965–1985). At the University of Pennsylvania she became associate dean of minority affairs and director of the teen clinic. The recipient of a large variety of awards, Dickens was the first black recipient of the Distinguished Daughters of Pennsylvania Award (1971). Her lifelong work on teen pregnancy has been essential to developments in the field.

● **Lena Frances Edwards** (1900–1986) spent a lifetime of service addressing the needs of the poor, women, students, and the aged. In 1964, she received a Presidential Medal of Freedom from President Lyndon B. Johnson. (See individual entry: Edwards, Lena Frances.)

● **Artishia Garcia Gilbert** (1869–?) was the first African American woman to pass the medical boards and become a doctor in Kentucky. She attended Kentucky's State Normal and Theological Institute, graduating when she was only sixteen. She moved on to the State University of Kentucky (BA, 1889, and MA, 1892) and Louisville National Medical College (MD). She graduated from the Howard University medical program in 1897 and returned to Kentucky to teach obstetrics at the state university. Among her many activities, she lectured for the Baptist Educational Convention, was superintendent of the Red Cross Sanitarium, and served on the board of Orphans Home in Louisville.

● **Sophia Bethene Jones** (1857–1932), one of the first black women doctors in America, was also the first black woman to teach at Spelman College. She was born in Ontario, Canada, and attended the University of Toronto, graduating in 1879. Approximately two years later she entered the medical school of the University of Michigan and became its first black woman graduate in 1885. She then moved to Atlanta, Georgia, and joined the faculty of Spelman. While there she also ran the infirmary and established a nurses' training course. In 1888 Jones left Spelman and practiced first in St. Louis, then in Philadelphia, and finally in Kansas. Because of ill health she migrated to California in 1915 and died there in 1932.

● **Verina Morton Harris Jones** (1865–1943) became one of the earliest black women doctors in the country when she received her MD in 1888. She was also the first woman, black or white, to practice medicine in the state of Mississippi. (See individual entry: Jones, Verina Harris Morton.)

● **Francis M. Kneeland** (1873–?) was one of the first black women physicians to graduate from Meharry Medical College in Nashville, Tennessee. Little is known of her life except that she was born in Tennessee and graduated from Meharry with honors in 1898. She established a private practice in Memphis and, after the death of Georgia E. L. Patton Washington in 1900, was the only African American woman doctor in the city. In addition to her immensely successful practice, she was the head instructor of the nursing program at the University of West Tennessee in Memphis. A prominent woman in the city, she purchased her own home. At some point, though it is unknown exactly when, Kneeland left Memphis and moved to Chicago.

● **Myra Adele Logan** (1908–1977) was the first female physician to perform open-heart surgery. Born in Tuskegee, Alabama, she was the daughter of Warren and Adella Hunt Logan. Her father was the treasurer of the Tuskegee Institute, and her mother was a noted activist in health care and the suffrage movement. Myra Logan attended Atlanta University (BA, 1927) and Columbia University (MS, psychology). She received her medical training from New York's Flower Fifth Avenue Hospital School of Medicine (MD, 1933). Her internship and residency were both served at Harlem Hospital, where she spent most of her career. In 1943 she became the first woman to perform open-heart surgery. In 1951 she was the second black woman fellow of the American College of Surgeons. Later in her career, she did important research on antibiotics such as Aureomycin. The results were published in *Archives of Surgery* and *Journal of American Medical Surgery*. In the 1960s she developed a slower X-ray process to detect breast cancer, one that showed differences in the density of tissue more effectively and was therefore more accurate in detecting tumors. She was a member of the Upper Manhattan Medical Group, one of the first group practices in the United States. In addition to her medical work, Logan was a member of the New York State Committee on Discrimination (until she resigned in protest in 1944), as well as Planned Parenthood and the NAACP. She retired from practice in 1970 and died of cancer in 1977.

● **Muriel Marjorie Petioni** (1914–) made notable contributions in substance abuse treatment and the organization of black women physicians. (See individual entry: Petioni, Muriel Marjorie.)

● **Maude Sanders** (1903–1995) spent most of her life serving African Americans in the city of Peoria, Illinois. Born in New Orleans, she initially became a teacher but had difficulty finding a position. For years she worked as a substitute teacher and in a tailor's shop. At the age of thirty-two she decided to go to medical school. After attending Xavier and New Orleans University for two years she had earned enough science credits to be accepted into Meharry Medical School, although she never received her BA. She graduated in 1939 and, with her classmate Doris Sanders, was one of the first two women to intern at City Hospital (Homer G. Phillips) in St. Louis, Missouri.

In 1942 Maude Sanders moved to Peoria, replacing the city's only black physician, who was leaving. She maintained her practice there, serving the community, whatever the hour and without regard for the patient's ability to pay, for the next forty-eight years. After she retired in 1990, the mayor of Peoria declared a Maude Sanders Day in her honor. She died five years later in 1995.

● **Ruth Janetta Temple** (1892–1984) was a pioneering black physician in Los Angeles, California. Born in Natchez, Mississippi, and raised in Los Angeles, she was the first African American to receive a medical degree from Loma Linda University (1918) and then interned with the Los Angeles City Maternity Service (1923–1928). When Temple graduated from medical school she became the first black woman doctor in Los Angeles County. In 1928 she established her own clinic, the Temple Health Institute, in East Los Angeles. At the time it was the only one in the area. In addition to the medical services provided by the clinic, Temple realized there was a need to educate the public on health issues. To answer this need, she started the Health Study Club program. In 1941 Temple returned to school, receiving a master's degree from the Yale University School of Public Health. The following year, she became the first health officer in the city of Los Angeles. Over the course of her twenty-year career with the Los Angeles health department, she helped create the city's public health program and was a founder of the Southeast District Health Center. She died in Los Angeles in 1984.

● **Georgia E. L. Patton Washington** (1864–1900) was the first black woman in Tennessee to be licensed to practice medicine and surgery, as well as one of the first two black women to graduate from Meharry Medical College. She was born in slavery in Grundy County, Tennessee, and attended Central Tennessee College in Nashville (1890). In 1893 she became one of the first two women to receive a medical degree from Meharry Medical College (The other was Annie D. Gregg). The same year, she set out for Liberia as a medical missionary. However, she had no official sponsorship and had to pay for the trip herself. Soon, with her own money running out and suffering from ill health, she returned to Memphis. She started a private practice and, in 1897, married. She died only a few years later, in 1900.

● **Jane Cooke Wright** (1919–) is a noted cancer researcher and medical educator. Her work with Jewel Plummer Cobb led to important insights on the effects of different drugs on living and test culture tissue. Wright also explored innovative methods of chemotherapy administration. (See individual entry: Wright, Jane Cooke.)

author. During the 1920s, the Children's Bureau, a federal child welfare agency, hired her to assist its efforts to reduce infant and maternal mortality in the South. Her responsibilities included training midwives, registering births, and conducting child health classes. In 1931, she organized the Lend-A-Hand Club, a campaign to establish a home for black unwed mothers in Washington, DC. At the time, any existing homes did not accept black women. In 1941, the Ionia R. Whipper Home for Unwed Mothers opened, and Whipper maintained the facility until her death in 1953.

Not all these early black women physicians came from privileged backgrounds. For example, Eliza Anna Grier (1864–1902) was born into slavery. It took her seven years to work and study her way through Fisk University, from which she graduated in 1891. In December 1890, she wrote to the Woman's Medical College of Pennsylvania about admission to its program. She stated that she was without the funds to pursue medical studies and that she desired to be a physician to work for the benefit of her race. Grier later noted that she had decided to become a physician "when [she] saw colored women doing all the work in cases of accouchement and all the fee going to some white doctor who merely looked on." She wondered why she herself should not receive the fee.

Grier matriculated at the Woman's Medical College in 1893 and graduated four years later. This "coal Black negress," as the *North American Medical Review* called her in 1898, went on to become the first black woman licensed to practice in Georgia. She set up practices in Atlanta and later in Greenville, South Carolina. She did not prosper financially because she worked mostly among the very poor and in neglected districts. Grier's professional career was short-lived. She died in 1902, only five years after her medical school graduation.

Education and Careers of Later Black Women Physicians

Racial and sexual discrimination limited educational opportunities for black women, and until the late twentieth century most received their medical degrees from either black or women's medical schools. It was not until the advent of affirmative action programs in the 1970s that black women entered coed majority medical schools in significant numbers.

In 1900, there were ten black medical schools. By 1923, only two remained—Howard University in Washington, DC, and Meharry Medical College in Nashville, Tennessee. These two schools were essential for the development of black women as physicians. Of the sixty-five black women who practiced in 1920, more than two-thirds had graduated from these two schools. The Howard University Medical Department opened in 1869 and graduated its first woman, Mary Sparkman, three

years later. Sparkman was white. It graduated its first black woman, Eunice Shadd, a former teacher, in 1877. Most of the early black women physicians received their medical education at Meharry, founded in 1876. By 1920, thirty-nine had graduated. The first black women, Annie D. Gregg and Georgia Washington Patton, received their degrees in 1891. After her graduation, Patton, who had been born a slave, became the first black woman physician licensed in Tennessee and worked as a medical missionary for two years in Liberia.

At the turn of the twentieth century, most black women who attended a women's medical college attended the Woman's Medical College of Pennsylvania. By 1900, the school had graduated ten African American women, including Verina Morton-Jones (1888), Lucy Hughes Brown

VERINA MORTON-JONES was the first woman to practice medicine in Mississippi. She began her practice there in 1888. (Moorland-Spingarn Research Center, Howard University.)

(1894), and Lulu Cecilia Fleming (1895). In smaller numbers black women received their degrees from other women's medical colleges. Emma Reynolds, a former nurse, graduated from Northwestern University Woman's Medical School in 1895. Earlier, her exclusion from Chicago nursing schools prompted the 1891 establishment of Provident Hospital, the first black hospital. In 1915, Isabella Vandervall graduated from another women's medical college, the New York Medical College for Women.

By the late nineteenth century, a few black women had gained admission to coed majority institutions. In 1885, Sophia Bethena Jones (1857–1932) became the first black woman to earn a medical degree at the University of Michigan. In 1920, Dorothy B. Ferebee (1898–1980) entered Tufts Medical School where she was one of five women and the only African American in a class of 137. She was named a member of the woman's honor society, elected class historian, and graduated at the top of her class.

Frequently, extended periods of time existed between the admission of black male and black female medical students to coed majority schools. Harvard Medical School, for example, graduated its first black man in 1869 and its first black woman, Mildred Jefferson, in 1951. The University of Pennsylvania graduated its first black man in 1882 and its first black woman, Arlene Bennett, in 1964. The gap between these graduation dates highlights the historical distinctions between the career paths of African American male physicians and African American female physicians.

At the end of World War II, medical education remained rigorously segregated. One-third of accredited medical schools—twenty-six out of seventy-eight—barred African American students. In 1948, 84 percent of black medical students attended either Howard or Meharry. On 10 September 1948, Edith Irby Jones took a major step at chiseling away segregation in medical education when she entered the University of Arkansas School of Medicine and became the first black person admitted to a southern medical school. Jones, the daughter of sharecroppers, entered the school without incident. In 1948, educational officials at the University of Arkansas, eager to avoid possible lawsuits, had decided to admit black students to programs for which alternatives for black students did not exist. They acknowledged that the establishment of a racially separate medical school was financially untenable. Jones gained admission because she ranked twenty-eighth out of 230 applicants on the medical school's aptitude test. (The school admitted the top ninety applicants.) Jones was allowed to attend classes on a nonsegregated basis, but she had to use a separate restroom and dining area. Jones did well in medical school and in 1952 became the first black intern at University Hospital in Little Rock and in 1959 the first black internal medicine resident at Houston's Baylor Hospital. Afterward, the University of Arkansas continued to accept black students, including Joycelyn Elders, who in 1993 became the first black woman surgeon general of the United States. Elders credited Jones as her inspiration to become a physician.

Racism and sexism limited not only the educational options available to black women but also their postgraduate and career opportunities. In contrast to white women, who began to graduate from Howard at the turn of the twentieth century, many black women did not actually practice medicine. Instead, they used their medical degrees to progress in the segregated Washington school system because the degree was one of their few advanced training options. For example, Lucy Moten (1851–1933), an 1897 graduate, became a school principal, and Mary Louise Brown, an 1898 graduate, taught school.

At times, black women were the first women of any race to practice medicine in a given area. In 1888, Verina Morton-Jones (1865–1943) became the first woman to practice medicine in Mississippi. Sarah G. Boyd Jones (1865–1905), an 1893 graduate of the Howard University Medical Department, was the first woman to pass the Virginia medical board examinations. When Halle Tanner Dillon Johnson (1864–1901) in 1891 became the first woman to pass the strenuous ten-day Alabama medical board examination, even the *New York Times* heralded her accomplishment. After her 1891 graduation from the Woman's Medical College of Pennsylvania, Johnson went to work at Tuskegee Institute as the school's first resident physician. At the time, working as a resident physician at a black college was one of the few career options open to black women doctors.

Until the mid-twentieth century, most black women physicians had general practices because of their limited opportunities to obtain specialty training. After World War II, however, a greater number entered the more prestigious and financially rewarding medical specialties. In 1946, Helen O. Dickens (1909–2001), the daughter of a former slave and a 1934 graduate of the University of Illinois School of Medicine, received her certification from the American Board of Obstetrics and Gynecology. Four years later, she became the first black woman admitted to the American College of Surgeons. The American Board of Surgery certified its first black woman, Hughenna L. Gauntlett, in 1968; the American Board of Neurological Surgery certified its first, Dr. Alexa Canady, in 1984; and the American Board of Thoracic Surgery, Dr. Rosalyn Sterling Scott, in 1986.

Finding a Place in Medicine: Maneuvering Racial and Sexual Obstacles

After 1920, hospitals became increasingly important to physicians' careers. In contrast to their nineteenth-century counterparts, twentieth-century black women physicians had to secure access to hospitals. Hospitals had become essential for medical education, medical practice, and medical specialization. Several states had even passed laws requiring the completion of an internship as a prerequisite for medical licensure.

These changes in medical practice threatened the future of black physicians and placed an additional burden on black women's advancement in the profession. African American physicians seeking internships and residencies were expected to pursue them at black hospitals, which usually had inferior programs. Black hospitals, however, preferred to admit black men for their few existing slots. In addition, the small number of women's hospitals did not always welcome black women.

The opportunities, therefore, for black women to obtain hospital appointments and specialty training were severely limited. Isabella Vandervall was rejected for an internship by four hospitals, including the one affiliated with her medical school, not because she was unqualified—she had graduated first in her class—but because of her race. She was able to practice only because she had obtained a license before the laws on compulsory internship went into effect. In 1923, Lillian Atkins Moore, a senior medical student at the Woman's Medical College of Pennsylvania, applied for an internship at the college's hospital. She, too, was rejected because she was black. The hospital's medical director admitted that race had been the deciding factor in the hospital's action and offered to get her an appointment at one of the "colored" hospitals. Moore finally secured a position at Douglass Hospital, a black hospital in Philadelphia.

A few black women were able to gain admission to programs at government hospitals. Dorothy Ferebee, after several rejections from white hospitals, secured an internship at Freedmen's Hospital in Washington, DC. In 1926, May Chinn (1896–1980) became the first black woman intern at Harlem Hospital. This was not the first time that Chinn had been a pioneer. She was also the first black woman to graduate from Bellevue Hospital Medical College, later New York University School of Medicine.

Featuring Contemporary Physicians

● **Patricia E. Bath** (1942–) was the first black woman to patent a medical invention. She has spent her life working to prevent blindness and to ensure that treatment reaches all people, not just the wealthy. Born and raised in New York City she completed high school in only two and a half years. By the age of sixteen she was becoming known for her cancer research. She attended Hunter College (BS, Chemistry, 1964) and Howard University Medical School (MD, 1968). Her medical education continued at Harlem Hospital, Columbia University, and New York University. While at Columbia she developed Community Ophthalmology, which combined public health, community medicine, and ophthalmology. In 1974 she joined the UCLA Medical Center. While there she established and chaired its ophthalmology resident training program (1983), and served as chair of the department of ophthalmology (1983–1986). She has been on the faculty of the UCLA Jules Stein Eye Institute, served as chief of ophthalmology at Nigeria's Mercy Hospital, and co-founded the American Institute for the Prevention of Blindness, among many other accomplishments. In 1988 she revolutionized cataract surgery when she patented her invention, the Laserphaco Probe. Since her retirement from UCLA in 1993 she has been active in developing the use of telecommunications to provide health care to underserved people. In 2001 she was inducted into the International Women in Medicine Hall of Fame.

● **Alexa Canady** (1950–) is the first African American woman to become a neurosurgeon. Born in Lansing, Michigan, she attended the University of Michigan at Ann Arbor (BS, 1971) and the University of Michigan College of Medicine (MD, cum laude, 1975). She interned at New Haven Hospital and did her neurosurgery residency at the University of Minnesota (1976–1981). She was the first woman and the first African American ever to be admitted to the program. She then went on to a fellowship in pediatric neurosurgery at Philadelphia's Children's Hospital, and served as an instructor in neurosurgery at the University of Pennsylvania (1981–1982). She became a staff member and instructor at Detroit's Henry Ford Hospital in 1982, and a year later became a pediatric neurosurgeon at Children's Hospital of Michigan. In 1984 she received her certification from the American Board of Neurological Surgery. She served as chief of neurosurgery at Children's from 1987 through 1997. She has also served as a clinical instructor at Wayne State University School of Medicine (1985–1997), a professor of neurosurgery (1997–2001), and vice chair of the department of neurosurgery (1991–2001). She served as president of the Michigan Association of Neurological Surgeons from 1994 to 1995. In 1993 She was named Woman of the Year by the American Women's Medical Association. She retired in 2001.

● **Sharon Henry** (?) is the first black woman to be a member of the American Association for the Surgery of Trauma (AAST). Born

Chinn also found that racial discrimination prohibited black physicians from appointments to private hospitals. Margaret Lawrence also completed her internship at Harlem Hospital. She had not been allowed to work at New York's Babies' Hospital, ostensibly because housing could not be provided for a black woman in the nurses' dormitory where female interns were housed. This was not the first time that Lawrence encountered racial barriers. She was denied admission to Cornell Medical School because a black man who had been admitted twenty-five years earlier had failed to graduate after contracting tuberculosis. Lawrence eventually gained admission to Columbia Medical School. In 1946, she was to become the first black trainee at the Columbia Psychoanalytic Clinic.

Racism was not the only obstacle in the professional paths of twentieth-century black women physicians, who were also forced to battle sexism. When Chinn opened her practice in Harlem, she encountered resistance from her black male colleagues. When Margaret Lawrence taught at Meharry Medical College in the 1940s, she was the only woman on the faculty and encountered blatant sexism. She was excluded from intellectual camaraderie, overburdened with responsibilities, and poorly paid in comparison with her male colleagues. Dorothy Ferebee, who spent most of her professional life at male-dominated Howard University, contended that sexism, rather than racism, had been her greatest professional challenge.

Black Women Physicians as Activists and Leaders

Many African American women physicians engaged in social uplift activities and often crafted careers that combined medicine and social with political activism. Their efforts helped improve the health and lives of black Americans.

At a time when racial segregation severely restricted the options available to black patients, black women physicians established facilities to tend to the sick. Matilda Evans (1872–1935), the first black woman to practice in South Carolina, established three hospitals in Columbia between 1898 and 1916. In 1920, Georgia Dwelle

---

in Berlin, Maryland, she attended Duke University (BA, 1981) and University of Maryland Medical School (MD, 1985). She served her residency at the State University of New York's Health Science Center in Brooklyn. Her critical care fellowship was with the University of Minnesota in Minneapolis. She went on to become an assistant professor of surgery at the University of Maryland School of Medicine. She is a trauma surgeon and physician-in-chief at the R. Adams Cowley Shock Trauma Center at the University of Maryland Medical Center. She is also the director and a trauma surgeon of the Division of Wound Healing and Metabolism.

● **Mae Carol Jemison** (1956–) is a physician as well as the first black woman astronaut. (See individual entry: Jemison, Mae Carol.)

● **Agnes D. Lattimer** (1928–) was the medical director of one of the country's biggest public health organizations, Cook County Hospital, in Chicago. Born in Memphis, she attended Fisk University (BS, Biology, magna cum laude, 1949), and the Chicago Medical School (MD, 1954). Her internship and residency in pediatrics were at Cook County Hospital, and she later became the director of ambulatory pediatrics at Michael Reese Hospital (1966–1971). She returned to Cook County as the director of ambulatory care (1971–1984), and then director of the Fantus Health Center (1984–1985). She became the hospital's medical director in 1986, the highest medical post attained by a black woman in any major hospital in the United States. In addition to her career as a pediatrician and hospital administrator she has taught at the University of Illinois School of Public Health and the University of Chicago. She was president of the Illinois chapter of American Academy of Pediatrics from 1983 to 1986.

● **Vivian Pinn** (1941–) is the first director of the Office of Research on Women's Health (ORWH) at the National Institutes of Health (NIH). As director, she lobbies to ensure both that women are represented in the institute's studies and that more women become biomedical researchers. Raised in Lynchburg, Virginia, she attended Wellesley College (BA, 1963) and went on to become the first black woman to graduate from the University of Virginia School of Medicine (MD, 1967). She served her residency in pathology at Massachusetts General Hospital and at the same time was a teaching fellow at Harvard Medical School (1967–1970). She was a member of the faculty of Tufts University School of Medicine (1970–1982) and professor and chair of the department of pathology at Howard University College of Medicine (1982–1991). She became the director of ORWH in 1991 and a fellow of the American Academy of Arts and Sciences in 1994. Among her many awards she has received the Elizabeth Blackwell Award from the American Medical Women's Association.

(1884–1977) established Dwelle Infirmary—the first obstetrical hospital for black women in Atlanta and Georgia's first venereal disease clinic for African Americans. Virginia Alexander (1899–1949), a 1925 graduate of Woman's Medical College of Pennsylvania, established the Aspiranto Health Home in 1931 to provide health care for the poor women and children of North Philadelphia. She also conducted research to document the poor health status of African Americans and used her membership in the predominantly white Society of Friends (Quakers) to push for the elimination of inequities in health care.

Dorothy Ferebee conducted much of her medical and social activism through black women's organizations. From 1940 to 1951, she served as the national president of Alpha Kappa Alpha (AKA), a black sorority, and steered the organization to increase its lobbying efforts in health, child welfare, racial discrimination, and economic security. For seven summers between 1935 and 1942, she led the AKA Mississippi Health Project, a program to bring health care to poor African American communities in Mississippi. In 1949, she succeeded Mary McLeod Bethune as the second president of the National Council of Negro Women and served in that position until 1953. Ferebee was not the first black physician to achieve prominence in a black women's organization. The Chicago physician Mary Fitzbutler Waring served as president of the National Association of Colored Women from 1933 until 1937.

The activism of black women physicians included work in political parties and political organizations. Philadelphian Ethel Allen (1929–1981) described herself as a "BFR—a Black female Republican, an entity as rare as a Black elephant, and just as smart." In addition to her medical practice, Allen, who graduated from the Philadelphia College of Osteopathic Medicine in 1963, pursued a political career. In 1975, she was elected to an at-large seat on the Philadelphia City Council, and *Esquire* named her one of the nation's outstanding politicians. Donna Christian-Christensen, a family physician, likewise found prominence in the political arena. In 1996, with her election as the U.S. Delegate from the Virgin Islands, she became the first woman physician to become a member of Congress. After 1998, she chaired the Congressional Black Caucus's Health Braintrust and took an active role in minority health issues. In the 1970s, Mildred Jefferson emerged as a prominent leader of the pro-life movement. In 1975, she began a three-year tenure as the president of the National Right to Life Committee.

By the late twentieth century, black women began to assume leadership roles within the medical profession. In 1985, Edith Irby Jones was elected the first woman president of the National Medical Association. By 2004, six additional women—Vivian Pinn, Alma George, Yvonnecris Veal, Javette Orgain, Lucille Perez, and L. Natalie Carroll—

DR. EDITH IRBY JONES, photographed in 1977. In 1948, she became the first African American admitted to a southern medical school, the University of Arkansas School of Medicine; in 1952, she became its first African American graduate. (Arkansas History Commission.)

held the position. In 1991, Pinn, was appointed the first permanent director of the National Institutes of Health Office of Women's Health Research. Roselyn Payne Epps in 1990 became the first black physician to be president of the American Medical Women's Association. Two years later, she was elected the first black woman president of the Medical Society of the District of Columbia. In 1995, Regina Benjamin became the first African American woman named to the Board of Trustees of the American Medical Association, and in 2002, she was elected the first African American and first woman president of the State Medical Society of Alabama. In 1993, Barbara Ross-Lee, upon her appointment as dean of the Ohio University College of Osteopathic Medicine, became the first black woman to head an American medical school. In 2002, PonJola Coney became the first black woman physician to head an allopathic medical school when she was named senior vice president for health affairs and dean of Meharry Medical School. That same year, Risa Lavizzo-Mourey became the first woman and first African American to be president and chief executive officer of the Robert Wood Johnson Foundation, the nation's largest health-care philanthropy.

Medicine as Black Women's Work

In their pursuit of medical careers, black women physicians have had to challenge stereotypical notions about black women and their work. May Chinn recalled that a black woman patient wept when she approached because "she felt she had been denied the privilege of having a white doctor wait on her." While Margaret Lawrence was in medical school, white women often stopped her on the street to offer her day work as a maid. In 1980, Jackson, Mississippi, police arrested Gloria Frelix for false pretense and possession of a controlled substance after she picked up a prescription for a patient. Although she had identified herself as a physician she was arrested because, in the words of one white police officer, "She didn't look like no doctor." Vanessa Northington Gamble and Cheryl Rucker wrote about how when they attended medical school in the 1970s and the 1990s, respectively, they were misidentified as maids and cooks.

Despite obstacles based on their race and gender, the number of black women in medicine increased steadily throughout the twentieth century. In 1920, there were sixty-five black women physicians. By 1930, the number had grown to ninety-two. Fifty years later, in 1980, they numbered three thousand. Ten years later, as a result of affirmative action, the total had more than doubled to over seven thousand. The 2000 Census reported that there were 12,500 black women physicians working in the United States—1.8 percent of all physicians. Significantly, after 1985 the number of black women entering medical school outpaced the number of black men doing so.

Black women physicians have made significant contributions to medicine and their communities. These women founded hospitals, established civic organizations, practiced medicine among the underserved, and broke down barriers in a profession that has been and continues to be white and, although the demographics are changing, male-dominated. And by so doing, they have challenged racist and sexist presumptions about the abilities of black women.

See also Jemison, Mae Carol; Jones, Verina Harris Morton; Petioni, Muriel Marjorie; Steward, Susan McKinney; *and* Wright, Jane Cooke.

BIBLIOGRAPHY

Blount, Melissa. "Surpassing Obstacles: Black Women in Medicine." *Journal of the American Medical Women's Association* 39 (1984): 6–9.

"Changing the Face of Medicine." http://www.nlm.nih.gov/changing thefaceofmedicine/exhibition/index.html. This National Library of Medicine site explores the lives of American women physicians, including sixty black women, since the nineteenth century; click on the box labeled physicians, then search for physicians by ethnicity.

Davis, George. "A Healing Hand in Harlem." *New York Times Magazine*, 22 April 1979, 40.

Dawson, Patricia L. *Forged by the Knife: The Experience of Surgical Residency from the Perspective of a Woman of Color.* Seattle, WA: Open Hand Publishing, Inc, 1999.

Gamble, Vanessa Northington. "On Becoming a Physician: A Dream Not Deferred." In *The Black Women's Health Book: Speaking for Ourselves*, edited by Evelyn C. White. Seattle, WA: Seal Press, 1994.

Hine, Darlene Clark. "Co-Laborers in the Work of the Lord: Nineteenth Century Black Women Physicians." In *Send Us a Lady Physician: Women Doctors in America, 1835–1920*, edited by Ruth J. Abram. New York: Norton, 1985.

Lightfoot, Sara Lawrence. *Balm in Gilead: Journey of a Healer.* Reading, MA: Addison-Wesley, 1988.

Moldow, Gloria. *Women Doctors in Gilded Washington: Race, Gender, and Professionalization.* Urbana: University of Illinois Press, 1987.

More, Ellen. *Restoring the Balance: Women Physicians and the Profession of Medicine, 1850–1995.* Cambridge, MA: Harvard University Press, 1999.

Sammons, Vivian Ovelton, ed. *Blacks in Science and Medicine.* New York: Hemisphere Publishing Corporation, 1990.

Smith, Susan L. *Sick and Tired of Being Sick and Tired: Black Women's Health Activism in America, 1890–1950.* Philadelphia: University of Pennsylvania Press, 1965.

Sterling, Rosalyn P. "Female Surgeons: The Dawn of a New Era." In *A Century of Black Surgeons: The U.S.A. Experience*, edited by Claude H. Organ and Margaret Kosiba. Norman, OK: Transcript Press, 1987.

Thornton, Yvonne S. *The Ditchdigger's Daughters: A Black Family's Astonishing Success Story.* New York: Birch Lane Press, 1996.

—VANESSA NORTHINGTON GAMBLE

PLAYER, WILLA B. (b. 9 August 1909; d. 27 August 2003), educator. Player was the first in a number of areas concerning black women in the field of education. She was the first black woman to run a four-year, fully accredited liberal arts college in the United States; the first woman president of the National Association of Schools and Colleges of the Methodist Church, and the first black woman to serve as trustee of Ohio Wesleyan University.

Player was born in Jackson, Mississippi. Her parents, Beatrice Day and Clarence Cromwell Player, moved the family to Akron, Ohio, in 1917. There Willa attended public schools and eventually Akron University and then Ohio Wesleyan. While at Akron University she served as the first black cadet/practice teacher in the public schools of Akron, Ohio, in 1929. In that same year she graduated with a bachelor's degree from Ohio Wesleyan. In 1930 she completed a master of arts degree at Oberlin College. At twenty-one years of age, Player was hired to teach Latin and French by David Dallas Jones at Bennett College in Greensboro, North Carolina. This initial employment was the beginning of a long and lasting career in higher education.

Player's desire to learn and teach led her to complete her PhD in 1948 at Columbia University. During her academic pursuits, Player studied and traveled abroad. As a result, she received the *certificat d'études* from the University of Grenoble, France, in 1935. Concurrently, her dedication to Bennett College continued; eventually she was made director of religious activities, director of admissions at the college, and acting dean. In 1952, twenty-six years after her initial teaching appointment, she was named coordinator of instruction at Bennett. Her move through the administrative offices of Bennett College led her to the presidency in 1956.

Her presidency at Bennett is unique for many reasons. First, she was the first African American women appointed to the presidency of any four-year college institution in America, and she was also an ardent advocate for the civil rights movement. In 1958 she organized and scheduled an appearance of Martin Luther King Jr. for the Greensboro community in general and the Bennett campus in particular. This polite invitation was seen as a high-handed political move by several prominent organizations and institutions that dreaded the attention and the overt challenge of the coming civil rights leader and his movement.

This event drew at least two thousand people and resulted in protests. According to Bennett history, at the zenith of events approximately 40 percent of Bennett's student body was arrested for trying to integrate restaurants and theaters in Greensboro. Player led several professors to the jails to hold classes and exams. She also tended to injured students after convincing the jail guards to grant access to the Bennett medical personnel. Her advocacy and open support for student activism in the civil rights movement allowed the world to see that educated black women had a strong role in the struggle for civil rights. Beyond access to restaurants and theaters, the deepest desire was total human respect.

Player served as president of Bennett until 1966. Eventually her desire for academic administration and education led her to resign from Bennett College to become an educational consultant. Upon her retirement, the Bennett College trustees proudly designated her president emerita. During this period of her educational career, Player worked with the Agency for International Development. While there she worked with fellow women educators in Kenya and Nigeria. She was director of the Division of College Support, U.S. Office of Education, and the Department of Health, Education, and Welfare, where she served until her retirement in 1986.

According to Linda Beatrice Brown, Player's niece and her biographer, during "her life of dedicated service in the field of higher education," Player received numerous awards and honors, including eight honorary doctorates and many citations from national, federal, and local organizations. Among her awards, says Brown, are the Superior Service and Distinguished Service awards from the U.S. Department of Health, Education, and Welfare and the Award for Outstanding Achievement in the field of higher education from the twenty-eighth annual convention of the National Council for Negro Women. The National Conference of Christians and Jews also presented her the Silver Medallion Award.

Toward the end of her life, Player said in an interview,

> our new found pride in preserving our heritage is going to be a tremendous contribution to our children and our children's children. And that's why it's important to preserve our history. And I have a feeling that one of these days, way down there after we have all gone, we will come into our own as a people. In my view, that's my interpretation of the coming of the kingdom of God on earth   (Obituary and Interview).

Player died at the age of ninety-four. She was memorialized on 4 September 2003 in the Annie Merner Pfeiffer Chapel on the Bennett College Campus.

See also Education.

BIBLIOGRAPHY

Brown, Linda Beatrice. *The Long Walk: The Story of the Presidency of Willa B. Player at Bennett College*. Greensboro, NC: Bennett College, 1998. This work examines Player's professional career. Her papers are in the Bennett College archives and currently unprocessed.

Obituary and Interview. Bennett College. http://www.bennett.edu/ABOUT/player_memorial.htm. Offers an excellent interview transcript with Player. One moving segment talks about her vision of the future.

—IDA E. JONES

PLAYWRITING. "Sing a black girl's song. . . ./she's half-notes scattered/without rhythm/no tune. . . ./sing the song of her possibilities." These lines from Ntozake Shange's 1975 play, *for colored girls who have considered suicide when the rainbow is enuf*, poeticize the challenges black women have faced in their efforts to represent their stories onstage. Like other black Americans, they have had to confront racist representations and discriminatory employment practices. For much of the twentieth century, if they sought a professional career outside black communities, they also had to battle producers and audiences who assumed their lives were of no dramatic interest. Despite these formidable obstacles, black women persevered, increasing their numbers on and behind the stage, and diversifying their subject matter and dramatic approaches.

Early Inroads

Against blackface minstrelsy's depiction of fun-loving blacks totally devoted to their white masters, the earliest black playwrights sought to present alternative views. In

FOR COLORED GIRLS WHO HAVE CONSIDERED SUICIDE WHEN THE RAINBOW IS ENUF, a poster by Paul Davis for Ntozake Shange's play, 1976. Among other awards, the play won an Obie in 1977. (Library of Congress.)

1880, at age twenty, Pauline Elizabeth Hopkins (1859–1930) wrote the four-act musical drama *Slaves' Escape; or the Underground Railroad*, which she and her family, known as the Hopkins Colored Troubadours, performed to favorable reviews. Though Hopkins had not been a

slave, her play—later re-titled *Peculiar Sam; or the Underground Railroad*—seemed to have been modeled on a play written by the fugitive slave William Wells Brown, whose works were well known on northern abolitionist stages. Hopkins dramatized not only a daring escape but, unlike Brown, also portrayed blacks as conductors on the Underground Railroad and as free people living in the North.

Katherine Davis Chapman Tillman (1870–1947?) celebrated the black progress that followed slavery in such plays as *Thirty Years of Freedom* (1902), *Fifty Years of Freedom* (1910), *Aunt Betsy's Thanksgiving* (1914), and *The Spirit of Allen* (1922). Published by the A.M.E. Book Concern, these plays dramatize a world in which hard work, professional training, disavowal of the materialistic "gaiety" of urban life, and strong family networks lead to racial progress. By performing these plays, members of the African Methodist Episcopal Church learned and reaffirmed an uplift agenda, but interestingly, moral integrity alone does not account for the success of Davis's characters, for at a crucial moment, the female protagonist—a former slave mother or a devoted daughter, for example—must overcome racism by relying on a personal relationship with a well-intentioned white person.

Theater as Propaganda or Entertainment?

The first three decades of the twentieth century saw an impressive increase in the numbers of women writing plays. Angelina Weld Grimké (1880–1958), Georgia Douglas Johnson (1877?–1966), Mary P. Burrill (1884–1946), and Myrtle Smith Livingston (1901–1973) tackled such issues as the extralegal practice of lynching, women's access to birth control, girls' education, and interracial liaisons; while Alice Dunbar-Nelson (1875–1935), May Miller (1899–1995), and Eulalie Spence (1894–1981) dramatized the discrimination that faced returning World War I veterans, scripted history plays as a response to racist representations, and poked gentle fun at blacks' foibles.

Angelina Weld Grimké's play *Rachel* is noteworthy because it pioneered a tradition of lynching plays and sparked controversy about the very purposes of theater when the NAACP Drama Committee first produced it in Washington, DC, in 1916. Active in the antilynching movement, Grimké used her play to tell the story of a northern teenager's growth toward adulthood. In the beginning, Rachel is bubbly and confident in her future, but when she grows older, she learns her father and older brother were lynched for resisting southern racism. Additionally, she encounters employment discrimination and tries in vain to protect children from internalizing racial hatred. As a consequence, Rachel rejects marriage and motherhood, vowing never to inflict such suffering on innocent babies. Though applauded by some for its propagandistic objective of spotlighting conditions endured by

ANGELINA GRIMKÉ. Her play *Rachel* is significant as an early use of drama to address the evils of lynching; she is also known for her lyric poetry. (Austin/Thompson Collection, by permission of Moorland-Spingarn Research Center.)

proponents and scholars contended. Women sought dramatic training with Alain Locke at Howard University and production opportunities through W. E. B. Du Bois's editorial sponsorship of playwriting contests in the NAACP's *Crisis* magazine, even though those men were popularly identified, respectively, with the opposing folk and propaganda philosophies of art. Georgia Douglas Johnson's representations of southern, rural religiosity in *A Sunday Morning in the South* (1925) and in *Plumes* (1927) or May Miller's depiction of festival practices among Baltimore blacks in *Riding the Goat* (1929) seem to conform to the folk play's goal of offering aesthetically pleasing and socially inoffensive fare, but they also dramatize issues of critical importance to black communities. *A Sunday Morning in the South* deals with the lynching of a young man falsely accused of rape; *Plumes* depicts a poor mother who must choose between expensive, inadequate Western medicine for her sick daughter or burial practices that seem superstitious because their African roots are unrecognized; while *Riding the Goat* raises subtle questions about the relationship of Du Bois's "talented tenth," or professional black class, to the masses it is supposed to "uplift" from their quaint practices into greater social acceptability.

Better known as a Harlem Renaissance novelist than as a playwright, Zora Neale Hurston (1891–1960) used her experiences of growing up in the all-black town of Eatonville, Florida, to represent rural people with a complexity that delved below their seemingly simple ways and easy laughter. As its name suggests, *Color Struck*—which placed second in the National Urban League's *Opportunity* magazine contest in 1925—dramatizes the deadly consequences of colorism, or prejudice based upon skin color, within black communities. In its contrast of this serious issue with the verbal banter and displays of dance agility among cakewalk contestants, Hurston merged the folk and race play genres. In 1930 Hurston collaborated with the poet Langston Hughes on *Mule Bone: A Comedy of Negro Life* to dramatize tensions over religious practices and gender-based roles of women in a small, southern town. Unfortunately, just as in the play in which former friends become enemies, so too did Hurston and Hughes quarrel about plot development and authorship. The play was never produced in their lifetimes.

Reconstructed from drafts left dormant in university archives, *Mule Bone* finally was produced in 1991 at the Ethel Barrymore Theatre on Broadway, where it garnered mixed reviews. Hurston and Hughes had hoped to pioneer a theater in which the "blues stance" of black people or their laughing-to-keep-from-crying approach to life could be dramatized, but some sixty years later, it appeared that audiences, still haunted by the grinning faces of blackface minstrelsy, could not discern the gritty

black people, the production caused an uproar because many interpreted it as advocating a self-induced genocide and disavowing the NAACP's hallowed assumptions about the possibilities for black advancement. Grimké responded that she hoped the play's focus on blighted motherhood would encourage white women to join the antilynching campaign then being waged. (Doing so, she identified an issue that would recur particularly around second-wave feminism in the 1960s, namely the extent to which black and white women could unite around gender or would remain divided around race.) So disturbed were some viewers by *Rachel*'s avowedly political stance that they argued the stage should offer more artistically crafted "folk plays" aimed at entertaining; in pursuit of that goal, they created Howard University's drama program, one of the first in the United States.

The debate about the desirability of "race" or "propaganda" plays over "folk" plays would later dominate scholarly discussion about black theater, but a close look at the women's networks of association and dramas indicates that these categories were never as distinct as significance behind the laughter. Within the last decade of the twentieth century, Hurston's theater career received more critical attention when a number of her one-act plays were rediscovered in the Library of Congress, and scholars reconstructed Hurston's translations of her anthropological research in the southern United States and the Caribbean into such diasporic dance-dramas as *The Great Day* (1932), subsequently revised as *From Sun to Sun* and *Singing Steel*.

Departures from Form. Marita Bonner's (1899–1971) *The Purple Flower* (1928) and *Exit: An Illusion* (1929) departed radically from the realistic style used by both the so-called propaganda and folk dramatists. Winner of the 1927 *Crisis* best play award, *The Purple Flower* is a highly abstract representation of the black "U.S.'s" struggles against appealing, though wily "Sundry White Devils" in order to move up the hill to where the purple "Flower-of-Life-at-Its-Fullest" grows. In its allegorical allusiveness and overt militancy, the play seems typical of the black arts nationalism of the 1960s. Bonner's essay, "On Being Young—a Woman—and Colored" (1925), registered the intersection of race and gender, contending that in order to be viewed as respectable, a black woman had to "sit quietly without a [racial] chip" on her shoulder, observe life flowing into herself, and wait for the moment when she could rise to her full potential. Unrecognized in the essay is the possibility that in remaining still "like Buddha," the woman may find that her creative gifts have atrophied.

In contrast to Bonner's position, the theater career of Shirley Graham Du Bois (1896–1977) suggests a greater intellectual and physical mobility than was available to some black women in the 1930s. Long before she married W. E. B. Du Bois in 1951, Graham studied music at the Sorbonne in Paris. She chaired the Fine Arts department at Tennessee A&I State College in Nashville before heading the Federal Theatre Project in Chicago from 1936 to 1938; after completing a creative writing fellowship at Yale University in Connecticut, she wrote five plays in only two years: *Dust to Earth*, *I Gotta Home*, *It's Morning*, *Track Thirteen*, and *Elijah's Raven*. Graham also composed the first black opera in the United States to be performed by a professional cast. Her *Tom-Tom* was produced in 1932 at the Municipal Stadium in Cleveland, where some ten thousand people saw the opera that featured five hundred blacks recruited from local church choirs. Sketching black history from pastoral African beginnings, through American slavery, to the desired return to Africa represented by Marcus Garvey's United Negro Improvement Association (UNIA), the opera skillfully represents philosophically diverse black communities in which, for example, Africans abjure traditional rituals, and their African American descendants adopt the UNIA

program for reasons both noble and selfish. Because Graham's father and brother had worked in Liberia, and Graham had befriended Senegalese musicians in Paris, she was able to incorporate authentic African music into *Tom-Tom*. While she focused on political causes after her marriage to Du Bois, Shirley Graham maintained an interest in performance even in Ghana, to which the couple emigrated in 1961.

Realism and Social Change

Though her career as a dramatist lasted four decades, Alice Childress (1916–1994) is often overshadowed by Lorraine Hansberry's meteoric trajectory and, later, by the public's lack of interest in the realistic style that both women employed. Like Hurston before her, Childress focused on the dignity of ordinary black folks. But unlike Hurston, she favored realism, a literary genre in which characters onstage behave in much the same way as do people offstage, the relationship between the cause of social problems and their effects is clear, and spectators can identify ways to improve conditions. In addition, Childress often situated her social critique within the world of art. For example, her first play, *Florence*, produced in 1949 by New York's American Negro Theatre, concerns a mother who decides to travel "up North" to convince her adult daughter, an aspiring actress, to return home and pursue occupations deemed more suitable for black women. An encounter with a white actress in a segregated waiting room changes the mother's resolve as she realizes that whites, based on biased observations, will only continue to produce demeaning dramatic representations of black life, and so the mother comes to see the validity of her daughter's choice of profession.

The critical role that black women played in articulating more positive visions is also apparent in *Trouble in Mind*, which premiered in 1955 and made Childress the first black woman playwright to win an Obie (off-Broadway) Award. Set backstage among a group of black actors and a white director, *Trouble in Mind* critiques lynching as imagined by the white mainstream. But Childress's play extends her critique to northern middle class blacks, for among the characters is a young actor who, ignorant of black traditions of resistance, is willing to embrace stereotypical behavior as the price of his hoped-for entry into professional theater. Ironically, Childress was pressured by her white producers to rewrite the ambiguous ending so that audiences might experience a happy picture of racial unity. Mirroring the racial militancy of the period, Childress in *Wine in the Wilderness* (1969) told the story of a painter who, though he espouses nationalist rhetoric, holds such stereotypical views of working class black folk that he cannot see their dignity, wit, and survival skills. *Wedding Band: A Love/Hate Story in Black and White* (1966) explores interracial marriage in 1918 in Charleston, South Carolina, where it was legally forbidden. Though the play dramatizes the painful legacy of racism, it seemed curiously out of step with its contemporary audience, as black communities in the 1960s and 1970s became increasingly invested in a separate black identity. During the 2002–2003 theater season, however, after more multicultural perspectives had achieved dominance, *Wedding Band* was successfully revived by the Congo Square Theatre Company in association with the Steppenwolf Theatre of Chicago. Childress was recognized in 1993 with a Lifetime Achievement Award from the Association for Theatre in Higher Education.

Lorraine Hansberry (1930–1965) is often regarded as the mother of contemporary black theater. Her *Raisin in the Sun* won the 1959 New York Drama Critics Circle Award for best drama and was the first play by a black woman to be produced on Broadway. The story of a Chicago family struggling to break out of the emotional and physical confines of its tenement apartment, *Raisin* brought ordinary black folk's aspirations for full citizenship into the national spotlight only five years after the landmark Supreme Court decision outlawing segregated public schools. The play was visionary in its inclusion of such women's issues as abortion and entry into male-dominated professions and in its positive representation of newly independent African nations. In the years after *Raisin*, Hansberry surprised everyone by authoring *The Sign in Sidney Brustein's Window* (1964), an attack on the glib disavowal of social concerns by white bohemians living in New York City's Greenwich Village. The critical reception of this work was decidedly less than enthusiastic, and despite the valiant efforts of artist-activists, it closed after a relatively short run. Hansberry's other dramatic works include *The Drinking Gourd*, written for television in 1960 but never produced because of studio fears that her representation of slaveholders would alienate some viewers. Hansberry returned to the topic of African liberation struggles in *Les Blancs*, adapted and brought to the stage in 1970 by her former husband and literary executor Robert Nemiroff five years after her death from cancer at age thirty-four. *To Be Young, Gifted and Black*, compiled from her writings, was produced posthumously in 1969. *What Use Are Flowers?* was written in 1961 but not fully produced until the 1994 National Black Arts Festival in Atlanta, Georgia.

An Avant-Garde Feminism. Hansberry's contemporary, Adrienne Kennedy (1931–), pursued a radically different conception of theater. Considered a poet of the theater, she eschewed linear plot development, preferring instead to create characters who surrealistically metamorphose into different personae, inhabit shifting worlds of the real and the fantasized, and struggle with their gendered, racial,

ADRIENNE KENNEDY is considered a poet of the theater. Her early play *Funnyhouse of a Negro* received an Obie Award. (Courtesy of University of Minnesota Press, by permission of Adrienne Kennedy.)

and cultural identities. Her early plays—Obie winner *Funnyhouse of a Negro* (1964), *The Owl Answers* (1965), and *The Rat's Mass* (1966)—won recognition from avant-garde audiences but were largely ignored by black theatergoers who, during that period of the Black Power and Black Arts movements, were not prepared to engage the seemingly hallucinatory narratives of women deeply troubled by their antithetical African and European cultural heritages or by sexism within both black and white communities. After the "second-wave" of feminism of the 1970s and 1980s had opened a space for women to examine gender, black and white feminists rediscovered Kennedy, giving her, so she later said, the inspiration to continue writing for the theater. Interweaving elements of her fictionalized biography, fragments from her own plays, current events, and popular culture, Kennedy wrote such other plays as *A Movie Star Has to Star in Black and White* (1976) and *The Alexander Plays* (1992), a cycle with character Suzanne Alexander re-appearing in *She Talks to Beethoven* (1989), *The Ohio State Murders* (1992), and *The Film Club*, a monologue re-scripted for radio as *The Dramatic Circle*.

The Next Wave

To a limited extent, one can view Lorraine Hansberry and Adrienne Kennedy as two ends of a continuum along which later women playwrights could locate themselves. Hansberry was the realist for whom theater was a public sphere in which issues of social importance could be debated and performances served as a catalyst for action. Kennedy offered a denser, imagistic theater, in which the elusiveness of character and form meant that spectators are less likely to align performances with a political project.

Younger women learned from these elders and produced work indebted to them in novel ways. For example, Ntozake Shange (1948–) devised what she termed a "choreopoem," a combination of narrative poetry and dance, to celebrate young women's freedom and action. Her Obie-winning *for colored girls who have considered suicide when the rainbow is enuf* burst onto the national scene in 1976 when it was produced off Broadway at Woodie King Jr.'s New Federal Theatre and later on Broadway at the Booth Theatre. This all-female play ignited debate within black communities. Proponents lauded its articulation of gender issues, silenced during the Black Power and Black Arts period, while detractors equated its woman-centered viewpoint with racial betrayal and confirmation of already dominant, largely negative stereotypes about black men. Though subsequent dramas like *A Photograph* (1977) and *Spell #7* (1979) include men's narratives, Shange continued to center on women (*Liliane*, 1994), experiment with nonlinear forms (*The Love Space Demands*, 1992), and provocatively juxtapose the real and the magical. But like Hansberry, Shange was committed to theater as a medium for social change.

Playwright-performers like Anna Deavere Smith (1950–) and Robbie McCauley (1942–) also blended Kennedy's and Hansberry's visions in their works. Best known for her one-woman shows in which she performed across gender and race, Smith repeats verbatim sections of interviews conducted with various members of a community in crisis in *Fires in the Mirror: Crown Heights, Brooklyn, and Other Identities* (1992). The play explores deadly tensions between African American and Caribbean residents on the one hand and their Hasidic Jewish neighbors on the other, while *Twilight: Los Angeles, 1992* (1993) probes, in nonlinear fashion, tensions between whites, blacks, Koreans, and Latinos in the aftermath of urban rebellions. Smith won Obies for both plays and in 1996 was honored with a MacArthur Foundation Fellows Award (the "Genius Award"). While indebted to Kennedy for demonstrating that language, rather than character-centered psychological realism, can offer a route to identity, Smith's objective of fostering civic dialogue about race draws from Hansberry's insistence that all art is political.

Robbie McCauley, who acted in a number of Kennedy plays and in the first Broadway cast of *for colored girls*, merged painful familial and national histories in such works as *My Father and the Wars* (1985) and the Obie-winning *Sally's Rape* (1992). Her site-specific pieces, like "The Mississippi Project" (1992) or the "Stories Exchange Project" (1994), which deals with the Czech and Romany peoples, aim to promote individual introspection and community dialogue as part of both the rehearsal process and the performance itself. Similarly, the playwright-performer Rhodessa Jones sought to empower women prisoners to enact their own narratives with her San Francisco–based Medea Project: Theater for Incarcerated Women, and she performed some of their stories in *Big Butt Girls, Hard-Headed Women* (1989). As a solo performance artist, creating ephemeral, process-oriented work that challenges the assumed boundary between the deeply personal and the artistic, Jones produced such pieces as *The Legend of Lily Overstreet* (1979) and *Hot Flashes, Power Surges, and Private Summers* (2000).

Cheryl West (1950–), Pearl Cleage (1948–), and Kia Cothron (1961–) continued in Hansberry's realist tradition. West, who is also an adept comic writer, addressed family issues in the context of AIDS, homosexuality, and child abuse in such plays as *Before It Hits Home* (1991), *Jar the Floor* (1992), *Holiday Heart* (1993), and *Puddin n' Pete* (1993). Pearl Cleage often infuses seemingly contemporary perspectives into historical plays. Her *Flyin' West* (1992) focuses on a family of women who move to the American West in the 1890s; *Blues for an Alabama Sky* (1995) tells the story of a gay designer and a birth control advocate during the twilight years of the Harlem Renaissance; while *Bourbon at the Border* (1997) examines the silenced legacy of the psychological trauma suffered by civil rights activists. In a hyperrealistic style replete with sociological data and a somewhat incongruous cinematic structure, Kia Corthron tackled current issues like family planning, the medication of supposedly violent black boys, and police brutality in plays like *Come Down Burning* (1993), *Seeking the Genesis* (1996), and *Force Continuum* (2001).

Closer to the Kennedy end of the continuum is the work of Aishah Rahman (1936–), Regina Taylor (c. 1960–) and Suzan-Lori Parks (1964–). Translating the polyrhythmic structures of jazz to theater and dramatizing the spiritual as a powerful, transformative energy, Rahman wrote such plays as *Unfinished Women Cry in No Man's Land While a Bird Dies in a Gilded Cage* (1977), *The Mojo and the Sayso* (1987), and later, *Public Spaces*, a collection of one-acts. Of all the dramatists working in theater at the turn of the twenty-first century, Regina Taylor was unique in her additional roles as a stage and film actress, an adapter of European texts, and an artistic associate who introduced new work to Goodman Theatre audiences in Chicago. Her plays include the one-acts *Watermelon Rinds* and *Inside the Belly of the Beast*, collectively titled *The Ties that Bind* (1994). Her 1999 *Oo-Blah-Dee*, about a World War II women's jazz band, escapes the strictures of realism in its use of a timeless muse figure and through elliptical reference to the Bette Davis film, *Now, Voyager*, which had also served as the setting for Kennedy's meditations on women's mobility and subjectivity in *A Movie Star*. In 2000 Taylor signaled her interest in Kennedy even more directly when she performed a collage of monologues by Kennedy, Shange, Corthron, and Parks entitled *Millennium Mambo* and later re-titled *Urban Zulu Mambo*.

In 2002, a year after receiving a MacArthur "Genius Award," Suzan-Lori Parks became the first black woman to win a Pulitzer Prize in drama and cited the novelist James Baldwin's challenge to consider writing for the theater as one of her inspirations. In plays such as the Obie-winning *Imperceptible Mutabilities in the Third Kingdom* (1989), *The Death of the Last Black Man in the Whole Entire World* (1990), and *The America Play* (1994), Parks sardonically reexamined the Middle Passage, racist, scientific taxonomies, such cultural icons as the Black Man with a Watermelon, or Abraham Lincoln's assassination, subjecting them to linguistic and gesture-based "rep and rev," or repetition and revision that challenged audiences to discern how meaning is contingent upon context, potentially shifting with each iteration. Thus, the Last Black Man in the Whole Entire World, though he is lynched, shot, and subjected to all kinds of violence, continues to re-appear and recite his story. Likewise, the Lincoln impersonator of *The America Play* reappears in *Topdog/Underdog* (2001), this time located in the contemporary historical moment but feuding with his brother Booth in a reenactment of the rivalry of Cain and Abel. Like Kennedy before her, Parks often distributed one personality among several characters. Furthermore, characters often describe themselves in the third person so that, for example, the Kin-Seer in *Imperceptible Mutabilities* . . . reports waving at his "uther me" and discovering that his "uther me was wavin at my Self." This subversion of conventional identity, in addition to the device of allowing characters to narrate to audiences while watching "themselves" in action insistently raises the question of what constitutes reality. Parks's answer appears to be that reality resides only in performance, which is not fiction, but rather the often-repeated behavior and narratives we enact for ourselves and others. Centering her dramas in black history, yet radically destabilizing concepts of narrative and identity, Parks seemed to deny the material

consequences of socially constructed definitions of race and challenged her audience to reconsider the idea of theater as an arena for public dialogue about pressing social issues.

Against significant obstacles, black women have fashioned a range of styles to dramatize their understandings of the world. Despite limited opportunities to have their plays produced or published, black women playwrights have persisted. They remain confident in the unique perspective and artistic strength of their voices.

See also **Black Theater Movement; Hansberry, Lorraine; Harlem Renaissance; Parks, Suzan-Lori; Smith, Anna Deavere;** *and* **Theater.**

BIBLIOGRAPHY

Brown-Guillory, Elizabeth. *Wines in the Wilderness: Plays by African American Women from the Harlem Renaissance to the Present.* New York: Greenwood Press, 1990.

Cleage, Pearl. *Flyin' West and Other Plays.* New York: Theatre Communications Group, 1999.

Elam, Harry J., Jr., and Robert Alexander, eds. *Colored Contradictions: An Anthology of Contemporary African-American Plays.* New York: Penguin Books, 1996.

Hamalian, Leo, and James V. Hatch, eds. *Lost Plays of the Harlem Renaissance, 1920–1940.* Detroit MI: Wayne State University Press, 1996.

Hamalian, Leo, and James V. Hatch, eds. *The Roots of African American Drama: An Anthology of Early Plays, 1858–1938.* Detroit, MI: Wayne State University Press, 1991.

Hansberry, Lorraine. *Les Blancs: The Collected Last Plays of Lorraine Hansberry.* New York: Random House, 1972.

Hansberry, Lorraine, and Robert Nemiroff. *A Raisin in the Sun and The Sign in Sidney Brustein's Window.* New York: New American Library, 1987.

Hatch, James V., and Ted Shine, eds. *Black Theater U.S.A.: Plays by African Americans, 1847 to Today.* New York: Free Press, 1996.

Hughes, Langston, and Zora Neale Hurston. *Mule Bone: A Comedy of Negro Life.* New York: HarperPerennial, 1991.

Kennedy, Adrienne. *Adrienne Kennedy in One Act.* Minneapolis: University of Minnesota Press, 2001.

Mahone, Sydne, ed. *Moon Marked and Touched by Sun: Plays by African American Women.* New York: Theatre Communications Group, 1994.

Parks, Suzan-Lori. *America Play and Other Works.* New York: Theatre Communications Group, 1995.

Parks, Suzan-Lori. *Topdog/Underdog.* New York: Theatre Communications Group, 2001.

Perkins, Kathy A., ed. *Black Female Playwrights: An Anthology of Plays before 1950.* Bloomington: Indiana University Press, 1989.

Perkins, Kathy A., and Judith Stephens, eds. *Strange Fruit: Plays on Lynching by American Women.* Bloomington: Indiana University Press, 1998.

Perkins, Kathy A., and Roberta Uno, eds. *Contemporary Plays by Women of Color, an Anthology.* New York: Routledge, 1996.

Shange, Ntozake. *for colored girls who have considered suicide when the rainbow is enuf.* New York: Macmillan, 1977.

Turner, Darwin, ed. *Black Drama in America, an Anthology.* Washington, DC: Howard University Press, 1994.

Wilkerson, Margaret B. *Nine Plays by Black Women.* New York: Penguin Books, 1986.

—S. L. RICHARDS

PLEASANT, MARY ELLEN (b. 19 August 1814; d. 1904), abolitionist. Mary Ellen Pleasant arrived in San Francisco during the Gold Rush, probably sometime in 1852. For the next fifty years, she worked as cook, accountant, abolitionist, and entrepreneur in the bustling town on the bay. Histories of the West describe her as madam, voodoo queen, and prostitute. Pleasant herself requested that the words "she was a friend of John Brown's" be printed on her gravestone, indicating her own desire to be remembered as an abolitionist. She was the target of what one historian has called an "avid conspiracy" that sought to silence her, and it was said that she harbored the skeletons of San Francisco's elite in her closet.

The folklore about Pleasant reveals conflicting stories of her background (some say she was from Georgia, others Virginia), but Pleasant herself claimed she was born in Philadelphia. She described her mother as a free colored woman and her father as a wealthy planter. Pleasant was educated on Nantucket by the Hussey family. She appeared to have spent time in Boston where she met William Lloyd Garrison and other abolitionists, including Alexander Smith, whom she married. Smith was a wealthy Cuban planter and, upon his death, willed Pleasant a considerable sum, perhaps as much as $45,000. Smith intended her to use the money for abolitionist causes. Pleasant's second husband, John James Pleasant, joined her in San Francisco sometime between 1848 and 1852. Pleasant had one child, Elizabeth Smith, but little is known of her beyond an 1866 report in a black newspaper, the *Elevator*, that Pleasant sponsored a lavish wedding for her daughter at the African Methodist Episcopal Zion Church in San Francisco.

Pleasant moved to Canada West in the late 1850s, working in the community of black abolitionists and fugitive slaves stationed near Chatham. She and John Pleasant, along with Mary Ann Shadd Cary, Martin Delaney, and other members of the Chatham Vigilance Committee, organized to aid escaped slaves after the passage of the 1850 Fugitive Slave Act. Pleasant also bought real estate in Chatham in 1858. She reported that she met John Brown in Chatham, where the raid on Harpers Ferry was planned, and that she gave him financial support for his activities.

By the 1860s, she had returned to San Francisco and become a restaurateur and investor. San Francisco's thriving elite provided an eager market for her elegant restaurants and boardinghouses, where she entertained some of the West's most famous financiers. Her best-known establishment, at 920 Washington Street (in the heart of twenty-first century Chinatown) was the meeting place for some of the city's most prominent politicians, including Newton Booth, elected as governor of California in 1871. In the private domain of Pleasant's

MARY ELLEN PLEASANT at age eighty-seven. This photograph of "Mammy Pleasant" appeared in *The Pandex*, a magazine published briefly in San Francisco. (Austin/Thompson Collection, by permission of Schomburg Center for Research in Black Culture.)

kitchens and dining rooms, she was privy to information about San Francisco's most powerful businessmen and politicians.

Pleasant also operated laundries in which she employed black men and women. She operated an extensive employment network for the black population of the city, supplying the chief employers of African Americans— mining moguls turned hotel owners—with most of their labor force. In this way, she functioned as a city boss, running an informal employment agency in black San Francisco. Her efforts to improve conditions for African Americans in the West extended beyond the workplace; she harbored fugitive slaves and fought for passage of an 1863 law guaranteeing black Americans the right to testify in court. Pleasant also challenged Jim Crow laws in her landmark 1868 case against the North Beach Railroad Company. She was awarded $500 in damages after drivers refused to allow her to board the streetcar, but the verdict was overturned on appeal.

In 1884, Pleasant again appeared in court. This time it was as a witness in the highly publicized trial *Sharon v. Sharon*. Stories of the trial and Pleasant's testimony were common fare in national as well as local papers, indicating that Pleasant's entrepreneurial reputation was well known. Further, her role in the trial was pivotal as she testified to the authenticity of a marriage contract between the mining mogul and Nevada Senator William Sharon and Sarah Althea Hill. Pleasant reportedly funded Hill's case, and press coverage of Pleasant likened her to a scheming voodoo queen.

Pleasant was well aware of the distortions her character suffered in the press: "You tell those newspaper people that they may be smart, but I'm smarter. They deal with words. Some folks say that words were made to reveal thought. That ain't so. Words were made to conceal thought." Pleasant died in San Francisco. All that remains of the mansion she had built, on the corner of Octavia and Bush streets in San Francisco, are the eucalyptus trees she planted. Her legend—although tangled—reveals the financial genius of a nineteenth-century African American woman whose power, at the very least, inspired mythology and imagination.

See also Abolition Movement *and* Enterpreneurs.

BIBLIOGRAPHY

Bennett, Lerone. "A Historical Detective Story: The Mystery of Mary Ellen Pleasant. Parts I and II." *Ebony,* April and May 1979.

Holdredge, Helen. *Mammy Pleasant*. New York: Putnam, 1953.

Hudson, Lynn M. *The Making of "Mammy Pleasant": A Black Entrepreneur in Nineteenth-Century San Francisco*. Urbana: University of Illinois Press, 2003.

—LYNN HUDSON

POETRY. Despite popular belief, the African American literary tradition did not begin in 1773, when Phillis Wheatley, a well-educated slave, published a poetry collection entitled *Poems on Various Subjects, Religious and Moral*. Rather, it began a year earlier, when Wheatley, who was able to translate Ovid's tales from Latin by age ten, was called before a group of eighteen Boston aristocrats to prove that she had written the book. No transcript of the meeting was taken, so scholars can only speculate that Wheatley was asked about the book's various Greek and Latin allusions and the obvious influences of Milton and Pope. She was certainly confronted with the collective skepticism about her ability to craft such accomplished poems. Whatever she said, it convinced the panel to draft and sign a two-paragraph "Attestation" as well as an open letter to readers of Wheatley's book, "To the Publick," that reads in part: "We whose Names are under-written, do assure the World, that the Poems specified in the following Page, were (as we verily believe) written by Phillis, a

young Negro girl . . . She has been examined by some of the best Judges, and is thought qualified to write them."

And so began the practice, which would continue for more than a century, of established white people (usually editors) including prefatory material at the beginning of books written by African Americans. Such prefaces and letters, which testified to the author's intelligence, trustworthiness, and generally good character, would accompany the publication of books ranging from poetry collections to novels and from short story collections to fugitive slave narratives. It is important to note that African American literature found its first publishing home not in the United States, but in London, where John Wheatley had taken his slave Phillis to recuperate from an illness and where the Countess of Huntington (to whom the book is dedicated) and the Earl of Dartmouth, convinced by the prefatory information, aided Phillis and her master in securing a publisher. Phillis and her master's son, Nathaniel Wheatley, had

"A POEM" BY PHILLIS WHEATLEY, cover. This work, published in 1770, was widely printed in broadside in America and Britain and is Wheatley's most famous elegy. (Beinecke Rare Book and Manuscript Library, Yale University.)

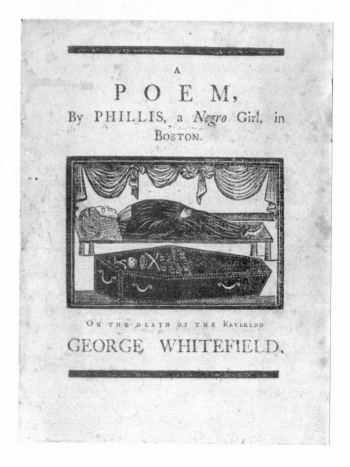

tried a year before to find Boston publisher for a similar collection, but, without the judges' comments, no one believed her capable of writing the poems.

Wheatley's poems rely on the conventions she learned from classic literature. They address "proper" poetic subjects such as "Imagination," allude to Greek and Roman mythology, and include invocations to the muse. In addition, they contain a consistent meter (usually iambic pentameter), rhyming couplets, personification, and epigrams, and were often written for and dedicated to prominent citizens like George Washington and leading business and religious leaders. Many critics are quick to point out that Wheatley was not simply a mimic, but rather an intelligent poet who used neoclassical conventions because they suited her purposes. In the words of Erlene Stetson, editor of the important anthology *Black Sister: Poetry by Black American Women 1746–1980*, "the strength of her poetics lies in the mastery, skill, perception, and black female consciousness that she fuses with these conventional models."

Many of Wheatley's strongest poems are about the illness, death, and dying that were such a part of women's lives at the time she was writing. Wheatley was often inspired by the deaths of women and children, and she paid particular attention to the suffering of mothers. These poems examine the overwhelming sense of loss that accompanies death and address the personal struggles that women were forced to endure alone. She often writes for and to her white patrons in such poems. Stetson interprets Wheatley's poetic stance in such pieces as "characteristically deferential[. S]he insisted on observing the proper social distance between herself and her masters. She accepted the world of masters and servants and acted according to the accepted code that demanded that she be 'humble, modest, wise.'" Wheatley was criticized and even dismissed as a literary figure by some in subsequent generations of African American poets (especially poets of the Black Arts Movement) for the absence of social protest in her work. Others, however, such as Elaine Stetson and Henry Louis Gates Jr., see Wheatley as an African American icon, a literary and historical matriarch.

Gates sees Wheatley's oral examination as part of a larger reexamination of sixteenth-century assumptions. Since at least that time, Europeans had been unsure whether or not the "African species of man" could ever "master the arts and sciences." If they could, according to the argument, then Africans were fundamentally related to Europeans. If not, then Africans seemed destined to be slaves. This was the burden that Wheatley carried into the meeting. Gates sees her successful defense as the launching point for two literary traditions at once: the African American literary tradition and the African American *woman's* literary tradition. In his view, Phillis Wheatley's

struggle to get published and find an audience, and the subsequent indifference she received from patrons and acquaintances after returning from England, *is* the history of African American literature and literary criticism.

Early African American writers seemed keenly aware of Wheatley's importance. Jupiter Hammon, for example, author of the first poem ("An Evening Thought. Salvation by Christ, With Penitential Cries") published by an African American, acknowledged her influence by making her the subject of his 1778 broadside "An Address to Miss Phillis Wheatly [*sic*], Ethiopian Poetess, in Boston." Also, George Horton, the second African American to publish a book of poetry in English—a startling *fifty-six* years after Wheatley—published an 1838 edition of his 1829 collection *The Hope of Liberty*, bound with Wheatley's.

While Wheatley was the first African American poet to publish an entire volume, she was not the first to be recognized as a poet. That honor belongs to then-sixteen-year-old Lucy Terry (1730–1821), of Deerfield, Massachusetts, who in 1746 wrote "Bars Fight, August 28, 1746." Her poem chronicles a Native American raid on a camp of white settlers. In the poem, she takes a decidedly pro-settler stance, casting most, but not all of them in a positive light: one man was killed after fighting "like a hero"; one woman was "tommyhawked . . . on her head" as she tried to flee; another man "fled across the water" and escaped; yet another was "taken and carried to Canada." While Terry's poem is far less refined and technically accomplished than any of Wheatley's, it is far more overtly intense and emotional.

In Wheatley's Shadow: Nineteenth-Century African American Women's Poetry

One poet who is perhaps more important historically than artistically is Ann Plato. Little is known about her; historians are certain only, through the records of the Reverend J. W. C. Pennington, that she was a member of the Colored Congregational Church of Hartford, Connecticut, in 1841 and that she put together the wide-ranging *Essays; Including Biographies and Miscellaneous Pieces, in Prose and Poetry* (Hartford, 1841), which, after Wheatley's collection, was one of the first books by an African American woman. While no definitive conclusion has yet been reached, scholars believe that Plato was relatively young when she wrote her book. Her age has been offered as an excuse, in fact, for some of the book's shortcomings: it is at times excessively sentimental and melodramatic, and it is cluttered with forced rhymes, missed rhymes, misspellings, and punctuation errors. Another important characteristic of the book is that it deals very little with complex issues such as race. In fact, only one of the twenty poems in the book addresses slavery. "To the First of August" celebrates the 1 August 1838 abolition of slavery in the British West Indies. Another, "The Natives of America," shows a father telling his child about the mistreatment of Native Americans. The majority of the book's poetry superficially addresses situations such as visiting a grave ("Reflections, Written on Visiting the Grave of a Venerated Friend") and talking in syrupy, gushing terms to one's love ("Forget Me Not").

Another important literary figure in nineteenth-century African American women's poetry is H.(enrietta) Cordelia Ray (1850–1916). One of two daughters born to the distinguished minister and abolitionist, Charles B. Ray, she was raised in New York City and received an exceptional education, graduating from New York University with a degree in Pedagogy and from the Sauveueur School of Languages, where she became fluent in Greek, Latin, French, and German in addition to developing into an English scholar. After completing her education, Ray became a teacher at grammar school No. 80. She quickly grew bored there, though, and quit, dedicating most of the rest of her life to tending to her physically challenged older sister, Florence; tutoring in music, mathematics, and languages; teaching literature classes to teachers; and supporting her father's antislavery work. Her debut as a poet occurred at the dedication of the Freedman's Monument, a sculpture unveiled by President Ulysses S. Grant in 1876, when a reading of her "Commemoration Ode on Lincoln/written for the occasion of the unveiling of the Freedman's monument/in Memory of Abraham Lincoln/April 14, 1876" was part of the ceremony. (The poem was eventually published in 1893.) Ray's academic background led her toward an intellectual writing style that tended to emphasize technique and form over emotion. Some of her more accomplished poems were inspired by historical and literary figures: "Oedipus and Antigone," "Milton," "Shakespeare," and "Robert G. Shaw." Her other published works include *Sonnets* (New York, 1893); *Poems* (1887); and, with her sister, *Sketch of the Life of Rev. Charles B. Ray* (New York, 1887).

After Phillis Wheatley, Frances E. W. Harper (1825–1911) is perhaps the most important nineteenth-century African American female poet. She was a novelist in addition to being a poet; her novel, *Iola Leroy, or Shadows Uplifted* (1892), was thought to be the first by an African American woman until Henry Louis Gates discovered Harriet E. Wilson's *Our Nig*. Harper's poems, which are usually narratives, are rooted in religion and the struggle against racism and gender discrimination. The tone of her poems ranges from furious to sentimental to humorous. Her subjects range, too, as exemplified by the following list: "A Grain of Sand," "Mary at the Feet of Christ," "A Mother's Blessing," "The Dying Bondsman," "The Sparrow's Fall," "Dandelions," "The Hermit's Sacrifice," "The Slave Auction," and "The Dying Mother."

In contrast to Wheatley, Harper wrote much of her poetry about the lower classes. She attacked the institution of slavery and upbraided white Christians who failed to show charity toward African Americans. As Frederick Douglass does brilliantly in the Appendix to his 1845 *Narrative of the Life of Frederick Douglass, An American Slave*, Harper often points out, in poems such as "Simon's Countrymen," the hypocrisy implicit within a societal structure that embraces both Christianity and slavery. Harper's passion emanated from her faith. Religion not only gave Harper the moral basis for her position, but also offered her images of hope. By adapting stories and parables from the Bible to address her audiences, Harper found a way to get through to African Americans who may have been illiterate, but who may have heard such stories growing up.

In addition, Harper fought for the rights of women to disregard unfair laws. Poems such as "Vashti" and books such as *Moses: A Story of the Nile* (1869), celebrate brave, strong women who face banishment rather than submit to the authority of unjust men. Harper also used the metaphor of the flower to exemplify the female condition. In "The Crocuses" and "The Mission of the Flowers," Harper praises the beauty, strength, and determination of African American women. Furthermore, Harper wrote a variety of other kinds of poems, including odes, lyrics, and eulogies. *Sketches of Southern Life* (1872) even contains several narrative poems written in dialect, in which Harper uses humor and irony to address subjects close to her heart: suffrage and slavery.

While Wheatley and Harper have long been fixtures in the African American literary canon, many African American woman poets of the eighteenth and nineteenth centuries have gone unrecognized because they could not find book publishers during their lifetimes. As a result, their work was forgotten until a resurgence in African American Studies has led historians and literary scholars to search through diaries, letters, and journals on a quest for un- or underappreciated writers. One woman who has recently earned recognition among scholars is Charlotte Forten [Grimké] (1837–1914). In what is the earliest known journal kept by an African American woman, Forten wrote an entry on 28 June 1854, in which she writes admiringly of Phillis Wheatley. Other African American women published anonymously or under a pen name. For example, anti-slavery poems by "Ada" appeared regularly in William Lloyd Garrison's abolitionist newspaper, *The Liberator*, between 1836 and 1855. Later revealed to be a woman named Sarah Louisa Forten, "Ada" was known only as "a young and intelligent lady of color" and was reportedly from Philadelphia. Little else is known of her. Learning much more about such writers is further complicated by the fact that these women published in periodicals with very small circulations—religious pamphlets, temperance and antislavery magazines, African American newspapers, and then-popular journals and weeklies—including *A.M.E. Church Review, Anglo-American, Women's Era, Atlantic Monthly, Golden Days, Ringwood's Magazine, Free Speech* (edited by Ida B. Wells), *Woman's Light and Love, Waverly Magazine, the Boston Herald,* and the *Philadelphia Press*. Most of the records and much of the poetry published in these small journals, which were among the few publications who accepted poetry by African American women, have unfortunately been lost. Aside from the single volume by Wheatley and a few others by Harper, there were no book-length collections of poems by an African American woman published in the United States before 1890.

The dearth of poetry collections had nothing to do with a lack of intellect, imagination, or energy among black women. Eighteenth- and nineteenth-century African American writers—both male and female—struggled to be recognized as artists. Most did not yet have the societal or economic resources to publish their own work or the work of other African American writers. Furthermore, their paths toward publication were blocked by the business interests of the publishing industry. Books by African American women had no track record: none had ever sold well, so publishers did not want to risk investing in an unproven commodity. Refusing to publish works by African American women guaranteed, of course, that such writers remained unpublished, obscure, and, in effect, voiceless. The political climate of the writer–publisher relationship would be one of the key issues in such important twentieth-century literary movements as the Harlem Renaissance and the Black Arts Movement.

African American Women's Poetry of The Harlem Renaissance

Also known as the New Negro Movement, the New Negro Renaissance, and the Negro Renaissance, the Harlem Renaissance began roughly at the end of World War I, peaked in the mid-1920s, and ended in the middle of the 1930s. During that time, African Americans migrated in unprecedented numbers from the South to the North, fleeing oppressive working conditions and hoping to capitalize on the increased opportunities created by World War I in cities such as Baltimore, Chicago, Cleveland, Philadelphia, and New York City. This demographic shift, known as "The Great Migration," brought African Americans together in concentrated areas and led to new political, intellectual, and artistic possibilities. Moving to the North did not eliminate racial tension, however. During this time, African Americans frequently found themselves threatened in both the North and the South. In 1919 alone, African Americans were attacked in twenty-five cities and seventy people were

lynched, with fourteen burned alive. The Ku Klux Klan, founded in 1915, was gaining strength, D. W. Griffith had just filmed *Birth of a Nation,* and the racist parodying of African American culture, the blackface minstrel show, was the hit of vaudeville. In the midst of this climate, Harlem emerged as a mecca of African American culture and thought. Writers such as Langston Hughes, James Weldon Johnson, Zora Neale Hurston, Countee Cullen, and Claude McKay formed what would become known as the "bumper crop" of Harlem Renaissance artists. This generation of writers sought, in a variety of styles, to empower themselves and their race by creating work that speaks to various aspects of the African American condition. While the Harlem Renaissance was primarily a literary movement, it was part of a larger transformation of African American thought that included the fields of music, photography, painting, theater, and politics.

In recent years, the female poets of the Harlem Renaissance have received increased attention. Originally dismissed by many critics as capable of writing only in anachronistic styles and about hackneyed subjects, writers such as Georgia Douglas Johnson, Jessie Fauset, Angelina Weld Grimké, Alice Dunbar-Nelson, and Virginia Houston are now appreciated for their use of metaphor and development of themes of great significance to women, such as family, nature, heritage, protest, and intellectual as well as sexual liberation.

Georgia Douglas Johnson (1886–1966) was born in Atlanta and educated at Atlanta University and Oberlin Conservatory in Ohio. Also a playwright, fiction writer, songwriter, and journalist, she was the best-known African American woman poet between Frances E. W. Harper, whose last book of poems was published in 1872, and Margaret Walker, whose first collection was published in 1942. Johnson, who once had aspirations of being a composer, wrote four volumes of poetry. Three of her books were modeled on the sonata form, which she saw as a perfect vehicle through with to show the close relationship between poetry and music. Her first volume, *The Heart of a Woman* (1918), is a personal collection that connects springtime to a young woman's emerging sense of self. Then came *Bronze* (1922), which looks at the struggles and triumphs associated with womanhood. Next, the poems of *An Autumn Love Cycle* (1928) present the speaker as an older woman who looks back at her life after "love's triumphant day is done." Each volume includes many references to stringed instruments and represents different aspects of the sonata form, serving respectively as beginning, development, and resolution. Her fourth book, *Share My World,* appeared in 1962.

Johnson's good friend, Jessie Redmon Fauset (1882–1961), was credited with midwifing the Harlem Renaissance through her discovery of several major poets, including Langston Hughes, during her tenure as literary editor of W. E. B. Du Bois's journal, *The Crisis*. Her work as an editor shaped her professional and social life, but Fauset saw herself first as a writer. In addition to important poems such as "Oriflamme," "Stars in Alabama," and "Fragment," she wrote four novels, most famously *There Is Confusion* (1924), which offered a glimpse of middle-class African American life from a female perspective. She and Johnson mentored a new generation of African American writers, both men and women, in addition to making significant contributions to the African American canon through their own writing.

Angelina Weld Grimké (1880–1958) was born in Boston, the only child of a freed slave and a Harvard Law School graduate, Archibald Henry Grimké, and a wealthy white woman, Sarah Stanley, who left the family when Angelina was very young. Her father was the nephew of the famous Grimké sisters from South Carolina. As a result of her close relationship with them, she became involved with progressive issues at a young age. In addition to poetry, she wrote stories and plays, including *Rachel*, an outstanding, powerful drama about a woman's struggle for an individual identity in the early twentieth century. Never married, she lived alone after her father's death, after which she did not continue her writing career. Her love poems to other women have been praised in recent years as groundbreaking and technically accomplished works of early lesbian writing.

Alice Dunbar-Nelson (1875–1935), born in New Orleans to a seamstress and a merchant marine, was a teacher, suffragist, fiction writer, and journalist in addition to being a poet. She was very well educated, having attended Straight, Cornell, and Columbia Universities, in addition to the University of Pennsylvania. She lived in Washington, DC, during a brief marriage to one of the most influential African American writers of the late-nineteenth and early-twentieth century, Paul Laurence Dunbar. When their marriage ended, she moved to Wilmington, Delaware, where she married Robert Nelson, a journalist, with whom she published *The Wilmington Advocate* from 1920 to 1922. She also became active in women's political issues and worked as a suffrage organizer in the mid-Atlantic region and was active in the National Association of Colored Women (NACW). While she published poems only in periodicals during her lifetime, she was the earliest of the women of the Harlem Renaissance to publish works of fiction, producing *Violets and Other Tales* at age twenty in 1894 and another collection of short stories, *The Goodness of St. Rocque and Other Stories*, in 1899. *Give Us This Day: The Diary of Alice Dunbar-Nelson*, edited by Gloria Hull, was published in 1984.

Anne Spencer (1882–1975) had to overcome a tumultuous childhood before her career as a writer could get started. She was born on a Virginia plantation and lived with her parents in Martinsville, Virginia, where her father was a bar owner, until her mother and she ran away, living briefly in various places before settling in Bramwell, West Virginia, a predominantly white community, where her mother worked as a cook. While Spencer did not go to school until age eleven, she flourished in her young adulthood after she and her mother moved again—this time to Lynchburg, Virginia, where Anne attended the Virginia Seminary—with Edward Spencer, a postal worker. With her mother looking after the house, Anne was able to dedicate her life to reading, writing, and talking with the most prominent writers and artists of her day. She found a mentor in James Weldon Johnson, a key political and literary figure in the Harlem Renaissance, who helped Spencer publish her poems and introduced her to well-known writers. Spencer made a novel decision in 1931—one that previous generations of African American women writers were in no position to make: she decided to stop publishing. She lived forty-four more years and did not change her mind: after 1931, she did not publish another book. She did not stop working, though. She kept writing until her death at age ninety-three.

Gwendolyn B. Bennett (1902–1981) lived, after her parents' separation, primarily with her father. Raised in Nevada and Washington, DC, she went to high school in Brooklyn, then attended the School of Fine Arts at Columbia University before she graduated from Pratt Institute in 1924. Soon afterward, Bennett began a promising career in academe when she was hired as an assistant professor of art by Howard University, where she taught design, watercolor, and crafts. When she won a fellowship to study painting in Paris in 1925, Howard agreed to hold her position. Around this time, she became an assistant editor for Charles S. Johnson's *Opportunity*, for which she wrote a column entitled "Ebony Flute"; she also collaborated with close friends Wallace Thurman, Langston Hughes, Zora Neale Hurston, Aaron Douglass, Richard Bruce, and John Davis in publishing *Fire!!*, "A Quarterly Devoted to the Younger Negro Artists." Unfortunately, they were unable to obtain sponsors and published only one issue. Although she never published a book of her own poetry, Bennett firmly establish herself as a poet during the Harlem Renaissance. Her poems appeared regularly in *The Crisis*, *Opportunity*, *American Mercury*, *Howard University Record*, and *Southern Workman*; they were also reprinted in some of the most popular anthologies of the time, including *Caroling Dusk*, edited by Countee Cullen, *Ebony and Topaz*, edited by Charles S. Johnson, and William Stanley Braithwaite's *Anthology of American Verse for 1927*. Her college teaching career came to a premature end when Howard fired her in 1927 for marrying a medical student. The couple left Washington, DC, for Florida, where

Bennett taught high school, and later moved to Long Island. She gave up on her career as an artist after her husband died and in 1935 moved to Harlem, where she worked as assistant to the director Augusta Savage in the Harlem Community Art Center. Bennett remarried in 1940. She retired in 1968 to bucolic Kutztown, Pennsylvania, where she spent her remaining years running an antiques shop with her husband.

Helene Johnson (1906–1995), a socialite, was well known in New York and Boston literary circles in the 1920s and 30s. A member of the Boston Quill Club, she was published in nearly every major journal and anthology of her day. Poems such as "Sonnet to a Negro in Harlem," "A Missionary Brings a Young Native to America," and "A Southern Road" show an impressive command of form and idiom and stand as some of the most beautiful imagistic verse of the Harlem Renaissance. Like several female poets of the Harlem Renaissance, Johnson's publication record ends abruptly; in Johnson's case, the poem "Let Me Sing My Song" in the May 1935 issue of *Challenge*, a Boston journal edited by Dorothy West was her final published work. Around the time of that poem's appearance, family considerations took precedence. During the 1940s and 1950s, she worked as a correspondent for Consumers Union in Mount Vernon, New York. With the exception of a short stay in Onset, Massachusetts, she spent the rest of her life with her family in New York City.

A native Philadelphian, Mae V. Cowdery (1909–1953) was raised in a comfortable middle class home. As a senior at the Philadelphia High School for Girls (a school also attended by Jessie Fauset) in 1927, she won first prize in a poetry contest run by *The Crisis*, as well as the Krigwa Poetry Prize for another poem. After graduation, she, like Gwendolyn B. Bennett, attended Pratt Institute. She quickly took to New York City and enjoyed Harlem and Greenwich Village cabarets. Cowdery was one of the few women of her time to publish a book of her own poems, *We Lift Our Voices and Other Poems* (1936). Despite early success and earning the respect of some of the most influential figures of the Harlem Renaissance, Alain Locke and Langston Hughes, Cowdery fell silent after the book's publication. Her final years are shrouded in mystery. She took her own life at the age of forty-four.

A number of factors contributed to the end of the Harlem Renaissance in the mid-1930s. First, the Great Depression was especially hard on African American communities. Second, organizations such as the NAACP and the Urban League shifted their interests away from artistic concerns toward economic and social ones. Along with the lack of organized support, Harlem Renaissance leaders such as James Weldon Johnson, Langston Hughes, Charles S. Johnson, and W. E. B. Du Bois left

Harlem to pursue varied interests elsewhere. Perhaps most devastating was the Harlem Riot of 1935, which was set off by frustrations with an economic structure—white owners serving black neighborhoods—that limited the access of African Americans to positions of financial independence within their own communities. Still, the creative energy swirling in Harlem throughout the Renaissance did not die. Roughly one-third of the books published during the Renaissance were published after the stock market crash of 1929. In the end, though, most who had gathered there either left or stopped writing. The Harlem Renaissance changed the landscape of African American art and literature. Because it had no one agenda other than to celebrate the artistic and intellectual capabilities of African Americans, the Harlem Renaissance left a panoply of styles, subjects, and themes from which subsequent generations of artists, both inside and outside the United States, could draw inspiration.

African American Women's Poetry after the Harlem Renaissance

The Harlem Renaissance served as proof that the white race did not own the fields of literature, politics, and art. Whatever subsequent generations of African American writers, artists, and activists (such as those involved in the Black Arts Movement) may point out as shortcomings within the Harlem Renaissance, they must acknowledge that the Renaissance offered a new range of possibilities, a multitude of voices that had previously been rendered silent. It picked up an artistic dialogue—a response to a call—that began with the precocious poems of Phillis Wheatley and continued through poems and slave narratives of the eighteenth century. It continued with the work of writers such as Richard Wright in the late 1930s and the 1940s and with Ralph Ellison in the early 1950s.

It had a particularly liberating effect on African American women writers, who now worked not from a tradition of slavery followed by servile domesticity, but from one in which women sought to reexamine and affirm in new ways the African American female experience. It is not a coincidence that the longest, most varied, and most successful careers for African American women poets began in the decades after the Harlem Renaissance and, in many cases, continued until or beyond the end of the millennium. The Harlem Renaissance set the stage for powerful literary and cultural figures such as Maya Angelou, Nikki Giovanni, and Lucille Clifton and for award-winning and best-selling novelists such as Alice Walker and Toni Morrison, who have routinely drawn inspiration from the work of Harlem Renaissance writers and artists.

Margaret Abigail Walker (1915–1998) was born in Birmingham, Alabama, the daughter of a Methodist minister. She graduated from Northwestern University in

1935 and earned a graduate degree from the University of Iowa, where she submitted a collection of poems for her master's thesis, and *Jubilee*, a historical novel set around the time of the Civil War, for her doctorate. Both books were eventually published. She is best known for *For My People* (1942), winner of the Yale Series of Younger Poets competition, which includes poems that address issues such as race and family pride, personal struggles, and which express interests in Africa and Negro folklore. While much of her work—especially poems such as "For My People" "Molly Means," and "Lineage"—has been praised for its honesty, clarity, directness, and intensity, some of it has been criticized for being too direct and for having a racial consciousness so pronounced that it overshadows the effectiveness of the poems as works of art.

In 1950 Gwendolyn Brooks (1917–2000) became the first African American to win the Pulitzer Prize for poetry for *Annie Allen* (1949). Although born in Topeka, Kansas, Brooks was raised in Chicago, where she completed her formal education at Wilson Junior College. She was a housewife for many years before she took teaching positions at several colleges in Chicago and at the University of Wisconsin. Brooks's first volume, *A Street in Bronzeville*, was published in 1945. Subsequent books include *Maud Martha* (1953), a poetic novel about an African American girl's coming of age, *Bronzeville Boys and Girls* (poems for children, 1956), *The Bean Eaters* (1960), *Selected Poems* (1963), and *In the Mecca* (1963).

Gwendolyn Brooks earned praise for her poetic brilliance and for her revelations of African American life. She often wrote about "Bronzeville," an appellation for the predominantly African American South Side of Chicago. She wrote some of the most powerful poems of the twentieth century about the African American condition—including "To DeWitt Clinton in His Way to Lincoln Cemetery," "A Bronzeville Mother Loiters in Mississippi. Meanwhile, a Mississippi Mother Burns Bacon," "Winnie," and "To an Old Black Woman, Homeless and Indistinct"—as well as a number of equally remarkable poems that do not directly address race, such as "We Real Cool," "The Mother," "Boy Breaking Glass," and "The Lovers of the Poor." Revealing influences spanning from Dickinson, Robinson, and Frost to Dunbar, Cullen, and Melvin Tolson, she successfully used all of the traditional forms of short poetry as well as free verse. In the words of Michael S. Harper and Anthony Walton, editors of *Every Shut Eye Ain't Asleep: An Anthology of Poetry by African-Americans Since 1945* (1994), "Taken as a whole, Mrs. Brooks's poems represent a long novel of the experiences of African Americans in Chicago, Russian in scope, emotion and complexity, American and modern, even cubist at times, in their compression and technical wizardry."

Margaret Danner (1915–), like Gwendolyn Brooks, lived in Chicago for most of her life. She was educated at Loyola and Roosevelt Universities and was once an assistant editor of *Poetry*, arguably the most influential poetry journal of its time. Many of her poems, "These Beasts and the Benin Bronze," "Sadie's Playhouse," and "Through the Varied Patterned Lace," are full of vibrant imagery that is inspired by African folklore. Her poems have been published in many journals and anthologies, and readings of her work have been recorded. A booklet of her poems, *To Flower: Poems*, was published in the Counterpoise Series in 1963. In addition to her writing, Danner has also enjoyed a successful career in academia. In 1960 Danner became the first Poet in Residence at Wayne State (MI) University in Detroit. At that time, she founded Boone House, a poetry and art center for budding African American artists and writers. In 1966 she was part of the First World Festival of Negro Arts held in Dakar, Senegal.

Gloria Catherine Oden (1923–), who grew up the daughter of a minister in Yonkers, New York, has been mentioned alongside great women poets of the past century like Marianne Moore, Louise Bogan, and Elizabeth Bishop, as a writer who can combine the literal and the symbolic, the real and the fanciful. Her work is routinely grounded in a sense of loss. However, it appeals primarily to the intellect. There is an ironic detachment in her work that moves readers away from pathos and distinguishes Oden from many of her contemporaries. She was a professor of English at the University of Maryland, Baltimore County, and has been honored by many organizations, including the National Endowment for the Humanities.

Naomi Long Madgett (1923–), also the daughter of a minister, was born in Norfolk, Virginia, and educated at Virginia State College and Wayne State (MI) University. She has published three volumes of poetry: *Songs of the Phantom Nightingale* (1941), *One and the Many* (1956), and *Star by Star* (1965). Her poems are largely free-verse and focus on racial identity and injustice and, in poems like "Alabama Centennial," on the need for change in the American political system. Robert Hayden and other literary critics have written favorably of Madgett's race-related work, but many more critics have been drawn to her lyric poems on the enduring themes of personal experience, love, nature, and death.

Mari Evans (1923–) has composed songs and studied fashion design in addition to writing poems. Her free-flowing poems, driven by sparse conversational language, are akin to Langston Hughes's jazz poetry—indeed, to jazz itself—in their improvisational, elliptical nature. Many of her poems contain direct and/or indirect musical references. She has been Writer-in-Residence and Assistant Professor in Black Literature at Indiana University and has also taught at Spelman College, the State

University of New York at Albany, and Cornell, Northwestern, and Purdue Universities. Her poems have been anthologized in *Beyond the Blues* (1962), *American Negro Poetry* (1963), and *New Negro Poets: U.S.A.* (1964); her books include *Where Is All the Music?* (1968) and *I Am a Black Woman* (1970). In addition, she contributed to and edited *Black Women Writers (1950-1980): A Critical Evaluation* (1984).

Dolores Kendrick (1927–), the poet laureate of Washington, DC, has published three books of poetry: *Through the Ceiling* (1975), *Now Is the Thing to Praise* (1984), and *The Women of Plums: Poems in the Voices of Slave Women* (c. 1989). Her ability to articulate, without sentimentality, the struggles facing nineteenth-century African American women makes her writing especially engaging and valuable. Poems such as "Jenny in Love," (which reads, in its entirety: "Danced in the evenin'/while/the supper/burn;/ whupped/in the morning:/danced again!") speak to the perseverance, humor, and deep humanity of Kendrick's subjects; such poems have earned her a position as a matriarchal figure for late-twentieth-century African American women poets. Kendrick has received the Anisfield-Wolf Award, the George Kent Award for Literature, New York Library's Best Book for Teenagers Award for *The Women of Plums*, a Fulbright Fellowship, and a National Endowment for the Arts Award. Her stage adaptation of *The Women of Plums* won the New York Playwrights Award in 1997 and was produced at the Kennedy Center in 1997–1998. She is Vira I. Heinz Professor Emerita at Phillips Exeter Academy.

Maya Angelou (1928–) was born Marguerite Johnson in St. Louis, Missouri. An author, poet, historian, songwriter, dancer, playwright, stage and screen producer, director, performer, singer, and civil rights activist, she grew up in St. Louis, San Francisco, and Stamps, Arkansas. She has written critically and commercially successful books in several genres, including autobiography: *All God's Children Need Traveling Shoes* (1986), *The Heart of a Woman* (1981), and *I Know Why the Caged Bird Sings* (1969), which was nominated for the National Book Award; and poetry: *A Brave and Startling Truth* (1995), *The Complete Collected Poems of Maya Angelou* (1994), *Shaker, Why Don't You Sing?* (1983), and *Just Give Me a Cool Drink of Water 'fore I Die* (1971), nominated for the Pulitzer Prize.

Angelou's list of accomplishments has an awe-inspiring degree of depth and range. In 1959 Maya Angelou became northern coordinator for the Southern Christian Leadership Conference at the request of Dr. Martin Luther King Jr. From 1961 to 1962 she was associate editor of *The Arab Observer* in Cairo, Egypt, the only English-language news weekly in the Middle East, and from 1964 to 1966 she was feature editor of the *African Review* in Accra, Ghana. After she returned to the U.S. in 1974, Gerald Ford appointed her to the Bicentennial Commission. Later, Jimmy Carter appointed her to the Commission for International Woman of the Year. She accepted a lifetime appointment in 1981 as Reynolds Professor of American Studies at Wake Forest University. In 1993 Angelou wrote and delivered a poem, "On the Pulse of Morning," at the inauguration of President William Jefferson Clinton at his request.

Angelou was the first black woman director in Hollywood. She has written, produced, and starred in productions for stage, film, and television. In 1971 she wrote the original screenplay and musical score for the film *Georgia, Georgia*, and was both author and executive producer of a five-part television miniseries *Three Way Choice*. In addition, she has written and produced several prize-winning documentaries, including "Afro-Americans in the Arts," a PBS special for which she received the Golden Eagle Award. Maya Angelou was twice nominated for a Tony Award in acting: once for her Broadway debut in *Look Away* (1973) and again for her portrayal of Nyo Boto in the television adaptation of the best-selling novel *Roots* (1977). Past her seventy-fifth birthday, Angelou continued to travel extensively, giving readings and speeches, serving as an inspiration to several generations.

Sonia Sanchez (1934–) described herself in *Black Spirits: A Festival of New Black Poets in America* (1972) as a "blk/woman/mother/poet/playwright/teacher who tries to teach the truth." One of the best poets to emerge from the Black Arts Movement of the late 1960s and early 1970s, she has the rare talent of being able to write effective poems in a variety of tones and about subjects ranging from personal depression to historical events (the 1985 MOVE bombing in Philadelphia, for example). Her poems address the tensions between white and black, old and young, women and men. Many of her poems, such as "right on: white america," are intended to be controversial, to serve as political rallying cries and wake-up calls. In the words of Michael S. Harper and Anthony Walton, editors of *Every Shut Eye Ain't Asleep* (1994), Sanchez's work "searingly narrates the passions and concerns of an astute and aware black woman in the late twentieth century."

Audre Lorde (1934–1992) was born in Harlem to Caribbean immigrants. She graduated from Hunter College, received an MLS from Columbia University, and worked as a librarian and schoolteacher before becoming Professor of English at Hunter College in 1981. Her poems address the variety of societally imposed roles—black, wife, teacher—that she encountered over the course of her life. They also offer an emotional map of sorts to her life as a complete person: a poet, feminist, lesbian, and political activist. Perhaps most interesting about Lorde's work is the way it examines how we describe and label the

Spoken Word

The origin of spoken word may be traced to the 1970s work of Sonia Sanchez, Gil Scott Heron, and Amiri Baraka and even further back to the African griot. A kind of performance poetry, it often makes use of improvisation, imitation of musical instruments, ambient silence, humming, scatting, singing, dancing, or accompaniment by musical instruments. Spoken word is typically most popular among young people and works best in performance settings rather than on the printed page. As a result, many spoken word artists and performance poets are unlikely to be published by conventional publishers.

Jessica Care Moore is a performance poet who won New York's Apollo Theater's Amateur Competition five times. This highly visible artist plays international venues and enjoys commercial success. Credits include appearances in the movie *Slam Nation*, HBO's *Def Poetry Jam*, and the International Poetry Festival in Berlin—where she and the Nobel Laureate Derek Wolcott represented the United States. Yet Moore's manuscripts are rejected repeatedly by publishers who feel her poetry fails on the printed page. As a result, the Detroit native founded Moore Black Press in Atlanta.

Medusa and her backup group/spoken word artists/singers, Feline Science, have appeared regularly at the hip-hop club Fais Do-Do in Los Angeles. She has also been featured on Black Entertainment TV's *Lyric Café*. Rah Goddess, alias Rhamelle Green, describes her work as "flowetry," because she often improvises on a given theme. She was featured in the pilot for *Def Poetry Jam* and often appears in venues throughout Los Angeles.

Many spoken word poets achieve fame through poetry slams, open-microphone competitions wherein the audience or judges select a winner. Poetry slams were born in a Chicago nightclub, the Get Me High Lounge, in 1984. By 1986, the Uptown Poetry Slam—the mother of all slams—was being held at the Green Mill Club, also in Chicago. Although most cities hold regular slams, Chicago remains the national slam headquarters.

New York Women of Word enjoy increasing visibility. The poet Liza Jessie Patterson appeared in the films *Slam Nation* and *Bamboozled*.

Yolanda Wilkinson is the VH-1 Poetry Slam Champion. Amanda Diva appeared in HBO's *Def Poetry Jam*. The Women of Word member Asha Bandele also appeared on *Def Poetry Jam*. She is best known for her book *Prisoner's Wife*, an autobiography that tells how Bandele volunteered to read poetry to inmates. In doing so, she met and married Rashid, who is serving a twenty-to-life sentence.

Women Out Loud is a Chicago women's poetry collective founded in 2000 by Tara Betts and Nikki Patin. They meet monthly in a club called Square One. The co-host Tara Betts is a Cave Canem fellow who won the 1999 Gwendolyn Brooks Poetry Award. Her poetry has appeared in Steppenwolf Theatre's production of *Words on Fire*; *Obsidian III*, *Columbia Poetry Review*, *Poetry Slam*, *Power Lines*, *Bum Rush the Page*, *Mosaic*, and *That Takes Ovaries*. Betts co-founded GirlSpeak, a weekly mentoring workshop for young girls and represented Chicago in the 1999 and 2000 National PoetrySlam.

Nikki Patin is a writer, vocalist, performance poet, and co-founder of Women Out Loud. She has won poetry slams at the Mad Bar and Green Mill Lounge in Chicago and appears regularly at Mental Graffiti and Café Metro. Patin was a finalist in the 2000 Chicago Poetry Slam.

Heather Marie Walker is a member of Women Out Loud. Her "Lipstick Lesbian" describes the persona of a woman-loving woman who defies homosexual labels. Walker's use of sophisticated, womanish language, and vivid imagery makes "Lipstick" a favorite at Dike Mikes, lesbian open-microphone sessions.

Mars Gamba-Adisa Caulton is a native of rural Massachusetts who calls Chicago home. She holds a degree in Early Childhood Education and established herself as spoken word poet-musician-activist. Caulton co-hosted open mikes for Sister Sense and Gourmand Coffee shop in Chicago's South Loop, featuring the singer-poet Sharon Klopner. *She Laughs* is a CD of all-female poetry and music featuring Caulton, Carolyn Aguila, Elon Cameron, Kate Hers, Genine Coleman, Liz Marino, Melysha Sargis, Nicole Mitchell, and Shannon Morrow.

—Regina Harris Baiocchi

world. Equally important is the way Lorde's sense of self expanded as she developed a deeper understanding of personal and cultural history.

The poems of Lucille Clifton (1936–), built of sparse, precise language and exact rhythms, may appear, if skimmed, to be slight, even simple. When read carefully, however, especially when read aloud, the clear, profound voice within her poems asserts a depth of emotional and social intelligence that can be found nowhere else in contemporary poetry. Clifton frequently writes about personal and societal tragedy, with a focus on overcoming setbacks and continuing to live a strong, happy, even joyous life. Her books of poetry include *Mercy* (2004), *Blessing the*

Boats: New and Selected Poems, 1988-2000 (2000), winner of the National Book Award; *The Terrible Stories*, nominated for the National Book Award; *The Book of Light* (1993); *Quilting: Poems 1987-1990* (1991); *Next: New Poems* (1987); *Good Woman: Poems and a Memoir 1969–1980* (1987), nominated for the Pulitzer Prize; and *Two Headed-Woman* (1980), also a Pulitzer Prize nominee and winner of the University of Massachusetts Press's Juniper Prize. In addition, she has written sixteen books for children. Other honors include an Emmy Award, a Lannon Literary Award, and two National Endowment for the Arts poetry fellowships. In 1999 she was elected a Chancellor of the Academy of American Poets. She has served as Poet Laureate for the State of Maryland and as of 2005 was distinguished professor of Humanities at St. Mary's College of Maryland.

June Jordan (1936–2002) was born in New York City on 9 July. A political activist and award-winning poet and essayist, Jordan distinguished herself in several genres, including poetry, fiction, nonfiction, and writing for children. She earned praise from critics for addressing the personal struggles and political oppression facing African Americans. Her books of poetry include *Who Look at Me* (1969), a poem accompanied by paintings that addresses black-white relationships and the nature of racial identity, *Some Changes* (1971), *Things That I Do in the Dark* (1977), *Passion* (1980), *Living Room* (1985), *Naming Our Destiny: New and Selected Poems* (1989), *Haruko/Love Poems* (1994), *Kissing God Goodbye: Poems 1991–1997* (1997). She is also the author of children's books, plays, a novel, and *Poetry for the People: A Blueprint for the Revolution* (1995), a guide to writing, teaching, and publishing poetry. Her prose collections include *Affirmative Acts: Political Essays* (1998), *Technical Difficulties* (1994), and *Soldier: Poet's Childhood* (2000). In addition, she was a frequent contributor to *The Progressive*. Jordan received a Rockefeller Foundation grant, a National Association of Black Journalists Award, and fellowships from the Massachusetts Council for the Arts, the National Endowment for the Arts, and the New York Foundation for the Arts. She taught African American studies and women's studies at the University of California, Berkeley, where she founded Poetry for the People.

Jayne Cortez (c. 1936–) grew up in Arizona and California, and her roots, as well as her love of jazz and blues, are an important component of her poetry. Her poems examine various aspects of Latin, South American, and aboriginal American culture. They have been praised for their strong narrative voices that weave together in interesting ways, and they have had great impacts on audiences. She has written seven collections of poems and has made five recordings of her poetry. In addition, she has been the recipient of two National Endowment for the Arts grants and has been on the Executive Board for the Pen American Center.

Toi Derricotte (1941–) was born in Detroit and educated at Wayne State University and NYU. Her work is characterized by an understated lyricism that illuminates the tenuous nature of human relationships. Her work celebrates family and romantic love, addresses unflinchingly the world's capacity for beauty as well as horror, and focuses often on her experiences as an African American woman in the twentieth and twenty-first centuries. She has taught at George Mason University, NYU, Old Dominion University, and the University of Pittsburgh and has published several volumes of poetry, including *Tender*

(1997) and *Captivity* (1989). She has also published a well-received work of nonfiction, *The Black Notebooks*.

Nikki Giovanni (1943–), also known as the "Princess of Black Poetry," has enjoyed a remarkably prolific and varied career: in addition to several collections of poetry, she has written an autobiography of her first twenty-five years, edited a volume of poetry, recorded her poetry to musical accompaniment, and held distinguished positions at several universities. In addition, her "raps" with Margaret Walker and James Baldwin have been published as books.

Giovanni's work often addresses opposites: white and black, past and present, love and hate, personal and communal, stasis and change. Her themes of unity, love, respect for community and self, and the importance of one's heritage are at once universal and particular to the African American experience. Her work is clearly pro-black, but just as clearly not anti-white. It seeks relentlessly to recognize beauty in the face of ugliness. For example, much of Giovanni's "protest poetry"—a label usually reserved for bitter, angry rants that respond to specific incidents—contains some of her most lovely images and ideas.

In addition to racial injustice, Giovanni writes powerfully about womanhood, family, sexuality, and nature. She breaks down traditional boundaries between readers and writers by relying heavily on a conversational tone. Rather than rejecting slang, dialect, or musical elements, Giovanni fuses them with traditional English to create a distinctive and clear poetic voice that often ignores the traditional roles of line breaks, form, punctuation, grammar, and even spelling. Her rhythms often rely on jazz and blues riffs, on African drumming rhythms and chants. By capturing patterns of African American music and speech, Giovanni has created an authentic language for her black audience. Her work expresses an appreciation for black speech and respects traditions within African and African American cultures.

Sherley Anne Williams (1944–1999) was born in Bakersfield, California, and raised in Fresno. She earned a BA from the University of California at Fresno and studied at Fisk and Howard Universities before earning an MA from Brown University. For many years, she was a professor of English at the University of California, San Diego. She is the author of two poetry collections, a book of criticism, a play, and two novels, the second of which, *Dessa Rose* (1986), won wide critical acclaim. Her poetry covers a range of styles, from elegant, precise formalism to modernist works grounded in the blues. Many of her poems are concerned with history, music, and the sisterhood of African American women.

Marilyn Nelson (1946–) was born in Cleveland. She received her bachelor's degree from the University of

California, Davis, her master's from the University of Pennsylvania, and her PhD at the University of Minnesota. She is the author of seven books of poetry, including *The Field of Praise* (1997) and *The Homeplace* (1985), a National Book Award nominee. Nelson's poems are probing and sparse, blending a painter's attention to small, telling details with unpretentious diction and resonant themes. She often finds inspiration within her own family, as in poems like "My Grandfather Walks in the Woods" and, based on her father's experiences as a member of the first group of African Americans allowed to fly in the United States, "Tuskegee Airfield."

Before committing to poetry, Wanda Coleman (1946–) worked as a medical secretary, editor, journalist, and scriptwriter. Coleman's style is characterized by her lack of capitalization and punctuation. Her poems address the myriad trials facing African American women in inner city Los Angeles at the turn of the twenty-first century. They are driven by precise, direct language that transcends strict narrative and lyric impulses and commands one to read them aloud. Coleman won the 1999 Lenore Marshall Poetry Prize for *Bathwater Wine* (1998). The judge, Marilyn Hacker, wrote in her citation that Coleman's work is "[d]emotic, idiosyncratic, at once celebratory and embittered . . . Coleman's poems are not always easy or reassuring reading. But the generosity of their larger-than-life extravagance, their careful tempering of self-mockery, their elastic balance of overstatement and control, make them a continual, renewable reward." Coleman is a prolific poet; she published ten books of poetry in nineteen years. She has received poetry fellowships from the Guggenheim Foundation and the National Endowment for the Arts. Her collections include *Mercurochrome: New Poems* (2001), *Native in a Strange Land: Trials & Tremors* (1996); *Hand Dance* (1993); *African Sleeping Sickness* (1990); *A War of Eyes & Other Stories* (1988); *Heavy Daughter Blues: Poems & Stories 1968–1986* (1988). She has also written *Mambo Hips & Make Believe: A Novel* (1999).

Cheryl Clarke (1947–) earned her BA from Howard University and her MA, MSW, and PhD from Rutgers University. She has written four books of poetry: *Experimental Love* (1993), a 1994 Lambda Literary Award nominee; *Humid Pitch* (1989); *Living as a Lesbian* (1986); and *Narratives: Poems in the Tradition of Black Women* (1983). Clarke's writing focuses on questions of sexual, racial, and political identity. Her work has appeared in numerous feminist, lesbian, gay, "straight," and African American publications, including *The Black Scholar*, *The Kenyon Review*, *Belles Lettres*, *A Journal for Jewish Feminists and Our Friends*, *The World in Us: An Anthology of Lesbian and Gay Poetry*, *The Arc of Love: An Anthology of Lesbian Love Poetry*, and *Persistent Desire: A Femme-Butch Reader* (1992). She has served as a member of the board of directors of New York Women Against Rape, was a founding member and fund-raiser for New Jersey Women and AIDS Network, and has served as co-chairperson of the board of the Center for Lesbian and Gay Studies at the CUNY Graduate School. Clarke works at Rutgers, the State University of New Jersey, New Brunswick campus, as the director of the Office of Diverse Community Affairs and Lesbian-Gay Concerns.

Ntozake Shange (1948–), a poet, performance artist, playwright, and novelist, was born Paulette Williams on 18 October 1948, in Trenton, New Jersey. She earned a BA from Barnard College and an MA from UCLA. She is known for crafting multilayered texts, rich in feminist, racial, and sexual themes, that often abandon conventions such as plot and character development. Her books of poetry include *Ridin' the Moon in Texas* (1997), *From Okra to Greens* (1984), *A Daughter's Geography* (1983), *Nappy Edges* (1978), *Natural Disasters and Other Festive Occasions* (1977), and *Melissa & Smith* (1976). Among her plays are *Daddy Says* (1989), *Spell #7* (1985), *From Okra to Greens/A Different Kinda Love Story* (1983), and *for colored girls who have considered suicide/when the rainbow is enuf* (1977), a group of twenty poems for seven actors that dramatize the power that African American women must summon in order to survive in the face of heartbreak, depression, and pain. *for colored girls* made Shange famous, earning Tony, Grammy, and Emmy award nominations. Shange is also the author of the prose works: *If I Can Cook You Know God Can* (1998), *See No Evil: Prefaces, Essays, & Accounts 1976-1983* (1984), *Sassafass, Cypress & Indigo: A Novel* (1982) and *The Black Book* (1986, with Robert Mapplethorpe). Among her numerous honors are fellowships from the Guggenheim Foundation and the Lila Wallace–Reader's Digest Fund, and a Pushcart Prize.

Gayl Jones (1949–) was born in Lexington, Kentucky. Her early experiences with Southern culture are reflected in her writing, which spans several genres, including poetry, novels, short fiction, drama, and literary criticism. Jones moved from the South to attend Connecticut College, where she received a BA in English in 1971. She then earned an MFA and a PhD in Creative Writing at Brown University, where her first play, *Chile Woman*, was produced. Jones's writing career began with two published novels, *Corregidora* (1975) and *Eva's Man* (1976). After publishing a book of short stories called *White Rat* (1977), Jones turned to poetry, writing a volume-length poem, *Songs for Anninho* (1981), which was followed by two other poetry volumes, *The Hermit-Woman* (1983) and *Xarque & Other Poems* (1985).

Much of Jones's work focuses on how contradictory emotions can coexist within oppressed people. The complex blend of love–hate, confidence–paranoia, beauty–ugliness makes Jones's work intellectually and emotionally demanding. Another feature of Jones's work is the emphasis she places on storytelling—a key component of the African American tradition and an indispensable source of family history. Jones's other books include two novels, *Mosquito* (1999) and *The Healing* (1998), and a book of criticism, *Liberating Voices: Oral Tradition in African American Literature* (1991),

Rita Dove (1952–) has emerged as one of the most influential black poets of the late twentieth century. After graduating summa cum laude from Miami University of Ohio with her BA in 1973, she attended the University of Tubingen, in Germany, on a Fulbright Fellowship and completed her MFA in Creative Writing from the University of Iowa in 1977. She began her academic career in 1981 at Arizona State University, and in 1989 she became Commonwealth Professor of English at the University of Virginia.

Dove was named poet laureate of the United States in 1993, the first African American and then the youngest person to hold that title. She was also the second African American to receive the Pulitzer Prize for poetry, which she won for *Thomas and Beulah* (1986). Dove's brush-stroke attention to detail, tight rhythms, and unfailing music reveal the influence of other art forms on her poetry. Equally at ease writing about the hardships of rural Ohio as about the elegance of ballroom dancing, in employing strict villanelles and sonnets as in using sweeping free-verse stanzas, Rita Dove has amassed a truly impressive and resonant body of work.

Like many of her contemporaries, Dove has enjoyed success in multiple genres. In addition to her eight poetry collections, which include *American Smooth* (2004), *Grace Notes* (1989), *The Museum* (1983), and *The Yellow House in the Corner* (1980), she has published a novel, *Through the Iron Gate* (1992), a short story collection, *Fifth Sunday* (1985), and a verse drama, *The Darker Face of the Earth* (1994).

Thylias Moss (1954–) is a poet gifted with startling ability to write effectively in a range of voices, from comic to elegiac, and to deal in direct yet novel ways with issues like racial oppression, identity, and sexuality. Her best poems draw comparisons to, as well as inspiration from, the greatest poets of the last two centuries. In "A Reconsideration of the Blackbird," for example, she invokes not only the imagination of Wallace Stevens, but also the political spirit of Allen Ginsberg and Gwendolyn Brooks: "Let's call him *Jim Crow*./Let's call him *Nigger* and see if he rises/faster than when we say *abracadabra*./Guess who's *coming to dinner?*/Score ten points if you said blackbird./Score twenty points if you were more specific, as in the first line./ . . . /Problem: No one's in love with the blackbirds./Solution: Paint them white, call them visions, everyone will want one." Her

books of poetry include *Last Chance for the Tarzan Holler* (1998), *Small Congregations: New and Selected Poems* (1993), *Rainbow Remnants in Rock Bottom Ghetto Sky* (1991), *Pyramid of Bone* (1988), and *Hosiery Seams on a Bowlegged Woman* (1983).

The Future of African American Women's Poetry

Since the days of Phillis Wheatley, African American women poets have emerged as a cornerstone of American literature. Their struggle from obscurity to prominence reflects the great social and political progress that our country has made since its inception, and their perseverance through racial and gender discrimination reflects great pride and an unbreakable collective will. African American women poets currently enjoy freedoms and honors that their predecessors could only dream of, and many have accepted prestigious academic appointments at colleges and universities across the country. Equally remarkable, African American women poets now have the creative freedom to write about themes beyond race and gender and still have reason to hope that their work might be published. Indeed, many literary journals, writing organizations, and book publishers now actively support poetry by African American women.

Perhaps as a result of greater support, a number of impressive African American female poets have emerged within the past fifteen years. Elizabeth Alexander (1962–) writes poems that address identity, gender, race, and motherhood. Her poetry collections are *Antebellum Dream Book* (2001), *Body of Life* (1996), and *The Venus Hottentot* (1990). Natasha Trethewey (1966–) has written beautifully about African American history and culture. Her books are *Bellocq's Ophelia* (2002) and *Domestic Work* (2000), selected by Rita Dove as winner of the inaugural Cave Canem Poetry Prize for the best first book by an African American poet. Allison Joseph (1967–) has written five collections of poetry, *Worldly Pleasures* (2004), *Imitation of Life* (2003), *Soul Train* (1997), *In Every Seam* (1997), and *What Keeps Us Here* (1992). Her poems explore issues of empowerment, race, and motherhood with a clarity and precision akin to Brooks, Clifton, and Dove.

While African American women's poetry currently enjoys its most venerated position to date, its best days lie ahead. The range of subjects, themes, styles, and voices in African American women's poetry will become even more plentiful as social opportunities and critical attention continue to increase. Because their voices were silenced by the white male voice for too long, African American women poets, as well as other marginalized groups such as Asian, Jewish, Latino, and Chicano Americans, need to be highlighted as the United States moves into the twenty-first century. While still far from being free from prejudice, the United States, more mosaic than melting

Women of Cave Canem

For nearly a decade, Cave Canem, co-founded by the poets Toi Derricotte and Cornelius Eady, has sponsored workshops, retreats, readings, and an annual prize: $500 and publication of a book of poems. Participating publishers include the University of Georgia Press, Graywolf, and the University of Pittsburgh Press. Competition judges and workshop faculty include the black poets Rita Dove, Marilyn Nelson, Lucille Clifton, Elizabeth Alexander, Nikky Finney, Harryette Mullen, Cheryl Clarke, and Sonja Sanchez. Women who have won the prize include Natasha Trethewey, Tracy K. Smith, and Lyrae Van Clief-Stefanon.

In 1999 Natasha Trethewey won the first Cave Canem Award for her *Domestic Work, 1937*, which is now in its second printing. She has since published a second book of poetry, *Bellocq's Ophelia*. Her awards include a Pushcart Prize and a fellowship from the National Endowment for the Arts. Tretheway has published poetry in *New England Review*, *American Poetry Review*, *Southern Humanities Review*, and *Callaloo*. She teaches at Emory University.

Tracy K. Smith was awarded the 2002 Cave Canem Prize for her book *The Body's Question*. Smith holds degrees in English and creative writing from Harvard and Columbia universities, and was a poetry fellow at Stanford University. Her work appears in *Callaloo*, *Boulevard*, and *PN Review*. Smith teaches at Marymount and Medgar Evers colleges in New York.

In 2001 Lyrae Van Clief-Stefanon received the Cave Canem Award for *Black Swan*. Clief-Stefanon holds an MFA from Penn State, and her poetry is included in *African American Review*, *Callaloo*, and *Crab Orchard Review*. Her second book of poetry, *The Buffet Dream*, is forthcoming.

Toni Asante Lightfoot is a graduate of Cave Canem workshops. She was raised in Washington, DC, and co-founded the Modern Urban Griots. She divides her time between Caribbean travels, during which she collects stories she weaves into poetry, and Chicago, where she is business and outreach manager for the Guild Complex and Tia Chucha Press. One of Lightfoot's strong poems, "Between the Thighs of the Sky," is a tribute to conga drummer Skai Shadow.

Another workshop graduate is the Detroit native Shayla Hawkins. She has won the Detroit Writer's Guild Paul Laurence Dunbar Award, Geraldine Dodge Poetry Festival Award, and an Art Serve Michigan Creative Artist Grant. Her poetry enjoys international exposure in *Drumvoices*, *Graffiti Rag*, *Paris/Atlantic*, *Obsidian II*, and *Calabash*.

Renée K. Moore is also a Cave Canem graduate. A native Chicagoan with New Orleans roots, she has published poetry in *Callaloo* and *Obsidian III*. Moore is a poet, fiction writer, and technical communications consultant. She conducts workshops for the Afro-American Genealogical and Historical Society, and the Guild Complex. Moore judged the Gwendolyn Brooks Annual Poetry Contest and Ndugu Poetry Prize. She appeared with her mentor, Cornelius Eady, in Writers Across the Generations, Poets for Peace, Words to Rhythms, and the Women Writer's Conference for the Guild Complex. Moore wrote a series of haiku on Mardi Gras, including the untitled "Batons beat Tuesday/sober brush sweeps drunken beads/ashes silence lust."

Robin Michel Caudell's poetry appears in three Cave Canem anthologies. Born and raised in Maryland, she earned her bachelor's degree in Journalism from the University of Maryland, College Park, and an MFA from Goddard College. Caudell served as a counselor for the National Book Foundation Summer Writing Camp and writes for the *Press Republican* in Plattsburgh, NY.

Duriel E. Harris has received grants from Cave Canem. She holds a PhD from the University of Illinois, an MA from New York University, and a BA from Yale University. Harris was featured in the 2002 Insight Arts Women's Performance Jam, *African American Review*, and *Fence* magazine. Chicago's National Public Radio station, WBEZ, dubbed her "Poet for the 21st Century." Harris is poetry editor for *Obsidian III* and author of *DRAG* a book of poetry forthcoming as of 2005.

—REGINA HARRIS BAIOCCHI

pot, and its literature have never been more receptive to a greater plurality of voices or a wider-ranging polyphony of songs.

See also Autobiography; Fiction; *and* Playwriting.

BIBLIOGRAPHY

Davies, Carole Boyce. *Black Women, Writing, and Identity: Migrations on the Subject*. New York: Routledge, 1994. A complex work of feminist theory that attempts to broaden the discussion surrounding issues of representation of and by African American women.

Evans, Mari, ed. *Black Women Writers (1950–1980): A Critical Evaluation*. Garden City, NY: Anchor Press/Doubleday, 1984. A comprehensive critical history of fifteen authors, including Maya Angelou, Gwendolyn Brooks, Lucille Clifton, Mari Evans, Nikki Giovanni, Audre Lorde, Toni Morrison, Sonia Sanchez, Alice Walker, and Margaret Walker.

Gabbin, Joanne V., ed. *Furious Flower: American Poetry from the Black Arts Movement to the Present*. Charlottesville: University of Virginia Press, 2004. A collection of forty-six poets over three generations, from established figures like Gwendolyn Brooks and Nikki Giovanni to an array of spoken word performers.

Gilbert, Derrick I. M. (D-Knowledge), ed. *Catch the Fire!!!: A Cross-Generational Anthology of Contemporary African-American Poetry*. New York: Riverhead Books, 1998. The book includes a diverse group, from established writers like June Jordan, Ntozake Shange and Amiri Baraka to the NBA star Shaquille O'Neal, *The Cosby Show*'s Malcolm Jamal-Warner, and Kevin Powell from MTV's *Real World*.

Gilyard, Keith, ed. *Spirit & Flame: An Anthology of Contemporary African American Poetry*. Syracuse, NY: Syracuse University Press, 1997. Contains more than two hundred pieces by African American poets from the last decade. The work is diverse, ranging from formal verse to performance pieces influenced by jazz, hip hop, and rap.

Gray, Janet, ed. *She Wields a Pen: American Woman Poets of the Nineteenth Century*. Iowa City: University of Iowa Press, 1997. A good overview of female poets, regardless of ethnicity, of the 1800s.

Harper, Michael S., and Anthony Walton, eds. *Every Shut Eye Ain't Asleep: An Anthology of Poetry by African-Americans Since 1945*. Boston: Little, Brown, 1994. A wide-ranging anthology that highlights African American poetry after World War II. Valuable for its thoughtful introductions to featured poets.

Harper, Michael S., and Anthony Walton, eds. *The Vintage Book of African American Poetry*. New York: Vintage, 2000. A comprehensive anthology that includes poets from Phillis Wheatley to Yusef Komunyakaa. Particularly valuable for its generous selections of lesser-known but important poets such as Sterling A. Brown and Jay Wright.

Hayden, Robert. *Kaleidoscope: Poems by American Negro Poets*. New York: Harcourt, Brace, and World, 1967. A wide-ranging anthology that includes poets from Phillis Wheatley to Leroi Jones (Amiri Baraka).

Honey, Maureen, ed. *Shadowed Dreams: Women's Poetry of the Harlem Renaissance*. New Brunswick, NJ: Rutgers University Press, 1989. A good, in-depth anthology focusing on African American women poets of the Harlem Renaissance. Honey offers a generous sampling of each poet's work, as well as thorough introductions.

King, Woodie, Jr. ed. *Black Spirits: A Festival of New Black Poets in America*. New York: Random House, 1972. An anthology that captures the spirit of the Black Arts Movement. See Nikki Giovanni's Foreward and Don L. Lee's Introduction.

King, Woodie, Jr. ed. *The Forerunners: Black Poets in America*. Washington, DC: Howard University Press, 1981. A unique anthology that bridges the years from the end of the Harlem Renaissance to the activists of the 1960s and 1970s. Most interesting is each poet's short reflections on African American poetry at the time of the book's publication.

Miller, E. Ethelbert, ed. *Beyond the Frontier: African-American Poetry for the 21st Century*. Baltimore, MD: Black Classic Press, 2002. Includes generous selections from contemporary African American poets, many of whom will be new to most readers.

Sherman, Joan R., ed. *Collected Black Women's Poetry*. New York: Oxford University Press, 1988. Three volumes of previously out-of-print poetry collections by African American female poets, including Mary Weston Fordham, H. Cordelia Ray, and Priscilla Jane Thompson.

Stetson, Erlene, ed. *Black Sister: Poetry by Black American Women, 1746–1980*. Bloomington: Indiana University Press, 1981. A good reference for understanding the evolution of African American women's poetry.

Valade, Roger M., III, ed. with Denise Kasinec. *The Schomburg Center Guide to Black Literature*. Detroit, MI: Gale Research, 1996. As defined in its preface, this book serves as a "ready reference source on the authors, works, characters, general themes and topics, and literary theories relating to black literature."

Wolosky, Shira, ed. *Major Voices: 19th Century American Women's Poetry*. New Milford, CT: Toby Press, 2003. A recent anthology that offers a generous sampling of the work of ten significant nineteenth-century women writers, as well as a good introduction to each writer's life and career.

www.poets.org. The Academy of American Poets Web site. A very good resource for major poems and biographical material related to a range of American poets.

—DANIEL DONAGHY

POLITICAL PARTIES. Black women's political activism took many forms in American history and does not fit easily into traditional political culture or the professionally organized political party framework. The unique social and economic status of black women affected the ways in which their participation took shape before and after slavery and in every region of the country. Racism and sexism inhibited black women's inclusion into mainstream politics prior to emancipation and locked them out of political parties until the later half of the twentieth century.

By design political parties frame platforms, groom potential nominees, endorse and market candidates, provide funding, and advance the agendas of specific voting blocs. Locked out of these conventional methods of political activity, black women found a number of ways to define politics, participating in the political culture and commanding recognition.

Background for a Revolution

Prior to emancipation, race defined one's status as citizen or alien, free or otherwise. Gender determined status in relationship to men and the state. As cotton production expanded and its profitability increased, black female bondage became more entrenched as an institution in the South. State and local legislatures enacted slave codes to prohibit meetings and curtail all social activity not approved by the owners and mandated laws that determined the status of bondswomen in America, effectively usurping any autonomy for black women. As a result, slave women were increasingly brutalized and limited in their ability to assist themselves and their families. Still, they sought redress and made political statements by meeting secretly, running away, participating in slave revolts, and aborting pregnancies that would produce more slaves.

Freedom from bondage, however, did not grant political access. The lives of black women residing in the free states of the North and the territories of the West were circumscribed by racism and sexism as well. But the freedom of movement and limited government interference in their private lives enabled them to publicly engage in an alternative political culture. Church membership, voluntary associations, mutual aid societies, and women's organizations afforded them the opportunity to build a strong race-conscious, female-centered community. They created strategies to attack racial discrimination and slavery, sought ways to alleviate social ills, and joined with their men and sympathetic whites in the fight for justice. Several engaged in the local, state, and national convention movement held between 1830 and 1860. Often stressing black self-reliance, temperance, morality, and education, black women viewed these meetings as effective methods of voicing their concerns. Although rarely in leadership

WOMEN'S DIVISION OF NATIONAL REPUBLICAN COMMITTEE. Left to right: Mrs. Gainer, Illinois; Miss Eartha M. White, Florida; Mrs. C. McDowell, Missouri; Mrs. Emma Holcomb, Georgia; Mrs. V. Clay Haley, Missouri; Col. H. L. Johnson, Georgia; Mrs. George S. Williams, Georgia; Mrs. H. R. Butler, Georgia; Mrs. Blanche Beatty, Louisiana; Mrs. M. A. McCurdy, Indiana; Mrs. William Francis, Minnesota. (Moorland-Spingarn Research Center.)

positions, the black women who attended the conventions had the opportunity to join with black men in seeking redress for discrimination, advocating suffrage, and voicing objections against slavery. Many also joined the growing membership of antislavery societies. With particular empathy for black female slaves, women like Sarah M. Douglass, Sarah Forten, and Margaretta Forten became powerful forces. They held leadership roles and highlighted their ability to assist with shaping the structure and ideology of the groups by espousing solutions to the problems that faced the black community.

The antislavery movement proved to be a pivotal aspect of crucial training for African American women in the struggle for political equality. The suffrage movement that officially began at the Seneca Falls, New York, convention in 1848 was primarily assembled and supported by black and white women and men who were involved in the abolitionist movement. Black women found this venue to be a unique opportunity to build and defend a platform that included supporting suffrage, ending slavery, and calling attention to their distinctive problems.

During Reconstruction, black women expanded their voluntary activism and played a strong supporting role to black male political prowess. While legal statutes enacted by the Fifteenth Amendment enabled black men to vote, hold membership in political parties, and be elected to political office, black women found themselves excluded from mainstream political culture. Still, black male loyalty to the Radical Republicans generated interest among black women. The Republicans had paved the way for the emancipation of nearly 4 million African Americans, citizenship rights, and civil rights legislation. Although still unable to participate in conventional politics through the ballot or party membership, black women found the Republican leadership to be favorable to their progressive agenda. Women's benevolence associations through churches and secular organizations assumed an even greater activist role than before emancipation and engendered a powerful gender-consciousness among black women. United by common causes and diligent in their commitment to blacks and women, they worked to increase literacy rates; fed, clothed, and sheltered the needy; combated immoral behavior; and pushed for reform laws that provided better economic opportunities. In many of these organizations, women expanded the boundaries of traditional women's activities by creating business models of association building. They drew up constitutions, elected officers, held formal meetings, and kept formal records such as minutes and treasury reports. Some black women also joined with white women and began to publicly challenge the limits on women's access to the vote and to political parties. Women like Mary Ann Shadd Cary, who registered to vote in 1871 in Washington, DC, defied the laws limiting their access. Others found organizational affiliation their best means of bringing about change.

Legal restraints at the end of Reconstruction and the restoration of home rule created a solid white southern Democratic base that enforced rules and regulations designed to restrict black men's political access and inhibited black women's attempt to gain access to electoral politics. Northern acquiescence to white southern domination and discriminatory practices and views among whites in the region left blacks isolated. The incidence of lynching escalated; black men lost their political offices and disappeared from most southern voting rolls. Poverty levels increased as more blacks were caught in the cycle of sharecropping and crop lien. Illiteracy rates increased because of the lack of adequate education. State-enacted segregation laws, though challenged, were upheld by the Supreme Court's 1896 *Plessy v. Ferguson* decision. Jim Crow challenged every social, political, and economic facet of black life. Moreover, white women joined in the assault on the black community. When the National Woman Suffrage Association and the American Woman Suffrage Association joined their powerful forces in 1890 to form the National American Woman Suffrage Association (NAWSA), the rhetoric of the organization became much more hostile to blacks and immigrants. Nativism and racism engaged white women in the racist overtone of the period and encouraged them to argue against the black female ballot. Even the General Federation of Women's Clubs, the umbrella of white women's local and state associations, refused to directly admit black women to membership. For most black women, attempts at interracial cooperation failed. In the face of these issues, black women independently and through new voluntary associations acted on their own behalf, broadening their agendas, creating new opportunities for themselves and the black community, highlighting the effect of racism and sexism on women and girls, and establishing the largest network of black female club women in American history.

Suffragists and Club Women

One of the most famous and important suffragists and clubwomen was Ida Bell Wells-Barnett. A native of Holly Springs, Mississippi, she gained notoriety as the leading antilynching expert in the country. A writer, reporter, and part owner of a newspaper, she was exiled by an angry mob of whites from her home and forced to abandon her newspaper in Memphis, Tennessee. Landing in New York, she compiled statistics and published essays railing against the injustice of lynching for the *New York Age*. In the early 1890s she moved her crusade to an international stage by traveling to England on several occasions to organize antilynching societies and to persuade the English to pressure the American government to end lynching.

Other women such as Adella Hunt Logan and Mary Ann Shadd Cary also reflected the expanded agenda of black women. Logan, a Tuskegee Institute teacher, championed black women's access to the ballot and spoke out against NAWSA's blatant hostility to black female suffrage. Cary, the first black female newspaper editor in North America, tied black female suffrage to the economic viability and stability of the black community. She encouraged women to increase the number of employment opportunities for women and tend to the social welfare needs of black youth.

Collectively, the black women's club movement gained popularity among many middle-class and some working-class women. The middle class often formed elite social clubs mainly for cultural purposes. The working class often found church auxiliaries the best means of pushing its agenda. Still, they honed their leadership and managerial skills by holding weekly and monthly meetings that included lectures and entertainment and managing funds that were distributed to the needy. Eventually, many of these local clubs in every region moved beyond the cultural to embrace civic and political reform as well. As more women joined forces in similar causes, the clubs proliferated. Suffrage clubs in every region of the country attracted hundreds of black women to their ranks. As western states became the first to extend the ballot to women, black women enjoyed political freedoms not accessible to eastern and southern women. However, their limited numbers and racism denied them any real gains as electorates or in political parties.

Common ground and broader perspectives among black women generated increased interest and encouraged the growth of national associations. The National League of Colored Women and the National Federation of Afro-American Women were two of the first. In 1895, the National Federation of Afro-American Women met in Boston under the leadership of Josephine St. Pierre Ruffin. Among the themes of the convention was political equality. In 1896, the League and the Federation joined their resources to form the National Association of Colored Women (NACW). Acting as the umbrella for black women's associations, it broadened and expanded the race and gender agenda, boosted much-needed resources, and provided African American women with a central location to seek social, political, and economic reform. Under the leadership of Mary Church Terrell, the NACW merged social activism with political activism. Every aspect of the black community that involved women and girls gained an audience among these women. Lectures and meetings on female suffrage were juxtaposed with women's roles in alleviating poverty. Discussions about lynching and ways to combat it were interspersed with lessons on mothering. The women in the NACW and the local associations proved to be the lifeblood of the social and political welfare network in the black community. By World War I, more than fifty thousand women held membership in the organization.

The migration of thousands of African Americans out of the South altered the political landscape of many northern and midwestern cities between 1910 and 1930. The persistence of Jim Crow segregation, hostility, and dismal job opportunities pushed blacks out of the South. The lure of better race relations, less oppression, and more employment prospects pulled blacks to urban centers like Chicago, Detroit, New York, and Philadelphia. Settling in predominantly black ghettos, blacks gained political power unavailable to them in the South. Unlike in the South, black men voted, belonged to political clubs, and held political offices. Black men had the freedom to choose their party affiliation without the threat of violence. Most black men remained committed to the Republican Party. A few, however, pledged loyalty to the Democrats. Although still unable to cast ballots, black women were as politically interested as were men. In addition to their gender-segregated associations, they had influential supporting roles as members in political club auxiliaries. As a result, the black woman's views and influence were key to the success of any black or white politician seeking office in black majority districts.

The political landscape was further changed by the midwestern and northeastern state legislatures that began to grant women limited access to the ballot. African American women understood the ballot's usefulness as a weapon in the battle for social reform in the black community and its power to promote economic and political viability for blacks in traditional politics. In most major cities, white-run political machines monopolized the landscape. Few blacks held key posts inside the party, and none were elected to positions of power. Black women recognized that their ability to participate in the political process would enable them to change that dynamic. Their first opportunity came in Chicago. In 1913, the state of Illinois became the first state east of the Mississippi to empower women with access to municipal politics, nearly doubling the black vote on the South Side. Black women took advantage of the privilege and created their own suffrage clubs, taught women how to register, adopted platforms, and demanded the presence of potential candidates. The Alpha Suffrage Club, organized by Ida B. Wells-Barnett and Belle Squire, a white colleague, was the first of its kind in the area. Wells-Barnett envisioned the club as a training ground to raise the consciousness of black women by teaching them how to take advantage of the political process. This linking of voting to racial responsibility and duty elevated black women's status to that of the male electorate. Members canvassed neighborhoods, developed their own platforms, and endorsed candidates. Because the women were tied to issues rather than to parties, not all the candidates they endorsed were members of the two ruling parties, the Democrats and Republicans. Instead, women often found that the best candidate was from the ranks of a third party. As a result, the political machines and their candidates often found themselves actively seeking the women's endorsement. In 1915, the clout of the Alpha Suffrage Club in mainstream politics produced the first black alderman in Chicago, Oscar DePriest.

The ballot encouraged black women in Texas to develop voter leagues to educate their constituents and enable black women to register to vote for the first time in 1917. In New York, black women gained access to the New York State Republican convention and ran for political office. Two delegates to the convention were Gertrude E. Curtis and Laura B. Fisher. Others in Seattle, Washington, and New Jersey enjoyed the fruits of being elected to school boards. Often, they ran on third party tickets that ran counter to the black community's political allegiance. Again, issues rather than parties remained the priority.

When the Nineteenth Amendment was ratified in 1920, African American women throughout the country had already developed the interest and skills to become full participants in the traditional political process. Eager to become full citizens and gain admittance to political parties they joined predominantly white leagues, created their own leagues, canvassed their communities, and held voter registration and citizenship classes to encourage voting among black women. Several held membership in the newly formed League of Women Voters while others established separate black leagues. By 1924, the National League of Republican Colored Women had formed to become a permanent political force in party politics and for black women. Members raised money, endorsed and campaigned for candidates, and educated other black women on the political process. Throughout the South, the majority registered under the Republican Party in opposition to the solid white southern Democrat stronghold. Still, their gains inside mainstream political parties remained few in part because black men and women in the South lost their ability to participate in the political landscape. The threat of violence and lack of economic opportunity exacerbated the multitude of issues facing black women and the black community. For almost four decades, most southern black women did not find formal politics a favorable setting for advancement.

In the North, black women promoted their causes by merging their voluntary efforts with the traditional party structure. Through their positions in Republican conventions and clubs, they rallied black female voters to support party candidates. They also played a key role in the increase in the number of black men running for political office. Black female political prowess, massive migration, and race consciousness in urban centers such as Philadelphia, New York, Chicago, and Detroit forced the party to recognize black women's significance as a constituent bloc. In 1928, the black women's vote helped make Oscar DePriest the first northern black member elected to the House of Representatives.

Still, prior to the voting rights legislation of 1965, black women remained marginal to party politics and on the periphery of much of the political discourse. Most continued to find themselves locked out of mainstream political parties. Racism and sexism within the ranks of the two major parties exacerbated this trend. The white Democratic and Republican parties deterred black women from joining in the political scene. So they continued their long tradition of joining and building organizations, defining a political context that fit their needs, and creating social and political opportunity for their communities. They held membership in school groups, teacher associations, labor unions, and civil rights organizations. Many found a political space in a number of nationally recognized civil rights and local grassroots organizations. The National Association for the Advancement of Colored People (NAACP), organized in 1908 as a bulwark against the assault on African American civil rights, provided major figures like Septima Clark, Constance Baker Motley, and Ella Baker with leadership roles. Some found places in

the National Council of Negro Women, the Congress for Racial Equality (CORE), and the Student Nonviolent Coordinating Committee (SNCC). Each of these organizations utilized its resources to work toward the social, civic, and political welfare of people of every age.

Third Party Movement

Grassroots organizations and third party affiliations offered women alternatives to the limited access offered by mainstream political parties. Most women found that grassroots organizations in their local communities gave them the greatest flexibility. For example, Fannie Lou Hamer, a sharecropper born in Montgomery County, Mississippi, disenfranchised, worked tirelessly to register blacks to vote. She became a field secretary for SNCC, assisted with the creation of the Mississippi Freedom Democratic Party, an alternative to the all-white Democratic Party, and spoke at the 1964 Democratic National Convention. Hamer articulated the plight of the disenfranchised black voter and highlighted the political determination of black women.

Individually, some women found third parties the best alternative to the limitations placed on them by mainstream party politics. For example, Charlotta A. Bass, a Republican Party western regional director in 1940, ran unsuccessfully as an Independent candidate for the Los Angeles City Council in 1945 and as an Independent Progressive Party nominee in 1950. By 1952, she had secured the endorsement of the Progressive Party's vice presidential nominee. Though the party lost its bid, Bass's platform highlighted the under-representation of blacks and women in the local, state, and federal legislative branches.

Others rebelled from within the existing political party structure by seeking to increase black people's ability to control their own fate. The tight control of traditional parties and urban machines played a major part in the unsuccessful efforts to mobilize impoverished and disillusioned blacks. The creation of all-black political entities, segregated from the all-white Democratic machines, increased registration, promoted black candidates, and offered the most viable opportunities for blacks. Increasingly, these alternatives to the traditional parties enabled black men and women to gain political positions in local, state, and national elections. Shirley Chisholm's involvement in politics began when she joined two alternative Democratic organizations that were created for the sole purpose of electing black officials in predominantly black districts. Elected to the New York State Assembly in 1964, she became the first black woman to be elected to the House of Representatives. In 1972, she became the first African American to make a bid for the presidential nomination under the auspices of the Democratic Party. Underfunded and shunned by the party, black men, white women's organizations, and the mainstream press, Chisholm lost her bid. Her campaign reflected the gender and racial polarization that existed within the two-party system and in the country. It also highlighted the evolution of black women's involvement in party politics.

As more black women and men engaged in electoral politics, the major parties began to encourage people of color to seek office and to help shape party platforms. In 1966, Barbara Jordan, a Texan, became the first black elected to the Texas Senate since 1883. Her impressive record as a state senator solidified her voting constituency and garnered her the attention, funding, and backing of the Democratic Party. In 1972, she successfully won a seat in the U.S. House of Representatives. Understanding the link between race, gender, and poverty, she sponsored bills that championed the welfare and rights of minorities and the poor. Her compelling presence at the impeachment of President Richard Nixon catapulted her to national prominence. Maxine Waters, born in St. Louis, became a delegate to the Democratic National Convention in 1980. A proponent of black advancement, she built a solid base among disillusioned blacks in the Twenty-ninth District of California. In 1990, she was elected to the U.S. House of Representatives.

Perhaps the most significant changes in black women's access to traditional parties was the nomination and election of the first African American woman to the U.S. Senate under the banner of the Democratic Party. Born in Chicago in 1947, Carol Moseley Braun began her professional career as a prosecutor in the U.S. Attorney's office. Her desire to shape the dynamics of black and female participatory politics in the city and the state drew her to the political stage. For fourteen years, she cultivated her constituency, vocalized issues important to blacks and women, and skillfully maneuvered within the circles of the Democratic Party. In 1978, she won a seat in the Illinois House of Representatives, her first elected public office. Nine years later, in 1987, she was elected the Cook County Recorder of Deeds. With a secure local base, she honed her skills, maximized her political prowess within the party, broadened her platform, and appealed to a statewide voting constituency. She won the party's nomination in the primary and was elected to the U.S. Senate in November 1992.

Most of the collective successes for black women came through the Democratic Party. Many were elected mayors, city council representatives, and to state legislative posts. In those positions, they were instrumental in shaping policies for city and state governments. They also played key roles in major presidential, senatorial, and legislative campaigns, sat on central legislative committees, and held significant posts in major political parties. Long viewed with suspicion by African Americans, the Republican Party did not have the same influence among black women. Its anti–affirmative action rhetoric and the implementation of policies that seem most favorable to wealthy whites isolated the party from the black community. Still, a few black women gained some plum positions among the Republicans. Regardless of their party affiliation, black women were an astute and an accomplished component of the electorate. They became vital to the success of parties and candidates in many areas of the country where they wielded political clout.

See also Baker, Ella Josephine; Bass, Charlotta Spears; Cary, Mary Ann Shadd; Chisholm, Shirley; Clark, Septima Poinsette; Hamer, Fannie Lou; Jordan, Barbara Charline; Moseley Braun, Carol; Motley, Constance Baker; National Association of Colored Women; Terrell, Mary Eliza Church; *and* Wells-Barnett, Ida B.

BIBLIOGRAPHY

Clark, Septima. *Ready from Within: Septima Clark and the Civil Rights Movement*. Navarro, CA: Wild Tree Press, 1986.

Gill, Gerald R. *"Win or Lose—We Win": The 1952 Vice Presidential Campaign of Charlotta A. Bass*. In *The Afro-American Woman: Struggles and Images*, edited by Sharon Harley and Rosalyn Terborg-Penn. Port Washington, NY: National University Publications, 1978.

Hendricks, Wanda A. "Ida B. Wells-Barnett and the Alpha Suffrage Club of Chicago." In *One Woman, One Vote: Rediscovering the Woman Suffrage Movement*, edited by Marjorie Spruill Wheeler. Troutdale, OR: NewSage Press, 1995.

Higginbotham, Evelyn Brooks. "In Politics to Stay: Black Women Leaders and Party Politics in the 1920s." In *Women, Politics, and Change*, edited by Louise A. Tilly and Patricia Gurin. New York: Russell Sage Foundation, 1990.

Lee, Chana Kai. *For Freedom's Sake: The Life of Fannie Lou Hamer*. Chicago: University of Illinois Press, 1999.

Prestage, Jewell L. "In Quest of African American Political Women." *Annals, AAPSS* (May 1991): 88–103.

Rogers, Mary Beth. *Barbara Jordan: American Hero*. New York: Bantam Books, 1998.

Terborg-Penn, Rosalyn. *African American Women in the Struggle for the Vote, 1850–1920*. Bloomington: Indiana University Press, 1998.

Ransby, Barbara. *Ella Baker and the Black Freedom Movement: A Radical Democratic Vision*. Chapel Hill: University of North Carolina Press, 2003.

Schechter, Patricia A. *Ida B. Wells-Barnett and American Reform 1880–1920*. Chapel Hill: University of North Carolina Press, 2001.

—WANDA A. HENDRICKS

POLITICAL RESISTANCE. The personal was political for black women in the United States well before the 1960s women's movements. Activities that would normally be considered outside the realm of politics—such as learning to read and write, running boardinghouses for young women, or sitting at the front of the bus—were inherently political. From the antebellum era to the present day, efforts to obtain and maintain equal access to housing, employment, and education, as well as freedom from sexual and economic exploitation, have been expressly political endeavors for blacks living in the United States.

Through it all, black women have developed and implemented distinctively female political strategies for racial survival, uplift, and equality.

Understanding black women's political activism in the United States requires understanding that politics is more than what happens within the institutional arena of formal governmental processes. It requires expanding the definition of politics to include strategies and activities employed individually or collectively to resist domination and control based on race, gender, class, sexuality, citizenship, and other categories of difference.

As scholars have increasingly noted in the past two decades, racism, sexism, classism, homophobia, and other institutionalized forms of control are interrelated

FLORYNCE KENNEDY speaking outside the Democratic Convention, in support of the Equal Rights Amendment, in 1976. Kennedy, a celebrity activist, advocated black civil rights and gay rights as well as feminism and also took up the cause of prostitutes and the poor. (© Bettye Lane.)

sites of domination and resistance deeply rooted in the history and social consciousness of the United States. Some categories of difference are more or less pronounced than others, depending on the historical period. Likewise, some power relations result in widely disparate effects on members of the same group ("women" or "blacks"), depending on individuals' memberships in other dominant or subordinate groups. Consequently, categories of difference may be sources of cohesion and unity, or sources of fractiousness and discord, and even marginalized groups may wield an unequal balance of power against certain of their own group members.

These dynamics of oppression and resistance play themselves out across the field of history and simultaneously constrain and expand contemporary life. Identifying and understanding power relations across categories of difference is essential to any analysis of black women's political activism in the United States.

The Slave Era

Understanding black women's political activism in the United States begins with understanding the gendered dimensions of the slave trade and of slavery itself. In the early stages of the slave trade, African men were more often seized and transported for slavery than were African women because of the labor-driven premium placed on physical strength. However, with increased efforts to outlaw the slave trade, slave owners eventually valued African women more highly than they had previously because of their reproductive capacity.

The relative treatment of captive men and women during the transatlantic voyage was another gendered aspect of the slave trade. While men were chained together in the ship's hold like livestock, women were often housed unshackled on the quarterdeck. This gendered "freedom" had its price, however, as women were routinely subjected to rape and other forms of physical cruelty by the ship's crew. Nonetheless, the horrors of the middle passage gave rise to some of the first expressions of black women's resistance, for captive African women were sometimes known to incite insurrections at sea or throw themselves overboard rather than endure enslavement.

The men and women who lived through the transatlantic voyage quickly found themselves embroiled in the "invisible politics" of physical and psychic survival. Though linked by the trauma of displacement and enslavement, men and women experienced and resisted slavery in significantly different ways. For instance, slave women experienced untold sexual violence at the hands of slave masters, who then justified their wholesale rape and reproductive exploitation by developing stereotypes depicting black women as sexually loose, indiscriminate, and insatiable. Also, in contrast to male slaves, female slaves were less likely to leave the confines of the plantation, and their relative lack of mobility, coupled with childbearing and child rearing responsibilities, made it less likely they would resist slavery by running away.

Nonetheless, slave women resisted efforts to dehumanize and commodify them in a variety of ways—many of which were circumscribed by gender. Some resisted sexual exploitation and enslavement by murdering their masters, committing arson, participating in or initiating work stoppages or slowdowns, feigning illness, or inducing miscarriages. Others exercised more passive forms of resistance by simply surviving, nurturing their children, and creating a sense of community. The mere fact that slave women were restricted in their movements—whether by custom or biology—often rendered them bearers and transmitters of culture, as well as "sites" of community coalescence. Given the tenuous presence of males in the lives of slave families, the community that coalesced around slave women was largely made up of other slave women, their children, and elders. According to Gayle T. Tate, "Slave women reconstituted their 'workplace' to address the needs of its members, distribute the workload more effectively, and engender female solidarity." In so doing, they were engaging in inherently political acts of survival and resistance.

Not all black women living in the United States prior to Emancipation were enslaved. Indeed, by the start of the Civil War—due to a variety of factors, including manumission and rising birthrates among freed blacks—there were a quarter of a million freed black women in the United States. Though liberated from the bondage imposed on their enslaved sisters, most freed black women enjoyed only limited autonomy as a result of race, sex, and class oppression. At the same time that northern industrialization was giving rise to the "cult of domesticity" (the belief that women's place was in the home), economic necessity required most black women to seek outside employment. Excluded by their race and gender from more lucrative jobs in factories and skilled trades, black women were forced to accept menial, labor-intensive, underpaid work as domestic servants, cooks, and washerwomen.

Relegated to the lowest rung of paid labor, black women who worked outside the home had no hope of aspiring to Victorian notions of womanhood, which, at least partially, equated female morality with middle- and upper-class leisure. As a result, the bodies of free black women—like those of their enslaved sisters—continued to be marked for both economic and sexual exploitation, and both free and enslaved black women continued to be blamed for their own degradation.

Even those black women fortunate enough to have been neither enslaved nor subjected to menial paid labor found themselves in tenuous social and political positions as a result of their race and gender. Tarred by the common brush of assumed black inferiority and lasciviousness, black women who had the means to do so resisted the debilitating and dehumanizing influences of white supremacy by founding their own self-help and self-improvement societies—many of which had such stereotype-defying names as "Colored Female Religious and Moral Society," "Literary Ladies Society," and "Afric-American Intelligence Society." Despite the bow to Victorian rectitude suggested by the names of these groups, black women's organizations were more than sites of acculturation to nineteenth-century middle-class values. They were also sites of resistance to both the system of slavery and the disfranchisement of free blacks. Moreover, in a society with strict gender role expectations regarding traditional leadership roles, these organizations often provided space for "legitimate" black female political inclusion.

Abolition

Free black women resisted slavery and racial discrimination on a variety of fronts. Those with literary talents—such as Harriet Jacobs, Francis Ellen Watkins Harper, and Mary Ann Shadd Cary—wrote poems, newspaper articles, and books condemning the "peculiar institution." Those with oratorical skills—such as Maria Stewart, Sojourner Truth, and Sarah Remond—used the lecture circuit to speak against slavery, as well as racism and sexism. By doing so, they often risked being targets for the very behaviors they criticized. For instance, a male heckler once called upon Sojourner Truth to reveal her breasts to prove she was not a man (and to the shame of the heckler, she did), and Maria Stewart's stint on the lecture circuit was cut short by ad hominem attacks on her virtue by members of her own community.

Other free black women undermined the system of slavery in more direct ways, such as hiding or transporting runaways, or—as was the case in the Abolition Riot of 1836—mobilizing to rescue fugitives from slave hunters. In this category of direct resistance strategies, no one is better known than Harriet Tubman. An escaped slave herself, Tubman returned to the South more than a dozen times to guide others to freedom. Not content with this record of resistance against slavery, she went on to spy for the North and to nurse wounded black soldiers during the Civil War.

Black free women also took the lead in creating and sustaining female antislavery societies that functioned to raise money to finance abolitionist lectures and newspapers. Some antislavery societies were mixed race or mixed gender. In many instances, however, the antislavery sentiments of European Americans did not translate into antiracist attitudes or behaviors. Many white abolitionists did not subscribe to either racial equality or integration and, in fact, some of the most liberal among them advocated repatriating free blacks to Africa. Black women who attempted to integrate white female antislavery groups often found themselves cut out of leadership positions—if they were allowed to join at all. Likewise, black women were relegated to subordinate positions in black mixed gender abolitionist groups. Black men assumed the local leadership and headed state and national societies, while black women, true to the gender role expectations of the time, formed separate, auxiliary organizations.

Significantly, for bodies that were marked both "black" and "female," the crosscurrents and tensions between black rights and women's rights came to a head in the middle of the nineteenth century. Given the organically false, but historically real, dichotomy between race and gender, black women were faced with choosing whether to give primacy to their race or to their sex. In most instances, as Paula Giddings notes, race consciousness won out, and black women's political activism was directed largely toward eliminating slavery and obtaining political, social, and economic equality for the race as a whole.

Reconstruction and Jim Crow

For the fleeting historical period known as Reconstruction, it appeared that the uneven balance between blacks and whites was finally on the verge of being righted. In December 1865—eight months after the official end of the Civil War—slavery was formally abolished by the Thirteenth Amendment, and the Fourteenth and Fifteenth Amendments were ratified soon after. Although the latter two additions to the U.S. Constitution secured citizenship and suffrage for men only, black women shared informally in the franchise and wielded considerable political influence through association with male members of their households. In fact, the vote accorded to black men was a family vote, cast in accordance with communal wishes. Black women had considerable political influence outside of the home during this period, as well. They organized women's political groups, participated in campaigns, and raised money for candidates. They were even known to stand guard outside men's political meetings and to serve as armed escorts for male family members going to the polls on Election Day.

For nearly a decade, freed black men and women enjoyed a taste of freedom and a degree of self-determination. With the withdrawal of federal troops from the South in 1877, however, Reconstruction collapsed, and in its place rushed a new tide of racism so virulent that it threatened to roll back every gain blacks had made in the South. New laws were enacted to strip black men of their recently won rights; black men, women, and children were routinely terrorized by the Ku Klux Klan; and a quasi slave system of sharecropping was introduced by plantation owners to ensure blacks's continued vulnerability to economic and sexual exploitation.

Faced with a new version of an old tyranny, recently emancipated southern blacks were forced to develop new strategies for resistance, and—as they had been since the inception of American slavery—black women were in the thick of it. One of the most outstanding exemplars of black female resistance to Jim Crow was Ida B. Wells. Although she participated in numerous political struggles and helped found many activist organizations during the course of her life, she is probably best known for three major acts of post-Reconstruction resistance: biting the hand of a railway conductor who tried to remove her from the ladies' coach car, and subsequently suing—and winning an award against—the Chesapeake and Ohio Railroad; exposing the rape myth behind the lynching of black males, and taking her antilynching campaign to the United Kingdom in order to shame the United States into passing antilynching legislation; and convincing several thousand Memphis blacks to sell their property and move west in protest of the greed-motivated lynching of three black Memphis grocers.

Other resistance strategies employed by black women in response to the ravages of the post-Reconstruction era included black business development and entrepreneurship. One of the most well-known black female entrepreneurs of the period, Madam C. J. Walker, invested in the black community by establishing franchises for her beauty care products that employed thousands of other black women. Around the same time, finding it inherently contradictory for blacks to financially support white businesses that discriminated against them, Richmond-born Maggie Lena Walker established an emporium, an insurance company, and a bank where blacks could invest their earnings within their own community.

As illustrated by the account of the six thousand Memphis blacks who moved west at the urging of Ida B. Wells, migration was another form of resistance to the post-Reconstruction efforts to deny blacks the freedom and rights so recently conferred on them. In addition to migrating west and to urban centers in the South, blacks also moved to industrialized cities in the North, although on a lesser scale than during the period from 1910 to 1930 known as the Great Migration. Black women and girls made their way to these urban centers to escape the triple bind of poverty, race discrimination, and sexual violence they experienced in the rural South. Because the cult of domesticity and the custom of slavery had marked black women's bodies for sexual predation, whenever possible women would travel directly to their destination and be met and taken in by family members who would then try to help them get jobs. Finding work, however—especially more pleasant or better paying jobs in factories, shops, hospitals, or department stores—was an uphill battle. Like the majority of free black women who had sought outside employment before Emancipation, former slave women who migrated to urban industrial centers at the end of Reconstruction were channeled mostly into domestic service.

Perhaps because of the plight of these black women and girls—newly emancipated but essentially rudderless in a sea fraught more with perils than possibilities—one of the most effective forms of black women's resistance to the collapse of Reconstruction was the black club women's movement. Black women's clubs were formed in response to the political, economic, and social setbacks to both men and women caused by the collapse of Reconstruction, as well as to the negative stereotyping of women that was carried over from slavery. Rooted in black women's self-help and self-improvement societies that proliferated in the North before the Civil War, the black club women's movement promoted collective self-help programs, as well as moral and social uplift of black women and advancement of the race as a whole. It also provided a hugely successful training ground for political organizing and collective action against racist policies and practices, including racist depictions of black women.

In the beginning, black club women focused on the immediate survival needs of newly emancipated people—distributing food and clothing, housing orphans and the elderly, and organizing free health clinics. By the 1890s, however, black women's clubs began extending their activities to community development, establishing kindergartens, settlement houses, hospitals, and other social institutions designed to meet the needs of their communities. Black women's clubs rapidly became a strong base for political organizing, with one of the most momentous events in the history of black women's political activism occurring in 1896, when the League of Colored Women, a coalition of 113 clubs, and the National Federation of Afro-American Women, representing 85 clubs, merged to form the National Association of Colored Women (NACW). Under the influential leadership of Mary Church Terrell, Josephine St. Pierre Ruffin, and Margaret Murray Washington, the NACW grew to fifty thousand members by 1914. As the umbrella organization for hundreds of clubs and thousands of members, the NACW became a powerful political voice for black women throughout the United States and remained so for decades to come.

Black Women's Political Activism between the Wars

As in previous periods, black women's political activism was expressed in a variety of ways between 1920 and 1940. During the 1920s, black women's club movements continued to be the major platform for the political expression of black middle-class women. But the 1920s also ushered in a new era of political expression for poor and working class black women who found a voice in labor organizing, the music and arts of the Harlem Renaissance, black nationalism, and the development of a black lesbian and gay subculture.

The music, poetry, theater, and other cultural and artistic expressions of the Harlem Renaissance promoted black pride and a fierce resistance to the debilitating impact of poverty, family dissolution, racism, and social and political ostracism. Black women poets and writers of the period—such as Nella Larsen, Alice Dunbar-Nelson, and Zora Neale Hurston—used their creative talents to awaken a love for distinctively black culture and art. Blues women used song and intonation to articulate the psychic, social, and economic sufferings of black people, particularly black women, who labored under class and race exploitation, gendered racism, and male domination. Unlike black club women who appeared—at least on the surface—to emulate white obsessions with the "cult of domesticity" and white female standards of beauty and morality, blues women generated musical lyrics that implored women to be self-reliant and independent. Blues women like Bessie Smith, Ida Cox, Ma Rainey, and Billie Holiday refused to give husbands and children "any best place" in their lives. Rather—in sharp contrast to sexist and heterosexist gender role expectations generated by both the cult of domesticity and the culture of secrecy and dissemblance designed to shield black women from the judgmental eyes of white society—blues women sang lyrics that embraced female sexual license, including same-sex sexuality, and spoke of women's rights to free themselves from abusive relationships with men. In fact, as Angela Davis argues, women's blues of the 1920s marked the beginning of feminist insurgency against domestic violence and a willingness to air publicly what is still too often characterized as "dirty laundry."

During this same time frame, poor and working class men and women also found refuge and empowerment in radical protest movements, such as Marcus Garvey's grassroots Universal Negro Improvement Association (UNIA). Despite its patriarchal roots and aspirations, this black nationalist organization proved a rich ideological and political training ground for a number of black women activists, not the least of whom was Garvey's second wife, Amy Jacques. Amy Jacques Garvey ran the UNIA while Marcus Garvey was in prison and applied a markedly black feminist philosophy in the process. According to Paula Giddings in *When and Where I Enter*, when male members of the UNIA began to suggest that female members were stepping out of their assigned roles, Amy Jacques Garvey responded:

We serve notice on our men that Negro women will demand equal opportunity to fill any position in the Universal Negro Improvement Association or anywhere else without discrimination because of sex. We are very sorry if it hurts your old-fashioned tyrannical feelings, and we not only make the demand but we intend to enforce it.

Moreover, when the UNIA's appeal to militant nationalism appeared to dissipate in the mid 1920s, Amy Jacques Garvey warned male leaders that they needed to put their words into action or prepare to be displaced by women. This warning was consistent with Amy Jacques Garvey's repeated message that black women were the "burden bearers of their race" and should prepare to assume leadership positions in the struggle for black liberation in the United States and abroad.

Arguably, these multiple strands of resistance, ranging from the blues to black nationalism to the omnipresent black women's club movement, girded African American women to endure the ravages of the Great Depression of the 1930s. Although thousands of citizens of all races were reduced to poverty by this catastrophic event, black families—long victimized by racist efforts to prevent black economic self-sufficiency—were among those hardest hit. As always, black women were at the forefront of efforts to ensure the survival of black people during these hard times. Black women mobilized within their communities to feed and shelter their families—working, whenever possible, alongside black men in industry, or, when necessary, alone or with other women in sex and race segregated jobs. Many black women in the North worked with economic development programs and consumer action groups to keep their families' earnings within black communities. For example, at the start of the Great Depression, the Housewives League of Detroit was established to promote black self-sufficiency by encouraging housewives to patronize only black-owned businesses or businesses employing black workers. This strategy of directed spending spread nationwide, largely due to the political organizing already accomplished by the black club women's movement.

By the mid-1930s, black club women redoubled their efforts to integrate blacks into the social, political, and economic fabric of American life. There was no stronger champion of these efforts than Mary McLeod Bethune, who remains one of the most important figures in national black political history. Remembered largely for her incomparable contributions to the education of black women and girls, Bethune was also a savvy political strategist. As the president of the National Association of Colored Women (NACW)—which was part of the otherwise all white National Council of Women (NCW)—Bethune negotiated for desegregated seating at the 1925 international women's conference in Washington, DC.

When the promise of desegregated seating failed to materialize, Bethune and other members of the NACW walked out of the conference—and into the waiting arms of the press. Leveraging the power of the press and capitalizing on an international presence at the conference, Bethune shamed conference conveners into honoring their commitment by suggesting that a public display of discrimination against black citizens would disgrace the United States in the eyes of the world. In so doing, she not only won the day for black women at the conference but also won recognition as an advocate and spokesperson for black women throughout the United States.

A decade later, Bethune parlayed this recognition into leadership of the National Council of Negro Women, a "superorganization" representing half a million black women. This status—along with a burgeoning friendship with Eleanor Roosevelt—won Bethune a post in President Franklin Roosevelt's National Youth Administration (NYA), where she served, formally, as director of the Negro Division and, informally—along with other members of the "black cabinet"—as a conduit to greater opportunity for thousands of other black women, men, and youth.

Black Women's Political Activism during World War II

While blacks made some economic, political, and social advances under President Franklin Roosevelt's first two terms, they were by no means close to achieving parity with whites. This was made resoundingly clear at the advent of World War II, when the majority of jobs in the defense industry went to white women, while black women continued to be employed predominantly as agricultural and domestic workers. When black women were allowed to partake of the wartime economy, they were often relegated to the dirtiest, heaviest, and worst paying jobs. Even these minimal advances were made possible only through political organizing, agitation, and persistence in the face of racist and sexist exclusionary practices designed to keep black women "in their place" and stereotyped by race and gender. Whether factory workers or skilled professionals, black women had to fight constantly for inclusion in jobs created by the wartime economy. Frequently, they had to fight discrimination by both management and organized labor.

Equally—perhaps more—significant, black women also had to fight for inclusion on their own terms, terms that promoted their self-respect and worth as contributing members of the skilled trades and professions they had trained for. The struggle of black female nurses is a case in point. Black female nurses had to battle quotas mandating limited participation of black women in the Armed Forces Nurse Corps, the exclusionary practices of nursing associations, and attempts to use black nurses as sexual capital, rather than as skilled professionals. Nowhere was this latter practice more evident than in the attempts of the U.S. military to recruit black nurses to go overseas during World War II so that they could serve as a sexual buffer between black male soldiers and white British women. It took political resistance from black nurses and the NAACP to force the U.S. military to abandon this "wartime strategy" for preserving the assumed racial purity of English stock.

Nonetheless, the war years—which Paula Giddings characterizes as a time of "two steps forward and one step back" for black women—did see significant gains for black women, both in terms of occupational categories and in terms of wages.

Modern Civil Rights Period

Although the media and black male leaders of the time ignored or downplayed the contributions of black women to the civil rights struggles of the 1950s and 1960s, black women often served as both catalysts and agents of the modern civil rights movement. For instance, the Montgomery bus boycott is widely recognized as the event that precipitated the modern black civil rights era. While Rosa Parks is often given credit for her role in the boycott, little, if any, attention is given to Jo Ann Robinson who mobilized the bus riders' strike, the working-class black women who stopped using the bus system to get to their jobs as domestics, or the Women's Political Caucus who helped devise alternative forms of transportation. Likewise, Diane Nash—the Chicago-born Fisk undergraduate who gave up the relative privilege of her black middle-class upbringing to join the Freedom movement—has been given little coverage in the movement literature, despite her leadership roles in several major civil rights organizations, as well as her direct involvement in the Freedom Rides and student sit-ins.

Although there are countless—and well-deserved—books, articles, and documentaries about the role of Dr. Martin Luther King Jr. and other black male leaders in the civil rights struggles of the 1950s and 1960s, we are just now beginning to see a wider accounting of the contributions that women like Daisy Bates, Ella Baker, and Fannie Lou Hamer made to those very same events. Bates, Baker, Hamer, and countless unidentified, or simply overlooked, black women were at the heart of the massive grassroots movements, the bus boycotts, the sit-ins, the 1963 March on Washington, and other nonviolent protests and legal efforts that rocked the U.S. political landscape. And black churchwomen, working behind the scenes, prodded black ministers into the center of social justice activism.

Moreover, like their movement foremothers, black female activists of the 1950s and 1960s often saw the intersectional quality of race, class, and gender struggles in ways that male leaders did not. For instance, Ella Baker, who helped found the Student Nonviolent Coordinating Committee, advocated a group-centered—rather than hierarchical and patriarchal—approach to decision making and encouraged constructive engagement in civil rights activism across race, gender, class, and age differences. Another exemplar of intersectional thinking and action is Fannie Lou Hamer, a sharecropper with only a sixth-grade education whose name is synonymous with the working-class–led Mississippi Freedom Democratic Party. Though ultimately betrayed by backroom maneuvering at the highest level of the Democratic Party—in collusion with the male leadership of the civil right's movement—Hamer made political history with her televised testimony at the 1964 Democratic National Convention, where she exposed the interconnectedness of racial violence and economic injustice.

Numerous events shaping black women's political activism in the late 1950s and 1960s sprang from seeds planted by black women in previous decades. When Ida B. Wells refused to leave the ladies' coach of the Chesapeake and Ohio Railway in 1884, she prefigured Rosa Parks's famous act of civil disobedience in 1955. Likewise, student sit-ins of the 1960s had their roots in the 22 April 1944 sit-in organized by Pauli Murray and three other Howard activists at Thompson's cafeteria in Washington, DC. More broadly, the collective activism of the 1950s and 1960s—whether defined by actions like boycotts and sit-ins or strategic organizations such as the Southern Christian Leadership Conference and the Student Nonviolent Coordinating Committee—were integrally connected to the local and national organizing work already set in motion by previous generations of black club women.

The intergenerational nature of black women's resistance strategies is not surprising, given the intergenerational nature of black women's struggles for racial and gender equality. Like their foremothers, black women in the 1950s and 1960s continued to resist segregation in public transportation and accommodations, racial inequities within public education, discriminatory labor practices, race-based criminal prosecutions—and racist constructions of black women's bodies as damaged and inferior to those of white women. As it was with their foremothers, every aspect of black women's bodies in the 1950s and 1960s—from hair to sexuality—was highly politicized and scrutinized. Curiously, one of the most virulent assaults against black womanhood came not from a southern apologist for segregation, but from a northern white liberal, Daniel Patrick Moynihan. The 1965 Moynihan Report, which blamed black women for everything from the prevalence of pathology-ridden black families to the emasculation of black men, precipitated renewed attacks on black womanhood by the dominant society, as well as by some prominent members of the black community. Even though several decades have passed since the report was issued, black women still live under its cloud—whether in the form of the ongoing racial libel that black women are impervious to rape or in the form of the constant drumbeat that black women are outstripping black men in educational attainment.

Immediately after the passage of the Civil Rights Act of 1964 and the Voting Rights Act of 1965, there was a degree of optimism regarding racial progress in the United States. This optimism was short-lived, however, since—despite the passage of federal non-discrimination laws—extralegal systems of exclusion and segregation persisted or intensified. A number of nationalist organizations sprang up across the United States in response to wrenching poverty, unemployment, educational and housing inequities, and police brutality. Among the most prominent of these organizations were the Revolutionary Action movement, the Organization for Afro-American Unity, and the Black Panther Party for Self Defense, all of which embraced the nationalist perspectives associated with Malcolm X and the Black Power movement. Black women like Elaine Brown, Angela Davis, and Kathleen Cleaver played vital roles in these nationalist efforts, though they often endured virulent sexism and sexual violence from male counterparts who told them, "stand *behind* your man," or "have babies for the revolution." Sexism was also rampant in the Student Nonviolent Coordinating Committee. Indeed, it was so pervasive that several female organizational leaders created the Black Women's Liberation Caucus, which later became the Third World Women's Alliance—reputed to be the first truly black feminist organization of the 1960s.

Ongoing racism catapulted black women into new forms of protests that included politicizing black women's beauty. Because physical attractiveness had been based on white beauty standards that had long been associated with inner morality and worth, establishing the legitimacy of black women as beauty contestants and beauty pageant winners was seen as a way of establishing the worth of black people, in general. In 1968, largely in response to the exclusion of black women from the Miss America pageant, the NAACP launched the Miss Black America pageant. The winner of the first pageant, Saundra Williams, used her beauty, civil rights activism, and African-centered identity as a means of racial protest and as a way to embody the nationalist slogan, "black is beautiful." In a very real sense, "the personal was political" for pageant winners like Williams and her supporters who believed that any challenge to white-dominated enterprises was a blow for black civil rights.

Black women's political activism advanced to a new level in the 1970s with the emergence of black feminism and the formation of the National Welfare Rights Organization and the National Black Feminist Organization (NBFO). Within these organizations, black women openly focused on issues and concerns that had previously been relegated to the margins by male-dominated black civil rights movements and white-dominated women's organizations. For instance, the National Welfare Rights Organization, though short-lived, championed the right of poor women to have autonomy over their own bodies and reproductive capacities, their right to a monthly stipend that ensured a decent quality of life for themselves and their children, and their right to hold leadership positions within the organization, rather than simply being objects of the organization's beneficence.

The National Black Feminist Organization also heralded a new phase in black women's political activism by tackling such issues as sexual harassment and class oppression. Offshoots of the national organization went even further. For example, the Combahee River Collective, a Boston chapter of the National Black Feminist Organization, explicitly addressed homophobia and called for "sisterhood among black women of various sexual orientations." The Combahee River Collective also issued a position statement in 1977 that has served as a general blueprint for black women's political activism for the 1980s, 1990s, and beyond:

> We are actively committed to struggling against racial, sexual, heterosexual, and class oppression, and see as our particular task the development of integrated analysis and practice based upon the fact that the major systems of oppression are interlocking. The synthesis of these oppressions creates the conditions of our lives. As black women we see black feminism as the logical political movement to combat the manifold and simultaneous oppression that all women of color face.

The black lesbian scholar activist Barbara Smith provided more specific guidance regarding the appropriate arena of black women's political activism by noting the following areas of concern: reproductive rights, sterilization abuse, equal access to abortion, health care, child care, the rights of the disabled, violence against women, rape, battering, sexual harassment, welfare rights, lesbian and gay rights, aging, police brutality, labor organizing, anti-imperialist struggles, antiracist organizing, nuclear disarmament, and preserving the environment.

Events of the 1980s, 1990s, and—at least preliminarily—the 2000s have done nothing to lessen the urgency of the concerns raised by Smith. Indeed, a cursory review of events taking place over the 1980s and 1990s would suggest that Smith was prophetic. The 1980s saw a number of civil rights rollbacks, including the first generation of attacks on affirmative action; the onslaught of AIDS; ongoing efforts to chip away at *Roe v. Wade*; and deep cuts

AIDS DEMONSTRATION at City Hall Plaza, New York City, seeking funding for research from the city government. (© Bettye Lane.)

to social welfare programs that especially affected the lives of poor women. The 1990s saw renewed assaults on the poor in the guise of welfare reform; an increased incidence of HIV/AIDS in communities of color (with a shockingly high prevalence of HIV/AIDS among heterosexual black women and Latinas); and an ever-widening gap between technological advances and black people's access to those advances. The 1990s also highlighted the spectacle of black women under assault from within their own communities—Desiree Washington and Anita Hill being the most publicized examples. Hill's testimony against Clarence Thomas, in particular, precipitated an antifemale backlash that fueled the already fractious issue of sexual politics within the black community and breathed new life into the raced and gendered sexual libel that had shadowed black women since the slave era. On the credit side of the ledger, the antifemale backlash

in the black community also served as a catalyst for one of the most pronounced black feminist acts of resistance in modern times—the historic "African American Women in Defense of Ourselves" statement in support of Anita Hill that appeared 18 November 1991 in the *New York Times*.

Events on this side of the "new millennium"—from the 11 September 2001 attacks on the World Trade Center to the war in Iraq and the debate surrounding same-sex marriage—are perhaps too recent to pass objective judgment on. Nonetheless, they, too, fall squarely within Barbara Smith's list of intersectional concerns and will undoubtedly shape black women's political activism for years to come.

See also Abolition Movement; Antilynching Movement; Civil Rights Movement; The Left; *and* Political Parties.

BIBLIOGRAPHY

Craig, Maxine Leeds. *Ain't I a Beauty Queen?: Black Women, Beauty, and the Politics of Race*. New York: Oxford University Press, 2002.

Davis, Angela Y. *Blues Legacies and Black Feminism: Gertrude "Ma" Rainey, Bessie Smith, and Billie Holiday*. New York: Pantheon Books, 1998.

Davis, Angela Y. *Women, Race and Class*. New York: Vintage, 1983.

Duster, Alfreda M., ed. *Crusade for Justice: The Autobiography of Ida B. Wells*. Chicago: University of Chicago Press, 1970.

Enloe, Cynthia H. *Bananas, Beaches and Bases: Making Feminist Sense of International Politics*. London: Pandora, 1989.

Giddings, Paula. *When and Where I Enter: The Impact of Black Women on Race and Sex in America*. New York: Morrow, 1984.

Gilmore, Glenda Elizabeth. *Gender and Jim Crow: Women and the Politics of White Supremacy in North Carolina, 1896–1920*. Chapel Hill: University of North Carolina, 1996.

Hardy, Gayle J. *American Women Civil Rights Activists: Biobibliographies of Sixty-eight Leaders, 1825–1992*. Jefferson, NC: McFarland, 1993.

Hine, Darlene Clark. *Hine Sight: Black Women and the Re-Construction of American History*. New York: Carlson, 1994.

Hine, Darlene Clark, and Kathleen Thompson. *A Shining Thread of Hope: The History of Black Women in America*. New York: Broadway Books, 1998.

hooks, bell. *Black Looks: Race and Representation*. Boston: South End Press, 1992.

hooks, bell. *Yearning: Race, Gender, and Cultural Politics*. Boston: South End Press, 1990.

Ransby, Barbara. *Ella Baker and the Black Freedom Movement: A Radical Democratic Vision*. Chapel Hill: University of North Carolina Press, 2003.

St. Jean, Yanick, and Joe R. Feagin. *Double Burden: Black Women and Everyday Racism*. Armonk, NY: M.E. Sharpe, 1998.

Tate, Gayle T. *Unknown Tongues: Black Women's Political Activism in the Antebellum Era, 1830–1860*. East Lansing: Michigan State University Press, 2003.

White, Deborah Gray. *Ar'n't I a Woman? Female Slaves in the Plantation South*. New York: Norton, 1985.

White, Deborah Gray. *Too Heavy a Load: Black Women in Defense of Themselves, 1894–1994*. New York: Norton, 1999.

Wyatt, Gail Elizabeth. *Stolen Women: Reclaiming Our Sexuality, Taking Back Our Lives*. New York: Wiley, 1997.

—PATRICIA WASHINGTON

POWERS, HARRIET (b. 29 October 1837; d. c. 1911), quilter. Quilts and the act of quilt making have played important roles in the history of African America. Rife with symbolism, quilts represent comfort, resistance, self-expression, poverty, and a dozen other aspects of the lives of black Americans. Most quilters are not known outside their own circle of friends and family, but there is one woman who stood out. Her quilts, startling in their quality and originality, and having caught the world's attention, were displayed in the Smithsonian Institution and the Museum of Fine Arts in Boston, where the name of their creator, Harriet Powers, is preserved.

Powers was born a slave in Georgia. Her maiden name is unknown, as are the circumstances of her birth and childhood. She was married to Armstead Powers and had three children, two of whom were born in slavery; the third was born in 1866, just after the end of the Civil War. Most of this information comes from the 1870 census, which also states that Powers's occupation was keeping house and that her husband was a farmhand.

The family was fairly prosperous. They owned animals and tools and, sometime in the 1880s, bought two two-acre plots of land. In 1873, they were living in the Buck Branch, Winterville district of Clarke County, Georgia. At other times between 1870 and 1894, when Armstead seems to have left the farm, they lived in the Sandy Creek district. Powers remained in that district, living an independent and reasonably comfortable life until her death.

Powers's existence and her quilts are known to us because of Jennie Smith, a white artist from Athens, Georgia, who was head of the art department of the Lucy Cobb School. Smith first saw a Powers quilt at the Athens Cotton Fair of 1886. She was enormously impressed and resolved at once to find its maker. She visited Powers at her farm and offered to buy the quilt, but Powers refused to sell. Then, in 1890, the Powers family went through a difficult time financially. A year later, they were forced to sell off one of their pieces of land. Smith received word that she could now buy the quilt. Unfortunately, she was unable to do so. The next year, Smith sent word to Powers

CREATION OF THE ANIMALS, dated 1895–1898, detail. Powers made this quilt in Athens, Georgia, of pieced cotton with plain and metallic yarns; the square shown here is one of fifteen different scenes. (Photograph © 2004 Museum of Fine Arts, Boston.)

HARRIET POWERS, c. 1900. The artist Jennie Smith brought Powers's work to the attention of the public. (Photograph © 2004 Museum of Fine Arts, Boston.)

had raised $10,000 for a special building at the exposition, and there were exhibits from eleven southern states. Powers's name is not on the list of exhibitors, but there is evidence that her quilt was there. In 1898, a group of faculty wives from Atlanta University commissioned Powers to create a second quilt as a gift for the Reverend Charles Cuthbert Hall, president of Union Theological Seminary.

The quilt owned by Smith passed, at her death, into the hands of a friend, Hal Heckman. He kept the quilt for some time and then gave it to the Smithsonian Institution, where it was placed on exhibit.

The quilt owned by Hall was inherited by his son, the Reverend Basil Douglas Hall, who sold it to the collector Maxim Karolik, who in turn gave it to the Museum of Fine Arts in Boston in 1964. It was entitled *The Creation of the Animals*. Powers dictated her explanations of this quilt to Jennie Smith as well. In the summer of 2001, it was the centerpiece of a major exhibition of folk art at the museum.

Looking at these two quilts causes profoundly mixed feelings. It is wonderful to see the work of an artist preserved, but it is impossible not to feel great sadness that Powers was denied the opportunity to fulfill her potential.

See also Quilting.

BIBLIOGRAPHY

Adams, Marie Jeanne. "The Harriet Powers Pictorial Quilts." *Black Art* (1979).

Bowen, Nancy Bunker. "American Tapestry: Story Quilts of Harriet Powers Reveal Remarkable Artistry." *Athens Banner-Herald*, 2 September 2001.

Fry, Gladys-Marie. "Harriet Powers: Portrait of a Black Quilter." *Sage* (Spring 1987).

McDaniel, M. Akua. "Black Women: Making Quilts of Their Own." *Art Papers* (September/October 1987).

—KATHLEEN THOMPSON

that she was ready to buy the quilt if it was still for sale. At the end of this back-and-forth, Powers brought the quilt, carefully wrapped, to Smith's home and handed it over in return for $5. Before she left, she related to Smith the story of each of the quilt's fifteen squares. The quilt depicts events of her lifetime that Powers considered significant, such as a dark day apparently caused by forest fires in New York and Canada. Smith wrote down and preserved what she had been told. Powers returned a number of times to Smith's house to visit her quilt.

It was Smith's purpose to exhibit the quilt in Atlanta at the Cotton States Exposition of 1895. The black community

PRICE, FLORENCE SMITH (b. 9 April 1888; d. 3 June 1953), composer. The life story of Florence Smith Price is one filled with amazing accomplishments in the music world during the first half of the twentieth century. Not only would her music career have been a model of success on its own merit, but the historical and cultural contexts of Florence Price's work especially establish a unique persona worthy of acclaim. Price's legacy was grounded in the pride and fortitude of her parentage, propelling her through a rich array of pursuits in music education and composition. Thus, Florence Price is remembered in the music world as the first black American woman composer to earn international recognition. Her works have been performed by major orchestras as well as by numerous renowned solo artists.

Florence Price was born in Little Rock, Arkansas, the daughter of a politically and socially well-connected family.

Her father, James H. Smith, was a dentist who opened his office on Main Street in Little Rock, the first black to claim that distinction in this southern town in the late1800s. He had been born in the state of Delaware in the year 1843. His parents, both free blacks, moved their family to New Jersey, where Smith remained until the 1850s. Smith had worked in New York City before. Unable to gain admission to medical school, he sought dental studies in Philadelphia. Even though he was able to overcome this rejection by studying with several members of the dental profession in Philadelphia, this was an early indication that the strides blacks had been making during the Reconstruction period were beginning to erode.

James Smith married Florence Gulliver, who had been a teacher in the Indianapolis area. Their union was to produce three children, one son and two daughters. Florence Beatrice was the youngest, born after her brother Charles and sister Gertrude. At a very early age Florence

FLORENCE SMITH PRICE, in a photograph inscribed to her friend Camille Nickerson. Price was one of the first African American women composers to achieve widespread recognition. (Moorland-Spingarn Research Center.)

began studying piano with her mother. Mrs. Smith presented Florence in public performance when she was four years old. Encouraged in her musical studies throughout her childhood, Florence Price soon began composing her own music. By the time she was eleven, one of her pieces was in print, and when she was sixteen one of her compositions earned her a fee.

Shortly thereafter, Florence Price left Little Rock to study piano, organ, and composition at the New England Conservatory in Boston. She studied with George Chadwick and Frederick Converse before graduating in 1906 at the age of eighteen. For the next four years she taught at the Cotton Plant–Arkadelphia Academy and Shorter College in her hometown. In 1910 Price moved to Atlanta where she had accepted a position as head of the music department at Clark University.

It was in 1912 that Florence returned to Little Rock for an extended stay. There she married Thomas Price, a young attorney who for several years had been a partner in a law firm but soon opened his own office. After the death of their first baby, a son, the Prices had two daughters, Florence Louise, born 1917, and Edith, 1921. Florence became well established as a teacher in her hometown. Along with piano and organ, Price also offered lessons in violin, another instrument she had studied as a child. She soon began to earn recognition for her creative work. She won her first Holstein composition award in 1925 and repeated this success two years later. Unfortunately, race relations had been on a steady decline in Arkansas, a circumstance that had a disturbing impact on the Price family, both as observers of history and as individuals. By the mid-1920s it was obvious that Florence Price would have difficulty expanding upon her career if the family remained in the area. For example, Price's application for membership in the Arkansas Music Teachers Association, the primary music organization dedicated to maintaining standards for the private instruction of students, was denied. Then, the lynching of a black man accused of assaulting a white woman had a great impact on the lives of many black families. Thus, in 1927 the family moved to Chicago, where Florence Price remained until her death in 1953. Her career blossomed during her years in the Chicago area and reflected the versatility of her talents and training. She was an example of a professional woman who enjoyed the support of her husband, who took pride in her accomplishments until his death in 1942.

In Chicago, Price engaged in additional studies, working with composers and theorists in such institutions as the Chicago Musical College, the American Conservatory of Music, the Chicago Teachers College, and the University of Chicago. Soon her compositions were receiving attention from the leading players in Chicago's musical life. Her piano sonata and the Symphony in E Minor were winners of the Rodman Wanamaker Foundation Award in 1932. The Symphony in E Minor was premiered by the Chicago Symphony Orchestra under the direction of Frederick Stock at the 1933 Chicago World's Fair. With this performance Price made history, becoming the first black woman to have a symphony performed by a major American orchestra. She became one of three black American composers to accomplish a similar feat in this decade. William Grant Still (1895–1978) heard his Afro-American Symphony performed by the Rochester Symphony in 1931. Three years after Price's premiere the Philadelphia Orchestra presented the Negro Folk Symphony by William Dawson (1899–1990).

Price's successes, as well as those of contemporaries such as Still and Dawson, occurred during what is known as the Negro Renaissance, a particularly favorable time in U.S. history for black Americans to express their creative ideas. Black composers during this Renaissance found a broader acceptance of their work than others who followed them in the next decades of the twentieth century. During this period, a number of composers were influenced by the folk elements of their culture. This particular approach to the creative process has been labeled "nationalism" and had permeated musical language of composers across the globe at various levels for centuries. The black American composers of the early 1900s incorporated folk music from their culture into their original compositions. Price and those in her circle who pursued formal studies of music composition brought a new approach to the manner in which nationalistic elements were folded into the fabric of their creations. Rather than including literal quotes of specific songs from their culture, the melodic, harmonic, and rhythmic flavor of their heritage intermingled with the traditions of western classical music. Price was one of the earliest black American composers to successfully bridge the gap between these two worlds. The combination of the two languages intrigued the music world and helped create a positive environment for Price to thrive with her teaching and composition.

Price enjoyed a multifaceted career as a music educator, performer and composer. In the 1920s she became an active church organist, using the training she received at the New England Conservatory in her organ performance. Through these experiences in her life she developed associations with such influential people as Estella C. Bonds, the mother of Margaret Bonds, who also built a career in music. Margaret Bonds became a pupil of Price's and reached such a level of proficiency as a composer and classical pianist that she too earned a place in history. Price remained active as a piano teacher throughout her career, from her private teaching in Arkansas to her later years in Chicago. She also taught organ and violin. She wrote many piano pieces appropriate for the pedagogical work in which she was so heavily involved. A number of these have piqued the interest of recent scholars. For example, "Three Little Negro Dances," published by Presser, originally appeared as solo piano pieces and was later arranged by Price for two pianos as well as for symphonic band. Other piano titles that reflected Price's intent to write for younger students were "The Gnat and the Bee," "Rock-a-Bye," and "Doll Waltz."

The mature concert pianist would be attracted to other compositions from Price's output. Along with the Sonata in E Minor, the winner of the Wanamaker Prize, Price also left a piano concerto and a work completed in 1935, *Tecumseh*, which was published by Carl Fischer. The piano collaborated with vocalists in many songs, including the well-known "My Soul's Been Anchored in de Lord." In addition to her symphony, Price contributed a number of other major works for orchestra. There are three numbered symphonies (the E minor symphony is number one). She also wrote several concertos for orchestra and either piano or violin. The Violin Concerto No. 2 was written just one year before her death. The Chicago Symphony Orchestra and the Chicago Women's Orchestra performed her Piano Concerto in One Movement. Along with Presser and Fischer, Summy, Clayton, Oxford Piano Course, and Silver Burdette have published her works.

Price was not only known for her classical compositions but also for writing commercials for radio, a lucrative aspect of the music business, yet less of an expectation among the more "traditional" classical composers of our time. While Price had suffered a snub by the Arkansas music teachers' group years earlier, she did become a member of the prestigious American Society of Composers, Authors and Publishers (ASCAP). Other major performing groups and soloists that have performed her music include the Detroit Symphony Orchestra, the Pittsburgh Symphony Orchestra, the United States Marine Band, and the artists Marian Anderson, Roland Hayes, Leontyne Price, Todd Duncan, and William Warfield.

The music of Florence Beatrice Price was particularly known among the audiences in Chicago during her lifetime. Today scholars are continuing to engage in research on her life and works. While her music may not have become standard repertoire among pianists, American symphony orchestras, or other performers since her death, it is to the benefit of the music world that her contributions have not become lost to history. In 1986 her Symphony in E Minor was given rebirth through a performance by the North Arkansas Symphony Orchestra, perhaps as a birthday remembrance since it was performed during Price's birth month of April. This performance was held at the University of Arkansas, the home of more than eighty scores by Price in the Special Collections Division of the university library. The life and music of Florence Price may have come full circle. Everything began in Arkansas, peaked in Chicago, and returned home for the final stage of development—settling into a place in music history.

See also **Composers** *and* **Concert Music.**

BIBLIOGRAPHY

Brown, Rae Linda. "William Grant Still, Florence Price, and William Dawson: Echoes of the Harlem Renaissance." In *Black Music in the Harlem Renaissance: A Collection of Essays*, edited by Samuel Floyd. Westport, CT: Greenwood Press, 1990.

Green, Mildred Denby. *Black Women Composers: A Genesis*. Boston: Twayne, 1983.

Jackson, Barbara Garvey. "Florence Price, Composer." *Black Perspectives in Music* 5.1 (Spring 1977): 31–43.

Southall, Geneva. "In Celebration of Black Women Composers." Program notes, Fourth Annual "Music of the Black American Composer" Program. Washington, DC: Smithsonian Institution, National Museum of American History, May, 1988.

Southern, Eileen. *The Music of Black Americans: A History*. 3rd ed. New York: Norton, 1997.

Walker-Hill, Helen, "Music by Black Women Composers at the American Music Research Center." *American Music Research Center Journal* 2 (1992): 23–51.

—MELLASENAH MORRIS

LEONTYNE PRICE AS AIDA, 1967. The production was by the Metropolitan Opera in New York City. In 1985, again at the Met, this was the role in which she gave her last opera performance. (Library of Congress.)

PRICE, LEONTYNE (b. 10 February 1927), opera singer. The superlatives required to describe the voice and career of Leontyne Price must inevitably stretch credulity. To one who has never heard her, it must seem impossible that anyone could really have been as good as this singer has been. She was born with a miracle of a voice, and then she became its caretaker for the rest of her life, working and training and protecting. The world will probably never know all the sacrifices she made for her achievement. It can only acknowledge and, thanks to her many remarkable recordings, enjoy the result.

Mary Violet Leontyne Price was born in Laurel, Mississippi, to James and Kate Price. Her father worked in a sawmill and her mother was a midwife. Both were interested in music and encouraged the same interest in their daughter. Young Price played the piano at four and sang in the choir at St. Paul's Methodist Church only a few years later. In 1936, when she was nine, she went to a Marian Anderson concert and decided she wanted a life in music. However, she believed she would be a teacher. After graduating from Oak Park High School in 1944, she attended the College of Education and Industrial Arts (now Central State College) in Wilberforce, Ohio.

In Ohio, Price's remarkable talents were soon recognized. Her professors encouraged her to pursue a career as a singer, rather than as a teacher. Before she graduated, she applied for and received a four-year, full-tuition scholarship to New York's Juilliard School of Music, beginning in 1949. While there, she began to fear she would have to take work singing in clubs in order to pay the rest of her expenses, but a family friend from Laurel, Elizabeth Chisholm, helped out financially. She was therefore able to concentrate entirely on her studies with Florence Kimball.

When Price performed the role of Mistress Ford in a production of Verdi's *Falstaff*, she caught the eye of composer Virgil Thomson. He was looking for singers for a revival of his opera *Four Saints in Three Acts*, which requires an all-black cast. Price appeared as Cecilia in the opera in New York in 1952 and then at the Paris International Arts Festival. The role led to her casting as Bess in a revival of George Gershwin's *Porgy and Bess*, with which she toured from 1952 to 1954. Price saw the capitals of Europe and married her costar, William C. Warfield. The marriage was not happy and they soon separated, although they did not divorce until the early 1970s.

Price made her concert debut at Town Hall, in New York, in 1954 and was hailed by critics. The next year, she became the first black singer to appear in an opera on television when she sang *Tosca* on NBC. She was a popular and critical success, and NBC invited her back to do Mozart's *Magic Flute*, Poulenc's *Dialogues des Carmélites*, and Mozart's *Don Giovanni*.

In 1957, Price debuted in San Francisco in the Poulenc opera under the baton of Kurt Herbert Adler. To Price's great good fortune, while she was in San Francisco, Antoinetta Stella was taken ill before a performance of *Aida*, and Price was asked to step into the role. It became an important part of her repertoire from that time on. She also appeared with the San Francisco Opera in *Il trovatore* and *Madama Butterfly* and went on, during the same year, to perform in a number of venues in Europe, thus consolidating her reputation. She was introduced to Europe by the conductor Herbert von Karajan. She debuted in Chicago in 1959 in *Turandot*.

Price's formal debut at the Metropolitan Opera in New York came in 1961. She sang Leonora in *Il trovatore* and received a standing ovation that lasted for forty-two minutes. It was the longest ovation the Met had ever seen, and Price became one of the company's great stars. She opened the season the following year in *La fanciulla del west*. Then she opened the next season with *Aida*. In 1966, when the Met moved to Lincoln Center, she opened it with an opera written especially for her by Samuel Barber, *Antony and Cleopatra*. Although the opera was not particularly successful, Price's performance was stunning. She had committed to her preparation with unparalleled zeal, and the effort was rewarded with the performance of a lifetime.

After her 1962 performance of *La fanciulla del west*, she experienced vocal problems that made it clear the role was not for her. As a result, she cut it out of her repertoire and began being more cautious about her voice. Nonetheless, in the years between 1961 and 1969, she appeared in 118 Metropolitan Opera productions. In the 1970s, she cut back her opera appearances and began to focus on concert performances and recordings. In the process, she alienated some opera purists and developed a reputation for being difficult. But, while a number of other Met stars of the 1960s found themselves with ruined or badly compromised voices, Price continued to soar vocally.

In 1985, Price gave her last opera performance, in *Aida* at the Met, but she continued to be quite active into the twenty-first century. Among her other accomplishments is *Aida: A Picture Book for All Ages*, which she published in 1990. She also sang at the centennial celebration of Carnegie Hall in 1991. She has won thirteen Grammy Awards, the Presidential Medal of Freedom, and the Kennedy Center Honors for lifetime achievement in the arts. RCA released *The Essential Leontyne Price* in 1996.

The eleven-disc set, which covers twenty-five years, was met with raptures by critics and the millions of aficionados for whom Leontyne Price has been a true diva and a source of great joy.

See also **Concert Music.**

BIBLIOGRAPHY

Blier, Steven. "Time after Time: Throughout Her Long Career, Leontyne Price Has Inspired Fans and a New Generation of Singers." *Opera News*, October 1996.

Price, Reynolds. "Bouquet for Leontyne." *Opera News*, 1 April 1995.

Southern, Eileen. *The Biographical Dictionary of Afro-American and African Musicians*. Westport, CT: Greenwood Press, 1982.

Steins, Richard. *Leontyne Price: Opera Superstar*. Woodbridge, CT: Blackbirch Press, 1993.

—HILARY MAC AUSTIN

PRIMUS, PEARL (b. 29 November 1919; d. 29 October 1994), dancer, choreographer, and teacher. Pearl Primus set out to be a doctor and became a dancer. In her lifelong study of dance she also became a choreographer, an anthropologist, an educator, and a cultural ambassador. And in her hands dance became a language, a medium of social comment, a channel for anger and frustration, a teaching tool, and an instrument of healing.

Primus was born in Trinidad to Edward and Emily (Jackson) Primus. In 1921 the family moved to New York, where she attended Hunter College High School and graduated from Hunter College in 1940 with a major in biology and premedical sciences. At that time there were no jobs available to blacks in New York's laboratories, so she turned to the National Youth Administration (NYA) for help finding work while she began her graduate studies at night.

The NYA, unable to find the kind of job Primus was looking for, sent her into one of its dance groups as an understudy. Her progress was so rapid that, in the summer of 1941, she auditioned for and won a scholarship to study with New York's New Dance group. There she studied classical and preclassical dance forms with some of the most influential dancers of the time, including Martha Graham, Hanya Holm, Doris Humphrey, Charles Weidman, and Beryl McBurnie. At the same time Primus began researching African dances, visiting museums and consulting published sources, leading up to her first composition, *African Ceremonial*.

On 14 February 1943, in her first professional appearance, Primus presented *African Ceremonial* and three other dances, including an interpretation of Abel Meeropol's antilynching song "Strange Fruit." The response, including a rave review in the *New York Times*, was so encouraging that she decided to embark upon a career in dance. After a ten-month engagement as an entertainer at Café Society Downtown, Primus presented

PEARL PRIMUS, shown here in a dance pose. In addition to her work as a dancer, she was a choreographer, an anthropologist, an educator, and a cultural ambassador. (Scurlock Collection, Archives Center, National Museum of American History, Smithsonian Institution.)

her first solo concert performance, in April 1944 at the Young Men's Hebrew Association.

Primus spent two months of the summer of 1944 in Georgia picking cotton with sharecroppers and attending black churches. She also studied African traditions brought over by slaves and how those traditions evolved in the United States. By the time of her Broadway debut at the Belasco Theater, in October of that year, Primus had developed a set of original works concentrating on her lifelong interests in the lives of black people and in the culture and traditions of Africa.

At the Belasco, Primus appeared for ten days with a troupe that included four male dancers, two drummers, two singers, a five-piece jazz band, a narrator, and folk singer Josh White. The concert included dances of African and Haitian origin, as well as "Slave Market," which portrayed the slave custom of using spirituals to send messages about the Underground Railroad. "The Negro Speaks of Rivers," set to the poem by Langston

Hughes; the jazz number "Rock Daniel"; "Strange Fruit"; and a setting of Josh White's song "Hard Times Blues" were also on the program. In December, Primus began a month-long engagement at the Roxy (movie) Theatre, performing an expanded version of *African Ceremonial* with an ensemble of fourteen dancers.

In 1945 Primus performed concerts in several American cities. For the first ten months of 1946, she appeared as a featured dancer in the second revival of the Broadway musical *Show Boat*, and from November 1946 to February 1947 she toured with her own company.

In 1948 Primus was granted a fellowship from the Rosenwald fund, which enabled her to travel through Africa, living with the peoples of Liberia, Senegal, Ghana, the Gold Coast, Nigeria, Cameroon, Zaire, Angola, and the Congo, among others. In Nigeria she was renamed "Omowale," which means "child returned home." In Liberia she was awarded the Order of the Star of Africa medal by then-president William V. S. Tubman. Everywhere she went in Africa, Primus performed her own dances and observed, studied, and took part in the local native dances. After returning from Africa, Primus wrote and lectured about African dance and began to perform new works informed by her firsthand experience of African dance.

In 1953 in Trinidad, researching West Indian folklore, Primus met Percival Borde, whom she married the following year. Their son, Onwin Borde, born in 1955, grew up to become a master drummer who accompanied and stage-managed some of his mother's later programs. Percival Borde, a distinguished dancer in his own right, made his stage debut in 1958. A few years later Primus and Borde founded the Primus-Borde Dance Studio in New York, where they taught many members of the next generation of African-influenced dancers, until Borde's death in 1979.

In 1959 Primus and Borde moved to Liberia for two years, where Primus performed, taught, studied, and served as the director of Liberia's Performing Arts Center. They returned to New York for a year before setting off on a tour of Africa, sponsored by the Rebekah Harkness Foundation and the U.S. State Department.

During the 1960s and 1970s, education became an increasingly important part of Primus's work. In 1966 her study "A Pilot Study in the Integration of Visual Form and Anthropological Content for Use in Teaching Children Ages Six to Eleven about Cultures and Peoples of the World" resulted in dance classes being introduced into several New York public schools. In 1978 she earned her doctorate in anthropology from New York University.

In addition to teaching dance and choreography at the studio that became the Pearl Primus Dance Language Institute in 1979, Pearl Primus taught anthropology, anatomy, and ethnic dance at major colleges and universities. She served as a consultant to museums and published articles and lectured throughout most of the world. She received awards and honors from a host of universities, organizations, and governments, including the Medal of Art, presented to her by President George H. W. Bush in 1991.

Primus died at her home in New Rochelle, New York, in 1994.

See also Dancers and Choreographers, Modern.

BIBLIOGRAPHY

Emery, Lynn Fauley. *Black Dance in the United States from 1619 to 1970.* Princeton, NJ: Princeton Book, 1988.

Johns, Robert L. "Pearl Primus." In *Notable Black American Women,* edited by Jessie Carney Smith. Detroit, MI: Gale Research, 1992.

McLaren, Joseph. *The African American Encyclopedia,* vol. 5, edited by Michael W. Williams. North Bellmore, NY: Marshall Cavendish, 1993.

Murray, James Briggs. "Pearl Primus." In *International Encyclopedia of Dance: A Project of Dance Perspectives Foundation, Inc.,* edited by Selma Jeanne Cohen. New York: Oxford University Press, 1998.

Rothe, Anna, ed. *Current Biography: Who's News and Why.* New York: H. W. Wilson, 1944.

Sussman, Alison Carb. *Profiles from the International Black Community,* vol. 6, edited by Barbara Carlisle Bigelow. Contemporary Black Biography. Detroit, MI: Gale Research, 1994.

—ROBERT W. LOGAN

PRINCE, LUCY TERRY (b. c. 1724; d. 21 August 1821), poet. Until the archival work of David R. Proper, important details of Lucy Terry Prince's life were undocumented and guesses about them were inaccurate. Unfortunately, gaps in her biography persist, but the information that is available reveals that Prince led a remarkable life as an advocate, devoted mother, wife, and poet.

It seems certain that Lucy Terry was born in Africa, enslaved there, transported first to Bristol, Rhode Island, and later to Enfield, Connecticut, when she was about five years old. Terry's surname suggests that she was probably first purchased by Samuel Terry, a linen weaver and prominent landowner in Enfield and a year later, by some means not clear, became the property of Ebenezer Wells, an innkeeper in Deerfield, Massachusetts. Wells and his wife, Abigail, were childless. Records show that Wells had her baptized in his home on 15 June 1735. Lucy Terry remained in slavery until 1756, at which time she married Abijah Prince, a freeman. Whether Terry was freed by Wells or purchased from him by Prince is not known.

Lucy Terry Prince, or Luce as she was called, was perhaps best known for her thirty-line rhymed poem, "Bars Fight," which was sometimes called the most accurate contemporary account of the Indian raid that occurred on 25 August 1746 in that part of Deerfield known as "The Bars," so named for a common type of field fence with a set of slip-bars. As the poem makes clear, many of Prince's neighbors perished in the attack, which occurred not long after the French and Indian capture of Fort Massachusetts

at North Adams. Although Prince's poem was not published until 1855 in Josiah Gilbert Holland's *History of Western Massachusetts,* it was composed—if not written; there is only slim evidence that Prince was literate—over a century earlier in the year of the raid and almost certainly makes Prince the first black poet in America. Proper argued that as an oral poet, having kept her verse alive, perhaps through repeated performance over the generations, Lucy Prince embodied the tradition of African griot, a singer of history.

"Bars Fight" was Prince's single poem, but it was not the only accomplishment in her long, full life. She was thirty-two when she married Abijah, eighteen years her

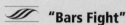 **"Bars Fight"**

The following is one of at least three versions of Lucy Terry Prince's poem, "Bars Fight." Versions vary in orthography and length. Lines five and six are often not included. No manuscript text exists.

BARS FIGHT

August 'twas the twenty-fifth,
Seventeen hundred forty-six
The Indians did in ambush lay,
Some very valiant men to slay,
'Twas nigh unto Sam Dickinson's mill,
The Indians there five men did kill.
The names of whom I'll not leave out.
Samuel Allen like a hero fout,
And though he was so brave and bold,
His face no more shall we behold.
Eleazer Hawks was killed outright,
Before he had time to fight,
Before he did the Indians see,
Was shot and killed immediately.
Oliver Amsden he was slain,
Which caused his friends much grief and pain.
Simeon Amsden they found dead
Not many rods from Oliver's head.
Adonijah Gillett, we do hear,
Did lose his life which was so dear.
John Sadler fled across the water,
And thus escaped the dreadful slaughter.
Eunice Allen see the Indians coming
And hopes to save herself by running;
And had not her petticoats stopped her,
The awful creatures had not catched her,
Nor tommy hawked her on the head,
And left her on the ground for dead.
Young Samuel Allen, Oh! Lack-a-day!
Was taken and carried to Canada.

senior and by all accounts an extraordinary man. Abijah, also known as Bijah, had served four years in the militia during the French and Indian War (1744–1748), and perhaps because of this military service was granted his freedom and three parcels of land in Northfield, Massachusetts. The Princes paid taxes in Northfield but remained in Deerfield until they moved in the 1760s to Guilford, Vermont, on a hundred-acre lot that had been left to Abijah by an employer, Dean Samuel Field. Later, Abijah became one of the sixty-four original grantees and founders of the town of Sunderland, Vermont, where he owned about three hundred acres. Between 1757 and 1769, Lucy and Abijah had six children. Their two oldest sons, Caesar and Festus, enlisted in the militia during the American Revolution. Festus, aged sixteen, appears to have served about three years, including at least five months as an artilleryman at West Point, New York. After the war he married a white woman and settled on a farm in Sunderland. Not much is known of the other children.

It was while she lived in Guilford that Lucy Prince first demonstrated a willingness to defend her rights in a public debate. In 1785, white neighbors, the Noyes family, threatened the Princes' lives and property. Lucy appealed in person to Governor Thomas Chittenden and his Council for protection from these assaults, and on 7 June 1785, the Council ordered the selectmen of the town to defend the Princes. One of her sons, probably Festus, was the impetus for another of Prince's appeals to public authority, when she tried, unsuccessfully, to gain her son's admission to the Free School in Williamstown, which became Williams College in October 1793. Although there is no record of the incident in school archives, Prince is said to have importuned the trustees on her son's behalf, recounting her family's military contributions, quoting the law and the Bible, and reminding her audience of what she considered her friendship with the late Colonel Ephraim Williams, whose property bequeathal had established the Free School. Despite her efforts, however, Prince's son was not admitted.

A short time later, Prince once again seems to have engaged in public debate to establish her rights by pleading a property dispute case in court. Her neighbor, Colonel Eli Bronson, had claimed part of the Sunderland lot that Abijah had been granted by King George III. The town could not settle the matter, and tradition has it that Bronson's lawsuit eventually reached the Supreme Court. Prince was represented by Isaac Tichnor, who later became governor of Vermont, but, according to George Sheldon, a nineteenth-century historian, it was Prince who presented the argument before the court with Justice Samuel Chase of Baltimore presiding. Sheldon wrote that the court ruled in her favor and Justice Chase declared her argument exceptional, "better than he had heard from any lawyer at the Vermont bar." Although widely accepted as fact, the event has never been authenticated. Indeed, new archival research by Proper revealed that the United States Supreme Court was never in session in Vermont. Proper speculated that perhaps Prince argued her case against Bronson in the U.S. Circuit Court during May 1796, since records show that Justice Chase opened a session of the Circuit Court at nearby Bennington that year. According to Proper, "there is probably some truth behind this anecdote, although it defies documentation despite its plausibility."

In 1808, at age seventy-nine, Prince moved to Sunderland from Guilford. Abijah had died fourteen years earlier and was buried at Bennington, some eighteen miles from Sunderland. As evidence of her fortitude and strength, Prince made an annual visit by horseback to her husband's grave up until 1821, the year of her death. The 21 August 1821 obituary that appeared in the *Franklin Herald* of Greenfield, Massachusetts, was a fitting summary of Lucy Prince's life:

> In this remarkable woman there was an assemblage of qualities rarely to be found among her sex. Her volubility was exceeded by none, and in general the fluency of her speech captivated all around her, and was not destitute of instruction and edification. She was much respected among her acquaintance, who treated her with a degree of deference.

See also Poetry.

BIBLIOGRAPHY

Dannett, Sylvia G. L. "America's First Negro Poet." In *Profiles of Negro Womanhood*. New York: Negro Heritage Library, 1966.

Kaplan, Sidney, and Emma Nogrady Kaplan. "Lucy Terry Prince." In *The Black Presence in the Era of the American Revolution, 1770–1800*, edited by Sidney Kaplan. Amherst: University of Massachusetts Press, 1989.

Katz, William Loren. "Lucy and Abijah Prince." *The Black West*. Garden City, NY: Anchor Press, 1973.

Proper, David R. *Lucy Terry Prince—Singer of History*. Deerfield, MA: Pocumtuck Valley Memorial Association, 1997.

Robinson, William H., Jr. "Lucy Terry." In *Early Black American Poets*, edited by William Henry Robinson. Dubuque, IA: W. C. Brown, 1969.

Sheldon, George. *A History of Deerfield, Massachusetts* (1895–1896). Somersworth, NH: New Hampshire Publishing Company, 1972.

Sheldon, George. "Negro Slavery in Old Deerfield," *New England Magazine*, 8 March 1893.

—Jan Furman

PRINCE, NANCY GARDNER

PRINCE, NANCY GARDNER (b. 15 September 1799; d. c. 1856), author, abolitionist, and human-rights activist. Prince's autobiography, *Narrative of the Life and Travels of Mrs. Nancy Prince, Written by Herself* (1850), is distinctive for several reasons. Its narrator wrote it as evidence of her energy, leadership, and agency during the antebellum era, when few black American women wrote or traveled beyond the locations where they were enslaved. It is textual evidence of the presence of a limited number of blacks living in czarist Russia. It defines Prince's leadership, spiritual prowess, and transnational awareness as a black woman traveler, missionary, and reporter across lands and cultures outside the experience of most nineteenth-century African Americans and whites as well. Prince's narrative authenticates her family background, its multiracial origins, the history of traveling seamen, and the extreme difficulties of being nominally free in a slave society.

Prince was born free in Newburyport, Massachusetts, the second of eight children. Although her narrative does not name her mother, her maternal grandfather, Tobias Wornton, was "stolen" from Africa, and her maternal grandmother was a Native American. Her father, of African descent, was Thomas Gardner. Prince grew up hearing the tale of her stepfather, whose life evolved as a traveler. As an African captive, he escaped the slave ship he was on when it reached one of the American colonies' eastern ports. He was later impressed into service at sea for a number of years and died under English control. Two of Prince's brothers also became seamen.

Although Prince seldom lost heart, her young life was mired in poverty and harsh domestic service to help support her mentally deranged, widowed mother and her siblings. Despite her own limited circumstances and intermittent illness from overwork, Prince was determined to fight the kind of poverty that led to prostitution. At fifteen, she endured freezing weather to travel from Salem to Boston to rescue her sister from a brothel. Prince, with the aid of a Mr. Brown, engaged in a strenuous tussle with the madam to rescue her sister successfully. Although struggles to help her rescued sister and mentally ill mother continued, Prince nevertheless took up training for sewing and later married Nero Prince on 15 February 1824.

Having decided to leave America, on 14 April 1824, Prince began her journey to St. Petersburg, Russia, with her husband, who had been a guard for the Russian court and Czar Alexander I. Nero Prince, like other black seamen during the antebellum period, found more opportunities at sea than on land. He first sailed to Russia in 1810. Ever mindful of the conditions marking people of color because she witnessed slavery firsthand in America, Prince was pleased to note the absence of color discrimination in Russia. Her narrative takes the form of a travelogue as she recounts being received at court as a new bride and given a gold watch as a wedding gift. She notes the character of holiday celebrations, burial, and religious practices in Russia. Prince details major events: the Flood of 1824, in which she almost drowned; the St. Petersburg cholera outbreak, which claimed 9,255 victims; and the Decembrist Revolt, where the revolutionists attempted to overthrow Nicholas I and were brutally punished.

As in Massachusetts, Prince was seldom idle. She established a sewing shop and orphanage and participated in the distribution of Bibles through the Russian Bible Society. After nine and one-half years in Russia, Prince's illness caused her to return to the United States, leaving Nero Prince behind to acquire the financial means for a new start in America. Nero Prince died before he was able to join his wife in Massachusetts.

Before and during the second phase of her travels, to Jamaica as a missionary, Prince made her presence felt in the Boston area as a speaker about her Russian experience, as a co-founder of an orphanage for black children (which failed because of limited funds), and as an abolitionist and civil-rights advocate. Her 17 September 1841 letter to William Lloyd Garrison in the *Liberator*, an abolitionist newspaper, exposes the racism of the captain and the rudeness of the black chambermaids on the *Massachusetts*, a steamboat traveling from New York to Providence, Rhode Island. The journey on the *Massachusetts* was perhaps one made on Prince's return from Jamaica in 1841 to raise funds for a free labor school for poor Jamaican girls.

Prince's objective in her first trip to Jamaica in 1840 emerged in part from an activist, reformist, and religious consciousness. But she was also aware of the continuum of black oppression across geographies and was determined to prove the value of emancipation. Her intent in the 1840 trip was to help the Reverend Ingraham with emancipated slaves in Kingston. She was persuaded instead to support Mr. Abbott in St. Ann's Bay until she confronted power- and money-conscious church officials. When she arrived in Kingston, Prince decided to return to America to seek funds for a free labor school where girls could receive an education in exchange for work. Prince was unable to continue her efforts for the school because when she returned to Jamaica in 1842, there was an insurrection preventing any protection of Prince and her co-missionaries. During a difficult journey back to America, Prince survived storms, a threat of piracy, and kidnapping into slavery. Although Prince continued abolitionist activities, little is known about her after 1854.

Prince's autobiographical travel narrative, published again in 1853 and 1856, offers a rare female perspective of a genre dominated by male writers. It reinforces Prince's self-empowerment, liberation, and self-making, even in the face of physical debilitation and social and racial oppression.

See also Autobiography.

BIBLIOGRAPHY

Foster, Frances Smith. *Written by Herself: Literary Production by African American Women, 1746–1892*. Bloomington: Indiana University Press, 1993. Excellent for placing Nancy Prince in a larger context of early African American women writers.

Mason, Mary O. "Travel as Metaphor and Reality in Afro-American Women's Autobiography, 1850–1972." *Black American Literature Forum* 24 (Summer 1990): 337–356. A helpful comparative study of the journey theme in Nancy Prince, Ida B. Wells, and Mary Church Terrell.

Prince, Nancy Gardner. *A Narrative of the Life and Travels of Mrs. Nancy Prince, Written by Herself.* 1850. Reprinted in *Collected Black Women's Narratives*, edited by Henry Louis Gates Jr. New York: Oxford University Press, 1988. Also reprinted in *A Black Woman's Odyssey through Russia and Jamaica*, edited by Ronald G. Walters. New York: Markus Wiener, 1990.

—AUSTRALIA TARVER

PROFESSIONALISM AND PROFESSIONALIZATION.

Professionalism as it pertains to African American women entails three distinct ideas. The first is the significance of African American women's participation in the professions throughout history. The second is the notion of a professional approach to their work. Finally, the idea of professionalization includes the attempts by African American women professionals to increase the skills and expertise of their members, as well as the attempts of white organizations to exclude African Americans by changing standards for inclusion in professions.

Participation in the Professions

Throughout the history of the United States, African American women have had a major influence on the working world. At first, they were not paid for their work, and after they were freed from slavery, they had to fight off racism and sexism to be successful. It is a tribute to the strength and dedication of these women that they were able to overcome insurmountable obstacles and enter the professions. In the early twenty-first century, African American women were members of all the professions, although their greatest numbers were in teaching, nursing, and social work. There is a critical mass of African American women lawyers and physicians, and there is a great history of their involvement in these professions. More and more black women have entered the fields of science, engineering, the clergy, and other professions that are nontraditional for African Americans and women. In fact, the number of African American women in the professions from 1982 to 1992 increased 125 percent, an increase that far surpasses that of African American men over the same period. In the early part of the twenty-first century, more African American women than men had attended colleges and universities in pursuit of graduate degrees and professional careers. Most of the women who paved the way pursued careers in teaching, nursing, and social work.

Teaching. The first African American women professionals were teachers. The guardians of American slavery outlawed the teaching of slaves to read and write because they knew that education was an important avenue toward freedom, even if it was only the freedom of the mind. So it is fitting that the first women professionals were dedicated to helping their own people obtain an education and expand their physical freedom. It is also no mystery

AFRICAN AMERICAN PROFESSIONAL WOMEN. This undated photograph includes Betty Hall, a staunch Republican; De Voda Sommerville, the first black woman graduate at the University of Southern California, in beauty; and the attorney Martha Jefferson Louis, the wife of Joe Louis. (Los Angeles Public Library, SPNB Collection.)

that African Americans valued education highly, as it was for them a means to gain prestige and affluence. It was also the manner by which African American women could leave traditional jobs, such as domestic laborer.

Eleanor Harris and Magaretta Forten were among the first African American teachers. Other pioneers began their own schools. For example, a former slave, Katy (Catherine) Ferguson, started an integrated Sunday school in her New York home in 1793. Sarah Mapps Douglass opened the first school for black girls in Philadelphia and trained many teachers for public schools. In fact, she was one of the first educators to teach science to female students. The American Missionary Association was responsible for creating many elementary and secondary schools for African Americans, and most teachers at those schools were trained at private black institutions supported by religious organizations. Teaching grew as a profession because it was one of the few professions open to women, and it was a way of actively investing in the future of the race.

African American women also have a history of involvement with higher education. Mary McLeod Bethune founded the Daytona Normal and Industrial School for Negro Girls in 1904 that, because of her ingenuity and tireless efforts, merged with Cookman Institute to become Bethune-Cookman College in 1923. The first African American woman to graduate from a recognized American college was Mary Jane Patterson, who graduated in 1862 from Oberlin College in Ohio. The first women to receive PhDs found it difficult to obtain employment in their fields. Though she received her degree in 1921, Eva Beatrice Dykes was not hired by Howard University until 1929. Georgiana R. Simpson also completed her doctorate in 1921 but joined the professorate in 1931. However, Sadie Tanner Mossell Alexander was faced with so much discrimination that she was never able to find employment in the field of economics but went on to law school. Postsecondary teaching remained a nontraditional field for women of any race, and because of continued racism and sexism, African American women account for only a little over 2 percent of the faculty in higher education. A milestone was achieved, however, when Johnnetta Betsch Cole became the first African American woman to be named president of Spelman College.

Nursing. Another profession that African American women entered early in the history of this country was nursing. Because their work as slaves included taking care of the household, many nursing duties fell to the women slaves. Nursing, therefore, was a natural outgrowth of their work and provided women with employment when they were freed from slavery. For the most part, however, their nursing ministrations were delivered primarily to their own families and their white employers. Susie Baker King Taylor was one of the first African American nurses.

She worked closely with Clara Barton during the Civil War, and for four years she cared for wounded soldiers and others. Formal training for all women was elusive in the beginning stages of the profession. Although training did become available for white women, African American women were denied access to equivalent hospital programs. However, Mary Eliza Mahoney was able to gain access to training, and in 1879 she graduated from the New England Hospital for Women and Children in Boston, Massachusetts. She was the first African American nursing graduate. It was not until 1886 that Atlanta Baptist Seminary (later Spelman College) opened the first black school of nursing, which was funded by John D. Rockefeller. Hospital nursing schools were started in the 1890s by black physicians and women's clubs. Even as late as the mid-1920s, of eighteen hundred accredited nursing schools, only fifty-eight admitted African Americans.

 Parallel Professionalism in Medicine

Beginning in the 1890s, a period the historian Rayford Logan referred to as "the nadir" because of the deplorable state of race relations, the black community produced a class of professional men and women who would work across the generations to meet the race's survival needs, promote and nurture its advancement agenda, and in so doing provide a crucial link to the freedom struggles of the 1950s and 1960s. Three concepts capture the process of black professional class development from the Progressive Era through the Great Depression and New Deal and World War II: (1) white separatism, (2) black parallelism, and (3) freedom of opportunity.

The historian Leon Litwack observes that with the emergence of Jim Crow in the 1890s, the white South "segregate[d] the races by law and enforced custom in practically every conceivable situation in which whites and blacks might come into social contact. . . . Not only were the races to be kept apart in hospitals . . . but some denied admission to blacks altogether." Rayford Logan noted ironically that the "doctrine of 'separate but equal' first sanctioned by the United States Supreme Court in *Plessy v. Ferguson* (1896) was a 'radical' concept. But, perhaps unwittingly, Negroes continued to use segregation as a weapon to remove segregation."

Given white southerners' grim determination to separate from black people, the latter were forced to pursue a strategy of parallel institutional development. African Americans created an array of organizations, schools, and healthcare facilities as the grip of legal discrimination and political disfranchisement tightened. The black community invented its own social welfare system and a national network of associations. In 1895 the National Medical Association was formed. Just as the American Medical Association denied membership to African Americans, so did the American Nurses Association. In 1908 black nurses developed the National Association of Colored Graduate Nurses.

The growth of nursing has an important connection with military service, especially where African American women are concerned. The first black woman to work for the military was Namahyoke Sockum Curtis, who recruited others to attend to soldiers with yellow fever and malaria in the Spanish-American War. During World War I, Martha Minerva Franklin led the fight to gain acceptance of black nurses by the army through the American Red Cross, which enrolled army nurses at that time. In 1917, the American Red Cross voted to accept black nurses, but it was not until 1918 that the army assigned African American women to work as nurses in army camps. During World War II, black nurses were accepted into the military on a quota system. Phyllis Daley was the first black woman to receive induction into the nurse corps, but by 1979 Hazel W. Johnson had been made the first female brigadier general of the U.S. Army Nurse Corps.

Following the aftershocks of the 1910 Flexner Report on the quality of medical education and its recommendations for reform that were supported by the American Medical Association, only two black medical schools remained out of the dozen that had been founded in the last third of the nineteenth century. For the next fifty years, Howard University School of Medicine in Washington, DC, and Meharry Medical School in Nashville, Tennessee, bore the burden for training approximately 90 percent of black physicians. Only one of a score of female medical colleges remained viable after the reform impulse subsided, the Woman's Medical College of Pennsylvania.

The numbers of black hospitals and nurse training schools exploded to nearly three hundred by the end of the 1920s. Every white nursing school in the South barred black women, and many in other sections imposed rigid quotas. The black hospital and nursing school network therefore provided career opportunities for black women as well as healthcare to adjacent black communities.

Public or municipal hospitals in the South, and in many states in the country, denied black physicians staff appointments and visiting privileges. One newspaper editor put it bluntly, "most white [medical] practitioners just are not interested in whether Negroes live or die." Black physicians therefore opened proprietary institutions in order to have places in which to attend their own patients with dignity and, of course, to generate income.

Officials of an array of uplift organizations, newspapers, fraternal and mutual aid societies, club women auxiliaries, and educational institutions welcomed affiliation with professionals who had much to gain from connections with prominent civic and religious leaders. Thus black professionals cemented a multifaceted socioeconomic and political agenda grounded in self-interest, to be sure, but fueled by the imperative to forge solidarity within the larger black community.

—DARLENE CLARK HINE

Social Work. From 1898 to 1918, African American social workers made significant contributions to the care of their communities. They were primarily concerned with fostering self-pride, race pride, self-help, and mutual aid. Since African Americans were systematically excluded from the greater social systems in the United States, African Americans were determined to take care of their own. One of the first social workers was most likely Catherine (Katy) Ferguson. Usually noted as a leader in education because of the school she started for girls, Ferguson offered her services not only to African American students but also to poor white children and would certainly qualify as a pioneer in social welfare.

African American women have been involved in lifting up others as they climb to success throughout U.S. history. The most notable of these contributions was the network of black women's clubs most active in the late 1800s and early 1900s. Women in these clubs (often church related) organized schools and day care facilities, homes for girls, job training, moral instruction, and community support for hospitals and nursing schools. Most of the women involved in the clubs were middle class, and many were of the elite classes of African Americans dedicated to helping the poor and less fortunate. In fact, the middle and upper classes were socialized to believe that because they were privileged, they had an obligation to help advance the race and to give back to their communities. The women in these clubs embraced this concept and went on to make major contributions to public health, mental health, truancy, and recreation.

Sarah A. Collins Fernandis, a leader in women's clubs, established the first African American settlement house in Washington, DC, and Rhode Island. Lugenia Burns Hope was a key figure in the network of women's clubs that helped the poor in Atlanta, Georgia, and that evolved into the Neighborhood Union. Using her influence as the wife of the president of Morehouse College, Lugenia Burns Hope helped establish the first School of Social Work for African Americans at Atlanta University in 1920. Janie Porter Barrett turned her own home into a place for needy people in Hampton, Virginia—the Locust Street Social Settlement. She went on to become a superintendent of a school for girls in legal difficulty. By the mid-1920s, the school was ranked as one of the five best institutions of its kind. Many of the most prominent African American social work pioneers donated money and sponsored fund-raising activities to help provide services to people in need.

The National Urban League, founded in 1911, was one of the most significant black organizations of social reform of its time, pursuing numerous social and economic opportunities for blacks. For example, the National Urban League, with its fellowship program, supported many individuals pursuing degrees in social work, including Inabel Burns Lindsay, who was the founding dean of the Howard University School of Social Work. In the 1920s, schools of social work for African Americans were established in Georgia and North Carolina. In the early twenty-first century, many African American colleges, businesses, and churches continued to provide social service programs. Dedication of time and money was still a focus of African American sororities and other women's groups. Black social workers also continued the fight for black families and children as they struggled to sensitize social workers of other races and nationalities to the issues important in the black community.

Other Professions. Nontraditional professions for women in general and African American women in particular include medicine and law. It was difficult enough for African American women to enter professions, and those that chose nontraditional professions had to be especially brave and committed. The earliest records of African American female physicians indicate that twenty-five years after slavery there were 115 women practicing medicine in hospitals, clinics, and black colleges, and by 1900 there were more than 7,000. The first African American woman to receive a medical degree was Rebecca Lee Crumpler, who graduated from the New England Female Medical College of Boston in 1864. Though there had been four black medical schools, by 1914 only Meharry Medical College in Nashville, Tennessee, and Howard University School of Medicine remained open as a result of ever-changing medical school standards. However, gaining a medical degree was only the beginning. Many medical school graduates were discriminated against not only for their race but also for their gender. Black female doctors were primarily involved in treating African American women. Over the decades, African American women physicians not only served their communities with professional skills but they have also founded hospitals, clinics, and training programs for nurses.

In the early twenty-first century, African American women made up a large proportion of black lawyers in the United States. In 1872, Charlotte E. Ray was the first black woman to graduate from law school (Howard University Law School) and to be admitted to the bar in the District of Columbia. She may have been able to practice law, but because of sexism and racism, she was unable to make a living as a lawyer. In 1926, Violette N. Anderson became the first black woman to practice law before the U.S. Supreme Court, and Jane Bolin became the first black woman judge in the court of domestic relations in 1939. Other milestones for black women in the legal profession include the appointment of Constance Baker Motley to serve on the federal bench in 1966 and Pamela Fanning Carter as the first state attorney general (Indiana)

in 1992. Charlotte E. Ray, the first woman lawyer, was not even able to vote, and Constance Baker Motley would have had to sit in the back of the bus the same year she argued against the board of trustees of the University of Alabama in Birmingham.

Because of discrimination, African American women with law degrees found that government employment held more opportunities and security than did private practice.

A Strong Work Ethic

The stereotype of African Americans as lazy emerged and was promoted during slavery to get more work from slaves. To counteract that stereotype, African Americans over the decades have promoted a work ethic that encouraged young people to work hard and to do their best regardless of the task. As Dr. Martin Luther King Jr. is often quoted as saying, "if a man is called to be a street sweeper, he should sweep streets even as Michelangelo painted, or Beethoven played music, or Shakespeare wrote poetry." This kind of work ethic has been enthusiastically endorsed among African Americans.

This work ethic is most relevant to those who would compete professionally with white Americans. African American parents, teachers, church leaders, and other mentors in the African American community admonished young people against mediocrity as a defense against racist and discriminatory practices. In fact, youngsters were warned that they must outperform their white counterparts to be perceived as merely competent. For women, the challenge was even greater because they were discriminated against both for gender and race. African American girls and women were warned that they must be twice as good as their white counterparts. Affirmative action caused many to harbor the belief that African Americans were hired to meet a quota and could not be qualified for the job. African American women who met two affirmative action criteria often found that being twice as good as one's colleagues was sound advice. For many African American women in the professions, this pressure for outstanding performance was present not only in their profession but also in the home. They had to do it all and do it all well, which is the legacy of the African American woman.

Professionalization

The effort to be better than white counterparts was monumental during segregation. African Americans were barred from training institutions with the best facilities, creating the African American tradition to make a way out of no way. African American professionals had to use their creativity and hard work to make their dreams come true. They had to found their own schools and professional organizations. By doing so, they were able not only to train their own people but also to offer quality services to the African American community—a community typically ignored by white professionals. To uplift the quality of training and improve service to African Americans, teachers, nurses, social workers, and other professionals formed professional organizations. These organizations provided training, standards, and, more importantly, an activist agenda to encourage the acceptance of their members into the greater community of professionals in their fields.

Teaching. The early teachers did not attend colleges and universities, yet they were vital to the progress of blacks. In fact, African American women were often encouraged to teach because teaching was seen as the most significant contribution they could make to their people. The schools in which these teachers worked were often inadequate, but teachers persevered and provided the best education they possibly could. One of the ways that education was professionalized was through the teaching methods advocated by the Jeanes Fund. A Quaker heiress, Anna Jeanes, established a fund to improve small southern black schools. The teachers in the program were told to teach cooking, laundering, and sewing, but the Jeanes supervisors were able to help them work in academic curriculum to ready students for higher education. The industrial skills were used to improve conditions of the schools and community, and the academic skills prepared students to be able to leave domestic and field work.

Black teachers like Septima Poinsette Clark worked tirelessly with lawyers and others to integrate schools. However, after the Civil Rights Act passed and schools were ordered to integrate, the schools that served the African American populations were closed, and students were transferred to the previously all-white buildings. Over thirty thousand African American teachers in the southern states lost their jobs as a result of this process. In hindsight, many argued that the closing of the predominantly black schools and the integration of black children into virtually all-white schools—where they did not learn about black history, and they did not have black role models or the black community's involvement in their education—became more of a hindrance than a help to the development of black students.

Nursing, Social Work. African American nurses both gained and lost because of professionalization. Initially, women of all races learned by working in hospitals. They were treated more like domestic help than professionals. In 1896, white nurses organized to form what would eventually become the American Nurses Association to upgrade nursing into a profession. As white women were able to professionalize nursing, they also created barriers for African American nurses to continue in the field. African American nurses, with limited resources, worked hard to improve their own nurse training. They were aware that their training programs were not ideal and sought funding to improve. In her speech to the National Association of Colored Graduate Nurses in 1921, Adah Belle Samuels Thoms encouraged nurses to pursue higher education and to take up specialized training in prenatal care and social service work. Nurses were so badly needed, however, that there were varying requirements for admission to and graduation from black nursing schools. In 1935, Estelle G. Massey-Riddle reported that in her visits to nursing schools she saw some that were so poorly run that she did not know how they could have met the requirements for the board of examiners that approved them. Other schools, though, were pioneers in nursing education.

The American Nurses Association (ANA) continued to push for professionalization but also continued to exclude African American nurses from its roster. In an effort to address the needs of black graduate nurses, Martha Minerva Franklin and Adah Belle Samuels Thoms created the National Association of Colored Graduate Nurses (NACGN) in 1908. The NACGN played a vital role in gaining acceptance for black nurses in the military during the world wars. As a result of their struggles and their persistence, black nurses were able to gain membership into the ANA, and the NACGN was dissolved in 1951.

African Americans also played an important part in professionalizing social work for blacks. Many people practicing social work in the early 1920s received no training, but it was preferable to have it. Several historically black colleges and universities trained social workers. The efforts of professionalization, however, were most evident in the insistence that all workers adopt an Afrocentric paradigm for their work with African Americans. Black social workers encouraged their colleagues to tap the resources of the black community and the extended family. They were vocal in their fight for the preservation of the black family and the culture.

Assessment

The involvement of African American women in the professions over the course of history is awe inspiring. They overcame incomprehensible barriers to reach their achievements. Many of those barriers disappeared, some remained, and new ones developed. The heritage of hard work, dedication, and perseverance will sustain many more African American women in their future endeavors.

See also Alexander, Sadie Tanner Mossell; Bethune, Mary McLeod; Bolin, Jane Mathilda; Clark, Septima Poinsette; Cole, Johnnetta Betsch; Douglass, Sarah Mapps; Ferguson, Catherine; Forten Sisters; Franklin, Martha Minerva; Hope, Lugenia Burns; Johnson, Hazel Winnifred; Mahoney, Mary Eliza; Motley, Constance Baker; Ray, Charlotte E.; Taylor, Susie Baker King; *and* Thoms, Adah Belle Samuels.

BIBLIOGRAPHY

Bolden, Tonya. *The Book of African-American Women: 150 Crusaders, Creators, and Uplifters*. Holbrook, MA: Adams Media, 1996.

Comas-Díaz, Lillian, and Beverly Greene, eds. *Women of Color: Integrating Ethnic and Gender Identities in Psychotherapy*. New York: Guilford Press, 1994.

Edwards, R. L., et al, eds. *Encyclopedia of Social Work*, vol. 1. Washington, DC: NASW Press, 1995.

Greene, B. A. "What Has Gone Before: The Legacy of Racism and Sexism in the Lives of Black Mothers and Daughters." In *Diversity and Complexity in Feminist Therapy*, edited by Laura S. Brown and Maria P. P. Root. New York: Haworth Press, 1990.

Higginbotham, Elizabeth. *Too Much to Ask: Black Women in the Era of Integration*. Chapel Hill: University of North Carolina Press, 2001.

Hine, Darlene Clark, ed. *Black Women in the Nursing Profession: A Documentary History*. New York: Garland, 1985.

Hine, Darlene Clark, ed. *Black Women in United States History, From Colonial Times to the Present*. 16 vols. New York: Carlson, 1990.

Hine, Darlene Clark. "Culture, Consciousness, and Community: The Making of the African-American Woman's History." In *The Lawrence F. Brewster Lecture in History*. Greenville, NC: East Carolina University, 1994.

Hine, Darlene Clark, Elsa Barkley Brown, and Rosalyn Terborg-Penn, eds. *Black Women in America: An Historical Encyclopedia*. 2 vols. New York: Carlson, 1993.

Jackson, Cynthia L. *African American Education: A Reference Handbook*. Santa Barbara, CA: ABC-CLIO, 2001.

Reeser, Linda Cherrey, and Irwin Epstein. *Professionalism and Activism in Social Work: The Sixties, the Eighties, and the Future*. New York: Columbia University Press, 1989.

Robinson, Tracy L., and Mary F. Howard-Hamilton. *The Convergence of Race, Ethnicity, and Gender: Multiple Identities in Counseling*. Upper Saddle River, NJ: Merrill, 2000.

—Kathy Evans

PROGRESSIVE ERA. Many black women made formidable advancements in their education, professional lives, and leadership roles during the Progressive Era. At the same time, black women experienced what has been referred to as the nadir of black history—systematic discrimination and segregation through Jim Crow laws and virulent violence, including lynching. This essay discusses black women's lives from 1890 to 1920, with attention to differences in social class, nativity, educational and occupational attainment, and church and organizational affiliations.

Social Class and Employment

To be expected, there were differences in social class membership during this period, expressed in the material conditions of black women's lives. There was a small group of urban elite whose level of education, wealth, and ancestry gave them privilege not accorded to most blacks. However, their status also required of them certain obligations in terms of exemplary deportment, character, and charity to those less fortunate. To illustrate, Fannie Barrier

Williams had studied painting at the New England Conservatory; following her marriage to lawyer S. Laing Williams, she settled in Chicago, where she became a member of the elite Prudence Crandall Study Club as well as the prestigious, all-white Chicago Woman's Club. At the same time, though, she assisted in numerous fundraisers for the only black hospital in Chicago, helped young working women residing at the Phyllis [*sic*] Wheatley Home, and participated in other forms of social uplift.

In the early 1890s, the black middle class expanded to include businessmen and businesswomen, teachers, clerks, and government workers. Many black women of this social class were college-educated or had completed normal schools and were employed as teachers or other professionals. Given their education and relative privilege, middle-class women, along with the elite, joined mutual women's clubs and community organizations and participated in civic and charity events. As such, they constituted part of the "talented tenth," those who assumed leadership roles in their communities.

By and large, however, the majority of black women during the Progressive Era were working-class and poor. Most, in fact, were agricultural workers and domestic servants who lived in the rural South, as did nearly 90 percent of blacks as of 1910. These women led dramatically different lives from their middle-class counterparts: their work day was extremely long and physically exhausting and their wages were meager. Most had little choice but to leave their children while they worked. Given these conditions, some chose to work in their homes as laundry women or seamstresses so they could care for their children as well as avoid the demanding supervision of white employers.

Some also chose to migrate to the North. Between 1910 and 1920, over 300,000 blacks migrated to the North to secure better employment, exercise their political rights, and escape sexual and physical violence. By 1920, nearly 40 percent of the northern black population lived in the urban centers of New York City, Chicago, Detroit, and Philadelphia. Despite black migrant women's hopes for better employment, many still remained as domestic and laundry workers because of discrimination and false promises from employment agencies. Nonetheless, these women formed the backbone of the working-class black communities, supporting their families and providing better opportunities for their children.

Given discrimination in employment, some black women chose to become entrepreneurs, for example, starting their own sewing or millinery businesses. Black women within the communities supported these businesses, including club women, whose charity balls provided occasions for new dresses and hats as well as the services of hairdressers and beauty culturists. Others became businesswomen by selling beauty products, especially those of

EARTHA M. M. WHITE (seated on steps at left) with her mother, Clara White (seated on steps at right), and residents of the Clara White Old Folks home. Eartha White, an educator and publisher, was active in a number of progressive causes. (Florida State Archives.)

Madam C. J. Walker. Walker had learned her skills while working under Annie Turnbo Malone, the first black beautician and chemist to develop her own line of face and hair products. Walker exemplified the bootstrap ideology of the industrial educator Booker T. Washington as much as anyone. A daughter of slaves, Walker had worked as a domestic worker and laundress. With less than two dollars she started her own beauty business in 1905. Her hair grower and scalp treatments were especially popular among black women because of the prevalence of scalp disease due to poor nutrition and hygiene, ill health, and the use of chemical hair treatments. For "Walker agents," selling these products provided a viable alternative to domestic service. Further, agents developed a sense of pride in selling "race" products that were created for them by a black woman who had become a millionaire by 1910. By 1916, nearly twenty thousand agents worked for Walker and her company.

Some working-class black women also secured jobs in factories. As of 1900, only 3 percent of black women worked in segregated factory lines, compared to seven times as many foreign-born women and nearly ten times as many native-born white women. This pattern of discrimination would persist even though the next generation of black women was more educated overall than the other two groups. Most factory workers were employed on embroidery, bed making, needlework, and garment lines in the North. However, only 2 percent of black women employed in nonagricultural work in the South were employed in

factories as of 1910. Most worked in cotton mills, tobacco and cigar factories, and oyster-shucking businesses.

In professional employment, black women also made progress. As of 1890, black women constituted only 25 percent of all black professionals. By 1910, that percentage had increased to 40, although only 3 to 4 percent of black women employed in southern states were categorized as such. Although many professionals became social workers, probation officers, librarians, nurses, journalists, and doctors, most were teachers. In fact, by 1919 nearly 80 percent of black teachers nationally were female. This pattern was especially prevalent in the South, where most taught in segregated, overcrowded schools for considerably lower salaries than their white female counterparts. Other southern teachers were employed through the Anna T. Jeanes Fund. In this capacity, they functioned as intermediaries between schools, families, and communities in their efforts to improve conditions for students. Some black female teachers also became principals and deans, such as Margaret Murray Washington of Tuskegee Institute. Even fewer became professors at historically black colleges, including Hallie Quinn Brown of Wilberforce College and Anna Julia Cooper of Lincoln University, who had received her doctorate at the Sorbonne.

Black women also entered the health professions as nurses and doctors. Because most hospitals, even in the North, refused health care to blacks, there was clearly a great need for qualified medical staff. Because black nurses nonetheless found their employment limited, they founded the National Association of Colored Graduate Nurses in 1908 to improve nursing education and provide a national employment registry. Regardless, black nurses received lower wages and worked longer hours than white nurses. Likewise, black female doctors' employment opportunities were restricted to black hospitals, social settlements, and agencies that segregated health services for blacks. To serve black communities better, some opened their own clinics and dispensaries, such as Fannie Emanuel of Chicago. Others, such as Dr. Rebecca Cole, visited the tenements, giving mothers instructions in health and hygiene. Several also founded hospitals and training schools. One was Sarah Boyd Jones, who founded the Richmond Hospital and Training School of Nurses after completing her medical degree at Howard University in 1893. Despite the prodigious work of black female doctors, there were far too few to serve their communities—only sixty-five as of 1920.

The increasing number of black newspapers and journals provided opportunities for women as journalists and writers. Pauline Hopkins, playwright and novelist, published frequently in the *Colored American Magazine*, as did novelist Jessie Fauset in the *Crisis*. Perhaps the most eminent of black female journalists, Ida B. Wells-Barnett, became known nationally and internationally for her articles decrying lynching and other acts of white mob violence. Wells-Barnett herself was literally driven out of Memphis and threatened with lynching because of her strong condemnation of the murder of three innocent black men. Thereafter she worked for the *New York Age* as well as continuing her antilynching campaign in England and Scotland, publishing a pamphlet, *Southern Horrors: Lynch Law in All Its Phases*, in 1892. One year later, she protested the absence of black representation in the Chicago World's Fair's administration in her co-publication, *The Reason Why the Colored American Is Not in the World's Columbian Exposition*. She would continue her investigative publishing with her husband, Ferdinand Barnett, through their newspaper, the *Chicago Conservator*.

Black women also trained as social workers and probation officers during the early twentieth century. The growth in these professions coincided with the expansion of various courts, including juvenile, morals, and municipal, as well as legislative provisions to protect dependent, orphaned, and delinquent children. Although some of these professionals were hired by the courts, most worked in their own communities' social settlements, nurseries, and homes for children and youth. Others were employed through the National Urban League (NUL), which had established training fellowships for social workers as well as acting as a clearinghouse for their employment. However,

since there was a dearth of trained social workers and probation officers, community institutions often relied upon the volunteerism of club and church women.

Social welfare professionals' work was compromised by the limited social services they could offer their clients, since many state and municipal institutions refused to give blacks assistance. For example, few black mothers received mothers' pensions (the precursor to Aid for Dependent Children) compared to immigrant and native-born women, in large part because court officials claimed that black mothers did not meet the criterion of moral fitness. Here, single black mothers fueled stereotypes about black women's promiscuity and "disorganized" family life.

Further, black mothers' morality was questioned because they often took in lodgers to offset high rents. Given the menial salaries of many black mothers who worked as cooks and domestic maids, lodgers were a necessary supplement to their wages. Moreover, female lodgers usually assisted mothers with child care. But social workers saw things differently. Their adherence to the nuclear family model ran counter to the strength and resilience of black extended families; as such, they found these housing arrangements "disorganized" and "immoral."

These stereotypes also led to a disproportionate number of black girls being classified as delinquent. Black women, keenly aware of this problem, engaged in protective work. They met girls and young women at the railway station, then directed them to the black YWCAs or other safe residencies. They organized recreational programs and supervised dances to provide wholesome alternatives to public dance halls, roadhouses, and nickelodeons. And knowing that most reformatories refused to admit delinquent girls, black women founded their own community facilities.

Clearly, black women made strides in their employment. But regardless of their type of work, black women worked five times more than any other group of ethnic women, at least as of 1920. Further, they generally remained in the workforce for a longer time and in more menial and lower-paying jobs. Black women would turn to education as one way to improve their living conditions.

Black Women's Education

As of 1890, there were a number of higher educational institutions attended by black women. Some chose to enroll in predominantly white institutions, including Oberlin College, the Seven Sisters colleges, and land-grant universities. But there they often faced discrimination; for example, they were not allowed to live in the dormitories and so had to make other boarding arrangements. Most black females, though, chose to enroll in historically black colleges such as Wilberforce University, Spelman and Fisk colleges, black land-grant universities, and the Tuskegee and Hampton institutes. These schools did more than prepare young black women as teachers, nurses, social workers, and librarians. Certainly, Spelman's express mission was to prepare teachers and missionaries. But its goals also included the cultivation of respectability and Christian morality, the very foundation of race progress. Similarly, although Tuskegee's primary mission was teacher preparation, it offered sewing, cooking, millinery, and laundry classes to prepare female students for their future roles as mothers and housewives. The staff there also held female students to the highest standards of behavior and deportment. Young women were under strict supervision and chaperoned to all public events.

The need for black teachers led to the creation of black normal schools such as Palmer Memorial Institute; established by Charlotte Hawkins Brown, it was the first normal school in North Carolina. Following in the tradition of other black school founders—Mary McLeod Bethune of Bethune-Cookman College in Florida and Lucy Laney of Haines Normal and Industrial Institute in Georgia—Brown gave up her marriage and a family life to devote herself to her vision of educating young black women. Like Bethune, Brown expanded her school through prodigious fund-raising, securing monies from the northern philanthropists. And like Bethune and Laney, Brown was deeply involved in the black women's club movement and the black teachers' association. For all three women, the activities of teaching and club work were mutual enterprises.

For nursing, Spelman had established the first black nurses' training department in 1886; by 1900 the college had added a hospital and infirmary. Other nurses' training schools were established at Provident Hospital in Chicago, the Tuskegee and Hampton institutes, and the Freedmen's Hospital and the Meharry Nurse Training School in Washington, DC. Most black female physicians, too, received their medical training at black colleges, such as Meharry Medical College and Howard Medical School; only a few attended the predominantly white Woman's Medical College of Pennsylvania.

Many black female social workers trained at Fisk and Atlanta universities, known for their model schools of social work. Additionally, these students engaged in social and activist work at the affiliate black settlement houses, Bethlehem House in Nashville and Atlanta Neighborhood Union in Atlanta. Lugenia Burns Hope, founder of the latter settlement, nurtured a community perspective amongst the students, who organized classes, made home visits to the sick, provided child care in the nursery, and advocated for better school facilities in Atlanta. As such, social work was indelibly connected to social uplift.

In order to professionalize domestic workers as well as to increase their wages, notable black female educators—including Nannie Burroughs, Mary McLeod Bethune, Jane Edna Harris Hunter, and Lucy Laney—founded domestic training schools. Their curricula also struck a moral chord, for homes were the very source of race progress. At the National Training School for Girls in Washington, DC, Burroughs became known for her motto of the three Bs, "the Bible, the bath, the broom," which carried the obligation of respectable and Christian behavior. Because of white men's sexual assaults, Burroughs insisted that domestic servants be beyond their reproach. She and other educators were well aware of the stereotypes black domestics often faced: the mammy, as portrayed in the film *Birth of a Nation*, or Jezebel, an image promoted by white men to justify their sexual behavior.

Schools were not the only institutions that educated women. The black women's club movement promoted educational opportunities for women and their children through the establishment of social settlements, kindergartens, and other community facilities.

Black Women's Club Movement

If any one word spoke to black women's collective sense of identity and how they wanted to be perceived by others, it was "respectability." Given the double discrimination of race and gender faced by black women, the concern for respectability permeated every aspect of their lives: their employment, their education, and their important roles as mothers, wives, and members of their communities. The rhetoric of the "cult of true womanhood," circumscribed around native-born white women's lives, did not adequately address the historic and economic conditions of most black women's lives. Nonetheless, black women and men did advance arguments about respectable behavior. Black men, especially ministers, stated that because family life and motherhood were paramount, black women's education should be of a Christian and moral nature. Because of the emphasis on moral character, their descriptions of black mothers sometimes tended to be idealized versions, often masking the difficult economic and social conditions faced by many black women. Such attitudes prompted the black educator Anna Julia Cooper, in *A Voice from the South*, to conclude that black men's elevation of black women was archaic.

Black women instead sought uplift, not elevation; they sought an education that instructed them, not idealized them. They were also keenly aware of the historical effects of slavery, especially the aspersions cast upon their moral character. And because they had been historically denied their own expressions of motherhood and home, they immediately began the task of articulating their own visions. This was accomplished through the establishment of black colleges, mothers' and women's clubs, and black women's involvement in social and religious institutions. In their roles as "other mothers," a term from

Patricia Hill Collins's *Black Feminist Thought*, black middle-class women taught other women through their clubs and their exemplary behavior and deeds.

It was, in fact, the concern for respectability that ushered in the black women's national club movement. Prior to the formation of the National Association of Colored Women (NACW), there were black women's clubs in some cities. One of the better known was the Woman's Era Club, established in Boston in 1893 by Josephine St. Pierre Ruffin. Composed mostly of teachers, the club published the *Woman's Era*, the first American magazine by black women. In 1895 Ruffin published a copy of a southern journalist's letter that castigated black women. It cast aspersions on their moral character and so incensed them that they decided to form a national organization.

Club women convened and organized the National Federation of Afro-American Women, which joined the Colored Women's League to became the NACW in 1896. The NACW's departments reflected the club women's twinned concerns of home life and motherhood: child welfare, kindergarten, mothers' meetings, day nurseries, temperance, domestic science, and hygiene. Building upon women's traditional roles as caretakers, the members extended their influence to promoting political issues such as antilynching legislation and suffrage, as well as protesting discrimination in railway transportation and employment. Through state, regional, and city affiliations, black club women collectively formed a critical mass of informed citizens. By 1914, the NACW had a membership of fifty thousand women in over one thousand clubs and twenty-eight state federations.

Linda Gordon has astutely noted the similarities between black and white club women. That is, most were middle-class, although some black clubs did include working-class women, such as the Salisbury Colored Women's Civic League of North Carolina. Likewise, many club women were or had been teachers or held other professional jobs. Last, many were married, often to professionals such as doctors and lawyers. Such women, in Fannie Barrier's estimation, were needed to help change public opinion about black women. However, as Gordon also emphasizes, there were significant differences between black and white club women. Although black club women may have held more status and privilege than their poorer sisters, there was less distinction between rich and poor blacks. Almost all blacks, regardless of their social class, faced residential segregation and discrimination in employment and access to public facilities.

Nonetheless, club women drew class distinctions in activities reserved for them only. In their meetings, they studied and discussed literature for self-edification. They listened to Wagner's operas as well as black composers and performers. They wrote poetry, performed plays, and gave dramatic readings and oratories to cultivate their talents. However, most club members also used these skills to organize fund-raising activities for community institutions. And in the spirit of the NACW's motto, "lifting as we climb," they generally reached down, not across, to those less fortunate.

Given the segregation of most social welfare institutions during the Progressive Era, one of the most enduring legacies of the black club women's movement was the establishment of kindergartens, nurseries, social settlements, employment bureaus, libraries, mothers' and girls' clubs, and homes for single working women, orphans, dependents, and the elderly and infirm. To illustrate, club women visited homes as teachers and volunteers in kindergartens, providing mothers with instructions on child and home care. At Tuskegee Institute, Margaret Murray Washington established a kindergarten as well as mothers' meetings, which attracted nearly three hundred women each Saturday at a local grocery store. There mothers learned about domestic and social matters, including dressmaking, their duties to their homes, temperance, and canning food. Such activities reflected black club women's belief that the home was the foundation and future of all race progress. As the first NACW president, Mary Church Terrell, espoused, "Homes, more homes, better homes, purer homes."

Washington also organized the Tuskegee Woman's Club, composed of the female teachers and faculty wives of Tuskegee Institute. Like most clubs, members engaged in literary and musical programs. But they also established the E. A. Russell Settlement House, with its own agricultural and industrial school. They started a small library, a night school, and a Sunday school, as well as "social purity" clubs for girls and a woman's conference, where women continued their nonformal education. This club illustrated how successful the outreach of black women's clubs was.

Throughout southern and northern cities, club women also organized Phyllis (or Phillis, both spellings used in various cities) Wheatley Homes for young working women. These homes served a number of purposes. First, they provided affordable housing for single working women. Second, the homes provided camaraderie and recreational activities for young women after a day's work. Third, many of the homes offered industrial classes and had employment bureaus, thereby assisting young women in finding work or in improving their job prospects. Lastly, according to their advertisements, the homes offered protection from the vices of cities. It is not entirely clear, though, how the young working women responded to the staff's supervision. To be sure, there were competing entertainments and images of sexuality for young women in the dance halls, vaudeville, and minstrel shows, where ragtime and blues were made popular by performers such as Ma Rainey and Bessie Smith.

Black club women also fought for political causes, as exemplified by one organization, the Negro Fellowship League. Aware of the need for a reading room, employment bureau, and legal representation, Ida B. Wells-Barnett established this settlement in Chicago. She continued to use her journalism to publicize the mistreatment of black prisoners; she also visited the prisoners on behalf of their families. Arguing that there should be a complete investigation of the race riots in East St. Louis, Wells-Barnett printed the testimony and photographs of the riot. The league also engaged in letter-writing campaigns, advocating for an antilynching law and publicizing the discriminatory practices of businesses.

Black club women fought for suffrage as well, advancing various arguments. Fannie Barrier Williams and Mary Church Terrell emphasized that black women were better prepared than black men had been when they received the right to vote. The club woman and YWCA worker Adella Hunt Logan stressed that women could make more significant social changes if given the vote. More specifically, they could help improve the conditions of black schools and homes by creating legislation to protect children and families. Nannie Burroughs, too, insisted that suffrage would give black women access to legal redress against white men's assaults. Significantly, black women, especially in the South, hoped that suffrage would help to redress the violence and disenfranchisement their men faced.

Accordingly, black women established their own suffrage clubs and associations, given the exclusion of white women's organizations. Indeed, white northern suffragists, including Susan B. Anthony, more often sided with white southern women at the expense of black women's involvement. For example, at a national suffrage parade in 1913 sponsored by the National Woman Suffrage Association, Ida B. Wells-Barnett was prohibited from marching with the white Illinois delegation. Wells-Barnett nonetheless refused to honor the association's orders and marched with the delegation. In addition to marching in suffrage parades, black women signed petitions and helped to register voters. When granted the right to vote, they educated one another about political candidates, created voting blocs, and later became delegates at state conventions.

Clearly, the black women's clubs were remarkable in their scope of social and political activities. Through their volunteerism and organizational skills, they created and sustained community institutions, fought discrimination on various fronts, and gained the right to vote. Further, the black women's clubs created a space where black women could receive recognition. Many of the club women had also been active members of black national organizations, especially the National Association for the Advancement of Colored People (NAACP) and the NUL. But they did not usually receive credit for their work, nor were they accorded leadership positions. Kathryn Johnson, for one, canvassed throughout the country to establish NAACP branches yet was summarily dismissed three years later, in 1916. Similarly, black women volunteered for the NUL's chapters, distributing information to southern migrants, offering advice on housing and employment, and teaching mothers hygiene, cleanliness, and thrift, yet official positions remained closed to them.

The club women worked in tandem not only with these organizations but also with black women's church groups, the Black Young Women's Christian Association (YWCA), and Women Christian Temperance Union (WCTU). To be sure, most black club women were active in their churches, the YWCAs, and the WCTUs. In fact, networking and joint memberships were vital for successful fund-raisers and for co-sponsoring events.

Black Women in Church and Christian Organizations

Like other women's organizations, most black YWCAs were segregated, operating as branches of the white YWCAs or independently of them. The first black YWCA opened in 1893 in Dayton, Ohio, followed by others in eastern and mid-Atlantic cities and on college campuses such as Spelman, Wilberforce, and Tuskegee. Like the Phyllis Wheatley Homes, they provided safe accommodations for working women of the domestic and industrial classes and assistance in securing employment.

Under the leadership of Eva Bowles, secretary for the YWCA's Department of Colored Work, the number of black YWCA chapters grew to forty-five during World War I. In the spirit of patriotism, these chapters sponsored hostess houses where black soldiers and their families could visit together. The black YWCAs also organized fund-raisers for the Liberty Loan drives and participated in the thrift savings stamp program. They provided comfort kits for soldiers as well as continuing to assist women with securing wartime employment. Some YWCA workers also engaged in war work overseas. Addie Hunton, for one, traveled to France to give support to black soldiers.

As with the YWCAs, black women formed their own segregated WCTU chapters, with a Department of Colored Work at the national level. Nonetheless, some black and white chapters worked together, as was the case in North Carolina, where members supported a public health program. For these and other WCTU members, temperance was connected to social purity, respectability, and a strong family life. These issues were the core of the NACW's and the YWCA's work as well. Not surprisingly, prominent club and church women supported temperance work. Hallie

Quinn Brown, a noted elocutionist, professor, and, later, NACW president, lectured throughout Europe from 1894 to 1899 on behalf of a British temperance group. Lucinda "Lucy" Thurman, superintendent of the Department of Colored Work and NACW president in 1908, continued her temperance work in both organizations.

Church women, too, were active in temperance, providing instruction in temperance and organizing temperance clubs. However, the church women were active in various political and social programs as well. Like the club women, black women in the Baptist Church created a space wherein they could enact progressive reform by organizing a woman's auxiliary at the 1900 National Baptist Convention. Evelyn Higginbotham has closely examined how black Baptist women emphasized issues similar to the NACW clubs, such as education, hygiene, child care, and industrial training. Similarly, these women espoused middle-class ideologies in their roles as teachers and missionaries. And finally, they organized at the state and local levels, sponsoring programs as various as publishing houses, schools, mothers' clubs and classes, and homes for orphans, the infirm, and the elderly. In their 1913 convention's manifesto they turned to more political issues: improving housing conditions, equalizing school funds, advocating for better prisons, and protesting lynching and segregated railway transportation.

Similarly, women's roles in the African Methodist Episcopal (AME) Church expanded so that some became stewardesses, preachers, and missionaries. The establishment of the Women's Home and Foreign Missionary Society in 1904 was one catalyst. However, even before 1904, some women were active in the missionary movement. Amanda Smith, a preacher and revivalist for the AME Church, traveled to the British Isles, where she participated in temperance conferences. She then went to India and Liberia, where she continued her temperance and missionary work. In the midst of her work, she reflected on how she had not done enough missionary work in her own country. Returning to the United States, she started an orphanage in Harvey, Illinois, in 1899. Fanny Jackson Coppin, teacher and principal of the Institute for Colored Youth in Philadelphia, traveled with her husband, an AME bishop, to South Africa, where she organized temperance societies and assisted with the establishment of an AME school.

Culture of Disemblance

The lives of black women during the Progressive Era were complex and varied. In the face of threats, insults, and assaults, they were resilient and utilized multiple strategies. Poor southern black women resisted the intrusion of white employers by creating what Darlene Clark Hine has called a "culture of disemblance"; that is, black women created a mask of sociability with their white supervisors while protecting their own true identities. Middle-class black women, too, resisted much: black men's chivalrous attitudes; a white male's slanderous remarks about their morality; and the divisive approaches of white women's organizations that played to the southern etiquette of race relations.

ISABELLA DORSEY on the front steps of the Dorsey Home for Dependent Colored Children. This photograph was printed in the *Rochester Herald* on 15 May 1921. (Albert R. Stone Negative Collection, Rochester Museum and Science Center, New York.)

Through the establishment of industrial and preparatory schools, black women ensured that a younger generation of females would assume their future roles as mothers and community leaders. Through their professional involvement in colleges, libraries, hospitals, and courts, black women advanced the race while providing services that would have otherwise been absent. Through their clubs, churches, and Christian-affiliated groups, black women created community institutions, fought for political inclusion, and protested Jim Crow laws and practices. Through their own national organizations, black women created a visible place where they were recognized for their formidable achievements.

See also Bethune, Mary McLeod; National Association of Colored Women; Physicians; Terrell, Mary Eliza Church; Wells-Barnett, Ida B.; *and* Young Women's Christian Association.

BIBLIOGRAPHY

Bundles, A'Lelia. *On Her Own Ground: The Life and Times of Madam C. J. Walker*. New York: Scribners, 2001.

Collins, Patricia Hill. *Black Feminist Thought*. New York: Routledge, 1990.

Gilmore, Glenda Elizabeth. *Gender and Jim Crow: Women and the Politics of White Supremacy in North Carolina, 1896–1920*. Chapel Hill: University of North Carolina Press, 1996.

Gordon, Linda. "Black and White Visions of Welfare: Women's Welfare Activism, 1890–1945." *Journal of American History* 78 (February 1991): 559–590.

Hendricks, Wanda A. *Gender, Race, and Politics in the Midwest: Black Club Women in Illinois*. Bloomington: Indiana University Press, 1998.

Hewitt, Nancy A. *Southern Discomfort: Women's Activism in Tampa, Florida, 1880s–1920s*. Urbana: University of Illinois Press, 2001. This book painstakingly examines the activism of various ethnic women's groups in one southern city.

Higginbotham, Evelyn Brooks. *Righteous Discontent: The Women's Movement in the Black Baptist Church, 1880–1920*. Cambridge, MA: Harvard University Press, 1993. The definitive book on black Baptist women's activism.

Hine, Darlene Clark. *Hine Sigh: Black Women and the Re-Construction of American History*. Brooklyn, NY: Carlson, 1994. This collection of essays portrays the scope and depth of Hine's work.

Hine, Darlene Clark, and Kathleen Thompson. *A Shining Thread of Hope: The History of Black Women in America*. New York: Broadway Books, 1998. A history that is accessible but does not compromise the complexity of the subject.

Jones, Jacqueline. *Labor of Love, Labor of Sorrow: Black Women, Work and the Family, from Slavery to the Present*. New York: Basic Books, 1985. Still the most complete history about black women's employment and working conditions.

Knupfer, Anne Meis. *Toward a Tenderer Humanity and a Nobler Womanhood: African American Women's Clubs in Turn-of-the-Century Chicago*. New York: New York University Press, 1996.

Lasch-Quinn, Elisabeth. *Black Neighbors: Race and the Limits of Reform in the American Settlement House Movement, 1890–1945*. Chapel Hill: University of North Carolina Press, 1993.

Neverdon-Morton, Cynthia. *African American Women in the Struggle for the Vote, 1850–1920*. Bloomington: Indiana University Press, 1998.

Neverdon-Morton, Cynthia. *Afro-American Women of the South and the Advancement of the Race, 1895–1925*. Knoxville: University of Tennessee Press, 1989.

Salem, Dorothy C. *To Better Our World: Black Women in Organized Reform, 1890–1920*. Brooklyn, NY: Carlson, 1990. Remains one of the most thorough studies of the black women's club movement.

Shaw, Stephanie. *What a Woman Ought to Be and to Do: Black Professional Women Workers during the Jim Crow Era*. Chicago: University of Chicago Press, 1996.

Weisenfeld, Judith. *African American Women and Christian Activism: New York's Black YWCA, 1905–1945*. Cambridge, MA: Harvard University Press, 1997.

Wesley, Charles Harris. *The History of the National Association of Colored Women's Clubs: A Legacy of Service*. Washington, DC: National Association of Colored Women's Clubs, 1984.

White, Deborah Gray. *Too Heavy a Load: Black Women in Defense of Themselves, 1894–1994*. New York: Norton, 1999. The only book that examines the major black women's organizations from the club movement to the present.

—Anne Meis Knupfer

PROTESTANT CHURCHES, BLACK.

The Protestant arm of black Christianity was forged out of a desire to seek the Lord for sincere worship and to establish safe sanctuary from a hostile chattel slave environment. The Protestant church is defined as any order of Christians who do not belong to the Roman Catholic Church or the Orthodox Eastern Church. The Protestant Reformation began in sixteenth-century Europe, when religious purists opposed the rising secularism and materialistic spirit that the Renaissance had brought to the Roman Catholic Church. Toward this end, in 1517, Martin Luther challenged the church to address their bifurcated interests. His challenge led to a revival of faith among individual believers. Luther translated the Bible into German and espoused a priesthood of believers, rather than a priesthood based on a hierarchy.

African American religious expression and experience in early America had roots in Methodist and Baptist congregations across the eastern seaboard. The Methodist Church was primarily located in the mid-Atlantic and northeastern United States, while the Baptist Church remained a southeastern stronghold.

When women are added to the equation of African American religious freedom and expression, the story of liberation becomes more complex. Black women faced challenges to their calling from within the African American community as well as from the dominant society. From the eighteenth century until the beginning of the twenty-first, African American women religious activists confronted these obstacles. Despite opposition, black women in the Methodist, Baptist, Quaker, Episcopal, and Sanctified Churches, among others, wrestled in the spirit realm to find the place that God called them to occupy. Some found it in historically black denominations such as the African Methodist Episcopal (AME) Church, founded in 1816; the African Methodist Episcopal Zion (AME Zion)

BAPTISM IN THE JAMES RIVER, c. 1900–1925. According to a note on the photograph, this was an annual baptizing by Bishop "Daddy" Grace. (Valentine Richmond History Center, Virginia.)

Church, founded in 1822; the Christian Methodist Episcopal (CME) Church, founded in 1870; and the Church of God in Christ (COGIC), founded in 1895. Others found their place in denominations with interracial origins such as the Black Baptists founded in 1773–1775, the Black Holiness Movement founded in 1877, and the Pentecostal denomination founded in 1906. Many of these churches eventually developed independent local and regional black congregations. Another group of female leaders answered their call in historically white denominations with a significant African American following such as the Shakers, the United Methodists, and the Episcopalians.

Three Epochs

The contributions of notable women of faith can be placed in three epochs: the Genesis Generation, 1787– 1850; the Exodus Explorers, 1855–1930; and the Era of Elizabeth, 1935–2000. During these three eras, women's involvement in domestic and international ministry expanded as Protestant women utilized their religious fervor to create church auxiliaries, schools, and organizations that employed the social Gospel. According to the scholar Gayle Tate, "The centeredness of spirituality in the lives of these gospel pioneers allowed them to transcend all of the conventional bonds of womanhood, imbuing them with vision, courage, and fortitude."

The Genesis Generation, 1787–1850. As in Scripture, the Genesis Generation established the beginning of the black church movement. Operating in the wake of the American Revolution and the First Great Awakening, these women witnessed American liberty firsthand. They also came of age during a time of increased nationalism and an emphasis on Republican motherhood. Many of the African American religious leaders of this period were enslaved or the offspring of enslaved parents. Women of the Genesis Generation included the itinerant preacher Elizabeth (1766–1866); the AME member Jarena Lee (1783–1850); the AME member Zilpha Elaw (1790–1845?); the Shaker elder Rebecca Cox Jackson (1795–1871); the AME Zion member Sojourner Truth (1799–1883); and the Methodist Julia Foote (1823–1900).

The earliest documented African American Protestant was an enslaved woman named Elizabeth who heard God's calling to ministry, despite her status. Answering His call, she spread the Gospel and converted several groups of people to Christianity. Elizabeth wrote about her calling and her years as a minister in a narrative written and published when she was in her late eighties. In *Elizabeth, A Colored Minister of the Gospel Born in Slavery*, she wrote "I often felt the overshadowing of the Lord's Spirit." She was sold away from her family at age eleven and experienced extreme loneliness. After receiving a severe beating from an overseer, Elizabeth recalled her mother's words and found strength knowing that there was no one to look to but God:

> I betook myself to prayer, and in every lonely place I found an altar. . . . My spirit was then *taught* to pray, Lord have mercy on me Christ save me. . . . The next day, when I had come to myself, I felt like a new creature in Christ, and all my desire was to see the Saviour.
>
> (Elizabeth, p. 3)

Jarena Lee, another religious activist from this generation, was the first woman to petition the AME Church for a license to preach. She submitted the petition in 1809 and it was denied. However, this did not stop her and she continued to preach and share the gospel with anyone willing to listen. She made a conscious effort to talk about her conversion to let people know that the Christian God was real. In 1849 she made a second request for a license to preach; this time, Bishop Richard Allen, recognizing her special talent for religious work, granted her request.

Unlike Lee, Rebecca Cox Jackson was born to a free family. Her religious experience differed because she belonged to a Shaker community in Pennsylvania. By the time she reached her early fifties, she had received permission to establish her own congregation of African American Shaker women. She spent the years preceding this milestone as an itinerant preacher, sharing God's message with a diverse audience of men and women, blacks and whites. In 1831 the AME Bishop Morris Brown attended one of her meetings with the intention of stopping her, but after listening, he declared, "If ever the Holy Ghost was in any place, it was in that meeting. Let her alone now."

 Methodist Women

The African Methodist Episcopal (AME) denomination is the oldest and largest of the predominantly African American churches in the Methodist tradition, founded as a single church in 1794 and becoming a denomination in 1816. It was slow to give official acceptance to female clergy, first ordaining them as deacons in 1948 but not as ministers until 1960. Rev. Carrie T. Hooper in 1964 was the first female candidate for bishop in the AME Church. Her candidacy had little support. In the following years, a few women obtained positions in the AME Church administration or were appointed pastor of one of the large congregations. Rev. Carolyn Tyler Guidry, a Presiding Elder supervising nineteen churches in Los Angeles, received considerable support as a candidate for bishop in both 1996 and 2000 but was unsuccessful.

In 1980 Rev. Marjorie Swank Matthews, a white woman, was the first female elected bishop in the United Methodist Church. In 1984, Rev. Leontine T. C. Kelly, an African American, was elected as the second female bishop in the United Methodist Church. Subsequently, several other women were elected United Methodist bishops, including three African Americans in 2000: Revs. Linda Lee, Violet Fisher, and Beverly Shamana. Rev. Barbara Harris became a Suffragan (Assistant) Bishop in the Episcopal Church in 1989, the first African American woman to do so.

In July 2000, Vashti McKenzie was one of forty-two candidates for four open seats as bishop in the AME Church. She was elected the first female AME bishop on 11 July 2000 and assigned to the Eighteenth Episcopal District, supervising two hundred churches with ten thousand members in Lesotho, Swaziland, Botswana, and Mozambique. Bishop McKenzie set forth an agenda emphasizing spiritual growth and increased church membership in addition to aid to children of AIDS victims, and expanding educational and economic opportunity.

—De Witt S. Dykes Jr.

The Genesis Generation included women who experienced separation from family through their sale as slaves or the death of loved ones. Dealing with abandonment and loss allowed the Lord to become central in their lives. Through their faith and testimony, the Genesis Generation established a solid foundation for future women preachers of the Gospel of Jesus Christ. By speaking publicly against injustice, these women created a place at the altar for women in ministry. Their lives and ability to survive insurmountable challenges of gender and race, both in the pulpit and in public, provided them with the tangible evidence that God did indeed hear their cries and concerns.

The Exodus Explorers 1855–1930. The book of Exodus details the Hebrew people's escape from bondage. Likewise, the women in this second generation experienced the miraculous work of the Lord as He led black people out of slavery and into freedom. During this era, the black church was no longer a northern anomaly. There were congregations within white denominations in the mid-Atlantic region, and several independent black congregations throughout the South. Black liberation theology and radical black ministers also emerged in this generation as they overtly confronted the pro-slavery and colonization movements.

By the close of the century, the black church witnessed the formation of the National Baptist Convention and the rise of the interracial Holiness Movement. Black women of this era were speaking out and being heard, and their concerns were being incorporated into regional and national agendas. These women also formed church auxiliaries, literary clubs, women's clubs, and at times their own denominations and churches. Exodus Explorer women included the AME and Holiness Amanda Smith (1837–1915); the AME Zion Florence Spearing Randolph (1866–1951); the Holiness-Pentecostal Mary Magdalene Tate (1871–1930); the Baptist Nannie Helen Burroughs (1879–1961); and the Holiness-Pentecostal Ida Bell Robinson (1891–1946).

Following in the footsteps of Jarena Lee, Florence Spearing Randolph was ordained a deacon in the AME Zion Church in 1889 and therefore granted permission to preach and lead services. Born in Charleston, South Carolina, to John and Anna Smith Spearing, Randolph came from a long line of antebellum free blacks. Growing up in a financially stable family allowed her to attend school and pursue an educational rather than a vocational career. However, Randolph still faced covert gender discrimination and she was doubtful about her calling. She took Bible classes for a deeper understanding of God's word for missionary work, not to preach. Despite these obstacles, in 1886, she joined the Monmouth AME Zion Church in Virginia. Through exposure, experience, and answered prayer, Randolph realized the call on her life to preach the Gospel and began preaching holiness in church and temperance through the Women's Christian Temperance Union.

Nearly a decade after Randolph was born, Mary Magdalene Tate entered the world in Dickson, Tennessee. Like many other women Exodus Explorers leaders, Tate experienced sanctification at an early age. People who knew Tate called her "Miss Do Right." In 1903, along with her two sons, Walter Curtis Lewis and Feliz Early Lewis, she founded the Church of the Living God, Pillar and Ground of the Truth denomination—a name said to be revealed by God to her sons, and supported by Scripture in 1 Timothy 3:15–16. The early history of the church is vague, but it is well known that Mother Tate proclaimed she was ordained by God and was therefore the first Bishop of the Church she founded. Affectionately known as Mother Tate, she organized and presided over the First General Assembly of the Church from 25 June to 5 July 1908.

Ida Bell Robinson, the final woman of the Exodus Explorers, was born in Hazelhurst, Georgia. In 1919 she was appointed pastor of Mount Olive, in Philadelphia, Pennsylvania. In 1920 she was publicly ordained at the national convocation of the United Holy Church of America. Although successful as a woman minister, Robinson was aware that the brewing controversy regarding women and ordination could affect her ministry. Troubled by the controversy, and knowing that God had called her to preach the Gospel, she prayed and fasted for ten days until God spoke the following words to her: "Come out on Mount Sinai and loose the women." In 1924 she secured a charter and established a denomination under the name Mount Sinai Holy Church of America, Incorporated.

Subsequently, in 1924 she was elevated to Bishop Robinson when her denomination opened new churches along the east coast from Florida to New York. Bishop Robinson nurtured the spiritual gifts of people and she served as their mentor. She held services five nights a week; on Mondays women preached; on Wednesdays men preached; the Friday sermon focused on young people; and on Saturdays she held meetings for Sunday school teachers. By catering to all members of the congregation, she was able to develop a ministry among men and women, young and old.

The women of the Exodus Explorers advanced the credibility of the call to ministry for women in mainstream denominations such as the Methodist and the Baptist churches. The rise of the Holiness Movement afforded these women the opportunity to work in egalitarian settings, where they helped change the perception of women in ministry. The formation of storefront churches and independent denominations allowed the church community

to observe the divine favor and determination of godly women. These advancements occurred during the height of racial discrimination through Jim Crow segregation, lynching, and disenfranchisement. Yet African American women in ministry continued to preach, prophesize, and worship God. In a 1909 sermon entitled "Hope," Florence Spearing Randolph stated that as black people in general and Christian women in particular,

> We must try and hold up our women, if we desire to see the race rise to a higher standard; for it is not the Negro's color but his condition that is the most detrimental; it is not the man or woman's color, but their merit, character and worth, and this has been proven by many of the race.
>
> (Collier-Thomas, p. 121)

The Era of Elizabeth 1935–2000. The sixty-five year period between the third and fourth Great Awakenings gave rise to yet another generation of African American religious leaders. During the third religious shift in U.S. history, religious leaders changed their emphasis from personal to social sin in response to poverty following the stock market crash of 1929. The fourth religious shift began in 1960, and represented a return to an intimate relationship with God and a reassertion of the experiential content of the Bible. World War II enabled more women to receive a formal education, and as a result, many of these women were active in helping their churches expand into international arenas through increased foreign missions work, broader social services, and civic education. The early civil rights movement of the 1950s fostered an air of protest within the black community. The black Protestant church led the crusade against injustice, Christian hypocrisy, and racial hatred. Ministers, both male and female, preached the beloved community doctrine of Jesus Christ.

The women of this era included the COGIC Lillian Brooks-Coffey (1896–1964); the Episcopalian Pauli Murray (1910–1985); the United Methodist Leontine Turpeau Current Kelly (1920–); the Holiness-Pentecostal Shirley Caesar (1938–); the AME Vashti McKenzie (1947–). Each of these women followed their foremothers in preaching sermons and singing songs of liberation and equality, even as they challenged Christians in America to demonstrate their creed of liberty and justice for all.

Lillian Brooks-Coffey was born in Memphis, Tennessee, in 1896. She and her grandmother joined the COGIC in 1903 when she was seven years old. Over the course of her life, Mother Coffey recalls that her family and husband were concerned about her membership in the church; ultimately, she was abandoned by them because of her decision to make the church her life's work. She organized prayer bands, one of which led to the establishment of the first COGIC in Chicago. She developed an evangelistic team that spread the Gospel in Illinois, Indiana, Wisconsin, and Minnesota. At the age of twenty-nine, she was appointed state supervisor for women in Michigan. In addition, she served as national supervisor of women for the COGIC, responsible for eighty-nine state supervisors. Upon the death of its founder C. H. Mason, the church experienced several transitions, and Mother Coffey kept the women's department intact and advanced it to new heights.

Leontine Turpeau Current Kelly was born in the historic Mount Zion United Methodist Church parsonage in the Georgetown neighborhood of Washington, DC, in 1920. Her father, the Reverend David DeWitt Turpeau Sr., served as pastor of Mount Zion, and he appreciated the rich history of the city's oldest black congregation, established in 1814. The family moved to Ohio when Reverend Turpeau was assigned another church, and Leontine opted for a career in teaching ministry as a secondary field. Ultimately, the ministry called her, and she was ordained to the episcopacy in 1984 by the Western Jurisdictional Conference of the United Methodist Church. She the first African American woman to be elected bishop of any major denomination.

Vashti McKenzie was born in 1947 into the Murphy publishing family. Her grandfather John Murphy, an early African American publisher, started *The Afro-American* newspaper in 1892. Raised in the Episcopal Church, McKenzie followed in the footsteps of the family business. After a period of consecration, she joined the Bethel AME Church in Baltimore and eventually pursued religious instruction. At the AME quadrennial convention in July 2000, she was ordained as bishop of the 18th district, which comprised some ten thousand members and two hundred churches in Africa. McKenzie was the first female AME bishop.

The Era of Elizabeth women received a legacy of faith, were imbued with a sense of works, and anointed with opportunities to expand Christian ministry beyond church walls. These women worked during the systematic dismantling of the 1960s civil rights agenda, and like earlier generations, they spoke truth to power. Their rise to leadership in traditional and new denominations made them a visible presence and permanent fixture in African American and mixed congregations. Many of these women openly engaged in political debates as they did their best to establish an egalitarian ministry. Pauli Murray, for example, the first black woman ordained to clergy in the Episcopal Church, preached a sermon titled "Male and Female: He Created Them," in which she reaffirmed the concept that both men and women were created equal by God, Who gave them dominion over the earth. This exegesis was used to dissolve the walls that divided Christians over race, gender, and class issues.

Legacy

The history of black Protestant women is a story of faith and conviction. From slavery, to Jim Crow segregation, to the modern civil rights movement, women of faith answered the call of their Lord. They preached sermons on salvation, temperance, deliverance, and damnation during challenging historical periods. Some questioned their call, while others embraced it, and all submitted to the sovereign authority of God.

See also Lee, Jarena; Religion; Sanctified Churches; *and* Womanist Theology.

BIBLIOGRAPHY

Alexander, Estrelda Y. "Gender and Leadership in the Theology and Practice of Three Pentecostal Women Pioneers: Mary Magdalena Lewis Tate, Aimee Semple McPherson, Ida Robinson." PhD diss., Catholic University of America, 2003.

Clemmons, Ithiel C. *Bishop C. H. Mason and the Roots of the Church of God in Christ*. Bakersfield, CA: Pneuma Life Publishing, 1996.

Collier-Thomas, Bettye. *Daughters of Thunder: Black Women Preachers and Their Sermons, 1850–1979*. San Francisco: Jossey-Bass, 1998.

Current, Angella. *Breaking Barriers: An African American Family and the Methodist Story*. Nashville, TN: Abingdon Press, 2001.

Elaw, Zilpha. *Memoirs of Life, Religious Experience Ministerial Travels, and Labours of Mrs. Zilpha Elaw, An American Female of Color; Together with Some Accounts of the Great Religious Revivals in America [Written by Herself]* (1841). Reprinted in *Sisters of the Spirit: Three Black Women's Autobiographies of the Nineteenth Century*, edited by William Andrews. Bloomington: Indiana University Press, 1986.

Elliott, Bishop J. C. *100th Annual General Assembly*. Nashville, TN: The House of God, Which Is the Pillar and Ground of Truth Without Controversy, Inc., 2003.

Elizabeth. *Elizabeth, A Colored Minister of the Gospel Born in Slavery*. Philadelphia: The Tract Association of Friends, 1889.

Fulop, Timothy E., and Albert J. Raboteau, eds. *African American Religion: Interpretive Essays in History and Culture*. New York: Routledge, 1997.

Gilkes, Cheryl Townsend. *If It Wasn't for the Women. . . . Black Women's Experience and Womanist Culture in Church and Community*. Maryknoll, NY: Orbis Books, 2000.

Higginbotham, Evelyn Brooks. *Righteous Discontent: The Women's Movement in Black Baptist Church, 1880–1920*. Cambridge, MA: Harvard University Press, 1994.

Lee, Jarena. *Religious Experience and Journal of Mrs. Jarena Lee, Giving an Account of Her Call to Preach the Gospel* (1849). Reprinted in *Sisters of the Spirit: Three Black Women's Autobiographies of the Nineteenth Century*, edited by William L. Andrews. Bloomington: Indiana University Press, 1986.

Lincoln, C. Eric, and Lawrence H. Mamiya, eds. *The Black Church in the African American Experience*. Durham, NC: Duke University Press, 1990.

Montgomery, William E. *Under Their Own Vine and Fig Tree: The African American Church in the South, 1865–1900*. Baton Rouge: Louisiana State University Press, 1993.

Murphy, Larry G., ed. *Down by the Riverside: Readings in African American Religion*. New York: New York University Press, 2000.

Raboteau, Albert J. *Canaan Land: A Religious History of African Americans*. New York: Oxford University Press, 2001.

Ross, Rosetta E. *Witnessing and Testifying: Black Women, Religion, and Civil Rights*. Minneapolis, MN: Fortress Press, 2003.

Tate, Gayle T. *Unknown Tongues: Black Women's Political Activism in the Antebellum Era*. East Lansing: Michigan State University Press, 2003.

Williams, Richard E. *Called and Chosen: The Story of Mother Rebecca Jackson and the Philadelphia Shakers*. Metuchen, NJ: The Scarecrow Press, Inc., and the American Theological Library Association, 1981.

—IDA E. JONES

QUAKERS. The relationships between Quakerism, women's rights, and African American women are complex. Since its beginnings in seventeenth-century England, the Religious Society of Friends has had a well-deserved reputation for treating women with equality and fairness. This Christian-based sect—whose early adherents came to be known as Quakers because they would often shake or quake when they felt the presence of God—quickly acquired what would become its signature characteristic: engaging the political controversies of the day with the goal of protecting human life and resisting injustice in whatever form these controversies might take. Speaking out against war and violence and protesting certain elements of social inequality are among the issues for which Friends, or Quakers, have become widely known.

Unlike that of many other Christian denominations, the internal history of the Quakers was unmarred by witch hunts or persecutions against outspoken or influential women. Indeed, from the earliest years of its existence, Quakerism consistently encouraged women to preach, to take leadership in public affairs, and to travel in the ministry, while husbands or congregation members back home assumed their household duties. Until late in the nineteenth century, local meetings generally separated men's and women's business meetings, allowing women to develop leadership roles unfettered by men's interference, but the division was amicable, and women's meetings combined or consulted with men's meetings when appropriate.

Racial Politics

Some Quakers also early voiced disapproval of the prevailing racial policies of their world, but the format, context, and agenda for addressing racial inequality were less forceful and consistent than were the Friends' policies concerning women's equality. Lacking a central authority such as a pope or synod, Quakers organized into regional groupings known as "Yearly Meetings," which helped to structure and organize local congregations, but had no authority over theology or behavior. As a consequence, Quakers soon came to rely on "epistles"—letters circulated among the independent Quaker meetings around the world—to encourage theological uniformity. It was in these epistles that as early as 1671, Friends expressed concern about race relations and the practice of slavery. At first, such protestations consisted of encouraging members to treat slaves well and to give them religious training. But by the end of the seventeenth century, some North American Quakers were suggesting that slavery itself should be outlawed, because, among other things, it violated the Golden Rule. By the era of the American Revolution, a vocal minority of Quakers was leading a growing chorus of abolitionists who began by defending the rights of African Americans who were already free, then quickly expanded their agenda to include agitation for the ending of slavery. By 1800, many American yearly meetings advised against slaveholding among their members.

Nevertheless, there is little evidence to suggest that many Friends translated their antislavery posture into social acceptance for African Americans. Rather, among white Quakers, attitudes toward slavery and African Americans lay along a continuum. At the conservative end of the spectrum were Quakers who abandoned the Religious Society of Friends rather than relinquish their slaves. Probably more numerous were white Quakers who took the middle ground, advocating the abolition of slavery because slaveholding, and the violence it implied, jeopardized the integrity of white Quakers' doctrines of nonviolence. These members held that while black people were not the social or religious equals of white people, there was no sufficient justification for enslaving

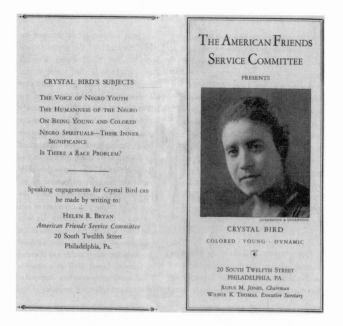

CRYSTAL BIRD, presented in a pamphlet of the American Friends Service Committee, c. 1927. The committee arranged numerous speaking engagements for her in several cities and in Indiana. (Courtesy of American Friends Service Committee.)

them. Nevertheless, while black people should not be enslaved, they also should not be incorporated into Quaker communities.

Sometimes black people were invited to attend Friends' meetings, but they were seated in a separate section, and they usually were discouraged from seeking membership. In the last decades of the eighteenth century, several mixed-race women were accepted into Friends' meetings in the Philadelphia area, but their applications to join were so contested that it took up to three years to approve the membership. Still, the Quakers' theological emphasis on mysticism and an ever-present and available God appealed to many African Americans, as did the Friends' focus on social justice. The family of the New England African American shipper Paul Cuffe, members of a Quaker meeting, may be a rare exception to the ostracism African Americans faced from white Quakers during the Revolutionary era. But Cuffe's interest in returning to Africa raises questions about whether Quakers embraced him only in order to help him prepare to carry Christianity—and African Americans—to Africa.

Schism

This diversity of religious perspectives contributed to a schism among Quakers in the 1820s, out of which developed not only a competing array of theological positions but also an accompanying variety of Quaker opinions about how to address slavery. Some anti-slavery Friends focused on alleviating the dislocation of free black people or on purchasing slaves in order to free them. Others advocated political agitation and civil disobedience in pursuit of abolition. The most vocal, radical, and best-remembered perspective is that of the Hicksite faction of Quakers, who took their cue from Elias Hicks of Long Island, New York. As early as 1803, Hicks had published a pamphlet expressing his disapproval of "The Keeping of Negroes."

With the development of the transatlantic radical abolitionist movement in the 1830s, the American women's rights movement—in which Quaker women were prominent—began to overlap with the anti-slavery cause. A few of the most radical Quakers, mostly followers of Elias Hicks, many of them women, advocated the radical view that African Americans should be treated with equality not only in American society but also within the Religious Society of Friends. Moreover, these women took the position that women's freedom and that of African Americans were in fact the same cause: both were silenced, disempowered, and disenfranchised by unfair laws. Leaders in this movement included the Philadelphians Lucretia Mott, Sarah Pugh, and Angelina Grimké, who insisted that not only were African Americans' souls equal before God but that they also were entitled to full equality within

society. Outspoken abolitionists, Mott and Grimké often sat with black women in Quaker worship gatherings, and in 1838, Grimké included a black Quaker woman among her wedding guests, a decision that elicited the disapproval of many in her Quaker meeting. Indeed, many Quaker meetings frowned on abolitionism and on Quaker women's public engagement with it.

Nevertheless, these radical women found allies among the black Philadelphian women who shared their views. In 1833, more than two dozen women founded the Philadelphia Female Antislavery Society (PFASS). The co-founders in this endeavor included at least nine black women, among them Sarah Douglass and her mother, Grace Douglass, who had grown up in a family that attended Quaker meeting regularly, both of whom dressed and spoke in the unique manner of Quakers. Other African American founders included Charlotte, Margaretta, and Sarah Forten, the wife and two unmarried daughters of the prominent black businessman James Forten. Forten's married daughter, Harriet Purvis, also was among the group. Predominantly young, unmarried, and unencumbered by family responsibilities, this group launched petitions, arranged lectures, and developed programs to educate the public about the evils of slavery. The group also supported the Free Produce Movement, which opened stores to promote products made with non–slave labor. Over the course of the next three decades, PFAAS programming narrowed to focus more on raising funds to assist fugitive slaves, and to travel to England to promote abolition there.

Though divided over abolition during the antebellum period, the Philadelphia Yearly Meeting, which was among the strongest of nearly a dozen American yearly meetings, helped dozens of women mount programs to assist free black people and fugitive slaves, as well as Native Americans. Their philanthropy included orphanages, adult job-skill training programs, and schools for children. One such school, the Institute for Colored Youth, grew into an enduring teacher-training institute, which evolved into Cheyney Teachers' College.

In other yearly meetings, white Quakers sometimes were more welcoming to black women. Examples of this could be found in northern New York, where Friends such as the Post family hosted the fugitive slave Harriet Jacobs. Another family took in several black children, whom they raised and who, after some slight resistance on the part of the meeting, attended meetings with their foster parents. In Indiana, strong Underground Railroad support among Friends sometimes resulted in numbers of black women and men becoming part of local meetings. In New England, a few black women worked closely with Quaker abolitionists like Connecticut's Prudence Crandall, whose property was burned by irate neighbors when she accepted black girls into her school. The black women who established the New England Female Antislavery Society soon found support among white Quaker women as well as the Congregationalists who backed William Lloyd Garrison's immediate-abolition coalition. Such white Quaker women learned from and enjoyed the company of African Americans, though sometimes romanticizing what they saw as the ennobling effects of black suffering.

Beginning in the late 1860s, with the close of the Civil War, more alliances developed between black women and white Quaker women as they went South to staff a number of schools supported by Friends. For northern women, white and black, this was often a first opportunity for independence and fulfillment, and women of both races worked side by side to educate freed people. Charlotte Forten, granddaughter and namesake of a PFASS founder, was among the black women who worked with white philanthropists to establish such a school near Beaufort, South Carolina. Out of such exposure to Quaker values grew a few all-black meetings in places such as Maryville, Tennessee; Lost Creek, North Carolina; and Southland, Indiana. While some Quakers insisted that black worshippers would not be comfortable in the silence of traditional Quaker worship, Alida Clark, a white member of the Southland meeting aimed to have her meeting do whatever might be necessary to make Quakerism attractive to black members. In Ohio, Walter and Emma Malone's evangelist Quaker college accepted and encouraged black men and women to study alongside white students, particularly if they planned to be missionaries in the African outposts established by Quakers between 1865 and 1920.

In the last decades of the nineteenth century, Quaker schools for black children often were led by black women who used their authority to expand opportunities for their students. For example, the Oberlin graduate Fanny Jackson Coppin, who headed Philadelphia's Institute for Colored Youth in the 1880s, successfully lobbied the white Quaker governing board to add classics, music, and foreign languages to the school's curriculum. Coppin's cooperative relationship with her board was typical of the working alliance between African Americans and Quakers who had a continuing concern for social and gender justice. This alliance was strengthened by the development of the American Friends Service Committee, founded in 1917, and expanded over the next two decades to focus on racial and gender justice.

In the 1940s, Quaker housing cooperatives and study centers sought to attract black membership and leadership, including black women. But it was a few white leaders of Quaker schools who pushed the integration of black women into membership and leadership roles among the Religious Society of Friends. Beginning in the 1940s, Sidwell Friends' School in Washington, DC, Pennsylvania's Westtown, Friends' Central, and Germantown Friends schools began to accept black students. Slowly black membership in the Religious Society of Friends increased, and at the beginning of the twenty-first century a number of Quaker institutions were headed by black Quaker women.

See also Abolition Movement.

BIBLIOGRAPHY

Bacon, Margaret Hope. "New Light on Sarah Mapps Douglass and Her Reconciliation with Friends." *Quaker History* 90.1 (Spring 2001).

Barbour, Hugh, et al., eds. *Quaker Crosscurrents: Three Hundred Years of Friends in the New York Yearly Meetings*. Syracuse, NY: Syracuse University Press, 1995.

Sterling, Dorothy. *We Are Your Sisters: Black Women in the Nineteenth Century*. New York: Norton, 1984.

Winch, Julie. *The Elite of Our People: Joseph Willson's Sketches of Black Upper-Class Life in Antebellum Philadelphia*. University Park: Pennsylvania State University Press, 2000.

Yee, Shirley. *Black Women Abolitionists: A Study in Activism, 1828–1860*. Knoxville: University of Tennessee Press, 1992.

Yellin, Jean Fagan. *The Abolitionist Sisterhood: Women's Political Culture in Antebellum America*. Ithaca, NY: Cornell University Press, 1994.

—EMMA J. LAPSANSKY-WERNER

QUEEN LATIFAH (b. 18 March 1970), entertainer. As of 2003, ten black women had been nominated for Academy Awards. Queen Latifah was one of them. Three situation comedies on television had starred black women. She starred in one of them. One black woman rapper had made the move to movie stardom. She was that woman. Queen Latifah won Grammies, hosted a talk show, and garnered an NAACP Image Award. She has owned a record production company and a talent management agency. Moreover, Queen Latifah emerged from a rap culture riddled with sexism and, without rejecting that culture, created an image for herself and other black women that was profoundly proud, strong, and race conscious. Queen Latifah has not just been a talented entertainer. She has been a presence in entertainment and in American society.

Queen Latifah was born Dana Elaine Owens in Newark, New Jersey. Her mother, Rita Owens, a high school teacher, and her father, Lancelot Owens, an armed forces veteran and Newark police officer, raised her with her older brother "Winki" (Lancelot Owens Jr.). Despite her parents' eventual separation in 1978, her family provided a nurturing environment for her future endeavors and accomplishments.

Rita Owens remembered her daughter as an active and independent child, not content to do, or restricted to doing, only things that little girls "were expected to do." Her interests ranged from the martial arts to guitar to ballet lessons. Refusing to accept the label of "tomboy,"

QUEEN LATIFAH signing autographs. She has been not just a talented performer but a significant presence in entertainment and in American society. (© Salimah Ali. All rights reserved.)

she was nonetheless interested in athletics, which she often played in the neighborhoods alongside her brother, one of her closest friends.

It was the search for independence that led her to adopt the name "Latifah." Looking through a book of Muslim names with her cousin, Owens chose the name that means "delicate, sensitive, kind." In her mind, this simple act was not a rejection of her family name, but rather one of her earliest efforts to define herself on her own terms. However, it would be several more years before she added "Queen" to her name, in memory of the African queens she considered her foremothers.

In high school, Latifah continued to hone her independence. Her athleticism became more pronounced as a member of Newark's Irvington High School basketball team, which won two state championships during her tenure. In addition, Latifah participated in various talent shows and was popular among her peers. Despite this successful high school experience, Latifah simultaneously sought more out of life beyond New Jersey.

One of the most important factors contributing to her transformation to "Queen Latifah" was her coming of age during the mid to late 1980s boom in hip-hop culture and rap music. Although these forces had been present for several years, during this era rap grew in both stature and artistic expression. Centered in such places as the Latin Quarters in New York City, rap entered what is often described as an era of "consciousness." Although the fun and entertaining side of the music remained, much of it focused on social messages such as black history, black pride, and the continued struggle against racism.

Latifah became engrossed in this culture. Using her employment at a local Burger King for money, she traveled back and forth to New York City through the Lincoln Tunnel, helping spread the movement to some of her peers in New Jersey. It was during this time that she became interested in performing. Following in the footsteps of such female rappers as Roxanne Shante, MC Lyte, Salt-n-Pepa, and Jazzy Joyce and Sweet T, Latifah began to rap with some of her New Jersey friends, who would eventually form the basis for her Flavor Unit company. What began as a source of fun soon became much more.

After her high school graduation, however, Latifah was not thinking of a career as a rapper; it was simply a hobby. She attended the Borough of Manhattan Community College the following year, where she briefly studied broadcast journalism. However, she soon decided to drop out and, with the blessing of her mother and the support of her brother and friends, put all of her energy into becoming a rapper. It was not long before Latifah signed a major recording contract and released her first album, *All Hail the Queen* (1989).

One of the most successful singles from this album, "Ladies First," reflected many of her own values as well as those of rap's consciousness movement. This combination became a trademark for Queen Latifah, who was determined to be both entertaining and informative. Her lyrics sought to uplift and enlighten all of her listeners but particularly the women, whom she hoped would adopt such attributes as self-confidence and self-esteem. Latifah's second album, *Nature of a Sista* (1991), continued to carry these messages.

In 1992, with success building, Queen Latifah's life virtually came apart with the death of her brother Winki in a motorcycle accident. Because they were so close, this tragedy was painful and damaging to Latifah both physically and mentally for some time. However, after a period of grieving, she was able to rebound and, with her brother as her inspiration, finish her third album, *Black Reign* (1993). This album included the single "U.N.I.T.Y.," a protest of both verbal and physical abuse against women. The song eventually brought Queen Latifah a Grammy for Best Rap Solo Performance, an NAACP Image Award, and a Soul Train Music Award.

At the same time that Queen Latifah reclaimed her position in music, she began to make a mark in the music, television, and movie industries. In 1993, she co-founded Flavor Unit Entertainment, which included a recording and management company. Latifah's status as an actress grew through a combination of television and movie roles. Beginning with guest appearances on such sitcoms as the *Fresh Prince of Bel Air*, Queen Latifah soon found a starring role as Khadijah James in the Fox Network hit sitcom *Living Single*. In film, she rose from minor roles in *Jungle Fever*, *House Party 2*, and *Juice* to more prominent roles in films such as *My Life*, *Set It Off*, and *Living Out Loud*. With this increased acting schedule, she was still able to complete her fourth album in 1998 (*Order in the Court*) and host her own talk show in 1999 (*The Queen Latifah Show*).

In 2002–2003, Queen Latifah reached heights in the movie industry that, other than Will Smith and Ice Cube, no rappers-turned-actors had attained. In a stunning performance as Matron Mama Morton in *Chicago*, Latifah sang and acted her way to nominations for the 2003 Academy Award for Best Supporting Actress, the 2003 Golden Globe Award for Best Supporting Actress in a Musical or Comedy, and the 2003 Screen Actors Guild Award for Outstanding Performance by a Female Actor in a Supporting Role. She eventually won a 2003 Screen Actors Guild Award for Best Ensemble along with the rest of the cast from *Chicago*. In addition to her role in *Chicago*, Latifah was executive producer and co-starred in the comedy *Bringing Down the House*. She also continued work on a fifth album, *First Love*.

The accolades continued to mount, including the 2003 Essence Award as Entertainer of the Year and being chosen as one of *People* magazine's Most Beautiful People of 2003. However, remembering her rise from the Burger King on High Street in Newark to the Oscars, Latifah was determined to remain grounded and to continue to be a role model for a broad section of the United States. While she achieved great success, she always remembered that the fight against racism and sexism continued, and she supported the struggle against them. In doing so, Queen Latifah followed in the footsteps of many African American women who defended both their race and gender.

See also **Hip Hop (Rap) Music.**

BIBLIOGRAPHY

Austin, Hilary Mac. "Queen Latifah." *Facts on File Encyclopedia of Black Women in America*, edited by Darlene Clark Hine. New York: Facts on File, 1997.

Ferran, Christine. "Queen Latifah." In *Contemporary Black Biography*, Volume 1, edited by Michael L. LaBlanc. Detroit, MI: Gale Research, 1992.

Johns, Robert L. "Queen Latifah." *Notable Black American Women*, Book II, edited by Jessie Carney Smith. Detroit, MI: Gale Research, 1996.

Latifah, Queen. *Ladies First: Revelations of a Strong Woman*. New York: Quill, 2000.

Norment, Lynn. "Queen Latifah's Roller-Coaster Ride to the Top." *Ebony* 58 (April 2003): 152–155.

"Queen Latifah." TV People. *TV Tome*. http://www.tvtome.com/tvtome/servlet/PersonDetail/personid-54643.

—Eric D. Duke

QUILTING. African Americans began to quilt well over a hundred years before scholars began to earnestly document this important folk tradition. But since the late 1970s folklorists, art historians, journalists, historians, and quilters themselves have pieced together the history and culture of black quilting with the same confident care and bold technique deployed by the multitude of black quilters who assembled often disparate scraps of fabric into warm bedding and works of art. Their words tell the story of a tenacious tradition, rooted in antebellum slavery, one that continued into the early twenty-first century.

Slavery

During the era of slavery, black women and men made quilts both for their white mistresses as well as for their own family members. After painstakingly searching through the collections at southern historical societies, scrutinizing diaries and newspapers, and mining the Works Progress Administration (WPA) narratives collected from former slaves during the Depression, the folklorist Gladys-Marie Fry offered the most complete history of quilting practices during slavery. The archival record is nearly as thin as a frequently washed quilt. Since documenting any woman's domestic practices was scorned during the nineteenth century, no reputable scholar sought to chronicle the handiwork of black women. Still, by probing obscure sources, Fry was able to track down and authenticate many examples of black women's stitchery. New World slavery resulted in the forced schooling of black women in textile practices so that they could stock the mistress's chests with clothing, needlework, and quilts. Using scraps garnered from the making of these quilts as well as leftovers from the coarse, heavy fabric allotted for slaves' clothing, black women made quilts for their own families.

Link to Underground Railroad

One of the most fascinating but difficult to document rumors about slavery-era quilts concerns the possible connection to the Underground Railroad. African American folklore has long held that certain quilt patterns were symbols used to guide slaves to safe houses or stations along the trail to freedom. In many of these stories, it is the log-cabin quilt square that signaled safety. The story usually goes that runaways were given other clues to combine with the presence of a log cabin quilt in the yard as a final signal that a particular house was owned by abolitionists willing to risk their own security to hide slaves. In other, more elaborate texts, quilts themselves were maps that disclosed the routes runaways could use to guide them to Canada or free northern states. Unfortunately, the archival trail on these texts is virtually nonexistent, and the early ethnographers who interviewed former slaves were unaware of the stories. The historians Jacqueline L. Tobin and Raymond G. Dobard endeavored to piece together the fragile support evidence for these texts.

Men Learned to Quilt

While African American slave women were expected to assume the domestic responsibilities assigned to white women, black men also learned to quilt, and even in the early twenty-first century, it was probably easier to locate black male quilters than white ones. Fry, who curated an exhibit entitled Made by Men and authored the companion volume, *Man Made: African-American Men and Quilting Traditions*, made the case that slave women fortunate enough to labor in the house instead of in the field were eager to make their sons valuable as house servants, as well. To protect their offspring from the brutal and insecure conditions of field slavery, black mothers taught their daughters and sons quilt making, embroidery, cooking, and similar domestic practices. By perfecting these skills, young slaves had a somewhat improved chance of securing their futures in the preferred indoor environs of the peculiar institution. But, as Fry's exhibit documented, quilt making offered aesthetic satisfaction to black men long after the end of slavery. The inventor George Washington Carver included quilting in his impressive list of talents. Within the pantheon of black art quilters whose pieces were celebrated at the end of the twentieth and the beginning of the twenty-first century, Michael Cummings enjoyed wide acclaim.

Reconstruction and After

Slavery's demise did not trigger the end of black quilting. Indeed, in addition to making quilts for utilitarian purposes, black women more frequently used quilting to express themselves artistically and politically as well as to achieve economic empowerment. Elizabeth Keckley, best known as the mulatto seamstress for Mary Todd Lincoln, was one of the first of many advocates for black financial autonomy who organized recently freed black women to make their quilts and then sell them for a profit. Even a century later, black women's groups such as the Alabama Freedom Quilting Bee and the Tutwiler Quilters in Mississippi used their traditional quilt-making prowess as a means to reach aesthetic satisfaction and economic improvement. Although there were exceptions, communally made black quilts were more likely to be made for fundraising, while individually made quilts were more likely to be made for family and friends.

Migration

In the century or so between Reconstruction and the late 1960s, African American women and men continued to quilt. Particularly in environments in which waste was economically unviable and ideologically abhorred, old clothes and bedding were made over into new quilts. But quilting was not completely restricted to southern rural communities. Just as surely as they brought their recipes for soul food and call-and-response-based worship, blacks who migrated to the North brought their textile practices. But two factors contributed to the fact that northern African American women did not take up their needles and scissors as frequently as their southern sisters did. First, urban occupational opportunities took women from the home, cutting down the amount of time available for quilting. Second, in many households, store-bought commodities were welcome symbols of an improved social

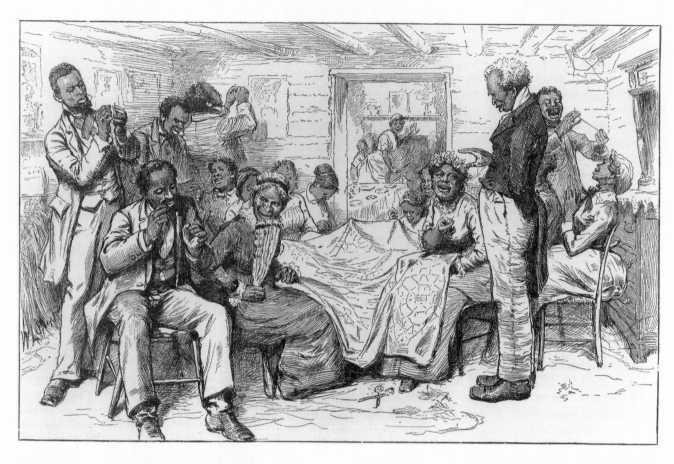

"THE 'BROTHERS' ASSISTED IN THE QUILTING." This drawing of women quilting and men threading the needles appeared in *Harper's Weekly*, 21 April 1883. (Schomburg Center for Research in Black Culture, New York Public Library.)

status. Still, many urban black women in the North returned to quilting in their later years, after raising their children and leaving the workforce.

African Survivals

Most scholars agree that quilting bed covers was not a custom practiced in sub-Saharan Africa, where keeping cool at night was a challenge. However, the techniques of quilting can be seen in some forms of African armor. Weaving was a common African textile technique, and in most West African cultures, men were assigned the responsibility for transforming threads into cloth and cloth into goods. More important than the techniques themselves, what survived from Africa was an underlying aesthetic sensibility informed by preferences for bold colors and clashing color combinations, rectangular strip structures, and coarse textures. As so many students of African American quilting have noted, the language used to describe black music also

suits descriptions of black textile practices. Whereas jazz musicians talk about wanting to tease the ear, quilters talk about wanting to fool the eye. With loud primary colors, audacious patterned fabrics, and large design elements, many African American quilts reflect the same impulse for improvisation evident in other genres of black folk expression.

For many years, most African American folk practices were described as inferior imitations of European traditions. Early twentieth-century scholars maintained that the horrors of the Middle Passage erased collective black cultural memory, leaving American blacks aesthetic blank slates. Whether blacks made music, danced, preached sermons, or crafted fabric into quilts, the ultimate products were believed to be substandard, failed imitations of an idealized European standard. By the middle of the twentieth century, as scholars began to study Africa and its aesthetics, a debate ensued over whether black cultural productions were imitations of white ones or whether they reflected an alternative not at all inferior in aesthetic sensibility. Over time, the most accepted theory was that African Americans syncretized what they learned from other cultures (including non-European ones) with an African-inspired worldview to forge art unique to the African American experience.

Within quilt scholarship, this proved to be a particularly tenacious and provocative debate. Cuesta Benberry, Carolyn Mazloomi, Eli Leon, John Vlach, Maude Wahlman, Roland Freeman, and many others concurred that blacks made quilts that were different from white ones. Leon coined the term *Afro-traditional* to describe the attributes he and others believed characterize the majority of black quilts. Afro-traditional quilts are improvisational and asymmetrical. They feature strongly contrasting primary colors, with red as the most common. Like kente cloth, Afro-traditional quilts tend to be constructed with long, rectangular strips, and *strip quilts* is a label that fits a large category of black quilts. Quilts within the utilitarian Afro-traditional quilt sphere tend to be constructed from leftover clothing, as opposed to purchased fabrics. The basic nine-patch is the most frequently used block in these quilts. Many black quilters have said that the first block they learned to quilt was a nine-patch. Upon inspecting older Afro-traditional quilts, one often finds an older, more worn quilt used as the base for a newer one. Black quilters tended to use a wide range of fabric types. While many mainstream quilters limited their quilts to 100 percent cotton fabrics, black quilters used corduroy, velvet, silk, and even man-made fabrics such as polyester and Dacron in their quilts. By the end of the twentieth century, many black quilters were eager to incorporate African and African-inspired fabrics into their quilts.

However, it would be misleading to suggest that all African American quilters embraced Afro-traditional tastes and techniques. Just as some African American musicians eschew jazz and blues to perform classical music, some African Americans made quilts that are indistinguishable from those pieced by mainstream quilters.

Private to Public Spheres

For more than a century, black quilters have taken their quilts from the privacy of bedrooms to more public spaces such as church fund-raisers, regional fairs, and expositions. Measure the Harriet Powers quilts in the custody of Boston's Museum of Fine Arts and the Smithsonian Institution and one discovers that they will not fit a conventional bed. Dominated by evocative Old Testament symbolism, these quilts tell the story of a quilter entranced by the miracles revealed in the Bible's most compelling narratives. Powers clearly wanted to share her quilts with the public, and when she faced financial difficulties, she sold her quilts to supplement her family's meager income.

In the last two decades of the twentieth century and the first decade of the twenty-first, more and more African American quilts were featured artifacts in galleries and museums. Some exhibits displayed utilitarian quilts made by blacks who did not identify themselves as artists. The well-documented Gee's Bend exhibit that included the elite Whitney Museum of American Art as one of its locales featured well-used, functional quilts.

Other exhibits featured quilts rendered by black artists who intentionally selected quilts as alternative canvases for their chosen mode of aesthetic expression. The quilts of Faith Ringgold, Carolyn Mazloomi, EdJohnetta Miller, Michael Cummings, and others were created as works of art. These quilts commanded extensive critical attention and boasted the serious price tags commensurate with other examples of highly praised contemporary art. Such quilts were featured in Stitching Memories: African American Story Quilts mounted at the Williams College Museum of Art. Still other quilters such as Arbie Williams, Nora Ezell, and Clementine Hunter are often labeled as "outsider artists." Firmly rooted in black folk art traditions, their quilts are well documented and displayed and often fetch handsome prices.

Legacy

African American interest in understanding the history of, reading about, decorating with, making, giving, and receiving quilts remains strong. Some young black quilters still learn to quilt in a direct line, linking them to their mothers, grandmothers, and great-grandmothers. Others learn in courses offered at fabric stores or churches, from books, or from online sources. Many young black quilters learn in integrated settings, where they might cut their first fabric strips while seated next to a young white quilting enthusiast. African Americans have transformed what started as one of the forced labor requirements demanded of enslaved blacks into a highly valued mode of cultural expression, one that can be shaped to reflect a range of individual and collective aesthetic impulses as wide and as varied as the people they have become.

See also Powers, Harriet.

BIBLIOGRAPHY

Benberry, Cuesta. *Always There: The African-American Presence in American Quilts*. Louisville: Kentucky Quilt Project, 1992.

Ezell, Nora McKeown. *My Quilts and Me: The Diary of an American Quilter*. Montgomery, AL: Black Belt Press, 1999.

Freeman, Roland L. *A Communion of the Spirits: African-American Quilters, Preservers, and Their Stories*. Nashville, TN: Rutledge Hill Press, 1996.

Fry, Gladys-Marie. *Stitched from the Soul: Slave Quilts from the Antebellum South*. Chapel Hill: University of North Carolina Press, 2002.

Hicks, Kyra E. *Black Threads: An African American Quilting Sourcebook*. Jefferson, NC: McFarland, 2003.

Leon, Eli. *Who'd a Thought It: Improvisation in African-American Quiltmaking; December 31, 1987, to February 28, 1988*. San Francisco: San Francisco Craft and Folk Art Museum, 1987.

Mazloomi, Carolyn. *Spirits of the Cloth: Contemporary African-American Quilts*. New York: Clarkson Potter, 1998.

Tobin, Jacqueline L., and Raymond G. Dobard. *Hidden in Plain View: The Secret Story of Quilts and the Underground Railroad*. New York: Doubleday, 1999.

—PATRICIA A. TURNER